W9-BZC-728

COLLINS

QUOTATION FINDER

COLLINS

QUOTATION
FINDER

COLLINS

QUOTATION FINDER

A catalogue record for this book is available from the British Library

All rights reserved. No part of this publication may be reproduced, stored in a retrieval system or transmitted, in any form or by any means, without the prior permission of the publisher.

This book is sold subject to the conditions that it shall not, by way of trade or otherwise, be lent, resold, hired out or otherwise circulated without the publisher's prior consent in any form of binding or cover other than that in which it is published and without a similar condition including this condition being imposed on the subsequent publisher.

Printed and bound in Great Britain by the Bath Press

HarperCollins*Publishers*
P.O. Box, Glasgow G4 ONB

This compilation © HarperCollins 1999

www.**fire**and**water**.com

Foreword © Reginald Hill 1999

ISBN 0 00 472384 8
Reprint 10 9 8 7 6 5 4 3 2 1 0

A catalogue record for this book is available from the British Library

All rights reserved. No part of this publication may be reproduced, stored in a retrieval system or transmitted, in any form or by any means, without the prior permission of the publisher.

This book is sold subject to the conditions that it shall not, by way of trade or otherwise, be lent, resold, hired out or otherwise circulated without the publisher's prior consent in any form of binding or cover other than that in which it is published and without a similar condition including this condition being imposed on the subsequent publisher.

Printed and bound in Great Britain by the Bath Press

CONTENTS

CONTENTS

FOREWORD

BY

REGINALD HILL

A year ago or so I had the pleasure of introducing the HarperCollins *Concise Dictionary of Quotations* to an eager public. My theme then was, you can't have too much of a good thing, and, being a practitioner as well as a preacher, here I am again, beating the drum for HarperCollins' latest contribution to this admittedly crowded field.

I make no apology.

After all, is not quotation our national vice, making it almost a patriotic duty to indulge in it as deeply as possible? And have we not been assured by the highest authority that it is a good thing for uneducated persons to read books of quotations? And will they not learn there that only the uneducated show off their knowledge while those who are truly widely read keep mum or at least take care never to quote accurately?

Uncertain to which group I have just proved I belong to, but certain, dear reader, that you belong to the second, let me urge upon you the peculiar merits of the present work, which has much more to offer than suggested by its title, the *Quotation Finder*. For this is a long way from being a simple source book, answering the question *Who said that*? No, it is rather a box of delights, a bran-tub of phrases – wise and witty, comic and curious, pathetic and pithy, sentimental and cynical – into which you can dip at leisure with all the confidence of Prince Serendip.

And to those of you who may be reading these words ensconced in one of those sybaritic coffee houses which are now a feature of so many bookshops, do not be tempted to toy lightly with this handsome volume before tossing it aside, having got what you want out of it, and leaving the shop empty handed, though not as empty headed, as you came in. This is no mere general reference tool – nor, I might add, are you sitting in a public reference library! Someone somewhere needs to own this book. It's probably you.

Go on. Buy it.

Or at the very least, dear reader, if I cannot persuade you to become a still dearer purchaser, brush off the crumbs and erase the jammy fingerprints before you return it to the shelf.

INTRODUCTION

The compilation of a dictionary of quotations is an unchancy business, not least because all compilers are uneasily aware that the compilations they produce may say as much about the compilers as the individual quotations may reveal about the source of the quotation.

Does one really need the source of a Chinese quotation given, as a sort of bonus, in the original Mandarin? Why does that seemingly innocuous little paperback contain so many references to leather-related subjects? And why, in heaven's name, does *that* one have so many references to Arsenal football club?

Here, then, is a compilation of quotations arranged by subject that is entirely free of personal prejudice and obsession. Or here it would be, if one could find one.

Compilers of quotation books are always asked 'What makes yours so different from all the rest? What have you got that the others haven't?' The most honest reply to this dreaded question is one you will rarely hear, 'a recent publication date'. Instead you will hear of teams of eagle-eyed observers monitoring all human utterances, and of wise arbiters calmly sifting through the wit of humanity for pithy expressions of lasting wisdom.

If only. This dictionary, too, has its team of observers, and its arbiters. Alas, however, the most common – and often heated – disputes concern not pearls of wisdom, but whether or not, for example, 'Time for Tubby Bye-byes' is a valid quotation. Like many problems in life, such arguments disappear over time if you can summon up the apathy to ignore them. Thus, thankfully, it has become apparent that the only people apart from doting mothers and four-year olds who ever said 'Time for Tubby Bye-Byes' were drunken students, so you will not find that particular quotation in here.

One quotation you will find, a quotation that no one else has until the next dictionary of quotations comes along, is Jeremy Paxman's question to Henry Kissinger (see POLITICS), which resulted in Kissinger's flight from a BBC studio in late June 1999. It's not here because we like Jeremy Paxman and we don't like Henry Kissinger, though that thought may well occur to you (note that Dr Kissinger's own thoughts can be found in ARMY, POLITICS and POWER). It's here because it's a question most of us, left or right, would like answered, and it's expressed in a way that is memorable and to our liking.

Apart from recent quotations, we have also, as a result of our continual revision process, included some gems which should have been in our quotation corpus a long time ago, from the movie *Get Carter* (see EYES), to the humble army attorney Joseph Welch's astounding outburst against Joseph McCarthy (which effectively ended McCarthy's career; see POLITICIANS). If these are the sort of quotations you like, then you'll love the *Collins Quotation Finder* – it's a book designed for you.

Edwin Moore
Managing Editor

ACKNOWLEDGEMENTS

The Publishers would like to give special thanks to Callum Brines, Alice Goldie and Hazel Mills for their sterling work in the compilation of this dictionary.

A

ABSENCE

ASHFORD, Daisy (1881–1972)
My life will be sour grapes and ashes without you.

[*The Young Visiters* (1919)]

BEHAN, Brendan (1923–1964)
When I came back to Dublin, I was courtmartialled in my absence and sentenced to death in my absence, so I said they could shoot me in my absence.

[*The Hostage* (1958)]

CLOUGH, Arthur Hugh (1819–1861)
That out of sight is out of mind
Is true of most we leave behind.

[*Songs in Absence* (1849)]

LA ROCHEFOUCAULD (1613–1680)
L'absence diminue les médiocres passions, et augmente les grandes, comme le vent éteint les bougies, et allume le feu.
Absence diminishes mediocre passions and increases great ones, as the wind extinguishes candles and kindles fire.

[*Maximes*, (1678)]

NORTON, Caroline (1808–1877)
I do not love thee! – no! I do not love thee!
And yet when thou art absent I am sad;
And envy even the bright blue sky above thee,
Whose quiet stars may see thee and be glad.

[*The Sorrows of Rosalie* (1829)]

SHAH, Idries (1924–)
A certain person may have, as you say, a wonderful presence: I do not know. What I do know is that he has a perfectly delightful absence.

[*Reflections*]

See SEPARATION

ACCIDENTS

ARNO, Peter (1904–1968)
Well, back to the old drawing board.

[*The New Yorker*, caption to cartoon of designers walking away from crashed plane]

CHESTERFIELD, Lord (1694–1773)
The chapter of knowledge is very short, but the chapter of accidents is a very long one.

[Letter to Solomon Dayrolles, 1753]

COREN, Alan (1938–)
The Act of God designation on all insurance policies; which means, roughly, that you cannot be insured for the accidents that are most likely to happen to you.

[*The Lady from Stalingrad Museum* (1977)]

GRAHAM, Harry (1874–1936)
'There's been an accident!' they said,
'Your servant's cut in half; he's dead!'
'Indeed!' said Mr Jones, 'and please
Send me the half that's got my keys.'

[*Ruthless Rhymes for Heartless Homes* (1899)]

MARQUIS, Don (1878–1937)
now and then
there is a person born
who is so unlucky
that he runs into accidents
which started out to happen
to somebody else.

[*archys life of mehitabel* (1933)]

MCGONAGALL, William (c.1830–1902)
Beautiful Railway Bridge of the Silv'ry Tay!
Alas, I am very sorry to say
That ninety lives have been taken away
On the last Sabbath day of 1879,
Which will be remember'd for a very long time.

['The Tay Bridge Disaster' (1890)]

POTTER, Beatrix (1866–1943)
You may go into the field or down the lane,

but don't go into Mr McGregor's garden: your Father had an accident there; he was put in a pie by Mrs McGregor.

[*The Tale of Peter Rabbit* (1902)]

PUNCH

What is better than presence of mind in a railway accident? Absence of body.

[1849]

SIMPSON, N.F. (1919–)

Knocked down a doctor? With an ambulance? How could she? It's a contradiction in terms!

[*One-Way Pendulum* (1960)]

SMOLLETT, Tobias (1721–1771)

I have met with so many axidents, suprisals, and terrifications, that I am in a pafeck fantigo, and I believe I shall never be my own self again.

[*The Expedition of Humphry Clinker* (1771)]

WILKES, John (1727–1797)

The chapter of accidents is the longest chapter in the book.

[Attr.]

See ADVERSITY; CHANCE

ACHIEVEMENT

CONFUCIUS (c.550–c.478 BC)

Our greatest glory is not in never falling, but in rising every time we fall.

[*Analects*]

HUXLEY, Aldous (1894–1963)

Those who believe that they are exclusively in the right are generally those who achieve something.

[*Proper Studies* (1927)]

LONGFELLOW, Henry Wadsworth (1807–1882)

Let us, then, be up and doing,
With a heart for any fate;
Still achieving, still pursuing,
Learn to labour and to wait.

['A Psalm of Life' (1838)]

The heights by great men reached and kept
Were not attained by sudden flight,
But they, while their companions slept,
Were toiling upward in the night.

['The Ladder of Saint Augustine' (1850)]

STEVENSON, Robert Louis (1850–1894)

Is there anything in life so disenchanting as attainment?

[*New Arabian Nights* (1882)]

See SUCCESS

ACTING

BAYLIS, Lilian (1874–1937)

[On a less than adequate performance in *King Lear*]

Quite a sweet little Goneril, don't you think?

[*The Guardian*,1976]

FIELDING, Henry (1707–1754)

He the best player! … Why, I could act as well as he himself. I am sure, if I had seen a ghost, I should have looked in the very same manner, and done just as he did … The king for my money! He speaks all his words distinctly, half as loud again as the other. Anybody may see he is an actor.

[*Tom Jones* (1749)]

GIELGUD, Sir John (1904–)

Being another character is more interesting than being yourself.

[Attr.]

HULL, Josephine (1886–1957)

Playing Shakespeare is very tiring. You never get to sit down, unless you're a King.

[In Cooper and Hartman, *Violets and Vinegar* (1980)]

LUNT, Alfred (1892–1977)

[On acting]

Speak in a loud clear voice and try not to bump into the furniture.

[In Halliwell, *Filmgoer's Book of Quotes* (1973)]

MOORE, George (1852–1933)

Acting is therefore the lowest of the arts, if it

is an art at all.

[*Impressions and Opinions* (1891)]

RICHARDSON, Sir Ralph (1902–1983)
The art of acting consists in keeping people from coughing.

[*The Observer*]

The most precious things in speech are pauses.

[Attr.]

SHAKESPEARE, William (1564–1616)
[On the power of acting]
He would drown the stage with tears,
And cleave the general ear with horrid speech;
Make mad the guilty, and appal the free,
Confound the ignorant, and amaze indeed
The very faculties of eyes and ears.

[*Hamlet*, II.ii]

SHERIDAN, Richard Brinsley (1751–1816)
Burleigh comes forward, shakes his head, and exit.
Sneer: He is very perfect indeed. Now pray, what did he mean by that?
Puff: Why, by that shake of the head, he gave you to understand that even though they had more justice in their cause and wisdom in their measures, yet, if there was not a greater spirit shown on the part of the people, the country would at last fall a sacrifice to the hostile ambition of the Spanish monarchy.
Sneer: The devil! – did he mean all that by shaking his head?
Puff: Every word of it. If he shook his head as I taught him.

[*The Critic* (1779)]

I wish, sir, you would practise this without me. I can't stay dying here all night.

[*The Critic* (1779)]

TERRY, Dame Ellen (1847–1928)
Imagination! imagination! I put it first years ago, when I was asked what qualities I thought necessary for success upon the stage.

[*The Story of My Life* (1933)]

ZE AMI (1363–1443)
In the act of imitation there is the level of no-imitation. When the act of imitation is perfectly accomplished and the actor becomes the thing itself, the actor will no longer have the desire to imitate.

[*Fúshi kaden* (1400–1418)]

See ACTORS; THEATRE

ACTION

AMIEL, Henri-Frédéric (1821–1881)
Action is but coarsened thought – thought become concrete, obscure, and unconscious.

[*Journal*,1850]

ARISTOTLE (384–322 BC)
Our actions determine our dispositions.

[*Nicomachean Ethics*]

BEERBOHM, Sir Max (1872–1956)
Anything that is worth doing has been done frequently. Things hitherto undone should be given, I suspect, a wide berth.

[*Mainly on the Air* (1946)]

CANETTI, Elias (1905–1994)
Was immer ihre Tätigkeit ist, die Tätigen halten sich für besser.
Whatever their activity is, the active think they are better.

[*The Human Province* (1969)]

CARLYLE, Thomas (1795–1881)
The end of man is an Action and not a Thought, though it were the noblest.

[*Sartor Resartus* (1834)]

CERNUDA, Luis (1902–1963)
¿Es toda acción humana, como estimas ahora,
Fruto de imitación y de inconsciencia?
Is every human action, as you now think,
The fruit of imitation and thoughtlessness?

[*La realidad y el deseo*, 1964)]

CHESTERFIELD, Lord (1694–1773)

It is an undoubted truth, that the less one has to do, the less time one finds to do it in. One yawns, one procrastinates, one can do it when one will, and therefore one seldom does it at all.

[Letter]

CONFUCIUS (c.550–c.478 BC)

Chi Wen Tzu always thought three times before taking action. Twice would have been quite enough.

[Analects]

CORNFORD, F.M. (1874–1943)

Every public action which is not customary, either is wrong or, if it is right, is a dangerous precedent. It follows that nothing should ever be done for the first time.

[Microcosmographia Academica (1908)]

DE GAULLE, Charles (1890–1970)

Deliberation is the work of many men. Action, of one alone.

[War Memoirs]

ELIOT, George (1819–1880)

Our deeds determine us, as much as we determine our deeds.

[Adam Bede (1859)]

EMERSON, Ralph Waldo (1803–1882)

The manly part is to do with might and main what you can do.

[Conduct of Life (1860)]

We are taught by great actions that the universe is the property of every individual in it.

[Nature (1836)]

The reward of a thing well done, is to have done it.

['New England Reformers' (1844)]

FLETCHER, John (1579–1625)

Deeds, not words shall speak me.

[The Lover's Progress (1647)]

GIDE, André (1869–1951)

M'est avis ... que le profit n'est pas toujours ce qui mène l'homme; qu'il y a des actions désintéressées.

... Par désintéressé j'entends: gratuit. Et que le mal, ce que l'on appelle: le mal, peut être aussi gratuit que le bien.

I believe ... that profit is not always what motivates man; that there are disinterested actions. ... By disinterested I mean: gratuitous. And that evil acts, what people call evil, can be as gratuitous as good acts.

[Les Caves du Vatican, (1914)]

HAZLITT, William (1778–1830)

We never do anything well till we cease to think about the manner of doing it.

[Atlas (1830)]

HERBERT, Sir A.P. (1890–1971)

Let's find out what everyone is doing,
And then stop everyone from doing it.

[Ballads for Broadbrows (1930)]

HUXLEY, T.H. (1825–1895)

The great end of life is not knowledge but action.

[Science and Culture (1877)]

JOWETT, Benjamin (1817–1893)

The way to get things done is not to mind who gets the credit for doing them.

[Attr.]

KANT, Immanuel (1724–1804)

Ich soll niemals anders verfahren als so, dass ich auch wollen könne, meine Maxime solle ein allgemeines Gesetz werden.

I should always act in such a way that I may want my maxim to become a general law.

[Outline of the Metaphysics of Morals (1785)]

KEMPIS, Thomas á (c.1380–1471)

Certe adveniente die iudicii non quaeretur a nobis quid legimus sed quid fecimus.

Truly, when the day of judgement comes, it will not be a question of what we have read, but what we have done.

[De Imitatione Christi (1892)]

LA ROCHEFOUCAULD (1613–1680)

Nous aurions souvent honte de nos plus belles actions, si le monde voyait les motifs qui les produisent.

We would often be ashamed of our finest

actions if the world could see the motives behind them.

[*Maximes* (1678)]

PÉREZ GALDOS, Benito (1843–1920)

El hombre de pensamiento descubre la Verdad; pero quien goza de ella y utiliza sus celestiales dones es el hombre de acción.

The man of reflection discovers Truth; but the one who enjoys it and makes use of its heavenly gifts is the man of action.

[*Friend Manso* (1882)]

SHAW, George Bernard (1856–1950)

Activity is the only road to knowledge.

[*Man and Superman* (1903)]

SHENSTONE, William (1714–1763)

People in high or in distinguished life ought to have a greater circumspection in regard to their most trivial actions. For instance, I saw Mr Pope … to the best of my memory, he was picking his nose.

[*The Selected Works in Verse and Prose of William Shenstone* (1770)]

SPINOZA, Baruch (1632–1677)

Sedula curavi, humanas actiones non ridere, non lugere, neque detestare, sed intelligere.

I have taken great care not to laugh at human actions, not to weep at them, nor to hate them, but to understand them.

[*Tractatus Politicus* (1677)]

SZASZ, Thomas (1920–)

Men are rewarded and punished not for what they do, but rather for how their acts are defined. This is why men are more interested in better justifying themselves than in better behaving themselves.

[*The Second Sin* (1973)]

TAWNEY, R.H. (1880–1962)

It is a commonplace that the characteristic virtue of Englishmen is their power of sustained practical activity, and their characteristic vice a reluctance to test the quality of that activity by reference to principles.

[*The Acquisitive Society* (1921)]

WHITEFIELD, George (1714–1770)

I had rather wear out than rust out.

[Attr.]

ACTORS

ANONYMOUS

[On a performance of Cleopatra by Sarah Bernhardt]

How different, how very different from the home life of our own dear Queen!

[Remark]

Totus mundus agit histrionem.

The whole world plays the actor.

[Motto of Globe playhouse]

BENCHLEY, Robert (1889–1945)

[Suggesting an epitaph for an actress]

She sleeps alone at last.

[Attr.]

BERNHARDT, Sarah (1844–1923)

For the theatre one needs long arms; it is better to have them too long than too short. An artiste with short arms can never, never make a fine gesture.

[Attr.]

BETTERTON, Thomas (1635–1710)

[Reply to the Archbishop of Canterbury]

Actors speak of things imaginary as if they were real, while you preachers too often speak of things real as if they were imaginary.

[Attr.]

BRANDO, Marlon (1924–)

An actor's a guy who, if you ain't talking about him, ain't listening.

[*The Observer*, 1956]

BROWN, John Mason (1900–1969)

[On Tallulah Bankhead's performance as Shakespeare's Cleopatra in 1937]

Tallulah Bankhead barged down the Nile last night and sank. As the Serpent of the Nile she proves to be no more dangerous than a garter snake.

[In *Current Biography* (1941)]

CAMPBELL, Mrs Patrick (1865–1940)

Watching Tallulah Bankhead on stage is like watching somebody skating over very thin ice – and the English want to be there when she falls through.

[In Gavin Lambert, *On Cukor*]

COLERIDGE, Samuel Taylor (1772–1834)

[Of Edmund Kean]
To see him act is like reading Shakespeare by flashes of lightning.

[*Table Talk* (1835)]

COWARD, Sir Noël (1899–1973)

[Comment on a child star, in a long-winded play]
Two things should be cut: the second act and the child's throat.

[In Richards, *The Wit of Noël Coward*]

DILLER, Phyllis (1917–1974)

[Of Arnold Schwarzenegger]
He has so many muscles that he has to make an appointment to move his fingers.

[Attr.]

DUNDY, Elaine (1927–)

The question actors most often get asked is how they can bear saying the same things over and over again night after night, but God knows the answer to that is, don't we all anyway; might as well get paid for it.

[*The Dud Avocado* (1958)]

FIELD, Eugene (1850–1895)

[Of Creston Clarke as *King Lear*]
He played the King as though under momentary apprehension that someone else was about to play the ace.

[Attr.]

FORD, John (1895–1973)

It is easier to get an actor to be a cowboy than to get a cowboy to be an actor.

[Attr.]

GOLDSMITH, Oliver (c.1728–1774)

[Of Garrick]
Here lies David Garrick, describe me who can,
An abridgment of all that was pleasant in man ...
On the stage he was natural, simple, affecting,
'Twas only that, when he was off, he was acting ...
He cast off his friends as a huntsman his pack,
For he knew, when he pleased, he could whistle them back.

['Retaliation' (1774)]

HITCHCOCK, Alfred (1899–1980)

I deny that I ever said that actors are cattle. What I said was, 'Actors should be treated like cattle'.

[Attr.]

Nobody can really like an actor.

[*The New Yorker*, 1992]

HOPPER, Hedda (1890–1966)

At one time I thought he wanted to be an actor. He had certain qualifications, including no money and a total lack of responsibility.

[*From Under My Hat* (1953)]

JOHNSON, Samuel (1709–1784)

Players, Sir! I look upon them as no better than creatures set upon tables and joint stools to make faces and produce laughter, like dancing dogs.

[In Boswell, *The Life of Samuel Johnson* (1791)]

[To Garrick]
I'll come no more behind your scenes, David: for the silk stockings and white bosoms of your actresses excite my amorous propensities.

[In Boswell, *The Life of Samuel Johnson* (1791)]

KAUFMAN, George S. (1889–1961)

[On Raymond Massey's interpretation of Abraham Lincoln]
Massey won't be satisfied until somebody assassinates him.

[In Meredith, *George S. Kaufman and the Algonquin Round Table* (1974)]

LANCHESTER, Elsa (1902–1986)

[Of Maureen O'Hara]
She looked as though butter wouldn't melt in her mouth – or anywhere else.

[Attr.]

LEVANT, Oscar (1906–1972)

Romance on the High Seas was Doris Day's first picture; that was before she became a virgin.

[*Memoirs of an Amnesiac* (1965)]

LLOYD, Robert (1733–1764)

Who teach the mind its proper face to scan,
And hold the faithful mirror up to man.

['The Actor']

MALOUF, David (1934–)

Actors don't pretend to be other people; they become themselves by finding other people inside them.

[*Harland's Half Acre* (1984)]

OLIVIER, Laurence, Baron (1907–1989)

[To Dustin Hoffman, who had stayed up all night to play a character in the film *Marathon Man* (1976) who had stayed up all night]
Why not try acting? It's much easier.

PARKER, Dorothy (1893–1967)

[Remark on a performance by Katherine Hepburn]
She ran the whole gamut of the emotions from A to B.

[In Carey, *Katherine Hepburn* (1985)]

Scratch an actor and you'll find an actress.

[Attr.]

SHAKESPEARE, William (1564–1616)

Like a dull actor now,
I have forgot my part and I am out,
Even to a full disgrace.

[*Coriolanus*, V.iii]

TREE, Sir Herbert Beerbohm (1853–1917)

[Directing a group of sophisticated actresses]
Ladies, just a little more virginity, if you don't mind.

[In H. Teichmann, *Smart Aleck*]

WARHOL, Andy (c.1926–1987)

[Of James Dean]
He is not our hero because he was perfect. He is our hero because he perfectly represented the damaged and beautiful soul of our time.

[In Brandreth, *Great Theatrical Disasters*]

WILDE, Oscar (1854–1900)

[Referring to Beerbohm Tree's unconscious adoption of some of the mannerisms of a character he was playing in one of Wilde's plays]
Ah, every day dear Herbert becomes *de plus en plus Oscarié*. It is a wonderful case of nature imitating art.

WILLIAMSON, Nicol (1938–)

[Of Sean Connery]
Guys like him and Caine talk about acting as if they knew what it was.

[Interview, Daily *Mail*,1996]

WINCHELL, Walter (1897–1972)

[Referring to a show starring Earl Carroll]
I saw it at a disadvantage – the curtain was up.

[In Whiteman, *Come to Judgement*]

See ACTING; THEATRE

ADDICTION

BANKHEAD, Tallulah (1903–1968)

Cocaine isn't habit-forming. I know, because I've been taking it for years.

[Attr.]

JUNG, Carl Gustav (1875–1961)

Jede Form von Süchtigkeit ist von übel, gleichgültig, ob es sich um Alkohol oder Morphium oder Idealismus handelt.
Every form of addiction is a bad thing, irrespective of whether it is to alcohol, morphine or idealism.

[*Memories, Dreams, Thoughts* (1962)]

ADULTERY

AUSTEN, Jane (1775–1817)

I am proud to say that I have a very good eye at an Adultress, for tho' repeatedly assured that another in the same party was the She, I fixed upon the right one from the first.

[Letter to Cassandra Austen, 1801]

BENCHLEY, Robert (1889–1945)

[Comment on an office shared with Dorothy Parker]

One cubic foot less of space and it would have constituted adultery.

[Attr.]

BYRON, Lord (1788–1824)

What men call gallantry, and gods adultery,
Is much more common where the climate's sultry.

[*Don Juan* (1824)]

Merely innocent flirtation.
Not quite adultery, but adulteration.

[*Don Juan* (1824)]

CARTER, Jimmy (1924–)

I've looked on a lot of women with lust. I've committed adultery in my heart many times. God recognizes I will do this and forgives me.

[Interview with *Playboy*,1976]

CARY, Joyce (1888–1957)

Sara could commit adultery at one end and weep for her sins at the other, and enjoy both operations at once.

[*The Horse's Mouth* (1944)]

DRING, Philip (1924–)

[Preacher of the Assembly of God Mission]

I may commit adultery again if God moves me to it.

[*The Observer*,1980]

HUXLEY, Aldous (1894–1963)

There are few who would not rather be taken in adultery than in provincialism.

[*Antic Hay* (1923)]

JOHN PAUL II (1920–)

Adultery in your heart is committed not only when you look with excessive sexual desire at a woman who is not your wife, but also if you look in the same manner at your wife.

[*The Observer*,1990]

MAUGHAM, William Somerset (1874–1965)

You know, of course, that the Tasmanians, who never committed adultery, are now

extinct.

[*The Bread-Winner*]

RICHELIEU, Duc de (1766–1822)

[On discovering his wife with her lover]

Madame, you must really be more careful. Suppose it had been someone else who found you like this.

[In Wallechinsky, *The Book of Lists* (1977)]

SHAKESPEARE, William (1564–1616)

Adultery?
Thou shalt not die. Die for adultery? No.
The wren goes to't, and the small gilded fly
Does lecher in my sight.
Let copulation thrive.

[*King Lear*, IV.vi]

See MARRIAGE; SEX

ADULTS

BEAUVOIR, Simone de (1908–1986)

Qu'est-ce qu'un adulte? Un enfant gonflé d'âge.
What is an adult? A child blown up by age.

[*The Woman Destroyed* (1969)]

HARRIS, Sydney J. (1917–)

We have not passed that subtle line between childhood and adulthood until we move from the passive voice to the active voice – that is, until we have stopped saying 'It got lost', and say, 'I lost it'.

[Attr.]

MILLAY, Edna St Vincent (1892–1950)

Was it for this I uttered prayers,
And sobbed and cursed and kicked the stairs,
That now, domestic as a plate,
I should retire at half-past eight?

['Grown-up' (1920)]

ROSTAND, Jean (1894–1977)

Etre adulte, c'est être seul.
To be an adult is to be alone.

[*Thoughts of a Biologist* (1939)]

SHAKESPEARE, William (1564–1616)

Your lordship, though not clean past your

youth, hath yet some smack of age in you, some relish of the saltness of time.

[*Henry IV, Part 2*, I.ii]

SZASZ, Thomas (1920–)

A child becomes an adult when he realizes that he has a right not only to be right but also to be wrong.

[*The Second Sin* (1973)]

ADVENTURE

CHURCHILL, Jennie Jerome (1854–1921)

… and we owe something to extravagance, for thrift and adventure seldom go hand in hand …

[*Pearson's*, 1915]

DUKES, Ashley (1885 –1959)

Adventure must be held in delicate fingers. It should be handled, not embraced. It should be sipped, not swallowed at a gulp.

[*The Man with a Load of Mischief* (1924)]

ADVERSITY

CARLYLE, Thomas (1795–1881)

Adversity is sometimes hard upon a man; but for one man who can stand prosperity, there are a hundred that will stand adversity.

[*On Heroes, Hero-Worship, and the Heroic in History* (1841)]

CHAUCER, Geoffrey (c.1340–1400)

For of fortunes sharpe adversitee
The worste kynde of infortune is this,
A man to han ben in prosperitee,
And it remembren, whan it passed is.

[*Troilus and Criseyde*, III]

ADVERTISING

DOUGLAS, Norman (1868–1952)

You can tell the ideals of a nation by its advertisements.

[*South Wind* (1917)]

HUXLEY, Aldous (1894–1963)

It is far easier to write ten passably effective Sonnets, good enough to take in the not too inquiring critic, than one effective advertisement that will take in a few thousand of the uncritical buying public.

[*On the Margin* (1923)]

JEFFERSON, Thomas (1743–1826)

Advertisements contain the only truths to be relied on in a newspaper.

[Letter, 1819]

JOHNSON, Samuel (1709–1784)

Promise, large promise, is the soul of an advertisement.

[*The Idler* (1758–1760)]

LEACOCK, Stephen (1869–1944)

Advertising may be described as the science of arresting the human intelligence long enough to get money from it.

[In Prochow, *The Public Speaker's Treasure Chest*]

LEVERHULME, Viscount (1851–1925)

Half the money I spend on advertising is wasted, and the trouble is I don't know which half.

[In Ogilvy, *Confessions of an Advertising Man* (1963)]

MCDERMOTT, John W. (1937–)

Ninety-Mile Beach was obviously named by one of New Zealand's first advertising copywriters … It is fifty-six miles long.

[*How to Get Lost and Found in New Zealand* (1976)]

MCLUHAN, Marshall (1911–1980)

Ads are the cave art of the twentieth century.

[*Culture Is Our Business* (1970)]

NASH, Ogden (1902–1971)

I think that I shall never see
A billboard lovely as a tree.
Indeed, unless the billboards fall
I'll never see a tree at all.

['Song of the Open Road' (1933)]

Beneath this slab
John Brown is stowed.
He watched the ads,
And not the road.

['Lather as You Go' (1942]

ADVICE

ADAMS, Douglas (1952–)
Don't panic.

[*The Hitch Hiker's Guide to the Galaxy* (1979)]

ADDISON, Joseph (1672–1719)
A woman seldom asks advice before she has bought her wedding clothes.

[*The Spectator*, September 1712]

AUDEN, W.H. (1907–1973)
Read *The New Yorker*, trust in God;
And take short views.

[*Collected Poems, 1939–1947*]

AVERY, Oswald Theodore (1877–1955)
Whenever you fall, pick up something.

[Attr.]

BIERCE, Ambrose (1842–c.1914)
Advice: The smallest current coin.

[*The Cynic's Word Book* (1906)]

BISMARCK, Prince Otto von (1815–1898)
To youth I have but three words of counsel – work, work, work.

[Attr.]

BORROW, George (1803–1881)
Fear God, and take your own part.

[*The Romany Rye* (1857)]

BURTON, Robert (1577–1640)
Who cannot give good counsel? 'tis cheap, it costs them nothing.

[*Anatomy of Melancholy* (1621)]

CHESTERFIELD, Lord (1694–1773)
In matters of religion and matrimony I never give any advice; because I will not have anybody's torments in this world or the next laid to my charge.

[Letter to A.C. Stanhope, 1765]

Advice is seldom welcome; and those who want it the most, always like it the least.

[Letter to his son, 1748]

COLLINS, John Churton (1848–1908)
To ask advice is in nine cases out of ten to tout for flattery.

[In L.C. Collins, *Life of John Churton Collins* (1912)]

EDWARD VIII (later Duke of Windsor) (1894–1972)
Perhaps one of the only positive pieces of advice that I was ever given was that supplied by an old courtier who observed: 'Only two rules really count. Never miss an opportunity to relieve yourself; never miss a chance to sit down and rest your feet.'

[*A King's Story* (1951)]

EMERSON, Ralph Waldo (1803–1882)
It was a high counsel that I once heard given to a young person, – 'Always do what you are afraid to do.'

[*Essays, First Series* (1841)]

GAY, John (1685–1732)
Can Love be controll'd by advice?

[*The Beggar's Opera* (1728)]

GROENING, Matt
[Instruction in Homer Simpson's brain to Homer during communal crisis]
Keep looking shocked and move slowly towards the cakes.

[*The Simpsons*, TV cartoon series]

HARRIS, George (1844–1922)
[In his address to students at the beginning of a new academic year]
I intended to give you some advice but now I remember how much is left over from last year unused.

[In Braude, *Braude's Second Encyclopedia* (1957)]

LA ROCHEFOUCAULD (1613–1680)
On ne donne rien si libéralement que ses conseils.
One gives nothing so generously as advice.

[*Maximes* (1678)]

PYTHAGORAS
Abstain from beans.

RUNCIE, Robert (1921–)
[On his discussions with the Prince and Princess of Wales prior to marrying them]
My advice was delicately poised between the

cliché and the indiscretion.

[*The Times*, 1981]

SMITH, Sydney (1771–1845)

Take short views, hope for the best, and trust in God.

[In Holland, *A Memoir of the Reverend Sydney Smith* (1855)]

SORKIN, Aaron

Walk softly and carry an armoured tank division, I always say.

[*A Few Good Men*, film, 1992]

STEINBECK, John (1902–1968)

No one wants advice – only corroboration.

[Attr.]

SULLIVAN, Annie (1866–1936)

It's queer how ready people always are with advice in any real or imaginary emergency, and no matter how many times experience has shown them to be wrong, they continue to set forth their opinions, as if they had received them from the Almighty!

[Letter, 1887]

THACKERAY, William Makepeace (1811–1863)

They tell me not to drink, and I do drink … They tell me not to eat, and I do eat.

[*The Letters and Private Papers of William Makepeace Thackeray* (1946)]

THOREAU, Henry David (1817–1862)

I have lived some thirty years on this planet, and I have yet to hear the first syllable of valuable or even earnest advice from my seniors.

[*Walden* (1854)]

WELLINGTON, Duke of (1769–1852)

[Advice when asked by Queen Victoria how to remove sparrows from the Crystal Palace]
Sparrowhawks, Ma'am.

[Attr.]

WEST, Nathaniel (1903–1940)

Are you in trouble? Do you need advice? Write to Miss Lonelyhearts and she will help.

[*Miss Lonelyhearts* (1933)]

AFRICA

Malcolm X (1925–1965)

The soul of Africa is still reflected in the music played by the black man. In everything else we do we still are African in color, feeling, everything. And we will always be that whether we like it or not.

[Speech, Harvard Law School, 1964]

PLINY THE ELDER (AD 23–79)

Ex Africa semper aliquid novi.
There is always something new out of Africa.

[*Historia Naturalis*]

PLOMER, William (1903–1973)

Men being absent, Africa is good.

['The Wild Doves at Louis Trichardt' (1960)]

Africa is not the white man's country.

[*Turbott Wolfe* (1926)]

VAN DER POST, Sir Laurens (1906–1996)

Africa has always walked in my mind proudly upright, an African giant among the other continents, toes well dug into the final ocean of one hemisphere, rising to its full height in the greying skies of the other; head and shoulders broad, square and enduring, making light of the bagful of blue Mediterranean slung over its back as it marches patiently through time.

[*Flamingo Feather* (1955)]

THE AFTERLIFE

BECKETT, Samuel (1906–1989)

Clov: Do you believe in the life to come?
Hamm: Mine was always that.

[*Endgame*]

COWARD, Sir Noël (1899–1973)

We have no reliable guarantee that the afterlife will be any less exasperating than this one, have we?

[*Blithe Spirit* (1941)]

GREGORY, Lady Isabella Augusta (1852–1932)

I believe we shall meet again after death …
but if we don't you will have the worst of it,
for you can't say anything to me, and if we
do, I will say 'I told you so!'.

[In Mary-Lou Kohfeldt, *Lady Gregory* (1985)]

SHINRAN (1173–1263)

Even good people achieve their rebirth in
the Land of Perfect Bliss; then how much
more so should the case be with evil
persons!

[*Tannishó* (c. 1290)]

See DEATH; HEAVEN

AGE

ADAMS, John Quincy (1767–1848)

I inhabit a weak, frail, decayed tenement;
battered by the winds and broken in on by
the storms, and, from all I can learn, the
landlord does not intend to repair.

[Attr.]

ADENAUER, Konrad (1876–1967)

[To his doctor]
I haven't asked you to make me young again.
All I want is to go on getting older.

[Attr.]

ALLEN, Dave (1936–)

I still think of myself as I was 25 years ago.
Then I look in a mirror and see an old bastard
and I realise it's me.

[*The Independent*, 1993]

ALLEN, Woody (1935–)

I recently turned sixty. Practically a third of
my life is over.

[*The Observer Review*, 1996]

ANONYMOUS

In ancient times a woman was considered
old at the age of forty. Today a woman of
that age is only twenty-nine.

ARISTOPHANES (c.445–385 BC)

Old age is a second childhood.

[*Clouds*, 1417]

ARNOLD, Matthew (1822–1888)

I am past thirty, and three parts iced over.

[Letter to A.H. Clough, 1853]

AUBER, Daniel François Esprit (1782–1871)

Ageing seems to be the only available way to
live a long time.

[Attr.]

BAINBRIDGE, Beryl (1934–)

The older one becomes the quicker the
present fades into sepia and the past looms
up in glorious technicolour.

[*The Observer*, 1998]

BARUCH, Bernard M. (1870–1965)

I will never be an old man. To me, old age is
always fifteen years older than I am.

[*The Observer*,1955]

BINYON, Laurence (1869–1943)

They shall grow not old, as we that are left
grow old:
Age shall not weary them, nor the years
condemn.
At the going down of the sun and in the
morning
We will remember them.

['For the Fallen' (1914)]

BLAKE, Eubie (1883–1983)

[He died five days after his hundredth birthday]
If I'd known I was gonna live this long, I'd
have taken better care of myself.

[*The Observer*, 1983]

BRENAN, Gerald (1894–1987)

Old age takes away from us what we have
inherited and gives us what we have earned.

[*Thoughts in a Dry Season* (1978)]

BROWNING, Robert (1812–1889)

Grow old along with me!
The best is yet to be,
The last of life for which the first was made:
Our times are in His hand
Who saith, 'A whole I planned,
Youth shows but half; trust God: see all, nor
be afraid!'.

['Rabbi Ben Ezra' (1864)]

BUCK, Pearl S. (1892–1973)
Ah well, perhaps one has to be very old before one learns how to be amused rather than shocked.
[*China, Past and Present* (1972)]

BURKE, Edmund (1729–1797)
The arrogance of age must submit to be taught by youth.
[Letter to Fanny Burney, 1782]

BYRON, Lord (1788–1824)
What is the worst of woes that wait on age?
What stamps the wrinkle deeper on the brow?
To view each loved one blotted from life's page,
And be alone on earth, as I am now.
[*Childe Harold's Pilgrimage* (1818)]

I am ashes where once I was fire.
['To the Countess of Blessington' (1823)]

Years steal
Fire from the mind as vigour from the limb;
And life's enchanted cup but sparkles near the brim.
[*Childe Harold's Pilgrimage* (1818)]

CALMENT, Jeanne (1875–)
[Reply to someone who asked what she would like for her 121st birthday]
Respect.
[*The Mail on Sunday*,1996]

CAMPBELL, Joseph (1879–1944)
As a white candle
In a holy place,
So is the beauty
Of an aged face.
['The Old Woman' (1913)]

CARROLL, Lewis (1832–1898)
'You are old, Father William,' the young man said,
'And your hair has become very white;
And yet you incessantly stand on your head –
Do you think, at your age, it is right?'

'In my youth,' Father William replied to his son,

'I feared it might injure the brain;
But now that I'm perfectly sure I have none,
Why, I do it again and again.'
[*Alice's Adventures in Wonderland* (1865)]

CHEVALIER, Maurice (1888–1972)
I'm over eighty in a world where the young reject the old with more intensity than ever before … Now I'd like my old age to be my best performance. Death is the best exit.
[In Behr, *Thank Heaven for Little Girls* (1993)]

I prefer old age to the alternative.
[Attr.]

CHURCHILL, Charles (1731–1764)
Old-age, a second child, by Nature curs'd
With more and greater evils than the first,
Weak, sickly, full of pains; in ev'ry breath
Railing at life, and yet afraid of death.
[*Gotham* (1764)]

COLLINS, Mortimer (1827–1876)
A man is as old as he's feeling,
A woman as old as she looks.
['The Unknown Quantity']

COMPTON-BURNETT, Dame Ivy (1884–1969)
[Describing a certain woman's age]
Pushing forty? She's clinging on to it for dear life.
[Attr.]

DE RONSARD, Pierre (1524–1585)
Quand vous serez bien vieille, au soir á la chandelle,
Assise auprès du feu dévidant et filant,
Direz, chantant mes vers, en vous émerveillant,
Ronsard me célébrait du temps que j'étais belle.
When you are very old, at night, in the candle-light, sitting spinning by the fire, you will say as you sing my verses, marvelling, 'Ronsard sang of me in the time of my beauty.'
[*Sonnets pour Hélène* (1578)]

DEWEY, John (1859–1952)
It is strange that the one thing that every person looks forward to, namely old age, is the one thing for which no preparation is made.
[Attr.]

DISRAELI, Benjamin (1804–1881)

When a man fell into his anecdotage it was a sign for him to retire from the world.

[*Lothair* (1870)]

DRYDEN, John (1631–1700)

None would live past years again,
Yet all hope pleasure in what yet remain;
And, from the dregs of life, think to receive,
What the first sprightly running could not give.

[*Aureng-Zebe* (1675)]

EDMOND, James (1859–1933)

[Caption to a drawing of three women by Norman Lindsay]

We walk along the gas-lit street in a dreadful row, we three,
The woman I was, the woman I am, and the woman I'll one day be.

[In Moore, *The Story of Australian Art*]

ELIOT, T.S. (1888–1965)

I grow old … I grow old …
I shall wear the bottoms of my trousers rolled.

Shall I part my hair behind? Do I dare to eat a peach?
I shall wear white flannel trousers, and walk upon the beach.
I have heard the mermaids singing, each to each.
I do not think that they will sing to me.

['The Love Song of J. Alfred Prufrock' (1917)]

EMERSON, Ralph Waldo (1803–1882)

Old age brings along with its ugliness the comfort that you will soon be out of it, – which ought to be a substantial relief to such discontented pendulums as we are. To be out of the war, out of debt, out of the drouth, out of the blues, out of the dentist's hands, out of the second thoughts, mortifications, and remorses that inflict such twinges and shooting pains, – out of the next winter, and the high prices, and company below your ambition, – surely these are soothing hints.

[*Journals*, 1864]

Spring still makes spring in the mind,
When sixty years are told.

[*Poems* (1847)]

ESTIENNE, Henri (1531–1598)

Si jeunesse savoit; si vieillesse pouvoit.
If only youth knew; if only age could.

[*Les Prémices* (1594)]

FAIRBURN, A.R.D. (1904–1957)

The years have stolen
all her loveliness,
her days are fallen
in the long wet grass
like petals shaken
from the lilac's bosom.

[*Collected Poems* (1966)]

FRANKLIN, Benjamin (1706–1790)

At twenty years of age, the will reigns; at thirty, the wit; and at forty, the judgement.

[*Poor Richard's Almanac* (1741)]

GIBBON, Edward (1737–1794)

I must reluctantly observe that two causes, the abbreviation of time, and the failure of hope, will always tinge with a browner shade the evening of life.

[*Memoirs of My Life and Writings* (1796)]

GOGOL, Nicolai Vasilyevich (1809–1852)

Threatening, terrifying is oncoming old age, but nothing will reverse and return!

[*Dead Souls* (1835–1842)]

GOLDSMITH, Oliver (c.1728–1774)

I love every thing that's old: old friends, old times, old manners, old books, old wine.

[*She Stoops to Conquer* (1773)]

GONNE, Maud (1865–1953)

Oh how you hate old age – well so do I … but I, who am more a rebel against man than you, rebel less against nature, and accept the inevitable and go with it gently into the unknown.

[Letter to W.B. Yeats]

GRANT, Cary (1904–1986)

[Responding to a telegram received by his agent

inquiring: 'How old Cary Grant?']
'Old Cary Grant fine. How you?'.

[In Halliwell, *Filmgoer's Book of Quotes* (1973)]

HALL, Sir Peter (1930–)

We do not necessarily improve with age: for better or worse we become more like ourselves.

[*The Observer*, 1988]

HAMILTON, Elizabeth (1758–1816)

With expectation beating high,
Myself I now desired to spy;
And straight I in a glass surveyed
An antique lady, much decayed.

[In Sarah Hale, *Biography of Distinguished Women* (1876)]

HARRISON, Tony (1937–)

Perhaps with age I've learned to let go of things and people, not to possess or confine them.

[Attr.]

HILTON, James (1900–1954)

Anno domini … that's the most fatal complaint of all, in the end.

[*Goodbye, Mr Chips* (1934)]

HOLMES, Oliver Wendell (1809–1894)

For him in vain the envious seasons roll
Who bears eternal summer in his soul.

['The Old Player' (1861)]

To be seventy years young is sometimes far more cheerful and hopeful than to be forty years old.

['On the Seventieth Birthday of Julia Ward Howe' (1889)]

HOLMES, Oliver Wendell, Jr (1841–1935)

[At the age of 86, on seeing a pretty girl]
Oh, to be seventy again!

[In Fadiman, *The American Treasury*]

IRVING, Washington (1783–1859)

Whenever a man's friends begin to compliment him about looking young, he may be sure that they think he is growing old.

[*Bracebridge Hall* (1822)]

JAMES, Alice (1848–1892)

It is so comic to hear oneself called old, even at ninety I suppose!

[In Leon Edel (ed.), *The Diary of Alice James*, 1889]

JOHNSON, Samuel (1709–1784)

At seventy-seven it is time to be in earnest.

[*A Journey to the Western Islands of Scotland* (1775)]

There is a wicked inclination in most people to suppose an old man decayed in his intellects. If a young or middle-aged man, when leaving a company, does not recollect where he laid his hat, it is nothing; but if the same inattention is discovered in an old man, people will shrug up their shoulders, and say, 'His memory is going.'

[In Boswell, *The Life of Samuel Johnson* (1791)]

LANG, Andrew (1844–1912)

Our hearts are young 'neath wrinkled rind:
Life's more amusing than we thought.

['Ballade of Middle Age']

LARKIN, Philip (1922–1985)

Perhaps being old is having lighted rooms
Inside your head, and people in them, acting.
People you know, yet can't quite name.

['The Old Fools' (1974)]

LAURENCE, Margaret (1926–1987)

If, as you grow older, you feel you are also growing stupider, do not worry. This is normal, and usually occurs around the time when your children, now grown, are discovering the opposite – they now see that you aren't nearly as stupid as they had believed when they were young teenagers. Take heart from that.

[Address at Trent University, 1983, quoted in *The Globe and Mail*, 1989]

LENCLOS, Ninon de (1620–1705)

La vieillesse est l'enfer des femmes.
Old age is woman's hell.

[Attr.]

LLOYD, Harold (1893–1971)

[Reply when, aged 77, he was asked his age]
I am just turning forty and taking my time

about it.

[*The Times*, 1970]

MAUGHAM, William Somerset (1874–1965)

[Said on his ninetieth birthday]
I am sick of this way of life. The weariness and sadness of old age make it intolerable. I have walked with death in hand, and death's own hand is warmer than my own. I don't wish to live any longer.

[In M.B. Strauss, *Familiar Medical Quotations*]

From the earliest times the old have rubbed it into the young that they are wiser than they, and before the young had discovered what nonsense this was they were old too, and it profited them to carry on the imposture.

[*Cakes and Ale* (1930)]

MEIR, Golda (1898–1978)

Being seventy is not a sin.

[*Reader's Digest*, 1971]

MOLIÈRE (1622–1673)

L'âge amènera tout, et ce n'est pas le temps, Madame, comme on sait, d'être prude à vingt ans.
Everything comes with age, and everyone knows, Madame, that twenty is not the time to be a prude.

[*Le Misanthrope* (1666)]

NASH, Ogden (1902–1971)

I prefer to forget both pairs of glasses and pass my declining years
Saluting strange women and grandfather clocks.

[*The Private Dining Room and Other New Verses* (1952)]

Do you think my mind is maturing late,
Or simply rotted early?

['Lines on Facing Forty' (1942)]

NAYLOR, James Ball (1860–1945)

King David and King Solomon
Led merry, merry lives,
With many, many lady friends
And many, many wives;
But when old age crept over them,

With many, many qualms,
King Solomon wrote the Proverbs
And King David wrote the Psalms.

['King David and King Solomon' (1935)]

ORWELL, George (1903–1950)

At 50, everyone has the face he deserves.

[*Notebook*, 1949]

PARKES, Sir Henry (1815–1896)

[On being congratulated when he was eighty years old on the birth of his last child]
Don't say my last, you damned fool! Say my latest.

[In Randolph Bedford, *Naught to Thirty-three*]

PATERSON, Jennifer (1928?–)

At 70, I'm in fine fettle for my age, sleep like a babe and feel around 12. The secret? Lots of meat, drink and cigarettes and not giving in to things.

[*The Times*, 1998]

PATTEN, Brian (1946–)

Mr Old Age, would catch you in his deadly trap
And come finally to polish you off,
His machine-gun dripping with years.

['where are you now, Batman?']

PATTISON, Ian (1950–)

Rab C. Nesbitt: I hate middle age. Too young for the bowling green, too old for Ecstasy.

[*Rab C. Nesbitt*, television series]

PEELE, George (c.1558–c.1597)

His golden locks time hath to silver turn'd;
O time too swift, O swiftness never ceasing!
His youth 'gainst time and age hath ever spurn'd
But spurn'd in vain; youth waneth by increasing:
Beauty, strength, youth, are flowers but fading seen;
Duty, faith, love, are roots, and ever green.

His helmet now shall make a hive for bees,
And, lovers' sonnets turn'd to holy psalms,
A man-at-arms must now serve on his knees,
And feed on prayers, which are age his alms:

But though from court to cottage he depart,
His saint is sure of his unspotted heart …

Goddess, allow this aged man his right,
To be your beadsman now that was your
knight.

['Sonnet. A Farewell to Arms'
(1590)]

PHILLIPS, Stephen (1864–1915)
A man not old, but mellow, like good wine.

[*Ulysses* (1902)]

PICASSO, Pablo (1881–1973)
Age only matters when one is ageing. Now
that I have arrived at a great age, I might just
as well be twenty.

[In J. Richardson, *The Observer, Shouts and
Murmurs*]

PINERO, Sir Arthur Wing (1855–1934)
From forty to fifty a man is at heart either a
stoic or a satyr.

[*The Second Mrs Tanqueray*
(1893)]

PITKIN, William B. (1878–1953)
Life Begins at Forty.

[Title of book, 1932]

POUND, Ezra (1885–1972)
One of the pleasures of middle age is to find
out that one WAS right, and that one was
much righter than one knew at say 17 or 23.

[*ABC of Reading* (1934)]

POWELL, Anthony (1905–)
Growing old is like being increasingly
penalized for a crime you haven't committed.

[*A Dance to the Music of Time* (1973)]

POWER, Marguerite, Countess of Blessington (1789–1849)
Tears fell from my eyes – yes, weak and
foolish as it now appears to me, I wept for my
departed youth; and for that beauty of which
the faithful mirror too plainly assured me, no
remnant existed.

[*The Confessions of an Elderly Lady*
(1838)]

REAGAN, Ronald (1911–)
[On his challenger, Walter Mondale, in the 1984
election campaign]
I will not make age an issue of this campaign.
I am not going to exploit for political
purposes my opponent's youth and
inexperience.

[TV debate, 1984]

I am delighted to be with you. In fact, at my
age, I am delighted to be anywhere.

[Speech at the Oxford Union, 1992]

REED, Henry (1914–1986)
As we get older we do not get any younger.
Seasons return, and today I am fifty-five,
And this time last year I was fifty-four,
And this time next year I shall be sixty-two.

['Chard Whitlow (Mr Eliot's Sunday Evening
Postscript)' (1941)]

REXFORD, Eben (1848–1916)
Darling, I am growing old,
Silver threads among the gold.

['Silver Threads Among the Gold' (1873)]

ROCHESTER, Earl of (1647–1680)
Ancient person, for whom I
All the flattering youth defy,
Long be it ere thou grow old,
Aching, shaking, crazy, cold;
But still continue as thou art,
Ancient person of my heart.

['A Song of a Young Lady to her Ancient Lover'
(1691)]

ROOSEVELT, Franklin Delano (1882–1945)
[After Churchill had congratulated him on his 60th
birthday]
It is fun to be in the same decade with you.

[In Winston S. Churchill, *The Hinge of Fate*]

RUBINSTEIN, Helena (c.1872–1965)
I have always felt that a woman has a right to
treat the subject of her age with ambiguity
until, perhaps, she passes into the realm of
over ninety. Then it is better she be candid
with herself and with the world.

[*My Life for Beauty* (1965)]

SAKI (1870–1916)

The young have aspirations that never come to pass, the old have reminiscences of what never happened. It's only the middle-aged who are really conscious of their limitations.

[*Reginald* (1904)]

SANTAYANA, George (1863–1952)

The young man who has not wept is a savage, and the old man who will not laugh is a fool.

[*Dialogues in Limbo* (1925)]

SARTON, May (1912–)

Old age is not an illness, it is a timeless ascent. As power diminishes, we grow toward the light.

[*Ms* magazine, 1982]

SATIE, Erik (1866–1925)

When I was young, I was told: 'You'll see, when you're fifty.' I am fifty and I haven't seen a thing.

[In Pierre-Daniel Templier, *Erik Satie*, 2, Letter to his brother]

SEXTON, Anne (1928–1974)

In a dream you are never eighty.

['Old' (1962)]

SHAKESPEARE, William (1564–1616)

Unregarded age in corners thrown.

[*As You Like It*, II.iii]

O, sir, you are old;
Nature in you stands on the very verge
Of her confine.

[*King Lear*, II.iv]

A good old man, sir, he will be talking; as they say 'When the age is in the wit is out.'

[*Much Ado About Nothing*, III.v]

That time of year thou mayst in me behold
When yellow leaves, or none, or few, do hang
Upon those boughs which shake against the cold,
Bare ruin'd choirs where late the sweet birds sang.
In me thou seest the twilight of such day
As after sunset fadeth in the west,

Which by and by black night doth take away,
Death's second self, that seals up all in rest.

[Sonnet 73]

Crabbed age and youth cannot live together:
Youth is full of pleasance, age is full of care ...

Age, I do abhor thee; youth, I do adore thee.

[*The Passionate Pilgrim*, xii]

SHAW, George Bernard (1856–1950)

Old men are dangerous: it doesn't matter to them what is going to happen to the world.

[*Heartbreak House* (1919)]

Every man over forty is a scoundrel.

[*Man and Superman* (1903)]

SMITH, Logan Pearsall (1865–1946)

There is more felicity on the far side of baldness than young men can possibly imagine.

['Last Words' (1933)]

SOLON (c.638–c.559 BC)

I grow old ever learning many things.

[In Bergk (ed.), *Poetae Lyrici Graeci*]

SOUTHEY, Robert (1774–1843)

You are old, Father William, the young man cried,
The few locks which are left you are grey;
You are hale, Father William, a hearty old man,
Now tell me the reason, I pray ...

In the days of my youth I remembered my God!
And He hath not forgotten my age.

['The Old Man's Comforts, and how he Gained them' (1799)]

SPARK, Muriel (1918–)

Being over seventy is like being engaged in a war. All our friends are going or gone and we survive amongst the dead and the dying as on a battlefield.

[*Memento Mori*]

SPARROW, John (1906–1992)

Chill on the brow and in the breast
The frost of years is spread –
Soon we shall take our endless rest
With the unfeeling dead.
Insensibly, ere we depart,
We grow more cold, more kind:
Age makes a winter in the heart,
An autumn in the mind.

['Grave Epigrams']

STEELE, Sir Richard (1672–1729)

There are so few who can grow old with a good grace.

[*The Spectator*, 263, 1712]

STEPHEN, James Kenneth (1859–1892)

Ah! Matt: old age has brought to me
Thy wisdom, less thy certainty:
The world's a jest, and joy's a trinket:
I knew that once: but now – I think it.

[*Lapsus Calami* (1891), 'Senex to Matt. Prior']

STEPHEN, James (1882–1950)

Men come of age at sixty, women at fifteen.

[*The Observer*, 1944]

STEVENSON, Robert Louis (1850–1894)

By the time a man gets well into the seventies his continued existence is a mere miracle.

[*Virginibus Puerisque* (1881)]

Our frailties are invincible, our virtues barren; the battle goes sore against us to the going down of the sun.

[*Across the Plains* (1892)]

STONE, I.F. (1907–1989)

If you live long enough, the venerability factor creeps in; you get accused of things you never did and praised for virtues you never had.

[In Laurence J. Peter, *Peter's Quotations*]

SWIFT, Jonathan (1667–1745)

Old men and comets have been reverenced for the same reason; their long beards, and pretences to foretell events.

[*Thoughts on Various Subjects* (1711)]

Every man desires to live long; but no man would be old.

[*Thoughts on Various Subjects* (1711)]

I'm as old as my tongue, and a little older than my teeth.

[*Polite Conversation* (1738)]

TALLEYRAND, Charles-Maurice de (1754–1838)

[Remark to young man who boasted that he did not play whist]
Quelle triste vieillesse vous vous préparez.
What a sad old age you are preparing for yourself.

[In J. Amédée Pichot, *Souvenirs intimes sur M. de Talleyrand* (1870)]

THOMAS, Dylan (1914–1953)

Do not go gentle into that good night,
Old age should burn and rave at close of day;
Rage, rage against the dying of the light.

['Do Not Go Gentle into that Good Night' (1952)]

TROTSKY, Leon (1879–1940)

Old age is the most unexpected of all the things that happen to a man.

[*Diary in Exile*, 8 May 1935]

TUCKER, Sophie (1884–1966)

[Asked, when 80, the secret of longevity]
Keep breathing.

[Attr.]

WALPOLE, Horace (1717–1797)

What has one to do, when one grows tired of the world, as we both do, but to draw nearer and nearer, and gently waste the remains of life with friends with whom one began it?

[Letter to George Montagu, 1765]

Old age is no such uncomfortable thing if one gives oneself up to it with a good grace, and doesn't drag it about 'To midnight dances and the public show'.

[Letter, 1774]

WEBB, Sidney (1859–1947)

Old people are always absorbed in something, usually themselves; we prefer to be absorbed in the Soviet Union.

[Attr.]

WHITE, Patrick (1912–1990)

The aged are usually tougher and more calculating than the young, provided they keep enough of their wits about them. How could they have lived so long if there weren't steel buried inside them?

[*The Eye of the Storm* (1973)]

WHITMAN, Walt (1819–1892)

Women sit or move to and fro, some old, some young.
The young are beautiful – but the old are more beautiful than the young.

['Beautiful Women' (1871)]

WILDE, Oscar (1854–1900)

One should never trust a woman who tells one her real age. A woman who would tell one that would tell one anything.

[*A Woman of No Importance* (1893)]

Mrs Allonby: I delight in men over seventy. They always offer one the devotion of a lifetime.

[*A Woman of No Importance* (1893)]

The old believe everything: the middle-aged suspect everything: the young know everything.

[*The Chameleon*,1894]

No woman should ever be quite accurate about her age. It looks so calculating.

[*The Importance of Being Earnest* (1895), IV]

WILLIAMS, William Carlos (1883–1963)

In old age
the mind
casts off
rebelliously
an eagle
from its crag.

[*Paterson* (1946–1958)]

WODEHOUSE, P.G. (1881–1975)

He was either a man of about a hundred and fifty who was rather young for his years or a man of about a hundred and ten who had

been aged by trouble.

[In Usborne, *Wodehouse at Work to the End* (1976)]

WORDSWORTH, William (1770–1850)

The wiser mind
Mourns less for what age takes away
Than what it leaves behind.

['The Fountain' (1800)]

YEATS, W.B. (1865–1939)

I thought no more was needed
Youth to prolong
Than dumb-bell and foil
To keep the body young.
O who could have foretold
That the heart grows old?

['A Song' 1918]

An aged man is but a paltry thing,
A tattered coat upon a stick, unless
Soul clap its hands and sing, and louder sing
For every tatter in its mortal dress.

['Sailing to Byzantium' (1927)]

You think it horrible that lust and rage
Should dance attention upon my old age;
They were not such a plague when I was young;
What else have I to spur me into song?

[In the *London Mercury*, 1938]

See LONGEVITY; MATURITY; YOUTH

AGREEMENT AND DISAGREEMENT

GIBRAN, Kahlil (1883–1931)

Disagreement may be the shortest cut between two minds.

[*Sand and Foam*]

HAMPTON, Christopher (1946–)

It's possible to disagree with someone about the ethics of non-violence without wanting to kick his face in.

[*Treats* (1976), Scene iv]

INGE, William Ralph (1860–1954)

It takes in reality only one to make a quarrel.

It is useless for the sheep to pass resolutions in favour of vegetarianism while the wolf remains of a different opinion.

[*Outspoken Essays: First Series* (1919)]

LA ROCHEFOUCAULD (1613–1680)

Nous ne trouvons guère de gens de bon sens que ceux qui sont de notre avis.

We rarely think people have good sense unless they agree with us.

[*Maximes*, (1678)]

SPAAK, Paul Henri (1899–1972)

[Concluding the first General Assembly meeting of the United Nations, 1946]

Our agenda is now exhausted. The secretary general is exhausted. All of you are exhausted. I find it comforting that, beginning with our very first day, we find ourselves in such complete unanimity.

WAUGH, Evelyn (1903–1966)

When Lord Copper was right he said, 'Definitely, Lord Copper'; when he was wrong, 'Up to a point'.

[*Scoop* (1938)]

WILDE, Oscar (1854–1900)

Ah! Don't say that you agree with me. When people agree with me I always feel that I must be wrong.

[*Intentions* (1891)]

AGRICULTURE

CRABBE, George (1754–1832)

Our farmers round, well pleased with constant gain,
Like other farmers, flourish and complain.

[*The Parish Register* (1807)]

DICKENS, Charles (1812–1870)

Cows are my passion.

[*Dombey and Son* (1848)]

GOLDSMITH, Oliver (c.1728–1774)

A time there was, ere England's griefs began,
When every rood of ground maintained its man;
For him light labour spread her wholesome store,

Just gave what life required, but gave no more.
His best companions, innocence and health;
And his best riches, ignorance of wealth.

[*The Deserted Village* (1770)]

RUSKIN, John (1819–1900)

Soldiers of the ploughshare as well as soldiers of the sword.

[*Unto this Last* (1862), Preface]

SWIFT, Jonathan (1667–1745)

And he gave it for his opinion, that whoever could make two ears of corn or two blades of grass to grow upon a spot of ground where only one grew before, would deserve better of mankind, and do more essential service to his country than the whole race of politicians put together.

[*Gulliver's Travels* (1726)]

THOMAS, Dylan (1914–1953)

This bread I break was once the oat,
This wine upon a foreign tree
Plunged in its fruit;
Man in the day or wind at night
Laid the crops low, broke the grape's joy.

['This bread I break' (1936)]

See COUNTRY

AIDS

ANNE, the Princess Royal (1950–)

It could be said that the Aids pandemic is a classic own-goal scored by the human race against itself.

[Remark, 1988]

ANONYMOUS

every time you sleep with a boy you sleep with all his old girlfriends.

[Government slogan, anti-Aids campaign, 1987]

CURRIE, Edwina (1946–)

My message to the businessmen of this country when they go abroad on business is that there is one thing above all they can take with them to stop them catching Aids, and that is the wife.

[*The Observer*, 1987]

ALCOHOL

AGA KHAN III (1877–1957)

[Justifying his liking for alcohol]
I'm so holy that when I touch wine, it turns
into water.

[Attr. in Compton Miller, *Who's Really Who* (1983)]

ALDRICH, Henry (1647–1710)

If all be true that I do think,
There are five reasons we should drink;
Good wine – a friend – or being dry –
Or lest we should be by and by –
Or any other reason why.

['Five Reasons for Drinking' (1689)]

ANONYMOUS

Hath wine an oblivious power?
Can it pluck out the sting from the brain?
The draught might beguile for an hour,
But still leaves behind it the pain.

['Farewell to England'; sometimes attr. to Byron]

[Menu translation]
Our wines leave you nothing to hope for.

[*The Times*, 1999]

ARCHPOET OF COLOGNE (fl. c.1205)

Meum est propositum in taberna mori,
ut sint vina proxima morientis ori.
Tunc cantabunt laetius angelorum chori:
'sit Deus propitius huic potatori!'
I am resolved to die in a tavern, so that wine
will be very near to my dying mouth. Then
the bands of angels will chant with greater
joy 'May God forgive this drinker.'

[*The Confession of Golias*]

BECON, Thomas (1512–1567)

For when the wine is in, the wit is out.

[*Catechism* (1560)]

BEHAN, Brendan (1923–1964)

I only take a drink on two occasions – when
I'm thirsty and when I'm not.

[In McCann, *The Wit of Brendan Behan*]

BELL, Ian (1881–1964)

There is no hangover on earth like the single
malt hangover. It roars in the ears, burns in
the stomach and sizzles in the brain like a
short circuit. Death is the easy way out.

[*The Observer*, 1991]

BELLOC, Hilaire (1870–1953)

Strong Brother in God and last Companion:
Wine.

[*Short Talks with the Dead and Others* (1926)]

BENCHLEY, Robert (1889–1945)

[Reply when asked if he realised that drinking was
a slow death]
So who's in a hurry?

[Attr.]

BENTLEY, Richard (1662–1742)

[Of claret]
It would be port if it could.

[Attr.]

BORROW, George (1803–1881)

Good ale, the true and proper drink of
Englishmen. He is not deserving of the name
of Englishman who speaketh against ale, that
is good ale.

[*Lavengro* (1851)]

BRIGID OF KILDARE (453–523)

I should like a great lake of ale
For the King of Kings.

[*The Feast of St Brigid of Kildare*]

BURNS, Robert (1759–1796)

Freedom and whisky gang thegither,
Tak aff your dram!

['The Author's Earnest Cry and Prayer'
(1786)]

BURTON, Robert (1577–1640)

I may not here omit those two main plagues,
and common dotages of human kind, wine
and women, which have infatuated and
besotted myriads of people. They go
commonly together.

[*Anatomy of Melancholy* (1621)]

CALVERLEY, C.S. (1831–1884)

The heart which grief hath canker'd

Hath one unfailing remedy – the Tankard.

['Beer' (1861)]

CHANDLER, Raymond (1888–1959)

Alcohol is like love: the first kiss is magic, the second is intimate, the third is routine. After that you just take the girl's clothes off.

[The Long Good-bye (1953)]

CHURCHILL, Sir Winston (1874–1965)

[Said during a lunch with the Arab leader Ibn Saud, when he heard that the king's religion forbade smoking and alcohol]
I must point out that my rule of life prescribed as an absolutely sacred rite smoking cigars and also the drinking of alcohol before, after, and if need be during all meals and in the intervals between them.

[Triumph and Tragedy]

CLARKE, Marcus (1846–1881)

No man has a right to inflict the torture of bad wine upon his fellow-creatures.

[The Peripatetic Philosopher (1867–1870)]

CONNOLLY, Billy (1942–)

A well-balanced person has a drink in each hand.

[Gullible's Travels]

COOPER, Derek (1925–)

[Highland saying]
One whisky is all right; two is too much; three is too few.

[A Taste of Scotch (1989)]

COPE, Wendy (1945–)

All you need is love, love
or, failing that, alcohol.

[Variation on a Lennon and McCartney song]

COREN, Alan (1938–)

Apart from cheese and tulips, the main product of the country [Holland] is advocaat, a drink made from lawyers.

[The Sanity Inspector (1974)]

CRABBE, George (1754–1832)

Lo! the poor toper whose untutor'd sense,
Sees bliss in ale, and can with wine dispense;
Whose head proud fancy never taught to

steer,
Beyond the muddy ecstasies of beer.

[Inebriety (1774)]

DE QUINCEY, Thomas (1785–1859)

It is most absurdly said, in popular language, of any man, that he is disguised in liquor; for, on the contrary, most men are disguised by sobriety.

[Confessions of an English Opium Eater (1822)]

DIBDIN, Charles (1745–1814)

Then trust me, there's nothing like drinking
So pleasant on this side the grave;
It keeps the unhappy from thinking,
And makes e'en the valiant more brave.

['Nothing like Grog']

DICKENS, Charles (1812–1870)

Bring in the bottled lightning, a clean tumbler, and a corkscrew.

[Nicholas Nickleby (1839)]

DISRAELI, Benjamin (1804–1881)

'I rather like bad wine,' said Mr Mountchesney; 'one gets so bored with good wine.'

[Sybil (1845)]

DOM PERIGNON

[On discovering champagne]
Come quickly, I am tasting stars!

DUNNE, Finley Peter (1867–1936)

There is wan thing an' on'y wan thing to be said in favour iv dhrink, an' that is that it has caused manny a lady to be loved that otherwise might've died single.

[Mr Dooley Says (1910)]

FARQUHAR, George (1678–1707)

I have fed purely upon ale; I have eat my ale, drank my ale, and I always sleep upon ale.

[The Beaux' Stratagem (1707)]

FITZGERALD, Edward (1809–1883)

Drink! for you know not whence you came, nor why:
Drink! for you know not why you go, nor where.

[The Rubáiyát of Omar Khayyám (1879)]

The Grape that can with Logic absolute
The Two-and-Seventy jarring Sects confute.

[*The Rubáiyát of Omar Khayyám* (1859)]

And much as Wine has play'd the Infidel,
And robb'd me of my Robe of Honour – Well,
I often wonder what the Vintners buy
One half so precious as the Goods they sell.

[*The Rubáiyát of Omar Khayyám* (1859)]

Here with a Loaf of Bread beneath the Bough,
A Flask of Wine, a Book of Verse – and Thou
Beside me singing in the Wilderness –
And Wilderness is Paradise enow.

[*The Rubáiyát of Omar Khayyám* (1859)]

FITZGERALD, F. Scott (1896–1940)

First you take a drink, then the drink takes a drink, then the drink takes you.

[In Jules Feiffer, *Ackroyd*]

FLETCHER, John (1579–1625)

And he that will go to bed sober,
Falls with the leaf still in October.

[*The Bloody Brother* (1616)]

FULLER, Thomas (1654–1734)

Bacchus hath drowned more men than Neptune.

[*Gnomologia*, 1732]

GOLDSMITH, Oliver (c.1728–1774)

Let school-masters puzzle their brain,
With grammar, and nonsense, and learning,
Good liquor, I stoutly maintain,
Gives genius a better discerning.

[*She Stoops to Conquer* (1773)]

HARRIS, Joel Chandler (1848–1908)

Licker talks mighty loud w'en it git loose fum de jug.

[*Uncle Remus* (1881)]

HERBERT, George (1593–1633)

Drink not the third glasse, – which thou canst not tame
When once it is within thee.

[*The Temple* (1633)]

HOLMES, Oliver Wendell (1809–1894)

Man wants but little drink below,

But wants that little strong.

['A Song of other Days' (1848)]

HOME, John (1722–1808)

[On the high duty on French wine, claret being 'the only wine drunk by gentlemen in Scotland']
Firm and erect the Caledonian stood,
Old was his mutton, and his claret good;
Let him drink port, an English statesman cried –
He drank the poison and his spirit died.

[In Mackenzie, *An Account of the Life and Writings of John Home, Esq.* (1822)]

HOOVER, Herbert Clark (1874–1964)

[On the Eighteenth Amendment, enacting Prohibition]
Our country has deliberately undertaken a great social and economic experiment, noble in motive and far-reaching in purpose.

[Letter to Senator Borah, 1928]

HOUSMAN, A.E. (1859–1936)

Oh many a peer of England brews
Livelier liquor than the Muse,
And malt does more than Milton can
To justify God's ways to man.
Ale, man, ale's the stuff to drink
For fellows whom it hurts to think.

[*A Shropshire Lad* (1896)]

HOWKINS, Alun (1947–)

Real ale is an odd concept, linked more to an imagined real pub with real fire and real bread and cheese, as much as to a scientific definition of a brewing process.

[*New Statesman and Society*, 1989]

HOWSE, Christopher

It is difficult to speak about proper beer, because its friends (just like the friends of G.K. Chesterton) are its worst enemies. 'Real ale' fans are just like train-spotters – only drunk.

[*The Spectator*, 1992]

IRVING, Washington (1783–1859)

They who drink beer will think beer.

[*The Sketch Book* (1820)]

JOHNSON, Samuel (1709–1784)

Claret is the liquor for boys; port for men; but
he who aspires to be a hero must drink
brandy.

[In Boswell, *The Life of Samuel Johnson* (1791)]

[Calling for a gill of whisky]
Come, let me know what it is that makes a
Scotchman happy!

[In Boswell, *Journal of a Tour to the Hebrides* (1785)]

He said that few people had intellectual
resources sufficient to forgo the pleasures of
wine. They would not otherwise contrive to
fill the interval between dinner and supper.

[In Boswell, *The Life of Samuel Johnson* (1791)]

JOYCE, James (1882–1941)
I was blue mouldy for the want of that pint.
Declare to God I could hear it hit the pit of
my stomach with a click.

[*Ulysses* (1922)]

KEATS, John (1795–1821)
Souls of poets dead and gone,
What Elysium have ye known,
Happy field or mossy cavern,
Choicer than the Mermaid Tavern?
Have ye tippled drink more fine
Than mine host's Canary wine?

['Lines on the Mermaid Tavern'
(1818)]

O for a beaker full of the warm South,
Full of the true, the blushful Hippocrene,
With beaded bubbles winking at the brim,
And purple-stainèd mouth;
That I might drink, and leave the world
unseen;
And with thee fade away into the forest dim.

['Ode to a Nightingale' (1819)]

LARDNER, Ring (1885–1933)
Frenchmen drink wine just like we used to
drink water before Prohibition.

[In R.E. Drennan, *Wit's End*]

LAUDER, Sir Harry (1870–1950)
Just a wee deoch-an-duoris
Before we gang awa' …
If y' can say
It's a braw brecht moonlecht necht,

Yer a' recht, that's a'.

[Song, 1912]

LAWSON, Henry (1867–1922)
Beer makes you feel as you ought to feel
without beer.

[In David Low, *Low's Autobiography*]

LLOYD GEORGE, David (1863–1945)
[To a deputation of ship owners urging a
campaign for prohibition during the First World
War]
We are fighting Germany, Austria, and drink,
and so far as I can see the greatest of these
deadly foes is drink.

[Speech, 1915]

MAP, Walter (c.1140–c.1209)
If die I must, let me die drinking in an inn.

[*De Nugis Curialium* (1182)]

MARTIN, Dean (1917–1995)
I feel sorry for people who don't drink. When
they wake up in the morning, that's the best
they are going to feel all day.

[Attr.]

MARX, Groucho (1895–1977)
I was T.T. until prohibition.

[Attr.]

MENCKEN, H.L. (1880–1956)
I've made it a rule never to drink by daylight
and never to refuse a drink after dark.

[*New York Post*,1945]

NASH, Ogden (1902–1971)
Candy
Is dandy
But liquor
Is quicker.

['Reflections on Ice-Breaking'
(1931)]

O'BRIEN, Flann (1911–1966)
When things go wrong and will not come
right,
Though you do the best you can,
When life looks black as the hour of night ñ
A PINT OF PLAIN IS YOUR ONLY MAN.

[*At Swim-Two-Birds* (1939)]

O'SULLIVAN, John L. (1813–1895)

[Of whisky]

A torchlight procession marching down your throat.

[Attr.]

OSLER, Sir William (1849–1919)

[His description of alcohol]

Milk of the elderly.

[*The Globe and Mail*,1988]

PASCAL, Blaise (1623–1662)

Too much and too little wine. Give him none, he cannot find truth; give him too much, the same.

[*Pensées*, 1670]

PEACOCK, Thomas Love (1785–1866)

[English satirical novelist, essayist and lyric poet]

There are two reasons for drinking; one is, when you are thirsty, to cure it; the other, when you are not thirsty, to prevent it … Prevention is better than cure.

[*Melincourt* (1817)]

PLINY THE ELDER (AD 23–79)

In vino veritas.

Wine brings out the truth!

[*Historia Naturalis*]

POTTER, Stephen (1900–1969)

It is WRONG to do what everyone else does – namely, to hold the wine list just out of sight, look for the second cheapest claret on the list, and say, 'Number 22, please'.

[*One-Upmanship* (1952)]

A good general rule is to state that the bouquet is better than the taste, and vice versa.

[*One-Upmanship* (1952)]

RABELAIS, François (c.1494–c.1553)

I drink for the thirst to come.

[*Gargantua* (1534)]

No noble man ever hated good wine.

[*Gargantua* (1534)]

RUSSELL, George William (1867–1935)

[Refusing a drink that was offered him]

No, thank you, I was born intoxicated.

[In L. Copeland, *10,000 Jokes, Toasts, and Stories*]

SAINTSBURY, George (1845–1933)

It is the unbroken testimony of all history that alcoholic liquors have been used by the strongest, wisest, handsomest, and in every way best races of all times.

[Attr.]

SELDEN, John (1584–1654)

'Tis not the drinking that is to be blamed, but the excess.

[*Table Talk* (1689)]

SHAW, George Bernard (1856–1950)

I'm only a beer teetotaller, not a champagne teetotaller.

[*Candida* (1898)]

Alcohol is a very necessary article … It enables Parliament to do things at eleven at night that no sane person would do at eleven in the morning.

[*Major Barbara* (1907)]

SHERIDAN, Richard Brinsley (1751–1816)

[On being warned that his drinking would destroy the coat of his stomach]

Well, then, my stomach must just digest in its waistcoat.

[In L. Harris, *The Fine Art of Political Wit* (1965)]

SITWELL, Dame Edith (1887–1964)

Another little drink wouldn't do us any harm.

['Scotch Rhapsody' (1922)]

STEVENSON, William (1546?–1575)

I can not eat but little meat,
My stomach is not good;
But sure I think, that I can drink
With him that wears a hood.
Though I go bare, take ye no care,
I am nothing a-cold:
I stuff my skin, so full within,
Of jolly good ale and old.

[*Gammer Gurton's Needle*, Song]

STILL, John (c.1543–c.1608)

Back and side go bare, go bare,

Both foot and hand go cold;
But, belly, God send thee good ale enough,
Whether it be new or old.

[*Gammer Gurton's Needle*, song]

SURTEES, R.S. (1805–1864)

Champagne certainly gives one werry gentlemanly ideas, but for a continuance, I don't know but I should prefer mild hale.

[*Jorrocks's Jaunts and Jollities* (1838)]

TARKINGTON, Booth (1869–1946)

There are two things that will be believed of any man whatsoever, and one of them is that he has taken to drink.

[*Penrod* (1914)]

THATCHER, Denis (1915–)

[Reply to someone who asked if he had a drinking problem.]
Yes, there's never enough.

[*Daily Mail*, 1996]

THOMAS, Dylan (1914–1953)

An alcoholic is someone you don't like who drinks as much as you do.

[Attr.]

THURBER, James (1894–1961)

It's a naïve domestic Burgundy, without any breeding, but I think you'll be amused by its presumption.

[Cartoon caption in *The New Yorker*, 1937]

WARD, Artemus (1834–1867)

I prefer temperance hotels – although they sell worse kinds of liquor than any other kind of hotels.

WODEHOUSE, P.G. (1881–1975)

It was my Uncle George who discovered that alcohol was a food well in advance of modern medical thought.

[*The Inimitable Jeeves* (1923)]

WRIGHT, Ian

[On his Arsenal teammate's alcoholism]
It took a lot of bottle for Tony [Adams] to own up.

YOUNG, George W. (1846–1919)

Your lips, on my own, when they printed 'Farewell',
Had never been soiled by the 'beverage of hell';
But they come to me now with the bacchanal sign,
And the lips that touch liquor must never touch mine.

['The lips that touch liquor must never touch mine' (c. 1870)]

See DRUNKENNESS

AMBITION

AESCHYLUS (525–456 BC)

He wishes not to seem but to be the best.

[*The Seven against Thebes*, 592]

ALEXANDER THE GREAT (356–323 BC)

Alexander wept on hearing from Anaxarchus that there was an infinite number of worlds … 'Do you not think it lamentable that with such an infinite number, we have not yet conquered one?'.

[In Plutarch, *On the Tranquillity of the Mind*]

BLAKE, William (1757–1827)

Ambition is the growth of ev'ry clime.

[*Poetical Sketches* (1783)]

BROWNING, Robert (1812–1889)

'Tis not what man does which exalts him, but what a man would do!

['Saul' (1855)]

BURKE, Edmund (1729–1797)

Well is it known that ambition can creep as well as soar.

[*Third Letter … on the Proposals for Peace with the Regicide Directory of France* (1797)]

CAESAR, Gaius Julius (c.102–44 BC)

I would rather be the first man here (in Gaul) than second in Rome.

[Attr. in Plutarch, *Lives*]

CONRAD, Joseph (1857–1924)

All ambitions are lawful except those which climb upward on the miseries or credulities of mankind.

[*A Personal Record* (1912)]

GILBERT, W.S. (1836–1911)

If you wish in this world to advance
Your merits you're bound to enhance,
You must stir it and stump it,
And blow your own trumpet,
Or, trust me, you haven't a chance!

[*Ruddigore* (1887)]

HERBERT, George (1593–1633)

Who aimeth at the sky
Shoots higher much than he that means a tree.

[*The Temple* (1633)]

JUVENAL (c.60–130)

I, demens, et saevas curre per Alpes
Ut pueris placeas et declamatio fias.
Go climb the Alps, ambitious fool,
To please the boys, and be a theme at school.

[*Satires*, X; trans. Dryden]

KEATS, John (1795–1821)

I am ambitious of doing the world some good: if I should be spared, that may be the work of maturer years – in the interval I will assay to reach to as high a summit in Poetry as the nerve bestowed upon me will suffer.

[Letter to Richard Woodhouse, 1818]

KENEALLY, Thomas (1935–)

It's only when you abandon your ambitions that they become possible.

[*Australian*, 1983]

LONGFELLOW, Henry Wadsworth (1807–1882)

If you would hit the mark, you must aim a little above it;
Every arrow that flies feels the attraction of earth.

['Elegiac Verse' (1880)]

MASSINGER, Philip (1583–1640)

Ambition, in a private man a vice,
Is, in a prince, the virtue.

[*The Bashful Lover* (1636)]

POPE, Alexander (1688–1744)

Get Place and Wealth, if possible, with Grace;
If not, by any means get Wealth and Place.

[*Imitations of Horace* (1737–1738)]

RALEIGH, Sir Walter (c.1552–1618)

[Written on a window-pane, and referring to his ambitions at the court of Elizabeth I]
Fain would I climb, yet fear I to fall.

[Attr.]

SHAKESPEARE, William (1564–1616)

I charge thee, fling away ambition:
By that sin fell the angels. How can man then,
The image of his Maker, hope to win by it?

[*Henry VIII*, III.ii]

'Tis a common proof
That lowliness is young ambition's ladder,
Whereto the climber-upward turns his face;
But when he once attains the upmost round,
He then unto the ladder turns his back,
Looks in the clouds, scorning the base degrees
By which he did ascend.

[*Julius Caesar*, II.i]

Thou wouldst be great;
Art not without ambition, but without
The illness should attend it. What thou wouldst highly,
That wouldst thou holily; wouldst not play false,
And yet wouldst wrongly win.

[*Macbeth*, I.v]

I have no spur
To prick the sides of my intent, but only
Vaulting ambition, which o'er-leaps itself,
And falls on th' other.

[*Macbeth*, I.vii]

SHAW, George Bernard (1856–1950)

The Gospel of Getting On.

[*Mrs Warren's Profession* (1898)]

SIDNEY, Sir Philip (1554–1586)

Who shoots at the midday sun, though he be sure he shall never hit the mark, yet as sure he is he shall shoot higher than who aims but at a bush.

[*New Arcadia* (1590)]

SMITH, Adam (1723–1790)

And thus, place, that great object which

divides the wives of aldermen, is the end of half the labours of human life; and is the cause of all the tumult and bustle, all the rapine and injustice, which avarice and ambition have introduced into this world.

[*The Theory of Moral Sentiments* (1759)]

SPENSER, Edmund (c.1522–1599)

And he that strives to touch the starres,
Oft stombles at a strawe.

[*The Shepheardes Calender* (1579)]

WAGNER, Jane (1927–)

All my life I always wanted to be somebody. Now I see that I should have been more specific.

[Attr.]

WEBSTER, Daniel (1782–1852)

[On being advised not to join the overcrowded legal profession]
There is always room at the top.

[Attr.]

See DESIRE

AMERICA

ANONYMOUS

[On GIs in Britain]
Overpaid, overfed, oversexed, and over here.

[Remark during World War II]

A man went looking for America and couldn't find it anywhere.

[Advertisement for the film *Easy Rider*, 1969]

APPLETON, Thomas Gold (1812–1884)

Good Americans, when they die, go to Paris.

[In Oliver Wendell Holmes, *The Autocrat of the Breakfast Table* (1858)]

ARNOLD, Matthew (1822–1888)

Our society distributes itself into Barbarians, Philistines, and Populace; and America is just ourselves, with the Barbarians quite left out, and the Populace nearly.

[*Culture and Anarchy* (1869)]

AUDEN, W.H. (1907–1973)

God bless the U.S.A., so large,
So friendly, and so rich.

['On the Circuit']

AYKROYD, Dan (1952–)

What the American public doesn't know is what makes it the American public.

[*Tommy Boy*, film, 1995]

BAILEY, Philip James (1816–1902)

America, thou half-brother of the world;
With something good and bad of every land.

[*Festus* (1839)]

BATES, Katherine Lee (1859–1929)

America! America!
God shed His grace on thee
And crown thy good with brotherhood
From sea to shining sea!

['America the Beautiful', song, 1895]

BUTLER, Nicholas Murray (1862–1947)

… a society like ours [USA] of which it is truly said to be often but three generations 'from shirt-sleeves to shirt-sleeves'.

[*True and False Democracy*]

CANNING, George (1770–1827)

I called the New World into existence, to redress the balance of the Old.

[Speech, 1826]

CHEEVER, John (1912–1982)

We travel by plane, oftener than not, and yet the spirit of our country seems to have remained a country of railroads.

[*Bullet Park* (1969)]

CLEMENCEAU, Georges (1841–1929)

America is the only nation in history which miraculously has gone directly from barbarism to degeneration without the usual interval of civilization.

[Attr.]

COOLIDGE, Calvin (1872–1933)

The business of America is business.

[Speech, 1925]

DÍAZ, Porfirio (1830–1915)

Poor Mexico, so far from God and so near to

the United States!

[Attr.]

EDWARD VIII (later Duke of Windsor) (1894–1972)

The thing that impresses me most about America is the way parents obey their children.

[In *Look*, 1957]

EISENHOWER, Dwight D. (1890–1969)

Whatever America hopes to bring to pass in this world must first come to pass in the heart of America.

[Inaugural address, 1953]

EMERSON, Ralph Waldo (1803–1882)

America is a country of young men.

[*Society and Solitude* (1870)]

The Americans have little faith. They rely on the power of a dollar.

[Lecture, 1841, 'Man the Reformer']

FITZGERALD, F. Scott (1896–1940)

Americans, while willing, even eager, to be serfs, have always been obstinate about being peasantry.

[*The Great Gatsby* (1926)]

FORD, Gerald R. (1913–)

[Referring to his own appointment as President]
I guess it proves that in America anyone can be President.

[In Reeves, *A Ford Not a Lincoln*]

FUENTES, Carlos (1928–)

What America does best is to understand itself. What it does worst is to understand others.

[*Time*, 1986]

GREY, Edward, Viscount of Fallodon (1862–1933)

The United States is like a gigantic boiler. Once the fire is lighted under it there is no limit to the power it can generate.

[In Winston S. Churchill, *Their Finest Hour*]

HARDING, Gilbert (1907–1960)

Before he [Gilbert Harding] could go to New York he had to get a US visa at the American consulate in Toronto. He was called upon to fill in a long form with many questions, including 'Is it your intention to overthrow the Government of the United States by force?' By the time Harding got to that one he was so irritated that he answered:'Sole purpose of visit.'

[In W. Reyburn, *Gilbert Harding* (1978)]

HARDING, Warren G. (1865–1923)

America's present need is not heroics but healing, not nostrums but normalcy.

[Speech, Boston, May 1920]

HOBSON, Sir Harold (1904–1992)

The United States, I believe, are under the impression that they are twenty years in advance of this country; whilst, as a matter of actual verifiable fact, of course, they are just about six hours behind it.

[*The Devil in Woodford Wells*]

JOHNSON, Samuel (1709–1784)

I am willing to love all mankind, except an American.

[In Boswell, *The Life of Samuel Johnson* (1791)]

KENNEDY, John F. (1917–1963)

The United States has to move very fast to even stand still.

[*The Observer*, 1963]

And so, my fellow Americans: ask not what your country can do for you – ask what you can do for your country. My fellow citizens of the world: ask not what America will do for you, but what together we can do for the freedom of man.

[Inaugural address, 1961]

LAWRENCE, D.H. (1885–1930)

And suddenly she craved again for the more absolute silence of America. English stillness was so soft, like an inaudible murmur of voices, of presences.

[*St Mawr* (1925)]

LEWIS, Sinclair (1885–1951)

In other countries, art and literature are left to a lot of shabby bums living in attics and feeding on booze and spaghetti, but in

America the successful writer or picture-painter is indistinguishable from any other decent business man.

[*Babbit* (1922)]

MCCARTHY, Senator Joseph (1908–1957)

McCarthyism is Americanism with its sleeves rolled.

[Speech, 1952]

MADARIAGA, Salvador de (1886–1978)

First, the sweetheart of the nation, then her aunt, woman governs America because America is a land where boys refuse to grow up.

['Americans are Boys']

MENCKEN, H.L. (1880–1956)

No one ever went broke underestimating the intelligence of the American people.

[Attr.]

MINIFIE, James M. (1900–1974)

The United States is the glory, jest, and terror of mankind.

[In Purdy (ed.), *The New Romans* (1988)]

PITT, William (1708–1778)

I rejoice that America has resisted. Three millions of people, so dead to all the feelings of liberty, as voluntarily to submit to be slaves, would have been fit instruments to make slaves of the rest.

[Speech, House of Commons, 1766]

ROOSEVELT, Eleanor (1884–1962)

I think if the people of this country can be reached with the truth, their judgment will be in favour of the many, as against the privileged few.

[Ladies' Home Journal]

ROOSEVELT, Theodore (1858–1919)

There can be no fifty-fifty Americanism in this country. There is room here for only hundred per cent Americanism, only for those who are Americans and nothing else.

[Speech, 1918]

We have room in this country for but one flag, the Stars and Stripes … We have room for but one loyalty, loyalty to the United States … We have room for but one language, the language of the Declaration of Independence and the Gettysburg speech.

[In Lord Charnwood, *Theodore Roosevelt* (1923)]

There is no room in this country for hyphenated Americanism.

[Speech, 1915]

RUSSELL, Bertrand (1872–1970)

America … where law and custom alike are based upon the dreams of spinsters.

[*Marriage and Morals* (1929)]

In America everybody is of the opinion that he has no social superiors, since all men are equal, but he does not admit that he has no social inferiors.

['Ideas that have harmed mankind' (1950)]

SMITH, Samuel Francis (1808–1895)

My country, 'tis of thee,
Sweet land of liberty,
Of thee I sing:
Land where my fathers died,
Land of the pilgrims' pride,
From every mountain-side
Let freedom ring.

['America' (1832)]

STAPLEDON, Olaf (1886–1950)

That strange blend of the commercial traveller, the missionary, and the barbarian conqueror, which was the American abroad.

[*Last and First Men* (1930)]

STEIN, Gertrude (1874–1946)

In the United States there is more space where nobody is than where anybody is. That is what makes America what it is.

[*The Geographical History of America* (1936)]

TALLEYRAND, Charles-Maurice de (1754–1838)

[Of America]

I found there a country with thirty-two religions and only one sauce.

[In Pedrazzini, *Autant en apportent les mots*]

TOYNBEE, Arnold (1889–1975)

America is a large, friendly dog in a very small room. Ever time it wags its tail it knocks over a chair.

[Broadcast news summary, 1954]

TRINDER, Tommy (1909–1989)

[Referring to the GIs in World War II]

Overpaid, overfed, oversexed and over here.

[The Sunday Times, 1976]

TROLLOPE, Anthony (1815–1882)

[On Frances Trollope's Domestic Manners of the Americans]

What though people had plenty to eat and clothes to wear, if they put their feet upon the tables and did not reverence their betters? The Americans were to her rough, uncouth, and vulgar, – and she told them so.

[An Autobiography (1883)]

VIDAL, Gore (1925–)

The land of the dull and the home of the literal.

[Reflections upon a Sinking Ship (1969)]

WALPOLE, Horace (1717–1797)

The next Augustan age will dawn on the other side of the Atlantic. There will, perhaps, be a Thucydides at Boston, a Xenophon at New York, and, in time, a Virgil at Mexico, and a Newton at Peru. At last, some curious traveller from Lima will visit England and give a description of the ruins of St Paul's, like the editions of Balbec and Palmyra.

[Letter to Sir Horace Mann, 1774]

WELLS, H.G. (1866–1946)

Every time Europe looks across the Atlantic to see the American eagle, it observes only the rear end of an ostrich.

[America]

WHITMAN, Walt (1819–1892)

The United States themselves are essentially the greatest poem.

[Leaves of Grass (1855 edition), Preface]

WILDE, Oscar (1854–1900)

Of course, America had often been discovered before, but it had always been hushed up.

[Personal Impressions of America (1883)]

The youth of America is their oldest tradition. It has been going on now for three hundred years.

[A Woman of No Importance (1893)]

WILSON, Woodrow (1856–1924)

America … is the prize amateur nation of the world. Germany is the prize professional nation.

[Speech, 1917]

America is the only idealistic nation in the world.

[Speech, 1919]

ZANGWILL, Israel (1864–1926)

America is God's Crucible, the great Melting-Pot where all the races of Europe are melting and re-forming!

[The Melting Pot (1908)]

ANARCHY

ANONYMOUS

Anarchy may not be the best form of government, but it's better than no government at all.

BENNETT, Alan (1934–)

We started off trying to set up a small anarchist community, but people wouldn't obey the rules.

[Getting On (1972)]

See GOVERNMENT; POLITICS

ANCESTORS

ADAMS, John Quincy (1767–1848)

Think of your forefathers! Think of your posterity!

[Speech, December 1802]

CERVANTES, Miguel de (1547–1616)

Dos linajes solos hay en el mundo, como decía una agüela mía, que son el tener y el no tener.

There are only two lineages in the world, as a grandmother of mine used to say, the Haves and the Have-nots.

[*Don Quixote*, II (1615)]

FORRO, (Rev. Fr) Francis Stephen (1914–1974)

[Response to a journalist's comment on the scruffiness of Hungarian refugees arriving at Mascot aerodrome, Australia, in 1956]

Ah, yes, but they will make fine ancestors.

[Attr.]

GILBERT, W.S. (1836–1911)

I can trace my ancestry back to a protoplasmal primordial atomic globule. Consequently, my family pride is something inconceivable.

[*The Mikado* (1885)]

JUNOT, Andoche, Duc d'Abrantes (1771–1813)

[On being made a duke]

I am my own ancestor.

[Attr.]

PLUTARCH (c.46–c.120)

It is indeed desirable to be well descended, but the glory belongs to our ancestors.

[*On the Training of Children*]

SENECA (c.4 BC–AD 65)

Qui genus joctat suum
Aliena laudat.

Who boasts his ancestry, praises others' worth.

[*Hercules Furens*, line 340, trans. Milton]

SHERIDAN, Richard Brinsley (1751–1816)

Our ancestors are very good kind of folks; but they are the last people I should choose to have a visiting acquaintance with.

[*The Rivals* (1775)]

SQUIRE, Sir J.C. (1884–1958)

At last incapable of further harm.
The lewd forefathers of the village sleep.

['If Gray had had to write his Elegy in the Cemetery of Spoon River']

STEVENSON, Robert Louis (1850–1894)

Each has his own tree of ancestors, but at the top of all sits Probably Arboreal.

[*Memories and Portraits* (1887)]

See ARISTOCRACY; FAMILY

ANGELS

CHESTERTON, G.K. (1874–1936)

Angels can fly because they can take themselves lightly.

[*Orthodoxy* (1908)]

FIRBANK, Ronald (1886–1926)

There was a pause – just long enough for an angel to pass, flying slowly.

[*Vainglory* (1915)]

POPE, Alexander (1688–1744)

Men would be Angels, Angels would be Gods.
Aspiring to be Gods, if Angels fell,
Aspiring to be Angels, Men rebel.

[*An Essay on Man* (1733)]

ANGER

ALBERTANO OF BRESCIA (c.1190–c.1270)

Iratus semper plus putat posse facere quam possit.
The angry man always thinks he can do more than he can.

[*Liber Consolationis*]

ARISTOTLE (384–322 BC)

The man who is angry on the right grounds and with the right people, and in the right manner and at the right moment and for the right length of time, is to be praised.

[*Nicomachean Ethics*]

BACON, Francis (1561–1626)

Anger makes dull men witty, but it keeps them poor.

['Apophthegms' (1679)]

BECKFORD, William (1760–1844)

When he was angry, one of his eyes became so terrible, that no person could bear to behold it; and the wretch upon whom it was fixed, instantly fell backward, and sometimes expired. For fear, however, of depopulating his dominions and making his palace desolate, he but rarely gave way to his anger.

[*Vathek* (1787)]

THE BIBLE
(King James Version)

A soft answer turneth away wrath.

[*Proverbs*,15:1]

Be ye angry, and sin not; let not the sun go down upon your wrath.

[*Ephesians*, 4:26]

BLAKE, William (1757–1827)

The tygers of wrath are wiser than the horses of instruction.

[*The Marriage of Heaven and Hell* (c. 1790–1793)]

I was angry with my friend:
I told my wrath, my wrath did end.
I was angry with my foe:
I told it not, my wrath did grow.

[*Songs of Experience* (1794)]

BURNS, Robert (1759–1796)

We think na on the lang Scots miles,
The mosses, waters, slaps, and styles,
That lie between us and our hame,
Whare sits our sulky, sullen dame,
Gathering her brows like gathering storm,
Nursing her wrath to keep it warm.

['Tam o' Shanter' (1790)]

CONGREVE, William (1670–1729)

Heav'n has no rage, like love to hatred turned,
Nor Hell a fury, like a woman scorn'd.

[*The Mourning Bride* (1697)]

CONNOLLY, Cyril (1903–1974)

There is no fury like an ex-wife searching for a new lover.

[*The Unquiet Grave* (1944)]

DILLER, Phyllis (1917–1974)

Never go to bed mad. Stay up and fight.

[*Phyllis Diller's Housekeeping Hints*]

DRYDEN, John (1631–1700)

Beware the fury of a patient man.

[*Absalom and Achitophel* (1681)]

FULLER, Thomas (1608–1661)

Anger is one of the sinews of the soul; he that wants it hath a maimed mind.

[*The Holy State and the Profane State* (1642)]

HALIFAX, Lord (1633–1695)

Anger is never without an Argument, but seldom with a good one.

[*Thoughts and Reflections* (1750)]

HAZLITT, William (1778–1830)

Spleen can subsist on any kind of food.

['On Wit and Humour' (1819)]

IRVING, Washington (1783–1859)

A tart temper never mellows with age, and a sharp tongue is the only edged tool that grows keener with constant use.

['Rip Van Winkle' (1820)]

SHAW, George Bernard (1856–1950)

Beware of the man who does not return your blow: he neither forgives you nor allows you to forgive yourself.

[*Man and Superman* (1903)]

SIDNEY, Sir Philip (1554–1586)

O heavenly Foole, thy most kisse worthy face
Anger invests with such a lovely grace,
That Anger's selfe I needes must kisse againe.

[*Astrophel and Stella* (1591)]

SPYRI, Johanna (1827–1901)

Anger has overpowered him, and driven him to a revenge which was rather a stupid one, I must acknowledge, but anger makes us all stupid.

[*Heidi*, 23]

TWAIN, Mark (1835–1910)

When angry count four; when very angry swear.

[*Pudd'nhead Wilson's Calendar* (1894)]

ANIMALS

ARCHILOCHUS (fl. c.650 BC)

The fox knows many things but the hedgehog one big one.

[In Plutarch, *Moralia*]

BLAKE, William (1757–1827)

Tyger Tyger, burning bright
In the forests of the night:
What immortal hand or eye
Could frame thy fearful symmetry?

['The Tyger' (1794)]

CANETTI, Elias (1905–1994)

Immer wenn man ein Tier genau betracht, hat man das Gefühl, ein Mensch, der drin sitzt, macht sich über einen lustig.

Whenever you observe an animal closely, you have the feeling that a person sitting inside is making fun of you.

[*The Human Province*]

CHESTERTON, G.K. (1874–1936)

When fishes flew and forests walked
And figs grew upon thorn,
Some moment when the moon was blood
Then surely I was born.

With monstrous head and sickening cry
And ears like errant wings,
The devil's walking parody
On all four-footed things …

Fools! For I also had my hour;
One far fierce hour and sweet:
There was a shout about my ears,
And palms before my feet.

[*The Wild Knight and Other Poems* (1900)]

COLERIDGE, Samuel Taylor (1772–1834)

Poor little Foal of an oppressed race!
I love the languid patience of thy face.

['To a Young Ass' (1794)]

ELIOT, George (1819–1880)

Animals are such agreeable friends – they ask no questions, they pass no criticisms.

[*Scenes of Clerical Life* (1858)]

ENNIUS, Quintus (239–169 BC)

Simia, quam similis turpissima bestia, nobis.

How like us is the ape, most horrible of beasts.

[In Cicero, *De Natura Deorum*]

FOYLE, Christina (1911–1999)

Animals are always loyal and love you, whereas with children you never know where you are.

[*The Times*,1993]

FROUDE, James Anthony (1818–1894)

Wild animals never kill for sport. Man is the only one to whom the torture and death of his fellow creatures is amusing in itself.

[*Oceana, or England and her Colonies* (1886)]

GOLDSMITH, Oliver (c.1728–1774)

Brutes never meet in bloody fray,
Nor cut each other's throats, for pay.

['Logicians Refuted' (1759)]

KEATS, John (1795–1821)

I go among the Fields and catch a glimpse of a Stoat or a fieldmouse peeping out of the withered grass – the creature hath a purpose and its eyes are bright with it. I go amongst the buildings of a city and I see a Man hurrying along – to what? the Creature has a purpose and his eyes are bright with it.

[Letter to George and Georgiana Keats, 14 February–3 May 1819]

LAWRENCE, D.H. (1885–1930)

Be a good animal, true to your animal instincts.

[*The White Peacock* (1911)]

NASH, Ogden (1902–1971)

The turtle lives 'twixt plated decks
Which practically conceal its sex.
I think it clever of the turtle
In such a fix to be so fertile.

[*Hard Lines* (1931)]

The cow is of the bovine ilk;
One end is moo, the other, milk.

[*Free Wheeling* (1931)]

PEACOCK, Thomas Love (1785–1866)

Nothing can be more obvious than that all

animals were created solely and exclusively for the use of man.

[*Headlong Hall* (1816)]

POPE, Alexander (1688–1744)

The spider's touch, how exquisitely fine!
Feels at each thread, and lives along the line.

[*An Essay on Man* 1733)]

PUNCH

Cats is 'dogs' and rabbits is 'dogs' and so's Parrats, but this 'ere 'Tortis' is an insect, and there ain't no charge for it.

[1869]

QUILLER-COUCH, Sir Arthur ('Q') (1863–1944)

The lion is the beast to fight:
He leaps along the plain,
And if you run with all your might,
He runs with all his mane.

['Sage Counsel']

SHAKESPEARE, William (1564–1616)

No beast so fierce but knows some touch of pity.

[*Richard III*, I.ii]

SOLZHENITSYN, Alexander (1918–)

Nowadays we don't think much of a man's love for an animal; we mock people who are attached to cats. But if we stop loving animals, aren't we bound to stop loving humans too?

[*Cancer Ward* (1968)]

SPENCER, Herbert (1820–1903)

People are beginning to see that the first requisite to success in life, is to be a good animal.

[*Education* (1861)]

VOLTAIRE (1694–1778)

There are two things for which animals are to be envied: they know nothing of future evils, or of what people say about them.

[Letter, 1739]

WHITMAN, Walt (1819–1892)

I think I could turn and live with animals, they are so placid and self-contain'd,
I stand and look at them long and long.

They do not sweat and whine about their condition,
They do not lie awake in the dark and weep for their sins,
They do not make me sick discussing their duty to God,
Not one is dissatisfied, not one is demented with the mania of owning things,
Not one kneels to another, nor to his kind that lived thousands of years ago,
Not one is respectable or unhappy over the whole earth.

['Song of Myself' (1855), 32]

SELLAR, Walter (1898–1951) and YEATMAN, Robert Julian (1897–1968)

To confess that you are totally Ignorant about the Horse, is social suicide: you will be despised by everybody, especially the horse.

[*Horse Nonsense* (1933)]

See BIRDS; CATS; DOGS

APOLOGIES

DICKENS, Charles (1812–1870)

'Not to put too fine a point upon it' – a favourite apology for plain-speaking with Mr Snagsby.

[*Bleak House* (1853)]

SHAW, George Bernard (1856–1950)

I never apologise.

[*Arms and the Man* (1898)]

WODEHOUSE, P.G. (1881–1975)

It is a good rule in life never to apologize. The right sort of people do not want apologies, and the wrong sort take a mean advantage of them.

[*The Man Upstairs* (1914)]

See REGRET

APPEARANCE

AESOP (6th century BC)

It is not only fine feathers that make fine

birds.

[Fables]

AMIS, Kingsley (1922–1995)

Outside every fat man there was an even fatter man trying to close in.

[One Fat Englishman (1963)]

AUDEN, W.H. (1907–1973)

Only God can tell the saintly from the suburban,
Counterfeit values always resemble the true;
Neither in Life nor Art is honesty bohemian,
The free behave much as the respectable do.

['New Year Letter' (1941)]

CAMUS, Albert (1913–1960)

Hélas! après un certain âge, tout homme est responsable de son visage.
Alas! after a certain age every man is responsible for the face he has.

[The Fall, 1956]

DICKENS, Charles (1812–1870)

He might have brought an action against his countenance for libel, and won heavy damages.

[Oliver Twist (1838)]

GOLDSMITH, Oliver (c.1728–1774)

Is it one of my well looking days, child? Am I in face to-day?

[She Stoops to Conquer (1773)]

LARDNER, Ring (1885–1933)

[Speaking to a flamboyantly dressed stranger who walked into the club where he was drinking]
How do you look when I'm sober?

[In J. Yardley, Ring]

LINCOLN, Abraham (1809–1865)

The Lord prefers common-looking people. That is why he makes so many of them.

[In James Morgan, Our President (1928)]

OVID (43 BC–AD 18)

Delectant etiam castas praeconia formae;
Virginibus curae grataque forma sua est.
Even respectable girls delight in hearing their beauty praised; even the innocent are worried and pleased by their appearance.

[Ars Amatoria, I, line 623]

PLATO (c.429–347 BC)

The imitator or maker of the images knows nothing of true existence; he knows appearances only.

[The Republic, X]

ROBINSON, Robert (1927–)

Certain people are born with natural false teeth.

[Stop the Week, BBC radio programme, 1977]

ROSTAND, Edmond (1868–1918)

…norme, mon nez!
– Vil camus, sot camard, tête plate, apprenez
Que je m'enorgueillis d'un pareil appendice,
Attendu qu'un grand nez est proprement l'indice
D'un homme affable, bon, courtois, spirituel,
Libéral, courageux, tel que je suis.
Enormous, my nose! Vile pug-nose, flat-nose, flat-head, let me inform you that I pride myself in such an appendage, considering that a big nose is the proper sign of a friendly, good, courteous, witty, liberal, courageous brave man, such as I am.

[Cyrano de Bergerac (1897)]

SARTRE, Jean-Paul (1905–1980)

Les choses sont tout entières ce qu'elles paraissent – et derrière elles … il n'y a rien.
Things are entirely what they appear to be and behind them … there is nothing.

[La Nausée, 1938)]

WILDE, Oscar (1854–1900)

It is only shallow people who do not judge by appearances.

[The Picture of Dorian Gray (1891)]

WINDSOR, Duchess of (Wallis Simpson) (1896–1986)

One can never be too thin or too rich.

[Attr.]

See BEAUTY; EYES; VANITY

ARCHITECTURE

AUSTEN, Jane (1775–1817)

Nothing can be said in his vindication, but

that his abolishing Religious Houses and leaving them to the ruinous depredations of time has been of infinite use to the landscape of England in general.

[*The History of England* (1791)]

BACON, Francis (1561–1626)

Houses are built to live in and not to look on; therefore let use be preferred before uniformity, except where both may be had.

[*Essays* (1625)]

BETJEMAN, Sir John (1906–1984)

Ghastly Good Taste, or A Depressing Story of the Rise and Fall of English Architecture.

[Title of book, 1933]

BOYD, Robin Gerard Penleigh (1919–1971)

The Australian town-dweller spent a century in the acquisition of his toy: an emasculated garden, a five-roomed cottage of his very own, different from its neighbours by a minor contortion of window or porch – its difference significant to no-one but himself.

[*Australia's Home* (1952)]

CHARLES, Prince of Wales (1948–)

[On the proposed extension to the National Gallery]

A kind of vast municipal fire station … like a monstrous carbuncle on the face of a much-loved and elegant friend.

[Speech, 1984, to the Royal Institute of British Architects]

COWARD, Sir Noël (1899–1973)

[Of the Taj Mahal]

It didn't look like a biscuit box did it? I've always felt that it might.

[*Private Lives* (1930)]

DE WOLFE, Elsie (1865–1950)

[On first sighting the Acropolis]

It's beige! My color!

[In J. Smith, *Elsie de Wolfe*]

FULLER, Thomas (1608–1661)

Light (God's eldest daughter) is a principal beauty in building.

[*The Holy State and the Profane State* (1642)]

GOETHE (1749–1832)

Ich [nenne] die Baukunst eine erstarrte Musik.

I [call] architecture a kind of petrified music.

[*Gespräche mit Eckermann*, 1829.]

GOGOL, Nicolai Vasilyevich (1809–1852)

I always feel sad when I look at new buildings which are constantly being built and on which millions are spent … Has the age of architecture passed without hope of return?

[Attr.]

LANCASTER, Sir Osbert (1908–1986)

'Fan vaulting' … an architectural device which arouses enormous enthusiasm on account of the difficulties it has all too obviously involved but which from an aesthetic standpoint frequently belongs to the 'Last-supper-carved-on-a-peach-stone' class of masterpiece.

[*Pillar to Post* (1938)]

A hundred and fifty accurate reproductions of Anne Hathaway's cottage, each complete with central heating and garage.

[*Pillar to Post* (1938)]

LE CORBUSIER (1887–1965)

Une maison est une machine-à-habiter.

A house is a machine for living in.

[*Vers une architecture* (1923)]

LETTE, Kathy

Inner-city council estates make you believe the world was really built in six days.

[*Mad Cows* (1996)]

MCGREGOR, Craig (1933–)

A house is a machine for loving in.

[In Ian McKay et al., *Living and Partly Living*]

MIES VAN DER ROHE, Ludwig (1886–1969)

Less is more.

[*New York Herald Tribune*, 1959]

NAIRN, Ian (1930–1983)

If what is called development is allowed to multiply at the present rate, then by the end of the century Great Britain will consist of isolated oases of preserved monuments in a desert of wire, concrete roads, cosy plots and bungalows ... Upon this new Britain the Review bestows a name in the hope that it will stick – SUBTOPIA.

[Architectural Review, 1955]

PRINGLE, John Martin Douglas (1912–)

[On Sydney Opera House]
There it stands, like Santa Maria della Salute on the lagoon in Venice, a perfect symbol linking the city to the sea ... I believe it is a building of which all Australians may rightly be proud, perhaps the only true work of architecture on this continent.

[*On Second Thoughts* (1971)]

REYNOLDS, Malvina (1900–1978)

[Describing newly built houses south of San Francisco]
They're all made out of ticky-tacky,
And they all look just the same.

['Little Boxes', song, 1962]

RUSKIN, John (1819–1900)

Better the rudest work that tells a story or records a fact, than the richest without meaning. There should not be a single ornament put upon great civic buildings, without some intellectual intention.

[*The Seven Lamps of Architecture* (1849)]

When we build, let us think that we build for ever.

[*The Seven Lamps of Architecture* (1849)]

You know there are a great many odd styles of architecture about; you don't want to do anything ridiculous; you hear of me, among others, as a respectable architectural man-milliner; and you send for me, that I may tell you the leading fashion.

[*The Crown of Wild Olive* (1866)]

No person who is not a great sculptor or painter can be an architect. If he is not a sculptor or painter, he can only be a builder.

[*Lectures on Architecture and Painting* (1854)]

SCHELLING, Friedrich von (1775–1854)

Architektur ... [ist] gleichsam die erstarrte Musik.
Architecture is, as it were, petrified music.

[*Philosophy of Art* (1803)]

WOTTON, Sir Henry (1568–1639)

In Architecture as in all other Operative Arts, the end must direct the Operation. The end is to build well. Well building hath three Conditions: Commodity, Firmness, and Delight.

[*Elements of Architecture* (1624)]

WRIGHT, Frank Lloyd (1869–1959)

The physician can bury his mistakes, but the architect can only advise his client to plant vines.

[*New York Times Magazine*, 1953]

See ART; TRAGEDY

ARGUMENT

ADDISON, Joseph (1672–1719)

Our disputants put me in mind of the skuttle fish, that when he is unable to extricate himself, blackens all the water about him, till he becomes invisible.

[*The Spectator*, 1712]

Arguments out of a pretty mouth are unanswerable.

[*Women and Liberty*]

ANONYMOUS

This is a rotten argument, but it should be good enough for their lordships on a hot summer afternoon.

[Annotation in ministerial brief]

BILLINGS, Josh (1818–1885)

Thrice is he armed that hath his quarrel just,
But four times he who gets his blow in fust.

[*Josh Billings, his Sayings* (1865)]

ESSEX, Robert Devereux, Earl of (1566–1601)

[To Lord Willoughby]
Reasons are not like garments, the worse for

wearing.

[Attr., c. 1599]

FERGUSSON, Sir James (1832–1907)

I have heard many arguments which influenced my opinion, but never one which influenced my vote.

[Attr.]

GAY, John (1685–1732)

Those, who in quarrels interpose,
Must often wipe a bloody nose.

[Fables (1727)]

HERBERT, George (1593–1633)

Be calm in arguing; for fiercenesse makes
Errour a fault, and truth discourtesie.

[The Temple (1633)]

INGE, William Ralph (1860–1954)

It takes in reality only one to make a quarrel. It is useless for the sheep to pass resolutions in favour of vegetarianism while the wolf remains of a different opinion.

[Outspoken Essays (1919)]

JOHNSON, Samuel (1709–1784)

I dogmatize and am contradicted, and in this conflict of opinions and sentiments I find delight.

[In Sir John Hawkins, Life of Samuel Johnson (1787)]

Though we cannot out-vote them we will out-argue them.

[In Boswell, The Life of Samuel Johnson (1791)]

LA ROCHEFOUCAULD (1613–1680)

Les querelles ne dureraient pas longtemps si le tort n'était que d'un côté.
Quarrels would not last long if the fault were on one side only.

[Maximes (1678)]

LOWELL, James Russell (1819–1891)

There is no good in arguing with the inevitable. The only argument available with an east wind is to put on your overcoat.

[Democracy and Other Addresses (1887)]

POTTER, Stephen (1900–1969)

[A blocking phrase for conversation]
'Yes, but not in the South', with slight

adjustments will do for any argument about any place, if not about any person.

[Lifemanship (1950)]

ROSTAND, Jean (1894–1977)

A married couple are well suited when both partners usually feel the need for a quarrel at the same time.

[Le Mariage]

SHERIDAN, Richard Brinsley (1751–1816)

The quarrel is a very pretty quarrel as it stands – we should only spoil it by trying to explain it.

[The Rivals (1775)]

STERNE, Laurence (1713–1768)

Heat is in proportion to the want of true knowledge.

[Tristram Shandy (1759–1767)]

YEATS, W.B. (1865–1939)

We make out of the quarrel with others, rhetoric; but of the quarrel with ourselves, poetry.

['Anima Hominis' (1917)]

ARISTOCRACY

AILESBURY, Maria, Marchioness of (d. 1893)

My dear, my dear, you never know when any beautiful young lady may not blossom into a Duchess!

[In Portland, Men, Women, and Things (1937)]

AUSTEN, Jane (1775–1817)

Sir Walter Elliot, of Kellynch Hall, in Somersetshire, was a man who, for his own amusement, never took up any book but the Baronetage; there he found occupation for an idle hour and consolation in a distressed one … this was the page at which the favourite volume always opened: – ELLIOT OF KELLYNCH-HALL.

[Persuasion (1818)]

BEAUMARCHAIS (1732–1799)

Because you are a great lord, you think

yourself a great genius! You took the trouble to be born, but nothing more.

[*Mariage de Figaro* (1784)]

BURKE, Edmund (1729–1797)
Nobility is a graceful ornament to the civil order. It is the Corinthian capital of polished society.

[*Reflections on the Revolution in France and on the Proceedings in Certain Societies in London* (1790)]

CHARLES, Prince of Wales (1948–)
The one advantage about marrying a princess – or someone from a royal family – is that they do know what happens.

[Attr.]

HALDANE, J.B.S. (1892–1964)
If human beings could be propagated by cutting, like apple trees, aristocracy would be biologically sound.

[*The Inequality of Man and Other Essays* (1932)]

HOPE, Anthony (1863–1933)
'Bourgeois,' I observed, 'is an epithet which the riff-raff apply to what is respectable, and the aristocracy to what is decent.'

[*The Dolly Dialogues* (1894)]

LÉVIS, Duc de (1764–1830)
Noblesse oblige.
Nobility has its obligations.

[*Maximes et réflexions* (1812)]

LLOYD GEORGE, David (1863–1945)
A fully equipped duke costs as much to keep up as two Dreadnoughts; and dukes are just as great a terror and they last longer.

[Speech, 1909]

MACHIAVELLI (1469–1527)
For titles do not reflect honour on men, but rather men on their titles.

[*Dei Discorsi*]

MANNERS, Lord (1818–1906)
Let wealth and commerce, laws and learning die,
But leave us still our old nobility!

[*England's Trust* (1841)]

MILL, John Stuart (1806–1873)
Persons require to possess a title, or some other badge of rank, or of the consideration of people of rank, to be able to indulge somewhat in the luxury of doing as they like without detriment to their estimation.

[*On Liberty* (1859)]

MITFORD, Nancy (1904–1973)
An aristocracy in a republic is like a chicken whose head had been cut off: it may run about in a lively way, but in fact it is dead.

[*Noblesse Oblige* (1956)]

MOSLEY, Charles
Did you know that a peer condemned to death had the right to be hanged with a silken cord? A bit like insisting that the electric chair had to be Chippendale.

[*The Observer*, 1999]

NORTHCLIFFE, Lord (1865–1922)
When I want a peerage, I shall buy one like an honest man.

[Attr.]

PEARSON, Hesketh (1887–1964)
There is no stronger craving in the world than that of the rich for titles, except that of the titled for riches.

[Attr.]

SEITZ, Raymond
In the British aristocracy, the gene pool has always had a shallow end.

[*The Observer*, 1998]

SHAW, George Bernard (1856–1950)
Titles distinguish the mediocre, embarrass the superior, and are disgraced by the inferior.

[*Man and Superman* (1903)]

I've been offered titles, but I think they get one into disreputable company.

[In Barrow, *Gossip*]

TALLEYRAND, Charles-Maurice de (1754–1838)
[Comment on exiled French aristocrats]
Ils n'ont rien appris, ni rien oublié.

They have learnt nothing, and forgotten nothing.

[Attr.]

TENNYSON, Alfred, Lord (1809–1892)

From yon blue heavens above us bent
The gardener Adam and his wife
Smile at the claims of long descent.
Howe'er it be, it seems to me,
'Tis only noble to be good.
Kind hearts are more than coronets,
And simple faith than Norman blood.

['Lady Clara Vere de Vere' (c. 1835)]

THACKERAY, William Makepeace (1811–1863)

Nothing like blood, sir, in hosses, dawgs, and men.

[Vanity Fair (1848)]

WELLINGTON, Duke of (1769–1852)

I believe I forgot to tell you I was made a Duke.

[Postscript to a letter to his nephew, 1814]

WILDE, Oscar (1854–1900)

You should study the Peerage, Gerald. It is the one book a young man about town should know thoroughly, and it is the best thing in fiction the English have ever done.

[A Woman of No Importance (1893), III]

WODEHOUSE, P.G. (1881–1975)

Unlike the male codfish which, suddenly finding itself the parent of three million five hundred thousand little codfish, cheerfully resolves to love them all, the British aristocracy is apt to look with a somewhat jaundiced eye on its younger sons.

[In R. Usborne, Wodehouse at Work to the End (1976)]

WOOLF, Virginia (1882–1941)

Those comfortably padded lunatic asylums which are known, euphemistically, as the stately homes of England.

[The Common Reader (1925)]

See CLASS

THE ARMY

ANONYMOUS

[Definition of NAAFI]
Where you can eat dirt cheap.

[In Frank Muir, A Kentish Lad (1997)]

Any officer who shall behave in a scandalous manner, unbecoming the character of an officer and a gentleman shall … be CASHIERED.

[Articles of War]

[The words of a soldier in the Peninsular War]
I looked along the line; it was enough to assure me. The steady determined scowl of my companions assured my heart and gave me determination.

[In Richardson, Fighting Spirit: Psychological Factors in War (1978)]

BAXTER, James K. (1926–1972)

The boy who volunteered at seventeen
At twenty-three is heavy on the booze.

['Returned Soldier' (1946)]

BRODSKY, Joseph (1940–1996)

It is the army that finally makes a citizen of you; without it, you still have a chance, however slim, to remain a human being.

['Less Than One' (1986)]

CAMBRONNE, GENERAL (1770–1842)

La Garde meurt, et ne se rend pas.
The Guard dies and does not surrender.

[Attr., Waterloo, June 1815]

CHURCHILL, Sir Winston (1874–1965)

[On the Chiefs of Staffs system, 1943]
You may take the most gallant sailor, the most intrepid airman, or the most audacious soldier, put them at a table together – what do you get? The sum of their fears.

[In Macmillan, The Blast of War]

FREDERICK THE GREAT (1712–1786)

An army, like a serpent, goes on its belly.

[Attr.]

GERRISH, Theodore (1712–1786)

The ties that bound us together were of the

most sacred nature: they had been gotten in hardship and baptised in blood.

[*Army Life: A Private's Reminiscence of the Civil War* (1882)]

GERRY, Elbridge (1744–1814)

A standing army is like a standing member: an excellent assurance of domestic tranquillity but a dangerous temptation to foreign adventure.

[The *Observer*, 'Soundbites', 1998]

GREEN, Michael (1927–)

Fortunately, the army has had much practice in ignoring impossible instructions.

[*The Boy Who Shot Down an Airship* (1988)]

HELLER, Joseph (1923–)

I had examined myself pretty thoroughly and discovered that I was unfit for military service.

[*Catch-22* (1961)]

HOFFMANN, Max (1869–1927)

[Referring to the performance of the British army in World War I]

Ludendorff: The English soldiers fight like lions.

Hoffman: True. But don't we know that they are lions led by donkeys.

[In Falkenhayn, *Memoirs*]

HULL, General Sir Richard, (1907–)

National Service did the country a lot of good but it darned near killed the army.

[Attr.]

KIPLING, Rudyard (1865–1936)

O, it's Tommy this, an' Tommy that, an' 'Tommy, go away';
But it's 'Thank you, Mister Atkins,' when the band begins to play …

Then it's Tommy this, an' Tommy that, an' 'Tommy 'ow's yer soul?'
But it's 'Thin red line of 'eroes' when the drums begin to roll …

For it's Tommy this, an' Tommy that, an' ''Chuck him out, the brute!'

But it's 'Saviour of 'is country' when the guns begin to shoot.

[*Barrack-Room Ballads and Other Verses* (1892)]

KISSINGER, Henry (1923–)

The conventional army loses if it does not win. The guerilla wins if he does not lose.

['Foreign Affairs', XIII (1969)]

LINCOLN, Abraham (1809–1865)

If you don't want to use the army, I should like to borrow it for a while. Yours respectfully, A. Lincoln.

[Letter to General George B. McClellan during the US Civil War, 1862]

MANNING, Frederic (1882–1935)

[Of the men in his battalion]

These apparently rude and brutal natures comforted, encouraged, and reconciled each other to fate, with a tenderness and tact which was more moving than anything in life.

[*Her Privates We* (1929)]

MARLBOROUGH, Duke of (1650–1722)

No soldier can fight unless he is properly fed on beef and beer.

[Attr.]

MILLIGAN, Spike (1918–)

The Army works like this: if a man dies when you hang him, keep hanging him until he gets used to it.

[Attr.]

MONASH, Sir John (1865–1931)

Leadership counts for something, of course, but it cannot succeed without the spirit, élan and morale of those led. Therefore I count myself the most fortunate of men in having been placed at the head of the finest fighting machine the world has ever known.

[*Argus*, 1927]

A man of character in peace is a man of courage in war.

[*The Anatomy of Courage* (1945)]

NAPIER, Sir William (1785–1860)

[British general and historian]

Then was seen with what a strength and majesty the British soldier fights.

[*History of the War in the Peninsula*]

NAPOLEON I (1769–1821)

An army marches on its stomach. [*See* Frederick The Great]

[Attr.]

[Of his generals]
I made most of mine *de la boue* [out of mud]. Wherever I found talent and courage, I rewarded it. My principle was *la carrière ouverte aux talens* [sic] [career open to talent], without asking whether there were any quarters of nobility to show.

[In O'Meara, *Napoleon in Exile* (1822)]

NAPOLEON III (1808–1873)

The army is the true nobility of our country.

[Speech, March 1855]

PATTON, General George S. (1885–1945)

Untutored courage is useless in the face of educated bullets.

[*Cavalry Journal*, 1922]

QUARLES, Francis (1592–1644)

Our God and soldiers we alike adore
Ev'n at the brink of danger; not before:
After deliverance, both alike requited,
Our God's forgotten, and our soldiers slighted.

['Of Common Devotion' (1632)]

ROSTEN, Norman (1914–)

And there's the outhouse poet, anonymous:
Soldiers who wish to be a hero
Are practically zero
But whose who wish to be civilians
Jesus they run into millions.

['The Big Road']

SASSOON, Siegfried (1886–1967)

Soldiers are citizens of death's gray land,
Drawing no dividend from time's tomorrows …

Soldiers are dreamers; when the guns begin
They think of firelit homes, clean beds, and wives.

I see them in foul dug-outs, gnawed by rats,
And in the ruined trenches, lashed with rain,
Dreaming of things they did with balls and bats.

['Dreamers' (1917)]

SELLAR, Walter (1898–1951) and YEATMAN, Robert Julian (1897–1968)

Napoleon's armies always used to march on their stomachs, shouting: 'Vive l'Intérieur!' and so moved about very slowly.

[*1066 And All That* (1930)]

SHAKESPEARE, William (1564–1616)

That in the captain's but a choleric word
Which in the soldier is flat blasphemy.

[*Measure For Measure*, II.ii]

SHAW, George Bernard (1856–1950)

I never expect a soldier to think.

[*The Devil's Disciple* (1901)]

When the military man approaches, the world locks up its spoons and packs off its womankind.

[*Man and Superman* (1903)]

You can always tell an old soldier by the inside of his holsters and cartridge boxes. The young ones carry pistols and cartridges: the old ones, grub.

[*Arms and the Man* (1898)]

SMITHERS, Alan Jack (1919–)

[Of Sir John Monash, Australian military commander]
He was, above all, the first twentieth-century general, a man with petrol in his veins and a computer in his head.

STERNE, Laurence (1713–1768)

'A soldier,' cried my uncle Toby, interrupting the corporal, 'is no more exempt from saying a foolish thing, Trim, than a man of letters.' – 'But not so often, and please your honour,' replied the corporal.

[*Tristram Shandy* (1759–1767)]

TOLSTOY, Leo (1828–1910)

The chief attraction of military service has been and will remain this compulsory and irreproachable idleness.

[*War and Peace* (1868–1869)]

TRUMAN, Harry S. (1884–1972)

[Of General MacArthur]

I didn't fire him because he was a dumb son of a bitch, although he was, but that's not against the law for generals. If it was, half to three-quarters of them would be in gaol.

[In Miller, *Plain Speaking* (1974)]

TUCHOLSKY, Kurt (1890–1935)

Der französische Soldat ist ein verkleideter Zivilist, der deutsche Zivilist ist ein verkleideter Soldat.

The French soldier is a civilian in disguise, the German civilian is a soldier in disguise.

['Ocean of Pain' (1973)]

USTINOV, Sir Peter (1921–)

As for being a General, well, at the age of four with paper hats and wooden swords we're all Generals. Only some of us never grow out of it.

[*Romanoff and Juliet* (1956)]

VIGNY, Alfred de (1797–1863)

L'armée est une nation dans la nation; c'est un vice de notre temps.

The army is a nation within the nation; it is one of the vices of our times.

[*The Military Condition*, 1835]

WASHINGTON, George (1732–1799)

Discipline is the soul of an army. It makes small numbers formidable; procures success to the weak, and esteem to all.

[Letter of Instructions to the Captains of the Virginia Regiments, 1759]

WELLINGTON, Duke of (1769–1852)

When I reflect upon the characters and attainments of some of the general officers of this army, and consider that these are the persons on whom I am to rely to lead columns against the French, I tremble; and as Lord Chesterfield said of the generals of his day, 'I only hope that when the enemy reads the list of their names, he trembles as I do.'

[Letter to Torrens, 29 August 1810; usually quoted as 'I don't know what effect these men will

have upon the enemy, but, by God, they frighten me.']

[Of his troops]

The mere scum of the earth.

[In Stanhope, *Conversations with the Duke of Wellington* (1888)]

WELLS, H.G. (1866–1946)

The army ages men sooner than the law and philosophy; it exposes them more freely to germs, which undermine and destroy, and it shelters them more completely from thought, which stimulates and preserves.

[*Bealby* (1915)]

WILDE, Lady Jane (1826–1896)

There's a proud array of soldiers –
what do they round your door?
They guard our master's granaries
from the thin hands of the poor.

['The Famine Years']

See NAVY; WAR; WEAPONS

ART

ALBERT, Prince Consort (1819–1861)

The works of art, by being publicly exhibited and offered for sale, are becoming articles of trade, following as such the unreasoning laws of markets and fashion; and public and even private patronage is swayed by their tyrannical influence.

[Speech to the Royal Academy, May 1851]

ALEXANDER, Hilary (1818–1895)

To the accountants, a true work of art is an investment that hangs on the wall.

[*Sunday Telegraph*, 1993]

ANONYMOUS

We would prefer to see the Royal Opera House run by a philistine with the requisite financial acumen than by the succession of opera and ballet lovers who have brought a great and valuable institution to its knees.

[Select Committe Report into the Royal Opera House, 1997]

ANOUILH, Jean (1910–1987)

C'est très jolie la vie, mais elle n'a pas de forme. L'art a pour objet de lui en donner une précisément.
Life is very nice, but it has no shape. It is the purpose of art to give it shape.

[*The Rehearsal* (1950)]

ARTAUD, Antonin (1896–1948)

No one has ever written, painted, sculpted, modelled, built or invented except literally to get out of hell.

[In Lewis Wolpert, *Malignant Sadness* (1999)]

BACON, Francis (1909–1993)

The job of the artist is always to deepen the mystery.

[*Sunday Telegraph*,1964]

BEAVERBROOK, Lord (1879–1964)

Buy old masters. They fetch a better price than old mistresses.

[Attr.]

BEERBOHM, Sir Max (1872–1956)

The lower one's vitality, the more sensitive one is to great art.

['Enoch Soames' (1912)]

BELL, Clive (1881–1964)

It would follow that 'significant form' was form behind which we catch a sense of ultimate reality.

[*Art* (1914)]

BELLOW, Saul (1915–)

I feel that art has something to do with the achievement of stillness in the midst of chaos. A stillness which characterizes prayer, too, and the eye of the storm. I think that art has something to do with an arrest of attention in the midst of distraction.

[In Plimpton (ed.), *Writers at Work* (1967)]

BING, Rudolf (1902–)

It is so much worse to be a mediocre artist than to be a mediocre post office clerk.

[*5000 Nights at the Opera* (1972)]

BLAKE, William (1757–1827)

When Sr Joshua Reynolds died
All Nature was degraded:

The King dropd a tear into the Queens Ear:
And all his Pictures Faded.

[Annotations to Sir Joshua Reynolds' Works (c. 1808)]

BOWEN, Elizabeth (1899–1973)

Art is the only thing that can go on mattering once it has stopped hurting.

[*The Heat of the Day* (1949)]

BOWEN, Stella (1893–1947)

Any artist knows that after a good bout of work one is both too tired and too excited to be of any use to anyone. … What one wants … is for other people to occupy themselves with one's own moods and requirements; to lie on a sofa and listen to music, and to have things brought to one on a tray!

[*Drawn from Life* (1941)]

BRACK, (Cecil) John (1920–)

I know all about art, but I don't know what I like.

[In Stephen Murray-Smith (ed.), *The Dictionary of Australian Quotations*]

BRAQUE, Georges (1882–1963)

L'Art est fait pour troubler, la Science rassure.
Art is meant to disturb, science reassures.

[*Day and Night, Notebooks* (1952)]

BRAY, John Jefferson (1912–)

A hundred canvasses and seven sons
He left, and never got a likeness once.

['Epitaph on a Portrait Painter']

BRODSKY, Joseph (1940–1996)

Art is not a better, but an alternative existence; it is not an attempt to escape reality but the opposite, an attempt to animate it. It is a spirit seeking flesh but finding words.

[*Less Than One* (1986)]

BUÑUEL, Luis (1900–1983)

In any society, the artist has a responsibility. His effectiveness is certainly limited and a painter or writer cannot change the world. But they can keep an essential margin of non-conformity alive. Thanks to them, the powerful can never affirm that everyone agrees with their acts. That small difference is very important.

[Quoted by Anthony Hill in *Contemporary Artists* (1977)]

BUTLER, Samuel (1835–1902)

An art can only be learned in the workshop of those who are winning their bread by it.

[*Erewhon* (1872)]

CALMAN, Mel (1931–1994)

[In answer to the criticism of his cartoons that 'any child could do better']
Yes, but it takes courage for an adult to draw as badly as that.

[*The Independent*, 1994]

CARY, Joyce (1888–1957)

Remember I'm an artist. And you know what that means in a court of law. Next worst to an actress.

[*The Horse's Mouth* (1944)]

CERVANTES, Miguel de (1547–1616)

Digo que los buenos pintores imitaban a naturaleza; pero que los malos la vomitaban.
I say that good painters imitated nature; but that bad ones vomited it.

[*Exemplary Novels*, 1613]

CHEKHOV, Anton (1860–1904)

The artist may not be a judge of his characters, only a dispassionate witness.

[Attr.]

CHESTERTON, G.K. (1874–1936)

The artistic temperament is a disease that afflicts amateurs.

[*Heretics* (1905)]

CONNOLLY, Cyril (1903–1974)

It is closing time in the gardens of the West and from now on an artist will be judged only by the resonance of his solitude or the quality of his despair.

[*Horizon*, 1949–1950]

There is no more sombre enemy of good art than the pram in the hall.

[*Enemies of Promise* (1938)]

CONRAD, Joseph (1857–1924)

A work that aspires, however humbly, to the condition of art should carry its justification in every line.

[*The Nigger of the Narcissus* (1897)]

CONSTABLE, John (1776–1837)

[Description of Watteau's 'Plaisirs du Bal']
As if painted in honey.

[In *The Times Literary Supplement*, 1993]

In Claude's landscape all is lovely – all amiable – all is amenity and repose; – the calm sunshine of the heart.

[In C.R. Leslie, *Memoirs of the Life of John Constable* (1843)]

The amiable but eccentric Blake … said of a beautiful drawing of an avenue of fir trees … 'Why, this is not drawing, but inspiration.' … [Constable] replied, 'I never knew it before; I meant it for drawing'.

[In C.R. Leslie, *Memoirs of the Life of John Constable* (1843)]

The sound of water escaping from mill-dams, etc, willows, old rotten planks, slimy posts, and brickwork, I love such things … those scenes made me a painter and I am grateful.

[Letter to John Fisher, 1821]

CONSTANT, Benjamin (1767–1834)

Dîner avec Robinson, écolier de Schelling. Son travail sur l'esthétique du Kant. Idées très ingénieuses. L'art pour l'art et sans but; tout but dénature l'art. Mais l'art atteint au but qu'il n'a pas.
Dinner with Robinson, a pupil of Schelling. His work on the aesthetics of that man Kant. Very ingenious ideas. Art for art's sake, without a purpose; every purpose distorts the true nature of art. But art achieves a purpose which it does not have.

[*Journal intime*, 1804]

CORREGGIO (c.1489–1534)

[On seeing Raphael's 'St Cecilia' in Bologna, c. 1525]
Anch'i io sono pittore!
I, too, am an artist.

[In L. Pungileoni, *Memorie Istoriche de … Correggio* (1817)]

CROCE, Benedetto (1866–1952)

Art is ruled uniquely by the imagination.

[*Esthetic*]

CROMWELL, Oliver (1599–1658)

Mr Lely, I desire you would use all your skill to paint my picture freely like me, and not flatter me at all; but remark all these roughnesses, pimples, warts, and everything as you see me, otherwise I will never pay a farthing for it.

[In Horace Walpole, *Anecdotes of Painting in England* (1763)]

DAVY, Sir Humphry (1778–1829)

[His opinion of the art galleries in Paris]

The finest collection of frames I ever saw.

[Attr.]

DEBUSSY, Claude (1862–1918)

L'art est le plus beau des mensonges.

Art is the most beautiful of all lies.

[*Monsieur Croche, antidilettante*]

DEGAS, Edgar (1834–1917)

Art is vice. You don't marry it legitimately, you rape it.

[In Paul Lafond, *Degas* (1918)]

DEMARCO, Richard (1930–)

Art is for everyone – paint, like a piece of music, is the most international thing I know.

[Attr.]

ELIOT, T.S. (1888–1965)

The only way of expressing emotion in the form of art is by finding an 'objective correlative'; in other words, a set of objects, a situation, a chain of events which shall be the formula of that particular emotion; such that when the external facts, which must terminate in sensory experience, are given, the emotion is immediately evoked.

['Hamlet' (1919)]

No poet, no artist of any sort, has his complete meaning alone. His significance, his appreciation is the appreciation of his relation to the dead poets and artists.

['Tradition and the Individual Talent' (1919)]

No artist produces great art by a deliberate attempt to express his own personality.

['Four Elizabethan Dramatists' (1924)]

ELLIS, Havelock (1859–1939)

Every artist writes his own autobiography.

[*The New Spirit* (1890)]

EMERSON, Ralph Waldo (1803–1882)

Art is a jealous mistress, and, if a man have a genius for painting, poetry, music, architecture, or philosophy, he makes a bad husband and an ill provider.

[*Conduct of Life* (1860)]

Artists must be sacrificed to their art. Like bees, they must put their lives into the sting they give.

[*Letters and Social Aims* (1875)]

EYRE, Richard (1943–)

I would like to see the good in art made popular and the popular made good.

[BBC radio interview, 1998]

[Commenting on the Government's decision to freeze spending on the arts.]

Art is all the things that politics isn't: it's passionate, ambiguous, complex, mysterious and thrilling. It's our means of redemption, it's the image of our humanity.

[*The Observer*,1996]

FADIMAN, Clifton (1904–)

[Of Gertrude Stein]

I encountered the mama of dada again.

[*Appreciations* (1955)]

FIELDING, Henry (1707–1754)

It hath been thought a vast commendation of a painter to say his figures seem to breathe; but surely it is much greater and nobler applause, that they appear to think.

[*Joseph Andrews* (1742)]

FLAUBERT, Gustave (1821–1880)

L'artiste doit être dans son œuvre comme Dieu dans la création, invisible et tout-puissant; qu'on le sente partout, mais qu'on ne le voie pas.

The artist must be in his work as God is in creation, invisible and all-powerful; his presence should be felt everywhere, but he should never be seen.

[Letter to Mlle Leroyer de Chantepie, 1857]

FORSTER, E.M. (1879–1970)

To make us feel small in the right way is a function of art. Men can only make us feel small in the wrong way.

[Attr.]

Works of art, in my opinion, are the only objects in the material universe to possess internal order, and that is why, though I don't believe that only art matters, I do believe in Art for Art's sake.

[*Two Cheers for Democracy* (1951)]

FRIEL, Brian (1929–)

The hell of it seems to be, when an artist starts saving the world, he starts losing himself.

[*Extracts from a Sporadic Diary*]

FRY, Roger (1866–1934)

Mr Fry … brought out a screen upon which there was a picture of a circus. The interviewer was puzzled by the long waists, bulging necks and short legs of the figures. 'But how much wit there is in those figures,' said Mr Fry. 'Art is significant deformity.'

[In Virginia Woolf, *Roger Fry* (1940)]

GAUGUIN, Paul (1848–1903)

Art is either a plagiarist or a revolutionist.

[In Huneker, *Pathos of Distance* (1913)]

GAUTIER, Théophile (1811–1872)

Oui, l'œuvre sort plus belle
D'une forme au travail
Rebelle,
Vers, marbre, onyx, émail.

Yes, creation comes out more beautiful from a form rebellious to work: verse, marble, onyx, enamel.

[*Emaux et Camées* (1932)]

GEORGE I (1660–1727)

I hate all Boets and Bainters.

[In Campbell, *Lives of the Chief Justices* (1849)]

GOETHE (1749–1832)

Wenn es eine Freude ist, das Gute zu geniessen, so ist es eine grössere, das Bessere zu empfinden, und in der Kunst ist das Beste gut genug. Neapel, den 3. März, 1787.

If it is a joy to enjoy what is good, then it is a greater one to feel what is better, and in art the best is good enough. Naples, 3rd March, 1787.

[*Italian Journey*, published 1816–17)]

Im übrigen ist es zuletzt die grösste Kunst, sich zu beschränken und zu isolieren.

Incidentally, however, ultimately the greatest art is in limiting and isolating oneself.

[*Gespräche mit Eckermann*, 1825]

Das Klassische nenne ich das Gesunde, und das Romantische das Kranke.

Classicism I call health, and romanticism disease.

[*Gespräche mit Eckermann*,1829]

HEPWORTH, Dame Barbara (1903–1975)

I rarely draw what I see. I draw what I feel in my body.

[Attr.]

HERBERT, Sir A.P. (1890–1971)

A highbrow is the kind of person who looks at a sausage and thinks of Picasso.

[Attr.]

As my poor father used to say
In 1863,
Once people start on all this Art
Good-bye, moralitee!
And what my father used to say
Is good enough for me.

['Lines for a Worthy Person' (1930)]

HERSHAW, William (1957–)

[On Damien Hirst's entry for the Turner Prize for contemporary art]
A coo and a cauf
Cut in hauf.

[*The Cowdenbeath Man*]

HEYSEN, Sir Hans William (1877–1968)

Why don't they draw, draw and draw? Their

one idea is to cultivate the emotional sense, under the plea that they are expressing their personality.

[In Colin Thiele, *Haysen of Hahndorf*]

HIRST, Damien (1965–)

[On winning the Turner Prize]
It's amazing what you can do with an E in A-level art, twisted imagination and a chainsaw.

[*The Observer Review*, 1995]

I sometimes feel that I have nothing to say and I want to communicate this.

[Attr.]

HUXLEY, Aldous (1894–1963)

In the upper and the lower churches of St Francis, Giotto and Cimabue showed that art had once worshipped something other than itself.

[*Those Barren Leaves* (1925)]

INGRES, J.A.D. (1780–1867)

Le dessin est la probité de l'art.
Drawing is the true test of art.

[*Pensées d'Ingres* (1922)]

JAMES, Henry (1843–1916)

It is art that makes life, makes interest, makes importance, for our consideration and application of these things, and I know of no substitute whatever for the force and beauty of its process.

[Letter to H.G. Wells, 1915]

JOYCE, James (1882–1941)

The artist, like the God of creation, remains within or behind or beyond or above his handiwork, invisible, refined out of existence, indifferent, paring his fingernails.

[*A Portrait of the Artist as a Young Man* (1916)]

KEATS, John (1795–1821)

The excellence of every art is its intensity, capable of making all disagreeables evaporate, from their being in close relationship with Beauty and Truth.

[Letter to George and Tom Keats, 21 December 1817]

KENNEDY, John F. (1917–1963)

In free society art is not a weapon … Artists are not engineers of the soul.

[Speech, 1963]

KIPLING, Rudyard (1865–1936)

Till the Devil whispered behind the leaves,
'It's pretty, but is it Art?' …

We know that the tail must wag the dog, for the horse is drawn by the cart;
But the Devil whoops, as he whooped of old:
'It's clever, but is it Art?'.

['The Conundrum of the Workshops' (1890)]

KLEE, Paul (1879–1940)

Eine aktive Linie, die sich frei ergeht, ein Spaziergang um seiner selbst willen, ohne Ziel. Das Agens ist ein Punkt, der sich verschiebt.
An active line going for a stroll, freely, aimlessly, a walk for its own sake. The agent is a point which moves around.

[*Pedagogical Sketchbook*, 1925]

Kunst gibt nicht das Sichtbare wieder, sondern macht sichtbar.
Art does not reproduce what is visible; it makes things visible.

['Creative Credo' (1920)]

KRAUS, Karl (1874–1936)

Künstler ist nur einer, der aus der Lösung ein Rätsel machen kann.
The only person who is an artist is the one that can make a puzzle out of the solution.

[*By Night* (1919)]

LANDSEER, Sir Edwin Henry (1802–1873)

If people only knew as much about painting as I do, they would never buy my pictures.

[In Campbell Lennie, *Landseer the Victorian Paragon*]

LAWRENCE, D.H. (1885–1930)

Never trust the artist. Trust the tale. The proper function of a critic is to save the tale from the artist who created it.

[*Studies in Classic American Literature* (1923)]

LOW, Sir David (1891–1963)

I do not know whether he draws a line himself. But I assume that his is the direction … It makes Disney the most significant figure in graphic art since Leonardo.

[In R. Schickel, *Walt Disney*]

MARLBOROUGH, Sarah, First Duchess of (1660–1744)

For painters, poets and builders have very high flights, but they must be kept down.

[Letter to the Duchess of Bedford, 1734]

MARON, Monika (1941–)

Der Künstler als Bürger kann Demokrat sein, so gut und so schlecht wie alle anderen. Der Künstler als Künstler darf kein Demokrat sein.

The artist as a citizen can be a democrat, just as well and as badly as everybody else. The artist as an artist may not be a democrat.

[Interview in *Der Spiegel*, 1994]

MAYAKOVSKY, Vladimir (1893–1930)

Art is not a mirror to reflect the world, but a hammer with which to shape it.

[*The Guardian*, 1974]

MOORE, George (1852–1933)

Art must be parochial in the beginning to be cosmopolitan in the end.

[*Hail and Farewell: Ave* (1911)]

MOSES, Grandma (1860–1961)

[Of painting]
I don't advise any one to take it up as a business proposition, unless they really have talent, and are crippled so as to deprive them of physical labor.

[Attr.]

MUMFORD, Lewis (1895–1990)

The artist has a special task and duty – the task of reminding men of their humanity and the promise of their creativity.

[Attr.]

MURDOCH, Iris (1919–1999)

All art deals with the absurd and aims at the simple. Good art speaks truth, indeed is truth, perhaps the only truth.

[*The Black Prince* (1989)]

MUSSET, Alfred de (1810–1857)

Les grands artistes n'ont pas de patrie.

Great artists have no homeland.

[*Lorenzaccio* (1834)]

NIETZSCHE, Friedrich Wilhelm (1844–1900)

Als Artist hat man keine Heimat in Europa ausser in Paris.

As an artist, one has no home in Europe except Paris.

[*Ecco Homo* (1888)]

NOLAN, Sir Sidney Robert (1917–)

A successful artist would have no trouble being a successful member of the Mafia.

[*Good Weekend*, 1985]

OPIE, John (1761–1807)

[Asked how he mixed his colours]
I mix them with my brains, sir.

[In Samuel Smiles, *Self-Help* (1859)]

ORTEGA Y GASSET, José (1883–1955)

El arte es incapaz de soportar el peso de nuestra vida. Cuando lo intenta, fracasa, perdiendo su gracia esencial.

Art is incapable of bearing the burden of our lives. When it tries, it fails, losing its essential grace.

[*The Theme of our Time*, 1923]

PALMER, Samuel (1805–1881)

A picture has been said to be something between a thing and a thought.

[In Arthur Symons, *Life of Blake*]

PAOLOZZI, Eduardo (1924–)

Modernism is the acceptance of the concrete landscape and the destruction of the human soul.

['Junk and the new Arts and Crafts Movement']

PATER, Walter (1839–1894)

The love of art for art's sake.

[*Studies in the History of the Renaissance* (1873)]

All art constantly aspires towards the condition of music.

[*Studies in the History of the Renaissance* (1873)]

PICASSO, Pablo (1881–1973)

Painting is a blind man's profession. He paints not what he sees, but what he feels, what he tells himself about what he has seen.

[In Jean Cocteau, *Journals* (1929), 'Childhood']

[Explaining why a Renoir in his apartment was hung crooked]

It's better like that, if you want to kill a picture all you have to do is to hang it beautifully on a nail and soon you will see nothing of it but the frame. When it's out of place you see it better.

[In Roland Penrose, *Picasso: His Life and Work* (1958)]

There's no such thing as a bad Picasso, but some are less good than others.

[In A. Whitman, *Come to Judgement*]

[Remark made at an exhibition of children's drawings]

When I was their age, I could draw like Raphael, but it took me a lifetime to learn to draw like them.

[In Penrose, *Picasso: His Life and Work* (1958)]

RENOIR, Pierre Auguste (1841–1919)

[Of the lifelike flesh tones of his nudes]

I just keep painting till I feel like pinching. Then I know it's right.

[Attr.]

[On why he still painted although he had arthritis of his hands]

The pain passes, but the beauty remains.

[Attr.]

REYNOLDS, Sir Joshua (1723–1792)

A mere copier of nature can never produce anything great.

[*Discourses on Art* (1770)]

ROSS, Harold W. (1892–1951)

I've never been in there [the Louvre] … but there are only three things to see, and I've seen colour reproductions of all of them.

[In Ernest Hemingway, *A Farewell to Arms* (1929)]

ROSSETTI, Dante Gabriel (1828–1882)

Conception, my boy, fundamental brainwork,

is what makes the difference in all art.

[Letter to Hall Caine]

RÜCKRIEM, Ulrich (1938–)

People don't want art, they want football.

[*Scala*,1992]

RUSKIN, John (1819–1900)

I believe the right question to ask, respecting all ornament, is simply this: Was it done with enjoyment – was the carver happy while he was about it?

[*The Seven Lamps of Architecture* (1849)]

Nobody cares much at heart about Titian; only there is a strange undercurrent of everlasting murmur about his name, which means the deep consent of all great men that he is greater than they.

[*The Two Paths* (1859)]

Fine art is that in which the hand, the head, and the heart of man go together.

[*The Two Paths* (1859)]

[Of one of Whistler's works]

I have seen, and heard, much of Cockney impudence before now; but never expected to hear a coxcomb ask two hundred guineas for flinging a pot of paint in the public's face.

[*Fors Clavigera*, Letter 79, 1877]

SAATCHI, Charles (1943–)

Ninety per cent of the art I buy will probably be worthless in ten years' time.

[*The Observer*,1997]

SAND, George (1804–1876)

L'art n'est pas une étude de la réalité positive; c'est une recherche de la vérité idéale.

Art is not a study of positive reality; it is a search for ideal truth.

[*The Devil's Pond* (1846)]

L'art est une démonstration dont la nature est la preuve.

Art is a demonstration of which nature is the proof.

[*François le Champi*]

SANTAYANA, George (1863–1952)

Nothing is really so poor and melancholy as art that is interested in itself and not in its subject.

[*The Life of Reason* (1906)]

SARGENT, John Singer (1856–1925)

Every time I paint a portrait I lose a friend.

[In Bentley and Esar, *Treasury of Humorous Quotations* (1951)]

SHAHN, Ben (1898–1969)

[Outlining the difference between professional and amateur painters]
An amateur is an artist who supports himself with outside jobs which enable him to paint. A professional is someone whose wife works to enable him to paint.

[Attr.]

SHAW, George Bernard (1856–1950)

The true artist will let his wife starve, his children go barefoot, his mother drudge for his living at seventy, sooner than work at anything but his art.

[*Man and Superman* (1903)]

SMITH, Logan Pearsall (1865–1946)

How often my soul visits the National Gallery, and how seldom I go there myself!

[*Afterthoughts* (1931)]

SONTAG, Susan (1933–)

A photograph is not only an image (as a painting is an image), an interpretation of the real; it is also a trace, something directly stencilled off the real, like a footprint or a death mask.

[*New York Review of Books*,1977]

SPALDING, Julian (1948–)

The professional art world is becoming a conspiracy against the public.

[*The Daily Mail*,1996]

STEVENSON, Robert Louis (1850–1894)

A little amateur painting in water-colours shows the innocent and quiet mind.

[*Virginibus Puerisque* (1881)]

STOPPARD, Tom (1937–)

Skill without imagination is craftsmanship and gives us many useful objects such as wickerwork picnic baskets. Imagination without skill gives us modern art.

[*Artist Descending a Staircase* (1973)]

What is an artist? For every thousand people there's nine hundred doing the work, ninety doing well, nine doing good, and one lucky bastard who's the artist.

[*Travesties* (1975)]

STORR, Dr Anthony (1920–)

By creating a new unity in a poem or other work of art, the artist is attempting to restore a lost unity, or to find a new unity, within the inner world of the psyche, as well as producing work which has a real existence in the external world.

[*Solitude* (1989)]

TERTZ, Abram (1925–1997)

Fairy-tales interest me as a manifestation of pure art, perhaps the very first instance of art detaching itself from real life, and also because – like pure art – they enhance reality, remaking it in their own likeness, separating good from evil, and bringing all fears and terrors to a happy conclusion.

[*A Voice From the Chorus* (1973)]

TOLSTOY, Leo (1828–1910)

Art is not a handicraft, it is a transmission of feeling which the artist has experienced.

[*What is Art?* (1898)]

Art is a human activity which has as its purpose the transmission to others of the highest and best feelings to which men have risen.

[*What is Art?* (1898)]

TURNER, Joseph Mallord William (1775–1851)

[His customary remark following the sale of one of his paintings]
I've lost one of my children this week.

[In E. Chubb, *Sketches of Great Painters*]

USTINOV, Sir Peter (1921–)

If Botticelli were alive today he'd be working for Vogue.

[*The Observer*, 1962]

VIDAL, Gore (1925–)

He will lie even when it is inconvenient, the sign of the true artist.

[*Two Sisters* (1970)]

WARHOL, Andy (c.1926–1987)

An artist is someone who produces things that people don't need to have but that he – for some reason – thinks it would be a good idea to give them.

[*From A to B and Back Again* (1975)]

WEST, Dame Rebecca (1892–1983)

… any authentic work of art must start an argument between the artist and his audience.

[*The Court and the Castle* (1958)]

WHARTON, Edith (1862–1937)

Another unsettling element in modern art is that common symptom of immaturity, the dread of doing what has been done before.

WHISTLER, James McNeill (1834–1903)

Listen! There never was an artistic period. There never was an Art-loving nation.

[*Mr Whistler's 'Ten O'Clock'* (1885)]

[To a lady who said the two greatest painters were himself and Velasquez]

'Why,' answered Whistler in dulcet tones, 'why drag in Velasquez?'.

[In Seitz, *Whistler Stories* (1913)]

[Replying to the question 'For two days' labour, you ask two hundred guineas?']

No, I ask it for the knowledge of a lifetime.

[In Seitz, *Whistler Stories* (1913)]

WHITEHEAD, A.N. (1861–1947)

Art is the imposing of a pattern on experience, and our aesthetic enjoyment is recognition of the pattern.

[*Dialogues* (1954)]

WILDE, Oscar (1854–1900)

Art never expresses anything but itself.

[*The Nineteenth Century*, 1889]

Art is the most intense mode of individualism that the world has known.

[*The Fortnightly Review*, 1891, 'The Soul of Man under Socialism']

All art is quite useless.

[*The Picture of Dorian Gray* (1891)]

WYLLIE, George (1921–)

[On modern art]

Art is like soup. There will be some vegetables you don't like but as long as you get some soup down you it doesn't matter.

[*The Daily Mail*, 1996]

Public art is art that the public can't avoid.

[Attr.]

YEVTUSHENKO, Yevgeny (1933–)

A tremendous part in strengthening friendship between our peoples must be played by art, whose eternal role is the uniting of human hearts in the name of goodness and justice.

[*Yevtushenko Poems* (1966)]

See DESIGN; NATURE

ARTIFICIAL INTELLIGENCE

ANONYMOUS

Artificial Intelligence is the study of how to make real computers act like the ones in movies.

Artificial Intelligence is no match for natural stupidity.

Computers are not intelligent. They only think they are.

See COMPUTERS

ATHEISM

BACON, Francis (1561–1626)

I had rather believe all the fables in the

legend, and the Talmud, and the Alcoran, than that this universal frame is without a mind.

[*Essays* (1625)]

God never wrought miracle to convince atheism, because his ordinary works convince it.

[*Essays* (1625)]

It is true, that a little philosophy inclineth man's mind to atheism; but depth in philosophy bringeth men's minds about to religion.

[*Essays* (1625)]

BUCHAN, John (1875–1940)

An atheist is a man who has no invisible means of support.

[Attr.]

BUÑUEL, Luis (1900–1983)

I am still an atheist, thank God.

[Attr.]

BURKE, Edmund (1729–1797)

Man is by his constitution a religious animal; … atheism is against, not only our reason, but our instincts.

[*Reflections on the Revolution in France …* (1790)]

COWPER, William (1731–1800)

Blind unbelief is sure to err,
And scan his work in vain;
God is his own interpreter,
And he will make it plain.

[*Olney Hymns* (1779)]

CUMMINGS, William Thomas (1903–1945)

There are no atheists in the foxholes.

[In Romulo, *I Saw the Fall of the Philippines* (1943)]

DIDEROT, Denis (1713–1784)

Voyez-vous cet œuf. C'est avec cela qu'on renverse toutes les écoles de théologie, et tous les temples de la terre.
See this egg. It is with this that one overturns all the schools of theology and all the temples on earth.

[*Le Rêve de d'Alembert* (1769)]

ORWELL, George (1903–1950)

He was an embittered atheist (the sort of atheist who does not so much disbelieve in God as personally dislike Him).

[*Down and Out in Paris and London* (1933)]

OTWAY, Thomas (1652–1685)

These are rogues that pretend to be of a religion now!
Well, all I say is, honest atheism for my money.

[*The Atheist* (1683)]

PROUST, Marcel (1871–1922)

On a même pu dire que la louange la plus haute de Dieu est dans la négation de l'athée qui trouve la Création assez parfaite pour se passer d'un créateur.
It has been said that the highest praise of God consists in the denial of Him by the atheist, who finds creation so perfect that he has no need of a creator.

[*Le Cote de Guermantes* (1921)]

ROSSETTI, Dante Gabriel (1828–1882)

The worst moment for the atheist is when he is really thankful and has nobody to thank.

[Attr.]

RUSSELL, Bertrand (1872–1970)

I was told that the Chinese say they would bury me by the Western Lake and build a shrine to my memory. I have some slight regret that this did not happen, as I might have become a god, which would have been very chic for an atheist.

[*The Autobiography of Bertrand Russell* (1969)]

SARTRE, Jean-Paul (1905–1980)

Elle ne croyait á rien; seul, son scepticisme l'empêchait d'être athée.
She didn't believe in anything; only her scepticism kept her from being an atheist.

[*Words* (1964)]

TURGENEV, Ivan (1818–1883)

The courage to believe in nothing.

[*Fathers and Sons* (1862)]

YOUNG, Edward (1683–1765)
By Night an Atheist half believes a God.

[*Night-Thoughts on Life, Death and Immortality*]

See GOD; RELIGION

AUSTRALIA

BLAINEY, Geoffrey Norman (1930–)
The Tyranny of Distance: How Distance Shaped Australia's History.

[Title of book, 1966]

The physical mastering of Australia was swift and often dramatic, but the emotional conquest was slow.

[*A Land Half Won*]

BOYD, Robin Gerard Penleigh (1919–1971)
The ugliness I mean is skin deep. If the visitor to Australia fails to notice it immediately, fails to respond to the surfeit of colour, the love of advertisements, the dreadful language, the ladylike euphemisms outside public lavatory doors, the technical competence, but the almost uncanny misjudgement in floral arrangements, or if he thinks that things of this sort are too trivial to dwell on, then he is unlikely to enjoy modern Australia.

[*The Australian Ugliness* (1960)]

BRAGG, William Henry (1862–1942)
Going to Australia was like sunshine and fresh invigorating air.

[In G.M. Caroe, *William Henry Bragg* (1978)]

CUSACK, Dymphna (1902–1981)
If the Spirit of the Bush walked down Martin Place it would be raped before it got ten feet.

[Remark at the Adelaide Arts Festival, March 1964]

ELLIS, Havelock (1859–1939)
But for my everlasting good fortune I was flung into the wide sea of Australian bush alone, to sink or to swim.

[*My Life* (1940)]

ESSON, Louis (1879–1943)
Australia is the only country in the world where the peasantry make the laws.

[*The Time Is Not Yet Ripe* (1912)]

FITZGERALD, Alan John (1935–)
In Canberra, even the mistakes are planned by the National Capital Development Commission.

[*Life in Canberra*]

GALBRAITH, J.K. (1908–)
The Australians were wise to choose such a large country, for of all the people in the world they clearly require the most space.

[*Annals of an Abiding Liberal* (1980)]

GREEN, Marshall (1916–)
Lyndon B. Johnson always thought that Australia was the next large rectangular State beyond El Paso, and treated it accordingly.

[Interview in film *Allies*]

HANCOCK, Sir William Keith (1898–1988)
The little exclusive circles, which in Melbourne and Sydney had politely imitated English gentility, looked askance at the lucky upstarts – and intermarried with them. In the second half of the nineteenth century Australia became familiar with a new vulgarity and a new vigour.

[*Australia* (1930)]

HERBERT, Xavier (1901–1984)
[On returning from the war]
There's no place like home, Mum. Have me head read if ever I leave this gawd's own lovely land again. You dunno what a lovely land it is till you've seen them other crowded, foggy, frozen, furrin holes.

[*Capricornia* (1938)]

[On the plight of the Aborigines]
Until we give back to the Blackman just a bit of the land that was his and give it back without provisos, without strings to snatch it back, without anything but complete generosity of spirit in concession for the evil we have done him – until we do that, we

shall remain what we have always been so far, a people without integrity; not a nation but a community of thieves.

[*Poor Fellow My Country* (1975]

HOGAN, Paul (1939–)
We're a nation of punters and party-goers.

[Bicentenary television programme, 'Australia Live', 1988]

HOPE, Alec (Derwent) (1907–)
And her five cities, like teeming sores,
Each drains her: a vast parasite robber-state
Where second-hand Europeans pullulate
Timidly on the edge of alien shores.

['Australia' (1939)]

HORNE, Donald Richmond (1921–)
Australia is a lucky country run mainly by second-rate people who share its luck.

[*The Lucky Country: Australia in the Sixties* (1964)]

LAWRENCE, D.H. (1885–1930)
And all lying mysteriously within the Australian underdark, that peculiar, lost weary aloofness of Australia. There was the vast town of Sydney. And it didn't seem to be real, it seemed to be sprinkled on the surface of a darkness into which it never penetrated.

[*Kangaroo* (1923)]

LAWSON, Henry (1867–1922)
And the sun sank on the grand Australian bush – the nurse and tutor of eccentric minds, the home of the weird, and of much that is different from things in other lands.

['Rats' (1893)]

LENIN, V.I. (1870–1924)
[On Australia]
What sort of peculiar capitalist country is this, in which the workers' representatives predominate in the Upper House and, till recently, did so in the Lower House as well, and yet the capitalist system is in no danger?

[*Collected Works* (1963)]

MOFFITT, Ian Lawson (1929–)
The Australian's loving relationship with his car has become a commonplace: he fondles each nut and bolt in interminable

conversations in the pub; strips it, lays it on the lawn, and greases its nipples while his wife wonders whether he will ever better his indoor average of one-a-month.

[*The U-Jack Society* (1972)]

MURRAY, Les A. (1938–)
Much of the hostility to Australia … shown by English people above a certain class can be traced to the fact that we are, to a large extent, the poor who got away.

[*Sydney Morning Herald*, 1974]

PHILLIP, Arthur (1738–1814)
[From a letter to Lord Sydney, 1788]
Nor do I doubt but that this country will prove the most valuable acquisition Great Britain ever made.

[*Historical Records of New South Wales*]

PRINGLE, John Martin Douglas (1912–)
Only one profound book has been written about Australia. It is D. H. Lawrence's novel *Kangaroo*. … Most of it is as true today as when it was written thirty-five years ago. I can think of no more convincing proof of the superiority of the creative writer over the journalist or historian.

[*Australian Accent*]

ROYCE, Phillip (1903–)
… as an Australian I was brought up in an Anglo-Irish country – part of the weirdness of our personality is that inside every Australian there's an Irishman fighting an Englishman.

[*The Independent*, 1992]

WHITE, Patrick (1912–1990)
The ideal Australia I visualised during any exile and which drew me back, was always, I realise, a landscape without figures.

[*Flaws in the Glass* (1981)]

WILDE, Oscar (1854–1900)
Do you know, Mr Hopper, dear Agatha and I are so much interested in Australia. It must be so pretty with all the dear little kangaroos flying about.

[*Lady Windermere's Fan* (1892)]

B

BABIES

CHURCHILL, Sir Winston (1874–1965)
There is no finer investment for any community than putting milk into babies.

[Radio broadcast, March 1943]

COLERIDGE, Samuel Taylor (1772–1834)
So for the mother's sake the child was dear,
And dearer was the mother for the child.

['Sonnet to a Friend Who Asked How I felt When the Nurse First Presented My Infant to Me' (1797)]

DICKENS, Charles (1812–1870)
Every baby born into the world is a finer one than the last.

[*Nicholas Nickleby* (1839)]

JONSON, Ben (1572–1637)
Rest in soft peace, and, ask'd say here doth lye
Ben Jonson his best piece of poetrie.

[*Epigrams* (1616)]

MARRYAT, Frederick (1792–1848)
[Of an illegitimate baby]
If you please, ma'am, it was a very little one.

[*Mr Midshipman Easy* (1836)]

NASH, Ogden (1902–1971)
A bit of talcum
Is always walcum.

[*Free Wheeling* (1931)]

PLATH, Sylvia (1932–1963)
[On seeing her newborn baby]
What did my fingers do before they held him?
What did my heart do, with its love?
I have never seen a thing so clear.
His lids are like the lilac flower
And soft as a moth, his breath.
I shall not let go.
There is no guile or warp in him. May he

keep so.

['Three Women: A Poem for Three Voices' (1962)]

RUNYON, Damon (1884–1946)
I once knew a chap who had a system of just hanging the baby on the clothes line to dry and he was greatly admired by his fellow citizens for having discovered a wonderful innovation on changing a diaper.

[*Short Takes* (1946)]

See BIRTH; CHILDREN; PREGNANCY

BEAUTY

BACON, Francis (1561–1626)
There is no excellent beauty, that hath not some strangeness in the proportion.

[*Essays* (1625)]

BLAKE, William (1757–1827)
Exuberance is Beauty.

['Proverbs of Hell' (1793)]

BRIDGES, Robert (1844–1930)
I love all beauteous things,
I seek and adore them;
God hath no better praise,
And man in his hasty days
Is honoured for them.

I too will something make
And joy in the making;
Altho' to-morrow it seem
Like the empty words of a dream
Remembered on waking.

['I Love All Beauteous Things' (1890)]

For beauty being the best of all we know
Sums up the unsearchable and secret aims
Of nature.

['The Growth of Love' (1876)]

BUCHANAN, Robert Williams (1841–1901)
All that is beautiful shall abide,

All that is base shall die.

['Balder the Beautiful' (1877)]

Beauty and Truth, though never found, are worthy to be sought.

['To David in Heaven' (1865)]

BUCK, Pearl S. (1892–1973)

It is better to be first with an ugly woman than the hundredth with a beauty.

[*The Good Earth* (1931)]

BURKE, Edmund (1729–1797)

Beauty in distress is much the most affecting beauty.

[*A Philosophical Enquiry into the Origin of our Ideas of the Sublime and Beautiful* (1757)]

BYRON, Lord (1788–1824)

She walks in beauty, like the night
Of cloudless climes and starry skies;
And all that's best of dark and bright
Meet in her aspect and her eyes.

['She Walks in Beauty' (1815)]

CONFUCIUS (c.550–c.478 BC)

Everything has its beauty but not everyone sees it.

[*Analects*]

CONGREVE, William (1670–1729)

Beauty is the lover's gift.

[*The Way of the World* (1700)]

CONSTABLE, John (1776–1837)

There is nothing ugly; I never saw an ugly thing in my life: for let the form of an object be what it may, – light, shade, and perspective will always make it beautiful.

[In C.R. Leslie, *Memoirs of the Life of John Constable* (1843)]

COUSIN, Victor (1792–1867)

Il faut de la religion pour la religion, de la morale pour la morale, comme de l'art pour l'art … le beau ne peut être la voie ni de l'utile, ni du bien, ni du saint; il ne conduit qu'à lui-même.

There must be religion for religion's sake, morality for morality's sake, as there is art for art's sake … the beautiful cannot be the way to what is useful, nor to what is good, nor to

what is holy; it leads only to itself.

[Lecture, 1818]

DRYDEN, John (1631–1700)

When beauty fires the blood, how love exalts the mind.

[*Cymon and Iphigenia* (1700)]

ELLIS, Havelock (1859–1939)

Beauty is the child of love.

[*The New Spirit* (1890)]

The absence of flaw in beauty is itself a flaw.

[*Impressions and Comments* (1914)]

EMERSON, Ralph Waldo (1803–1882)

Though we travel the world over to find the beautiful we must carry it with us or we find it not.

[*Essays, First Series* (1841)]

FARQUHAR, George (1678–1707)

No woman can be a beauty without a fortune.

[*The Beaux' Stratagem* (1707)]

GAINSBOURG, Serge (1928–1991)

Ugliness is, in a way, superior to beauty because it lasts.

[*The Scotsman*, 1998]

GALSWORTHY, John (1867–1933)

He [Jolyon] was afflicted by the thought that where Beauty was, nothing ever ran quite straight, which, no doubt, was why so many people looked on it as immoral.

[*In Chancery* (1920)]

HOPKINS, Gerard Manley (1844–1889)

Glory be to God for dappled things …

All things counter, original, spare, strange;
Whatever is fickle, freckled (who knows how?)
With swift, slow; sweet, sour; adazzle, dim;
He fathers-forth whose beauty is past change:
Praise him.

['Pied Beauty' (1877)]

HUGO, Victor (1802–1885)

Le beau est aussi utile que l'utile. Plus peut-être.

Beauty is as useful as usefulness. Maybe more so.

[*Les Misérables* (1862)]

HUME, David (1711–1776)

Beauty is no quality in things themselves: It exists merely in the mind which contemplates them; and each mind perceives a different beauty.

[*Essays, Moral, Political, and Literary* (1742)]

HUNGERFORD, Margaret Wolfe (c.1855–1897)

Beauty is altogether in the eye of the beholder.

[*Molly Bawn* (1878)]

JOHNSON, Samuel (1709–1784)

What ills from beauty spring.

[*The Vanity of Human Wishes* (1749)]

KEATS, John (1795–1821)

'Beauty is truth, truth beauty,' – that is all
Ye know on earth, and all ye need to know.

['Ode on a Grecian Urn' (1819)]

A thing of beauty is a joy for ever:
Its loveliness increases; it will never
Pass into nothingness; but still will keep
A bower quiet for us, and a sleep
Full of sweet dreams, and health, and quiet breathing.

['Endymion' (1818)]

I never can feel certain of any truth but from a clear perception of its Beauty.

[Letter to George and Georgiana Keats, 16 December 1818–4 January 1819]

KING, William (1663–1712)

Beauty from order springs.

[*Art of Cookery* (1708)]

MARLOWE, Christopher (1564–1593)

Was this the face that launch'd a thousand ships,
And burnt the topless towers of Ilium?

[*Doctor Faustus* (1604)]

O, thou art fairer than the evening's air
Clad in the beauty of a thousand stars.

[*Doctor Faustus* (1604)]

MOLIÈRE (1622–1673)

La beauté du visage est un frêle ornement,
Une fleur passagère, un éclat d'un moment,
Et qui n'est attaché qu'á la simple épiderme.
The beauty of a face is a frail ornament, a passing flower, a moment's brightness belonging only to the skin.

[*Les Femmes savantes* (1672)]

MORTIMER, John (1923–)

Beauty is handed out as undemocratically as inherited peerages, and beautiful people have done nothing to deserve their astonishing reward.

[*The Observer*, 1999]

PHILIPS, Ambrose (c.1675–1749)

The flowers anew, returning seasons bring!
But beauty faded has no second spring.

[*The First Pastoral* (1710)]

PICASSO, Pablo (1881–1973)

I hate that aesthetic game of the eye and the mind, played by these connoisseurs, these mandarins who 'appreciate' beauty. What is beauty, anyway? There's no such thing. I never 'appreciate', any more than I 'like'. I love or I hate.

[In Françoise Gilot and Carlton Lake, *Life with Picasso* (1964)]

PUSHKIN, Aleksandr (1799–1837)

I remember a wonderful moment:
Before me you appeared,
Like a fleeting apparition,
Like a spirit of pure beauty.

['To –' (1825)]

RODÓ, José Enrique (1872–1917)

Lo bello nace de la muerte de lo útil; lo útil se convierte en bello cuando ha caducado su utilidad.
What is beautiful has its origin in the death of what is useful; what is useful becomes beautiful when it has outlived its usefulness.

[Letter to Miguel de Unamuno, 19 July 1903]

ROURKE, M.E. (20th century)

And when I told them how beautiful you are
They didn't believe me! They didn't believe me!

['They Didn't Believe Me', song, 1914]

RUSKIN, John (1819–1900)

Remember that the most beautiful things in the world are the most useless; peacocks and lilies for instance.

[*The Stones of Venice* (1851)]

RUSSELL, Bertrand (1872–1970)

Mathematics, rightly viewed, possesses not only truth, but supreme beauty –a beauty cold and austere, like that of sculpture.

[*Mysticism and Logic* (1918)]

SAKI (1870–1916)

I always say beauty is only sin deep.

['Reginald's Choir Treat' (1904)]

SAPPHO (fl. 7th–6th centuries BC)

[Greek lyric poet, known for her love poetry]

Beauty endures for only as long as it can be seen; goodness, beautiful today, will remain so tomorrow.

[In Naim Attallah, *Women* (1987)]

SCHILLER, Johann Christoph Friedrich (1759–1805)

Die Schönheit ist das Produkt der Zusammenstimmung zwischen dem Geist und den Sinnen.

Beauty is the product of harmony between the mind and the senses.

['On Naive and Sentimental Poetry', (1795–1796)]

SPENSER, Edmund (c.1522–1599)

That Beautie is not, as fond men misdeeme,
An outward shew of things, that onely seeme …

For of the soule the bodie forme doth take:
For soule is forme, and doth the bodie make.

[*Fowre Hymnes* (1596)]

STEVENS, Wallace (1879–1955)

I do not know which to prefer,
The beauty of inflections
Or the beauty of innuendoes,
The blackbird whistling
Or just after.

['Thirteen Ways of Looking at a Blackbird' (1923)]

Beauty is momentary in the mind –
The fitful tracing of a portal;

But in the flesh it is immortal.
The body dies; the body's beauty lives.
So evenings die, in their green going,
Aware, interminably flowing.

['Peter Quince at the Clavier' (1923)]

TOLSTOY, Leo (1828–1910)

It is amazing how complete is the delusion that beauty is goodness.

[*The Kreutzer Sonata* (1890)]

VIRGIL (70–19 BC)

O formose puer, nimium ne crede colori.

O beautiful boy, do not put too much trust in your beauty.

[*Eclogues*, II, line 17]

WALLACE, Lew (1827–1905)

Beauty is altogether in the eye of the beholder.

[*The Prince of India* (1893)]

WOLLSTONECRAFT, Mary (1759–1797)

Taught from their infancy that beauty is woman's sceptre, the mind shapes itself to the body, and roaming round its gilt cage, only seeks to adorn its prison.

[*A Vindication of the Rights of Woman* (1792)]

YEATS, W.B. (1865–1939)

O heart, we are old;
The living beauty is for younger men:
We cannot pay its tribute of wild tears.

[In the *Little Review*, 1918]

See APPEARANCE

BED

BENJAMIN, Walter (1892–1940)

Bücher und Dirnen kann man ins Bett nehmen.

Books and bimbos can be taken to bed.

[*One-way street*, 1928]

BRETON, Nicholas (c.1545–c.1626)

We rise with the lark and go to bed with the lamb.

['The Court and Country' (1618)]

BROOKE, Rupert (1887–1915)

The cool kindliness of sheets, that soon
Smooth away trouble; and the rough male
kiss of blankets.

['The Great Lover' (1914)]

DICKENS, Charles (1812–1870)

'It would make any one go to sleep, that
bedstead would, whether they wanted to or
not.'
'I should think,' said Sam, … 'poppies was
nothing to it.'

[The Pickwick Papers (1837), 41]

FRANKLIN, Benjamin (1706–1790)

Early to bed and early to rise,
Makes a man healthy, wealthy and wise.

[Poor Richard's Almanac (1758)]

FRY, Christopher (1907–)

It doesn't do a man any good, daylight.
It means up and doing, and that means up to
no good.
The best life is led horizontal.

[Thor, with Angels (1949)]

HERBERT, George (1593–1633)

When boyes go first to bed,
They step into their voluntarie graves.

[The Temple (1633)]

HUXLEY, Aldous (1894–1963)

Lady Capricorn, he understood, was still
keeping open bed.

[Antic Hay (1923)]

'Bed,' as the Italian proverb succinctly puts it,
'is the poor man's opera.'

[Heaven and Hell (1956)]

JENNINGS, Elizabeth (1926–)

Now deep in my bed I turn
And the world turns on the other side.

['In the Night']

JOHNSON, Samuel (1709–1784)

I have, all my life long, been lying till noon;
yet I tell all young men, and tell them with
great sincerity, that nobody who does not
rise early will ever do any good.

[In Boswell, Journal of a Tour to the Hebrides (1785)]

LAUDER, Sir Harry (1870–1950)

O! it's nice to get up in the mornin',
But it's nicer to stay in bed.

[Song, 1913]

PEPYS, Samuel (1633–1703)

And mighty proud I am (and ought to be
thankful to God Almighty) that I am able to
have a spare bed for my friends.

[Diary, August 1666]

PROUST, Marcel (1871–1922)

Longtemps, je me suis couché de bonne heure.
For a long time I used to go to bed early.

[Du côté de chez Swann (1913)]

RABELAIS, François (c.1494–c.1553)

Lever matin n'est poinct bon heur;
Boire matin est le meilleur.
Getting up in the morning is no pleasure;
Drinking in the morning is the best.

[Gargantua (1534)]

RUNYON, Damon (1884–1946)

At such an hour the sinners are still in bed
resting up from their sinning of the night
before, so they will be in good shape for
more sinning a little later on.

[Runyon á la carte (1944), 'The Idyll of Miss Sarah
Brown']

SIDNEY, Sir Philip (1554–1586)

Take thou of me smooth pillows, sweetest
bed;
A chamber deaf to noise and blind to light,
A rosy garland and a weary head.

[Astrophel and Stella (1591)]

STERNE, Laurence (1713–1768)

'My brother Toby,' quoth she, 'is going to be
married to Mrs Wadman.'
'Then he will never,' quoth my father, 'be able
to lie diagonally in his bed again as long as
he lives.'

[Tristram Shandy (1759–1767)]

STEVENSON, Robert Louis (1850–1894)

Must we to bed indeed? Well then,
Let us arise and go like men,
And face with an undaunted tread

The long black passage up to bed.

[*A Child's Garden of Verses* (1885)]

SURTEES, R.S. (1805–1864)

When at length they rose to go to bed, it struck each man as he followed his neighbour upstairs that the one before him walked very crookedly.

[*Mr Sponge's Sporting Tour* (1853), 35]

THOMAS, Dylan (1914–1953)

He was sitting straight up in bed and rocking from side to side as though the bed were on a rough road; the knotted edges of the counterpane were his reins; his invisible horses stood in a shadow beyond the bedside candle. Over a white flannel nightshirt he was wearing a red waistcoat with walnut-sized brass buttons.

[*Portrait of the Artist as a Young Dog* (1940)]

THURBER, James (1894–1961)

I suppose that the high-water mark of my youth in Columbus, Ohio, was the night the bed fell on my father.

[*My Life and Hard Times* (1933)]

A man's bed is his resting-place, but a woman's is often her rack.

[*Further Fables for Our Time* (1956)]

Early to rise and early to bed makes a male healthy and wealthy and dead.

[*The New Yorker*, 1939]

WAUGH, Evelyn (1903–1966)

I haven't been to sleep for over a year. That's why I go to bed early. One needs more rest if one doesn't sleep.

[*Decline and Fall* (1928)]

See IDLENESS AND UNEMPLOYMENT; SLEEP

BEGINNING

CARROLL, Lewis (1832–1898)

'Begin at the beginning,' the King said, very gravely, 'and go on till you come to the end:

then stop.'

[*Alice's Adventures in Wonderland* (1865)]

CHURCHILL, Sir Winston (1874–1965)

[On the Battle of Egypt]
This is not the end. It is not even the beginning of the end. But it is, perhaps, the end of the beginning.

[Speech, Mansion House, November 1942.]

DU DEFFAND, Marquise (1697–1780)

[Commenting on the legend of St Denis, who is believed to have carried his severed head for six miles after his execution]
The distance isn't important; it is only the first step that is difficult.

[Letter to d'Alembert, 1763]

HORNE, Richard Henry (1803–1884)

'Tis always morning somewhere in the world.

[*Orion* (1843)]

KEATS, John (1795–1821)

There is an old saying 'well begun is half done' – 'tis a bad one. I would use instead – 'Not begun at all until half done'.

[Letter to B.R. Haydon, 10–11 May, 1817]

LAO-TZU (c.604–531 BC)

A journey of a thousand miles must begin with a single step.

[*Tao Te Ching*]

MARY, Queen of Scots (1542–1587)

En ma fin git mon commencement.
In my end is my beginning.

[Motto embroidered with her mother's emblem]

BELIEF

AMIEL, Henri-Frédéric (1821–1881)

A belief is not true because it is useful.

[*Journal*, 1876]

ARNOLD, Matthew (1822–1888)

The Sea of Faith
Was once, too, at the full, and round earth's shore
Lay like the folds of a bright girdle furl'd.
But now I only hear

Its melancholy, long, withdrawing roar,
Retreating, to the breath
Of the night-wind, down the vast edges
drear
And naked shingles of the world.

['Dover Beach' (1867)]

AUGUSTINE, Saint (354–430)

Nisi credideritis, non intelligitis.
Unless you believe, you will not understand.

[*De Libero Arbitrio*]

BAGEHOT, Walter (1826–1877)

So long as there are earnest believers in the
world, they will always wish to punish
opinions, even if their judgement tells them it
is unwise, and their conscience that it is wrong.

[*Literary Studies* (1879)]

THE BIBLE
(King James Version)

Lord, I believe; help thou mine unbelief.

[*Mark*, 9:24]

Blessed are they that have not seen, and yet
have believed.

[*John*, 20:29]

Faith is the substance of things hoped for,
the evidence of things not seen.

[*Hebrews*, 11:1]

Faith without works is dead.

[*James*, 2:20]

BROWNE, Sir Thomas (1605–1682)

To believe only possibilities, is not faith, but
mere Philosophy.

[*Religio Medici* (1643)]

BUCK, Pearl S. (1892–1973)

I feel no need for any other faith than my
faith in human beings.

[*I Believe* (1939)]

CAESAR, Gaius Julius (c.102–44 BC)

Fere libenter homines id quod volunt credunt.
Men generally believe what they wish.

[*De Bello Gallico*]

CARROLL, Lewis (1832–1898)

If you'll believe in me, I'll believe in you.

[*Through the Looking-Glass* (1872)]

'There's no use trying,' she said: 'one can't
believe impossible things.'
'I dare say you haven't had much practice,'
said the Queen. 'When I was your age, I
always did it for half an hour a day. Why,
sometimes I've believed as many as six
impossible things before breakfast.'

[*Through the Looking-Glass* (1872)]

CHESTERTON, G.K. (1874–1936)

Reason is itself a matter of faith. It is an act of
faith to assert that our thoughts have any
relation to reality at all.

[*Orthodoxy* (1908)]

COWARD, Sir Noël (1899–1973)

Life without faith is an arid business.

[*Blithe Spirit* (1941)]

FORSTER, E.M. (1879–1970)

I do not believe in Belief … Lord I disbelieve
– help thou my unbelief.

[*Two Cheers for Democracy* (1951)]

FRANK, Anne (1929–1945)

In spite of everything I still believe that
people are good at heart.

[*The Diary of Anne Frank* (1947)]

FREUD, Sigmund (1856–1939)

The more the fruits of knowledge become
accessible to men, the more widespread is
the decline of religious belief.

[*The Future of an Illusion* (1927)]

GRANT, George (1918–)

We listen to others to discover what we
ourselves believe.

[*CBC Times*, 1959]

GREENE, Graham (1904–1991)

My belief certainly seems to get stronger in
the presence of people whose goodness
seems of almost supernatural origin.

[Attr.]

HASKINS, Minnie Louise (1875–1957)

[Quoted by King George VI in his Christmas
broadcast, 1939]
And I said to a man who stood at the gate of

the year: 'Give me a light that I may tread safely into the unknown.' And he replied: 'Go out into the darkness and put your hand into the hand of God. That shall be to you better than a light, and safer than a known way.'

[*The Desert* (1908)]

IBSEN, Henrik (1828–1906)

It's not just what we inherit from our mothers and fathers that haunts us. It's all kinds of old defunct theories, all sorts of old defunct beliefs, and things like that. It's not that they actually live on in us; they are simply lodged there, and we cannot get rid of them. I've only to pick up a newspaper and I seem to see ghosts gliding between the lines.

[*Ghosts* (1881)]

JENKINS, David (1925–)

As I get older I seem to believe less and less and yet to believe what I do believe more and more.

[*The Observer*, 1988]

JOWETT, Benjamin (1817–1893)

My dear child, you must believe in God in spite of what the clergy tell you.

[In M. Asquith, *Autobiography* (1922)]

KANT, Immanuel (1724–1804)

Es ist nur eine (wahre) Religion; aber es kann vielerlei Arten des Glaubens geben.
There is only one (true) religion; but there can be many different kinds of belief.

[*Religion within the Boundaries of Mere Reason* (1793)]

LAMB, Charles (1775–1834)

Credulity is the man's weakness, but the child's strength.

[*Essays of Elia* (1823)]

MADAN, Geoffrey (1895–1947)

The dust of exploded beliefs may make a fine sunset.

[*Livre sans nom: Twelve Reflections* (1934)]

MENCKEN, H.L. (1880–1956)

Faith may be defined briefly as an illogical belief in the occurrence of the improbable.

[*Prejudices* (1927)]

NEWMAN, John Henry, Cardinal (1801–1890)

Though you can believe what you choose, you must believe what you ought.

[Letter, 1848]

It is as absurd to argue men, as to torture them, into believing.

[Sermon, 1831]

We can believe what we choose. We are answerable for what we choose to believe.

[Letter to Mrs Froude, 1848]

ORWELL, George (1903–1950)

Doublethink means the power of holding two contradictory beliefs in one's mind simultaneously, and accepting both of them.

[*Nineteen Eighty-Four* (1949)]

POPE, Alexander (1688–1744)

The most positive men are the most credulous.

[*Miscellanies* (1727)]

RUSSELL, Bertrand (1872–1970)

It is undesirable to believe a proposition when there is no ground whatever for supposing it true.

[*Sceptical Essays* (1928)]

Every man, wherever he goes, is encompassed by a cloud of comforting convictions, which move with him like flies on a summer day.

[*Sceptical Essays* (1928)]

[On being asked if he would be willing to die for his beliefs]
Of course not. After all, I may be wrong.

[Attr.]

SITWELL, Dame Edith (1887–1964)

During the writing … of this book, I realized that the public will believe anything – so long as it is not founded on truth.

[*Taken Care Of* (1965), Preface]

STEVENSON, Robert Louis (1850–1894)

Life is not all Beer and Skittles. The inherent tragedy of things works itself out from white to black and blacker, and the poor things of a day look ruefully on. Does it shake my cast iron faith? I cannot say it does. I believe in an ultimate decency of things; ay, and if I woke in hell, should still believe it!

[Letter to Sidney Colvin, 1893]

STORR, Dr Anthony (1920–)

One man's faith is another man's delusion.

[*Feet of Clay* (1996)]

TURGENEV, Ivan (1818–1883)

The courage to believe in nothing.

[*Fathers and Sons* (1862)]

UNAMUNO, Miguel de (1864–1936)

Creer en Dios es anhelar que le haya y es además conducirse como si le hubiera.

To believe in God is to yearn for his existence and, moreover, it is to behave as if he did exist.

[*The Tragic Sense of Life* (1913)]

VALÉRY, Paul (1871–1945)

Ce qui a été cru par tous, et toujours, et partout, a toutes les chances d'être faux.

What has always been believed by everyone, everywhere, will most likely turn out to be false.

[*Moralities*, 1932]

VOLTAIRE (1694–1778)

La foi consiste à croire ce que la raison ne croit pas … Il ne suffit pas qu'une chose soit possible pour la croire.

Faith consists in believing what reason does not believe … It is not enough that a thing may be possible for it to be believed.

[*Questions sur l'Encyclopédie* (1770–1772)]

WARBURTON, William (1698–1779)

Orthodoxy is my doxy; heterodoxy is another man's doxy.

[In Joseph Priestley, *Memoirs* (1807)]

See FAITH; RELIGION

BAGEHOT, Walter (1826–1877)

The most melancholy of human reflections, perhaps, is that, on the whole, it is a question whether the benevolence of mankind does most good or harm.

[*Physics and Politics* (1872)]

CHAMFORT, Nicolas (1741–1794)

Our gratitude to most benefactors is the same as our feeling for dentists who have pulled our teeth. We acknowledge the good they have done and the evil from which they have delivered us, but we remember the pain they occasioned and do not love them very much.

[*Maximes et pensées* (1796)]

COMPTON-BURNETT, Dame Ivy (1884–1969)

At any time you might act for my good. When people do that, it kills something precious between them.

[*Manservant and Maidservant* (1947)]

CONNOLLY, Billy (1942–)

[Of Andrew Carnegie]

It was said that he gave money away as silently as a waiter falling down a flight of stairs with a tray of glasses.

[*Gullible's Travels*]

CREIGHTON, Mandell (1843–1901)

No people do so much harm as those who go about doing good.

[*The Life and Letters of Mandell Creighton* (1904)]

GILBERT, W.S. (1836–1911)

I love my fellow creatures – I do all the good I can –
Yet everybody says I'm such a disagreeable man!

[*Princess Ida* (1884)]

GOLDSMITH, Oliver (c.1728–1774)

And learn the luxury of doing good.

['The Traveller' (1764)]

JOHNSON, Samuel (1709–1784)

Patron. Commonly a wretch who supports

with insolence, and is paid with flattery.

[*A Dictionary of the English Language* (1755)]

Is not a Patron, my Lord, one who looks with unconcern on a man struggling for life in the water, and, when he has reached ground, encumbers him with help? The notice which you have been pleased to take of my labours, had it been early, had been kind; but it has been delayed till I am indifferent, and cannot enjoy it; till I am solitary, and cannot impart it; till I am known, and do not want it.

[Letter to Lord Chesterfield, 1755]

MACHIAVELLI (1469–1527)

It is the nature of men to be bound by the benefits they confer as much as by those they receive.

[*The Prince* (1532)]

TITUS VESPASIANUS (AD 39–81)

Recordatus quondam super cenam, quod nihil cuiquam toto die praestitisset, memorabilem illam meritoque laudatam vocem edidit: 'Amici, diem perdidi.'
Recalling once after dinner that he had done nothing to help anyone all that day, he gave voice to that memorable and praiseworthy remark: 'Friends, I have lost a day.'

[In Suetonius, *Lives of the Caesars*]

WORDSWORTH, William (1770–1850)

On that best portion of a good man's life;
His little, nameless, unremembered acts
Of kindness and of love.

['Lines composed a few miles above Tintern Abbey' (1798)]

See GOODNESS

BETRAYAL

CHURCHILL, Sir Winston (1874–1965)

It is all right to rat, but you can't re-rat.

[Attr.]

CONGREVE, William (1670–1729)

Man was by Nature Woman's cully made:
We never are, but by ourselves, betrayed.

[*The Old Bachelor* (1693)]

BIBLE

CHILLINGWORTH, William (1602–1644)

The Bible and the Bible only is the religion of Protestants.

[*The Religion of Protestants* (1637)]

SELDEN, John (1584–1654)

Scrutamini scripturas. [Let us look at the Scriptures]. These two words have undone the world.

[*Table Talk* (1689)]

WHATELY, Richard (1787–1863)

[To a meeting of his diocesan clergy]
'Never forget, gentlemen,' he said, to his astonished hearers, as he held up a copy of the 'Authorised Version' of the Bible, 'never forget that this is not the Bible,' then, after a moment's pause, he continued, 'This, gentlemen, is only a translation of the Bible.'

[In H. Solly, *These Eighty Years* (1893)]

See RELIGION

BIOGRAPHY

AMIS, Martin (1949–)

[Of biography]
To be more interested in the writer than the writing is just eternal human vulgarity.

[*The Observer Review*, 1996]

ANDERSEN, Hans Christian (1805–1875)

Every man's life is a fairy-tale written by God's fingers.

[*Works* (c. 1843), Preface]

ARBUTHNOT, John (1667–1735)

[Of biography]
One of the new terrors of death.

[In Carruthers, *Life of Pope* (1857)]

BENTLEY, Edmund Clerihew (1875–1956)

The art of Biography
Is different from Geography.
Geography is about Maps,

But Biography is about chaps.

[*Biography for Beginners* (1905)]

BRONTË, Rev. Patrick (1777–1861)

[About her agreeing to write the life of Charlotte Brontë]

No quailing, Mrs Gaskell! no drawing back!

[Letter to Ellen Nussey, 1855]

CARLYLE, Thomas (1795–1881)

There is no life of a man, faithfully recorded, but is a heroic poem of its sort, rhymed or unrhymed.

[*Critical and Miscellaneous Essays* (1839)]

A well-written Life is almost as rare as a well-spent one.

[*Critical and Miscellaneous Essays* (1839)]

CRISP, Quentin (1908–)

An autobiography is an obituary in serial form with the last instalment missing.

[*The Naked Civil Servant* (1968)]

DAVIES, Robertson (1913–1995)

Biography at its best is a form of fiction.

[*The Lyre of Orpheus* (1988)]

DISRAELI, Benjamin (1804–1881)

Read no history: nothing but biography, for that is life without theory.

[*Contarini Fleming* (1832)]

EMERSON, Ralph Waldo (1803–1882)

There is properly no history; only biography.

[*Essays, First Series* (1841)]

FRYE, Northrop (1912–1991)

There's only one story, the story of your life.

[In Ayre, *Northrop Frye: A Biography* (1989)]

GLADSTONE, William (1809–1898)

[On J.W. Cross's *Life of George Eliot*]

It is not a Life at all. It is a Reticence, in three volumes.

[In E.F. Benson, *As We Were* (1930)]

GRANT, Cary (1904–1986)

Nobody is ever truthful about his own life. There are always ambiguities.

[*The Observer*, 1981]

GUEDALLA, Philip (1889–1944)

Biography, like big-game hunting, is one of the recognized forms of sport, and it is as unfair as only sport can be.

[*Supers and Supermen* (1920)]

JOHNSON, Samuel (1709–1784)

Nobody can write the life of a man, but those who have eat and drunk and lived in social intercourse with him.

[In Boswell, *The Life of Samuel Johnson* (1791)]

LEE, Robert E. (1807–1870)

[Refusing to write his memoirs]

I should be trading on the blood of my men.

[In M. Ringo, *Nobody Said It Better*]

MACAULAY, Lord (1800–1859)

[Refusing to write his memoirs]

Biographers, translators, editors, all, in short, who employ themselves in illustrating the lives or writings of others, are peculiarly exposed to the Lues Boswelliana, or disease of admiration.

[*Collected Essays* (1843)]

SALINGER, J.D. (1919–)

If you really want to hear about it, the first thing you'll probably want to know is where I was born and what my lousy childhood was like, and how my parents were occupied and all before they had me, and all that David Copperfield kind of crap.

[*The Catcher in the Rye* (1951)]

STOCKS, Mary, Baroness (1891–1975)

Biographies are like anthologies, especially anthologies of poetry. One's eyes are magnetically directed to what ought to be there but isn't, as well as to what oughtn't to be there but is.

[*Still More Commonplace* (1973)]

TROLLOPE, Anthony (1815–1882)

In these days a man is nobody unless his biography is kept so far posted up that it may be ready for the national breakfast-table on the morning after his demise.

[*Doctor Thorne* (1858)]

WALPOLE, Horace (1717–1797)

The life of any man written under the direction of his family, did nobody honour.

[Letter, 1778]

WEST, Dame Rebecca (1892–1983)

Just how difficult it is to write biography can be reckoned by anybody who sits down and considers just how many people know the real truth about his or her love affairs.

[Vogue, 1952]

WILDE, Oscar (1854–1900)

Every great man has his disciples, but it is always Judas who writes the biography.

[Attr.]

BIRDS

ARISTOPHANES (c.445–385 BC)

[Suggestion for the name of the Birds' capital city]
What do you think of 'Cloudcuckooland'?

[Birds, 819]

ARLEN, Michael (1895–1956)

There is a tale that is told in London about a nightingale, how it did this and that and, finally for no apparent reason, rested and sang in Berkeley Square.

[These Charming People (1924)]

BRIDGES, Robert (1844–1930)

I heard a linnet courting
His lady in the spring.

['I heard a linnet' (1890)]

BROWNING, Elizabeth Barrett (1806–1861)

Near all the birds
Will sing at dawn, – and yet we do not take
The chaffering swallow for the holy lark.

[Aurora Leigh (1857)]

CLARE, John (1793–1864)

The crow will tumble up and down
At the first sight of spring
And in old trees around the town
Brush winter from its wing.

['Crows in Spring']

CUPPY, Will (1884–1949)

The Dodo never had a chance. He seems to have been invented for the sole purpose of becoming extinct and that was all he was good for.

[How to Become Extinct (1941)]

GIBBONS, Orlando (1583–1625)

The silver swan, who, living had no note,
When death approached unlocked her silent throat.

['The Silver Swan' (1612)]

GILMORE, Dame Mary (1865–1962)

I never knew how wide the dark,
I never knew the depth of space,
I never knew how frail a bark,
How small is man within his place,

Not till I heard the swans go by,
Not till I marked their haunting cry,
Not till, within the vague on high,
I watched them pass across the sky.

['Swans at Night']

HARDY, Thomas (1840–1928)

A little ball of feather and bone.

['Shelley's Skylark' (1887)]

At once a voice arose among
The bleak twigs overhead
In a full-hearted evensong
Of joy illimited;
An aged thrush, frail, gaunt, and small,
In blast-beruffled plume,
Had chosen thus to fling his soul
Upon the growing gloom.

So little cause for carolings
Of such ecstatic sound
Was written on terrestrial things
Afar or nigh around,
That I could think there trembled through
His happy good-night air
Some blessed Hope, whereof he knew
And I was unaware.

['The Darkling Thrush' (1900)]

ISHERWOOD, Christopher (1904–1986)

The common cormorant or shag

Lays eggs inside a paper bag
The reason you will see no doubt
It is to keep the lightning out.

But what these unobservant birds
Have never noticed is that herds
Of wandering bears may come with buns
And steal the bags to hold the crumbs.

['The Common Cormorant' (c. 1925)]

JEFFERS, Robinson (1887–1962)
… I gave him the lead gift in the twilight.
What fell was relaxed,
Owl-downy, soft feminine feathers; but what
Soared: the fierce rush: the night-heron by
the flooded river cries fear at its rising
Before it was quite unsheathed from reality.

[*Hunt Hawks* (1928)]

KEATS, John (1795–1821)
Where the nightingale doth sing
Not a senseless, trancèd thing,
But divine melodious truth.

['Ode' (1818)]

Thou wast not born for death, immortal Bird!
No hungry generations tread thee down;
The voice I hear this passing night was heard
In ancient days by emperor and clown:
Perhaps the self-same song that found a
path
Through the sad heart of Ruth, when sick for
home,
She stood in tears amid the alien corn;
The same that oft-times hath
Charm'd magic casements, opening on the
foam
Of perilous seas, in faery lands forlorn.

['Ode to a Nightingale' (1819)]

LEAR, Edward (1812–1888)
There was an Old Man with a beard,
Who said, 'It is just as I feared! –
Two Owls and a Hen,
Four Larks and a Wren,
Have all built their nests in my beard!'.

[*A Book of Nonsense* (1846)]

LEE, Harper (1926–)
Shoot all the bluejays you want, if you can hit

'em, but remember it's a sin to kill a
mockingbird.

[*To Kill a Mockingbird* (1960)]

LYLY, John (c.1554–1606)
What bird so sings, yet does so wail?
O 'tis the ravish'd nightingale.
Jug, jug, jug, jug, tereu, she cries,
And still her woes at midnight rise.

[*Campaspe* (1584)]

[The lark]
How at heaven's gates she claps her wings,
The morn not waking till she sings.

[*Campaspe* (1584)]

MANSFIELD, Katherine (1888–1923)
The ostrich burying its head in the sand does
at any rate wish to convey the impression
that its head is the most important part of it.

[*Journal of Katherine Mansfield* (1954)]

MEREDITH, George (1828–1909)
Lovely are the curves of the white owl
sweeping
Wavy in the dusk lit by one large star.
Lone in the fir-branch, his rattle-note
unvaried,
Brooding o'er the gloom, spins the brown
eve-jar.

['Love in the Valley' (1883), V]

MERRITT, Dixon Lanier (1879–1972)
A wonderful bird is the pelican,
His bill will hold more than his belican.
He can take in his beak
Food enough for a week,
But I'm damned if I see how the helican.

[*Nashville Banner*, 1913]

NASH, Ogden (1902–1971)
The song of canaries
Never varies,
And when they're moulting
They're pretty revolting.

[*The Face is Familiar* (1940)]

ROCHE, Sir Boyle (1743–1807)
He regretted that he was not a bird, and
could not be in two places at once.

[Attr.]

SHELLEY, Percy Bysshe (1792–1822)

Hail to thee, blithe Spirit!
Bird thou never wert,
That from Heaven, or near it,
Pourest thy full heart
In profuse strains of unpremeditated art.

['To a Skylark' (1820)]

SPENSER, Edmund (c.1522–1599)

The merry Cuckow, messenger of Spring,
His trompet shrill hath thrise already
sounded.

[*Amoretti, and Epithalamion* (1595),
Sonnet 19]

THOREAU, Henry David (1817–1862)

I once had a sparrow alight upon my
shoulder for a moment while I was hoeing in
a village garden, and I felt that I was more
distinguished by that circumstance than I
should have been by any epaulet I could
have worn.

[*Walden* (1854)]

WEBSTER, John (c.1580–c.1625)

We think caged birds sing, when indeed they
cry.

[*The White Devil* (1612)]

WILLIAMS, Tennessee (1911–1983)

Caged birds accept each other but flight is
what they long for.

[*Camino Real* (1953)]

WILLIAMS, William Carlos (1883–1963)

On a tissue-thin monotone of blue-grey buds
two blue-grey birds, chasing a third,
at full cry! Now they are
flung outward and up – disappearing
suddenly!

['Spring Strains' (1917)]

WORDSWORTH, William (1770–1850)

O blithe new-comer! I have heard,
I hear thee and rejoice.
O Cuckoo! Shall I call thee bird,
Or but a wandering voice?

['To the Cuckoo' (1807)]

BIRTH

ACKERLEY, J.R. (1896–1967)

I was born in 1896, and my parents were
married in 1919.

[*My Father and Myself* (1968)]

AUSTEN, Jane (1775–1817)

The stain of illegitimacy, unbleached by
nobility or wealth, would have been a stain
indeed.

[*Emma* (1816)]

BHAGAVADGITA

For that which is born death is certain, and
for the dead birth is certain. Therefore grieve
not over that which is unavoidable.

[Ch. II]

BLAKE, William (1757–1827)

My mother groand! my father wept.
Into the dangerous world I leapt:
Helpless, naked, piping loud:
Like a fiend hid in a cloud.

Struggling in my father's hands:
Striving against my swadling bands:
Bound and weary I thought best
To sulk upon by mothers breast.

[*Songs of Experience* (1794)]

CALDERÓN DE LA BARCA, Pedro (1600–1681)

Pues el delito mayor del hombre es haber nacido.
For man's greatest offence is to have been
born.

[*Life is a Dream* (1636)]

CONGREVE, William (1670–1729)

I came upstairs into the world; for I was born
in a cellar.

[*Love for Love* (1695)]

FROMM, Erich (1900–1980)

Man's main task in life is to give *birth* to
himself.

[*Man for Himself*]

GUEST, Edgar A. (1945–)

Whoe'er has paced the floor
And lived those years of fearful thoughts,

and then been swept from woe
Up to the topmost height of bliss that's given
man to know,
Will tell you there's no phrase so sweet, so
charged with human joy
As that the doctor brings from God – that
message: 'It's a boy!'.

['It's a Boy']

LETTE, Kathy

Childbirth was the moment of truth in my
life. Suddenly you realise that you are having
the greatest love affair of your life (but you
also realise that God's a bloke).

[*The Observer*, June 1999]

LILLIE, Beatrice (1894–1989)

I'll simply say here that I was born Beatrice
Gladys Lillie at an extremely tender age
because my mother needed a fourth at
meals.

[*Every Other Inch a Lady* (1973)]

MACNEICE, Louis (1907–1963)

I am not yet born; O fill me
With strength against those who would
freeze my
humanity, would dragoon me into a lethal
automaton,
would make me a cog in a machine, a thing
withone face, a thing, and against all those
who would dissipate my entirety, would
blow me like thistledown hither and
thither or hither and thither
like water held in the
hands would spill me.

Let them not make me a stone and let them
not spill me.
Otherwise kill me.

['Prayer before Birth' (1944)]

MADONNA (1958–)

[Requesting an epidural in advance of childbirth,
1996]
I'm not interested in being Wonder Woman
in the delivery room. Give me drugs.

MITCHELL, MARGARET (1900–1949)

Death and taxes and childbirth! There's never
any convenient time for any of them.

[*Gone With The Wind* (1936)]

PLATO (c.429–347 BC)

You must consider this too, that we are born,
each of us, not for ourselves alone but partly
for our country, partly for our parents and
partly for our friends.

[*Epistles*, IX]

SOPHOCLES (496–406 BC)

Not to be born is the best of all; next best is,
having been born, to return as quickly as
possible whence we came.

[*Oedipus at Colonus*, line 1225]

STOWE, Harriet Beecher (1811–1896)

'Who was your mother?' 'Never had none!'
said the child, with another grin. 'Never had
any mother? What do you mean? Where
were you born?' 'Never was born!' persisted
Topsy.

[*Uncle Tom's Cabin* (1852)]

WISDOM, Norman (1918–)

I was born in very sorry circumstances. My
mother was sorry and my father was sorry as
well.

[*The Observer*, 1998]

WORDSWORTH, William (1770–1850)

Our birth is but a sleep and a forgetting.
The Soul that rises with us, our life's Star,
Hath had elsewhere its setting,
And cometh from afar;
Not in entire forgetfulness,
And not in utter nakedness,
But trailing clouds of glory do we come
From God, who is our home.

['Ode: Intimations of Immortality' (1807)]

See BABIES; PREGNANCY

THE BODY

BLAKE, Wiliam (1757–1827)

Man has no Body distinct from his Soul for
that called Body is a portion of Soul discernd
by the five Senses, the chief inlets of Soul in

this age.

[*The Marriage of Heaven and Hell* (c. 1790–1793)]

ORTON, Joe (1933–1967)

I'd the upbringing a nun would envy and that's the truth. Until I was fifteen I was more familiar with Africa than my own body.

[*Entertaining Mr Sloane* (1964)]

SANGER, Margaret (1879–1966)

No woman can call herself free who does not own and control her own body.

[In Rosalind Miles, *The Women's History of the World* (1988)]

STERNE, Laurence (1713–1768)

A man's body and his mind … are exactly like a jerkin and a jerkin's lining; – rumple the one, – you rumple the other.

[*Tristram Shandy* (1759–1767)]

SWIFT, Jonathan (1667–1745)

Thus finishing his grand survey,
The swain disgusted slunk away,
Repeating in his amorous fits,
'Oh! Celia, Celia, Celia shits!'.

['The Lady's Dressing Room' (1732)]

TRAHERNE, Thomas (c.1637–1674)

The hands are a sort of feet, which serve us in our passage towards Heaven, curiously distinguished into joints and fingers, and fit to be applied to any thing which reason can imagine or desire.

[*Meditations on the Six Days of Creation* (1717)]

WHEELER, Hugh (1912–1987)

To lose a lover or even a husband or two during the course of one's life can be vexing. But to lose one's teeth is a catastrophe.

[*A Little Night Music* (1974)]

WHITMAN, Walt (1819–1892)

If anything is sacred the human body is sacred.

['I Sing the Body Electric' (1855)]

See APPEARANCE; VANITY

BOLDNESS

LIVY (59 BC–AD 17)

In rebus asperis et tenui spe fortissima quaeque consilia tutissima sunt.

In harsh circumstances when there is little hope, the boldest measures are the safest.

[*History*,XXV]

MARMION, Shackerley (1603–1639)

Familiarity begets boldness.

[*The Antiquary* (1641)]

SPENSER, Edmund (c.1522–1599)

And as she lookt about, she did behold,
How over that same dore was likewise writ,
Be bold, be bold, and every where Be bold …
At last she spyde at that roome's upper end,
Another yron dore, on which was writ,
Be not too bold.

[*The Faerie Queene* (1596)]

SWIFT, Jonathan (1667–1745)

He was a bold man that first eat an oyster.

[*Polite Conversation* (1738)]

VIRGIL (70–19 BC)

Audentis Fortuna iuvat.

Fortune helps those who dare.

[*Aeneid*, X, line 284]

BOOKS

ADDISON, Joseph (1672–1719)

A reader seldom peruses a book with pleasure until he knows whether the writer of it be a black man or a fair man, of a mild or choleric disposition, married or a bachelor.

[*The Spectator*, 1711]

ARNOLD, Matthew (1822–1888)

He [the translator] will find one English book and one only, where, as in the Iliad itself, perfect plainness of speech is allied with perfect nobleness; and that book is the Bible.

[*On Translating Homer* (1861)]

AUDEN, W.H. (1907–1973)

Some books are undeservedly forgotten;

none are undeservedly remembered.

[*The Dyer's Hand* (1963)]

BACON, Francis (1561–1626)

Books will speak plain when counsellors blanch.

['Of Counsel' (1625)]

Some books are to be tasted, others to be swallowed, and some few to be chewed and digested; that is, some books are to be read only in parts; others to be read but not curiously; and some few to be read wholly, and with diligence and attention.

['Of Studies' (1625)]

BELLOC, Hilaire (1870–1953)

When I am dead, I hope it may be said: 'His sins were scarlet, but his books were read.'

[*Sonnets and Verse* (1923)]

BOORSTIN, Daniel J. (1914–)

A best-seller was a book which somehow sold well simply because it was selling well.

[*The Image* (1962)]

BRODSKY, Joseph (1940–1996)

There are worse crimes than burning books. One of them is not reading them.

[Remark, 1991]

BROWNE, Sir Thomas (1605–1682)

They do most by Books, who could do much without them, and he that chiefly owes himself unto himself, is the substantial man.

[*Christian Morals* (1716)]

BROWNING, Elizabeth Barrett (1806–1861)

Of writing many books there is no end.

[*Aurora Leigh* (1857)]

BURGESS, Anthony (1917–1993)

The possession of a book becomes a substitute for reading it.

[*New York Times Book Review*]

BYRON, Lord (1788–1824)

'Tis pleasant, sure, to see one's name in print;
A Book's a Book, altho' there is nothing in't.

[*English Bards and Scotch Reviewers* (1809)]

CALLIMACHUS (c.305–c.240 BC)

A great book is like great evil.

[In R. Pfeiffer (ed.), *Fragments*]

CAMPBELL, Baron (1799–1861)

So essential did I consider an Index to be to every book, that I proposed to bring a Bill into parliament to deprive an author who publishes a book without an Index of the privilege of copyright; and, moreover, to subject him, for his offence, to a pecuniary penalty.

[*Lives of the Chief Justices*, Preface to Vol. III]

CARROLL, Lewis (1832–1898)

'What is the use of a book,' thought Alice, 'without pictures or conversations?'.

[*Alice's Adventures in Wonderland* (1865)]

CHANDLER, Raymond (1888–1959)

If my books had been any worse I should not have been invited to Hollywood, and … if they had been any better, I should not have come.

[Letter to C.W. Morton, 1945]

CHESTERFIELD, Lord (1694–1773)

Due attention to the inside of books, and due contempt for the outside, is the proper relation between a man of sense and his books.

[Letter to his son, 1749]

COWPER, William (1731–1800)

Books are not seldom talismans and spells.

[*The Task* (1785)]

CRABBE, George (1754–1832)

Books cannot always please, however good;
Minds are not ever craving for their food.

[*The Borough* (1810)]

Lo! all in silence, all in order stand,
And mighty folios first, a lordly band,
Then quartos, their well-order'd ranks maintain,
And light octavos fill a spacious plain;
See yonder, ranged in more frequented rows,
A humbler band of duodecimos.

[*The Library* (1808), line 128]

With awe around these silent walks I tread:
These are the lasting mansions of the dead.

[*The Library* (1808)]

This, books can do – nor this alone: they give
New views to life, and teach us how to live;
They soothe the grieved, the stubborn they
chastise;
Fools they admonish, and confirm the wise,
Their aid they yield to all: they never shun
The man of sorrow, nor the wretch undone;
Unlike the hard, the selfish, and the proud,
They fly not from the suppliant crowd;
Nor tell to various people various things,
But show to subjects, what they show to
kings.

[*The Library* (1808)]

DAVIES, Robertson (1913–1995)

A truly great book should be read in youth,
again in maturity, and once more in old age,
as a fine building should be seen by morning
light, at noon, and by moonlight.

[In Grant, *The Enthusiasms of Robertson Davies*]

DESCARTES, René (1596–1650)

La lecture de tous les bons livres est comme une
conversation avec les plus honnêtes gens des siècles
passés.

The reading of all good books is like a
conversation with the finest men of past
centuries.

[*Discours de la Méthode* (1637)]

DIODORUS SICULUS (c.1st century BC)

[Inscription over library door in Alexandria]
Medicine for the soul.

[*History*]

EVANS, Dame Edith (1888–1976)

[On being told that Nancy Mitford had been lent a
villa to enable her to finish a book]
Oh really. What exactly is she reading?

[Attr.]

FLAUBERT, Gustave (1821–1880)

Les livres ne se font pas comme les enfants, mais
comme les pyramides … et ça ne sert á rien! et ça
reste dans le désert! … Les chacals pissent au bas et
les bourgeois montent dessus.

Books are made not like children but like the
pyramids … and they're good for nothing!
and they stay in the desert! Jackals piss at
their foot and the bourgeois climb up on
them.

[Letter to Ernest Feydeau, 1857]

FORSTER, E.M. (1879–1970)

I suggest that the only books that influence
us are those for which we are ready, and
which have gone a little farther down our
particular path than we have yet got
ourselves.

[*Two Cheers for Democracy* (1951)]

FRANKLIN, Benjamin (1706–1790)

If you would not be forgotten as soon as you
are dead, either write things worth reading
or do things worth writing.

[Attr.]

FRYE, Northrop (1912–1991)

The book is the world's most patient
medium.

[*The Scholar in Society*, film, 1984]

FULLER, Thomas (1608–1661)

Learning hath gained most by those books
by which the printers have lost.

[*The Holy State and the Profane State*
(1642)]

GLOUCESTER, William, Duke of (1743–1805)

Another damned, thick, square book. Always
scribble, scribble, scribble! Eh! Mr. Gibbon?

[In Henry Best, *Personal and Literary Memorials*
(1829)]

GOLDSMITH, Oliver (c.1728–1774)

I…shewed her that books were sweet
unreproaching companions to the miserable,
and that if they could not bring us to enjoy
life, they would at least teach us to endure it.

[*The Vicar of Wakefield* (1766)]

A book may be amusing with numerous
errors, or it may be very dull without a single
absurdity.

[*The Vicar of Wakefield* (1766)]

HEINE, Heinrich (1797–1856)

Dort, wo man Bücher
Verbrennt, verbrennt man auch am Ende Menschen.
It is there, where they
Burn books, that eventually they burn people
too.

[*Almansor: A Tragedy* (1821)]

HEMINGWAY, Ernest (1898–1961)

For a true writer each book should be a new
beginning, where he tries again for
something that is beyond attainment.

[Speech for the presentation of the Nobel Prize,
1954]

HORACE (65–8 BC)

Delere licebit
Quod non edideris; nescit vox missa reverti.
You can destroy what you haven't published;
the word once out cannot be recalled.

[*Ars Poetica*]

HUXLEY, Aldous (1894–1963)

A bad book is as much of a labour to write as
a good one; it comes as sincerely from the
author's soul … its sincerities will be …
uninterestingly expressed, and the labour
expended on the expression will be wasted.
Nature is monstrously unjust. There is no
substitute for talent. Industry and all the
virtues are of no avail.

[*Point Counter Point* (1928)]

The proper study of mankind is books.

[*Crome Yellow* (1921)]

INNES, Hammond (1913–)

[On growing trees]
I'm replacing some of the timber used up by
my books. Books are just trees with squiggles
on them.

[*Radio Times*, 1984]

JAMES, Brian (1892–1972)

The book of my enemy has been
remaindered
And I am pleased.

['The Book of My Enemy Has Been Remaindered']

JOWETT, Benjamin (1817–1893)

One man is as good as another until he has

written a book.

[In E. Abbott and L. Campbell (eds), *Life and Letters
of Benjamin Jowett* (1897)]

KAFKA, Franz (1883–1924)

*Ich glaube, man sollte überhaupt nur solche Bücher
lesen, die einen beissen und stechen.*
I think you should only read those books
which bite and sting you.

[Letter to Oskar Pollak, 1904]

*… ein Buch muss die Axt sein für das gefrorene Meer
in uns.*
… a book must be the axe for the frozen sea
within us.

[Letter to Oskar Pollak, 1904]

KENNEDY, A.L. (1965–)

[Definition of a classic]
… a book which in some manner celebrates
and encourages the human imagination,
which renders possible the impossible, which
sustains the interior life of the reader and
which speaks to and of the human spirit.

[*What makes a classic a classic? The test of time*]

KORAN

Every age hath its book.

[Chapter 13]

LA BRUYÈRE, Jean de (1645–1696)

*C'est un métier que de faire un livre, comme de faire
une pendule: il faut plus que de l'esprit pour être
auteur.*
The making of a book, like the making of a
clock, is a craft; it takes more than wit to be
an author.

[*Les caractères ou les moeurs de ce siècle* (1688)]

LAING, R.D. (1927–1989)

Few books today are forgivable.

[*The Politics of Experience* (1967)]

LAMB, Charles (1775–1834)

I mean your borrowers of books – those
mutilators of collections, spoilers of the
symmetry of shelves, and creators of odd
volumes.

[*Essays of Elia* (1823)]

I love to lose myself in other men's minds.

When I am not walking, I am reading; I cannot sit and think. Books think for me.

[*Last Essays of Elia* (1833)]

LARKIN, Philip (1922–1985)

Get stewed:
Books are a load of crap.

['A Study of Reading Habits' (1964)]

LEBOWITZ, Fran (1946–)

Never judge a book by its cover.

[*Metropolitan Life* (1978)]

LICHTENBERG, Georg (1742–1799)

There can hardly be a stranger commodity in the world than books. Printed by people who don't understand them; sold by people who don't understand them; bound, criticized and read by people who don't understand them, and now even written by people who don't understand them.

[A Doctrine of Scattered Occasions]

MACAULAY, Dame Rose (1881–1958)

It was a book to kill time for those who like it better dead.

[Attr.]

MARTIAL (c.AD 40–c.104)

Lasciva est nobis pagina, vita proba.
My book is licentious, but my life is pure.

[*Epigrammata*]

MAUGHAM, William Somerset (1874–1965)

There is an impression abroad that everyone had it in him to write one book; but if by this is implied a good book the impression is false.

[*The Summing Up* (1938)]

MILTON, John (1608–1674)

As good almost kill a Man as kill a good Book; who kills a Man kills a reasonable creature, God's Image; but hee who destroyes a good Booke, kills reason it selfe, kills the Image of God, as it were in the eye. Many a man lives a burden to the Earth; but a good Booke is the pretious life-blood of a master spirit, imbalm'd and treasur'd up on purpose

to a life beyond life.

[*Areopagitica* (1644)]

MURDOCH, Sir Walter Logie Forbes (1874–1970)

A second-hand bookshop is the sign and symbol of a civilized community … and the number and quality of these shops give you the exact measure of a city's right to be counted among the great cities of the world … Show me a city's second-hand bookshops, and I will tell you what manner of citizens dwell there, and of what ancestry sprung.

[*Collected Essays* (1940)]

POWELL, Anthony (1905–)

Books Do Furnish a Room.

[Title of novel, 1971]

RALEIGH, Sir Walter A. (1861–1922)

An anthology is like all the plums and orange peel picked out of a cake.

[Letter to Mrs Robert Bridges, 1915]

REED, Henry (1914–1986)

I have known her pass the whole evening without mentioning a single book, or in fact anything unpleasant, at all.

[*A Very Great Man Indeed* (1953)]

ROGERS, Samuel (1763–1855)

When a new book is published, read an old one.

[Attr.]

ROOSEVELT, Franklin Delano (1882–1945)

We all know that books burn – yet we have the greater knowledge that books cannot be killed by fire. People die, but books never die. No man and no force can abolish memory … In this war, we know, books are weapons.

[*Publisher's Weekly*, 1942, 'Message to the American Booksellers Association']

RUSKIN, John (1819–1900)

All books are divisible into two classes: the books of the hour, and the books of all time.

[*Sesame and Lilies* (1865)]

What do we, as a nation, care about books?

How much do you think we spend altogether on our libraries, public or private, as compared with what we spend on our horses?

[*Sesame and Lilies* (1865)]

If a book is worth reading, it is worth buying.

[*Sesame and Lilies* (1865)]

SAMUEL, Lord (1870–1963)

A library is thought in cold storage.

[*A Book of Quotations* (1947)]

SINGER, Isaac Bashevis (1904–1991)

Children… have no use for psychology. They detest sociology. They still believe in God, the family, angels, devils, witches, goblins, logic, clarity, punctuation, and other such obsolete stuff … When a book is boring, they yawn openly. They don't expect their writer to redeem humanity, but leave to adults such childish illusions.

[Nobel Prize acceptance speech, 1978]

SMITH, Logan Pearsall (1865–1946)

A best-seller is the gilded tomb of a mediocre talent.

[*Afterthoughts* (1931)]

SMITH, Sydney (1771–1845)

No furniture so charming as books, even if you never open them, or read a single word.

[In Holland, *A Memoir of the Reverend Sydney Smith* (1855)]

SPENSER, Edmund (c.1522–1599)

The generall end therefore of all the booke is to fashion a gentleman or noble person in vertuous and gentle discipline.

[*The Faerie Queene* (1596)]

STEINBECK, John (1902–1968)

It is wonderful that even today, with all the competition of radio, television, films, and records, the book has kept its precious character. A book is somehow sacred. A dictator can kill and maim people, can sink to any kind of tyranny, and only be hated. But when books are burnt the ultimate in tyranny has happened. This we cannot forgive.

[Attr.]

STEVENSON, Robert Louis (1850–1894)

Books are good enough in their own way, but they are a mighty bloodless substitute for life.

[*Virginibus Puerisque* (1881)]

SWIFT, Jonathan (1667–1745)

Books, like men their authors, have no more than one way of coming into the world, but there are ten thousand to go out of it, and return no more.

[*A Tale of a Tub* (1704)]

TROLLOPE, Anthony (1815–1882)

Of all the needs a book has the chief need is that it be readable.

[*Autobiography* (1883)]

TUPPER, Martin (1810–1889)

A good book is the best of friends, the same today and for ever.

[*Proverbial Philosophy* (1838)]

VALÉRY, Paul (1871–1945)

Les livres ont les mêmes ennemis que l'homme: le feu, l'humide, les bêtes, le temps; et leur propre contenu.
Books have the same enemies as man: fire, damp, animals, time; and their own contents.

[*Littérature*]

WAUGH, Evelyn (1903–1966)

Particularly against books the Home Secretary is. If we can't stamp out literature in the country, we can at least stop it being brought in from outside.

[*Vile Bodies* (1930)]

WESLEY, John (1703–1791)

Beware you be not swallowed up in books! An ounce of love is worth a pound of knowledge.

[In Southey, *Life of Wesley* (1820)]

WEST, Dame Rebecca (1892–1983)

God forbid that any book should be banned. The practice is as indefensible as infanticide.

[*The Strange Necessity* (1928)]

WILDE, Oscar (1854–1900)

There is no such thing as a moral or an

immoral book. Books are well written, or badly written. That is all.

[*The Picture of Dorian Gray* (1891)]

WODEHOUSE, P.G. (1881–1975)
[Dedication]
To my daughter Leonora without whose never-failing sympathy and encouragement this book would have been finished in half the time.

[*The Heart of a Goof* (1926)]

See CENSORSHIP; CRITICISM; FICTION; LITERATURE; PUBLISHING; READING; WRITERS; WRITING

BOREDOM

AUSTIN, Warren Robinson (1877–1962)
[On being asked if he found long debates at the UN tiring]
It is better for aged diplomats to be bored than for young men to die.

[Attr.]

BIERCE, Ambrose (1842–c.1914)
Bore: A person who talks when you wish him to listen.

[*The Cynic's Word Book* (1906)]

BRIDIE, James (1888–1951)
Boredom is a sign of satisfied ignorance, blunted apprehension, crass sympathies, dull understanding, feeble powers of attention and irreclaimable weakness of character.

[*Mr Bolfry* (1943)]

BRYSON, Bill (1951–)
I mused for a few moments on the question of which was worse, to lead a life so boring that you are easily enchanted or a life so full of stimulus that you are easily bored.

[*The Lost Continent* (1989)]

BYRON, Lord (1788–1824)
Society is now one polish'd horde,
Form'd of two mighty tribes, the Bores and
Bored.

[*Don Juan* (1819–1824)]

CARTER, Angela (1940–1992)
[Rationalization of the Japanese veneration of boredom]
He loved to be bored; don't think he was contemptuously dismissive of the element of boredom inherent in sexual activity. He adored and venerated boredom. He said that dogs, for example, were never bored, nor birds, so, obviously, the capacity that distinguished man from the other higher mammals, from the scaled and feathered things, was that of boredom. The more bored one was, the more one expressed one's humanity.

['The Quilt Maker']

CHESTERTON, G.K. (1874–1936)
There is no such thing on earth as an uninteresting subject; the only thing that can exist is an uninterested person.

[*Heretics* (1905)]

DE VRIES, Peter (1910–1993)
I wanted to be bored to death, as good a way to go as any.

[*Comfort me with Apples* (1956)]

DURRELL, Lawrence (1912–1990)
No more about sex, it's too boring.

[*Tunc* (1968)]

EMERSON, Ralph Waldo (1803–1882)
Every hero becomes a bore at last.

[*Representative Men* (1850)]

FREUD, Clement (1924–)
If you resolve to give up smoking, drinking and loving, you don't actually live longer; it just seems longer.

[*The Observer*, 1964]

GAUTIER, Théophile (1811–1872)
Plutôt la barbarie que l'ennui.
Sooner barbarity than boredom.

[Attr.]

HALSEY, Margaret (1910–)
… it takes a great deal to produce ennui in

an Englishman and if you do, he only takes it as convincing proof that you are well-bred.

[*With Malice Toward Some* (1938)]

HOWELLS, W.D. (1837–1920)

Some people can stay longer in an hour than others can in a week.

[In Esar, *Treasury of Humorous Quotations* (1951)]

HUGO, Victor (1802–1885)

La symétrie, c'est l'ennui, et l'ennui est le fond même du deuil. Le désespoir baille.
Symmetry is boredom, and boredom is the very source of death. Despair yawns.

[*Les Misérables* (1862)]

HUXLEY, Aldous (1894–1963)

I can sympathize with people's pains, but not with their pleasures. There is something curiously boring about somebody else's happiness.

[*Limbo* (1920)]

INGE, William Ralph (1860–1954)

The effect of boredom on a large scale in history is underestimated. It is a main cause of revolutions, and would soon bring to an end all the static Utopias and the farmyard civilization of the Fabians.

[*End of an Age* (1948)]

JERROLD, Douglas William (1803–1857)

[Remark to a small thin man who was boring him]
Sir, you are like a pin, but without either its head or its point.

[Attr.]

LA ROCHEFOUCAULD (1613–1680)

On s'ennuie presque toujours avec les gens avec qui il n'est pas permis de s'ennuyer.
We are almost always bored by the very people whom we are not allowed to find boring.

[*Maximes*, (1678)]

NIETZSCHE, Friedrich Wilhelm (1844–1900)

Ist das Leben nicht hundert Mal zu kurz, sich in ihm – zu langweilen?

Is life not a hundred times too short – to get bored?

[*Beyond Good and Evil*, (1886)]

SAKI (1870–1916)

'I believe I take precedence,' he said coldly; 'you are merely the club Bore; I am the club Liar.'

[*Beasts and Super-Beasts* (1914)]

SHAKESPEARE, William (1564–1616)

Life is as tedious as a twice-told tale
Vexing the dull ear of a drowsy man.

[*King John*, III.iv]

STEELE, Sir Richard (1672–1729)

It is to be noted, That when any Part of this Paper appears dull, there is a Design in it.

[*The Tatler*, 38, 1709]

TAYLOR, Bert Leston (1866–1921)

A bore is a man who, when you ask him how he is, tells you.

[*The So-Called Human Race* (1922)]

THOMAS, Dylan (1914–1953)

Dylan talked copiously, then stopped. 'Somebody's boring me,' he said, 'I think it's me.'

[In Heppenstall, *Four Absentees* (1960)]

TREE, Sir Herbert Beerbohm (1853–1917)

[Of Israel Zangwill]
He is an old bore; even the grave yawns for him.

[In Pearson, *Beerbohm Tree* (1956)]

UPDIKE, John (1932–)

A healthy male adult bore consumes one and a half times his own weight in other people's patience.

[*Assorted Prose* (1965)]

VOLTAIRE (1694–1778)

Le secret d'ennuyer est celui de tout dire.
The secret of being boring is to say everything.

[*Discours en vers sur l'homme* (1737)]

BORROWING AND LENDING

LAMB, Charles (1775–1834)
The human species, according to the best theory I can form of it, is composed of two distinct races, the men who borrow, and the men who lend.

[*Essays of Elia* (1823)]

PROVERB
Lend only what you can afford to lose.

SURTEES, R.S. (1805–1864)
Three things I never lends – my 'oss, my wife, and my name.

[*Hillingdon Hall* (1845)]

TUSSER, Thomas (c.1524–1580)
Who goeth a borrowing
Goeth a sorrowing.
Few lend (but fools)
Their working tools.

[*Five Hundred Points of Good Husbandry* (1557)]

BREVITY

BRABAZON OF TARA, Lord (1910–1974)
I take the view, and always have done, that if you cannot say what you have to say in twenty minutes, you should go away and write a book about it.

[Attr.]

FONTAINE, Jean de la (1621–1695)
Mais les ouvrages les plus courts
Sont toujours les meilleurs.
But the shortest works are always the best.

[*Fables*, 'Les lapins']

HORACE (65–8 BC)
Brevis esse laboro,
Obscurus fio.
I labour to be brief, and I become obscure.

[*Ars Poetica*, line 25]

JONSON, Ben (1572–1637)
In small proportions we just beauties see;
And in short measures, life may perfect be.

[*The Underwood* (1640), 'To the Immortal Memory … of … Sir Lucius Carey and Sir H. Morison']

THOREAU, Henry David (1817–1862)
Not that the story need be long, but it will take a long while to make it short.

[Letter to Harrison Blake, 1857]

See DEBT

BRITAIN

ACHESON, Dean (1893–1971)
Great Britain … has lost an Empire and not yet found a role. The attempt to play a separate power role – that is, a role apart from Europe, a role based on a 'special relationship' with the United States, a role based on being the head of a Commonwealth … this role is about to be played out … Her Majesty's Government is now attempting, wisely in my opinion, to re-enter Europe.

[Speech, 1962]

ARTLEY, Alexandra
[On the reprocessing of foreign nuclear waste in Britain]
This is not 'polite and tidy Britain' … It's Widow Twankey's Nuclear Laundry.

[In *Britain in the Eighties* (1989)]

ATTLEE, Clement (1883–1967)
I think the British have the distinction above all other nations of being able to put new wine into old bottles without bursting them.

[*Hansard*, 1950]

BORROW, George (1803–1881)
There are no countries in the world less known by the British than these selfsame British Islands.

[*Lavengro* (1851)]

BULLOCK, Alan, Baron (1914–)
The people Hitler never understood, and whose actions continued to exasperate him to the end of his life, were the British.

[*Hitler, A Study in Tyranny* (1952)]

CAMP, William (1926–)

What annoys me about Britain is the rugged will to lose.

[Attr.]

CASSON, Sir Hugh (1910–)

The British love permanence more than they love beauty.

[*The Observer*, 1964]

CHESTERFIELD, Lord (1694–1773)

It must be owned that the Graces do not seem to be natives of Great Britain; and, I doubt, the best of us here have more of the rough than the polished diamond.

[Letter to his son, 1748]

CHURCHILL, Sir Winston (1874–1965)

[Of the British]

They are the only people who like to be told how bad things are – who like to be told the worst.

[Speech, 1921]

When I warned them [the French Government] that Britain would fight on alone whatever they did, their Generals told their Prime Minister and his divided Cabinet, 'In three weeks England will have her neck wrung like a chicken'. Some chicken! Some neck!

[Speech, December 1941]

The British Empire and the United States will have to be somewhat mixed up together in some of their affairs for mutual and general advantage. For my own part, looking out for the future, I do not view the process with any misgivings. I could not stop it if I wished; no one can stop it. Like the Mississippi, it just keeps rolling along. Let it roll. Let it roll on full flood, inexorable, irresistible, benignant, to broader lands and better days.

[Speech, House of Commons, August 1940]

The maxim of the British people is 'Business as usual'.

[Speech, November 1914]

COLERIDGE, Samuel Taylor (1772–1834)

[Of Britain]

A vain, speech-mouthing, speech-reporting guild,
One benefit-club for mutual flattery.

['Fears in Solitude' (1798)]

EDMOND, James (1859–1933)

I had been told by Jimmy Edmond in Australia that there were only three things against living in Britain: the place, the climate and the people.

[In Low, *Low Autobiography*]

GAITSKELL, Hugh (1906–1963)

[On Britain's joining the European Community]

It does mean, if this is the idea, the end of Britain as an independent European state … it means the end of a thousand years of history.

[Speech, 1962]

HAMILTON, William (Willie) (1917–)

Britain is not a country that is easily rocked by revolution … In Britain our institutions evolve. We are a Fabian Society writ large.

[*My Queen and I* (1975)]

HARLECH, Lord (1918–1985)

In the end it may well be that Britain will be honoured by historians more for the way she disposed of an empire than for the way in which she acquired it.

[*New York Times*, 1962]

LEVIN, Bernard (1928–)

Once, when a British Prime Minister sneezed, men half a world away would blow their noses. Now when a British Prime Minister sneezes nobody else will even say 'Bless You'.

[*The Times*, 1976]

LLOYD GEORGE, David (1863–1945)

What is our task? To make Britain a fit country for heroes to live in.

[Speech, 1918]

SHAW, George Bernard (1856–1950)

He [the Briton] is a barbarian, and thinks that the custom of his tribe and island are the laws of nature.

[*Caesar and Cleopatra* (1901)]

SMITH, Adam (1723–1790)

If any of the provinces of the British empire cannot be made to contribute towards the support of the whole empire, it is surely time that Great Britain should free herself from the expense of defending those provinces in time of war, and of supporting any part of their civil or military establishments in time of peace, and endeavour to accommodate her future views and designs to the real mediocrity of her circumstances.

[*Wealth of Nations* (1776)]

SOMERVILLE, William (1675–1742)

Hail, happy Britain! highly favoured isle, And Heaven's peculiar care!

[*The Chase* (1735)]

THOMSON, James (1700–1748)

When Britain first, at heaven's command, Arose from out the azure main, This was the charter of the land, And guardian angels sung this strain: 'Rule, Britannia, rule the waves; Britons never will be slaves.'

[*Alfred: A Masque* (1740)]

See EMPIRE; ENGLAND; IRELAND; PATRIOTISM; SCOTLAND; WALES

BUREAUCRACY

ACHESON, Dean (1893–1971)

A memorandum is written not to inform the reader but to protect the writer.

[Attr.]

ADENAUER, Konrad (1876–1967)

Es gibt nichts, was durch Beamte nicht wieder kaputtgemacht werden kann. There's nothing which cannot be made a mess of again by officials.

[*Der Spiegel*, 1975]

ALLEN, Fred (1894–1956)

A conference is a gathering of important people who singly can do nothing, but together can decide that nothing can be done.

[Attr]

ANONYMOUS

A committee is a cul-de-sac down which ideas are lured and then quietly strangled.

[*New Scientist*, 1973]

A camel is a horse designed by a committee.

DICKENS, Charles (1812–1870)

Whatever was required to be done, the Circumlocution Office was beforehand with all the public departments in the art of perceiving – HOW NOT TO DO IT.

[*Little Dorrit* (1857)]

FONDA, Jane (1937–)

You can run the office without a boss, but you can't run an office without the secretaries.

[*The Observer*, 1981]

FOOT, Michael (1913–)

A Royal Commission is a broody hen sitting on a china egg.

[Speech, House of Commons, 1964]

GOWERS, Sir Ernest (1880–1966)

It is not easy nowadays to remember anything so contrary to all appearances as that officials are the servants of the public; and the official must try not to foster the illusion that it is the other way round.

[*Plain Words*]

HUXLEY, Aldous (1894–1963)

Official dignity tends to increase in inverse ratio to the importance of the country in which the office is held.

[*Beyond the Mexique Bay* (1934)]

KELLY, Bert (1912–1997)

Always remember that if a civil servant had the ability to … correctly foresee the demand situation for any product he would not be working for the government for long. He would shortly be sitting in the south of France with his feet in a bucket of champagne!

[*Economics Made Easy*]

MCCARTHY, Mary (1912–1989)

Bureaucracy, the rule of no one, has become the modern form of despotism.

[*The New Yorker*, 1958]

MCLUHAN, Marshall (1911–1980)

An administrator in a bureaucratic world is a man who can feel big by merging his non-entity with an abstraction. A real person in touch with real things inspires terror in him.

[Letter to Ezra Pound, 1951]

SAMPSON, Anthony (1926–)

[Of the Civil Service]

Members rise from CMG (known sometimes in Whitehall as 'Call Me God') to the KCMG ('Kindly Call Me God') to … the GCMG ('God Calls Me God').

[*The Anatomy of Britain* (1962)]

SAMUEL, Lord (1870–1963)

[Referring to the Civil Service]

A difficulty for every solution.

[Attr.]

SANTAYANA, George (1863–1952)

The working of great institutions is mainly the result of a vast mass of routine, petty malice, self interest, carelessness, and sheer mistake. Only a residual fraction is thought.

[*The Crime of Galileo*]

THOMAS, Gwyn (1913–1981)

My life's been a meeting, Dad, one long meeting. Even on the few committees I don't yet belong to, the agenda winks at me when I pass.

[*The Keep* (1961)]

TREE, Sir Herbert Beerbohm (1853–1917)

A committee should consist of three men, two of whom are absent.

[In Pearson, *Beerbohm Tree*]

VIDAL, Gore (1925–)

There is something about a bureaucrat that

does not like a poem.

[*Sex, Death and Money* (1968)]

BUSINESS

ANONYMOUS

A Company for carrying on an undertaking of Great Advantage, but no one to know what it is.

[*The South Sea Company Prospectus*]

Our company absorbs the cost.

[Useful Arab phrase in modern Arab–English phrase book for American oil engineers]

AUSTEN, Jane (1775–1817)

Business, you know, may bring money, but friendship hardly ever does.

[*Emma* (1816)]

BAGEHOT, Walter (1826–1877)

Business is really more agreeable than pleasure; it interests the whole mind, the aggregate nature of man more continuously, and more deeply. But it does not look as if it did.

[*The English Constitution* (1867)]

BALZAC, Honoré de (1799–1850)

Generous people make bad shopkeepers.

[*Illusions perdues* (1843)]

BARNUM, Phineas T. (1810–1891)

Every crowd has a silver lining.

[Attr.]

BETJEMAN, Sir John (1906–1984)

You ask me what it is I do. Well
actually, you know,
I'm partly a liaison man and partly
P.R.O.
Essentially I integrate the current
export drive
And basically I'm viable from ten
o'clock till five.

['Executive' (1974)]

CHARLES, Prince of Wales (1948–)

British management doesn't seem to

understand the importance of the human factor.

[Speech, 1979]

COHEN, Sir Jack (1898–1979)

Pile it high, sell it cheap.

[Business motto]

DENNIS, C.J. (1876–1938)

It takes one hen to lay an egg,
But seven men to sell it.

['The Regimental Hen']

DICKENS, Charles (1812–1870)

Here's the rule for bargains. 'Do other men, for they would do you.' That's the true business precept. All others are counterfeit.

[*Martin Chuzzlewit* (1844)]

FRANKLIN, Benjamin (1706–1790)

No nation was ever ruined by trade.

[*Essays*]

GALBRAITH, J.K. (1908–)

The salary of the chief executive of the large corporation is not a market award for achievement. It is frequently in the nature of a warm personal gesture by the individual to himself.

[*Annals of an Abiding Liberal* (1980)]

GANDHI (1869–1948)

It is difficult but not impossible to conduct strictly honest business. What is true is that honesty is incompatible with the amassing of a large fortune.

[*Non–Violence in Peace and War* (1948)]

GOLDWYN, Samuel (1882–1974)

Chaplin is no business man – all he knows is that he can't take anything less.

[Attr.]

KHRUSHCHEV, Nikita (1894–1971)

[Remark to British businessmen]
When you are skinning your customers, you should leave some skin on to heal so that you can skin them again.

[*The Observer*, 1961]

LLOYD GEORGE, David (1863–1945)

Love your neighbour is not merely sound

Christianity; it is good business.

[*The Observer*, 1921]

MACMILLAN, Harold (1894–1986)

[Macmillan and Company Limited] propose to carry on their business at St Martin's Street, London W.C.2 until they are either taxed, insured, ARP'd or bombed out of existence.

[Announcement, 17 September 1939]

MENCKEN, H.L. (1880–1956)

[Referring to the businessman]
He is the only man who is ever apologizing for his occupation.

[*Prejudices* (1927)]

NAPOLEON I (1769–1821)

L'Angleterre est une nation de boutiquiers.
England is a nation of shopkeepers.

[In O'Meara, *Napoleon in Exile* (1822)]

ONASSIS, Aristotle (1906–1975)

The secret of business is to know something that nobody else knows.

[*The Economist*, 1991]

PUZO, Mario (1920–)

He's a businessman. I'll make him an offer he can't refuse.

[*The Godfather* (1969)]

REVSON, Charles (1906–1975)

In the factory we make cosmetics. In the store we sell hope.

[In Tobias, *Fire and Ice* (1976)]

ROOSEVELT, Theodore (1858–1919)

We demand that big business give the people a square deal; in return we must insist that when any one engaged in big business honestly endeavors to do right he shall himself be given a square deal.

[*Theodore Roosevelt: an Autobiography* (1913)]

SHEEN, J. Fulton (1895–1979)

[Referring to his contract for a television appearance]
The big print giveth and the fine print taketh away.

[Attr.]

SMITH, Adam (1723–1790)

People of the same trade seldom meet together, even for merriment and diversion, but the conversation ends in a conspiracy against the public, or in some contrivance to raise prices.

[*Wealth of Nations* (1776)]

THURLOW, Edward, First Baron (1731–1806)

Did you ever expect a corporation to have a conscience, when it has no soul to be damned, and no body to be kicked?

[Attr.]

WARHOL, Andy (c.1926–1987)

Being good in business is the most fascinating kind of art.

[*The Observer*, 1987]

WILDER, Thornton (1897–1975)

A living is made, Mr Kemper, by selling something that everybody needs at least once a year. Yes, sir! And a million is made by producing something that everybody needs every day. You artists produce something that nobody needs at any time.

[*The Merchant of Yonkers* (1939)]

WILSON, Charles E. (1890–1961)

What is good for the country is good for General Motors, and vice versa.

[Remark to Congressional Committee, 1953]

WILSON, Woodrow (1856–1924)

Business underlies everything in our national life, including our spiritual life. Witness the fact that in the Lord's Prayer the first petition is for daily bread. No one can worship God or love his neighbour on an empty stomach.

[Speech, 1912]

YOUNG, Andrew (1932–)

Nothing is illegal if one hundred businessmen decide to do it.

[Attr.]

See BUYING AND SELLING; CAPITALISM; ECONOMICS; MONEY AND WEALTH

C

CAPITALISM

ANONYMOUS
Capitalism is the exploitation of man by man.
Communism is the complete opposite.

[Described by Laurence J. Peter as a 'Polish
proverb']

CONNOLLY, James (1868–1916)
Governments in a capitalist society are but
committees of the rich to manage the affairs
of the capitalist class.

[*Irish Worker*, 1914]

GALBRAITH, J.K. (1908–)
You must now speak always of the market
system. The word 'capitalism', once the
common reference, has acquired a
deleterious Marxist sound.

[*The Observer*, 1998]

GONNE, Maud (1865–1953)
To me judges seem the well paid watch-dogs
of Capitalism, making things safe and easy
for the devil Mammon.

[Letter to W.B. Yeats]

HAMPTON, Christopher (1946–)
If I had to give a definition of capitalism I
would say: the process whereby American
girls turn into American women.

[*Savages* (1973)]

HEATH, Sir Edward (1916–)
[On the Lonrho affair (involving tax avoidance)]
The unpleasant and unacceptable face of
capitalism.

[Speech, House of Commons, 1973]

ILLICH, Ivan (1926–)
In a consumer society there are inevitably
two kinds of slaves: the prisoners of
addiction and the prisoners of envy.

[*Tools for Conviviality* (1973)]

KELLER, Helen (1880–1968)
Militarism ... is one of the chief bulwarks of
capitalism, and the day that militarism is
undermined, capitalism will fail.

[*The Story of My Life* (1902)]

KEYNES, John Maynard (1883–1946)
I think that Capitalism, wisely managed, can
probably be made more efficient for
attaining economic ends than any
alternative system yet in sight, but that in
itself it is in many ways extremely
objectionable.

['The End of Laissez-Faire' (1926)]

LENIN, V.I. (1870–1924)
Under capitalism we have a state in the
proper sense of the word, that is, a special
machine for the suppression of one class by
another.

[*The State and Revolution* (1917)]

MALCOLM X (1925–1965)
You show me a capitalist, I'll show you a
bloodsucker.

[*Malcolm X Speaks*, 1965]

MARCUSE, Herbert (1898–1979)
Not every problem someone has with his
girlfriend is necessarily due to the capitalist
mode of production.

[*The Listener*]

MARX, Karl (1818–1883)
Capitalist production creates, with the
inexorability of a law of nature, its own
negation.

[*Das Kapital* (1867)]

**ORTEGA SPOTTORNO, José
(1870–1924)**
*Estoy ... convencido de que la forma actual del
capitalismo dejará paso a otra más humana y menos
especulativa.*
I'm convinced that the present form of
capitalism will make way for another one
which will be more human and less
speculative.

[*El País*, 1994]

PANKHURST, Sylvia (1882–1960)

I have gone to war too … I am going to fight capitalism even if it kills me. It is wrong that people like you should be comfortable and well fed while all around you people are starving.

[In David Mitchell, *The Fighting Pankhursts*]

RICHLER, Mordecai (1931–)

Remember this, Griffin. The revolution eats its own. Capitalism re-creates itself.

[*Cocksure* (1968)]

SAKI (1870–1916)

When she inveighed eloquently against the evils of capitalism at drawing-room meetings and Fabian conferences she was conscious of a comfortable feeling that the system, with all its inequalities and iniquities, would probably last her time. It is one of the consolations of middle-aged reformers that the good they inculcate must live after them if it is to live at all.

[*Beasts and Super-Beasts* (1914)]

STRETTON, Hugh (1924–)

Is it really good for policy-makers to act as if everything has its price, and as if policies should be judged chiefly by their effects in delivering material benefits to selfish citizens? … It does not ask those individuals whether they also have other values which are not revealed by their shopping.

[*Capitalism, Socialism and the Environment* (1976)]

TAYLOR, A.J.P. (1906–1990)

Lenin was the first to discover that capitalism 'inevitably' caused war; and he discovered this only when the First World War was already being fought. Of course he was right. Since every great state was capitalist in 1914, capitalism obviously 'caused' the First World War; but just as obviously it had 'caused' the previous generation of Peace.

[*The Origins of the Second World War* (1961)]

WAUGH, Evelyn (1903–1966)

Pappenhacker says that every time you are polite to a proletarian you are helping to bolster up the capitalist system.

[*Scoop* (1938)]

WELSH, Irvine (1957–)

Consumer capitalism has eaten up the Church, the state, trade unions, extended families, everywhere that people learn morality.

[*The Observer*, 1998]

See BUSINESS

CAREERS

BACON, Francis (1561–1626)

I hold every man a debtor to his profession.

[*The Elements of Common Law* (1596)]

BALFOUR, A.J. (1848–1930)

[On being asked whether he was going to marry Margot Tennant]

I rather think of having a career of my own.

[In Asquith, *Autobiography* (1920)]

BENTLEY, Nicolas (1907–1978)

His was the sort of career that made the Recording Angel think seriously about taking up shorthand.

[Attr.]

COLBY, Frank Moore (1865–1925)

I have found some of the best reasons I ever had for remaining at the bottom simply by looking at the men at the top.

[*Essays*]

DISRAELI, Benjamin (1804–1881)

To do nothing and get something, formed a boy's ideal of a manly career.

[*Sybil* (1845)]

EAMES, Emma (1865–1952)

[On giving up her operatic career at 47]

I would rather be a brilliant memory than a curiosity.

[Attr.]

FRANKLIN, Miles (1879–1954)

This was life – my life – my career, my brilliant career! I was fifteen – fifteen! A few fleeting hours and I would be old as those around me. I looked at them as they stood there, weary, and turning down the other side of the hill of life. When young, no doubt they had hoped for, and dreamed of, better things – had even known them, but here they were. This had been their life; this was their career. It was, and in all probability would be, mine too. My life – my career – my brilliant career!

[*My Brilliant Career* (1901)]

See AMBITION; WORK

CATS

ARNOLD, Matthew (1822–1888)
Cruel, but composed and bland,
Dumb, inscrutable and grand,
So Tiberius might have sat,
Had Tiberius been a cat.

['Poor Matthias']

CHAUCER, Geoffrey (c.1340–1400)
Lat take a cat, and fostre hym wel with milk
And tendre flessh, and make his couche of silk,
And lat hym seen a mous go by the wal,
Anon he weyveth milk and flessh and al,
And every deyntee that is in that hous,
Swich appetit hath he to ete a mous.

[*The Canterbury Tales* (1387)]

DE LA MARE, Walter (1873–1956)
In Hans' old Mill his three black cats
Watch the bins for the thieving rats.
Whisker and claw, they crouch in the night,
Their five eyes smouldering green and bright: ...

Then up he climbs to his creaking mill
Out come his cats all grey with meal –
Jekkel, and Jessup, and one-eyed Jill.

['Five Eyes' (1913)]

ELIOT, T.S. (1888–1965)
Macavity, Macavity, there's no one like Macavity,

There never was a Cat of such deceitfulness and suavity.
He always has an alibi, and one or two to spare:
At whatever time the deed took place –
MACAVITY WASN'T THERE!

['Macavity: the Mystery Cat', (1939)]

The Naming of Cats is a difficult matter,
It isn't just one of your holiday games;
You may think at first I'm as mad as a hatter
When I tell you a cat must have THREE
DIFFERENT NAMES ...

When you notice a cat in profound meditation,
The reason, I tell you, is always the same:
His mind is engaged in a rapt contemplation
Of the thought, of the thought, of the thought of his name:
His ineffable effable
Effanineffable
Deep and inscrutable singular Name.

['The Naming of Cats', (1939)]

HARE, Maurice Evan (1886–1967)
Alfred de Musset
Used to call his cat Pusset.
His accent was affected.
That was only to be expected.

['Byway in Biography']

HOUSEHOLD, Geoffrey (1900–1988)
I have noticed that what cats most appreciate in a human being is not the ability to produce food which they take for granted – but his or her entertainment value.

[*Rogue Male* (1939)]

JOHNSON, Samuel (1709–1784)
When I observed he was a fine cat, saying, 'why yes, Sir, but I have had cats whom I liked better than this'; and then as if perceiving Hodge to be out of countenance, adding, 'but he is a very fine cat, a very fine cat indeed.'

[In Boswell, *The Life of Samuel Johnson* (1791)]

MARQUIS, Don (1878–1937)
the great open spaces

0# CAUTION

0

where cats are cats.

0[*archys life of mehitabel* (1927)]

MONTAIGNE, Michel de (1533–1592)

Quand je me joue à ma chatte, qui sait si elle passe son temps de moi plus que je ne fais d'elle?
When I play with my cat, who knows whether she isn't amusing herself with me more than I am with her?

[*Essais* (1580)]

PORTER, Peter Neville Frederick (1929–)

Moving one paw out and yawning,
he closes his eyes. Everywhere
people are in despair. And he is dancing.

[*Collected Poems* (1983)]

PROVERBS

A cat may look at a king.

All cats are grey in the dark.

A cat has nine lives.

ROWBOTHAM, David Harold (1924–)

Let some of the tranquillity of the cat
Curl into me.

['The Creature in the Chair']

SACKVILLE-WEST, Vita (1892–1962)

The greater cats with golden eyes
Stare out between the bars.
Deserts are there, and different skies,
And night with different stars.

[*The King's Daughter* (1929)]

SMART, Christopher (1722–1771)

For I will consider my Cat Jeoffry.
For he is the servant of the Living God, duly and daily serving Him.
For at the first glance of the glory of God in the East he worships in his way.
For this is done by wreathing his body seven times round with elegant quickness.

[*Jubilate Agno*]

For the English Cats are the best in Europe.

[*Jubilate Agno*]

For he counteracts the powers of darkness by his electrical skin and glaring eyes.

For he counteracts the Devil, who is death, by brisking about the life.

[*Jubilate Agno*]

SMITH, Stevie (1902–1971)

Oh I am a cat that likes to
Gallop about doing good.

['The Galloping Cat' (1972)]

TESSIMOND, A.S.J. (1902–1962)

Cats, no less liquid than their shadows,
Offer no angles to the wind.
They slip, diminished, neat, through loopholes
Less than themselves.

[*Cats* (1934)]

See ANIMALS

CAUTION

ANONYMOUS

Quidquid agas, prudenter agas, et respice finem.
Whatever you do, do it warily, and take account of the end.

[*Gesta Romanorum*]

ARMSTRONG, Dr John (1709–1779)

Distrust yourself, and sleep before you fight.
'Tis not too late tomorrow to be brave.

[*The Art of Preserving Health* (1744)]

BACON, Francis (1561–1626)

A man ought warily to begin charges which once begun will continue.

['Of Expense' (1625)]

BELLOC, Hilaire (1870–1953)

And always keep a-hold of Nurse
For fear of finding something worse.

[*Cautionary Tales* (1907)]

COWPER, William (1731–1800)

To combat may be glorious, and success
Perhaps may crown us; but to fly is safe.

[*The Task* (1785)]

DRYDEN, John (1631–1700)

But now the world's o'er stocked with

prudent men.

[*The Medal* (1682)]

FONTAINE, Jean de la (1621–1695)

Il m'a dit qu'il ne faut jamais
Vendre la peau de l'ours qu'on ne l'ait mis par terre.
He told me never to sell the bear's skin
before killing the beast.

[Fables, 'L'ours et les deux compagnons']

LINCOLN, Abraham (1809–1865)

When you have got an elephant by the hind
leg, and he is trying to run away, it's best to
let him run.

[Remark, 1865]

SHAW, George Bernard (1856–1950)

Self-denial is not a virtue: it is only the effect
of prudence on rascality.

[*Man and Superman* (1903)]

TWAIN, Mark (1835–1910)

It is by the goodness of God that in our
country we have those three unspeakably
precious things: freedom of speech, freedom
of conscience, and the prudence never to
practise either of them.

[*Following the Equator* (1897)]

CELEBRITY

JACKSON, Michael (1958–)

I was a veteran, before I was a teenager.

MENCKEN, H.L. (1880–1956)

A celebrity is one who is known to many
persons he is glad he doesn't know.

See FAME; REPUTATION

CENSORSHIP

BOROVOY, A. Alan

It is usually better to permit a piece of trash
than to suppress a work of art.

[*When Freedoms Collide* (1988)]

EMERSON, Ralph Waldo (1803–1882)

Every burned book enlightens the world.

[Attr.]

GRIFFITH-JONES, Mervyn (1909–1979)

[At the trial of D.H. Lawrence's novel *Lady
Chatterley's Lover*]
Is it a book you would even wish your wife or
your servants to read?

[*The Times*, 1960]

HEINE, Heinrich (1797–1856)

Dort, wo man Bücher
Verbrennt, verbrennt man auch am Ende Menschen.
It is there, where they
Burn books, that eventually they burn people
too.

[*Almansor: A Tragedy* (1821)]

MILL, John Stuart (1806–1873)

We can never be sure that the opinion we
are endeavouring to stifle is a false opinion;
and if we were sure, stifling it would be an
evil still.

[*On Liberty* (1859)]

MILTON, John (1608–1674)

As good almost kill a Man as kill a good
Book; who kills a Man kills a reasonable
creature, God's Image; but hee who destroyes
a good Booke, kills reason it selfe, kills the
Image of God, as it were in the eye. Many a
man lives a burden to the Earth; but a good
Booke is the pretious life-blood of a master
spirit, imbalm'd and treasur'd up on purpose
to a life beyond life.

[*Areopagitica* (1644)]

PINTER, Harold (1930–)

[On the execution of Nigerian writer Ken Saro-
Wiwa]
Murder is the most brutal form of censorship.

[*The Observer*, 1995]

Censorship in the UK reveals a deeply
conservative country still in thrall to its strict
Protestant values.

[*Index on Censorship*, 1996]

RUSHDIE, Salman (1946–)

Means of artistic expression that require
large quantities of finance and sophisticated

technology – films, plays, records – become, by virtue of that dependence, easy to censor and to control. But what one writer can make in the solitude of one room is something no power can easily destroy.

[*Index on Censorship*, 1996]

SIDDIQUE, Dr Kalim

We cannot live in this country together with *The Satanic Verses* and Salman Rushdie. They will have to go.

[*The Independent*, 1989]

STROMME, Sigmund (1946–)

Strict censorship cannot be maintained without terrorism.

[*Index on Censorship*, 1996]

See BOOKS; PORNOGRAPHY

CERTAINTY

BARNFIELD, Richard (1574–1627)

Nothing more certain than incertainties;
Fortune is full of fresh variety:
Constant in nothing but inconstancy.

['The Shepherd's Content' (1594)]

BISSELL, Claude T. (1916–)

I prefer complexity to certainty, cheerful mysteries to sullen facts.

[Address, University of Toronto, 1969]

CAMUS, Albert (1913–1960)

Là était la certitude, dans le travail de tous les jours…
L'essentiel était de bien faire son métier.
That was where certainty lay, in everyday work … The essential thing was to do one's job well.

[*The Plague* (1947)]

FRANKLIN, Benjamin (1706–1790)

But in this world nothing can be said to be certain, except death and taxes.

[Letter to Jean Baptiste Le Roy, 1789]

GUEDALLA, Philip (1889–1944)

People who jump to conclusions rarely alight on them.

[*The Observer*, 1924]

JOHNSON, Samuel (1709–1784)

He is no wise man who will quit a certainty for an uncertainty.

[*The Idler* (1758–1760)]

PLINY THE ELDER (AD 23–79)

The only certainty is that nothing is certain.

[Attr.]

TERTULLIAN (c.AD 160–c.225)

Certum est quia impossibile.
It is certain because it is impossible.

[*De Carne Christi*]

YEATS, W.B. (1865–1939)

The best lack all conviction, while the worst
Are full of passionate intensity.

See DOUBT

CHANCE

FRANCE, Anatole (1844–1924)

Le hasard c'est peut-être le pseudonyme de Dieu,
quand il ne veut pas signer.
Chance might be God's pseudonym when He does not want to sign his name.

[*Le Jardin d'Epicure* (1894)]

OVID (43 BC–AD 18)

Chance is always powerful. Let your hook be always cast. In the pool where you least expect it, will be fish.

PROVERB

Throw out a sprat to catch a mackerel.

See ACCIDENTS; LUCK; OPPORTUNITY

CHANGE

ANONYMOUS

Change imposed is change opposed.

[Management slogan, Deloitte and Touche, 1999]

Tempora mutantur, et nos mutamur in illis.
Times change, and we change with them.

[In Harrison, *Description of Britain* (1577)]

ARNOLD, Matthew (1822–1888)

Wandering between two worlds, one dead,
The other powerless to be born,
With nowhere yet to rest my head,
Like these, on earth I wait forlorn …

Years hence, perhaps, may dawn an age,
More fortunate, alas! than we,
Which without hardness will be sage,
And gay without frivolity.

['The Grande Chartreuse' (1855)]

AURELIUS, Marcus (121–180)

The universe is change; life is what thinking makes of it.

[*Meditations*]

BACON, Francis (1561–1626)

That all things are changed, and that nothing really perishes, and that the sum of matter remains exactly the same, is sufficiently certain.

[*Thoughts on the Nature of Things* (1604)]

BEAUVOIR, Simone de (1908–1986)

Si l'on vit assez longtemps, on voit que toute victoire se change un jour en défaite.
If you live long enough, you'll find that every victory turns into a defeat.

[*All Men are Mortal* (1955)]

BRITTAIN, Vera (1893–1970)

It is probably true to say that the largest scope for change still lies in men's attitude to women, and in women's attitude to themselves.

[*Lady into Woman* (1953)]

It is said I am against change. I am not against change. I am in favour of change in the right circumstances. And those circumstances are when it can no longer be resisted.

[Attr. by Paul Johnson in *The Spectator*, May 1996]

CHESTERTON, G.K. (1874–1936)

All conservatism is based upon the idea that if you leave things alone you leave them as they are. But you do not. If you leave a thing

alone you leave it to a torrent of change.

[*Orthodoxy* (1908)]

CONFUCIUS (c.550–c.478 BC)

They must often change who would be constant in happiness or wisdom.

[*Analects*]

DISRAELI, Benjamin (1804–1881)

Change is inevitable. In a progressive country change is constant.

[Speech, Edinburgh, 1867]

FALKLAND, Viscount (c.1610–1643)

When it is not necessary to change, it is necessary not to change.

[Speech concerning Episcopacy, 1641]

HERACLITUS (c.540–c.480 BC)

You cannot step twice into the same river.

[In Plato, *Cratylus*]

HOOKER, Richard (c.1554–1600)

Change is not made without inconvenience, even from worse to better.

[In Johnson, *Dictionary of the English Language* (1755)]

HORACE (65–8 BC)

Immortalia ne speres, monet annus et almum
Quae rapit hora diem.
The changing year and the passing hour that takes away genial day warns you not to build everlasting hopes.

[*Odes*]

IRVING, Washington (1783–1859)

There is a certain relief in change, even though it be from bad to worse; as I have found in travelling in a stage-coach, that it is often a comfort to shift one's position and be bruised in a new place.

[*Tales of a Traveller* (1824)]

KARR, Alphonse (1808–1890)

Plus ça change, plus c'est la même chose.
The more things change the more they remain the same.

[*Les Guêpes* (1849)]

KEATS, John (1795–1821)

There is nothing stable in the world; uproar's

your only music.

[Letter to George and Tom Keats, 13 January 1818]

LLOYD GEORGE, David (1863–1945)

[On being asked how he maintained his cheerfulness when beset by numerous political obstacles]

Well, I find that a change of nuisances is as good as a vacation.

[Attr.]

LUCRETIUS (c.95–55 BC)

Augescunt aliae gentes, aliae minuuntur,
Inque brevi spatio mutantur saecla animantum
Et quasi cursores vitai lampada tradunt.

Some groups increase, others diminish, and in a short space the generations of living creatures are changed and like runners pass on the torch of life.

[*De Rerum Natura*]

MCCARTNEY, Paul (1942–)

The issues are the same. We wanted peace on earth, love, and understanding between everyone around the world. We have learned that change comes slowly.

[*The Observer*, 1987]

MALCOLM X (1925–1965)

Usually when people are sad, they don't do anything. They just cry over their condition. But when they get angry, they bring about a change.

[*Malcolm X Speaks*, 1965]

ROCHESTER, Earl of (1647–1680)

Since 'tis Nature's law to change,
Constancy alone is strange.

['A Dialogue between Strephon and Daphne' (1691)]

SPENSER, Edmund (c.1522–1599)

What man that sees the ever-whirling wheele
Of Change, the which all mortall things doth sway,
But that therby doth find, and plainly feele,
How Mutability in them doth play
Her cruell sports, to many men's decay?

[*The Faerie Queene* (1596)]

SWIFT, Jonathan (1667–1745)

There is nothing in this world constant, but inconstancy.

[*A Critical Essay upon the Faculties of the Mind* (1709)]

TENNYSON, Alfred, Lord (1809–1892)

Forward, forward let us range,
Let the great world spin for ever down the ringing grooves of change.

['Locksley Hall' (1838)]

The old order changeth, yielding place to new,
And God fulfils himself in many ways,
Lest one good custom should corrupt the world.

[*The Idylls of the King*]

THOREAU, Henry David (1817–1862)

Things do not change; we change.

[*Walden* (1854)]

TOFFLER, Alvin (1928–)

Future shock … the shattering stress and disorientation that we induce in individuals by subjecting them to too much change in too short a time.

[*Future Shock* (1970)]

TUSSER, Thomas (c.1524–1580)

The stone that is rolling can gather no moss;
For master and servant oft changing is loss.

[*Five Hundred Points of Good Husbandry* (1557)]

See CONSERVATISM; TIME

CHARACTER

EDGEWORTH, Maria (1767–1849)

We cannot judge either of the feelings or of the characters of men with perfect accuracy, from their actions or their appearance in public; it is from their careless conversations, their half-finished sentences, that we may hope with the greatest probability of success to discover their real character.

[*Castle Rackrent* (1800)]

ELIOT, George (1819–1880)

'Character', says Novalis, in one of his questionable aphorisms – 'character is destiny.'

[*The Mill on the Floss* (1860)]

EMERSON, Ralph Waldo (1803–1882)

Character is nature in the highest form. It is of no use to ape it, or to contend with it.

[*Essays, Second Series* (1844)]

FRISCH, Max (1911–1991)

Jede Uniform verdirbt den Charakter.

Every uniform corrupts one's character.

[*Diary*, 1948]

GOETHE (1749–1832)

Es bildet ein Talent sich in der Stille,
Sich ein Charakter in dem Strom der Welt.

Talent is formed in quiet retreat,
Character in the headlong rush of life.

[*Torquato Tasso* (1790)]

JAMES, Henry (1843–1916)

What is character but the determination of incident? What is incident but the illustration of character?

[*Partial Portraits* (1888)]

KARR, Alphonse (1808–1890)

Every man has three characters: that which he exhibits, that which he has, and that which he thinks he has.

[Attr.]

KING, Martin Luther (1929–1968)

The ultimate measure of a man is not where he stands in moments of comfort and convenience, but where he stands at times of challenge and controversy.

[*Strength to Love*, 1963]

LINCOLN, Abraham (1809–1865)

Character is like a tree and reputation like its shadow. The shadow is what we think of it; the tree is the real thing.

[In Gross, *Lincoln's Own Stories*]

MURRAY, Les A. (1938–)

In the defiance of fashion is the beginning of character.

[*The Boy who Stole the Funeral* (1979)]

REAGAN, Ronald (1911–)

You can tell a lot about a fellow's character by the way he eats jelly beans.

[*Daily Mail*, 1981]

SHERIDAN, Richard Brinsley (1751–1816)

I'm called away by particular business. But I leave my character behind me.

[*The School for Scandal* (1777)]

WILSON, Woodrow (1856–1924)

Character is a by-product; it is produced in the great manufacture of daily duty.

[Speech, 1915]

See REPUTATION

CHARITY

ARNOLD, George (1834–1865)

The living need charity more than the dead.

[*The Jolly Old Pedagogue* (1866)]

BACON, Francis (1561–1626)

In charity there is no excess.

['Of Goodness, and Goodness of Nature' (1625)]

BROWNE, Sir Thomas (1605–1682)

Charity begins at home, is the voice of the world.

[*Religio Medici* (1643)]

CARNEGIE, Andrew (1835–1919)

Of every thousand dollars spent in so-called charity today, it is probable that nine hundred and fifty dollars is unwisely spent.

['Wealth' (1889)]

FULLER, Thomas (1608–1661)

He that feeds upon charity has a cold dinner and no supper.

[Attr.]

POPE, Alexander (1688–1744)

For Forms of Government let fools contest;
Whate'er is best administer'd is best:
For Modes of Faith, let graceless zealots fight;

His can't be wrong whose life is in the right:
In Faith and Hope the world will disagree,
But all Mankind's concern is Charity.

[*Essay on Man* (1733)]

In Faith and Hope the world will disagree,
But all Mankind's concern is Charity.

[*Essay on Man* (1733)]

PROVERB
Charity begins at home.

PUBLILIUS, Syrus (1st century BC)
Inopi beneficium bis dat qui dat celeriter.
He does the poor man two favours who
gives quickly.

[*Sententiae*]

**ROUSSEAU, Jean-Jacques
(1712–1778)**
The feigned charity of the rich man is for him
no more than another luxury; he feeds the
poor as he feeds dogs and horses.

[Letter to M. Moulton]

**<$ISHERIDAN, Richard Brinsley
(1751–1816)**
Rowley: I believe there is no sentiment he has
more faith in than that 'charity begins at
home'.
Sir Oliver Surface: And his, I presume, is of that
domestic sort which never stirs abroad at all.

[*The School for Scandal* (1777)]

SMART, Christopher (1722–1771)
Charity is cold in the multitude of
possessions, and the rich are covetous of
their crumbs.

[*Jubilate Agno* (c. 1758–63)]

VOLTAIRE (1694–1778)
The man who leaves money to charity in his
will is only giving away what no longer
belongs to him.

[Letter, 1769]

WEST, Dame Rebecca (1892–1983)
[Of charity]
It is an ugly trick. It is a virtue grown by the
rich on the graves of the poor. Unless it is
accompanied by sincere revolt against the

present social system, it is cheap moral
swagger.

[*The Clarion*]

See BENEFACTORS; GENEROSITY

CHARM

BARRIE, Sir J.M. (1860–1937)
[On charm]
It's a sort of bloom on a woman. If you have
it, you don't need to have anything else; and
if you don't have it, it doesn't much matter
what else you have.

[*What Every Woman Knows* (1908)]

BIERCE, Ambrose (1842–c.1914)
Please: To lay the foundation for a
superstructure of imposition.

[*The Enlarged Devil's Dictionary* (1961)]

CAMUS, Albert (1913–1960)
*Vous savez ce que c'est le charme: une manière de
s'entendre répondre oui sans avoir posé aucune
question claire.*
You know what charm is: a way of getting
the answer yes without having asked any
clear question.

[*The Fall* (1956)]

CONNOLLY, Cyril (1903–1974)
All charming people have something to
conceal, usually their total dependence on
the appreciation of others.

[*Enemies of Promise* (1938)]

FARQUHAR, George (1678–1707)
Charming women can true converts make,
We love the precepts for the teacher's sake.

[*The Constant Couple* (1699)]

LERNER, Alan Jay (1918–1986)
Oozing charm from every pore,
He oiled his way around the floor.

[*My Fair Lady* (1956)]

MACNALLY, Leonard (1752–1820)
On Richmond Hill there lives a lass,
More sweet than May day morn,
Whose charms all other maids surpass,

A rose without a thorn.

['The Lass of Richmond Hill' (1789)]

WOLLSTONECRAFT, Mary (1759–1797)

The woman who has only been taught to please will soon find that her charms are oblique sunbeams, and that they cannot have much effect on her husband's heart when they are seen every day.

[*A Vindication of the Rights of Woman* (1792)]

CHILDREN

AMIS, Kingsley (1922–1995)

It was no wonder that people were so horrible when they started life as children.

[*One Fat Englishman* (1963)]

ANONYMOUS

Children are natural mimics who act like their parents despite every effort to teach them good manners.

AUDEN, W.H. (1907–1973)

Only those in the last stages of disease could believe that children are true judges of character.

[*The Orators* (1932)]

AUSTEN, Jane (1775–1817)

On every formal visit a child ought to be of the party, by way of provision for discourse.

[*Sense and Sensibility* (1811)]

BACON, Francis (1561–1626)

Children sweeten labours, but they make misfortunes more bitter.

[*Essays* (1625)]

BALDWIN, James (1924–1987)

Children have never been very good at listening to their elders, but they have never failed to imitate them. They must, they have no other models.

[*Nobody Knows My Name* (1961)]

BEHAN, Brendan (1923–1964)

I am married to Beatrice Salkeld, a painter. We have no children, except me.

[Attr.]

BOWEN, Elizabeth (1899–1973)

There is no end to the violations committed by children on children, quietly talking alone.

[*The House in Paris* (1935)]

BROWNING, Elizabeth Barrett (1806–1861)

Do you hear the children weeping, O my brothers,
Ere the sorrow comes with years?

['The Cry of the Children' (1844)]

CAMPBELL, David (1915–1979)

In the heart of dew we lie
Drowned in brief immortality
And watch our fair-haired children play.

['Hearts and Children']

CARROLL, Lewis (1832–1898)

I am fond of children (except boys).

[Letter to Kathleen Eschwege, 1879]

CARTER, ('Miz') Lillian (1902–1983)

I love all my children, but some of them I don't like.

[In *Woman*, 1977]

Sometimes when I look at my children I say to myself, 'Lillian, you should have stayed a virgin.'

[Remark, 1980]

CONNOLLY, Cyril (1903–1974)

Boys do not grow up gradually. They move forward in spurts like the hands of clocks in railway stations.

[*Enemies of Promise* (1938)]

DE GAULLE, Charles (1890–1970)

[After the death of his retarded daughter Anne]
Et maintenant elle est comme les autres.
And now she is like everyone else.

[Attr.]

DE LA MARE, Walter (1873–1956)

Angel of Words, in vain I have striven with thee,
Nor plead a lifetime's love and loyalty;
Only, with envy, bid thee watch this face,

That says so much, so flawlessly,
And in how small a space!

['A Child Asleep']

DICKENS, Charles (1812–1870)

In the little world in which children have their existence ... there is nothing so finely perceived and so finely felt as injustice.

[*Great Expectations* (1861)]

DUMAS, Alexandre (Fils) (1824–1895)

It is only rarely that one can see in a little boy the promise of a man, but one can almost always see in a little girl the threat of a woman.

[Attr.]

GANDHI, Indira (1917–1984)

To bear many children is considered not only a religious blessing but also an investment. The greater their number, some Indians reason, the more alms they can beg.

[In Fallaci, *New York Review of Books*]

GEORGE V (1865–1936)

My father was frightened of his mother. I was frightened of my father, and I'm damned well going to make sure that my children are frightened of me.

[In R. Churchill, *Lord Derby – 'King of Lancashire'* (1959)]

GIBBON, Edward (1737–1794)

Few, perhaps, are the children who, after the expiration of some months or years, would sincerely rejoice in the resurrection of their parents.

[*Memoirs of My Life and Writings* (1796)]

GIBRAN, Kahlil (1883–1931)

Your children are not your children.
They are the sons and daughters of Life's longing for itself.
They came through you but not from you,
And though they are with you yet they belong not to you.

You may give them your love but not your thoughts,
For they have their own thoughts.

You may house their bodies but not their souls,
For their souls dwell in the house of tomorrow, which you cannot visit, not even in your dreams.
You may strive to be like them, but seek not to make them like you.
For life goes not backward nor tarries with yesterday.
You are the bows from which your children as living arrows are sent forth.

[*The Prophet* (1923)]

HARWOOD, Gwen (1920–)

'It's so sweet
to hear their chatter, watch them grow and thrive,'
she says to his departing smile. Then, nursing the youngest child, sits staring at her feet.
To the wind she says, 'They have eaten me alive.'

[*Poems* (1968)]

INGE, William Ralph (1860–1954)

The proper time to influence the character of a child is about a hundred years before he is born.

[*The Observer*, 1929]

JONSON, Ben (1572–1637)

Rest in soft peace, and, ask'd say here doth lye
Ben Jonson his best piece of poetrie.

['On My First Son' (1616)]

KEY, Ellen (1849–1926)

At every step the child should be allowed to meet the real experiences of life; the thorns should never be plucked from his roses.

[*The Century of the Child* (1909)]

KIPLING, Rudyard (1865–1936)

These were our children who died for our lands ...
But who shall return us the children?

['The Children' (1917)]

KNOX, Ronald (1888–1957)

[Definition of a baby]
A loud noise at one end and no sense of

responsibility at the other.

[Attr.]

LAMB, Charles (1775–1834)

Boys are capital fellows in their own way, among their mates; but they are unwholesome companions for grown people.

[*Essays of Elia* (1823)]

Riddle of destiny, who can show
What thy short visit meant, or know
What thy errand here below?

['On an Infant Dying as soon as Born']

LAMB, Mary (1764–1847)

A child's a plaything for an hour.

[*Parental Recollections*]

LEBOWITZ, Fran (1946–)

Remember that as a teenager you are at the last stage in your life when you will be happy to hear that the phone is for you.

[*Social Studies* (1981)]

LONGFELLOW, Henry Wadsworth (1807–1882)

You are better than all the ballads
That ever were sung or said;
For ye are living poems,
And all the rest are dead.

['Children' (1849)]

MILLAY, Edna St Vincent (1892–1950)

Childhood is not from birth to a certain age
and at a certain age
The child is grown, and puts away childish things,
Childhood is the kingdom where nobody dies.
Nobody that matters, that is.

[*Wine from these Grapes* (1934)]

MILLER, Alice

Society chooses to disregard the mistreatment of children, judging it to be altogether normal because it is so commonplace.

[*Pictures of a Childhood* (1986)]

MITFORD, Nancy (1904–1973)

I love children – especially when they cry, for then someone takes them away.

[Attr.]

MONTAIGNE, Michel de (1533–1592)

Il faut noter, que les jeux d'enfants ne sont pas jeux: et les faut juger en eux, comme leurs plus sérieuses actions.

It should be noted that children at play are not merely playing; their games should be seen as their most serious actions.

[*Essais* (1580)]

NASH, Ogden (1902–1971)

Children aren't happy with nothing to ignore,
And that's what parents were created for.

['The Parent' (1933)]

PATTEN, Brian (1946–)

Growing up's wonderful if you keep your eyes closed tightly,
[and, if you manage to grow,
take your soul with you,
nobody wants it.].

[*Grinning Jack* (1990)]

PAVESE, Cesare (1908–1950)

One stops being a child when one realizes that telling one's trouble does not make it better.

[*The Business of Living: Diaries 1935–50*]

PENN, William (1644–1718)

Men are generally more careful of the breed of their horses and dogs than of their children.

[*Some Fruits of Solitude, in Reflections and Maxims relating to the Conduct of Humane Life* (1693)]

PLATH, Sylvia (1932–1963)

[On seeing her newborn baby]
What did my fingers do before they held him?
What did my heart do, with its love?
I have never seen a thing so clear.
His lids are like the lilac flower
And soft as a moth, his breath.
I shall not let go.

There is no guile or warp in him. May he keep so.

['Three Women: A Poem for Three Voices' (1962)]

POPE, Alexander (1688–1744)
Behold the child, by Nature's kindly law,
Pleas'd with a rattle, tickled with a straw.

[An Essay on Man (1733)]

SAKI (1870–1916)
Children with Hyacinth's temperament don't know better as they grow older; they merely know more.

[The Toys of Peace (1919)]

SMITH, Sir Sydney (1883–1969)
No child is born a criminal: no child is born an angel: he's just born.

[Remark]

STEVENSON, Robert Louis (1850–1894)
The child that is not clean and neat,
With lots of toys and things to eat,
He is a naughty child, I'm sure –
Or else his dear papa is poor.

[A Child's Garden of Verses (1885)]

A child should always say what's true,
And speak when he is spoken to,
And behave mannerly at table:
At least as far as he is able.

[A Child's Garden of Verses (1885)]

SWIFT, Jonathan (1667–1745)
I have been assured by a very knowing American of my acquaintance in London, that a young healthy child well nursed is, at a year old, a most delicious, nourishing, and wholesome food, whether stewed, roasted, baked, or boiled; and I make no doubt that it will equally serve in a fricassee, or a ragout.

[A Modest Proposal for Preventing the Children of Ireland from being a Burden to their Parents or Country (1729)]

TAYLOR, Bishop Jeremy (1613–1667)
No man can tell but he that loves his children, how many delicious accents make a man's heart dance in the pretty conversation of those dear pledges; their childishness, their stammering, their little angers, their innocence, their imperfections, their necessities are so many little emanations of joy and comfort to him that delights in their persons and society.

[XXV Sermons Preached at Golden Grove (1653)]

VIDAL, Gore (1925–)
Never have children, only grandchildren.

[Two Sisters (1970)]

WATTS, Isaac (1674–1748)
Birds in their little nests agree
And 'tis a shameful sight,
When children of one family
Fall out, and chide, and fight.

[Divine Songs for Children (1715)]

WILDE, Oscar (1854–1900)
Children begin by loving their parents. After a time they judge them. Rarely, if ever, do they forgive them.

[A Woman of No Importance (1893)]

WOOD, Anne
We are gearing our programmes at two to eight-year-olds. We feel that nine-year-olds can no longer be considered children.

[The Times, 'Quotes of the Week', 1999]

YANKWICH, Léon R. (1888–1975)
[Decision, State District Court, Southern District of California, June 1928, quoting columnist O.O. McIntyre]
There are no illegitimate children – only illegitimate parents.

[Attr.]

See BABIES; FAMILIES; INNOCENCE; PARENTS; YOUTH

CHINA

SAKI (1870–1916)
Even the Hooligan was probably invented in China centuries before we thought of him.

[Reginald (1904)]

SMITH, Adam (1723–1790)
China, though it may perhaps stand still, does not seem to go backwards.

[*Wealth of Nations* (1776)]

CHRISTIANITY

ARNOLD, Matthew (1822–1888)
But there remains the question: what righteousness really is. The method and secret and sweet reasonableness of Jesus.

[*Literature and Dogma* (1873)]

BARTON, Bruce (1886–1967)
[Jesus] picked up twelve men from the bottom ranks of business and forged them into an organization that conquered the world.

[*The Man Nobody Knows: A Discovery of the Real Jesus* (1924)]

BRECHT, Bertolt (1898–1956)
Da konnt [unser Herr] auch verlangen, dass man seinen Nächsten liebt, denn man war satt. Heutzutage ist das anders.
In those days [our Lord] could demand that men love their neighbour, because they'd had enough to eat. Nowadays it's different.

[*Mother Courage and her Children* (1941)]

BRUCE, Lenny (1925–1966)
[Referring to the Crucifixion]
It was just one of those parties which got out of hand.

[*The Guardian*, 1979]

BUTLER, Samuel (1835–1902)
They would have been equally horrified at hearing the Christian religion doubted, and at seeing it practised.

[*The Way of All Flesh* (1903)]

CARLYLE, Thomas (1795–1881)
If Jesus Christ were to come to-day, people would not even crucify him. They would ask him to dinner, and hear what he had to say, and make fun of it.

[In Wilson, *Carlyle at his Zenith* (1927)]

CHESTERTON, G.K. (1874–1936)
Carlyle said that men were mostly fools. Christianity, with a surer and more reverend realism, says that they are all fools.

[*Heretics* (1905)]

The Christian ideal has not been tried and found wanting. It has been found difficult; and left untried.

[*What's Wrong with the World* (1910)]

COLERIDGE, Samuel Taylor (1772–1834)
He who begins by loving Christianity better than Truth will proceed by loving his own sect or church better than Christianity, and end by loving himself better than all.

[*Aids to Reflection* (1825)]

CONSTANTINE, Emperor (c.288–337)
[His motto, in memory of a vision of the Cross which appeared to him on the eve of his defeat of Maxentius and victorious entry into Rome, 312]
In hoc signo vinces.
In this sign thou shalt conquer.

[In Eusebius, *Vita Constantini*]

DE BLANK, Joost (1908–1968)
[Of South Africa]
Christ in this country would quite likely have been arrested under the Suppression of Communism Act.

[*The Observer*, 1963]

DISRAELI, Benjamin (1804–1881)
His Christianity was muscular.

[*Endymion* (1880)]

A Protestant, if he wants aid or advice on any matter, can only go to his solicitor.

[*Lothair* (1870)]

DUNBAR, William (c.1460–c.1525)
Done is a battell on the dragon blak;
Our campioun Christ counfoundit hes his force;
The yettis of hell ar brokin with a crak,
The signe triumphall rasit is of the croce.

['On the Resurrection of Christ']

ELLIS, Bob (1942–)
Show me a Wednesday wencher and a

Sunday saint, and I'll show you a Roman Catholic.

[*The Legend of King O'Malley* (1974)]

FRANCE, Anatole (1844–1924)

Le Christianisme a beaucoup fait pour l'amour en en faisant un péché.

Christianity has done a great deal for love by making a sin of it.

[*Le Jardin d'Epicure* (1894)]

HALE, Sir Matthew (1609–1676)

Christianity is part of the laws of England.

[In Blackstone, *Commentaries on the Laws of England* (1769)]

HARDY, Thomas (1840–1928)

A local cult called Christianity.

[*The Dynasts*, Part I (1903)]

HOOD, Thomas (1799–1845)

[Of Quakers]

The sedate, sober, silent, serious, sad-coloured sect.

[*The Comic Annual* (1839)]

HUXLEY, Aldous (1894–1963)

Christianity accepted as given a metaphysical system derived from several already existing and mutually incompatible systems.

[*Grey Eminence* (1941)]

KINGSLEY, Charles (1819–1875)

We have used the Bible as if it was a constable's handbook – an opium-dose for keeping beasts of burden patient while they are being overloaded.

['Letters to Chartists' (1848)]

KIPLING, Rudyard (1865–1936)

The Three in One, the One in Three? Not so!
To my own Gods I go.
It may be they shall give me greater ease
Than your cold Christ and tangled Trinities.

[*Plain Tales from the Hills* (1888)]

LENNON, John (1940–1980)

We're more popular than Jesus Christ now. I don't know which will go first. Rock and roll

or Christianity.

[*The Beatles Illustrated Lyrics*]

LUTHER, Martin (1483–1546)

Esto peccator et pecca fortiter, sed fortius fide et gaude in Christo.

Be a sinner and sin strongly, but believe and rejoice in Christ even more strongly.

[Letter to Melanchton]

MCCARTHY, Mary (1912–1989)

I don't believe in God – that's just a fact, it's not an act of will … But ethics came to me in the frame of Christian teaching, and even though I don't believe in an afterlife, I'm still concerned with the salvation of my soul.

[In Carol Gelderman, *Mary McCarthy* (1988)]

MENCKEN, H.L. (1880–1956)

Puritanism - The haunting fear that someone, somewhere, may be happy.

[*A Mencken Chrestomathy* (1949)]

The chief contribution of Protestantism to human thought is its massive proof that God is a bore.

[*Notebooks* (1956)]

MONTESQUIEU, Charles (1689–1755)

Il n'y a jamais eu de royaume où il y ait eu tant de guerres civiles que dans celui du Christ.

No kingdom has ever had as many civil wars as the kingdom of Christ.

[*Lettres persanes* (1721)]

NIETZSCHE, Friedrich Wilhelm (1844–1900)

Ich heisse das Christentum den einen grossen Fluch, die eine grosse innerlichste Verdorbenheit, den einen grossen Instinkt der Rache, dem kein Mittel giftig, heimlich, unterirdisch, klein genug ist – ich heisse es den einen unsterblichen Schandfleck der Menschheit.

I call Christianity the one great curse, the one great innermost form of depravity, the one great instinct for revenge, for which no means is poisonous, furtive, underground, petty enough – I call it the one immortal blemish of humanity.

[*Der Antichrist* (1888)]

Der christliche Entschluss, die Welt hässlich und
schlecht zu finden, hat die Welt hässlich und schlecht
gemacht.
The Christian decision to find the world ugly
and bad has made the world ugly and bad.

[*The Gay Science* (1887)]

PENN, William (1644–1718)

No pain, no palm; no thorns, no throne; no
gall, no glory; no cross, no crown.

[*No Cross, No Crown* (1669)]

RUSSELL, Bertrand (1872–1970)

There's a Bible on that shelf there. But I keep
it next to Voltaire – poison and antidote.

[In Harris, *Kenneth Harris Talking To:* (1971)]

SAKI (1870–1916)

People may say what they like about the
decay of Christianity; the religious system
that produced green Chartreuse can never
really die.

[*Reginald* (1904)]

SANTAYANA, George (1863–1952)

The Bible is literature, not dogma.

[Introduction to Spinoza's *Ethics*]

SITWELL, Dame Edith (1887–1964)

Who dreamed that Christ has died in vain?
He walks again on the Seas of Blood, he
comes in the terrible Rain.

[*The Shadow of Cain* (1947)]

STRACHEY, John St Loe (1901–1963)

Becoming an Anglo-Catholic must surely be
a sad business – rather like becoming an
amateur conjurer.

[*The Coming Struggle for Power*]

SWIFT, Jonathan (1667–1745)

I conceive some scattered notions about a
superior power to be of singular use for the
common people, as furnishing excellent
materials to keep children quiet when they
grow peevish, and providing topics of
amusement in a tedious winter-night.

[*An Argument Against Abolishing Christianity* (1708)]

TEMPLE, William (1881–1944)

Christianity is the most materialistic of all

great religions.

[*Readings in St John's Gospel* (1939)]

TUTU, Archbishop Desmond (1931–)

For the Church in any country to retreat from
politics is nothing short of heresy.
Christianity is political or it is not
Christianity.

[*The Observer*, 1994]

TWAIN, Mark (1835–1910)

Most people are bothered by those passages
in Scripture which they cannot understand;
but as for me, I always noticed that the
passages in Scripture which trouble me most
are those that I do understand.

[In Simcox, *Treasury of Quotations on Christian Themes*]

VAN DER POST, Sir Laurens (1906–1996)

Organized religion is making Christianity
political rather than making politics
Christian.

[*The Observer*, 1986]

WILSON, Sir Angus (1913–1991)

'God knows how you Protestants can be
expected to have any sense of direction,' she
said. 'It's different with us. I haven't been to
mass for years, I've got every mortal sin on
my conscience, but I know when I'm doing
wrong. I'm still a Catholic.'

[*The Wrong Set* (1949)]

YBARRA, Thomas Russell (1880–)

A Christian is a man who feels
Repentance on a Sunday
For what he did on Saturday
And is going to do on Monday.

['The Christian' (1909)]

ZANGWILL, Israel (1864–1926)

Scratch the Christian and you find the pagan
– spoiled.

[*Children of the Ghetto* (1892)]

See BIBLE; RELIGION

CHRISTMAS

ADDISON, Joseph (1672–1719)
I have often thought, says Sir Roger, it happens very well that Christmas should fall out in the Middle of Winter.

[*The Spectator*, January 1712]

BARRY, Dave
In the old days, it was not called the Holiday Season; the Christians called it 'Christmas' and went to church; the Jews called it 'Hanukka' and went to synagogue; the atheists went to parties and drank. People passing each other on the street would say 'Merry Christmas!' or 'Happy Hanukka!' or (to the atheists) 'Look out for the wall!'.

[*Christmas Shopping: A Survivor's Guide*]

BERLIN, Irving (1888–1989)
I'm dreaming of a white Christmas.

['White Christmas', song, 1942; in film *Holiday Inn*]

BETJEMAN, Sir John (1906–1984)
And girls in slacks remember Dad,
And oafish louts remember Mum,
And sleepless children's hearts are glad,
And Christmas morning bells say 'Come!'
Even to shining ones who dwell
Safe in the Dorchester Hotel.

And is it true? And is it true,
This most tremendous tale of all,
Seen in a stained-glass window's hue,
A Baby in an ox's stall?

[*A Few Late Chrysanthemums* (1954)]

CLARKE, Marcus (1846–1881)
A very merry Christmas, with roast beef in a violent perspiration, and the thermometer 110° in the shade!

[*Australasian*, 1868]

COPE, Wendy (1945–)
Bloody Christmas, here again,
Let us raise a loving cup:
Peace on earth, goodwill to men,
And make them do the washing-up.

['Another Christmas Poem']

FRANKLIN, Benjamin (1706–1790)
How many observe Christ's birthday! How few, his precepts! O! 'tis easier to keep holidays than commandments.

[*Poor Richard's Almanack*, 1732–57]

FRY, Stephen (1957–)
Christmas to a child is the first terrible proof that to travel hopefully is better than to arrive.

[*Paperweight*]

HARDY, Thomas (1840–1928)
If someone said on Christmas Eve,
'Come; see the oxen kneel

In the lonely barton by yonder coomb
Our childhood used to know,'
I should go with him in the gloom,
Hoping it might be so.

['The Oxen' (1915)]

MILLIGAN, Spike (1918–)
I'm walking backwards for Christmas.

[*The Goon Show*]

MOORE, Clement C. (1779–1863)
'Twas the night before Christmas, when all through the house
Not a creature was stirring, not even a mouse;
The stockings were hung by the chimney with care,
In hopes that St Nicholas soon would be there …

'Happy Christmas to all, and to all a goodnight!'.

['A Visit from St Nicholas' (1823)]

NASH, Ogden (1902–1971)
People can't concentrate properly on blowing other people to pieces properly if their minds are poisoned by thoughts suitable to the twenty-fifth of December.

[*I'm a Stranger Here Myself*, 1938]

PROVERB
Christmas comes but once a year.

SCOTT, Sir Walter (1771–1832)

Heap on more wood! – the wind is chill;
But let it whistle as it will,
We'll keep our Christmas merry still …

England was merry England, when
Old Christmas brought his sports again.
'Twas Christmas broach'd the mightiest ale;
'Twas Christmas told the merriest tale;
A Christmas gambol oft could cheer
The poor man's heart through half the year.

[*Marmion* (1808)]

SIMS, George R. (1847–1922)

It is Christmas Day in the Workhouse.

['In the Workhouse – Christmas Day' (1879)]

TUSSER, Thomas (c.1524–1580)

At Christmas play and make good cheer,
For Christmas comes but once a year.

[*Five Hundred Points of Good Husbandry* (1557)]

WHITE, E.B. (1899–1985)

To perceive Christmas through its wrapping
becomes more difficult with every year.

[*The Second Tree from the Corner* (1954)]

ZARNACK, August (1777–1827)

O Tannenbaum, O Tannenbaum,
Wie treu sind deine Blätter!
O Christmas tree, O Christmas tree,
How faithful are thy branches!

[Adaptation of an old folk-song, 1820]

See CHRISTIANITY

THE CHURCH

AMBROSE, Saint (c.340–397)

Ubi Petrus, ibi ergo ecclesia.
Where Peter is, there of necessity is the Church.

[*Explanatio psalmi 40*]

ANDREWES, Bishop Lancelot (1555–1626)

The nearer the Church the further from God.

[Sermon 15, *Of the Nativity* (1629)]

AUGUSTINE, Saint (354–430)

Salus extra ecclesiam non est.
Outside the church there is no salvation.

[*De Baptismo*]

BANCROFT, Richard (1544–1610)

Where Christ erecteth his Church, the devil in
the same churchyard will have his chapel.

[Sermon, 1588]

BELLOC, Hilaire (1870–1953)

I always like to associate with a lot of priests
because it makes me understand anti-clerical
things so well.

[Attr.]

THE BIBLE
(King James Version)

Thou art Peter, and upon this rock I will build
my church; and the gates of hell shall not
prevail against it.

[*Matthew*, 16:18]

BLAKE, William (1757–1827)

But if at the Church they would give us some
Ale,
And a pleasant fire our souls to regale:
We'd sing and we'd pray all the live-long day;
Nor ever once wish from the Church to stray.

[*Songs of Experience* (1794)]

BLYTHE, Ronald (1922–)

As for the British churchman, he goes to
church as he goes to the bathroom, with the
minimum of fuss and no explanation if he
can help it.

[*The Age of Illusion* (1963)]

BRONTË, Charlotte (1816–1855)

Of late years an abundant shower of curates
has fallen upon the North of England.

[*Shirley* (1849)]

BURKE, Edmund (1729–1797)

Politics and the pulpit are terms that have
little agreement. No sound ought to be
heard in the church but the healing voice of
Christian charity.

[*Reflections on the Revolution in France* … (1790)]

CHARLES II (1630–1685)

He told me, he had a chaplain [Woolly, later
made a bishop] … a very great blockhead …

he said he was a very silly fellow: but that, he believed, his nonsense suited their nonsense, for he had brought them all [the non-conformists] to church.

[In Burnet, *The History of His Own Time* (1724)]

CHESTERFIELD, Lord (1694–1773)

[When asked what could be done to control the evangelical preacher George Whitefield]
Make him a bishop, and you will silence him at once.

[Attr.]

CYPRIAN, Saint (c.200–258)

Salus extra ecclesiam non est.
There is no salvation outside the Church.

[Letter]

Habere non potest Deum patrem qui ecclesiam non habet matrem.
Who has not the Church as his mother cannot have God as his father.

[*De Unitate Ecclesiae*]

D'ALPUGET, Blanche (1944–)

Convent girls never leave the church, they just become feminists. I learned that in Australia.

[*Turtle Beach* (1981)]

DEVLIN, Bernadette (1947–)

Among the best traitors Ireland has ever had, Mother Church ranks at the very top, a massive obstacle in the path to equality and freedom.

[*The Price of My Soul*]

EMERSON, Ralph Waldo (1803–1882)

I like the silent church before the service begins, better than any preaching.

[*Essays, First Series* (1841)]

FIELDING, Henry (1707–1754)

For clergy are men as well as other folks.

[*Joseph Andrews* (1742)]

There is not in the universe a more ridiculous, nor a more contemptible animal, than a proud clergyman.

[*Amelia* (1751)]

HERBERT, George (1593–1633)

Kneeling ne're spoil'd silk stocking. Quit thy state.
All equall are within the churches gate.

[*The Temple* (1633)]

HIGTON, Tony (19th century)

The church is not a mere ecclesiastical wing of the state which benignly blesses what an increasingly secular society does. Its function is primarily to represent God to the nation.

[*The Times*, 1992]

JOWETT, Benjamin (1817–1893)

Nowhere probably is there more true feeling, and nowhere worse taste, than in a churchyard – both as regards the monuments and the inscriptions. Scarcely a word of the true poetry anywhere.

[In E. Abbott and L. Campbell (eds), *Life and Letters of Benjamin Jowett* (1897)]

LAMB, William, Lord (1779–1848)

While I cannot be regarded as a pillar, I must be regarded as a buttress of the church, because I support it from the outside.

[Attr.]

MACAULAY, Lord (1800–1859)

[Of the Roman Catholic Church]
She may still exist in undiminished vigour when some traveller from New Zealand shall, in the midst of a vast solitude, take his stand on a broken arch of London Bridge to sketch the ruins of St Paul's.

[*Collected Essays* (1843)]

MILLER, Arthur (1915–)

There are many who stay away from church these days because you hardly ever mention God any more.

[*The Crucible* (1952)]

MUGGERIDGE, Malcolm (1903–1990)

[On Punch, which he once edited]
Very much like the Church of England. It is doctrinally inexplicable but it goes on.

[Attr.]

PAISLEY, Rev. Ian (1926–)

The Roman Catholic Church is getting nearer

to communism every day.

[*The Irish Times,* 1969]

PRIESTLEY, J.B. (1894–1984)

It is hard to tell where the MCC ends and the Church of England begins.

[*New Statesman,* 1962]

PROVERB

If there's a hen or a goose, it's on the priest's table you'll find it.

[Irish proverb]

SABIA, Laura (1903–1990)

I'm a Roman Catholic and I take a dim view of 2,500 celibates shuffling back and forth to Rome to discuss birth control and not one woman to raise a voice.

[*The Toronto Star,* 1975]

SHORTHOUSE, J.H. (1834–1903)

'The Church of England,' I said, seeing that Mr Inglesant paused, 'is no doubt a compromise.'

[*John Inglesant* (1880)]

SMITH, Sydney (1771–1845)

A Curate – there is something which excites compassion in the very name of a Curate!!!

[*Edinburgh Review,* 1822]

What Bishops like best in their Clergy is a droppingdown-deadness of manner.

[*The Works of the Rev. Sydney Smith* (1839)]

I have seen nobody since I saw you, but persons in orders. My only varieties are vicars, rectors, curates, and every now and they (by way of turbot) an archdeacon.

[*Letters,* To Miss Berry, 1843]

STALIN, Joseph (1879–1953)

[Reply to Laval, French Foreign Minister, who asked Stalin in 1935 to do something to encourage the Catholic religion in Russia in order to help him gain the support of the Pope]
The Pope! How many divisions has he got?

[In W.S. Churchill, *The Gathering Storm* (1948)]

SWIFT, Jonathan (1667–1745)

I never saw, heard, nor read, that the clergy were beloved in any nation where

Christianity was the religion of the country. Nothing can render them popular, but some degree of persecution.

[*Thoughts on Religion* (1765)]

TEMPLE, Frederick, Archbishop (1821–1902)

There is a certain class of clergyman whose mendicity is only equalled by their mendacity.

[Attr.]

TEMPLE, William (1881–1944)

The Church exists for the sake of those outside it.

[Attr.]

I believe in the Church, One Holy, Catholic and Apostolic, and I regret that it nowhere exists.

[Attr.]

TUCHOLSKY, Kurt (1890–1935)

Was die Kirche nicht verhindern kann, das segnet sie.
What the church can't prevent, it blesses.

[*Scraps* (1973)]

UPDIKE, John (1932–)

In general the churches, visited by me too often on weekdays … bore for me the same relation to God that billboards did to Coca-Cola: they promoted thirst without quenching it.

[*A Month of Sundays* (1975)]

WAUGH, Evelyn (1903–1966)

There is a species of person called a 'Modern Churchman' who draws the full salary of a beneficed clergyman and need not commit himself to any religious belief.

[*Decline and Fall* (1928)]

I have noticed again and again since I have been in the Church that lay interest in ecclesiastical matters is often a prelude to insanity.

[*Decline and Fall* (1928)]

See RELIGION

CINEMA

ALTMAN, Robert (1922–)

What's a cult? It just means not enough people to make a minority.

[*The Observer*, 1981]

BERRYMAN, John (1914–1972)

I seldom go to films. They are too exciting, Said the Honourable Possum.

[*Dream Songs* (1964), 53]

BROWN, Geoff (1949–)

Dictators needed a talking cinema to twist nations round their fingers: remove the sound from Mussolini and you are left with a puffing bullfrog.

[*The Times*, 1992]

CAMERON, James (1954–)

[On winning an oscar for Best Director for *Titanic*]
I'm the king of the world!

[*Scotland on Sunday*]

COLTRANE, Robbie (1950–)

[On film acting]
If anyone asked me what I was doing, I'd say 'I've come 1500 miles to a foreign country to pretend to be someone else in front of a machine'.

[*Arena*, 1991]

DISNEY, Walt (1901–1966)

Girls bored me – they still do. I love Mickey Mouse more than any woman I've ever known.

[In Wagner, *You Must Remember This*]

FELLINI, Federico (1920–1994)

Sono vent'anni che sempre più stancamente tento di dire che 'La dolce vita' era un titolo goffo e patetico.
I have been trying to say for over twenty years that 'La dolce vita' was a pathetic and awkward title.

[In *Corriere della Sera*, 1993]

GIBSON, Mel (1956–)

I'll tell you what really turns my toes up – love scenes with 68-year-old men and young actresses. I promise you, when I get to that age I will say no.

[*The Sunday Times*, 1999]

GODARD, Jean-Luc (1930–)

Of course a film should have a beginning, a middle and an end. But not necessarily in that order.

[Attr.]

La photographie, c'est la vérité. Le cinéma: la vérité vingt-quatre fois par seconde.
Photography is truth. Cinema is truth twenty-four times a second.

[*Le Petit Soldat*, film, 1960]

GOLDWYN, Samuel (1882–1974)

[On being warned that a story was too caustic]
To hell with the cost. If it's a sound story, we'll make a picture of it.

[In Zierold, *Moguls* (1969)]

Tell me, how did you love my picture?

[Attr.]

A wide screen just makes a bad film twice as bad.

[Attr.]

[Before the opening of his film *The Best Years of Our Lives* in 1946]
I don't care if it doesn't make a nickel, I just want every man, woman, and child in America to see it.

[In Zierold, *Moguls* (1969)]

Why should people go out and pay money to see bad films when they can stay at home and see bad television for nothing?

[*The Observer*, 1956]

The trouble with this business is the dearth of bad pictures.

[Attr.]

GRADE, Lew (1906–1994)

[To Franco Zeffirelli who had explained that the high cost of the film Jesus of Nazareth was partly because there had to be twelve apostles]
Twelve! So who needs twelve! Couldn't we make do with six?

[*Radio Times*, 1983]

GRIFFITH, D.W. (1874–1948)

[Said when directing an epic film]
Move those ten thousand horses a trifle to the right. And that mob out there, three feet forward.

[Attr.]

HITCHCOCK, Alfred (1899–1980)

Cinema is life with the dull bits cut out.

The length of a film should be directly related to the endurance of the human bladder.

[In Simon Rose, *Classic Film Guide* (1995)]

JUNG, Carl Gustav (1875–1961)

The cinema, like the detective story, makes it possible to experience without danger all the excitement, passion and desire which must be repressed in a humanitarian ordering of life.

[Attr.]

KAUFMAN, George S. (1889–1961)

[At a rehearsal of Animal Crackers (1930), for which he wrote the script]
Excuse me for interrupting but I actually thought I heard a line I wrote.

[In Meredith, George S. Kaufman and the Algonquin Round Table (1974)]

LUCAS, George (1944–)

[On *Star Wars*]
I thought it was too wacky for the general public.

MARX, Groucho (1895–1977)

[Explaining why he didn't go to films starring Victor Mature]
I never go to movies where the hero's bust is bigger than the heroine's.

[Attr.]

We in this industry know that behind every successful screenwriter stands a woman. And behind her stands his wife.

[Attr.]

MINGHELLA, Anthony

[On winning an oscar for Best Director for *The English Patient*]

It's a great day for the Isle of Wight.

[*Scotland on Sunday*, 1999]

ROGERS, Will (1879–1935)

The movies are the only business where you can go out front and applaud yourself.

[In Halliwell, *Filmgoer's Book of Quotes* (1973)]

TRACY, Spencer (1900–1967)

[Defending his demand for equal billing with Katherine Hepburn]
This is a movie, not a lifeboat.

[Attr.]

TREE, Sir Herbert Beerbohm (1853–1917)

[Objecting to the presence of a camera while performing in a silent film]
Take that black box away. I can't act in front of it.

[In K. Brownlow, *Hollywood: The Pioneers*]

WALLACH, Eli (1915–)

[Remarking upon the long line of people at the box office before one of his performances]
There's something about a crowd like that that brings a lump to my wallet.

[Attr.]

See HOLLYWOOD; SHOWBUSINESS

CITIES

ARNOLD, Matthew (1822–1888)

And that sweet city with her dreaming spires,
She needs not June for beauty's heightening.

['Thyrsis' (1866)]

BURGON, John William (1813–1888)

Match me such marvel save in Eastern clime,
A rose-red city 'half as old as Time'!

['Petra' (1845)]

CAESAR, Augustus (63 BC–AD 14)

Urbem…excoluit adeo, uti iure sit gloriatus marmoream se relinquere, quam latericiam accepisset.
He so beautified the city that he justly boasted that he found it brick and left it

marble.

[In Suetonius, *Lives of the Caesars*]

COLTON, Charles Caleb (c.1780–1832)
If you would be known, and not know,
vegetate in a village; if you would know, and
not be known, live in a city.

[*Lacon* (1820)]

COWPER, William (1731–1800)
God made the country, and man made the
town.

[*The Task* (1785)]

KEATS, John (1795–1821)
To one who has been long in city pent,
'Tis very sweet to look into the fair
And open face of heaven.

['To one who has been long in city pent' (1816)]

KIPLING, Rudyard (1865–1936)
Cities and Thrones and Powers,
Stand in Time's eye,
Almost as long as flowers,
Which daily die:
But, as new buds put forth,
To glad new men,
Out of the spent and unconsidered Earth,
The Cities rise again.

['Cities and Thrones and Powers' (1906)]

MILTON, John (1608–1674)
Towred Cities please us then,
And the busie humm of men.

['L'Allegro' (1645)]

MOORE, Brian (1921–1999)
This city was full of lunatics, people who
went into muttering fits on the bus, others
who shouted obscenities in automats, lost
souls who walked the pavements alone,
caught up in imaginary conversations.

[*An Answer From Limbo* (1994)]

MORRIS, Charles (1745–1838)
A house is much more to my taste than a
tree,
And for groves, oh! a good grove of
chimneys for me.

['Country and Town', 1840]

MORRIS, Desmond (1928–)
Clearly, then, the city is not a concrete jungle,
it is a human zoo.

[*The Human Zoo* (1969)]

THOMSON, James (1834–1882)
The City is of Night; perchance of Death,
But certainly of Night; for never there
Can come the lucid morning's fragrant breath
After the dewy dawning's cold grey air …

The City is of Night, but not of Sleep;
There sweet sleep is not for the weary brain;
The pitiless hours like years and ages creep,
A night seems termless hell.

[*The City of Dreadful Night* (1880)]

CITIES: BATH

AUSTEN, Jane (1775–1817)
Oh! who can ever be tired of Bath?

[*Northanger Abbey* (1818)]

CITIES: BELFAST

CRAIG, Maurice James (1919–)
Red bricks in the suburbs, white horse on the
wall,
Eyetalian marbles in the City Hall:
O stranger from England, why stand so aghast?
May the Lord in his mercy be kind to Belfast.

['Ballad to a traditional Refrain']

CITIES: BIRMINGHAM

AUSTEN, Jane (1775–1817)
One has not great hopes from Birmingham. I
always say there is something direful in the
sound.

[*Emma* (1816)]

CITIES: BOSTON

APPLETON, Thomas Gold (1812–1884)
A Boston man is the east wind made

flesh.

[Attr.]

BOSSIDY, John Collins (1860–1928)
And this is good old Boston,
The home of the bean and the cod,
Where the Lowells talk only to Cabots,
And the Cabots talk only to God.

[Toast at Harvard dinner, 1910]

EMERSON, Ralph Waldo (1803–1882)
We say the cows laid out Boston. Well, there
are worse surveyors.

[Conduct of Life (1860)]

CITIES: CAMBRIDGE

BAEDEKER, Karl (1801–1859)
Oxford is on the whole more attractive than
Cambridge to the ordinary visitor; and the
traveller is therefore recommended to visit
Cambridge first, or to omit it altogether if he
cannot visit both.

[Baedeker's Great Britain (1887)]

RAPHAEL, Frederic (1931–)
This is the city of perspiring dreams.

[The Glittering Prizes (1976)]

CITIES: CHICAGO

CAPONE, Al (1899–1947)
[Talking about suburban Chicago]
This is virgin territory for whorehouses.

[In Kenneth Allsop, The Bootleggers (1961)]

CITIES: EDINBURGH

GARIOCH, Robert (1909–1981)
In simmer, whan aa sorts foregether
in Embro to the ploy,
fowk seek out friens to hae a blether,
or faes they'd fain annoy;
smorit wi British Railways' reek
frae Glesca or Glen Roy
or Wick, they come to hae a week
of cultivatit joy,

or three,
in Embro to the ploy.

[Selected Poems (1966)]

GOEBBELS, Joseph (1897–1945)
[Of Edinburgh]
enchanting … it shall make a delightful
summer capital when we invade Britain.

[Attr.]

CITIES: GLASGOW

BRIDIE, James (1888–1951)
You must not look down on … Glasgow
which gave the world the internal
combustion engine, political economy,
antiseptic and cerebral surgery, the balloon,
the mariner's compass, the theory of Latent
Heat, Tobias Smollett and James Bridie.

[Letter to St John Ervine]

CERNUDA, Luis (1902–1963)
[On leaving Glasgow, where he had lived from
1939 to 1943]
Rara vez me he ido tan a gusto de sitio alguno.
Rarely have I been so pleased to leave a place.

[Chronicle of a book (1958)]

MCGONAGALL, William (c.1830–1902)
Beautiful city of Glasgow, I now conclude my
muse,
And to write in praise of thee my pen does
not refuse;
And, without fear of contradiction, I will
venture to say
You are the second grandest city in Scotland
at the present day.

['Glasgow' (1890)]

SMITH, Alexander (1830–1867)
City! I am true son of thine;
Ne'er dwelt I where great mornings shine
Around the bleating pens;
Ne'er by the rivulets I strayed,
And ne'er upon my childhood weighed
The silence of the glens.
Instead of shores where ocean beats,
I hear the ebb and flow of streets.
Thou hast my kith and kin:

My childhood, youth, and manhood brave;
Thou hast that unforgotten grave
Within thy central din.
A sacredness of love and death
Dwells in thy noise and smoky breath.

[*City Poems* (1857)]

CITIES: LONDON

AUSTEN, Jane (1775–1817)

Nobody is healthy in London. Nobody can be.

[*Emma* (1816)]

BLAKE, William (1757–1827)

I wander thro' each charter'd street,
Near where the charter'd Thames does flow
And mark in every face I meet
Marks of weakness, marks of woe.

['London' (1794)]

BLÜCHER, Prince (1742–1819)

[Remark made on seeing London in June, 1814]
Was für Plunder!
What junk!

[Attr.]

BRIDIE, James (1888–1951)

London! Pompous Ignorance sits enthroned there and welcomes Pretentious Mediocrity with flattery and gifts. Oh, dull and witless city! Very hell for the restless, inquiring, sensitive soul. Paradise for the snob, the parasite and the prig; the pimp, the placeman and the cheapjack.

[*The Anatomist* (1931)]

CHAMBERLAIN, Joseph (1836–1914)

Provided that the City of London remains as it is at present, the clearing-house of the world, any other nation may be its workshop.

[Speech, London, 1904]

COBBETT, William (1762–1835)

[Of London]
But what is to be the fate of the great wen of all? The monster, called…'the metropolis of the empire'?

['Rural Rides', 1822]

COLMAN, the Younger, George (1762–1836)

Oh, London is a fine town,
A very famous city,
Where all the streets are paved with gold,
And all the maidens pretty.

[*The Heir at Law* (1797)]

DISRAELI, Benjamin (1804–1881)

London; a nation, not a city.

[*Lothair* (1870)]

DOYLE, Sir Arthur Conan (1859–1930)

London, that great cesspool into which all the loungers of the Empire are irresistibly drained.

[*A Study in Scarlet* (1887)]

DUNBAR, William (c.1460–c.1525)

London, thou art the flower of cities all!
Gemme of all joy, jasper of jocunditie.

['London' (1834)]

GIBBON, Edward (1737–1794)

Crowds without company, and dissipation without pleasure.

[*Memoirs of My Life and Writings* (1796)]

JOHNSON, Samuel (1709–1784)

When a man is tired of London, he is tired of life; for there is in London all that life can afford.

[In Boswell, *The Life of Samuel Johnson* (1791)]

MEYNELL, Hugo (1727–1780)

The chief advantage of London is, that a man is always so near his burrow.

[In Boswell, *The Life of Samuel Johnson* (1791)]

MORRIS, William (1834–1896)

Forget six counties overhung with smoke,
Forget the snorting steam and piston stroke,
Forget the spreading of the hideous town;
Think rather of the pack-horse on the down,
And dream of London, small and white and clean,
The clear Thames bordered by its gardens green.

[*The Earthly Paradise* (1868–1870)]

SWIFT, Jonathan (1667–1745)
It is the folly of too many to mistake the echo of a London coffee house for the voice of the kingdom.

[*The Conduct of the Allies* (1711)]

WORDSWORTH, William (1770–1850)
Earth has not anything to show more fair;
Dull would he be of soul who could pass by
A sight so touching in its majesty:
This city now doth, like a garment, wear

The beauty of the morning; silent, bare,
Ships, towers, domes, theatres, and temples lie
Open unto the fields, and to the sky,
All bright and glittering in the smokeless air …

Dear God! the very houses seem asleep;
And all that mighty heart is lying still!

['Sonnet composed upon Westminster Bridge' (1807)]

CITIES: MANCHESTER

BOLITHO, William (1890–1930)
The shortest way out of Manchester is notoriously a bottle of Gordon's gin.

[*The Treasury of Humorous Quotations*]

CITIES: MELBOURNE

BEVEN, Rodney Allan (1916–1982)
The people of Melbourne
Are frightfully well-born.

['Observation Sociologique']

BYGRAVES, Max (1922–)
I've always wanted to see a ghost town. You couldn't even get a parachute to open here after 10 p.m.

[*Melbourne Sun*, 1965]

JILLETT, Neil (1933–)
[A phrase wrongly attributed to Ava Gardner, who starred in the film *On the Beach*, adapted from

Nevil Shute's novel of that name (1957)]
On the Beach is a story about the end of the world, and Melbourne sure is the right place to film it.

[Attr.]

CITIES: NAPLES

GLADSTONE, William (1809–1898)
This is a negation of God erected into a system of government.

[*Letter to Lord Aberdeen*, 1851]

CITIES: NEW YORK

GILMAN, Charlotte Perkins (1860–1935)
New York … that unnatural city where every one is an exile, none more so than the American.

[*The Living of Charlotte Perkins Gilman* (1935)]

KOCH, Ed
Being a New Yorker is a state of mind. If, after living there for six months, you find that you walk faster, talk faster and think faster, you are a New Yorker.

[*The Observer*, 1999]

MCALLISTER, Ward (1827–1895)
There are only about four hundred people in New York society.

[Interview with Charles H. Crandall in the *New York Tribune*, 1888]

SIMON, Neil (1927–)
New York … is not Mecca. It just smells like it.

[*California Suite* (1976)]

STOUT, Rex Todhunter (1886–1975)
I like to walk around Manhattan, catching glimpses of its wild life, the pigeons and cats and girls.

[*Three Witnesses*, 'When a Man Murders']

CITIES: OXFORD

Beautiful city! so venerable, so lovely, so

unravaged by the fierce intellectual life of our century, so serene! … whispering from her towers the last enchantments of the Middle Age … home of lost causes, and forsaken beliefs, and unpopular names, and impossible loyalties!

[*Essays in Criticism* (1865)]

CITIES: PARIS

ELMS, Robert (1927–)
Paris is the paradise of the easily-impressed – the universal provincial mind.

[In Burchill, *Sex and Sensibility* (1992)]

HAMMERSTEIN II, Oscar (1895–1960)
The last time I saw Paris,
Her heart was warm and gay,
I heard the laughter of her heart in ev'ry street café.

['The Last Time I Saw Paris', song, 1940, from *Lady Be Good*]

HEMINGWAY, Ernest (1898–1961)
If you are lucky enough to have lived in Paris as a young man, then wherever you go for the rest of your life, it stays with you, for Paris is a moveable feast.

[*A Moveable Feast* (1964)]

HENRI IV (1553–1610)
Paris vaut bien une messe.
Paris is well worth a mass.

[Attr.]

KURTZ, Irma (1935–)
Cities are only human. And I had begun to see Paris for the bitch she is: a stunning transvestite – vain, narrow-minded and all false charm.

[*Daily Mail*, 1996]

CITIES: PHILADELPHIA

FIELDS, W.C. (1880–1946)
Last week, I went to Philadelphia, but it was closed.

[Attr.]

CITIES: PRAGUE

PROWSE, William Jeffrey (1836–1870)
Though the latitude's rather uncertain,
And the longitude also is vague,
The persons I pity who know not the city,
The beautiful city of Prague.

['The City of Prague']

CITIES: ROME

BURGESS, Anthony (1917–1993)
Rome's just a city like anywhere else. A vastly overrated city, I'd say. It trades on belief just as Stratford trades on Shakespeare.

[*Inside Mr Enderby* (1968)]

CLOUGH, Arthur Hugh (1819–1861)
Rome, believe me, my friend, is like its own Monte Testaceo,
Merely a marvellous mass of broken and castaway wine-pots.

[*Amours de Voyage* (1858)]

HORACE (65–8 BC)
Fumum et opes strepitumque Romae.
The smoke and wealth and noise of Rome.

[*Odes*]

CITIES: ST ANDREWS

LANG, Andrew (1844–1912)
St Andrews by the Northern Sea,
A haunted town it is to me!

['Almae Matres' (1884)]

CITIES: SYDNEY

SLESSOR, Kenneth (1901–1971)
[On Sydney's ferry-boats]
At sunset, when the Harbour is glazed with pebbles of gold and white, and the sun is burning out like a bushfire behind Balmain, the ferry-boats put on their lights. They turn into luminous water-beetles, filed with a gliding, sliding reflected glitter that bubbles

on the water like phosphorus.

[*Bread and Wine* (1970)]

unhappy everywhere.

[*The Guardian*, 1968]

CITIES: VENICE

BENCHLEY, Robert (1889–1945)
[Telegram sent on arriving in Venice]
Streets flooded. Please advise.

[Attr.]

CAPOTE, Truman (1924–1984)
Venice is like eating an entire box of chocolate liqueurs in one go.

[*The Observer*, 1961]

MORRIS, James (later Jan Morris) (1926–)
There's romance for you! There's the lust and dark wine of Venice! No wonder George Eliot's husband fell into the Grand Canal.

[*Venice* (1960)]

See COUNTRY

CITIZENS

AUDEN, W.H. (1907–1973)
Our researchers into Public Opinion are content
That he held the proper opinions for the time of year;
When there was peace, he was for peace; when there was war, he went.

[*Collected Poems, 1939–1947*]

BRYAN, William Jennings (1860–1925)
The humblest citizen of all the land, when clad in the armour of a righteous cause is stronger than all the hosts of error.

[Speech, Chicago, 1896]

SOCRATES (469–399 BC)
I am not an Athenian nor a Greek, but a citizen of the world.

[Attr. in Plutarch, *On Exile*, 600]

VIZINCZEY, Stephen (1933–)
I was told I am a true cosmopolitan. I am

CIVILIZATION

ADDAMS, Jane (1860–1935)
Civilization is a method of living, an attitude of equal respect for all men.

[Speech, Honolulu, 1933]

ALCOTT, Bronson (1799–1888)
Civilization degrades the many to exalt the few.

[Table Talk (1877)]

ANONYMOUS
[Local resident on the opening of the first Russian McDonalds Restaurant, Moscow, 1990]
It's like the coming of civilization.

BAGEHOT, Walter (1826–1877)
The whole history of civilization is strewn with creeds and institutions which were invaluable at first, and deadly afterwards.

[*Physics and Politics* (1872)]

BATES, Daisy May (1863–1951)
The Australian native can withstand all the reverses of nature, fiendish droughts and sweeping floods, horrors of thirst and enforced starvation – but he cannot withstand civilisation.

[*The Passing of the Aborigines* ... (1938)]

BUCK, Pearl S. (1892–1973)
Nothing and no one can destroy the Chinese people. They are relentless survivors. They are the oldest civilized people on earth. Their civilization passes through phases but its basic characteristics remain the same. They yield, they bend to the wind, but they never break.

[*China, Past and Present* (1972)]

CARLYLE, Thomas (1795–1881)
The three great elements of modern civilization, Gunpowder, Printing, and the Protestant Religion.

[*Critical and Miscellaneous Essays* (1839)]

DISRAELI, Benjamin (1804–1881)

Increased means and increased leisure are the two civilizers of man.

[Speech, Manchester, 1872]

ELLIS, Havelock (1859–1939)

The more rapidly a civilisation progresses, the sooner it dies for another to rise in its place.

[*The Dance of Life*]

FOWLES, John (1926–)

In essence the Renaissance was simply the green end of one of civilization's hardest winters.

[*The French Lieutenant's Woman* (1969)]

GANDHI (1869–1948)

[When asked what he thought of Western civilization]

I think it would be an excellent idea.

[Attr.]

GARROD, Heathcote William (1878–1960)

[In response to criticism that, during World War I, he was not fighting to defend civilization]

Madam, I am the civilization they are fighting to defend.

[In Balsdon, *Oxford Now and Then* (1970)]

GAUGUIN, Paul (1848–1903)

Civilization is paralysis.

[In Cournos, *Modern Plutarch* (1928)]

HILLARY, Sir Edmund (1919–)

There is precious little in civilization to appeal to a Yeti.

[*The Observer*,1960]

HUGO, Victor (1802–1885)

Jésus a pleuré, Voltaire a souri; c'est de cette larme divine et de ce sourire humain qu'est faite la douceur de la civilisation actuelle.

Jesus cried; Voltaire smiled. From that divine tear, from that human smile was born the sweetness of civilisation today.

[Centenary oration on Voltaire, 1878]

JAMES, William (1842–1910)

Our civilization is founded on the shambles,

and every individual existence goes out in a lonely spasm of helpless agony.

[*Varieties of Religious Experience* (1902)]

KNOX, Ronald (1888–1957)

It is so stupid of modern civilization to have given up believing in the devil when he is the only explanation of it.

[Attr.]

MANSFIELD, Katherine (1888–1923)

How idiotic civilization is! Why be given a body if you have to keep it shut up in a case like a rare, rare fiddle?

[*Bliss and Other Stories* (1920)]

MILL, John Stuart (1806–1873)

I am not aware that any community has a right to force another to be civilized.

[*On Liberty* (1859)]

PAGLIA, Camille (1947–)

If civilisation had been left in female hands, we would still be living in grass huts.

[*Sex, Art and American Culture: Essays* (1992)]

PARK, Mungo (1771–1806)

[Remark on finding a gibbet in an unexplored part of Africa]

The sight of it gave me infinite pleasure, as it proved that I was in a civilized society.

[Attr.]

POPPER, Sir Karl (1902–1994)

Our civilization … has not yet fully recovered from the shock of its birth – the transition from the tribal or 'closed society', with its submission to magical forces, to the 'open society' which sets free the critical powers of man.

[*The Open Society and its Enemies* (1945)]

RAND, Ayn (1905–1982)

Civilization is the progress toward a society of privacy. The savage's whole existence is public, ruled by the laws of his tribe.

Civilization is the process of setting man free from men.

[*The Fountainhead* (1943)]

ROGERS, Will (1879–1935)
You can't say civilization don't advance, however, for in every war they kill you a new way.

[*New York Times*, 1929]

SANTAYANA, George (1863–1952)
Civilisation is perhaps approaching one of those long winters that overtake it from time to time. Romantic Christendom – picturesque, passionate, unhappy episode – may be coming to an end. Such a catastrophe would be no reason for despair.

[*Characters and Opinions in the United States*]

TREVELYAN, G.M. (1876–1962)
Disinterested intellectual curiosity is the life blood of real civilization.

[*English Social History* (1942)]

YEATS, W.B. (1865–1939)
A civilisation is a struggle to keep self-control.

[*A Vision* (1925)]

See CULTURE

CLASS

ARNOLD, Matthew (1822–1888)
Philistine gives the notion of something particularly stiff-necked and perverse in the resistance to light and its children; and therein it specially suits our middle class.

[*Culture and Anarchy* (1869)]

I often, therefore, when I want to distinguish clearly the aristocratic class from the Philistines proper, or middle class, name the former, in my own mind, the Barbarians.

[*Culture and Anarchy* (1869)]

But that vast portion, lastly, of the working-class which, raw and half-developed, has long lain half-hidden amidst its poverty and squalor, and is now issuing from its hiding-place to assert an Englishman's heaven-born privilege of doing as he likes, and is beginning to perplex us by marching where it likes, meeting where it likes, bawling what it likes, breaking what it likes – to this vast residuum we may with great propriety give the name of Populace.

[*Culture and Anarchy* (1869)]

One has often wondered whether upon the whole earth there is anything so unintelligent, so unapt to perceive how the world is really going, as an ordinary young Englishman of our upper class.

[*Culture and Anarchy* (1869)]

ASHFORD, Daisy (1881–1972)
My dear Clincham, The bearer of this letter is an old friend of mine not quite the right side of the blanket as they say in fact he is the son of a first rate butcher but his mother was a decent family called Hyssopps of the Glen so you see he is not so bad and is desireus of being the correct article.

[*The Young Visiters* (1919)]

BELLOC, Hilaire (1870–1953)
Like many of the Upper Class
He liked the Sound of Broken Glass.

[*New Cautionary Tales* (1930)]

BRENAN, Gerald (1894–1987)
Poets and painters are outside the class system, or rather they constitute a special class of their own, like the circus people and the gipsies.

[*Thoughts in a Dry Season* (1978)]

BROUGH, Robert Barnabas (1828–1860)
My Lord Tomnoddy is thirty-four;
The Earl can last but a few years more.
My Lord in the Peers will take his place:
Her Majesty's councils his words will grace.
Office he'll hold and patronage sway;
Fortunes and lives he will vote away;
And what are his qualifications? – ONE!
He's the Earl of Fitzdotterel's eldest son.

['My Lord Tomnoddy' (1855)]

BROUGHAM, Lord Henry (1778–1868)
The great Unwashed.

[Attr.]

BURGESS, Anthony (1917–1993)

Without class differences, England would cease to be the living theatre it is.

[Remark, 1985]

CALVERLEY, C.S. (1831–1884)

For I've read in many a novel that, unless they've souls that grovel,
Folks prefer in fact a hovel to your dreary marble halls.

['In the Gloaming' (1872)]

CARTLAND, Barbara (1902–)

[When asked in a radio interview whether she thought that British class barriers had broken down]
Of course they have, or I wouldn't be sitting here talking to someone like you.

[In J. Cooper, *Class* (1979)]

CHELSEA, Jenny, Viscountess

[Introducing a seminar on upper class behaviour]
So many people don't know how to behave at a shooting party.

[*The Observer*, 1998]

CURZON, Lord (1859–1925)

[On seeing some soldiers bathing]
I never knew the lower classes had such white skins.

[Attr.]

DEFOE, Daniel (c.1661–1731)

He bid me observe ... that the calamities of life were shared among the upper and lower part of mankind; but that the middle station had the fewest disasters.

[*The Life and Adventures of Robinson Crusoe* (1719)]

DOYLE, Roddy (1958–)

'You're working class, right?'
'We would be if there was any work.'

[*The Commitments*, film, 1991]

EDWARD, Prince (1964–)

We are forever being told we have a rigid class structure. That's a load of codswallop.

[*Daily Mail*, 1996]

ELIZABETH, the Queen Mother (1900–)

My favourite programme is 'Mrs Dale's Diary'. I try never to miss it because it is the only way of knowing what goes on in a middle-class family.

[Attr.]

ENGELS, Friedrich (1820–1895)

The history of all hitherto existing society is the history of class struggles.

[*The Communist Manifesto* (1848)]

FRIEL, Brian (1929–)

The result is that people with a culture of poverty suffer much less repression than we of the middle-class suffer and indeed, if I may make the suggestion with due qualification, they often have a lot more fun than we have.

[*The Freedom of the City* (1973)]

HAILSHAM, Quintin Hogg, Baron (1907–)

I don't see any harm in being middle class, I've been middle class all my life and have benefited from it.

[*The Observer*, 1983]

HOWARD, Philip (1933–)

Every time an Englishman opens his mouth, he enables other Englishmen if not to despise him, at any rate to place him in some social and class pigeonhole.

[*The Times*, 1992]

IPHICRATES (419–353 BC)

[Responding to a descendant of Harmodius (an Athenian hero), who had mocked Iphicrates for being the son of a shoemaker]
The difference between us is that my family begins with me, whereas yours ends with you.

[Attr.]

LERNER, Alan Jay (1918–1986)

An Englishman's way of speaking absolutely classifies him.

[*My Fair Lady* (1956)]

LEWIS, John Llewellyn (1880–1969)

I'm not interested in classes ... Far be it from

me to foster inferiority complexes among the workers by trying to make them think they belong to some special class. That has happened in Europe but it hasn't happened here yet.

[In A.M. Schlesinger Jr., *The Coming of the New Deal*]

LILLIE, Beatrice (1894–1989)

[Commenting on her childhood in Toronto]
We were located half way up the social ladder. Or half way down. It depends on which way you're looking.

[*The Toronto Star*, 1989]

MACNEICE, Louis (1907–1963)

Take, for instance, the question of class. There were many undergraduates like myself who theoretically conceded that all men were equal, but who, in practice, while only too willing to converse, or attempt to, with say Normandy peasants or shopkeepers, would wince away in their own college halls from those old grammar school boys who with impure vowels kept admiring Bernard Shaw or Noël Coward while grabbing their knives and forks like dumb-bells.

[*The Saturday Book* (1961)]

MARX, Karl (1818–1883)

What I did that was new was prove … that the class struggle necessarily leads to the dictatorship of the proletariat.

[Letter, 1852]

MIKES, George (1912–1987)

The one class you do not belong to and are not proud of at all is the lower-middle class. No one ever describes himself as belonging to the lower-middle class.

[*How to be an Inimitable*]

PARSONS, Tony (1953–)

The working class has come a long way in recent years, all of it downhill. They look like one big Manson family.

[*Arena*, 1989]

[Of the working class in the 1980s]
They are the real class traitors, betrayers of the men who fought the Second World War,

those men who fought for Churchill but voted for Clement Attlee. But in the tattooed jungle they have no sense of history. The true unruly children of Thatcherism, they know their place and wallow in their peasanthood.

[*Arena*, 1989]

RATTIGAN, Terence (1911–1977)

You can be in the Horse Guards and still be common, dear.

[*Separate Tables* (1955)]

SCARGILL, Arthur (1941–)

[On John Prescott's description of himself as middle class]
I have little or no time for people who aspire to be members of the middle class.

[Remark at the launch of the Socialist Labour Party, 1996]

STANTON, Elizabeth Cady (1815–1902)

It is impossible for one class to appreciate the wrongs of another.

[In Anthony and Gage, *History of Woman Suffrage* (1881)]

THEROUX, Paul (1941–)

The ship follows Soviet custom: it is riddled with class distinctions so subtle, it takes a trained Marxist to appreciate them.

[*The Great Railway Bazaar* (1975)]

THIERS, Louis Adolphe (1797–1877)

[Defending his social status after someone had remarked that his mother had been a cook]
She was – but I assure you that she was a very bad cook.

[Attr.]

THOMPSON, E.P. (1924–1993)

I am seeking to rescue the poor stockinger, the Luddite cropper, the 'obsolete' handloom weaver, the 'utopian' artisan, and even the deluded follower of Joanna Southcott, from the enormous condescension of posterity.

[*The Making of the English Working Class*, quoted in *The Guardian*]

WILDE, Oscar (1854–1900)

Really, if the lower orders don't set us a good

example, what on earth is the use of them? They seem, as a class, to have absolutely no sense of moral responsibility.

[*The Importance of Being Earnest* (1895)]

WRAN, Neville Kenneth (1926–)
There's what being in the working-class is all about – how to get out of it.

[*Sydney Morning Herald*, 1982]

See ARISTOCRACY; EQUALITY; SNOBBERY

CLONING

ANONYMOUS
[After Scottish scientists pioneered the cloning of a sheep, Dolly.]
There'll never be another ewe? Don't count on it!

[News headline, 1997]

CLUBS

DICKENS, Charles (1812–1870)
[Of the House of Commons]
I think … that it is the best club in London.

[*Our Mutual Friend* (1865)]

JOHNSON, Samuel (1709–1784)
Boswell is a very clubbable man.

[In Boswell, *The Life of Samuel Johnson* (1791)]

MARX, Groucho (1895–1977)
Please accept my resignation. I don't want to belong to any club that would have me as a member.

[*Groucho and Me* (1959)]

MORTIMER, John (1923–)
One enlightened member said that in the past the Garrick Club excluded lunatics, gays and women: now the first two classes have been let in there's no conceivable reason to bar the third.

[Attr.]

SURTEES, R.S. (1805–1864)
Every man shouting in proportion to the amount of his subscription.

[*Jorrock's Jaunts and Jollities* (1838)]

WILDE, Oscar (1854–1900)
[Refusing to attend a function at a club whose members were hostile to him]
I should be like a lion in a cage of savage Daniels.

[Attr.]

See BOREDOM

COFFEE

CHELEBI, Katib (1609–1657)
Coffee is a cold dry food, suited to the ascetic life and sedative of lust.

[In G.L. Lewis (trans.), *The Balance of Truth* (1957)]

POPE, Alexander (1688–1744)
Coffee, which makes the politician wise, And see through all things with his half-shut eyes.

[*The Rape of the Lock*, 1712]

THACKERAY, William Makepeace (1811–1863)
Why do they always put mud into coffee on board steamers? Why does the tea generally taste of boiled boots?

[*The Kickleburys on the Rhine* (1850)]

TWAIN, Mark (1835–1910)
The best coffee in Europe is Vienna coffee, compared to which all other coffee is fluid poverty.

[*Greatly Exaggerated*]

COMEDY

CHAPLIN, Charlie (1889–1977)
All I need to make a comedy is a park, a policeman and a pretty girl.

[*My Autobiography* (1964)]

I remain just one thing, and one thing only – and that is a clown. It places me on a far higher plane than any politician.

[*The Observer*, 1960]

FELDMAN, Marty (1933–1982)
Comedy, like sodomy, is an unnatural act.

[*The Times*, 1969]

MOLIÈRE (1622–1673)

C'est une étrange entreprise que celle de faire rire les honnêtes gens.
It's a strange job, making decent people laugh.

[*L'Ecole des Femmes* (1662)]

PRIESTLEY, J.B. (1894–1984)

Comedy, we may say, is society protecting itself – with a smile.

[*George Meredith* (1926)]

ROGERS, Will (1879–1935)

A comedian can only last till he either takes himself serious or his audience takes him serious.

[Newspaper article, 1931]

COMMON SENSE

DESCARTES, René (1596–1650)

Le bon sens est la chose du monde la mieux partagée, car chacun pense en être bien pourvu.
Common sense is the best distributed thing in the world, for we all think we possess a good share of it.

[*Discours de la Méthode* (1637)]

EINSTEIN, Albert (1879–1955)

Common sense is the collection of prejudices acquired by age eighteen.

[Attr.]

EMERSON, Ralph Waldo (1803–1882)

Nothing astonishes men so much as common-sense and plain dealing.

['Art' (1841)]

LA BRUYÈRE, Jean de (1645–1696)

Entre le bon sens et le bon goût il y a la différence de la cause et son effet.
Between good sense and good taste there is the same difference as between cause and effect.

[*Les caractères ou les moeurs de ce siècle* (1688)]

SALISBURY, Lord (1830–1903)

No lesson seems to be so deeply inculcated by the experience of life as that you never should trust experts. If you believe the doctors, nothing is wholesome: if you believe the theologians, nothing is innocent: if you believe the soldiers, nothing is safe. They all require to have their strong wine diluted by a very large admixture of insipid common sense.

[Letter to Lord Lytton, 1877]

COMMUNISM

ATTLEE, Clement (1883–1967)

Russian Communism is the illegitimate child of Karl Marx and Catherine the Great.

[*The Observer*, 1956]

BEVAN, Aneurin (1897–1960)

[Of the Communist Party]
Its relationship to democratic institutions is that of the death watch beetle – it is not a Party, it is a conspiracy.

[Attr.]

CHURCHILL, Sir Winston (1874–1965)

Beware, for the time may be short. A shadow has fallen across the scenes so lately lighted by the Allied victory. Nobody knows what Soviet Russia and its Communist international organization intend to do in the immediate future. From Stettin in the Baltic to Trieste in the Adriatic an Iron Curtain has descended across the Continent.

[Speech, Fulton, Missouri, March 1946]

ELLIOTT, Ebenezer (1781–1849)

What is a communist? One who hath yearnings
For equal division of unequal earnings.

[*Epigram*, 1850]

ENGELS, Friedrich (1820–1895)

A spectre is haunting Europe – the spectre of Communism.

[*The Communist Manifesto* (1848)]

GALLACHER, William (1881–1965)

We are for our own people. We want to see them happy, healthy and wise, drawing strength from cooperation with the peoples of other lands, but also contributing their full share to the general well-being. Not a broken-down pauper and mendicant, but a strong, living partner in the progressive advancement of civilization.

[*The Case for Communism* (1949)]

KHRUSHCHEV, Nikita (1894–1971)

[On the possibility that the Soviet Union might one day reject communism]
Those who wait for that must wait until a shrimp learns to whistle.

[Attr.]

LENIN, V.I. (1870–1924)

Communism is Soviet power plus the electrification of the whole country.

[Report at the Congress of Soviets, 1920]

MCCARTHY, Senator Joseph (1908–1957)

I have here in my hand a list of two hundred and five [people] that were known to the Secretary of State as being members of the Communist Party and who nevertheless are still working and shaping the policy of the State Department.

[Speech, Wheeling, West Virginia, Febuary 9, 1950]

[Of someone alleged to have communist sympathies]
It makes me sick, sick, sick way down inside.

[In Lewis, *The Fifties* (1978)]

[On how to spot a communist]
It looks like a duck, walks like a duck, and quacks like a duck.

[Attr.]

MORLEY, Robert (1908–1992)

There's no such thing in Communist countries as a load of old cod's wallop, the cod's wallop is always fresh made.

[*Punch*, 1974]

ROGERS, Will (1879–1935)

Communism is like prohibition, it's a good idea but it won't work.

[*Weekly Articles* (1981)]

SMITH, F.E. (1872–1930)

[On Bolshevism]

Nature has no cure for this sort of madness, though I have known a legacy from a rich relative work wonders.

[*Law, Life and Letters* (1927)]

SOLZHENITSYN, Alexander (1918–)

For us in Russia, communism is a dead dog, while for many people in the West, it is still a living lion.

[*The Listener*, 1979]

Every communist has a fascist frown, every fascist a communist smile.

[*The Girls of Slender Means*]

STALIN, Joseph (1879–1953)

The party is the rallying-point for the best elements of the working class.

[Attr.]

TAYLOR, A.J.P. (1906–1990)

Communism continued to haunt Europe as a spectre – a name men gave to their own fears and blunders. But the crusade against Communism was even more imaginary than the spectre of Communism.

[*The Origins of the Second World War* (1961)]

See CAPITALISM; SOCIALISM

COMPASSION

THE BIBLE
(King James Version)
Blessed are the merciful: for they shall obtain mercy.

[*Matthew*, 5:7]

BLAKE, William (1757–1827)

Can I see anothers woe,
And not be in sorrow too?
Can I see anothers grief,
And not seek for kind relief?

[*Songs of Innocence* (1789)]

Can I see another's woe,
And not be in sorrow too?
Can I see another's grief,
And not seek for kind relief?

['On Another's Sorrow' (1789)]

BRADFORD, John (c.1510–1555)
[Remark on criminals going to the gallows]
But for the grace of God there goes John
Bradford.
[Attr.]

BURNS, Robert (1759–1796)
Then gently scan your brother man,
Still gentler sister woman;
Tho' they may gang a kennin wrang,
To step aside is human.
['Address to the Unco Guid' (1786)]

CHAUCER, Geoffrey (c.1340–1400)
For pitee renneth soone in gentil herte.
[*The Canterbury Tales* (1387)]

CROMWELL, Oliver (1599–1658)
The dimensions of this mercy are above my
thoughts. It is, for aught I know, a crowning
mercy.
[Letter to William Lenthall, 1651]

DALAI LAMA (1935–)
Compassion and love are not mere luxuries.
As the source of both inner and external
peace, they are fundamental to the
continued survival of our species.
[*The Times*, June 1999]

DESMOULINS, Camille (1760–1794)
La clémence aussi est une mesure révolutionnaire.
Clemency is also a revolutionary measure.
[Speech, 1793]

ELIOT, George (1819–1880)
We hand folks over to God's mercy, and show
none ourselves.
[*Adam Bede* (1859)]

GAY, John (1685–1732)
He best can pity who has felt the woe.
[*Dione* (1720)]

GIBBON, Edward (1737–1794)
Our sympathy is cold to the relation of
distant misery.
[*Decline and Fall of the Roman Empire* (1788)]

HOPKINS, Gerard Manley (1844–1889)
My own heart let me more have pity on; let
Me live to my sad self hereafter kind,

Charitable; not live this tormented mind
With this tormented mind tormenting yet.
['My own Heart let me more have Pity on' (c. 1885)]

HUXLEY, Aldous (1894–1963)
She was a machine-gun riddling her hostess
with sympathy.
[*Mortal Coils* (1922)]

KINNOCK, Neil (1942–)
Compassion is not a sloppy, sentimental
feeling for people who are underprivileged
or sick … it is an absolutely practical belief
that, regardless of a person's background,
ability or ability to pay, he should be
provided with the best that society has to
offer.
[Maiden speech, House of Commons, 1970]

LAZARUS, Emma (1849–1887)
Give me your tired, your poor,
Your huddled masses yearning to breathe
free.
['The New Colossus' (1883); verse inscribed on the
Statue of Liberty]

**NIETZSCHE, Friedrich Wilhelm
(1844–1900)**
*Mitleiden äussern wird als ein Zeichen der
Verachtung empfunden, weil man ersichtlich
aufgehört hat, ein Gegenstand der Furcht zu sein,
sobald einem Mitleiden erwiesen wird.*
To show pity is felt to be a sign of scorn,
because one has obviously stopped being an
object of fear as soon as one is pitied.
[*Human, All too Human* (1886)]

RICHARDSON, Samuel (1689–1761)
Pity is but one remove from love.
[*The History of Sir Charles Grandison* (1754)]

SHAKESPEARE, William (1564–1616)
The quality of mercy is not strain'd;
It droppeth as the gentle rain from heaven
Upon the place beneath. It is twice blest:
It blesseth him that gives and him that takes.
[*The Merchant of Venice*, IV.i]

SMOLLETT, Tobias (1721–1771)
Any man of humane sentiments … would
have been prompted to offer his services to

the forlorn stranger: but … our hero was devoid of all these infirmities of human nature.

[*The Adventures of Ferdinand Count Fathom* (1753)]

VILLON, François (b. 1431)

Frères humains qui après nous vivez,
N'ayez les coeurs contre nous endurcis,
Car, si pitié de nous pauvres avez,
Dieu en aura plus tôt de vous mercis …
Mais priez Dieu que tous nous veuille absoudre!
Brothers in humanity who live after us, don't let your hearts be hardened against us, for, if you take pity on us poor souls, God will be more likely to have mercy on you. But pray to God that he may be willing to absolve us all!

['Ballad of the Hanged Men' (1462)]

VIRGIL (70–19 BC)

Non ignara mali miseris succurrere disco.
No stranger to misery myself, I am learning to befriend the wretched.

[*Aeneid*]

WHITE, Patrick (1912–1990)

And remember Mother's practical ethics: *one can drown in compassion if one answers every call it's another way of suicide.*

[*The Eye of the Storm* (1973)]

WILDE, Oscar (1854–1900)

I can sympathize with everything, except suffering.

[*The Picture of Dorian Gray* (1891)]

Anybody can sympathise with the sufferings of a friend, but it requires a very fine nature to sympathise with a friend's success.

['The Soul of Man under Socialism' (1881)]

COMPLAINT

BERKELEY, Bishop George (1685–1753)

We have first raised a dust and then complain we cannot see.

[*A Treatise Concerning the Principles of Human Knowledge* (1710)]

DISRAELI, Benjamin (1804–1881)

Never complain, never explain.

[Attr.]

GILMORE, Dame Mary (1865–1962)

Never admit the pain,
Bury it deep;
Only the weak complain,
Complaint is cheap.

[*The Wild Swan* (1930)]

MARX, Groucho (1895–1977)

I want to register a complaint. Do you know who sneaked into my room at three o'clock this morning? – Who?
Nobody, and that's my complaint.

[*Monkey Business*, film, 1931]

MELBOURNE, Lord (1779–1848)

[After his dismissal by William IV]
I have always thought complaints of ill-usage contemptible, whether from a seduced disappointed girl or a turned out Prime Minister.

[In a letter from Emily Eden to Mrs Lister, 1834]

SAKI (1870–1916)

There are so many things to complain of in this household that it would never have occurred to me to complain of rheumatism.

[*The Chronicles of Clovis* (1911)]

SEMPLE, Robert (1873–1955)

[A favourite term of abuse for whingeing complainants or opponents]
Snivelling snufflebusters.

[A Semple-ism, first recorded 1905]

COMPUTERS

ANDERSON, Jeremy S.

There are two major products that come out of Berkeley: LSD and UNIX. We don't believe this to be a coincidence.

ANONYMOUS

Putting a computer in front of a child and expecting it to teach him is like putting a book under his pillow, only more expensive.

Applying computer technology is simply finding the right wrench to pound in the correct screw.

WARNING: Keyboard Not Attached. Press F10 to Continue.

Press any key … no, no, no, NOT THAT ONE!

What goes up must come down. Ask any system administrator.

Intel has announced its next chip: the Repentium.

I speak BASIC to clients, 1-2-3 to management, and mumble to myself.

A program is a spell cast over a computer, turning input into error messages.

There are two ways to write error-free programs. Only the third one works.

Any given program, when running, is obsolete.

[Laws of Computer Programming I]

Any given program costs more and takes longer.

[Laws of Computer Programming II]

If a program is useful, it will have to be changed.

[Laws of Computer Programming, III]

If a program is useless, it will have to be documented.

[Laws of Computer Programming, IV]

Any program will expand to fill available memory.

[Laws of Computer Programming, V]

The value of a program is proportional to the weight of its output.

[Laws of Computer Programming, VI]

Program complexity grows until it exceeds the capabilities of the programmer who must maintain it.

[Laws of Computer Programming, VII]

Any non-trivial program contains at least one bug.

[Laws of Computer Programming, VIII]

Undetectable errors are infinite in variety, in contrast to detectable errors, which by definition are limited.

[Laws of Computer Programming, IX]

Adding manpower to a late software project makes it later.

[Laws of Computer Programming, X]

If a computer cable has one end, then it has another.

[Lyall's Conjecture]

AVISHAI, Bernard

The danger from computers is not that they will eventually get as smart as men, but we will meanwhile agree to meet them halfway.

BUSH, Vannevar (1890–1974)

The world has arrived at an age of cheap complex devices of great reliability, and something is bound to come of it.

CRINGELY, Robert X.

If the automobile had followed the same development cycle as the computer, a Rolls-Royce would today cost $100, get one million miles to the gallon, and explode once a year, killing everyone inside.

DAWKINS, Richard (1941–)

Personally, I rather look forward to a computer program winning the world chess championship. Humanity needs a lesson in humility.

HAWKING, Stephen (1942–)

I think computer viruses should count as life. I think it says something about human nature that the only form of life we have created so far is purely destructive. We've created life in our own image.

KULAWIEC, Rich

Any sufficiently advanced bug is indistinguishable from a feature.

MINOR, Janet

I have a spelling checker

It came with my PC;
It plainly marks four my revue
Mistakes I cannot sea.
I've run this poem threw it,
I'm sure your pleased too no,
Its letter perfect in it's weigh,
My checker tolled me sew.

ONDAATJE, Michael (1943–)

[Comment after accepting a computer at the Wang International Festival of Authors; the author writes with a fountain pen]
I think giving this computer to the last Luddite is ridiculous. It's like giving a Porsche to someone who just discovered the bicycle.

[Attr.]

SALOMOM, Dan

Sometimes it pays to stay in bed on Monday, rather than spending the rest of the week debuging Monday's code.

SEGAL, Erich (1937–)

The OED database is one of the wonders of the modern world – to paraphrase Christopher Marlowe, 'infinite riches in a little ROM'.

[*The Times Literary Supplement*, 1992]

STOLL, Clifford

Why is it drug addicts and computer afficionados are both called users?

STROUSTRUP, Bjarne

C makes it easy to shoot yourself in the foot. C++ makes it harder, but when you do, it blows away your whole leg.

WATSON, Thomas J. (1874–1956)

[The founder of IBM on the prospects for desktop computers]
I think there's a world market for about five computers.

[In Martin Moskovits *Science and Society*, 1995]

WOZNIAK, Steve

Never trust a computer you can't throw out a window.

See ARTIFICIAL INTELLIGENCE;
   INNOVATION; TECHNOLOGY

CONSCIENCE

ANONYMOUS

Conscience is what hurts when everything else feels so good.

DE QUINCEY, Thomas (1785–1859)

Better to stand ten thousand sneers than one abiding pang, such as time could not abolish, of bitter self-reproach.

[*Confessions of an English Opium Eater* (1822)]

HENDERSON, Arthur (1863–1935)

The plural of conscience is conspiracy.

[*The Independent*, 1992]

HOBBES, Thomas (1588–1679)

A man's conscience and his judgement is the same thing, and as the judgement, so also the conscience, may be erroneous.

[Attr.]

MENCKEN, H.L. (1880–1956)

Conscience is the inner voice that warns us somebody may be looking.

[*A Mencken Chrestomathy* (1949)]

NASH, Ogden (1902–1971)

He who is ridden by a conscience
Worries about a lot of nonscience;
He without benefit of scruples
His fun and income soon quadruples.

['Reflection on the Fallibility of Nemesis' (1940)]

SHAKESPEARE, William (1564–1616)

A peace above all earthly dignities,
A still and quiet conscience.

[*Henry VIII*, III.ii]

My conscience hath a thousand several tongues,
And every tongue brings in a several tale,
And every tale condemns me for a villain.

[*Richard III*, V.iii]

Conscience is but a word that cowards use,
Devis'd at first to keep the strong in awe.

[*Richard III*, V.iii]

SHERIDAN, Richard Brinsley (1751–1816)

Conscience has no more to do with gallantry

than it has with politics.

[*The Duenna* (1775)]

WASHINGTON, George (1732–1799)

Labour to keep alive in your breast that little spark of celestial fire, called conscience.

[*Rules of Civility and Decent Behaviour*]

CONSERVATISM

DISRAELI, Benjamin (1804–1881)

Conservatism discards Prescription, shrinks from Principle, disavows Progress: having rejected all respect for antiquity, it offers no redress for the present, and makes no preparation for the future.

[*Coningsby* (1844)]

A sound Conservative government … Tory men and Whig measures.

[*Coningsby* (1844)]

It seems to me a barren thing this Conservatism – an unhappy cross-breed, the mule of politics that engenders nothing.

[*Coningsby* (1844)]

A Conservative government is an organized hypocrisy.

[Speech, 1845]

EMERSON, Ralph Waldo (1803–1882)

Men are conservatives when they are least vigorous, or when they are most luxurious. They are conservatives after dinner. … when they hear music, or when they read poetry, they are radicals.

[*Essays, Second Series* (1844)]

LINCOLN, Abraham (1809–1865)

What is conservatism? Is it not adherence to the old and tried, against the new and untried?

[Speech, 1860]

MONTAIGNE, Michel de (1533–1592)

Pour les affaires publiques, il n'est aucun si mauvais train, pourvu qu'il ait de l'âge et de la constance, qui ne vaille mieux que le changement et le remuement.
There is, in public affairs, no state so bad,

provided it has age and stability on its side, that is not preferable to change and disturbance.

[*Essais* (1580)]

TWAIN, Mark (1835–1910)

The radical invents the views. When he has worn them out, the conservative adopts them.

[*Notebooks* (1935)]

WATSON, Sir William (1858–1936)

The staid conservative,
Came-over-with-the-Conqueror type of mind.

['A Study in Contrasts' (1905)]

See CHANGE; CONVENTION; POLITICIANS

CONSUMER SOCIETY

GALBRAITH, J.K. (1908–)

In a community where public services have failed to keep abreast of private consumption things are very different. Here, in an atmosphere of private opulence and public squalor, the private goods have full sway.

[*The Affluent Society* (1958)]

GITLIN, Todd

There is a misunderstanding by marketers in our culture about what freedom of choice is. In the market, it is equated with multiplying choice. This is a misconception. If you have infinite choice, people are reduced to passivity.

[*New York Times*, 1990]

ILLICH, Ivan (1926–)

In both rich and poor nations consumption is polarized while expectation is equalized.

[*Celebration of Awareness* (1970)]

JAMES, Clive (1939–)

The last stage of fitting the product to the market is fitting the market to the product.

[*The Observer*, 1989]

LARKIN, Philip (1922–1985)

Recognising that if you haven't got the money for something you can't have it – this is a concept that's vanished for many years.

[Interview, *The Observer*, 1979]

NICHOLSON, Vivian (1936–)

[Reply when asked what she would do with the £152,000 she won on the pools in 1961]

I'm going to spend, spend, spend, that's what I'm going to do.

[In V. Nicholson and S. Smith, *I'm Going to Spend, Spend, Spend*]

STRETTON, Hugh (1924–)

Is it really good for policy-makers to act as if everything has its price, and as if policies should be judged chiefly by their effects in delivering material benefits to selfish citizens? … It does not ask those individuals whether they also have other values which are not revealed by their shopping.

[*Capitalism, Socialism and the Environment* (1976)]

THEROUX, Paul (1941–)

There must be something in the Japanese character that saves them from the despair Americans feel in similar throes of consuming. The American, gorging himself on merchandise, develops a sense of guilty self-consciousness; if the Japanese have these doubts they do not show them. Perhaps hesitation is not part of the national character, or perhaps the ones who hesitate are trampled by the crowds of shoppers – that natural selection that capitalist society practises against the reflective.

[*The Great Railway Bazaar* (1975)]

VEBLEN, Thorstein (1857–1929)

Conspicuous consumption of valuable goods is a means of reputability to the gentleman of leisure.

[*The Theory of the Leisure Class* (1899)]

See CAPITALISM; GREED; MONEY AND WEALTH; SHOPPING

CONTEMPT

ALBERTANO OF BRESCIA (c.1190–c.1270)

Qui omnes despicit, omnibus displicet.
Who despises all, displeases all.

[*Liber Consolationis*]

ASHFORD, Daisy (1881–1972)

Ethel patted her hair and looked very sneery.

[*The Young Visiters* (1919)]

AUSTEN, Jane (1775–1817)

She was nothing more than a mere good-tempered, civil and obliging young woman; as such we could scarcely dislike her – she was only an Object of Contempt.

[*Love and Freindship* (1791)]

BIERCE, Ambrose (1842–c.1914)

Contempt: The feeling of a prudent man for an enemy who is too formidable safely to be oppoosed.

[*The Enlarged Devil's Dictionary* (1961)]

CAREW, Thomas (c.1595–1640)

I was foretold, your rebell sex,
Nor love, nor pitty knew.
And with what scorne, you use to vex
Poore hearts, that humbly sue.

['A deposition from love']

CHATEAUBRIAND, François-René (1768–1848)

One is not superior merely because one sees the world in an odious light.

[Attr.]

CONGREVE, William (1670–1729)

A little disdain is not amiss; a little scorn is alluring.

[*The Way of the World* (1700)]

JOHNSON, Samuel (1709–1784)

Of all the griefs that harrass the distress'd,
Sure the most bitter is a scornful jest;
Fate never wounds more deep the gen'rous heart,
Than when a blockhead's insult points the dart.

[*London: A Poem* (1738)]

PALEY, Rev. William (1743–1805)

Who can refute a sneer?

[*Principles of Moral and Political Philosophy* (1785)]

PROVERB

Familiarity breeds contempt.

ROOSEVELT, Theodore (1858–1919)

The poorest way to face life is to face it with a sneer.

[Attr.]

SHAW, George Bernard (1856–1950)

I have never sneered in my life. Sneering doesn't become either the human face or the human soul.

[*Pygmalion* (1916)]

STEINBECK, John (1902–1968)

Okie use' ta mean you was from Oklahoma. Now it means you're a dirty son-of-a-bitch. Okie means you're scum. Don't mean nothing itself, it's the way they say it.

[*The Grapes of Wrath* (1939)]

See RIDICULE

CONTRACEPTION

ALLEN, Woody (1935–)

I want to tell you a terrific story about oral contraception. I asked this girl to sleep with me and she said 'no'.

[Attr.]

LOWRY, Malcolm (1909–1957)

Where are the children I might have had? You may suppose I might have wanted them. Drowned to the accompaniment of the rattling of a thousand douche bags.

[*Under the Volcano* (1947)]

MENCKEN, H.L. (1880–1956)

It is now quite lawful for a Catholic woman to avoid pregnancy by a resort to mathematics, though she is still forbidden to resort to physics and chemistry.

[*Notebooks* (1956)]

MILLIGAN, Spike (1918–)

Contraceptives should be used on every conceivable occasion.

[*The Last Goon Show of All*]

RUSSELL, Dora (1894–1986)

We want far better reasons for having children than not knowing how to prevent them.

[*Hypatia*]

SHARPE, Tom (1928–)

Skullion had little use for contraceptives at the best of times. Unnatural, he called them, and placed them in the lower social category of things along with elastic-sided boots and made-up bow ties. Not the sort of attire for a gentleman.

[*Porterhouse Blue* (1974)]

THOMAS, Irene (1920–)

Protestant women may take the Pill. Roman Catholic woman must keep taking *The Tablet*.

[*The Guardian*, 1990]

See SEX

CONVENTION

BRONTË, Charlotte (1816–1855)

Conventionality is not morality. Self-righteousness is not religion. To attack the first is not to assail the last. To pluck the mask from the face of the Pharisee, is not to lift an impious hand to the Crown of Thorns.

[*Jane Eyre* (1847)]

CONVERSATION

ACHEBE, Chinua (1930–)

Among the Ibo the art of conversation is regarded very highly and proverbs are the palm-oil with which words are eaten.

[*Things Fall Apart* (1958)]

BAGEHOT, Walter (1826–1877)

The habit of common and continuous speech is a symptom of mental deficiency.

[*Literary Studies* (1879)]

BOSWELL, James (1740–1795)

Johnson: Well, we had a good talk.
Boswell: Yes, Sir; you tossed and gored several persons.

[*The Life of Samuel Johnson* (1791)]

BRYAN, William Jennings (1860–1925)

An orator is a man who says what he thinks and feels what he says.

[Attr.]

CARLYLE, Thomas (1795–1881)

Speech is human, silence is divine, yet also brutish and dead: therefore we must learn both arts.

[Attr.]

CHURCHILL, Sir Winston (1874–1965)

[Of Lord Charles Beresford]
He is one of those orators of whom it was well said, 'Before they get up they do not know what they are going to say; when they are speaking, they do not know what they are saying; and when they sit down, they do not know what they have said.'

[Speech, House of Commons, 1912]

To jaw-jaw is better than to war-war.

[Speech, Washington, 1954]

COLERIDGE, Samuel Taylor (1772–1834)

I am glad you came in to punctuate my discourse, which I fear has gone on for an hour without any stop at all.

[*Table Talk* (1835), 29 June 1833]

CONFUCIUS (c.550–c.478 BC)

For one word a man is often deemed to be wise, and for one word he is often deemed to be foolish. We should be careful indeed what we say.

[*Analects*]

DARWIN, Erasmus (1731–1802)

[Reply when asked whether he found his stammer inconvenient]
No, Sir, because I have time to think before I speak, and don't ask impertinent questions.

[In Sir Francis Darwin, *Reminiscences of My Father's Everyday Life*]

DISRAELI, Benjamin (1804–1881)

I grew intoxicated with my own eloquence.

[*Contarini Fleming* (1832)]

DRYDEN, John (1631–1700)

But far more numerous was the herd of such
Who think too little and who talk too much.

[*Absalom and Achitophel* (1681)]

ELIOT, George (1819–1880)

Half the sorrows of women would be averted if they could repress the speech they know to be useless; nay, the speech they have resolved not to make.

[*Felix Holt* (1866)]

EMERSON, Ralph Waldo (1803–1882)

Conversation is a game of circles. In conversation we pluck up the termini which bound the common of silence on every side.

[*Essays, First Series* (1841)]

HALIFAX, Lord (1633–1695)

Most Men make little other use of their Speech than to give evidence against their own Understanding.

['Of Folly and Fools' (1750)]

HOBBES, Thomas (1588–1679)

True and false are attributes of speech, not of things. And where speech is not, there is neither truth nor falsehood.

[*Leviathan* (1651)]

HOLMES, Oliver Wendell (1809–1894)

And, when you stick on conversation's burrs,
Don't strew your pathway with those dreadful urs.

['A Rhymed Lesson' (1848)]

JOHNSON, Samuel (1709–1784)

That is the happiest conversation where there is no competition, no vanity, but a calm quiet interchange of sentiments.

[In Boswell, *The Life of Samuel Johnson* (1791)]

Questioning is not the mode of conversation among gentlemen.

[In Boswell, *The Life of Samuel Johnson* (1791)]

JONSON, Ben (1572–1637)

Talking and eloquence are not the same: to

speak, and to speak well, are two things.

[*Timber, or Discoveries made upon Men and Matter* (1641)]

LA BRUYÈRE, Jean de (1645–1696)

Il y a des gens qui parlent un moment avant que d'avoir pensé.

There are people who speak one moment before they think.

[*Les caractères ou les moeurs de ce siècle* (1688)]

MACAULAY, Lord (1800–1859)

The object of oratory alone is not truth, but persuasion.

['Essay on Athenian Orators' (1898)]

MEREDITH, George (1828–1909)

Speech is the small change of silence.

[*The Ordeal of Richard Feverel* (1859)]

MOORE, Lorrie

Overheard or recorded, all marital conversation sounds as if someone must be joking, though usually no one is.

[*Birds of America* (1998)]

O'BRIAN, Patrick (1828–1909)

Question and answer is not a civilized form of conversation.

[*Clarissa Oakes* (1992)]

POST, Emily (1873–1960)

Ideal conversation must be an exchange of thought, and not, as many of those who worry most about their shortcomings believe, an eloquent exhibition of wit or oratory.

[*Etiquette* (1922)]

SENECA (c.4 BC–AD 65)

Conversation has a kind of charm about it, an insinuating and insidious something that elicits secrets from us just like love or liquor.

[*Epistles*]

SHAKESPEARE, William (1564–1616)

He draweth out the thread of his verbosity finer than the staple of his argument.

[*Love's Labour Lost*, V.i]

SMITH, Sydney (1771–1845)

One of the greatest pleasures in life is

conversation.

[*Essays* (1877)]

TALLEYRAND, Charles-Maurice de (1754–1838)

La parole a été donnée á l'homme pour déguiser sa pensée.

Speech was given to man to disguise his thoughts.

[Attr.]

TANNEN, Deborah (1945–)

Each person's life is lived as a series of conversations.

[*The Observer*, 1992]

TROLLOPE, Anthony (1815–1882)

For the most of us, if we do not talk of ourselves, or at any rate of the individual circles of which we are the centres, we can talk of nothing. I cannot hold with those who wish to put down the insignificant chatter of the world.

[*Framley Parsonage* (1860)]

WEST, Dame Rebecca (1892–1983)

There is no such thing as conversation. It is an illusion. There are intersecting monologues, that is all.

[*There is No Conversation* (1935)]

See SILENCE

COOKERY

ACTON, Eliza (1799–1859)

The difference between good cookery and bad cookery can scarcely be more strikingly shown than in the manner in which sauces are prepared and served.

[*Modern Cookery for Private Families* (1845)]

BRILLAT-SAVARIN, Anthelme (1755–1826)

La découverte d'un mets nouveau fait plus pour le bonheur du genre humain que la découverte d'une étoile.

The discovery of a new dish does more for the happiness of mankind than the discovery of a star.

[*Physiologie du Goût* (1825)]

CLEESE, John (1939–)

The English contribution to world cuisine – the chip.

[*A Fish Called Wanda*, film, 1988]

DAVID, Elizabeth (1913–1992)

Even more than long hours in the kitchen, fine meals require ingenious organization and experience which is a pleasure to acquire. A highly developed shopping sense is important, so is some knowledge of the construction of a menu with a view to the food In season, the manner of cooking, the texture and colour of the dishes to be served in relation to each other.

[*French Country Cooking* (1951)]

Delicious meals can, as everybody knows, be cooked with the sole aid of a blackened frying-pan over a primus stove, a camp fire, a gas-ring, or even a methylated spirit lamp.

[*French Country Cooking* (1951)]

FERN, Fanny (Sara Payson Parton) (1811–1872)

The way to a man's heart is through his stomach.

[*Willis Parton*]

GALSWORTHY, John (1867–1933)

The French cook; we open tins.

[*Treasury of Humorous Quotations*]

GAUGUIN, Paul (1848–1903)

Many excellent cooks are spoiled by going into the arts.

[In Cournos, *Modern Plutarch* (1928)]

HARNEY, Bill (1895–1962)

[Advice on bush cooking]
You always want to garnish it when it's orf.

['Talkabout', c.1960]

HOOD, Thomas (1799–1845)

Home-made dishes that drive one from home.

[*Miss Kilmansegg and her Precious Leg* (1840)]

KING, William (1663–1712)

'Tis by his cleanliness a cook must please.

[*Art of Cookery* (1708)]

LANDOR, Walter Savage (1775–1864)

[Having thrown his cook out of an open window into the flowerbed below]
Good God, I forgot the violets!

[In F. Muir, *An Irreverent Companion to Social History* (1976)]

LEITH, Prue (1940–)

Cuisine is when things taste like what they are.

[Lecture, 'The Fine Art of Food', 1987]

MEREDITH, George (1828–1909)

Kissing don't last: cookery do!

[*The Ordeal of Richard Feverel* (1859)]

MEREDITH, Owen (1831–1891)

We may live without poetry, music and art;
We may live without conscience, and live without heart;
We may live without friends; we may live without books;
But civilized man cannot live without cooks.

['Lucile' (1860)]

POST, Emily (1873–1960)

To the old saying that man built the house but woman made of it a 'home' might be added the modern supplement that woman accepted cooking as a chore but man has made of it a recreation.

[*Etiquette* (1922)]

ROBINSON, Robert (1927–)

The national dish of America is menus.

[BBC TV programme, *Robinson's Travels*, 1977]

SAKI (1870–1916)

The cook was a good cook, as cooks go; and as cooks go she went.

[*Reginald* (1904)]

SALA, G.A.

The Milanese, be it remarked, are undoubtedly the best cooks in Italy.

[*The Thorough Good Cook*]

SCOTT, Sir Walter (1771–1832)

Man is a cooking animal.

[*St Ronan's Well* (1823)]

SLATER, Nigel (1870–1916)

Cooking is about not cheating yourself of pleasure.

[*Slice of Life*, BBC TV programme]

SMITH, Delia (1941–)

If you look at France now, after *nouvelle cuisine* and all the rest, you find that they are going crazy about what they call *cuisine grandmère*: just like granny used to make. I suppose that's what I'm about.

[Interview by Libby Purves, *The Times*, 1990]

I truly have tried and we had a microwave to heat things in the filming – but, actually, we mainly use it to keep the ashtrays in. I think it takes the soul out of food. Cooking is about ingredients being put together, and having time to amalgamate.

[Interview, *The Times*, 1990]

ULLMAN, Tracey

The most remarkable thing about my mother is that for 30 years she served nothing but leftovers. The original meal was never found.

[*The Observer*, 1999]

See DIETS; DINING; FOOD

THE COUNTRY

BRODERICK, John (1927–)

The city dweller who passes through a country town, and imagines it sleepy and apathetic is very far from the truth: it is watchful as the jungle.

[*The Pilgrimage* (1961)]

CONGREVE, William (1670–1729)

I nauseate walking; 'tis a country diversion, I

loathe the country.

[*The Way of the World* (1700)]

CONN, Stewart (1936–)

[On John Muir, naturalist]
What better than a Wilderness, to liberate the mind.

[*In the Blood* (1995)]

COWPER, William (1731–1800)

God made the country, and man made the town.

[*The Task* (1785)]

DOYLE, Sir Arthur Conan (1859–1930)

It is my belief, Watson, founded upon my experience, that the lowest and vilest alleys of London do not present a more dreadful record of sin than does the smiling and beautiful countryside.

['Copper Beeches' (1892)]

GIBBON, Lewis Grassic (1901–1935)

Nothing endured at all, nothing but the land … The land was forever, it moved and changed below you, but was forever.

[*Sunset Song* (1932)]

HAZLITT, William (1778–1830)

When I am in the country, I wish to vegetate like the country.

[*Table-Talk* (1822)]

There is nothing good to be had in the country, or, if there is, they will not let you have it.

[*The Round Table* (1817)]

KILVERT, Francis (1840–1879)

It is a fine thing to be out on the hills alone. A man could hardly be a beast or a fool alone on a great mountain.

[*Diary*, 1871]

SACKVILLE-WEST, Vita (1892–1962)

The country habit has me by the heart,
For he's bewitched for ever who has seen,

Not with his eyes but with his vision, Spring
Flow down the woods and stipple leaves
with sun.

['Winter' (1926)]

SMITH, Sydney (1771–1845)

It is a place with only one post a day … In
the country I always fear that creation will
expire before tea-time.

[In H. Pearson, *The Smith of Smiths* (1934)]

I have no relish for the country; it is a kind of
healthy grave.

[Letter to Miss G. Harcourt, 1838]

STEVENSON, Robert Louis (1850–1894)

In the highlands, in the country places,
Where the old plain men have rosy faces,
And the young fair maidens
Quiet eyes.

[*Songs of Travel* (1896)]

WILDE, Oscar (1854–1900)

Anybody can be good in the country.

[*The Picture of Dorian Gray* (1891)]

See CITIES

COURAGE

ANONYMOUS

Never share a foxhole with anyone braver
than you are.

ARISTOTLE (384–322 BC)

I count him braver who overcomes his
desires than him who overcomes his
enemies.

[In Stobaeus, *Florilegium*]

BARRIE, Sir J.M. (1860–1937)

Courage is the thing. All goes if courage
goes.

[Address, St Andrews University, 1922]

BLAIR, Robert (1699–1746)

The schoolboy, with his satchel in his hand,
Whistling aloud to bear his courage up.

['The Grave' (1743)]

CARROLL, Lewis (1832–1898)

'I'm very brave generally,' he went on in a low
voice: 'only to-day I happen to have a
headache.'

[*Through the Looking-Glass (and What Alice Found There)* (1872)]

CHANDLER, Raymond (1888–1959)

Down these mean streets a man must go
who is not himself mean, who is neither
tarnished nor afraid.

[*Atlantic Monthly* (1944)]

DAY LEWIS, C. (1904–1972)

I sang as one
Who on a tilting deck sings
To keep men's courage up, though the wave
hangs
That shall cut off their sun.

['The Conflict' (1935)]

EARHART, Amelia (1898–1937)

Courage is the price that Life exacts for
granting peace.

['Courage' (1927)]

HEMINGWAY, Ernest (1898–1961)

[Definition of 'guts']
Grace under pressure.

[Attr.]

HOWARD, Michael (1922–)

The important thing when you are going to
do something brave is to have someone on
hand to witness it.

[*The Observer*, 1980]

IBÁRRURI, Dolores ('La Pasionaria') (1895–1989)

Il vaut mieux mourir debout que vivre á genoux!
It is better to die on your feet than to live on
your knees.

[Speech, Paris, 1936]

KIERKEGAARD, Soren (1813–1855)

It takes moral courage to grieve, but it takes
religious courage to rejoice.

[Attr. by Jonathan Sacks in *The Times*, 1998]

LEACOCK, Stephen (1869–1944)

It takes a good deal of physical courage to

ride a horse. This, however, I have. I get it at about forty cents a flask, and take it as required.

[*Literary Lapses* (1910)]

NAPOLEON I (1769–1821)

Quant au courage moral, il avait trouvé fort rare, disait-il, celui de deux heures après minuit; c'est-á-dire le courage de l'improviste.

As for moral courage, he said he had very rarely encountered two o'clock in the morning courage; that is, the courage of the unprepared.

[*Mémorial de Sainte Hélène*]

NIXON, Richard (1913–1994)

Courage – or putting it more accurately, lack of fear – is a result of discipline. By an act of will, a man refuses to think of the reasons for fear, and so concentrates entirely on winning the battle.

[*The Independent*,1994]

SCOTT, Sir Walter (1771–1832)

The stubborn spear-men still made good
Their dark impenetrable wood,
Each stepping where his comrade stood,
The instant that he fell.

[*Marmion* (1808)]

SHAKESPEARE, William (1564–1616)

Courage mounteth with occasion.

[*King John*, II.i]

SHERIDAN, Richard Brinsley (1751–1816)

My valour is certainly going! – it is sneaking off! – I feel it oozing out as it were at the palms of my hands!

[*The Rivals* (1775)]

THOREAU, Henry David (1817–1862)

The three-o'-clock in the morning courage, which Bonaparte thought was the rarest.

[*Walden* (1854)]

TROLLOPE, Anthony (1815–1882)

Those who have courage to love should have courage to suffer.

[*The Bertrams* (1859)]

USTINOV, Sir Peter (1921–)

Courage is often lack of insight, whereas cowardice in many cases is based on good information.

[Attr.]

WALPOLE, Sir Hugh (1884–1941)

'Tisn't life that matters! 'Tis the courage you bring to it.

See PATRIOTISM

COURTESY

BACON, Francis (1561–1626)

If a man be gracious and courteous to strangers, it shews he is a citizen of the world.

[*Essays*]

DUHAMEL, Georges (1884–1966)

Courtesy is not dead – it has merely taken refuge in Great Britain.

[*The Observer*, 1953]

PROVERB

Civility cost nothing.

See MANNERS; RESPECT

COURTSHIP

BRAISTED, Harry (19th century)

If you want to win her hand,
Let the maiden understand
That's she's not the only pebble on the beach.

['You're Not the Only Pebble on the Beach']

BRAY, John Jefferson (1912–)

When your grape was green you denied me.
When your grape was ripe you despised me.
Can I have a nibble at the old sultana?

['After Long Absence']

CAMPBELL, Thomas (1777–1844)

Better be courted and jilted
Than never be courted at all.

['The Jilted Nymph' (1843)]

CONGREVE, William (1670–1729)

Courtship to marriage, as a very witty prologue to a very dull Play.

[*The Old Bachelor* (1693)]

DACRE, Harry (d. 1922)

Daisy, Daisy, give me your answer, do!
I'm half crazy, all for the love of you!
It won't be a stylish marriage,
I can't afford a carriage,
But you'll look sweet upon the seat
Of a bicycle made for two!

['Daisy Bell', song, 1892]

GAY, John (1685–1732)

Would you gain the tender Creature?
Softly, gently, kindly treat her;
Suff'ring is the Lover's Part.
Beauty by Constraint possessing,
You enjoy but half the Blessing,
Lifeless Charms, without the Heart.

[*Acis and Galatea* (1718)]

JONSON, Ben (1572–1637)

Follow a shadow, it still flies you,
Seem to fly it, it will pursue:
So court a mistress, she denies you;
Let her alone, she will court you.
Say, are not women truly, then,
Styl'd but the shadows of us men?

[*The Forest* (1616)]

MEREDITH, George (1828–1909)

She whom I love is hard to catch and conquer,
Hard, but O the glory of the winning were she won!

['Love in the Valley' (1883)]

PRIOR, Matthew (1664–1721)

I court others in verse: but I love thee in prose:
And they have my whimsies, but thou hast my heart.

['A Better Answer' (1718)]

WILDE, Oscar (1854–1900)

I am not in favour of long engagements.
They give people the opportunity of finding out each other's character before marriage,
which I think is never advisable.

[*The Importance of Being Earnest* (1895)]

See MARRIAGE; SEX

COWARDICE

BRONTË, Emily (1818–1848)

No coward soul is mine,
No trembler in the world's storm-troubled sphere:
I see Heaven's glories shine,
And faith shines equal, arming me from fear.

['Last Lines' (1846)]

ELIZABETH I (1533–1603)

If thy heart fails thee, climb not at all.

[In Fuller, *The History of the Worthies of England* (1662)]

GRANVILLE, George (1666–1735)

Cowards in scarlet pass for men of war.

[*The She Gallants* (1696)]

HOUSMAN, A.E. (1859–1936)

The man that runs away
Lives to die another day.

[*A Shropshire Lad* (1896)]

JOHNSON, Samuel (1709–1784)

It is thus that mutual cowardice keeps us in peace. Were one half of mankind brave and one half cowards, the brave would be always beating the cowards. Were all brave, they would lead a very uneasy life; all would be continually fighting; but being all cowards, we go on very well.

[In Boswell, *The Life of Samuel Johnson* (1791)]

JOHNSTON, Brian (1912–1994)

[When asked by his commanding officer what steps he would take if he came across a German battalion]
Long ones, backwards.

[Quoted in his obituary, *The Sunday Times*]

KIPLING, Rudyard (1865–1936)

I could not look on Death, which being known,

Men led me to him, blindfold and alone.

[*The Years Between* (1919)]

ROCHESTER, Earl of (1647–1680)

For all men would be cowards if they durst.

['A Satire Against Reason and Mankind' (1679)]

SHAKESPEARE, William (1564–1616)

Instinct is a great matter: I was now a coward on instinct.

[*Henry IV, Part 1*, II.iv]

SHAW, George Bernard (1856–1950)

As an old soldier I admit the cowardice: it's as universal as sea sickness, and matters just as little.

[*Man and Superman* (1903)]

VOLTAIRE (1694–1778)

Marriage is the only adventure open to the cowardly.

[Attr.]

WEBSTER, John (c.1580–c.1625)

Cowardly dogs bark loudest.

[*The White Devil* (1612)]

CRIME

ADLER, Freda (1934–)

[On rape]

Perhaps it is the only crime in which the victim becomes the accused and, in reality, it is she who must prove her good reputation, her mental soundness, and her impeccable propriety.

[*Sisters in Crime* (1975)]

ALLEN, Fred (1894–1956)

He's a good boy; everything he steals he brings right home to his mother.

[Attr.]

ANONYMOUS

The fault is great in man or woman
Who steals a goose from off a common;
But what can plead that man's excuse
Who steals a common from a goose?

[*The Tickler Magazine*, 1821]

BACON, Francis (1561–1626)

Opportunity makes a thief.

[Letter to Essex, 1598]

THE BIBLE
(King James Version)

Whoso sheddeth man's blood, by man shall his blood be shed.

[*Genesis*, 9:6]

BOCCA, Giorgio (1920–)

The mafia is rational, it wants to reduce homicides to the minimum.

[*Hell* (1992)]

<$IBOYLE, Jimmy (1944–)

Society has a choice: it either has a prison system based on punitive measures or one that rehabilitates. Do people want to sleep with a shotgun under their bed and go shopping in an armoured van, or do they want to live in a safer, fairer community? .

[Interview, *The Big Issue*, May 1996]

When you've got nothing, being a great thief or a respected fighter really counts for something.

[Interview, *The Big Issue*, May 1996]

BRECHT, Bertolt (1898–1956)

Was ist ein Einbruch in eine Bank gegen die Gründung einer Bank?

What is robbing a bank compared with founding a bank?

[*The Threepenny Opera* (1928)]

BULWER-LYTTON, Edward (1803–1873)

[English novelist, dramatist, poet and politician]

In other countries poverty is a misfortune – with us it is a crime.

[*England and the English* (1833)]

CAMUS, Albert (1913–1960)

Combien de crimes commis simplement parce que leur auteur ne pouvait supporter d'être en faute!

How many crimes committed simply because their authors could not endure being wrong!

[*The Fall*, 1956]

CAPONE, AL (1899–1947)

I've been accused of every death except the casualty list of the World War.

[In Allsop, *The Bootleggers* (1961)]

CHAUCER, Geoffrey (c.1340–1400)

Mordre wol out, that se we day by day.

[*The Canterbury Tales* (1387)]

CHESTERTON, G.K. (1874–1936)

Thieves respect property; they merely wish the property to become their property that they may more perfectly respect it.

[Attr.]

CONGREVE, William (1670–1729)

He that first cries out stop thief, is often he that has stolen the treasure.

[*Love for Love* (1695)]

DE QUINCEY, Thomas (1785–1859)

If a man once indulges himself in murder, very soon he comes to think little of robbing; and from robbing he comes next to drinking and sabbath-breaking, and from that to incivility and procrastination.

['Murder Considered as One of the Fine Arts' (1839)]

DOYLE, Sir Arthur Conan (1859–1930)

Singularity is almost invariably a clue. The more featureless and commonplace a crime is, the more difficult it is to bring it home.

['The Boscombe Valley Mystery' (1892)]

FARBER, Barry (1859–1930)

Crime expands according to our willingness to put up with it.

[Attr.]

FARQUHAR, George (1678–1707)

Crimes, like virtues, are their own rewards.

[*The Inconstant* (1702)]

FRY, Elizabeth (1780–1845)

[English social and prison reformer]
Punishment is not for revenge, but to lessen crime and reform the criminal.

[Journal entry]

GOLDMAN, Emma (1869–1940)

Crime is naught but misdirected energy.

[*Anarchism* (1910)]

GREENE, Graham (1904–1991)

Catholics and Communists have committed great crimes, but at least they have not stood aside, like an established society, and been indifferent. I would rather have blood on my hands than water like Pilate.

[*The Comedians* (1966)]

HANCOCK, Sir William Keith (1898–1988)

Were it possible to compel the prison warders of this past age to produce for our inspection a 'typical' transported convict, they would show us, not the countryman who snared rabbits, but the Londoner who stole spoons.

[*Australia* (1930)]

HAWTHORNE, Nathaniel (1804–1864)

By the sympathy of your human hearts for sin ye shall scent out all the places – whether in church, bedchamber, stret, field or forest – where crime has been committed, and shall exult to behold the whole earth one stain of guilt, one mighty blood spot.

[*Young Goodman Brown* (1835)]

HENRY, O. (1862–1910)

A burglar who respects his art always takes his time before taking anything else.

[*Makes the Whole World Kin*]

LA BRUYÈRE, Jean de (1645–1696)

Si la pauvreté est la mère des crimes, le défaut d'esprit en est le père.
If poverty is the mother of crime, lack of intelligence is its father.

[*Les caractères ou les moeurs de ce siècle* (1688)]

LEWES, G.H. (1817–1878)

Murder, like talent, seems occasionally to run in families.

[*The Physiology of Common Life* (1859)]

LIGHTNER, Candy (1946–)

Death by drunken driving is a socially acceptable form of homicide.

[*San José Mercury*, April 1981]

MEIR, Golda (1898–1978)

[Replying to a member of her Cabinet who proposed a curfew on women after dark in response to a recent outbreak of assaults on women]

But it's the men who are attacking the women. If there's to be a curfew, let the men stay at home, not the women.

[Attr.]

RACINE, Jean (1639–1699)

Ainsi que la vertu, le crime a ses degrés.

Crime has its degrees, as virtue does.

[*Phèdre* (1677)]

RAINS, Claude (1889–1967)

Major Strasser has been shot. Round up the usual suspects.

[*Casablanca*, film, 1942]

ROOSEVELT, Theodore (1858–1919)

[Dismissing a cowboy who had put Roosevelt's brand on a steer belonging to a neighbouring ranch]

A man who will steal for me will steal from me.

[In Hagedorn, *Roosevelt in the Bad Lands* (1921)]

ROSS, Nick (1947–)

[British broadcaster]

We're barking mad about crime in this country. We have an obsession with believing the worst, conning ourselves that there was a golden age – typically forty years before the one we're living in.

[*Radio Times*, 1993]

ROSTAND, Jean (1894–1977)

Tue un homme, on est un assassin. On tue des millions d'hommes, on est conquérant. On les tue tous, on est un dieu.

Kill one man, and you are a murderer. Kill millions of men, and you are a conqueror. Kill them all, and you are a god.

[*Thoughts of a Biologist* (1939)]

SHAKESPEARE, William (1564–1616)

[Of stealing]

Why, Hal, 'tis my vocation, Hal; 'tis no sin for a man to labour in his vocation.

[*Henry IV, Part 1*, I.ii]

The robb'd that smiles steals something from the thief.

[*Othello*, I.iii]

SPENCER, Herbert (1820–1903)

A clever theft was praiseworthy amongst the Spartans; and it is equally so amongst Christians, provided it be on a sufficiently large scale.

[*Social Statics* (1850)]

TAKAYAMA, Tokutaro

[Kyoto mob boss defending the reputation of Japan's yakuza following the attack on film director Juzo Itami]

We haven't used our power only for doing bad things. I myself personally wounded the head of the local Communist party after the police asked us for help.

[*Newsweek*, 1992]

WAUGH, Evelyn (1903–1966)

I came to the conclusion many years ago that almost all crime is due to the repressed desire for aesthetic expression.

[*Decline and Fall* (1928)]

See MURDER; PUNISHMENT; THEFT

CRITICISM

ANTIPHANES OF MACEDONIA (fl. 360 BC)

Idly inquisitive tribe of grammarians, who dig up the poetry of others by the roots … Get away, bugs that secretly bite the eloquent.

[*Greek Anthology*]

ARNOLD, Matthew (1822–1888)

I am bound by my own definition of criticism: a disinterested endeavour to learn and propagate the best that is known and thought in the world.

[*Essays in Criticism* (1865)]

ATWOOD, Margaret (1939–)

Once upon a time I thought there was an old man with a grey beard somewhere who knew the truth, and if I was good enough, naturally he would tell me that this was it. That person doesn't exist, but that's who I write for. The great critic in the sky.

[In Ingersoll, *Margaret Atwood: Conversations* (1990)]

AUDEN, W.H. (1907–1973)

One cannot review a bad book without showing off.

[*The Dyer's Hand and Other Essays* (1963)]

BELL, Clive (1881–1964)

I will try to account for the degree of my aesthetic emotion. That, I conceive, is the function of the critic.

[*Art* (1914)]

BROWNE, Sir Thomas (1605–1682)

He who discommendeth others obliquely commendeth himself.

[*Christian Morals* (1716)]

BULLET, Gerald (1893–1958)

So, when a new book comes his way,
By someone still alive to-day,
Our Honest John, with right good will,
Sharpens his pencil for the kill.

['A Reviewer']

BURGESS, Anthony (1917–1993)

I know how foolish critics can be, being one myself.

[*The Observer*, 1980]

BUTLER, Samuel (1835–1902)

Talking it over, we agreed that Blake was no good because he learnt Italian at over 60 to study Dante, and we knew Dante was no good because he was so fond of Virgil, and Virgil was no good because Tennyson ran him, and as for Tennyson – well, Tennyson goes without saying.

[*The Note-Books of Samuel Butler* (1912)]

BYRON, Lord (1788–1824)

A man must serve his time to every trade
Save censure – critics all are ready made.
Take hackney'd jokes from Miller, got by rote,
With just enough of learning to misquote.

[*English Bards and Scotch Reviewers* (1809)]

CASTRO, Fidel (1927–)

All criticism is opposition. All opposition is counter-revolutionary.

[In John Newhouse, 'Socialism of Death', *The New Yorker*, 1992]

CHESTERTON, G.K. (1874–1936)

A great deal of contemporary criticism reads to me like a man saying: 'Of course I do not like green cheese; I am very fond of brown sherry.'

[*All I Survey* (1933)]

CHURCHILL, Charles (1731–1764)

Though by whim, envy, or resentment led,
They damn those authors whom they never read.

[*The Candidate* (1764)]

CHURCHILL, Sir Winston (1874–1965)

I do not resent criticism, even when, for the sake of emphasis, it parts for the time with reality.

[Speech, 1941]

COLERIDGE, Samuel Taylor (1772–1834)

That passage is what I call the sublime dashed to pieces by cutting too close with the fiery four-in-hand round the corner of nonsense.

[*Table Talk* (1835), 20 January 1834]

Reviewers are usually people who would have been poets, historians, biographers, etc., if they could; they have tried their talents at one or at the other, and have failed; therefore they turn critics.

[*Seven Lectures on Shakespeare and Milton* (1856)]

COLLINS, Jackie

The biggest critics of my books are people who never read them.

COLLINS, William (1721–1759)

Too nicely Jonson knew the critic's part,
Nature in him was almost lost in Art.

['Verses Addressed to Sir Thomas Hanmer' (1743)]

CONRAN, Shirley (1932–)

[On Julie Burchill]

I cannot take seriously the criticism of someone who doesn't know how to use a semicolon.

[Attr.]

DISRAELI, Benjamin (1804–1881)
You know who the critics are? The men who have failed in literature and art.

[*Lothair* (1870)]

This shows how much easier it is to be critical than to be correct.

[Speech, 1860]

Cosmopolitan critics, men who are the friends of every country save their own.

[Speech, 1877]

DONATUS, Aelius (fl. 4th century AD)
[Donatus was a commentator on texts]
Pereant, inquit, qui ante nos nostra dixerunt.
Confound those who have made our comments before us.

[In St Jerome, *Commentaries on Ecclesiastes*]

ELIOT, T.S. (1888–1965)
The critic, one would suppose, if he is to justify his existence, should endeavour to discipline his personal prejudices and cranks – tares to which we are all subject – and compose his differences with as many of his fellows as possible, in the common pursuit of true judgement.

['The Function of Criticism' (1923)]

FRANCE, Anatole (1844–1924)
Le bon critique est celui qui raconte les aventures de son âme au milieu des chefs-d'oeuvre.
A good critic is one who tells of his own soul's adventures among masterpieces.

[*La Vie Littéraire* (1888)]

FRY, Christopher (1907–)
I sometimes think
His critical judgement is so exquisite
It leaves us nothing to admire except his opinion.

[*The Dark is Light Enough* (1954)]

HAMPTON, Christopher (1946–)
Asking a working writer what he thinks about critics is like asking a lamp-post how it feels about dogs.

[*The Sunday Times Magazine*, 1977]

HELLER, Joseph (1923–)
When I read something saying I've not done anything as good as *Catch 22* I'm tempted to reply, 'who has?'.

[*The Times*, 1993]

HOOD, Thomas (1799–1845)
What is a modern poet's fate?
To write his thoughts upon a slate;
The critic spits on what is done,
Gives it a wipe – and all is gone.

[In Hallam Tennyson, *Alfred Lord Tennyson, A Memoir* (1897)]

HUXLEY, Aldous (1894–1963)
Parodies and caricatures are the most penetrating of criticisms.

[*Point Counter Point* (1928)]

JAMES, Henry (1843–1916)
We must grant the artist his subject, his idea, his donnée: our criticism is applied only to what he makes of it.

[*Partial Portraits* (1888)]

JOHNSON, Samuel (1709–1784)
[Replying to Maurice Morgann who asked him whether Derrick or Smart was the better poet]
Sir, there is no settling the point of precedency between a louse and a flea.

[In Boswell, *The Life of Samuel Johnson* (1791)]

There are two things which I am confident I can do very well: one is an introduction to any literary work, stating what it is to contain, and how it should be executed in the most perfect manner; the other is a conclusion, shewing from various causes why the execution has not been equal to what the author promised himself and to the public.

[In Boswell, *The Life of Samuel Johnson* (1791)]

[Of literary criticism]
You may abuse a tragedy, though you cannot write one, You may scold a carpenter who has made you a bad table, though you cannot make a table. It is not your trade to

make tables.

[In Boswell, *The Life of Samuel Johnson* (1791)]

The man who is asked by an author what he thinks of his work, is put to the torture, and is not obliged to speak the truth.

[In Boswell, *The Life of Samuel Johnson* (1791)]

LA BRUYÈRE, Jean de (1645–1696)

Le plaisir de la critique nous ôte celui d'être vivement touchés de très belles choses.

The pleasure of criticizing takes away from us the pleasure of being moved by some very fine things.

[*Les caractères ou les moeurs de ce siècle* (1688)]

LANDOR, Walter Savage (1775–1864)

Fleas know not whether they are upon the body of a giant or upon one of ordinary size.

[*Imaginary Conversations* (1824)]

He who first praises a good book becomingly, is next in merit to the author.

[*Imaginary Conversations* (1824–1829)]

LEAVIS, F.R. (1895–1978)

Literary criticism provides the test for life and concreteness; where it degenerates, the instruments of thought degenerate too, and thinking, released from the testing and energizing contact with the full living consciousness, is debilitated, and betrayed to the academic, the abstract and the verbal.

[*Towards Standards in Criticism* (1930)]

MARX, Groucho (1895–1977)

I was so long writing my review that I never got around to reading the book.

[Attr.]

MAUGHAM, William Somerset (1874–1965)

People ask you for criticism, but they only want praise.

[*Of Human Bondage* (1915)]

MOORE, George (1852–1933)

The lot of critics is to be remembered by what they failed to understand.

[*Impressions and Opinions* (1891)]

ORWELL, George (1903–1950)

Prolonged, indiscriminate reviewing of books … not only involves praising trash … but constantly inventing reactions towards books about which one has no spontaneous feelings whatever.

[*Shooting an Elephant* (1950)]

PARKER, Dorothy (1893–1967)

[On A. A. Milne's *The House at Pooh Corner* in her column 'Constant Reader']
Tonstant Weader fwowed up.

[Attr.]

This is not a novel to be tossed aside lightly. It should be thrown with great force.

[In Gaines, *Wit's End*]

POPE, Alexander (1688–1744)

Turn what they will to Verse, their toil is vain,
Critics like me shall make it Prose again.

[*The Dunciad* (1742)]

Nor in the Critic let the Man be lost.
Good-nature and good-sense must ever join;
To err is human, to forgive, divine.

[*An Essay on Criticism* (1711)]

PORSON, Richard (1759–1808)

[Giving his opinion of Southey's poems]
Your works will be read after Shakespeare and Milton are forgotten – and not till then.

[In Meissen, *Quotable Anecdotes*]

POTTER, Stephen (1900–1969)

Donsmanship … 'the art of criticizing without actually listening'.

[*Lifemanship* (1950)]

PRIESTLEY, J.B. (1894–1984)

They will review a book by a writer much older than themselves as if it were an over-ambitious essay by a second-year student … It is the little dons I complain about, like so many corgis trotting up, hoping to nip your ankles.

[*Outcries and Asides*]

QUILLER-COUCH, Sir Arthur ('Q') (1863–1944)

The best is the best, though a hundred

judges have declared it so.

[*Oxford Book of English Verse* (1900)]

REGER, Max (1873–1916)

[Letter written to Rudolf Louis in response to his criticism of Reger's *Sinfonietta*, 1906]

Ich sitze in dem kleinsten Zimmer in meinem Hause. Ich habe Ihre Kritik vor mir. Im nächsten Augenblick wird sie hinter mir sein.

I am sitting in the smallest room in my house. I have your review in front of me. In a moment it will be behind me.

[In Slonimsky, *The Lexicon of Musical Invective*]

RIVAROL, Antoine de (1753–1801)

[On a couplet by a mediocre poet]

C'est bien, mais il y a des longueurs.

Very good, but it has its longueurs.

[*Rivaroliana*]

SHAW, George Bernard (1856–1950)

A dramatic critic … leaves no turn unstoned.

[*New York Times*, 1950]

You don't expect me to know what to say about a play when I don't know who the author is, do you? … If it's by a good author, it's a good play, naturally. That stands to reason.

[*Fanny's First Play* (1911)]

SIBELIUS, Jean (1865–1957)

Pay no attention to what the critics say. No statue has ever been put up to a critic.

[Attr.]

SMITH, Sydney (1771–1845)

I never read a book before reviewing it; it prejudices a man so.

[In Pearson, *The Smith of Smiths* (1934)]

SONTAG, Susan (1933–)

Interpretation is the revenge of the intellect upon art.

[*Evergreen Review*, 1964]

STEINBECK, John (1902–1968)

[On critics]

Unless the bastards have the courage to give you unqualified praise, I say ignore them.

[In J.K. Galbraith, *A Life in Our Times* (1981)]

STERNE, Laurence (1713–1768)

Of all the cants which are canted in this canting world, – though the cant of hypocrites may be the worst, – the cant of criticism is the most tormenting!

[*Tristram Shandy* (1759–1767)]

STOPPARD, Tom (1937–)

I doubt that art needed Ruskin any more than a moving train needs one of its passengers to shove it.

[*The Times Literary Supplement*, 1977]

STRAVINSKY, Igor (1882–1971)

I had another dream the other day about music critics. They were small and rodent-like with padlocked ears, as if they had stepped out of a painting by Goya.

[*The Evening Standard*, 1969]

SWIFT, Jonathan (1667–1745)

So, naturalists observe, a flea
Hath smaller fleas that on him prey;
And these have smaller fleas to bite 'em,
And so proceed ad infinitum.
Thus every poet, in his kind,
Is bit by him that comes behind.

['On Poetry' (1733)]

TYNAN, Kenneth (1927–1980)

A good drama critic is one who perceives what is happening in the theatre of his time. A great drama critic also perceives what is not happening.

[*Tynan Right and Left* (1967)]

A critic is a man who knows the way but can't drive the car.

[*New York Times Magazine*, 1966]

VOLTAIRE (1694–1778)

[Reviewing Rousseau's poem 'Ode to Posterity']

I do not think this poem will reach its destination.

[Attr.]

VORSTER, John (1915–1983)

As far as criticism is concerned, we don't resent that unless it is absolutely biased, as it is in most cases.

[*The Observer*, 1969]

WHISTLER, James McNeill (1834–1903)

You shouldn't say it is not good. You should say, you do not like it; and then, you know, you're perfectly safe.

[In D.C. Seitz, *Whistler Stories* (1913)]

WILDE, Oscar (1854–1900)

[On a notice at a dancing saloon]
I saw the only rational method of art criticism I have ever come across ... 'Please do not shoot the pianist. He is doing his best.' The mortality among pianists in that place is marvellous.

['Impressions of America' (1906)]

The man who sees both sides of a question is a man who sees absolutely nothing at all.

['The Critic as Artist' (1891)]

See ACTORS; INSULTS; POETS; WRITERS

CRUELTY

BLAKE, William (1757–1827)

Cruelty has a Human Heart
And Jealousy a Human Face,
Terror the Human Form Divine,
And Secrecy the Human Dress.

['A Divine Image' (c. 1832)]

CALIGULA (12–41)

Ita feri ut se mori sentiat.
Strike him so that he may feel that he is dying.

[In Suetonius, *Lives of the Caesars*]

COWPER, William (1731–1800)

I would not enter on my list of friends
(Tho' grac'd with polish'd manners and fine sense,
Yet wanting sensibility) the man
Who needlessly sets foot upon a worm.

[*The Task* (1785)]

DANIELS, Dr Anthony

Cruelty is like hope: it springs eternal.

[*The Observer*, 1998]

FROUDE, James Anthony (1818–1894)

Fear is the parent of cruelty.

[*Short Studies on Great Subjects* (1877)]

GIDE, André (1869–1951)

La cruauté, c'est le premier des attributs de Dieu.
Cruelty is the first of God's attributes.

[*The Counterfeiters*]

SHELLEY, Percy Bysshe (1792–1822)

Cruel he looks, but calm and strong,
Like one who does, not suffers wrong.

[*Prometheus Unbound* (1820)]

TROTSKY, Leon (1879–1940)

In a serious struggle there is no worse cruelty than to be magnanimous at an inappropriate time.

[*The History of the Russian Revolution* (1933)]

See PURITANS; VIOLENCE

CRYING

BLAKE, William (1757–1827)

For a Tear is an Intellectual thing!
And a Sigh is the Sword of an Angel King
And the bitter groan of a Martyrs woe
Is an Arrow from the Almighties Bow.

[*Jerusalem* (1804–1820)]

BYRON, Lord (1788–1824)

[English Romantic poet, satirist and traveller]
Oh! too convincing – dangerously dear –
In woman's eye the unanswerable tear!

[*The Corsair* (1814)]

CHURCHILL, Charles (1731–1764)

With the persuasive language of a tear.

['The Times' (1764)]

CRISP, Quentin (1908–)

Tears were to me what glass beads are to African traders.

[*The Naked Civil Servant* (1968)]

CROMPTON, Richmal (1890–1969)

Violet Elizabeth dried her tears. She saw that they were useless and she did not believe in wasting her effects. 'All right,' she said calmly,

'I'll thcream then. I'll thcream, an' thcream, an' thcream till I'm thick.'

[*Still William* (1925)]

DICKENS, Charles (1812–1870)

We need never be ashamed of our tears.

[*Great Expectations* (1861)]

'It opens the lungs, washes the countenance, exercises the eyes, and softens down the temper', said Mr Bumble. 'So cry away.'

[*Oliver Twist* (1838)]

FLETCHER, Phineas (1582–1650)

Drop, drop, slow tears,
And bathe those beauteous feet,
Which brought from Heav'n
The news and Prince of Peace.

[*Poetical Miscellanies* (1633), 'An Hymn']

LIBERACE, Wladziu Valentino (1919–1987)

[Remark made after hostile criticism]
I cried all the way to the bank.

[*Autobiography* (1973)]

MUSSET, Alfred de (1810–1857)

Le seul bien qui me rest au monde
Est d'avoir quelquefois pleuré.
The only good things the world has left me are the times that I have wept.

['Tristesse' (1841)]

RHYS, Jean (1894–1979)

I often want to cry. That is the only advantage women have over men – at least they can cry.

[*Good Morning, Midnight* (1939)]

SAINT-EXUPÉRY, Antoine de (1900–1944)

C'est tellement mystérieux, le pays des larmes.
It is such a mysterious place, the land of tears.

[*The Little Prince* (1943)]

WEBSTER, John (c.1580–c.1625)

There's nothing sooner dry than women's tears.

[*The White Devil* (1612)]

WEST, Dame Rebecca (1892–1983)

[English novelist, journalist, critic and feminist]
But there are other things than dissipation that thicken the features. Tears, for example.

[*Black Lamb and Grey Falcon* (1942)]

See EYES

CULTURE

ARNOLD, Matthew (1822–1888)

Philistinism! – We have not the expression in English. Perhaps we have not the word because we have so much of the thing.

[*Essays in Criticism* (1865)]

… the aim which is the great aim of culture, the aim of setting ourselves to ascertain what perfection is and to make it prevail.

[*Culture and Anarchy* (1869)]

The pursuit of perfection, then, is the pursuit of sweetness and light. He who works for sweetness and light, works to make reason and the will of God prevail.

[*Culture and Anarchy* (1869)]

The men of culture are the true apostles of equality.

[*Culture and Anarchy* (1869)]

Hebraism and Hellenism – between these two points of influence moves our World … they are, each of them, contributions to human development.

[*Culture and Anarchy* (1869)]

The governing idea of Hellenism is spontaneity of consciousness; that of Hebraism, strictness of conscience.

[*Culture and Anarchy* (1869)]

Culture being a pursuit of our total perfection by means of getting to know, on all the matters which most concern us, the best which has been thought and said in the world.

[*Culture and Anarchy* (1869)]

Culture, the acquainting ourselves with the

best that has been known and said in the world, and thus the history of the human spirit.

[*Literature and Dogma*]

BANDA, Dr Hastings (1905–)

I wish I could bring Stonehenge to Nyasaland to show there was a time when Britain had a savage culture.

[*The Observer*, 1963]

BAUDELAIRE, Charles (1821–1867)

Il faut épater le bourgeois.
One must shock the bourgeois.

[Attr.]

BELLOW, Saul (1915–)

If culture means anything, it means knowing what value to set upon human life; it's not somebody with a mortarboard reading Greek. I know a lot of facts, history. That's not culture. Culture is the openness of the individual psyche … to the news of being.

[*The Glasgow Herald*, 1985]

We are in the position of savage men who have been educated into believing there are no mysteries.

[*The Independent*, 1990]

BERLIN, Isaiah (1909–1997)

To belong to a given community, to be connected with its members by indissoluble and impalpable ties of a common language, historical memory, habit, tradition and feeling, is a basic human need no less natural than that for food or drink and security or procreation. One nation can under-stand and sympathize with the institutions of another only because it knows how much its own mean to itself. Cosmopolitanism is the shedding of all that makes one most human, most oneself.

['The Counter-Enlightenment']

CARLYLE, Thomas (1795–1881)

The great law of culture is: let each become all that he was created capable of being.

['Jean Paul Friedrich Richter' (1839)]

DARWIN, Charles (1809–1882)

The highest possible stage in moral culture is when we recognize that we ought to control our thoughts.

[*The Descent of Man* (1871)]

FRYE, Northrop (1912–1991)

Creative culture is infinitely porous – it absorbs influences from all over the world.

[*Maclean's*, 1991]

GOERING, Hermann (1893–1946)

When I hear anyone talk of Culture, I reach for my revolver.

[Attr.]

HELPMAN, Sir Robert Murray (1909–1986)

I don't despair about the cultural scene in Australia because there isn't one here to despair about.

[In Dunstan, *Knockers* (1972)]

JOHST, Hanns (1890–1978)

Wenn ich Kultur höre … entsichere ich meinen Browning!
When I hear the word 'culture' … I take the safety-catch off my Browning!

[*Schlageter* (1933)]

KENNY, Mary (1944–)

Decadent cultures usually fall in the end, and robust cultures rise to replace them. Our own cultural supermarket may eventually be subject to a takeover bid: the most likely challenger being, surely, Islam.

[*Sunday Telegraph*, 1993]

KOESTLER, Arthur (1905–1983)

Two half-truths do not make a truth, and two half-cultures do not make a culture.

[*The Ghost in the Machine* (1961)]

LAWLESS, Emily (1845–1913)

We are all children of our environment – the good no less than the bad, – products of that particular group of habits, customs, traditions, ways of looking at things, standards of right and wrong, which chance has presented to our still growing and expanding consciousness.

[*Hurrish* (1886)]

MCLUHAN, Marshall (1911–1980)

In a culture like ours, long accustomed to splitting and dividing all things as a means of control, it is sometimes a bit of a shock to be reminded that, in operational and practical fact, the medium is the message.

[*Understanding Media* (1964)]

MANTEL, Hilary (1952–)

[On travel]

I saw the world as some sort of exchange scheme for my ideals, but the world deserves better than this. When you come across an alien culture you must not automatically respect it. You must sometimes pay it the compliment of hating it.

['Last Months in Al Hamra' (1987)]

MENAND, Louis (1953–)

Culture isn't something that comes with one's race or sex. It comes only through experience; there isn't any other way to acquire it. And in the end everyone's culture is different, because everyone's experience is different.

[*The New Yorker*, 1992]

MUSSOLINI, Benito (1883–1945)

In un uomo di stato, la cosidetta 'cultura' è in fin dei conti un lusso inutile.

In a statesman so-called 'culture' is, after all, a useless luxury.

[*Il Populo d'Italia*, 1919]

SHAFFER, Peter (1926–)

All my wife had ever taken from the Mediterranean – from that whole vast intuitive culture – are four bottles of Chianti to make into lamps, and two china condiment donkeys labelled Sally and Peppy.

[*Equus* (1973)]

WALLACE, Edgar (1875–1932)

What is a highbrow? He is a man who has found something more interesting than women.

[*New York Times*, 1932]

WEIL, Simone (1909–1943)

La culture est un instrument manié par des professeurs pour fabriquer des professeurs qui á leur tour fabriqueront des professeurs.

Culture is an instrument wielded by teachers to manufacture teachers, who, in their turn, will manufacture teachers.

[*The Need for Roots* (1949)]

WHARTON, Edith (1862–1937)

Mrs Ballinger is one of the ladies who pursue Culture in bands, as though it were dangerous to meet it alone.

[*Xingu and Other Stories* (1916)]

See CIVILIZATION; SCIENCE

CUNNING

BLAKE, William (1757–1827)

The weak in courage is strong in cunning.

[*The Marriage of Heaven and Hell* (c. 1790–1793)]

CHESTERFIELD, Lord (1694–1773)

Cunning is the dark sanctuary of incapacity.

[Letter to his godson and heir (to be delivered after his own death)]

CURIOSITY

BACON, Francis (1561–1626)

They are ill discoverers that think there is no land, when they can see nothing but sea.

[*The Advancement of Learning* (1605)]

THE BIBLE
(King James Version)

Be not curious in unnecessary matters: for more things are shewed unto thee than men understand.

[*Apocrypha, Ecclesiasticus*, 3:23]

BAX, Sir Arnold (1883–1953)

One should try everything once, except incest and folk-dancing.

[*Farewell my Youth* (1943)]

CARROLL, Lewis (1832–1898)

'If everybody minded their own business,'

said the Duchess in a hoarse growl, 'the world would go round a deal faster than it does.'

[*Alice's Adventures in Wonderland* (1865)]

JOHNSON, Samuel (1709–1784)

A generous and elevated mind is distinguished by nothing more certainly than an eminent degree of curiosity.

[In Boswell, *The Life of Samuel Johnson* (1791)]

LAMB, Charles (1775–1834)

Not many sounds in life, and I include all urban and all rural sounds, exceed in interest a knock at the door.

['Valentine's Day' (1823)]

MORITA, Akio (1920–)

Curiosity is the key to creativity.

[*Made in Japan* (1986)]

PERELMAN, S.J. (1904–1979)

[Giving his reasons for refusing to see a priest as he lay dying]

I am curious to see what happens in the next world to one who dies unshriven.

[Attr.]

PROVERB

Curiosity killed the cat.

CURSES

BLAKE, William (1757–1827)

Damn braces: Bless relaxes.

[*The Marriage of Heaven and Hell* (c. 1790–1793)]

SIDNEY, Sir Philip (1554–1586)

Though I will not wish unto you the Ass's eares of Midas, nor to be driven by a Poet's verses as Bubonax was, to hang himselfe, nor to be rimed to death as is said to be done in Ireland; yet thus much Curse I must send you in the behalfe of all Poets, that while you live, you live in love, and never get favour, for lacking skill of a Sonet, and when you die, your memorie die from the earth for want of an Epitaphe.

[*The Defence of Poesie* (1595)]

SOUTHEY, Robert (1774–1843)

Curses are like young chickens, they always come home to roost.

[*The Curse of Kehama* (1810)]

And Sleep shall obey me,
And visit thee never,
And the Curse shall be on thee
For ever and ever.

[*The Curse of Kehama* (1810)]

SYNGE, J.M. (1871–1909)

[To the sister of an enemy of the author who disapproved of *The Playboy of the Western World*]

Lord, confound this surly sister,
Blight her brow with blotch and blister,
Cramp her larynx, lung and liver,
In her guts a galling give her.

Let her live to earn her dinners
In Mountjoy with seedy sinners:
Lord, this judgement quickly bring,
And I'm your servant, J.M. Synge.

['The Curse']

THEROUX, Paul (1941–)

A foreign swear-word is practically inoffensive except to the person who has learnt it early in life and knows its social limits.

[*Saint Jack*]

TWAIN, Mark (1835–1910)

Some of his words were not Sunday-school words.

[*A Tramp Abroad* (1880)]

CURTAINS

ANONYMOUS

The first pull on the cord ALWAYS sends the curtains in the wrong direction.

[Boyle's Other Law]

POPE, Alexander (1688–1744)

Lo! thy dread empire, Chaos! is restored;
Light dies before thy uncreating word:
Thy hand, great Anarch! lets the curtain fall;

And universal darkness buries all.

[*The Dunciad* (1742)]

RABELAIS, François (c.1494–c.1553)

[Last words]

I am going to seek a great perhaps ...Bring down the curtain, the farce is played out.

[Attr.]

CUSTOM

BAILLIE, Joanna (1762–1851)

What custom hath endear'd
We part with sadly, though we prize it not.

[*Basil* (1798)]

BECKETT, Samuel (1906–1989)

The air is full of our cries. But habit is a great deadener.

[*Waiting for Godot* (1955)]

BURKE, Edmund (1729–1797)

Custom reconciles us to everything.

[*A Philosophical Enquiry into the Origin of our Ideas of the Sublime and Beautiful* (1757)]

CRABBE, George (1754–1832)

Habit with him was all the test of truth,
'It must be right: I've done it from my youth.'

[*The Borough* (1810)]

Habit with him was all the test of truth,
'It must be right: I've done it from my youth.'

[*The Borough* (1810)]

DAVENANT, Charles (1656–1714)

Custom, that unwritten law,
By which the people keep even kings in awe.

[*Circe* (1677)]

HUME, David (1711–1776)

Custom, then, is the great guide of human life.

[*Philosophical Essays Concerning Human Understanding* (1748)]

JAMES, William (1842–1910)

Habit is the enormous fly-wheel of society, its most precious conservative agent.

[*Principles of Psychology* (1890)]

MORE, Hannah (1745–1833)

Small habits, well pursued betimes,
May reach the dignity of crimes.

PÉGUY, Charles (1873–1914)

La mémoire et l'habitude sont les fourriers de la mort.
Memory and habit are the harbingers of death.

[*Note conjointe sur M. Descartes*]

SHAKESPEARE, William (1564–1616)

Age cannot wither her, nor custom stale
Her infinite variety. Other women cloy
The appetites they feed, but she makes hungry
Where most she satisfies.

[*Antony and Cleopatra*, II.ii]

Custom calls me to't.
What custom wills, in all things should we do't.

[*Coriolanus* II.iii]

It is a custom
More honour'd in the breach than the observance.

[*Hamlet*, I.iv]

How use doth breed a habit in a man!

[*The Two Gentlemen of Verona*, V.iv]

SHERIDAN, Richard Brinsley (1751–1816)

There's nothing like being used to a thing.

[*The Rivals* (1775)]

WORDSWORTH, William (1770–1850)

Not choice
But habit rules the unreflecting herd.

['Grant that by this unsparing hurricane' (1822)]

See HABIT

CYNICISM

ALLEN, Woody (1935–)

The lion and the calf shall lie down together but the calf won't get much sleep.

[*Without Feathers* (1976)]

BIERCE, Ambrose (1842–c.1914)
Cynic: A blackguard whose faulty vision sees things as they are, not as they ought to be.

[*The Enlarged Devil's Dictionary* (1961)]

CHEKHOV, Anton (1860–1904)
After all, the cynicism of real life can't be outdone by any literature: one glass won't get someone drunk when he's already had a whole barrel.

[Letter to M.V. Kiseleva, 1887]

COZZENS, James Gould (1903–1978)
A cynic is just a man who found out when he was about ten that there wasn't any Santa Claus, and he's still upset.

[Attr.]

HARRIS, Sydney J. (1917–)
A cynic is not merely one who reads bitter lessons from the past, he is one who is prematurely disappointed in the future.

[*On the Contrary* (1962)]

HELLMAN, Lillian (1905–1984)
Cynicism is an unpleasant way of saying the truth.

[*The Little Foxes* (1939)]

HURST, Fannie (1889–1968)
It takes a clever man to turn cynic, and a wise man to be clever enough not to.

[Attr.]

MEREDITH, George (1828–1909)
Cynicism is intellectual dandyism.

[*The Egoist* (1879)]

WILDE, Oscar (1854–1900)
[In a lecture on Dickens]
One would have to have a heart of stone to read the death of Little Nell without laughing.

[In H. Pearson, *Lives of the Wits*]

Cecil Graham: What is a cynic?
Lord Darlington: A man who knows the price of everything and the value of nothing.

[*Lady Windermere's Fan* (1892)]

D

DANCING

AUSTEN, Jane (1775–1817)

Fine dancing, I believe, like virtue, must be its own reward.

[*Emma* (1816)]

BANKHEAD, Tallulah (1903–1968)

[Said on dropping fifty dollars into a tambourine held out by a Salvation Army collector]
Don't bother to thank me. I know what a perfectly ghastly season it's been for you Spanish dancers.

[Attr.]

BURNEY, Fanny (1752–1840)

Dancing? Oh, dreadful! How it was ever adopted in a civilized country I cannot find out; 'tis certainly a Barbarian exercise, and of savage origin.

[*Cecilia* (1782)]

BURNS, Robert (1759–1796)

But the ae best dance ere cam to the land
Was The Deil's Awa wi' th' Exciseman!

['The Deil's Awa wi' th' Exciseman' (1792)]

CHESTERFIELD, Lord (1694–1773)

Custom has made dancing sometimes necessary for a young man; therefore mind it while you learn it, that you may learn to do it well, and not be ridiculous, though in a ridiculous act.

[Letter to his son, 1746]

CICERO (106–43 BC)

Nemo enim fere saltat sobrius, nisi forte insanit.
No sober man dances, unless he happens to be mad.

[*Pro Murena*]

DE VALOIS, Dame Ninette (1898–)

Ladies and gentlemen, it takes more than one to make a ballet.

[*The New Yorker*]

DUNCAN, Isadora (1878–1927)

I have discovered the dance. I have discovered the art which has been lost for two thousand years.

[*My Life* (1927)]

HARRIS, Charles (1865–1930)

Many a heart is aching, if you could read them all,
Many the hopes that have vanished, after the ball.

['After the Ball', 1892]

HELPMAN, Sir Robert Murray (1909–1986)

Aren't all ballets sexy? I think they should be. I can thing of nothing more kinky than a prince chasing a swan around all night.

[In Jonathon Green (ed.), *A Dictionary o f Contemporary Quotations* (1982)]

PAVLOVA, Anna (1881–1931)

Although one may fail to find happiness in theatrical life, one never wishes to give it up after having once tasted its fruits. To enter the School of the Imperial Ballet is to enter a convent whence frivolity is banned, and where merciless discipline reigns.

[In A.H. Franks (ed.), *Pavlova: A Biography*]

SALLUST (86–c.34 BC)

[Roman historian and statesman]
Psallere et saltare elegantius, quam necesse est probae.
To play the lyre and dance more beautifully than a virtuous woman need.

[*Catiline*]

SHAKESPEARE, William (1564–1616)

You and I are past our dancing days.

[*Romeo and Juliet*, I.v]

When you do dance, I wish you
A wave o' th' sea, that you might ever do
Nothing but that; move still, still so,
And own no other function.

[*The Winter's Tale*, IV.iv]

SUCKLING, Sir John (1609–1642)

Her feet beneath her petticoat,
Like little mice, stole in and out,
As if they fear'd the light:
But O she dances such a way!
No sun upon an Easter-day
Is half so fine a sight.

['A Ballad upon a Wedding' (1646)]

SURTEES, R.S. (1805–1864)

These sort of boobies think that people
come to balls to do nothing but dance;
whereas everyone knows that the real
business of a ball is either to look out for a
wife, to look after a wife, or to look after
somebody else's wife.

[Mr Facey Romford's Hounds (1865)]

YEATS, W.B. (1865–1939)

When I play on my fiddle in Dooney,
Folk dance like a wave of the sea …

For the good are always the merry,
Save by an evil chance,
And the merry love the fiddle,
And the merry love to dance.

[In the Bookman, 1892]

All men are dancers and their tread
Goes to the barbarous clangour of a gong.

['Nineteen Hundred and Nineteen' (1921)]

O chestnut-tree, great-rooted blossomer,
Are you the leaf, the blossom or the bole?
O body swayed to music, O brightening
glance,
How can we know the dancer from the
dance?

['Among School Children' (1927)]

DANGER

BURKE, Edmund (1729–1797)

Dangers by being despised grow great.

[Speech on the Petition of the Unitarians, 1792]

CHAPMAN, George (c.1559–c.1634)

Danger (the spurre of all great mindes) is
ever

The curbe to your tame spirits.

[Revenge of Bussy D'Ambois (1613)]

CORNEILLE, Pierre (1606–1684)

A vaincre sans péril, on triomphe sans gloire.
When we conquer without danger our
triumph is without glory.

[Le Cid (1637)]

CURNOW, Allen (1911–)

Always to islanders danger
Is what comes over the sea.

[Collected Poems 1933–1973
(1974)]

EARHART, Amelia (1898–1937)

[Of her flight in the 'Friendship']
Of course I realized there was a measure of
danger. Obviously I faced the possibility of
not returning when first I considered going.
Once faced and settled there really wasn't
any good reason to refer to it.

[20 Hours: 40 Minutes – Our Flight in the Friendship
(1928)]

EMERSON, Ralph Waldo (1803–1882)

In skating over thin ice, our safety is in our
speed.

['Prudence' (1841)]

As soon as there is life there is danger.

[Society and Solitude (1870)]

GAY, John (1685–1732)

How, like a moth, the simple maid,
Still plays about the flame!

[The Beggar's Opera (1728)]

JORDAN, Thomas (c.1612–1685)

Our God and soldier we alike adore,
Just at the brink of ruin, not before:
The danger past, both are alike requited;
God is forgotten, and our soldier slighted.

[Epigram]

MACCARTHY, Cormac (1933–)

There are dragons in the wings of the world.

[The Guardian, 1995]

PROVERB

Danger and delight grow on one stalk.

SALINGER, J.D. (1919–)

What I have to do, I have to catch everybody if they start to go over the cliff – I mean if they're running and they don't look where they're going I have to come out from somewhere and catch them … I'd just be the catcher in the rye and all.

[*The Catcher in the Rye* (1951)]

SALVANDY, Narcisse Achille (1795–1856)

Nous dansons sur un volcan.

We are dancing on a volcano.

[Remark made before July Revolution, 1830]

SHAKESPEARE, William (1564–1616)

Out of this nettle, danger, we pluck this flower, safety.

[*Henry IV, Part 1*, II.iii]

STEVENSON, Robert Louis (1850–1894)

The bright face of danger.

['The Lantern-Bearers' (1892)]

WASHINGTON, George (1732–1799)

I heard the bullets whistle, and believe me, there is something charming in the sound.

[In P. Boller, *Presidential Anecdotes*]

DEADLINES

ADAMS, Scott (1957–)

I love deadlines. I especially love the swooshing sound they make as they go flying by.

[*The Dilbert Principle*]

ANONYMOUS

The remaining work to finish in order to reach your goal increases as the deadline approaches.

[Bove's Theorem]

DEATH

Addison, Joseph (1672–1719)

When I read the several dates of the tombs, of some that died yesterday, and some six hundred years ago, I consider that great day when we shall all of us be contemporaries, and make our appearance together.

[*Thoughts in Westminster Abbey*]

AUBER, Daniel François Esprit (1782–1871)

[Remark made at a funeral]
This is the last time I will take part as an amateur.

[Attr.]

BACON, Francis (1561–1626)

Men fear death as children fear to go in the dark; and as that natural fear in children is increased with tales, so is the other.

[*Essays* (1625)]

I have often thought upon death, and I find it the least of all evils.

[*The Remaines of … Lord Verulam* (1648)]

BALZAC, Honoré de (1799–1850)

La fin est le retour de toutes choses á l'unite qui est Dieu.

The end is when all things return to unity, that is to say, God.

[*Louis Lambert* (1832)]

Que signifie adieu, à moins de mourir? Mais la mort serait-elle un adieu?

What does farewell mean, unless one is dying? But is death itself a farewell?

[*Louis Lambert* (1832)]

BHAGAVADGITA

I am become death, the destroyer of worlds.

[Quoted by J. Robert Oppenheimer on seeing the first nuclear explosion]

BION (fl. 280 BC)

Though boys throw stones at frogs in sport, the frogs do not die in sport, but in earnest.

[Quoted by *Plutarch*]

BOWRA, Sir Maurice (1898–1971)

Any amusing deaths lately?

[Attr.]

BRIDGES, Robert (1844–1930)

When Death to either shall come, –

I pray it be first to me.

['When Death to Either Shall Come']

BRONTË, Emily (1818–1848)

I lingered round them, under that benign sky: watched the moths fluttering among the heath and harebells; listened to the soft wind breathing through the grass; and wondered how anyone could ever imagine unquiet slumbers for the sleepers in that quiet earth.

[*Wuthering Heights* (1847), last lines]

BROOKE, Rupert (1887–1915)

Oh! Death will find me long before I tire
Of watching you; and swing me suddenly
Into the shade and loneliness and mire
Of the last land!

['Oh! Death will find me' (1909)]

BROWNE, Sir Thomas (1605–1682)

He forgets that he can die who complains of misery – we are in the power of no calamity while death is in our own.

[*Religio Medici* (1643)]

I am not so much afraid of death, as ashamed thereof; 'tis the very disgrace and ignominy of our natures, that in a moment can so disfigure us that our nearest friends, wife, and children, stand afraid and start at us.

[*Religio Medici* (1643)]

BUCK, Pearl S. (1892–1973)

Euthanasia is a long, smooth-sounding word, and it conceals its danger as long, smooth words do, but the danger is there, nevertheless.

[*The Child Who Never Grew* (1950)]

BURKE, Edmund (1729–1797)

I would rather sleep in the southern corner of a little country church-yard, than in the tomb of the Capulets. I should like, however, that my dust should mingle with kindred dust.

[Letter to Matthew Smith, 1750]

BUTLER, Samuel (1835–1902)

When you have told anyone you have left him a legacy the only decent thing to do is

to die at once.

[In Festing Jones, *Samuel Butler: A Memoir*]

CATULLUS (84–c.54 BC)

Qui nunc it per iter tenebricosum
Illuc, unde negant redire quemquam.

Now he goes along the shadowy path, there, from which they say no one returns.

[*Carmina*]

CERVANTES, Miguel de (1547–1616)

Ahora bien: todas las cosas tienen remedio, si no es la muerte.

Well, now: there's a remedy for everything, except death.

[*Don Quixote* (1615)]

CHATEAUBRIAND, François-René (1768–1848)

On n'apprend pas á mourir en tuant les autres.

One does not learn how to die by killing others.

[*Memoirs* (1826–1841)]

CHESTERFIELD, Lord (1694–1773)

[Said when Tyrawley was old and infirm]
Tyrawley and I have been dead these two years; but we don't choose to have it known.

[In Boswell, *The Life of Samuel Johnson* (1791)]

CLARE, John (1793–1864)

Pale death, the grand physician, cures all pain;
The dead rest well who lived for joys in vain.

['Child Harold' (1841)]

DIBDIN, Charles (1745–1814)

What argufies pride and ambition?
Soon or late death will take us in tow:
Each bullet has got its commission,
And when our time's come we must go.

['Each Bullet has its Commission']

DICKINSON, Emily (1830–1886)

Because I could not stop for Death –
He kindly stopped for me –
The Carriage held but just Ourselves –
And Immortality.

['Because I could not stop for Death' (c. 1863)]

This quiet Dust was Gentlemen and Ladies

And Lads and Girls –
Was laughter and ability and Sighing
And Frocks and Curls.

['This quiet Dust was Gentlemen and Ladies' (c. 1864)]

DONNE, John (1572–1631)

Think then, my soul, that death is but a groom,
Which brings a taper to the outward room.

[*Of the Progress of the Soul* (1612)]

One short sleep past, we wake eternally,
And death shall be no more; death, thou shalt die.

[*Holy Sonnets* (1609–1617)]

[On Death]
It comes equally to us all, and makes us all equal when it comes. The ashes of an Oak in the Chimney, are no epitaph of that Oak, to tell me now high or how large that was; It tells me not what flocks it sheltered while it stood, nor what men it hurt when it fell. The dust of great persons' graves is speechless too, it says nothing, it distinguishes nothing: As soon the dust of a wretch whom thou wouldest not, as of a Prince whom thou couldest not look upon, will trouble thine eyes, if the wind blow it thither; and when a whirlwind hath blown the dust of the Churchyard into the Church, and the man sweeps out the dust of the Church into the Churchyard, who will undertake to sift those dusts again, and to pronounce, This is the Patrician, this is the noble flower, and this is the yeomanly, this the Plebeian bran.

[*LXXX Sermons* (1640)]

DRYDEN, John (1631–1700)

Death, in itself, is nothing; but we fear,
To be we know not what, we know not where.

[*Aureng-Zebe* (1675)]

DUNBAR, William (c.1460–c.1525)

I that in heill wes and gladnes
Am trublit now with gret seiknes
And feblit with infirmitie:
Timor mortis conturbat me …

Our plesance here is all vain glory,
This fals world is but transitory,
The flesh is bruckle, the Feynd is slee:
Timor Mortis conturbat me …

Unto the deid gois all Estatis,
Princis, prelatis, and potestatis,
Baith rich and poor of all degree:
Timor Mortis conturbat me.

['Lament for the Makaris' (1834)]

ELIOT, T.S. (1888–1965)

Webster was much possessed by death
And saw the skull beneath the skin;
And breastless creatures under ground
Leaned backward with a lipless grin.

['Whispers of Immortality' (1920)]

Phlebas the Phoenician, a fortnight dead,
Forgot the cry of gulls, and the deep sea swell
And the profit and loss.

[*The Waste Land* (1922)]

FITZGERALD, Edward (1809–1883)

Strange, is it not? that of the myriads who
Before us pass'd the door of Darkness through,
Not one returns to tell us of the Road,
Which to discover we must travel too.

[*The Rubáiyát of Omar Khayyám* (1879)]

FLETCHER, John (1579–1625)

Death hath so many doors to let out life.

[*The Custom of the Country* (1647)]

FONTAINE, Jean de la (1621–1695)

La Mort ne surprend point le sage;
Il est toujours prêt á partir.
Death does not take the wise man by surprise, he is always prepared to leave.

['La Mort et le mourant']

FORSTER, E.M. (1879–1970)

Death destroys a man; the idea of Death saves him.

[*Howard's End* (1910)]

GOLDSMITH, Oliver (c.1728–1774)

I'm told he makes a very handsome corpse,

and becomes his coffin prodigiously.

[*The Good Natur'd Man* (1768)]

GORDON, Adam Lindsay (1833–1870)

Let me slumber in the hollow where the
wattle blossoms wave,
With never stone or rail to fence my bed;
Should the sturdy station children pull the
bush flowers on my grave,
I may chance to hear them romping
overhead.

['The Sick Stockrider']

GRAY, John

There are nearly as many human beings alive
as ever lived up to the start of this century.
Soon, the Greek catchword for death –
joining the majority – will cease to be
accurate.

[*The Observer*, 1998]

GRAY, Patrick (d. 1612)

[Advocating the execution of Mary, Queen of
Scots]

A dead woman bites not.

[Oral tradition, 1587]

GRAY, Thomas (1716–1771)

The boast of heraldry, the pomp of pow'r,
And all that beauty, all that wealth e'er gave,
Awaits alike th' inevitable hour,
The paths of glory lead but to the grave.

['Elegy Written in a Country Churchyard' (1751)]

HASTINGS, Lady Flora (1806–1839)

Grieve not that I die young. Is it not well
To pass away ere life hath lost its brightness?

['Swan Song']

HAWTHORNE, Nathaniel (1804–1864)

We sometimes congratulate ourselves at the
moment of waking from a troubled dream; it
may be so the moment after death.

[*American Notebooks*]

HENDRIX, Jimi (1942–1970)

Once you're dead, you're made for life.

[Attr.]

HENLEY, William Ernest (1849–1903)

Madam Life's a piece in bloom

Death goes dogging everywhere:
She's the tenant of the room,
He's the ruffian on the stair.

[*Echoes* (1877)]

HERBERT, George (1593–1633)

Death is still working like a mole,
And digs my grave at each remove.

[*The Temple* (1633)]

HOLLAND, Canon Henry Scott (1847–1918)

Death is nothing at all. It does not count. I
have only slipped away into the next room.
Nothing has happened. Everything remains
exactly as it was. I am I, and you are you,
and the old life that we lived so fondly
together is untouched, unchanged.
Whatever we were to each other, that we
are still. Call me by the old familiar name.
Speak of me in the easy way which you
always used. Put no difference into your
tone. Wear no forced air of solemnity or
sorrow. Laugh as we always laughed at the
little jokes that we enjoyed together. Play,
smile, think of me, pray for me. Let my
name be ever the household word that it
always was. Let my name be ever the
household word that it always was. Let it be
spoken without an effort, without the
ghost of a shadow upon it. Life means all
that it ever meant. It is the same as it ever
was. There is absolute and unbroken
continuity. What is death but a negligible
accident? Why should I be out of mind
because I am out of sight? I am but waiting
for you, for an interval, somewhere very
near, just round the corner. All is well.

[*Facts of the faith* (1919)]

HORACE (65–8 BC)

*Pallida Mors, aequo pulsat pede pauperum tabernas
Regumque turris.*

Pale Death strikes with impartial foot at the
cottages of the poor and the turrets of kings.

[*Odes*]

HUXLEY, Aldous (1894–1963)

Death ... It's the only thing we haven't

succeeded in completely vulgarizing.

[*Eyeless in Gaza* (1936)]

HUXLEY, Henrietta (1825–1915)

And if there be no meeting past the grave,
If all is darkness, silence, yet 'tis rest.
Be not afraid ye waiting hearts that weep;
For still He giveth His beloved sleep,
And if an endless sleep He wills, so best.

[Lines on the grave of her husband, 1895]

JUVENAL (c.60–130)

Mors sola fatetur
Quantula sint hominum corpuscula.
Death only this mysterious truth unfolds,
The mighty soul, how small a body holds.

[*Satires*]

KÜBLER-ROSS, Elisabeth (1926–)

Watching the peaceful death of a human
being reminds us of a falling star; one of a
million lights in a vast sky that flares up for a
brief moment only to disappear into the
endless night forever.

[*On Death and Dying* (1969)]

KEATS, John (1795–1821)

Darkling I listen; and, for many a time
I have been half in love with easeful Death,
Call'd him soft names in many a musèd
rhyme,
To take into the air my quiet breath;
Now more than ever seems it rich to die,
To cease upon the midnight with no pain,
While thou art pouring forth thy soul abroad
In such an ecstasy!
Still wouldst thou sing, and I have ears in
vain –
To thy high requiem become a sod.

['Ode to a Nightingale' (1819)]

KEYES, Sidney (1922–1943)

At this twelfth hour of unrelenting summer
I think of those whose ready mouths are
stopped,
I remember those who crouch in narrow
graves,
I weep for those whose eyes are full of sand.

[*Two Offices of a Sentry* (1942)]

KIPLING, Rudyard (1865–1936)

[To a magazine which incorrectly reported his
death]
I've just read that I am dead. Don't forget to
delete me from your list of subscribers.

[Attr.]

KOESTLER, Arthur (1905–1983)

[Of the atomic bomb]
Hitherto man had to live with the idea of
death as an individual; from now onward
mankind will have to live with the idea of its
death as a species.

[Attr.]

LAMB, Charles (1775–1834)

Gone before
To that unknown and silent shore.

['Hester' (1803)]

LANDOR, Walter Savage (1775–1864)

Death stands above me, whispering low
I know not what into my ear;
Of his strange language all I know
Is, there is not a word of fear.

[*Epigrams* (1853)]

LARKIN, Philip (1922–1985)

[On death]
The anaesthetic from which none come round.

['Aubade' (1988)]

LAWRENCE, D.H. (1885–1930)

The dead don't die. They look on and help.

[Letter to J. Middleton Murry, 1923]

LEWIS, D.B. Wyndham (1891–1969)

I am one of those unfortunates to whom
death is less hideous than explanations.

[*Welcome to All This*]

LUCRETIUS (c.95–55 BC)

Nil igitur mors est ad nos neque pertinet hilum,
Quandoquidem natura animi mortalis habetur.
What has this bugbear death to frighten man
If souls can die as well as bodies can?

[*De Rerum Natura*]

MAETERLINCK, Maurice (1862–1949)

The living are just the dead on holiday.

[Attr.]

MANKIEWICZ, Herman J. (1897–1953)

[Of death]
It is the only disease you don't look forward to being cured of.

[*Citizen Kane*, film, 1941]

MANN, Thomas (1875–1955)

Vom Tode wüsste Ihnen keiner, der wiederkäme, was Rechtes zu erzählen, denn man erlebt ihn nicht. Wir kommen aus dem Dunkel und gehen ins Dunkel, dazwischen liegen Erlebnisse, aber Anfang und Ende, Geburt und Tod, werden von uns nicht erlebt, sie haben keinen subjektiven Charakter.

No one who could come back from death would be able to tell you anything about it, because we do not experience it. We come out of the dark and go into the dark, and in between we have experiences, but beginning and end, birth and death, are not experienced by us, they have no subjective character.

[*The Magic Mountain* (1924)]

MARX, Groucho (1895–1977)

Either he's dead or my watch has stopped.

[*A Day at the Races*, film, 1937]

MASEFIELD, John (1878–1967)

Death opens unknown doors. It is most grand to die.

[*Pompey the Great* (1910)]

MASSINGER, Philip (1583–1640)

Death has a thousand doors to let out life:
I shall find one.

[*A Very Woman* (1634)]

MILLAY, Edna St Vincent (1892–1950)

Down, down, down into the darkness of the grave
Gently they go, the beautiful, the tender, the kind;
Quietly they go, the intelligent, the witty, the brave.
I know. But I do not approve. And I am not resigned.

['Dirge without Music' (1928)]

MOLIÈRE (1622–1673)

On ne meurt qu'une fois, et c'est pour si longtemps!

One dies only once, and then for such a long time!

[*Le Dépit Amoureux* (1656)]

MONTAIGNE, Michel de (1533–1592)

Je veux ... que la mort me trouve plantant mes choux, mais nonchalant d'elle, et encore plus de mon jardin imparfait.

I want death to find me planting my cabbages, but caring little for it, and even less for my imperfect garden.

[*Essais* (1580)]

NAPOLEON I (1769–1821)

Oh well, no matter what happens, there's always death.

[Attr.]

OUIDA (1839–1908)

Even of death Christianity has made a terror which was unknown to the gay calmness of the Pagan.

[*Views and Opinions* (1895)]

OWEN, Wilfred (1893–1918)

What passing-bells for these who die as cattle?
Only the monstrous anger of the guns.
Only the stuttering rifles' rapid rattle
Can patter out their hasty orisons.

['Anthem for Doomed Youth' (1917)]

PATTEN, Brian (1946–)

Death is the only grammatically correct full-stop ...

['Schoolboy' (1990)]

Death does not necessarily diminish us, it also deepens our awareness of what it means to be alive.

['Grave gossip']

Between himself and the grave his parents stand,
monuments that will crumble.

['Schoolboy' (1990)]

PETRONIUS ARBITER (d. AD 66)

[Speaking of someone who has died]
Abiit ad plures.

He has joined the great majority.

[*Satyricon*]

POWER, Marguerite, Countess of Blessington (1789–1849)

It is better to die young than to outlive all one loved, and all that rendered one lovable.

[*The Confessions of an Elderly Gentleman* (1836)]

PROVERBS

Death is the great leveller.

Fear of death is worse than death itself.

A man can die but once.

RALEIGH, Sir Walter (c.1552–1618)

Only we die in earnest, that's no jest.

['On the Life of Man']

O eloquent, just and mighty Death! … thou hast drawn together all the far-stretched greatness, all the pride, cruelty, and ambition of man, and covered it all over with these two narrow words, *Hic jacet*.

[*The History of the World* (1614)]

ROBINSON, Edwin Arlington (1869–1935)

I shall have more to say when I am dead.

[*The Three Taverns* (1920)]

ROS, Amanda (1860–1939)

Holy Moses! Have a look!
Flesh decayed in every nook.
Some rare bits of brain lie here,
Mortal loads of beef and beer.

['Lines on Westminster Abbey']

ROSS, Sir Ronald (1857–1932)

O Death, where is thy sting?
Thy victory, O Grave?

[*Philosophies* (1910)]

ROSSETTI, Christina (1830–1894)

O Earth, lie heavily upon her eyes;
Seal her sweet eyes weary of watching, Earth.

['Rest' (1862)]

ROWE, Nicholas (1674–1718)

Death is the privilege of human nature,

And life without it were not worth our taking.

[*The Fair Penitent* (1703)]

SAKI (1870–1916)

Waldo is one of those people who would be enormously improved by death.

[*Beasts and Super-Beasts* (1914)]

SASSOON, Siegfried (1886–1967)

Stumbling along the trench in the dusk, dead men and living lying against the sides of the trenches – one never knew which were dead and which living. Dead and living were nearly one, for death was in all our hearts.

[*Diary*, April 1917]

The place was rotten with dead: green clumsy legs
High-booted, sprawled and grovelled along the saps
And trunks, face downward, in the sucking mud
Wallowed like trodden sandbags loosely filled;
And naked sodden buttocks, mats of hair,
Bulged, clotted heads slept in the plastering slime.
And then the rain began – the jolly old rain!

['Counter-Attack' (1917)]

SCHOPENHAUER, Arthur (1788–1860)

After your death you will be what you were before your birth.

[*Parerga and Paralipomena* (1851)]

SCOTT, Ridley

[Dying speech of replicant Roy Batty]
I've seen things you wouldn't believe. Attack ships on fire off the shoulder of Orion. I watched C-beams glitter in the dark near the Tannhauser gate. All those moments will be lost in time, like tears in rain. Time to die.

[Film *Blade Runner* (1982)]

SCOTT, Sir Walter (1771–1832)

And come he slow, or come he fast,
It is but Death who comes at last.

[*Marmion* (1808)]

His morning walk was beneath the elms in

the churchyard; 'for death,' he said, 'had been his next-door neighbour for so many years, that he had no apology for dropping the acquaintance.'

[*A Legend of Montrose* (1819)]

SEEGER, Alan (1888–1916)

I have a rendezvous with Death,
At some disputed barricade,
At midnight in some flaming town.

['I Have a Rendezvous with Death' (1916)]

SENECA (c.4 BC–AD 65)

Eripere vitam nemo non homini potest,
At nemo mortem; mille ad hanc aditus patent.

Anyone can take away a man's life, but no one his death; to this a thousand doors lie open.

[*Phoenissae*]

Illi mors gravis incubat
Qui notus nimis omnibus
Ignotus moritur sibi.

For him death grippeth right hard by the crop
That know of all, but to himself, alas
Doth die unknown, dazed with dreadful face.

[*Thyestes*]

SÉVIGNÉ, Marquise de (1626–1696)

Je trouve la mort si terrible, que je hais plus la vie
parce qu'elle m'y mène, que par les épines qui s'y
rencontrent.

I find death so terrible that I hate life more for leading me towards it than for the thorns encountered on the way.

[Letter to Mme de Grignan, 1672]

SHAKESPEARE, Nicholas

The dead are surprised by too many friends.

[*Sunday Telegraph*, 1993]

SHAKESPEARE, William (1564–1616)

Fear no more the heat o' th' sun
Nor the furious winter's rages;
Thou thy worldly task hast done,
Home art gone, and ta'en thy wages.
Golden lads and girls all must,
As chimney-sweepers, come to dust.

[*Cymbeline*, IV.ii]

O, that this too too solid flesh would melt,
Thaw, and resolve itself into a dew!
Or that the Everlasting had not fix'd
His canon 'gainst self-slaughter! O God! God!
How weary, stale, flat, and unprofitable,
Seem to me all the uses of this world!
Fie on't! Ah, fie! 'tis an unweeded garden,
That grows to seed; things rank and gross in nature
Possess it merely.

[*Hamlet*, I.ii]

To be, or not to be – that is the question;
Whether 'tis nobler in the mind to suffer
The slings and arrows of outrageous fortune,
Or to take arms against a sea of troubles,
And by opposing end them? To die, to sleep –
No more; and by a sleep to say we end
The heart-ache and the thousand natural shocks
That flesh is heir to. 'Tis a consummation
Devoutly to be wish'd. To die, to sleep;
To sleep, perchance to dream. Ay, there's the rub;
For in that sleep of death what dreams may come,
When we have shuffled off this mortal coil,
Must give us pause.

[*Hamlet*, III.i]

This fell sergeant Death
Is strict in his arrest.

[*Hamlet*, V.ii]

Cowards die many times before their deaths:
The valiant never taste of death but once.

[*Julius Caesar*, II.ii]

Men must endure
Their going hence, even as their coming hither:
Ripeness is all.

[*King Lear*, V.ii]

The weariest and most loathed worldly life
That age, ache, penury, and imprisonment,
Can lay on nature is a paradise
To what we fear of death.

[*Measure For Measure*, III.i]

SHAW, George Bernard (1856–1950)

Life levels all men: death reveals the eminent.

[*Man and Superman* (1903)]

SHELLEY, Percy Bysshe (1792–1822)

Death is the veil which those who live call life:
They sleep, and it is lifted.

[*Prometheus Unbound* (1820)]

SHIRLEY, James (1596–1666)

The glories of our blood and state
Are shadows, not substantial things;
There is no armour against fate;
Death lays his icy hand on kings:
Sceptre and crown
Must tumble down,
And in the dust be equal made
With the poor crooked scythe and spade.

[*The Contention of Ajax and Ulysses* (1659)]

How little room
Do we take up in death that living know
No bounds!

[*The Wedding* (1629)]

SLESSOR, Kenneth (1901–1971)

Softly and humbly to the Gulf of Arabs
The convoys of dead sailors come;
At night they sway and wander in the waters far under,
But morning rolls them in the foam.

Between the sob and clubbing of the gunfire
Someone, it seems, has time for this,
To pluck them from the shallows and bury them in burrows
And tread the sand upon their nakedness;

And each cross, the driven stake of tidewood,
Bears the last signature of men,
Written with such perplexity, with such bewildered pity,
The words choke as they begin –

'Unknown seaman' - the ghostly pencil
Wavers and fades, the purple drips,
The breath of the wet season has washed their inscriptions
As blue as drowned men's lips,

Dead seamen, gone in search of the same landfall,
Whether as enemies they fought,
Or fought with us, or neither; the sand joins them together,
Enlisted on the other front.

['Beach Burial' (1942)]

SMITH, Stevie (1902–1971)

If there wasn't death, I think you couldn't go on.

[*The Observer*, 1969]

SMITH, Sydney (1771–1845)

Death must be distinguished from dying, with which it is often confused.

[In H. Pearson, *The Smith of Smiths* (1934), 11]

SOCRATES (469–399 BC)

Death is one of two things. Either it is nothingness, and the dead have no consciousness of anything; or, as people say, it is a change and migration of the soul from this place to another.

[Attr. in Plato, *Apology*]

SOPHOCLES (496–406 BC)

Death is not the worst thing; rather, when one who craves death cannot attain even that wish.

[*Electra*]

SOUTHEY, Robert (1774–1843)

My name is Death: the last best friend am I.

[*Carmen Nuptiale* (1816)]

SPOONER, William (1844–1930)

Poor soul, very sad; her late husband, you know, a very sad death – eaten by missionaries – poor soul!

[In William Hayter, *Spooner* (1977)]

SWIFT, Jonathan (1667–1745)

You think, as I ought to think, that it is time for me to have done with the world, and so I would if I could get into a better before I was called into the best, and not die here in a rage, like a poisoned rat in a hole.

[Letter to Bolingbroke, 1729]

TATE, Allen (1899–1979)

Row upon row with strict impunity
The headstones yield their names to the element.

['Ode to the Confederate Dead' (1926)]

TENNYSON, Alfred, Lord (1809–1892)

Do we indeed desire the dead
Should still be near us at our side?
Is there no baseness we would hide?
No inner vileness that we dread?

[*In Memoriam A. H. H.* (1850)]

THOMAS, Dylan (1914–1953)

Though they go mad they shall be sane,
Though they sink through the sea they shall rise again;
Though lovers be lost love shall not;
And death shall have no dominion.

['And death shall have no dominion' (1936)]

TURGENEV, Ivan (1818–1883)

Go and try to disprove death. Death will disprove you, and that's all there is to it!

[*Fathers and Sons* (1862), 27]

Death is an old jest but it comes to everyone.

[In Jennifer Johnston, *The Old Jest*]

TWAIN, Mark (1835–1910)

Whoever has lived long enough to find out what life is, knows how deep a debt of gratitude we owe to Adam, the first great benefactor of our race. He brought death into the world.

[*Pudd'nhead Wilson* (1894)]

The report of my death was an exaggeration.

[Cable, 1897]

VAUGHAN, Henry (1622–1695)

Dear, beauteous death! the Jewel of the Just,
Shining nowhere, but in the dark;
What mysteries do lie beyond thy dust;
Could man outlook that mark!

[*Silex Scintillans* (1650–1655)]

VOLTAIRE (1694–1778)

On doit des égards aux vivants; on ne doit aux morts que la vérité.
We owe respect to the living; we owe nothing but truth to the dead.

['Première Lettre sur Oedipe' (1785)]

WEBSTER, John (c.1580–c.1625)

I know death hath ten thousand several doors
For men to take their exits.

[*The Duchess of Malfi* (1623)]

O, that it were possible,
We might but hold some two days' conference
With the dead!

[*The Duchess of Malfi* (1623)]

WEISS, Peter (1916–1982)

Jeder Tod auch der grausamste
ertrinkt in der völligen Gleichgültigkeit der Natur
Nur wir verleihen unserm Leben irgendeinen Wert.
Every death, even the cruellest, drowns in Nature's complete indifference. We are the only ones who bestow a value on our lives.

[*The Hunting Down and Murder of Jean Paul Marat* (1964)]

WHITMAN, Walt (1819–1892)

Has anyone supposed it lucky to be born?
I hasten to inform him or her it is just as lucky to die, and I know it.

['Song of Myself' (1855)]

WRIGHT, Judith (1915–)

Death marshals up his armies round us now.
Their footsteps crowd too near.
Lock your warm hand above the chilling heart
and for a time I live without my fear.
Grope in the night to find me and embrace,
for the dark preludes of the drums begin,
and round us, round the company of lovers,
death draws his cordons in.

['The Company of Lovers' (1946)]

YEATS, W.B. (1865–1939)

Nor dread nor hope attend
A dying animal;

A man awaits his end
Dreading and hoping all.

['Death' (1933)]

YOUNG, Edward (1683–1765)

Life is the desert, life the solitude;
Death joins us to the great majority.

[*The Revenge* (1721)]

See AFTERLIFE; EPITAPHS; FUNERALS;
GRIEF; LAST WORDS; MORTALITY;
MOURNING; MURDER; SLEEP;
SUICIDE

DEATH: Dying

ADDISON, Joseph (1672–1719)

See in what peace a Christian can die.

[Dying words]

ALEXANDER THE GREAT (356–323 BC)

I am dying with the help of too many
physicians.

[Attr.]

ALLEN, Woody (1935–)

It's not that I'm afraid to die. I just don't want
to be there when it happens.

[*Without Feathers* (1976)]

BACON, Francis (1561–1626)

I do not believe that any man fears to be
dead, but only the stroke of death.

[*The Remaines of … Lord Verulam* (1648)]

BARRIE, Sir J.M. (1860–1937)

To die will be an awfully big adventure.

[*Peter Pan* (1904)]

BETJEMAN, Sir John (1906–1984)

There was sun enough for lazing upon
beaches,
There was fun enough for far into the night.
But I'm dying now and done for,
What on earth was all the fun for?
For I'm old and ill and terrified and tight.

['Sun and Fun' (1954)]

BROWNE, Sir Thomas (1605–1682)

The long habit of living indisposeth us for

dying.

[*Hydriotaphia: Urn Burial* (1658)]

BUTLER, Samuel (1835–1902)

It costs a lot of money to die comfortably.

[*The Note-Books of Samuel Butler* (1912)]

CHARLES II (1630–1685)

He had been, he said, a most unconscionable
time dying; but he hoped that they would
excuse it.

[In Macaulay, *The History of England* (1849)]

CHILDERS, Erskine (1870–1922)

[Writing about his imminent execution]
It seems perfectly simple and inevitable, like
lying down after a long day's work.

[Prison letter to his wife]

CRASHAW, Richard (c.1612–1649)

And when life's sweet fable ends,
Soul and body part like friends;
No quarrels, murmurs, no delay;
A kiss, a sigh, and so away.

['Temperance' (1652)]

DARROW, Clarence (1857–1938)

I have never killed a man, but I have read
many obituaries with a lot of pleasure.

[*Medley*]

DICKINSON, Emily (1830–1886)

I heard a Fly buzz – when I died …
With Blue – uncertain stumbling Buzz –
Between the light – and me –
And then the Windows failed – and then
I could not see to see.

['I heard a Fly buzz – when I died'
(c. 1862)]

EDWARDS, Jonathan (1703–1758)

The bodies of those that made such a noise
and tumult when alive, when dead, lie as
quietly among the graves of their
neighbours as any others.

[*Works* (1834)]

FARMER, Edward (c.1809–1876)

I have no pain, dear mother, now;
But oh! I am so dry:
Just moisten poor Jim's lips once more;

And, mother, do not cry!

['The Collier's Dying Child']

FIELDING, Henry (1707–1754)

It hath been often said, that it is not death, but dying, which is terrible.

[*Amelia* (1751)]

HALL, Rodney (1935–)

They're dying just the same in station homesteads
they're dying in Home Beautiful apartments
in among their lovely Danish furniture
on and across the furniture they're dying
spewing blood or stiffening dry and seeming never
to have been alive.

[*Black Bagatelles* (1978)]

JOHNSON, Samuel (1709–1784)

It matters not how a man dies, but how he lives. The act of dying is not of importance, it lasts so short a time.

[In Boswell, *The Life of Samuel Johnson* (1791)]

MAUGHAM, William Somerset (1874–1965)

Dying is a very dull, dreary affair. And my advice to you is to have nothing whatever to do with it.

[In R. Maugham, *Escape from the Shadows* (1972)]

MILLAY, Edna St Vincent (1892–1950)

Down, down, down into the darkness of the grave
Gently they go, the beautiful, the tender, the kind;
Quietly they go, the intelligent, the witty, the brave.
I know. But I do not approve. And I am not resigned.

[*Buck in the Snow* (1928)]

PLATH, Sylvia (1932–1963)

Dying
Is an art, like everything else.
I do it exceptionally well.

['Lady Lazarus' (1963)]

PASCAL, Blaise (1623–1662)

On mourra seul.

We shall die alone.

[*Pensées* (1670)]

POPE, Alexander (1688–1744)

I mount! I fly!
O Grave! where is thy victory?
O Death! where is thy sting?

['The Dying Christian to his Soul' (1730)]

SHAKESPEARE, William (1564–1616)

Nothing in his life
Became him like the leaving it: he died
As one that had been studied in his death
To throw away the dearest thing he ow'd
As 'twere a careless trifle.

[*Macbeth*, I.iv]

Dar'st thou die?
The sense of death is most in apprehension;
And the poor beetle that we tread upon
In corporal sufferance finds a pang as great
As when a giant dies.

[*Measure For Measure*, III.i]

SMITH, Logan Pearsall (1865–1946)

I cannot forgive my friends for dying; I do not find these vanishing acts of theirs at all amusing.

[*Afterthoughts* (1931)]

THOMAS, Dylan (1914–1953)

Do not go gentle into that good night,
Old age should burn and rave at close of day;
Rage, rage against the dying of the light.

['Do Not Go Gentle into that Good Night' (1952)]

TWAIN, Mark (1835–1910)

All say, 'How hard it is to die' – a strange complaint to come from the mouths of people who have had to live.

[*Pudd'nhead Wilson's Calendar* (1894)]

See AFTERLIFE; EPITAPHS; FUNERALS; GRIEF; LAST WORDS; MORTALITY; MOURNING; MURDER; SUICIDE

DEBT

CAESAR, Augustus (63 BC–AD 14)

[Said of those who never pay their debts. The term

Kalends was Roman and did not exist in Greek]
Ad Kalendas Graecas soluturos.
It will be paid at the Greek Kalends.

[In Suetonius, *Lives of the Caesars*]

COOLIDGE, Calvin (1872–1933)
[Of Allied war debts]
They hired the money, didn't they?

[Remark, 1925]

FOX, Henry Stephen (1791–1846)
[Remark after an illness]
I am so changed that my oldest creditors would hardly know me.

[Quoted by Byron in a letter to John Murray, 1817]

FRANKLIN, Benjamin (1706–1790)
Creditors have better memories than debtors.

[*Poor Richard's Almanac* (1758)]

IBSEN, Henrik (1828–1906)
Home life ceases to be free and beautiful as soon as it is founded on borrowing and debt.

[*A Doll's House* (1879)]

MUMFORD, Ethel (1878–1940)
In the midst of life we are in debt.

[*Altogether New Cynic's Calendar* (1907)]

SHAKESPEARE, William (1564–1616)
I can get no remedy against this consumption of the purse; borrowing only lingers and lingers it out, but the disease is incurable.

[*Henry IV Part II*, I.ii]

SHERIDAN, Richard Brinsley (1751–1816)
[To his tailor when he requested payment of a debt, or at least the interest on it]
It is not my interest to pay the principal, nor my principle to pay the interest.

[Attr.]

[Handing one of his creditors an IOU]
Thank God, that's settled.

[In Shriner, *Wit, Wisdom, and Foibles of the Great* (1918)]

[After being refused a loan of £25 from a friend who asked him to repay the £500 he had

already borrowed]
My dear fellow, be reasonable; the sum you ask me for is a very considerable one, whereas I only ask you for twenty-five pounds.

[Attr.]

WARD, Artemus (1834–1867)
Let us all be happy, and live within our means, even if we have to borrer the money to do it with.

['Science and Natural History']

WILDE, Oscar (1854–1900)
It is only by not paying one's bills that one can hope to live in the memory of the commercial classes.

[*The Chameleon*, 1894]

WODEHOUSE, P.G. (1881–1975)
I don't owe a penny to a single soul – not counting tradesmen, of course.

['Jeeves and the Hard-Boiled Egg' (1919)]

See BORROWING AND LENDING

DECEPTION

AESOP (6th century BC)
The lamb that belonged to the sheep whose skin the wolf was wearing began to follow the wolf in the sheep's clothing.

[Fables, 'The Wolf in Sheep's Clothing']

ALLEN, Woody (1935–)
I was thrown out of NYU my freshman year for cheating in my metaphysics final. I looked into the soul of the boy sitting next to me.

[*Annie Hall*, film, 1977]

BERKELEY, Bishop George (1685–1753)
It is impossible that a man who is false to his friends and neighbours should be true to the public.

[*Maxims Concerning Patriotism* (1750)]

CARSWELL, Catherine (1879–1946)
It wasn't a woman who betrayed Jesus with a kiss.

[*The Savage Pilgrimage* (1932)]

CHAUCER, Geoffrey (c.1340–1400)

The carl spak oo thing, but he thoghte another.

[*The Canterbury Tales* (1387)]

The smylere with the knyf under the cloke.

[*The Canterbury Tales* (1387)]

COLMAN, the Younger, George (1762–1836)

Says he, 'I am a handsome man, but I'm a gay deceiver.'

[*Love Laughs at Locksmiths* (1808)]

CONGREVE, William (1670–1729)

Man was by Nature Woman's cully made:
We never are, but by ourselves, betrayed.

[*The Old Bachelor* (1693)]

DEMOSTHENES (c.384–322 BC)

There is a great deal of wishful thinking in such cases; it is the easiest thing of all to deceive one's self.

[*Olynthiac*]

FADIMAN, Clifton (1904–)

Experience teaches you that the man who looks you straight in the eye, particularly if he adds a firm handshake, is hiding something.

[*Enter, Conversing*]

FONTAINE, Jean de la (1621–1695)

C'est double plaisir de tromper le trompeur.
It is a double pleasure to trick the trickster.

['Le coq et le renard']

GAY, John (1685–1732)

To cheat a man is nothing; but the woman must have fine parts indeed who cheats a woman!

[*The Beggar's Opera* (1728)]

HENRY, O. (1862–1910)

It was beautiful and simple as all truly great swindles are.

['The Octopus Marooned' (1908)]

HILL, Joe (1879–1914)

You will eat (You will eat)
Bye and bye (Bye and bye)
In that glorious land above the sky (Way up high)

Work and pray (Work and pray)
Live on hay (Live on hay)
You'll get pie in the sky when you die (That's a lie.).

['The Preacher and the Slave', song, 1911]

SCOTT, Sir Walter (1771–1832)

O what a tangled web we weave,
When first we practise to deceive!

[*Marmion* (1808)]

SHAKESPEARE, William (1564–1616)

O villain, villain, smiling, damned villain!
My tables – meet it is I set it down
That one may smile, and smile, and be a villain.

[*Hamlet*, I.v]

False face must hide what the false heart doth know.

[*Macbeth*, I.vii]

So may the outward shows be least themselves;
The world is still deceiv'd with ornament.

[*The Merchant of Venice*, III.ii]

SWIFT, Jonathan (1667–1745)

This is the sublime and refined point of felicity, called the possession of being well deceived; the serene peaceful state of being a fool among knaves.

[*A Tale of a Tub* (1704)]

TAYLOR, Bishop Jeremy (1613–1667)

In the matter of interest we are wary as serpents, subtle as foxes, vigilant as the birds of the night, rapacious as kites, tenacious as grappling-hooks and the weightiest anchors, and, above all, false and hypocritical as a thin crust of ice spread upon the face of a deep, smooth, and dissembling pit.

[*XXV Sermons Preached at Golden Grove* (1653)]

THURBER, James (1894–1961)

It is not so easy to fool little girls today as it used to be.

[*Fables for Our Time* (1940)]

You can fool too many of the people too

much of the time.

[*The New Yorker*, 1939]

VIRGIL (70–19 BC)

Quis fallere possit amantem?

Who may deceive a lover?

[*Aeneid*]

See APPEARANCE; HYPOCRISY; LIES

DECISIONS

CAESAR, Gaius Julius (c.102–44 BC)

[Remark on crossing the Rubicon]

Iacta alea est.

The die is cast.

[In Suetonius, *Lives of the Caesars*]

DENNING, Lord (1899–1999)

A wrong decision can make me very miserable. But I have trust in God. If you have this trust you don't have to worry, as you don't have the sole responsibility.

[Speech on his retirement, 1982]

PARKINSON, C. Northcote (1909–1993)

The man who is denied the opportunity of taking decisions of importance begins to regard as important the decisions he is allowed to take.

[*Parkinson's Law* (1958)]

QUARLES, Francis (1592–1644)

The road to resolution lies by doubt:
The next way home's the farthest way about.

[*Emblems* (1643)]

RIFKIN, Jeremy (c.1860–1930)

When the Iroquois made a decision, they said, 'How does it affect seven generations in the future?'.

[*New York Times Magazine*, 1988]

DEFEAT

LINCOLN, Abraham (1809–1865)

[On losing an election]

Like a little boy who has stubbed his toe in the dark … too old to cry, but it hurt too much to laugh.

[Attr. by Adlai Stevenson]

LIVY (59 BC–AD 17)

Vae victis.

Woe to the vanquished.

[*History*]

LOUIS XIV (1638–1715)

[On hearing of the French defeat at Malplaquet]

Dieu, a-t-il donc oublié ce que j'ai fait pour lui?

Has God then forgotten what I have done for him?

[Attr.]

STEVENSON, Adlai (1900–1965)

[Said after losing an election, quoting a story told by Abraham Lincoln]

He said that he was too old to cry, but it hurt too much to laugh.

[Speech, 1952]

TAFT, William Howard (1857–1930)

[Referring to his disastrous defeat in the 1912 presidential election]

Well, I have one consolation. No candidate was ever elected ex-president with such a large majority!

[Attr.]

DEMOCRACY

ANONYMOUS

Democracy is mob rule, but with income taxes.

[Chinese Student during protests in Tiananmen Square, Beijing, 1989]

I don't know exactly what democracy is. But we need more of it.

ATTLEE, Clement (1883–1967)

Democracy means government by discussion but it is only effective if you can stop people talking.

[Speech, 1957]

BEVERIDGE, William Henry (1879–1963)

The trouble in modern democracy is that

men do not approach to leadership until they have lost the desire to lead anyone.

[*The Observer*, 1934]

CARTWRIGHT, John (1740–1824)

One man shall have one vote.

[*The People's Barrier Against Undue Influence* (1780)]

CHESTERTON, G.K. (1874–1936)

You can never have a revolution in order to establish a democracy. You must have a democracy in order to have a revolution.

[*Tremendous Trifles*]

Democracy means government by the uneducated, while aristocracy means government by the badly educated.

[*New York Times*, 1931]

CHURCHILL, Sir Winston (1874–1965)

Many forms of government have been tried, and will be tried in this world of sin and woe. No one pretends that democracy is perfect or all-wise. Indeed, it has been said that democracy is the worst form of Government except all those other forms that have been tried from time to time.

[*Speech*, 1947]

DEMOSTHENES (c.384–322 BC)

There is one safeguard, which is an advantage and security for all, but especially to democracies against despots. What is it? Distrust.

[*Philippics*]

FLERS, Marquis de (1872–1927) and Caillavet, Arman de (1869–1915)

Démocratie est le nom que nous donnons au peuple toutes les fois que nous avons besoin de lui.
Democracy is the name we give the people whenever we need them.

[*L'habit vert*]

FO, Dario (1926–)

Giusto! L'ha detto! Lo scandalo è il concime della democrazia.
Correct! You said it! Scandal is the manure of democracy.

[*Accidental Death of an Anarchist* (1974)]

FORSTER, E.M. (1879–1970)

So Two cheers for Democracy: one because it admits variety and two because it permits criticism. Two cheers are quite enough: there is no occasion to give three. Only Love the Beloved Republic deserves that.

[*Two Cheers for Democracy* (1951)]

IBSEN, Henrik (1828–1906)

The most dangerous foe to truth and freedom in our midst is the compact majority. Yes, the damned, compact liberal majority.

[*An Enemy of the People* (1882)]

INGE, William Ralph (1860–1954)

Democracy is only an experiment in government, and it has the obvious disadvantage of merely counting votes instead of weighing them.

[*Possible Recovery?* (c. 1922)]

JUNIUS (1769–1772)

The right of election is the very essence of the constitution.

[*Letters* (1769–1771)]

LINCOLN, Abraham (1809–1865)

No man is good enough to govern another man without that other's consent.

[*Speech*, 1854]

The ballot is stronger than the bullet.

[*Speech*, 1856]

MACAULAY, Lord (1800–1859)

Thus our democracy was, from an early period, the most aristocratic, and our aristocracy the most democratic in the world.

[*History of England* (1849)]

NIEBUHR, Reinhold (1892–1971)

Man's capacity for justice makes democracy possible, but man's inclination to injustice makes democracy necessary.

[*The Children of Light and the Children of Darkness* (1944)]

PERICLES (c.495–429)

We enjoy a constitution that does not follow the customs of our neighbours; we are rather an example to them than they to us. Our government is called a democracy because power is in the hands not of the few but of the many.

[In Thucydides, *Histories*]

PRESTON, Keith (1884–1927)

[Of democracy]
An institution in which the whole is equal to the scum of all the parts.

[*Pot Shots from Pegasus*]

SAND, George (1804–1876)

Il faut s'avouer impuissant devant cette fatalité politique d'un nouvel ordre dans l'histoire: le suffrage universel.
One must admit one is powerless in the face of the political inevitability of this new order in history: universal suffrage.

[Letter to Joseph Mazzini, 1848]

SELLAR, Walter (1898–1951) and YEATMAN, Robert Julian (1897–1968)

Magna Charter was … the cause of Democracy in England, and thus a Good Thing for everyone (except the Common People).

[*1066 And All That* (1930)]

SHAW, George Bernard (1856–1950)

Our political experiment of democracy, the last refuge of cheap misgovernment.

[*Man and Superman* (1903), Epistle Dedicatory]

Our political experiment of democracy, the last refuge of cheap misgovernment.

[*Man and Superman* (1903)]

Democracy substitutes election by the incompetent many for appointment by the corrupt few.

[*Man and Superman* (1903)]

TOCQUEVILLE, Alexis de (1805–1859)

I sought the image of democracy, in order to learn what we have to fear and to hope from its progress.

[*De la Démocratie en Amérique* (1840)]

WEBSTER, Daniel (1782–1852)

The people's government, made for the people, made by the people, and answerable to the people.

[Speech, 1830]

WILDE, Oscar (1854–1900)

Democracy means simply the bludgeoning of the people by the people for the people.

[*The Fortnightly Review*, 1891]

WILLIAMS, Tennessee (1911–1983)

Knowledge – Zzzzzp! Money – Zzzzzp! – Power! That's the cycle democracy is built on!

[*The Glass Menagerie* (1945)]

WILSON, Woodrow (1856–1924)

The world must be made safe for democracy.

[Speech, 1917]

See CLASS; GOVERNMENT

DESIGN

ANONYMOUS

Design flaws travel in groups.

[Fifth Law of Design]

Information necessitating a change of design will be conveyed to the designer after and only after the design is complete.

['Now They Tell Us' Law]

The more innocuous the modification appears to be, the further its influence will extend and the more the design will have to be redrawn.

[Law of Revision I]

If, when completion of a design is imminent, field dimensions are finally supplied as they actually are, instead of as they were meant to be, it is always simpler to start over from scratch.

[Law of Revision II]

See ART; ARCHITECTURE

DESIRE

BLAKE, William (1757–1827)

Those who restrain desire, do so because

DESPAIR

180

theirs is weak enough to be restrained.

[*The Marriage of Heaven and Hell* (c. 1790–1793)]

Man's desires are limited by his perceptions; none can desire what he has not perceiv'd.

[*There is No Natural Religion* (c. 1788)]

The desire of Man being Infinite the possession is Infinite and himself Infinite.

[*There is No Natural Religion* (c. 1788)]

Abstinence sows sand all over
The ruddy limbs & flaming hair
But Desire Gratified
Plants fruits of life & beauty there.

['Abstinence sows sand all over' (c. 1793)]

What is it men in women do require?
The lineaments of Gratified Desire.
What is it women do in men require?
The lineaments of Gratified Desire.

['What is it men in women do require']

BROWNE, Sir Thomas (1605–1682)

My desires only are, and I shall be happy therein, to be but the last man, and bring up the rear in heaven.

[*Religio Medici* (1643)]

CONGREVE, William (1670–1729)

O, she is the antidote to desire.

[*The Way of the World* (1700)]

DRAYTON, Michael (1563–1631)

Thus when we fondly flatter our desires,
Our best conceits do prove the greatest liars.

[*The Barrons' Wars* (1603)]

JOYCE, James (1882–1941)

[Commenting on the interruption of a music recital when a moth flew into the singer's mouth]
The desire of the moth for the star.

[In Ellmann, *James Joyce* (1958)]

KIPLING, Rudyard (1865–1936)

The depth and dream of my desire,
The bitter paths wherein I stray –
Thou knowest Who hast made the Fire,
Thou knowest Who hast made the Clay.

[*Life's Handicap* (1888)]

PATTEN, Brian (1946–)

Not all that you want and ought not to have is forbidden to you,
Not all that you want and are allowed to want Is acceptable.

[*Vanishing Trick*]

PROUST, Marcel (1871–1922)

Le désir fleurit, la possession flétrit toutes choses.
Desire makes everything blossom; possession makes everything wither and fade.

[*Les Plaisirs et les Jours* (1896)]

Il n'y a rien comme le désir pour empêcher les choses qu'on dit d'avoir aucune ressemblance avec ce qu'on a dans la pensée.
There is nothing like desire for preventing the things one says from bearing any resemblance to what one has in mind.

[*Le Côté de Guermantes* (1921)]

SHAW, George Bernard (1856–1950)

There are two tragedies in life. One is to lose your heart's desire. The other is to gain it.

[*Man and Superman* (1903)]

SWIFT, Jonathan (1667–1745)

The stoical scheme of supplying our wants, by lopping off our desires, is like cutting off our feet when we want shoes.

[*Thoughts on Various Subjects* (1711)]

SWINBURNE, Algernon Charles (1837–1909)

The delight that consumes the desire,
The desire that outruns the delight.

['Dolores' (1866)]

See HUNGER

DESPAIR

ALLEN, Woody (1935–)

More than any other time in history, mankind faces a crossroads. One path leads to despair and utter hopelessness. The other, to total extinction. Let us pray we have the wisdom to choose correctly.

[*Side Effects*]

CAMUS, Albert (1913–1960)

He who despairs over an event is a coward,
but he who holds hopes for the human
condition is a fool.

[*The Rebel* (1951)]

CLARE, John (1793–1864)

My life hath been one chain of
contradictions,
Madhouses, prisons, whore-shops …

Pale death, the grand physician, cures all
pain;
The dead rest well who lived for joys in
vain …

Hopeless hope hopes on and meets no end,
Wastes without springs and homes without a
friend.

['Child Harold' (1841)]

FITZGERALD, F. Scott (1896–1940)

In the real dark night of the soul it is always
three o'clock in the morning.

[*The Crack-Up* (1945)]

GREENE, Graham (1904–1991)

Despair is the price one pays for setting
oneself an impossible aim.

[*Heart of the Matter* (1948)]

HOPKINS, Gerard Manley (1844–1889)

Not, I'll not, carrion comfort, Despair, not feast
on thee;
Not untwist – slack they may be – these last
strands of man
In me or, most weary, cry I can no more. I can;
Can something, hope, wish day come, not
choose not to be.

['Carrion Comfort' (1885)]

I wake and feel the fell of dark, not day.
What hours, O what black hours we have
spent
This night!

['I wake and Feel the Fell of dark, not day'
(c. 1885)]

KAFKA, Franz (1883–1924)

*Nicht verzweifeln, auch darüber nicht, dass du nicht
verzweifelst.*

Do not despair, not even about the fact that
you do not despair.

[*Diary*, 1913]

SHAKESPEARE, William (1564–1616)

I shall despair. There is no creature loves me;
And if I die no soul will pity me:
And wherefore should they, since that I
myself
Find in myself no pity to myself?

[*Richard III*, V.iii]

SHAW, George Bernard (1856–1950)

He who has never hoped can never despair.

[*Caesar and Cleopatra*
(1901)]

ST JOHN OF THE CROSS (1542–1591)

Noche oscura del alma
The dark night of the soul.

[Title of poem]

THOREAU, Henry David (1817–1862)

The mass of men lead lives of quiet
desperation.

[*Walden* (1854)]

WALSH, William (1663–1708)

I can endure my own despair,
But not another's hope.

['Song: Of All the Torments']

See SUFFERING

DESTINY

AESCHYLUS (525–456 BC)

Things are where things are, and, as fate has
willed,
So shall they be fulfilled.

[*Agamemnon*, trans. Browning]

ARNOLD, Matthew (1822–1888)

Yet they, believe me, who await
No gifts from chance, have conquered fate.

['Resignation' (1849)]

AURELIUS, Marcus (121–180)

That 'all that happens, happens as it should', if you observe carefully, you will find to be the case.

[*Meditations*]

Whatever may happen to you was prepared for you from all eternity; and the thread of causes was spinning from eternity both your being and this which is happening to you.

[*Meditations*]

Nothing happens to any thing which that thing is not made by nature to bear.

[*Meditations*]

BACON, Francis (1561–1626)

If a man look sharply, and attentively, he shall see Fortune: for though she be blind, yet she is not invisible.

[*Essays* (1625)]

BOWEN, Elizabeth (1899–1973)

Fate is not an eagle, it creeps like a rat.

[*The House in Paris* (1935)]

BÜCHNER, Georg (1813–1837)

Puppen sind wir von unbekannten Gewalten am Draht gezogen; nichts, nichts wir selbst!
We are puppets on strings worked by unknown forces; we ourselves are nothing, nothing!

[*Danton's Death* (1835)]

BURNS, Robert (1759–1796)

The best-laid schemes o' mice an' men
Gang aft agley,
An' lea'e us nought but grief an' pain,
For promis'd joy!

['To a Mouse' (1785)]

CHURCHILL, Sir Winston (1874–1965)

Which brings me to my conclusion upon Free Will and Predestination, namely – let the reader mark it – that they are identical.

[*My Early Life* (1930)]

I felt as if I were walking with destiny, and that all my past life had been but a preparation for this hour and this trial.

[*The Gathering Storm*]

CLAUDIUS CAECUS, Appius (4th–3rd century BC)

Faber est suae quisque fortunae.
Each man is the architect of his own destiny.

[In Sallust, *Ad Caesarem*]

CLIVE, Lord (1725–1774)

[Said when his pistol failed to go off twice, in his attempt to commit suicide]
I feel that I am reserved for some end or other.

[In Gleig, *The Life of Robert, First Lord Clive* (1848)]

CRISP, Quentin (1908–)

Believe in fate, but lean forward where fate can see you.

[Attr.]

DEFOE, Daniel (c.1661–1731)

The best of men cannot suspend their fate:
The good die early, and the bad die late.

['Character of the late Dr S. Annesley' (1697)]

DELILLE, Abbé Jacques (1738–1813)

Le sort fait les parents, le choix fait les amis.
Relations are made by fate, friends by choice.

[*Malheur et pitié* (1803)]

DRYDEN, John (1631–1700)

[Of Fortune]
I can enjoy her while she's kind;
But when she dances in the wind,
And shakes the wings, and will not stay,
I puff the prostitute away.

[*Sylvae* (1685)]

ELIOT, George (1819–1880)

[Of Fortune]
'Character', says Novalis, in one of his questionable aphorisms – 'character is destiny.'

[*The Mill on the Floss* (1860)]

EMERSON, Ralph Waldo (1803–1882)

The bitterest tragic element in life to be derived from an intellectual source is the belief in a brute Fate or Destiny.

[*Natural History of Intellect* (1893)]

FITZGERALD, Edward (1809–1883)

'Tis all a Chequer-board of Nights and Days
Where Destiny with Men for Pieces plays:
Hither and thither moves, and mates, and slays,
And one by one back in the Closet lays.

[*The Rubáiyát of Omar Khayyám* (1859)]

The Moving Finger writes; and, having writ,
Moves on: nor all thy Piety nor Wit
Shall lure it back to cancel half a Line,
Nor all thy Tears wash out a Word of it.

[*The Rubáiyát of Omar Khayyám* (1859)]

FORD, John (c.1586–1639)

Tempt not the stars, young man, thou canst not play
With the severity of fate.

[*The Broken Heart* (1633)]

GAY, John (1685–1732)

'Tis a gross error, held in schools,
That Fortune always favours fools.

[*Fables* (1738)]

HARE, Maurice Evan (1886–1967)

There once was a man who said, 'Damn!
It is borne in upon me I am
An engine that moves
In predestinate grooves,
I'm not even a bus, I'm a tram.'

['Limerick', 1905]

HITLER, Adolf (1889–1945)

Ich gehe mit traumwandlerischer Sicherheit den Weg, den mich die Vorsehung gehen heisst.
I go the way that Providence bids me go with the certainty of a sleepwalker.

[Speech, Munich, 1936]

HORACE (65–8 BC)

Tu ne quaesieris, scire nefas, quem mihi, quem tibi Finem di dederint.
Do not ask – it is forbidden to know – what end the gods have in store for me or for you.

[*Odes*]

JONSON, Ben (1572–1637)

Blind Fortune still

Bestows her gifts on such as cannot use them.

[*Every Man out of His Humour* (1599)]

LOOS, Anita (1893–1981)

Fate keeps on happening.

[*Gentlemen Prefer Blondes* (1925)]

MACAULAY, Lord (1800–1859)

[Of Rumbold]
He never would believe that Providence had sent a few men into the world ready booted and spurred to ride, and millions ready saddled and bridled to be ridden.

[*History of England* (1849)]

MACHIAVELLI (1469–1527)

La fortuna, come donna, è amica de giovani, perché sono meno respettivi, più feroci e con più audacia la comandano.
Fortune, like a woman, is friendly to the young, because they show her less respect, they are more daring and command her with audacity.

[*The Prince* (1532)]

MALLARMÉ, Stéphane (1842–1898)

Un coup de dés jamais n'abolira le hasard.
A throw of the dice will never eliminate chance.

[Title of work, 1897]

POPPER, Sir Karl (1902–1994)

We may become the makers of our fate when we have ceased to pose as its prophets.

[*The Observer*, 1975]

READE, Charles (1814–1884)

Sow an act, and you reap a habit. Sow a habit, and you reap a character. Sow a character, and you reap a destiny.

[Attr.]

SARRAUTE, Nathalie (1900–)

Je ne crois pas aux rencontres fortuites.
I don"t believe in chance encounters.

[*Martereau*]

SCHOPENHAUER, Arthur (1788–1860)

Das Schicksal mischt die Karten und wir spielen.

Fate shuffles the cards and we play.

['Aphorisms for Wisdom' (1851)]

SHAKESPEARE, William (1564–1616)

Let us sit and mock the good housewife
Fortune from her wheel, that her gifts may
henceforth be bestowed equally.

[*As You Like It*, I.ii]

Men at some time are masters of their fates:
The fault, dear Brutus, is not in our stars,
But in ourselves, that we are underlings.

[*Julius Caesar*, I.ii]

Fortune is merry,
And in this mood will give us any thing.

[*Julius Caesar*, III.ii]

There is a tide in the affairs of men
Which, taken at the flood, leads on to
fortune;
Omitted, all the voyage of their life
Is bound in shallows and in miseries.

[*Julius Caesar*, IV.iii.]

SIMPSON, N.F. (1919–)

Each of us as he receives his private
trouncings at the hands of fate is kept in
good heart by the moth in his brother's
parachute, and the scorpion in his
neighbour's underwear.

[*A Resounding Tinkle* (1958)]

SINGER, Isaac Bashevis (1904–1991)

We have to believe in free will. We've got no
choice.

[*The Times*, 1982]

STEELE, Sir Richard (1672–1729)

Every Man is the Maker of his own Fortune.

[*The Tatler*, 52, 1709]

TEMPLE, Frederick, Archbishop (1821–1902)

'My aunt was suddenly prevented from
going a voyage in a ship what went down –
would you call that a case of Providential
interference?'
'Can't tell: didn't know your aunt.'

[In Sandford, *Memoirs of Archbishop Temple*]

TERENCE (c.190–159 BC)

Fortis fortuna adiuvat.
Fortune favours the brave.

[*Phormio*]

WEBSTER, John (c.1580–c.1625)

Fortune's a right whore:
If she give aught, she deals it in small parcels,
That she may take away all at one swoop.

[*The White Devil* (1612)]

We are merely the stars' tennis-balls, struck
and bandied,
Which way please them.

[*The Duchess of Malfi* (1623)]

See PURPOSE

DESTRUCTION

BAKUNIN, Mikhail (1814–1876)

Die Lust der Zerstörung ist zugleich eine schaffende Lust!
The desire for destruction is, at the same
time, a creative desire.

[In *Jahrbuch für Wissenschaft und Kunst*, 1842]

BETJEMAN, Sir John (1906–1984)

Come, friendly bombs, and fall on Slough
It isn't fit for humans now,
There isn't grass to graze a cow
Swarm over, Death! …

Come, friendly bombs, and fall on Slough
To get it ready for the plough.

[*Continual Dew* (1937)]

CHEKHOV, Anton (1860–1904)

Human beings have been endowed with
reason and a creative power so that they can
add to what thay have been given. But until
now they have been not creative, but
destructive. Forests are disappearing, rivers
are drying up, wildlife is becoming extinct,
the climate's being ruined and with every
passing day the earth is becoming poorer
and uglier.

[*Uncle Vanya* (1897)]

CONNOLLY, Cyril (1903–1974)
Whom the gods wish to destroy they first call promising.

[*Enemies of Promise* (1938)]

EURIPIDES (c.485–406 BC)
Those whom God wishes to destroy, he first makes mad.

[*Fragment*]

THE DEVIL

BAUDELAIRE, Charles (1821–1867)
My dear brothers, never forget when you hear the progress of the Enlightenment praised, that the Devil's cleverest ploy is to persuade you that he doesn't exist.

[Attr.]

**THE BIBLE
(King James Version)**
Resist the devil, and he will flee from you.

[*James*, 4:7]

BLAKE, William (1757–1827)
Truly My Satan thou art but a Dunce
And dost not know the Garment from the Man.
Every Harlot was a Virgin once
Nor canst thou ever change Kate into Nan.

[*For the Sexes: The Gates of Paradise* (c. 1810)]

BROWNE, Sir Thomas (1605–1682)
Thus the devil played at chess with me, and yielding a pawn, thought to gain a queen of me, taking advantage of my honest endeavours.

[*Religio Medici* (1643)]

**BROWNING, Elizabeth Barrett
(1806–1861)**
The devil's most devilish when respectable.

[*Aurora Leigh* (1857)]

BUTLER, Samuel (1835–1902)
An apology for the devil: it must be remembered that we have heard only one side of the case; God has written all the books.

[*The Note-Books of Samuel Butler* (1912)]

**COLERIDGE, Samuel Taylor
(1772–1834)**
From his brimstone bed at break of day
A walking the Devil is gone,
To visit his snug little farm the Earth,
And see how his stock goes on …

His jacket was red and his breeches were blue,
And there was a hole where the tail came through …

He saw a Lawyer killing a viper
On a dunghill hard by his own stable;
And the Devil smiled, for it put him in mind
Of Cain and his brother, Abel …

He saw a cottage with a double coach-house,
A cottage of gentility;
And the Devil did grin, for his darling sin
Is pride that apes humility …

As he went through Cold-Bath Fields he saw
A solitary cell;
And the Devil was pleased, for it gave him a hint
For improving his prisons in Hell.

['The Devil's Thoughts' (1799)]

CONGREVE, William (1670–1729)
The Devil watches all opportunities.

[*The Old Bachelor* (1693)]

DEFOE, Daniel (c.1661–1731)
Wherever God erects a house of prayer,
The Devil always builds a chapel there;
And 'twill be found, upon examination,
The latter has the largest congregation.

[*The True-Born Englishman* (1701)]

DOSTOEVSKY, Fyodor (1821–1881)
I think if the devil doesn't exist, and man has created him, he has created him in his own image and likeness.

[*The Brothers Karamazov* (1880)]

HILL, Rowland (1744–1833)
[Referring to his writing of hymns]
He did not see any reason why the devil

should have all the good tunes.

[In Broome, *The Rev. Rowland Hill* (1881)]

LAWRENCE, D.H. (1885–1930)

It is no good casting out devils. They belong to us, we must accept them and be at peace with them.

['The Reality of Peace' (1936)]

LUTHER, Martin (1483–1546)

Der alt böse Feind
Mit Ernst er's itzt meint,
Gross Macht und viel List,
Sein grausam Rüstung ist,
Auf Erd ist nicht seins gleichen.

The ancient prince of hell
Hath risen with purpose fell;
Strong mail of craft and power
He weareth in this hour;
On earth is not his fellow.

[Hymn, c. 1527–1528; trans. Carlyle]

MILTON, John (1608–1674)

Abasht the Devil stood,
And felt how awful goodness is.

[*Paradise Lost* (1667)]

MOTTEUX, Peter Anthony (1660–1718)

The devil was sick, the devil a monk would be;
The devil was well, and the devil a monk he'd be.

[Translation of Rabelais, *Gargantua and Pantagruel* (1693)]

PROVERBS

The devil is not so black as he is painted.

The devil looks after his own.

He who sups with the devil should have a long spoon.

Talk of the devil, and he is bound to appear.

READE, Charles (1814–1884)

Courage, mon ami, le diable est mort.
Courage, my friend, the devil is dead.

[*The Cloister and the Hearth* (1861)]

SHAKESPEARE, William (1564–1616)

The devil can cite Scripture for his purpose.

[*The Merchant of Venice*, I.iii]

SHAW, George Bernard (1856–1950)

Is the devil to have all the passions as well as all the good tunes?

[*Man and Superman* (1903)]

STEVENSON, Robert Louis (1850–1894)

The devil, depend upon it, can sometimes do a very gentlemanly thing.

[*New Arabian Nights* (1882)]

WILDE, Oscar (1854–1900)

We are each our own devil, and we make
This world our hell.

[*The Duchess of Padua* (1883)]

See HELL

DIARIES

BANKHEAD, Tallulah (1903–1968)

Only good girls keep diaries. Bad girls don't have the time.

[Attr.]

TERRY, Dame Ellen (1847–1928)

What is a diary as a rule? A document useful to the person who keeps it, dull to the contemporary who reads it, invaluable to the student, centuries afterwards, who treasures it!

[*The Story of My Life* (1933)]

TOLSTOY, Sophie (1844–1919)

[Of Tolstoy]

He would like to destroy his old diaries and to appear before his children and the public only in his patriarchal robes. His vanity is enormous!

[*A Diary of Tolstoy's Wife*, 1860–1891]

DIET

MONTAGU, Lady Mary Wortley (1689–1762)

Be plain in dress, and sober in your diet;

In short, my deary! kiss me, and be quiet.

[*Summary of Lord Lyttleton's Advice*]

SMITH, Sydney (1771–1845)

[On his convalescent diet]

If you hear of sixteen or eighteen pounds of human flesh, they belong to me. I look as if a curate has been taken out of me.

[Letter to Lady Carlisle, 1844]

See COOKERY; DINING; FOOD

DINING

BOWRA, Sir Maurice (1898–1971)

I'm a man
More dined against than dining.

[In Betjeman, *Summoned by Bells* (1960)]

EDWARDS, Oliver (1711–1791)

For my part now, I consider supper as a turnpike through which one must pass, in order to get to bed.

[In Boswell, *The Life of Samuel Johnson* (1791)]

EVARTS, William Maxwell (1818–1901)

[Of a dinner given by US President and temperance advocate Rutherford B. Hayes]

It was a brilliant affair; water flowed like champagne.

[Attr.]

GULBENKIAN, Nubar (1896–1972)

The best number for a dinner party is two: myself and a damn good head waiter.

[*The Observer*, 1965]

JOHNSON, Samuel (1709–1784)

We could not have had a better dinner had there been a Synod of Cooks.

[In Boswell, *The Life of Samuel Johnson* (1791)]

This was a good dinner enough, to be sure; but it was not a dinner to ask a man to.

[In Boswell, *The Life of Samuel Johnson* (1791)]

A man seldom thinks with more earnestness of anything than he does of his dinner.

[In Piozzi, *Anecdotes of the Late Samuel Johnson* (1786)]

A man is in general better pleased when he has a good dinner upon his table, than when his wife talks Greek.

[In Hawkins, *Life of Samuel Johnson* (1787)]

LANDOR, Walter Savage (1775–1864)

I shall dine late; but the dining-room will be well lighted, the guests few and select.

[*Imaginary Conversations* (1853)]

LANE, George Martin (1823–1897)

The waiter roars it through the hall:
'We don't give bread with one fish-ball!'.

['Lay of the Lone Fish-Ball' (1855)]

MARTIAL (c.AD 40–c.104)

Caenae fercula nostrae malim convivis quam placuisse cocis.

I prefer that the courses at our banquet should give pleasure to the guests rather than to the cooks.

[*Epigrammata*]

MAUGHAM, William Somerset (1874–1965)

At a dinner party one should eat wisely but not too well, and talk well but not too wisely.

[*A Writer's Notebook* (1949)]

PEPYS, Samuel (1633–1703)

Strange to see how a good dinner and feasting reconciles everybody.

[*Diary*, 1665]

POWELL, Anthony (1905–)

Dinner at the Huntercombes' possessed 'only two dramatic features – the wine was a farce and the food a tragedy'.

[*A Dance to the Music of Time: The Acceptance World* (1955)]

SCOTT, William (1745–1836)

A dinner lubricates business.

[In Boswell, *The Life of Samuel Johnson* (1791)]

SMITH, Sydney (1771–1845)

Most London dinners evaporate in whispers to one's next-door neighbour. I make it a rule never to speak a word to mine, but fire across the table; though I broke it once … I turned suddenly round and said, 'Madam, I have been looking for a person who disliked gravy all my life; let us swear eternal friendship.'

[In Holland, *A Memoir of the Reverend Sydney Smith* (1855)]

[From his recipe for salads]
Serenely full, the epicure would say,
Fate cannot harm me, I have dined today.

[In Holland, *A Memoir of the Reverend Sydney Smith* (1855)]

SWIFT, Jonathan (1667–1745)

We were to do more business after dinner; but after dinner is after dinner – an old saying and a true, 'much drinking, little thinking'.

[*Journal to Stella*, 1711]

He showed me his bill of fare to tempt me to dine with him; Poh, said I, I value not your bill of fare; give me your bill of company.

[*Journal to Stella*, 1711]

WILDE, Oscar (1854–1900)

[Said to Frank Harris who was listing the houses he had dined at]
Dear Frank, we believe you; you have dined in every house in London – once.

[Attr.]

See FOOD

DIPLOMACY

CROMWELL, Oliver (1599–1658)

A man-of-war is the best ambassador.

[Attr.]

DENNING, Lord (1899–1999)

[His views on the difference between a diplomat and a lady]
When a diplomat says yes, he means perhaps. When he says perhaps he means no. When he says no, he is not a diplomat. When a lady says no, she means perhaps. When she says perhaps, she means yes. But when she says yes, she is no lady.

[Speech at meeting of Magistrates Association, 14 October 1982]

FROST, Robert (1874–1963)

A diplomat is a man who always remembers a woman's birthday but never remembers her age.

[Attr.]

GRANT, Bruce Alexander (1925–)

I recall at least two Australian ambassadors who complained to me in the past about the constraints which the inherited British style placed on Australian diplomacy, but, when their time came to resist the invitation of knighthood, their resolve buckled under the terrible strain.

[*Gods and Politicians* (1982)]

PEARSON, Lester B. (1897–1972)

Diplomacy is letting someone else have your way.

[*The Observer*, 1965]

USTINOV, Sir Peter (1921–)

A diplomat these days is nothing but a head-waiter who's allowed to sit down occasionally.

[*Romanoff and Juliet* (1956)]

WOTTON, Sir Henry (1568–1639)

Legatus est vir bonus peregre missus ad mentiendum rei publicae causa.
An ambassador is an honest man sent to lie abroad for the good of his country.

[Written in an album, 1606]

DISABILITY

SASSOON, Siegfried (1886–1967)

Does it matter? – losing your legs? …
For people will always be kind,
And you need not show that you mind
When others come in after hunting
To gobble their muffins and eggs.

Does it matter? – losing your sight? …
There's such splendid work for the blind;
And people will always be kind,
As you sit on the terrace remembering
And turning your face to the light.

['Does it Matter?' (1917)]

DISAPPOINTMENT

ELIOT, George (1819–1880)
Nothing is so good as it seems beforehand.
[*Silas Marner* (1861)]

GOLDSMITH, Oliver (c.1728–1774)
As for disappointing them, I should not so
much mind; but I can't abide to disappoint
myself.
[*She Stoops to Conquer* (1773)]

MOORE, Thomas (1779–1852)
Like Dead Sea fruits, that tempt the eye,
But turn to ashes on the lips!
[*Lalla Rookh* (1817)]

POPE, Alexander (1688–1744)
'Blessed is the man who expects nothing, for
he shall never be disappointed,' was the
ninth beatitude which a man of wit (who like
a man of wit was a long time in gaol) added
to the eighth.
[Letter to William Fortescue,
1725]

DISCOVERY

ARCHIMEDES (c.287–212 BC)
Eureka!
I've got it!
[In Vitruvius Pollio, *De Architectura*]

KEATS, John (1795–1821)
Much have I travell'd in the realms of gold,
And many goodly states and kingdoms
seen ...

Then felt I like some watcher of the skies
When a new planet swims into his ken;
Or like stout Cortez when with eagle eyes
He star'd at the Pacific – and all his men
Look'd at each other with a wild surmise –
Silent, upon a peak in Darien.
['On First Looking into Chapman's Homer' (1816)]

SMILES, Samuel (1812–1904)
We often discover what will do, by finding
out what will not do; and probably he who

never made a mistake never made a
discovery.
[*Self-Help* (1859)]

**TEILHARD DE CHARDIN, Pierre
(1881–1955)**
*Rien ne vaut la peine d'être trouvé que ce qui n'a
jamais existé encore.*
Nothing is worth discovering except that
which has not yet existed.
[*La Vision du passé*]

See SCIENCE

DISTANCE

CAMPBELL, Thomas (1777–1844)
'Tis distance lends enchantment to the view,
And robes the mountain in its azure hue.
[*Pleasures of Hope* (1799)]

WHITE, Patrick (1912–1990)
Anyone who stares long enough into the
distance is bound to be mistaken for a
philosopher or mystic in the end.
[*Happy Valley* (1939)]

WORDSWORTH, William (1770–1850)
Sweetest melodies
Are those by distance made more sweet.
[*Personal Talk* (1807)]

DIVORCE

PARKER, Dorothy (1893–1967)
[Said of her husband on the day their divorce
became final]
Oh, don't worry about Alan ... Alan will
always land on somebody's feet.
[In J. Keats, *You Might As Well Live* (1970)]

**THORNDIKE, Dame Sybil
(1882–1976)**
[Replying to a query as to whether she had ever
considered divorce during her long marriage to Sir
Lewis Casson]
Divorce? Never. But murder often!
[Attr.]

WEST, Dame Rebecca (1892–1983)

If our divorce laws were improved, we could at least say that if marriage does nobody much good it does nobody any harm.

[*The Clarion*]

DIY

ANONYMOUS

Don't force it; get a larger hammer.

[Anthony's Law of Force]

Any tool when dropped, will roll into the least accessible corner of the workshop.

[Anthony's Law of the Workshop]

On the way to the corner, any dropped tool will first strike your toes.

[Corollary to Anthony's Law of the Workshop]

Interchangeable parts won't.

[Laws of Assembly]

Any product cut to length will be too short.

[Klipstein's Observation]

If you need four screws for the job, the first three are easy to find.

[The N-1 Law]

PROVERB

A bad workman always blames his tools.

See DESIGN

DOCUMENTATION

ANONYMOUS

If it should exist, it doesn't.

[Arnold's First Law of Documentation]

If it does exist, it's out of date.

[Arnold's Second Law of Documentation]

DOGS

BEERBOHM, Sir Max (1872–1956)

You will find that the woman who is really kind to dogs is always one who has failed to inspire sympathy in men.

[*Zuleika Dobson* (1911)]

BENNETT, Alan (1934–)

It's the one species I wouldn't mind seeing vanish from the face of the earth. I wish they were like the white rhino – six of them left in the Serengeti National Park, and all males.

[Attr.]

ELIOT, George (1819–1880)

Though, as we know, she was not fond of pets that must be held in the hands or trodden on, she was always attentive to the feelings of dogs, and very polite if she had to decline their advances.

[*Middlemarch* (1872)]

HUXLEY, Aldous (1894–1963)

To his dog, every man is Napoleon; hence the constant popularity of dogs.

[Attr.]

MACAULAY, Lord (1800–1859)

We were regaled by a dogfight … How odd that people of sense should find any pleasure in being accompanied by a beast who is always spoiling conversation.

[In Trevelyan, *Life and Letters of Macaulay* (1876)]

MUIR, Frank (1920–1998)

Dogs, like horses, are quadrupeds. That is to say, they have four rupeds, one at each corner, on which they walk.

[*You Can't Have Your Kayak and Heat It*, with Dennis Norden]

NASH, Ogden (1902–1971)

A door is what a dog is perpetually on the wrong side of.

['A Dog's Best Friend Is His Illiteracy' (1952)]

SPARROW, John (1906–1992)

That indefatigable and unsavoury engine of pollution, the dog.

[Letter to *The Times*, 1975]

STREATFIELD, Sir Geoffrey Hugh Benbow (1897–1978)

I loathe people who keep dogs. They are cowards who haven't got the guts to bite

people themselves.
[*A Madman's Diary*]

See ANIMALS; CHILDREN

DOUBT

AUSTEN, Jane (1775–1817)
Where so many hours have been spent in convincing myself that I am right, is there not some reason to fear I may be wrong?
[*Sense and Sensibility* (1811)]

BACON, Francis (1561–1626)
If a man will begin with certainties, he shall end in doubts; but if he will be content to begin with doubts, he shall end in certainties.
[*The Advancement of Learning* (1605)]

THE BIBLE (King James Version)
How long halt ye between two opinions?
[*I Kings*, 18:21]

O thou of little faith, wherefore didst thou doubt?
[*Matthew*, 14:31]

BLAKE, William (1757–1827)
He who Doubts from what he sees
Will neer Believe do what you Please.
If the Sun & Moon should doubt,
Theyd immediately Go out.
['Auguries of Innocence' (c. 1803)]

BORGES, Jorge Luis (1899–1986)
He conocido io que ignoran los griegos: la incertidumbre.
I have known what the Greeks knew not: uncertainty.
[*The Garden of Paths which Diverge* (1941)]

BOYD, William (1952–)
What now? What next? All these questions. All these doubts. So few certainties. But then I have taken new comfort and refuge in the doctrine that advises one not to seek tranquillity in certainty, but in permanently

suspended judgement.
[*Brazzaville Beach* (1990)]

BROWNING, Robert (1812–1889)
All we have gained then by our unbelief
Is a life of doubt diversified by faith,
For one of faith diversified by doubt:
We called the chess-board white, – we call it black.
['Bishop Blougram's Apology' (1855)]

BUTLER, Samuel (1835–1902)
My Lord, I do not believe. Help thou mine unbelief.
[*Samuel Butler's Notebooks* (1951)]

CHESTERTON, G.K. (1874–1936)
John Grubby, who was short and stout
And troubled with religious doubt,
Refused about the age of three
To sit upon the curate's knee.
[*Poems* (1915)]

DARROW, Clarence (1857–1938)
[Remark during the trial of John Scopes, 1925, for teaching evolution in school]
I do not consider it an insult but rather a compliment to be called an agnostic. I do not pretend to know where many ignorant men are sure – that is all that agnosticism means.
[Attr.]

DENT, Alan (1905–1978)
This is the tragedy of a man who could not make up his mind.
[Introduction to film *Hamlet*, 1948]

EMERSON, Ralph Waldo (1803–1882)
I am the doubter and the doubt,
And I the hymn the Brahmin sings.
['Brahma' (1867)]

HARDWICKE, Philip Yorke, Earl of (1690–1764)
[Referring to Dirleton's Doubts]
His doubts are better than most people's certainties.
[In Boswell, *The Life of Samuel Johnson* (1791)]

HUXLEY, Aldous (1894–1963)
Defined in psychological terms, a fanatic is a

man who consciously overcompensates a secret doubt.

[*Proper Studies* (1927)]

HUXLEY, T.H. (1825–1895)

I am too much of a sceptic to deny the possibility of anything.

[Letter to Herbert Spencer, 1886]

KORAN

There is no doubt in this book.

[Chapter 1]

LICHTENBERG, Georg (1742–1799)

Zweifle an allem wenigstens einmal, und wäre es auch der Satz: zweimal zwei ist vier.

Doubt everything at least once – even the proposition that two and two are four.

[*Miscellaneous Writings*]

NEWMAN, John Henry, Cardinal (1801–1890)

Ten thousand difficulties do not make one doubt.

[*Apologia pro Vita Sua* (1864)]

PIRSIG, Robert (1928–)

You are never dedicated to something you have complete confidence in. No one is fanatically shouting that the sun is going to rise tomorrow. They know it's going to rise tomorrow. When people are fanatically dedicated to political or religious faiths or any other kind of dogmas or goals, it's always because these dogmas or goals are in doubt.

[*Zen and the Art of Motorcycle Maintenance* (1974)]

TENNYSON, Alfred, Lord (1809–1892)

There lives more faith in honest doubt, Believe me, than in half the creeds.

[*In Memoriam A. H. H.* (1850)]

For nothing worthy proving can be proven, Nor yet disproven: wherefore thou be wise, Cleave ever to the sunnier side of doubt.

['The Ancient Sage' (1885)]

UNAMUNO, Miguel de (1864–1936)

Una fe que no duda es una fe muerta.

A faith which does not doubt is a dead faith.

[*La agonía del cristianismo* (1931)]

See UNCERTAINTY

DREAMS

BACON, Francis (1561–1626)

Dreams and predictions of astrology … ought to serve but for winter talk by the fireside.

[*Essays* (1625)]

BEDDOES, Thomas Lovell (1803–1849)

If there were dreams to sell, What would you buy? Some cost a passing bell; Some a light sigh, That shakes from Life's fresh crown Only a roseleaf down. If there were dreams to sell, Merry and sad to tell, And the crier rung the bell, What would you buy?

['Dream-Pedlary' (1851)]

BROWNE, Sir Thomas (1605–1682)

That children dream not in the first half year, that men dream not in some countries, are to me sick men's dreams, dreams out of the ivory gate, and visions before midnight.

[In S. Wilkin (ed.), *Sir Thomas Browne's Works* (1835)]

BUNN, Alfred (1796–1860)

I dreamt that I dwelt in marble halls, With vassals and serfs at my side.

[*The Bohemian Girl* (1843)]

CALDERÓN DE LA BARCA, Pedro (1600–1681)

Aun en sueños
no se pierde el hacer bien.
Even in dreams doing good is not wasted.

[*Life is a Dream* (1636)]

Pues veo estando dormido,
que sueñe estando despierto.
For I see, since I am asleep, that I dream while

I am awake.

[*Life is a Dream* (1636)]

CHUANG TSE (c.369–286 BC)

I do not know whether I was then a man
dreaming I was a butterfly, or whether I am
now a butterfly dreaming I am a man.

[*Chuang Tse* (1889)]

CLARKE, Arthur C. (1917–)

[Voice of computer HAL 2000]
Dr Chandra, will I dream?

[Film *2001, A Space Odyssey*, (1969)]

COLERIDGE, Mary (1861–1907)

Egypt's might is tumbled down
Down a-down the deeps of thought;
Greece is fallen and Troy town,
Glorious Rome hath lost her crown,
Venice' pride is nought.

But the dreams their children dreamed
Fleeting, unsubstantial, vain.
Shadowy as the shadows seemed
Airy nothing, as they deemed,
These remain.

[*Poems* (1894), 'Egypt's Might is Tumbled
Down']

DONNE, John (1572–1631)

So, if I dream I have you, I have you,
For, all our joys are but fantastical.

[*Elegies* (c. 1600)]

HERRICK, Robert (1591–1674)

With thousand such enchanting dreams, that
meet
To make sleep not so sound, as sweet.

[*Hesperides* (1648)]

LAWRENCE, T.E. (1888–1935)

All men dream: but not equally. Those who
dream by night in the dusty recesses of their
minds wake in the day to find that it was
vanity; but the dreamers of the day are
dangerous men, for they may act their dream
with open eyes, to make it possible.

[*The Seven Pillars of Wisdom* (1926)]

MILLER, Arthur (1915–)

Nobody dast blame this man. A salesman is

got to dream, boy. It comes with the territory.

[*Death of a Salesman* (1949)]

MONTAIGNE, Michel de (1533–1592)

*Ceux qui ont apparié notre vie á un songe, ont eu de
la raison, á l'aventure plus qu'ils ne pensaient …
Nous veillons dormants, et veillants dormons.*
Those who have compared our life to a
dream were, by chance, more right than they
thought … We are awake while sleeping, and
sleeping while awake.

[*Essais* (1580)]

PATTEN, Brian (1946–)

Sink then dreamer into what might have
been!

['Lethargy']

POE, Edgar Allan (1809–1849)

All that we see or seem
Is but a dream within a dream.

['A Dream within a Dream' (1849)]

ROSTAND, Edmond (1868–1918)

*Le seul rêve intéresse,
Vivre sans rêve, qu'est-ce?
Et j'aime la Princesse
Lointaine.*
Only dreaming is of interest. What is life,
without dreams? And I love the Far-away
Princess.

[*La Princesse Lointaine*
(1895)]

SHAKESPEARE, William (1564–1616)

O God, I could be bounded in a nutshell and
count myself a king of infinite space, were it
not that I have bad dreams.

[*Hamlet*, II.ii]

O, I have pass'd a miserable night,
So full of fearful dreams, of ugly sights,
That, as I am a Christian faithful man,
I would not spend another such a night
Though 'twere to buy a world of happy
days –
So full of dismal terror was the time!

[*Richard III*, I.iv]

We are such stuff
As dreams are made on; and our little life

Is rounded with a sleep.

[*The Tempest*, IV.i]

Weary with toil, I haste me to my bed,
The dear repose for limbs with travel tired;
But then begins a journey in my head
To work my mind when body's work's
expired.

[Sonnet 27]

SMITH, Alexander (1830–1867)

Looking into a dream is like looking into the
interior of a watch; you see the processes at
work by which results are obtained. A man
thus becomes his own eavesdropper, he
plays the spy on himself. Hope and fear, and
the other passions, are all active; but the
activity is uncontrolled by the will, and in
remembering dreams one has the somewhat
peculiar feeling of being one's own spiritual
anatomist.

[*On Dreams and Dreaming*]

TENNYSON, Alfred, Lord (1809–1892)

Dreams are true while they last, and do we
not live in dreams?

['The Higher Pantheism' (1867)]

VIRGIL (70–19 BC)

Sunt geminae Somni portae; quarum altera fertur
Cornea, qua veris facilis datur exitus umbris,
Altera candenti perfecta nitens elephanto,
Sed falsa ad caelum mittunt insomnia Manes.
Two gates the silent house of Sleep adorn;
Of polished ivory this, that of transparent horn:
True visions through transparent horn arise;
Through polished ivory pass deluding lies.

[*Aeneid*]

YEATS, W.B. (1865–1939)

In dreams begins responsibility.

[*Responsibilities* (1914)]

See BED; SLEEP

DRESS

AESOP (6th century BC)

It is not only fine feathers that make fine

birds.

['The Jay and the Peacock']

ASHFORD, Daisy (1881–1972)

You look rather rash my dear your colors
dont quite match your face.

[*The Young Visiters* (1919)]

BONGAY, Amy

[Commenting on the fact that the fashion industry
had begun to find supermodels too demanding]
It's a terrible sign. It will be the death of this
profession if designers start using real
people on the catwalks and in their
advertising.

[*Daily Mail*, 1995]

CHANEL, Coco (1883–1971)

Fashion is architecture: it is a matter of
proportions.

[In Haedrich, *Coco Chanel, Her Life, Her Secrets*
(1971)]

[On Dior's New Look]
These are clothes by a man who doesn't
know women, never had one and dreams of
being one.

[*Scotland on Sunday*, 1995]

CLOUGH, Arthur Hugh (1819–1861)

Petticoats up to the knees, or even, it might
be, above them,
Matching their lily-white legs with the
clothes that they trod in the wash-tub!

[*The Bothie of Tober-na-Vuolich* (1848)]

CURIE, Marie (1867–1934)

[Referring to a wedding dress]
I have no dress except the one I wear every
day. If you are going to be kind enough to
give me one, please let it be practical and
dark so that I can put it on afterwards to go
to the laboratory.

[Letter to a friend, 1894]

DARROW, Clarence (1857–1938)

I go to a better tailor than any of you and
pay more for my clothes. The only difference
is that you probably don't sleep in yours.

[In E. Fuller, *2500 Anecdotes*]

DICKENS, Charles (1812–1870)

Any man may be in good spirits and good temper when he's well drest. There ain't much credit in that.

[*Martin Chuzzlewit* (1844)]

If you could see my legs when I take my boots off, you'd form some idea of what unrequited affection is.

[*Dombey and Son* (1848)]

EBNER-ESCHENBACH, Marie von (1830–1916)

'Himmel!', ruft er, 'wenn es Kleider sind, die uns in der Welt möglich machen, wie hoch müssen wir den halten, der sie verfertigt!'

'Goodness,' he cried, 'if it is our clothes which fit us for this world, in what high esteem must we hold those who make them!'.

[*The Two Countesses*, 'Countess Muschi' (1884)]

EDWARD VII (1841–1910)

I thought everyone must know that a short jacket is always worn with a silk hat at a private view in the morning.

[In Sir P. Magnus, *Edward VII*]

EMERSON, Ralph Waldo (1803–1882)

I have heard with admiring submission the experience of the lady who declared that 'the sense of being well-dressed gives a feeling of inward tranquillity which religion is powerless to bestow.'

[*Letters and Social Aims* (1875)]

[Of the English]
They think him the best dressed man, whose dress is so fit for his use that you cannot notice or remember to describe it.

[*English Traits* (1856)]

The Frenchman invented the ruffle, the Englishman added the shirt.

[*English Traits* (1856)]

It is only when the mind and character slumber that the dress can be seen.

[*Letters and Social Aims* (1875)]

FARQUHAR, George (1678–1707)

A lady, if undrest at Church, looks silly,

One cannot be devout in dishabilly.

[*The Stage Coach* (1704)]

FORBES, Miss C.F. (1817–1911)

The sense of being well-dressed gives a feeling of inward tranquillity which religion is powerless to bestow.

[In Emerson, *Social Aims* (1876)]

GASKELL, Elizabeth (1810–1865)

[The Cranford ladies'] dress is very independent of fashion; as they observe, 'What does it signify how we dress here at Cranford, where everybody knows us?' And if they go from home, their reason is equally cogent, 'What does it signify how we dress here, where nobody knows us?'.

[*Cranford* (1853)]

HERRICK, Robert (1591–1674)

When as in silks my Julia goes,
Then, then (me thinks) how sweetly flowes
That liquefaction of her clothes.
Next, when I cast mine eyes and see
That brave Vibration each way free;
O how that glittering taketh me!

[*Hesperides* (1648)]

A sweet disorder in the dresse
Kindles in cloathes a wantonnesse:
A Lawne about the shoulders thrown
Into a fine distraction …

A winning wave (deserving Note)
In the tempestuous petticote:
A carelesse shooe-string, in whose tye
I see a wilde civility:
Doe more bewitch me, than when Art
Is too precise in every part.

['Delight in Disorder' (1648)]

HEWETT, Dorothy (1923–)

Gentlemen may remove any garment consistent with decency.
Ladies may remove any garment consistent with charm.

['Beneath the Arches']

JONSON, Ben (1572–1637)

Still to be neat, still to be drest,

As you were going to a feast;
Still to be powder'd, still perfum'd,
Lady, it is to be presumed,
Though art's hid causes are not found,
All is not sweet, all is not sound.
Give me a look, give me a face,
That makes simplicity a grace;
Robes loosely flowing, hair as free:
Such sweet neglect more taketh me,
Than all the adulteries of art;
They strike mine eyes, but not my heart.

[*Epicoene* (1609)]

JULIA (39 BC–AD 14)

[On being complimented by her father on the modest dress she was wearing that day]
Today I dressed to meet my father's eyes;
yesterday it was for my husband's.

[In Macrobius, *Saturnalia*]

KAUFMAN, Jean-Claude

The sock is a highly sensitive conjugal object.

[*The Observer*, 1992]

LOOS, Anita (1893–1981)

You have got to be a Queen to get away with a hat like that.

[*Gentlemen Prefer Blondes* (1925)]

MASTERS, John (1914–)

Join a Highland regiment, me boy. The kilt is an unrivalled garment for fornication and diarrhoea.

[*Bugles and a Tiger*]

MOORE, Brian (1921–1999)

So the years hang like old clothes, forgotten in the wardrobe of our minds. Did I wear that? Who was I then?

[*No Other Life* (1993)]

NASH, Ogden (1902–1971)

There was a young belle of old Natchez
Whose garments were always in patchez.
When comment arose
On the state of her clothes,
She drawled, When Ah itchez, Ah scratchez!

[*I'm a Stranger Here Myself* (1935)]

Sure, deck your lower limbs in pants;
Yours are the limbs, my sweeting.

You look divine as you advance –
Have you seen yourself retreating?

['What's the Use?' (1940)]

O'ROURKE, P.J. (1947–)

The only really firm rule of taste about cross dressing is that neither sex should ever wear anything they haven't yet figured out how to go to the bathroom in.

[*Modern Manners* (1984)]

PARKER, Dorothy (1893–1967)

Where's the man could ease a heart,
Like a satin gown?

['The Satin Dress' (1937)]

Brevity is the soul of lingerie.

[In Woollcott, *While Rome Burns* (1934)]

PARTON, Dolly (1946–)

You'd be surprised how much it costs to look this cheap.

[In Carole McKenzie, *Quotable Women* (1992)]

RIMBAUD, Arthur (1854–1891)

Je m'en allais, les poings dans mes poches crevées;
Mon paletot aussi devenait idéal.

I was walking along, fists in my torn pockets;
my overcoat also was entering the realm of the ideal.

['Ma Bohème' (1870)]

SAKI (1870–1916)

His shoes exhaled the right soupçon of harness-room; his socks compelled one's attention without losing one's respect.

[*The Chronicles of Clovis* (1911)]

SURTEES, R.S. (1805–1864)

No one knows how ungentlemanly he can look, until he has seen himself in a shocking bad hat.

[*Mr Facey Romford's Hounds* (1865)]

SWIFT, Jonathan (1667–1745)

She wears her clothes, as if they were thrown on with a pitchfork.

[*Polite Conversation* (1738)]

TAYLOR, John (20th century)

The only man who really needs a tail coat is a

man with a hole in his trousers.

[*The Observer*, 'Shouts and Murmurs']

THOREAU, Henry David (1817–1862)
Beware of all enterprises that require new clothes.

[*Walden* (1854)]

WATTS, Isaac (1674–1748)
The tulip and the butterfly
Appear in gayer coats than I:
Let me be dressed fine as I will,
Flies, worms, and flowers, exceed me still.

['Against Pride in Clothes' (1715)]

WHITEHORN, Katherine (1926–)
Hats divide generally into three classes: offensive hats, defensive hats, and shrapnel.

[*Shouts and Murmurs* (1963)]

WILDE, Oscar (1854–1900)
A well-tied tie is the first serious step in life.

[*A Woman of No Importance* (1893)]

The only way to atone for being occasionally a little over-dressed is by being always absolutely over-educated.

[*The Chameleon*, 1894]

WODEHOUSE, P.G. (1881–1975)
The Right Hon was a tubby little chap who looked as if he had been poured into his clothes and had forgotten to say 'When!'.

[*Very Good, Jeeves* (1930)]

DRUNKENNESS

BYRON, Lord (1788–1824)
Man, being reasonable, must get drunk;
The best of life is but intoxication:
Glory, the grape, love, gold, in these are sunk
The hopes of all men, and of every nation.

[*Don Juan* (1824)]

CHAUCER, Geoffrey (c.1340–1400)
For dronkenesse is verray sepulture
Of mannes wit and his discrecioun.

[*The Canterbury Tales* (1387)]

CHURCHILL, Randolph (1911–1968)
[In a letter to a hostess after ruining her dinner party with one of his displays of drunken rudeness]
I should never be allowed out in private.

[In B. Roberts, *Randolph: a Study of Churchill's Son* (1984)]

CHURCHILL, Sir Winston (1874–1965)
[To Bessie Braddock MP who told him he was drunk]
And you, madam, are ugly. But I shall be sober in the morning.

[Attr.]

DICKENS, Charles (1812–1870)
It's my opinion, sir, that this meeting is drunk, sir.

[*The Pickwick Papers* (1837)]

LIGHTNER, Candy (1946–)
Death by drunken driving is a socially acceptable form of homicide.

[*San José Mercury*, April 1981]

FRANKLIN, Benjamin (1706–1790)
There are more old drunkards than old doctors.

[Attr.]

HALIFAX, Lord (1633–1695)
It is a piece of Arrogance to dare to be drunk, because a Man sheweth himself without a Vail.

['Drunkenness' (1750)]

JAMES, William (1842–1910)
If merely 'feeling good' could decide, drunkenness would be the supremely valid human experience.

[*Varieties of Religious Experience* (1902)]

JOHNSON, Samuel (1709–1784)
A man who exposes himself when he is intoxicated, has not the art of getting drunk.

[In Boswell, *The Life of Samuel Johnson* (1791)]

JUNELL, Thomas
The Finns have a very different alcohol culture from other European countries. Basically, it's nothing to do with socialising – it's about getting drunk.

[*Daily Mail*,1996]

PROVERB

Qu'il faut á chaque mois,
Du moins s'enivrer une fois.

Every month one should get drunk at least once.

[French proverb]

RUSSELL, Bertrand (1872–1970)

Drunkenness is temporary suicide: the happiness that it brings is merely negative, a momentary cessation of unhappiness.

[*The Conquest of Happiness* (1930)]

SENECA (c.4 BC–AD 65)

Drunkenness doesn't create vices, but it brings them to the fore.

[*Letters to Lucilius*, 100 A.D.]

SQUIRE, Sir J.C. (1884–1958)

But I'm not so think as you drunk I am.

['Ballade of Soporific Absorption' (1931)]

TYNAN, Kenneth (1927–1980)

What, when drunk, one sees in other women, one sees in Garbo sober.

[*The Sunday Times*, 1963]

See ALCOHOL

DUTY

ANONYMOUS

Straight is the line of Duty
Curved is the line of Beauty
Follow the first and thou shallt see
The second ever following thee.

BIERCE, Ambrose (1842–c.1914)

Duty: That which sternly impels us in the direction of profit, along the line of desire.

[*The Enlarged Devil's Dictionary* (1967)]

COBBETT, William (1762–1835)

From a very early age, I had imbibed the opinion, that it was every man's duty to do all that lay in his power to leave his country as good as he had found it.

[*Political Register*, 1832]

CORNEILLE, Pierre (1606–1684)

Faites votre devoir et laissez faire aux dieux.

Do your duty, and put yourself into the hands of the gods.

[*Horace* (1640)]

ELIOT, George (1819–1880)

She, stirred somewhat beyond her wont, and taking as her text the three words which have been used so often as the inspiring trumpet-calls of men – the words God, Immortality, Duty – pronounced, with terrible earnestness, how inconceivable was the first, how unbelievable the second, and yet how peremptory and absolute the third. Never, perhaps, have the sterner accents affirmed the sovereignty of impersonal and unrecompensing Law.

[In F.W.H. Myers, 'George Eliot' (1881)]

EMERSON, Ralph Waldo (1803–1882)

So nigh is grandeur to our dust,
So near is God to man,
When Duty whispers low, Thou must,
The youth replies, I can.

[*May-Day* (1867)]

GIBBON, Edward (1737–1794)

Dr Winchester well remembered that he had a salary to receive, and only forgot that he had a duty to perform.

[*Memoirs of My Life and Writings* (1796)]

GILBERT, W.S. (1836–1911)

The question is, had he not been a thing of beauty,
Would she be swayed by quite as keen a sense of duty?

[*The Pirates of Penzance* (1880)]

GOETHE (1749–1832)

Du kannst, denn du sollst!
You can, for you ought to!

['An eighth' (1796); written with Schiller]

GRANT, Ulysses S. (1822–1885)

No personal consideration should stand in the way of performing a public duty.

[Note on letter, 1875]

HOOPER, Ellen Sturgis (1816–1841)

I slept, and dreamed that life was Beauty;
I woke, and found that life was Duty.

['Beauty and Duty' (1840)]

IBSEN, Henrik (1828–1906)

What's a man's first duty? The answer's brief:
To be himself.

[*Peer Gynt* (1867)]

JOHNSON, Samuel (1709–1784)

It is our first duty to serve society, and, after
we have done that, we may attend wholly to
the salvation of our own souls. A youthful
passion for abstracted devotion should not
be encouraged.

[In Boswell, *The Life of Samuel Johnson* (1791)]

LEE, Robert E. (1807–1870)

Duty then is the sublimest word in our
language. Do your duty in all things. You
cannot do more. You should never wish to do
less.

[Inscription in the Hall of Fame]

LINCOLN, Abraham (1809–1865)

Let us have faith that right makes might; and
in that faith let us to the end, dare to do our
duty as we understand it.

[Speech, 1860]

MILNER, Alfred (1854–1925)

If we believe a thing to be bad, and if we
have a right to prevent it, it is our duty to try
to prevent it and to damn the consequences.

[Speech, 1909]

NELSON, Lord (1758–1805)

[Nelson's last signal at the Battle of Trafalgar, 1805]
England expects every man to do his duty.

[In Southey, *The Life of Nelson* (1860)]

PEACOCK, Thomas Love (1785–1866)

Sir, I have quarrelled with my wife; and a man
who has quarrelled with his wife is absolved
from all duty to his country.

[*Nightmare Abbey* (1818)]

SALISBURY, Lord (1830–1903)

Our first duty is towards the people of this
country, to maintain their interests and their
rights; our second duty is to all humanity.

[Speech, 1896]

SHAKESPEARE, William (1564–1616)

Every subject's duty is the King's; but every
subject's soul is his own.

[*Henry V*, IV.i]

SHAW, George Bernard (1856–1950)

When a stupid man is doing something he is
ashamed of, he always declares that it is his
duty.

[*Caesar and Cleopatra* (1901)]

**STEVENSON, Robert Louis
(1850–1894)**

There is no duty we so much underrate as
the duty of being happy.

[*Virginibus Puerisque* (1881)]

TENNYSON, Alfred, Lord (1809–1892)

O hard, when love and duty clash!

[*The Princess* (1847)]

WASHINGTON, George (1732–1799)

To persevere in one's duty and be silent is
the best answer to calumny.

[*Moral Maxims*]

WILDE, Oscar (1854–1900)

Duty is what one expects of others, it is not
what one does oneself.

[*A Woman of No Importance* (1893)]

E

ECONOMICS

BAGEHOT, Walter (1826–1877)
No real English gentleman, in his secret soul, was ever sorry for the death of a political economist.

['The First Edinburgh Reviewers' (1858)]

BLAIR, Tony (1953–)
I want Britain to be a stake-holder economy where everyone has a chance to get on and succeed, where there is a clear sense of national purpose and where we leave behind some of the battles between Left and Right which really are not relevant in the new global economy of today.

[Speech in Singapore, 1996]

CARLYLE, Thomas (1795–1881)
[Of Political Economics]
And the Social Science, – not a 'gay science', … no, a dreary, desolate, and indeed quite abject and distressing one; what we might call …the dismal science.

[Latter-Day Pamphlets (1850)]

DOUGLAS-HOME, Sir Alec (1903–1995)
When I have to read economic documents I have to have a box of matches and start moving them into position to illustrate and simplify the points to myself.

[Interview in The Observer, 1962]

EDEN, Anthony (1897–1977)
Everybody is always in favour of general economy and particular expenditure.

[The Observer, 1956]

EISENHOWER, Dwight D. (1890–1969)
Every gun that is made, every warship launched, every rocket fired signifies, in the final sense, a theft from those who hunger and are not fed, those who are cold and are not clothed. This world in arms is not spending money alone. It is spending the sweat of its labourers, the genius of its scientists, the hopes of its children.

[Speech, 1953]

FRIEDMAN, Milton (1912–)
There's no such thing as a free lunch.

[Title of book]

GALBRAITH, J.K. (1908–)
Economics is extremely useful as a form of employment for economists.

[Attr.]

If all else fails, immortality can always be assured by spectacular error.

[Attr.]

GEORGE, Eddie (1938–)
There are three kinds of economist. Those who can count and those who can't.

[The Observer Review, 1996]

HELLER, Walter (1915–)
[Definition of an economist]
Someone who can't see something working in practice without asking whether it would work in theory.

[Attr.]

HENDERSON, Leon (1895–1986)
Having a little inflation is like being a little pregnant.

[Attr.]

JONES, Barry Owen (1932–)
Academic economists have about the status and reliability of astrologers or the readers of Tarot cards. If the medical profession was as lacking in resources as the economics we would not have advanced very far beyond the provision of splints for broken arms.

[In John Wilkes (ed.), The Future of Work]

KEYNES, John Maynard (1883–1946)
But this long run is a misleading guide to current affairs. In the long run we are all dead. Economists set themselves too easy, too useless a task if in tempestuous seasons

they can only tell us that when the storm is long past the ocean will be flat again.

[*A Tract on Monetary Reform* (1923)]

It is better that a man should tyrannize over his bank balance than over his fellow-citizens.

[*The General Theory of Employment, Interest and Money* (1936)]

Practical men, who believe themselves to be quite exempt from any intellectual influences, are usually the slaves of some defunct economist. Madmen in authority, who hear voices in the air, are distilling their frenzy from some academic scribbler of a few years back.

[*The General Theory of Employment, Interest and Money* (1936)]

LEVIN, Bernard (1928–)
Inflation in the Sixties was a nuisance to be endured, like varicose veins or French foreign policy.

[*The Pendulum Years* (1970)]

MACLEOD, Iain (1913–1970)
We now have the worst of both worlds – not just inflation on the one side or stagnation on the other side, but both of them together. We have a sort of 'stagflation' situation.

[Speech, 1965]

MALTHUS, Thomas Robert (1766–1834)
Population, when unchecked, increases in a geometrical ratio. Subsistence only increases in an arithmetical ratio.

[*Essay on the Principle of Population* (1798)]

MELLON, Andrew William (1855–1937)
A nation is not in danger of financial disaster merely because it owes itself money.

[Attr.]

ROOSEVELT, Franklin Delano (1882–1945)
We have always known that heedless self-interest was bad morals; we know now that it

is bad economics.

[First Inaugural Address, 1933]

RUTSKOI, Alexander (1947–)
The dollar is Russia's national currency now, the rouble is just a sweetie paper. We've handed our sword to America.

[*Newsweek*, 1994]

SCHUMACHER, E.F. (1911–1977)
Small is Beautiful. A study of economics as if people mattered.

[Title of book, 1973]

SELLAR, Walter (1898–1951) and **YEATMAN, Robert Julian (1897–1968)**
The National Debt is a very Good Thing and it would be dangerous to pay it off, for fear of Political Economy.

[*1066 And All That* (1930)]

SHAW, George Bernard (1856–1950)
Whether you think Jesus was God or not, you must admit that he was a first-rate political economist.

[*Androcles and the Lion* (1915)]

If all economists were laid end to end, they would not reach a conclusion.

[Attr.]

TRUMAN, Harry S. (1884–1972)
It's a recession when your neighbour loses his job; it's a depression when you lose your own.

[*The Observer*, 1958]

WILSON, Harold (1916–1995)
It does not mean, of course, that the pound here in Britain, in your pocket or purse or in your bank, has been devalued.

[Television broadcast, 1967]

YELTSIN, Boris (1931–)
I am for the market, not for the bazaar.

[*The Times*, 1992]

EDITING

ALLEN, Fred (1894–1956)
[Remark to writers who had heavily edited one of

his scripts]

Where were you fellows when the paper was blank?

[Attr.]

AUBREY, John (1626–1697)

He [Shakespeare] was wont to say that he 'never blotted out a line of his life'; said Ben Jonson, 'I wish he had blotted out a thousand.'

[*Brief Lives* (c. 1693)]

BOILEAU-DESPRÉAUX, Nicolas (1636–1711)

Si j'écris quatre mots, j'en effacerai trois.

If I write four words, I shall strike out three.

[*Satires* (1666)]

CHANDLER, Raymond (1888–1959)

Would you convey my compliments to the purist who reads your proofs and tell him or her that I write in a sort of broken-down patois which is something like the way a Swiss waiter talks, and that when I split an infinitive, God damn it, I split it so it will stay split.

[Letter to Edward Weeks, his English publisher, 1947]

CHEEVER, John (1912–1982)

Trust your editor, and you'll sleep on straw.

[In Susan Cheever, *Home Before Dark* (1984)]

HUBBARD, Elbert (1856–1915)

Editor: a person employed by a newspaper whose business it is to separate the wheat from the chaff and to see that the chaff is printed.

[*A Thousand and One Epigrams* (1911)]

JOHNSON, Samuel (1709–1784)

Read over your compositions, and where ever you meet with a passage which you think is particularly fine, strike it out.

[In Boswell, *The Life of Samuel Johnson* (1791)]

MAYER, Louis B. (1885–1957)

[Comment to writers who had objected to changes in their work]

The number one book of the ages was written by a committee, and it was called The Bible.

[In Halliwell, *The Filmgoer's Book of Quotes* (1973)]

PASCAL, Blaise (1623–1662)

Je n'ai fait celle-ci plus longue que parce que je n'ai pas eu le loisir de la faire plus courte.

I have made this letter longer only because I have not had time to make it shorter.

[*Lettres Provinciales* (1657)]

ROSS, Harold W. (1892–1951)

[Upon founding *The New Yorker* in 1925]

The New Yorker will not be edited for the old lady from Dubuque.

[Remark]

TWAIN, Mark (1835–1910)

As to the Adjective: when in doubt, strike it out.

[*Pudd'nhead Wilson's Calendar* (1894)]

See BOOKS; NEWSPAPERS; PUBLISHING

EDUCATION

ADE, George (1866–1944)

'Whom are you?' said he, for he had been to night school.

[Attr.]

AMIS, Kingsley (1922–1995)

[On 'the delusion' that thousands of young people were capable of benefiting from university but had somehow failed to find their way there]

I wish I could have a little tape-and-loudspeaker arrangement sewn into the binding of this magazine, to be triggered off by the light reflected from the reader's eyes on to this part of the page, and set to bawl out at several bels: MORE WILL MEAN WORSE.

[*Encounter*, 1960]

ARISTOTLE (384–322 BC)

The roots of education are bitter, but the fruit is sweet.

[In Diogenes Laertius, *Lives of Philosophers*]

ARNOLD, Thomas (1795–1842)

My object will be, if possible, to form

Christian men, for Christian boys I can scarcely hope to make.

[Letter, 1828]

ASCHAM, Roger (1515–1568)

I said … how, and why, young children were sooner allured by love, than driven by beating, to attain good learning.

[*The Scholemaster* (1570)]

BACON, Francis (1561–1626)

Reading maketh a full man; conference a ready man; and writing an exact man.

[*Essays* (1625)]

BIERCE, Ambrose (1842–c.1914)

Education: That which discloses to the wise and disguises from the foolish their lack of understanding.

[*The Cynic's Word Book* (1906)]

BROUGHAM, Lord Henry (1778–1868)

Education makes a people easy to lead, but difficult to drive; easy to govern, but impossible to enslave.

[Attr.]

BUCHAN, John (1875–1940)

To live for a time close to great minds is the best kind of education.

[*Memory Hold the Door*]

CARROLL, Lewis (1832–1898)

'Reeling and Writhing, of course, to begin with,' the Mock Turtle replied; 'and then the different branches of Arithmetic – Ambition, Distraction, Uglification, and Derision.'

[*Alice's Adventures in Wonderland* (1865)]

'That's the reason they're called lessons,' the Gryphon remarked: 'because they lessen from day to day.'

[*Alice's Adventures in Wonderland* (1865)]

CHESTERTON, G.K. (1874–1936)

Education is simply the soul of a society as it passes from one generation to another.

[*The Observer*, 1924]

CODY, Henry John (1868–1951)

Education is casting false pearls before real swine.

[Attr.]

COOPER, Roger

[After five years in an Iranian prison]
I can say that anyone who, like me, has been educated in English public schools and served in the ranks of the British Army is quite at home in a Third World prison.

[*Newsweek*, 1991]

COWARD, Sir Noël (1899–1973)

I've over-educated myself in all the things I shouldn't have known at all.

[*Mild Oats* (1931)]

D'SOUZA, Dinesh (1961–)

If education cannot help separate truth from falsehood, beauty from vulgarity, right from wrong, then what can it teach us?

[*Atlantic Monthly*, 1991]

DICKENS, Charles (1812–1870)

Now, what I want is, Facts. Teach these boys and girls nothing but Facts. Facts alone are wanted in life. Plant nothing else, and root out everything else … Stick to Facts, sir!

[*Hard Times* (1854)]

DIOGENES (THE CYNIC) (c.400–325 BC)

Education is something that tempers the young and consoles the old, gives wealth to the poor and adorns the rich.

[In Diogenes Laertius, *Lives of Eminent Philosophers*]

DISRAELI, Benjamin (1804–1881)

Upon the education of the people of this country the fate of this country depends.

[Speech, 1874]

DRYDEN, John (1631–1700)

By education most have been misled;
So they believe, because they so were bred.
The priest continues what the nurse began,
And thus the child imposes on the man.

[*The Hind and the Panther* (1687)]

EMERSON, Ralph Waldo (1803–1882)

I pay the schoolmaster, but 'tis the schoolboys that educate my son.

[*Journals*]

HAZLITT, William (1778–1830)

It is better to be able neither to read nor write than to be able to do nothing else.

[*The Edinburgh Magazine*, 1818, 'On the Ignorance of the Learned']

HELVÉTIUS, Claude Adrien (1715–1771)

L'éducation nous faisait ce que nous sommes.
Education made us what we are.

[*De l'esprit* (1758)]

HUXLEY, Aldous (1894–1963)

The solemn foolery of scholarship for scholarship's sake.

[*The Perennial Philosophy* (1945)]

JOHNSON, Samuel (1709–1784)

Example is always more efficacious than precept.

[*Rasselas* (1759)]

All intellectual improvement arises from leisure.

[In Boswell, *The Life of Samuel Johnson* (1791)]

KANT, Immanuel (1724–1804)

Der Mensch ist das einzige Geschöpf, das erzogen werden muss.
Man is the only creature which must be educated.

[*On Pedagogy* (1803)]

KRAUS, Karl (1874–1936)

Bildung ist das, was die meisten empfangen, viele weitergeben und wenige haben.
Education is what most people receive, many pass on and few actually have.

[*Pro domo et mundo* (1912)]

LODGE, David (1935–)

Four times, under our educational rules, the human pack is shuffled and cut – at eleven-plus, sixteen-plus, eighteen-plus and twenty-plus – and happy is he who comes top of the deck on each occasion, but especially the last. This is called Finals, the very name of which implies that nothing of importance can happen after it. The British postgraduate student is a lonely forlorn soul … for whom nothing had been real since the Big Push.

[*Changing Places* (1975)]

MCIVER, Charles D. (1860–1906)

When you educate a man you educate an individual; when you educate a woman you educate a whole family.

[Address at women's college]

MELBOURNE, Lord (1779–1848)

[To the Queen]
I don't know, Ma'am, why they make all this fuss about education; none of the Pagets can read or write, and they get on well enough.

[Attr.]

MILTON, John (1608–1674)

… the right path of a vertuous and noble Education, laborious indeed at the first ascent, but else so smooth, so green, so full of goodly prospect, and melodious sounds on every side, that the harp of Orpheus was not more charming.

[*Of Education: To Master Samuel Hartlib* (1644)]

MORAVIA, Alberto (1907–1990)

The ratio of literacy to illiteracy is constant, but nowadays the illiterates can read and write.

[*The Observer*, 1979]

ROGERS, Will (1879–1935)

Instead of giving money to found colleges to promote learning, why don't they pass a constitutional amendment prohibiting anybody from learning anything? If it works as good as the Prohibition one did, why, in five years we would have the smartest race of people on earth.

ROUSSEAU, Jean-Jacques (1712–1778)

On n'est curieux qu'à proportion qu'on est instruit.
One is only curious in proportion to one's level of education.

[*Émile ou De l'éducation* (1762)]

RUSKIN, John (1819–1900)
To make your children capable of honesty is
the beginning of education.
[*Time and Tide by Weare and Tyne* (1867)]

SCOTT, Alexander (1920–)
I tellt ye
I tellt ye.
[*Scotched*, 'Scotch Education']

SCOTT, Sir Walter (1771–1832)
All men who have turned out worth
anything have had the chief hand in their
own education.
[*Letter to J.G. Lockhart*, 1830]

SITWELL, Osbert (1892–1969)
My education [takes place] during the
holidays from Eton.
[*Who's Who* (1929)]

SKINNER, B.F. (1904–1990)
Education is what survives when what has
been learned has been forgotten.
[*New Scientist*, 1964]

Indeed one of the ultimate advantages of an
education is simply coming to the end of it.
[*The Technology of Teaching* (1968)]

SMITH, Adam (1723–1790)
There are no public institutions for the
education of women, and there is accordingly
nothing useless, absurd, or fantastical in the
common course of their education.
[*Wealth of Nations* (1776)]

SPARK, Muriel (1918–)
To me education is a leading out of what is
already there in the pupil's soul. To Miss
Mackay it is a putting in of something that is
not there, and that is not what I call
education, I call it intrusion.
[*The Prime of Miss Jean Brodie* (1961)]

SPENCER, Herbert (1820–1903)
Education has for its object the formation of
character.
[*Social Statics* (1850)]

STEELE, Sir Richard (1672–1729)
The truth of it is, the first rudiments of

education are given very indiscreetly by
most parents.
[*The Tatler*, 173]

STOCKS, Mary, Baroness (1891–1975)
Today we enjoy a social structure which
offers equal opportunity in education. It is
indeed regrettably true that there is no equal
opportunity to take advantage of the equal
opportunity.
[*Still More Commonplace* (1973)]

TREVELYAN, G.M. (1876–1962)
Education … has produced a vast population
able to read but unable to distinguish what
is worth reading.
[*English Social History* (1942)]

USTINOV, Sir Peter (1921–)
People at the top of the tree are those
without qualifications to detain them at the
bottom.
[Attr.]

WHITE, Patrick (1912–1990)
'I dunno,' Arthur said. 'I forget what I was
taught. I only remember what I've learnt.'
[*The Solid Mandala* (1966)]

WILDE, Oscar (1854–1900)
Education is an admirable thing, but it is well
to remember from time to time that nothing
that is worth knowing can be taught.
['The Critic as Artist' (1891)]

See EXAMINATIONS; KNOWLEDGE;
    LEARNING; SCHOOL; TEACHERS;
    UNIVERSITY

EGOISM

ADLER, Alfred (1870–1937)
[On hearing that an egocentric had fallen in love]
Against whom?
[Attr.]

ALI, Muhammad (1942–)
I am the greatest.
[Catchphrase]

I'm the greatest golfer. I just have not played yet.

[Attr.]

BACON, Francis (1561–1626)

[English philosopher, essayist, politician, lawyer and courtier]

It was prettily devised of Aesop, 'The fly sat upon the axletree of the chariot-wheel and said, what a dust do I raise.'

['Of Vain-Glory' (1625)]

BARNES, Peter (1931–)

I know I am God because when I pray to him I find I'm talking to myself.

[The Ruling Class (1968)]

BEERBOHM, Sir Max (1872–1956)

To give an accurate and exhaustive account of that period would need a far less brilliant pen than mine.

[Attr.]

BIERCE, Ambrose (1842–c.1914)

Egotist: A person of low taste, more interested in himself than in me.

[The Cynic's Word Book (1906)]

BULMER-THOMAS, Ivor (1905–)

[Of Harold Wilson]

If ever he went to school without any boots it was because he was too big for them.

[Remark, 1949]

BUTLER, Samuel (1835–1902)

The advantage of doing one's praising for oneself is that one can lay it on so thick and exactly in the right places.

[The Way of All Flesh (1903)]

CHAMFORT, Nicolas (1741–1794)

Quelqu'un disait d'un homme très personnel; il brûlerait votre maison pour se faire cuire deux oeufs. Someone said of a great egotist: 'He would burn your house down to cook himself a couple of eggs.'

[Caractères et anecdotes]

CHURCHILL, Charles (1731–1764)

[Of Thomas Franklin, Professor of Greek, Cambridge]

He sicken'd at all triumphs but his own.

[The Rosciad (1761)]

CICERO (106–43 BC)

O fortunatam natam me consule Romam! O happy Rome, born when I was consul!

[In Juvenal, Satires]

DISRAELI, Benjamin (1804–1881)

Every day when he looked into the glass, and gave the last touch to his consummate toilette, he offered his grateful thanks to Providence that his family was not unworthy of him.

[Lothair (1870)]

DULLES, John Foster (1888–1959)

[Reply when asked if he had ever been wrong]

Yes, once – many, many years ago. I thought I had made a wrong decision. Of course, it turned out that I had been right all along. But I was wrong to have thought that I was wrong.

[Attr.]

ELIOT, George (1819–1880)

He was like a cock, who thought the sun had risen to hear him crow.

[Adam Bede (1859)]

I've never any pity for conceited people, because I think they carry their comfort about with them.

[The Mill on the Floss (1860)]

GORTON, John Grey (1911–)

I am always prepared to recognize that there can be two points of view – mine, and one that is probably wrong.

[In Trengove, John Grey Gorton]

HARTLEY, L.P. (1895–1972)

'Should I call myself an egoist?' Miss Johnstone mused. 'Others have called me so. They merely meant I did not care for them.'

[Simonetta Perkins (1925)]

HAWKE, Bob (1929–)

[On first entering Parliament, 1979]

Well, I don't want to be any more egotistical

than possible. I have total confidence in my ability.

[In Thomson and Butel, *The World According to Hawke*]

JAMES, Brian (1892–1972)
A dominant personality doesn't believe in its own will. All it needs is the inability to recognise the existence of anybody else's.

[*Falling Towards England*]

JEROME, Jerome K. (1859–1927)
Conceit is the finest armour a man can wear.

[*Idle Thoughts of an Idle Fellow* (1886)]

KEITH, Penelope (1940–)
Shyness is just egotism out of its depth.

[*The Observer*, 1988]

KOURNIKOVA, Anna
Frankly, I am beautiful, famous and gorgeous.

[*Scotland on Sunday*, 1998]

MEREDITH, George (1828–1909)
In … the book of Egoism, it is written, Possession without obligation to the object possessed approaches felicity.

[*The Egoist* (1879)]

ROUX, Joseph (1834–1886)
The egoist does not tolerate egoism.

[*Meditations of a Parish Priest* (1886)]

SITWELL, Dame Edith (1887–1964)
I have often wished I had time to cultivate modesty … But I am too busy thinking about myself.

[*The Observer*, 1950]

STRACHEY, Lytton (1880–1932)
[Of Hurrell Froude]
The time was out of joint, and he was only too delighted to have been born to set it right.

[*Eminent Victorians* (1918)]

SUZUKI, D.T. (1870–1966)
The individual ego asserts itself strongly in the West. In the East, there is no ego. The ego is non-existent and, therefore, there is no ego to be crucified.

[*Mysticism Christian and Buddhist* (1957)]

TROLLOPE, Anthony (1815–1882)
As for conceit, what man will do any good who is not conceited? Nobody holds a good opinion of a man who has a low opinion of himself.

[*Orley Farm* (1862)]

WEBB, Beatrice (1858–1943)
If I ever felt inclined to be timid as I was going into a room full of people, I would say to myself, 'You're the cleverest member of one of the cleverest families in the cleverest class of the cleverest nation in the world, why should you be frightened?'.

[In Russell, *Portraits from Memory* (1956)]

WHISTLER, James McNeill (1834–1903)
[Replying to the pointed observation that it was as well that we do not see ourselves as others see us]
Isn't it? I know in my case I would grow intolerably conceited.

[In Pearson, *The Man Whistler*]

WILDE, Oscar (1854–1900)
I am the only person in the world I should like to know thoroughly.

[*Lady Windermere's Fan* (1892)]

See PRIDE; SELF

EMPIRE

CHAMBERLAIN, Joseph (1836–1914)
Learn to think Imperially.

[Speech, London, 1904]

The day of small nations has long passed away. The day of Empires has come.

[Speech, Birmingham, 1904]

CHURCHILL, Sir Winston (1874–1965)
I have not become the King's First Minister in order to preside over the liquidation of the British Empire.

[Speech, Mansion House, November 1942]

DISRAELI, Benjamin (1804–1881)
You are not going, I hope, to leave the

destinies of the British Empire to prigs and pedants.

[Speech, House of Commons, 1863]

KIPLING, Rudyard (1865–1936)

Take up the White Man's burden –
Send forth the best ye breed –
Go, bind your sons to exile
To serve your captives' need;
To wait in heavy harness
On fluttered folk and wild –
Your new-caught, sullen peoples,
Half devil and half child …

By all ye cry or whisper,
By all ye leave or do,
The silent, sullen peoples
Shall weigh your Gods and you.

['The White Man's Burden' (1899)]

MACAULAY, Lord (1800–1859)

The reluctant obedience of distant provinces generally costs more than it [the territory] is worth.

[*Collected Essays* (1843), 'War of the Succession in Spain']

MAO TSE-TUNG (1893–1976)

Imperialism is a paper tiger.

[*Quotations from Chairman Mao Tse-Tung*]

MONTESQUIEU, Charles (1689–1755)

Un empire fondé par les armes a besoin de se soutenir par les armes.
An empire founded by war has to maintain itself by war.

[*Considérations sur les causes de la grandeur des Romains et de leur décadence* (1734)]

RICHTER, Jean Paul Friedrich (1763–1825)

Providence has given to the French the empire of the land, to the English that of the sea, and to the Germans that of – the air!

[In Thomas Carlyle, 'Jean Paul Friedrich Richter' (1827)]

ROSEBERY, Earl of (1847–1929)

The Empire is a Commonwealth of Nations.

[Speech, Adelaide, 1884]

Imperialism, sane Imperialism, as distinguished from what I may call wild-cat Imperialism, is nothing but this – a larger patriotism.

[Speech at a City Liberal Club dinner, 1899]

SMITH, Adam (1723–1790)

To found a great empire for the sole purpose of raising up a people of customers, may at first sight appear a project fit only for a nation of shopkeepers. It is, however, a project altogether unfit for a nation of shopkeepers; but extremely fit for a nation whose government is influenced by shopkeepers.

[*Wealth of Nations* (1776)]

See ENGLAND

ENEMIES

BEVIN, Ernest (1881–1951)

[When told that another Labourite was 'his own worst enemy']
Not while I'm alive, he ain't.

[In M. Foot, *Aneurin Bevan 1945–60* (1975)]

THE BIBLE
(King James Version)

Love your enemies, bless them that curse you, do good to them that hate you, and pray for them which despitefully use you, and persecute you.

[*Matthew*, 5:44]

BRETON, Nicholas (c.1545–c.1626)

I wish my deadly foe, no worse
Than want of friends, and empty purse.

['A Farewell to Town' (1577)]

BURKE, Edmund (1729–1797)

He that wrestles with us strengthens our nerves, and sharpens our skill. Our antagonist is our helper.

[*Reflections on the Revolution in France* (1790)]

CONRAD, Joseph (1857–1924)

You shall judge of a man by his foes as well

[*Lord Jim* (1900)]

LESAGE, Alain-René (1668–1747)

On nous réconcilia: nous nous embrassâmes, et depuis ce temps-lá nous sommes ennemis mortels.
They made peace between us; we embraced, and since that time we have been mortal enemies.

[*Le Diable boiteux*]

LINKLATER, Eric (1899–1974)

With a heavy step Sir Matthew left the room and spent the morning designing mausoleums for his enemies.

[*Juan in America* (1931)]

MONTAGU, Lady Mary Wortley (1689–1762)

People wish their enemies dead – but I do not; I say give them the gout, give them the stone!

[In a letter from Horace Walpole to the Earl of Harcourt, 1778]

NARVÁEZ, Ramón María (1800–1868)

[On his deathbed, when asked by a priest if he forgave his enemies]
I do not have to forgive my enemies, I have had them all shot.

[Attr.]

PUZO, Mario (1920–)

Keep your friends close, but your enemies closer.

[*The Godfather, Part II*, film, 1974]

ROOSEVELT, Franklin Delano (1882–1945)

I ask you to judge me by the enemies I have made.

[*The Observer*, 1932]

WHITMAN, Walt (1819–1892)

Beautiful that war and all its deeds of carnage must in time be utterly lost,
That the hands of the sisters Death and Night incessantly softly wash again, and ever again, this soil'd world;
For my enemy is dead, a man as divine as myself is dead,

I look where he lies white-faced and still in the coffin – I draw near,
Bend down and touch lightly with my lips the white face in the coffin.

['Reconciliation' (1865)]

WILDE, Oscar (1854–1900)

A man cannot be too careful in the choice of his enemies.

[*The Picture of Dorian Gray* (1891)]

ENGLAND

ADDISON, Joseph (1672–1719)

The Knight in the triumph of his heart made several reflections on the greatness of the British Nation; as, that one Englishman could beat three Frenchmen; that we cou'd never be in danger of Popery so long as we took care of our fleet; that the Thames was the noblest river in Europe; that London Bridge was a greater piece of work than any of the Seven Wonders of the World; with many other honest prejudices which naturally cleave to the heart of a true Englishman.

[*The Spectator*, May 1712]

AGATE, James (1877–1947)

The English instinctively admire any man who has no talent and is modest about it.

[Attr.]

BAGEHOT, Walter (1826–1877)

Of all nations in the world the English are perhaps the least a nation of pure philosophers.

[*The English Constitution* (1867)]

BEHAN, Brendan (1923–1964)

He was born an Englishman and remained one for years.

[*The Hostage* (1958)]

BOSSUET, Jacques-Bénigne (1627–1704)

L'Angleterre, ah, la perfide Angleterre, que le rempart de ses mers rendoit inaccessible aux Romains, la foi du Sauveur y est abordée.
England, ah, perfidious England, which the

bulwarks of the sea rendered inaccessible to the Romans, the faith of the Saviour made landfall even there.

[*Oeuvres de Bossuet* (1816)]

BRADBURY, Malcolm (1932–)

I like the English. They have the most rigid code of immorality in the world.

[*Eating People is Wrong* (1954)]

BRIGHT, John (1811–1889)

England is the mother of Parliaments.

[Speech, 1865]

BROOKE, Rupert (1887–1915)

If I should die, think only this of me:
That there's some corner of a foreign field
That is for ever England.

['The Soldier' (1914)]

BROWNE, Sir Thomas (1605–1682)

All places, all airs make unto me one country;
I am in England, everywhere, and under any meridian.

[*Religio Medici* (1643)]

BROWNING, Robert (1812–1889)

Oh, to be in England
Now that April's there,
And whoever wakes in England
Sees, some morning, unaware,
That the lowest boughs and the brushwood sheaf
Round the elm-tree bole are in tiny leaf,
While the chaffinch sings on the orchard bough
In England – now!

['Home Thoughts, from Abroad' (1845)]

BUTLER, Samuel (1835–1902)

The wish to spread those opinions that we hold conducive to our own welfare is so deeply rooted in the English character that few of us can escape its influence.

[*Erewhon* (1872)]

BYRON, Lord (1788–1824)

The English winter – ending in July,
To recommence in August.

[*Don Juan* (1824)]

I am sure my bones would not rest in an English grave, or my clay mix with the earth of that country. I believe the thought would drive me mad on my deathbed, could I suppose that any of my friends would be base enough to convey my carcass back to your soil. I would not even feed your worms if I could help it.

[Letter to John Murray, 1819]

CARLYLE, Thomas (1795–1881)

[When asked what the population of England was] Thirty millions, mostly fools.

[Attr.]

CARROLL, Lewis (1832–1898)

He's an Anglo-Saxon Messenger – and those are Anglo-Saxon attitudes.

[*Through the Looking-Glass (and What Alice Found There)* (1872)]

CHARLES, Hughie (1907–)

There'll always be an England
While there's a country lane.

['There'll always be an England', song, 1939]

CHESTERTON, G.K. (1874–1936)

Smile at us, pay us, pass us; but do not quite forget.
For we are the people of England, that never have spoken yet.

[*Poems* (1915), 'The Secret People']

CHURCHILL, Charles (1731–1764)

Be England what she will,
With all her faults, she is my country still.

['The Farewell' (1764)]

COMPTON-BURNETT, Dame Ivy (1884–1969)

Well, the English have no family feelings. That is, none of the kind you mean. They have them, and one of them is that relations must cause no expense.

[*Parents and Children* (1941)]

COWARD, Sir Noël (1899–1973)

Mad dogs and Englishmen go out in the mid-day sun;
The Japanese don't care to, the Chinese wouldn't dare to;

Hindus and Argentines sleep firmly from
twelve to one,
But Englishmen detest a
Siesta …

In the mangrove swamps where the python
romps
There is peace from twelve till two.
Even caribous lie around and snooze,
For there's nothing else to do.
In Bengal, to move at all
Is seldom, if ever done.

['Mad Dogs and Englishmen', song, 1931]

COWPER, William (1731–1800)

England, with all thy faults, I love thee still –
My country!

[*The Task* (1785)]

CUNNINGHAM, Peter Miller (1789–1864)

A young girl, when asked how she would like
to go to England, replied with great naïveté, 'I
should be afraid to go, from the number of
thieves there,' doubtless conceiving England
to be a downright hive of such, that threw off
its annual swarms to people the wilds of this
colony.

[*Two Years in New South Wales* (1827)]

DEFOE, Daniel (c.1661–1731)

Your Roman-Saxon-Danish-Norman English.

[*The True-Born Englishman* (1701)]

DICKENS, Charles (1812–1870)

'This Island was Blest, Sir, to the Direct
Exclusion of such Other Countries as – as
there may happen to be. And if we were all
Englishmen present, I would say,' added Mr
Podsnap … 'that there is in the Englishman a
combination of qualities, a modesty, an
independence, a responsibility, a repose,
combined with an absence of everything
calculated to call a blush into the cheek of a
young person, which one would seek in vain
among the Nations of the Earth.'

[*Our Mutual Friend* (1865)]

DRYDEN, John (1631–1700)

But 'tis the talent of our English nation,

Still to be plotting some new reformation.

[*Prologue at Oxford* (1680)]

FORSTER, E.M. (1879–1970)

It is not that the Englishman can't feel – it is
that he is afraid to feel. He has been taught
at his public school that feeling is bad form.
He must not express great joy or sorrow, or
even open his mouth too wide when he talks
– his pipe might fall out if he did.

[*Abinger Harvest* (1936)]

GOLDING, William (1911–1993)

We've got to have rules and obey them. After
all, we're not savages. We're English; and the
English are best at everything. So we've got
to do the right things.

[*Lord of the Flies* (1954)]

HALSEY, Margaret (1910–)

The attitude of the English … toward English
history reminds one a good deal of the
attitude of a Hollywood director toward love.

[*With Malice Toward Some* (1938)]

Living in England, provincial England, must
be like being married to a stupid but
exquisitely beautiful wife.

[*With Malice Toward Some* (1938)]

HAZLITT, William (1778–1830)

The English (it must be owned) are rather a
foul-mouthed nation.

[*Table-Talk* (1822)]

HERBERT, Sir A.P. (1890–1971)

The Englishman never enjoys himself except
for a noble purpose.

[*Uncommon Law* (1935)]

HILL, Reginald (1936–)

Nobody has ever lost money by
overestimating the superstitious credulity of
an English jury.

[*Pictures of Perfection* (1994)]

HOWARD, Philip (1933–)

Every time an Englishman opens his mouth,
he enables other Englishmen if not to
despise him, at any rate to place him in some

social and class pigeonhole.

[*The Times*, 1992]

HOWKINS, Alun (1947–)

The English pub is, we are told from childhood, a unique institution. Nothing 'quite like it' exists anywhere else. That's true. The pub uniquely represents, even in metropolitan England, the precise inequalities of gender, race and class that construct our society. From the inclusive white, male and proletarian 'public' of many northern pubs to the parasitic blazer and cotton dress 'locals' of the home counties, our unique institution divides our society and our social life.

[*New Statesman and Society*, 1989]

HUGO, Victor (1802–1885)

England has two books: the Bible and Shakespeare. England made Shakespeare but the Bible made England.

[*Attr.*]

JOAD, C.E.M. (1891–1953)

It will be said of this generation that it found England a land of beauty and left it a land of beauty spots.

[*The Observer*, 1953]

JOYCE, James (1882–1941)

We feel in England that we have treated you Irish rather unfairly. It seems history is to blame.

[*Ulysses* (1922)]

KINGSLEY, Charles (1819–1875)

'Tis the hard grey weather
Breeds hard English men.

['Ode to the North-East Wind' (1854)]

KIPLING, Rudyard (1865–1936)

For Allah created the English mad – the maddest of all mankind!

[*The Five Nations* (1903)]

[Of the English]
For undemocratic reasons and for motives not of State,
They arrive at their conclusions – largely inarticulate.

Being void of self-expression they confide their views to none;
But sometimes in a smoking-room, one learns why things were done.

[*Actions and Reactions* (1909)]

The Saxon is not like us Normans. His manners are not so polite.
But he never means anything serious till he talks about justice and right,
When he stands like an ox in the furrow with his sullen set eyes on your own,
And grumbles, 'This isn't fair dealing,' my son, leave the Saxon alone.

[Songs written for C.R.L. Fletcher's *A History of England* (1911)]

LAWRENCE, D.H. (1885–1930)

It was one of those places where the spirit of aboriginal England still lingers, the old savage England, whose last blood flows still in a few Englishmen, Welshmen, Cornishmen.

[*St Mawr* (1925)]

MACAULAY, Lord (1800–1859)

The history of England is emphatically the history of progress.

['Sir James Mackintosh' (1843)]

MACINNES, Colin (1914–1976)

England is … a country infested with people who love to tell us what to do, but who very rarely seem to know what's going on.

[*England, Half English*]

MARY, Queen of Scots (1542–1587)

England is not all the world.

[Said at her trial, 1586]

MIKES, George (1912–1987)

On the Continent people have good food; in England people have good table manners.

[*How to be an Alien* (1946)]

An Englishman, even if he is alone, forms an orderly queue of one.

[*How to be an Alien* (1946)]

MONTESQUIEU, Charles (1689–1755)

Les Anglais sont occupés; ils n'ont pas le temps d'être polis.

The English are busy; they don't have the time to be polite.

[*Pensées et fragments inédits* (1899)]

NAPOLEON I (1769–1821)

L'Angleterre est une nation de boutiquiers.
England is a nation of shopkeepers.

[In O'Meara, *Napoleon in Exile* (1822)]

NASH, Ogden (1902–1971)

Let us pause to consider the English
Who when they pause to consider
themselves they get all reticently thrilled and
tinglish.
Englishmen are distinguished by their
traditions and ceremonials,
And also by their affection for their colonies
and their condescension to their colonials.

['England Expects' (1929)]

O'CONNELL, Daniel (1775–1847)

The Englishman has all the qualities of a
poker except its occasional warmth.

[Attr.]

ORWELL, George (1903–1950)

England is not the jewelled isle of
Shakespeare's much-quoted passage, nor is it
the inferno depicted by Dr Goebbels. More
than either it resembles a family, a rather
stuffy Victorian family, with not many black
sheep in it but with all its cupboards
bursting with skeletons. It has rich relations
who have to be kow-towed to and poor
relations who are horribly sat upon, and
there is a deep conspiracy about the source
of the family income. It is a family in which
the young are generally thwarted and most
of the power is in the hands of irresponsible
uncles and bedridden aunts. Still, it is a family
… A family with the wrong members in
control.

['England, Your England' (1941)]

PARSONS, Tony (1953–)

To be born an Englishman – ah, what an easy
conceit that builds in you, what a self-
righteous nationalism, a secure xenophobia,
what a pride in your ignorance. No other
people speak so few languages. No other

people – certainly not the Germans, Italians
or French, and not even the multi-ethnic
Americano – have an expression that is the
equivalent of 'greasy foreign muck'. The
noble, wisecracking savages depicted
everywhere from *Eastenders* to *Boys from the
Blackstuff* are exercises in nostalgia who no
longer exist.

[*Arena*, 1989]

PEPYS, Samuel (1633–1703)

But Lord! to see the absurd nature of
Englishmen, that cannot forbear laughing
and jeering at everything that looks strange.

[*Diary*, 1662]

PITT, William (1759–1806)

England has saved herself by her exertions,
and will, as I trust, save Europe by her
example.

[Speech, 1805]

RHODES, Cecil (1853–1902)

Remember that you are an Englishman, and
have consequently won first prize in the
lottery of life.

[In Ustinov, *Dear Me* (1977)]

ROUSSEAU, Jean-Jacques (1712–1778)

The English people imagine themselves to
be free, but they are wrong: it is only during
the election of members of parliament that
they are so.

[*Du Contrat Social* (1762)]

SANTAYANA, George (1863–1952)

England is the paradise of individuality,
eccentricity, heresy, anomalies, hobbies, and
humours.

[*Soliloquies in England* (1922)]

SEELEY, Sir John Robert (1834–1895)

We [the English] seem as it were to have
conquered and peopled half the world in a
fit of absence of mind.

[*The Expansion of England* (1883)]

SELLAR, Walter (1898–1951) and
YEATMAN, Robert Julian (1897–1968)

Pope Gregory … made the memorable joke

–'Non Angli, sed Angeli' ('not Angels, but Anglicans').

[*1066 And All That* (1930)]

SHAKESPEARE, William (1564–1616)

This royal throne of kings, this scept'red isle,
This earth of majesty, this seat of Mars,
This other Eden, demi-paradise,
This fortress built by Nature for herself
Against infection and the hand of war,
This happy breed of men, this little world,
This precious stone set in the silver sea,
Which serves it in the office of a wall,
Or as a moat defensive to a house,
Against the envy of less happier lands;
This blessed plot, this earth, this realm, this England.

[*Richard II*, II.i]

SHAW, George Bernard (1856–1950)

There is nothing so bad or so good that you will not find Englishmen doing it; but you will never find an Englishman in the wrong. He does everything on principle. He fights you on patriotic principles; he robs you on business principles; he enslaves you on imperial principles; he bullies you on manly principles; he supports his king on loyal principles and cuts off his king's head on republican principles.

[*The Man of Destiny* (1898)]

SMITH, Sydney (1771–1845)

What a pity it is that we have no amusements in England but vice and religion!

[In H. Pearson, *The Smith of Smiths* (1934)]

STEINER, George (1929–)

This land is blessed with a powerful mediocrity of mind. It has saved you from communism and from fascism.

[*The Observer*, 1998 from a review of Paxman's *The English*]

SULLY, Duc de (1559–1641)

Les Anglais s'amusent tristement, selon l'usage de leur pays.
The English enjoy themselves sadly,

according to the custom of their country.

[*Memoirs* (1638)]

TREE, Sir Herbert Beerbohm (1853–1917)

The national sport of England is obstacle-racing. People fill their rooms with useless and cumbersome furniture, and spend the rest of their lives trying to dodge it.

[In Hesketh Pearson, *Beerbohm Tree* (1956)]

VOLTAIRE (1694–1778)

Le sombre Anglais, même dans ses amours,
Veut raisonner toujours.
On est plus raisonnable en France.
The gloomy Englishman, even in love, always wants to reason. We are more reasonable in France.

[*Les Originaux, Entrée des Diverses Nations*]

WELLS, H.G. (1866–1946)

In England we have come to rely upon a comfortable time-lag of fifty years or a century intervening between the perception that something ought to be done and a serious attempt to do it.

[*The Work, Wealth and Happiness of Mankind* (1931)]

WILDE, Oscar (1854–1900)

Those things which the English public never forgives – youth, power, and enthusiasm.

[In R. Ross (ed.), *Collected Works of Oscar Wilde* (1908)]

The English have a miraculous power of turning wine into water.

[Attr.]

WORDSWORTH, William (1770–1850)

I travelled among unknown men
In lands beyond the sea;
Nor, England! did I know till then
What love I bore to thee.

['I travelled among unknown men' (1807)]

Milton! thou shouldst be living at this hour:
England hath need of thee; she is a fen
Of stagnant waters: altar, sword, and pen,
Fireside, the heroic wealth of hall and bower,
Have forfeited their ancient English dower

Of inward happiness.

['Milton! thou shouldst be living at this hour' (1807)]

YEATS, W.B. (1865–1939)

The Irish mind has still in country rapscallion or in Bernard Shaw an ancient, cold, explosive, detonating impartiality. The English mind, excited by its newspaper proprietors and its schoolmasters, has turned into a bed-hot harlot.

['Ireland after the Revolution' (1939)]

See CITIES; PATRIOTISM

ENVIRONMENT

BOTTOMLEY, Gordon (1874–1948)

When you destroy a blade of grass
You poison England at her roots:
Remember no man's foot can pass
Where evermore no green life shoots.

['To Ironfounders and Others' (1912)]

CARSON, Rachel Louise (1907–1964)

As man proceeds towards his announced goal of the conquest of nature, he has written a depressing record of destruction, directed not only against the earth he inhabits but against the life that shares it with him.

[The Silent Spring (1962)]

Over increasingly large areas of the United States, spring now comes unheralded by the return of the birds, and the early mornings are strangely silent where once they were filled with the beauty of bird song.

[The Silent Spring (1962)]

CHEKHOV, Anton (1860–1904)

Human beings have been endowed with reason and a creative power so that they can add to what thay have been given. But until now they have been not creative, but destructive. Forests are disappearing, rivers are drying up, wildlife is becoming extinct, the climate's being ruined and with every passing day the earth is becoming poorer

and uglier.

[Uncle Vanya (1897)]

LAWRENCE, D.H. (1885–1930)

It is the hideous rawness of the world of men, the horrible desolating harshness of the advance of the industrial world upon the world of nature, that is so painful … If only we could learn to take thought for the whole world instead of for merely tiny bits of it.

[Twilight in Italy (1916)]

MCLEAN, Joyce (1860–1904)

There's an old saying which goes: Once the last tree is cut and the last river poisoned, you will find you cannot eat your money.

[The Globe and Mail, 1989]

MEAD, Margaret (1901–1978)

We are living beyond our means. As a people we have developed a life-style that is draining the earth of its priceless and irreplaceable resources without regard for the future of our children and people all around the world.

[Redbook]

STRETTON, Hugh (1924–)

People can't change the way they use resources without changing their relations with one another. … How to conserve is usually a harder question than whether, or what, to conserve.

[Capitalism, Socialism and the Environment (1976)]

See COUNTRY

ENVY

BEERBOHM, Sir Max (1872–1956)

The dullard's envy of brilliant men is always assuaged by the suspicion that they will come to a bad end.

[Zuleika Dobson (1911)]

THE BIBLE
(King James Version)

Through envy of the devil came death into

the world.

[*Apocrypha, Wisdom of Solomon*, 2:24]

BRONTË, Charlotte (1816–1855)

Had I been in anything inferior to him, he would not have hated me so thoroughly, but I knew all that he knew, and, what was worse, he suspected that I kept the padlock of silence on mental wealth in which he was no sharer.

[*The Professor* (1857)]

CHURCHILL, Charles (1731–1764)

Who wit with jealous eye surveys,
And sickens at another's praise.

[*The Ghost* (1763)]

FIELDING, Henry (1707–1754)

Some folks rail against other folks because other folks have what some folks would be glad of.

[*Joseph Andrews* (1742)]

GAY, John (1685–1732)

Fools may our scorn, not envy raise,
For envy is a kind of praise.

[*Fables* (1727)]

MOORE, Brian (1921–1999)

How many works of the imagination have been goaded into life by envy of an untalented contemporary's success.

[*An Answer from Limbo* (1994)]

PROVERB

Better be envied than pitied.

SHAKESPEARE, William (1564–1616)

[Of Cassius]
Such men as he be never at heart's ease
Whiles they behold a greater than themselves,
And therefore are they very dangerous.

[*Julius Caesar*, I.ii]

The general's disdain'd
By him one step below, he by the next,
That next by him beneath; so every step,
Exampl'd by the first pace that is sick
Of his superior, grows to an envious fever

Of pale and bloodless emulation.

[*Troilus and Cressida*, I.iii]

See DISAPPOINTMENT; JEALOUSY

EPITAPHS

ANONYMOUS

All who come my grave to see
Avoid damp beds and think of me.

[Epitaph of Lydia Eason, St Michael's, Stoke]

[On a child dead of snake-bite]
From a subtle serpents Bite he cride
our RoseBud cut he drup'd his head and died,
He was his Fathers glorey
And Mothers pride.

[Memorial to John Howorth, died 8 October 1804 at 11 years, St John's Churchyard, Wilberforce, New South Wales]

God took our flour,
Our little Nell;
He thought He too
Would like a smell.

[In Thomas Wood, *Cobbers*]

Here lie I and my four daughters,
Killed by drinking Cheltenham waters.
Had we but stuck to Epsom salts,
We wouldn't have been in these here vaults.

['Cheltenham Waters']

Here lie I by the chancel door;
They put me here because I was poor.
The further in, the more you pay,
But here lie I as snug as they.

[Epitaph, Devon churchyard]

Here lies a child that took one peep of Life
And viewed its endless troubles with dismay,
Gazed with an anguish'd glance upon the strife
And sickening at the sight flew fast away.
What though for many the gate of Heaven is shut,
It stands wide open for this little Butt.

[Epitaph on Allena Butt, who had died when only 6 weeks old]

Here lies a man who was killed by lightning;
He died when his prospects seemed to be brightening.
He might have cut a flash in this world of trouble,
But the flash cut him, and he lies in the stubble.

[Epitaph, Torrington, Devon]

Here lies a poor woman who always was tired,
For she lived in a place where help wasn't hired.
Her last words on earth were, Dear friends I am going
Where washing ain't done nor sweeping nor sewing,
And everything there is exact to my wishes,
For there they don't eat and there's no washing of dishes …
Don't mourn for me now, don't mourn for me never,
For I'm going to do nothing for ever and ever.

[Epitaph in Bushey churchyard]

Here lies Fred,
Who was alive and is dead;
Had it been his father,
I had much rather;
Had it been his brother,
Still better than another;
Had it been his sister,
No one would have missed her;
Had it been the whole generation,
Still better for the nation:
But since 'tis only Fred,
Who was alive and is dead, –
There's no more to be said.

[In Horace Walpole, *Memoirs of George II* (1847)]

Here lies my wife,
Here lies she;
Hallelujah!
Hallelujee!

[Epitaph, Leeds churchyard]

Here lies the body of Mary Ann Lowder,
She burst while drinking a seidlitz powder.
Called from the world to her heavenly rest,

She should have waited till it effervesced.

[Epitaph]

Here lies the body of Richard Hind,
Who was neither ingenious, sober, nor kind.

[Epitaph]

Here lies Will Smith – and, what's something rarish,
He was born, bred, and hanged, all in the same parish.

[Epitaph]

Lo, Huddled up, together Lye
Gray Age, Grene youth, White Infancy.
If Death doth Nature's Laws dispence,
And reconciles All Difference
Tis Fit, One Flesh, One House Should have
One Tombe, One Epitaph, One Grave:
And they that Liv'd and Lov'd Either,
Should Dye and Lye and Sleep together.

Good reader, whether go or stay
Thou must not hence be Long Away.

[Epitaph, of William Bartholomew (died 1662), his wife and some of their children, St John the Baptist, Burford]

Mary Ann has gone to rest,
Safe at last on Abraham's breast,
Which may be nuts for Mary Ann,
But is certainly rough on Abraham.

[Epitaph]

My sledge and anvil lie declined
My bellows too have lost their wind
My fire's extinct, my forge decayed,
And in the Dust my Vice is laid
My coals are spent, my iron's gone
My Nails are Drove, My Work is done.

[Epitaph in Nettlebed churchyard]

Reader, one moment stop and think,
That I am in eternity, and you are on the brink.

[Tombstone inscription at Perth, Scotland]

Remember man, as thou goes by,
As thou art now so once was I,
As I am now so must thou be,

Remember man that thou must die.

[Headstone in Straiton, Ayrshire]

Rest in peace – until we meet again.

[Widow's epitaph for husband; in Mitford, *The American Way of Death*]

Sacred to the memory of
Captain Anthony Wedgwood
Accidentally shot by his gamekeeper
Whilst out shooting
'Well done thou good and faithful servant'.

[Epitaph]

Stranger! Approach this spot with gravity!
John Brown is filling his last cavity.

[Epitaph of a dentist]

That we spent, we had:
That we gave, we have:
That we left, we lost.

[Epitaph of the Earl of Devonshire]

This is the grave of Mike O'Day
Who died maintaining his right of way.
His right was clear, his will was strong.
But he's just as dead as if he'd been wrong.

[Epitaph]

Warm summer sun shine kindly here:
Warm summer wind blow softly here:
Green sod above lie light, lie light:
Good-night, Dear Heart: good-night, good-night.

[Memorial to Clorinda Haywood, St Bartholomew's, Edgbaston]

ARBUTHNOT, John (1667–1735)

Here continueth to rot the body of Francis Chartres.

[First line of epitaph]

ATKINSON, Surgeon-Captain E.L. (1882–1929)

Hereabouts died a very gallant gentleman, Captain L.E.G. Oates of the Inniskilling Dragoons. In March 1912, returning from the Pole, he walked willingly to his death in a blizzard, to try and save his comrades, beset by hardships.

[Epitaph on a cairn and cross erected in the Antarctic, November 1912]

AUDEN, W.H. (1907–1973)

Perfection, of a kind, was what he was after,
And the poetry he invented was easy to understand;
He knew human folly like the back of his hand,
And was greatly interested in armies and fleets;
When he laughed, respectable senators burst with laughter,
And when he cried the little children died in the streets.

[*Collected Poems, 1933–1938*, 'Epitaph on a Tyrant']

To save your world you asked this man to die:
Would this man, could he see you now, ask why?

['Epitaph for the Unknown Soldier' (1955)]

He disappeared in the dead of winter:
The brooks were frozen, the airports almost deserted,
And snow disfigured the public statues;
The mercury sank in the mouth of the dying day.
What instruments we have agree
The day of his death was a dark cold day …

[*Collected Poems, 1939–1947*, 'In Memory of W.B. Yeats']

BARHAM, Rev. Richard Harris (Thomas Ingoldsby) (1788–1845)

Though I've always considered Sir Christopher Wren,
As an architect, one of the greatest of men;
And, talking of Epitaphs, – much I admire his,
'Circumspice, si Monumentum requiris';
Which an erudite Verger translated to me,
'If you ask for his Monument, Sir-come-spy-see!'.

[*The Ingoldsby Legends* (1840–1847), 'The Cynotaph']

BARNFIELD, Richard (1574–1627)

[In memory of Sir John Hawkins]

The waters were his winding sheet, the sea was made his tomb;
Yet for his fame the ocean sea, was not sufficient room.

[*The Encomion of Lady Pecunia* (1598), 'To the Gentlemen Readers']

BELLOC, Hilaire (1870–1953)

When I am dead, I hope it may be said:
'His sins were scarlet, but his books were read.'

[*Sonnets and Verse* (1923), 'On His Books']

BENCHLEY, Robert (1889–1945)

[Suggesting an epitaph for an actress]
She sleeps alone at last.

[Attr.]

BLAUVELDT, Robert R.

[On the cairn dedicated to the memory of the United Empire Loyalists, Tusket, Yarmouth County, N.S.; words chosen by Blauveldt who is of U.E.L. descent]
They Sacrificed Everything Save Honour.

[Inscription, 1964]

BRAY, John Jefferson (1912–)

A hundred canvasses and seven sons
He left, and never got a likeness once.

['Epitaph on a Portrait Painter']

BROWNE, William (c.1591–1643)

Underneath this sable hearse
Lies the subject of all verse,
Sidney's sister, Pembroke's mother;
Death! ere thou hast slain another,
Fair and learn'd, and good as she,
Time shall throw a dart at thee.

['Epitaph on the Countess of Pembroke' (1623)]

BURKE, Edmund (1729–1797)

His virtues were his arts.

[Inscription on the statue of the Marquis of Rockingham in Wentworth Park]

BURNS, Robert (1759–1796)

Here lie Willie Michie's banes:
O Satan, when ye tak him,
Gie him the schulin' o' your weans,
For clever Deils he'll mak them!

['Epitaph for William Michie.

Schoolmaster of Cleish Parish, Fifeshire' (1787)]

BYRON, Lord (1788–1824)

With death doomed to grapple,
Beneath this cold slab, he
Who lied in the chapel
Now lies in the Abbey.

['Epitaph for William Pitt' (1820)]

CAMDEN, William (1551–1623)

My friend, judge not me,
Thou seest I judge not thee.
Betwixt the stirrup and the ground
Mercy I asked, mercy I found.

[*Remains Concerning Britain* (1605), 'Epitaph for a Man Killed by Falling from His Horse']

CAREW, Thomas (c.1595–1640)

Here lyes a King, that rul'd, as he thought fit
The Universal Monarchie of wit,
Here lyes two Flamens, and both those, the best,
Apollo's first, at last, the true God's Priest.

['An Elegy upon the death of Doctor Donne' (1640)]

So though a Virgin, yet a Bride
To every Grace, she justifi'd
A chaste Poligamie, and dy'd.

['Inscription on Tomb of Lady Mary Wentworth' (1640)]

CARLYLE, Thomas (1795–1881)

[Epitaph for Jane Welsh Carlyle in Haddington Church]
For forty years she was the true and ever-loving helpmate of her husband, and, by act and word, unweariedly forwarded him as none else could, in all of worthy that he did or attempted. She died at London, 21st April 1866, suddenly snatched away from him, and the light of his life as if gone out.

[In Hector C. Macpherson, *Thomas Carlyle* (1896)]

CLEVELAND, John (1613–1658)

Here lies wise and valiant dust,
Huddled up, 'twixt fit and just:
Strafford, who was hurried hence
'Twixt treason and convenience.

He spent his time here in a mist,
A Papist, yet a Calvinist.
His Prince's nearest joy and grief;
He had, yet wanted, all relief:
The Prop and Ruin of the State,
The people's violent love and hate:
One in extremes lov'd and abhor'd.
Riddles lie here, or in a word,
Here lies blood; and let it lie
Speechless till, and never cry.

['Epitaph on the Earl of Strafford' (1647)]

COLERIDGE, Samuel Taylor (1772–1834)

Ere sin could blight or sorrow fade,
Death came with friendly care:
The opening bud to Heaven convey'd
And bade it blossom there.

['Epitaph on an Infant' (1794)]

CORNFORD, Frances Crofts (1886–1960)

Whoso maintains that I am humbled now
(Who wait the Awful Day) is still a liar;
I hope to meet my Maker brow to brow
And find my own the higher.

['Epitaph for a Reviewer' (1954)]

CRASHAW, Richard (c.1612–1649)

To these, Whom Death again did wed,
This Grave's the second Marriage-Bed …
Peace, good Reader, doe not weepe;
Peace, the Lovers are asleepe:
They (sweet Turtles) folded lye,
In the last knot that love could tye.

[*Steps to the Temple* (1646), 'An Epitaph upon Husband and Wife, which died, and were buried together']

DAY LEWIS, C. (1904–1972)

Now we lament one
Who danced on a plume of words,
Sang with a fountain's panache,
Dazzled like slate roofs in sun
After rain, was flighty as birds
And alone as a mountain ash.
The ribald, inspired urchin
Leaning over the lip
Of his world, as over a rock pool

Or a lucky dip,
Found everything brilliant and virgin.

['In Memory of Dylan Thomas']

DOUGLAS, James, Earl of Morton (c.1516–1581)

[Said during the burial of John Knox, 1572]
Here lies he who neither feared nor flattered any flesh.

[Attr.]

DRYDEN, John (1631–1700)

Here lies my wife: here let her lie!
Now she's at rest, and so am I.

['Epitaph intended for his wife']

EMMET, Robert (1778–1803)

[Before his execution]
When my country takes her place among the nations of the earth, then and not till then, let my epitaph be written. I have done.

[Attr.]

EVANS, Abel (1679–1737)

Under this stone, Reader, survey
Dead Sir John Vanbrugh's house of clay.
Lie heavy on him, Earth! for he
Laid many heavy loads on thee!

['Epitaph on Sir John Vanbrugh, Architect of Blenheim Palace' (died 1726)]

FIELDS, W.C. (1880–1946)

On the whole, I'd rather be in Philadelphia.

[His own epitaph]

FRANKLIN, Benjamin (1706–1790)

The body of
Benjamin Franklin, printer,
(Like the cover of an old book,
Its contents worn out,
And stript of its lettering and gilding)
Lies here, food for worms!
Yet the work itself shall not be lost,
For it will, as he believed, appear once more
In a new
And more beautiful edition,
Corrected and amended
By its Author!

[Epitaph for himself, 1728]

FROST, Robert (1874–1963)

I would have written of me on my stone:
I had a lover's quarrel with the world.

['The Lesson for Today' (1942)]

GARRICK, David (1717–1779)

Here lies Nolly Goldsmith, for shortness call'd Noll,
Who wrote like an angel, but talk'd like poor Poll.

['Impromptu Epitaph on Goldsmith', 1774]

HALLECK, Fitz-Greene (1790–1867)

Green be the turf above thee,
Friend of my better days!
None knew thee but to love thee,
Nor named thee but to praise.

['On the Death of J.R. Drake' (1820)]

HOPE, Alec (Derwent) (1907–)

[An ironic parody of the Greek epitaph commemorating the Spartans who died at Thermopylae in 480 bc]
Go tell those old men, safe in bed,
We took their orders and are dead.

['Inscription for Any War']

HOPE, Anthony (1863–1933)

His foe was folly and his weapon wit.

[Inscription on the tablet to W.S. Gilbert, Victoria Embankment, London, 1915]

HOUSMAN, A.E. (1859–1936)

These, in the day when heaven was falling,
The hour when earth's foundations fled,
Followed their mercenary calling
And took their wages and are dead.

Their shoulders held the sky suspended;
They stood, and earth's foundations stay;
What God abandoned, these defended,
And saved the sum of things for pay.

[*Last Poems* (1922)]

HUME, David (1711–1776)

Within this circular idea
Call'd vulgarly a tomb,
The ideas and impressions lie
That constituted Hume.

[Epitaph on his monument on Calton Hill, Edinburgh]

HUXLEY, Henrietta (1825–1915)

And if there be no meeting past the grave,
If all is darkness, silence, yet 'tis rest.
Be not afraid ye waiting hearts that weep;
For still He giveth His beloved sleep,
And if an endless sleep He wills, so best.

[Lines on the grave of her husband, 1895, in Deighton, *Huxley, His Life and Work* (1904)]

JOHNSON, Samuel (1709–1784)

In lapidary inscriptions a man is not upon oath.

[In Boswell, *The Life of Samuel Johnson* (1791)]

Olivarii Goldsmith, Poetae, Physici, Historici, Qui nullum fere scribendi genus non tetigit, Nullum quod tetigit non ornavit.
To Oliver Goldsmith, A Poet, Naturalist, and Historian, who left scarcely any style of writing untouched, and touched none that he did not adorn.

[In Boswell, *The Life of Samuel Johnson* (1791)]

[On the death of Mr Levett]
Officious, innocent, sincere,
Of every friendless name the friend.
Yet still he fills affection's eye,
Obscurely wise, and coarsely kind.

[In Boswell, *The Life of Samuel Johnson* (1791)]

JONSON, Ben (1572–1637)

Weep with me, all you that read
This little story:
And know for whom a tear you shed
Death's self is sorry.
'Twas a child that so did thrive
In grace and feature,
As Heaven and Nature seem'd to strive
Which own'd the creature.
Years he number'd scarce thirteen
When Fates turn'd cruel,
Yet three fill'd Zodiacs had he been
The stage's jewel;
And did act, what now we moan,
Old men so duly,
As sooth the Parcae thought him one,
He play'd so truly.

So, by error, to his fate
They all consented;
But viewing him since, alas, too late!
They have repented;
And have sought (to give new birth)
In baths to steep him;
But being so much too good for earth,
Heaven vows to keep him.

    [*Epigrams* (1616),'An Epitaph on Salomon Pavy, a
    Child of Queen Elizabeth's Chapel']

Rest in soft peace, and, ask'd say here doth
lye
Ben Jonson his best piece of poetrie.

    [*Epigrams* (1616),'On My First Son']

O rare Ben Jonson.

    [Epitaph in Westminster Abbey]

KAUFMAN, George S. (1889–1961)

[Suggestion for his own epitaph]
Over my dead body!

                [Attr.]

KEATS, John (1795–1821)

Here lies one whose name was writ in water.
    [Epitaph for himself]

KIPLING, Rudyard (1865–1936)

A Soldier of the Great War Known unto God.

  [Inscription on the graves of unidentified soldiers,
1919]

I could not look on Death, which being
known,
Men led me to him, blindfold and alone.

    [*The Years Between* (1919),'Epitaphs – The
Coward']

KNOX, John (1505–1572)

Un homme avec Dieu est toujours dans la majorité.
A man with God is always in the majority.

    [Inscription on the Reformation Monument,
Geneva, Switzerland]

LEE, Henry (1756–1818)

[Of Washington]
A citizen, first in war, first in peace, and first in
the hearts of his countrymen.

  [Resolution adopted by Congress on the death of
George Washington, 1799]

LOCKHART, John Gibson (1794–1854)

Here lies that peerless peer Lord Peter,
Who broke the laws of God and man and
metre.

    [Epitaph for Patrick ('Peter'), Lord Robertson, 1890]

MACAULAY, Lord (1800–1859)

To my true king I offer'd free from stain
Courage and faith; vain faith, and courage
vain …

By those white cliffs I never more must see,
By that dear language which I spake like
thee,
Forget all feuds, and shed one English tear
O'er English dust. A broken heart lies here.

            ['A Jacobite's Epitaph' (1845)]

MACDONALD, George (1824–1905)

Here lie I, Martin Elginbrodde:
Hae mercy o' my soul, Lord God;
As I wad do, were I Lord God,
And you were Martin Elginbrodde.

            [*David Elginbrod* (1863)]

MARVELL, Andrew (1621–1678)

Who can foretell for what high cause
This Darling of the Gods was born! …

Gather the flowers, but spare the buds.

  ['The Picture of Little T.C. in a Prospect of Flowers'
(1681)]

MENCKEN, H.L. (1880–1956)

If, after I depart this vale, you ever remember
me and have thought to please my ghost,
forgive some sinner and wink your eye at
some homely girl.

        [*Smart Set*, 1921, Epitaph]

MILL, John Stuart (1806–1873)

Were there but a few hearts and intellects
like hers this earth would already become
the hoped-for heaven.

        [Epitaph for his wife, Harriet,
1859]

MOORE, George (1852–1933)

[What he would like on his tombstone]
Here lies George Moore, who looked upon

corrections as the one morality.

[Conversation with Geraint Goodwin]

NEWCASTLE, Margaret, Duchess of (c.1624–1674)

Her name was Margaret Lucas youngest daughter of Lord Lucas, earl of Colchester, a noble family, for all the brothers were valiant, and all the sisters virtuous.

[Epitaph in Westminster Abbey; quoted by Joseph Addison]

PARKER, Dorothy (1893–1967)

He lies below, correct in cypress wood, And entertains the most exclusive worms.

[*Not So Deep as a Well* (1937), 'Epitaph for a Very Rich Man']

[Suggesting words for tombstone]
This is on me.

[In J. Keats, *You Might As Well Live* (1970)]

[Her own epitaph]
Excuse my dust.

[In Alexander Woollcott, *While Rome Burns* (1934)]

PEACOCK, Thomas Love (1785–1866)

Long night succeeds thy little day
Oh blighted blossom! can it be,
That this gray stone and grassy clay
Have closed our anxious care of thee?

[In Henry Cole (ed.), *Works of Peacock* (1875), 'Epitaph on his Daughter']

POPE, Alexander (1688–1744)

Nature, and Nature's laws lay hid in night:
God said, Let Newton be! and all was light.

['Epitaph for Sir Isaac Newton' (1730)]

Of manners gentle, of affections mild;
In wit, a man; simplicity, a child:
With native humour temp'ring virtuous rage,
Formed to delight at once and lash the age.

['Epitaph: On Mr. Gay in Westminster Abbey', 1733]

PRIOR, Matthew (1664–1721)

Nobles and heralds, by your leave,
Here lies what once was Matthew Prior;
The son of Adam and of Eve,
Can Bourbon or Nassau go higher?

['Epitaph' (1702)]

ROCHESTER, Earl of (1647–1680)

Here lies our sovereign lord the King
Whose word no man relies on,
Who never said a foolish thing,
Nor ever did a wise one.

[Epitaph written for Charles II (1706)]

ROSSETTI, Christina (1830–1894)

O Earth, lie heavily upon her eyes;
Seal her sweet eyes weary of watching.

['Rest' (1862)]

SASSOON, Siegfried (1886–1967)

Here sleeps the Silurist; the loved physician;
The face that left no portraiture behind;
The skull that housed white angels and had vision
Of daybreak through the gateways of the mind.

[*The Heart's Journey* (1928)]

SCOTT, Sir Walter (1771–1832)

Here lies one who might be trusted with untold gold, but not with unmeasured whisky.

[Epitaph for his favourite servant, Tom Purdie]

SHAKESPEARE, William (1564–1616)

[Epitaph on his tomb]
Good friend, for Jesu's sake forbear,
To dig the dust enclosed here.
Blest be the man that spares these stones,
And curst be he that moves my bones.

[Attr.]

SIMONIDES (c.556–468 BC)

[Epitaph for the three hundred Spartans under Leonidas who died at Thermopylae in 480]
Go, tell the Spartans, thou who passest by,
That here, obedient to their laws, we lie.

[In Herodotus, *Histories*]

SMITH, Joseph (1805–1844)

No man knows my history.

[Funeral sermon, written by himself]

STEVENSON, Robert Louis (1850–1894)

Under the wide and starry sky
Dig the grave and let me lie.
Glad did I live and gladly die,

And I laid me down with a will.
This be the verse you grave for me:
'Here he lies where he longed to be;
Home is the sailor, home from sea,
And the hunter home from the hill.'

[*Underwoods* (1887), 'Requiem']

STURGES, Preston (1898–1959)

[Suggested epitaph for himself]
Now I've laid me down to die
I pray my neighbours not to pry
Too deeply into sins that I
Not only cannot here deny
But much enjoyed as time flew by.

[In Halliwell, *The Filmgoer's Book of Quotes* (1973)]

SURREY, Henry Howard, Earl of (c.1517–1547)

But to the heavens that simple soule is fled:
Which left with such, as covet Christ to know,
Witnesse of faith, that never shall be ded:
Sent for our helth, but not received so.
Thus, for our gilte, this jewel have we lost:
The earth his bones, the heavens possesse
his gost.

['Of the death of Sir T.W. Thomas Wyatt']

SWIFT, Jonathan (1667–1745)

Poor Pope will grieve a month, and Gay
A week, and Arbuthnot a day.
St John himself will scarce forbear
To bite his pen, and drop a tear.
The rest will give a shrug, and cry,
'I'm sorry – but we all must die!' ...

Yet malice never was his aim;
He lash'd the vice, but spared the name;
No individual could resent,
Where thousands equally were meant ...

He gave the little wealth he had
To build a house for fools and mad;
And show'd, by one satiric touch,
No nation wanted it so much.
That kingdom he hath left a debtor,
I wish it soon may have a better.

['Verses on the Death of Dr. Swift' (1731)]

Where fierce indignation can no longer tear
his heart.

[Epitaph]

TURGOT, A.-R.-J. (1727–1781)

[Inscription for a bust of Benjamin Franklin, who invented the lightning conductor]
Eripuit coelo fulmen, sceptrumque tyrannis.
He snatched the lightning shaft from heaven,
and the sceptre from tyrants.

[In A.N. de Condorcet, *Vie de Turgot*]

WILDE, Oscar (1854–1900)

All her bright golden hair
Tarnished with rust,
She that was young and fair
Fallen to dust.

['Requiescat' (1881)]

WORDSWORTH, William (1770–1850)

Three years she grew in sun and shower,
Then Nature said, 'A lovelier flower
On earth was never sown;
This child I to myself will take;
She shall be mine, and I will make
A Lady of my own'.

['Three years she grew' (1800)]

WOTTON, Sir Henry (1568–1639)

He first deceased; she for a little tried
To live without him: liked it not, and died.

['Death of Sir Albertus Moreton's Wife' (c. 1610)]

WREN, Sir Christopher (1632–1723)

Si monumentum requiris, circumspice.
If you are looking for his memorial, look
around you.

[Inscription written by his son, in St Paul's Cathedral, London]

YEATS, W.B. (1865–1939)

Swift has sailed into his rest;
Savage indignation there
Cannot lacerate his breast.
Imitate him if you dare,
World-besotted traveller; he
Served human liberty.

[In the *Dublin Magazine*, 1931, 'Swift's Epitaph']

Under bare Ben Bulben's head

In Drumcliff churchyard Yeats is laid …
On limestone quarried near the spot
By his command these words are cut:
Cast a cold eye
On life, on death.
Horseman, pass by!

[In *The Irish Times*, *Irish Independent*, and *Irish Press*, 1939, (Yeats' epitaph)]

EQUALITY

ANTHONY, Susan B. (1820–1906)
There never will be complete equality until women themselves help to make laws and elect lawmakers.

[*The Arena*, 1897]

ARISTOTLE (384–322 BC)
Inferiors agitate in order that they may be equal and equals that they may be superior. Such is the state of mind which creates party strife.

[*Politics*]

BAKUNIN, Mikhail (1814–1876)
[Anarchist declaration, Lyon, 1870]
We wish, in a word, equality – equality in fact as corollary, or rather, as primordial condition of liberty. From each according to his faculties, to each according to his needs; that is what we wish sincerely and energetically.

[In J. Morrison Davidson, *The Old Order and the New* (1890)]

BALZAC, Honoré de (1799–1850)
Equality may perhaps be a right, but no power on earth can ever turn it into a fact.

[*La Duchesse de Langeais* (1834)]

BARRIE, Sir J.M. (1860–1937)
His Lordship may compel us to be equal upstairs, but there will never be equality in the servants' hall.

[*The Admirable Crichton* (1902)]

BURNS, Robert (1759–1796)
The rank is but the guinea's stamp,
The man's the gowd for a' that …

For a' that, an' a' that,
It's comin yet for a' that,
That man to man the world o'er
Shall brithers be for a' that.

['A Man's a Man for a' that' (1795)]

EMERSON, Ralph Waldo (1803–1882)
There is a little formula, couched in pure Saxon, which you may hear in the corners of the streets and in the yard of the dame's school, from very little republicans: 'I'm as good as you be,' which contains the essence of the Massachusetts Bill of Rights and of the American Declaration of Independence.

[*Natural History of Intellect* (1893)]

FORSTER, E.M. (1879–1970)
All men are equal – all men, that is to say, who possess umbrellas.

[*Howard's End* (1910)]

GILBERT, W.S. (1836–1911)
They all shall equal be!
The Earl, the Marquis, and the Dook,
The Groom, the Butler, and the Cook,
The Aristocrat who banks with Coutts,
The Aristocrat who cleans the boots.

[*The Gondoliers* (1889)]

HUXLEY, Aldous (1894–1963)
That all men are equal is a proposition to which, at ordinary times, no sane human being has ever given his assent.

[*Proper Studies* (1927)]

JOHNSON, Samuel (1709–1784)
Your levellers wish to level down as far as themselves; but they cannot bear levelling up to themselves.

[In Boswell, *The Life of Samuel Johnson* (1791)]

It is better that some should be unhappy than that none should be happy, which would be the case in a general state of equality.

[In Boswell, *The Life of Samuel Johnson* (1791)]

KING, Martin Luther (1929–1968)
Now, I say to you today my friends, even though we face the difficulties of today and

tomorrow, I still have a dream. It is a dream deeply rooted in the American dream. I have a dream that one day this nation will rise up and live out the true meaning of its creed: – 'We hold these truths to be self-evident, that all men are created equal'.

[Speech at Civil Rights March on Washington, August 28, 1963]

MANDELA, Nelson (1918–)

I have fought against white domination, and I have fought against black domination. I have cherished the ideal of a democratic and free society in which all persons will live together in harmony and with equal opportunities. It is an ideal which I hope to live for and achieve. But, if needs be, it is an ideal for which I am prepared to die.

[Statement in the dock, 1964]

MILL, John Stuart (1806–1873)

The principle which regulates the existing social relations between the two sexes – the legal subordination of one sex to the other – is wrong in itself, and now one of the chief hindrances to human improvement; and … it ought to be replaced by a principle of perfect equality, admitting no power or privilege on the one side, nor disability on the other.

[*The Subjection of Women* (1869)]

MURDOCH, Iris (1919–1999)

The cry of equality pulls everyone down.

[*The Observer*, 1987]

ORWELL, George (1903–1950)

All animals are equal, but some animals are more equal than others.

[*Animal Farm* (1945)]

PROVERB

The beak of the goose is no longer than that of the gander.

RAINBOROWE, THOMAS (d. 1648)

The poorest he that is in England hath a life to live as the greatest he.

[Speech in Army debates, 1647]

WEDGWOOD, Josiah (1730–1795)

Am I not a man and a brother?

[Motto adopted by Anti-Slavery Society]

WILLKIE, Wendell (1892–1944)

The Constitution does not provide for first and second class citizens.

[*An American Program* (1944)]

WILSON, Harold (1916–1995)

Everybody should have an equal chance – but they shouldn't have a flying start.

[*The Observer*, 1963]

See CLASS; FEMINISM

ERROR

AESCHYLUS (525–456 BC)

Even he who is wiser than the wise may err.

[*Fragments*]

ANONYMOUS

In any collection of data, the figure most obviously correct, beyond all need of checking, is the mistake.

[Finagle's Third Law]

Once a job is fouled up, anything done to improve it only makes it worse.

[Finagle's Fourth Law]

BANVILLE, Théodore Faullain de (1823–1891)

Et ceux qui ne font rien ne se trompent jamais.
Those who do nothing are never wrong.

[*Odes funambulesques*]

BIDAULT, Georges (1899–1983)

The weak have one weapon: the errors of those who think they are strong.

[*The Observer*, 1962]

BOLINGBROKE, Henry (1678–1751)

Truth lies within a little and certain compass, but error is immense.

[*Reflections upon Exile* (1716)]

BOULAY DE LA MEURTHE, Antoine (1761–1840)

[On the execution of the Duc d'Enghien, 1804]
C'est pire qu'un crime, c'est une faute.
It is worse than a crime; it is a mistake.

[Attr.]

BROWNE, Sir Thomas (1605–1682)

Many … have too rashly charged the troops of error, and remain as trophies unto the enemies of truth.

[*Religio Medici* (1643)]

CROMWELL, Oliver (1599–1658)

I beseech you, in the bowels of Christ, think it possible you may be mistaken.

[Letter to the General Assembly of the Church of Scotland, 1650]

DESTOUCHES, Philippe Néricault (1680–1754)

Les absents ont toujours tort.
The absent are always in the wrong.

[*L'Obstacle Imprévu* (1717)]

DOYLE, Sir Arthur Conan (1859–1930)

It is a capital mistake to theorize before one has data.

[*The Adventures of Sherlock Holmes* (1892)]

DRYDEN, John (1631–1700)

Errors, like straws, upon the surface flow;
He who would search for pearls must dive below.

[*All for Love* (1678)]

ELIOT, George (1819–1880)

Errors look so very ugly in persons of small means – one feels they are taking quite a liberty in going astray; whereas people of fortune may naturally indulge in a few delinquencies.

[*Scenes of Clerical Life* (1858)]

Among all forms of mistake, prophecy is the most gratuitous.

[*Middlemarch* (1872)]

GOETHE (1749–1832)

Es irrt der Mensch, solang' er strebt.

Man errs as long as he strives.

[*Faust*, (1808)]

HALIFAX, Lord (1633–1695)

It is a general Mistake to think the Men we like are good for every thing, and those we do not, good for nothing.

[*Political, Moral and Miscellaneous Thoughts and Reflections* (1750)]

HUBBARD, Elbert (1856–1915)

The greatest mistake you can make in life is to be continually fearing you will make one.

JOHNSON, Samuel (1709–1784)

[Asked the reason for a mistake in his Dictionary]
Ignorance, madam, sheer ignorance.

[In Boswell, *The Life of Samuel Johnson* (1791)]

LOCKE, John (1632–1704)

It is one thing to show a man that he is in an error, and another to put him in possession of truth.

[*Essay concerning Human Understanding* (1690)]

All men are liable to error; and most men are, in many points, by passion or interest, under temptation to it.

[*Essay concerning Human Understanding* (1690)]

MALESHERBES, Chrétien Guillaume de Lamoignonde (1721–1794)

A new maxim is often a brilliant error.

[*Pensées et maximes*]

MARKHAM, Beryl (1902–1986)

Who thinks it just to be judged by a single error?

[*West with the Night* (1942)]

METTERNICH, Prince Clement (1773–1859)

L'erreur n'a jamais approché de mon esprit.
Error has never even come close to my mind.

[Remark, 1848]

PHELPS, E.J. (1822–1900)

The man who makes no mistakes does not usually make anything.

[Speech, 1899]

POPE, Alexander (1688–1744)

A man should never be ashamed to own he has been in the wrong, which is but saying, in other words, that he is wiser today than he was yesterday.

[*Miscellanies* (1727)]

PROVERB

To err is human.

REAGAN, Ronald (1911–)

You know, by the time you reach my age, you've made plenty of mistakes if you've lived your life properly.

[*The Observer*, 1987]

SCHOPENHAUER, Arthur (1788–1860)

Es gibt nur einen angeborenen Irrtum, und es ist der, dass wir dasind, um glücklich zu sein.

There is only one innate error, and that is that we are here in order to be happy.

[*The World as Will and Idea* (1859)]

SHIRLEY, James (1596–1666)

I presume you're mortal, and may err.

[*The Lady of Pleasure* (1637)]

SMILES, Samuel (1812–1904)

We often discover what will do, by finding out what will not do; and probably he who never made a mistake never made a discovery.

[*Self-Help* (1859)]

STRAW, Jack

The only people who never make mistakes are those who have never taken a decision.

[*The Observer*, May 1999]

TELLER, Edward (1908–)

An expert is a man who has made all the mistakes which can be made in a very narrow field.

[Remark, 1972]

WEST, Mae (1892–1980)

To err is human, but it feels divine.

[In Simon Rose, *Classic Film Guide* (1995)]

See TRUTH

ETERNITY

AURELIUS, Marcus (121–180)

All things from eternity are of similar forms and come round in a circle.

[*Meditations*]

BLAKE, William (1757–1827)

To see a World in a Grain of Sand
And a Heaven in a Wild Flower
Hold Infinity in the palm of your hand
And Eternity in an hour.

['Auguries of Innocence' (c. 1803)]

BROWNE, Sir Thomas (1605–1682)

Who can speak of eternity without a solecism, or think thereof without an ecstasy? Time we may comprehend, 'tis but five days elder than ourselves.

[*Religio Medici* (1643)]

CONGREVE, William (1670–1729)

Eternity was in that moment.

[*The Old Bachelor* (1693)]

CRISP, Quentin (1908–)

It may be true that preoccupation with time has been the downfall of Western man, but it can also be argued that conjecture about eternity is a waste of time.

[In Guy Kettlehack (ed.), *The Wit and Wisdom of Quentin Crisp*]

DICKINSON, Emily (1830–1886)

Our journey had advanced –
Our feet were almost come
To that odd Fork in Being's Road –
Eternity – by term.

['Our Journey had Advanced' (c. 1862)]

DOSTOEVSKY, Fyodor (1821–1881)

We keep imagining eternity as an idea that can't be understood, as something enormous … instead of all that there will just be one little room, somewhat like a country bath-house, with spiders in all the corners – that's eternity.

[*Crime and Punishment* (1865)]

SERVETUS, Michael (1511–1553)

[Comment to the judges of the Inquisition after

being condemned to be burned at the stake]
I will burn, but this is a mere incident. We
shall continue our discussion in eternity.

[Attr.]

See TIME

EUROPE

ASCHERSON, Neal (1932–)
Europe and the United States together
invented representative democracy and
human rights. But Europe invented fascism
and communism all by itself.

[Article, *The Observer*, June 1998]

BALDWIN, James (1924–1987)
Europe has what we do not have yet, a sense
of the mysterious and inexorable limits of
life, a sense, in a word, of tragedy. And we
have what they sorely need: a sense of life's
possibilities.

[Attr.]

BALDWIN, Stanley (1867–1947)
When you think of the defence of England
you no longer think of the chalk cliffs of
Dover. You think of the Rhine. That is where
our frontier lies today.

[Speech, 1934]

BENES, Eduard (1884–1948)
To make peace in Europe possible, the last
representative of the pre-war generation
must die and take his pre-war mentality into
the grave with him.

[Interview, 1929]

BEVIN, Ernest (1881–1951)
[On the Council of Europe]
If you open that Pandora's Box you never
know what Trojan 'orses will jump out.

[In Sir Roderick Barclay, *Ernest Bevin and the Foreign
Office* (1975)]

CHASE, Ilka (1905–1978)
That is what is so marvellous about Europe;
the people long ago learned that space and
beauty and quiet refuges in a great city,

where children may play and old people sit
in the sun, are of far more value to the
inhabitants than real estate taxes and
contractors' greed.

[*Fresh From the Laundry* (1967)]

CHURCHILL, Sir Winston (1874–1965)
We must build a kind of United States of
Europe.

[Speech, Zurich, September 1946]

COHN-BENDIT, Daniel (1945–)
*Europa soll aus Bosnien ein neues Westberlin
machen.*
Europe should make a new West-Berlin out
of Bosnia.

[Interview in *Süddeutsche Zeitung,* 1994]

DELORS, Jacques (1925–)
Europe is not just about material results, it is
about spirit. Europe is a state of mind.

[*The Independent*, May 1994]

The hardest thing is to convince European
citizens that even the most powerful nation
is no longer able to act alone.

[*The Independent*, May 1994]

FANON, Frantz (1925–1961)
When I search for man in the technique and
style of Europe, I see only a succession of
negations of man, and an avalanche of
murders.

[*The Wretched of the Earth* (1961)]

FISHER, H.A.L. (1856–1940)
Purity of race does not exist. Europe is a
continent of energetic mongrels.

[*History of Europe* (1935)]

GLADSTONE, William (1809–1898)
We are part of the community of Europe, and
we must do our duty as such.

[Speech, 1888]

GOLDSMITH, James (1933–)
Brussels is madness. I will fight it from within.

[*The Times*, June 1994]

GOLDSMITH, Oliver (c.1728–1774)
On whatever side we regard the history of
Europe, we shall perceive it to be a tissue of

crimes, follies, and misfortunes.

[*The Citizen of the World* (1762)]

HAZZARD, Shirley (1931–)

Going to Europe, someone had written, was about as final as going to heaven. A mystical passage to another life, from which no one returned the same.

[*The Transit of Venus* (1980)]

HEALEY, Denis (1917–)

[Of Conservatives]

Their Europeanism is nothing but imperialism with an inferiority complex.

[*The Observer*, 1962]

HEATH, Sir Edward (1916–)

Nor would it be in the interests of the [European] Community that its enlargement should take place except with the full-hearted consent of the Parliament and people of the new member countries.

[Speech to the Franco-British Chamber of Commerce, Paris, 1970]

HUGO, Victor (1802–1885)

I represent a party which does not yet exist: the party of revolution, civilisation. This party will make the twentieth century. There will issue from it first the United States of Europe, then the United States of the World.

[Written on the wall of the room in which Hugo died, Paris, 1885]

KOHL, Helmut (1930–)

[On plans for a single currency]

economic and political union … is the next step toward a United States of Europe.

[Comment, 1990]

MCCARTHY, Mary (1912–1989)

When an American heiress wants to buy a man, she at once crosses the Atlantic. The only really materialistic people I have ever met have been Europeans.

[*On the Contrary* (1961)]

The immense popularity of American movies abroad demonstrates that Europe is the

unfinished negative of which America is the proof.

[*On the Contrary* (1961)]

NICHOLSON, Sir Bryan (1932–)

[On the government's non-cooperation with Europe over the ban on exporting British beef]

In this pungent atmosphere of romantic nationalism and churlish xenophobia, I sometimes wonder if there are some among us who have failed to notice that the war with Germany has ended.

[*The Observer*, May 1996]

PITT, William (1759–1806)

[Commenting on the map of Europe, after the Battle of Austerlitz, 1805]

Roll up that map; it will not be wanted these ten years.

[In Lord Stanhope, *Life of the Rt. Hon. William Pitt*, (1862)]

SALISBURY, Lord (1830–1903)

We are part of the community of Europe and we must do our duty as such.

[Speech, 1888]

SCANLON, Hugh, Baron (1913–)

[Referring to his union's attitude to the Common Market]

Here we are again with both feet firmly planted in the air.

[*The Observer*, 1973]

SHERMAN, Alfred (1919–)

Britain does not wish to be ruled by a conglomerate in Europe which includes Third World nations such as the Greeks and Irish, nor for that matter the Italians and French, whose standards of political morality are not ours, and never will be.

[*The Independent*, August 1990]

SOAMES, Nicholas (1948–)

[Comment during a Commons debate, the topics of which included positive discrimination for women in the armed forces and a European Union directive on equality]

All that EC nonsense is beyond me.

[The *Mail on Sunday*, 1996]

THATCHER, Margaret (1925–)

Historians will one day look back and think it a curious folly that just as the Soviet Union was forced to recognize reality by dispersing power to its separate states and by limiting the powers of its central government, some people in Europe were trying to create a new artificial state by taking powers from national states and concentrating them at the centre.

[Speech, 1994]

VICTORIA, Queen (1819–1901)

I am sick of all this horrid business of politics, and Europe in general, and I think you will hear of me going with the children to live in Australia, and to think of Europe as the Moon!

[Letter to her daughter, the Princess Royal, 1859]

See BRITAIN; ENGLAND; FRANCE; GERMANY; IRELAND; ITALY; RUSSIA; SCOTLAND; SWITZERLAND; WALES

EVIL

ANONYMOUS

Honi soit qui mal y pense.
Evil be to him who evil thinks.

[Motto of the Order of the Garter]

ARENDT, Hannah (1906–1975)

[Of Eichmann]
It was as though in those last minutes he was summing up the lessons that this long course in human wickedness had taught us – the lesson of the fearsome, word-and-thought-defying banality of evil.

[*Eichmann in Jerusalem* (1963)]

THE BIBLE (King James Version)

The heart is deceitful above all things, and desperately wicked.

[*Jeremiah*, 17:9]

BOILEAU-DESPRÉAUX, Nicolas (1636–1711)

Souvent la peur d'un mal nous conduit dans un pire.
The fear of one evil often leads us into a greater one.

[*L'Art Poétique* (1674)]

BRECHT, Bertolt (1898–1956)

Die Gemeinheit der Welt ist gross, und man muss sich die Beine ablaufen, damit sie einem nicht gestohlen werden.
The wickedness of the world is so great that you have to run your legs off so you don't get them stolen from you.

[*The Threepenny Opera* (1928)]

BURKE, Edmund (1729–1797)

The only thing necessary for the triumph of evil is for good men to do nothing.

[Attr.]

CONRAD, Joseph (1857–1924)

The belief in a supernatural source of evil is not necessary; men alone are quite capable of every wickedness.

[*Under Western Eyes* (1911)]

CRISP, Quentin (1908–)

Vice is its own reward.

[*The Naked Civil Servant* (1968)]

DELBANCO, Andrew

The idea of evil is something on which the health of society depends. We have an obligation to name evil and oppose it in ourselves as well as in others.

[*The Guardian*, 1995]

GOLDSMITH, Oliver (c.1728–1774)

Don't let us make imaginary evils, when you know we have so many real ones to encounter.

[*The Good Natur'd Man* (1768)]

HATTERSLEY, Roy (1932–)

Familiarity with evil breeds not contempt but acceptance.

[*The Guardian*, 1993]

HAZLITT, William (1778–1830)

Wrong dressed out in pride, pomp, and

circumstance, has more attraction than abstract right.

[*Characters of Shakespeare's Plays* (1817)]

To great evils we submit, we resent little provocations.

[*Table-Talk* (1822)]

HOOD, Thomas (1799–1845)

But evil is wrought by want of Thought,
As well as want of Heart!

['The Lady's Dream' (1844)]

KEMPIS, Thomas á (c.1380–1471)

De duobus malis minus est semper eligendum.
Of two evils the lesser is always to be chosen.

[*De Imitatione Christi* (1892)]

LA ROCHEFOUCAULD (1613–1680)

Il n'y a guère d'homme assez habile pour connaître tout le mal qu'il fait.
There is scarcely a single man clever enough to know all the evil he does.

[*Maximes* (1678)]

MCCARTHY, Mary (1912–1989)

If someone tells you he is going to make 'a realistic decision', you immediately understand that he has resolved to do something bad.

[*On the Contrary* (1961)]

NEWMAN, John Henry, Cardinal (1801–1890)

Whatever is the first time persons hear evil, it is quite certain that good has been beforehand with them, and they have a something within them which tells them it is evil.

[*Parochial and Plain Sermons*]

NIETZSCHE, Friedrich Wilhelm (1844–1900)

Wer mit Ungeheurn kämpft, mag zusehn, dass er nicht dabei zum Ungeheuer wird. Und wenn du lange in einen Abgrund blickst, blickt der Abgrund auch in dich hinein.
Whoever struggles with monsters might watch that he does not thereby become a monster. When you stare into an abyss for a long time, the abyss also stares into you.

[*Beyond Good and Evil* (1886)]

POPE, Alexander (1688–1744)

Vice is a monster of so frightful mien,
As, to be hated, needs but to be seen;
Yet soon too oft, familiar with her face,
We first endure, then pity, then embrace.

[*An Essay on Man* (1733)]

ROOSEVELT, Theodore (1858–1919)

No man is justified in doing evil on the ground of expediency.

[*The Strenuous Life* (1900)]

SARTRE, Jean-Paul (1905–1980)

On ne peut vaincre un mal que par un autre mal.
One can only overcome an evil by means of another evil.

[*Les Mouches* (1943)]

SHAKESPEARE, William (1564–1616)

How oft the sight of means to do ill deeds
Make deeds ill done!

[*King John*, IV.ii]

Through tatter'd clothes small vices do appear;
Robed and furr'd gowns hide all.

[*King Lear*, IV.vi]

Oftentimes to win us to our harm,
The instruments of darkness tell us truths,
Win us with honest trifles, to betray's
In deepest consequence.

[*Macbeth*, I.iii]

An evil soul producing holy witness
Is like a villain with a smiling cheek,
A goodly apple rotten at the heart.
O, what a goodly outside falsehood hath!

[*The Merchant of Venice*, I.iii]

SOCRATES (469–399 BC)

No evil can befall a good man either in life or death.

[Attr. in Plato, *Apology*]

VEGA, Garcilaso de la (c.1501–1536)

Aquéste es de los hombres el oficio:
tentar el mal, y si es malo el suceso,
pedir con humildad perdón del vicio.

This is man's rôle:
to try evil, and if the outcome be evil,
to ask humbly for forgiveness for the act of
depravity.

[*Second Eclogue*]

WEST, Mae (1892–1980)

Whenever I'm caught between two evils, I
take the one I've never tried.

[*Klondike Annie*, film, 1936]

WILDE, Oscar (1854–1900)

Wickedness is a myth invented by good
people to account for the curious
attractiveness of others.

[*The Chameleon*, 1894]

WOLLSTONECRAFT, Mary (1759–1797)

No man chooses evil because it is evil; he only
mistakes it for happiness, the good he seeks.

[*A Vindication of the Rights of Men* (1790)]

See GOOD AND EVIL; SIN

EVOLUTION

BLACKWELL, Antoinette Brown (1825–1921)

Mr Darwin … has failed to hold definitely
before his mind the principle that the
difference of sex, whatever it may consist in,
must itself be subject to natural selection
and to evolution.

[*The Sexes Throughout Nature* (1875)]

CONGREVE, William (1670–1729)

I confess freely to you, I could never look
long upon a monkey, without very
mortifying reflections.

[*Letter to Mr Dennis*, 1695]

DARWIN, Charles (1809–1882)

The expression often used by Mr Herbert
Spencer of the Survival of the Fittest is more
accurate, and is sometimes equally
convenient.

[*The Origin of Species* (1859)]

We will now discuss in a little more detail the
struggle for existence.

[*The Origin of Species* (1859)]

It is interesting to contemplate an entangled
bank, clothed with many plants of many
kinds, with birds singing on the bushes, with
various insects flitting about, and with
worms crawling through the damp earth,
and to reflect that these elaborately
constructed forms, so different from each
other, and dependent upon each other in so
complex a manner, have all been produced
by laws acting around us … Growth with
Reproduction; Inheritance … Variability … a
Ratio of Increase so high as to lead to a
Struggle for Life, and as a consequence to
Natural Selection, entailing Divergence of
Character and the Extinction of less-
improved forms.

[*The Origin of Species* (1859)]

Believing as I do that man in the distant
future will be a far more perfect creature
than he now is, it is an intolerable thought
that he and all other sentient beings are
doomed to complete annihilation after such
long-continued slow progress. To those who
fully admit the immortality of the human
soul, the destruction of our world will not
appear so dreadful.

[*Life and Letters* (1973)]

I have called this principle, by which each
slight variation, if useful, is preserved, by the
term of Natural Selection.

[*The Origin of Species* (1859)]

We must, however, acknowledge, as it seems
to me, that man with all his noble qualities
… still bears in his bodily frame the indelible
stamp of his lowly origin.

[*The Descent of Man* (1871)]

DARWIN, Charles Galton (1887–1962)

The evolution of the human race will not be
accomplished in the ten thousand years of
tame animals, but in the million years of wild
animals, because man is and will always be a
wild animal.

[*The Next Ten Million Years*]

DISRAELI, Benjamin (1804–1881)

Is man an ape or an angel? Now I am on the side of the angels.

[Speech, 1864]

HUXLEY, T.H. (1825–1895)

[Reply to Bishop Wilberforce during debate on Darwin's theory of evolution]

I asserted – and I repeat – that a man has no reason to be ashamed of having an ape for his grandfather. If there were an ancestor whom I should feel shame in recalling it would rather be a man – a man of restless and versatile intellect – who, not content with an equivocal success in his own sphere of activity, plunges into scientific questions with which he has no real acquaintance, only to obscure them by an aimless rhetoric, and distract the attention of his hearers from the real point at issue by eloquent digressions and skilled appeals to religious prejudice.

[Speech, Oxford, 1860]

ROGERS, Will (1879–1935)

Coolidge is a better example of evolution than either Bryan or Darrow, for he knows when not to talk, which is the biggest asset the monkey possesses over the human.

[*Saturday Review*, 'A Rogers Thesaurus', 1962]

SPENCER, Herbert (1820–1903)

Evolution … is – a change from an indefinite, incoherent homogeneity, to a definite coherent heterogeneity.

[*First Principles* (1862)]

It cannot but happen … that those will survive whose functions happen to be most nearly in equilibrium with the modified aggregate of external forces … This survival of the fittest implies multiplication of the fittest.

[*The Principles of Biology* (1864)]

WILBERFORCE, Bishop Samuel (1805–1873)

[To T.H. Huxley]

And, in conclusion, I would like to ask the gentleman … whether the ape from which

he is descended was on his grandmother's or his grandfather's side of the family.

[Speech at Oxford, 1860]

See SURVIVAL

EXAMINATIONS

COLTON, Charles Caleb (c.1780–1832)

Examinations are formidable even to the best prepared, for the greatest fool may ask more than the wisest man can answer.

[*Lacon* (1820)]

SAINTSBURY, George (1845–1933)

[From an examination paper]

Without remarking that the thing became a trumpet in his hands, say something relevant about Milton's sonnets.

[In Stephen Potter, *The Muse in Chains* (1937)]

SELLAR, Walter (1898–1951) and YEATMAN, Robert Julian (1897–1968)

Do not on any account attempt to write on both sides of the paper at once.

[*1066 And All That* (1930)]

WILDE, Oscar (1854–1900)

In examinations the foolish ask questions that the wise cannot answer.

[*The Chameleon*, 1894]

See EDUCATION

EXCESS

BEST, George (1946–)

I spent a lot of money on booze, birds and fast cars. The rest I just squandered.

[Attr.]

BLAKE, William (1757–1827)

The road of excess leads to the palace of Wisdom.

['Proverbs of Hell' (1793)]

GOLDWATER, Barry (1909–1998)

I would remind you that extremism in the defence of liberty is no vice. And let me remind you also that moderation in the pursuit of justice is no virtue!

[Speech, 1964]

LETTERMAN, David (1947–)

Sometimes something worth doing is worth overdoing.

[CBS Late Show, 1994]

WILDE, Oscar (1854–1900)

Moderation is a fatal thing, Lady Hunstanton. Nothing succeeds like excess.

[A Woman of No Importance (1893)]

See MODERATION

EXERCISE

DRYDEN, John (1631–1700)

Better to hunt in fields, for health unbought,
Than fee the doctor for a nauseous draught.
The wise, for cure, on exercise depend;
God never made his work, for man to mend.

[Epistles (1700)]

HUTCHINS, Robert M. (1899–1977)

Whenever I feel like exercise, I lie down until the feeling passes.

[In Jarman, The Guinness Dictionary of Sports Quotations (1990)]

O'TOOLE, Peter (1932–)

The only exercise I get these days is from walking behind the coffins of friends who took too much exercise.

[The Observer, 'Sayings of the Year', 1998]

SKELTON, Red (1913–1997)

I get plenty of exercise carrying the coffins of my friends who exercise.

See HEALTH

EXILE

AYTOUN, W.E. (1813–1865)

They bore within their breasts the grief
That fame can never heal –
The deep, unutterable woe

Which none save exiles feel.

['The Island of the Scots' (1849)]

The earth is all the home I have,
The heavens my wide roof-tree.

['The Wandering Jew' (1867)]

THE BIBLE
(King James Version)

I have been a stranger in a strange land.

[Exodus, 2:22]

BIERCE, Ambrose (1842–c.1914)

Exile: One who serves his country by residing abroad, yet is not an ambassador.

[The Enlarged Devil's Dictionary (1967)]

BROWN, Ford Madox (1821–1893)

The last of England! O'er the sea, my dear,
Our homes to seek amid Australian fields.
Us, not our million-acred island yields
The space to dwell in. Thrust out, forced to hear
Low ribaldry from sots, and share rough cheer
From rudely nurtured men.

['Sonnet']

GALT, John (1779–1839)

From the lone shieling of the misty island
Mountains divide us, and the waste of seas –
Yet still the blood is strong, the heart is Highland,
And we in dreams behold the Hebrides!
Fair these broad meads, these hoary woods are grand;
But we are exiles from our fathers' land.

[Attr. in Blackwoods Edinburgh Magazine, 1829]

GREGORY VII (c.1020–1085)

[Last words]
I have loved righteousness and hated iniquity: therefore I die in exile.

[In Bowden, The Life and Pontificate of Gregory VII (1840)]

SANTAYANA, George (1863–1952)

People who feel themselves to be exiles in this world are mightily inclined to believe themselves citizens of another.

[Attr.]

SCOTT, Sir Walter (1771–1832)

From the lone shieling of the misty island
Mountains divide us and the waste of the
seas –
Yet still the blood is strong, the heart is
Highland,
And we in dreams behold the Hebrides!

['Canadian Boat Song' (1829)]

SPARK, Muriel (1918–)

It was Edinburgh that bred within me the
conditions of exiledom; and what have I
been doing since then but moving from exile
to exile? It has ceased to be a fate, it has
become a calling.

['What Images Return']

STEVENSON, Robert Louis (1850–1894)

Blows the wind today, and the sun and the
rain are flying,
Blows the wind on the moors today and
now,
Where about the graves of the martyrs the
whaups are crying,
My heart remembers how! …

Be it granted to me to behold you again in
dying,
Hills of home! and to hear again the call;
Hear about the graves of the martyrs the
peewees crying,
And hear no more at all.

[Songs of Travel (1896)]

EXPERIENCE

ANONYMOUS

Experience is the comb that nature gives us
when we are bald.

ANTRIM, Minna (1861–1950)

Experience is a good teacher, but she sends
in terrific bills.

[Naked Truth and Veiled Allusions (1902)]

BEERBOHM, Sir Max (1872–1956)

You will think me lamentably crude: my

experience of life has been drawn from life
itself.

[Zuleika Dobson (1911)]

BLAKE, William (1757–1827)

What is the price of Experience? do
men buy it for a song?
Or wisdom for a dance in the street?
No, it is bought with the price
Of all that a man hath, his house, his
wife, his children.
Wisdom is sold in the desolate market
where none come to buy,
And in the wither'd field where the
farmer plows for bread in vain.

[Vala, or the Four Zoas]

BOWEN, Elizabeth (1899–1973)

Experience isn't interesting till it begins to
repeat itself – in fact, till it does that, it hardly
is experience.

[The Death of the Heart (1938)]

CONGREVE, William (1670–1729)

Ay, ay, I have experience: I have a wife, and so
forth.

[The Way of the World (1700)]

DISRAELI, Benjamin (1804–1881)

Experience is the child of Thought, and
Thought is the child of Action. We cannot
learn men from books.

[Vivian Grey (1826)]

EMERSON, Ralph Waldo (1803–1882)

The years teach much which the days never
know.

['Experience' (1844)]

FADIMAN, Clifton (1904–)

Experience teaches you that the man who
looks you straight in the eye, particularly if he
adds a firm handshake, is hiding something.

[Enter, Conversing]

FROUDE, James Anthony (1818–1894)

Experience teaches slowly, and at the cost of
mistakes.

[Short Studies on Great Subjects (1877)]

HALIFAX, Lord (1633–1695)

The best way to suppose what may come, is to remember what is past.

[*Political, Moral and Miscellaneous Thoughts and Reflections* (1750)]

HEGEL, Georg Wilhelm (1770–1831)

Was die Erfahrung aber und die Geschichte lehren, ist dieses, dass Völker und Regierungen niemals etwas aus der Geschichte gelernt haben.

What experience and history teach us, however, is this, that peoples and governments have never learned anything from history.

[*Lectures on the Philosophy of History* (1837)]

HOLMES, Oliver Wendell (1809–1894)

A moment's insight is sometimes worth a life's experience.

[*The Professor at the Breakfast-Table* (1860)]

HUXLEY, Aldous (1894–1963)

experience is not what happens to a man. It is what a man does with what happens to him.

[Attr.]

JAMES, Henry (1843–1916)

Experience is never limited, and it is never complete; it is an immense sensibility, a kind of huge spider-web of the finest silken threads suspended in the chamber of consciousness, and catching every air-borne particle in its tissue.

[*Partial Portraits* (1888)]

KEATS, John (1795–1821)

Nothing ever becomes real till it is experienced – Even a Proverb is no proverb to you till your Life has illustrated it.

[Letter to George and Georgiana Keats, 1819]

MACCAIG, Norman (1910–1996)

Experience teaches that it doesn't.

[*A World of Difference* (1983)]

MEREDITH, George (1828–1909)

We spend our lives in learning pilotage, And grow good steersmen when the vessel's crank!

['The Wisdom of Eld']

POMFRET, John (1667–1702)

We live and learn, but not the wiser grow.

['Reason' (1700)]

PROVERBS

Experience is the mother of wisdom.

Experience is the best teacher.

WALLER, Edmund (1606–1687)

The soul's dark cottage, batter'd and decay'd
Lets in new light through chinks that time has made;
Stronger by weakness, wiser men become,
As they draw nearer to their eternal home.
Leaving the old, both worlds at once they view,
That stand upon the threshold of the new.

['Of the Last Verses in the Book' (1685)]

WILDE, Oscar (1854–1900)

Dumby: Experience is the name every one gives to their mistakes.
Cecil Graham: One shouldn't commit any.
Dumby: Life would be very dull without them.

[*Lady Windermere's Fan* (1892)]

Experience is the name every one gives to their mistakes.

[*Lady Windermere's Fan* (1892)]

See HISTORY; PAST

EXPERTS

BOHR, Niels Henrik David (1885–1962)

An expert is a man who has made all the mistakes which can be made in a very narrow field.

[Attr.]

DOYLE, Sir Arthur Conan (1859–1930)

All other men are specialists, but his specialism is omniscience.

[*His Last Bow* (1917)]

HEISENBERG, Werner (1901–1976)

Ein Fachmann ist ein Mann, der einige der größten

*Fehler kennt, die man in dem betreffenden Fach
machen kann, und der sie deshalb zu vermeiden
versteht.*

An expert is a man who knows some of the
worst errors that can be made in the subject
in question and who therefore understands
how to avoid them.

[*The Part and the Whole*,
(1969)]

MAYO, William James (1861–1939)

Specialist – A man who knows more and
more about less and less.

[Attr.]

MORGAN, Elaine (1920–)

The trouble with specialists is that they tend
to think in grooves.

[*The Descent of Woman*]

EXPLANATIONS

BARRIE, Sir J.M. (1860–1937)

I do loathe explanations.

[*My Lady Nicotine* (1890)]

CARROLL, Lewis (1832–1898)

'Why,' said the Dodo, 'the best way to explain
it is to do it.'

[*Alice's Adventures in Wonderland* (1865)]

'I can't explain myself, I'm afraid, sir,' said
Alice, 'because I'm not myself, you see.' 'I don't
see,' said the Caterpillar.

[*Alice's Adventures in Wonderland* (1865)]

I can explain all the poems that ever were
invented – and a good many that haven't
been invented just yet.

[*Through the Looking-Glass (and What Alice Found
There)* (1872)]

GRAYSON, Victor (1881–c.1920)

Never explain: your friends don't need it and
your enemies won't believe it.

[Attr.]

MARX, Chico (1886–1961)

[Explanation given when his wife caught him
kissing a chorus girl]

But I wasn't kissing her. I was whispering in
her mouth.

[In G. Marx and R. Anobile, *The Marx Brothers
Scrapbook* (1974)]

EYES

ARNOLD, Matthew (1822–1888)

Let beam upon my inward view
Those eyes of deep, soft, lucent hue –
Eyes too expressive to be blue,
Too lovely to be grey.

['Faded Leaves' (1852)]

BAGEHOT, Walter (1826–1877)

There is a glare in some men's eyes which
seems to say, 'Beware, I am dangerous; *Noli
me tangere*.' Lord Brougham's face has this. A
mischievous excitability is the most obvious
expression of it. If he were a horse, nobody
would buy him; with that eye no one could
answer for his temper.

[*Historical Essays*]

BEERBOHM, Sir Max (1872–1956)

It needs no dictionary of quotations to
remind me that the eyes are the windows of
the soul.

[*Zuleika Dobson* (1911)]

COBORN, Charles (1852–1945)

Two lovely black eyes,
Oh, what a surprise!
Only for telling a man he was wrong.
Two lovely black eyes!

['Two Lovely Black Eyes', song,
1886]

CRASHAW, Richard (c.1612–1649)

Two walking baths; two weeping motions;
Portable, and compendious oceans.

['Saint Mary Magdalene, or The Weeper' (1652)]

DICKENS, Charles (1812–1870)

'Yes, I have a pair of eyes,' replied Sam, 'and
that's just it. If they wos a pair o' patent
double million magnifyin' gas microscopes of
hextra power, p'raps I might be able to see
through a flight o' stairs and a deal door; but

bein' only eyes, you see my wision's limited.'

[*The Pickwick Papers* (1837)]

FLETCHER, Phineas (1582–1650)

Love's tongue is in the eyes.

['Piscatory Eclogues' (1633)]

HERRICK, Robert (1591–1674)

Sweet, be not proud of those two eyes,
Which Star-like sparkle in their skies …

That Rubie which you weare,
Sunk from the tip of your soft eare,
Will last to be a precious Stone,
When all your world of Beautie's gone.

[*Hesperides* (1648)]

HODGES, Mike

CARTER: So you're doing all right then, Eric.
You're making good … Do you know, I'd
almost forgotten what your eyes looked like.
They're still the same. Piss holes in the snow.

[*Get Carter*, film, 1971]

MERCER, Johnny (1909–1976)

Jeepers Creepers – where'd you get them
peepers?

['Jeepers Creepers', song, 1938]

POPE, Alexander (1688–1744)

Bright as the sun, her eyes the gazers strike,
And, like the sun, they shine on all alike.

[*The Rape of the Lock* (1714)]

POUND, Ezra (1885–1972)

Free us, for we perish
In this ever-flowing monotony
Of ugly print marks, black
Upon white parchment.

['The Eyes' (1908)]

SPARK, Muriel (1918–)

But I did not remove my glasses, for I had not
asked for her company in the first place, and
there is a limit to what one can listen to with
the naked eye.

[*Voices at Play* (1961)]

STERNE, Laurence (1713–1768)

'I am half distracted, Captain Shandy,' said
Mrs Wadman, … 'a mote – or sand – or
something – I know not what, has got into
this eye of mine – do look in to it.'… In
saying which, Mrs Wadman edged herself
close in beside my uncle Toby, … 'Do look
into it,' – said she …
If thou lookest, uncle Toby, in search of this
mote one moment longer – thou art undone.

[*Tristram Shandy* (1759–1767)]

An eye full of gentle salutations – and soft
responses – … whispering soft – like the last
low accents of an expiring saint … It did my
uncle Toby's business.

[*Tristram Shandy* (1759–1767)]

See APPEARANCE; CRYING

F

FACTS

BARRIE, Sir J.M. (1860–1937)
Facts were never pleasing to him. He acquired them with reluctance and got rid of them with relief. He was never on terms with them until he had stood them on their heads.

[*The Greenwood Hat* (1937)]

BURNS, Robert (1759–1796)
But facts are chiels that winna ding,
And downa be disputed.

['A Dream' (1786)]

DOYLE, Sir Arthur Conan (1859–1930)
'I should have more faith,' he said; 'I ought to know by this time that when a fact appears opposed to a long train of deductions it invariably proves to be capable of bearing some other interpretation.'

[*A Study in Scarlet* (1887)]

HUXLEY, Aldous (1894–1963)
Facts do not cease to exist because they are ignored.

[*Proper Studies* (1927)]

JAMES, Henry (1843–1916)
The fatal futility of Fact.

[*Prefaces* (1897)]

JERROLD, Douglas William (1803–1857)
Talk to him of Jacob's ladder, and he would ask the number of the steps.

[*Wit and Opinions of Douglas Jerrold* (1859)]

RYLE, Gilbert (1900–1976)
A myth is, of course, not a fairy story. It is the presentation of facts belonging to one category in the idioms appropriate to another. To explode a myth is accordingly not to deny the facts but to re-allocate them.

[*The Concept of Mind* (1949)]

TINDAL, Matthew (1657–1733)
Matters of fact, which as Mr Budgell somewhere observes, are very stubborn things.

[*The Will of Matthew Tindal* (1733)]

See TRUTH

FAILURE

CIANO, Count Galeazzo (1903–1944)
As always, victory finds a hundred fathers, but defeat is an orphan.

[*Diary*, 1942]

COWARD, Sir Noël (1899–1973)
[On Randolph Churchill]
Dear Randolph, utterly unspoiled by failure.

[Attr.]

DYLAN, Bob (1941–)
She knows there's no success like failure
And that failure's no success at all.

['Love Minus Zero/No Limit', song, 1965]

HARE, Augustus (1792–1834)
Half the failures in life arise from pulling in one's horse as he is leaping.

[*Guesses at Truth* (1827)]

HEALEY, Denis (1917–)
Examining one's entrails while fighting a battle is a recipe for certain defeat.

[*The Observer*, 1983]

HELLER, Joseph (1923–)
He was a self-made man who owed his lack of success to nobody.

[*Catch-22* (1961)]

HEMINGWAY, Ernest (1898–1961)
But man is not made for defeat … A man can be destroyed but not defeated.

[*The Old Man and the Sea* (1952)]

KEATS, John (1795–1821)
I would sooner fail than not be among the

greatest.

[Letter to James Hessey, 1818]

NEWMAN, Paul (1925–)

Show me a good loser and I'll show you a loser.

[*The Observer*, 1982]

ROCKNE, Knut (1888–1931)

Show me a good and gracious loser and I'll show you a failure.

[Attr.]

SHAKESPEARE, William (1564–1616)

Macbeth: If we should fail?
Lady Macbeth: We fail!
But screw your courage to the sticking place,
And we'll not fail.

[*Macbeth*, I.vii]

STEVENSON, Robert Louis (1850–1894)

Here lies one who meant well, tried a little, failed much: – surely that may be his epitaph, of which he need not be ashamed.

[*Across the Plains* (1892)]

VICTORIA, Queen (1819–1901)

[Said of the Boer War in 'Black Week', 1899]
We are not interested in the possibilities of defeat; they do not exist.

[In Cecil, *Life of Robert, Marquis of Salisbury* (1931)]

VOLTAIRE (1694–1778)

Never having been able to succeed in the world, he took his revenge by speaking ill of it.

[*Zadig, or Fate* (1747)]

WILDE, Oscar (1854–1900)

We women adore failures. They lean on us.

[*A Woman of No Importance* (1893)]

See SUCCESS

FAME

ALLEN, Fred (1894–1956)

A celebrity is a person who works hard all his life to become known, then wears dark

glasses to avoid being recognized.

[Attr.]

ANONYMOUS

Fame is a mask that eats the face.

BENNETT, Alan (1934–)

My claim to literary fame is that I used to deliver meat to a woman who became T.S. Eliot's mother-in-law.

[*The Observer*, 'Sayings of the Year', 1992]

BERNERS, Lord (1883–1950)

[Of T.E. Lawrence]
He's always backing into the limelight.

[Attr.]

BOORSTIN, Daniel J. (1914–)

The celebrity is a person who is known for his well-knownness.

[*The Image* (1962)]

BRIDGES, Robert (1844–1930)

Rejoice ye dead, where'er your spirits dwell,
Rejoice that yet on earth your fame is bright,
And that your names, remembered day and night,
Live on the lips of those who love you well.

['Ode to Music' (1896)]

BURKE, Edmund (1729–1797)

Passion for fame; a passion which is the instinct of all great souls.

[Speech on American Taxation (1774)]

BYRON, Lord (1788–1824)

[Remark on the instantaneous success of Childe Harold]
I awoke one morning and found myself famous.

[In Moore, *Letters and Journals of Lord Byron* (1830)]

CALDERÓN DE LA BARCA, Pedro (1600–1681)

Fame, like water, bears up the lighter things, and lets the weighty sink.

[Attr.]

CAREW, Thomas (c.1595–1640)

Know, Celia (since thou art so proud,)
'Twas I that gave thee thy renowne:

Thou had'st in the forgotten crowd
Of common beauties, liv'd unknowne,
Had not my verse exhal'd thy name,
And with it imped the wings of fame.

['Ingratefull Beauty Threatened'
(1640)]

CATO THE ELDER (234–149 BC)

I would much rather have men ask why I
have no statue than why I have one.

[In Plutarch, *Lives*]

DANTE ALIGHIERI (1265–1321)

Ché, seggendo in piuma,
In fama non si vien, né sotto coltre.

For fame is not achieved by sitting on feather
cushions or lying in bed.

[*Divina Commedia* (1307)]

DANTON, Georges (1759–1794)

[Response to formal questions during his trial in
Paris, 2 April 1794]

My address will soon be Annihilation. As for
my name you will find it in the Pantheon of
History.

[Attr.]

DOBSON, Henry Austin (1840–1921)

Fame is a food that dead men eat, –
I have no stomach for such meat.

['Fame is a Food' (1906)]

GOETHE (1749–1832)

Die Tat ist alles, nichts der Ruhm.

The deed is all, the glory is naught.

[*Faust* (1832)]

GRAINGER, James (c.1721–1766)

What is fame? an empty bubble;
Gold? a transient, shining trouble.

['Solitude' (1755)]

GREENE, Graham (1904–1991)

Fame is a powerful aphrodisiac.

[*Radio Times*, 1964]

HEPBURN, Katharine (1907–)

I don't care what is written about me as long
as it isn't true.

[In Cooper and Hartman, *Violets and Vinegar*
(1980)]

HILLEL, 'The Elder' (c.60 BC–c.10 AD)

A name made great is a name destroyed.

[In Taylor (ed.), *Sayings of the Jewish Fathers* (1877)]

HUGO, Victor (1802–1885)

La popularité? c'est la gloire en gros sous.

Fame? It's glory in small change.

[*Ruy Blas* (1838)]

HUXLEY, Aldous (1894–1963)

I'm afraid of losing my obscurity.
Genuineness only thrives in the dark. Like
celery.

[*Those Barren Leaves* (1925)]

HUXLEY, T.H. (1825–1895)

[Remark to George Howell]

Posthumous fame is not particularly
attractive to me, but, if I am to be
remembered at all, I would rather it should
be as 'a man who did his best to help the
people' than by any other title.

[In L. Huxley, *Life and Letters of Thomas Henry
Huxley* (1900)]

KEATS, John (1795–1821)

Fame, like a wayward girl, will still be coy
To those who woo her with too slavish
knees.

['On Fame (1)' (1819)]

MELBA, Dame Nellie (1861–1931)

[To the editor of the Argus]

I don't care what you say, for me or against
me, but for heaven's sake say something
about me.

[In Thompson, *On Lips of Living Men*]

MONTAIGNE, Michel de (1533–1592)

*La gloire et le repos sont choses qui ne peuvent loger
en même gîte.*

Fame and tranquillity cannot dwell under the
same roof.

[*Essais* (1580)]

MURDOCH, Iris (1919–1999)

'What are you famous for?'
'For nothing. I am just famous.'

[*The Flight from the Enchanter*
(1955)]

PECK, Gregory (1916–)

[On the fact that no-one in a crowded restaurant recognized him]
If you have to tell them who you are, you aren't anybody.

[In S. Harris, *Pieces of Eight*]

PERICLES (c.495–429)

For the whole earth is the supulchre of famous men.

[In Thucydides, *Histories*]

PINDAR, Peter (John Wolcot) (1738–1819)

What rage for fame attends both great and small!
Better be damned than mentioned not at all!

['To the Royal Academicians' (1782–1785)]

POPE, Alexander (1688–1744)

Then teach me, Heav'n! to scorn the guilty bays,
Drive from my breast that wretched lust of praise,
Unblemished let me live, or die unknown;
Oh grant an honest fame, or grant me none!

[*The Temple of Fame* (1715)]

ROOSEVELT, Theodore (1858–1919)

It is better to be faithful than famous.

[In Riis, *Theodore Roosevelt, the Citizen*]

SALINGER, J.D. (1919–)

They didn't act like people and they didn't act like actors. It's hard to explain. They acted more like they knew they were celebrities and all. I mean they were good, but they were too good.

[*The Catcher in the Rye* (1951)]

SITWELL, Dame Edith (1887–1964)

A pompous woman of his acquaintance, complaining that the head-waiter of a restaurant had not shown her and her husband immediately to a table, said 'We had to tell him who we were.' Gerald, interested, enquired, 'And who were you?'.

[*Taken Care Of* (1965)]

SPENSER, Edmund (c.1522–1599)

One day I wrote her name upon the strand,

But came the waves and washed it away:
Agayne I wrote it with a second hand,
But came the tyde, and made my paynes his pray.
Vayne man, sayd she, that doest in vaine assay,
A mortall thing so to immortalize,
For I my selfe shall lyke to this decay,
And eek my name bee wyped out lykewise.
Not so, (quod I) let baser things devize
To dy in dust, but you shall live by fame:
My verse your vertues rare shall eternize,
And in the hevens wryte your glorious name.
Where whenas death shall all the world subdew,
Our love shall live, and later life renew.

[*Amoretti, and Epithalamion* (1595)]

TACITUS (AD c.56–c.120)

The desire for fame is the last thing to be put aside, even by the wise.

[*Histories*]

WARHOL, Andy (c.1926–1987)

In the future everyone will be world famous for fifteen minutes.

[Catalogue for an exhibition, 1968]

WILDE, Oscar (1854–1900)

There is only one thing in the world worse than being talked about, and that is not being talked about.

[*The Picture of Dorian Gray* (1891)]

See CELEBRITY; POPULARITY; REPUTATION

FAMILIARITY

STEIN, Gertrude (1874–1946)

I like familiarity. In me it does not breed contempt. Only more familiarity.

[*Dale Carnegie's Scrapbook*]

PROVERB

Familiarity breeds contempt.

FAMILIES

BEERBOHM, Sir Max (1872–1956)

They were a tense and peculiar family, the Oedipuses, weren't they?

[Attr.]

BELLOC, Hilaire (1870–1953)

Mothers of large families (who claim to common sense)
Will find a Tiger well repays the trouble and expense.

[*The Bad Child's Book of Beasts* (1896)]

BROWNE, Sir Thomas (1605–1682)

Generations pass while some tree stands, and old families last not three oaks.

[*Hydriotaphia: Urn Burial* (1658)]

BUTLER, Samuel (1835–1902)

I believe that more unhappiness comes from this source than from any other – I mean from the attempt to prolong family connection unduly and to make people hang together artificially who would never naturally do so. The mischief among the lower classes is not so great, but among the middle and upper classes it is killing a large number daily. And the old people do not really like it much better than the young.

[*The Note-Books of Samuel Butler* (1912)]

CONGREVE, William (1670–1729)

A branch of one of your antediluvian families, fellows that the flood could not wash away.

[*Love for Love* (1695)]

DICKENS, Charles (1812–1870)

It is a melancholy truth that even great men have their poor relations.

[*Bleak House* (1853)]

Accidents will occur in the best-regulated families.

[*David Copperfield* (1850)]

FORSTER, E.M. (1879–1970)

I felt for a moment that the whole Wilcox family was a fraud, just a wall of newspapers and motor-cars and golf-clubs, and that if it

fell I should find nothing behind it but panic and emptiness.

[*Howard's End* (1910)]

FRAZER, Sir James (1854–1941)

The awe and dread with which the untutored savage contemplates his mother-in-law are amongst the most familiar facts of anthropology.

[*The Golden Bough* (1900)]

FREUD, Sigmund (1856–1939)

Philosophers and politicians have agreed that the bonding together in family groups is both instinctive and necessary to human welfare – and therefore essential to the health of a society. The family is the microcosm.

[Attr. in *The Times*, May 1996]

HAZLITT, William (1778–1830)

A person may be indebted for a nose or an eye, for a graceful carriage or a voluble discourse, to a great-aunt or uncle, whose existence he has scarcely heard of.

[*London Magazine*, 1821]

HOPE, Anthony (1863–1933)

Good families are generally worse than any others.

[*The Prisoner of Zenda* (1894)]

JOHN PAUL II (1920–)

Treasure your families – the future of humanity passes by way of the family.

[Speech, 1982]

JUVENAL (c.60–130)

Desperanda tibi salva concordia socru.
Despair of peace as long as your mother-in-law is alive.

[*Satires*]

LAMB, Charles (1775–1834)

A poor relation – is the most irrelevant thing in nature.

[*Last Essays of Elia* (1833)]

LEACH, Sir Edmund (1910–1989)

Far from being the basis of the good society, the family, with its narrow privacy and tawdry secrets, is the source of all our discontents.

[BBC Reith Lecture, 1967]

LENNON, John (1940–1980)

She's leaving home after living alone for so many years.

['She's Leaving Home', song, 1967, with Paul McCartney]

LINCOLN, Abraham (1809–1865)

I don't know who my grandfather was; I am much more concerned to know what his grandson will be.

[In Gross, *Lincoln's Own Stories*]

MACAULAY, Dame Rose (1881–1958)

A group of closely related persons living under one roof; it is a convenience, often a necessity, sometimes a pleasure, sometimes the reverse; but who first exalted it as admirable, an almost religious ideal?

[*The World My Wilderness* (1950)]

MARX, Groucho (1895–1977)

You're a disgrace to our family name of Wagstaff, if such a thing is possible.

[*Horse Feathers*, film, 1932]

MITCHELL, Julian (1935–)

The sink is the great symbol of the bloodiness of family life. All life is bad, but family life is worse.

[*As Far as You Can Go* (1963)]

MONTAIGNE, Michel de (1533–1592)

Il n'y a guère moins de tourment au gouvernement d'une famille que d'un état entier … et, pour être les occupations domestiques moins importantes, elles n'en sont pas moins importunes.

There is scarcely any less trouble in running a family than in governing an entire state … and domestic matters are no less importunate for being less important.

[*Essais* (1580)]

MOONEY, Bel

[On the need for family life]

I find myself surprised at how its realism actually unites morality with – yes – romance. It is that need that draws us to nest

in rows, separated by thin walls, hoping to be tolerated and loved forever – and to go on reproducing ourselves in family patterns, handing on some misery (perhaps), but untold happiness too.

[*The Times*, 1996]

NASH, Ogden (1902–1971)

One would be in less danger
From the wiles of a stranger
If one's own kin and kith
Were more fun to be with.

['Family Court' (1931)]

POUND, Ezra (1885–1972)

Oh how hideous it is
To see three generations of one house gathered together!
It is like an old tree with shoots,
And with some branches rotted and falling.

['Commission' (1916)]

PROVERB

Every family has a skeleton in the cupboard.

ROSSETTI, Christina (1830–1894)

For there is no friend like a sister
In calm or stormy weather;
To cheer one on the tedious way,
To fetch one if one goes astray,
To lift one if one totters down,
To strengthen whilst one stands.

['Goblin Market' (1862)]

THACKERAY, William Makepeace (1811–1863)

If a man's character is to be abused, say what you will, there's nobody like a relation to do the business.

[*Vanity Fair* (1848)]

TOLSTOY, Leo (1828–1910)

All happy families resemble one another, but every unhappy family is unhappy in its own way.

[*Anna Karenina* (1877)]

WODEHOUSE, P.G. (1881–1975)

It is no use telling me that there are bad aunts and good aunts. At the core they are all alike. Sooner or later, out pops the cloven hoof.

[*The Code of the Woosters* (1938)]

See ANCESTORS; BABIES; BIRTH; CHILDREN; FATHERS; MARRIAGE; MOTHERS; PREGNANCY

FASCISM

BEVAN, Aneurin (1897–1960)

Fascism is not in itself a new order of society. It is the future refusing to be born.

[Attr.]

CASTELLANI, Maria (fl 1930s)

Fascism recognises women as part of the life force of the country, laying down a division of duties between the two sexes, without putting obstacles in the way of those women who by their intellectual gifts reach the highest positions.

[*Italian Women, Past and Present* (1937)]

IBÁRRURI, Dolores ('La Pasionaria') (1895–1989)

Wherever they pass, they [the fascists] sow death and desolation.

[*Speeches and Articles* (1938)]

MCKENNEY, Ruth (1911–1972)

If modern civilisation had any meaning it was displayed in the fight against Fascism.

[In Seldes, *The Great Quotations* (1960)]

MOSLEY, Sir Oswald (1896–1980)

Before the organization of the Blackshirt movement free speech did not exist in this country.

[In *New Statesman, This England*]

MUSSOLINI, Benito (1883–1945)

[On Hitler's seizing power]
Fascism is a religion; the twentieth century will be known in history as the century of Fascism.

[In Seldes, *Sawdust Caesar*]

Per noi fascisti le frontiere, tutte le frontiere, sono sacre. Non si discutono: si defendono.

For us fascists, frontiers, all frontiers, are sacred. We do not dispute them: we defend them.

[Speech to the Lower House, 1938]

Fascism is not an article for export.

[Article in the German press, 1932]

PLATH, Sylvia (1932–1963)

Every woman adores a Fascist,
The boot in the face, the brute
Brute heart of a brute like you.

['Daddy' (1963)]

STRACHEY, John St Loe (1901–1963)

Fascism means war.

[Slogan, 1930s]

FASHION

AUSTEN, Jane (1775–1817)

A person and face, of strong, natural, sterling insignificance, though adorned in the first style of fashion.

[*Sense and Sensibility* (1811)]

CASSINI, Oleg (1913–)

Fashion anticipates, and elegance is a state of mind.

[*In My Own Fashion* (1987)]

CHANEL, Coco (1883–1971)

[Remark at a press conference, 1967]
Fashion is reduced to a question of hem lengths. Haute couture is finished because it's in the hands of men who don't like women.

[In Madsen, *Coco Chanel* (1990)]

A fashion for the young? That is a pleonasm: there is no fashion for the old.

[In Haedrich, *Coco Chanel, Her Life, Her Secrets* (1971)]

CHURCHILL, Charles (1731–1764)

Fashion – a word which knaves and fools may use,
Their knavery and folly to excuse.

[*The Rosciad* (1761)]

CIBBER, Colley (1671–1757)

One had as good be out of the world, as out of the fashion.

[*Love's Last Shift* (1696)]

GOLDSMITH, Oliver (c.1728–1774)

And, even while fashion's brightest arts decoy,

The heart distrusting asks, if this be joy.

[*The Deserted Village* (1770)]

STEELE, Sir Richard (1672–1729)

Fashion, the arbiter, and rule of right.

[*The Spectator*, 478]

WALPOLE, Horace (1717–1797)

It is charming to totter into vogue.

[Letter to George Selwyn, 1765]

See APPEARANCE; STYLE

FATHERS

AUBREY, John (1626–1697)

[Of Sir Walter Raleigh]

Sir Walter, being strangely surprised and put out of his countenance at so great a table, gives his son a damned blow over the face. His son, as rude as he was, would not strike his father, but strikes over the face the gentleman that sat next to him and said 'Box about:'twill come to my father anon.'

[*Brief Lives* (c. 1693)]

**THE BIBLE
(King James Version)**

The fathers have eaten sour grapes, and the children's teeth are set on edge.

[*Ezekiel*, 18:2]

BURTON, Robert (1577–1640)

Diogenes struck the father when the son swore.

[*Anatomy of Melancholy* (1621)]

CHESTERFIELD, Lord (1694–1773)

As fathers commonly go, it is seldom a misfortune to be fatherless; and considering the general run of sons, as seldom a misfortune to be childless.

[Attr.]

CODE NAPOLÉON

La recherche de la paternité est interdite.

Investigations into paternity are forbidden.

[Article 340]

COLMAN, the Younger, George (1762–1836)

My father was an eminent button maker – but I had a soul above buttons – I panted for a liberal profession.

[*Sylvester Daggerwood: or New Hay at the Old Market* (1795)]

HARRISON, Tony (1937–)

When the chilled dough of his flesh went in an oven

not unlike those he fuelled all his life,

I thought of his cataracts ablaze with Heaven

and radiant with the sight of his dead wife,

light streaming from his mouth to shape her name,

'not Florence and not Flo but always Florrie'.

[*Continuous* (1981)]

HOLMES, Oliver Wendell, Jr (1841–1935)

[In response to Andrew Lang's enquiring if he were the son of the celebrated Oliver Wendell Holmes]

No, he was my father.

[In C. Bowen, *Yankee from Olympus* (1945)]

MCAULEY, James Philip (1917–1976)

Small things can pit the memory like a cyst:

Having seen other fathers greet their sons,

I put my childish face up to be kissed

After an absence. The rebuff still stuns

My blood. The poor man's embarrassment

At such a delicate proffer of affection

Cut like a saw. But home the lesson went:

My tenderness thenceforth escaped detection.

[*Collected Poems* (1971)]

RUSSELL, Bertrand (1872–1970)

The fundamental defect of fathers is that they want their children to be a credit to them.

[Attr.]

SHAKESPEARE, William (1564–1616)

It is a wise father that knows his own child.

[*The Merchant of Venice*, II.ii]

TENNYSON, Alfred, Lord (1809–1892)

How many a father have I seen,
A sober man, among his boys,
Whose youth was full of foolish noise.

[*In Memoriam A. H. H.* (1850)]

TURNBULL, Margaret (fl. 1920s–1942)

No man is responsible for his father. That is entirely his mother's affair.

[*Alabaster Lamps* (1925)]

TWAIN, Mark (1835–1910)

When I was a boy of 14 my father was so ignorant I could hardly stand to have the old man around. But when I got to be 21, I was astonished at how much he had learned in seven years.

[In Mackay, *The Harvest of a Quiet Eye* (1977)]

See BABIES; CHILDREN; FAMILIES; MOTHERS

FAULTS

CARLYLE, Thomas (1795–1881)

The greatest of faults, I should say, is to be conscious of none.

[*On Heroes, Hero-Worship, and the Heroic in History*]

COLERIDGE, Samuel Taylor (1772–1834)

The faults of great authors are generally excellences carried to an excess.

[*Miscellanies*]

CONFUCIUS (c.550–c.478 BC)

When you have faults, do not fear to abandon them.

[*Analects*]

GOLDSMITH, Oliver (c.1728–1774)

All his faults are such that one loves him still the better for them.

[*The Good Natur'd Man* (1768)]

LA ROCHEFOUCAULD (1613–1680)

Si nous n'avions point de défauts, nous ne prendrions pas tant de plaisir á en remarquer dans les autres.
If we had no faults of our own, we should not take so much pleasure in noticing them in others.

[*Maximes*, (1678)]

Nous n'avouons de petits défauts que pour persuader que nous n'en avons pas de grands.
We only admit our little faults to persuade others that we have no great ones.

[*Maximes*, (1678)]

PROUST, Marcel (1871–1922)

People often say that, by pointing out to a man the faults of his mistress, you succeed only in strengthening his attachment to her, because he does not believe you; yet how much more so if he does!

[*A la recherche du temps perdu, Du côté de chez Swann* (1913)]

See ERROR; MISTAKES

FEAR

ALLEN, Woody (1935–)

I'm really a timid person – I was beaten up by Quakers.

[*Sleeper*, film, 1973]

BOWEN, Elizabeth (1899–1973)

Proust has pointed out that the predisposition to love creates its own objects: is this not true of fear?

[*Collected Impressions* (1950)]

BOYD, Martin a'Beckett (1893–1972)

The only effect the atomic age has had on man had been to give him an underlying sense of nervous apprehension, which must also have been felt during the Black Death, and by the Christians under Diocletian.

[*Day of My Delight* (1965)]

BURKE, Edmund (1729–1797)

No passion so effectually robs the mind of all its powers of acting and reasoning as fear.

[*A Philosophical Enquiry into the Origin of our Ideas of the Sublime and Beautiful* (1757)]

The concessions of the weak are the concessions of fear.

[*Speech on Conciliation with America* (1775)]

BURTON, Robert (1577–1640)

The fear of some divine and supreme powers, keeps men in obedience.

[*Anatomy of Melancholy* (1621)]

CERVANTES, Miguel de (1547–1616)

Tiene el miedo muchos ojos, y vee las cosas debajo de tierra.
Fear has many eyes and can see things which are underground.

[*Don Quixote* I (1605)]

CHURCHILL, Sir Winston (1874–1965)

When I look back on all these worries I remember the story of the old man who said on his deathbed that he had had a lot of trouble in his life, most of which had never happened.

[*Their Finest Hour*]

CLOUGH, Arthur Hugh (1819–1861)

If hopes were dupes, fears may be liars.

['Say Not the Struggle Naught Availeth' (1855)]

COWPER, William (1731–1800)

He has no hope who never had a fear.

['Truth' (1782)]

CURIE, Marie (1867–1934)

Nothing in life is to be feared, it is only to be understood. Now is the time to understand more, so that we may fear less.

[Attr.]

DELANEY, Shelagh (1939–)

I'm not frightened of the darkness outside. It's the darkness inside houses I don't like.

[*A Taste of Honey* (1959)]

DRYDEN, John (1631–1700)

I am devilishly afraid, that's certain; but … I'll sing, that I may seem valiant.

[*Amphitryon* (1690)]

EMERSON, Ralph Waldo (1803–1882)

Fear is an instructor of great sagacity, and the herald of all revolutions.

[*Essays, First Series* (1841)]

FOCH, Ferdinand (1851–1929)

None but a coward dares to boast that he has never known fear.

[Attr.]

FROUDE, James Anthony (1818–1894)

Fear is the parent of cruelty.

[*Short Studies on Great Subjects* (1877)]

JONSON, Ben (1572–1637)

Tell proud Jove,
Between his power and thine there is no odds:
'Twas only fear first in the world made gods.

[*Sejanus* (1603)]

KIERKEGAARD, Søren (1813–1855)

Dread is a sympathetic antipathy and an antipathetic sympathy.

[In W.H. Auden, *Kierkegaard*]

MTSHALI, Oswald (1940–)

Man is
a great wall builder …
but the wall
most impregnable
has a moat
flowing with fright
around his heart.

[*Sounds of a Cowhide Drum* (1971)]

PARRIS, Matthew (1949–)

Terror of discovery and fear of reproval slip into our unconscious minds during infancy and remain there forever, always potent, usually unacknowledged.

[*The Spectator*, 1996]

PLATO (c.429–347 BC)

Nothing in the affairs of men is worthy of great anxiety.

[*Republic*]

ROOSEVELT, Franklin Delano (1882–1945)

The only thing we have to fear is fear itself.

[First Inaugural Address, 1933]

SHAKESPEARE, William (1564–1616)

I have almost forgot the taste of fears.
The time has been my senses would have
cool'd
To hear a night-shriek, and my fell of hair
Would at a dismal treatise rouse and stir
As life were in't. I have supp'd full with
horrors;
Direness, familiar to my slaughterous thoughts,
Cannot once start me.

[Macbeth, V.v]

SHAW, George Bernard (1856–1950)

There is only one universal passion: fear.

[The Man of Destiny (1898)]

SPENSER, Edmund (c.1522–1599)

Still as he fled, his eye was backward cast,
As if his feare still followed him behind.

[The Faerie Queene (1596)]

STEPHENS, James (1882–1950)

Curiosity will conquer fear even more than
bravery will.

[The Crock of Gold (1912)]

THOMAS, Lewis (1913–)

Worrying is the most natural and
spontaneous of all human functions. It is
time to acknowledge this, perhaps even to
learn to do it better.

[More Notes of a Biology Watcher]

VOLTAIRE (1694–1778)

La crainte suit le crime, et c'est son châtiment.
Fear follows crime, and is its punishment.

[Sémiramis (1748)]

See DEATH

FEELINGS

AUSTEN, Jane (1775–1817)

It was too pathetic for the feelings of Sophia
and myself – we fainted Alternately on a
Sofa.

[Love and Freindship (1791)]

HARRIS, Max (1921–1995)

In an atmosphere of reciprocal banter or
rubbishing Australians can express mutual
affection without running into risk of
indecently exposing states of feeling.

[In Keith Dunstan, Knockers (1972)]

RIDDING, Bishop George (1828–1904)

I feel a feeling which I feel you all feel.

[Sermon, 1885]

FEMINISM

ANTHONY, Susan B. (1820–1906)

Men their rights and nothing more; women
their rights and nothing less.

[Motto of The Revolution, 1868]

ATKINSON, Ti-Grace (c.1938–)

Feminism is the theory: lesbianism is the
practice.

[Attr. in Amazons, Bluestockings and Crones: A
Feminist Dictionary]

BROWN, Arnold

Uncle Harry was an early feminist … Our
family would often recount how, at a race-
meeting in Ayr, he threw himself under a
suffragette.

[Are You Looking at Me, Jimmy?]

DWORKIN, Andrea (1946–)

We imagined, in our ignorance, that we
might be novelists and philosophers… We
did not know that our professors had a
system of beliefs and convictions that
designated us as an inferior gender class, and
that that system of beliefs and convictions
was virtually universal – the cherished
assumption of most of the writers,
philosophers, and historians we were so
ardently studying.

[Our Blood: Prophecies and Discourses on Sexual
Politics (1976)]

FAIRBAIRN, Sir Nicholas (1933–1995)

[On feminism]
It's a cover for lesbian homosexuality.

[Daily Mail, 1993]

FAUST, Beatrice Eileen (1939–)

If the women's movement can be summed up in a single phrase, it is 'the right to choose'.

[*Women, Sex and Pornography* (1980)]

FOURIER, François Charles Marie (1772–1837)

L'extension des privilèges des femmes est le principe général de tous progrès sociaux.

The extension of women's privileges is the basic principle of all social progress.

[*Théorie des Quatre Mouvements* (1808)]

FRIEDAN, Betty (1921–)

I hope there will come a day when you, daughter mine, or your daughter, can truly afford to say 'I'm not a feminist. I'm a person' – and a day, not too far away, I hope, when I can stop fighting for women and get onto other matters that interest me now.

[Letter to her daughter, in Cosmopolitan, 1978]

GREER, Germaine (1939–)

If women understand by emancipation the adoption of the masculine role then we are lost indeed.

[*The Female Eunuch* (1970)]

JOHNSTON, Jill (1929–)

Until all women are lesbians there will be no true political revolution.

[*Lesbian Nation: The Feminist Solution* (1973)]

Feminists who still sleep with men are delivering their most vital energies to the oppressor.

[*Lesbian Nation: The Feminist Solution* (1973)]

No one should have to dance backwards all their life.

[In Miles, *The Women's History of the World* (1988)]

KEY, Ellen (1849–1926)

The emancipation of women is practically the greatest egoistic movement of the nineteenth century, and the most intense affirmation of the right of the self that history has yet seen.

[*The Century of the Child* (1909)]

LIVERMORE, Mary Ashton (c.1820–1905)

Above the titles of wife and mother, which, although dear, are transitory and accidental, there is the title human being, which precedes and out-ranks every other.

[*What Shall We Do with Our Daughters*]

LOOS, Anita (1893–1981)

I'm furious about the Women's Liberationists. They keep getting up on soapboxes and proclaiming that women are brighter than men. That's true, but it should be kept very quiet or it ruins the whole racket.

[*The Observer*, 1973]

MARTINEAU, Harriet (1802–1876)

Is it to be understood that the principles of the Declaration of Independence bear no relation to half of the human race?

[*Society in America* (1837)]

MILL, John Stuart (1806–1873)

The most important thing women have to do is to stir up the zeal of women themselves.

[Letter to Alexander Bain, 1869]

O'BRIEN, Edna (1936–)

The vote, I thought, means nothing to women. We should be armed.

[In Erica Jong, *Fear of Flying* (1973)]

ORBACH, Susie (1946–)

Fat is a Feminist Issue.

[Title of book, 1978]

PAGLIA, Camille (1947–)

Women and children first is an unscientific sentimentality which must be opposed.

[*The Observer*, 1998]

PANKHURST, Dame Christabel (1880–1958)

We are here to claim our right as women, not only to be free, but to fight for freedom. It is our privilege, as well as our pride and our joy, to take some part in this militant movement, which, as we believe, means the regeneration of all humanity.

[Speech, 1911]

PANKHURST, Emmeline (1858–1928)

We have taken this action, because as women … we realize that the condition of our sex is so deplorable that it is our duty even to break the law in order to call attention to the reasons why we do so.

[Speech in court, 1908]

PARTON, Dolly (1946–)

When women's lib started I was the first to burn my bra and it took three days to put out the fire.

[In Simon Rose, *Essential Film Guide* (1993)]

RILKE, Rainer Maria (1875–1926)

Eines … Tages wird das Mädchen da sein und die Frau, deren Name nicht mehr nur einen Gegensatz zum Männlichen bedeuten wird, sondern etwas für sich, etwas, wobei man an keine Ergänzung und Grenze denkt, nur an Leben und Dasein, – der weibliche Mensch. Dieser Fortschritt wird das Liebe-Erleben … zu einer Beziehung umbilden, die von Mensch zu Mensch gemeint ist, nicht mehr von Mann und Weib. Und diese menschlichere Liebe … wird jener ähneln, … die darin besteht, dass zwei Einsamkeiten einander schützen, grenzen und grüssen.

One day … there will be the girl and the woman, whose name will no longer signify merely a contrast to masculinity, but something of value in itself, something in respect of which one thinks not of a complement and a limitation, but only of life and existence: the female person. This progress will make the experience of love … become a relationship which is one of person to person, no longer one of man and wife. And this more human love … will resemble one … which consists in this, that two solitary people protect and limit and greet each other.

[*Letters to a Young Poet* (1929)]

ROBERTSON, Pat

It is about a socialist, anti-family movement that encourages women to leave their husbands, kill their children, practice witchcraft and become lesbians.

[*The World Almanac and Book of Facts*, 1993]

SHAW, George Bernard (1856–1950)

Give women the vote, and in five years there will be a crushing tax on bachelors.

[*Man and Superman* (1903)]

SOLANAS, Valerie (1940–1998)

[SCUM (Society for Cutting Up Men), manifesto, 1968]

Every man, deep down, knows he's a worthless piece of shit.

[In Bassnett, *Feminist Experiences: The Women's Movement in Four Cultures* (1986)]

STANTON, Elizabeth Cady (1815–1902)

[On Genesis]

As to woman's subjection, on which both the canon and the civil law delight to dwell, it is important to note that equal dominion is given to woman over every living thing, but not one word is said giving man dominion over woman.

[*The Woman's Bible* (1895)]

Womanhood is the great fact in her life; wifehood and motherhood are but incidental relations.

[In Anthony and Gage (eds), *History of Woman Suffrage* (1881)]

… we still wonder at the stolid incapacity of all men to understand that woman feels the invidious distinctions of sex exactly as the black man does those of color, or the white man the more transient distinctions of wealth, family, position, place, and power; that she feels as keenly as man the injustice of disfranchisement.

[In Anthony and Gage (eds), *History of Woman Suffrage* (1881)]

We hold these truths to be self-evident, that all men and women are created equal.

['Declaration of Sentiments', 1848]

STEAD, Christina (1902–1983)

I don't believe in segregation of any kind, and I think men and women should unite to fight the battle. All the men I've known have been in favour of women's success.

[Interview with Rodney Wetherell, first broadcast by Australian Broadcasting Commission, 1980]

STEINEM, Gloria (1934–)

Some of us have become the men we wanted to marry.

[*The Observer*, 1982]

VICTORIA, Queen (1819–1901)

The Queen is most anxious to enlist every one who can speak or write to join in checking this mad, wicked folly of 'Women's Rights', with all its attendant horrors, on which her poor feeble sex is bent, forgetting every sense of womanly feeling and propriety … It is a subject which makes the Queen so furious that she cannot contain herself. God created men and women different – then let them remain each in their own position.

[Letter to Sir Theodore Martin, 1870]

WELDON, Fay (1931–)

There has to be a halt in the gender war and feminism must extend its remit to include the rights of men.

[*The Observer* debate on feminism, 1998]

WEST, Dame Rebecca (1892–1983)

People call me a feminist whenever I express sentiments that differentiate me from a doormat or a prostitute.

[In Anne Stibbs (ed.), *Hell Hath No Fury*]

WHITTLESEY, Faith

Remember, Ginger Rogers did everything Fred Astaire did, but she did it backwards and in high heels.

WOLLSTONECRAFT, Mary (1759–1797)

The divine right of husbands, like the divine right of kings, may, it is hoped, in this enlightened age, be contested without danger.

[*A Vindication of the Rights of Woman* (1792)]

[Of women]
I do not wish them to have power over men; but over themselves.

[*A Vindication of the Rights of Woman* (1792)]

See EQUALITY; MEN AND WOMEN; WOMEN

FICTION

ALDISS, Brian (1925–)

Science fiction is no more written for scientists than ghost stories are written for ghosts.

[*Penguin Science Fiction* (1961)]

AUDEN, W.H. (1907–1973)

Political history is far too criminal and pathological to be a fit subject of study for the young. All teachers know this. In consequence, they bowdlerize, but to bowdlerize political history is not to simplify but to falsify it. Children should acquire their heroes and villains from fiction.

[*A Certain World* (1970)]

AUSTEN, Jane (1775–1817)

'And what are you reading, Miss ––?' 'Oh! it is only a novel!' replies the young lady; while she lays down her book with affected indifference, or momentary shame. It is only *Cecilia*, or *Camilla*, or *Belinda*; or, in short, only some work in which the greatest powers of the mind are displayed, in which the most thorough knowledge of human nature, the happiest delineation of its varieties, the liveliest effusions of wit and humour, are conveyed to the world in the best chosen language.

[*Northanger Abbey* (1818)]

BARTH, John (1930–)

If you are a novelist of a certain type of temperament, then what you really want to do is re-invent the world. God wasn't too bad a novelist, except he was a Realist.

[Attr.]

CECIL, Lord David (1902–1986)

It does not matter that Dickens' world is not lifelike: it is alive.

[*Early Victorian Novelists* (1934)]

CHANDLER, Raymond (1888–1959)

When I started out to write fiction I had the

great disadvantage of having absolutely no talent for it … If more than two people were on scene I couldn't keep one of them alive.

[Letter to Paul Brooks, 1949]

CHESTERTON, G.K. (1874–1936)

It is the art in which the conquests of woman are quite beyond controversy … The novel of the nineteenth century was female.

[*The Victorian Age in Literature* (1913)]

A good novel tells us the truth about its hero; but a bad novel tells us the truth about its author.

[*Heretics* (1905)]

DAVISON, Frank Dalby (1893–1970)

You need a skin as thin as a cigarette paper to write a novel and the hide of an elephant to publish it.

[*Meanjin*, 1982]

DISRAELI, Benjamin (1804–1881)

When I want to read a novel I write one.

[Attr.]

EMERSON, Ralph Waldo (1803–1882)

Novels are as useful as Bibles, if they teach you the secret, that the best of life is conversation, and the greatest success is confidence.

[*Conduct of Life* (1860)]

FORSTER, E.M. (1879–1970)

Yes – oh dear, yes – the novel tells a story.

[*Aspects of the Novel* (1927)]

That [the story] is the highest factor common to all novels, and I wish that it was not so, that it could be something different – melody, or perception of the truth, not this low atavistic form.

[*Aspects of the Novel* (1927)]

FOWLES, John (1926–)

There are many reasons why novelists write, but they all have one thing in common – a need to create an alternative world.

[*The Sunday Times Magazine*, 1977]

GARCÍA MÁRQUEZ, Gabriel (1928–)

El periodismo es un género literario, muy parecido a la novela, y tiene la gran ventaja de que el reportero puede inventar cosas. Y eso el novelista lo tiene totalmente prohibido.

Journalism is a literary genre very similar to that of the novel, and has the great advantage that the reporter can invent things. And that is completely forbidden to the novelist.

[Speech, April 1994, reported in *El País*]

GIBBON, Edward (1737–1794)

The romance of Tom Jones, that exquisite picture of human manners, will outlive the palace of the Escurial and the imperial eagle of the house of Austria.

[*Memoirs of My Life and Writings* (1796)]

GONCOURT, Edmond de (1822–1896)

Les historiens sont des raconteurs du passé, les romanciers des raconteurs du présent.

Historians tell stories of the past, novelists stories of the present.

[*Journal*]

JAMES, Henry (1843–1916)

The only obligation to which in advance we may hold a novel, without incurring the accusation of being arbitrary, is that it be interesting.

[*Partial Portraits* (1888)]

I remember once saying to Henry James, in reference to a novel of the type that used euphemistically to be called 'unpleasant': 'You know, I was rather disappointed; that book wasn't nearly as bad as I expected'; to which he replied, with his incomparable twinkle: 'Ah, my dear, the abysses are all so shallow.'

[In Edith Wharton, *The House of Mirth* (1936)]

LARKIN, Philip (1922–1985)

[Referring to modern novels]
Far too many relied on the classic formula of a beginning, a muddle, and an end.

[*New Fiction*, 1978]

LAWRENCE, D.H. (1885–1930)

I am a man, and alive … For this reason I am
a novelist. And being a novelist, I consider
myself superior to the saint, the scientist, the
philosopher, and the poet, who are all great
masters of different bits of man alive, but
never get the whole hog.

[*Phoenix* (1936)]

The novel is the one bright book of life.

[*Phoenix* (1936)]

NABOKOV, Vladimir (1899–1977)

A novelist is, like all mortals, more fully at
home on the surface of the present than in
the ooze of the past.

[*Strong Opinions* (1973)]

POWELL, Anthony (1905–)

People think that because a novel's invented,
it isn't true. Exactly the reverse is the case.
Biography and memoirs can never be wholly
true, since they cannot include every
conceivable circumstance of what happened.
The novel can do that.

[*Hearing Secret Harmonies* (1975)]

READE, Charles (1814–1884)

[Programme for a serial novel]
Make 'em laugh; make 'em cry; make 'em
wait.

[Attr.]

SAYERS, Dorothy L. (1893–1957)

My impression is that I was thinking about
writing a detective story, and that he walked
in, complete with spats.

[*Harcourt Brace News*, 1936, 'How I came to Invent
the Character of Lord Peter']

[On *Whose Body?*, 1923, her first book]
One cannot write a novel unless one has
something to say about life, and I had
nothing to say about it, because I knew
nothing.

[In Hone, *Dorothy L. Sayers: A Literary Biography*
(1979)]

SCOTT, Sir Walter (1771–1832)

But I must say to the Muse of fiction, as the
Earl of Pembroke said to the ejected nun of

Wilton, 'Go spin, you jade, go spin!'.

[*Journal*, 1826]

SHAW, George Bernard (1856–1950)

It is clear that a novel cannot be too bad to
be worth publishing … It certainly is
possible for a novel to be too good to be
worth publishing.

[*Plays Pleasant and Unpleasant* (1898)]

SHERIDAN, Richard Brinsley (1751–1816)

I hate Novels, and love Romances. The Praise
of the best of the former, their being natural,
as it is called, is to me their greatest Demerit.

[Letter, 1772]

STENDHAL (1783–1842)

*Un roman est un miroir qui se promène sur une
grande route.*
A novel is a mirror walking along a wide
road.

[*Le Rouge et le Noir* (1830)]

TYNAN, Kenneth (1927–1980)

A novel is a static thing that one moves
through; a play is a dynamic thing that
moves past one.

[*Curtains* (1961)]

WAUGH, Auberon (1939–)

It is a sad feature of modern life that only
women for the most part have time to write
novels, and they seldom have much to write
about.

[*The Observer*, 1981]

WILDE, Oscar (1854–1900)

The good ended happily, and the bad
unhappily. That is what Fiction means.

[*The Importance of Being Earnest* (1895)]

WOOLF, Virginia (1882–1941)

A woman must have money and a room of
her own if she is to write fiction.

[*A Room of One's Own* (1929)]

See BOOKS; LITERATURE; WRITERS;
  WRITING

FIRE

BRENNAN, Christopher (1870–1932)

Fire in the heavens, and fire along the hills,
and fire made solid in the flinty stone,
thick-mass'd or scatter'd pebble, fire that fills
the breathless hour that lives in fire alone.

[*Poems* (1914)]

GRAHAM, Harry (1874–1936)

Billy, in one of his nice new sashes,
Fell in the fire and was burnt to ashes;
Now, although the room grows chilly,
I haven't the heart to poke poor Billy.

[*Ruthless Rhymes for Heartless Homes* (1899)]

GREVILLE, Fulke (1554–1628)

Fire and people do in this agree,
They both good servants, both ill masters be.

['An Inquisition upon Fame and Honour' (1633)]

SHERIDAN, Richard Brinsley (1751–1816)

[At a coffee house, during the fire which destroyed his Drury Lane theatre, 1809]
A man may surely be allowed to take a glass of wine by his own fireside.

[In Moore, *Memoirs of the Life of Sheridan* (1825)]

SITWELL, Dame Edith (1887–1964)

The fire was furry as a bear.

['Dark Song' (1922)]

FLATTERY

AUSTEN, Jane (1775–1817)

It is happy for you that you possess the talent of flattering with delicacy. May I ask whether these pleasing attentions proceed from the impulse of the moment, or are the result of previous study?

[*Pride and Prejudice* (1813)]

BIERCE, Ambrose (1842–c.1914)

Flatter: To impress another with a sense of one's own merit.

[*The Enlarged Devil's Dictionary* (1961)]

COLTON, Charles Caleb (c.1780–1832)

Imitation is the sincerest form of flattery.

[*Lacon* (1820)]

CONGREVE, William (1670–1729)

She lays it on with a trowel.

[*The Double Dealer* (1694)]

DISRAELI, Benjamin (1804–1881)

[To Queen Victoria]
We authors, Ma'am.

[Attr.]

DUNBAR, William (c.1460–c.1525)

Flattery wearis ane furrit gown,
And falsett with the lord does roun,
And truth stands barrit at the dure.

['Into this World May None Assure' (1834 edition)]

FONTAINE, Jean de la (1621–1695)

Mon bon Monsieur,
Apprenez que tout flatteur
Vit au dépens de celui qui l'écoute.
My dear Monsieur, know that every flatterer lives at the expense of the one who listens to him.

['Le corbeau et le renard']

HALIFAX, Lord (1633–1695)

It is flattering some Men to endure them.

['Of Company' (1750)]

JOHNSON, Samuel (1709–1784)

[Remark to Hannah More]
Madam, before you flatter a man so grossly to his face, you should consider whether or not your flattery is worth his having.

[*Diary and Letters of Madame d'Arblay* (1842)]

PROVERBS

Fine words butter no parsnips.

Imitation is the sincerest form of flattery.

SCOTT, Sir Walter (1771–1832)

For ne'er
Was flattery lost on poet's ear:
A simple race! they waste their toil
For the vain tribute of a smile.

[*The Lay of the Last Minstrel* (1805), IV]

SHAW, George Bernard (1856–1950)

What really flatters a man is that you think him worth flattering.

[*John Bull's Other Island* (1907)]

STEVENSON, Adlai (1900–1965)

I suppose flattery hurts no one – that is, if he doesn't inhale.

[*Meet the Press, TV broadcast*, 1952]

See PRAISE

FLIRTATION

CHESTERFIELD, Lord (1694–1773)

I assisted at the birth of that most significant word flirtation, which dropped from the most beautiful mouth in the world.

[*The World*, 1754]

SMITH, Sydney (1771–1845)

How can a bishop marry? How can he flirt? The most he can say is, 'I will see you in the vestry after service.'

[In Holland, *A Memoir of the Reverend Sydney Smith* (1855)]

STERNE, Laurence (1713–1768)

Vive l'amour! et vive la bagatelle!
Long live love! Long live philandering!

[*A Sentimental Journey* (1768)]

WILDE, Oscar (1854–1900)

The amount of women in London who flirt with their own husbands is perfectly scandalous. It looks so bad. It is simply washing one's clean linen in public.

[*The Importance of Being Earnest* (1895)]

FLOWERS

KAWABATA, Yasunari (1899–1972)

A single flower could impress you with more gorgeousness than one hundred such.

['Japan the Beautiful and I' (1968)]

KEATS, John (1795–1821)

I cannot see what flowers are at my feet,
Nor what soft incense hangs upon the boughs,
But, in embalmed darkness, guess each sweet
Wherewith the seasonable month endows
The grass, the thicket, and the fruit-tree wild –
White hawthorn, and the pastoral eglantine;
Fast fading violets cover'd up in leaves;
And mid-May's eldest child,
The coming musk-rose, full of dewy wine,
The murmurous haunt of flies on summer eves.

['Ode to a Nightingale' (1819)]

SEEGER, Pete (1919–)

Where have all the flowers gone?
The girls have picked them every one.
Oh, when will you ever learn?

['Where Have All the Flowers Gone?', song, 1961]

SKELTON, John (c.1460–1529)

She is the vyolet,
The daysy delectable,
The columbyn commendable
This jelofer amyable;
For this most goodly floure,
This blossom of fressh colour,
So Jupiter me succour,
She florysheth new and new
In beautie and vertew.

['Phyllyp Sparowe: The Commendacions']

SPENSER, Edmund (c.1522–1599)

Bring hether the Pincke and purple Cullambine,
With Gelliflowres:
Bring Coronations, and Sops in wine,
Worne of Paramoures.
Strowe me the ground with Daffadowndillies,
And Cowslips, and Kingcups, and loved Lillies:
The pretie Pawnce,
And the Chevisaunce,
Shall match with the fayre flowre Delice.

[*The Shepheardes Calender* (1579)]

See GARDENS

FOOD

ATWOOD, Margaret (1939–)

Eating is our earliest metaphor, preceding our consciousness of gender difference, race, nationality, and language. We eat before we talk.

[*The CanLit Foodbook: From Pen to Palate – A Collection of Tasty Literary Fare* (1987)]

BAREHAM, Lindsey (1948–)

Good mashed potato is one of the great luxuries of life and I don't blame Elvis for eating it every night for the last year of his life.

[*In Praise of the Potato* (1989)]

THE BIBLE
(King James Version)

Better is a dinner of herbs where love is, than a stalled ox and hatred therewith.

[*Proverbs*, 15:17]

BRILLAT-SAVARIN, Anthelme (1755–1826)

Dis-moi ce que tu manges, je te dirai ce que tu es.
Tell me what you eat and I will tell you what you are.

[*Physiologie du Goût* (1825)]

CARROLL, Lewis (1832–1898)

Beautiful Soup, so rich and green,
Waiting in a hot tureen!
Who for such dainties would not stoop?
Soup of the evening, beautiful Soup!

[*Alice's Adventures in Wonderland* (1865)]

CERVANTES, Miguel de (1547–1616)

La mejor salsa del mundo es la hambre.
Hunger is the best sauce in the world.

[*Don Quixote* (1615)]

DAHL, Roald (1916–1990)

Do you know what breakfast cereal is made of? It's made of all those little curly wooden shavings you find in pencil sharpeners!

[*Charlie and the Chocolate Factory* (1964)]

DAVID, Elizabeth (1913–1992)

To eat figs off the tree in the very early morning, when they have been barely

touched by the sun, is one of the exquisite pleasures of the Mediterranean.

[*Italian Food* (1954)]

DAVIES, David (1742–1819)

Though the potato is an excellent root, deserving to be brought into general use, yet it seems not likely that the use of it should ever be normal in the country.

[*The Case of the Labourers in Husbandry* (1795)]

DE VRIES, Peter (1910–1993)

Gluttony is an emotional escape, a sign something is eating us.

[*Comfort me with Apples* (1956)]

DURRELL, Lawrence (1912–1990)

The whole Mediterranean, the sculpture, the palms, the gold beads, the bearded heroes, the wine, the ideas, the ships, the moonlight, the winged gorgons, the bronze men, the philosophers – all of it seems to rise in the sour, pungent taste of these black olives between the teeth. A taste older than meat, older than wine. A taste as old as cold water.

[*Prospero's Cell* (1945)]

FADIMAN, Clifton (1904–)

Cheese – milk's leap toward immortality.

[*Any Number Can Play* (1957)]

FEUERBACH, Ludwig (1804–1872)

Man is what he eats.

[In Moleschott, *Lehre der Nahrungsmittel: Für das Volk* (1850)]

FRANKLIN, Benjamin (1706–1790)

To lengthen thy life, lessen thy meals.

[*Poor Richard's Almanac* (1733)]

FULLER, Thomas (1608–1661)

He was a very valiant man who first ventured on eating of oysters.

[*The History of the Worthies of England* (1662)]

GROENING, Matt

Groundskeeper Willie: Get yer haggis right here! Chopped heart and lungs, boiled in a wee sheep's stomach! Tastes as good as it sounds!

[*The Simpsons*, TV cartoon series]

HERBERT, George (1593–1633)

A cheerful look makes a dish a feast.

[*Jacula Prudentum* (1640)]

HERBERT, Sir A.P. (1890–1971)

Bring porridge, bring sausage, bring fish, for a start,

Bring kidneys, and mushrooms, and partridges' legs,

But let the foundation be bacon and eggs.

[In Catherine Brown, *Scottish Cookery* (1985)]

HOLMES, Oliver Wendell (1809–1894)

That most wonderful object of domestic art called trifle – with its charming confusion of cream and cake and almonds and jam and jelly and wine and cinnamon and froth.

[*Elsie Venner* (1861)]

JOHNSON, Samuel (1709–1784)

I look upon it, that he who does not mind his belly will hardly mind anything else.

[In Boswell, *The Life of Samuel Johnson* (1791)]

LAMB, Charles (1775–1834)

[Of food]

I hate a man who swallows it, affecting not to know what he is eating. I suspect his taste in higher matters.

[*Essays of Elia* (1823)]

LEBOWITZ, Fran (1946–)

Food is an important part of a balanced diet.

[*Metropolitan Life* (1978)]

LLEWELLYN, Richard (1907–1983)

And there is good fresh trout for supper. My mother used to put them on a hot stone over the fire, wrapped in breadcrumbs, butter, parsley and lemon rind, all bound about with the fresh leaves of leeks. If there is better food in heaven, I am in a hurry to be there.

[*How Green Was My Valley* (1939)]

LUTYENS, Sir Edwin Landseer (1869–1944)

[Comment made in a restaurant]

This piece of cod passes all understanding.

[In Robert Lutyens, *Sir Edwin Lutyens* (1942)]

MOLIÈRE (1622–1673)

Il faut manger pour vivre et non pas vivre pour manger.

One should eat to live, not live to eat.

[*L'Avare* (1669)]

MONROE, Marilyn (1926–1962)

[On having matzo balls for supper at Arthur Miller's parents]

Isn't there another part of the matzo you can eat?

[Attr.]

ORWELL, George (1903–1950)

We may find in the long run that tinned food is a deadlier weapon than the machine-gun.

[*The Road to Wigan Pier* (1937)]

PETER, Laurence J. (1919–1990)

The noblest of all dogs is the hot-dog; it feeds the hand that bites it.

[*Quotations for Our Time* (1977)]

PIGGY, Miss

Never eat anything at one sitting that you can't lift.

[*Woman's Hour*, 1992]

POOLE, Shona Crawford (1943–)

Ice cream is the most evocative of puddings. It brings back summer holidays and the bicycle bell call of the hokey-cokey man with his tricycle cart, and rushing down the garden path with grandpa's big mug to have it filled for the ice cream sodas which were invariably constructed in tall sundae glasses.

[*The New Times Cookbook*]

POPE, Alexander (1688–1744)

Fame is at best an unperforming cheat;
But 'tis substantial happiness, to eat.

['Prologue for Mr D'Urfey's Last Play' (1727)]

PORTLAND, Sixth Duke of (1857–1943)

[On being told to reduce his expenses by dispensing with one of his two Italian pastry cooks]

What! Can't a fellow even enjoy a biscuit any more?

[In Winchester, *Their Noble Lordships*]

PRIOR, Matthew (1664–1721)

Salads, and eggs, and lighter fare,
Tune the Italian spark's guitar.
And, if I take Dan Congreve right,
Pudding and beef make Britons fight.

[*Alma* (1718)]

PROVERB

There is much meat in God's storehouse.

[Danish proverb]

RABELAIS, François (c.1494–c.1553)

L'appétit vient en mangeant, … la soif s'en va en beuvant.
Appetite comes with eating … thirst goes with drinking.

[*Gargantua* (1534)]

RALEIGH, Sir Walter A. (1861–1922)

We would not lead a pleasant life,
And 'twould be finished soon,
If peas were eaten with the knife,
And gravy with the spoon.
Eat slowly: only men in rags
And gluttons old in sin
Mistake themselves for carpet bags
And tumble victuals in.

['Stans puer ad mensam' (1923)]

RAMSAY, Allan (1686–1758)

… bannocks and a share of cheese
Will make a breakfast that a laird might please.

['The Gentle Shepherd' (1725)]

RAPHAEL, Frederic (1931–)

Great restaurants are, of course, nothing but mouth-brothels. There is no point in going to them if one intends to keep one's belt buckled.

[*The Sunday Times Magazine*, 1977]

ROUSSEAU, Émile (1929–)

Les grands mangeurs de viande sont en général cruels et féroces plus que les autres hommes … La barbarie anglaise est connue.
Great eaters of meat are in general more cruel and ferocious than other men. The English are known for their cruelty.

[Attr.]

RUNYON, Damon (1884–1946)

These citizens are always willing to bet that what Nicely-Nicely dies of will be over-feeding and never anything small like pneumonia, for Nicely-Nicely is known far and wide as a character who dearly loves to commit eating.

[*Take it Easy* (1938)]

SAKI (1870–1916)

Oysters are more beautiful than any religion … There's nothing in Christianity or Buddhism that quite matches the sympathetic unselfishness of an oyster.

[*The Chronicles of Clovis* (1911)]

I believe I once considerably scandalized her by declaring that clear soup was a more important factor in life than a clear conscience.

[*Beasts and Super-Beasts* (1914)]

SECOMBE, Sir Harry (1921–)

My advice if you insist on slimming: Eat as much as you like – just don't swallow it.

[*Daily Herald*, 1962]

SHAKESPEARE, William (1564–1616)

Methinks sometimes I have no more wit than a Christian or an ordinary man has; but I am a great eater of beef, and I believe that does harm to my wit.

[*Twelfth Night*, I.iii]

SHAW, George Bernard (1856–1950)

There is no love sincerer than the love of food.

[*Man and Superman* (1903)]

SHELLEY, Percy Bysshe (1792–1822)

There are two Italies – the one is the most sublime and lovely contemplation that can be conceived by the imagination of man; the other is the most degraded, disgusting and odious. What do you think? Young women of rank actually eat – you will never guess what – garlic!

[Attr.]

ST LEGER, Warham (1850–c.1915)

There is a fine stuffed chavender,

A chavender, or chub,
That decks the rural pavender,
The pavender, or pub,
Wherein I eat my gravender,
My gravender, or grub.

['The Chavender, or Chub']

STEVENSON, Robert Louis (1850–1894)

Many's the long night I [Ben Gunn] have dreamed of cheese – toasted mostly, and woke up again and here I were … You might not happen to have a piece of cheese about you now?

[*Treasure Island* (1883)]

VOLTAIRE (1694–1778)

[On learning that coffee was considered a slow poison]

I think it must be so, for I have been drinking it for sixty-five years and I am not dead yet.

[Attr.]

WEBSTER, John (c.1580–c.1625)

I saw him even now going the way of all flesh, that is to say towards the kitchen.

[*Westward Hoe* (1607)]

WODEHOUSE, P.G. (1881–1975)

The lunches of fifty-seven years had caused his chest to slip down to the mezzanine floor.

[*The Heart of a Goof* (1926)]

See COOKERY; DINING; VEGETARIANISM

FOOLISHNESS

ANONYMOUS

When I was a little boy, I had but a little wit,
'Tis a long time ago, and I have no more yet;
Nor ever ever shall, until that I die,
For the longer I live the more fool am I.

[In *Wit and Mirth, an Antidote against Melancholy* (1684)]

ANTRIM, Minna (1861–1950)

A fool bolts pleasure, then complains of moral indigestion.

[*Naked Truth and Veiled Allusions* (1902)]

BARNUM, Phineas T. (1810–1891)

There's a sucker born every minute.

[Attr.]

BEECHER, Henry Ward (1813–1887)

[On receiving a note containing only one word: 'Fool']

I have known many an instance of a man writing a letter and forgetting to sign his name, but this is the only instance I have ever known of a man signing his name and forgetting to write the letter.

[Attr.]

BLAKE, William (1757–1827)

If the fool would persist in his folly he would become wise.

['Proverbs of Hell' (1793)]

BOILEAU-DESPRÉAUX, Nicolas (1636–1711)

Un sot trouve toujours un plus sot qui l'admire.
A fool will always find a greater fool to admire him.

[*L'Art Poétique* (1674)]

CERVANTES, Miguel de (1547–1616)

…l es un entreverado loco, lleno de lúcidos intervalos.
He's an intermittent fool, full of lucid intervals.

[*Don Quixote* (1615)]

COWPER, William (1731–1800)

A fool must now and then be right, by chance.

['Conversation' (1782)]

DARWIN, Erasmus (1731–1802)

A fool … is a man who never tried an experiment in his life.

[In a letter from Maria Edgeworth to Sophy Ruxton, 1792]

ELIOT, T.S. (1888–1965)

When lovely woman stoops to folly and
Paces about her room again, alone,
She smoothes her hair with automatic hand,
And puts a record on the gramophone.

[*The Waste Land* (1922)]

FIELDING, Henry (1707–1754)

One fool at least in every married couple.

[*Amelia* (1751)]

FRANKLIN, Benjamin (1706–1790)

Experience keeps a dear school, but fools will learn in no other.

[*Poor Richard's Almanac* (1743)]

GOLDSMITH, Oliver (c.1728–1774)

In my time, the follies of the town crept slowly among us, but now they travel faster than a stage-coach.

[*She Stoops to Conquer* (1773)]

GRACIÁN, Baltasar (1601–1658)

No es necio el que hace la necedad, sino el que, hecha, no la sabe encubrir.

It is not the one who commits an act of foolishness who is foolish, but the one who, once such an act has been committed, does not know how to cover it up.

[*Handbook-Oracle and the Art of Prudence*, 1647)]

HORACE (65–8 BC)

Misce stultitiam consiliis brevem:

Dulce est desipere in loco.

Mix a little folly with your plans: it is sweet to be silly at the right moment.

[*Odes*]

IBSEN, Henrik (1828–1906)

Fools are in a terrible, overwhelming majority, all the wide world over.

[*An Enemy of the People* (1882)]

MOLIÈRE (1622–1673)

C'est une folie á nulle autre seconde,

De vouloir se mêler á corriger le monde.

The greatest folly of all is wanting to busy oneself in setting the world to rights.

[*Le Misanthrope* (1666)]

Un sot savant est sot plus qu'un sot ignorant.

A knowledgeable fool is more foolish than an ignorant fool.

[*Les Femmes savantes* (1672)]

POPE, Alexander (1688–1744)

For Fools rush in where Angels fear to tread.

[*An Essay on Criticism* (1711)]

PROVERBS

Fools build houses, and wise men buy them.

There's no fool like an old fool.

ROWLAND, Helen (1875–1950)

The follies which a man regrets most in his life are those which he didn't commit when he had the opportunity.

[*A Guide to Men* (1922)]

SCHILLER, Johann Christoph Friedrich (1759–1805)

Mit der Dummheit kämpfen Götter selbst vergebens.

Gods themselves struggle in vain with stupidity.

[*The Maid of Orleans* (1801)]

SHADWELL, Thomas (c.1642–1692)

The haste of a Fool is the slowest thing in the World.

[*A True Widow* (1679), III]

SHAKESPEARE, William (1564–1616)

He uses his folly like a stalking-horse, and under the presentation of that he shoots his wit.

[*As You Like It*, V.iv]

SHENSTONE, William (1714–1763)

A fool and his words are soon parted; a man of genius and his money.

[*Essays on Men and Manners*]

SPENCER, Herbert (1820–1903)

The ultimate result of shielding men from the effects of folly, is to fill the world with fools.

[*Essays* (1891)]

STEVENSON, Robert Louis (1850–1894)

It is better to be a fool than to be dead.

[*Virginibus Puerisque* (1881),

For God's sake give me the young man who has brains enough to make a fool of himself!

[*Virginibus Puerisque* (1881)]

SWIFT, Jonathan (1667–1745)

Hated by fools, and fools to hate,

Be that my motto and my fate.

['To Mr Delany' (1718)]

THE BIBLE
(King James Version)

Answer a fool according to his folly.

[*Proverbs*, 26:5]

THOREAU, Henry David (1817–1862)

Any fool can make a rule and every fool will mind it.

[Attr.]

TUSSER, Thomas (c.1524–1580)

A fool and his money be soon at debate.

[*Five Hundred Points of Good Husbandry* (1557)]

WHATELY, Richard (1787–1863)

It is a folly to expect men to do all that they may reasonably be expected to do.

[*Apophthegms* (1854)]

YOUNG, Edward (1683–1765)

Be wise with speed;
A fool at forty is a fool indeed.

[*Love of Fame, the Universal Passion* (1728)]

See IGNORANCE; STUPIDITY

FORCE

ASIMOV, Isaac (1920–1992)

Violence is the last refuge of the incompetent.

[*Foundation* (1951)]

BRIEN, Alan (1925–)

Violence is the repartee of the illiterate.

[*Punch*, 1973]

BRIGHT, John (1811–1889)

Force is not a remedy.

[Speech, 1880]

BRONOWSKI, Jacob (1908–1974)

The wish to hurt, the momentary intoxication with pain, is the loophole through which the pervert climbs into the minds of ordinary men.

[*The Face of Violence* (1954)]

BURKE, Edmund (1729–1797)

The use of force alone is but temporary. It may subdue for a moment; but it does not remove the necessity of subduing again: and a nation is not governed, which is perpetually to be conquered.

[Speech on Conciliation with America (1775)]

FONTAINE, Jean de la (1621–1695)

La raison du plus fort est toujours la meilleure.
The reason of the strongest is always the best.

['Le loup et l'agneau']

HORACE (65–8 BC)

Vis consili expers mole ruit sua.
Brute force without judgement collapses under its own weight.

[*Odes*]

INGE, William Ralph (1860–1954)

A man may build himself a throne of bayonets, but he cannot sit upon it.

[*Philosophy of Plotinus* (1923)]

KING, Martin Luther (1929–1968)

A riot is at bottom the language of the unheard.

[*Chaos or Community* (1967)]

KORAN

Let there be no violence in religion.

[Chapter 2]

MACKENZIE, Sir Compton (1883–1972)

There is little to choose morally between beating up a man physically and beating him up mentally.

[*On Moral Courage* (1962)]

MILTON, John (1608–1674)

… who overcomes
By force, hath overcome but half his foe.

[*Paradise Lost* (1667)]

ROOSEVELT, Theodore (1858–1919)

There is a homely old adage which runs, 'Speak softly and carry a big stick; you will go far.'

[Speech, 1903]

SAINT-PIERRE, Bernardin de (1737–1814)

Les femmes sont fausses dans les pays où les hommes sont des tyrans. Partout la violence produit la ruse.

Women are false in countries where men are tyrants. Violence everywhere leads to deception.

[*Paul et Virginie* (1788)]

TROTSKY, Leon (1879–1940)

Where force is necessary, one should make use of it boldly, resolutely, and right to the end. But it is as well to know the limitations of force; to know where to combine force with manoeuvre, assault with conciliation.

[*What Next?* (1932)]

UNAMUNO, Miguel de (1864–1936)

[Of Franco's supporters]
Vencer no es convencer.
To conquer is not to convince.

[Speech, 1936]

See POWER; VIOLENCE

FOREIGNERS

BRADBURY, Malcolm (1932–)

Sympathy – for all these people, for being foreigners – lay over the gathering like a woolly blanket; and no one was enjoying it at all.

[*Eating People is Wrong* (1954)]

BOTHAM, Ian (1955–)

[On Pakistan]
The sort of place everyone should send his mother-in-law for a month, all expenses paid.

[BBC Radio 2 interview, March 1984]

BROWNE, Sir Thomas (1605–1682)

I feel not in myself those common antipathies that I can discover in others; those national repugnances do not touch me, nor do I behold with prejudice the French, Italian, Spaniard, or Dutch; but where I find their actions in balance with my countrymen's, I honour, love and embrace

them in the same degree.

[*Religio Medici* (1643)]

CRISP, Quentin (1908–)

I don't hold with abroad and think that foreigners speak English when our backs are turned.

[*The Naked Civil Servant* (1968)]

DU BELLOY, P.-L.B. (1727–1775)

Plus je vis d'étrangers, plus j'aimai ma patrie.
The more foreigners I saw, the more I loved my native land.

[*Le Siège de Calais* (1765)]

ERASMUS (c.1466–1536)

Is not the Turk a man and a brother?

[*Querela Pacis*]

GOLDSMITH, Oliver (c.1728–1774)

The Scotch may be compared to a tulip planted in dung, but I never see a Dutchman in his own house, but I think of a magnificent Egyptian Temple dedicated to an ox.

[Letter from Leyden to Rev. Thomas Contarine, 1754]

MEYNELL, Hugo (1727–1780)

For anything I see, foreigners are fools.

[In Boswell, *The Life of Samuel Johnson* (1791)]

MITFORD, Nancy (1904–1973)

I loathe abroad, nothing would induce me to live there … and, as for foreigners, they are all the same, and they all make me sick.

[*The Pursuit of Love* (1945)]

Abroad is unutterably bloody and foreigners are fiends.

[*The Pursuit of Love* (1945)]

TROLLOPE, Anthony (1815–1882)

We cannot bring ourselves to believe it possible that a foreigner should in any respect be wiser than ourselves. If any such point out to us our follies, we at once claim those follies as the special evidences of our wisdom.

[*Orley Farm* (1862)]

TWAIN, Mark (1835–1910)

They spell it Vinci and pronounce it Vinchy;

foreigners always spell better than they pronounce.

[*The Innocents Abroad* (1869)]

See TRAVEL

FORGETTING

BROWNE, Sir Thomas (1605–1682)

But the iniquity of oblivion blindly scattereth her poppy, and deals with the memory of men without distinction to merit of perpetuity.

[*Hydriotaphia: Urn Burial* (1658)]

Oblivion is a kind of Annihilation.

[*Christian Morals* (1716)]

CALVERLEY, C.S. (1831–1884)

I cannot sing the old songs now!
It is not that I deem them low;
'Tis that I can't remember how
They go.

['Changed' (1872)]

CARROLL, Lewis (1832–1898)

'The horror of that moment,' the King went on, 'I shall never, never forget!'
'You will, though,' the Queen said, 'if you don't make a memorandum of it.'

[*Through the Looking-Glass (and What Alice Found There)* (1872)]

DISRAELI, Benjamin (1804–1881)

Nobody is forgotten when it is convenient to remember him.

[Attr.]

When I meet a man whose name I can't remember, I give myself two minutes; then, if it is a hopeless case, I always say, And how is the old complaint?

[Attr.]

FENTON, James (1949–)

How comforting it is, once or twice a year
To get together and forget the old times.

[*The Memory of War. Poems 1968–1982* (1983)]

MARX, Groucho (1895–1977)

I never forget a face, but I'll make an exception in your case.

[*The Guardian*, 1965]

SAKI (1870–1916)

Women and elephants never forget an injury.

[*Reginald* (1904)]

SHERIDAN, Richard Brinsley (1751–1816)

Illiterate him, I say, quite from your memory.

[*The Rivals* (1775)]

STEVENSON, Robert Louis (1850–1894)

I've a grand memory for forgetting, David.

[*Kidnapped* (1886)]

SVEVO, Italo (1861–1928)

There are three things I always forget. Names, faces and – the third I can't remember.

[Attr.]

See MEMORY

FORGIVENESS

AUSTEN, Jane (1775–1817)

You ought certainly to forgive them as a Christian, but never to admit them in your sight, or allow their names to be mentioned in your hearing.

[*Pride and Prejudice* (1813)]

THE BIBLE (King James Version)

Father, forgive them; for they know not what they do.

[*Luke*, 23:34]

BROWNING, Robert (1812–1889)

Good, to forgive;
Best, to forget!
Living, we fret;
Dying, we live.

[*La Saisiaz* (1878)]

CATHERINE THE GREAT (1729–1796)

Moi, je serai autocrate: c'est mon métier. Et le bon

Dieu me pardonnera: c'est son métier.
I shall be an autocrat: that's my job. And the good Lord will forgive me: that's his job.

[Attr.]

CHURCHILL, Sir Winston (1874–1965)

Men will forgive a man anything except bad prose.

[Election speech, Manchester, 1906]

DIETRICH, Marlene (1901–1992)

Once a woman has forgiven her man, she must not reheat his sins for breakfast.

[*Marlene Dietrich's ABC* (1962)]

DRYDEN, John (1631–1700)

Forgiveness to the injured does belong;
But they ne'er pardon, who have done the wrong.

[*The Conquest of Granada* (1670)]

FROST, Robert (1874–1963)

Forgive, O Lord, my little jokes on Thee
And I'll forgive Thy great big one on me.

['Cluster of Faith' (1962)]

GAY, John (1685–1732)

Well, Polly; as far as one woman can forgive another, I forgive thee.

[*The Beggar's Opera* (1728)]

HEINE, Heinrich (1797–1856)

We should forgive our enemies, but only after they have been hanged first.

KENNEDY, Robert F. (1925–1968)

Always forgive your enemies – but never forget their names.

PROVERBS

To err is human; to forgive divine.

Forgive and forget.

YEATS, W.B. (1865–1939)

Only the dead can be forgiven;
But when I think of that my tongue's a stone.

['A Dialogue of Self and Soul' (1933)]

FRANCE

ANONYMOUS

The overall impression from the British and the Germans is that they love France itself but would rather that the French didn't live there.

[Paris Chamber of Commerce spokesman commenting on the results of a tourist survey]

ARNOLD, Matthew (1822–1888)

France, famed in all great arts, in none supreme.

['To a Republican Friend' (1849)]

CAESAR, Gaius Julius (c.102–44 BC)

Gallia est omnis divisa in partes tres.
The whole territory of Gaul is divided into three parts.

[*De Bello Gallico*]

CARLYLE, Thomas (1795–1881)

France was long a despotism tempered by epigrams.

[*History of the French Revolution* (1837)]

CHURCHILL, Sir Winston (1874–1965)

The Almighty in His infinite wisdom did not see fit to create Frenchmen in the image of Englishmen.

[Speech, House of Commons, December 1942]

COWARD, Sir Noël (1899–1973)

There's always something fishy about the French.

[*Conversation Piece* (1934)]

DE GAULLE, Charles (1890–1970)

On ne peut rassembler les Français que sous le coup de la peur. On ne peut pas rassembler á froid un pays qui compte 265 spécialités de fromage.
One can only unite the French under the threat of danger. One cannot simply bring together a nation that produces 265 kinds of cheese.

[Speech, 1951]

When I want to know what France thinks, I ask myself.

[Attr.]

DU BELLAY, Joachim (1522–1560)

France, mère des arts, des armes et des lois.

France, mother of arts, of arms, and of laws.

[*Les Regrets* (1558)]

GALLICO, Paul (1897–1976)

The words Liberté, Egalité, Fraternité rimming their coins might well be replaced by the slogan 'It can be arranged'.

[*The Zoo Gang* (1971)]

GRAHAM, Harry (1874–1936)

Weep not for little Léonie
Abducted by a French Marquis!
Though loss of honour was a wrench
Just think how it's improved her French.

[*More Ruthless Rhymes for Heartless Homes* (1930)]

JOAN OF ARC (c.1412–1431)

You think when you have slain me you will conquer France, but that you will never do. Though there were a hundred thousand God-dammees more in France than there are, they will never conquer that kingdom.

[Attr.]

JOHNSON, Samuel (1709–1784)

A Frenchman must be always talking, whether he knows anything of the matter or not; an Englishman is content to say nothing, when he has nothing to say.

[In Boswell, *The Life of Samuel Johnson* (1791)]

NAPOLEON I (1769–1821)

France has more need of me than I have need of France.

[Speech, 1813]

NOVELLO, Ivor (1893–1951)

There's something Vichy about the French.

[In Marsh, *Ambrosia and Small Beer*]

RIVAROL, Antoine de (1753–1801)

Ce qui n'est pas clair n'est pas français.
What is not clear is not French.

[*Discours sur l'Universalité de la Langue Française* (1784)]

SIDNEY, Sir Philip (1554–1586)

That sweet enemy, France.

[*Astrophel and Stella* (1591)]

SPENCER, Herbert (1820–1903)

French art, if not sanguinary, is usually obscene.

[In *Home Life with Herbert Spencer* (1906)]

STERNE, Laurence (1713–1768)

[Of the French]
They are a loyal, a gallant, a generous, an ingenious, and good tempered people as is under heaven – if they have a fault, they are too serious.

[*A Sentimental Journey* (1768)]

TOCQUEVILLE, Alexis de (1805–1859)

L'esprit français est de ne pas vouloir de supérieur. L'esprit anglais de vouloir des inférieurs. Le Français lève les yeux sans cesse au-dessus de lui avec inquiétude. L'Anglais les baisse au-dessous de lui avec complaisance. C'est de part et d'autre de l'orgueil, mais entendu de manière différente.
The French want no-one to be their superior. The English want inferiors. The Frenchman constantly looks above him with anxiety. The Englishman looks beneath him with complacency. On either side it is pride, but understood in a different manner.

[*Voyage en Angleterre et en Irlande de 1835* (1835)]

WALPOLE, Horace (1717–1797)

I do not dislike the French from the vulgar antipathy between neighbouring nations, but for their insolent and unfounded airs of superiority.

[Letter, 1787]

WILDER, Billy (1906–)

France is a country where the money falls apart in your hands and you can't tear the toilet paper.

[In Halliwell, *Filmgoer's Book of Quotes* (1973)]

FREEDOM

ADDISON, Joseph (1672–1719)

A day, an hour of virtuous liberty
Is worth a whole eternity in bondage.

[*Cato* (1713)]

ANONYMOUS

As a general rule, the freedom of any people can be judged by the volume of their laughter.

[Declaration sent to Pope John XXII by the Scottish barons]
For so long as but a hundred of us remain alive, we will in no way yield ourselves to the dominion of the English. For it is not for glory, nor riches, nor honour that we fight, but for Freedom only, which no good man lays down but with his life.

[Declaration of Arbroath, 1320]

ARISTOTLE (384–322 BC)

Where we are free to act, we are also free not to act, and where we are able to say No, we are also able to say Yes.

[Nicomachean Ethics]

AURELIUS, Marcus (121–180)

Remember that to change your mind and follow someone who puts you right is to be none the less free than you were before.

[Meditations]

BALDWIN, Stanley (1867–1947)

There is a wind of nationalism and freedom blowing round the world, and blowing as strongly in Asia as elsewhere.

[Speech, London, 4 December 1934]

BARBOUR, John (c.1316–1395)

A! fredome is a noble thing!
Fredome mayss man to haiff liking;
Fredome all solace to man giffio:
He levys at ess that frely levys!

[The Bruce (1375)]

BELL, Clive (1881–1964)

Only reason can convince us of those three fundamental truths without a recognition of which there can be no effective liberty: that what we believe is not necessarily true; that what we like is not necessarily good; and that all questions are open.

[Civilisation (1928)]

BERLIN, Isaiah (1909–1997)

Liberty is liberty, not equality or fairness or justice or culture, or human happiness or a quiet conscience.

[Four Essays on Liberty (1969)]

Rousseau asks why it is that man, who was born free, is nevertheless everywhere in chains; one might as well ask, says Maistre, why it is that sheep, who are born carnivorous, nevertheless everywhere nibble grass. Men are not born for freedom, nor for peace.

['The Counter-Enlightenment']

BURKE, Edmund (1729–1797)

Abstract liberty, like other mere abstractions, is not to be found.

[Speech on Conciliation with America (1775)]

Freedom and not servitude is the cure of anarchy; as religion, and not atheism, is the true remedy for superstition.

[Speech on Conciliation with America (1775)]

Liberty, too, must be limited in order to be possessed.

[Letter to the Sheriffs of Bristol on the Affairs of America (1777)]

The only liberty I mean, is a liberty connected with order; that not only exists along with order and virtue, but which cannot exist at all without them.

[Speech, 1774]

BURNS, Robert (1759–1796)

Scots, wha hae wi' Wallace bled,
Scots, wham Bruce has aften led,
Welcome to your gory bed
Or to victorie! ...

Lay the proud usurpers low!
Tyrants fall in ev'ry foe!
Liberty's in every blow!
Let us do, or die!

['Scots, Wha Hae' (1793)]

BYRON, Lord (1788–1824)

Yet, Freedom! yet thy banner, torn, but flying,
Streams like the thunder-storm against the wind.

[Childe Harold's Pilgrimage (1812–18)]

COLERIDGE, Hartley (1796–1849)
But what is Freedom? Rightly understood,
A universal licence to be good.
['Liberty' (1833)]

COLERIDGE, Samuel Taylor (1772–1834)
With what deep worship I have still adored
The spirit of divinest Liberty.
['France' (1798)]

For what is freedom, but the unfettered use
Of all the powers which God for use had
given?
['The Destiny of Nations']

COLUMBANUS, Saint (c.543–615)
[To the Pope]
Liberty was ever the tradition of my fathers,
and, among us, no person avails, but rather
reason.
[In Brendan Lehane, *Early Celtic Christianity* (1994)]

CONNOLLY, James (1868–1916)
Apostles of Freedom are ever idolised when
dead, but crucified when alive.
[*Workers Republic*, 1898]

COWPER, William (1731–1800)
Freedom has a thousand charms to show,
That slaves, howe'er contented, never know.
[*Table Talk* (1782)]

CURRAN, John Philpot (1750–1817)
The condition upon which God hath given
liberty to man is eternal vigilance; which
condition if he break, servitude is at once the
consequence of his crime, and the
punishment of his guilt.
[Speech, 1790]

DIDEROT, Denis (1713–1784)
Men will never be free until the last king is
strangled with the entrails of the last priest.
[*Dithyrambe sur la Fête des Rois*]

ENGELS, Friedrich (1820–1895)
Freedom is the recognition of necessity.
[In Mackay, *The Harvest of a Quiet Eye* (1977)]

EWER, William Norman (1885–1976)
I gave my life for freedom – This I know:

For those who bade me fight had told me so.
['The Souls' (1917)]

GEORGE, Dan (1899–1982)
O Freedom, what liberties are taken in thy
name!
[In Sagittarius and D. George, *Perpetual Pessimist* (1963)]

GIBBON, Edward (1737–1794)
Corruption, the most infallible symptom of
constitutional liberty.
[*Decline and Fall of the Roman Empire* (1776–88)]

HALIFAX, Lord (1633–1695)
Power is so apt to be insolent and Liberty to
be saucy, that they are very seldom upon
good Terms.
[*Political, Moral and Miscellaneous Thoughts and Reflections* (1750)]

When the people contend for their Liberty,
they seldom get any thing by their Victory
but new Masters.
[*Political, Moral and Miscellaneous Thoughts and Reflections* (1750)]

HATTERSLEY, Roy (1932–)
The proposition that Muslims are welcome in
Britain if, and only if, they stop behaving like
Muslims is incompatible with the principles
of a free society.
[*The Independent*, 1995]

HAZLITT, William (1778–1830)
The love of liberty is the love of others; the
love of power is the love of ourselves.
[*Political Essays* (1819)]

HENRY, Patrick (1736–1799)
Give me liberty, or give me death!
[Speech, 1775]

HOFFER, Eric (1902–1983)
When people are free to do as they please,
they usually imitate each other.
[*The Passionate State of Mind* (1955)]

HORACE (65–8 BC)
Quisnam igitur liber? Sapiens qui sibi imperiosus,
Quem neque pauperies neque mors neque vincula
terrent. Responsare cupidinibus, contemnere honores

Fortis, et in se ipso totus, teres, atque rotundus.
Who then is free? The wise man who commands himself, whom neither poverty nor death nor chains can terrify, who is strong enough to defy his passions and to despise distinctions, a man who is complete in himself, polished and well-rounded.

[*Satires*]

JAMES I OF SCOTLAND (1394–1437)

The bird, the beast, the fish eke in the sea,
They live in freedom everich in his kind;
And I a man, and lackith liberty.

[*The Kingis Quair*]

JEFFERSON, Thomas (1743–1826)

The tree of liberty must be refreshed from time to time with the blood of patriots and tyrants. It is its natural manure.

[Letter to W.S. Smith, 1787]

KAFKA, Franz (1883–1924)

Es ist oft besser, in Ketten, als frei zu sein.
It's often better to be in chains than to be free.

[*The Trial* (1925)]

KIERKEGAARD, Søren (1813–1855)

People hardly ever make use of the freedom they have, for example, the freedom of thought; instead they demand freedom of speech as a compensation.

[In *The Faber Book of Aphorisms* (1962)]

KING, Martin Luther (1929–1968)

Free at last, free at last, thank God Almighty, we are free at last!

[Speech, 1963]

KRISTOFFERSON, Kris (1936–)

Freedom's just another word for nothing left to lose.

['Me and Bobby McGee', song, 1969]

LENIN, V.I. (1870–1924)

It is true that liberty is precious – so precious that it must be rationed.

[In Sidney and Beatrice Webb, *Soviet Communism* (1936)]

LINCOLN, Abraham (1809–1865)

I leave you, hoping that the lamp of liberty will burn in your bosoms, until there shall no longer be a doubt that all men are created free and equal.

[Speech, 1858]

Those who deny freedom to others, deserve it not for themselves.

[Speech, 1856]

MACAULAY, Lord (1800–1859)

There is only one cure for the evils which newly acquired freedom produces; and that is freedom.

[*Collected Essays* (1843)]

Many politicians of our time are in the habit of laying it down as a self-evident proposition, that no people ought to be free till they are fit to use their freedom. The maxim is worthy of the fool in the old story, who resolved not to go into the water till he had learnt to swim. If men are to wait for liberty till they become wise and good in slavery, they may indeed wait for ever.

[*Collected Essays* (1843)]

MALCOLM X (1925–1965)

You can't separate peace from freedom because no one can be at peace unless he has his freedom.

[*Malcolm X Speaks*, 1965]

MANDELA, Nelson (1918–)

I cannot and will not give any undertaking at a time when I, and you, the people, are not free. Your freedom and mine cannot be separated.

[Message to a rally in Soweto, 1985]

A sudden access of psychological freedom often turns from sheer excitement to deep panic.

[*The Man Who Dreamed of Tomorrow* (1980)]

MILL, John Stuart (1806–1873)

The liberty of the individual must be thus far limited; he must not make himself a nuisance to other people.

[*On Liberty* (1859)]

Liberty consists in doing what one desires.

[*On Liberty* (1859)]

The sole end for which mankind are warranted, individually or collectively, in interfering with the liberty of action of any of their number, is self-protection.

[*On Liberty* (1859)]

MILTON, John (1608–1674)

Give me the liberty to know, to utter, and to argue freely according to conscience, above all liberties.

[*Areopagitica* (1644)]

None can love freedom heartilie, but good men; the rest love not freedom, but licence.

[*The Tenure of Kings and Magistrates* (1649)]

MONTESQUIEU, Charles (1689–1755)

La liberté est le droit de faire tout ce que les lois permettent.
Freedom is the right to do whatever the laws permit.

[*De l'esprit des lois* (1748)]

MUSSOLINI, Benito (1883–1945)

Ci sono le libertá; la libertá non è mai esistita.
There are freedoms; freedom has never existed.

[Speech, 1923]

ORWELL, George (1903–1950)

I sometimes think that the price of liberty is not so much eternal vigilance as eternal dirt.

[*The Road to Wigan Pier* (1937)]

PANKHURST, Dame Christabel (1880–1958)

What we suffragettes aspire to be when we are enfranchised is ambassadors of freedom to women in other parts of the world, who are not so free as we are.

[Speech, 1915]

PITT, William (1759–1806)

Necessity is the plea for every infringement of human freedom. It is the argument of tyrants; it is the creed of slaves.

[Speech, 1783]

POPPER, Sir Karl (1902–1994)

We must plan for freedom, and not only for security, if for no other reason than that only freedom can make security secure.

[*The Open Society and its Enemies* (1945)]

RAND, Ayn (1905–1982)

Intellectual freedom cannot exist without political freedom; political freedom cannot exist without economic freedom; a free mind and a free market are corollaries.

[*For The New Intellectual*]

ROLAND, Madame (1754–1793)

[Remark on mounting the scaffold]
O liberté! O liberté! que de crimes on commet en ton nom!
O liberty! O liberty! how many crimes are committed in your name!

[In Lamartine, *Histoire des Girondins* (1847)]

ROOSEVELT, Franklin Delano (1882–1945)

In the future days, which we seek to make secure, we look forward to a world founded upon four essential human freedoms. The first is freedom of speech and expression – everywhere in the world. The second is freedom of every person to worship God in his own way – everywhere in the world. The third is freedom from want … The fourth is freedom from fear.

[Address, 1941]

ROUSSEAU, Jean-Jacques (1712–1778)

Man was born free, and everywhere he is in chains.

[*Du Contrat Social* (1762)]

SARTRE, Jean-Paul (1905–1980)

Quand une fois la liberté a explosé dans une âme d'homme, les Dieux ne peuvent plus rien contre lui.
Once freedom has exploded in the soul of a man, the gods have no more power over him.

[*The Flies* (1943)]

Man is condemned to be free.

[*Existentialism and Humanism*]

SHAW, George Bernard (1856–1950)

Liberty means responsibility. That is why most men dread it.

[Man and Superman (1903)]

SMITH, Sydney (1771–1845)

I love liberty, but hope that it can be so managed that I shall have soft beds, good dinners, fine linen, etc., for the rest of my life. I am too old to fight or to suffer.

[Letter to J.A. Murray, Jan. 3rd, 1830]

SOLZHENITSYN, Alexander (1918–)

You took my freedom away long ago and you can't give it back to me because you haven't got it yourself.

[The First Circle (1968)]

You only have power over people as long as you don't take everything away from them. But when you've robbed a man of everything he's no longer in your power – he's free again.

[The First Circle (1968)]

STEVENSON, Adlai (1900–1965)

My definition of a free society is a society where it is safe to be unpopular.

[Speech, Detroit, 1952]

TWAIN, Mark (1835–1910)

It is by the goodness of God that in our country we have those three unspeakably precious things: freedom of speech, freedom of conscience, and the prudence never to practise either of them.

[Following the Equator (1897)]

VOLTAIRE (1694–1778)

La Liberté est née en Angleterre des querelles des tyrans.
Liberty was born in England from the quarrels of tyrants.

[Lettres philosophiques (1734)]

WASHINGTON, George (1732–1799)

Liberty, when it begins to take root, is a plant of rapid growth.

[Letter, 1788]

WILLKIE, Wendell (1892–1944)

Freedom is an indivisible word. If we want to enjoy it, and fight for it, we must be prepared to extend it to everyone, whether they are rich or poor, whether they agree with us or not, no matter what their race or the colour of their skin.

[One World (1943)]

WILSON, Woodrow (1856–1924)

The history of liberty is a history of resistance.

[Speech, 1912]

FRIENDSHIP

ADAMS, Henry (1838–1918)

A friend in power is a friend lost.

[The Education of Henry Adams (1918)]

One friend in a lifetime is much; two are many; three are hardly possible. Friendship needs a certain parallelism of life, a community of thought, a rivalry of aim.

[The Education of Henry Adams (1918)]

ADAMS, Victoria

[On her marriage to footballer David Beckham]
David and I haven't got that many friends. We could have our wedding in a postbox.

[The Observer, 1999]

ARISTOTLE (384–322 BC)

On being asked what is a friend, he said 'A single soul dwelling in two bodies.'

[In Diogenes Laertius, Lives of Philosophers]

AUBREY, John (1626–1697)

[Of Francis Beaumont]
There was a wonderful consimility of phansey between him and Mr John Fletcher, which caused that dearness of friendship between them … They lived together on the Bank side, not far from the Playhouse, both bachelors; lay together; had one wench in the house between them, which they did so admire; the same clothes and cloak, &c.; between them.

[Brief Lives (c. 1693)]

BACON, Francis (1561–1626)

A false friend is more dangerous than an open enemy.

> [*A Letter of Advice … to the Duke of Buckingham* (1616)]

It is the worst solitude, to have no true friendships.

> [*The Advancement of Learning* (1605)]

This communicating of a man's self to his friend works two contrary effects; for it redoubleth joys, and cutteth griefs in halves.

> [*Essays* (1625)]

BELLOC, Hilaire (1870–1953)

From quiet homes and first beginning,
Out to the undiscovered ends,
There's nothing worth the wear of winning,
But laughter and the love of friends.

> [*Verses* (1910)]

THE BIBLE
(King James Version)

A faithful friend is a sturdy shelter: he that has found one has found a treasure. There is nothing so precious as a faithful friend, and no scales can measure his excellence.

> [*Apocrypha, Ecclesiasticus*]

Forsake not an old friend; for the new is not comparable to him; a new friend is as new wine; when it is old, thou shalt drink it with pleasure.

> [*Apocrypha, Ecclesiasticus*]

BIERCE, Ambrose (1842–c.1914)

Antipathy: The sentiment inspired by one's friend's friend.

> [*The Enlarged Devil's Dictionary* (1961)]

BRADBURY, Malcolm (1932–)

I've noticed your hostility towards him … I ought to have guessed you were friends.

> [*The History Man* (1975)]

BRECHT, Bertolt (1898–1956)

Ich [trau] ihm nicht, wir sind befreundet.
I'm wary of him. We're friends.

> [*Mother Courage and her Children*, (1941)]

BRONTË, Emily (1818–1848)

Love is like the wild rose-briar,
Friendship like the holly-tree,
The holly is dark when the rose-briar blooms
But which will bloom most constantly?

> ['Love and Friendship']

BULWER-LYTTON, Edward (1803–1873)

There is no man so friendless but what he can find a friend sincere enough to tell him disagreeable truths.

> [*What Will He Do With It?* (1857)]

BYRON, Lord (1788–1824)

Friendship is Love without his wings.

> ['L'amitié est l'amour sans ailes' (1806)]

CANNING, George (1770–1827)

Give me the avowed, erect and manly foe;
Firm I can meet, perhaps return the blow;
But of all plagues, good Heaven, thy wrath can send,
Save me, oh, save me, from the candid friend.

> ['New Morality' (1821)]

CATHERWOOD, Mary (1847–1901)

Two may talk together under the same roof for many years, yet never really meet; and two others at first speech are old friends.

> [*Mackinac and Lake Stories*, 'Marianson']

CHURCHILL, Charles (1731–1764)

Greatly his foes he dreads, but more his friends;
He hurts me most who lavishly commends.

> ['The Apology, addressed to the Critical Reviewers' (1761)]

COLETTE (1873–1954)

My true friends have always given me that supreme proof of devotion, a spontaneous aversion for the man I loved.

> [*Break of Day* (1928)]

COLTON, Charles Caleb (c.1780–1832)

Friendship often ends in love; but love in friendship – never.

> [*Lacon* (1820)]

CONFUCIUS (c.550–c.478 BC)

Have no friends not equal to yourself.

[*Analects*]

CONGREVE, William (1670–1729)

O the pious friendships of the female sex!

[*The Way of the World* (1700)]

COWLEY, Abraham (1618–1667)

Acquaintance I would have, but when't depends

Not on the number, but the choice of friends.

[*Essays in Verse and Prose* (1668)]

DE GAULLE, Charles (1890–1970)

[Replying to Jacques Soustelle's complaint that he was being attacked by his own friends]

Changez vos amis.

Change your friends.

[Attr.]

ELIOT, George (1819–1880)

Friendships begin with liking or gratitude – roots that can be pulled up.

[*Daniel Deronda* (1876)]

EMERSON, Ralph Waldo (1803–1882)

Let the soul be assured that somewhere in the universe it should rejoin its friend, and it would be content and cheerful alone for a thousand years.

['Friendship' (1841)]

A friend is a person with whom I may be sincere. Before him I may think aloud.

['Friendship' (1841)]

A friend may well be reckoned the masterpiece of Nature.

['Friendship' (1841)]

The only reward of virtue is virtue; the only way to have a friend is to be one.

['Friendship' (1841)]

EPICURUS (341–270 BC)

It is not so much our friends' help that helps us as the confident knowledge that they will help us.

[Attr.]

GARCÍA MÁRQUEZ, Gabriel (1928–)

Un solo minuto de reconciliación tiene más mérito que toda una vida de amistad.

One single minute of reconciliation is worth more than an entire life of friendship.

[*One Hundred Years of Solitude* (1968)]

GAY, John (1685–1732)

A woman's friendship ever ends in love.

[*Dione* (1720)]

GOLDSMITH, Oliver (c.1728–1774)

Friendship is a disinterested commerce between equals; love, an abject intercourse between tyrants and slaves.

[*The Good Natur'd Man* (1768)]

HUMPHRIES, Barry (1934–)

Friendship is tested in the thick years of success rather than in the thin years of struggle.

[In Green, *A Dictionary of Contemporary Quotations* (1982)]

JOHNSON, Samuel (1709–1784)

The endearing elegance of female friendship.

[*Rasselas* (1759)]

If a man does not make new acquaintance as he advances through life, he will soon find himself left alone. A man, Sir, should keep his friendship in constant repair.

[In Boswell, *The Life of Samuel Johnson* (1791)]

How few of his friends' houses would a man choose to be at when he is sick.

[In Boswell, *The Life of Samuel Johnson* (1791)]

KINGSMILL, Hugh (1889–1949)

Friends are God's apology for relations.

[In Ingrams, *God's Apology* (1977)]

LA ROCHEFOUCAULD (1613–1680)

Dans l'adversité de nos meilleurs amis, nous trouvons toujours quelque chose qui ne nous déplait pas.

In the misfortunes of our closest friends, we always find something which is not displeasing to us.

[*Maximes* (1665)]

Il est plus honteux de se défier de ses amis que d'en être trompé.

There is more shame in distrusting one's friends than in being deceived by them.

[*Maximes* (1678)]

LEWIS, C.S. (1898–1963)

Friendship is unnecessary, like philosophy, like art. … It has no survival value; rather it is one of those things that give value to survival.

[*The Four Loves* (c. 1936)]

MEDICI, Cosimo de' (1389–1464)

We read that we ought to forgive our enemies; but we do not read that we ought to forgive our friends.

[In Bacon, *Apophthegms* (1625)]

MONTAIGNE, Michel de (1533–1592)

[Of his friend …tienne de la Boétie]
Si on me presse de dire pourquoi je l'aimais, je sens que cela ne se peut s'exprimer, qu'en répondant: 'Parce que c'était lui; parce que c'était moi.'
If I am pressed to say why I loved him, I feel it can only be explained by replying: 'Because it was he; because it was me.'

[*Essais* (1580)]

POPE, Alexander (1688–1744)

True friendship's laws are by this rule express'd,
Welcome the coming, speed the parting guest.

[*The Odyssey* (1726)]

How often are we to die before we go quite off this stage? In every friend we lose a part of ourselves, and the best part.

[Letter to Swift, 1732]

PROVERBS

One who looks for a friend without faults will have none.

A friend in need is a friend indeed.

A hedge between keeps friendship green.

SALLUST (86–c.34 BC)

Idem velle atque idem nolle, ea demum firma amicitia est.
To like and dislike the same things, this in the end is the basis of true friendship.

[*Catiline*]

SELDEN, John (1584–1654)

Old friends are best. King James used to call for his old shoes; they were easiest for his feet.

[*Table Talk* (1689)]

SHAKESPEARE, William (1564–1616)

Friendship is constant in all other things
Save in the office and affairs of love.

[*Much Ado About Nothing*, II.i]

I count myself in nothing else so happy
As in a soul rememb'ring my good friends.

[*Richard II*, II.iii]

SMITH, Logan Pearsall (1865–1946)

I might give my life for my friend, but he had better not ask me to do up a parcel.

[*Afterthoughts* (1931)]

I cannot forgive my friends for dying; I do not find these vanishing acts of theirs at all amusing.

[*Afterthoughts* (1931)]

TWAIN, Mark (1835–1910)

The holy passion of Friendship is of so sweet and steady and loyal and enduring a nature that it will last through a whole lifetime, if not asked to lend money.

[*Pudd'nhead Wilson's Calendar* (1894)]

The proper office of a friend is to side with you when you are in the wrong. Nearly anybody will side with you when you are in the right.

[Attr.]

VIDAL, Gore (1925–)

Whenever a friend succeeds, a little something in me dies.

[*The Sunday Times Magazine*, 1973]

WASHINGTON, George (1732–1799)

Be courteous to all, but intimate with few, and let those few be well tried before you give them your confidence. True friendship is a plant of slow growth, and must undergo and withstand the shocks of adversity before it is entitled to the appellation.

[Letter, 1783]

WAUGH, Evelyn (1903–1966)

We cherish our friends not for their ability to amuse us, but for our ability to amuse them.

[Attr.]

WHITMAN, Walt (1819–1892)

I no doubt deserved my enemies, but I don't believe I deserved my friends.

[In Bradford, *Biography and the Human Heart*]

WOOLF, Virginia (1882–1941)

I have lost friends, some by death … others through sheer inability to cross the street.

[*The Waves* (1931)]

YEATS, W.B. (1865–1939)

Always we'd have the new friend meet the old
And we are hurt if either friend seem cold.

[In the *English Review*, 1918]

Think where man's glory most begins and ends,
And say my glory was I had such friends.

['The Municipal Gallery Revisited' (1937)]

See ENEMIES

FUNERALS

BROWNE, Sir Thomas (1605–1682)

With rich flames, and hired tears, they solemnized their obsequies.

[*Hydriotaphia: Urn Burial* (1658)]

They carried them out of the world with their feet forward.

[*Hydriotaphia: Urn Burial* (1658)]

CATULLUS (84–c.54 BC)

Multas per gentes et multa per aequora vectus
Advenio has miseras, frater, ad inferias,
Ut te postremo donarem munere mortis
Et mutam nequiquam alloquerer cinerem.
Quandoquidem fortuna mihi tete abstulit ipsum,
Heu miser indigne frater adempte mihi,
Nunc tamen interea haec, prisco quae more

parentum
Tradita sunt tristi munere ad inferias,
Accipe fraterno multum manantia fletu,
Atque in perpetuum, frater, ave atque vale.

Having journeyed through many peoples and over many a sea I come, my brother, for these sad funeral rites, that I may present to you a last gift in death and vainly address your dumb ashes, since fortune has taken you from me – alas, poor brother cruelly snatched from me – but now accept these offerings which by our parents' custom have been handed down as a funeral gift, bedewed with many fraternal tears, and for all time, my brother, hail and farewell.

[*Carmina*]

DAY, Clarence Shepard (1874–1935)

'If you don't go to other men's funerals,' he told Father stiffly, 'they won't go to yours.'

[*Life with Father* (1935),
'Father plans']

MANN, Thomas (1875–1955)

Man sollte, statt in die Kirche, zu einem Begräbnis gehen, wenn man sich ein bisschen erbauen will. Die Leute haben gutes schwarzes Zeug an und nehmen die Hüte ab und sehen auf den Sarg und halten sich ernst und andächtig, und niemand darf faule Witze machen.

Instead of going to church you should go to a funeral when you wish to be uplifted. The people have got good black clothes on, they take their hats off, look at the coffin and are serious and reverent, and no-one dares make bad jokes.

[*The Magic Mountain*, (1924)]

MILLER, Arthur (1915–)

[When asked if he would attend Marilyn Monroe's funeral]
Why should I go? She won't be there.

[Attr.]

MITFORD, Jessica Lucy (1917–)

I have nothing against undertakers personally. It's just that I wouldn't want one to bury my sister.

[Attr. in *Saturday Review*, 1964]

MOUNTBATTEN OF BURMA, First Earl (1900–1979)
I can't think of a more wonderful thanksgiving for the life I have had than that everyone should be jolly at my funeral.
[TV interview, shown after his death in August 1979]

PITTS, William (1900–1980)
It is the overtakers who keep the undertakers busy.
[The Observer, 1963]

THE FUTURE

ADDISON, Joseph (1672–1719)
'We are always doing,' says he, 'something for Posterity, but I would fain see Posterity do something for us.'
[The Spectator, August 1714]

BACON, Francis (1561–1626)
Men must pursue things which are just in present, and leave the future to the divine Providence.
[The Advancement of Learning (1605)]

BALDWIN, James (1924–1987)
The future is … black.
[The Observer, 1963]

BALFOUR, A.J. (1848–1930)
The energies of our system will decay, the glory of the sun will be dimmed, and the earth, tideless and inert, will no longer tolerate the race which has for a moment disturbed its solitude. Man will go down into the pit, and all his thoughts will perish.
[The Foundations of Belief (1895)]

BENNETT, Arnold (1867–1931)
The people who live in the past must yield to the people who live in the future. Otherwise the world would begin to turn the other way round.
[Attr.]

BIERCE, Ambrose (1842–c.1914)
Future: That period of time in which our affairs prosper, our friends are true and our happiness is assured.
[The Cynic's Word Book (1906)]

BURKE, Edmund (1729–1797)
People will not look forward to posterity, who never look backward to their ancestors.
[Reflections on the Revolution in France (1790)]

You can never plan the future by the past.
[Letter to a Member of the National Assembly (1791)]

CAMUS, Albert (1913–1960)
The future is the only kind of property that the masters willingly concede to slaves.
[The Rebel (1951)]

CHURCHILL, Sir Winston (1874–1965)
The empires of the future are empires of the mind.
[Speech, 1943]

CLARK, Lord Kenneth (1903–1983)
One may be optimistic, but one can't exactly be joyful at the prospect before us.
[End of TV series, Civilization]

COLERIDGE, Samuel Taylor (1772–1834)
Often do the spirits
Of great events stride on before the events,
And in to-day already walks to-morrow.
['Death of Wallenstein' (1800)]

CONFUCIUS (c.550–c.478 BC)
Study the past, if you would divine the future.
[Analects]

COWARD, Sir Noël (1899–1973)
I don't give a hoot about posterity. Why should I worry about what people think of me when I'm dead as a doornail anyway?
[Present Laughter (1943)]

CRISP, Quentin (1908–)
I still lived in the future – a habit which is the death of happiness.
[The Naked Civil Servant (1968)]

DISRAELI, Benjamin (1804–1881)
He seems to think that posterity is a pack-

horse, always ready to be loaded.

[Speech, House of Commons, 1862]

DIX, Dorothy (1870–1951)

I have learned to live each day as it comes, and not to borrow trouble by dreading tomorrow. It is the dark menace of the future that makes cowards of us.

[Dorothy Dix, Her Book (1926)]

EINSTEIN, Albert (1879–1955)

I never think of the future. It comes soon enough.

[Interview, 1930]

HILL, Reginald (1936–)

I have seen the future and it sucks.

[Pictures of Perfection (1994)]

HUGO, Victor (1802–1885)

In the twentieth century, war will be dead, the scaffold will be dead, hatred will be dead, frontier boundaries will be dead, dogmas will be dead; man will live. He will possess something higher than all these – a great country, the whole earth, and a great hope, the whole heaven.

[The Future of Man]

JOHNSON, Samuel (1709–1784)

The future is purchased by the present.

[Attr.]

LEWIS, C.S. (1898–1963)

The Future is something which everyone reaches at the rate of sixty minutes an hour, whatever he does, whoever he is.

[The Screwtape Letters (1942)]

MITCHELL, Margaret (1900–1949)

After all, tomorrow is another day.

[Gone with the Wind (1936)]

ORTEGA Y GASSET, José (1883–1955)

You don't fight hand-to-hand with the past. The future conquers it because it swallows it. If it leaves part of it outside, it is lost.

[The Rebellion of the Masses (1930)]

ORWELL, George (1903–1950)

If you want a picture of the future, imagine a boot stamping on a human face – for ever.

[Nineteen Eighty-Four (1949)]

PROUST, Marcel (1871–1922)

Nous appelons notre avenir l'ombre de lui-même que notre passé projette devant nous.

What we call our future is the shadow which our past throws in front of us.

[A l'ombre des jeunes filles en fleurs (1918)]

ROCHE, Sir Boyle (1743–1807)

What has posterity done for us?

[Speech, 1780]

SNOW, C.P. (1905–1980)

[On industrialisation]

Common men can show astonishing fortitude in chasing jam tomorrow. Jam today, and men aren't at their most exciting: jam tomorrow, and one often sees them at their noblest.

[The Two Cultures and the Scientific Revolution (1959)]

STEFFENS, Lincoln (1866–1936)

[Remark after visiting Russia in 1919]

I have seen the future; and it works.

[Letter to Marie Howe, 1919]

WEIL, Simone (1909–1943)

The future is made of the same stuff as the present.

[On Science, Necessity, and the Love of God]

WELLS, H.G. (1866–1946)

One thousand years more. That's all Homo sapiens has before him.

[In H. Nicolson, Diary]

WILLIAMS, Tennessee (1911–1983)

The future is called 'perhaps', which is the only possible thing to call the future. And the important thing is not to allow that to scare you.

[Attr.]

See PAST; PRESENT; TIME

G

GARDENS

ADDISON, Joseph (1672–1719)

I value my garden more for being full of blackbirds than of cherries, and very frankly give them fruit for their songs.

[*The Spectator*, 1712]

BACON, Francis (1561–1626)

God Almighty first planted a garden. And indeed, it is the purest of human pleasures. It is the greatest refreshment to the spirits of man; without which, buildings and palaces are but gross handiworks.

['Of Gardens' (1625)]

BROWN, Thomas Edward (1830–1897)

A garden is a lovesome thing, God wot!

['My Garden' (1893)]

COWLEY, Abraham (1618–1667)

God the first garden made, and the first city Cain.

['The Garden' (1668)]

EMERSON, Ralph Waldo (1803–1882)

What is a weed? A plant whose virtues have not yet been discovered.

[*Fortune of the Republic* (1878)]

GARDINER, Richard (b. c.1533)

Sowe Carrets in your Gardens, and humbly praise God for them, as for a singular and great blessing.

[*Profitable Instructions for the Manuring, Sowing and Planting of Kitchen Gardens*]

GURNEY, Dorothy (1858–1932)

The kiss of the sun for pardon,
The song of the birds for mirth,
One is nearer God's Heart in a garden
Than anywhere else on earth.

['God's Garden' (1913)]

KIPLING, Rudyard (1865–1936)

Oh, Adam was a gardener, and God who made him sees

That half a proper gardener's work is done upon his knees,
So when your work is finished, you can wash your hands and pray
For the Glory of the Garden, that it may not pass away!
And the Glory of the Garden it shall never pass away!

[Songs written for C.R.L. Fletcher's *A History of England* (1911)]

MARVELL, Andrew (1621–1678)

I have a garden of my own,
But so with roses overgrown,
And lilies, that you would it guess
To be a little wilderness.

['The Nymph Complaining for the Death of her Fawn' (1681)]

Here at the fountain's sliding foot,
Or at some fruit-tree's mossy root,
Casting the body's vest aside,
My soul into the boughs does glide.

['The Garden' (1681)]

MILTON, John (1608–1674)

And add to these retired leisure,
That in trim gardens takes his pleasure.

['Il Penseroso' (1645)]

RUSSELL, Bertrand (1872–1970)

Every time I talk to a savant I feel quite sure that happiness is no longer a possibility. Yet when I talk to my gardener, I'm convinced of the opposite.

[Attr.]

SHAKESPEARE, William (1564–1616)

'Tis in ourselves that we are thus or thus. Our bodies are our gardens to the which our wills are gardeners.

[*Othello*, I.iii]

SHERIDAN, Richard Brinsley (1751–1816)

Won't you come into the garden? I would

like my roses to see you.

[*Attr.*]

SIMMONS, John (1937–)
A weed is simply a plant that you don't want.
[*The Observer*, 1983]

TENNYSON, Alfred, Lord (1809–1892)
Come into the garden, Maud,
For the black bat, night, has flown,
Come into the garden, Maud,
I am here at the gate alone;
And the woodbine spices are wafted abroad,
And the musk of the rose is blown.
[*Maud* (1855)]

VOLTAIRE (1694–1778)
Cela est bien dit, répondit Candide, mais il faut
cultiver notre jardin.
'That is well said,' replied Candide, 'but we
must cultivate our garden.'
[*Candide* (1759)]

See FLOWERS

GENEROSITY

BARRIE, Sir J.M. (1860–1937)
Never ascribe to an opponent motives
meaner than your own.
[Address, St Andrews University,
1922]

**THE BIBLE
(King James Version)**
It is more blessed to give than to receive.
[*Acts of the Apostles*, 20:35]

God loveth a cheerful giver.
[*II Corinthians*, 9:7]

BURNS, Robert (1759–1796)
To be overtopped in anything else, I can
bear: but in the tests of generous love, I defy
all mankind!
[*Letter to Clarinda*, 1788]

CORNEILLE, Pierre (1606–1684)
Le façon de donner vaut mieux que ce qu'on donne.
The manner of giving is worth more than the

gift.
[*Le Menteur* (1643)]

GIBBS, Sir Philip (1877–1962)
It is better to give than to lend, and it costs
about the same.
[*Attr.*]

LA BRUYÈRE, Jean de (1645–1696)
La liberalité consiste moins à donner beaucoup qu'à
donner à propos.
Liberality consists less in giving a great deal
than in gifts well timed.
[*Les caractères ou les moeurs de ce siècle* (1688)]

LOYOLA, St Ignatius (1491–1556)
Teach us, good Lord, to serve Thee as Thou
deservest:
To give and not to count the cost;
To fight and not to heed the wounds;
To toil and not to seek for rest;
To labour and not to ask for any reward
Save that of knowing that we do Thy will.
['Prayer for Generosity']

MUIR, Edwin (1887–1959)
I think it possible that all Scots are
illegitimate, Scotsmen being so mean and
Scotswomen so generous.
[*Scottish Journey* (1935)]

**TALLEYRAND, Charles-Maurice de
(1754–1838)**
Méfiez-vous du premier mouvement; il est toujours
généreux.
Don't trust first impulses; they are always
generous.
[*Attr.*]

See BENEFACTORS; CHARITY

GENETICALLY MODIFIED FOOD

CHARLES, Prince of Wales (1948–)
[On genetically modified food crops]
I happen to believe that this kind of genetic
modification takes mankind into the realms
that belong to God, and to God alone … do

we have the right to experiment with, and commercialise, the building blocks of life?

[*Daily Telegraph*, June 1998]

Are we going to allow the industrialisation of Life itself, redesigning the natural world for the sake of convenience and embarking on an Orwellian future? – Or should we be adopting a gentler, more considered approach, seeking always to work with the grain of Nature in making better, more sustainable use of what we have, for the long-term benefit of mankind as a whole?

[*Daily Mail*, June 1999]

MAY, Sir Robert

Properly handled, GM crops have the potential to be more wildlife-friendly than the ones we have now.

[*The Scotsman*, May 1999]

GENIUS

ALCOTT, Louisa May (1832–1888)

It takes people a long time to learn the difference between talent and genius, especially ambitious young men and women.

[*Little Women* (1869)]

ANONYMOUS

The difference between genius and stupidity is that genius has its limits.

No amount of genius can overcome a preoccupation with detail.

[*Levy's Eighth Law*]

ARNOLD, Matthew (1822–1888)

So we have the Philistine of genius in religion – Luther; the Philistine of genius in politics – Cromwell; the Philistine of genius in literature – Bunyan.

[*Mixed Essays* (1879)]

BEERBOHM, Sir Max (1872–1956)

I have known no man of genius who had not to pay, in some affliction or defect either physical or spiritual, for what the gods had given him.

[*And Even Now* (1920)]

BROWNING, Elizabeth Barrett (1806–1861)

Since when was genius found respectable?

[*Aurora Leigh* (1857)]

BUFFON, Comte de (1707–1788)

Le génie n'est qu'une plus grande aptitude á la patience.

Genius is merely a greater aptitude for patience.

[In *Hérault de Séchelles, Voyage á Montbar* (1803)]

BUTLER, Samuel (1835–1902)

Genius … has been defined as a supreme capacity for taking trouble … It might be more fitly described as a supreme capacity for getting its possessors into pains of all kinds, and keeping them therein so long as the genius remains.

[*The Note-Books of Samuel Butler* (1912)]

CARLYLE, Thomas (1795–1881)

'Genius' (which means transcendent capacity of taking trouble, first of all).

[*History of Frederick the Great* (1858–1865)]

CHURCHILL, Charles (1731–1764)

Genius is of no country.

[*The Rosciad* (1761)]

DALI, Salvador (1904–1989)

I'm going to live forever. Geniuses don't die.

[*The Observer*, 1986]

DOYLE, Sir Arthur Conan (1859–1930)

Mediocrity knows nothing higher than itself, but talent instantly recognizes genius.

[*The Valley of Fear* (1914)]

EDISON, Thomas Alva (1847–1931)

Genius is one per cent inspiration and ninety-nine per cent perspiration.

[*Life*, 1932]

EMERSON, Ralph Waldo (1803–1882)

To believe your own thought, to believe that what is true for you in your private heart is true for all men, – that is genius.

[*Essays, First Series* (1841)]

When Nature has work to be done, she creates a genius to do it.

[Lecture, 1841, 'Method of Nature']

GOLDSMITH, Oliver (c.1728–1774)

True Genius walks along a line, and, perhaps, our greatest pleasure is in seeing it so often near falling, without being ever actually down.

[The Bee (1759)]

HAZLITT, William (1778–1830)

Rules and models destroy genius and art.

['Thoughts on Taste' (1818)]

HOPE, Anthony (1863–1933)

Unless one is a genius, it is best to aim at being intelligible.

[The Dolly Dialogues (1894)]

HOPKINS, Jane Ellice (1836–1904)

Gift, like genius, I often think, only means an infinite capacity for taking pains.

[Work amongst Working Men, 1870]

HUBBARD, Elbert (1856–1915)

One machine can do the work of fifty ordinary men. No machine can do the work of one extraordinary man.

[A Thousand and One Epigrams (1911)]

JAMES, Henry (1843–1916)

[Of Thoreau]

Whatever question there may be of his talent, there can be none, I think, of his genius. It was a slim and crooked one; but it was eminently personal. He was imperfect, unfinished, inartistic; he was worse than provincial – he was parochial.

[Hawthorne (1879)]

JOHNSON, Samuel (1709–1784)

The true genius is a mind of large general powers, accidentally determined to some particular direction.

[The Lives of the Most Eminent English Poets (1779–1781)]

JOYCE, James (1882–1941)

A man of genius makes no mistakes. His

errors are volitional and are the portals of discovery.

[Ulysses (1922)]

KEATS, John (1795–1821)

So I do believe ... that works of genius are the first things in this world.

[Letter to George and Tom Keats, 13 January 1818]

KENNEDY, John F. (1917–1963)

[At a dinner held at the White House for Nobel prizewinners]

... probably the greatest concentration of talent and genius in this house, except for perhaps those times when Thomas Jefferson ate alone.

[New York Times, 1962]

MEREDITH, Owen (1831–1891)

Genius does what it must, and Talent does what it can.

['Last Words of a Sensitive Second-Rate Poet' (1868)]

PROVERB

Genius is an infinite capacity for taking pains.

STEPHEN, Sir James Fitzjames (1829–1894)

The way in which the man of genius rules is by persuading an efficient minority to coerce an indifferent and self-indulgent majority.

[Liberty, Equality and Fraternity (1873)]

SWIFT, Jonathan (1667–1745)

When a true genius appears in the world, you may know him by this sign, that the dunces are all in confederacy against him.

[Thoughts on Various Subjects (1711)]

[Of A Tale of a Tub]

Good God! what a genius I had when I wrote that book.

[In Sir Walter Scott, Works of Swift (1824)]

WHISTLER, James McNeill (1834–1903)

[Replying to a lady inquiring whether he thought genius hereditary]

I cannot tell you that, madam. Heaven has

granted me no offspring.

[In Seitz, *Whistler Stories* (1913)]

WILDE, Oscar (1854–1900)

[Spoken to André Gide]

Voulez-vous savoir le grand drame de ma vie? C'est que j'ai mis mon génie dans ma vie; je n'ai mis que mon talent dans mes oeuvres.

Do you want to know the great tragedy of my life? I have put all of my genius into my life; all I've put into my works is my talent.

[In Gide, *Oscar Wilde* (1910)]

[At the New York Customs]

I have nothing to declare except my genius.

[In Harris, *Oscar Wilde* (1918)]

See TALENT

GENTEEL BEHAVIOUR

BETJEMAN, Sir John (1906–1984)

Phone for the fish-knives, Norman
As Cook is a little unnerved;
You kiddies have crumpled the serviettes
And I must have things daintily served …

I know what I wanted to ask you;
Is trifle sufficient for sweet? …

Milk and then just as it comes dear?
I'm afraid the preserve's full of stones;
Beg pardon, I'm soiling the doileys
With afternoon tea-cakes and scones.

[*A Few Late Chrysanthemums* (1954)]

BOSWELL, James (1740–1795)

A man, indeed, is not genteel when he gets drunk; but most vices may be committed very genteelly: a man may debauch his friend's wife genteelly: he may cheat at cards genteelly.

[*The Life of Samuel Johnson* (1791)]

DICKINSON, Emily (1830–1886)

What Soft – Cherubic Creatures –
These Gentlewomen are –
One would as soon assault a Plush –
Or violate a Star –

Such Dimity Convictions –
A Horror so refined
Of freckled Human Nature –
Of Deity – ashamed.

['What Soft – Cherubic Creatures' (c. 1862)]

RIDGE, William Pett (c.1860–1930)

'How did you think I managed at dinner, Clarence?' 'Capitally!' 'I had a knife and two forks left at the end,' she said regretfully.

[*Love at Paddington Green*]

SAKI (1870–1916)

I think she must have been very strictly brought up, she's so desperately anxious to do the wrong thing correctly.

[*Reginald* (1904)]

SHAW, George Bernard (1856–1950)

I am a woman of the world, Hector; and I can assure you that if you will only take the trouble always to do the perfectly correct thing, and to say the perfectly correct thing, you can do just what you like.

[*Heartbreak House* (1919)]

SMITH, Stevie (1902–1971)

This Englishwoman is so refined
She has no bosom and no behind.

['This Englishwoman' (1937)]

THIRKELL, Angela Margaret (1890–1961)

[Major Bowen narrating]

'I don't mind if I do,' said I.
Mrs Jerry turned round to the girl and said:
'That means Major Bowen thanks me very much and is delighted to accept.'
I didn't tumble to what she meant, but I supposed it was all right.

[*Trooper to the Southern Cross*]

GENTLEMEN

ALLEN, Fred (1894–1956)

A gentleman is any man who wouldn't hit a woman with his hat on.

[Attr.]

ANONYMOUS

When Adam delved, and Eve span,
Who was then a gentleman?

[Attr. John Ball, 1381]

ASHFORD, Daisy (1881–1972)

I do hope I shall enjoy myself with you ... I am parshial to ladies if they are nice I suppose it is my nature. I am not quite a gentleman but you would hardly notice it.

[*The Young Visiters* (1919)]

BENCHLEY, Robert (1889–1945)

Even nowadays a man can't step up and kill a woman without feeling just a bit unchivalrous.

[Attr.]

BROME, Richard (c.1590–1652)

I am a gentleman, though spoiled i' the breeding. The Buzzards are all gentlemen. We came in with the Conqueror.

[*English Moor* (1637)]

BURKE, Edmund (1729–1797)

It is therefore our business carefully to cultivate in our minds, to rear to the most perfect vigour and maturity, every sort of generous and honest feeling that belongs to our nature. To bring the dispositions that are lovely in private life into the service and conduct of the commonwealth; so to be patriots, as not to forget we are gentlemen.

[*Thoughts on the Cause of the Present Discontents* (1770)]

Somebody has said, that a king may make a nobleman but he cannot make a Gentleman.

[Letter to William Smith, 1795]

CHIFLEY, Joseph Benedict (1885–1951)

My experience of gentlemen's agreements is that, when it comes to the pinch, there are rarely enough bloody gentlemen about.

[In Crisp, *Ben Chifley* (1960)]

CURZON, Lord (1859–1925)

Gentlemen do not take soup at luncheon.

[In Woodward, *Short Journey* (1942)]

EMERSON, Ralph Waldo (1803–1882)

Living blood and a passion of kindness does at last distinguish God's gentlemen from Fashion's.

['Manners' (1844)]

FURPHY, Joseph (1843–1912)

For there is no such thing as a democratic gentleman; the adjective and the noun are hyphenated by a drawn sword.

[*Such is Life* (1903)]

LINTON, W.J. (1812–1897)

For he is one of Nature's Gentlemen, the best of every time.

[*Nature's Gentleman*]

MATTHEWS, Brander (1852–1929)

A gentleman need not know Latin, but he should at least have forgotten it.

[Attr.]

NELSON, Lord (1758–1805)

[To his midshipmen]
Recollect that you must be a seaman to be an officer; and also, that you cannot be a good officer without being a gentleman.

[In Southey, *The Life of Nelson* (1860)]

NEWMAN, John Henry, Cardinal (1801–1890)

It is almost a definition of a gentleman to say that he is one who never inflicts pain.

['Knowledge and Religious Duty' (1852)]

SHAW, George Bernard (1856–1950)

I am a gentleman: I live by robbing the poor.

[*Man and Superman* (1903)]

STEVENSON, Robert Louis (1850–1894)

Between the possibility of being hanged in all innocence, and the certainty of a public and merited disgrace, no gentleman of spirit could long hesitate.

[*The Wrong Box* (1889)]

SURTEES, R.S. (1805–1864)

He was a gentleman who was generally spoken of as having nothing a-year, paid quarterly.

[*Mr Sponge's Sporting Tour* (1853)]

The only infallible rule we know is, that the man who is always talking about being a gentleman never is one.

[*Ask Mamma* (1858)]

GERMANY

BISMARCK, Prince Otto von (1815–1898)

[Describing Germany's role in peace negotiations]
Ich denke [mir die Macht des Deutschen Reiches] … mehr die eines ehrlichen Maklers.
I consider [the power of the German Empire] …to be more than that of an honest broker.

[Speech, Reichstag, 1878]

Legt eine möglichst starke militärische Kraft, mit anderen Worten möglichst viel Blut und Eisen in die Hand des Königs von Preussen, dann wird er die Politik machen können, die Ihr wünscht; mit Reden und Schützenfesten und Liedern macht sie sich nicht, sie macht sich nur durch 'Blut und Eisen'!
Put the strongest possible military power, in other words as much blood and iron as possible, in the hands of the King of Prussia, and then he will be able to carry out the policy you want; this cannot be achieved with speeches and shooting-matches and songs; it can only be achieved by 'blood and iron'!

[Speech, Prussian House of Deputies, 1886]

FISCHER, Joschka

[Commenting on the war in Serbia]
For the first time in its history, Germany is fighting on the right side.

[*The Times*, June 1999]

HÖLDERLIN, Friedrich (1770–1843)

Denn, ihr Deutschen, auch ihr seid Tatenarm und gedankenvoll.
For, you Germans, you too are Poor in deed and rich in thoughts.

['To the Germans' (1798)]

HUXLEY, Aldous (1894–1963)

How appallingly thorough these Germans always managed to be, how emphatic! In sex no less than in war – in scholarship, in

science. Diving deeper than anyone else and coming up muddier.

[*Time Must Have a Stop* (1944)]

LAWRENCE, D.H. (1885–1930)

It is as if the life had retreated eastwards. As if the Germanic life were slowly ebbing away from contact with western Europe, ebbing to the deserts of the east.

[*A Letter from Germany* (1924)]

LICHTENBERG, Georg (1742–1799)

Sagt, ist noch ein Land ausser Deutschland, wo man die Nase eher rümpfen lernt als putzen?
Tell me, is there a country besides Germany where you learn to turn up your nose rather than wipe it?

[*Aphorisms (Scrawlings)*, (1775–1776)]

SCHOPENHAUER, Arthur (1788–1860)

Ein eigentümlicher Fehler der Deutschen ist, dass sie, was vor ihren Füssen liegt, in den Wolken suchen.
It is a curious failing in the German people that they search in the clouds for what lies at their feet.

[*Parerga und Paralipomena* (1851)]

See EUROPE; WAR

GHOSTS

BETJEMAN, Sir John (1906–1984)

The gas was on in the Institute,
The flare was up in the gym,
A man was running a mineral line,
A lass was singing a hymn,
When Captain Webb the Dawley man,
Captain Webb from Dawley,
Came swimming along the old canal
That carried the bricks to Lawley …

We saw the ghost of Captain Webb,
Webb in a water sheeting,
Come dripping along in a bathing dress
To the Saturday evening meeting.
Dripping along –
Dripping along –
To the Congregational Hall;

Dripping and still he rose over the sill and faded away in a wall.

[*Old Lights for New Chancels* (1940)]

SHENSTONE, William (1714–1763)

Beneath a church-yard yew
Decay'd and worn with age,
At dusk of eve methought I spy'd
Poor Slender's ghost, that whimpering cry'd
O sweet, O sweet Anne Page!

['Slender's Ghost']

THOMAS, Dylan (1914–1953)

I, born of flesh and ghost, was neither
A ghost nor man, but mortal ghost.
And I was struck down by death's feather.

['Before I knocked' (1933)]

GIFTS

BROWNING, Elizabeth Barrett (1806–1861)

God's gifts put man's best gifts to shame.

[*Sonnets from the Portuguese* (1850)]

CARROLL, Lewis (1832–1898)

They gave it me … for an un-birthday present.

[*Through the Looking-Glass (and What Alice Found There)* (1872)]

CONRAD, Joseph (1857–1924)

The fatal imperfection of all the gifts of life, which makes of them a delusion and a snare.

[*Victory* (1915)]

LAMB, Charles (1775–1834)

'Presents,' I often say 'endear Absents.'

[*Essays of Elia* (1823)]

REED, Henry (1914–1986)

If one doesn't get birthday presents it can remobilize very painfully the persecutory anxiety which usually follows birth.

[*The Primal Scene, as it were* (1958)]

SOPHOCLES (496–406 BC)

Gifts from enemies are no gifts, and bring no good.

[*Ajax*, line 665]

See CHARITY; GENEROSITY; KINDNESS

GLORY

ANONYMOUS

Sic transit gloria mundi.
Thus passes the glory of the world.

[Spoken during the coronation of a new Pope]

BACON, Francis (1561–1626)

[Knowledge is] a rich storehouse for the glory of the Creator and the relief of man's estate.

[*The Advancement of Learning* (1605)]

BLAKE, William (1757–1827)

The pride of the peacock is the glory of God.

['Proverbs of Hell' (c. 1793)]

BYRON, Lord (1788–1824)

Glory, like the phoenix 'midst her fires,
Exhales her odours, blazes, and expires.

[*English Bards and Scotch Reviewers* (1809)]

Oh, talk not to me of a name great in story;
The days of our youth are the days of our glory;
And the myrtle and ivy of sweet two-and-twenty
Are worth all your laurels, though ever so plenty.

['Stanzas Written on the Road between Florence and Pisa, November 1821']

CAMPBELL, Thomas (1777–1844)

The combat deepens. On, ye brave,
Who rush to glory, or the grave!

['Hohenlinden']

DRAKE, Sir Francis (c.1540–1596)

There must be a beginning of any great matter, but the continuing unto the end until it be thoroughly finished yields the true glory.

[Dispatch to Sir Francis Walsingham, 1587]

FONTAINE, Jean de la (1621–1695)

Aucun chemin de fleurs ne conduit á la gloire.
No flowery path leads to glory.

['Les deux aventuriers et le talisman']

GRAY, Thomas (1716–1771)

The boast of heraldry, the pomp of pow'r,
And all that beauty, all that wealth e'er gave,
Awaits alike th' inevitable hour,
The paths of glory lead but to the grave … .

['Elegy Written in a Country Churchyard' (1751)]

KEMPIS, Thomas à (c.1380–1471)

O quam cito transit gloria mundi.
Oh, how quickly the glory in this world
passes away.

[*De Imitatione Christi* (1892)]

MORDAUNT, Thomas Osbert (1730–1809)

Sound, sound the clarion, fill the fife,
Throughout the sensual world proclaim,
One crowded hour of glorious life
Is worth an age without a name.

['Verses written during the War, 1756–1763' (1791)]

PROPERTIUS, Sextus Aurelius (c.50–c.15 BC)

Magnum iter ascendo, sed dat mihi gloria vires.
Great is the height that I must scale, but the
prospect of glory gives me strength.

[*Elegies*]

ROSSETTI, Christina (1830–1894)

'Come cheer up, my lads, 'tis to glory we
steer!'
As the soldier remarked whose post lay in
the rear.

[Untitled couplet (c. 1845)]

ROUGET DE LISLE, Claude-Joseph (1760–1836)

Allons, enfants de la patrie,
Le jour de gloire est arrivé!
Let us go, children of this land, the day of
glory has arrived!

['La Marseillaise', 1792]

SHAKESPEARE, William (1564–1616)

Like madness is the glory of this life.

[*Timon of Athens*, I.ii]

WEBSTER, John (c.1580–c.1625)

Glories, like glow-worms, afar off shine
bright,
But, looked too near, have neither heat nor
light.

[*The Duchess of Malfi* (1623)]

WORDSWORTH, William (1770–1850)

Not in entire forgetfulness,
And not in utter nakedness,
But trailing clouds of glory do we come
From God, who is our home:
Heaven lies about us in our infancy!

['Ode: Intimations of Immortality' (1807)]

YEATS, W.B. (1865–1939)

Think where man's glory most begins and
ends,
And say my glory was I had such friends.

[*A Speech and Two Poems* (1937)]

GOALS

BERLIN, Isaiah (1909–1997)

Injustice, poverty, slavery, ignorance – these
may be cured by reform or revolution. But
men do not live only by fighting evils. They
live by positive goals, individual and
collective, a vast variety of them, seldom
predictable, at times incompatible.

['Political Ideas in the Twentieth Century' (1969)]

KAFKA, Franz (1883–1924)

There is a goal but no way of reaching it;
what we call the way is hesitation.

[*Reflections on Sin, Sorrow, Hope and the True Way*]

LONGFELLOW, Henry Wadsworth (1807–1882)

If you would hit the mark, you must aim a
little above it;
Every arrow that flies feels the attraction of
earth.

['Elegiac Verse' (1880)]

SANTAYANA, George (1863–1952)

Fanaticism consists in redoubling your effort
when you have forgotten your aim.

[*The Life of Reason* (1906)]

SIDNEY, Sir Philip (1554–1586)

Who shoots at the midday sun, though he be sure he shall never hit the mark, yet as sure he is he shall shoot higher than who aims but at a bush.

[*New Arcadia* (1590)]

SMITH, Logan Pearsall (1865–1946)

When people come and talk to you of their aspirations, before they leave you had better count your spoons.

[*Afterthoughts* (1931)]

STEVENSON, Robert Louis (1850–1894)

To be honest, to be kind – to earn a little and to spend a little less, to make upon the whole a family happier for his presence, to renounce when that shall be necessary and not be embittered, to keep a few friends, but these without capitulation – above all, on the same grim condition, to keep friends with himself – here is a task for all that a man has of fortitude and delicacy.

[*Across the Plains* (1892)]

An aspiration is a joy forever.

[*Virginibus Puerisque* (1881)]

THATCHER, Margaret (1925–)

If you are going from A to B you do not always necessarily go in a straight line.

[*The Observer*, 1980]

WHITE, Patrick (1912–1990)

That is men all over … They will aim too low. And achieve what they expect.

[*Voss* (1957)]

YOUNG, Edward (1683–1765)

At thirty man suspects himself a Fool;
Knows it at forty, and reforms his Plan;
At fifty chides his infamous Delay,
Pushes his prudent Purpose to Resolve;
In all the magnanimity of Thought
Resolves; and re-resolves; then dies the same.

[*Night-Thoughts on Life, Death and Immortality* (1742–1746)]

See AMBITION

GOD

AGATHON (c.445–400 BC)

Even God is deprived of this one thing only: the power to undo what has been done.

[In Aristotle, *Nicomachean Ethics*]

AINGER, A.C. (1841–1919)

God is working His purpose out as year succeeds to year,
God is working His purpose out and the time is drawing near;
Nearer and nearer draws the time, the time that shall surely be,
When the earth shall be filled with the glory of God as the waters cover the sea.

[*Hymn*]

ALLEN, Woody (1935–)

Not only is there no God, but try getting a plumber on weekends.

[*Getting Even* (1971)]

[Of God]
The worst that can be said is that he's an under-achiever.

[*Love and Death*, film, 1976]

If only God would give me some clear sign! Like making a large deposit in my name at a Swiss bank.

[*Without Feathers* (1976)]

ANDREWES, Bishop Lancelot (1555–1626)

What gets God by nobiscum? Nothing He. What get we?

[*Sermon 9, Of the Nativity* (c. 1614)]

ANONYMOUS

The nature of God is a circle of which the centre is everywhere and the circumference is nowhere.

[Attr. to Empedocles]

ANOUILH, Jean (1910–1987)

Dieu est avec tout le monde … Et, en fin de compte, il est toujours avec ceux qui ont beaucoup d'argent, et de grosses arm»es.
God is on everyone's side … And, in the final analysis, he is on the side of those who have

plenty of money and large armies.

[*The Lark* (1953)]

ASTURIAS, Miguel Angel (1899–1974)

Para un pueblo hambriento e inactivo la sola forma en que Dios puede aparecer es en la de trabajo y comida.

For people who are hungry and inactive, God can only appear in the form of work and food.

[*The Little Rich Boy* (1961)]

AUGUSTINE, Saint (354–430)

Fecisti nos ad te, et inquietum est cor nostrum donec requiescat in te.

Thou hast created us for Thyself, and our heart is restless till it finds rest in Thee.

[*Confessions* (397–398)]

BALDWIN, James (1924–1987)

If the concept of God has any validity or any use, it can only be to make us larger, freer, and more loving. If God cannot do this, then it is time we got rid of Him.

[*The Fire Next Time* (1963)]

BAXTER, Richard (1615–1691)

Suppose you saw the Lord in glory continually before you; When you are hearing, praying, talking, jesting, eating, drinking, and when you are tempted to wilful sin: Suppose you saw the Lord stand over you, as verily as you see a man! Would you be godly or ungodly after it? As sure as you live, and see one another, God always seeth you.

['The Life of Faith' (1660)]

THE BIBLE
(King James Version)

In the beginning God created the heaven and the earth.
And the earth was without form, and void; and darkness was upon the face of the deep. And the Spirit of God moved upon the face of the waters.
And God said, Let there be light: and there was light.

[*Genesis*, 1:1–3]

For the Lord seeth not as man seeth: for man

looketh on the outward appearance, but the Lord looketh on the heart.

[*I Samuel*, 16:7]

God is a Spirit: and they that worship him must worship him in spirit and in truth.

[*John*, 4:24]

BONHOEFFER, Dietrich (1906–1945)

Ein Gott, der sich von uns beweisen liesse, wäre ein Götze.

A God who allowed us to prove his existence would be an idol.

['If you believe it, you have it' (1931)]

Der Mensch hat gelernt, in allen wichtigen Fragen mit sich selbst fertig zu werden ohne Zuhilfenahme der 'Arbeitshypothese: Gott.'

In all important questions, man has learned to cope without recourse to God as a working hypothesis.

[Letter to a friend, 1944]

BROOKE, Rupert (1887–1915)

Because God put His adamantine fate
Between my sullen heart and its desire,
I swore that I would burst the Iron Gate,
Rise up, and curse Him on His throne of fire.

['Failure' (1905–1908)]

BROWNE, Sir Thomas (1605–1682)

God is like a skilful Geometrician.

[*Religio Medici* (1643)]

BROWNING, Elizabeth Barrett (1806–1861)

God answers sharp and sudden on some prayers,
And thrusts the thing we have prayed for in our face,
A gauntlet with a gift in't.

[*Aurora Leigh* (1857)]

CLOUGH, Arthur Hugh (1819–1861)

'There is no God,' the wicked saith,
'And truly it's a blessing,
For what he might have done with us
It's better only guessing.' …

But country folks who live beneath
The shadow of the steeple;

The parson and the parson's wife,
And mostly married people;

Youths green and happy in first love,
So thankful for illusion;
And men caught out in what the world
Calls guilt, in first confusion;

And almost every one when age,
Disease, or sorrows strike him,
Inclines to think there is a God,
Or something very like Him.

[*Dipsychus* (1865)]

COWPER, William (1731–1800)

God moves in a mysterious way
His wonders to perform;
He plants his footsteps in the sea,
And rides upon the storm.

[*Olney Hymns* (1779)]

DE VRIES, Peter (1910–1993)

It is the final proof of God's omnipotence
that he need not exist in order to save us.

[*The Mackerel Plaza* (1958)]

DOSTOEVSKY, Fyodor (1821–1881)

It's not God that I don't accept, Alyosha, only
I most respectfully return the ticket to Him.

[*The Brothers Karamazov*
(1879–1880)]

DUHAMEL, Georges (1884–1966)

*Je respecte trop l'idée de Dieu pour la rendre
responsable d'un monde aussi absurde.*
I have too much respect for the idea of God
to make it responsible for such an absurd
world.

[*Chronique des Pasquier* (1948)]

DUMAS, Alexandre (Fils) (1824–1895)

*Si Dieu pouvait tout à coup être condamné à vivre de
la vie qu'il inflige à l'homme, il se tuerait.*
If God were suddenly condemned to live the
life which he had inflicted on men, He would
kill Himself.

[*Pensées d'album* (1847)]

DÜRRENMATT, Friedrich (1921–1990)

Gott ist ein unmenschlicher Begriff.

God is an inhuman concept.

[*The Marriage of Mr Mississippi* (1951)]

EINSTEIN, Albert (1879–1955)

Raffiniert ist der Herrgott, aber bashaft ist er nicht.
The Lord God is crafty but he is not spiteful.

[Inscription in the Mathematical Institute at
Princeton]

Gott würfelt nicht.
God does not play dice.

[Attr.]

Before God we are all equally wise – equally
foolish.

[Address, Sorbonne, Paris]

ELLIS, Havelock (1859–1939)

God is an unutterable Sigh in the Human
Heart, said the old German mystic. And
therewith said the last word.

[*Impressions and Comments* (1914)]

EMPEDOCLES (c.490–c.430 BC)

God is a circle whose centre is everywhere
and whose circumference is nowhere.

[Attr.]

FONTAINE, Jean de la (1621–1695)

Dieu fait bien ce qu'il fait.
What God does, He does well.

[*Fables*, 'Le gland et la citrouille']

FREUD, Sigmund (1856–1939)

At bottom God is nothing more than an
exalted father.

[*Totem and Taboo* (1919)]

FULLER, Richard Buckminster
(1895–1983)

God, to me, it seems,
is a verb
not a noun,
proper or improper.

[*No More Secondhand God* (1963)]

GALILEO GALILEI (1564–1642)

I do not feel obliged to believe that the same
God who has endowed us with sense,
reason, and intellect has intended us to forgo
their use.

[Attr.]

GREENE, Graham (1904–1991)

Those who marry God … can become domesticated too – it's just as hum-drum a marriage as all the others.

[*A Burnt-Out Case* (1961)]

HALDANE, J.B.S. (1892–1964)

[Reply when asked what inferences could be drawn about the nature of God from a study of his works]

The Creator … has a special preference for beetles.

[Lecture, 1951]

HEINE, Heinrich (1797–1856)

[Last words]

Dieu me pardonnera, c'est son métier.

God will forgive me. It is his profession.

[In Meissner, *H H Erinnerungen* (1856)]

HOOKER, Richard (c.1554–1600)

The earth may shake, the pillars of the world may tremble under us, the countenance of the heaven may be appalled, the sun may lose his light, the moon her beauty, the stars their glory; but concerning the man that trusteth in God … what is there in the world that shall change his heart, overthrow his faith, alter his affection towards God, or the affection of God to him?

[*Of the Laws of Ecclesiasticall Politie* (1593)]

HUGHES, Sean (1966–)

I'd like to thank God for fucking up my life and at the same time not existing, quite a special skill.

[*The Independent*, 1993]

HUGHES, Ted (1930–1998)

God is a good fellow, but His mother's against him.

[*Wodwo* (1967)]

HUXLEY, Sir Julian Sorell (1887–1975)

Operationally, God is beginning to resemble not a ruler but the last fading smile of a cosmic Cheshire cat.

[*Religion without Revelation* (1957)]

INGE, William Ralph (1860–1954)

Many people believe that they are attracted by God, or by Nature, when they are only repelled by man.

[*More Lay Thoughts of a Dean* (1931)]

JOWETT, Benjamin (1817–1893)

[Responding to a conceited young student's assertion that he could find no evidence for a God]

If you don't find a God by five o'clock this afternoon you must leave the college.

[Attr.]

KEMPIS, Thomas á (c.1380–1471)

Nam homo proponit, sed Deus disponit.

For man proposes, but God disposes.

[*De Imitatione Christi* (1892)]

KNOX, Ronald (1888–1957)

There was once a man who said 'God
Must think it exceedingly odd
If he finds that this tree
Continues to be
When there's no one about in the Quad.'

[Attr.]

O God, for as much as without Thee
We are not enabled to doubt Thee,
Help us all by Thy grace
To convince the whole race
It knows nothing whatever about Thee.

[Attr.]

KOESTLER, Arthur (1905–1983)

God seems to have left the receiver off the hook, and time is running out.

[*The Ghost in the Machine* (1961)]

LAPLACE, Pierre-Simon, Marquis de (1749–1827)

[Reply when asked by Napoleon why he had made no reference to God in his book about the universe, *Mécanique céleste*]

I have no need of that hypothesis.

[In E. Bell, *Men of Mathematics*]

LOGAU, Friedrich von (1605–1655)

Gottes Mühlen mahlen langsam, mahlen aber trefflich klein;
Ob aus Langmut er sich säumet, bringt mit Schärf' er alles ein.

Though the mills of God grind slowly, yet they grind extremely small;
Though his patience makes him tarry, with exactness grinds He all.

[*Epigrams* (1653), no. 638]

LUTHER, Martin (1483–1546)

Worauf du nun … dein Herz hängt und verlässt, das ist eigentlich dein Gott.
Whatever your heart clings to and relies upon, that is really your God.

[*Large Catechism* (1529)]

Ein feste Burg ist unser Gott,
Ein gute Wehr und Waffen.
A strong castle is our God,
A good defence and weapon.

[Hymn, first extant version, *Rauscher's Hymnal* (1531)]

MENCKEN, H.L. (1880–1956)

God is the immemorial refuge of the incompetent, the helpless, the miserable. They find not only sanctuary in His arms, but also a kind of superiority, soothing to their macerated egos; He will set them above their betters.

[*Notebooks* (1956)]

It takes a long while for a naturally trustful person to reconcile himself to the idea that after all God will not help him.

[*Notebooks* (1956)]

NERVAL, Gérard de (1808–1855)

Dieu est mort! le ciel est vide –
Pleurez! enfants, vous n'avez plus de père.
God is dead! Heaven is empty – Weep, children, you no longer have a father.

['Le Christ aux Oliviers']

NIETZSCHE, Friedrich Wilhelm (1844–1900)

Gott ist tot: aber so wie die Art der Menschen ist, wird es vielleicht noch jahrtausendelang Höhlen geben, in denen man seinen Schatten zeigt.
God is dead: but men's natures are such that for thousands of years yet there will perhaps be caves in which his shadow will be seen.

[*The Gay Science* (1887)]

OWEN, John (c.1560–1622)

God and the doctor we alike adore
But only when in danger, not before;
The danger o'er, both are alike requited,
God is forgotten, and the Doctor slighted.

[*Epigrams*]

PASCAL, Blaise (1623–1662)

Je ne puis pardonner á Descartes: il aurait bien voulu, dans toute sa philosophie, pouvoir se passer de Dieu; mais il n'a pu s'empêcher de lui faire donner une chiquenaude, pour mettre le monde en mouvement; après celá, il n'a plus eu que faire de Dieu.
I cannot forgive Descartes; in all his philosophy he did his best to dispense with God. But he could not avoid making Him set the world in motion with a flick of His finger; after that he had no more use for God.

[*Pensées* (1670)]

PHILLIPS, Wendell (1811–1884)

One, on God's side, is a majority.

[Lecture, 1859]

PICASSO, Pablo (1881–1973)

God is really only another artist. He invented the giraffe, the elephant, and the cat. He has no real style. He just goes on trying other things.

[In Françoise Gilot and Carlton Lake, *Life with Picasso* (1964)]

POPE, Alexander (1688–1744)

Nor God alone in the still calm we find,
He mounts the storm, and walks upon the wind.

[*An Essay on Man* (1733)]

PRÉVERT, Jacques (1900–1977)

Notre Père qui êtes aux cieux
Restez-y
Et nous nous resterons sur la terre.
Our Father which art in heaven, stay there; and as for us, we shall stay on earth.

[*Paroles* (1946)]

PRIESTLEY, J.B. (1894–1984)

God can stand being told by Professor Ayer and Marghanita Laski that He doesn't exist.

[*The Listener*, 1965]

SARTRE, Jean-Paul (1905–1980)

L'absence c'est Dieu. Dieu, c'est la solitude des hommes.

God is absence. God is the solitude of man.

[*Le Diable et le Bon Dieu* (1951)]

SHAKESPEARE, William (1564–1616)

There's a divinity that shapes our ends,
Rough-hew them how we will.

[*Hamlet*, V.ii]

As flies to wanton boys are we to th' gods –
They kill us for their sport.

[*King Lear*, IV.i]

SQUIRE, Sir J.C. (1884–1958)

God heard the embattled nations sing and shout
'Gott strafe England!' and 'God save the King!'
God this, God that, and God the other thing –
'Good God!' said God, 'I've got my work cut out.'

[*The Survival of the Fittest* (1916)]

STRACHEY, Lytton (1880–1932)

Yet her conception of God was certainly not orthodox. She felt towards Him as she might have felt towards a glorified sanitary engineer; and in some of her speculations she seems hardly to distinguish between the Deity and the Drains.

['Florence Nightingale' (1918)]

VAUGHAN, Henry (1622–1695)

There is in God (some say)
A deep, but dazzling darkness; as men here
Say it is late and dusky, because they
See not all clear;
O for that night! where I in him
Might live invisible and dim.

[*Silex Scintillans* (1650–1655)]

VIGNY, Alfred de (1797–1863)

Le vrai Dieu, le Dieu fort, est le Dieu des idées.

The true God, the mighty God, is the God of ideas.

['The Bottle in the Sea', 1847]

VOLTAIRE (1694–1778)

Dieu n'est pas pour les gros bataillons, mais pour ceux qui tirent le mieux.

God is not on the side of the big batallions, but of the best marksmen.

['The Piccini Notebooks' (c. 1735–1750)]

Si Dieu n'existait pas, il faudrait l'inventer.

If God did not exist, it would be necessary to invent him.

[*Epîtres*, 'A l'auteur du livre des trois imposteurs']

WALKER, Alice (1944–)

I think it pisses God off if you walk by the color purple in a field somewhere and don't notice it.

[*The Color Purple*, film, 1985]

WOLSEY, Thomas, Cardinal (c.1475–1530)

[Remark to Sir William Kingston]
Had I but served God as diligently as I have served the King, he would not have given me over in my grey hairs.

[In Cavendish, *Negotiations of Thomas Wolsey* (1641)]

YOUNG, Edward (1683–1765)

A God All mercy, is a God unjust.

[*Night-Thoughts on Life, Death and Immortality* (1742–1745)]

See ATHEISM; BELIEF

GOOD AND EVIL

THE BIBLE (King James Version)

Ye shall be as gods, knowing good and evil.

[*Genesis*, 3:5]

BRECHT, Bertolt (1898–1956)

Something must be wrong with your world. Why
Is a price set on wickedness, and why is the good man
Attended by such harsh punishments?

[*Good Woman of Setzuan* (1943)]

BURNS, Robert (1759–1796)

Whatever mitigates the woes or increases the happiness of others, this is my criterion of goodness; and whatever injures society at large, or any individual in it, this is my measure of iniquity.

[Attr.]

DANA, Charles Anderson (1819–1897)

All the goodness of a good egg cannot make up for the badness of a bad one.

[*The Making of a Newspaper Man*]

GOLDSMITH, Oliver (c.1728–1774)

We must touch his weaknesses with a delicate hand. There are some faults so nearly allied to excellence, that we can scarce weed out the vice without eradicating the virtue.

[*The Good Natur'd Man* (1768)]

HALIFAX, Lord (1633–1695)

Our Vices and Virtues couple with one another, and get Children that resemble both their Parents.

['Of the World' (1750)]

KING, Martin Luther (1929–1968)

I believe that unarmed truth and unconditional love will have the final word in reality. That is why right, temporarily defeated, is stronger than evil triumphant.

[Speech at Civil Rights March on Washington, August 28, 1963]

LERMONTOV, Mikhail (1814–1841)

What is the greatest good and evil? – two ends of an invisible chain which come closer together the further they move apart.

[*Vadim* (1834)]

PROVERB

Better be a fool than a knave.

SHAKESPEARE, William (1564–1616)

Men's evil manners live in brass: their virtues We write in water.

[*Henry VIII*, IV.ii]

The evil that men do lives after them;
The good is oft interred with their bones.

[*Julius Caesar*, III.ii]

Some rise by sin, and some by virtue fall.

[*Measure for Measure*, II.i]

Virtue that transgresses is but patch'd with sin, and sin that amends is but patch'd with virtue.

[*Twelfth Night*, I.v]

SPINOZA, Baruch (1632–1677)

Nam una eadem res potest eodem tempore bona et mala, e.g. Musica bona est Melancholico, mala Lugenti; Surdo autem neque bona neque mala.

One and the same thing can at the same time be good and bad, for example, music is good to the melancholy, bad to the mourner, and neither good nor bad to the deaf.

[*Ethics* (1677)]

SURTEES, R.S. (1805–1864)

More people are flattered into virtue than bullied out of vice.

[*The Analysis of the Hunting Field* (1846)]

VANBRUGH, Sir John (1664–1726)

Belinda: Ay, but you know we must return good for evil.
Lady Brute: That may be a mistake in the translation.

[*The Provok'd Wife* (1697)]

See GOODNESS

GOODNESS

ADDISON, Joseph (1672–1719)

Content thyself to be obscurely good.
When vice prevails, and impious men bear sway,
The post of honour is a private station.

[*Cato* (1713)]

ARISTOTLE (384–322 BC)

The good has been well said to be that at which all things aim.

[*Nicomachean Ethics*]

In all things the middle state is to be praised. But it is sometimes necessary to incline towards overshooting and sometimes to shooting short of the mark, since this is the easiest way of hitting the mean and the right course.

[*Nicomachean Ethics*]

BACON, Francis (1561–1626)

The inclination to goodness is imprinted deeply in the nature of man: insomuch, that if it issue not towards men, it will take unto other living creatures.

['Of Goodness, and Goodness of Nature' (1625)]

BAGEHOT, Walter (1826–1877)

The most melancholy of human reflections, perhaps, is that, on the whole, it is a question whether the benevolence of mankind does most good or harm.

[*Physics and Politics* (1872)]

BARTH, Karl (1886–1968)

Men have never been good, they are not good, they never will be good.

[*Time*, 1954]

BLAKE, William (1757–1827)

He who would do good to another must do it in Minute Particulars.
General Good is the plea of the Scoundrel hypocrite & flatterer.

[*Jerusalem* (1804–1820)]

BUDDHA (c.563–483 BC)

This Ayrian Eightfold Path, that is to say: Right view, right aim, right speech, right action, right living, right effort, right mindfulness, right contemplation.

[In Woodward, *Some Sayings of the Buddha*]

BURKE, Edmund (1729–1797)

When bad men combine, the good must associate; else they will fall, one by one, an unpitied sacrifice in a contemptible struggle.

[*Thoughts on the Cause of the Present Discontents* (1770)]

Good order is the foundation of all good things.

[*Reflections on the Revolution in France* (1790)]

BUTLER, Samuel (1835–1902)

Virtue and vice are like life and death or mind and matter: things which cannot exist without being qualified by their opposite.

[*The Way of All Flesh* (1903)]

When the righteous man turneth away from his righteousness that he hath committed and doeth that which is neither quite lawful nor quite right, he will generally be found to have gained in amiability what he has lost in holiness.

[*The Note-Books of Samuel Butler* (1912)]

CAMPION, Thomas (1567–1620)

The man of life upright,
Whose guiltlesse hart is free
From all dishonest deedes
Or thought of vanitie …

Good thoughts his onely friendes,
His wealth a well-spent age,
The earth his sober Inne
And quiet Pilgrimage.

[*A Booke of Ayres* (1601)]

COMPTON-BURNETT, Dame Ivy (1884–1969)

At any time you might act for my good. When people do that, it kills something precious between them.

[*Manservant and Maidservant* (1947)]

CONFUCIUS (c.550–c.478 BC)

True goodness springs from a man's own heart. All men are born good.

[*Analects*]

CRABBE, George (1754–1832)

He tried the luxury of doing good.

[*Tales of the Hall* (1819)]

CREIGHTON, Mandell (1843–1901)

No people do so much harm as those who go about doing good.

[*The Life and Letters of Mandell Creighton* (1904)]

GRACIÁN, Baltasar (1601–1658)

Lo bueno, si breve, dos veces bueno.
Good things, if they are short, are twice as good.

[Attr.]

GRELLET, Stephen (1773–1855)

I expect to pass through this world but once; any good thing therefore that I can do, or any kindness that I can show to any fellow-creature, let me do it now; let me not defer or neglect it, for I shall not pass this way again.

[Attr.]

HARDY, Thomas (1840–1928)

Good, but not religious-good.

[*Under the Greenwood Tree* (1872)]

HUTCHESON, Francis (1694–1746)

That action is best, which procures the greatest happiness for the greatest numbers.

[An Inquiry into the Original of our Ideas of Beauty and Virtue (1725)]

KINGSLEY, Charles (1819–1875)

Be good, sweet maid, and let who can be clever;
Do lovely things, not dream them, all day long;
And so make Life, and Death, and that For Ever,
One grand sweet song.

['A Farewell. To C.E.G.' (1856)]

LANDOR, Walter Savage (1775–1864)

Goodness does not more certainly make men happy than happiness makes them good.

[*Imaginary Conversations* (1853)]

MACHIAVELLI (1469–1527)

Gli uomini non operano mai nulla nel bene se non per necessitá.
Men never do anything good except out of necessity.

[*Discourse*]

MEREDITH, George (1828–1909)

Much benevolence of the passive order may be traced to a disinclination to inflict pain upon oneself.

[*Vittoria* (1866)]

PLATO (c.429–347 BC)

The good is the beautiful.

[*Lysis*]

PROVERBS

The good die young.

If you can't be good, be careful.

One good turn deserves another.

SALLUST (86–c.34 BC)

[Of Cato]
Esse quam videri bonus malebat.
He preferred to be rather than to seem good.

[*Catiline*]

SHAKESPEARE, William (1564–1616)

How far that little candle throws his beams!
So shines a good deed in a naughty world.

[*The Merchant of Venice*, V.i]

TOLSTOY, Leo (1828–1910)

But my life now, my whole life, independently of anything that can happen to me, every minute of it is no longer meaningless as it was before, but has a positive meaning of goodness with which I have the power to invest it.

[*Anna Karenina* (1875–7)]

VOLTAIRE (1694–1778)

Le mieux est l'ennemi du bien.
The best is the enemy of the good.

['Art dramatique' (1770)]

WELLS, H.G. (1866–1946)

He was quite sure that he had been wronged. Not to be wronged is to forgo the first privilege of goodness.

[*Bealby* (1915)]

WESLEY, John (1703–1791)

Do all the good you can,
By all the means you can,
In all the ways you can,
In all the places you can,
At all the times you can,
To all the people you can,
As long as ever you can.

[*Letters* (1915)]

WEST, Mae (1892–1980)

When I'm good I'm very good, but when I'm bad I'm better.

[*I'm No Angel*, film, 1933]

WILDE, Oscar (1854–1900)

It is better to be beautiful than to be good.
But … it is better to be good than to be ugly.

[*The Picture of Dorian Gray* (1891)]

WORDSWORTH, Dame Elizabeth (1840–1932)

If all the good people were clever,
And all clever people were good,
The world would be nicer than ever
We thought that it possibly could.
But somehow, 'tis seldom or never
The two hit it off as they should;
The good are so harsh to the clever,
The clever so rude to the good.

['The Clever and the Good' (1890)]

See BEAUTY; BENEFACTORS; GOOD AND
EVIL; MORALITY; VIRTUE

GOSSIP

BIERCE, Ambrose (1842–c.1914)

Backbite: To speak of a man as you find him
when he can't find you.

[*The Enlarged Devil's Dictionary* (1961)]

CHESTERFIELD, Lord (1694–1773)

In the case of scandal, as in that of robbery,
the receiver is always thought as bad as the
thief.

[Letter to his son, 1748]

CONGREVE, William (1670–1729)

Retired to their tea and scandal, according to
their ancient custom.

[*The Double Dealer* (1694)]

They come together like the Coroner's
Inquest, to sit upon the murdered
reputations of the week.

[*The Way of the World* (1700)]

ELIOT, George (1819–1880)

Gossip is a sort of smoke that comes from
the dirty tobacco-pipes of those who diffuse
it: it proves nothing but the bad taste of the
smoker.

[*Daniel Deronda* (1876)]

FARQUHAR, George (1678–1707)

I believe they talked of me, for they laughed
consumedly.

[*The Beaux' Stratagem* (1707)]

LONGWORTH, Alice Roosevelt (1884–1980)

[Embroidered on a cushion at her home in
Washington]
If you haven't anything nice to say about
anyone, come and sit by me.

[*New York Times*, 1980]

OUIDA (1839–1908)

A cruel story runs on wheels, and every hand
oils the wheels as they run.

[*Wisdom, Wit and Pathos*, 'Moths']

POPE, Alexander (1688–1744)

At ev'ry word a reputation dies.

[*The Rape of the Lock* (1714)]

PROVERB

Believe nothing of what you hear, and only
half of what you see.

ROGERS, Will (1879–1935)

So live that you wouldn't be ashamed to sell
the family parrot to the town gossip.

[Attr.]

RUSSELL, Bertrand (1872–1970)

No one gossips about other people's secret
virtues.

[*On Education, especially in early childhood* (1926)]

SHERIDAN, Richard Brinsley (1751–1816)

Tale-bearers are as bad as the tale-makers.

[*The School for Scandal* (1777)]

Here is the whole set! a character dead at
every word.

[*The School for Scandal* (1777)]

See SECRETS

GOVERNMENT

ACTON, Lord (1834–1902)

The danger is not that a particular class is

unfit to govern. Every class is unfit to govern.

[Letter to Mary Gladstone, 1881]

ANONYMOUS

Anarchy may not be the best form of government, but it's better than no government at all.

Government expands to absorb revenue and then some.

[Wiker's Law]

BAGEHOT, Walter (1826–1877)

The Crown is, according to the saying, the 'fountain of honour'; but the Treasury is the spring of business.

[*The English Constitution* (1867)]

It has been said that England invented the phrase, 'Her Majesty's Opposition'; that it was the first Government which made a criticism of administration as much a part of the polity as administration itself. This critical opposition is the consequence of Cabinet government.

[*The English Constitution* (1867)]

Royalty is a government in which the attention of the nation is concentrated on one person doing interesting actions. A Republic is a government in which that attention is divided between many, who are all doing uninteresting actions. Accordingly, so long as the human heart is strong and the human reason weak, royalty will be strong because it appeals to diffused feeling, and Republics weak because they appeal to the understanding.

[*The English Constitution* (1867)]

A severe though not unfriendly critic of our institutions said that 'the cure for admiring the House of Lords was to go and look at it.'

[*The English Constitution* (1867)]

BENTHAM, Jeremy (1748–1832)

It is with government as with medicine, its only business is the choice of evils. Every law is an evil, for every law is an infraction of liberty.

[*An Introduction to the Principles of Morals and Legislation* (1789)]

BEVERIDGE, William Henry (1879–1963)

The object of government in peace and in war is not the glory of rulers or of races, but the happiness of the common man.

[Report on Social Insurance and Allied Services (1942)]

BURKE, Edmund (1729–1797)

All government, indeed every human benefit and enjoyment, every virtue, and every prudent act, is founded on compromise and barter.

[*Speech on Conciliation with America* (1775)]

In all forms of Government the people is the true legislator.

[*Tracts on the Popery Laws* (1812)]

CAMPBELL-BANNERMAN, Sir Henry (1836–1908)

Good government could never be a substitute for government by the people themselves.

[Speech, 1905]

CARTER, Jimmy (1924–)

[Visiting Egypt in 1979, when told that it took only twenty years to build the Great Pyramid] I'm surprised that a government organization could do it that quickly.

[In *Time*, March 1979]

CHURCHILL, Lord Randolph (1849–1894)

The duty of an opposition is to oppose.

[In W.S. Churchill, *Lord Randolph Churchill* (1906)]

CONFUCIUS (c.550–c.478 BC)

An oppressive government is more to be feared than a tiger.

[*Analects*]

COOLIDGE, Calvin (1872–1933)

The governments of the past could fairly be characterized as devices for maintaining in perpetuity the place and position of certain privileged classes ... The Government of the

United States is a device for maintaining in perpetuity the rights of the people, with the ultimate extinction of all privileged classes.

[Speech, 1924]

DERBY, Earl of (1799–1869)

When I first came into Parliament, Mr Tierney, a great Whig authority, used always to say that the duty of an Opposition was very simple – it was, to oppose everything, and propose nothing.

[Speech, House of Commons, 1841]

DISRAELI, Benjamin (1804–1881)

No Government can be long secure without a formidable opposition.

[*Coningsby* (1844)]

I believe that without party Parliamentary government is impossible.

[Speech, Manchester, 1872]

FRIEDMAN, Milton (1912–)

Governments never learn. Only people learn.

[*The Observer*, 1996]

GIBBON, Edward (1737–1794)

The principles of a free constitution are irrecoverably lost, when the legislative power is nominated by the executive.

[*Decline and Fall of the Roman Empire* (1776–88)]

GOLDWATER, Barry (1909–1998)

A government that is big enough to give you all you want is big enough to take it all away.

[Bachman's *Book of Freedom Quotations*]

GORDIMER, Nadine (1923–)

I don't think any writers since the generation of Jean-Paul Sartre and Camus in France have influenced a government.

[Interview, *The Observer*, 1998]

HERBERT, Sir A.P. (1890–1971)

Well, fancy giving money to the Government!
Might as well have put it down the drain.
Fancy giving money to the Government!
Nobody will see the stuff again.
Well, they've no idea what money's for –
Ten to one they'll start another war.
I've heard a lot of silly things, but, Lor'!

Fancy giving money to the Government!

['Too Much!']

HOBBES, Thomas (1588–1679)

The only way to erect such a common power, as may be able to defend them from the invasion of foreigners, and the injuries of one another … is, to confer all their power and strength upon one man, or upon one assembly of men, that may reduce all their wills, by plurality of voices, unto one will … This is the generation of that great Leviathan, or rather, to speak more reverently, of that mortal god, to which we owe under the immortal God, our peace and defence.

[*Leviathan* (1651)]

They that are discontented under monarchy, call it tyranny; and they that are displeased with aristocracy, call it oligarchy: so also, they which find themselves grieved under a democracy, call it anarchy, which signifies want of government; and yet I think no man believes, that want of government, is any new kind of government.

[*Leviathan* (1651)]

HUME, David (1711–1776)

Nothing appears more surprising to those, who consider human affairs with a philosophical eye, than the easiness with which the many are governed by the few; and the implicit submission, with which men resign their own sentiments and passions to those of their rulers.

[*Essays, Moral, Political, and Literary* (1742)]

JAMES VI OF SCOTLAND AND I OF ENGLAND (1566–1625)

I will govern according to the common weal, but not according to the common will.

[Remark, 1621]

JOHNSON, Samuel (1709–1784)

I would not give half a guinea to live under one form of government rather than another. It is of no moment to the happiness of an individual.

[In Boswell, *The Life of Samuel Johnson* (1791)]

KEYNES, John Maynard (1883–1946)

The important thing for government is not to do things which individuals are doing already, and to do them a little better or a little worse; but to do those things which at present are not done at all.

['The End of Laissez-Faire' (1926)]

LÉVIS, Duc de (1764–1830)

Gouverner, c'est choisir.
To govern is to make choices.

[*Maximes et réflexions* (1812)]

MACKINTOSH, Sir James (1765–1832)

The Commons, faithful to their system, remained in a wise and masterly inactivity.

[*Vindiciae Gallicae* (1791)]

MAISTRE, Joseph de (1753–1821)

Toute nation a le gouvernement qu'elle mérite.
Each country has the government it deserves.

[Letter, 1811]

MENCKEN, H.L. (1880–1956)

The worst government is the most moral. One composed of cynics is often very tolerant and human. But when fanatics are on top there is no limit to oppression.

[*Notebooks* (1956)]

O'SULLIVAN, John L. (1813–1895)

Understood as a central consolidated power, managing and directing the various general interests of the society, all government is evil, and the parent of evil … The best government is that which governs least.

[*United States Magazine and Democratic Review*, 1837, Introduction]

PAINE, Thomas (1737–1809)

Government, even in its best state, is but a necessary evil; in its worst state, an intolerable one. Government, like dress, is the badge of lost innocence; the palaces of kings are built upon the ruins of the bowers of paradise.

[*Common Sense* (1776)]

As to religion, I hold it to be the indispensable duty of government to protect all conscientious professors thereof, and I know of no other business which government hath to do therewith.

[*Common Sense* (1776)]

Man is not the enemy of Man, but through the medium of a false system of government.

[*The Rights of Man* (1791)]

PASSMORE, John Arthur (1914–)

Never trust governments absolutely, and always do what you can to prevent them from doing too much harm.

[*The Limits of Government*]

PEMBROKE, Second Earl of (c.1534–1601)

A parliament can do any thing but make a man a woman, and a woman a man.

[Quoted in speech made by his son, the 4th Earl, 1648]

RIPPON, Geoffrey (1924–)

Governments don't retreat, they simply advance in another direction.

[*The Observer*, 1981]

ROBERTSON, George (1946–)

[On John Major's government]
If this government was an individual, it would be locked up in the interests of public safety.

[Speech, Labour Party Conference, 1993]

ROGERS, Will (1879–1935)

I don't make jokes – I just watch the government and report the facts.

[Attr.]

RUSKIN, John (1819–1900)

Government and cooperation are in all things the laws of life; anarchy and competition, the laws of death.

[*Unto this Last* (1862)]

SPENCER, Herbert (1820–1903)

The Republican form of government is the highest form of government; but because of this it requires the highest type of human nature – a type nowhere at present existing.

[*Essays* (1891)]

STEVENSON, Adlai (1900–1965)

Government by postponement is bad enough, but it is far better than government by desperation.

[*The Observer*, 1953]

THOREAU, Henry David (1817–1862)

I heartily accept the motto, 'That government is best which governs least'; and I should like to see it acted up to more rapidly and systematically. Carried out, it finally amounts to this, which I also believe, – 'That government is best which governs not at all.'

[*Civil Disobedience* (1849)]

TROLLOPE, Anthony (1815–1882)

A fainéant government is not the worst government that England can have. It has been the great fault of our politicians that they have all wanted to do something.

[*Phineas Finn* (1869)]

VOLTAIRE (1694–1778)

Il faut, dans le gouvernement, des bergers et des bouchers.

In governments there must be both shepherds and butchers.

['The Piccini Notebooks']

WASHINGTON, George (1732–1799)

Mankind, when left to themselves, are unfit for their own government.

[Letter, 1786]

See CAPITALISM; DEMOCRACY; MONARCHY AND ROYALTY; POLITICIANS; POLITICS

GRATITUDE

BLAKE, William (1757–1827)

To Mercy, Pity, Peace and Love
All pray in their distress,
And to these virtues of delight
Return their thankfulness.

[*Songs of Innocence* (1789)]

CATULLUS (84–c.54 BC)

Desine de quoquam quicquam bene velle mereri,
Aut aliquem fieri posse putare pium.

Stop wishing to merit anyone's gratitude or thinking that anyone can become grateful.

[*Carmina*]

LA ROCHEFOUCAULD (1613–1680)

La reconnaissance de la plupart des hommes n'est qu'une secrète envie de recevoir de plus grands bienfaits.

In most of mankind gratitude is merely a secret hope for greater favours.

[*Maximes*, (1678)]

GREATNESS

AMIEL, Henri-Frédéric (1821–1881)

The age of great men is going; the epoch of the ant-hill, of life in multiplicity, is beginning.

[*Journal*, 1851]

ASQUITH, Margot (1864–1945)

Mrs Asquith remarked indiscreetly that if Kitchener was not a great man, he was, at least, a great poster.

[In Sir Philip Magnus, *Kitchener: Portrait of an Imperialist* (1958)]

BACON, Francis (1561–1626)

All rising to great place is by a winding stair.

['Of Great Place' (1625)]

BEERBOHM, Sir Max (1872–1956)

Great men are but life-sized. Most of them, indeed, are rather short.

[Attr.]

BURKE, Edmund (1729–1797)

Great men are the guide-posts and landmarks in the state.

[*Speech on American Taxation* (1774)]

CAMPBELL, Thomas (1777–1844)

What millions died – that Caesar might be great!

[*Pleasures of Hope* (1799)]

CARLYLE, Thomas (1795–1881)

No sadder proof can be given by a man of

his own littleness than disbelief in great men.

[*On Heroes, Hero-Worship, and the Heroic in History*]

No great man lives in vain. The History of the world is but the Biography of great men.

['The Hero as Divinity' (1841)]

CHAPMAN, George (c.1559–c.1634)

They're only truly great who are truly good.

[*Revenge for Honour* (1654)]

EMERSON, Ralph Waldo (1803–1882)

It is easy in the world to live after the world's opinion; it is easy in solitude after our own; but the great man is he who, in the midst of the crowd, keeps with perfect sweetness the independence of solitude.

[*Essays, First Series* (1841)]

Nothing great was ever achieved without enthusiasm.

[*Essays, First Series* (1841)]

A foolish consistency is the hobgoblin of little minds, adored by little statesmen and philosophers and divines. With consistency a great soul has simply nothing to do.

[*Essays, First Series* (1841)]

Is it so bad, then, to be misunderstood? Pythagoras was misunderstood, and Socrates, and Jesus, and Luther, and Copernicus, and Galileo, and Newton, and every pure and wise spirit that ever took flesh. To be great is to be misunderstood.

[*Essays, First Series* (1841)]

FIELDING, Henry (1707–1754)

Greatness consists in bringing all manner of mischief on mankind, and goodness in removing it from them.

[*Jonathan Wild* (1743)]

FRAZER, Sir James (1854–1941)

The world cannot live at the level of its great men.

[*The Golden Bough* (1900)]

LA ROCHEFOUCAULD (1613–1680)

La gloire des grands hommes se doit toujours mesurer aux moyens dont ils se sont servis pour l'acquérir.

The glory of great men must always be measured by the means they have used to obtain it.

[*Maximes* (1678)]

LONGFELLOW, Henry Wadsworth (1807–1882)

Lives of great men all remind us
We can make our lives sublime,
And, departing, leave behind us
Footprints on the sands of time.

['A Psalm of Life' (1838)]

La gloire des grands hommes se doit toujours mesurer aux moyens dont ils se sont servis pour l'acquérir.

The heights by great men reached and kept
Were not attained by sudden flight,
But they, while their companions slept,
Were toiling upward in the night.

['The Ladder of Saint Augustine' (1850)]

PASTERNAK, Boris (1890–1960)

Only real greatness can be so misplaced and so untimely.

[*Doctor Zhivago* (1958)]

PROVERB

From small beginnings come great things.

SHAKESPEARE, William (1564–1616)

Be not afraid of greatness. Some are born great, some achieve greatness, and some have greatness thrust upon 'em.

[*Twelfth Night*, II.v]

SPENDER, Sir Stephen (1909–1995)

I think continually of those who were truly great.
The names of those who in their lives fought for life
Who wore at their hearts the fire's centre.
Born of the sun they travelled a short while towards the sun,
And left the vivid air signed with their honour.

['I think continually of those who were truly great' (1933)]

TWAIN, Mark (1835–1910)

Keep away from people who try to belittle

your ambitions. Small people always do that, but the really great make you feel that you, too, can become great.

WALPOLE, Horace (1717–1797)

They who cannot perform great things themselves may yet have a satisfaction in doing justice to those who can.

[Attr.]

GREED

AESOP (6th century BC)

Thinking to get all the gold that the goose could give in one go, he killed it, and opened it only to find – nothing.

[*Fables*, 'The Goose with the Golden Eggs']

PROVERB

The eye is bigger than the belly.

SELLERS, Peter (1925–1980)

People will swim through shit if you put a few bob in it.

[In Halliwell, *The Filmgoer's and Video Viewer's Companion*]

VIRGIL (70–19 BC)

Quid non mortalia pectora cogis,
Auri sacra fames!
O sacred hunger of pernicious gold!
What bands of faith can impious lucre hold?

[*Aeneid*]

See FOOD

GRIEF

ARNOLD, Matthew (1822–1888)

Strew on her roses, roses,
And never a spray of yew.
In quiet she reposes:
Ah! would that I did too.

['Requiescat' (1853)]

AUSTEN, Jane (1775–1817)

We met ... Dr Hall in such very deep mourning that either his mother, his wife, or himself must be dead.

[Letter to Cassandra Austen, 1799]

BAILLIE, Joanna (1762–1851)

But woman's grief is like a summer storm,
Short as it violent is.

[*Plays on the Passions* (1798)]

BRENAN, Gerald (1894–1987)

When we attend the funerals of our friends we grieve for them, but when we go to those of other people it is chiefly our own deaths that we mourn for.

[*Thoughts in a Dry Season* (1978)]

BRONTË, Emily (1818–1848)

Cold in the earth – and fifteen wild Decembers,
From those brown hills, have melted into spring ...

Sweet Love of youth, forgive if I forget thee
While the World's tide is bearing me along:
Sterner desires and darker hopes beset me,
Hopes which obscure but cannot do thee wrong! ...

But when the days of golden dreams had perished,
And even Despair was powerless to destroy,
Then did I learn how existence could be cherished,
Strengthened, and fed without the aid of joy ...

Once drinking deep of that divinest anguish,
How could I seek the empty world again?

['Remembrance' (1845)]

BROWNING, Elizabeth Barrett (1806–1861)

I tell you, hopeless grief is passionless.

[Sonnets, 'Grief' (1844)]

BYRON, Lord (1788–1824)

[A cypress]
Dark tree, still sad when others' grief is fled,
The only constant mourner o'er the dead!

['The Giaour' (1813)]

COWPER, William (1731–1800)

Grief is itself a med'cine.

['Charity' (1782)]

DICKENS, Charles (1812–1870)

Grief never mended no broken bones, and as good people's wery scarce, what I says is, make the most on 'em.

[*Sketches by Boz* (1836)]

DICKINSON, Emily (1830–1886)

After great pain, a formal feeling comes –
The Nerves sit ceremonious, like Tombs –
The stiff Heart questions was it He, that bore,
And Yesterday, or Centuries before? …

This is the Hour of Lead –
Remembered, if outlived,
As Freezing persons, recollect the Snow –
First – Chill – then Stupor – then the letting
go.

['After great pain, a formal feeling comes' (c. 1862)]

The Bustle in a House
The Morning after Death
Is solemnest of industries
Enacted upon Earth –

The Sweeping up the Heart
And putting Love away
We shall not want to use again
Until Eternity.

['The Bustle in a House' (c. 1866)]

ELLIOT, Jean (1727–1805)

I've heard them lilting, at our yowe-milking,
Lasses a' lilting before the dawn o' day;
But now they are moaning on ilka green loaning –
The Flowers of the Forest are a' wede away.

['The Flowers of the Forest' (1756)]

EMERSON, Ralph Waldo (1803–1882)

There are people who have an appetite for grief; pleasure is not strong enough and they crave pain.

[In *The Faber Book of Aphorisms* (1962)]

FORD, John (c.1586–1639)

They are the silent griefs which cut the heart-strings.

[*The Broken Heart* (1633)]

GASKELL, Elizabeth (1810–1865)

Bombazine would have shown a deeper sense of her loss.

[*Cranford* (1853)]

GRAVES, Robert (1895–1985)

His eyes are quickened so with grief,
He can watch a grass or leaf
Every instant grow …

Across two counties he can hear
And catch your words before you speak.
The woodlouse or the maggot's weak
Clamour rings in his sad ear,
And noise so slight it would surpass
Credence.

['Lost Love' (1921)]

HENRYSON, Robert (c.1425–1505)

Thar was na solace mycht his sobbing ces,
Bot cryit ay, with caris cald and kene,
'Quhar art thow gane, my luf Erudices?'.

['Orpheus and Eurydice' (1508)]

HUME, David (1711–1776)

Grief and disappointment give rise to anger, anger to envy, envy to malice, and malice to grief again, until the whole circle be completed.

[*A Treatise of Human Nature* (1739)]

JOHNSON, Samuel (1709–1784)

Grief is a species of idleness.

[Letter to Mrs. Thrale, 1773]

LOWELL, James Russell (1819–1891)

Sorrow, the great idealizer.

[Attr]

MACDIARMID, Hugh (1892–1978)

I met ayont the cairney
A lass wi' tousie hair
Singin' till a bairnie
That was nae langer there.

Wund wi' warlds to swing

Dinna sing sae sweet,
The licht that bends owre a' thing
Is less ta'en up wi't.

['Empty Vessel' (1926)]

MANN, Thomas (1875–1955)

Was wir Trauer nennen, ist vielleicht nicht sowohl der Schmerz über die Unmöglichkeit, unsere Toten ins Leben kehren zu sehen, als darüber, dies gar nicht wünschen zu können.

What we call mourning is perhaps not so much grief that it is impossible to see our dead return to life as grief that we are quite unable to wish to do so.

[*The Magic Mountain* (1924)]

MELVILLE, Herman (1819–1891)

In these flashing revelations of grief's wonderful fire, we see all things as they are; and though when the electric element is gone, the shadows once more descend, and the false outlines of objects again return; yet not with their former power to deceive.

[In Lewis Wolpert, *Malignant Sadness* (1999)]

MILTON, John (1608–1674)

Methought I saw my late espoused Saint
Brought to me like Alcestis from the grave …

But O as to embrace me she enclin'd,
I wak'd, she fled, and day brought back my night.

['Methought I saw my late espoused Saint' (1658)]

PROUST, Marcel (1871–1922)

Le bonheur seul est salutaire pour le corps, mais c'est le chagrin qui développe les forces de l'esprit.

Happiness alone is beneficial for the body, but it is grief that develops the powers of the mind.

[*Le Temps retrouvé* (1926)]

ROSSETTI, Dante Gabriel (1828–1882)

From perfect grief there need not be
Wisdom or even memory:
One thing then learnt remains to me, –
The woodspurge has a cup of three.

['The Woodspurge' (1870)]

SENECA (c.4 BC–AD 65)

Nothing becomes so offensive so quickly as grief. When fresh it finds someone to console it, but when it becomes chronic, it is ridiculed, and rightly.

[Attr.]

SHAKESPEARE, William (1564–1616)

Grief fills the room up of my absent child,
Lies in his bed, walks up and down with me,
Puts on his pretty looks, repeats his words,
Remembers me of all his gracious parts,
Stuffs out his vacant garments with his form;
Then have I reason to be fond of grief.

[*King John*, III.iv]

Howl, howl, howl, howl! O, you are men of stones!
Had I your tongues and eyes, I'd use them so
That heaven's vault should crack. She's gone for ever.

[*King Lear*, V.iii]

What, man! Ne'er pull your hat upon your brows;
Give sorrow words. The grief that does not speak
Whispers the o'erfraught heart and bids it break.

[*Macbeth*, IV.iii]

Every one can master a grief but he that has it.

[*Much Ado About Nothing*, III.ii]

What's gone and what's past help
Should be past grief.

[*The Winter's Tale*, III.ii]

SHELLEY, Percy Bysshe (1792–1822)

Ah, woe is me! Winter is come and gone,
But grief returns with the revolving year.

[*Adonais* (1821)]

SMITH, Sydney (1771–1845)

[Written in response to the death of one of Lady Holland's children]
The World is full of all sorts of sorrows and miseries – and I think it is better never to have been born – but when evils have happened turn away your mind from them

as soon as you can to everything of good which remains. Most people grieve as if grief were a duty or a pleasure, but all who can control it should control it – and remember that these renovations of sorrows are almost the charter and condition under which life is held.

[Letter to Lady Holland, November 1819]

STOWE, Harriet Beecher (1811–1896)

The bitterest tears shed over graves are for words left unsaid and deeds left undone.

[*Little Foxes* (1866)]

TENNYSON, Alfred, Lord (1809–1892)

I sometimes hold it half a sin
To put in words the grief I feel;
For words, like Nature, half reveal
And half conceal the Soul within.

But, for the unquiet heart and brain,
A use in measured language lies;
The sad mechanic exercise,
Like dull narcotics, numbing pain.

[*In Memoriam A. H. H.* (1850)]

Death has made
His darkness beautiful with thee.

[*In Memoriam A. H. H.* (1850)]

TWAIN, Mark (1835–1910)

[On receiving news of the death of a loved one]
It is one of the mysteries of our nature that man, all unprepared, can receive a thunder-stroke like that and live. There is but one reasonable explanation of it. The intellect is stunned by the shock and but gropingly gathers the meaning of the words. The power to realize their full import is mercifully lacking.

[*Autobiography*]

WHITMAN, Walt (1819–1892)

When lilacs last in the dooryard bloom'd,
And the great stars early droop'd in the western sky in the night,
I mourn'd, and yet shall mourn with ever-returning spring.

['When lilacs last in the dooryard bloom'd' (1865)]

WORDSWORTH, William (1770–1850)

Surprised by joy – impatient as the Wind
I turned to share the transport – Oh! with whom
But thee, deep buried in the silent tomb.

['Surprised by joy' (1815)]

GUILT

ARENDT, Hannah (1906–1975)

It is quite gratifying to feel guilty if you haven't done anything wrong: how noble! Whereas it is rather hard and certainly depressing to admit guilt and to repent.

[*Eichmann in Jerusalem: A Report on the Banality of Evil* (1963)]

BARKER, George (1913–1991)

My tall dead wives with knives in their breasts
Gaze at me, I am guilty, as they roll
Like derelicts in my tempests.

[*Eros in Dogma* (1944)]

GOETHE (1749–1832)

Denn alle Schuld rächt sich auf Erden.
For all guilt is avenged on earth.

[*Wilhelm Meister's Apprentice Years* (1796)]

GOLDSMITH, Oliver (c.1728–1774)

When lovely woman stoops to folly
And finds too late that men betray,
What charm can soothe her melancholy,
What art can wash her guilt away?

The only art her guilt to cover,
To hide her shame from every eye,
To give repentance to her lover
And wring his bosom – is to die.

[*The Vicar of Wakefield* (1766)]

HORACE (65–8 BC)

Hic murus aeneus esto,
Nil conscire sibi, nulla pallescere culpa.
This be your wall of brass, to have nothing on your conscience, no reason to grow pale with guilt.

[*Epistles*]

KAFKA, Franz (1883–1924)

'Ich bin aber nicht schuldig', sagte K., 'es ist ein Irrtum. Wie kann denn ein Mensch überhaupt schuldig sein.'
'But I'm not guilty,' said K., 'there's been a mistake. How can a man be guilty anyway.'

[*The Trial* (1925)]

KENNEDY, A.L. (1965–)

Guilt is of course not an emotion in the Celtic countries, it is simply a way of life – a kind of gleefully painful social anaesthetic.

[*So I am Glad* (1995)]

MCGOUGH, Roger (1937–)

You will put on a dress of guilt
and shoes with broken high ideals.

['Comeclose and Sleepnow' (1967)]

ORWELL, George (1903–1950)

Saints should always be judged guilty until they are proved innocent.

[*Shooting an Elephant* (1950)]

RUSKIN, John (1819–1900)

Life without industry is guilt.

['The Relation of Art to Morals' (1870)]

SHAKESPEARE, William (1564–1616)

And then it started like a guilty thing
Upon a fearful summons.

[*Macbeth*, I.i]

Will all great Neptune's ocean wash this blood
Clean from my hand? No; this my hand will rather
The multitudinous seas incarnadine,
Making the green one red.

[*Macbeth*, II.ii]

Out, damned spot! out, I say! One, two; why then 'tis time to do't. Hell is murky. Fie, my lord, fie! a soldier, and afeard? What need we fear who knows it, when none can call our pow'r to account? Yet who would have thought the old man to have had so much blood in him?

[*Macbeth*, V.i]

Here's the smell of the blood still. All the perfumes of Arabia will not sweeten this little hand. Oh, oh, oh!

[*Macbeth*, V.i]

STEVENSON, Robert Louis (1850–1894)

What hangs people … is the unfortunate circumstance of guilt.

[*The Wrong Box* (1889)]

See CONSCIENCE; REGRET

H

HABIT

BECKETT, Samuel (1906–1989)
The air is full of our cries. But habit is a great deadener.

[*Waiting for Godot* (1955)]

CHRISTIE, Dame Agatha (1890–1976)
Curious things, habits. People themselves never knew they had them.

[*Witness for the Prosecution* (1953)]

PROVERB
Old habits die hard.

See CUSTOM

HAPPINESS

ADAMS, Scott (1957–)
Smile, it confuses people.

[*The Dilbert Principle*]

ARISTOTLE (384–322 BC)
One swallow does not make a summer, neither does one fine day; similarly one day or brief time of happiness does not make a person entirely happy.

[*Nicomachean Ethics*]

AUSTEN, Jane (1775–1817)
Perfect happiness, even in memory, is not common.

[*Emma* (1816)]

Why not seize the pleasure at once? How often is happiness destroyed by preparation, foolish preparation!

[*Emma* (1816)]

BENTHAM, Jeremy (1748–1832)
[*Quoting Francis Hutcheson*]
… this sacred truth – that the greatest happiness of the greatest number is the foundation of morals and legislation.

[*Works*]

BERGMAN, Ingrid (1915–1982)
Happiness is good health – and a bad memory.

[In Simon Rose, *Classic Film Guide* (1995)]

**THE BIBLE
(King James Version)**
Beatus vir, qui timet Dominum, in mandatis eius cupit nimis!
Happy is the man who fears the Lord, who is only too willing to follow his orders.

[*Psalms*, 111:1]

BOETHIUS (c.475–524)
Nihil est miserum nisi cum putes; contraque beata sors omnis est aequanimitate tolerantis.
Nothing is miserable unless you think it so; conversely, every lot is happy to one who is content with it.

[*De Consolatione Philosophiae*]

BRADLEY, F.H. (1846–1924)
The secret of happiness is to admire without desiring. And that is not happiness.

[*Aphorisms* (1930)]

BROWNE, Sir Thomas (1605–1682)
Certainly there is no happiness within this circle of flesh, nor is it in the optics of these eyes to behold felicity; the first day of our Jubilee is death.

[*Religio Medici* (1643)]

CAMPBELL, Thomas (1777–1844)
One moment may with bliss repay
Unnumber'd hours of pain.

['The Ritter Bann']

CHESTERTON, G.K. (1874–1936)
Happiness is a mystery like religion, and should never be rationalized.

[*Heretics* (1905)]

COLERIDGE, Samuel Taylor (1772–1834)
We ne'er can be
Made happy by compulsion.

['The Three Graves' (1809)]

COLTON, Charles Caleb (c.1780–1832)

True contentment depends not on what we have; a tub was large enough for Diogenes, but a world was too little for Alexander.

[*Lacon* (1820)]

COWPER, William (1731–1800)

Domestic happiness, thou only bliss
Of Paradise that has surviv'd the fall!

[*The Task* (1785)]

DRYDEN, John (1631–1700)

For all the happiness mankind can gain
Is not in pleasure, but in rest from pain.

[*The Indian Emperor* (1665)]

Happy the man, and happy he alone,
He, who can call to-day his own:
He who, secure within, can say,
Tomorrow do thy worst, for I have lived to-day.

[*Sylvae* (1685)]

ELIOT, George (1819–1880)

The happiest women, like the happiest nations, have no history.

[*The Mill on the Floss* (1860)]

EMERSON, Ralph Waldo (1803–1882)

To fill the hour, – that is happiness.

[*Essays, Second Series* (1844)]

FRANKLIN, Benjamin (1706–1790)

Be in general virtuous, and you will be happy.

['On Early Marriages']

HORACE (65–8 BC)

Non possidentem multa vocaveris
Recte beatum: rectius occupat
Nomen beati, qui deorum
Muneribus sapienter uti
Duramque callet pauperiem pati
Peiusque leto flagitium timet.
You would not rightly call the man who has many possessions happy; he more rightly deserves to be called happy who knows how to use the gifts of the gods wisely, and can endure the hardship of poverty, and who fears dishonour more than death.

[*Odes*]

HUXLEY, Aldous (1894–1963)

Happiness is like coke – something you get as a by-product in the process of making something else.

[*Point Counter Point* (1928)]

JEROME, Jerome K. (1859–1927)

If you are foolish enough to be contented, don't show it, but grumble with the rest.

[*Idle Thoughts of an Idle Fellow* (1886)]

JOHNSON, Samuel (1709–1784)

That all who are happy, are equally happy, is not true. A peasant and a philosopher may be equally satisfied, but not equally happy. Happiness consists in the multiplicity of agreeable consciousness.

[In Boswell, *The Life of Samuel Johnson* (1791)]

There is nothing which has yet been contrived by man, by which so much happiness is produced as by a good tavern or inn.

[In Boswell, *The Life of Samuel Johnson* (1791)]

KANT, Immanuel (1724–1804)

… weil Glückseligkeit nicht ein Ideal der Vernunft, sondern der Einbildungskraft ist.
… because bliss is not an ideal of reason, but of the powers of imagination.

[*Outline of the Metaphysics of Morals* (1785)]

Tue das, wodurch du würdig wirst, glücklich zu sein.
Act in such a way that you will be worthy of being happy.

[*Critique of Pure Reason* (1787)]

KEATS, John (1795–1821)

It is a flaw
In happiness, to see beyond our bourn, –
It forces us in summer skies to mourn:
It spoils the singing of the nightingale.

['To J. H. Reynolds, Esq.' (1818)]

MARMION, Shackerley (1603–1639)

Great joys, like griefs, are silent.

[*Holland's Leaguer* (1632)]

MENCKEN, H.L. (1880–1956)

The only really happy people are married

women and single men.

[Attr.]

MILL, John Stuart (1806–1873)

Ask yourself whether you are happy, and you cease to be so.

[*Autobiography* (1873)]

PAINE, Thomas (1737–1809)

It is necessary to the happiness of man that he be mentally faithful to himself. Infidelity does not consist in believing, or in disbelieving, it consists in professing to believe what one does not believe.

[*The Age of Reason* (1794)]

PALACIO VALDÉS, Armando (1853–1938)

Si quieres ser feliz, aparenta ser desgraciado.

If you want to be happy, pretend to be miserable.

[*Doctor Angélico's Papers* (1911)]

POPE, Alexander (1688–1744)

Oh Happiness! our being's end and aim!

[*Essay on Man* (1734)]

ROUSSEAU, Jean-Jacques (1712–1778)

Happiness: a good bank account, a good cook, and a good digestion.

[*Treasury of Humorous Quotations*]

SAGAN, Françoise (1935–)

Quel mur s'impose donc toujours entre les êtres humains et leur désir le plus intime, leur effroyable volonté de bonheur? … Est-ce une nostalgie cultivée depuis l'enfance?

What is that wall that always rises up between human beings and their most intimate desire, their frightening will to be happy? … Is it a nostalgia nurtured from childhood?

[*Le Garde du coeur* (1968)]

SAINT-EXUPÉRY, Antoine de (1900–1944)

Si tu veux comprendre le mot de bonheur, il faut l'entendre comme récompense et non comme but.

If you want to understand the meaning of happiness, you must see it as a reward and

not as a goal.

[*Carnets*]

SAND, George (1804–1876)

One is happy as a result of one's own efforts, once one knows the necessary ingredients of happiness - simple tastes, a certain degree of courage, self denial to a point, love of work, and, above all, a clear conscience. Happiness is no vague dream, of that I now feel certain.

[*Correspondence*]

SANTAYANA, George (1863–1952)

Happiness is the only sanction of life; where happiness fails, existence remains a mean and lamentable experience.

[*The Life of Reason* (1905–1906)]

SHAKESPEARE, William (1564–1616)

O, how bitter a thing it is to look into happiness through another man's eyes!

[*As You Like It*, V.ii]

I swear 'tis better to be lowly born
And range with humble livers in content
Than to be perk'd up in a glist'ring grief
And wear a golden sorrow.

[*Henry VIII*, II.iii]

SHAW, George Bernard (1856–1950)

We have no more right to consume happiness without producing it than to consume wealth without producing it.

[*Candida* (1898)]

A lifetime of happiness! No man alive could bear it: it would be hell on earth.

[*Man and Superman* (1903)]

SMITH, Sydney (1771–1845)

This great spectacle of human happiness.

[*Essays* (1877)]

Mankind are always happy for having been happy, so that if you make them happy now, you make them happy twenty years hence by the memory of it.

[*Sketches of Moral Philosophy* (1849)]

SOLON (c.638–c.559 BC)

Until [a man] dies, be careful to call him not

happy but lucky.

[In Herodotus, *Histories*]

SPENSER, Edmund (c.1522–1599)
What more felicitie can fall to creature,
Than to enjoy delight with libertie.

[*Complaints* (1591)]

SURREY, Henry Howard, Earl of (c.1517–1547)
Martial, the things for to attain
The happy life be these, I find:
The riches left, not got with pain;
The fruitful ground, the quiet mind;
The equal friend; no grudge nor strife;
No charge or rule nor governance;
Without disease the healthful life;
The household of continuance.

The chaste wife wise, without debate;
Such sleeps as may beguile the night;
Content thyself with thine estate;
Neither wish death, nor fear his might.

['The Happy Life' (1547)]

SZASZ, Thomas (1920–)
Happiness is an imaginary condition,
formerly often attributed by the living to the
dead, now usually attributed by adults to
children, and by children to adults.

[*The Second Sin* (1973)]

TOLSTOY, Leo (1828–1910)
If you want to be happy, be.

[Attr.]

WAUGH, Evelyn (1903–1966)
I can't quite explain it, but I don't believe one
can ever be unhappy for long provided one
does just exactly what one wants to and
when one wants to.

[*Decline and Fall* (1928)]

WELDON, Fay (1931–)
I don't believe in happiness: why should we
expect to be happy? In such a world as this,
depression is rational, rage reasonable.

[*The Observer*, 1995]

WHATELY, Richard (1787–1863)

Happiness is no laughing matter.

[*Apophthegms* (1854)]

WORDSWORTH, William (1770–1850)
Happy is he, who, caring not for Pope,
Consul, or King, can sound himself to know
The destiny of Man, and live in hope.

[*Sonnets Dedicated to Liberty and Order* (1807)]

YEVTUSHENKO, Yevgeny (1933–)
The hell with it. Who never knew
the price of happiness will not be happy.

['Lies' (1955)]

See LAUGHTER; PLEASURE

HASTE

EMERSON, Ralph Waldo (1803–1882)
In skating over thin ice, our safety is in our
speed.

[*Essays* (1860)]

POPE, Alexander (1688–1744)
For fools rush in where angels fear to tread.

[*An Essay on Criticism* (1711)]

PROVERBS
Haste makes waste.

More haste, less speed

HATRED

ACCIUS, Lucius (170–86 BC)
Oderint dum metuant.
Let them hate provided that they fear.

[*Atreus*]

BACON, Francis (1561–1626)
Severity breedeth fear, but roughness
breedeth hate. Even reproofs from authority
ought to be grave, and not taunting.

['Of Great Place' (1625)]

BYRON, Lord (1788–1824)
Now hatred is by far the longest pleasure;
Men love in haste, but they detest at leisure.

[*Don Juan* (1824)]

DE VRIES, Peter (1910–1993)

Everybody hates me because I'm so universally liked.

[*The Vale of Laughter* (1967)]

FARQUHAR, George (1678–1707)

I hate all that don't love me, and slight all that do.

[*The Constant Couple* (1699)]

FIELDS, W.C. (1880–1946)

I am free of all prejudice. I hate everyone equally.

[Attr.]

GABOR, Zsa-Zsa (1919–)

I never hated a man enough to give him his diamonds back.

[*The Observer*, 1957]

HAZLITT, William (1778–1830)

Violent antipathies are always suspicious, and betray a secret affinity.

[*Table-Talk* (1822)]

The dupe of friendship, and the fool of love; have I not reason to hate and to despise myself? Indeed I do; and chiefly for not having hated and despised the world enough.

[*The Plain Speaker* (1826)]

Violent antipathies are always suspicious, and betray a secret affinity.

[*Table-Talk* (1822)]

We can scarcely hate any one that we know.

[*Table-Talk* (1825)]

HESSE, Hermann (1877–1962)

Wenn wir einen Menschen hassen, so hassen wir in seinem Bild etwas, was in uns selber sitzt. Was nicht in uns selber ist, das regt uns nicht auf.

If we hate a person, we hate something in our image of him that lies within ourselves. What is not within ourselves doesn't upset us.

[*Demian* (1919)]

HOFFER, Eric (1902–1983)

Passionate hatred can give meaning and purpose to an empty life.

[Attr.]

JUNG CHANG (1952–)

He [Mao Zedong] was, it seemed to me, really a restless fight promoter by nature and good at it. He understood ugly human instincts such as envy and resentment, and knew how to mobilize them for his ends. He ruled by getting people to hate each other.

[*Wild Swans* (1991)]

NASH, Ogden (1902–1971)

Any kiddie in school can love like a fool,
But hating, my boy, is an art.

[*Happy Days* (1933)]

NIXON, Richard (1913–1994)

Always give your best, never get discouraged, never be petty. Always remember, others may hate you, but those who hate you don't win unless you hate them, and then you destroy yourself.

[Farewell speech to his staff, 1974]

O'CASEY, Sean (1880–1964)

Sacred Heart of the Crucified Jesus, take away our hearts o' stone … an' give us hearts o' flesh! … Take away this murdherin' hate … an' give us Thine own eternal love!

[*Juno and the Paycock* (1924)]

ROSTEN, Leo (1908–1997)

[Of W.C. Fields; often attributed to him]
Any man who hates dogs and babies can't be all bad.

[Speech, 1939]

RUSSELL, Bertrand (1872–1970)

Few people can be happy unless they hate some other person, nation or creed.

[Attr.]

SCOTT, Sir Walter (1771–1832)

I never saw a richer company or to speak my mind a finer people. The worst of them is the bitter and envenomed dislike which they have to each other; their factions have been so long envenomed and have so little ground to fight their battle in that they are like people fighting with daggers in a hogshead.

[Letter to Joanna Baillie, 1825]

SWIFT, Jonathan (1667–1745)

I have ever hated all nations, professions and communities, and all my love is towards individuals … But principally I hate and detest that animal called man; although I heartily love John, Peter, Thomas, and so forth.

[Letter to Pope, 1725]

TACITUS (AD c.56–c.120)

Proprium humani ingenii est odisse quem laeseris.
It is part of human nature to hate those whom you have injured.

[*Agricola*]

THOREAU, Henry David (1817–1862)

It were treason to our love
And a sin to God above
One iota to abate
Of a pure impartial hate.

['Indeed, Indeed I Cannot Tell' (1852)]

See LOVE

HEALTH

ASHFORD, Daisy (1881–1972)

I am very pale owing to the drains in this house.

[*The Young Visiters* (1919)]

BUTLER, Samuel (1835–1902)

The healthy stomach is nothing if not conservative. Few radicals have good digestions.

[*The Note-Books of Samuel Butler* (1912)]

DRYDEN, John (1631–1700)

Better to hunt in fields, for health unbought,
Than fee the doctor for a nauseous draught.
The wise, for cure, on exercise depend;
God never made his work, for man to mend.

['To John Driden of Chesterton' (1700)]

JAY, Douglas (1907–)

For in the case of nutrition and health, just as in the case of education, the gentleman in Whitehall really does know better what is good for people than the people know

themselves.

[*The Socialist Case* (1947)]

JUVENAL (c.60–130)

Orandum est ut sit mens sana in corpore sano.
Your prayers should be for a healthy mind in a healthy body.

[*Satires*]

MARTIAL (c.AD 40–c.104)

Non est vivere, sed valere vita est.
It is not to live but to be healthy that makes a life.

[*Epigrammata*]

MÉNAGE, Gilles (1613–1692)

[Part of a conversation with Jean-Louis Guez de Balzac]
Comme nous nous entretenions de ce qui pouvait rendre heureux, je lui dis; Sanitas sanitatum, et omnia sanitas.
While we were talking about what could make one happy, I said to him: Sanitas sanitatum et omnia sanitas.

[In *Ménagiana* (1693)]

PROVERBS

Health is better than wealth.
The health of the salmon to you.

[Irish toast]

SMITH, Sydney (1771–1845)

I am convinced digestion is the great secret of life.

[Letter to Arthur Kinglake, 1837]

SWIFT, Jonathan (1667–1745)

I row after health like a waterman, and ride after it like a postboy, and find little success.

[Attr.]

TOLSTOY, Leo (1828–1910)

Our body is a machine for living. It is geared towards it, it is its nature. Let life go on in it unhindered and let it defend itself, it will be more effective than if you paralyse it by encumbering it with remedies.

[*War and Peace* (1869)]

TUSSER, Thomas (c.1524–1580)

Make hunger thy sauce, as a medicine for

health.

[*Five Hundred Points of Good Husbandry* (1557)]

WALTON, Izaak (1593–1683)

Look to your health; and if you have it, praise God, and value it next to a good conscience; for health is the second blessing that we mortals are capable of; a blessing money cannot buy.

[*The Compleat Angler* (1653)]

See ILLNESS; MEDICINE

HEART

BEDDOES, Thomas Lovell (1803–1849)

If thou wilt ease thine heart
Of love and all its smart,
Then sleep, dear, sleep …

But wilt thou cure thine heart
Of love and all its smart,
Then die, dear, die.

[*Death's Jest Book* (1850)]

BRIDGES, Robert (1844–1930)

Awake, my heart, to be loved, awake, awake!

['Awake, My Heart, To be Loved' (1890)]

BRIDIE, James (1888–1951)

The Heart of Man, we are told, is deceitful and desperately wicked. However that may be, it consists of four chambers, the right ventricle, the left ventricle, the left auricle, the right auricle.

[*The Anatomist* (1931)]

CAMPBELL, Thomas (1777–1844)

The proud, the cold untroubled heart of stone,
That never mused on sorrow but its own.

[*Pleasures of Hope* (1799)]

DAVIDSON, John (1857–1909)

'In shuttered rooms let others grieve,
And coffin thought in speech of lead;
I'll tie my heart upon my sleeve:
It is the Badge of Men,' he said.

['The Badge of Men' (1891)]

DIANA, Princess of Wales (1961–1997)

I want to be the queen of people's hearts.

[BBC Panorama interview, 1996]

DICKENS, Charles (1812–1870)

There are strings … in the human heart that had better not be wibrated.

[*Barnaby Rudge* (1841), 22]

DONNE, John (1572–1631)

A naked thinking heart, that makes no show,
Is to a woman, but a kind of ghost.

[*Songs and Sonnets* (1611)]

GRANVILLE, George (1666–1735)

I'll be this abject thing no more;
Love, give me back my heart again.

['Adieu l'Amour']

LONGFELLOW, Henry Wadsworth (1807–1882)

The secret anniversaries of the heart.

[*Sonnets* (1877)]

MACLEOD, Fiona (1855–1905)

My heart is a lonely hunter that hunts on a lonely hill.

['The Lonely Hunter' (1896)]

MEYNELL, Alice (1847–1922)

My heart shall be thy garden.

['The Garden' (1875)]

MUIR, Edwin (1887–1959)

The heart could never speak
But that the Word was spoken.
We hear the heart break
Here with hearts unbroken.
Time, teach us the art
That breaks and heals the heart.

['The heart could never speak' (1960)]

NEWMAN, John Henry, Cardinal (1801–1890)

Cor ad cor loquitur.
Heart speaks to heart.

[Motto adopted for his coat-of-arms as cardinal, 1879]

PROVERB

Cold hands, warm heart.

QUARLES, Francis (1592–1644)
The heart is a small thing, but desireth great matters.
It is not sufficient for a kite's dinner, yet the whole world is not sufficient for it.

[*Emblems* (1635)]

RALEIGH, Sir Walter (c.1552–1618)
[Reply when asked which way he would like to lay his head on the block]
So the heart be right, it is no matter which way the head lies.

[In W. Stebbing, *Sir Walter Raleigh* (1891)]

ROSSETTI, Christina (1830–1894)
My heart is like a singing bird
Whose nest is in a watered shoot;
My heart is like an apple-tree
Whose boughs are bent with thickset fruit;
My heart is like a rainbow shell
That paddles in a halcyon sea;
My heart is gladder than all these
Because my love is come to me.

['A Birthday' (1862)]

SCOTT, Sir Walter (1771–1832)
We shall never learn to feel and respect our real calling and destiny, unless we have taught ourselves to consider every thing as moonshine, compared with the education of the heart.

[Letter to J.G. Lockhart, 1825]

SIDNEY, Sir Philip (1554–1586)
My true Love hathe my harte and I have his,
By just exchaunge one for the other given,
I holde his deare, and myne hee can not misse,
There never was a better Bargayne driven.

[*Old Arcadia* (1581)]

SPENSER, Edmund (c.1522–1599)
The noble hart, that harbours vertuous thought,
And is with child of glorious great intent,
Can never rest, untill it forth have brought
Th' eternall brood of glorie excellent.

[*The Faerie Queene* (1596)]

SUCKLING, Sir John (1609–1642)
I prithee send me back my heart,
Since I cannot have thine
For if from yours you will not part,
Why then shouldst thou have mine?

['Song']

THOMAS, Dylan (1914–1953)
Light breaks where no sun shines;
Where no sea runs, the waters of the heart
Push in their tides.

['Light breaks where no sun shines' (1934)]

YEATS, W.B. (1865–1939)
Out-worn heart, in a time out-worn,
Come clear of the nets of wrong and right;
Laugh, heart, again in the grey twilight,
Sigh, heart, again in the dew of the morn.

[In the *National Observer*, 1893, 'Into the Twilight']

See LOVE

HEAVEN

BORGES, Jorge Luis (1899–1986)
Que el cielo exista, aunque mi lugar sea el infierno.
Let heaven exist, even if my place be hell.

['The Library of Babel' (1941)]

BROWN, Helen Gurley (1922–)
[Promotional line for *Cosmopolitan* magazine]
Good girls go to heaven, bad girls go everywhere.

[Attr.]

BROWNING, Robert (1812–1889)
On the earth the broken arcs; in the heaven, a perfect round.

['Abt Vogler' (1864)]

CARLYLE, Jane Welsh (1801–1866)
They must be comfortable people who have leisure to think about going to heaven! My most constant and pressing anxiety is to keep out of bedlam, that's all …

[*Letters and Memorials of Jane Welsh Carlyle* (1883)]

COLERIDGE, Samuel Taylor (1772–1834)
If a man could pass through Paradise in a

dream, and have a flower presented to him as a pledge that his soul had really been there, and if he found that flower in his hand when he awoke – Aye, and what then?

[*Anima Poetae* (1816)]

DE QUINCEY, Thomas (1785–1859)

Thou hast the keys of Paradise, oh just, subtle, and mighty opium!

[*Confessions of an English Opium Eater* (1822)]

FITZGERALD, Edward (1809–1883)

Here with a Loaf of Bread beneath the Bough,
A Flask of Wine, a Book of Verse – and Thou
Beside me singing in the Wilderness –
And Wilderness is Paradise enow.

[*The Rubáiyát of Omar Khayyám* (1859)]

LICHTENBERG, Georg (1742–1799)

Probably no invention came more easily to man than Heaven.

[*Aphorisms*]

MILTON, John (1608–1674)

Heav'n is for thee too high
To know what passes there; be lowlie wise:
Think onely what concerns thee and thy being.

[*Paradise Lost* (1667)]

PROUST, Marcel (1871–1922)

Les vrais paradis sont les paradis qu'on a perdus.
The true paradises are the paradises we have lost.

[*Le Temps retrouvé* (1926)]

SEDGWICK, Catharine Maria (1789–1867)

[Comparing heaven with her home town of Stockbridge, Massachussetts]
I expect no very violent transition.

[Attr.]

SHAKESPEARE, William (1564–1616)

Heaven is above all yet: there sits a Judge
That no king can corrupt.

[*Henry VIII*, III.i]

SHAW, George Bernard (1856–1950)

In heaven an angel is nobody in particular.

[*Man and Superman* (1903)]

Heaven, as conventionally conceived, is a place so inane, so dull, so useless, so miserable, that nobody has ever ventured to describe a whole day in heaven, though plenty of people have described a day at the seaside.

[*Misalliance* (1914)]

SMITH, Sydney (1771–1845)

My idea of heaven is, eating pâté de foie gras to the sound of trumpets.

[In H. Pearson, *The Smith of Smiths* (1934)]

SWIFT, Jonathan (1667–1745)

What they do in heaven we are ignorant of; what they do not we are told expressly, that they neither marry, nor are given in marriage.

[*Thoughts on Various Subjects* (1711)]

TINTORETTO (1518–1594)

[Arguing that he be allowed to paint the Paradiso at the Doge's palace in Venice, despite his advanced age]
Grant me paradise in this world; I'm not so sure I'll reach it in the next.

[Attr.]

WADDELL, Helen Jane (1889–1965)

Would you think Heaven could be so small a thing
As a lit window on the hills at night.

['I Shall Not Go To Heaven']

WILLIAMS, William Carlos (1883–1963)

Is it any better in Heaven, my friend Ford,
Than you found it in Provence?

['To Ford Madox Ford in Heaven' (1944)]

See AFTERLIFE

HELL

BECKFORD, William (1760–1844)

He did not think with the Caliph Omar Ben Adalaziz, that it was necessary to make a hell of this world to enjoy paradise in the next.

[*Vathek* (1787)]

BERNANOS, Georges (1888–1948)

L'enfer, madame, c'est de ne plus aimer.

Hell, madam, is to love no longer.

[*The Diary of a Country Priest*, 1936)]

BETJEMAN, Sir John (1906–1984)

Maud was my hateful nurse who smelt of soap …

She rubbed my face in messes I had made

And was the first to tell me about Hell,

Admitting she was going there herself.

[*Summoned by Bells* (1960)]

BUNYAN, John (1628–1688)

Then I saw there was a way to Hell, even from the gates of heaven.

[*The Pilgrim's Progress* (1678)]

BURTON, Robert (1577–1640)

If there is a hell upon earth, it is to be found in a melancholy man's heart.

[*Anatomy of Melancholy* (1621)]

CLARE, Dr Anthony (1942–)

Hell is when you get what you think you want.

[*The Observer*, 1983]

DANTE ALIGHIERI (1265–1321)

PER ME SI VA NELLA CITTA' DOLENTE,

PER ME SI VA NELL'ETERNO DOLORE,

PER ME SI VA TRA LA PERDUTA GENTE …

LASCIATE OGNI SPERANZA VOI CH'ENTRATE!

Through me one goes to the sorrowful city.

Through me one goes to eternal suffering.

Through me one goes among lost people …

Abandon all hope, you who enter!

[*Divina Commedia* (1307)]

Questi non hanno speranza di morte,

E la lor cieca vita è tanto bassa,

Che invidiosi son d'ogni altra sorte.

There is no hope of death for these souls, and their lost life is so low, that they are envious of any other kind.

[*Divina Commedia* (1307)]

ELIOT, T.S. (1888–1965)

Hell is oneself;

Hell is alone, the other figures in it

Merely projections. There is nothing to escape from

And nothing to escape to. One is always alone.

[*The Cocktail Party* (1950)]

LEWIS, C.S. (1898–1963)

There is wishful thinking in Hell as well as on earth.

[*The Screwtape Letters* (1942)]

MARLOWE, Christopher (1564–1593)

Hell hath no limits nor is circumscrib'd

In one self place, where we are is Hell,

And where Hell is, there must we ever be.

And to be short, when all the world dissolves,

And every creature shall be purified,

All places shall be hell that are not heaven.

[*Doctor Faustus* (1604)]

MILTON, John (1608–1674)

Here we may reign secure, and in my choice

To reign is worth ambition though in Hell:

Better to reign in Hell, then serve in Heav'n.

[*Paradise Lost* (1667)]

Long is the way

And hard, that out of Hell leads up to Light.

[*Paradise Lost* (1667)]

PROVERB

The road to hell is paved with good intentions.

SADE, Marquis de (1740–1814)

Il n'y a d'autre enfer pour l'homme que la bêtise ou la méchanceté de ses semblables.

There is no other hell for man than the stupidity and wickedness of his own kind.

[*Histoire de Juliette* (1797)]

SARTRE, Jean-Paul (1905–1980)

Alors, c'est ça l'enfer. Je n'aurais jamais cru … Vous vous rappelez: le soufre, le bûcher, le gril … Ah! quelle plaisanterie. Pas besoin de gril, l'enfer, c'est les Autres.

So that's what Hell is. I'd never have believed it … Do you remember, brimstone, the stake, the gridiron? … What a joke! No need of a gridiron, Hell is other people.

[*In Camera* (1944)]

SHAW, George Bernard (1856–1950)

A perpetual holiday is a good working definition of hell.

[Attr.]

TEILHARD DE CHARDIN, Pierre (1881–1955)

Vous m'avez dit, mon Dieu, de croire á l'enfer. Mais vous m'avez interdit de penser, avec absolue certitude, d'un seul homme, qu'il était damné.

You have told me, O God, to believe in hell. But you have forbidden me to think, with absolute certainty, of any man as damned.

[*Le Milieu divin*]

VIRGIL (70–19 BC)

Facilis descensus Averno:
Noctes atque dies patet atri ianua Ditis;
Sed revocare gradum superasque evadere ad auras,
Hoc opus, hic labor est.

The gates of Hell are open night and day;
Smooth the descent, and easy is the way:
But to return, and view the cheerful skies,
In this the task and mighty labour lies.

[*Aeneid*]

WATTS, Isaac (1674–1748)

There is a dreadful Hell,
And everlasting pains;
There sinners must with devils dwell
In darkness, fire and chains.

[*Divine Songs for Children* (1715)]

WILDE, Oscar (1854–1900)

We are each our own devil, and we make
This world our hell.

[*The Duchess of Padua* (1883)]

See DEVIL

HEROES

BRECHT, Bertolt (1898–1956)

Andrea: Unglücklich das Land, das keine Helden hat! …
Galileo: Nein. Unglücklich das Land, das Helden nötig hat.

Andrea: Unhappy the country that has no heroes! Galileo: No. Unhappy the country that needs heroes.

[*Life of Galileo* (1938–1939)]

CARLYLE, Thomas (1795–1881)

The Hero can be Poet, Prophet, King, Priest or what you will, according to the kind of world he finds himself born into.

['The Hero as Poet' (1841)]

CORNUEL, Madame Anne-Marie Bigot de (1605–1694)

Il n'y a point de grand homme pour son valet de chambre.

No man is a hero to his valet.

[In *Lettres de Mlle Aïssé á Madame C* (1787)]

GAMBETTA, Léon (1838–1882)

Les temps héroïques sont passés.

Heroic times have passed away.

[Saying]

HARRIS, Max (1921–1995)

The Australian world is peopled with good blokes and bastards, but not heroes.

[In Coleman (ed.), *Australian Civilization*]

HENDERSON, Hamish (1919–)

There were our own, there were the others. Their deaths were like their lives, human and animal.
There were no gods and precious few heroes.

[*Elegies for the Dead in Cyrenaica* (1948)]

LANDOR, Walter Savage (1775–1864)

Hail, ye indomitable heroes, hail!
Despite of all your generals ye prevail.

['The Crimean Heroes']

MACKENZIE, Sir Compton (1883–1972)

Ever since the first World War there has been an inclination to denigrate the heroic aspect of man.

[*On Moral Courage* (1962)]

MORELL, Thomas (1703–1784)

See, the conquering hero comes!

Sound the trumpets, beat the drums!

[*Joshua* (1748)]

ORWELL, George (1903–1950)
The high sentiments always win in the end, leaders who offer blood, toil, tears and sweat always get more out of their followers than those who offer safety and a good time. When it comes to the pinch, human beings are heroic.

[*Horizon*, 1941]

RILKE, Rainer Maria (1875–1926)
Wunderlich nah ist der Held doch den jugendlichen Toten.
Wondrous close is the hero to those who die young.

[*Duino Elegies* (1923)]

ROGERS, Will (1879–1935)
Heroing is one of the shortest-lived professions there is.

[In Grove, *The Will Rogers Book* (1961)]

See COURAGE; PATRIOTISM; WAR

HISTORY

ANGELOU, Maya (1928–)
History, faced with courage, need not be lived again.

[Speech at the Inauguration of President Clinton, 1993]

ANONYMOUS
Every time history repeats itself the price goes up.

AUSTEN, Jane (1775–1817)
N.B. There will be very few Dates in this History.

[*The History of England* (1791)]

History tells me nothing that does not either vex or weary me; the men are all so good for nothing, and hardly any women at all.

[Letter]

Real solemn history, I cannot be interested in … The quarrels of popes and kings, with wars or pestilences, in every page; the men all so good for nothing, and hardly any women at all, it is very tiresome.

[*Northanger Abbey* (1818)]

BALFOUR, A.J. (1848–1930)
History does not repeat itself. Historians repeat each other.

[Attr.]

BEECHAM, Sir Thomas (1879–1961)
When the history of the first half of this century comes to be written – properly written – it will be acknowledged the most stupid and brutal in the history of civilisation.

[Attr.]

BIRRELL, Augustine (1850–1933)
That great dust-heap called 'history'.

[*Obiter Dicta* (1884–1887)]

BOLINGBROKE, Henry (1678–1751)
I have read somewhere or other – in Dionysius of Halicarnassus, I think – that History is Philosophy teaching by examples.

[*Letters on Study and Use of History* (1752)]

[Of Thucydides and Xenophon]
They maintained the dignity of history.

[*Letters on Study and Use of History* (1752)]

BROWN, George MacKay (1921–1996)
History can show few benign mergings of people with people. Flame and blood is always the cement.

['The View from Orkney']

BUTLER, Samuel (1835–1902)
It has been said that though God cannot alter the past, historians can; it is perhaps because they can be useful to Him in this respect that He tolerates their existence.

[*Erewhon Revisited* (1901)]

CARLYLE, Thomas (1795–1881)
History a distillation of rumour.

[*History of the French Revolution* (1837)]

For, as I take it, Universal History, the history of what man has accomplished in this world, is at bottom the History of the Great Men who have worked here.

[*On Heroes, Hero-Worship, and the Heroic in History*]

History is the essence of innumerable biographies.

['*On History*' (1839)]

Happy the people whose annals are blank in history-books!

[*History of Frederick the Great* (1865)]

CATHER, Willa (1873–1947)

The history of every country begins in the heart of a man or a woman.

[*O Pioneers!* (1913)]

COLERIDGE, Samuel Taylor (1772–1834)

If men could learn from history, what lessons it might teach us! But passion and party blind our eyes, and the light which experience gives is a lantern on the stern, which shines only on the waves behind us!

[*Table Talk* (1835)]

DIONYSIUS OF HALICARNASSUS (fl. 30–7 BC)

History is philosophy teaching from examples.

[*Ars Rhetorica*]

DURRELL, Lawrence (1912–1990)

History is an endless repetition of the wrong way of living.

[*The Listener*, 1978]

EBAN, Abba (1915–)

History teaches us that men and nations behave wisely once they have exhausted all other alternatives.

[Speech, 1970]

FISHER, H.A.L. (1856–1940)

One intellectual excitement has, however, been denied me. Men wiser and more learned than I have discerned in history a plot, a rhythm, a predetermined pattern. These harmonies are concealed from me. I can see only one emergency following upon another as wave follows upon wave, only one great fact with respect to which, since it is

unique, there can be no generalizations, only one safe rule for the historian: that he should recognize in the development of human destinies the play of the contingent and the unforeseen.

[*History of Europe* (1935)]

FORD, Henry (1863–1947)

[Popularly remembered as 'History is bunk']
History is more or less bunk. It's tradition. We don't want tradition. We want to live in the present and the only history that is worth a tinker's damn is the history we make today.

[*Chicago Tribune*, 1916]

FORSTER, E.M. (1879–1970)

The historian must have … some conception of how men who are not historians behave. Otherwise he will move in a world of the dead.

[*Abinger Harvest* (1936)]

GIBBON, Edward (1737–1794)

If a man were called to fix the period in the history of the world during which the condition of the human race was most happy and prosperous, he would, without hesitation, name that which elapsed from the death of Domitian to the accession of Commodus.

[*Decline and Fall of the Roman Empire* (1776–88)]

History … is, indeed, little more than the register of the crimes, follies, and misfortunes of mankind.

[*Decline and Fall of the Roman Empire* (1776–88)]

JAMES, Henry (1843–1916)

It takes a great deal of history to produce a little literature.

[*Hawthorne* (1879)]

JOHNSON, Samuel (1709–1784)

Great abilities are not requisite for an Historian … Imagination is not required in any high degree.

[In Boswell, *The Life of Samuel Johnson* (1791)]

JOYCE, James (1882–1941)

History is a nightmare from which I am

trying to awake.

[*Ulysses* (1922)]

KHRUSHCHEV, Nikita (1894–1971)
Whether you like it or not, history is on our side.

[Speech to Western ambassadors, 1956]

KOESTLER, Arthur (1905–1983)
The most persistent sound which reverberates through men's history is the beating of war drums.

[*Janus: A Summing Up* (1978)]

LANG, Ian (1940–)
History is littered with dead opinion polls.

[*The Independent*, 1994]

MACLEOD, Iain (1913–1970)
History is too serious to be left to historians.

[*The Observer*, 1961]

MCLUHAN, Marshall (1911–1980)
The hydrogen bomb is history's exclamation point. It ends an age-long sentence of manifest violence.

[Attr.]

MARX, Karl (1818–1883)
Hegel says somewhere that all great events and personalities in world history reappear in one way or another. He forgot to add: the first time as tragedy, the second as farce.

[*The Eighteenth Brumaire of Louis Napoleon* (1852)]

ORWELL, George (1903–1950)
To a surprising extent the war-lords in shining armour, the apostles of the martial virtues, tend not to die fighting when the time comes. History is full of ignominious getaways by the great and famous.

['Who are the War Criminals?' (1941)]

PASTERNAK, Boris (1890–1960)
But what is history? It is the setting up, through the ages, of works which are consistently devoted to solving death and to overcoming it in the future.

[*Doctor Zhivago* (1958)]

PATTEN, Brian (1946–)
History's full of absurd mistakes.

King Arthur if he ever existed would only have farted and excused himself from the Round Table in a hurry.

[*Grinning Jack* (1990)]

PÉGUY, Charles (1873–1914)
It is impossible to write ancient history because we do not have enough sources, and impossible to write modern history because we have far too many.

[*Clio*]

POPPER, Sir Karl (1902–1994)
There is no history of mankind, there are only many histories of all kinds of aspects of human life. And one of these is the history of political power. This is elevated into the history of the world.

[*The Open Society and its Enemies* (1945)]

PROVERB
History repeats itself.

SAKI (1870–1916)
The people of Crete unfortunately make more history than they can consume locally.

[*The Chronicles of Clovis* (1911)]

SAMUEL, Lord (1870–1963)
Hansard is history's ear, already listening.

[*The Observer*, 1949]

SCHILLER, Johann Christoph Friedrich (1759–1805)
Die Weltgeschichte ist das Weltgericht.
The history of the world is its judgement.

['Resignation' (1786)]

SCHLEGEL, Friedrich von (1772–1829)
Anfang und Ende der Geschichte ist prophetisch, kein Objekt mehr der reinen Historie.
The beginning and end of history are prophetic, they are no longer the object of pure history.

[*Fragments on Literature and Poetry*]

Der Historiker ist ein rückwärts gekehrter Prophet.
A historian is a prophet in reverse.

[*Athenäum – Fragmente*]

SEELEY, Sir John Robert (1834–1895)
[Quoting E.A. Freeman]

History is past politics, and politics present history.

[*The Growth of British Policy* (1895)]

SELLAR, Walter (1898–1951) and
YEATMAN, Robert Julian (1897–1968)
A Bad Thing: America was thus clearly top nation, and History came to a .

[*1066 And All That* (1930)]

STALIN, Joseph (1879–1953)
History shows that there are no invincible armies.

[Speech on the declaration of war on Germany, 1941]

TAYLOR, A.J.P. (1906–1990)
History gets thicker as it approaches recent times.

[*English History*, 1914–1945 (1965), Bibliography]

[Of Napoleon III]
He was what I often think is a dangerous thing for a statesman to be – a student of history; and like most of those who study history, he learned from the mistakes of the past how to make new ones.

[*The Listener*, 1963]

TEBBITT, Norman (1931–)
Youngsters of all races born here should be taught that British history is their history, or they will forever be foreigners holding British passports, and this kingdom will become a Yugoslavia.

[Speech, Conservative Party Conference, 1997]

TOLSTOY, Leo (1828–1910)
History would be an excellent thing if only it were true.

[Attr.]

Historians are like deaf people who go on answering questions that no one has asked them.

[Attr.]

VOLTAIRE (1694–1778)
En effet, l'histoire n'est que le tableau des crimes et des malheurs.
Indeed, history is nothing but a tableau of crimes and misfortunes.

[*L'Ingénu* (1767)]

WALPOLE, Robert (1676–1745)
[On being asked whether he would like to be read to]
Anything but history, for history must be false.

[Attr.]

WEDGEWOOD, Cicely Veronica (1910–1997)
… truth can neither be apprehended nor communicated … history is an art like all other sciences.

[*Truth and Opinion* (1960)]

WELLS, H.G. (1866–1946)
Human history becomes more and more a race between education and catastrophe.

[*The Outline of History* (1920)]

YELTSIN, Boris (1931–)
[*Said after the failure of the communist coup*]
History will record that the twentieth century essentially ended on 19–21 August 1991.

[Article in *Newsweek*, 1994]

See EXPERIENCE; PAST

HOLLYWOOD

HAWN, Goldie (1945–)
There are only three ages for women in Hollywood – Babe, District Attorney, and Driving Miss Daisy.

HOLLAND, Agnieska
In Hollywood they don't feel guilt.

MATURE, Victor (1915–)
Hollywood: Where the stars twinkle until they wrinkle.

MIZNER, Wilson (1876–1933)
A trip through a sewer in a glass-bottomed boat.

MONROE, Marilyn (1926–1962)
Hollywood is a place where they'll pay you

$50,000 for a kiss and 50 cents for your soul.

[Attr.]

REED, Rex (1938–)
In Hollywood, if you don't have happiness, you send out for it.

ROWLAND, Richard (c.1881–1947)
[When United Artists was established in 1919 by Mary Pickford, Douglas Fairbanks, Charlie Chaplin and D.W. Griffith]
The lunatics have taken over the asylum.

[Attr.]

STALLINGS, Laurence (1894–1968)
Hollywood – a place where the inmates are in charge of the asylum.

[Attr.]

See CINEMA; SHOWBUSINESS

HOME

ACE, Jane (1905–1974)
Home wasn't built in a day.

[In G. Ace, *The Fine Art of Hypochondria* (1966)]

ANONYMOUS
[Graffiti in Notting Hill]
Dwelling unit sweet dwelling unit.

[In Nigel Rees, *Graffiti Lives, OK* (1979)]

Be it ever so humble there's no place like home for sending one slowly crackers.

There's no place like home, after the other places close.

BEAUVOIR, Simone de (1908–1986)
The ideal of happiness has always taken material form in the house, whether cottage or castle; it stands for permanence and separation from the world.

[*The Second Sex* (1949)]

CICERO (106–43 BC)
What is more agreeable than one's home?

[*Ad Familiares*]

CLARKE, John (fl. 1639)
Home is home, though it be never so homely.

[*Paraemiologia Anglo-Latina* (1639)]

COKE, Sir Edward (1552–1634)
The house of everyone is to him as his castle and fortress, as well for his defence against injury and violence, as for his repose.

[*Semayne's Case*]

DE WOLFE, Elsie (1865–1950)
It is the personality of the mistress that the home expresses. Men are forever guests in our homes, no matter how much happiness they may find there.

[*The House in Good Taste* (1920)]

DOUGLAS, Norman (1868–1952)
Many a man who thinks to found a home discovers that he has merely opened a tavern for his friends.

[*South Wind* (1917)]

FLETCHER, John (1579–1625)
Charity and beating begins at home.

[*Wit Without Money* (c. 1614)]

FORD, Lena (1870–1916)
Keep the home fires burning while your hearts are yearning,
Though your lads are far away, they dream of home.
There's a silver lining through the dark cloud shining:
Turn the dark cloud inside out, till the boys come home.

['Keep the Home Fires Burning' (1914)]

FROST, Robert (1874–1963)
'Home is the place where, when you have to go there,
They have to take you in.'
'I should have called it
Something you somehow haven't to deserve.'

['The Death of the Hired Man' (1914)]

FULLER, Margaret
A house is no home unless it contain food

and fire for the mind as well as for the body.

[*Woman in the Nineteenth Century* (1845)]

GROSSMITH, George and Weedon

What's the good of a home, if you are never in it?

[*Diary of a Nobody* (1894)]

HIGLEY, Brewster (19th century)

Oh give me a home where the buffalo roam,
Where the deer and the antelope play,
Where seldom is heard a discouraging word
And the skies are not cloudy all day.

['Home on the Range', song, c. 1873]

JEROME, Jerome K. (1859–1927)

I want a house that has got over all of its troubles; I don't want to spend the rest of my life bringing up a young and inexperienced house.

[Attr.]

KAUFMAN, Sue (1926–)

In violent and chaotic times such as these, our only chance for survival lies in creating our own little islands of sanity and order, in making little havens of our homes.

[*Falling Bodies* (1974)]

LUCE, Clare Boothe (1903–1987)

A man's home may seem to be his castle on the outside; inside, it is more often his nursery.

[Attr.]

MEYER, Agnes (1887–c.1970)

What the nation must realise is that the home, when both parents work, is non-existent. Once we have honestly faced the fact, we must act accordingly.

[*Washington Post*, 1943]

MORE, Hannah (1745–1833)

The sober comfort, all the peace which springs
From the large aggregate of little things;
On these small cares of daughter, wife, or friend,
The almost sacred joys of home depend.

['Sensibility' (1782)]

MORRIS, William (1834–1896)

If you want a golden rule that will fit everybody, this is it: Have nothing in your houses that you do not know to be useful, or believe to be beautiful.

[*Hopes and Fears for Art* (1882)]

PAYNE, J.H. (1791–1852)

Mid pleasures and palaces though we may roam,
Be it ever so humble, there's no place like home;
A charm from the skies seems to hallow us there,
Which, seek through the world, is ne'er met with elsewhere.
Home, home, sweet, sweet home!
There's no place like home! there's no place like home!

['Home, Sweet Home', song, 1823]

PITT, William (1708–1778)

The poorest man may in his cottage bid defiance to all the forces of the Crown. It may be frail – its roof may shake – the wind may blow through it – the rain may enter – but the King of England cannot enter – all his force dares not cross the threshold of the ruined tenement!

[Speech, c. 1763]

PROVERB

Home is where the heart is.

ROWLAND, Helen (1875–1950)

'Home' is any four walls that enclose the right person.

[*Reflections of a Bachelor Girl* (1909)]

SHAW, George Bernard (1856–1950)

Home is the girl's prison and the woman's workhouse.

[*Man and Superman* (1903)]

The great advantage of a hotel is that it's a refuge from home life.

[*You Never Can Tell* (1898)]

SITWELL, Dame Edith (1887–1964)

One's own surroundings mean so much to

one, when one is feeling miserable.
[*Selected Letters* (1970)]

STOWE, Harriet Beecher (1811–1896)
Home is a place not only of strong affections,
but of entire unreserve; it is life's undress
rehearsal, its backroom, its dressing room,
from which we go forth to more careful and
guarded intercourse, leaving behind us much
debris of cast-off and everyday clothing.
[*Little Foxes* (1866)]

THOREAU, Henry David (1817–1862)
I had three chairs in my house; one for
solitude, two for friendship, three for society.
[*Walden* (1854)]

TUSSER, Thomas (c.1524–1580)
Seek home for rest,
For home is best.
[*Five Hundred Points of Good Husbandry* (1557)]

See TRAVEL

HOMOSEXUALS

DUNSTAN, Keith (1925–)
[*On the opinion that Ned Kelly and his gang were
homosexuals, expressed by Sidney Baker in* The
Australian Language, *1966*]
It is all very well to call him a white-livered
cur, a bully, a coward, a liar and a psychotic
murderer but to actually name him as a
queer is going too far.
[*Knockers* (1972)]

FRYE, Marilyn (1934–)
Gay men generally are in significant ways,
perhaps in all important ways, more loyal to
masculinity and male-supremacy than other
men. The gay rights movement may be the
fundamentalism of the global religion which
is patriarchy.
[In Julie Burchill, *Sex and Sensibility*]

HALL, Radclyffe (1883–1943)
Acknowledge us, oh God, before the whole
world. Give us also the right to our existence!
[*The Well of Loneliness* (1928)]

LEWIS, Wyndham (1882–1957)
The 'homo' is the legitimate child of the
'suffragette'.
[*The Art of Being Ruled* (1926)]

MARX, Groucho (1895–1977)
Many years ago I chased a woman for almost
two years, only to discover her tastes were
exactly like mine: we were both crazy about
girls.
[Attr.]

See SEX

HONESTY

AUDEN, W.H. (1907–1973)
Only God can tell the saintly from the
suburban,
Counterfeit values always resemble the true;
Neither in Life nor Art is honesty bohemian,
The free behave much as the respectable do.
['New Year Letter' (1941)]

BLAKE, William (1757–1827)
Always be ready to speak your mind, and a
base man will avoid you.
[Attr.]

BROWNE, Sir Thomas (1605–1682)
I have tried if I could reach that great
resolution … to be honest without a thought
of Heaven or Hell.
[*Religio Medici* (1643)]

CARLYLE, Thomas (1795–1881)
Make yourself an honest man and then you
may be sure there is one rascal less in the
world.
[Attr.]

CROMWELL, Oliver (1599–1658)
A few honest men are better than numbers.
[Letter to Sir William Spring, 1643]

DEFOE, Daniel (c.1661–1731)
Necessity makes an honest man a knave.
[*Serious Reflections of Robinson Crusoe*
(1720)]

FITZGERALD, F. Scott (1896–1940)

I am one of the few honest people that I have ever known.

[*The Great Gatsby* (1926)]

JUVENAL (c.60–130)

Probitas laudatur et alget.

Honesty is praised and is left out in the cold.

[*Satires*]

MARQUIS, Don (1878–1937)

honesty is a good
thing but
it is not profitable to
its possessor
unless it is
kept under control.

['archygrams' (1933)]

PROVERB

Honesty is the best policy.

RUSKIN, John (1819–1900)

Your honesty is not to be based either on religion or policy. Both your religion and policy must be based on it. Your honesty must be based, as the sun is, in vacant heaven; poised, as the lights in the firmament, which have rule over the day and over the night.

[*Time and Tide by Weare and Tyne* (1867)]

SHAKESPEARE, William (1564–1616)

O wretched fool,
That liv'st to make thine honesty a vice!
O monstrous world! Take note, take note, O world,
To be direct and honest is not safe.

[*Othello*, III.iii]

Though I am not naturally honest, I am so sometimes by chance.

[*The Winter's Tale*, IV.iv]

WHATELY, Richard (1787–1863)

Honesty is the best policy, but he who is governed by that maxim is not an honest man.

[*Apophthegms* (1854)]

See TRUTH

HONOUR

BULGAKOV, Mikhail (1891–1940)

No man should break his word of honour.

[*The White Guard* (1925)]

EMERSON, Ralph Waldo (1803–1882)

The louder he talked of his honor, the faster we counted our spoons.

[*Conduct of Life* (1860)]

HARE, Augustus (1792–1834)

Purity is the feminine, Truth the masculine, of Honour.

[*Guesses at Truth* (1827)]

LOVELACE, Richard (1618–1658)

True; a new mistress now I chase,
The first foe in the field;
And with a stronger faith embrace
A sword, a horse, a shield.

Yet this inconstancy is such,
As you too shall adore;
I could not love thee (Dear) so much,
Lov'd I not honour more.

['To Lucasta, Going to the Wars' (1649)]

MARX, Groucho (1895–1977)

Remember, men, we're fighting for this woman's honour; which is probably more than she ever did.

[*Duck Soup*, film, 1933]

PROVERB

There is honour among thieves.

RACINE, Jean (1639–1699)

Sans argent l'honneur n'est qu'une maladie.

Without money, honour is no more than a disease.

[*Les Plaideurs* (1668)]

SHAKESPEARE, William (1564–1616)

Honour pricks me on. Yea, but how if honour prick me off when I come on? How then? Can honour set to a leg? No. Or an arm? No. Or take away the grief of a wound? No. Honour hath no skill in surgery, then? No. What is honour? A word. What is in that word? Honour. What is that honour? Air. A trim reckoning! Who hath it? He that died o' Wednesday. Doth he feel it? No. Doth he hear it? No. 'Tis insensible, then? Yea, to the dead. But will it not live with the living? No. Why? Detraction will not suffer it. Therefore I'll none of it. Honour is a mere scutcheon. And so ends my catechism.

[*Henry IV, Part 1*, V.i]

STEVENSON, Robert Louis (1850–1894)

Still obscurely fighting the lost fight of virtue, still clinging, in the brothel or on the scaffold, to some rag of honour, the poor jewel of their souls!

[*Across the Plains* (1892)

HOPE

ARNOLD, Matthew (1822–1888)

And the pale master on his spar-
strewn deck
With anguish'd face and flying hair
Grasping the rudder hard,
Still bent to make some port he knows
not where,
Still standing for some false,
impossible shore.

['A Summer Night' (1852)]

Still nursing the unconquerable hope,
Still clutching the inviolable shade.

['The Scholar-Gipsy' (1853)]

The foot less prompt to meet the morning
dew,
The heart less bounding at emotion new,
And hope, once crushed, less quick to spring
again.

['Thyrsis' (1866)]

BACON, Francis (1561–1626)

Hope is a good breakfast, but it is a bad supper.

['Apophthegms']

CHESTERTON, G.K. (1874–1936)

Hope is the power of being cheerful in circumstances which we know to be desperate.

[*Heretics* (1905)]

CLARE, John (1793–1864)

Hopeless hope hopes on and meets no end,
Wastes without springs and homes without a friend.

['Child Harold' (1841)]

COLERIDGE, Samuel Taylor (1772–1834)

Work without hope draws nectar in a sieve,
And hope without an object cannot live.

['Work Without Hope' (1828)]

FRANKLIN, Benjamin (1706–1790)

He that lives upon hope will die fasting.

[*Poor Richard's Almanac* (1758)]

HERBERT, George (1593–1633)

He that lives in hope danceth without music.

[*Jacula Prudentum* (1640)]

ILLICH, Ivan (1926–)

We must rediscover the distinction between hope and expectation.

[*Deschooling Society* (1971)]

KERR, Jean (1923–)

Hope is the feeling you have that the feeling you have isn't permanent.

[*Finishing Touches* (1973)]

OSBORNE, John (1929–1994)

[A notice in his bathroom]
Since I gave up hope I feel so much better.

[*The Independent*, 1994]

POPE, Alexander (1688–1744)

Hope springs eternal in the human breast;
Man never Is, but always To be blest.

[*An Essay on Man* (1733)]

PRIOR, Matthew (1664–1721)

For hope is but a dream of those that wake.

[Solomon *(1718)*]

PROVERB

Every cloud has a silver lining.

SHAKESPEARE, William (1564–1616)

True hope is swift and flies with swallow's

wings;
Kings it makes gods, and meaner creatures kings.

[*Richard III*, V.ii]

TERENCE (c.190–159 BC)

Modo liceat vivere, est spes.
Where there's life, there's hope.

[*Heauton Timoroumenos*]

See AMBITION; DESIRE; OPTIMISM

HOSTS AND GUESTS

COLERIDGE, Samuel Taylor (1772–1834)

Like some poor nigh-related guest,
That may not rudely be dismist;
Yet hath outstay'd his welcome while,
And tells the jest without the smile.

['Youth and Age' (1834)]

DAVIS, Thomas (1814–1845)

Come in the evening, or come in the morning,
Come when you're looked for, or come without warning.

['The Welcome' (1846)]

FITZGERALD, F. Scott (1896–1940)

I was one of the few guests who had actually been invited. People were not invited – they went there.

[*The Great Gatsby* (1925)]

I entertained on a cruising trip that was so much fun that I had to sink my yacht to make my guests go home.

[*The Crack-Up* (1945)]

HOMER (fl. c.8th century BC)

Alike he thwarts the hospitable end
Who drives the free or stays the hasty friend;
True friendship's laws are by this rule express'd,
Welcome the coming, speed the parting guest.

[*Odyssey*]

KENNEDY, A.L. (1965–)

[*On book promotion tours*]
You are put up in Five-Star-Hotel land, when you come from One-Star-Hotel land – you can't even afford to go out of the door. So you go to the bookshop, you drink sour wine, you talk to people who don't want to talk to you, and you go back to your hotel room with a club sandwich, and watch a documentary on East Timor …

[*Sunday Herald*, 1999]

LEACOCK, Stephen (1869–1944)

The landlady of a boarding-house is a parallelogram – that is, an oblong angular figure, which cannot be described, but which is equal to anything.

[*Literary Lapses* (1910)]

POPE, Alexander (1688–1744)

True friendship's laws are by this rule express'd,
Welcome the coming, speed the parting guest.

[*The Odyssey*]

PROVERB

A guest always brings pleasure: if not the arrival, the departure.

[Portuguese proverb]

The first day a guest, the second day a guest, the third day a calamity.

RUNYON, Damon (1884–1946)

A free-loader is a confirmed guest. He is the man who is always willing to come to dinner.

[*Short Takes* (1946)]

SAKI (1870–1916)

By insisting on having your bottle pointing to the north when the cork is being drawn, and calling the waiter Max, you may induce an impression on your guests which hours of laboured boasting might be powerless to achieve. For this purpose, however, the guests must be chosen as carefully as the wine.

[*The Chronicles of Clovis* (1911)]

SICKERT, Walter (1860–1942)

[To Denton Welch]

Come again when you can't stay so long.

[In D. Welch, 'Sickert at St Peter's', *Horizon*, 1942]

SMITH, Sydney (1771–1845)

Tory and Whig in turns shall be my host,
I taste no politics in boil'd and roast.

[Letters, To John Murray, 1834]

HOUSE OF LORDS

BAGEHOT, Walter (1826–1877)

The House of Peers has never been a House where the most important peers were most important.

[*The English Constitution* (1867)]

A severe though not unfriendly critic of our institutions said that 'the cure for admiring the House of Lords was to go and look at it.'

[*The English Constitution* (1867)]

CHARLES II (1630–1685)

[On the Debates in the House of Lords on Lord Ross's Divorce Bill, 1670]
Better than going to a play.

[In A. Bryant, *King Charles II* (1931)]

CRANBORNE, Robert Cecil, Lord (1946–)

[Member of the Cecil family, represented in the House of Lords since 1603]
Thanks to Mr Blair, my family and I will be leaving British politics after a limited period of involvement.

[*The Observer*, 'Sayings of the Year', 1998]

DISRAELI, Benjamin (1804–1881)

[*Said to a fellow peer when moving on to the House of Lords*]
I am dead: dead, but in the Elysian fields.

[In Monypenny and Buckle, *Life of Disraeli*, (1920)]

HAILSHAM, Quintin Hogg, Baron (1907–)

When I'm sitting on the Woolsack in the House of Lords I amuse myself by saying 'Bollocks' sotto voce to the bishops.

[*The Observer*, 1985]

LLOYD GEORGE, David (1863–1945)

The House of Lords is not the watchdog of

the constitution: it is Mr Balfour's poodle.

[Speech, 1908]

Every man has a House of Lords in his own head. Fears, prejudices, misconceptions – those are the peers, and they are hereditary.

[Speech, Cambridge, 1927]

NORFOLK, Lord (1746–1815)

I cannot be a good Catholic; I cannot go to heaven; and if a man is to go to the devil, he may as well go thither from the House of Lords as from any other place on earth.

[In Henry Best, *Personal and Literary Memorials* (1829)]

ONSLOW, Lord (1938–)

[Opposing plans to reform the House of Lords]
I will be sad, if I look up or down after my death and don't see my son asleep on the same benches on which I slept.

[*The Observer*, 'Sayings of the Year' 1998]

PARRIS, Matthew (1949–)

[*On the House of Lords*]
Bishops are the unguided missiles of the Upper Chamber – unguided by human agency, anyway: you can never know what a bishop is about to say because all too often he does not know himself.

[*The Times*, 1998]

See ARISTOCRACY; GOVERNMENT; POLITICS

HOUSEWORK

ALCOTT, Louisa May (1832–1888)

Housekeeping ain't no joke.

[*Little Women* (1868)]

CRISP, Quentin (1908–)

There was no need to do any housework at all. After the first four years the dirt doesn't get any worse.

[*The Naked Civil Servant* (1968)]

DILLER, Phyllis (1917–1974)

Cleaning your house while your kids are growing

Is like shoveling the walk before it stops snowing.

[*Phyllis Diller's Housekeeping Hints*]

GIBBONS, Stella (1902–1989)

There's nothing like a thorn twig for cletterin' dishes.

[*Cold Comfort Farm* (1932)]

GREGORY, Lady Isabella Augusta (1852–1932)

I am so tired of housekeeping I dreamed I was being served up for my guests and awoke only when the knife was at my throat.

[In Mary-Lou Kohfeldt, *Lady Gregory* (1985)]

THURBER, James (1894–1961)

I was seized by the stern hand of Compulsion, that dark, unreasonable Urge that impels women to clean house in the middle of the night.

[*Alarms and Diversions*]

WHITE, Patrick (1912–1990)

The tragedy of domesticity, that avalanche of overcoats and boots.

[*The Aunt's Story* (1948)]

See FEMINISM; WOMEN

HUMANITY AND HUMAN NATURE

AUDEN, W.H. (1907–1973)

Man is a history-making creature who can neither repeat his past nor leave it behind.

[*The Dyer's Hand* (1963)]

Alone, alone, about a dreadful wood
Of conscious evil runs a lost mankind,
Dreading to find its Father.

['For the Time Being' (1945)]

AUSTEN, Jane (1775–1817)

Human nature is so well disposed towards those who are in interesting situations, that a young person, who either marries or dies, is sure of being kindly spoken of.

[*Emma* (1816)]

BACON, Francis (1561–1626)

There is in human nature generally more of the fool than of the wise.

[*Essays* (1625)]

Nature is often hidden; sometimes overcome; seldom extinguished.

[*Essays* (1625)]

BEAUMARCHAIS (1732–1799)

Boire sans soif et faire l'amour en tout temps, madame, il n'y a que ça qui nous distingue des autres bêtes.

Drinking when we're not thirsty and making love all the time, madam, that is all there is to distinguish us from other animals.

[*Le Barbier de Seville* (1775)]

BEERBOHM, Sir Max (1872–1956)

Mankind is divisible into two great classes: hosts and guests.

[Attr.]

THE BIBLE
(King James Version)

Man is born unto trouble, as the sparks fly upward.

[*Job*, 5:7]

As for man, his days are as grass: as a flower of the field, so he flourisheth.

[*Psalms*, 103:15]

BLACKSTONE, Sir William (1723–1780)

Man was formed for society.

[*Commentaries on the Laws of England* (1765–1769)]

BORROW, George (1803–1881)

My favourite, I might say, my only study, is man.

[*The Bible in Spain* (1843)]

BRADLEY, F.H. (1846–1924)

It is good to know what a man is, and also what the world takes him for. But you do not understand him until you have learnt how he understands himself.

[*Aphorisms* (1930)]

BROWNE, Sir Thomas (1605–1682)

There is surely a piece of divinity in us,

something that was before the elements, and owes no homage unto the sun.

[*Religio Medici* (1643)]

BRONOWSKI, Jacob (1908–1974)

Every animal leaves traces of what it was; man alone leaves traces of what he created.

[*The Ascent of Man* (1973)]

BRONTË, Anne (1820–1849)

The human heart is like Indian rubber: a little swells it, but a great deal will not burst it.

[*Agnes Grey* (1847)]

BROWNE, Sir Thomas (1605–1682)

Man is a noble animal, splendid in ashes, and pompous in the grave.

[*Hydriotaphia: Urn Burial* (1658)]

BÜCHNER, Georg (1813–1837)

Puppen sind wir von unbekannten Gewalten am Draht gezogen; nichts, nichts wir selbst!
We are puppets on strings worked by unknown forces; we ourselves are nothing, nothing!

[*Danton's Death* (1835)]

BURNS, Robert (1759–1796)

Man's inhumanity to man
Makes countless thousands mourn!

['Man was made to Mourn, a Dirge' (1784)]

BUTLER, Samuel (1835–1902)

'Man wants but little here below' but likes that little good – and not too long in coming.

[*Further Extracts from the Note-Books of Samuel Butler* (1934)]

Man is the only animal that can remain on friendly terms with the victims he intends to eat until he eats them.

[*Samuel Butler's Notebooks* (1951)]

CAMPBELL, Roy (1901–1957)

I hate 'Humanity' and all such abstracts: but I love people. Lovers of 'Humanity' generally hate people and children, and keep parrots or puppy dogs.

[*Light on a Dark Horse* (1951)]

CAMUS, Albert (1913–1960)

A single sentence will suffice for modern

man: he fornicated and read the papers.

[*The Fall* (1956)]

CANNING, George (1770–1827)

Man, only – rash, refined, presumptuous man,
Starts from his rank, and mars creation's plan.

['Progress of Man' (1799)]

CARLYLE, Thomas (1795–1881)

Man is a Tool-using Animal … feeblest of bipeds! … Without Tools he is nothing, with Tools he is all.

[*Sartor Resartus* (1834)]

CASWALL, Rev. Edward (1814–1878)

Man's chief end is to glorify God, and to enjoy him forever.

[Question 1]

All mankind by their fall lost communion with God, are under his wrath and curse, and so made liable to all the miseries in this life, to death itself, and to the pains of hell for ever.

[Question 19]

No mere man since the fall is able in this life perfectly to keep the commandments of God, but doth daily break them in thought, word, and deed.

[Question 82]

CERVANTES, Miguel de (1547–1616)

Cada uno es como Dios le hizo, y aun peor muchas veces.
Every man is as God made him, and often even worse.

[*Don Quixote* (1615)]

CHARRON, Pierre (1541–1603)

La vraye science et la vray estude de l'homme, c'est l'homme.
The true science and the true study of man is man.

[*De la Sagesse* (1601)]

CHESTERTON, G.K. (1874–1936)

The human race, to which so many of my readers belong, has been playing at children's games from the beginning, and will probably do it till the end, which is a nuisance for the few people who grow up.

[*The Napoleon of Notting Hill* (1904)]

Individually, men may present a more or less rational appearance, eating, sleeping and scheming. But humanity as a whole is changeful, mystical, fickle and delightful. Men are men, but Man is a woman.

[*The Napoleon of Notting Hill* (1904)]

COLERIDGE, Samuel Taylor (1772–1834)

A Fall of some sort or other – the creation as it were, of the non-absolute – is the fundamental postulate of the moral history of man. Without this hypothesis, man is unintelligible; with it, every phenomenon is explicable.

[*Table-Talk* (1835)]

COLTON, Charles Caleb (c.1780–1832)

Man is an embodied paradox, a bundle of contradictions.

[*Lacon* (1820)]

CONFUCIUS (c.550–c.478 BC)

Men's natures are alike; it is their habits that carry them far apart.

[*Analects*]

DISRAELI, Benjamin (1804–1881)

[Addressed to Bishop Wilberforce]
Man, my Lord, is a being born to believe.

[Speech, Meeting of Society for Increasing Endowments of Small Livings in the Diocese of Oxford, 1864]

Man is only truly great when he acts from the passions.

[*Coningsby* (1844)]

DONLEAVY, J.P. (1926–)

I got disappointed in human nature as well and gave it up because I found it too much like my own.

[*Fairy Tales of New York* (1961)]

DONNE, John (1572–1631)

No man is an Island, entire of it self; every man is a piece of Continent, a part of the main; if a clod be washed away by the sea,

Europe is the less, as well as if a promontory were, as well as if a manor of thy friends or of thine own were; any man's death diminishes me, because I am involved in Mankind; And therefore never send to know for whom the bell tolls; it tolls for thee.

[*Devotions upon Emergent Occasions* (1624)]

ELIOT, George (1819–1880)

There is a great deal of unmapped country within us which would have to be taken into account in an explanation of our gusts and storms.

[*Daniel Deronda* (1876)]

ELIOT, T.S. (1888–1965)

Human kind
Cannot bear very much reality.

[*Four Quartets* (1944)]

FROUDE, James Anthony (1818–1894)

Wild animals never kill for sport. Man is the only one to whom the torture and death of his fellow creatures is amusing in itself.

[*Oceana, or England and her Colonies* (1886)]

GOLDSMITH, Oliver (c.1728–1774)

Man wants but little here below,
Nor wants that little long.

[*The Vicar of Wakefield* (1766)]

GORKY, Maxim (1868–1936)

Man and man alone is, I believe, the creator of all things and all ideas.

[Attr.]

GREVILLE, Fulke (1554–1628)

Oh wearisome Condition of Humanity!
Borne under one Law, to another, bound:
Vainely begot, and yet forbidden vanity,
Created sicke, commanded to be sound.

[*Mustapha* (1609)]

HAZLITT, William (1778–1830)

Man is an intellectual animal, and therefore an everlasting contradiction to himself. His senses centre in himself, his ideas reach to the ends of the universe; so that he is torn in pieces between the two, without a possibility of its ever being otherwise.

[*Characteristics* (1823)]

HERBERT, George (1593–1633)

Man is God's image, but a poore man is Christ's stamp to boot.

[*The Temple* (1633)]

JOHNSON, Samuel (1709–1784)

Sir, are you so grossly ignorant of human nature, as not to know that a man may be very sincere in good principles without having good practice?

[In Boswell, *Journal of a Tour to the Hebrides* (1785), 25 October 1773]

JUNG, Carl Gustav (1875–1961)

We need more understanding of human nature, because the only real danger that exists is man himself … We know nothing of man, far too little. His psyche should be studied because we are the origin of all coming evil.

[BBC television interview, 1959]

KANT, Immanuel (1724–1804)

Aus so krummen Holze, als woraus der Mensch gemacht ist, kann nichts ganz Gerades gezimmert werden.

No straight thing can ever be formed from timber as crooked as that from which humanity is made.

[*Idea for a General History with a Cosmopolitan purpose* (1784)]

Ob … der Mensch nun von Natur moralisch gut oder böse ist? Keines von beiden, denn er ist von Natur gar kein moralisches Wesen; er wird dieses nur, wenn seine Vernunft sich bis zu den Begriffen der Pflicht und des Gesetzes erhebt.

Is man by nature morally good or evil? Neither, for he is by nature not a moral being; he only becomes such when his reason is raised to the concepts of duty and law.

[‹On Pedagogy› (1803)]

KEATS, John (1795–1821)

Scenery is fine – but human nature is finer.

[Letter to Benjamin Bailey, 13 March 1818]

Upon the whole I dislike Mankind: whatever people on the other side of the question may advance they cannot deny that they are always surprised at hearing of a good action and never of a bad one.

[Letter to Georgiana Keats, 13–28 January, 1820]

KINGSMILL, Hugh (1889–1949)

It is difficult to love mankind unless one has a reasonable private income and when one has a reasonable private income one has better things to do than loving mankind.

[In R. Ingrams, *God's Apology* (1977)]

LA BRUYÈRE, Jean de (1645–1696)

La plupart des hommes emploient la meilleure partie de leur vie á rendre l'autre misérable.

Most men spend the best part of their lives in making their remaining years unhappy.

[*Les caractères ou les moeurs de ce siècle* (1688)]

LAWRENCE, D.H. (1885–1930)

Ideal mankind would abolish death, multiply itself million upon million, rear up city upon city, save every parasite alive, until the accumulation of mere existence is swollen to a horror.

[*St Mawr* (1925)]

LEE, Nathaniel (c.1653–1692)

Man, false man, smiling, destructive man.

[*Theodosius* (1680)]

LONGFELLOW, Henry Wadsworth (1807–1882)

Ships that pass in the night, and speak each other in passing;
Only a signal shown and a distant voice in the darkness;
So on the ocean of life we pass and speak one another,
Only a look and a voice; then darkness again and a silence.

[*Tales of a Wayside Inn* (1863–1874)]

MACHIAVELLI (1469–1527)

Dio fa gli uomini, è s'appaiono.

God creates men, but they choose each other.

[*The Mandrake* (1518)]

Men sooner forget the death of their father than the loss of their possessions.

[*The Prince*, 1532]

MAUGHAM, William Somerset (1874–1965)

I'll give you my opinion of the human race. … Their heart's in the right place, but their head is a thoroughly inefficient organ.

[*The Summing Up* (1938)]

MILLAY, Edna St Vincent (1892–1950)

Man has never been the same since God died.
He has taken it very hard. Why, you'd think it was only yesterday,
The way he takes it.
Not that he says much, but he laughs much louder than he used to,
And he can't bear to be left alone even for a minute, and he can't
Sit still.

[*Conversation at Midnight* (1937)]

MONASH, Sir John (1865–1931)

Nothing man does to the animal creation is equal to the cruelties he commits on his own kind.

[*The Seals*]

MONTAIGNE, Michel de (1533–1592)

L'homme est bien insensé. Il ne saurait forger un ciron, et forge des Dieux á douzaines.
Man is quite insane. He wouldn't know how to create a maggot, yet he creates Gods by the dozen.

[*Essais* (1580)]

NIETZSCHE, Friedrich Wilhelm (1844–1900)

Wie? ist der Mensch nur ein Fehlgriff Gottes? Oder Gott nur ein Fehlgriff des Meschen?
What? is man only a mistake made by God, or God only a mistake made by man?

[*Twilight of the Idols* (1889)]

O'BRIEN, Flann (1911–1966)

The pocket was the first instinct of humanity and was used long years before the human race had a trousers between them – the quiver for arrows is one example and the pocket of the kangaroo is another.

[*At Swim-Two-Birds* (1939)]

ORWELL, George (1903–1950)

The high sentiments always win in the end, leaders who offer blood, toil, tears and sweat always get more out of their followers than those who offer safety and a good time. When it comes to the pinch, human beings are heroic.

[*Horizon*, 1941]

Man is the only creature that consumes without producing.

[*Animal Farm* (1945)]

PASCAL, Blaise (1623–1662)

L'homme n'est qu'un roseau, le plus faible de la nature; mais c'est un roseau pensant.
Man is only a reed, the feeblest thing in nature; but he is a thinking reed.

[*Pensées* (1670)]

PLAUTUS, Titus Maccius (c.254–184 BC)

Lupus est homo homini.
Man is a wolf to man.

[*Asinaria*]

POPE, Alexander (1688–1744)

Know then thyself, presume not God to scan;
The proper study of Mankind is Man.
Plac'd on this isthmus of a middle state,
A being darkly wise, and rudely great:
With too much knowledge for the Sceptic side,
With too much weakness for the Stoic's pride,
He hangs between; in doubt to act or rest,
In doubt to deem himself a God, or Beast;
In doubt his Mind or Body to prefer,
Born but to die, and reas'ning but to err;
Alike in ignorance, his reason such,
Whether he thinks too little or too much.

[*An Essay on Man* (1733)]

Created half to rise, and half to fall;
Great lord of all things, yet a prey to all;
Sole judge of truth, in endless error hurl'd:
The glory, jest, and riddle of the world!

[*An Essay on Man* (1733)]

POUND, Ezra (1885–1972)

When I carefully consider the curious habits

of dogs
I am compelled to conclude
That man is the superior animal.

When I consider the curious habits of man
I confess, my friend, I am puzzled.

['Meditatio' (1916)]

PROTAGORAS (c.485–c.410 BC)

Man is the measure of all things.

[In Plato, *Theaetetus*]

QUARLES, Francis (1592–1644)

No man is born unto himself alone;
Who lives unto himself, he lives to none.

['Esther' (1621)]

Man is Heaven's masterpiece.

[*Emblems* (1635)]

Man is man's A.B.C. There is none that can
Read God aright, unless he first spell Man.

[*Hieroglyphics of the Life of Man* (1638)]

RALEIGH, Sir Walter A. (1861–1922)

I wish I loved the Human Race;
I wish I loved its silly face;
I wish I liked the way it walks;
I wish I liked the way it talks;
And when I'm introduced to one,
I wish I thought What Jolly Fun!

['Wishes of an Elderly Man' (1923)]

ROUSSEAU, Jean-Jacques (1712–1778)

La nature a fait l'homme heureux et bon, mais … la société le déprave et le rend misérable.
Nature made man happy and good, but … society corrupts him and makes him miserable.

[*Rousseau juge de Jean-Jacques*]

RUSKIN, John (1819–1900)

No human being, however great, or powerful, was ever so free as a fish.

[*The Two Paths* (1859)]

SARTRE, Jean-Paul (1905–1980)

Ainsi, il n'y a pas de nature humaine, puisqu'il n'y a pas de Dieu pour la concevoir.
So there is no human nature, since there is no God to conceive it.

[*Existentialism and Humanism* (1946)]

SCHILLER, Johann Christoph Friedrich (1759–1805)

Der zahlreichere Teil der Menschen wird durch den Kampf mit der Not viel zu sehr ermüdet und abgespannt, als dass er sich zu einem neuen und härtern Kampf mit dem Irrtum aufraffen sollte.
The greater part of humanity is far too weary and worn down by the struggle with want to rouse itself for a new and harder struggle with error.

[*On the Aesthetic Education of Man* (1793–1795)]

Das Herz und nicht die Meinung ehrt den Mann.
Man is honoured by his heart and not by his opinions.

[*Wallensteins Tod* (1801)]

SHAKESPEARE, William (1564–1616)

What a piece of work is a man! How noble in reason! how infinite in faculties! in form and moving, how express and admirable! in action, how like an angel! in apprehension, how like a god! the beauty of the world! the paragon of animals!

[*Hamlet*, II.ii]

Roses have thorns, and silver fountains mud;
Clouds and eclipses stain both moon and sun,
And loathsome canker lives in sweetest bud.
All men make faults.

[Sonnet 35]

SHAW, George Bernard (1856–1950)

Man can climb to the highest summits; but he cannot dwell there long.

[*Candida* (1898)]

SOPHOCLES (496–406 BC)

Of wonders there are many, but none more wonderful than man.

[*Antigone*]

TAINE, Hippolyte Adolphe (1828–1893)

On peut considérer l'homme comme un animal d'espèce supérieure qui produit des philosophies et des poèmes á peu près comme les vers á soie font

leurs cocons et comme les abeilles font leurs ruches.
Man can be considered as a superior animal
who produces philosophies and poems
much as silkworms construct their cocoons
and bees their hives.

[*La Fontaine and his Fables*, 1860]

TEMPLE, William (1881–1944)
It is not the ape, nor the tiger in man that I
fear, it is the donkey.

[Attr.]

TERENCE (c.190–159 BC)
Homo sum; humani nil a me alienum puto.
I am a man, I count nothing human
indifferent to me.

[*Heauton Timoroumenos*]

TERTZ, Abram (1925–1997)
Man is always both much worse and much
better than is expected of him. The fields of
good are just as limitless as the wastelands
of evil.

[*A Voice From the Chorus* (1973)]

THOREAU, Henry David (1817–1862)
The finest qualities of our nature, like the
bloom on fruits, can be preserved only by
the most delicate handling. Yet we do not
treat ourselves nor one another delicately.

[*Walden* (1854)]

TWAIN, Mark (1835–1910)
Adam was but human – this explains it all. He
did not want the apple for the apple's sake,
he wanted it only because it was forbidden.

[*Pudd'nhead Wilson* (1894)]

Man is the Only Animal that Blushes. Or
needs to.

[*Following the Equator* (1897)]

UNAMUNO, Miguel de (1864–1936)
*El hombre, por ser hombre, por tener conciencia, es
ya, respecto al burro o a un cangrejo, un animal
enfermo. La conciencia es una enfermedad.*
Man, because he is man, because he is
conscious, is, in relation to the ass or to a
crab, already a diseased animal.
Consciousness is a disease.

[*The Tragic Sense of Life* (1913)]

VALÉRY, Paul (1871–1945)
A man is infinitely more complicated than his
thoughts.

[In Auden, *A Certain World*]

VAUGHAN, Henry (1622–1695)
Man is the shuttle, to whose winding quest
And passage through these looms
God order'd motion, but ordain'd no rest.

[*Silex Scintillans* (1650–1655)]

VOLTAIRE (1694–1778)
*Si Dieu nous a fait á son image, nous le lui avons bien
rendu.*
If God has created us in his image, we have
repaid him well.

[*Le Sottisier* (c. 1778)]

WAUGH, Evelyn (1903–1966)
Instead of this absurd division into sexes
they ought to class people as static and
dynamic.

[*Decline and Fall* (1928)]

WILDE, Oscar (1854–1900)
It is absurd to divide people into good and
bad. People are either charming or tedious.

[*Lady Windermere's Fan* (1892)]

YEVTUSHENKO, Yevgeny (1933–)
In the final analysis, humanity has only two
ways out – either universal destruction or
universal brotherhood.

['The Spirit of Elbe' (1966)]

See LIFE

HUMILITY

DICKENS, Charles (1812–1870)
I am well aware that I am the umblest person
going … My mother is likewise a very umble
person. We live in a numble abode.

[*David Copperfield* (1850)]

STILLINGFLEET, Edward (1635–1699)
'My Lord,' a certain nobleman is said to have
observed, after sitting next to [Richard]
Bentley at dinner, 'that chaplain of yours is a
very extraordinary man.' Stillingfleet agreed,

adding, 'Had he but the gift of humility, he would be the most extraordinary man in Europe.'

[In R.J. White, *Dr Bentley*]

TROLLOPE, Anthony (1815–1882)

Not only humble but umble, which I look upon to be the comparative, or, indeed, superlative degree.

[*Doctor Thorne* (1858)]

HUMOUR

ADDISON, Joseph (1672–1719)

If we may believe our logicians, man is distinguished from all other creatures by the faculty of laughter.

[*The Spectator*, 1712]

AYCKBOURN, Alan (1939–)

Few women care to be laughed at and men not at all, except for large sums of money.

[*The Norman Conquests* (1975)]

BARKER, Ronnie (1929–)

The marvellous thing about a joke with a double meaning is that it can only mean one thing.

[Attr.]

BEAUMARCHAIS (1732–1799)

Je me presse de rire de tout, de peur d'être obligé d'en pleurer.
I make myself laugh at everything, for fear of having to cry.

[*Le Barbier de Seville* (1775)]

BERLIN, Irving (1888–1989)

[*Telegram message to Groucho Marx on his seventy-first birthday*]
The world would not be in such a snarl, had Marx been Groucho instead of Karl.

[Attr.]

BRACKEN, Brendan, First Viscount (1901–1958)

It's a good deed to forget a poor joke.

[*The Observer*, 1943]

BROWN, Thomas Edward (1830–1897)

A rich man's joke is always funny.

['The Doctor' (1887)]

BUTLER, Samuel (1835–1902)

The most perfect humour and irony is generally quite unconscious.

[*Life and Habit* (1877)]

CARLYLE, Thomas (1795–1881)

No man who has once heartily and wholly laughed can be altogether irreclaimably bad.

[*Sartor Resartus* (1834)]

CHAMFORT, Nicolas (1741–1794)

La plus perdue de toutes les journées est celle où l'on n'a pas ri.
The most wasted of all days is the day one did not laugh.

[*Maximes et pensées* (1796)]

CHESTERFIELD, Lord (1694–1773)

In my mind, there is nothing so illiberal and so ill-bred, as audible laughter … I am neither of a melancholy, nor a cynical disposition; and am as willing, and as apt, to be pleased as anybody; but I am sure that, since I have had the full use of my reason, nobody has ever heard me laugh.

[Letter to his son, 1748]

CHURCHILL, Charles (1731–1764)

A joke's a very serious thing.

[*The Ghost* (1763)]

COLBY, Frank Moore (1865–1925)

Men will confess to treason, murder, arson, false teeth, or a wig. How many of them will own up to a lack of humour?

[*Essays*]

COLETTE (1873–1954)

Une totale absence d'humour rend la vie impossible.
A total absence of humour makes life impossible.

[*Chance Acquaintances*]

CONGREVE, William (1670–1729)

It is the business of a comic poet to paint the vices and follies of human kind.

There is nothing more unbecoming a man of

quality than to laugh; Jesu, 'tis such a vulgar expression of the passion!

[*The Double Dealer* (1694)]

DENNIS, John (1657–1734)

A man who could make so vile a pun would not scruple to pick a pocket.

[*The Gentleman's Magazine*, 1781]

DODD, Ken (1931–)

[Commenting on Freud's theory that a good joke will lead to great relief and elation]
The trouble with Freud is that he never played the Glasgow Empire Saturday night after Rangers and Celtic had both lost.

[TV interview, 1965]

ELIOT, George (1819–1880)

A difference of taste in jokes is a great strain on the affections.

[*Daniel Deronda* (1876)]

GRIFFITHS, Trevor (1935–)

Comedy is medicine.

[*The Comedians* (1979)]

HOBBES, Thomas (1588–1679)

Laughter is nothing else but sudden glory arising from some sudden conception of some eminency in ourselves, by comparison with infirmity of others, or with our own formerly.

[*Human Nature* (1650)]

HUMPHRIES, Barry (1934–)

The only people really keeping the spirit of irony alive in Australia are taxi-drivers and homosexuals.

[*Australian Women's Weekly*, 1983]

LA BRUYÈRE, Jean de (1645–1696)

Il faut rire avant que d'être heureux, de peur de mourir sans avoir ri.
One must laugh before one is happy, for fear of dying without ever having laughed at all.

[*Les caractères ou les moeurs de ce siècle* (1688)]

LAMB, Charles (1775–1834)

[Referring to the nature of a pun]
It is a pistol let off at the ear; not a feather to

tickle the intellect.

[*Last Essays of Elia* (1833)]

LEWIS, C.S. (1898–1963)

The coarse joke proclaims that we have here an animal which finds its own animality either objectionable or funny.

[*Miracles* (c. 1936)]

LICHTENBERG, Georg (1742–1799)

A person reveals his character by nothing so clearly as the joke he resents.

[Attr.]

MUGGERIDGE, Malcolm (1903–1990)

It is not for nothing that, in the English language alone, to accuse someone of trying to be funny is highly abusive.

[*Tread Softly* (1966)]

ORWELL, George (1903–1950)

Whatever is funny is subversive, every joke is ultimately a custard pie … A dirty joke is not … a serious attack upon morality, but it is a sort of mental rebellion, a momentary wish that things were otherwise.

['The Art of Donald McGill' (1941)]

OWEN, Roderic (1921–)

The important thing is to know when to laugh, or since laughing is somewhat undignified, to smile.

[*The Golden Bubble*]

PRIESTLEY, J.B. (1894–1984)

Comedy, we may say, is society protecting itself – with a smile.

[*George Meredith* (1926)]

RENARD, Jules (1864–1910)

L'ironie est la pudeur de l'humanité.
Irony is humanity's sense of propriety.

[*Journal*, 1892]

ROGERS, Will (1879–1935)

Everything is funny as long as it is happening to someone else.

[*The Illiterate Digest* (1924)]

SHAW, George Bernard (1856–1950)

My way of joking is to tell the truth. It's the

funniest joke in the world.
[*John Bull's Other Island* (1907)]

STERNE, Laurence (1713–1768)

'Tis no extravagant arithmetic to say, that for every ten jokes, – thou hast got a hundred enemies.
[*Tristram Shandy*]

I live in a constant endeavour to fence against the infirmities of ill health, and other evils of life, by mirth; being firmly persuaded that every time a man smiles, – but much more so, when he laughs, it adds something to this Fragment of Life.
[*Tristram Shandy*]

STEVENSON, Robert Louis (1850–1894)

Nothing like a little judicious levity.
[*The Wrong Box* (1889)]

SWIFT, Jonathan (1667–1745)

Humour is odd, grotesque, and wild,
Only by affectation spoil'd;
'Tis never by invention got,
Men have it when they know it not.
['To Mr Delany' (1718)]

THURBER, James (1894–1961)

Humour is emotional chaos remembered in tranquillity.
[Attr.]

TUCHOLSKY, Kurt (1890–1935)

Humor ist ein Element, das dem deutschen Menschen abhanden gekommen ist.
Humour is an element which the German man has lost.
['What may Satire do –?' (1973)]

WALTON, Izaak (1593–1683)

I love such mirth as does not make friends ashamed to look upon one another next morning.
[*The Compleat Angler* (1653)]

WILCOX, Ella Wheeler (1850–1919)

Laugh and the world laughs with you;
Weep, and you weep alone;
For the sad old earth must borrow its mirth,

But has trouble enough of its own.
['Solitude' (1917)]

WODEHOUSE, P.G. (1881–1975)

She had a penetrating sort of laugh. Rather like a train going into a tunnel.
[*The Inimitable Jeeves* (1923)]

HUNGER

KENNEDY, John F. (1917–1963)

The war against hunger is truly mankind's war of liberation.
[Speech, 4 June 1963]

MARY-ANTOINETTE (1755–1793)

[On being told the people had no bread to eat] Let them eat cake.
[attr.]

PROVERBS

The full man doesn't understand the wants of the hungry.

Hunger finds no fault with the cookery.

Hunger is the best sauce.

See DESIRE; FOOD

HYPOCRISY

BACON, Francis (1561–1626)

It is the wisdom of the crocodiles, that shed tears when they would devour.
['Of Wisdom for a Man's Self' (1625)]

Even innocence itself has many a wile,
And will not dare to trust itself with truth,
And love is taught hypocrisy from youth.
[*Don Juan* (1824)]

CHAUCER, Geoffrey (c.1340–1400)

The smylere with the knyf under the cloke.
[*The Canterbury Tales* (1387)]

CHESTERTON, G.K. (1874–1936)

We ought to see far enough into a hypocrite to see even his sincerity.
[*Heretics* (1905)]

CHURCHILL, Charles (1731–1764)

Keep up appearances; there lies the test;
The world will give thee credit for the rest.
Outward be fair, however foul within;
Sin if thou wilt, but then in secret sin.

[*'Night'* (1761)]

DICKENS, Charles (1812–1870)

With affection beaming in one eye, and
calculation shining out of the other.

[*Martin Chuzzlewit* (1844)]

EMERSON, Ralph Waldo (1803–1882)

The book written against fame and learning
has the author's name on the title-page.

[*Journals*]

GAY, John (1685–1732)

An open foe may prove a curse,
But a pretended friend is worse.

[*Fables* (1727)]

HAWTHORNE, Nathaniel (1804–1864)

I have laughed in bitterness and agony of
heart, at the contrast between what I seem
and what I am!

[*The Scarlet Letter* (1850)]

KERR, Jean (1923–)

Man is the only animal that learns by being
hypocritical. He pretends to be polite and
then, eventually, he becomes polite.

[*Finishing Touches* (1973)]

LA ROCHEFOUCAULD (1613–1680)

*L'hypocrisie est un hommage que le vice rend á la
vertu.*

Hypocrisy is a homage that vice pays to
virtue.

[*Maximes* (1678)]

MAUGHAM, William Somerset (1874–1965)

Hypocrisy is the most difficult and nerve-
racking vice that any man can pursue; it
needs an unceasing vigilance and a rare
detachment of spirit. It cannot, like adultery
or gluttony, be practised at spare moments; it
is a whole-time job.

[*Cakes and Ale* (1930)]

MILTON, John (1608–1674)

For neither Man nor Angel can discern
Hypocrisie, the onely evil that walks
Invisible, except to God alone.

[*Paradise Lost* (1667)]

TOLSTOY, Leo (1828–1910)

Hypocrisy in anything whatever may deceive
the cleverest and most penetrating man, but
the least wide-awake of children recognizes
it, and is revolted by it, however ingeniously
it may be disguised.

[Attr.]

WILDE, Oscar (1854–1900)

I hope that you have not been leading a
double life, pretending to be wicked and
being really good all the time. That would be
hypocrisy.

[*The Importance of Being Earnest* (1895)]

See DECEPTION

IDEALISM

DALAI LAMA (1935–)
History shows that most of the positive or beneficial developments in human society have occurred as the result of care and compassion. Consider, for example, the abolition of the slave trade – Ideals are the engine of progress.
[*The Times*, June 1999]

KING, Martin Luther (1929–1968)
I submit to you that if a man hasn't discovered something he will die for, he isn't fit to live.
[Speech in Detroit, June 23, 1963]

LAWRENCE, D.H. (1885–1930)
Away with all ideals. Let each individual act spontaneously from the for ever incalculable prompting of the creative wellhead within him. There is no universal law.
[*Phoenix* (1936)]

MCCARTNEY, Paul (1942–)
The issues are the same. We wanted peace on earth, love, and understanding between everyone around the world. We have learned that change comes slowly.
[*The Observer*, 1987]

TARKINGTON, Booth (1869–1946)
An ideal wife is any woman who has an ideal husband.
[Attr.]

THATCHER, Margaret (1925–)
If a woman like Eva Peron with no ideals can get that far, think how far I can go with all the ideals that I have.
[*The Sunday Times*, 1980]

IDEAS

ALAIN (EMILE-AUGUSTE CHARTIER) (1868–1951)
Rien n'est plus dangereux qu'une idée, quand on n'a qu'une idée.
Nothing is more dangerous than an idea, when you only have one idea.
[*Remarks on Religion* (1938)]

There are only two kinds of scholars; those who love ideas and those who hate them.
[In Alan L. Mackay, *The Harvest of a Quiet Eye* (1977)]

BAGEHOT, Walter (1826–1877)
One of the greatest pains to human nature is the pain of a new idea.
[*Physics and Politics* (1872)]

BOWEN, Elizabeth (1899–1973)
One can live in the shadow of an idea without grasping it.
[*The Heat of the Day* (1949)]

EMERSON, Ralph Waldo (1803–1882)
It is a lesson which all history teaches wise men, to put trust in ideas, and not in circumstances.
[*Miscellanies* (1856)]

GEDDES, Patrick (1854–1932)
When an idea is dead it is embalmed in a textbook.
[In Boardman, *The Worlds of Patrick Geddes* (1978)]

HOLMES, Oliver Wendell, Jr (1841–1935)
Many ideas grow better when transplanted into another mind than in the one where they sprang up.
[In Bowen, *Yankee from Olympus* (1945)]

HUGO, Victor (1802–1885)
On résiste á l'invasion des armées; on ne résiste pas á l'invasion des idées.
One can resist the invasion of an army; but one cannot resist the invasion of ideas.
[*Histoire d'un Crime* (1852)]

JARRELL, Randall (1914–1965)
It is better to entertain an idea than to take it

home to live with you for the rest of your life.

[*Pictures from an Institution* (1954)]

KEYNES, John Maynard (1883–1946)

The difficulty lies, not in the new ideas, but in escaping the old ones, which ramify, for those brought up as most of us have been, into every corner of our minds.

[In K. Eric Drexler *Engines of Creation*, 1987]

The power of vested interests is vastly exaggerated compared with the gradual encroachment of ideas. Not, indeed, immediately … But, soon or late, it is ideas, not vested interests, which are dangerous for good or evil.

[*The General Theory of Employment, Interest and Money* (1936)]

LEWIS, Wyndham (1882–1957)

'Dying for an idea,' again, sounds well enough, but why not let the idea die instead of you?

[*The Art of Being Ruled* (1926)]

LORENZ, Konrad (1903–1989)

‹berhaupt ist es für den Forscher ein guter Morgensport, täglich vor dem Frühstück eine Lieblingshypothese einzustampfen – das erhält jung. In general it is a good morning exercise for a researcher to destroy a favourite hypothesis every day before breakfast – it keeps him young.

[*On Aggression* (1963)]

MACDONALD, Ramsay (1866–1937)

Society goes on and on and on. It is the same with ideas.

[Speech, 1935]

MARQUIS, Don (1878–1937)

An idea isn't responsible for the people who believe in it.

[*New York Sun*]

MEDAWAR, Sir Peter Brian (1915–1987)

The human mind treats a new idea the way the body treats a strange protein – it rejects it.

[Attr.]

MONTAGU, Lady Mary Wortley (1689–1762)

General notions are generally wrong.

[Letter to her husband, Edward Wortley Montagu, 1710]

PAXMAN, Jeremy (1950–)

The English way with ideas is not to kill them but to let them die of neglect.

[*The Observer*, 'Sayings of the Year', 1998]

SANTAYANA, George (1863–1952)

For an idea ever to be fashionable is ominous, since it must afterwards be always old-fashioned.

[*Winds of Doctrine* (1913)]

SHAW, George Bernard (1856–1950)

This creature Man, who in his own selfish affairs is a coward to the backbone, will fight for an idea like a hero.

[*Man and Superman* (1903)]

STERNE, Laurence (1713–1768)

It is the nature of an hypothesis, when once a man has conceived it, that it assimilates every thing to itself as proper nourishment; and, from the first moment of your begetting it, it generally grows the stronger by every thing you see, hear, read, or understand. This is of great use.

[*Tristram Shandy* (1759–1767)]

SWIFT, Jonathan (1667–1745)

A nice man is a man of nasty ideas.

[*Thoughts on Various Subjects* (1711)]

UNAMUNO, Miguel de (1864–1936)

No suelen ser nuestras ideas las que nos hacen optimistas o pesimistas, sino que es nuestro optimismo o nuestro pesimismo, de origen fisiológico o patológico quizás … el que hace nuestras ideas. It is not normally our ideas which make us optimists or pessimists, but it is our optimism or our pessimism, which is perhaps of a physiological or pathological origin … which makes our ideas.

[*The Tragic Sense of Life* (1913)]

See MIND; OPINIONS; THOUGHT

IDLENESS AND UNEMPLOYMENT

ADAMS, Scott (1957–)

Of course I don't look busy, I did it right the first time.

[*The Dilbert Principle*]

ANONYMOUS

Doing nothing gets pretty tiresome because you can't stop and rest.

BOILEAU-DESPRÉAUX, Nicolas (1636–1711)

Le pénible fardeau de n'avoir rien á faire!

What a terrible burden it is to have nothing to do!

[*Epitres* (c. 1690)]

BRASCH, Charles Orwell (1909–1973)

[On walking on a week-day in Dunedin, 1938, when he was unemployed]

It is not only an offence against society to be seen in the streets flaunting the fact that one does not work like everyone else; it challenges the settled order of things, a threat that no right thinking New Zealander could tolerate. It makes one an object of suspicion, and more, an enemy.

[*Indirections: A Memoir 1909–1947* (1980)]

BRUMMEL, Beau (1778–1840)

I always like to have the morning well-aired before I get up.

[In Macfarlane, *Reminiscences of a Literary Life* (1917)]

CHESTERFIELD, Lord (1694–1773)

Idleness is only the refuge of weak minds, and the holiday of fools.

[Letter to his son, 1749]

CICERO (106–43 BC)

Numquam se minus otiosum esse quam cum otiosus, nec minus solum quam cum solus esset.

Never less idle than when free from work, nor less lonely than when completely alone.

[*De Officiis*]

CONRAN, Shirley (1932–)

I make no secret of the fact that I would rather lie on a sofa than sweep beneath it.

But you have to be efficient if you're going to be lazy.

[*Superwoman* (1975)]

COWPER, William (1731–1800)

How various his employments, whom the world
Calls idle.

[*The Task* (1785)]

ELIOT, George (1819–1880)

There's many a one would be idle if hunger didn't pinch him; but the stomach sets us to work.

[*Felix Holt* (1866)]

EWART, Gavin (1916–1995)

After Cambridge – unemployment. No one wanted much to know.
Good degrees are good for nothing in the business world below.

['The Sentimental Education']

FARQUHAR, George (1678–1707)

Says little, thinks less, and does – nothing at all, faith.

[*The Beaux' Stratagem* (1707)]

FITZGERALD, F. Scott (1896–1940)

'What'll we do with ourselves this afternoon?' cried Daisy, 'and the day after that, and the next thirty years?'.

[*The Great Gatsby* (1925)]

FURPHY, Joseph (1843–1912)

Unemployed at last!

[*Such is Life* (1903)]

HEWETT, Dorothy (1923–)

For dole bread is bitter bread
Bitter bread and sour
There's grief in the taste of it
There's weevils in the flour.

['Weevils in the Flour']

HOOVER, Herbert Clark (1874–1964)

When a great many people are unable to find work, unemployment results.

[In Boller, *Presidential Anecdotes* (1981)]

JEROME, Jerome K. (1859–1927)

It is impossible to enjoy idling thoroughly

unless one has plenty of work to do.

[*Idle Thoughts of an Idle Fellow* (1886)]

George goes to sleep at a bank from ten to four each day, except Saturdays, when they wake him up and put him outside at two.

[*Three Men in a Boat* (1889)]

JOHNSON, Samuel (1709–1784)

Every man is, or hopes to be, an idler.

[*The Idler* (1758–1760)]

If you are idle, be not solitary; if you are solitary, be not idle.

[Letter to Boswell, 1779]

JOSEPH, Jenny

I was raised to feel that doing nothing was a sin. I had to learn to do nothing.

[*The Observer*, 1998]

JOWETT, Benjamin (1817–1893)

Research! A mere excuse for idleness; it has never achieved, and will never achieve any results of the slightest value.

[In Logan Pearsall Smith, *Unforgotten Years*]

KEMPIS, Thomas á (c.1380–1471)

Never be completely idle, but be either reading, or writing, or praying, or meditating, or working at something useful for the community.

[*De Imitatione Christi* (1892)]

LYNES, J. Russel (1910–1991)

Wasting time is negative, but there is something positive about idleness.

MADAN, Geoffrey (1895–1947)

The devil finds mischief still for hands that have not learnt how to be idle.

[*Livre sans nom: Twelve Reflections* (1934)]

MARX, Karl (1818–1883)

Without doubt machinery has greatly increased the number of well-to-do idlers.

[*Das Kapital* (1867)]

MAUGHAM, William Somerset (1874–1965)

It was such a lovely day I thought it was a

pity to get up.

[*Our Betters* (1923)]

NASH, Ogden (1902–1971)

I would live my life in nonchalance and insouciance
Were it not for making a living, which is rather a nouciance.

['Introspective Reflection' (1940)]

POPE, Alexander (1688–1744)

She marked thee there,
Stretch'd on the rack of a too easy chair,
And heard thy everlasting yawn confess
The Pains and Penalties of idleness.

[*The Dunciad* (1742)]

PROVERB

The devil finds work for idle hands to do.

SAMUEL, Lord (1870–1963)

To help the unemployed is not the same thing as dealing with unemployment.

[*The Observer*, 1933]

SHERIDAN, Richard Brinsley (1751–1816)

[On a notice fixed to his door when he was a Secretary to the Treasury]
No applications can be received here on Sundays, nor any business done during the remainder of the week.

[Attr. in Morwood, *The Life and Works of Sheridan* (1985)]

STEELE, Sir Richard (1672–1729)

The insupportable Labour of doing nothing.

[*The Spectator*, 54, 1711]

STEVENSON, Robert Louis (1850–1894)

Extreme busyness, whether at school or college, kirk or market, is a symptom of deficient vitality; and a faculty for idleness implies a catholic appetite and a strong sense of personal identity.

[*Virginibus Puerisque* (1881)]

THURBER, James (1894–1961)

It is better to have loafed and lost than never

to have loafed at all.

[*Fables for Our Time* (1940)]

WARD, Artemus (1834–1867)

I am happiest when I am idle. I could live for months without performing any kind of labour, and at the expiration of that time I should feel fresh and vigorous enough to go right on in the same way for numerous more months.

[*Artemus Ward in London* (1867)]

WATTS, Isaac (1674–1748)

In works of labour, or of skill,
I would be busy too;
For Satan finds some mischief still
For idle hands to do.

[*Divine Songs for Children* (1715)]

See BED

IGNORANCE

ANONYMOUS

What you don't know will always hurt you.

[First Law of Blissful Ignorance]

A little ignorance can go a long way.

[Gerrold's Law]

DISRAELI, Benjamin (1804–1881)

Mr Kremlin himself was distinguished for ignorance, for he had only one idea, – and that was wrong.

[*Sybil* (1845)]

DURRELL, Sir Gerald (1925–1995)

I said I liked being half-educated; you were so much more surprised at everything when you were ignorant.

[*My Family and Other Animals* (1956)]

GRAY, Thomas (1716–1771)

Where ignorance is bliss,
'Tis folly to be wise.

['Ode on a Distant Prospect of Eton College' (1742)]

HOPE, Anthony (1863–1933)

I wish you would read a little poetry sometimes. Your ignorance cramps my

conversation.

[*The Dolly Dialogues* (1894)]

KING, Martin Luther (1929–1968)

Nothing in all the world is more dangerous than sincere ignorance and conscientious stupidity.

[*Strength to Love*, 1963]

LOMBROSO, Cesare (1853–1909)

L'uomo ignorante ama ciò che non capisce.
The ignorant man always loves that which he cannot understand.

[*The Man of Genius* (1894)]

MARLOWE, Christopher (1564–1593)

I count religion but a childish toy,
And hold there is no sin but ignorance.

[*The Jew of Malta* (c. 1592)]

MONSARRAT, Nicholas (1910–1979)

You English … think we know damn nothing but I tell you we know damn all.

[*The Cruel Sea* (1951)]

PROVERB

What you don't know can't hurt you.

SMITH, Sydney (1771–1845)

What you don't know would make a great book.

[In Lady Holland, *Memoir* (1855)]

TOLSTOY, Leo (1828–1910)

The most powerful weapon of ignorance – the diffusion of printed material.

[*War and Peace* (1868–1869)]

WILDE, Oscar (1854–1900)

Ignorance is like a delicate exotic fruit; touch it, and the bloom is gone.

[*The Importance of Being Earnest* (1895)]

See FOOLISHNESS; STUPIDITY

ILLNESS

AUBREY, John (1626–1697)

Sciatica: he cured it, by boiling his buttock.

[*Brief Lives* (c. 1693)]

AUSTIN, Alfred (1835–1913)

[On the illness of the Prince of Wales]
Across the wires the electric message came:
'He is no better, he is much the same.'

[Attr.]

BACON, Francis (1561–1626)

The remedy is worse than the disease.

['Of Seditions and Troubles' (1625)]

BENNETT, Arnold (1867–1931)

'Ye can call it influenza if ye like,' said Mrs
Machin. 'There was no influenza in my young
days. We called a cold a cold.'

[The Card (1911)]

BROWNE, Sir Thomas (1605–1682)

We all labour against our own cure, for death
is the cure of all diseases.

[Religio Medici (1643)]

CHEKHOV, Anton (1860–1904)

If many remedies are suggested for a
disease, that means the disease is incurable.

[The Cherry Orchard (1904)]

DAVIES, Robertson (1913–1995)

Not to be healthy … is one of the few sins
that modern society is willing to recognise
and condemn.

[The Cunning Man (1994)]

EMERSON, Ralph Waldo (1803–1882)

A person seldom falls sick, but the
bystanders are animated with a faint hope
that he will die.

[Conduct of Life (1860)]

GALBRAITH, J.K. (1908–)

Much of the world's work, it has been said, is
done by men who do not feel quite well.
Marx is a case in point.

[The Age of Uncertainty]

HELLER, Joseph (1923–)

Hungry Joe collected lists of fatal diseases
and arranged them in alphabetical order so
that he could put his finger without delay on
any one he wanted to worry about.

[Catch-22 (1961)]

HIPPOCRATES (c.460–357 BC)

For extreme illnesses extreme remedies are
most fitting.

[Aphorisms]

HOOD, Thomas (1799–1845)

For that old enemy the gout
Had taken him in toe!

[Comic Melodies (1830)]

LAMB, Charles (1775–1834)

How sickness enlarges the dimensions of a
man's self to himself!

[Last Essays of Elia (1833)]

LAWRENCE, D.H. (1885–1930)

I am only half there when I am ill, and so
there is only half a man to suffer. To suffer in
one's whole self is so great a violation, that it
is not to be endured.

[Letter to Catherine Carswell, 1916]

MCAULEY, James Philip (1917–1976)

[After his first cancer operation; to a friend]
Well, better a semi-colon than a full stop!

[In Coleman, The Heart of James McAuley (1980)]

PERELMAN, S.J. (1904–1979)

I've got Bright's disease and he's got mine.

[Attr.]

PERSIUS FLACCUS, Aulus (AD 34–62)

Venienti occurrite morbo.
Confront disease at its onset.

[Satires]

PHILIP, Sir Robert (1857–1939)

Mankind is responsible for tuberculosis. What
an ignorant civilisation has introduced, an
educated civilisation can remove.

[Attr.]

PROUST, Marcel (1871–1922)

As soon as he ceased to be mad he became
merely stupid. There are maladies we must
not seek to cure because they alone protect
us from others that are more serious.

[A la recherche du temps perdu, Le Côté de
Guermantes (1921)]

SONTAG, Susan (1933–)

Illness is the night-side of life, a more

onerous citizenship. Everyone who is born holds dual citizenship, in the kingdom of the well and in the kingdom of the sick. Although we all prefer to use only the good passport, sooner or later each of us is obliged, at least for a spell, to identify ourselves as citizens of that other place.

[*Illness as Metaphor* (1978)]

STACPOOLE, H. de Vere (1863–1951)

In home-sickness you must keep moving – it is the only disease that does not require rest.

[*The Bourgeois* (1901)]

STEVENSON, Robert Louis (1850–1894)

Even if the doctor does not give you a year, even if he hesitates about a month, make one brave push and see what can be accomplished in a week.

[*Virginibus Puerisque* (1881)]

SWIFT, Jonathan (1667–1745)

We are so fond of one another, because our ailments are the same.

[*Journal to Stella*, 1711]

WOLFE, Thomas (1900–1938)

Most of the time we think we're sick, it's all in the mind.

[*Look Homeward, Angel* (1929)]

See AIDS; HEALTH; MEDICINE

IMAGINATION

AUSTEN, Jane (1775–1817)

A lady's imagination is very rapid; it jumps from admiration to love, from love to matrimony, in a moment.

[*Pride and Prejudice* (1813)]

BLAKE, William (1757–1827)

What is now proved was once only imagin'd.

['Proverbs of Hell', (c. 1793)]

CERVANTES, Miguel de (1547–1616)

[Don Quixote of his lady, Dulcinea del Toboso] I imagine that everything is as I say it is,

neither more or less, and I paint her in my imagination the way I want her to be.

[*Don Quixote* (1605)]

COLERIDGE, Samuel Taylor (1772–1834)

The primary imagination I hold to be the living power and prime agent of all human perception, and as a repetition in the finite mind of the eternal act of creation in the infinite I AM. The secondary imagination … dissolves, diffuses, dissipates, in order to recreate; or where this process is rendered impossible, yet still at all events it struggles to idealize and to unify.

[*Biographia Literaria* (1817)]

Fancy, on the contrary, has no other counters to play with, but fixities and definites. The fancy is indeed no other than a mode of memory emancipated from the order of time and space.

[*Biographia Literaria* (1817)]

EINSTEIN, Albert (1879–1955)

Imagination is more important than knowledge.

[*On Science*]

ELIOT, George (1819–1880)

He said he should prefer not to know the sources of the Nile, and that there should be some unknown regions preserved as hunting-grounds for the poetic imagination.

[*Middlemarch* (1872)]

JOHNSON, Samuel (1709–1784)

Were it not for imagination, Sir, a man would be as happy in the arms of a chambermaid as of a Duchess.

[In Boswell, *The Life of Samuel Johnson* (1791)]

JOUBERT, Joseph (1754–1824)

Imagination is the eye of the soul.

[Attr.]

KEATS, John (1795–1821)

The Imagination may be compared to Adam's dream – he awoke and found it truth.

[Letter to Benjamin Bailey, 22 November 1817]

I am certain of nothing but of the holiness of the Heart's affections and the truth of Imagination – What the imagination seizes as Beauty must be truth – whether it existed before or not.

[Letter to Benjamin Bailey, 22 November 1817]

MACAULAY, Lord (1800–1859)

His imagination resembled the wings of an ostrich. It enabled him to run, though not to soar.

['John Dryden' (1843)]

ROBINSON, Roland Edward (1912–1992)

Where does imagination start
but from primeval images
in man's barbaric heart?

['Mopoke']

STEAD, Christina (1902–1983)

I don't know what imagination is, if not an unpruned, tangled kind of memory.

[Letty Fox: Her Luck (1946)]

IMMORTALITY

ALLEN, Woody (1935–)

I don't want to achieve immortality through my work ... I want to achieve it by not dying.

[Attr.]

BECKETT, Samuel (1906–1989)

Clov: Do you believe in the life to come?
Hamm: Mine was always that.

[Endgame (1958)]

BUTLER, Bishop Joseph (1692–1752)

That which is the foundation of all our hopes and of all our fears; all our hopes and fears which are of any consideration: I mean a Future Life.

[The Analogy of Religion (1736)]

DOSTOEVSKY, Fyodor (1821–1881)

If you were to destroy in mankind the belief in immortality, not only love but every living force maintaining the life of the world would at once dry up. Moreover, nothing then would be immoral, everything would be

lawful, even cannibalism.

[The Brothers Karamazov (1879–1880)]

EMERSON, Ralph Waldo (1803–1882)

Other world! There is no other world! Here or nowhere is the whole fact.

['Natural Religion']

ERTZ, Susan (1894–1985)

Someone has somewhere commented on the fact that millions long for immortality who don't know what to do with themselves on a rainy Sunday afternoon.

[Anger in the Sky (1943)]

HAZLITT, William (1778–1830)

No young man believes he shall ever die.

['On the Feeling of Immortality in Youth' (1827)]

HELLER, Joseph (1923–)

He had decided to live forever or die in the attempt.

[Catch-22 (1961)]

KEATS, John (1795–1821)

There is an awful warmth about my heart like a load of Immortality.

[Letter to J.H. Reynolds, 22 September 1818]

I long to believe in immortality ... If I am destined to be happy with you here – how short is the longest Life. I wish to believe in immortality – I wish to live with you for ever.

[Letter to Fanny Brawne, July 1820]

KRAUS, Karl (1874–1936)

Die Unsterblichkeit ist das einzige, was keinen Aufschub verträgt.
Immortality is the only thing which doesn't tolerate being postponed.

[Sayings and Contradictions, (1909)]

PINDAR (518–438 BC)

Strive not, my soul, for an immortal life, but make the most of what is possible.

[Pythian Odes]

PLATO (c.429–347 BC)

Let us be persuaded ... to consider that the soul is immortal and capable of enduring all evil and all good, and so we shall always hold to the upward way and pursue justice with wisdom.

[*Republic*]

SPINOZA, Baruch (1632–1677)

Sentimus experimurque, nos aeternos esse.
We feel and know by experience that we are eternal.

[*Ethics* (1677)]

STASSINOPOULOS, Arianna (1950–)

Our current obsession with creativity is the result of our continued striving for immortality in an era when most people no longer believe in an afterlife.

[*The Female Woman* (1973)]

THOREAU, Henry David (1817–1862)

[*On being asked his opinion of the hereafter*]
One world at a time.

[Attr.]

UPANISHADS (c.800–300 BC)

When all desires that dwell within the human heart are cast away, then a mortal becomes immortal and here he attaineth to Brahman.

[*Katha Upanishad*]

VAUGHAN, Henry (1622–1695)

My Soul, there is a countrie
Far beyond the stars,
Where stands a winged Sentry
All skilfull in the wars;
There above noise and danger,
Sweet peace sits crown'd with smiles,
And one born in a Manger
Commands the Beauteous files.

[*Silex Scintillans* (1655)]

See ETERNITY; MORTALITY

IMPOSSIBILITY

ARISTOPHANES (c.445–385 BC)

You will never make a crab walk straight.

[*Peace*]

ARISTOTLE (384–322 BC)

Probable impossibilities are always to be preferred to improbable possibilities.

[*Poetics*]

CALONNE, Charles Alexandre de (1734–1802)

Madame, si c'est possible, c'est fait; impossible? cela se fera.
Madam, if it is possible, it has been done; impossible? It will be done.

[In J. Michelet, *Histoire de la Révolution Française* (1847)]

CARROLL, Lewis (1832–1898)

'There's no use trying,' she said: 'one can't believe impossible things.'
'I dare say you haven't had much practice,' said the Queen. 'When I was your age, I always did it for half an hour a day. Why, sometimes I've believed as many as six impossible things before breakfast.'

[*Through the Looking-Glass (and What Alice Found There)* (1872)]

GRAINGER, Percy (1882–1961)

Why be difficult when with a little extra effort you can make yourself impossible?

[*Anecdotes, Index Part I, Grainger Collection*]

TWAIN, Mark (1835–1910)

There ain't no way to find out why a snorer can't hear himself snore.

[*Tom Sawyer Abroad* (1894)]

INCOME

AUSTEN, Jane (1775–1817)

An annuity is a very serious business; it comes over and over every year, and there is no getting rid of it.

[*Sense and Sensibility* (1811)]

A large income is the best recipe for happiness I ever heard of. It certainly may secure all the myrtle and turkey part of it.

[*Mansfield Park* (1814)]

BUTLER, Samuel (1835–1902)

All progress is based upon a universal innate

desire on the part of every organism to live beyond its income.

[*The Note-Books of Samuel Butler* (1912)]

DICKENS, Charles (1812–1870)

Annual income twenty pounds, annual expenditure nineteen nineteen six, result happiness. Annual income twenty pounds, annual expenditure twenty pounds ought and six, result misery.

[*David Copperfield* (1850)]

LAMBTON, John, First Earl of Durham (1792–1840)

He said he considered £40,000 a year a moderate income – such a one as a man might jog on with.

[In *The Creevey Papers* (1903)]

MORLEY, John David (1812–1870)

For the average European a job was an income, for the average Japanese it was a home.

[*Pictures From the Water Trade - An Englishman in Japan*]

NASH, Ogden (1902–1971)

He who is ridden by a conscience
Worries about a lot of nonscience;
He without benefit of scruples
His fun and income soon quadruples.

['Reflection on the Fallibility of Nemesis' (1940)]

PARKINSON, C. Northcote (1909–1993)

Expenditure rises to meet income.

[Attr.]

SAKI (1870–1916)

I'm living so far beyond my income that we might almost be said to be living apart.

[Attr.]

All decent people live beyond their incomes nowadays, and those who aren't respectable live beyond other people's. A few gifted individuals manage to do both.

[*The Chronicles of Clovis* (1911)]

SAUNDERS, Ernest (1935–)

I was on a basic £100,000 a year. You don't make many savings on that.

[*The Observer*, 1987]

SHAKESPEARE, William (1564–1616)

Remuneration! O, that's the Latin word for three farthings.

[*Love's Labour Lost*, III.i]

SMITH, Logan Pearsall (1865–1946)

There are few sorrows, however poignant, in which a good income is of no avail.

[*Afterthoughts* (1931)]

See MONEY AND WEALTH

INDECISION

ASQUITH, Margot (1864–1945)

[*Of Sir Stafford Cripps*]
He has a brilliant mind until he makes it up.

[In *The Wit of the Asquiths*]

BEVAN, Aneurin (1897–1960)

We know what happens to people who stay in the middle of the road. They get run over.

[*The Observer*, 1953]

THE BIBLE
(King James Version)

How long halt ye between two opinions?

[*I Kings*, 18:21]

BROOKS, Mel (1926–)

He who hesitates is poor.

[*The Producers*, film, 1968]

DICKENS, Charles (1812–1870)

[On a performance of *Hamlet*]
Whenever that undecided Prince had to ask a question or state a doubt, the public helped him out with it – on the question whether 'twas nobler in the mind to suffer, some roared yes, and some no, and some inclining to both opinions said 'toss up for it'.

[*Great Expectations* (1861)]

JAMES, William (1842–1910)

There is no more miserable human being

than one in whom nothing is habitual but indecision.

[*Principles of Psychology* (1890)]

NASH, Ogden (1902–1971)
If I could but spot a conclusion, I should race to it.

['All, All Are Gone, The Old Familiar Quotations' (1952)]

SMITH, Sir Cyril (1928–)
If the fence is strong enough I'll sit on it.

[*The Observer*, 1974]

TWAIN, Mark (1835–1910)
I must have a prodigious quantity of mind; it takes me as much as a week, sometimes, to make it up.

[*The Innocents Abroad* (1869)]

See UNCERTAINTY

INDEPENDENCE

AESOP (6th century BC)
The gods help those who help themselves.

['Hercules and the Waggoner']

BRANCUSI, Constantin (1876–1957)
[*Refusing Rodin's invitation to work in his studio*]
Nothing grows well in the shade of a big tree.

[Attr.]

EMERSON, Ralph Waldo (1803–1882)
It is easy in the world to live after the world's opinion; it is easy in solitude after our own; but the great man is he who, in the midst of the crowd, keeps with perfect sweetness the independence of solitude.

['Self-Reliance' (1841)]

FONTAINE, Jean de la (1621–1695)
Aide-toi, le ciel t'aidera.
Help yourself, and heaven will help you.

[*Fables*, 'Le Chartier embourbé']

GIBBON, Edward (1737–1794)
The first of earthly blessings, independence.

[*Memoirs of My Life and Writings* (1796)]

IBSEN, Henrik (1828–1906)
The strongest man in the world is the man who stands alone.

[*An Enemy of the People* (1882)]

MARRYAT, Frederick (1792–1848)
I think it much better that … every man paddle his own canoe.

[*Settlers in Canada* (1844)]

SCOTT, Sir Walter (1771–1832)
[Refusing offers of help following his bankruptcy in 1826]
No! this right hand shall work it all off!

[In Cockburn, *Memorials of His Time* (1856)]

THOREAU, Henry David (1817–1862)
I would rather sit on a pumpkin and have it all to myself than be crowded on a velvet cushion.

[*Walden* (1854)]

INDIVIDUALITY

ARIOSTO, Ludovico (1474–1533)
Natura il fece, e poi roppe la stampa.
Nature first made him, and then smashed the mould.

[*Orlando furioso* (1516)]

BLAKE, William (1757–1827)
O why was I born with a different face?
Why was I not born like the rest of my race?

['Letter to Thomas Butts' (1803)]

BROWNE, Sir Thomas (1605–1682)
It is the common wonder of all men, how among so many millions of faces, there should be none alike.

[*Religio Medici* (1643)]

HUXLEY, T.H. (1825–1895)
One of the unpardonable sins, in the eyes of most people, is for a man to go about unlabelled. The world regards such a person as the police do an unmuzzled dog, not under proper control.

[*Evolution and Ethics* (1893)]

MILL, John Stuart (1806–1873)

Whatever crushes individuality is despotism, by whatever name it may be called.

[*On Liberty* (1859)]

SCHOPENHAUER, Arthur (1788–1860)

Aus seiner Individualität kann Keiner heraus.
No-one can escape from his individuality.

[*Parerga und Paralipomena* (1851)]

WILDE, Oscar (1854–1900)

Most people are other people. Their thoughts are someone else's opinions, their life a mimicry, their passions a quotation.

[Letter to Lord Alfred Douglas]

See OPINIONS; TASTE

INDUSTRIAL RELATIONS

ANONYMOUS

In his chamber, weak and dying,
While the Norman Baron lay,
Loud, without, his men were crying,
'Shorter hours and better pay.'

['A Strike among the Poets']

CASTLE, Ted (1907–1979)

In Place of Strife.

[Title of White Paper on industrial relations legislation, 1969]

COOK, A.J. (1885–1931)

Not a penny off the pay, not a minute on the day.

[Speech, 1926]

COOLIDGE, Calvin (1872–1933)

[Of the Boston police strike]
There is no right to strike against the public safety by anybody, anywhere, any time.

[Telegram to the President of the American Federation of Labour, 1919]

FEATHER, Vic, Baron (1906–1976)

Industrial relations are like sexual relations. It's better between two consenting parties.

[*Guardian Weekly*, 1976]

KEYNES, John Maynard (1883–1946)

There are the Trade Unionists, once the oppressed, now the tyrants, whose selfish and sectional pretensions need to be bravely opposed.

['Liberalism and Labour' (1926)]

MACMILLAN, Harold (1894–1986)

[Referring to privatization of profitable nationalized industries]
Selling the family silver.

[Speech, House of Lords, 1986]

MUIR, Frank (1920–1998)

Another fact of life that will not have escaped you is that, in this country, the twenty-four-hour strike is like the twenty-four-hour flu. You have to reckon on it lasting at least five days.

[*You Can't Have Your Kayak and Heat It*, 'Great Expectations', with Dennis Norden]

SHINWELL, Emanuel (1884–1986)

We know that you, the organized workers of the country, are our friends … As for the rest, they do not matter a tinker's curse.

[Speech at the Electrical Trades Union Conference, Margate, 1947]

SPEIGHT, Johnny (1920–1998)

Have you noticed, the last four strikes we've had, it's pissed down? It wouldn't be a bad idea to check the weather reports before they pull us out next time.

[*Till Death Do Us Part*, television programme]

WILSON, Harold (1916–1995)

We are redefining and we are restating our socialism in terms of the scientific revolution … the Britain that is going to be forged in the white heat of this revolution will be no place for restrictive practices or out-dated methods on either side of industry.

[Speech, 1963]

One man's wage rise is another man's price increase.

[*The Observer*, 1970]

See DIPLOMACY

INEQUALITY

ALEXANDER, Cecil Frances (1818–1895)

The rich man in his castle,
The poor man at his gate,
God made them, high or lowly,
And order'd their estate.

[*Hymn*, 1848]

BELLOW, Saul (1915–)

One part of mankind is in prison; another is starving to death; and those of us who are free and fed are not awake. What will it take to rouse us?

[*Critical Enquiry*, 1975, 'A World Too Much With Us']

BRECHT, Bertolt (1898–1956)

Der Sieg und Niederlagen der Grosskopfigen oben und der von unten fallen nämlich nicht immer zusammen.
Victories and defeats for the bigshots at the top aren't always victories and defeats for those at the bottom.

[*Mother Courage and her Children* (1941)]

FROUDE, James Anthony (1818–1894)

Men are made by nature unequal. It is vain, therefore, to treat them as if they were equal.

[*Short Studies on Great Subjects* (1877)]

GOLDSMITH, Oliver (c.1728–1774)

Ye friends to truth, ye statesmen, who survey
The rich man's joys increase, the poor's decay,
'Tis yours to judge, how wide the limits stand
Between a splendid and a happy land.

[*The Deserted Village* (1770)]

JOHNSON, Samuel (1709–1784)

Subordination tends greatly to human happiness. Were we all upon an equality, we should have no other enjoyment than mere animal pleasure.

[In Boswell, *The Life of Samuel Johnson* (1791)]

PENN, William (1644–1718)

It is a reproach to religion and government to suffer so much poverty and excess.

[*Some Fruits of Solitude, in Reflections and Maxims relating to the Conduct of Humane Life* (1693)]

SHELLEY, Percy Bysshe (1792–1822)

Many faint with toil,
That few may know the cares and woe of sloth.

[*Queen Mab* (1813)]

WATSON, Sir William (1858–1936)

Too long, that some may rest,
Tired millions toil unblest.

['New National Anthem']

See CLASS; FEMINISM

INFLUENCE

CARNEGIE, Dale (1888–1955)

How to Win Friends and Influence People.

[Book title]

EINSTEIN, Albert (1879–1955)

Setting an example is not the main means of influencing others, it is the only means.

[Attr.]

NAISBITT, John (1929 –)

The new source of power is not money in the hands of a few but information in the hands of many.

[*Megatrends*]

WILDE, Oscar (1854–1900)

The man who can dominate a London dinnertable can dominate the world.

[Attr.]

See INSPIRATION; POWER

INGRATITUDE

CHILLINGWORTH, William (1602–1644)

I once knew a man out of courtesy help a lame dog over a stile, and he for requital bit his fingers.

[*The Religion of Protestants* (1637)]

GARCÍA MÁRQUEZ, Gabriel (1928–)

La ingratitud humana no tiene límites.

There are no limits to human ingratitude.

[*No-one Writes to the Colonel* (1961)]

HUXLEY, Aldous (1894–1963)
Most human beings have an almost infinite capacity for taking things for granted.

[*Themes and Variations* (1950)]

LA ROCHEFOUCAULD (1613–1680)
Over-great haste to repay an obligation is a form of ingratitude.

[*Maximes* (1678)]

LOUIS XIV (1638–1715)
Toutes les fois que je donne une place vacante, je fais cent mécontents et un ingrat.
Every time I make an appointment, I make a hundred men discontented and one ungrateful.

[In Voltaire, *Siècle de Louis XIV*]

SHAKESPEARE, William (1564–1616)
Blow, blow, thou winter wind,
Thou art not so unkind
As man's ingratitude …
Thy tooth is not so keen,

Freeze, freeze, thou bitter sky,
That dost not bite so nigh
As benefits forgot.

[*As You Like It*, II.vii]

TWAIN, Mark (1835–1910)
There's plenty of boys that will come hankering and gruvvelling around when you've got an apple, and beg the core off you; but when they've got one, and you beg for the core and remind them how you give them a core one time, they make a mouth at you and say thank you 'most to death, but there ain't-a-going to be no core.

[*The Adventures of Tom Sawyer* (1876)]

INNOCENCE

BOWEN, Elizabeth (1899–1973)
No, it is not only our fate but our business to lose innocence, and once we have lost that, it

is futile to attempt a picnic in Eden.

[In R. Lehmann and others (eds.), *Orion III* (1946)]

GOLDING, William (1911–1993)
Ralph wept for the end of innocence, the darkness of man's heart, and the fall through the air of the true, wise friend called Piggy.

[*Lord of the Flies* (1954)]

PROVERB
Every one is innocent until he is proved guilty.

RACINE, Jean (1639–1699)
My innocence is at last becoming a burden to me.

[*Andromaque* (1667)]

YEATS, W.B. (1865–1939)
The innocent and the beautiful
Have no enemy but time.

[*The Winding Stair and Other Poems* (1933)]

See IGNORANCE

INNOVATION

ANONYMOUS
Every revolutionary idea – in science, politics, art, or whatever – evokes three stages of reaction in a hearer:
– It is completely impossible – don't waste my time.
– It is possible, but it is not worth doing.
– I said it was a good idea all along.

BACON, Francis (1561–1626)
He that will not apply new remedies must expect new evils; for time is the greatest innovator.

[*Essays* (1625)]

See CONSERVATISM; ORIGINALITY; PROGRESS

INSPIRATION

COLETTE (1873–1954)
On ne fait bien que ce qu'on aime. Ni la science, ni la

conscience ne modèlent un grand cuisinier. De quoi sert l'application où il faut l'inspiration?

One only does well what one loves doing. Neither science nor conscience makes a great cook. What use is application where inspiration is what's needed?

[*Prisons et paradis* (1932)]

PROVERB

Ninety per cent of inspiration is perspiration.

INSULTS

ALLEN, Dave (1936–)

If I had a head like yours, I'd have it circumcised.

[In Gus Smith, *God's Own Comedian*]

AUSTEN, Jane (1775–1817)

You have delighted us long enough.

[*Pride and Prejudice* (1813)]

BEVAN, Aneurin (1897–1960)

[Wishing to address Harold Macmillan, the Prime Minister, rather than Selwyn Lloyd, the Foreign Secretary, in the post-Suez debate]

I am not going to spend any time whatsoever in attacking the Foreign Secretary. Quite honestly I am beginning to feel extremely sorry for him. If we complain about the tune, there is no reason to attack the monkey when the organ grinder is present.

[Speech, House of Commons, 1957]

BRAHMS, Johannes (1833–1897)

[Said on leaving a gathering of friends]

If there is anyone here whom I have not insulted, I beg his pardon.

[Attr.]

BRUMMEL, Beau (1778–1840)

[Said of the Prince of Wales, 1813]

Who's your fat friend?

[In Gronow, *Reminiscences* (1862)]

CHESTERFIELD, Lord (1694–1773)

An injury is much sooner forgotten than an insult.

[Letter to his son, 1746]

CORNEILLE, Pierre (1606–1684)

He who allows himself to be insulted, deserves to be.

[*Héraclius* (1646)]

DISRAELI, Benjamin (1804–1881)

[Speaking to Lord Palmerston]

Your dexterity seems a happy compound of the smartness of an attorney's clerk and the intrigue of a Greek of the lower empire.

[Attr.]

If a traveller were informed that such a man [Lord John Russell] was leader of the House of Commons, he may well begin to comprehend how the Egyptians worshipped an insect.

[Attr.]

GILBERT, W.S. (1836–1911)

I shouldn't be sufficiently degraded in my own estimation unless I was insulted with a very considerable bribe.

[*The Mikado* (1885)]

GROSSMITH, Weedon (1854–1919)

I am a poor man, but I would gladly give ten shillings to find out who sent me the insulting Christmas card I received this morning.

[*Diary of a Nobody* (1894)]

JOHNSON, Samuel (1709–1784)

[To an abusive Thames waterman]

Sir, your wife, under pretence of keeping a bawdy-house, is a receiver of stolen goods.

[In Boswell, *The Life of Samuel Johnson* (1791)]

LLOYD GEORGE, David (1863–1945)

[Of Sir Douglas Haig]

He was brilliant to the top of his army boots.

[Attr.]

PARKER, Dorothy (1893–1967)

[Reply to the comment, 'Anyway, she's always very nice to her inferiors']

Where does she find them?

[In Lyttelton Hart-Davis, *Letters*]

SHERIDAN, Richard Brinsley (1751–1816)

If it is abuse, – why one is always sure to hear

of it from one damned good-natured friend or another!

[*The Critic* (1779)]

SITWELL, Dame Edith (1887–1964)

[On novelist Ethel Mannin]
I do not want Miss Mannin's feelings to be hurt by the fact that I have never heard of her … At the moment I am debarred from the pleasure of putting her in her place by the fact that she has not got one.

[In J. Pearson, *Façades* (1978)]

SMITH, F.E. (1872–1930)

Judge Willis: You are extremely offensive, young man.
F.E. Smith: As a matter of fact, we both are, and the only difference between us is that I am trying to be, and you can't help it.

[In Birkenhead, *Frederick Elwin, Earl of Birkenhead* (1933)]

SMITH, Sydney (1771–1845)

Let the Dean and Canons lay their heads together and the thing will be done. (It being proposed to surround St Paul's with a wooden pavement.).

[In H. Pearson, *The Smith of Smiths* (1934)]

THOMPSON, William Hepworth (1810–1886)

[Of Sir Richard Jebb, Professor of Greek at Cambridge]
What time he can spare from the adornment of his person he devotes to the neglect of his duties.

[In M.R. Bobbit, *With Dearest Love to All* (1960)]

THURBER, James (1894–1961)

A man should not insult his wife publicly, at parties. He should insult her in the privacy of the home.

[*Thurber Country* (1953)]

WILKES, John (1727–1797)

[Reply to Lord Sandwich, who had told him that he would die either on the gallows or of the pox]
That must depend on whether I embrace your lordship's principles or your mistress.

[Attr. in Sir Charles Petrie, *The Four Georges* (1935)]

See ACTORS; CRITICISM; POLITICIANS

INTELLECTUALS

AUDEN, W.H. (1907–1973)

To the man-in-the-street, who, I'm sorry to say,
Is a keen observer of life,
The word intellectual suggests straight away
A man who's untrue to his wife.

[*Collected Poems*, 1939–1947]

BANKHEAD, Tallulah (1903–1968)

I've been called many things, but never an intellectual.

[*Tallulah* (1952)]

BLAKE, William (1757–1827)

I care not whether a Man is Good or Evil; all that I care
Is whether he is a Wise Man or a Fool. Go! put off Holiness
And put on Intellect.

[*Jerusalem* (1804–1820)]

CAMUS, Albert (1913–1960)

Intellectuel? Oui. Et ne jamais renier. Intellectuel = celui qui se dédouble. «a me plaît. Je suis content d'être les deux.
An intellectual? Yes. And never deny it. An intellectual = one who splits himself in two. I like that. I am happy to be both [halves].

[*Carnets, 1935–1942* (1962)]

SCHWEITZER, Albert (1875–1965)

'Heda, Kamerad', rufe ich, 'willst du uns nicht ein wenig helfen?' 'Ich bin ein Intellektueller und trage kein Holz', lautete die Antwort. 'Hast du Glück', erwiderte ich; 'auch ich wollte ein Intellektueller werden, aber es ist mir nicht gelungen."
'Hello, friend,' I shout, 'Won't you help us?' 'I am an intellectual and don't carry wood around,' came the answer. 'You're lucky,' I replied. 'I too wanted to become an intellectual, but I didn't manage it.'

[*Mitteilungen aus Lambarene* (1928)]

SHORTIS, Gregory Brien (1945–)

I'm observing the golden mean and living

frugally
In the country without plumbing and only
A smoky, open fire, and things would be
perfect
If my wife wasn't an intellectual.

['To Malcolm from an Unemployed Youth']

STEVENSON, Adlai (1900–1965)
Eggheads of the world unite; you have
nothing to lose but your yolks.

[Attr.]

See INTELLIGENCE; MIND; THOUGHT

INTELLIGENCE

ALLEN, Woody (1935–)
My brain: it's my second favourite organ.

[Sleeper, film, 1973]

ASQUITH, Margot (1864–1945)
[On F.E. Smith]
He's very clever, but sometimes his brains go
to his head.

[Quoted by Baroness Asquith in TV programme, As I Remember, 30 April 1967]

BALDWIN, Stanley (1867–1947)
The intelligent are to the intelligentsia what
a gentleman is to a gent.

[Attr.]

BOGARDE, Dirk (1921–1999)
I'm not very clever, but I'm quite intelligent.

[Attr.]

BRENAN, Gerald (1894–1987)
Intellectuals are people who believe that
ideas are of more importance than values.
That is to say, their own ideas and other
people's values.

[Thoughts in a Dry Season (1978)]

CHRISTIE, Dame Agatha (1890–1976)
[Hercule Poirot] tapped his forehead. 'These
little gray cells, it is 'up to them' – as you say
over here.'

[The Mysterious Affair at Styles
(1920)]

COWPER, William (1731–1800)
His wit invites you by his looks to come,
But when you knock it is never at home.

['Conversation' (1782)]

DE VRIES, Peter (1910–1993)
We know the human brain is a device to
keep the ears from grating on one another.

[Comfort me with Apples (1956)]

DIDEROT, Denis (1713–1784)
[A retort which comes to mind too late]
L'esprit de l'escalier.
Staircase wit.

[Paradoxe sur le Comédien (c. 1778)]

DOYLE, Sir Arthur Conan (1859–1930)
I am a brain, Watson. The rest of me is a mere
appendix.

[The Case Book of Sherlock Holmes (1927)]

FREUD, Sigmund (1856–1939)
The voice of the intellect is a soft one, but it
does not rest till it has gained a hearing.

[The Future of an Illusion]

FRISCH, Max (1911–1991)
Wieso haben die Intellektuellen, wenn sie
scharenweise zusammenkommen, unweigerlich
etwas Komisches?
Why is there invariably something comic
about intellectuals when they meet together
in crowds?

[Diary, 1948]

**GOULBURN, Edward, Dean of Norwich
(1818–1897)**
Let the scintillations of your wit be like the
coruscations of summer lightning, lambent
but innocuous.

[Sermon at Rugby]

HERBERT, George (1593–1633)
Wit's an unruly engine, wildly striking
Sometimes a friend, sometimes the engineer.

[The Temple (1633)]

KEATS, John (1795–1821)
The only means of strengthening one's
intellect is to make up one's mind about
nothing – to let the mind be a thoroughfare

for all thoughts. Not a select party.

[Letter to George and Georgiana Keats, 1819]

LA ROCHEFOUCAULD (1613–1680)

On peut être plus fin qu'un autre, mais non pas plus fin que tous les autres.

One can be more astute than another, but not more astute than all the others.

[*Maximes*, (1678)]

C'est une grande habileté que de savoir cacher son habileté.

The height of cleverness is to be able to conceal it.

[*Maximes* (1678)]

MACAULAY, Lord (1800–1859)

The highest intellects, like the tops of mountains, are the first to catch and to reflect the dawn.

['Sir James Mackintosh' (1843)]

MANN, Thomas (1875–1955)

Every intellectual attitude is latently political.

[*The Observer*, 1974]

NIETZSCHE, Friedrich Wilhelm (1844–1900)

Der Witz ist das Epigramm auf dem Tod eines Gefühls.

Wit is the epigram for the death of an emotion.

[*Human, All too Human* (1886)]

PASCAL, Blaise (1623–1662)

A mesure qu'on a plus d'esprit, on trouve qu'il y a plus d'hommes originaux. Les gens du commun ne trouvent point de différence entre les hommes.

The more intelligence one has the more people one finds original. Commonplace people see no difference between men.

[*Pensées* (1670)]

SCHOPENHAUER, Arthur (1788–1860)

Intellect is invisible to the man who has none.

[*Aphorismen zur Lebensweisheit*]

SHAKESPEARE, William (1564–1616)

Brevity is the soul of wit.

[*Hamlet*, II.ii]

Look, he's winding up the watch of his wit; by and by it will strike.

[*The Tempest*, II.i]

This fellow is wise enough to play the fool; And to do that well craves a kind of wit.

[*Twelfth Night*, III.i]

SU TUNG-P'O (SU SHIH) (1036–1101)

Families, when a child is born
Want it to be intelligent.
I, through intelligence,
Having wrecked my whole life,
Only hope the baby will prove
Ignorant and stupid.
Then he will crown a tranquil life
By becoming a Cabinet Minister.

[In Waley, *170 Chinese Poems*]

WHITEHEAD, A.N. (1861–1947)

Intelligence is quickness to apprehend as distinct from ability, which is capacity to act wisely on the thing apprehended.

[*Dialogues* (1954)]

See INTELLECTUALS; KNOWLEDGE;
    MIND; PERCEPTION; THOUGHT;
    WISDOM

THE INTERNET

CHOMSKY, Noam (1928–)

The Internet is an élite organisation; most of the population of the world has never even made a phone call.

[*The Observer Review*, 1996]

FASULO, Tom

Surfing on the Internet is like sex; everyone boasts about doing more than they actually do. But in the case of the Internet, it's a lot more.

GERSTNER, Lou

The killer app[lication] will not be a shrink-wrapped program that sells in millions. The killer app will be a Web site that touches millions of people and helps them to do what they want to do.

GIBSON, William (1948–)

Cyberspace: A consensual hallucination experienced daily by billions of legitimate operators, in every nation.

[*Neuromancer* (1984)]

SIRIAM, M.G.

Looking at the proliferation of personal web pages on the net, it looks like very soon everyone on earth will have 15 Megabytes of fame.

See ARTIFICIAL INTELLIGENCE; COMPUTERS; MEDIA; TECHNOLOGY

INVENTION

BIERCE, Ambrose (1842–c.1914)

An inventor is a person who makes an ingenious arrangement of wheels, levers and springs, and believes it civilization.

[*The Devil's Dictionary*, 1958]

CARLYLE, Thomas (1795–1881)

He who first shortened the labour of Copyists by device of Movable Types was disbanding hired Armies, and cashiering most Kings and Senates, and creating a whole new Democratic world: he had invented the Art of Printing.

[*Sartor Resartus* (1834)]

EDISON, Thomas Alva (1847–1931)

To invent, you need a good imagination and a pile of junk.

[Attr.]

EMERSON, Ralph Waldo (1803–1882)

Invention breeds invention.

[*Society and Solitude* (1870)]

FLAUBERT, Gustave (1821–1880)

Tout ce qu'on invente est vrai, sois-en sûre. La poésie est une chose aussi précise que la géométrie.
Everything one invents is true, you can be sure of that. Poetry is as exact a science as geometry.

[Letter to Louise Colet, 1853]

FRANKLIN, Benjamin (1706–1790)

[On being asked the use of a new invention]
What is the use of a new-born child?

[In Parton, *Life and Times of Benjamin Franklin* (1864)]

PIOZZI, Miss

[Of a balloonist exhibiting in London]
Monsieur Garnevin goes up again tomorrow with an Umbrella Thing to hinder his Fall, he calls it for that Reason a Parachute. We shall see how it answers – taking so much money at such a Risk of breaking all his bones.

[Letter to Lady Williams, 2 July 1802]

PROVERB

Necessity is the mother of invention.

SWIFT, Jonathan (1667–1745)

He had been eight years upon a project for extracting sun-beams out of cucumbers, which were to be put into vials hermetically sealed, and let out to warm the air in raw inclement summers.

[*Gulliver's Travels* (1726)]

VOLTAIRE (1694–1778)

The most amazing and effective inventions are not those which do most honour to the human genius.

[*Lettres philosophiques* (1734)]

See INNOVATION; SCIENCE

INVESTMENTS

BUFFETT, Warren (1930–)

Put all your eggs in one basket, and then pay very close attention to that basket.

KEILLOR, Garrison (1942–)

Where I'm from we don't trust paper. Wealth is what's here on the premises. If I open a cupboard and see, say, 30 cans of tomato sauce and a five-pound bag of rice, I get a little thrill of well-being – much more so than if I take a look at the quarterly dividend report from my mutual fund.

See MONEY AND WEALTH

IRELAND

ALLEN, Dave (1936–)

The foreman says, 'You must have an intelligence test'. The Irishman says, 'All right.' So the foreman says, 'What is the difference between joist and girder?' And the Irishman says, 'Joyce wrote *Ulysses* and Goethe wrote *Faust*.'

[Retelling the only Irish joke he really liked, quoted in Gus Smith, *God's Own Comedian*]

ALLINGHAM, William (1824–1889)

Not men and women in an Irish street But Catholics and Protestants you meet.

[Attr.]

ASCHERSON, Neal (1932–)

Peace in Northern Ireland has to built on its divisions, not on a fiction of unity which does not yet exist.

[*The Observer*, 1998]

BATES, Daisy May (1863–1951)

There are a few fortunate races that have been endowed with cheerfulness as their main characteristic, the Australian Aborigine and the Irish being among these.

[*The Passing of the Aborigines* … (1938)]

BEHAN, Brendan (1923–1964)

Pat: He was an Anglo-Irishman.
Meg: In the blessed name of God, what's that?
Pat: A Protestant with a horse.

[*The Hostage* (1958)]

The English and Americans dislike only some Irish – the same Irish that the Irish themselves detest, Irish writers – the ones that think.

[*Richard's Cork Leg* (1972)]

Other people have a nationality. The Irish and the Jews have a psychosis.

[*Richard's Cork Leg* (1972)]

BLACKWOOD, Helen Selina (1807–1867)

And the red was on your lip, Mary,
The love-light in your eye …

I'm sitting on the stile, Mary,
Where we sat, side by side …

They say there's bread and work for all,
And the sun shines always there:
But I'll not forget old Ireland,
Were it fifty times as fair.

['Lament of the Irish Emigrant' (1845)]

CHESTERTON, G.K. (1874–1936)

For the great Gaels of Ireland
Are the men that God made mad,
For all their wars are merry,
And all their songs are sad.

[*Ballad of the White Horse* (1911)]

CHILD, Lydia M. (1802–1880)

Not in vain is Ireland pouring itself all over the earth … The Irish, with their glowing hearts and reverent credulity, are needed in this cold age of intellect and skepticism.

[*Letters from New York* (1842)]

CLARE, Dr Anthony (1942–)

The whole notion of holding a referendum on women's access to information is such a profound disgrace for a nation such as this that I … apologise to Irish women on behalf of what has been predominantly a male-dominated, male-driven male disgrace.

[*The Irish Times*, 1993]

CLINTON, Bill (1946–)

[On the IRA, shortly after they resumed their campaign of violence in February 1996]
We must not let the men of the past ruin the future of the children of Northern Ireland.

[*Daily Mail*, 1996]

COLLINS, Michael (1890–1922)

[Said on signing the agreement with Great Britain, 1921, that established the Irish Free State; he was assassinated some months later]
Think – what have I got for Ireland?
Something which she has wanted these past

seven hundred years. Will anyone be satisfied at the bargain? Will anyone? I tell you this – early this morning I signed my death warrant. I thought at the time how odd, how ridiculous – a bullet may just as well have done the job five years ago.

[Letter to John O'Kane, 1921]

DE VALERA, Eamon (1882–1975)

Whenever I wanted to know what the Irish people wanted, I had only to examine my own heart and it told me straight off what the Irish people wanted.

[Dáil Éireann, 1922]

… a land whose countryside would be bright with cosy homesteads, whose fields and villages would be joyous with the sounds of industry, with the romping of sturdy children, the contests of athletic youths and the laughter of comely maidens, whose firesides would be forums for the wisdom of serene old age.

[Radio broadcast, St Patrick's Day, 1943]

DISRAELI, Benjamin (1804–1881)

A starving population, an absentee aristocracy, and an alien Church, and in addition the weakest executive in the world. That is the Irish question.

[Speech, 1844]

DOYLE, Roddy (1958–)

The Irish are the niggers of Europe … An' Dubliners are the niggers of Ireland … An' the northside Dubliners are the niggers o' Dublin – Say it loud. I'm black an' I'm proud.

[The Commitments (1987)]

EMMET, Robert (1778–1803)

[Before his execution]

When my country takes her place among the nations of the earth, then and not till then, let my epitaph be written. I have done.

[Attr.]

GALLANT, Mavis (1922–)

The Irish were not English. God had sent them to Canada to keep people from

marrying Protestants.

[Across the Bridge (1993)]

GOGARTY, Oliver St John (1878–1957)

Politics is the chloroform of the Irish people, or rather the hashish.

[As I Was Going Down Sackville Street (1937)]

HEWITT, John (1907–1987)

The names of a land show the heart of the race;
They move on the tongue like the lilt of a song.
You say the name and I see the place –
Drumbo, Dungannon, or Annalong.
Barony, townland, we cannot go wrong.

['Ulster Names']

JOHNSON, Samuel (1709–1784)

The Irish are a fair people; – they never speak well of one another.

[In Boswell, The Life of Samuel Johnson (1791)]

JOYCE, James (1882–1941)

Ireland is the old sow that eats her farrow.

[A Portrait of the Artist as a Young Man (1916)]

My intention was to write a chapter of the moral history of my country and I chose Dublin for the scene because that city seemed to me the centre of paralysis.

[Letter to Grant Richards, 1905]

LEONARD, Hugh (1926–)

The problem with Ireland is that it's a country full of genius, but with absolutely no talent.

[Interview in The Times, 1977]

MAJOR, John (1943–)

[On the search for peace in Northern Ireland after the end of the IRA ceasefire in February 1996]

If we are pushed back, we will start again. If we are pushed back, we will start again. If we are pushed back a third time we will start again.

[The Observer Review, 1996]

MORRISON, Danny (1950–)

Who here really believes that we can win the war through the ballot box? But will anyone here object if with a ballot box in this hand and an Armalite in this hand we take power in Ireland.

[Provisional Sinn Féin Conference, 1981]

O'FAOLAIN, Sean (1900–1991)

An Irish Quaker is a fellow who prefers women to drink.

[Attr. on Nigel Rees' BBC programme, *Quote Unquote*, 1999]

O'LEARY, Father Joseph

[On the IRA, during the search for the bodies of the 'disappeared']

How could we tolerate for all those years the deeds of a fascist organisation dedicated to torture and murder? What cowardice or connivance prevented us from speaking out against these atrocities? Were we any better than the denizens of Buchenwald who couldn't smell the smoke from the crematoria?

[Letter to *The Irish Times*, June 1999]

ROBINSON, Mary (1944–)

As the elected choice of the people of this part of our island I want to extend the hand of friendship and of love to both communities in the other part.

[Inaugural speech as President, 1991]

SHAW, George Bernard (1856–1950)

An Irishman's heart is nothing but his imagination.

[*John Bull's Other Island* (1907)]

If you want to bore an Irishman, play him an Irish melody, or introduce him to another Irishman.

[In Holroyd, *Shaw* (1989)]

SMITH, Adam (1723–1790)

Without a union with Great Britain, the inhabitants of Ireland are not likely for many ages to consider themselves as one people.

[*Wealth of Nations* (1776)]

SMITH, Sydney (1771–1845)

The moment the very name of Ireland is mentioned, the English seem to bid adieu to common feeling, common prudence, and to

common sense, and to act with the barbarity of tyrants, and the fatuity of idiots.

[*Letters of Peter Plymley* (1807)]

WATSON, Sir William (1858–1936)

[Of Ireland]

The lovely and lonely bride,
Whom we have wedded but never won.

['Ode on the Coronation of Edward VII' (1902)]

YEATS, W.B. (1865–1939)

[Of Ireland]

This blind bitter land.

[*The Green Helmet and Other Poems* (1912)]

Behind Ireland fierce and militant, is Ireland poetic, passionate, remembering, idyllic, fanciful, and always patriotic.

['Popular Ballad Poetry of Ireland', 1889]

[From Yeats's speech on divorce, in which he stressed the contribution made by the Protestant minority to the literary and political life of Ireland]

We against whom you have done this thing are no petty people. We are one of the great stocks of Europe. We are the people of Burke; we are the people of Grattan; we are the people of Swift, the people of Emmett, the people of Parnell. We have created the most of the modern literature of this country. We have created the best of its political intelligence.

[Speech to the Senate, June 1925]

ITALY

BIAGI, Enzo (1920–)

[On the Italians]

Allora siamo i più disonesti? Credo proprio di no: ma probabilmente i più indifferenti.

Are we then the most dishonest people? I don't really think so: but probably we are the most indifferent ones.

[*The Good and the Bad*, 1989)]

[After the kidnapping and subsequent murder of Aldo Moro, Christian Democrat Premier, May 1978]

All'annuncio del rapimento l'Italia è come messa al tappeto da un colpo basso: non riesce a capire che cosa sta succedendo, le pare impossibile che il terrorismo sia cos' forte.

At the announcement of Moro's kidnapping, Italy looked as if she had been knocked out by a blow below the belt: she doesn't understand what's happening; it seems impossible to her that terrorism could be so powerful.

[*We Terrorists*, 1985)]

DI PIETRO, Antonio (1947–)

[Speaking of 'Mani pulite']

L'Italia si sta tirando fuori il suo dente; che ciascuno degli altri Paesi provi a cavare il suo di dente.

Italy is pulling out her own rotten tooth, let all other Countries pull out their own.

[Speech in Toronto, Canada, November 1993, reported in the magazine, EPOCA, 1994]

JOTTI, Nilde (1920–)

Quali difetti attribuisce al maschio italiano: Primo è prepotente. Secondo una vittima, un prodotto che non sa badare a se stesso.

Which faults do you attribute to the Italian male: First he's a bully. Second a victim, a product that cannot look after himself.

[In E. Biagi, *La Geografia di Italia* (1975)]

METTERNICH, Prince Clement (1773–1859)

Italien ist ein geographischer Begriff.

Italy is a geographical concept.

[Letter, 1849]

RUSH, Ian

I couldn't settle in Italy – it was like living in a foreign country.

TOMASI, Giuseppe di Lampedusa (1896–1957)

L'Italia era nata in quell'accigliata sera a Donnafugata, nata proprio lì in quel paese dimenticato.

Una fata cattiva però della quale non si conosceva il nome doveva essere stata presente.

Italy was born on that sombre evening at Donnafugata, she was indeed born in that forgotten village.

A bad fairy, however, whose name no one knew must have been there.

[*The Leopard*, 1958)]

J

JAPAN

HODSON, Peregrine
… Japan is like a quicksand – the more one tries to get out of it, the more it sucks one in – or a maze without a centre – a sphinx without a riddle – or like Peer Gynt's onion, peel away the layers one after another and in the end all there is left is mush and tears.

[*A Circle Round The Sun - A Foreigner in Japan*]

HYDE, Robin (1906–1939)
The Japanese are described as 'the most nostalgic people on earth,' but I think possibly the remark applies to all island people, who have the spirit of adventure, but also the feeling of being secure on a small place among the waters.

[*Mirror*, 1938]

MORISHIMA, Michio
The ability of the Japanese to assimilate Western technology and science with astonishing rapidity after the Meiji Restoration was due, at least in part, to their education under Confucianism; Western rationalist thinking was not entirely foreign.

['Why Has Japan Succeeded?, quoted in *Created in Japan*]

MORITA, Akio (1920–)
Whereas Americans and Europeans often develop complex, large-scale solutions to problems, the Japanese constantly pare down and reduce the complexity of products and ideas to the barest minimum. They streamline the design, reduce the number of parts, and simplify the inner workings and moving parts. The influence of Zen and haiku poetry are often evident in the simplicity and utility of Japanese designs.

[*Made in Japan* (1986)]

RAUCH, Jonathan
… Japan's social and economic systems conspire, not against foreigners, but against newcomers.

[*Business Magazine*, 1992]

THEROUX, Paul (1941–)
Outside the Nichigeki Music Hall, the Japanese men who had watched with fastidious languor and then so enthusiastically applauded the savage eroticism that could enjoy no encore – baring their teeth as they did so – these men, as I say, bowed deeply to one another, murmured polite farewells to their friends, linked arms with their wives with the gentleness of old-fashioned lovers, and, in the harsh lights of the street, smiled, looking positively cherubic.

[*The Great Railway Bazaar* (1975)]

It is with a kind of perverse pride that the Japanese point out how expensive their country has become. But this is as much a measure of wealth as of inflation.

[*The Great Railway Bazaar* (1975)]

JEALOUSY

HERBERT, Sir A.P. (1890–1971)
I'm not a jealous woman, but I can't see what he sees in her.

['I Can't Think What He Sees in Her']

MILTON, John (1608–1674)
Nor jealousie
Was understood, the injur'd Lover's Hell.

[*Paradise Lost* (1667)]

SAGAN, Françoise (1935–)
To jealousy nothing is more frightful than laughter.

[Attr.]

SHAKESPEARE, William (1564–1616)
O, beware, my lord, of jealousy;
It is the green-ey'd monster which doth mock

The meat it feeds on.

[*Othello*, III.iii]

Trifles light as air
Are to the jealous confirmations strong
As proofs of holy writ.

[*Othello*, III.iii]

Jealous souls will not be answer'd so;
They are not ever jealous for the cause,
But jealous for they are jealous.

[*Othello*, III.iv]

VANBRUGH, Sir John (1664–1726)

Jealousy's a city passion; 'tis a thing
unknown amongst people of quality.

[*The Confederacy* (1705)]

WELLS, H.G. (1866–1946)

Moral indignation is jealousy with a halo.

[*The Wife of Sir Isaac Harman* (1914)]

See ENVY

JEWELLERY

DICKENS, Charles (1812–1870)

It was not a bosom to repose upon, but it
was a capital bosom to hang jewels upon.

[*Little Dorrit* (1857)]

LENNON, John (1940–1980)

Those in the cheaper seats clap. The rest of
you rattle your jewellery.

[Remark, Royal Variety Performance, 15 November
1963]

LOOS, Anita (1893–1981)

Any girl who was a lady would not even
think of having such a good time that she
did not remember to hang on to her jewelry.

[*Gentlemen Prefer Blondes*
(1925)]

READE, Charles (1814–1884)

She wrenched from her brow a diamond and
eyed it with contempt, took from her pocket
a sausage and contemplated it with respect
and affection.

[*Peg Woffington* (1852)]

ROBIN, Leo (1899–)

Diamonds Are A Girl's Best Friend.

[Song title, 1949]

STEVENSON, Adlai (1900–1965)

As the girl said, 'A kiss on the wrist feels good,
but a diamond bracelet lasts forever.'

[Address to Chicago Council on Foreign Relations,
194]

WEST, Mae (1892–1980)

'Goodness, what beautiful diamonds!'
'Goodness had nothing to do with it!'.

[*Night After Night*, film,
1932]

JEWS

BALFOUR, A.J. (1848–1930)

His Majesty's Government views with favour
the establishment in Palestine of a national
home for the Jewish people.

['The Balfour Declaration', 1917]

BLUE, Rabbi Lionel (1930–)

There is always a danger in Judaism of
seeing history as a sort of poker game
played between Jews and God, in which the
presence of others is noted but not given
much importance.

[*The Observer*, 1982]

BROWNE, Cecil (1932–)

But not so odd
As those who choose
A Jewish God,
But spurn the Jews.

[Reply to William Norman Ewer: *How odd/Of
God/To choose/The Jews*]

DRYDEN, John (1631–1700)

The Jews, a headstrong, moody, murmuring
race
As ever tried the extent and stretch of grace,
God's pampered people, whom, debauched
with ease,
No king could govern nor no God could
please.
Gods they had tried of every shape and size

That godsmiths could produce or priests devise.

[*Absalom and Achitophel* (1681)]

HEINE, Heinrich (1797–1856)

When people talk about a wealthy man of my creed, they call him an Israelite; but if he is poor they call him a Jew.

[MS. Papers]

It is extremely difficult for a Jew to be converted, for how can he bring himself to believe in the divinity of – another Jew?

[Attr.]

JOHNSON, Paul (1928–)

For me this is a vital litmus test: no intellectual society can flourish where a Jew feels even slightly uneasy.

[*The Sunday Times Magazine*, 1977]

LAWRENCE, D.H. (1885–1930)

The very best that is in the Jewish blood: a faculty for pure disinterestedness, and warm, physically warm love, that seems to make the corpuscles of the blood glow.

[*Kangaroo* (1923)]

MARX, Groucho (1895–1977)

[When excluded, on racial grounds, from a beach club]

Since my daughter is only half-Jewish, could she go into the water up to her knees?

[*The Observer*, 1977]

MILLER, Jonathan (1934–)

I'm not really a Jew; just Jew-ish, not the whole hog.

[*Beyond the Fringe* (1961)]

MILLIGAN, Spike (1918–)

Q. Are you Jewish?
A. No, a tree fell on me.

[*Private Eye*, 1973]

RICHLER, Mordecai (1931–)

And furthermore did you know that behind the discovery of America there was a Jewish financier?

[*Cocksure* (1968)]

RODEN, Claudia

The real crystallisation of Jewish cuisine took place in the 16th century, when the Jews were confined to ghettos by edict. It may seem surprising that interest in food should blossom in a ghetto, especially one devoted to religious worship; but people focused on their home life as an antidote to the misery and degradation outside. Hospitality became a means of survival and the celebration of religious festivals … made it possible to remain indifferent to the world outside the gates.

[*The Good Food Guide*, 1985]

ROTH, Philip (1933–)

A Jewish man with parents alive is a fifteen-year-old boy, and will remain a fifteen-year-old boy until they die.

[*Portnoy's Complaint* (1969)]

SHAKESPEARE, William (1564–1616)

Hath not a Jew eyes? Hath not a Jew hands, organs, dimensions, senses, affections, passions, fed with the same food, hurt with the same weapons, subject to the same diseases, healed by the same means, warmed and cooled by the same winter and summer, as a Christian is? If you prick us, do we not bleed? If you tickle us, do we not laugh? If you poison us, do we not die? And if you wrong us, shall we not revenge? If we are like you in the rest, we will resemble you in that.

[*The Merchant of Venice*, III.i]

STEIN, Gertrude (1874–1946)

The Jews have produced only three originative geniuses: Christ, Spinoza, and myself.

[In Mellow, *Charmed Circle* (1974)]

USTINOV, Sir Peter (1921–)

I believe that the Jews have made a contribution to the human condition out of all proportion to their numbers: I believe them to be an immense people. Not only have they supplied the world with two leaders of the stature of Jesus Christ and Karl Marx, but they have even indulged in the luxury of following neither one nor the other.

[*Dear Me* (1977)]

ZANGWILL, Israel (1864–1926)

No Jew was ever fool enough to turn
Christian unless he was a clever man.

[*Children of the Ghetto* (1892)]

See PREJUDICE; RACE; RELIGION

JOY

BLAKE, William (1757–1827)

… I have no name
I am but two days old – '
What shall I call thee?
… I happy am,
Joy is my name, – '
Sweet joy befall thee!

[*Songs of Innocence* (1789)]

Joys impregnate. Sorrows bring forth.

[*The Marriage of Heaven and Hell* (c. 1790–1793)]

He who binds to himself a joy
Does the winged life destroy;
But he who kisses the joy as it flies
Lives in eternity's sun rise.

['Eternity' (c. 1793), from 'The Rossetti Manuscript']

LANG, Andrew (1844–1912)

There's a joy without canker or cark,
There's a pleasure eternally new,
'Tis to gloat on the glaze and the mark
Of China that's ancient and blue.

['Ballade of Blue China']

REID, Bill

Joy is a well-made object.

[*Maclean's*, 1989]

SCHILLER, Johann Christoph Friedrich (1759–1805)

Freude, schöner Götterfunken,
Tochter aus Elysium,
Wir betreten feuertrunken
Himmlische, dein Heiligtum.
Deine Zauber binden wieder,
Was die Mode streng geteilt,
Alle Menschen werden Brüder,

Wo dein sanfter Flügel weilt.
Joy, fair ray of the gods,
Daughter of Elysium,
Dazzled we enter,
Heavenly one, thy shrine.
Against thy charms join together
What custom has harshly divided,
All men become brothers,
Under thy gentle wing.

['To Joy', revised 1803); set to music by Beethoven in the last movement of his Ninth Symphony]

See HAPPINESS; LAUGHTER; PLEASURE

JUDGEMENT

ADDISON, Joseph (1672–1719)

Sir Roger told them, with the air of a man who would not give his judgement rashly, that much might be said on both sides.

[*The Spectator*, July 1711]

AUGUSTINE, Saint (354–430)

Securus iudicat orbis terrarum.
The judgement of the world is sure.

[*Contra Epistolam Parmeniani*]

BENTLEY, Edmund Clerihew (1875–1956)

Between what matters and what seems to matter, how should the world we know judge wisely?

[*Trent's Last Case* (1913)]

His judgement of persons was penetrating, but its process was internal; no-one felt on good behaviour with a man who seemed always to be enjoying himself.

[*Trent's Last Case* (1913)]

THE BIBLE
(King James Version)

Judge not, that ye be not judged.

[*Matthew*, 7:1]

By their fruits ye shall know them.

[*Matthew*, 7:20]

He that is without sin among you, let him

first cast a stone at her.

[*Luke*, 8:7]

BROWNING, Elizabeth Barrett (1806–1861)

Let no one till his death
Be called unhappy. Measure not the work,
Until the day's out and the labour done.

[*Aurora Leigh* (1857)]

BRUNO, Giordano (1548–1600)

[Said to the cardinals who excommunicated him]
Perhaps your fear in passing judgement is
greater than mine in receiving it.

[Attr.]

CAMUS, Albert (1913–1960)

N'attendez pas le jugement dernier. Il a lieu tous les jours.

Don't wait for the Last Judgement. It is taking
place every day.

[*The Fall* (1956)]

CELANO, Thomas de (c.1190–c.1260)

Tuba mirum sparget sonum
Per sepulchra regionum,
Coget omnes ante thronum.

Mors stupebit et natura,
Cum resurget creatura
Iudicanti responsura.

Liber scriptus proferetur,
In quo totum continetur
Unde mundus iudicetur.

The trumpet will fling out a stupendous
sound through the tombs of all regions, it
will drive everyone before the throne. Death
will be amazed and so will nature, when
creation rises again to make answer to the
judge. The written book will be brought
forward, in which everything is contained
whereby the world will be judged.

[*Dies irae*]

COMPTON-BURNETT, Dame Ivy (1884–1969)

Appearances are not held to be a clue to the
truth. But we seem to have no other.

[*Manservant and Maidservant* (1947)]

COWPER, William (1731–1800)

Judgment drunk, and brib'd to lose his way,
Winks hard, and talks of darkness at noon-
day.

['The Progress of Error' (1782)]

EDGEWORTH, Maria (1767–1849)

We cannot judge either of the feelings or of
the characters of men with perfect accuracy,
from their actions or their appearance in
public; it is from their careless conversations,
their half-finished sentences, that we may
hope with the greatest probability of success
to discover their real character.

[*Castle Rackrent* (1800)]

EURIPIDES (c.485–406 BC)

The wisest men follow their own
direction
And listen to no prophet guiding them.
None but the fools believe in oracles,
Forsaking their own judgement. Those
who know,
Know that such men can only come to
grief.

[*Iphigenia in Tauris*]

KAFKA, Franz (1883–1924)

Dann erinnere ich Sie an den alten Rechtsspruch: für den Verdächtigen ist Bewegung besser als Ruhe, denn der, welcher ruht, kann immer, ohne es zu wissen, auf einer Waagschale sein und mit seinen Sünden gewogen werden.

Then I shall remind you of the old verdict: the
person under suspicion is better to be
moving than at rest, for at rest one can,
without knowing it, be in the balance being
weighed together with one's sins.

[*The Trial* (1914)]

MAUROIS, André (1885–1967)

Aucun de nous ne vit à chaque instant toutes ses idées; mais il faut juger les êtres plus par leurs dépassements que par leurs défaillances.

None of us lives out, at every moment, all of
our ideas; but one should judge human
beings more by their excellence than by their
weaknesses.

[*Lélia ou la vie de George Sand* (1952)]

MONTAIGNE, Michel de (1533–1592)

It is a dangerous and serious presumption, and argues an absurd temerity, to condemn what we do not understand.

[*Essais* (1580)]

PLINY THE ELDER (AD 23–79)

Ne supra crepidam sutor iudicaret.

The cobbler should not judge beyond his last.

[*Historia Naturalis*]

POPE, Alexander (1688–1744)

'Tis with our judgements as our watches, none

Go just alike, yet each believes his own.

[*An Essay on Criticism* (1711)]

PROVERB

A judge knows nothing unless it has been explained to him three times.

SHAKESPEARE, William (1564–1616)

What judgment shall I dread, doing no wrong?

[*The Merchant of Venice*, IV.i]

JUSTICE AND INJUSTICE

BENNETT, Arnold (1867–1931)

The price of justice is eternal publicity.

[*Things That Have Interested Me*]

BINGHAM, Sir Thomas (1933–)

[As Master of the Rolls, discussing the rising costs of going to law]

We cannot for ever be content to acknowledge that in England justice is open to all – like the Ritz Hotel.

[*Independent on Sunday*, 1994]

BLACKSTONE, Sir William (1723–1780)

It is better that ten guilty persons escape than one innocent suffer.

[*Commentaries on the Laws of England* (1765–1769)]

BOWEN, Lord (1835–1894)

The rain it raineth on the just

And also on the unjust fella:

But chiefly on the just, because

The unjust steals the just's umbrella.

[In Sichel, *Sands of Time* (1923)]

CARLYLE, Jane Welsh (1801–1866)

When one has been threatened with a great injustice, one accepts a smaller as a favour.

[*Journal*, 1855]

CARROLL, Lewis (1832–1898)

'I'll be judge, I'll be jury,' said cunning old Fury:

'I'll try the whole cause, and condemn you to death.'

[*Alice's Adventures in Wonderland* (1865)]

'No! No!' said the Queen. 'Sentence first – verdict afterwards'.

[*Alice's Adventures in Wonderland* (1865)]

CONFUCIUS (c.550–c.478 BC)

Recompense injury with justice, and recompense kindness with kindness.

[*Analects*]

DISRAELI, Benjamin (1804–1881)

Justice is truth in action.

[Speech, House of Commons, 1851]

DÜRRENMATT, Friedrich (1921–1990)

Die Gerechtigkeit ist etwas Fürchterliches.

Justice is something terrible.

[*Romulus the Great* (1964)]

Die Gerechtigkeit ist nicht eine Hackmaschine, sondern ein Abkommen.

Justice is not a mincer but an agreement.

[*The Marriage of Mr Mississippi* (1951)]

FERDINAND I, Emperor (1503–1564)

Fiat justitia, et pereat mundus.

Let there be justice though the world perish.

FIELDING, Henry (1707–1754)

Thwackum was for doing justice, and leaving mercy to Heaven.

[*Tom Jones* (1749)]

FRANCE, Anatole (1844–1924)

Désarmer les forts et armer les faibles ce serait changer l'ordre social que j'ai mission de conserver. La justice est la sanction des injustices établies.

To disarm the strong and arm the weak would be to change a social order which I have been commissioned to preserve. Justice is the means whereby established injustices are sanctioned.

[Crainquebille (1904)]

HARDY, Thomas (1840–1928)

'Justice' was done, and the President of the Immortals, in Aeschylean phrase, had ended his sport with Tess.

[Tess of the D'Urbervilles (1891)]

HEWART, Gordon (1870–1943)

It is not merely of some importance but is of fundamental importance that justice should not only be done, but should manifestly and undoubtedly be seen to be done.

[Rex v. Sussex Justices, 1923]

JUNIUS (1769–1772)

The injustice done to an individual is sometimes of service to the public.

[Letters (1769–1771)]

JUSTINIAN, Emperor (c.482–565)

Justitia est constans et perpetua voluntas ius suum cuique tribuens.

Justice is the constant and perpetual wish to give to every one his due.

[Institutes]

KAFKA, Franz (1883–1924)

Sie können einwenden, dass es ja überhaupt kein Verfahren ist, Sie haben sehr recht, denn es ist ja nur ein Verfahren, wenn ich als solches anerkenne.

You may raise the objection that it really is not a trial at all; you are quite right, for it is only a trial if I recognise it as such.

[The Trial (1925)]

KELLY, Ned (1855–1880)

There never was such a thing as justice in the English laws but any amount of injustice to be had.

[In Overland, 1981]

KING, Martin Luther (1929–1968)

Injustice anywhere is a threat to justice everywhere.

[Letter from Birmingham Jail, April 16, 1963]

LA ROCHEFOUCAULD (1613–1680)

L'amour de la justice n'est, en la plupart des hommes, que la crainte de souffrir l'injustice.

The love of justice in most men is no more than the fear of suffering injustice.

[Maximes (1678)]

LINCOLN, Abraham (1809–1865)

The probability that we may fail in the struggle ought not to deter us from the support of a cause we believe to be just.

[Speech, 1859]

MAGNA CARTA (1215)

Nulli vendemus, nulli negabimus aut differemus, rectum aut justitiam.

To no one will we sell, to no one will we deny, or delay, right or justice.

[Clause 40]

MANSFIELD, William Murray, Earl of (1705–1793)

[Advice given to a new colonial governor]

Consider what you think justice requires, and decide accordingly. But never give your reasons; for your judgement will probably be right, but your reasons will certainly be wrong.

[In Campbell, Lives of the Chief Justices (1849)]

MENCKEN, H.L. (1880–1956)

Injustice is relatively easy to bear: what stings is justice.

[Attr.]

MILTON, John (1608–1674)

Yet I shall temper so
Justice with Mercie.

[Paradise Lost (1667)]

MOLIÈRE (1622–1673)

Ils commencent ici par faire pendre un homme et puis ils lui font son procès.

Here they have a man hanged, and then proceed to try him.

[Monsieur de Pourceaugnac (1670)]

OSBORNE, John (1929–1994)

The injustice of it is almost perfect! The wrong people going hungry, the wrong people being loved, the wrong people dying!

[*Look Back in Anger* (1956)]

PETERS, Ellis (1913–1995)

'It may well be,' said Cadfael, 'that our justice sees as in a mirror image, left where right should be, evil reflected back as good, good as evil, your angel as her devil. But God's justice, if it makes no haste, makes no mistakes.'

[*The Potter's Field* (1989)]

POPE, Alexander (1688–1744)

The hungry Judges soon the sentence sign,
And wretches hang that jury-men may dine.

[*The Rape of the Lock* (1714)]

PUBLILIUS, Syrus (1st century BC)

Iudex damnatur ubi nocens absolvitur.
The judge is condemned when the guilty party is acquitted.

[*Sententiae*]

PULTENEY, William, Earl of Bath (1684–1764)

Since twelve honest men have decided the cause,
And were judges of fact, though not judges of laws.

['The Honest Jury' (1729)]

RICHELIEU, Cardinal (1585–1642)

If you give me six lines written by the most honest man, I will find something in them to hang him.

[Attr.]

ROUX, Joseph (1834–1886)

We love justice greatly, and just men but little.

[*Meditations of a Parish Priest* (1886)]

SHAKESPEARE, William (1564–1616)

What stronger breastplate than a heart untainted?
Thrice is he arm'd that hath his quarrel just;
And he but naked, though lock'd up in steel,
Whose conscience with injustice is corrupted.

[*Henry VI, Part 2*, III.ii]

SHIRLEY, James (1596–1666)

Only the actions of the just
Smell sweet, and blossom in their dust.

[*The Contention of Ajax and Ulysses* (1659)]

STOPPARD, Tom (1937–)

This is a British murder inquiry and some degree of justice must be seen to be more or less done.

[*Jumpers* (1972)]

VERGNIAUD, Pierre (1753–1793)

When justice has spoken, humanity must have its turn.

[Speech, 1793]

WILDE, Oscar (1854–1900)

For Man's grim Justice goes its way,
And will not swerve aside:
It slays the weak, it slays the strong,
It has a deadly stride.

[*The Ballad of Reading Gaol* (1898)]

See JUDGEMENT; LAW

K

KINDNESS

ANONYMOUS
Be kind to unkind people – they need it the most.

BIRLEY, Mark
You never forget people who were kind to you when you were young.
[*The Observer*, 1989]

CAMUS, Albert (1913–1960)
Ils savaient maintenant que s'il est une chose qu'on puisse désirer toujours et obtenir quelquefois, c'est la tendresse humaine.
They now knew that if there is one thing which can always be desired and sometimes obtained, it is human tenderness.
[*The Plague* (1947)]

CONFUCIUS (c.550–c.478 BC)
Recompense injury with justice, and recompense kindness with kindness.
[*Analects*]

DAVIES, William Henry (1871–1940)
I love thee for a heart that's kind –
Not for the knowledge in thy mind.
[*Sweet Stay-at-Home*' (1913)]

GIDE, André (1869–1951)
True kindness presupposes the faculty of imagining as one's own the suffering and joy of others.
[Attr.]

JACKSON, F.J. Foakes (1855–1941)
[Advice given to a new don at Jesus College, Cambridge]
It's no use trying to be clever – we are all clever here; just try to be kind – a little kind.
[In *Benson's Commonplace Book*]

JOHNSON, Samuel (1709–1784)
Always, Sir, set a high value on spontaneous kindness. He whose inclination prompts him to cultivate your friendship of his own accord, will love you more than one whom you have been at pains to attach to you.
[In Boswell, *The Life of Samuel Johnson* (1791)]

MARSHALL, Alan John (1911–1968)
Beware of people you've been kind to.
[Remark to John Morrison]

SHAKESPEARE, William (1564–1616)
I must be cruel, only to be kind.
[*Hamlet*, III.iv]

WILCOX, Ella Wheeler (1850–1919)
So many gods, so many creeds,
So many paths that wind and wind,
While just the art of being kind
Is all the sad world needs.
['The World's Need' (1917)]

WILLIAMS, Tennessee (1911–1983)
I have always depended on the kindness of strangers.
[*A Streetcar Named Desire* (1947)]

WORDSWORTH, William (1770–1850)
On that best portion of a good man's life;
His little, nameless, unremembered acts
Of kindness and of love.
['Lines composed a few miles above Tintern Abbey' (1798)]

See CHARITY

KNOWLEDGE

ADAMS, Henry (1838–1918)
They know enough who know how to learn.
[*The Education of Henry Adams* (1918)]

ALEXANDER THE GREAT (356–323 BC)
I would rather excel in the knowledge of what is excellent, than in the extent of my power.
[In Plutarch, *Lives*]

ARISTOTLE (384–322 BC)
All men naturally desire knowledge.
[*Metaphysics*]

BACON, Francis (1561–1626)
Knowledge itself is power.
['Of Heresies' (1597)]

BEECHING, Rev. H.C. (1859–1919)
First come I; my name is Jowett.
There's no knowledge but I know it.
I am Master of this college:
What I don't know isn't knowledge.
['The Masque of Balliol' (late 1870s)]

BEHN, Aphra (1640–1689)
Of all that writ, he was the wisest bard, who
spoke this mighty truth –
He that knew all that ever learning writ,
Knew only this – that he knew nothing yet.
[*The Emperor of the Moon* (1687)]

THE BIBLE
(King James Version)
He that increaseth knowledge increaseth
sorrow.
[*Ecclesiastes*, 1:18]

CARLYLE, Thomas (1795–1881)
What is all knowledge too but recorded
experience, and a product of history; of
which, therefore, reasoning and belief, no less
than action and passion, are essential
materials?
[*Critical and Miscellaneous Essays* (1839)]

CHESTERFIELD, Lord (1694–1773)
The knowledge of the world is only to be
acquired in the world, and not in a closet.
[Letter to his son, 1746]

CLOUGH, Arthur Hugh (1819–1861)
Grace is given of God, but knowledge is
bought in the market.
[*The Bothie of Tober-na-Vuolich* (1848)]

COWPER, William (1731–1800)
Knowledge is proud that he has learn'd so
much;
Wisdom is humble that he knows no more.
[*The Task* (1785)]

DOYLE, Sir Arthur Conan (1859–1930)
A man should keep his little brain attic
stocked with all the furniture that he is likely
to use, and the rest he can put away in the
lumber-room of his library, where he can get
it if he wants it.
[*The Adventures of Sherlock Holmes* (1892)]

EMERSON, Ralph Waldo (1803–1882)
There is no knowledge that is not power.
[*Society and Solitude* (1870)]

FONTAINE, Jean de la (1621–1695)
Il connaît l'univers et ne se connaît pas.
He knows the world and does not know
himself.
[*Fables*]

HOLMES, Oliver Wendell (1809–1894)
It is the province of knowledge to speak and
it is the privilege of wisdom to listen.
[*The Poet at the Breakfast-Table* (1872)]

HUXLEY, T.H. (1825–1895)
The saying that a little knowledge is a
dangerous thing is, to my mind, a very
dangerous adage. If knowledge is real and
genuine, I do not believe that it is other than
a very valuable possession however
infinitesimal its quantity may be. Indeed, if a
little knowledge is dangerous, where is the
man who has so much as to be out of
danger?
[*Science and Culture* (1877)]

INGE, William Ralph (1860–1954)
The fruit of the tree of knowledge always
drives man from some para-dise or other.
[Attr.]

JOAD, C.E.M. (1891–1953)
There was never an age in which useless
knowledge was more important than in ours.
[*The Observer*, 1951]

JOHNSON, Samuel (1709–1784)
In my early years I read very hard. It is a sad
reflection, but a true one, that I knew almost
as much at eighteen as I do now.
[In Boswell, *The Life of Samuel Johnson*
(1791)]

Integrity without knowledge is weak and
useless, and knowledge without integrity is

dangerous and dreadful.

[*Rasselas* (1759)]

If it rained knowledge, I'd hold out my hand; but I would not give myself the trouble to go in quest of it.

[In Boswell, *The Life of Samuel Johnson* (1791)]

KEATS, John (1795–1821)
Knowledge enormous makes a God of me.

['Hyperion. A Fragment (1818)']

LINKLATER, Eric (1899–1974)
For the scientific acquisition of knowledge is almost as tedious as a routine acquisition of wealth.

[*White Man's Saga*]

LOCKE, John (1632–1704)
No man's knowledge here can go beyond his experience.

[*Essay concerning Human Understanding* (1690)]

MACAULAY, Lord (1800–1859)
Knowledge advances by steps, and not by leaps.

['History' (1828)]

MENÉNDEZ Y PELAYO, Marcelino (1856–1912)
Desde luego, es más cómodo saber poco que saber mucho.
Of course, knowing a little is more agreeable than knowing a lot.

[Spanish Literature Programme, 1934)]

MILTON, John (1608–1674)
The first and wisest of them all professd
To know this onely, that he nothing knew.

[*Paradise Regained* (1671)]

MOLIÈRE (1622–1673)
Ah, la belle chose que de savoir quelque chose.
Ah, what a fine thing it is, to know something.

[*Le Bourgeois Gentilhomme* (1671)]

MUMFORD, Ethel (1878–1940)
Knowledge is power if you know it about the right person.

[In Cowan, *The Wit of Women*]

POPPER, Sir Karl (1902–1994)
Our knowledge can only be finite, while our ignorance must necessarily be infinite.

[*Conjectures and Refutations* (1963)]

PROVERB
Knowledge is power.

RENAN, J. Ernest (1823–1892)
'Savoir c'est pouvoir' est le plus beau mot qu'on ait dit.
'Knowledge is power' is the finest idea ever put into words.

[*Dialogues et fragments philosophiques* (1876)]

SHARPE, Tom (1928–)
His had been an intellectual decision founded on his conviction that if a little knowledge was a dangerous thing, a lot was lethal.

[*Porterhouse Blue* (1974)]

SHERIDAN, Richard Brinsley (1751–1816)
Madam, a circulating library in a town is an ever-green tree of diabolical knowledge! – It blossoms through the year! – And depend on it, Mrs Malaprop, that they who are so fond of handling the leaves, will long for the fruit at last.

[*The Rivals* (1775)]

STERNE, Laurence (1713–1768)
The desire of knowledge, like the thirst of riches, increases ever with the acquisition of it.

[*Tristram Shandy* (1767)]

See EDUCATION; LEARNING; WISDOM

L

LAND

FROST, Robert (1874–1963)
The land was ours before we were the land's.
[*'The Gift Outright'* (1942)]

GIBBON, Lewis Grassic (1901–1935)
Nothing endured at all, nothing but the land
… The land was forever, it moved and
changed below you, but was forever.
[*Sunset Song* (1932)]

ROWSE, A.L. (1903–1997)
What is there in a Cornish hedge
The broken herring-bone pattern of stones,
The gorse, the ragged rick,
The way the little elms are,
Sea-bent, sea-shorn
That so affects the heart?
[*'Cornish Landscape'*]

TROLLOPE, Anthony (1815–1882)
It is a comfortable feeling to know that you
stand on your own ground. Land is about the
only thing that can't fly away.
[*The Last Chronicle of Barset* (1867)]

LANGUAGE

AUDEN, W.H. (1907–1973)
Time that is intolerant
Of the brave and innocent,
And indifferent in a week
To a beautiful physique,

Worships language and forgives
Everyone by whom it lives.
[*Collected Poems, 1939–1947*]

CHURCHILL, Sir Winston (1874–1965)
[Marginal comment on a document]
This is the sort of English up with which I will
not put.
[In Gowers, *Plain Words* (1948)]

Everybody has a right to pronounce foreign
names as he chooses.
[*The Observer*, 1951]

DALY, Mary (1928–)
The liberation of language is rooted in the
liberation of ourselves.
[*Beyond God The Father, Toward a Philosophy of Women's Liberation* (1973)]

DAY, Clarence Shepard (1874–1935)
Imagine the Lord talking French! Aside from a
few odd words in Hebrew, I took it completely
for granted that God had never spoken
anything but the most dignified English.
[*Life with Father* (1935)]

DICKENS, Charles (1812–1870)
There was no light nonsense about Miss
Blimber … She was dry and sandy with
working in the graves of deceased
languages. None of your live languages for
Miss Blimber. They must be dead – stone
dead – and then Miss Blimber dug them up
like a Ghoul.
[*Dombey and Son* (1848)]

DOBBS, Kildare (1923–)
My country is the English language.
[In Galt (ed.), *The Saturday Night Traveller* (1990)]

DUPPA, Richard (1770–1831)
In language, the ignorant have prescribed
laws to the learned.
[*Maxims* (1830)]

ELIOT, George (1819–1880)
Correct English is the slang of prigs who
write history and essays.
[*Middlemarch* (1872)]

EMERSON, Ralph Waldo (1803–1882)
Language is fossil poetry.
[*'The Poet'* (1844)]

FRANKLIN, Benjamin (1706–1790)
Write with the learned, pronounce with the vulgar.
[*Poor Richard's Almanac* (1738)]

GOETHE (1749–1832)

Wer fremde Sprachen nicht kennt, weiss nichts von seiner eigenen.

Whoever is not acquainted with foreign languages knows nothing of his own.

[*On Art and Antiquity* (1827)]

GOLDSMITH, Oliver (c.1728–1774)

The true use of speech is not so much to express our wants as to conceal them.

[*The Bee* (1759)]

GOLDWYN, Samuel (1882–1974)

Let's have some new clichés.

[*The Observer*, 1948]

HYDE, Douglas (1860–1949)

In order to de-Anglicise ourselves we must at once arrest the decay of the language.

['The Necessity for de-Anglicising Ireland' (1892)]

JESPERSEN, Otto (1860–1943)

In his whole life man achieves nothing so great and so wonderful as what he achieved when he learned to talk.

[*Language* (1904)]

JOHNSON, Samuel (1709–1784)

I am not yet so lost in lexicography, as to forget that words are the daughters of the earth, and that things are the sons of heaven. Language is only the instrument of science, and words are but the signs of ideas: I wish, however, that the instrument might be less apt to decay, and that signs might be permanent, like the things which they denote.

[*A Dictionary of the English Language* (1755)]

Language is only the instrument of science, and words are but the signs of ideas: I wish, however, that the instrument might be less apt to decay, and that signs might be permanent, like the things which they denote.

[*A Dictionary of the English Language* (1755)]

Language is the dress of thought.

[*The Lives of the Most Eminent English Poets* (1781)]

I am always sorry when any language is lost, because languages are the pedigree of nations.

[In Boswell, *Journal of a Tour to the Hebrides* (1785)]

LANGLAND, William (c.1330–c.1400)

Grammere, that grounde is of alle.

[*The Vision of William Concerning Piers the Plowman*]

LÉVI-STRAUSS, Claude (1908–)

La langue est une raison humaine qui a ses raisons, et que l'homme ne connaît pas.

Language is a kind of human reason, which has its own internal logic of which man knows nothing.

[*The Savage Mind* (1962)]

MACAULAY, Lord (1800–1859)

The English Bible, a book which, if everything else in our language should perish, would alone suffice to show the whole extent of its beauty and power.

['John Dryden' (1843)]

MILNE, A.A. (1882–1956)

If the English language had been properly organized ... then there would be a word which meant both 'he' and 'she', and I could write, 'If John or Mary comes heesh will want to play tennis,' which would save a lot of trouble.

[*The Christopher Robin Birthday Book*]

MURROW, Edward R. (1908–1965)

[Of Churchill]

He mobilized the English language and sent it into battle to steady his fellow countrymen and hearten those Europeans upon whom the long dark night of tyranny had descended.

[Broadcast, 1954]

NARAYAN, R. K. (1907–)

English is a very adaptable language. And it's so transparent it can take on the tint of any country.

[Radio conversation, 1968]

O'CONNOR, Mark (1945–)

Yet all world languages die at last:
Greek of grammar and factions; Latin

of clotted syntax and Renaissance purism;
French of bad admirals and over-subtle
vowels;
English and Chinese of their written forms;
Russian of subject people's hate.

['Lingua Romana']

PARKER, Dorothy (1893–1967)

[Of an acquaintance]
You know, she speaks eighteen languages.
And she can't say 'No' in any of them.

[In J. Keats, *You Might As Well Live* (1970)]

PAZ, Octavio (1914–)

*Las diferencias entre el idioma hablado o escrito y los
otros – plásticos o musicales – son muy profundas,
pero no tanto que nos hagan olvidar que todos son,
esencialmente, lenguaje: sistemas expresivos dotados
de poder significativo.*

The differences between the spoken or
written language and the other ones –
plastic or musical – are very profound, but
not to such an extent that they make us
forget that essentially they are all language:
expressive systems which possess a
significative power.

[*The Bow and the Lyre* (1956)]

PHILIP, Prince, Duke of Edinburgh (1921–)

I include 'pidgin-English' ... even though I am
referred to in that splendid language as 'Fella
belong Mrs Queen'.

[Speech, English-Speaking Union Conference,
Ottawa, 1958]

PORSON, Richard (1759–1808)

Life is too short to learn German.

[In Thomas Love Peacock, *Gryll Grange* (1861)]

ROSS, Alan S.C. (1907–1980)

U and Non-U. An Essay in Sociological
Linguistics.

[In Nancy Mitford (ed.), *Noblesse Oblige* (1956)]

SHAW, George Bernard (1856–1950)

The English have no respect for their
language, and will not teach their children to
speak it ... It is impossible for an Englishman
to open his mouth without making some

other Englishman hate or despise him.

[*Pygmalion* (1916)]

England and America are two countries
separated by the same language.

[*Reader's Digest*, 1942]

SHERIDAN, Richard Brinsley (1751–1816)

An aspersion upon my parts of speech! ... If I
reprehend anything in this world, it is the use
of my oracular tongue, and a nice
derangement of epitaphs!

[*The Rivals* (1775)]

SIGISMUND (1368–1437)

[Responding to criticism of his Latin]
I am the Roman Emperor, and am above
grammar.

[Attr.]

SMITH, F.E. (1872–1930)

[When the Labour MP J.H. Thomas complained he
"ad a 'eadache']
Try taking a couple of aspirates.

[Attr.]

SPENSER, Edmund (c.1522–1599)

So now they have made our English tongue,
a gallimaufray or hodgepodge of al other
speches.

[*The Shepheardes Calender* (1579)]

SPRAT, Thomas (1635–1713)

[Of the Royal Society]
They have exacted from all their members a
close, naked, natural way of speaking;
positive expressions; clear senses; a native
easiness: bringing all things as near the
mathematical plainness, as they can; and
preferring the language of artizans,
countrymen, and merchants, before that of
wits or scholars.

[*The History of the Royal Society* (1667)]

SULLIVAN, Annie (1866–1936)

Language grows out of life, out of its needs
and experiences ... Language and
knowledge are indissolubly connected; they
are interdependent. Good work in language
presupposes and depends on a real

knowledge of things.

[Speech, 1894]

SWIFT, Jonathan (1667–1745)

Nor do they trust their tongue alone,
But speak a language of their own;
Can read a nod, a shrug, a look,
Far better than a printed book;
Convey a libel in a frown,
And wink a reputation down.

['The Journal of a Modern Lady' (1729)]

TOMLIN, Lily (1939–)

Man invented language in order to satisfy his
deep need to complain.

[In Pinker, *The Language Instinct* (1994)]

TUCHOLSKY, Kurt (1890–1935)

*Das Englische ist eine einfache, aber schwere
Sprache. Es besteht aus lauter Fremdwörtern die
falsch ausgesprochen werden.*
English is a simple, yet hard language. It
consists entirely of foreign words
pronounced wrongly.

[*Scraps* (1973)]

TWAIN, Mark (1835–1910)

A verb has a hard time enough of it in this
world when it's all together. It's downright
inhuman to split it up. But that's just what
those Germans do. They take part of a verb
and put it down here, like a stake, and they
take the other part of it and put it away over
yonder like another stake, and between
these two limits they just shovel in German.

[Address, 1900]

VOLTAIRE (1694–1778)

*Je ne suis pas comme une dame de la cour de
Versailles, qui disait: c'est bien dommage que
l'aventure de la tour de Babel ait produit la confusion
des langues; sans cela tout le monde aurait toujours
parlé français.*
I am not like a lady at the court of Versailles,
who said: 'What a great pity it is that the
adventure at the tower of Babel should have
produced the confusion of languages; if it
weren't for that, everyone would always have
spoken French.'

[Letter to Catherine the Great, 1767]

A language is a dialect that has an army and
a navy.

[In Rosten, *The Joys of Yiddish* (1968)]

WHITMAN, Walt (1819–1892)

Language … is not an abstract construction
of the learned, or of dictionary-makers, but is
something arising out of the work, needs,
ties, joys, affections, tastes, of long
generations of humanity, and has its bases
broad and low, close to the ground.

[*November Boughs* (1888)]

WHORF, Benjamin (1897–1941)

We dissect nature along lines laid down by
our native language … Language is not
simply a reporting device for experience but
a defining framework for it.

[In Hoyer (ed.), *New Directions in the Study of
Language* (1964)]

WOOLLCOTT, Alexander (1887–1943)

Subjunctive to the last, he preferred to ask,
'And that, sir, would be the Hippodrome?'.

[*While Rome Burns* (1934), 'Our Mrs Parker']

See CLASS; STYLE; WORDS; WRITING

LAST WORDS

ADDISON, Joseph (1672–1719)

See in what peace a Christian can die.

[Dying words]

ALEXANDER THE GREAT (356–323 BC)

I am dying with the help of too many
physicians.

[Attr.]

APPEL, George (d.1928)

[Executed in electric chair in New York.]
Well, gentlemen, you are about to see a
baked Appel.

BAILLY, Jean Sylvain (1736–1793)

[Reflection on the evening before his execution]
It's time for me to enjoy another pinch of
snuff. Tomorrow my hands will be bound, so
as to make it impossible.

[Attr.]

BANKHEAD, Tallulah (1903–1968)

Codeine … bourbon.

[Attr.]

BARNUM, Phineas T. (1810–1891)

How were the receipts today at Madison Square Garden?

[Attr.]

BARRIE, Sir J.M. (1860–1937)

I can't sleep.

[Attr.]

BARRYMORE, Ethel (1879–1959)

Is everybody happy? I want everybody to be happy. I know I'm happy.

[Attr.]

BEETHOVEN, Ludwig van (1770–1827)

Friends applaud, the comedy is finished.

[Attr.]

BEHAN, Brendan (1923–1964)

Thank you, sister. May you be the mother of a bishop!

> [Remark from his deathbed to a nun who was nursing him]

BELL, Alexander Graham (1847–1922)

So little done. So much to do.

[Last words, 1922]

BISMARCK, Prince Otto von (1815–1898)

[Remark made just before he died]

If there is ever another war in Europe, it will come out of some damned silly thing in the Balkans.

[Attr.]

BOGART, Humphrey (1899–1957)

I should never have changed from scotch to martinis.

[In Simon Rose, *Classic Film Guide* (1995)]

GANDHI, Indira (1917–1984)

[Said 24 hours before she was assassinated]

Even if I die in the service of this nation, I would be proud of it. Every drop of my blood, I am sure, will contribute to the growth of this nation and make it strong and dynamic.

GEORGE V (1865–1936)

[To Lord Wigram, his secretary; sometimes quoted as his last words]

How is the Empire?

[Attr.]

GILLMORE, Gary (d.1977)

[Executed by firing squad, Utah.]

Let's do it!

[Attr.]

GOETHE (1749–1832)

Mehr Licht!

More light!

[Attr.]

GRAHAM, James, Marquis of Montrose (1612–1650)

May God have mercy upon this afflicted Kingdom.

[Last words]

GREGORY VII (c.1020–1085)

Dilexi justitiam et odivi iniquitatem: propterea morior in exilio.

I have loved righteousness and hated iniquity: therefore I die in exile.

> [In Bowden, *The Life and Pontificate of Gregory VII* (1840)]

GWENN, Edmund (1875–1959)

[Reply on his deathbed, when someone said to him, 'It must be very hard']

It is. But not as hard as farce.

[*Time*, 1984]

HALE, Nathan (1755–1776)

[Speech before he was executed by the British]

I only regret that I have but one life to lose for my country.

[In Johnston, *Nathan Hale* (1974)]

HAZLITT, William (1778–1830)

Well, I've had a happy life.

[In W.C. Hazlitt, *Memoirs of William Hazlitt* (1867)]

HEGEL, Georg Wilhelm (1770–1831)

[Said on his deathbed]

Only one man ever understood me. … And he didn't understand me.

[In B. Conrad, *Famous Last Words* (1962)]

HEINE, Heinrich (1797–1856)

Dieu me pardonnera, c'est son métier.
God will forgive me. It is his profession.

[In Meissner, *H H Erinnerungen* (1856)]

HENRY, O. (1862–1910)

[Attr. last words, quoting the song 'I'm Afraid to Go Home in the Dark']
Don't turn down the light, I'm afraid to go home in the dark.

[In Leacock, 'The Amazing Genius of O. Henry', 1916]

HOBBES, Thomas (1588–1679)

I am about to take my last voyage, a great leap in the dark.

[In Watkins, *Anecdotes of Men of Learning* (1808)]

HOKUSAI (1760–1849)

[Said on his deathbed]
If heaven had granted me five more years, I could have become a real painter.

[In B. Conrad, *Famous Last Words* (1962)]

HOLLAND, First Lord (Henry Fox) (1705–1774)

[Said during his last illness]
If Mr Selwyn calls, let him in: if I am alive I shall be very glad to see him, and if I am dead he will be very glad to see me.

[Attr.]

HOLT, Harold Edward (1908–1967)

I know this beach like the back of my hand.

[Last words, *Sydney Morning Herald*, 1967]

HUBBOCK, Chris (d.1970)

[US newsreader before shooting herself during a broadcast.]
And now, in keeping with Channel 40's policy of always bringing you the latest in blood and guts, in living color, you're about to see another first – an attempted suicide.

HUME, David (1711–1776)

I am dying as fast as my enemies, if I have any, could wish, and as cheerfully as my best friends could desire.

[Last words, 1776]

HUSS, Jan (c.1370–1415)

[At the stake, on seeing a peasant bringing wood]
O sancta simplicitas!
O holy simplicity!

[In Zincgreff and Weidner, *Apothegmata* (1653)]

IBSEN, Henrik (1828–1906)

[Ibsen's last words; his nurse had just remarked that he was feeling a little better]
On the contrary!

[Attr.]

JOHN XXIII (1881–1963)

[Remark made two days before he died]
I am able to follow my own death step by step. Now I move softly towards the end.

[*The Guardian*,1963]

JOHNSON, Samuel (1709–1784)

[On his deathbed]
I will be conquered; I will not capitulate.

[In Boswell, *The Life of Samuel Johnson* (1791)]

KEATS, John (1795–1821)

I shall soon be laid in the quiet grave – thank God for the quiet grave – O! I can feel the cold earth upon me – the daisies growing over me – O for this quiet – it will be my first.

[Attr.]

KELLY, Ned (1855–1880)

[On the scaffold, 11 November 1880]
'Ah well, I suppose it has come to this! … Such is life!'.

[Attr.]

LATIMER, Bishop Hugh (c.1485–1555)

[Said shortly before being put to death]
Be of good comfort, Master Ridley, and play the man. We shall this day light such a candle by God's grace in England, as (I trust) shall never be put out.

[In Foxe, *Actes and Monuments* (1562–1563)]

LE MESURIER, John (1912–1983)

It's all been rather lovely.

[Last words, quoted in *The Times*, 1983]

LOUIS XIV (1638–1715)

[Noticing as he lay on his deathbed that his attendants were crying]

Why are you weeping? Did you imagine that I was immortal?

[Attr.]

MARCO POLO (c.1254–1324)

I have not told half of what I saw.

[In W. Durant, *The Story of Civilization*, I]

MCALPINE, Sir Alfred (1881–1944)

Keep Paddy behind the big mixer.

[Attr.]

MONMOUTH, Duke of (1649–1685)

[Words to his executioner]

Do not hack me as you did my Lord Russell.

[In Macaulay, *History of England* (1849)]

MOORE, General Sir John (1761–1809)

I hope the people of England will be satisfied. I hope my country will do me justice.

[Attr.]

MORE, Sir Thomas (1478–1535)

After his head was upon the block, [he] lift it up again, and gently drew his beard aside, and said, This hath not offended the king.

[In Francis Bacon, *Apophthegms New and Old* (1625)]

MORRIS, William (1834–1896)

I want to get Mumbo-Jumbo out of the world.

[Attr.]

NELSON, Lord (1758–1805)

[Last words at the Battle of Trafalgar, 1805]

Thank God, I have done my duty.

[In Robert Southey, *The Life of Nelson* (1860)]

NERO (37–68)

Qualis artifex pereo!

What a great artist dies with me!

[In Suetonius, *Lives of the Caesars*, 'Nero']

O'NEILL, Eugene (1888–1953)

I knew it. I knew it. Born in a hotel room – and God damn it – died in a hotel room.

[Attr.]

OATES, Captain Lawrence (1880–1912)

I am just going outside, and may be some time.

[Last words, quoted in Captain Scott's diary]

PALMERSTON, Lord (1784–1865)

Die, my dear Doctor, that's the last thing I shall do!

[Attr. last words]

PAVLOVA, Anna (1881–1931)

Get my swan costume ready.

[Attr.]

PERELMAN, S.J. (1904–1979)

[Giving his reasons for refusing to see a priest as he lay dying]

I am curious to see what happens in the next world to one who dies unshriven.

[Attr.]

PHEIDIPPIDES (d. 490 BC)

[His last words, after he had run to Athens with news of the Battle of Marathon]

Greetings, we have won.

[In Lucian, 'Pro Lapsu inter salutandum']

PICASSO, Pablo (1881–1973)

Drink to me.

[Attr.]

PITT, William (1759–1806)

I think I could eat one of Bellamy's veal pies.

[Attr. last words]

POPE, Alexander (1688–1744)

Here am I, dying of a hundred good symptoms.

[In Spence, *Anecdotes*]

RABELAIS, François (c.1494–c.1553)

Je vais quérir un grand peut-être … Tirez le rideau, la farce est jouée.

I am going to seek a great perhaps …Bring down the curtain, the farce is played out.

[Attr.]

RALEIGH, Sir Walter (c.1552–1618)

[On feeling the edge of the axe before his execution]

'Tis a sharp remedy, but a sure one for all ills.

[Attr.]

REYNOLDS, Sir Joshua (1723–1792)

I should desire that the last words which I should pronounce in this Academy, and from this place, might be the name of – Michael Angelo.

[*Discourses on Art*, XV (1790)]

RHODES, Cecil (1853–1902)

So little done, so much to do!

[In Lewis Mitchell, *Life of Rhodes* (1910)]

SAKI (1870–1916)

[Last words, said by Corporal Munro to one of his men who had lit up; he was killed by a German sniper]

Put that bloody cigarette out!

[In A. J. Langguth, *Life of Saki*]

SANDERS, George (1906–1972)

Dear World, I am leaving you because I am bored. I feel I have lived long enough. I am leaving you with your worries in this sweet cesspool – good luck.

[Suicide note]

SARO-WIWA, Ken (d. 1995)

Lord take my soul, but the struggle continues.

[*The Observer*, 1995]

SAROYAN, William (1908–1981)

Everybody has got to die, but I have always believed an exception would be made in my case. Now what?

[*Time*, 1984]

SCARRON, Paul (1610–1660)

[As he lay dying]

At last I am going to be well!

[Attr.]

SCOTT, Captain Robert (1868–1912)

For God's sake look after our people.

[*Journal*, 25 March 1912]

Had we lived, I should have had a tale to tell of the hardihood, endurance, and courage of my companions which would have stirred the heart of every Englishman. These rough notes and our dead bodies must tell the tale.

[Message to the Public, 1912]

SEDGWICK, John (1813–1864)

[His last words, in response to a suggestion that he should not show himself over the parapet during the Battle of the Wilderness]

Nonsense, they couldn't hit an elephant at this dist –.

[Attr.]

SIDNEY, Sir Philip (1554–1586)

[Offering his water-bottle, despite his own injuries, to a dying soldier on the battlefield near Zutphen, 1586]

Thy necessity is yet greater than mine.

[In Sir Fulke Greville, *Life of Sir Philip Sidney* (1652)]

SMITH, Adam (1723–1790)

I believe we must adjourn this meeting to some other place.

[Last words]

SOCRATES (469–399 BC)

Crito, we owe a cock to Asclepius. Pay it and do not neglect it.

[Attr. in Plato, *Phaedo*,]

SPENCER, Sir Stanley (1891–1959)

[Thanking the nurse who had given him his nightly injection, just before he died]

Beautifully done.

[In Collis, *Stanley Spencer* (1962)]

SPENKELINK, John (d.1979)

[Executed in electric chair, Florida.]

Capital punishment: them without the capital get the punishment.

[Attr.]

STEIN, Gertrude (1874–1946)

Just before she [Stein] died she asked, 'What is the answer?' No answer came. She laughed and said, 'In that case, what is the question?' Then she died.

[In Sutherland, *Gertrude Stein* (1951)]

STRACHEY, Lytton (1880–1932)

If this is dying, then I don't think much of it.

[In Michael Holroyd, *Lytton Strachey: A Critical Biography* (1968)]

SWIFT, Jonathan (1667–1745)

[Learning of the arrival of Handel: Swift's last

words]

Ah, a German and a genius! a prodigy, admit him!

[Attr.]

THURBER, James (1894–1961)

God bless … God damn.

[Attr.]

TICHBORNE, Chidiock (c.1558–1586)

My prime of youth is but a frost of cares;
My feast of joy is but a dish of pain;
My crop of corn is but a field of tares;
And all my good is but vain hope of gain.
The day is past, and yet I saw no sun;
And now I live, and now my life is done.

['Elegy', written in the Tower of London before his
execution]

TOLSTOY, Leo (1828–1910)

[Refusing to reconcile himself with the Russian
Orthodox Church as he lay dying]
Even in the valley of the shadow of death,
two and two do not make six.

[Attr.]

**VEGA CARPIO, Félix Lope de
(1562–1635)**

[On learning that he was about to die]
All right, then, I'll say it: Dante makes me sick.

[Attr.]

VESPASIAN (AD 9–79)

[Last words]
Vae, puto deus fio.
Woe is me, I think I am becoming a god.

[In Suetonius, *Lives of the Caesars*]

WILDE, Oscar (1854–1900)

[Last words, as he lay dying in a drab Paris
bedroom]
Either that wallpaper goes, or I do.

[*Time*, 16 January 1984]

WILHELM I, Kaiser (1797–1888)

[Said during his last illness]
I haven't got time to be tired.

[Attr.]

WOLFE, James (1727–1759)

[Dying words]

Now God be praised, I will die in peace.

[In J. Knox, *Historical Journal of Campaigns* (1914
edition)]

LAUGHTER

**THE BIBLE
(King James Version)**

I said of laughter, It is mad: and of mirth,
What doeth it?

[*Ecclesiastes*, 2:2]

PROVERBS

Laughter is brightest where food is best.

Laughter is the best medicine.

Laugh and grow fat.

Laugh before breakfast, you'll cry before
supper.

WILCOX, Ella Wheeler (1850–1919)

Laugh, and the world laughs with you;
Weep, and you weep alone,
For the sad old earth must borrow its mirth,
But has trouble enough of its own.

[*Solitude*]

See HAPPINESS; HUMOUR

LAW

ADAMS, Richard (1846–1908)

You have been acquitted by a Limerick jury
and you may now leave the dock without
any other stain on your character.

[In Healy, *The Old Munster Circuit*]

ARBUTHNOT, John (1667–1735)

Law is a bottomless pit.

[*The History of John Bull* (c. 1712)]

BACON, Francis (1561–1626)

One of the Seven was wont to say: 'That laws
were like cobwebs; where the small flies
were caught, and the great brake through.'

[*Apophthegms New and Old* (1624)]

BENTHAM, Jeremy (1748–1832)

Lawyers are the only persons in whom

ignorance of the law is not punished.

[Attr.]

BIERCE, Ambrose (1842–c.1914)

Lawsuit: A machine which you go into as a pig and come out as a sausage.

[*The Cynic's Word Book* (1906)]

BRAXFIELD, Lord (1722–1799)

Let them bring me prisoners, and I'll find them law.

[Attr. by Cockburn]

BURKE, Edmund (1729–1797)

Laws, like houses, lean on one another.

[*Tracts on the Popery Laws* (1812)]

People crushed by law have no hopes but from power. If laws are their enemies, they will be enemies to laws; and those who have much to hope and nothing to lose will always be dangerous more or less.

[Letter to Charles James Fox, 1777]

There is but one law for all, namely, that law which governs all law – the law of our Creator, the law of humanity, justice, equity, the law of nature, and of nations.

[Speech, 1794]

CARROLL, Lewis (1832–1898)

'I'll be judge, I'll be jury,' said cunning
   old Fury:
'I'll try the whole cause, and condemn
   you to death.'

[*Alice's Adventures in Wonderland*
(1865)]

CHAPMAN, George (c.1559–c.1634)

I'me asham'd the law is such an Ass.

[*Revenge for Honour* (1654)]

COETZEE, J.M. (1940–)

All we can do is to uphold the laws, all of us, without allowing the memory of justice to fade.

[*Waiting for the Barbarians* (1980)]

DARLING, Charles (1849–1936)

The Law of England is a very strange one; it cannot compel anyone to tell the truth … But what the Law can do is to give you seven

years for not telling the truth.

[In Walker-Smith, *Lord Darling*]

DENNING, Lord (1899–1999)

To every subject of this land, however powerful, I would use Thomas Fuller's words over three hundred years ago, 'Be ye never so high, the law is above you'.

[High Court ruling against the Attorney-General, 1977]

EMERSON, Ralph Waldo (1803–1882)

Good men must not obey the laws too well.

['Politics' (1844)]

FRANCE, Anatole (1844–1924)

La majestueuse égalité des lois, qui interdit au riche comme au pauvre de coucher sous les ponts, de mendier dans les rues et de voler du pain.
The law, in its majestic equality, forbids the rich as well as the poor to sleep under bridges, to beg in the streets, and to steal bread.

[*Le Lys Rouge* (1894)]

GIRAUDOUX, Jean (1882–1944)

Nous savons tous ici que le droit est la plus puissante des écoles de l'imagination. Jamais poète n'a interprété la nature aussi librement qu'un juriste la realité.
All of us here know that there is no better way of exercising the imagination than the study of law. No poet has ever interpreted nature as freely as a lawyer interprets reality.

[*La Guerre de Troie n'aura pas lieu* (1935)]

GOETHE (1749–1832)

Wenn man alle Gesetze studieren sollte, so hätte man gar keine Zeit, sie zu übertreten.
If one were to study all the laws, one would have absolutely no time to break them.

['Experience and Life']

GOLDSMITH, Oliver (c.1728–1774)

Laws grind the poor, and rich men rule the law.

['The Traveller' (1764)]

GRANT, Ulysses S. (1822–1885)

I know no method to secure the repeal of bad or obnoxious laws so effective as their stringent execution.

[Inaugural Address, 1869]

HERBERT, Sir A.P. (1890–1971)

The Common Law of England has been laboriously built about a mythical figure – the figure of 'The Reasonable Man'.

[*Uncommon Law* (1935)]

HOLMES, Hugh (Lord Justice Holmes) (1840–1916)

An elderly pensioner on being sentenced to fifteen years' penal servitude cried 'Ah! my Lord, I'm a very old man, and I'll never do that sentence.' The judge replied 'Well try to do as much of it as you can'.

[In Healy, *The Old Munster Circuit* (1939)]

HORSLEY, Bishop Samuel (1733–1806)

In this country, my Lords, … the individual subject … 'has nothing to do with the laws but to obey them'.

[Speech, House of Lords, 1795]

INGRAMS, Richard (1937–)

I have come to regard the law courts not as a cathedral but rather as a casino.

[*The Guardian*, 1977]

JOHNSON, Samuel (1709–1784)

Johnson observed, that 'he did not care to speak ill of any man behind his back, but he believed the gentleman was an attorney.'

[In Boswell, *The Life of Samuel Johnson* (1791)]

KNOX, Philander Chase (1853–1921)

[Reply when Theodore Roosevelt requested legal justification for US acquisition of the Panama Canal Zone]

Oh, Mr President, do not let so great an achievement suffer from any taint of legality.

[Attr.]

LOCKE, John (1632–1704)

Wherever Law ends, Tyranny begins.

[*Second Treatise of Civil Government* (1690)]

MACHIAVELLI (1469–1527)

Li buoni esempi nascano dalla buona educazione; la buona educazione dalle buone leggi: e le buone leggi, da quei tumulti che molti inconsideratamente dannano.

Good examples are borne out of good education, which is the outcome of good legislation; and good legislation is borne out of those uprisings which are unduly damned by so many people.

[*Discourse*]

MAYNARD, Sir John (1602–1690)

[Reply to Judge Jeffreys' suggestion that he was so old he had forgotten the law]

I have forgotten more law than you ever knew, but allow me to say, I have not forgotten much.

[Attr.]

MORTIMER, John (1923–)

No brilliance is needed in the law. Nothing but common sense, and relatively clean finger nails.

[*A Voyage Round My Father* (1971)]

NORTH, Christopher (1785–1854)

Laws were made to be broken.

[*Blackwood's Edinburgh Magazine*, 1830]

PARKER, Hubert Lister (1900–1972)

A judge is not supposed to know anything about the facts of life until they have been presented in evidence and explained to him at least three times.

[*The Observer*, 1961]

PROVERBS

With a Scotsman or a priest, don't begin a lawsuit.

Possession is nine points of the law.

PUZO, Mario (1920–)

A lawyer with his briefcase can steal more than a thousand men with guns.

[*The Godfather* (1969)]

RICHELIEU, Cardinal (1585–1642)

Faire une loi et ne pas la faire exécuter, c'est autoriser la chose qu'on veut défendre.

To pass a law and not have it enforced is to authorize the very thing you wish to prohibit.

[*Mémoires*]

ROBESPIERRE, Maximilien (1758–1794)

Toute loi qui viole les droits imprescriptibles de l'homme, est essentiellement injuste et tyrannique; elle n'est point une loi.

Any law which violates the indefeasible rights of man is in essence unjust and tyrannical; it is no law.

[*Déclaration des Droits de l'homme* (1793)]

ROUSSEAU, Jean-Jacques (1712–1778)

Les lois sont toujours utiles á ceux qui possèdent et nuisibles á ceux qui n'ont rien.

Laws are always useful to those who have possessions, and harmful to those who have nothing.

[*Du Contrat Social* (1762)]

SCOTT, Sir Walter (1771–1832)

Mrs Bertram: That sounds like nonsense, my dear.

Mr Bertram: May be so, my dear; but it may be very good law for all that.

[*Guy Mannering* (1815)]

SELDEN, John (1584–1654)

Every law is a contract between the king and the people and therefore to be kept.

[*Table Talk* (1689)]

Ignorance of the law excuses no man; not that all men know the law, but because 'tis an excuse every man will plead, and no man can tell how to confute him.

[*Table Talk* (1689)]

SEWARD, William (1801–1872)

There is a higher law than the Constitution.

[Speech against Fugitive Slave Law, 1850]

SHAKESPEARE, William (1564–1616)

We must not make a scarecrow of the law,
Setting it up to fear the birds of prey,
And let it keep one shape till custom make it
Their perch, and not their terror.

[*Measure for Measure*, II.i]

SHENSTONE, William (1714–1763)

Laws are generally found to be nets of such a texture, as the little creep through, the great

break through, and the middle-sized are alone entangled in.

[*Works in Verse and Prose* (1764)]

SMITH, F.E. (1872–1930)

Judge Willis: What do you suppose I am on the Bench for, Mr Smith?

F.E. Smith: It is not for me to attempt to fathom the inscrutable workings of Providence.

[In Birkenhead, *Frederick Elwin, Earl of Birkenhead* (1933)]

[To a judge who complained that he was no wiser at the end than at the start of one of Smith's cases] Possibly not, My Lord, but far better informed.

[In Birkenhead, *Life of F.E. Smith* (1959)]

SOLON (c.638–c.559 BC)

Laws are like spider's webs, which hold firm when any light, yielding object falls upon them, while a larger thing breaks through them and escapes.

[In Diogenes Laertius, *Lives of the Eminent Philosophers*]

SWIFT, Jonathan (1667–1745)

Laws are like cobwebs, which may catch small flies, but let wasps and hornets break through.

[*A Critical Essay upon the Faculties of the Mind* (1709)]

See CRIME; JUSTICE

LEADERSHIP

ANONYMOUS

If it weren't for the last minute, nothing would ever get done.

BYRON, Lord (1788–1824)

And when we think we lead, we are most led.

[*The Two Foscari* (1821)]

COMPTON-BURNETT, Dame Ivy (1884–1969)

'She still seems to me in her own way a

person born to command,' said Luce …

'I wonder if anyone is born to obey,' said Isabel.

'That may be why people command rather badly, that they have no suitable material to work on.'

[*Parents and Children* (1941)]

LAW, Bonar (1858–1923)

I must follow them; I am their leader.

[In E.T. Raymond, *Mr Balfour*]

LEDRU-ROLLIN, Alexandre Auguste (1807–1874)

[Trying to force his way through a mob during the 1848 revolution, of which he was one of the chief instigators]

Eh! je suis leur chef, il fallait bien les suivre.

Ah well! I am their leader, I really should be following them!

[In E. de Mirecourt, *Histoire Contemporaine* (1857)]

MASSINGER, Philip (1583–1640)

He that would govern others, first should be The master of himself.

[*The Bondman: an Antient Story* (1624)]

MONTY PYTHON

Peasant: Look, you can't expect to wield supreme executive power just because some watery tart threw a sword at you!

[*Monty Python and the Holy Grail*, film, 1974]

MURRAY, Les A. (1938–)

Never trust a lean meritocracy
nor the leader who has been lean;
only the lifelong big have the knack of wedding
greatness with balance.

Never wholly trust the fat man
who lurks in the lean achiever
and the defeated, yearning to get out.

['Quintets for Robert Morley']

SARTRE, Jean-Paul (1905–1980)

Il est toujours facile d'obéir, si l'on rêve de commander.

It is always easy to obey, if one dreams of being in command.

[*Situations*]

SHAKESPEARE, William (1564–1616)

We were not born to sue, but to command.

[*Richard II*, I.i]

TACITUS (AD c.56–c.120)

[Of the Emperor Galba]

Omnium consensu capax imperii nisi imperasset.

No one would have doubted his ability to rule had he never been emperor.

[*Histories*]

LEARNING

ADDISON, Joseph (1672–1719)

The truth of it is, learning … makes a silly man ten thousand times more insufferable, by supplying variety of matter to his impertinence, and giving him an opportunity of abounding in absurdities.

[*The Man of the Town*]

ARISTOTLE (384–322 BC)

What we have to learn to do, we learn by doing.

[*Nicomachean Ethics*]

ARMSTRONG, Dr John (1709–1779)

Much had he read,
Much more had seen; he studied from the life,
And in th' original perus'd mankind.

[*The Art of Preserving Health* (1744)]

ASCHAM, Roger (1515–1568)

There is no such whetstone, to sharpen a good wit and encourage a will to learning, as is praise.

[*The Scholemaster* (1570)]

BACON, Francis (1561–1626)

Studies serve for delight, for ornament, and for ability.

['Of Studies' (1625)]

Crafty men contemn studies; simple men admire them; and wise men use them.

['Of Studies' (1625)]

CHESTERFIELD, Lord (1694–1773)

Wear your learning, like your watch, in a private pocket; and do not merely pull it out and strike it merely to show you have one. If you are asked what o'clock it is, tell it; but do not proclaim it hourly and unasked like the watchman.

[Letter to his son, 1748]

CONFUCIUS (c.550–c.478 BC)

Learning without thought is labour lost; thought without learning is perilous.

[Analects]

FOOTE, Samuel (1720–1777)

For as the old saying is,
When house and land are gone and spent
Then learning is most excellent.

[Taste (1752)]

GREGORY, Lady Isabella Augusta (1852–1932)

There's more learning than is taught in books.

[The Jester]

HUXLEY, T.H. (1825–1895)

Try to learn something about everything and everything about something.

[Memorial stone]

KNOX, Vicesimus (1752–1821)

That learning belongs not to the female character, and that the female mind is not capable of a degree of improvement equal to that of the other sex, are narrow and unphilosophical prejudices.

[Essays, Moral and Literary (1782)]

LESSING, Doris (1919–)

… that is what learning is. You suddenly understand something you've understood all your life, but in a new way.

[The Four-Gated City (1969)]

MILL, John Stuart (1806–1873)

As often as a study is cultivated by narrow minds, they will draw from it narrow conclusions.

[Auguste Comte and Positivism (1865)]

MILTON, John (1608–1674)

Where there is much desire to learn, there of necessity will be much arguing, much writing, many opinions; for opinion in good men is but knowledge in the making.

[Areopagitica (1644)]

OVID (43 BC–AD 18)

Adde quod ingenuas didicisse fideliter artes
Emollit mores nec sinit esse feros.

Add the fact that to have diligently studied the liberal arts refines behaviour and does not allow it to be savage.

[Epistulae Ex Ponto]

POPE, Alexander (1688–1744)

A little learning is a dangerous thing;
Drink deep, or taste not the Pierian spring:
There shallow draughts intoxicate the brain,
And drinking largely sobers us again.

[An Essay on Criticism (1711)]

WHITE, Patrick (1912–1990)

'I dunno,' Arthur said. 'I forget what I was taught. I only remember what I've learnt.'

[The Solid Mandala (1966)]

See EDUCATION; KNOWLEDGE; SCHOOL; UNIVERSITY

LETTERS

ADAMS, Abigail (1744–1818)

[Of letter-writing]
… a habit the pleasure of which increases with practice, but becomes more irksome with neglect.

[Letter to her daughter, 1808]

AUDEN, W.H. (1907–1973)

This is the Night Mail crossing the Border,
Bringing the cheque and the postal order,

Letters for the rich, letters for the poor,
The shop at the corner, the girl next door.

Pulling up Beattock, a steady climb:
The gradient's against her, but she's on time.

Past cotton-grass and moorland border,
Shovelling white steam over her shoulder …

Letters of thanks, letters from banks,
Letters of joy from girl and boy,
Receipted bills and invitations
To inspect new stock or to visit relations,
And applications for situations,
And timid lovers' declarations,
And gossip, gossip from all the nations.

[*Collected Poems, 1933–1938*, 'Night Mail']

JOHNSON, Samuel (1709–1784)

An odd thought strikes me: – we shall receive no letters in the grave.

[In Boswell, *The Life of Samuel Johnson* (1791)]

MORLEY, Lord (1838–1923)

[Of letter-writing]
That most delightful way of wasting time.

[*Critical Miscellanies* (1886), 'Life of George Eliot']

OSBORNE, Dorothy (Lady Temple) (1627–1695)

All letters, methinks, should be as free and easy as one's discourse, not studied as an oration, nor made up of hard words like a charm.

[Letter to Sir William Temple, 1653]

PRIOR, Matthew (1664–1721)

And oft the pangs of absence to remove
By letters, soft interpreters of love.

['Henry and Emma' (1708)]

STEELE, Sir Richard (1672–1729)

I have heard Will Honeycomb say, A Woman seldom Writes her Mind but in her Postscript.

[*The Spectator*, 79, 1711]

LIBERALS

FRAYN, Michael (1933–)

To be absolutely honest, what I feel really bad about is that I don't feel worse. There's the ineffectual liberal's problem in a nutshell.

[*The Observer*, 1965]

PATON, Alan (1903–1988)

By liberalism I don't mean the creed of any party or any century. I mean a generosity of spirit, a tolerance of others, an attempt to comprehend otherness, a commitment to the rule of law, a high ideal of the worth and dignity of man, a repugnance for authoritarianism and a love of freedom.

[Lecture on South Africa at Yale University, 1973]

LIES

ANONYMOUS

An abomination unto the Lord, but a very present help in time of trouble.

[Definition of a lie]

ARMSTRONG, Sir Robert (1927–)

[Replying to an allegation in court that a letter he had written on behalf of the British Government had contained a lie]
It contains a misleading impression, not a lie. It was being economical with the truth.

[*The Observer*, 1986]

ASQUITH, Margot (1864–1945)

[Of Lady Desborough]
She tells enough white lies to ice a wedding cake.

[Quoted by Lady Violet Bonham Carter in *The Listener*, June 1953]

BACON, Francis (1561–1626)

But it is not the lie that passeth through the mind, but the lie that sinketh in, and settleth in it, that doth the hurt.

['Of Truth' (1625)]

BELLOC, Hilaire (1870–1953)

Matilda told such Dreadful Lies,
It made one Gasp and Stretch one's Eyes;
Her Aunt, who, from her Earliest Youth,
Had kept a Strict Regard for Truth,
Attempted to Believe Matilda:
The effort very nearly killed her.

['Matilda' (1907)]

BENÉT, Stephen Vincent (1898–1943)

… the lounging mirth of cracker-barrel men,
Snowed in by winter, spitting at the fire,
And telling the disreputable truth

With the sad eye that marks the perfect liar.

['Poem']

THE BIBLE
(King James Version)

God is not a man, that he should lie.

[*Numbers*, 23:19]

BURKE, Edmund (1729–1797)

Falsehood has a perennial spring.

[*Speech on American Taxation* (1774)]

BUTLER, Samuel (1835–1902)

Any fool can tell the truth, but it requires a man of some sense to know how to lie well.

[*The Note-Books of Samuel Butler* (1912)]

BYRON, Lord (1788–1824)

And, after all, what is a lie? 'Tis but
The truth in masquerade.

[*Don Juan* (1824)]

CALLAGHAN, James (1912–)

A lie can be half-way round the world before the truth has got its boots on.

[Speech, 1976]

CORNEILLE, Pierre (1606–1684)

Il faut bonne mémoire après qu'on a menti.
One needs a good memory after telling lies.

[*Le Menteur* (1643)]

DAVIES, Robertson (1913–1995)

Better a noble lie than a miserable truth.

[In Twigg, *Conversations with Twenty-four Canadian Writers* (1981)]

EVANS, Harold (1928–)

The camera cannot lie. But it can be an accessory to untruth.

[Attr.]

GOLDSMITH, Oliver (c.1728–1774)

As ten millions of circles can never make a square, so the united voice of myriads cannot lend the smallest foundation to falsehood.

[*The Vicar of Wakefield* (1766), 27]

HAMPTON, Christopher (1946–)

You see, I always divide people into two groups. Those who live by what they know to be a lie, and those who live by what they

believe, falsely, to be the truth.

[*The Philanthropist* (1970)]

HERBERT, George (1593–1633)

The stormie working soul spits lies and froth.
Dare to be true. Nothing can need a ly.
A fault which needs it most grows two thereby.

[*The Temple* (1633)]

HERVEY, Lord (1696–1743)

Whoever would lie usefully should lie seldom.

[In Croker, *Memoirs of the Reign of George II* (1848)]

HOUSEHOLD, Geoffrey (1900–1988)

It's easy to make a man confess the lies he tells to himself; it's far harder to make him confess the truth.

[*Rogue Male* (1939)]

IBSEN, Henrik (1828–1906)

Take the saving lie from the average man and you take his happiness away, too.

[*The Wild Duck* (1884)]

JOWETT, Benjamin (1817–1893)

The lie in the Soul is a true lie.

[From the introduction to his translation (1871) of Plato's *Republic*]

MAUGHAM, William Somerset (1874–1965)

She's too crafty a woman to invent a new lie when an old one will serve.

[*The Constant Wife* (1927)]

MURDOCH, Iris (1919–1999)

He led a double life. Did that make him a liar? He did not feel a liar. He was a man of two truths.

[*The Sacred and Profane Love Machine* (1974)]

NIETZSCHE, Friedrich Wilhelm (1844–1900)

Wir haben die Lüge nötig, … um zu leben.
We need lies … in order to live.

[*Fragments* (1880–1889)]

PROUST, Marcel (1871–1922)

Une de ces dépêches dont M. de Guermantes avait spirituellement fixé le modèle: 'Impossible venir, mensonge suit'.

One of those telegrams of which M. de Guermantes had wittily fixed the formula: 'Cannot come, lie follows'.

[*Le Temps retrouvé* (1926)]

PROVERBS

Better a lie that heals than a truth that wounds.

A liar is worse than a thief.

QUINTILIAN (c.35–c.100)

Mendacem memorem esse oportere.

A liar must have a good memory.

[*Institutio Oratoria*, IV, 2, 91]

ROSSETTI, Dante Gabriel (1828–1882)

Was it a friend or foe that spread these lies?
Nay, who but infants question in such wise?
'Twas one of my most intimate enemies.

['Fragment']

RUSSELL, Bertrand (1872–1970)

I have never but once succeeded in making [George Moore] tell a lie, that was by a subterfuge. 'Moore,' I said, 'do you always speak the truth?' 'No,' he replied. I believe this to be the only lie he had ever told.

[*The Autobiography of Bertrand Russell* (1967–1969)]

SAKI (1870–1916)

A little inaccuracy sometimes saves tons of explanation.

[*The Square Egg* (1924)]

SALMON, George (1819–1904)

[Remark at the unveiling of a portrait of a colleague]

Excellent, excellent, you can just hear the lies trickling out of his mouth.

[Attr.]

SHAKESPEARE, William (1564–1616)

For my part, if a lie may do thee grace,
I'll gild it with the happiest terms I have.

[*Henry IV, Part 1*, V.iv]

SIDNEY, Algernon (1622–1683)

Liars ought to have good memories.

[*Discourses Concerning Government* (1698)]

SOLZHENITSYN, Alexander (1918–)

In our country the lie has become not just a moral category but a pillar of the State. In recoiling from the lie we are performing a moral act, not a political act.

[Interview in *Time* magazine, 1974]

This universal, compulsory, force-feeding with lies is now the most agonizing aspect of existence in our country – worse than all our material miseries, worse than any lack of civil liberties.

[*Letter to Soviet Leaders* (1974)]

STEAD, Christina (1902–1983)

A lie is real; it aims at success. A liar is a realist.

[*Letty Fox: Her Luck* (1946)]

STEVENSON, Adlai (1900–1965)

A lie is an abomination unto the Lord, and a very present help in trouble.

[Speech, Springfield, Illinois, 1951]

STEVENSON, Robert Louis (1850–1894)

The cruellest lies are often told in silence.

[*Virginibus Puerisque* (1881)]

SWIFT, Jonathan (1667–1745)

He replied that I must needs be mistaken, or that I said the thing which was not. (For they have no word in their language to express lying or falsehood.).

[*Gulliver's Travels* (1726)]

I mean, you lie – under a mistake.

[*Polite Conversation* (1738)]

TENNYSON, Alfred, Lord (1809–1892)

A lie which is all a lie may be met and fought with outright,
But a lie which is part a truth is a harder matter to fight.

['The Grandmother' (1859)]

TWAIN, Mark (1835–1910)

An experienced, industrious, ambitious, and often quite picturesque liar.

[*Private History of a Campaign that Failed* (1885)]

WASHINGTON, George (1732–1799)

[On being accused of cutting down a cherry tree]
Father, I cannot tell a lie; I did it with my little hatchet.

[Attr., probably apocryphal]

WELLS, H.G. (1866–1946)

The Social Contract is nothing more or less than a vast conspiracy of human beings to lie to and humbug themselves and one another for the general Good. Lies are the mortar that bind the savage individual man into the social masonry.

[*Love and Mr Lewisham* (1900)]

WILDE, Oscar (1854–1900)

The final revelation is that Lying, the telling of beautiful untrue things, is the proper aim of Art.

['The Decay of Lying' (1889)]

See ART; DECEPTION; HONESTY; TRUTH

LIFE

ADAMS, Douglas (1952–)

The Answer to the Great Question Of … Life, the Universe and Everything … Is … Forty-two.

[*The Hitch Hiker's Guide to the Galaxy* (1979)]

ADAMS, Henry (1838–1918)

Chaos often breeds life, when order breeds habit.

[*The Education of Henry Adams* (1918)]

ADAMS, Scott (1957–)

Accept that some days you're the pigeon, and some days you're the statue.

[*The Dilbert Principle*]

On the keyboard of life, always keep one finger on the escape key.

[*The Dilbert Principle*]

AMBROSE, Saint (c.340–397)

Si fueris Romae, Romano vivito more;
Si fueris alibi, vivito sicut ibi.
If you are in Rome, live in the Roman fashion;

if you are elsewhere, live as they do there.

[In Taylor, *Ductor Dubitantium* (1660)]

AMIEL, Henri-Frédéric (1821–1881)

Every life is a profession of faith, and exercises an inevitable and silent influence.

[*Journal*, 1852]

ANKA, Paul (1941–)

And now the end is near
And so I face the final curtain,
My friends, I'll say it clear,
I'll state my case of which I'm certain.
I've lived a life that's full, I've travelled each and evr'y high-way
And more, much more than this, I did it my way.

['My Way', song, 1969]

ANONYMOUS

Live well. It is the greatest revenge.

[*The Talmud*]

The reverse side also has a reverse side.

[Japanese Proverb]

Almost anything is easier to get into than out of.

[Allen's Law]

Hot glass looks the same as cold glass.

[Dominic Cirino's Law of Burnt Fingers]

When you need to knock on wood is when you realize that the world is composed of vinyl, naugahyde and aluminum.

[Flugg's Law]

If you knew what you were doing, you'd probably be bored.

[Fresco's Law]

It ain't necessarily so.

[Gershwin's Law]

Be happy while y'er leevin,
For y'er a lang time deid.

[Scottish motto]

ARISTOTLE (384–322 BC)

Just as at the Olympic games it is not the handsomest or strongest men who are crowned with victory but the successful competitors, so in life it is those who act rightly who carry off all the prizes and rewards.

[*Nicomachean Ethics*]

ARNOLD, Matthew (1822–1888)

For most men in a brazen prison live,
Where, in the sun's hot eye,
With heads bent o'er their toil, they languidly
Their lives to some unmeaning taskwork give,
Dreaming of nought beyond their prison-wall.

['A Summer Night' (1852)]

Is it so small a thing
To have enjoy'd the sun,
To have liv'd light in the spring,
To have lov'd, to have thought, to have done?

['Empedocles on Etna' (1852)]

When we are asked further, what is conduct? – let us answer: Three fourths of life.

[*Literature and Dogma* (1873)]

AURELIUS, Marcus (121–180)

Remember that no one loses any other life than this which he now lives, nor lives any other than this which he now loses.

[*Meditations*]

BACON, Francis (1561–1626)

But men must know, that in this theatre of man's life it is reserved only for God and angels to be lookers on.

[*The Advancement of Learning* (1605)]

BALFOUR, A.J. (1848–1930)

Nothing matters very much, and very few things matter at all.

[Attr.]

BARRIE, Sir J.M. (1860–1937)

The life of every man is a diary in which he means to write one story, and writes another; and his humblest hour is when he compares the volume as it is with what he vowed to make it.

[Attr.]

BECKETT, Samuel (1906–1989)

We always find something, eh, Didi, to give us the impression that we exist?

[*Waiting for Godot* (1955)]

BEDE, The Venerable (673–735)

When we compare the present life of man with that time of which we have no knowledge, it seems to me like the swift flight of a lone sparrow through the banqueting-hall where you sit in the winter months … This sparrow flies swiftly in through one door of the hall, and out through another … Similarly, man appears on earth for a little while, but we know nothing of what went on before this life, and what follows.

[*Ecclesiastical History*]

BEHAN, Beatrice (1931–1993)

I wonder why dreams must be broken, idylls lost and love forgotten? The transience of life has always exasperated me.

[*My Life with Brendan Behan* (1973)]

BENNETT, Alan (1934–)

You know life … it's rather like opening a tin of sardines. We are all of us looking for the key.

[*Beyond the Fringe* (1962)]

BENTLEY, Nicolas (1907–1978)

One should not exaggerate the importance of trifles. Life, for instance, is much too short to be taken seriously.

[Attr.]

BERRYMAN, John (1914–1972)

Life, friends, is boring. We must not say so.

[*Dream Songs* (1964)]

BLAKE, William (1757–1827)

For every thing that lives is holy, life delights in life.

[*America: a Prophecy* (1793)]

BRENAN, Gerald (1894–1987)

We should live as if we were going to live forever, yet at the back of our minds remember that our time is short.

[*Thoughts in a Dry Season* (1978)]

BRONTË, Charlotte (1816–1855)

Life, believe, is not a dream,
So dark as sages say;
Oft a little morning rain
Foretells a pleasant day!

['Life' (1846)]

BROWNE, Sir Thomas (1605–1682)

Life itself is but the shadow of death, and
souls but the shadows of the living. All things
fall under this name. The sun itself is but the
dark *simulacrum*, and light but the shadow of
God.

[*The Garden of Cyrus* (1658)]

The long habit of living indisposeth us for
dying.

[*Hydriotaphia: Urn Burial* (1658)]

BUCHAN, John (1875–1940)

It's a great life if you don't weaken.

[*Mr Standfast* (1919)]

BUTLER, Samuel (1835–1902)

Life is one long process of getting tired.

[*The Note-Books of Samuel Butler* (1912)]

To live is like love, all reason is against it, and
all healthy instinct for it.

[*The Note-Books of Samuel Butler* (1912)]

CHAMFORT, Nicolas (1741–1794)

*Vivre est une maladie dont le sommeil nous soulage
toutes les 16 heures. C'est un palliatif. La mort est le
remède.* Living is an illness to which sleep
provides relief every sixteen hours.
It's a palliative. Death is the remedy.

[*Maximes et pensées* (1796)]

CHAPLIN, Charlie (1889–1977)

Life is a tragedy when seen in close-up, but a
comedy in long-shot.

[In *The Guardian*, Obituary, 1977]

CLARE, John (1793–1864)

And what is Life? – an hour glass on
   the run
A mist retreating from the morning
   sun
A busy bustling still repeated dream

Its length? – A moment's pause, a
   moment's thought
And happiness? A Bubble on the
   stream
That in the act of seizing shrinks to
nought.

['What is Life?' (1820)]

If life had a second edition, how I would
correct the proofs.

[Letter to a friend]

COCTEAU, Jean (1889–1963)

Vivre est une chute horizontale.
Life is falling sideways.

[*Opium* (1930)]

COMPTON-BURNETT, Dame Ivy (1884–1969)

As regards plots I find real life no help at all.
Real life seems to have no plots.

[In R. Lehmann et al., *Orion I* (1945)]

CONRAN, Shirley (1932–)

Life is too short to stuff a mushroom.

[*Superwoman* (1975)]

CORY, William (1823–1892)

You promise heavens free from strife,
Pure truth, and perfect change of will;
But sweet, sweet is this human life,
So sweet, I fain would breathe it still;
Your chilly stars I can forgo,
This warm kind world is all I know …
All beauteous things for which we live
By laws of space and time decay.
But Oh, the very reason why
I clasp them, is because they die.

['Mimnermus in Church' (1858)]

COUBERTIN, Pierre de (1863–1937)

*L'important dans la vie ce n'est point le triomphe
mais le combat; l'essentiel ce n'est pas d'avoir vaincu
mais de s'être bien battu.*
The most important thing in life is not the
winning but the taking part; the essential
thing is not conquering but fighting well.

[Speech, 1908]

COWPER, William (1731–1800)

Variety's the very spice of life,

That gives all its flavour.

[*The Task* (1785)]

CROWFOOT (1821–1890)

What is life? It is the flash of a firefly in the night. It is the breath of a buffalo in the wintertime. It is the little shadow which runs across the grass and loses itself in the sunset.

[Last words]

DAVIES, William Henry (1871–1940)

What is this life if, full of care,
We have no time to stand and stare?

[*Songs of Joy* (1911)]

DICKENS, Charles (1812–1870)

'I am ruminating,' said Mr Pickwick, 'on the strange mutability of human affairs.'
'Ah, I see – in at the palace door one day, out at the window the next. Philosopher, sir?'
'An observer of human nature, sir,' said Mr Pickwick.

[*The Pickwick Papers* (1837)]

DISRAELI, Benjamin (1804–1881)

Next to knowing when to seize an opportunity, the most important thing in life is to know when to forego an advantage.

[Attr.]

DUNCAN, Isadora (1878–1927)

People do not live nowadays – they get about ten percent out of life.

[*This Quarter Autumn*, 'Memoirs']

EINSTEIN, Albert (1879–1955)

Only a life lived for others is a life worthwhile.

['Defining Success']

EMERSON, Ralph Waldo (1803–1882)

Life is good only when it is magical and musical, a perfect timing and consent, and when we do not anatomize it. You must treat the days respectfully, you must be a day yourself, and not interrogate it like a college professor ... You must hear the bird's song without attempting to render it into nouns and verbs.

[*Society and Solitude* (1870)]

FRANKLIN, Benjamin (1706–1790)

Dost thou love life? Then do not squander time, for that's the stuff life is made of.

[*Poor Richard's Almanac* (1746)]

FRY, Christopher (1907–)

What a minefield
Life is! One minute you're taking a stroll in the sun,
The next your legs and arms are all over the hedge.
There's no dignity in it.

[*A Yard of Sun* (1970)]

GAY, John (1685–1732)

Life is a jest; and all things show it.
I thought so once; but now I know it.

['My Own Epitaph' (1720)]

GIBBONS, Orlando (1583–1625)

What is our life? a play of passion,
Our mirth the music of derision,
Our mothers' wombs the tiring houses be,
Where we are dressed for this short comedy ...
Only we die in earnest, that's no jest.

[*The First Set of Madrigals and Motets of Five Parts* (1612)]

GOETHE (1749–1832)

Grau, teuer Freund, ist alle Theorie,
Und grün des Lebens goldner Baum.
Grey, dear friend, is all theory,
And green the golden tree of life.

[*Faust* (1808)]

GORDON, Adam Lindsay (1833–1870)

Life is mostly froth and bubble,
Two things stand like stone,
Kindness in another's trouble,
Courage in your own.

[*Ye Wearie Wayfarer* (1866)]

A little season of love and laughter,
Of light and life, and pleasure and pain,
And a horror of outer darkness after,
And dust returneth to dust again.

['The Swimmer' (1903)]

HARDY, Thomas (1840–1928)

'What do you think of it, Moon,

As you go?
Is Life much, or no?'
'O, I think of it, often think of it
As a show
God ought surely to shut up soon,
As I go.'

['To the Moon' (1917)]

HAWTHORNE, Nathaniel (1804–1864)

Life is made up of marble and mud.

[*The House of the Seven Gables* (1851)]

HENRY, O. (1862–1910)

Life is made up of sobs, sniffles, and smiles, with sniffles predominating.

[*The Four Million* (1906)]

HENSHAW, Bishop Joseph (1603–1679)

One doth but breakfast here, another dines, he that liveth longest doth but sup; we must all go to bed in another world.

[*Horae Succisivae* (1631)]

HOBBES, Thomas (1588–1679)

No arts; no letters; no society; and which is worst of all, continual fear, and danger of violent death; and the life of man, solitary, poor, nasty, brutish, and short.

[*Leviathan* (1651)]

HODSON, Peregrine

It shows hunger for life, like the Zen parable of a man holding on to a tree root over the edge of a cliff: below him rocks, above him a tiger, and a black and white mouse nibbling at the root: the man notices a strawberry beside him and picks it.

[*A Circle Round The Sun - A Foreigner in Japan*]

HUBBARD, Elbert (1856–1915)

Life is just one damned thing after another.

[*Philistine*, 1909]

HUXLEY, Aldous (1894–1963)

Living is an art; and to practise it well, men need, not only acquired skill, but also a native tact and taste.

[*Texts and Pretexts* (1932)]

Most of one's life … is one prolonged effort

to prevent oneself thinking.

[*Mortal Coils* (1922)]

HUXLEY, T.H. (1825–1895)

The chess-board is the world; the pieces are the phenomena of the universe; the rules of the game are what we call the laws of Nature. The player on the other side is hidden from us. We know that his play is always fair, just, and patient. But we also know, to our cost, that he never overlooks a mistake, or makes the smallest allowance for ignorance.

[*Macmillan's Magazine*, 1868]

JAMES, Henry (1843–1916)

Live all you can; it's a mistake not to. It doesn't so much matter what you do in particular, so long as you have your life. If you haven't had that then what have you had?

[*The Ambassadors* (1903)]

JEANS, Sir James Hopwood (1877–1946)

Life exists in the universe only because the carbon atom possesses certain exceptional properties.

[*The Mysterious Universe* (1930)]

JOHNSON, Samuel (1709–1784)

Life is a pill which none of us can bear to swallow without gilding.

[In Hester Lynch Piozzi, *Anecdotes of the Late Samuel Johnson* (1786)]

Human life is everywhere a state in which much is to be endured, and little to be enjoyed.

[*Rasselas* (1759)]

JUNG, Carl Gustav (1875–1961)

Soweit wir zu erkennen vermögen, ist er der einzige Sinn der menschlichen Existenz, ein Licht anzuzünden in der Finsternis des blossen Seins.
As far as we are able to understand, the only aim of human existence is to kindle a light in the darkness of mere being.

[*Memories, Dreams, Thoughts* (1962)]

KEATS, John (1795–1821)

But this is human life: the war, the deeds,

The disappointment, the anxiety,
Imagination's struggles, far and nigh,
All human.

['Endymion' (1818)]

I compare human life to a large Mansion of
Many Apartments, two of which I can only
describe, the doors of the rest being as yet
shut upon me.

[Letter to J.H. Reynolds, 3 May 1818]

A Man's life of any worth is a continual
allegory.

[Letter to George and Georgiana Keats, 1819]

KIERKEGAARD, Søren (1813–1855)

Life can only be understood backwards; but
it must be lived forwards.

[*Life*]

LA BRUYÈRE, Jean de (1645–1696)

*Il n'y a pour l'homme que trois événements: naître,
vivre, et mourir. Il ne se sent pas naître, il souffre à
mourir, et il oublie de vivre.*
There are only three events in a man's life;
birth, life, and death; he is not aware of being
born, he dies in suffering, and he forgets to
live.

[*Les caractères ou les moeurs de ce siècle* (1688)]

LAFORGUE, Jules (1860–1887)

Ah! que la vie est quotidienne!
Oh, what an everyday affair life is!

[*Les complaintes* (1885)]

LEHRER, Tom (1928–)

Life is like a sewer. What you get out of it
depends on what you put in.

[Record album, *An Evening Wasted with Tom Lehrer*
(1953)]

LENNON, John (1940–1980)

Life is what happens to you when you're
busy making other plans.

['Beautiful Boy', song, 1980]

LEONARDO DA VINCI (1452–1519)

While I thought that I was learning how to
live, I have been learning how to die.

[*Selections from the Notebooks of Leonardo da Vinci*
(1952 edition)]

LESSING, Gotthold Ephraim (1729–1781)

*Gestern liebt' ich,
Heute leid' ich,
Morgen sterb' ich.
Dennoch denk' ich
Heut und morgen
Gern an gestern.*
Yesterday I loved, today I suffer, tomorrow I
shall die. Nonetheless I still think with
pleasure, today and tomorrow, of yesterday.

['Song taken from the Spanish']

LEWIS, C.S. (1898–1963)

Term, holidays, term, holidays, till we leave
school, and then work, work, work till we die.

[*Surprised by Joy* (1955)]

LEWIS, Sir George Cornewall (1806–1863)

Life would be tolerable but for its
amusements.

[In *Dictionary of National Biography*]

LONGFELLOW, Henry Wadsworth (1807–1882)

Lives of great men all remind us
We can make our lives sublime,
And, departing, leave behind us
Footprints on the sands of time …

['A Psalm of Life' (1838)]

LUCRETIUS (c.95–55 BC)

Vitaque mancipio, nulli datur, omnibus usu.
For life is not confined to him or thee;
'Tis given to all for use, to none for property.

[*De Rerum Natura*]

MANN, Thomas (1875–1955)

*Der Mensch lebt nicht nur sein persönliches Leben als
Einzelwesen, sondern, bewusst oder unbewusst, auch
das seiner Epoche und Zeitgenossenschaft.*
Man does not only live his personal life as an
individual, but also, consciously or
unconsciously, the life of his era and of his
contemporaries.

[*The Magic Mountain* (1924)]

MARTIAL (c.AD 40–c.104)

Non est, crede mihi, sapientis dicere 'Vivam':

Sera nimis vita est crastina: vive hodie.
Believe me, 'I shall live' is not the saying of a wise man. Tomorrow's life is too late: live today.

[*Epigrammata*]

MAUGHAM, William Somerset (1874–1965)

Life is too short to do anything for oneself that one can pay others to do for one.

[*The Summing Up* (1938)]

MITCHELL, Joni (1943–)

I've looked at life from both sides now
From win and lose and still somehow
It's life's illusions I recall
I really don't know life at all.

['Both Sides Now', song, 1968]

MONTAIGNE, Michel de (1533–1592)

L'utilité de vivre n'est pas en l'espace, elle est en l'usage … Il gît en votre volonté, non au nombre des ans, que vous ayez assez vécu.'
The value of life does not lie in the number of years but in the use you make of them…
Whether you have lived enough depends on your will, not on the number of your years.

[*Essais* (1580)]

Mon métier et mon art, c'est vivre.
Living is both my job and my art.

[*Essais* (1580)]

NASH, Ogden (1902–1971)

When I consider how my life is spent,
I hardly ever repent.

['Reminiscent Reflection' (1931)]

NIETZSCHE, Friedrich Wilhelm (1844–1900)

Glaubt es mir! – das Geheimnis, um die grösste Fruchtbarkeit und den grössten Genuss vom Dasein einzuernten, heisst: gefährlich leben!
Believe me! – the secret of gathering in the greatest fruitfulness and the greatest enjoyment from existence is living dangerously!

[*The Gay Science* (1887)]

O'CASEY, Sean (1880–1964)

I am going where life is more like life than it

is here.

[*Cock-a-Doodle Dandy* (1949)]

O'KEEFFE, Georgia (1887–1986)

My feeling about life is a curious kind of triumphant feeling about seeing it bleak, knowing it is so, and walking into it fearlessly because one has no choice.

[Attr.]

O'NEILL, Eugene (1888–1953)

Our lives are merely strange dark interludes in the electric display of God the Father!

[*Strange Interlude* (1928)]

ORTEGA Y GASSET, José (1883–1955)

Poca cosa es la vida si no piafa en ella un afán formidable de ampliar sus fronteras. Se vive en la proporción en que se ans'a a vivir más.
Life is a petty thing unless there is pounding within it an enormous desire to extend its boundaries. We live in proportion to the extent to which we yearn to live more.

[*The Dehumanization of Art* (1925)]

PASCAL, Blaise (1623–1662)

Le dernier acte est sanglant, quelque belle que soit la comédie en tout le reste.
The last act is bloody, however delightful the rest of the play may be.

[*Pensées* (1670)]

PROUST, Marcel (1871–1922)

Good-bye, I've barely said a word to you, it is always like that at parties, we never see the people, we never say the things we should like to say, but it is the same everywhere in this life. Let us hope that when we are dead things will be better arranged.

[*A la recherche du temps perdu, Sodome et Gomorrhe* (1922)]

PROVERBS

Life begins at forty.

All's well that ends well.

The best things in life are free.

Life is just a bowl of cherries.

Life is sweet.

He that lives long suffers much.

RENARD, Jules (1864–1910)

Il faut dompter la vie par la douceur.
Life should be tamed with tenderness.

[*Journal*, 1892]

RUSSELL, Bertrand (1872–1970)

Brief and powerless is Man's life; on him and all his race the slow, sure doom falls pitiless and dark.

[*Mysticism and Logic* (1918)]

SANTAYANA, George (1863–1952)

There is no cure for birth and death save to enjoy the interval.

[*Soliloquies in England* (1922)]

Life is not a spectacle or a feast; it is a predicament.

[In Sagittarius and George, *The Perpetual Pessimist*]

SENECA (c.4 BC–AD 65)

Nil melius aeterna lex fecit, quam quod unum introitum nobis ad vitam dedit, exitus multos.
Eternal law has arranged nothing better than this, that it has given us one way in to life, but many ways out.

[*Epistulae Morales*]

Live among men as if God beheld you; speak to God as if men were listening.

[*Epistles*]

SHAKESPEARE, William (1564–1616)

All the world's a stage,
And all the men and women merely players;
They have their exits and their entrances;
And one man in his time plays many parts.

[*As You Like It*, II.vii]

O gentlemen, the time of life is short!
To spend that shortness basely were too long.

[*Henry IV, Part 1*, V.ii]

To-morrow, and to-morrow, and to-morrow,
Creeps in this petty pace from day to day
To the last syllable of recorded time,
And all our yesterdays have lighted fools
The way to dusty death. Out, out, brief candle!

Life's but a walking shadow, a poor player,
That struts and frets his hour upon the stage,
And then is heard no more; it is a tale
Told by an idiot, full of sound and fury,
Signifying nothing.

[*Macbeth*, V.v]

SHELLEY, Percy Bysshe (1792–1822)

Lift not the painted veil which those who live
Call Life.

['Sonnet' (1818)]

SMITH, Logan Pearsall (1865–1946)

There are two things to aim at in life: first, to get what you want; and, after that, to enjoy it. Only the wisest of mankind achieve the second.

[*Afterthoughts* (1931)]

SMOLLETT, Tobias (1721–1771)

What is life but a veil of affliction?

[*The Expedition of Humphry Clinker* (1771)]

SOCRATES (469–399 BC)

The unexamined life is not a life worth living for a human being.

[Attr. in Plato, *Apology*]

SOUTHEY, Robert (1774–1843)

Live as long as you may, the first twenty years are the longest half of your life.

[*The Doctor* (1812)]

STEINER, Rudolf (1861–1925)

The history of our spiritual life is a continuing search for the unity between ourselves and the world.

[*The Philosophy of Freedom* (1964)]

STEVENSON, Robert Louis (1850–1894)

To love playthings well as a child, to lead an adventurous and honourable youth, and to settle when the time arrives, into a green and smiling age, is to be a good artist in life and deserve well of yourself and your neighbour.

[*Virginibus Puerisque* (1881)]

STOPPARD, Tom (1937–)

Life is a gamble, at terrible odds – if it was a

bet, you wouldn't take it.

[*Rosencrantz and Guildenstern Are Dead* (1967)]

TAYLOR, Bishop Jeremy (1613–1667)

As our life is very short, so it is very miserable, and therefore it is well it is short.

[*The Rule and Exercise of Holy Dying* (1651)]

TEMPLE, Sir William (1628–1699)

When all is done, human life is, at the greatest and the best, but like a forward child, that must be play'd with and humoured a little to keep it quiet till it falls asleep, and then the care is over.

[*Miscellanea, The Second Part* (1690)]

TERENCE (c.190–159 BC)

Modo liceat vivere, est spes.

Where there's life, there's hope.

[*Heauton Timoroumenos*]

THALES (c.624–547 BC)

[His reply when asked why he chose to carry on living after saying there was no difference between life and death]

Because there is no difference.

[In Durant, *The Story of Civilization*]

THOREAU, Henry David (1817–1862)

I wanted to live deep and suck out all the marrow of life … to drive life into a corner, and reduce it to its lowest terms, and, if it proved to be mean, why then to get the whole and genuine meanness of it, and publish its meanness to the world; or if it were sublime, to know it by experience, and be able to give a true account of it in my next excursion.

[*Walden* (1854)]

Our life is frittered away by detail … Simplify, simplify.

[*Walden* (1854)]

TUCKER, Sophie (1884–1966)

Life begins at forty.

[Attr.]

TWAIN, Mark (1835–1910)

All say, 'How hard it is to die' – a strange complaint to come from the mouths of

people who have had to live.

[*Pudd'nhead Wilson's Calendar* (1894)]

VAUVENARGUES, Marquis de (1715–1747)

Pour exécuter de grandes choses, il faut vivre comme si on ne devait jamais mourir.

In order to achieve great things we must live as though we were never going to die.

[*Réflexions et Maximes* (1746)]

VILLIERS DE L'ISLE-ADAM, Philippe-Auguste (1838–1889)

Vivre? Les serviteurs feront cela pour nous.

Live? The servants will do that for us.

[*Axel* (1890)]

WELLS, H.G. (1866–1946)

I tell you, we're in a blessed drainpipe, and we've got to crawl along it till we die.

[*Kipps: the Story of a Simple Soul* (1905)]

WHITEHEAD, A.N. (1861–1947)

It is the essence of life that it exists for its own sake.

[*Nature and Life* (1934)]

WILDE, Oscar (1854–1900)

Lord Illingworth: The soul is born old but grows young. That is the comedy of life.
Mrs Allonby: And the body is born young and grows old. That is life's tragedy.

[*A Woman of No Importance* (1893)]

One can live for years sometimes without living at all, and then all life comes crowding into one single hour.

[*Vera, or The Nihilist* (1880)]

One's real life is so often the life that one does not lead.

['L'Envoi to Rose-Leaf and Apple-Leaf']

WODEHOUSE, P.G. (1881–1975)

I spent the afternoon musing on Life. If you come to think of it, what a queer thing Life is! So unlike anything else, don't you know, if you see what I mean.

[*My Man Jeeves* (1919)]

XERXES (c.519–465 BC)

[On surveying his army]

I was thinking, and I was moved to pity that the whole of human life is so short – not one of this great number will be alive a hundred years from now.

[In Herodotus, *Histories*]

YEATS, W.B. (1865–1939)

When I think of all the books I have read, and of the wise words I have heard spoken, and of the anxiety I have given to parents and grandparents, and of the hopes that I have had, all life weighed in the scales of my own life seems to me preparation for something that never happens.

[*Autobiographies* (1955)]

ZOLA, Emile (1840–1902)

Le seul intérêt à vivre est de croire à la vie, de l'aimer et de mettre toutes les forces de son intelligence à la mieux connaître.

The only interest in living comes from believing in life, from loving life and using all the power of your intelligence to know it better.

[*Le Docteur Pascal* (1893)]

See AFTERLIFE; HUMANITY AND HUMAN NATURE; MORTALITY; PURPOSE; TIME

LITERATURE

BRENAN, Gerald (1894–1987)

The cliché is dead poetry. English, being the language of an imaginative race, abounds in clichés, so that English literature is always in danger of being poisoned by its own secretions.

[*Thoughts in a Dry Season* (1978)]

CONNOLLY, Cyril (1903–1974)

Literature is the art of writing something that will be read twice; journalism what will be grasped at once.

[*Enemies of Promise* (1938)]

GAISFORD, Rev. Thomas (1779–1855)

Nor can I do better, in conclusion, than impress upon you the study of Greek literature, which not only elevates above the vulgar herd, but leads not infrequently to positions of considerable emolument.

[Christmas Day Sermon, Oxford Cathedral]

GOETHE (1749–1832)

Nationalliteratur will jetzt nicht viel sagen, die Epoche der Weltliteratur ist an der Zeit.

National literature does not now have much significance, it is time for the era of world literature.

[*Gespräche mit Eckermann*, 1827]

HELLER, Joseph (1923–)

He knew everything about literature except how to enjoy it.

[*Catch-22* (1961)]

HORACE (65–8 BC)

Inceptis gravibus plerumque et magna professis Purpureus, late qui splendeat, unus et alter Adsuitur pannus.

In serious works and ones that promise great things, one or two purple patches are often stitched in, to glitter far and wide.

[*Ars Poetica*]

INGE, William Ralph (1860–1954)

Literature flourishes best when it is half a trade and half an art.

['The Victorian Age' (1922)]

LEWIS, Sinclair (1885–1951)

Our American professors like their literature clear, cold, pure, and very dead.

[Address to Swedish Academy, 1930]

LODGE, David (1935–)

Literature is mostly about having sex and not much about having children; life is the other way round.

[*The British Museum is Falling Down* (1965)]

LOVER, Samuel (1797–1868)

When once the itch of literature comes over a man, nothing can cure it but the scratching of a pen.

[*Handy Andy* (1842)]

NABOKOV, Vladimir (1899–1977)

Literature and butterflies are the two

sweetest passions known to man.

[*Radio Times*, 1962]

PALMER, Nettie (1885–1964)

But is there, I wonder, any such thing as 'pure' literature? Isn't it just a conception of people who look on writing as an escape from the living world? Perhaps a painter, or musician, can cut himself off, in his work, from what's going on around him, but a writer can't.

[*Fourteen Years …*, Journal entry, 1939]

POUND, Ezra (1885–1972)

Great Literature is simply language charged with meaning to the utmost possible degree.

[*How to Read* (1931)]

Literature is news that STAYS news.

[*ABC of Reading* (1934)]

QUILLER-COUCH, Sir Arthur ('Q') (1863–1944)

Does it or does it not strike you as queer that the people who set you 'courses of study' in English Literature never include the Authorised Version, which not only intrinsically but historically is out and away the greatest book of English Prose? Perhaps they pay you the compliment of supposing that you are perfectly acquainted with it? … I wonder.

[*On the Art of Writing* (1916)]

SOUTHEY, Robert (1774–1843)

Your true lover of literature is never fastidious.

[*The Doctor* (1812)]

STEIN, Gertrude (1874–1946)

[Speaking to a friend she considered knew little about literature]

Besides Shakespeare and me, who do you think there is?

[In Mellow, *Charmed Circle* (1974)]

STENDHAL (1783–1842)

Le romantisme est l'art de présenter aux peuples les oeuvres littéraires qui, dans l'état actuel de leurs habitudes et de leurs croyances, sont susceptibles de leur donner le plus de plaisir possible. Le classicisme, au contraire, leur présente la littérature qui donnait le

plus grand plaisir possible á leurs arrière-grand-pères.

Romanticism is the art of presenting people with the literary works which are capable of giving them the greatest possible pleasure, in the present state of their customs and beliefs. Classicism, on the other hand, presents them with the literature that gave the greatest possible pleasure to their great-grandfathers.

[*Racine et Shakespeare* (1823)]

TOLSTOYA, Tatyana

Literature is written according to certain rules, but which rules?

[Interview, Waterstones, Glasgow]

TWAIN, Mark (1835–1910)

[Definition of a classic]

Something that everybody wants to have read and nobody wants to read.

['The Disappearance of Literature']

WILDE, Oscar (1854–1900)

Movement, that problem of the visible arts, can be truly realized by Literature alone. It is Literature that shows us the body in its swiftness and the soul in its unrest.

['The Critic as Artist' (1891)]

WILDER, Thornton (1897–1975)

Literature is the orchestration of platitudes.

[*Time*, 1953]

WOOLF, Virginia (1882–1941)

Literature is strewn with the wreckage of men who have minded beyond reason the opinions of others.

[*A Room of One's Own* (1929)]

YEATS, W.B. (1865–1939)

All folk literature, and all literature that keeps the folk tradition, delights in unbounded and immortal things.

['The Celtic Element in Literature' (1902)]

We have no longer in any country a literature as great as the literature of the old world, and that is because the newspapers, all kinds of second-rate books, the preoccupation of men with all kinds of practical changes, have driven the living imagination out of this world.

['First Principles' (1904)]

See ART; BOOKS; CRITICISM; FICTION; POETRY; POETS; READING; WRITERS; WRITING

LOGIC

ANONYMOUS
Logic is a systematic method of coming to the wrong conclusion with confidence.

[Manley's Maxim]

CHESTERTON, G.K. (1874–1936)
You can only find truth with logic if you have already found truth without it.

[The Man who was Orthodox]

WITTGENSTEIN, Ludwig (1889–1951)
Logic must look after itself.

[Tractatus Logico-Philosophicus (1922)]

See PHILOSOPHY

LONELINESS

ARNOLD, Matthew (1822–1888)
Yes! in the sea of life enisled,
With echoing straits between us thrown,
Dotting the shoreless watery wild,
We mortal millions live alone.

['To Marguerite – Continued' (1852)]

This truth – to prove, and make thine own:
'Thou hast been, shalt be, art, alone.'

['Isolation. To Marguerite' (1857)]

CONRAD, Joseph (1857–1924)
Who knows what true loneliness is – not the conventional word but the naked terror? To the lonely themselves it wears a mask.

[Attr.]

HAMMARSKJÖLD, Dag (1905–1961)
Pray that your loneliness may spur you into finding something to live for, great enough

to die for.

[Diaries, 1951]

HUBBARD, Elbert (1856–1915)
Loneliness is to endure the presence of one who does not understand.

[Attr.]

LENNON, John (1940–1980)
Waits at the window, wearing the face that she keeps in a jar by the door
Who is it for? All the lonely people, where do they all come from?
All the lonely people, where do they all belong?

['Eleanor Rigby', 1966, with Paul McCartney]

O'BRIEN, Edna (1936–)
I often get lonely for unrealistic things: for something absolute.

[The Observer, 1992]

SARTON, May (1912–)
Loneliness is the poverty of self; solitude is the richness of self.

[Mrs Stevens Hears the Mermaids Singing (1993)]

WILLIAMS, Hank
Hear that lonesome whippoorwill?
He sounds too blue to fly.
The midnight train is whining low,
I'm so lonesome I could cry.

['I'm So Lonesome I Could Cry', 1942]

See SOLITUDE

LOTTERY

JONES, Roger
I guess I think of lotteries as a tax on the mathematically challenged.

LOVE

ANONYMOUS
Western wind, when wilt thou blow,
The small rain down can rain?
Christ, if my love were in my arms

And I in my bed again!

[*New Oxford Book of 16th-Century Verse* (1991)]

ANOUILH, Jean (1910–1987)

Vous savez bien que l'amour, c'est avant tout le don de soi!

Love is, above all else, the gift of oneself.

[*Ardèle ou la Marguerite* (1949)]

AUDEN, W.H. (1907–1973)

When it comes, will it come without warning
Just as I'm picking my nose?
Will it knock on my door in the morning,
Or tread in the bus on my toes?
Will it come like a change in the weather?
Will its greeting be courteous or rough?
Will it alter my life altogether?
O tell me the truth about love.

['Twelve Songs']

Stop all the clocks, cut off the telephone,
Prevent the dog from barking with a juicy bone,
Silence the pianos and with muffled drum
Bring out the coffin, let the mourners come.

He was my North, my South, my East and West,
My working week and my Sunday rest,
My noon, my midnight, my talk, my song;
I thought that love would last for ever: I was wrong.

['Twelve Songs']

Reindeer are coming to drive you away
Over the snow on an ebony sleigh,
Over the mountains and over the sea
You shall go happy and handsome and free.

[Auden and Isherwood, *The Ascent of F.6* (1936)]

Lay your sleeping head, my love,
Human on my faithless arm;
Time and fevers burn away
Individual beauty from
Thoughtful children, and the grave
Proves the child ephemeral:
But in my arms till break of day
Let the living creature lie,
Mortal, guilty, but to me

The entirely beautiful.

[*Collected Poems, 1933–1938*, 'Lullaby']

In an upper room at midnight
See us gathered on behalf
Of love according to the gospel
Of the radio-phonograph.

[*Nones* (1951), 'The Love Feast']

AUGUSTINE, Saint (354–430)

Veni Karthaginem, et circumstrepebat me undique sartago flagitiosorum amorum. Nondum amabam, et amare amabam … quaerebam quid amarem, amans amare.

I came to Carthage where a whole frying pan full of abominable loves crackled about me on every side. I was not in love yet, yet I loved to be in love … I was looking for something to love, in love with love itself.

[*Confessions* (397–398)]

AUSTEN, Jane (1775–1817)

All the privilege I claim for my own sex … is that of loving longest, when existence or when hope is gone.

[*Persuasion* (1818)]

BACON, Francis (1561–1626)

They do best who, if they cannot but admit love, yet make it keep quarter; and sever it wholly from their serious affairs and actions of life: for if it check once with business, it troubleth men's fortunes, and maketh men, that they can no ways be true to their own ends.

['Of Love' (1625)]

BALZAC, Honoré de (1799–1850)

It is easier to be a lover than a husband, for the same reason that it is more difficult to show a ready wit all day long than to produce an occasional bon mot.

[Attr.]

BARNFIELD, Richard (1574–1627)

My flocks feed not, my ewes breed not,
My rams speed not, all is amiss:
Love is denying, Faith is defying,
Heart's renying, causer of this.

[In Nicholas Ling (ed.), *England's Helicon* (1600)]

BEHN, Aphra (1640–1689)

Oh, what a dear ravishing thing is the beginning of an Amour!

[*The Emperor of the Moon* (1687)]

BETJEMAN, Sir John (1906–1984)

'Let us not speak, for the love we bear one another –
Let us hold hands and look.'
She, such a very ordinary little woman;
He, such a thumping crook;
But both, for a moment, little lower than the angels
In the teashop's ingle-nook.

[*New Bats in Old Belfries* (1945)]

THE BIBLE
(King James Version)

And Jacob served seven years for Rachel; and they seemed unto him but a few days, for the love he had to her.

[*Genesis*, 29:20]

Intreat me not to leave thee, or to return from following after thee: for whither thou goest, I will go; and where thou lodgest, I will lodge: thy people shall be my people, and thy God my God.

[*Ruth*, 1:16–17]

Greater love hath no man than this, that a man lay down his life for his friends.

[*John*, 15:13]

He that loveth not knoweth not God; for God is love.

[*I John*, 4:8]

Perfect love casteth out fear.

[*I John*, 4:18]

BICKERSTAFFE, Isaac (c.1733–c.1808)

Perhaps it was right to dissemble your love,
But – why did you kick me downstairs?

['An Expostulation' (1789)]

BLAKE, William (1757–1827)

Love seeketh not Itself to please,
Nor for itself hath any care;
But for another gives its ease,

And builds a Heaven in Hells despair.

['The Clod & the Pebble' (1794)]

Children of the future Age,
Reading this indignant page:
Know that in a former time,
Love! sweet Love! was thought a crime.

['A Little Girl Lost' (1794)]

BLANCH, Lesley (1907–)

[Of Jane Digby who was successively Lady Ellenborough, Baroness Venningen, Countess Theotoky and the wife of Sheik Abdul Medjuel El Mezrab]
She was an Amazon. Her whole life was spent riding at breakneck speed towards the wilder shores of love.

[*The Wilder Shores of Love* (1954)]

BOETHIUS (c.475–524)

Quis legem dat amantibus? Major lex amor est sibi.
Who can give a law to lovers? Love is a greater law unto itself.

[*De Consolatione Philosophiae* (c. 522–524)]

BRENNAN, Christopher (1870–1932)

My heart was wandering in the sands,
a restless thing, a scorn apart;
Love set his fire in my hands,
I clasped the flame into my heart.

[*Poems* (1914)]

BRIDGES, Robert (1844–1930)

When first we met we did not guess
That Love would prove so hard a master.

['Triolet' (1890)]

BROOKE, Rupert (1887–1915)

I thought when love for you died, I
   should die.
It's dead. Alone, mostly strangely, I live on.

['The Life Beyond' (1910)]

BROWNING, Elizabeth Barrett (1806–1861)

How do I love thee? Let me count the ways.

[*Sonnets from the Portuguese* (1850)]

BURNS, Robert (1759–1796)

Ae fond kiss, and then we sever!
Ae fareweel, and then forever! …

But to see her was to love her,
Love but her, and love for ever.
Had we never lov'd sae kindly,
Had we never lov'd sae blindly,
Never met – or never parted –
We had ne'er been broken-hearted.

['Ae Fond Kiss' (1791)]

O, my luve's like a red, red, rose
That's newly sprung in June.
O, my luve's like the melodie,
That's sweetly play'd in tune.

['A Red Red Rose' (1794)]

BURTON, Robert (1577–1640)

No chord, nor cable can so forcibly draw, or
hold so fast, as love can do with a twined
thread.

[*Anatomy of Melancholy* (1621)]

BUTLER, Samuel (1612–1680)

For money has a power above
The stars and fate, to manage love.

[*Hudibras* (1678)]

All love at first, like generous wine,
Ferments and frets until 'tis fine;
But when 'tis settled on the lee,
And from th' impurer matter free,
Becomes the richer still the older,
And proves the pleasanter the colder.

[*Miscellaneous Thoughts*]

BUTLER, Samuel (1835–1902)

'Tis better to have loved and lost than never
to have lost at all.

[*The Way of All Flesh* (1903)]

God is Love, I dare say. But what a
mischievous devil Love is.

[*The Note-Books of Samuel Butler* (1912)]

BYRON, Lord (1788–1824)

In her first passion woman loves her
lover,
In all the others all she loves is love.

[*Don Juan* (1824)]

CHAMFORT, Nicolas (1741–1794)

L'amour, tel qu'il existe dans la société, n'est que
l'échange de deux fantaisies et le contact de deux
épidermes.
Love, as it exists in society, is nothing more
than the exchange of two fantasies and the
contact of two skins.

[*Maximes et pensées* (1796)]

CHER (1946–)

If grass can grow through cement, love can
find you at every time in your life.

[*The Times*, 1998]

CHEVALIER, Maurice (1888–1972)

Many a man has fallen in love with a girl in a
light so dim he would not have chosen a suit
by it.

[Attr.]

CLARE, John (1793–1864)

Language has not the power to speak
   what love indites:
The soul lies buried in the ink that
   writes.

[Attr.]

COLMAN, the Elder, George (1732–1794)

Love and a cottage! Eh, Fanny! Ah, give me
indifference and a coach and six!

[*The Clandestine Marriage* (1766)]

CONGREVE, William (1670–1729)

In my conscience I believe the baggage loves
me, for she never speaks well of me her self,
nor suffers any body else to rail me.

[*The Old Bachelor* (1693)]

COPE, Wendy (1945–)

2 cures for love
1. Don't see him. Don't phone or write a
letter.
2. The easy way: get to know him better.

[Attr.]

DIDEROT, Denis (1713–1784)

On a dit que l'amour qui ôtait l'esprit à ceux qui en
avaient en donnait à ceux qui n'en avaient pas.
They say that love takes wit away from those
who have it, and gives it to those who have
none.

[*Paradoxe sur le Comédien*]

DIETRICH, Marlene (1901–1992)

Latins are tenderly enthusiastic. In Brazil they throw flowers at you. In Argentina they throw themselves.

[*Newsweek*, 1959]

DONNE, John (1572–1631)

Love built on beauty, soon as beauty dies.

[*Elegies* (c. 1595)]

Who ever loves, if he do not propose
The right true end of love, he's one
   that goes
To sea for nothing but to make him sick.

[*Elegies* (c. 1600)]

Chang'd loves are but chang'd sorts of
   meat,
And when he hath the kernel eat,
Who doth not fling away the shell?

[*Songs and Sonnets* (1611)]

I wonder by my troth, what thou, and I
Did, till we lov'd?

[*Songs and Sonnets* (1611)]

DOUGLAS, Lord Alfred (1870–1945)

I am the Love that dare not speak its name.

['Two Loves' (1896)]

DRYDEN, John (1631–1700)

Pains of love be sweeter far
Than all other pleasures are.

[*Tyrannic Love* (1669)]

For, Heaven be thanked, we live in
   such an age,
When no man dies for love, but on the
   stage.

[*Mithridates* (1678)]

ELLIS, Havelock (1859–1939)

Love is friendship plus sex.

[Attr.]

ETHEREGE, Sir George (c.1635–1691)

When love grows diseased, the best thing we can do is put it to a violent death; I cannot endure the torture of a lingering and consumptive passion.

[*The Man of Mode* (1676)]

FARQUHAR, George (1678–1707)

Money is the sinews of love, as of war.

[*Love and a Bottle* (1698)]

FARRELL, J.G. (1935–1979)

Vera, who had carefully educated herself in the arts of love, did not believe that this sacred art, whose purpose was to unite her not only with her lover but with the earth and the firmament, too, should take place in the Western manner which to her resembled nothing so much as a pair of drunken rickshaw coolies colliding briefly at some foggy crossroads at the dead of night.

[*The Singapore Grip* (1979)]

FIELDING, Henry (1707–1754)

Love and scandal are the best sweeteners of tea.

[*Love in Several Masques* (1728)]

What is commonly called love, namely the desire of satisfying a voracious appetite with a certain quantity of delicate white human flesh.

[*Tom Jones* (1749)]

FLETCHER, Phineas (1582–1650)

Love is like linen often chang'd, the sweeter.

[*Sicelides* (1614)]

FLORIAN, Jean-Pierre Claris de (1755–1794)

Plaisir d'amour ne dure qu'un moment,
Chagrin d'amour dure toute la vie. Love's pleasure only lasts a moment; love's sorrow lasts one's whole life long.

['Célestine' (1784)]

FORSTER, E.M. (1879–1970)

Only connect! That was the whole of her sermon. Only connect the prose and the passion, and both will be exalted, and human love will be seen at its highest.

[*Howard's End* (1910)]

FRANKLIN, Benjamin (1706–1790)

The having made a young girl miserable may give you frequent bitter reflection; none of which can attend the making of an old woman happy.

[*On the Choice of a Mistress*]

FRY, Christopher (1907–)

Oh, the unholy mantrap of love!

[*The Lady's not for Burning* (1949)]

Try thinking of love, or something. Amor vincit insomnia.

[*A Sleep of Prisoners* (1951)]

GAY, John (1685–1732)

Then nature rul'd, and love, devoid of art, Spoke the consenting language of the heart.

[*Dione* (1720)]

She who has never lov'd, has never liv'd.

[*The Captives* (1724)]

Pretty Polly, say,
When I was away,
Did your fancy never stray
To some newer lover?

[*The Beggar's Opera* (1728)]

How happy could I be with either,
Were t'other dear charmer away!

[*The Beggar's Opera* (1728)]

GIBRAN, Kahlil (1883–1931)

Love has no other desire but to fulfil itself. But if you love and must needs have desires, let these be your desires:
To melt and be like the running brook that sings its melody to the night.
To know the pain of too much tenderness.
To be wounded by your own understanding of love;
And to bleed willingly and joyfully.
To wake at dawn with a winged heart and give thanks for another day of loving;
To rest at the noon hour and meditate love's ecstasy;
To return home at eventide with gratitude;
And then to sleep with a prayer for the beloved in your heart and a song of praise upon your lips ...

Love one another, but make not a bond of love:

Let it be rather a moving sea between the shores of your souls ...

Let each one of you be alone,
Even as the strings of the lute are alone though they quiver with the same music ...

Stand together yet not too near together:
For the pillars of the temple stand apart,
And the oak tree and the cypress grow not in each other's shadow.

[*The Prophet* (1923)]

GOGARTY, Oliver St John (1878–1957)

Only the Lion and the Cock;
As Galen says, withstand Love's shock.
So, dearest, do not think me rude
If I yield now to lassitude,
But sympathize with me. I know
You would not have me roar, or crow.

[*Collected Poems* (1951)]

GOLDSMITH, Oliver (c.1728–1774)

It seemed to me pretty plain, that they had more of love than matrimony in them.

[*The Vicar of Wakefield* (1766)]

GORKY, Maxim (1868–1936)

Love is always a bit deceitful,
Truth always struggles with it,
We wait long for a woman worthy of it,
And we wait in vain.

[In *Samara Gazette*, 1895]

GOWER, John (c.1330–1408)

It hath and schal ben evermor
That love is maister wher he wile.

['Confessio Amantis' (1390)]

GRANVILLE, George (1666–1735)

O Love! thou bane of the most generous souls!
Thou doubtful pleasure, and thou certain pain.

['Heroic Love']

GRAVES, Robert (1895–1985)

Down, wanton, down! Have you no shame
That at the whisper of Love's name,
Or Beauty's, presto! up you raise

Your angry head and stand at gaze?

['Down, Wanton, Down']

In love as in sport, the amateur status must be strictly maintained.

[*Occupation: Writer*]

GREER, Germaine (1939–)

Love, love, love – all the wretched cant of it, masking egotism, lust, masochism, fantasy under a mythology of sentimental postures, a welter of self induced miseries and joys, blinding and masking the essential personalities in the frozen gestures of courtship, in the kissing and the dating and the desire, the compliments and the quarrels which vivify its barrenness.

[*The Female Eunuch* (1970)]

HALM, Friedrich (1806–1871)

Mein Herz, ich will dich fragen:
Was ist denn Liebe? Sag'! –
'Zwei Seelen und ein Gedanke,
Zwei Herzen und ein Schlag!"
'My heart, I want to ask you:
What is love? Tell me!' –
'Two souls with just one thought,
Two hearts with just one beat.'

[*The Son of the Wilderness*, 1842)]

HARDY, Thomas (1840–1928)

Love is lame at fifty years.

['The Revisitation' (1904)]

A lover without indiscretion is no lover at all.

[*The Hand of Ethelberta* (1876)]

HARTLEY, L.P. (1895–1972)

Once she had loved her fellow human beings; she did not love them now, she had seen them do too many unpleasant things.

[*Facial Justice* (1960)]

HAZZARD, Shirley (1931–)

When we are young, she thought, we worship romantic love for the wrong reasons … and, because of that, subsequently repudiate it. Only later, and for quite other reasons, we discover its true importance. And by then it has become tiring even to observe.

[*The Evening of a Holiday* (1966)]

HEANEY, Seamus (1939–)

And in that dream I dreamt – how like you this? –
Our first night years ago in that hotel
When you came with your deliberate kiss
To raise us towards the lovely and painful
Covenants of flesh; our separateness;
The respite in our dewy dreaming faces.

[*Field Work* (1979)]

HEMINGWAY, Ernest (1898–1961)

Love is just another dirty lie. … I know about love. Love always hangs up behind the bathroom door. It smells like lysol. To hell with love.

[*To Have and Have Not* (1937)]

HERBERT, Edward (1583–1648)

O that our love might take no end,
Or never had beginning took! …

For where God doth admit the fair,
Think you that he excludeth Love?

['An Ode upon a Question moved, Whether Love should continue for ever?' (1665)]

HERBERT, George (1593–1633)

Love bade me welcome; yet my soul drew back,
Guiltie of dust and sinne.
But quick-ey'd Love, observing me grow slack
From my first entrance in,
Drew nearer to me, sweetly questioning
If I lack'd any thing …

Love took my hand, and smiling did reply,
Who made the eyes but I? …

You must sit down, sayes Love, and taste my meat:
So I did sit and eat.

[*The Temple* (1633)]

HERBERT, Sir A.P. (1890–1971)

I wouldn't be too ladylike in love if I were you.

['I Wouldn't be Too Ladylike']

HERRICK, Robert (1591–1674)

Love is a circle that doth restlesse move
In the same sweet eternity of love.

[*Hesperides* (1648)]

Give me a kiss, add to that kiss a score;
Then to that twenty, adde an hundred more:
A thousand to that hundred: so kiss on,
To make that thousand up a million.
Treble that million, and when that is done,
Let's kiss afresh, as when we first begun.

[*Hesperides* (1648)]

You say, to me-wards your affection's strong;
Pray love me little, so you love me long.

[*Hesperides* (1648)]

Thou art my life, my love, my heart,
The very eyes of me:
And hast command of every part,
To live and die for thee.

[*Hesperides* (1648)]

HEWETT, Dorothy (1923–)

My body turns to you as the earth turns.
O for such bitter need you've taken me,
To dub me lover, friend and enemy,
Take neither one can set the other free.
But still there is a loveliness that burns
That burns between us two so tenderly.

['There is a Loveliness that Burns']

HOGG, James (1770–1835)

O, love, love, love!
Love is like a dizziness;
It winna let a poor body
Gang about his biziness!

['Love is Like a Dizziness']

HUDSON, Louise (1958–)

Now I go to films alone
watch a silent telephone
send myself a valentine
whisper softly 'I am mine'.

['Men, Who Needs Them']

JAMES I OF SCOTLAND (1394–1437)

So far I fallen was in loves dance,
That suddenly my wit, my countenance,
My heart, my will, my nature, and my mind

Was changit right clean in another kind.

[*The Kingis Quair*]

JEROME, Jerome K. (1859–1927)

Love is like the measles; we all have to go through it.

[*Idle Thoughts of an Idle Fellow* (1886)]

JERROLD, Douglas William (1803–1857)

Love's like the measles – all the worse when it comes late in life.

[*Wit and Opinions of Douglas Jerrold* (1859)]

JONSON, Ben (1572–1637)

Drink to me only with thine eyes,
And I will pledge with mine;
Or leave a kiss upon the cup,
And I'll not look for wine.
The thirst that from the soul doth rise
Doth ask a drink divine;
But might I of Jove's nectar sup,
I would not change for thine.
I sent thee late a rosy wreath,
Not so much honouring thee,
As giving it a hope that there
It could not wither'd be.

[*The Forest* (1616)]

JULIANA of Norwich (c.1343–c.1429)

Wouldest thou wit thy Lord's meaning in this thing? Wit it well: Love was his meaning. Who shewed it thee? Love. What shewed He thee? Love. Wherefore shewed it He? for Love … Thus was I learned that Love is our Lord's meaning.

[*Revelations of Divine Love* (1393)]

KAFKA, Franz (1883–1924)

Liebe ist, dass Du mir das Messer bist, mit dem ich in mir wühle.
Love is, that you are the knife which I plunge into myself.

[Letter to Milena Jesenká, 1920]

KEATS, John (1795–1821)

I never was in love – yet the voice and the shape of a Woman has haunted me these two days.

[Letter to J.H. Reynolds, 22 September 1818]

KEY, Ellen (1849–1926)
Love is moral even without legal marriage,
but marriage is immoral without love.
[*'The Morality of Women'* (1911)]

KIDMAN, Nicole (1967–)
I'm past the seven-year itch. When you're
loved for your flaws, that's when you feel
really safe.
[*The Observer*, 1998]

KING, Bishop Henry (1592–1669)
Sleep on, my Love, in thy cold bed,
Never to be disquieted!
My last good night! Thou wilt not wake
Till I thy fate shall overtake:
Till age, or grief, or sickness must
Marry my body to that dust
It so much loves; and fill the room
My heart keeps empty in thy tomb.
Stay for me there; I will not fail
To meet thee in that hollow vale …

But hark! My pulse like a soft drum
Beats my approach, tells thee I come.
['Exequy upon his Wife'
(1651)]

LA ROCHEFOUCAULD (1613–1680)
*Si on juge de l'amour par la plupart de ses effets, il
ressemble plus á la haine qu'á l'amitié.*
If love is to be judged by most of its effects, it
looks more like hatred than like friendship.
[*Maximes*, (1678)]

*Il n'y a guère de gens qui ne soient honteux de s'être
aimés quand ils ne s'aiment plus.*
There are very few people who are not
ashamed of having loved one another once
they have fallen out of love.
[*Maximes* (1678)]

**LAMARTINE, Alphonse de
(1790–1869)**
Un seul être vous manque, et tout est dépeuplé.
Only one being is missing, and your whole
world is bereft of people.
[*Premières Méditations poétiques*
(1820)]

LARKIN, Philip (1922–1985)
What will survive of us is love.
['An Arundel Tomb' (1964)]

LAWRENCE, D.H. (1885–1930)
I'm not sure if a mental relation with a
woman doesn't make it impossible to love
her. To know the mind of a woman is to end
in hating her. Love means the pre-cognitive
flow … it is the honest state before the
apple.
[Letter to Dr Trigant Burrow, 1927]

LAWRENCE, T.E. (1888–1935)
I loved you, so I drew these tides of men into
my hands
and wrote my will across the sky in stars
To earn you Freedom, the seven pillared
worthy house,
that your eyes might be shining for me
When we came.
[*The Seven Pillars of Wisdom* (1926)]

LEWIS, Wyndham (1882–1957)
To give up another person's love is a mild
suicide.
[*Tarr* (1918)]

LINDSAY, Norman (1879–1969)
The best love affairs are those we never had.
[*Bohemians of the Bulletin* (1965)]

LODGE, Thomas (1558–1625)
Love, in my bosom, like a bee,
Doth suck his sweet.
['Love, In My Bosom' (1590)]

LOVELACE, Richard (1618–1658)
When Love with unconfined wings
Hovers within my gates;
And my divine Althea brings
To whisper at the grates:
When I lie tangled in her hair,
And fettered to her eye;
The Gods, that wanton in the air,
Know no such liberty.
['To Althea, From Prison'
(1649)]

LOVELL, Maria (1803–1877)
Two souls with but a single thought,

Two hearts that beat as one.

[*Ingomar the Barbarian*,II]

LOWRY, Malcolm (1909–1957)

How alike are the groans of love to those of the dying.

[*Under the Volcano* (1947)]

LYDGATE, John (c.1370–c.1451)

Love is mor than gold or gret richesse.

['The Story of Thebes' (c. 1420)]

MACDIARMID, Hugh (1892–1978)

It is very rarely that a man loves
And when he does it is nearly always fatal.

['The International Brigade' (1957)]

MARLOWE, Christopher (1564–1593)

Where both deliberate, the love is slight;
Who ever loved that loved not at first sight?

[*Hero and Leander* (1598), First Sestiad]

Come live with me, and be my love,
And we will all the pleasures prove.

['The Passionate Shepherd to his Love']

MARVELL, Andrew (1621–1678)

Therefore the love which us doth bind,
But Fate so enviously debars,
Is the conjunction of the mind,
And opposition of the stars.

['The Definition of Love' (1681)]

MCCUAIG, Ronald (1908–1990)

Love me, and never leave me,
Love, nor ever deceive me,
And I shall always bless you
If I may undress you:
This I heard a lover say
To his sweetheart where they lay.

He, though he did undress her,
Did not always bless her;
She, though she would not leave him,
Often did deceive him;
Yet they loved, and when they died
They were buried side by side.

['Love Me and Never Leave Me' (1930)]

MILLAY, Edna St Vincent (1892–1950)

This have I known always: Love is no more
Than the wide blossom which the wind assails,
Than the great tide that treads the shifting shore,
Strewing fresh wreckage gathered in the gales:
Pity me that the heart is slow to learn
What the swift mind beholds at every turn.

[*The Harp-Weaver and Other Poems* (1923)]

MITFORD, Nancy (1904–1973)

Like all the very young we took it for granted that making love is child's play.

[*The Pursuit of Love* (1945)]

MOLIÈRE (1622–1673)

On est aisément dupé par ce qu'on aime.
One is easily taken in by what one loves.

[*Tartuffe* (1664)]

MOORE, Thomas (1779–1852)

No, there's nothing half so sweet in life
As love's young dream.

[*Irish Melodies* (1807)]

MORRIS, William (1834–1896)

Love is enough: though the world be a-waning,
And the woods have no voice but the voice of complaining.

['Love is Enough' (1872)]

O'BRIEN, Edna (1936–)

Oh, shadows of love, inebriations of love, foretastes of love, trickles of love, but never yet the one true love.

[*Night* (1972)]

OVID (43 BC–AD 18)

Qui finem quaeris amoris,
Cedet amor rebus; res age, tutus eris.
You who seek an end to love, love will yield to business: be busy, and you will be safe.

[*Remedia Amoris*]

PARKER, Dorothy (1893–1967)

By the time you swear you're his,
Shivering and sighing,
And he vows his passion is
Infinite, undying –
Lady, make a note of this:

One of you is lying.

['Unfortunate Coincidence' (1937)]

PARNELL, Anna (1852–1911)

Two children playing by a stream
Two lovers walking in a dream
A married pair whose dream is o'er,
Two old folks who are quite a bore.

['Love's Four Ages']

PATTEN, Brian (1946–)

Love, smeared across his face, like a road accident.

[*Grinning Jack* (1990), 'Schoolboy']

PATTERSON, Johnny (1840–1889)

Have you ever been in love, me boys
Oh! have you felt the pain,
I'd rather be in jail, I would,
Than be in love again.

['The Garden where the Praties Grow']

PEELE, George (c.1558–c.1597)

What thing is love for (well I wot) love is a thing.
It is a prick, it is a sting,
It is a pretty, pretty thing;
It is a fire, it is a coal
Whose flame creeps in at every hole.

['The Hunting of Cupid'
(c.1591)]

POUND, Ezra (1885–1972)

And we knew all that stream,
And our two horses had traced out the valleys;
Knew the low flooded lands squared out with poplars,
In the young days when the deep sky befriended.
And great wings beat above us in the twilight,
And the great wheels in heaven
Bore us together … surging … and apart …
Believing we should meet with lips and hands,
High, high and sure … and then the counter-thrust:
'Why do you love me? Will you always love me?

But I am like the grass, I cannot love you.'

['Near Perigord' (1915)]

PROUST, Marcel (1871–1922)

There can be no peace of mind in love, since the advantage one has secured is never anything but a fresh starting-point for further desires.

[*A la recherche du temps perdu, A l'ombre des jeunes filles en fleurs* (1918)]

Une dame prétentieuse: Que pensez-vous de l'amour?
Mme Leroi: *L'amour? Je le fais souvent, mais je n'en parle jamais.*
A pretentious lady: What are your views on love?
Mme Leroi: I often make love but I never talk about it.

[*A la recherche du temps perdu, Le Côté de Guermantes* (1921)]

On a tort de parler en amour de mauvais choix, puisque dès qu'il y a choix il ne peut être que mauvais.
It is wrong to speak of making a bad choice in love, since as soon as there is choice, it can only be bad.

[*La Fugitive* (1923)]

PROVERBS

Love is blind.

All is fair in love and war.

All the world loves a lover.

In love, there is always one who kisses, and one who offers his cheek.

Love conquers all.

Love laughs at locksmiths.

Love me, love my dog.

Lucky at cards, unlucky in love.

No love like the first love.

True love never grows cold.

RACINE, Jean (1639–1699)

Je t'aimais inconstant, qu'aurais-je fait fidèle?

I loved you inconstant; what would I have done had you been faithful?

[*Andromaque* (1667)]

Ah! je l'ai trop aimé pour ne le point haïr!
Ah, I have loved him too much not to hate him!

[*Andromaque* (1667)]

RALEIGH, Sir Walter (c.1552–1618)

Now what is love? I pray thee, tell.
It is that fountain and that well,
Where pleasure and repentance dwell.
It is perhaps that sauncing bell,
That tolls all in to heaven or hell:
And this is love, as I hear tell.

['A Description of Love']

ROCHESTER, Earl of (1647–1680)

That cordial drop heaven in our cup has thrown
To make the nauseous draught of life go down.

['A letter from Artemisa in the Town to Chloe in the Country' (1679)]

ROGERS, Samuel (1763–1855)

Oh! she was good as she was fair.
None – none on earth above her!
As pure in thought as angels are,
To know her was to love her.

[*Jacqueline* (1814)]

But there are moments which he calls his own,
Then, never less alone than when alone,
Those whom he loved so long and sees no more,
Loved and still loves – not dead – but gone before,
He gathers round him.

['Human Life' (1819)]

RUSSELL, Bertrand (1872–1970)

Of all forms of caution, caution in love is perhaps the most fatal to true happiness.

[*Marriage and Morals* (1929)]

SAGAN, Françoise (1935–)

Every little girl knows about love. It is only her capacity to suffer because of it that increases.

[*Daily Express*]

SAINT-EXUPÉRY, Antoine de (1900–1944)

L'expérience nous montre qu'aimer ce n'est point nous regarder l'un l'autre mais regarder ensemble dans la même direction.
Experience shows us that love is not looking into one another's eyes but looking together in the same direction.

[*Wind, Sand and Stars* (1939)]

SAKI (1870–1916)

Romance at short notice was her speciality.

[*Beasts and Super-Beasts* (1914)]

SAND, George (1804–1876)

Liszt said to me today that God alone deserves to be loved. It may be true, but when one has loved a man it is very different to love God.

[*Intimate Journal*]

SCOTT, Alexander (c.1525–c.1584)

Luve is ane fervent fire,
Kendillit without desire;
Short pleisure, lang displeisure,
Repentence is the hire;
Ane puir treisure without meisure.
Luve is ane fervent fire.

['A Rondel of Luve' (c. 1568)]

SCOTT, Sir Walter (1771–1832)

In peace, Love tunes the shepherd's reed;
In war, he mounts the warrior's steed;
In halls, in gay attire is seen;
In hamlets, dances on the green.
Love rules the court, the camp, the grove,
And men below, and saints above;
For love is heaven, and heaven is love.

[*The Lay of the Last Minstrel* (1805)]

True love's the gift which God has given
To man alone beneath the heaven:
It is the secret sympathy,
The silver link, the silken tie,
Which heart to heart, and mind to mind,
In body and in soul can bind.

[*The Lay of the Last Minstrel* (1805)]

SEDLEY, Sir Charles (c.1639–1701)

Love still has something of the Sea
From whence his Mother rose.

['Song: Love still has Something']

Not, Celia, that I juster am
Or better than the rest,
For I would change each hour like them,
Were not my heart at rest …

Why then should I seek farther store,
And still make love anew;
When change itself can give no more,
'Tis easy to be true.

['To Celia']

SEGAL, Erich (1937–)

Love means never having to say you're sorry.

[*Love Story* (1970)]

SHAKESPEARE, William (1564–1616)

Doubt thou the stars are fire;
Doubt that the sun doth move;
Doubt truth to be a liar;
But never doubt I love.

[*Hamlet*, II.ii]

Ay me! for aught that I could ever read,
Could ever hear by tale or history,
The course of true love never did run
smooth.

[*A Midsummer Night's Dream*, I.i]

Love looks not with the eyes, but with the
mind;
And therefore is wing'd Cupid painted blind.

[*A Midsummer Night's Dream*, I.i]

I thank God, and my cold blood, I am of your
humour for that: I had rather hear my dog
bark at a crow than a man swear he loves
me.

[*Much Ado About Nothing*, I.i]

My bounty is as boundless as the sea,
My love as deep: the more I give to thee,
The more I have, for both are infinite.

[*Romeo and Juliet*, II.ii]

If music be the food of love, play on,
Give me excess of it, that, surfeiting,

The appetite may sicken and so die.
That strain again! It had a dying fall;
O, it came o'er my ear like the sweet sound
That breathes upon a bank of violets,
Stealing and giving odour! Enough, no more;
'Tis not so sweet now as it was before.

[*Twelfth Night*, I.i]

She never told her love,
But let concealment, like a worm i' th' bud,
Feed on her damask cheek. She pin'd in
thought;
And with a green and yellow melancholy
She sat like Patience on a monument,
Smiling at grief. Was not this love indeed?
We men may say more, swear more, but
indeed
Our shows are more than will; for still we
prove
Much in our vows, but little in our love.

[*Twelfth Night*, II.iv]

Love sought is good, but given unsought is
better.

[*Twelfth Night*, III.i]

Fie, fie, how wayward is this foolish love,
That like a testy babe will scratch the nurse,
And presently, all humbled, kiss the rod!

[*Two Gentlemen of Verona*, I.ii]

Let me not to the marriage of true minds
Admit impediments. Love is not love
Which alters when it alteration finds,
Or bends with the remover to remove.

[*Sonnet 116*]

When my love swears that she is made of
truth,
I do believe her, though I know she lies.

[*Sonnet 138*]

SHAW, George Bernard (1856–1950)

The fickleness of the women I love is only
equalled by the infernal constancy of the
women who love me.

[*The Philanderer* (1898)]

SHELLEY, Percy Bysshe (1792–1822)

Familiar acts are beautiful through love.

[*Prometheus Unbound* (1820)]

SIDNEY, Sir Philip (1554–1586)

They love indeede who dare not say they love.

[*Astrophel and Stella* (1591)]

SMOLLETT, Tobias (1721–1771)

[On being tongue-tied when alone with one's object of desire]

'Tis very surprising that love should act so inconsistent with itself, as to deprive its votaries of the use of their faculties, when they have most occasion for them.

[*The Adventures of Roderick Random* (1748)]

SPENSER, Edmund (c.1522–1599)

To be wise and eke to love,
Is graunted scarce to God above.

[*The Shepheardes Calender* (1579), 'March']

So let us love, deare love, lyke as we ought,
Love is the lesson which the Lord us taught.

[*Amoretti, and Epithalamion* (1595), Sonnet 68]

STEAD, Christina (1902–1983)

When women are free, we'll see other emotions, no love. Love is a slave emotion, like a dog's.

[*For Love Alone* (1944)]

STERNE, Laurence (1713–1768)

Love, an' please your honour, is exactly like war, in this; that a soldier, though he has escaped three weeks complete o' Saturday night, – may nevertheless be shot through his heart on Sunday morning.

[*Tristram Shandy*]

STODDARD, Elizabeth Drew (1823–1902)

A woman despises a man for loving her, unless she returns his love.

[Attr.]

STOW, Randolph (1935–)

The love of man is a weed of the waste places.
One may think of it as the spinifex of dry souls.

['The Land's Meaning' (1969)]

SUCKLING, Sir John (1609–1642)

Out upon it, I have loved
Three whole days together;
And am like to love three more
If it prove fair weather.

Time shall moult away his wings,
Ere he shall discover
In the whole wide world again
Such a constant lover …

Had it any been but she,
And that very face,
There had been at least ere this
A dozen dozen in her place.

['A Poem with the Answer' (1659)]

But love is such a mystery,
I cannot find it out:
For when I think I'm best resolv'd.
I then am in most doubt.

['Song']

SWINBURNE, Algernon Charles (1837–1909)

If love were what the rose is,
And I were like the leaf,
Our lives would grow together
In sad or singing weather,
Blown fields or flowerful closes,
Green pleasure or grey grief.

['A Match' (1866)]

SYMONS, Michael Brooke (1945–)

Love is what makes the world go around – that and clichés.

[*Sydney Morning Herald*, 1970]

TENNYSON, Alfred, Lord (1809–1892)

In the Spring a young man's fancy lightly turns to thoughts of love.

['Locksley Hall' (1838)]

I hold it true, whate'er befall;
I feel it, when I sorrow most;
'Tis better to have loved and lost
Than never to have loved at all.

[In Memoriam A. H. H. (1850)]

To love one maiden only, cleave to her,
And worship her by years of noble deeds,

Until they won her; for indeed I knew
Of no more subtle master under heaven
Than is the maiden passion for a maid,
Not only to keep down the base in man,
But teach high thought, and amiable words
And courtliness, and the desire of fame,
And love of truth, and all that makes a man.

[*The Idylls of the King*]

TERENCE (c.190–159 BC)

Amantium irae amoris integratio est.
Lovers' quarrels are the renewal of love.

[*Andria*]

THACKERAY, William Makepeace (1811–1863)

Some cynical Frenchman has said that there are two parties to a love transaction; the one who loves and the other who condescends to be so treated.

[*Vanity Fair* (1847–1848)]

We love being in love, that's the truth on't.

[*The History of Henry Esmond* (1852)]

Werther had a love for Charlotte
Such as words could never utter;
Would you know how first he met her?
She was cutting bread and butter.
Charlotte was a married lady,
And a moral man was Werther,
And for all the wealth of Indies,
Would do nothing for to hurt her.
So he sighed and pined and ogled,
And his passion boiled and bubbled,
Till he blew his silly brains out
And no more was by it troubled.
Charlotte, having seen his body
Borne before her on a shutter,
Like a well-conducted person,
Went on cutting bread and butter.

['Sorrows of Werther' (1855)]

TIBULLUS (c.54–19 BC)

Te spectem, suprema mihi cum venerit hora,
Et teneam moriens deficiente manu.
May I be looking at you when my last hour has come, and as I die may I hold you with my weakening hand.

[*Elegies*]

TOLSTOY, Leo (1828–1910)

Love is God, and when I die it means that I, a particle of love, shall return to the general and eternal source.

[*War and Peace* (1869)]

TROLLOPE, Anthony (1815–1882)

Love is like any other luxury. You have no right to it unless you can afford it.

[*The Way We Live Now* (1875)]

VIRGIL (70–19 BC)

Omnia vincit Amor: et nos cedamus Amori.
Love conquers all: let us also yield to love.

[*Eclogues*]

WAX, Ruby (1953–)

This 'relationship' business is one big waste of time. It is just Mother Nature urging you to breed, breed, breed. Learn from nature. Learn from our friend the spider. Just mate once and then kill him.

[*Spectator*, 1994]

WEBSTER, John (c.1580–c.1625)

Is not old wine wholesomest, old pippins toothsomest? Does not old wood burn brightest, old linen wash whitest? Old soldiers, sweethearts, are surest, and old lovers are soundest.

[*Westward Hoe* (1607)]

WESLEY, John (1703–1791)

Beware you be not swallowed up in books! An ounce of love is worth a pound of knowledge.

[In Southey, *Life of Wesley* (1820)]

WILCOX, Ella Wheeler (1850–1919)

We flatter those we scarcely know,
We please the fleeting guest,
And deal full many a thoughtless blow
To those who love us best.

['Life's Scars' (1917)]

WILDE, Oscar (1854–1900)

Yet each man kills the thing he loves,
By each let this be heard,
Some do it with a bitter look,
Some with a flattering word,
The coward does it with a kiss,

The brave man with a sword!

[*The Ballad of Reading Gaol* (1898)]

When one is in love one begins by deceiving oneself. And one ends by deceiving others.

[*A Woman of No Importance* (1893)]

WYCHERLEY, William (c.1640–1716)

A mistress should be like a little country retreat near the town, not to dwell in constantly, but only for a night and away.

[*The Country Wife* (1675)]

YEATS, W.B. (1865–1939)

A pity beyond all telling
Is hid in the heart of love.

['The Pity of Love' (1892)]

It seems to me that true love is a discipline, and it needs so much wisdom that the love of Solomon and Sheba must have lasted, for all the silence of the Scriptures.

[*Estrangement: Being some fifty Thoughts from a Diary kept in the year nineteen hundred and nine* (1926)]

See PASSION; SEX

LUCK

JERROLD, Douglas William (1803–1857)

Some people are so fond of ill-luck that they run half-way to meet it.

[*Wit and Opinions of Douglas Jerrold* (1859)]

NAPOLEON I (1769–1821)

[Question of potential officers]
Has he luck?

[Attr.]

PROVERB

It is better to be born lucky than rich.

STEAD, Christina (1902–1983)

A self-made man is one who believes in luck and sends his son to Oxford.

[*House of All Nations* (1938)]

WEBSTER, John (c.1580–c.1625)

And of all axioms this shall win the prize, –
'Tis better to be fortunate than wise.

[*The White Devil* (1612)]

WHITMAN, Walt (1819–1892)

Has anyone supposed it lucky to be born?
I hasten to inform him or her it is just as lucky to die, and I know it.

['Song of Myself' (1855)]

See CHANCE; SUPERSTIOTION

LUXURY

ASHFORD, Daisy (1881–1972)

It was a sumpshous spot all done up in gold with plenty of looking glasses.

[*The Young Visiters* (1919)]

KEATS, John (1795–1821)

I have two luxuries to brood over in my walks, your Loveliness and the hour of my death. O that I could have possession of them both in the same minute.

[Letter to Fanny Brawne, 25 July 1819]

MOTLEY, John Lothrop (1814–1877)

Give us the luxuries of life, and we will dispense with its necessities.

[In Oliver Wendell Holmes, *Autocrat of the Breakfast Table* (1857–1858)]

ORTON, Joe (1933–1967)

Every luxury was lavished on you – atheism, breast-feeding, circumcision. I had to make my own way.

[*Loot* (1967)]

WRIGHT, Frank Lloyd (1869–1959)

Give me the luxuries of life and I will willingly do without the necessities.

[Quoted in his obituary, April 9, 1959]

See MONEY AND WEALTH

M

MACHINES

GZOWSKI, Peter (1650–1687)
[Referring to the fax machine and cellular telephone]
I have seen the future and it's here.
[CBC Radio's *Morningside, 1988*]

O'BRIEN, Flann (1911–1966)
People who spend most of their natural lives riding iron bicycles over the rocky roadsteads of this parish get their personalities mixed up with the personalities of their bicycles as a result of the interchanging of the atoms of each of them and you would be surprised at the number of people in these parts who nearly are half people and half bicycles.
[*The Third Policeman* (1967)]

PATTEN, Brian (1946–)
I can imagine the night when waking from a nervous sleep
you find the telephone has dragged itself up the stairs one at a time
and sits mewing,
the electronic pet waiting for its bowl of words.
['I studied telephones constantly']

RUSSELL, Bertrand (1872–1970)
Machines are worshipped because they are beautiful, and valued because they confer power; they are hated because they are hideous, and loathed because they impose slavery.
[*Sceptical Essays* (1928)]

SLEZAK, Leo (1873–1946)
[When the mechanical swan left the stage without him during a performance of Lohengrin]
What time is the next swan?
[In W. Slezak, *What Time's the Next Swan?* (1962)]

SPENDER, Sir Stephen (1909–1995)
After the first powerful plain manifesto
The black statement of pistons, without more fuss
But gliding like a queen, she leaves the station.
['The Express' (1933)]

SWIFT, Jonathan (1667–1745)
[Describing a watch]
He put this engine to our ears, which made an incessant noise like that of a water-mill; and we conjecture it is either some unknown animal, or the god that he worships; but we are more inclined to the latter opinion.
[*Gulliver's Travels* (1726)]

WELLINGTON, Duke of (1769–1852)
[Referring to steam locomotives]
I see no reason to suppose that these machines will ever force themselves into general use.
[In J. Gere, *Geoffrey Madan's Notebooks*]

See TECHNOLOGY

MADNESS

BECKETT, Samuel (1906–1989)
We are all born mad. Some remain so.
[*Waiting for Godot* (1955)]

BEERBOHM, Sir Max (1872–1956)
Only the insane take themselves quite seriously.
[Attr.]

CHESTERTON, G.K. (1874–1936)
The madman is not the man who has lost his reason. The madman is the man who has lost everything except his reason.
[*Orthodoxy* (1908)]

CLARE, John (1793–1864)
Dear Sir, – I am in a Madhouse and quite forget your name or who you are.
[Letter, 1860]

DALI, Salvador (1904–1989)

There is only one difference between a madman and me. I am not mad.

[*The American*, 1956]

DAVIES, Scrope Berdmore (c.1783–1852)

Babylon in all its desolation is a sight not so awful as that of the human mind in ruins.

[Letter to Thomas Raikes, 1835]

DRYDEN, John (1631–1700)

Great wits are sure to madness near alli'd,
And thin partitions do their bounds divide.

[*Absalom and Achitophel* (1681)]

EURIPIDES (c.485–406 BC)

Whom God wishes to destroy, he first makes mad.

[Fragment]

GEORGE II (1683–1760)

[Reply to the Duke of Newcastle who complained that General Wolfe was a madman]

Mad, is he? Then I hope he will *bite* some of my other generals.

[In Wilson, *The Life and Letters of James Wolfe* (1909)]

GINSBERG, Allen (1926–1997)

I saw the best minds of my generation destroyed by madness, starving hysterical naked.

[*Howl* (1956)]

GREENE, Graham (1904–1991)

Innocence is a kind of insanity.

[The Quiet American (1955)]

HARRIS, Thomas

Wil Graham: I know that I'm not smarter than you.
Dr Hannibal Lector: Then how did you catch me?
Wil Graham: You had disadvantages.
Dr Hannibal Lector: What disadvantages?
Wil Graham: You're insane.

[*Manhunter*, film, 1986]

HELLER, Joseph (1923–)

Orr was crazy and could be grounded. All he had to do was ask; and as soon as he did, he would no longer be crazy and would have to fly more missions … Yossarian was moved very deeply by the absolute simplicity of this clause of Catch-22 and let out a respectful whistle.

[*Catch-22* (1961)]

JOHNSON, Samuel (1709–1784)

I inherited a vile melancholy from my father, which has made me mad all my life, at least not sober.

[In Boswell, *Journal of a Tour to the Hebrides* (1785)]

If a madman were to come into this room with a stick in his hand, no doubt we should pity the state of his mind; but our primary consideration would be to take care of ourselves. We should knock him down first, and pity him afterwards.

[In Boswell, *The Life of Samuel Johnson* (1791)]

JUNG, Carl Gustav (1875–1961)

Show me a sane man and I will cure him for you.

[*The Observer*, 1975]

KIPLING, Rudyard (1865–1936)

Every one is more or less mad on one point.

[*Plain Tales from the Hills* (1888)']

The mad all are in God's keeping.

[*Kim* (1901)]

KYD, Thomas (1558–1594)

I am never better than when I am mad. Then methinks I am a brave fellow; then I do wonders. But reason abuseth me, and there's the torment, there's the hell.

[*The Spanish Tragedy* (1592)]

LAING, R.D. (1927–1989)

Madness need not be all breakdown. It may also be break-through. It is potential liberation and renewal as well as enslavement and existential death.

[*The Politics of Experience* (1967)]

The statesmen of the world who boast and

threaten that they have Doomsday weapons are far more dangerous, and far more estranged from 'reality', than many of the people on whom the label 'psychotic' is affixed.

[*The Divided Self* (1960)]

Schizophrenia cannot be understood without understanding despair.

[*The Divided Self* (1960)]

LAMB, Charles (1775–1834)

The six weeks that finished last year and begun this, your very humble servant spent very agreeably in a madhouse at Hoxton. I am got somewhat rational now, and don't bite anyone.

[Letter to Coleridge, 1796]

LEE, Nathaniel (c.1653–1692)

[Objecting to being confined in Bedlam]
They called me mad, and I called them mad, and damn them, they outvoted me.

[In Porter, *A Social History of Madness*]

PROUST, Marcel (1871–1922)

Tout ce que nous connaissons de grand nous vient des nerveux. Ce sont eux et non pas d'autres qui ont fondé les religions et composé les chefs-d'úuvre.
Everything great in the world is done by neurotics; they alone founded our religions and composed our masterpieces.

[*Le Côté de Guermantes* (1921)]

Neurosis has an absolute genius for malingering. There is no illness which it cannot counterfeit perfectly … If it is capable of deceiving the doctor, how should it fail to deceive the patient?

[*Le Côté de Guermantes* (1921)]

RENOIR, Pierre Auguste (1841–1919)

[Of the men of the French Commune]
C'étaient des fous, mais ils avaient cette petite flamme qui ne s'éteint pas.
They were madmen; but they had in them that little flame which does not go out.

[In Jean Renoir, *Renoir, My Father* (1962)]

SHAKESPEARE, William (1564–1616)

And he repelled, a short tale to make,

Fell into a sadness, then into a fast,
Thence to a watch, thence into a weakness,
Thence to a lightness, and, by this declension,
Into the madness wherein now he raves
And all we mourn for.

[*Hamlet*, II.ii]

O, what a noble mind is here o'erthrown!
The courtier's, soldier's, scholar's, eye, tongue, sword;
Th' expectancy and rose of the fair state,
The glass of fashion and the mould of form,
Th' observ'd of all observers – quite, quite down!

[*Hamlet*, III.i]

O, let me not be mad, not mad, sweet heaven!
Keep me in temper; I would not be mad!

[*King Lear*, I.v]

Canst thou not minister to a mind diseas'd,
Pluck from the memory a rooted sorrow,
Raze out the written troubles of the brain,
And with some sweet oblivious antidote
Cleanse the stuff'd bosom of that perilous stuff
Which weighs upon the heart?

[*Macbeth*, V.iii]

It is the very error of the moon;
She comes more nearer earth than she was wont,
And makes men mad.

[*Othello*, V.ii]

SHERIDAN, Richard Brinsley (1751–1816)

O Lord, sir, when a heroine goes mad she always goes into white satin.

[*The Critic* (1779)]

SMOLLETT, Tobias (1721–1771)

I think for my part one half of the nation is mad – and the other not very sound.

[*The Adventures of Sir Launcelot Greaves* (1762)]

SZASZ, Thomas (1920–)

If you talk to God, you are praying; if God talks to you, you have schizophrenia. If the dead talk to you, you are a spiritualist; if God talks to you, you are a schizophrenic.

[*The Second Sin* (1973)]

Psychiatrists classify a person as neurotic if he suffers from his problems in living, and a psychotic if he makes others suffer.

[*The Second Sin* (1973)]

TILLICH, Paul (1886–1965)

Neurosis is the way of avoiding non-being by avoiding being.

[*The Courage to Be* (1952)]

VOLTAIRE (1694–1778)

Men will always be mad and those who think they can cure them are the maddest of all.

[Letter, 1762]

See PSYCHIATRY

MANNERS

BELLOC, Hilaire (1870–1953)

A manner rude and wild
Is common at your age …

Who take their manners from the Ape,
Their habits from the Bear,
Indulge the loud unseemly jape,
And never brush their hair.

[*The Bad Child's Book of Beasts* (1896)]

BRADBURY, Malcolm (1932–)

The English are polite by telling lies. The Americans are polite by telling the truth.

[*Stepping Westward* (1965)]

COWARD, Sir Noël (1899–1973)

Comedies of manners swiftly become obsolete when there are no longer any manners.

[*Relative Values* (1951)]

EASTMAN, Max (1883–1969)

[On chivalry]
It is but the courteous exterior of a bigot.

[*Woman Suffrage and Sentiment*]

EMERSON, Ralph Waldo (1803–1882)

Good manners are made up of petty sacrifices.

['Social Aims' (1875)]

JARRELL, Randall (1914–1965)

To Americans English manners are far more frightening than none at all.

[*Pictures from an Institution* (1954)]

KERR, Jean (1923–)

Man is the only animal that learns by being hypocritical. He pretends to be polite and then, eventually, he becomes polite.

[*Finishing Touches* (1973)]

LOUIS XVIII (1755–1824)

L'exactitude est la politesse des rois.
Punctuality is the politeness of kings.

[Attr.]

MANKIEWICZ, Herman J. (1897–1953)

[After being sick at the table of a fastidious host]
It's all right, Arthur. The white wine came up with the fish.

[Attr.]

MONTAGU, Lady Mary Wortley (1689–1762)

Civility costs nothing and buys everything.

[Letter to the Countess of Bute, 1756]

PROVERB

Manners maketh man.

SHERIDAN, Richard Brinsley (1751–1816)

He is the very pine-apple of politeness!

[*The Rivals* (1775)]

SMITH, Sydney (1771–1845)

Where etiquette prevents me from doing things disagreeable to myself, I am a perfect martinet.

[Letters, To Lady Holland]

SPENSER, Edmund (c.1522–1599)

The gentle minde by gentle deeds is knowne.
For a man by nothing is so well bewrayd,
As by his manners.

[*The Faerie Queene* (1596)]

STERNE, Laurence (1713–1768)
Hail ye small sweet courtesies of life.
[*A Sentimental Journey* (1768)]

THEROUX, Paul (1941–)
The Japanese have perfected good manners and made them indistinguishable from rudeness.
[*The Great Railway Bazaar* (1975)]

TWAIN, Mark (1835–1910)
Good breeding consists in concealing how much we think of ourselves and how little we think of other persons.
[*Notebooks* (1935)]

WAUGH, Evelyn (1903–1966)
Manners are especially the need of the plain. The pretty can get away with anything.
[*The Observer*, 1962]

WILLIAM OF WYKEHAM (1324–1404)
Manners maketh man.
[Motto of Winchester College and New College, Oxford]

See COURTESY; GENTEEL BEHAVIOUR; RESPECT

MARRIAGE

ALBERT, Prince Consort (1819–1861)
Tomorrow our marriage will be 21 years old! How many a storm has swept over it and still it continues green and fresh and throws out vigorous roots.
[Attr.]

ALLEN, Woody (1935–)
It was partially my fault that we got divorced … I tended to place my wife under a pedestal.
[At a nightclub in Chicago, 1964]

AMIN, Idi (1925–)
[Public message to Lord Snowdon, when his marriage to Princess Margaret broke up]
Your experience will be a lesson to all of us men to be careful not to marry ladies in very high positions.
[In A. Barrow, *International Gossip* (1983)]

ASQUITH, Margot (1864–1945)
To marry a man out of pity is folly; and, if you think you are going to influence the kind of fellow who has 'never had a chance, poor devil,' you are profoundly mistaken. One can only influence the strong characters in life, not the weak; and it is the height of vanity to suppose that you can make an honest man of anyone.
[*The Autobiography of Margot Asquith* (1920)]

ASTOR, Nancy, Viscountess (1879–1964)
I married beneath me – all women do.
[*Dictionary of National Biography*]

ATWOOD, Margaret (1939–)
Marriage is not
a house or even a tent
it is before that, and colder:
the edge of the forest, the edge
of the desert …
the edge of the receding glacier
where painfully and with wonder
at having survived even
this far
we are learning to make fire.
[*Procedures for Underground* (1970)]

AUBREY, John (1626–1697)
[Sir Thomas More's] daughters were then both together abed … asleep. He carries Sir [William Roper, who wished to marry one of More's daughters] into the chamber and takes the sheet by the corner and suddenly whips it off. They lay on their backs and their smocks up as high as their armpits. This awakened them, and immediately they turned on their bellies. Quoth Roper, I have seen both sides, and so gave a pat on her buttock he made choice of, saying 'Thou art mine.' Here was all the trouble of the wooing.
[*Brief Lives* (c. 1693)]

AUSTEN, Jane (1775–1817)
It is a truth universally acknowledged, that a single man in possession of a good fortune,

must be in want of a wife.

[*Pride and Prejudice* (1813)]

Happiness in marriage is entirely a matter of chance.

[*Pride and Prejudice* (1813)]

Matrimony, as the origin of change, was always disagreeable.

[*Emma* (1816)]

BACON, Francis (1561–1626)

He that hath wife and children, hath given hostages to fortune; for they are impediments to great enterprises, either of virtue or mischief.

['Of Marriage and Single Life' (1625)]

But the most ordinary cause of a single life, is liberty; especially in certain self-pleasing and humorous minds, which are so sensible of every restraint as they will go near to think their girdles and garters to be bonds and shackles.

['Of Marriage and Single Life' (1625)]

Wives are young men's mistresses, companions for middle age, and old men's nurses.

['Of Marriage and Single Life' (1625)]

What is it then to have or have no wife,
But single thraldom, or a double strife?

[The World (1629)]

BALZAC, Honoré de (1799–1850)

Le sort d'un mariage dépend de la première nuit.
The fate of a marriage depends on the first night.

[*La Physiologie du mariage* (1826)]

BARNARD, Lady Ann (1750–1825)

My father argued sair – my mother didna speak,
But she looked in my face till my heart was like to break;
They gied him my hand but my heart was in the sea;
And so auld Robin Gray, he was gudeman to me.

['Auld Robin Gray' (1771)]

BENNETT, Arnold (1867–1931)

Being a husband is a whole-time job. That is why so many husbands fail. They cannot give their entire attention to it.

[*The Title* (1918)]

BERNARD, Jessie (1932–)

Women at marriage move from the status of female to that of neuter being.

[*The Future of Marriage*]

THE BIBLE
(King James Version)

Therefore shall a man leave his father and his mother, and shall cleave unto his wife: and they shall be one flesh.

[*Genesis*, 2:24]

BLACKSTONE, Sir William (1723–1780)

Husband and wife are one, and that one is the husband.

[In Miles, *The Women's History of the World* (1988)]

BURTON, Robert (1577–1640)

One was never married, and that's his hell; another is, and that's his plague.

[*Anatomy of Melancholy* (1621)]

BYRON, Lord (1788–1824)

Though women are angels, yet wed-lock's the devil.

['To Eliza' (1806)]

Romances paint at full length people's
    wooings,
But only give a bust of marriages:
For no one cares for matrimonial
    cooings.
There's nothing wrong in a connubial
    kiss;
Think you, if Laura had been
    Petrarch's wife,
He would have written sonnets all his
    life?

[*Don Juan* (1824)]

CHAUCER, Geoffrey (c.1340–1400)

Experience, though noon auctoritee
Were in this world, is right ynogh for
    me

To speke of wo that is in mariage.

[*The Canterbury Tales* (1387)]

COLERIDGE, Samuel Taylor (1772–1834)

The most happy marriage I can picture or imagine to myself would be union of a deaf man to a blind woman.

[In Allsop, *Recollections* (1836)]

DIANA, Princess of Wales (1961–1997)

[Referring to the Prince of Wales' relationship with Camilla Parker-Bowles]
There were three of us in this marriage, so it was a bit crowded.

[BBC television interview, 1995]

DISRAELI, Benjamin (1804–1881)

I have always thought that every woman should marry – and no man.

[*Lothair* (1870)]

Marriage is the greatest earthly happiness when founded on complete sympathy.

[Letter to Gladstone]

EASTWOOD, Clint (1930–)

There's only one way to have a happy marriage and as soon as I learn what it is I'll get married again.

[Attr.]

ELIOT, George (1819–1880)

A woman dictates before marriage in order that she may have an appetite for submission afterwards.

[*Middlemarch* (1872)]

FARQUHAR, George (1678–1707)

It is a maxim that man and wife should never have it in their power to hang one another.
[*The Beaux' Stratagem* (1707)]

GABOR, Zsa-Zsa (1919–)

Husbands are like fires. They go out when unattended.

[*Newsweek*, 1960]

[Her answer to the question 'How many husbands have you had?']

You mean apart from my own?

[Attr.]

A man in love is incomplete until he has married. Then he's finished.

[*Newsweek*, 1960]

GAY, John (1685–1732)

Do you think your mother and I should have liv'd comfortably so long together, if ever we had been married?

[*The Beggar's Opera* (1728)]

Polly: Then all my sorrows are at an end.
Mrs Peachum: A mighty likely speech in troth, for a wench who is just married!

[*The Beggar's Opera* (1728)]

I am ready, my dear Lucy, to give you satisfaction – if you think there is any in marriage.

[*The Beggar's Opera* (1728)]

One wife is too much for most husbands to hear,
But two at a time there's no mortal can bear.
This way, and that way, and which way I will,
What would comfort the one, t'other wife would take ill.

[*The Beggar's Opera* (1728)]

GIBBONS, Stella (1902–1989)

[Mr Mybug] said that, by God, D.H. Lawrence was right when he had said there must be a dumb, dark, dull, bitter belly-tension between a man and a woman, and how else could this be achieved save in the long monotony of marriage?

[*Cold Comfort Farm* (1932)]

GOLDSMITH, Oliver (c.1728–1774)

I … chose my wife as she did her wedding gown, not for a fine glossy surface, but such qualities as would wear well.

[*The Vicar of Wakefield* (1766)]

HARDY, Rev. E.J. (1849–1920)

How To Be Happy Though Married.

[Title of book, 1885]

HUME, David (1711–1776)

I shall tell the women what it is our sex

complains of in the married state; and if they be disposed to satisfy us in this particular, all the other difficulties will easily be accommodated. If I be not mistaken, 'tis their love of dominion.

[*Essays, Moral, Political and Literary* (1742)]

JOHNSON, Samuel (1709–1784)

Supposing … a wife to be of a studious or argumentative turn, it would be very troublesome: for instance, – if a woman should continually dwell upon the subject of the Arian heresy.

[In Boswell, *The Life of Samuel Johnson* (1791)]

Marriage has many pains, but celibacy has no pleasures.

[*Rasselas* (1759)]

A gentleman who had been very unhappy in marriage married immediately after his wife died. Dr Johnson said, it was the triumph of hope over experience.

[In Boswell, *The Life of Samuel Johnson* (1791)]

It is so far from being natural for a man and woman to live in a state of marriage that we find all the motives which they have for remaining in that connection, and the restraints which civilized society imposes to prevent separation, are hardly sufficient to keep them together.

[In Boswell, *The Life of Samuel Johnson* (1791)]

Marriages would in general be as happy, and often more so, if they were all made by the Lord Chancellor … without the parties having any choice in the matter.

[In Boswell, *The Life of Samuel Johnson* (1791)]

KEATS, John (1795–1821)

The roaring of the wind is my wife and the Stars through the window pane are my Children. The mighty abstract Idea I have of Beauty in all things stifles the more divided and minute domestic happiness … the opinion I have of the generality of women – who appear to me as children to whom I would rather give a Sugar Plum than my time, forms a barrier against Matrimony

which I rejoice in.

[Letter to George and Georgiana Keats, 1818]

LA ROCHEFOUCAULD (1613–1680)

Il y a de bons mariages, mais il n'y en a point de délicieux.
There are good marriages, but no delightful ones.

[*Maximes*, (1678)]

LAMB, Charles (1775–1834)

Nothing to me is more distasteful than that entire complacency and satisfaction which beam in the countenance of a new-married couple.

[*Essays of Elia* (1823)]

LONGFELLOW, Henry Wadsworth (1807–1882)

The men that women marry,
And why they marry them, will always be
A marvel and a mystery to the world.

[*Michael Angelo* (1883)]

LOVETT, Lyle (1956–)

[On marrying actress Julia Roberts, 1994]
It's true that I did get the girl, but then my grandfather always said, 'Even a blind chicken finds a few grains of corn now and then.'

MACNEICE, Louis (1907–1963)

So they were married – to be the more together –
And found they were never again so much together,
Divided by the morning tea,
By the evening paper,
By children and tradesmen's bills.

['Les Sylphides' (1941)]

MARTINEAU, Harriet (1802–1876)

Any one must see at a glance that if men and women marry those whom they do not love, they must love those whom they do not marry.

[*Society in America* (1837)]

I am in truth very thankful for not having married at all.

[*Harriet Martineau's Autobiography* (1877)]

MILL, John Stuart (1806–1873)

The moral regeneration of mankind will only really commence, when the most fundamental of the social relations [marriage] is placed under the rule of equal justice, and when human beings learn to cultivate their strongest sympathy with an equal in rights and cultivation.

[*The Subjection of Women* (1869)]

MILTON, John (1608–1674)

Flesh of Flesh,
Bone of my Bone thou art, and from thy State
Mine never shall be parted, weal or woe.

[*Paradise Lost* (1667)]

MOLIÈRE (1622–1673)

Le mariage, Agnès, n'est pas un badinage.
Marriage, Agnès, is not a joke.

[*L'Ecole des Femmes* (1662)]

MURRAY, Jenni (1950–)

Marriage is an insult and women should not touch it.

[Attr.]

NEWMAN, Andrea

Women will only leave a marriage if it's unbearable, whereas men will split if they get a better offer.

[*The Observer*, 1999]

'What is the difference between marriage and prison?'
'In prison somebody else does the cooking.'

[*Love Hurts*, film, 1990]

PEACOCK, Thomas Love (1785–1866)

Marriage may often be a stormy lake, but celibacy is almost always a muddy horse-pond.

[*Melincourt* (1817)]

PEPYS, Samuel (1633–1703)

Strange to say what delight we married people have to see these poor fools decoyed into our condition.

[*Diary*, December 1665]

POPE, Alexander (1688–1744)

She who ne'er answers till a Husband cools,

Or, if she rules him, never shows she rules;
Charms by accepting, by submitting sways,
Yet has her humour most, when she obeys.

['Epistle to a Lady' (1735)]

PROVERBS

Marry in haste, and repent at leisure.

Marriages are made in heaven.

PUNCH

Advice to persons about to marry – 'Don't!'.

[1845]

RAMSAY, Allan (1686–1758)

Ane canna wive an' thrive baith in ae year.

[*A Collection of Scots Proverbs* (1737)]

ROGERS, Samuel (1763–1855)

It doesn't much signify whom one marries, for one is sure to find next morning that it was someone else.

[*Recollections of the Table-Talk of Samuel Rogers* (1856)]

ROSTAND, Jean (1894–1977)

Never feel remorse for what you have thought about your wife; she has thought much worse things about you.

[*Le Mariage*]

ROWLAND, Helen (1875–1950)

Before marriage, a man will lie awake thinking about something you said; after marriage, he'll fall asleep before you finish saying it.

[In Cowan, *The Wit of Women*]

SAIKAKU, Ihara (1642–1693)

Marrying off your daughter is a piece of business you may expect to do only once in a lifetime, and, bearing in mind that none of the losses are recoverable later, you should approach the matter with extreme caution.

[*The Japanese Family Storehouse* (1688)]

And why do people wilfully exhaust their strength in promiscuous living, when their wives are on hand from bridal night till old age – to be taken when required, like fish from a private pond.

[*The Japanese Family Storehouse* (1688)]

SAKI (1870–1916)

A woman who takes her husband about with her everywhere is like a cat that goes on playing with a mouse long after she's killed it.

[Attr.]

The Western custom of one wife and hardly any mistresses.

[*Reginald in Russia* (1910)]

SAMUEL, Lord (1870–1963)

It takes two to make a marriage a success and only one a failure.

[*A Book of Quotations* (1947)]

SELDEN, John (1584–1654)

Marriage is nothing but a civil contract.

[*Table Talk* (1689)]

SETH, Vikram (1952–)

'You will marry a boy I choose,' said Mrs Rupa Mehra firmly to her younger daughter.

[*A Suitable Boy* (1993)]

SHAKESPEARE, William (1564–1616)

Men are April when they woo, December when they wed: maids are May when they are maids, but the sky changes when they are wives.

[*As You Like It*, IV.i]

Let me give light, but let me not be light,
For a light wife doth make a heavy husband.

[*The Merchant of Venice*, V.i]

Thy husband is thy lord, thy life, thy keeper,
Thy head, thy sovereign; one that cares for thee,
And for thy maintenance commits his body
To painful labour both by sea and land.

[*The Taming of the Shrew*, V.ii]

Let still the woman take
An elder than herself; so wears she to him,
So sways she level in her husband's heart.
For, boy, however we do praise ourselves,
Our fancies are more giddy and unfirm,
More longing, wavering, sooner lost and won,

Than women's are.

[*Twelfth Night*, II.iv]

SHAW, George Bernard (1856–1950)

It is a woman's business to get married as soon as possible, and a man's to keep unmarried as long as he can.

[*Man and Superman* (1903)]

Marriage is popular because it combines the maximum of temptation with the maximum of opportunity.

[*Man and Superman* (1903)]

Those who talk most about the blessings of marriage and the constancy of its vows are the very people who declare that if the chain were broken and the prisoners left free to choose, the whole social fabric would fly asunder. You cannot have the argument both ways. If the prisoner is happy, why lock him in? If he is not, why pretend that he is?

[*Man and Superman* (1903)]

SHERIDAN, Richard Brinsley (1751–1816)

'Tis safest in matrimony to begin with a little aversion.

[*The Rivals* (1775)]

You had no taste when you married me.

[*The School for Scandal* (1777)]

SIMPSON, Ronald Albert (1929–)

She cannot say just when
The cooking first began within her mind –
But here she knows … like cakes or bread, a wife
Must lie content as if within a hand
And feel the teeth of time upon her life.

['Wife']

SMITH, Logan Pearsall (1865–1946)

Married women are kept women, and they are beginning to find it out.

[*Afterthoughts* (1931)]

SMITH, Sydney (1771–1845)

[On marriage]

It resembles a pair of shears, so joined that they cannot be separated; often moving in opposite directions, yet always punishing anyone who comes between them.

[In Holland, *A Memoir of the Reverend Sydney Smith* (1855)]

STEVENSON, Robert Louis (1850–1894)

In marriage, a man becomes slack and selfish, and undergoes a fatty degeneration of his moral being.

[*Virginibus Puerisque* (1881)]

Lastly (and this is, perhaps, the golden rule), no woman should marry a teetotaller, or a man who does not smoke.

[*Virginibus Puerisque* (1881)]

Marriage is like life in this – that it is a field of battle and not a bed of roses.

[*Virginibus Puerisque* (1881)]

To marry is to domesticate the Recording Angel. Once you are married, there is nothing left for you, not even suicide, but to be good.

[*Virginibus Puerisque* (1881)]

Even if we take matrimony at its lowest, even if we regard it as no more than a sort of friendship recognized by the police.

[*Virginibus Puerisque* (1881)]

Marriage is a step so grave and decisive that it attracts light-headed, variable men by its very awfulness.

[*Virginibus Puerisque* (1881)]

Times are changed with him who marries; there are no more by-path meadows, where you may innocently linger, but the road lies long and straight and dusty to the grave.

[*Virginibus Puerisque* (1881)]

Trusty, dusky, vivid, true,
With eyes of gold and bramble-dew,
Steel-true and blade-straight,
The great artificer
Made my mate.

['My Wife' (1896)]

SWIFT, Jonathan (1667–1745)

The reason why so few marriages are happy, is, because young ladies spend their time in making nets, not in making cages.

[*Thoughts on Various Subjects* (1711)]

TAYLOR, Bishop Jeremy (1613–1667)

He that loves not his wife and children, feeds a lioness at home and broods a nest of sorrows.

[*XXV Sermons Preached at Golden Grove* (1653)]

THACKERAY, William Makepeace (1811–1863)

And this I set down as a positive truth. A woman with fair opportunities, and without an absolute hump may marry whom she likes.

[*Vanity Fair* (1847–1848)]

THATCHER, Denis (1915–)

[Replying to the question 'Who wears the pants in this house?']
I do, and I also wash and iron them.

[*Times* (Los Angeles), 1981]

THOMAS, Irene (1920–)

It should be a very happy marriage – they are both so much in love with him.

[Attr.]

TOOKE, John Horne (1736–1812)

[Replying to the suggestion that he take a wife]
With all my heart. Whose wife shall it be?

[Attr.]

VANBRUGH, Sir John (1664–1726)

No man worth having is true to his wife, or can be true to his wife, or ever was, or ever will be so.

[*The Relapse, or Virtue in Danger* (1696)]

WARD, Artemus (1834–1867)

He is dreadfully married. He's the most married man I ever saw in my life.

[*Artemus Ward's Lecture* (1869)]

WEBB, Sidney (1859–1947)

Marriage is the waste-paper basket of the emotions.

[In Bertrand Russell, *Autobiography* (1967)]

WELDON, Fay (1931–)

… the great wonderful construct which is marriage – a construct made up of a hundred little kindnesses, a thousand little bitings back of spite, tens of thousands of minor actions of good intent – this must not, as an institution, be brought down in ruins.

[*Splitting* (1995)]

WERB, Mike

Most of the men in this town think monogamy is some kind of wood.

[*The Mask*, film, 1994]

WILDE, Oscar (1854–1900)

There's nothing in the world like the devotion of a married woman. It's a thing no married man knows anything about.

[*Lady Windermere's Fan* (1893)]

You don't seem to realise, that in married life three is company and two is none.

[*The Importance of Being Earnest* (1895)]

The real drawback to marriage is that it makes one unselfish. And unselfish people are colourless.

[*The Picture of Dorian Gray* (1891)]

Twenty years of romance make a woman look like a ruin; but twenty years of marriage make her something like a public building.

[*A Woman of No Importance* (1893)]

The amount of women in London who flirt with their own husbands is perfectly scandalous. It looks so bad. It is simply washing one's clean linen in public.

[*The Importance of Being Earnest* (1895)]

I am not in favour of long engagements. They give people the opportunity of finding out each other's character before marriage, which I think is never advisable.

[*The Importance of Being Earnest* (1895)]

WILDER, Thornton (1897–1975)

The best part of married life is the fights. The rest is merely so-so.

[*The Matchmaker* (1954)]

WODEHOUSE, P.G. (1881–1975)

All the unhappy marriages come from the husbands having brains. What good are

brains to a man? They only unsettle him.

[*The Adventures of Sally* (1920)]

Like so many substantial Americans, he had married young and kept on marrying, springing from blonde to blonde like the chamois of the Alps leaping from crag to crag.

[In Usborne, *Wodehouse at Work to the End* (1976)]

WYLIE, Betty Jane (1931–)

A marriage is really a nonstop conversation.

[*All in the Family: A Survival Guide for Living and Loving in a Changing World*]

See ADULTERY; FAMILY

MARTYRDOM

BOLEYN, Anne (1507–1536)

[Said on hearing that she was to be executed for adultery]
The king has been very good to me. He promoted me from a simple maid to be a marchioness. Then he raised me to be a queen. Now he will raise me to be a martyr.

[Attr.]

BROWNE, Sir Thomas (1605–1682)

Were the happiness of the next world as closely apprehended as the felicities of this, it were a martyrdom to live.

[*Hydriotaphia: Urn Burial* (1658)]

DRYDEN, John (1631–1700)

For all have not the gift of martyrdom.

[*The Hind and the Panther* (1687)]

IBÁRRURI, Dolores ('La Pasionaria') (1895–1989)

Il vaut mieux mourir debout que vivre à genoux!
It is better to die on your feet than to live on your knees.

[Speech, Paris, 1936]

KIERKEGAARD, Søren (1813–1855)

The tyrant dies and his rule is over; the martyr dies and his rule begins.

[Attr.]

LEWIS, C.S. (1898–1963)

She's the sort of woman who lives for others – you can tell the others by their hunted expression.

[*The Screwtape Letters* (1942)]

SMITH, Sydney (1771–1845)

The only way to deal with such a man as O'Connell is to hang him up and erect a statue to him under the gallows.

[In H. Pearson, *The Smith of Smiths* (1934)]

TERTULLIAN (c.AD 160–c.225)

Plures efficimur quoties metimur a vobis, semen est sanguis Christianorum.

As often as we are mown down by you, the more we grow in numbers; the blood of Christians is the seed.

[*Apologeticus*]

VOLTAIRE (1694–1778)

I am very fond of truth, but not at all of martyrdom.

[Letter to d'Alembert, 1776]

WILDE, Oscar (1854–1900)

A thing is not necessarily true because a man dies for it.

[*Sebastian Melmoth* (1904)]

MATHEMATICS

ABEL, Niels Henrik (1809–1829)

[Explaining how he had become a great mathematician at such a young age]
By studying the masters – not their pupils.

[In E.T. Bell, *Men of Mathematics* (1937)]

BARRIE, Sir J.M. (1860–1937)

What is algebra exactly; is it those three-cornered things?

[*Quality Street* (1901)]

BROWNE, Sir Thomas (1605–1682)

I have often admired the mystical way of Pythagoras, and the secret magic of numbers.

[*Religio Medici* (1643)]

CARLYLE, Thomas (1795–1881)

It is a mathematical fact that the casting of this pebble from my hand alters the centre of gravity of the Universe.

[*Sartor Resartus* (1834)]

EINSTEIN, Albert (1879–1955)

As far as the laws of mathematics refer to reality, they are not certain, and as far as they are certain, they do not refer to reality.

[In Capra, *The Tao of Physics* (1975)]

EUCLID (fl. c.300 BC)

A line is length without breadth.

[*Elements*]

[To Ptolemy I]
There is no royal road to geometry.

[In Proclus, *Commentaria in Euclidem*]

FLEMING, Marjory (1803–1811)

The most devilish thing is 8 times 8 and 7 times 7 it is what nature itselfe cant endure.

[In Esdaile, *Journals, Letters and Verses* (1934)]

GALILEO GALILEI (1564–1642)

This grand book, the universe, is written in the language of mathematics.

[Quoted by Melvyn Bragg, BBC radio, 1999]

HOBBES, Thomas (1588–1679)

Geometry … is the only science that it hath pleased God hitherto to bestow on mankind.

[*Leviathan* (1651)]

MILLIGAN, Spike (1918–)

Moriarty: How are you at Mathematics?
Harry Secombe: I speak it like a native.

[*The Goon Show*]

PLATO (c.429–347 BC)

[Inscription written over the entrance to the Academy]
Let no one ignorant of mathematics enter here.

[Attr.]

RAMANUJAN, Srinivasa (1887–1920)

[Reply to the mathematician, G.H. Hardy, who remarked that a cab's number –1729 – was dull]
No, it is a very interesting number; it is the

smallest number expressible as a sum of two cubes in two different ways.

[*Proceedings of the London Mathematical Society* (1921); the two ways are 13 + 123, and 93 + 103]

RUSSELL, Bertrand (1872–1970)
Mathematics may be defined as the subject in which we never know what we are talking about, nor whether what we are saying is true.

[*Mysticism and Logic* (1918)]

Mathematics, rightly viewed, possesses not only truth, but supreme beauty – a beauty cold and austere, like that of sculpture.

[*Mysticism and Logic* (1918)]

SMITH, Sydney (1771–1845)
What would life be without arithmetic, but a scene of horrors.

[Letters, To Miss – , 1835]

WEIL, Simone (1909–1943)
Algebra and money are essentially levellers; the first intellectually, the second effectively.

[Attr.]

MEANING

JUNG, Carl Gustav (1875–1961)
The least of things with a meaning is worth more in life than the greatest of things without it.

[*Modern Man in Search of a Soul*]

SMITH, Logan Pearsall (1865–1946)
[Contemplating whether life has any meaning, shortly before his death]
Yes, there is a meaning, at least for me, there is one thing that matters – to set a chime of words tinkling in the minds of a few fastidious people.

[*New Statesman*, 1946]

WALLAS, Graham (1858–1932)
The little girl had the makings of a poet in her who, being told to be sure of her meaning before she spoke, said: 'How can I know what I think till I see what I say?'.

[*The Art of Thought* (1926)]

See PURPOSE; WORDS

MEDIA

BAKEWELL, Joan (1933–)
The BBC is full of men appointing men who remind them of themselves when young, so you get the same backgrounds, the same education, and the same programmes.

[*The Observer*, 1993]

BJELKE-PETERSEN, Sir Johannes (1911–)
The greatest thing that could happen to the state and the nation is when we can get rid of all the media. Then we could live in peace and tranquillity, and no one would know anything.

[*The Spectator*, 1987]

HOWARD, Philip (1933–)
The proliferation of radio and television channels has produced a wilderness of cave-dwellers instead of the promised global village.

[*The Times*, 1992]

JACKSON, Robert (1946–)
To have open government you need mature media. It is more difficult for people to discuss complex issues than it used to be because of the destructive power of the tabloids. The TV sound bite also makes it impossible to communicate complex arguments. It is all black and white, cut and dried, yaa-boo.

[*Independent on Sunday*, 1994]

KAVANAU, 'Mad Dog'
[Statement of CNN editorial policy]
If it bleeds, it leads.

[*The Guardian*, 1999]

MCLUHAN, Marshall (1911–1980)
The medium is the message. This is merely to say that the personal and social consequences of any medium ... result from

the new scale that is introduced into our affairs by each extension of ourselves or by any new technology.

[*Understanding Media* (1964)]

MURDOCH, Rupert (1931–)

Monopoly is a terrible thing, till·you have it.

[*The New Yorker*, 1979]

[In reply to Ted Turner (*see below*)]

It is true that I am a low mean snake. But you could walk beneath me wearing a top hat.

[*The Guardian*, 1999]

REITH, Lord (1889–1971)

It was in fact the combination of public service motive, sense of moral obligation, assured finance and the brute force of monopoly which enabled the BBC to make of broadcasting what no other country has made of it.

[*Into the Wind* (1949)]

SHELLEY, Sir James

[As Director of Broadcasting]

There was once a wicked lady called Circe, who was reputed to turn human beings into swine. The object of broadcasting should be the exact opposite.

[In Hamish Keith and William Main (eds), *New Zealand Yesterdays: A Look at Our Recent Past*]

STEVENSON, Adlai (1900–1965)

The trouble with this country is that it has a two-party system and a one-party press.

[Speech, 1952]

STOPPARD, Tom (1937–)

The media. It sounds like a convention of spiritualists.

[*Night and Day* (1978)]

TURNER, Ted

[CNN Launch speech, 1980]

See we're gonna take the news and put it on satellite and then we're gonna beam it down to Russia, and we're gonna bring world peace and we're gonna get rich in the process!

[*The Guardian*, 1999]

[After launch of Rupert Murdoch's Fox news in 1996]

[Murdoch's] a schlockmeister. We're gonna squish Rupert like a bug.

[*The Guardian*, 1999]

WHITLAM, Gough (1916–)

Quite small and ineffectual demonstrations can be made to look like the beginnings of a revolution if the cameraman is in the right place at the right time.

[*A Dictionary of Contemporary Quotations* (1982)]

See INTERNET; MONEY AND WEALTH; NEWS; NEWSPAPERS; TELEVISION

MEDICINE

ARNOLD, Matthew (1822–1888)

Nor bring, to see me cease to live,
Some doctor full of phrase and fame,
To shake his sapient head and give
The ill he cannot cure a name.

['A Wish' (1867)]

ASQUITH, Margot (1864–1945)

The King told me he would never have died if it had not been for that fool Dawson of Penn.

[In K. Rose, *King George V* (1983)]

BELLOC, Hilaire (1870–1953)

Physicians of the Utmost Fame
Were called at once; but when they came
They answered, as they took their Fees,
'There is no Cure for this Disease.'

[*Cautionary Tales* (1907)]

THE BIBLE
(King James Version)

Physician, heal thyself.

[*Luke*, 4:23]

CHEKHOV, Anton (1860–1904)

Medicine is my lawful wife but literature is my mistress. When I'm bored with one, I spend the night with the other.

[Letter to Suvorin, 1888]

FLETCHER, John (1579–1625)

I find the medicine worse than the malady.

[*The Lover's Progress* (1623)]

FRANKLIN, Benjamin (1706–1790)

He's the best physician that knows the worthlessness of the most medicines.

[*Poor Richard's Almanac* (1733)]

GOLDSMITH, Oliver (c.1728–1774)

The doctor found, when she was dead, – Her last disorder mortal.

['Elegy on Mrs Mary Blaize' (1759)]

GOLDWYN, Samuel (1882–1974)

Any man who goes to a psychiatrist should have his head examined.

[In Zierold, *Moguls* (1969)]

HAHNEMANN, C.F.S. (1755–1843)

Similia similibus curantur.

Like cures like.

[Motto of homeopathic medicine]

HIPPOCRATES (c.460–357 BC)

[Of medicine]

Life is short, science is so long to learn, opportunity is elusive, experience is dangerous, judgement is difficult.

[*Aphorisms* (c. 415 BC)]

JAMES, Alice (1848–1892)

I suppose one has a greater sense of intellectual degradation after an interview with a doctor than from any human experience.

[In Leon Edel (ed.), *The Diary of Alice James*, 1890]

JOHNSON, Samuel (1709–1784)

It is incident to physicians, I am afraid, beyond all other men, to mistake subsequence for consequence.

[In Boswell, *The Life of Samuel Johnson* (1791)]

LA BRUYÈRE, Jean de (1645–1696)

Les médecins laissent mourir, les charlatans tuent.

Doctors allow us to die; charlatans kill us.

[*Les caractères ou les moeurs de ce siècle* (1688)]

LOOS, Anita (1893–1981)

So then Dr Froyd said that all I needed was to cultivate a few inhibitions and get some sleep.

[*Gentlemen Prefer Blondes* (1925)]

MCLUHAN, Marshall (1911–1980)

If the nineteenth century was the age of the editorial chair, ours is the century of the psychiatrist's couch.

[*Understanding Media* (1964)]

MOLIÈRE (1622–1673)

C'est un homme expéditif, qui aime á dépêcher ses malades; et quand on a á mourir, cela se fait avec lui le plus vite du monde.

He's an expeditious man, who likes to hurry his patients along; and when you have to die, he gets it over with quicker than anyone else.

[*Monsieur de Pourceaugnac* (1670)]

PROVERB

Prevention is better than cure.

QUARLES, Francis (1592–1644)

Physicians of all men are most happy; what good success soever they have, the world proclaimeth, and what faults they commit, the earth covereth.

[*Hieroglyphics of the Life of Man* (1638)]

ROLLESTON, Sir Humphrey (1862–1944)

[Of physicians]

First they get on, then they get honour, then they get honest.

[In David Ogilvy, *Confessions of an Advertising Man* (1963)]

SHAW, George Bernard (1856–1950)

If you are going to have doctors you had better have doctors well off; just as if you are going to have a landlord you had better have a rich landlord. Taking all the round of professions and occupations, you will find that every man is the worse for being poor; and the doctor is a specially dangerous man when poor.

[*The Socialist Criticism of the Medical Profession* (1909)]

Optimistic lies have such immense

therapeutic value that a doctor who cannot tell them convincingly has mistaken his profession.

[*Misalliance* (1914)]

WILLIAMS, Tennessee (1911–1983)

[Explaining why he had stopped seeing his psychoanalyst]
He was meddling too much in my private life.

[Attr.]

See HEALTH; ILLNESS; PSYCHIATRY

MELANCHOLY

BURTON, Robert (1577–1640)

If there is a hell upon earth, it is to be found in a melancholy man's heart.

[*Anatomy of Melancholy* (1621)]

LAMB, Charles (1775–1834)

The man must have a rare recipe for melancholy, who can be dull in Fleet Street.

[Letter to Thomas Manning, 1802]

ROGERS, Samuel (1763–1855)

Go – you may call it madness, folly;
You shall not chase my gloom away.
There's such a charm in melancholy,
I would not, if I could, be gay.

['To –', 1814']

See DESPAIR

MEMORY

ALLINGHAM, William (1824–1889)

Four ducks on a pond,
A grass-bank beyond,
A blue sky of spring,
White clouds on the wing:
What a little thing
To remember for years –
To remember with tears.

['A Memory' (1888)]

APOLLINAIRE, Guillaume (1880–1918)

Les souvenirs sont cors de chasse
Dont meurt le bruit parmi le vent.
Memories are hunting horns whose sound dies away in the wind.

['Cors de Chasse' (1913)]

ARNOLD, Matthew (1822–1888)

Ere the parting hour go by,
Quick, thy tablets, Memory!

['A Memory Picture' (1849)]

And we forget because we must
And not because we will.

['Absence' (1852)]

AUSTEN, Jane (1775–1817)

There seems something more speakingly incomprehensible in the powers, the failures, the inequalities of memory, than in any other of our intelligences.

[*Mansfield Park* (1814)]

BAUDELAIRE, Charles (1821–1867)

J'ai plus de souvenirs que si j'avais mille ans.
I have more memories than if I had lived for a thousand years.

[*Les Fleurs du mal* (1857)]

BRIDGES, Robert (1844–1930)

Rejoice ye dead, where'er your spirits
    dwell,
Rejoice that yet on earth your fame is
    bright,
And that your names, remembered day
    and night,
Live on the lips of those who love you
    well.

['Ode to Music' (1896)]

BRODSKY, Joseph (1940–1996)

What memory has in common with art is the knack for selection, the taste for detail … More than anything, memory resembles a library in alphabetical disorder, and with no collected works by anyone.

['In a Room and a Half' (1986)]

CAMPBELL, Thomas (1777–1844)

To live in hearts we leave behind

Is not to die.

['Hallowed Ground']

DISRAELI, Benjamin (1804–1881)
Nobody is forgotten when it is convenient to remember him.

[Attr.]

LA ROCHEFOUCAULD (1613–1680)
Tout le monde se plaint de sa mémoire, et personne ne se plaint de son jugement.
Everyone complains of his memory; nobody of his judgment.

[*Maximes* (1678)]

LAVIN, Mary (1912–)
What did they know about memory? What was it but another name for dry love and barren longing?

[*In the Middle of the Fields* (1967)]

PROUST, Marcel (1871–1922)
Et tout d'un coup le souvenir m'est apparu. Ce goût c'était celui du petit morceau de madeleine que le dimanche matin á Combray … ma tante Léonie m'offrait après l'avoir trempé dans son infusion de thé ou de tilleul.
And suddenly the memory came back to me. The taste was that of the little piece of madeleine which on Sunday mornings at Combray … my aunt Léonie used to give me, after dipping it first in her cup of tea or tisane.

[*A la recherche du temps perdu, Du côté de chez Swann* (1913)]

PROVERB
I hate a man with a memory at a drinking bout.

[Greek proverb]

SCHOPENHAUER, Arthur (1788–1860)
To expect a man to retain everything that he has ever read is like expecting him to carry about in his body everything that he has ever eaten.

[*Parerga and Paralipomena* (1851)]

SHAKESPEARE, William (1564–1616)
Praising what is lost

Makes the remembrance dear.

[*All's Well That Ends Well*, V.iii]

SHAW, George Bernard (1856–1950)
Reminiscences make one feel so deliciously aged and sad.

[*The Irrational Knot* (1905)]

See NOSTALIGIA; PAST

MEN AND WOMEN

ADAMS, Scott (1957–)
Needing someone is like needing a parachute. If he isn't there the first time you need him, chances are you won't be needing him again.

[*The Dilbert Principle*]

ALLRED, Gloria
The more I know about men the more I like dogs.

[*Politically Incorrect*, 1995]

ANONYMOUS
It's not what you call me, but what I answer to.

[African proverb]

AUSTEN, Jane (1775–1817)
There certainly are not so many men of large fortune in the world as there are pretty women to deserve them.

[*Mansfield Park* (1814)]

BARRIE, Sir J.M. (1860–1937)
I have always found that the man whose second thoughts are good is worth watching.

[*What Every Woman Knows* (1908)]

THE BIBLE
(King James Version)
It is not good that the man should be alone; I will make him an help meet for him.

[*Genesis*, 2:18]

BOMBECK, Erma (1927–1996)
What's wrong with you men? Would hair stop growing on your chest if you asked

directions somewhere?

[*When You Look Like Your Passport Photo, It's Time to Go Home* (1991)]

BURCHILL, Julie (1960–)

Men have charisma; women have vital statistics.

[*Sex and Sensibility* (1992)]

BYRON, Lord (1788–1824)

Man's love is of man's life a thing
  apart,
'Tis woman's whole existence.

[*Don Juan* (1824)]

The more I see of men, the less I like them. If I could but say so of women too, all would be well.

[*Journal*, 1814]

CHESTERFIELD, Lord (1694–1773)

Have you found out that every woman is infallibly to be gained by every sort of flattery, and every man by one sort or other?

[*Letter to his son*, 1752]

COLERIDGE, Samuel Taylor (1772–1834)

The man's desire is for the woman; but the woman's desire is rarely other than for the desire of the man.

[*Table Talk* (1835)]

CONNOLLY, Cyril (1903–1974)

The true index of a man's character is the health of his wife.

[*The Unquiet Grave* (1944)]

COPE, Wendy (1945–)

There are so many kinds of awful
  men –
One can't avoid them all. She often
  said
She'd never make the same mistake
  again:
She always made a new mistake
  instead.

['Rondeau Redoublé' (1986)]

DAVIES, Robertson (1913–1995)

Women tell men things that men are not very

likely to find out for themselves.

[In J. Madison Davis, *Conversations with Robertson Davies* (1989)]

DICKINSON, Angie (1931–)

Men should be the ones who succeed. It makes me feel comfortable if men are the ones in control.

[*Daily Mail*, 1995]

DIETRICH, Marlene (1901–1992)

The average man is more interested in a woman who is interested in him than he is in a woman – any woman – with beautiful legs.

News item, 1954]

Most women set out to try to change a man, and when they have changed him they do not like him.

[Attr.]

DRYDEN, John (1631–1700)

Men are but children of a larger
  growth;
Our appetites as apt to change as
  theirs,
And full as craving too, and full as
  vain.

[*All for Love* (1678)]

DWORKIN, Andrea (1946–)

Men love death. In everything they make, they hollow out a central place for death … Men especially love murder. In art they celebrate it. In life, they commit it.

[*The Independent*, 1992]

EBNER-ESCHENBACH, Marie von (1830–1916)

Eine gescheite Frau hat Millionen geborener Feinde – alle dummen Männer.
A clever woman has millions of born enemies – all stupid men.

[*Aphorisms* (1880)]

ELIOT, George (1819–1880)

I'm not denyin' the women are foolish: God Almighty made 'em to match the men.

[*Adam Bede* (1859)]

A man is seldom ashamed of feeling that he cannot love a woman so well when he sees a certain greatness in her: nature having intended greatness for men.

[*Middlemarch* (1872)]

EMERSON, Ralph Waldo (1803–1882)

Men are what their mothers made them.

[*The Conduct of Life* (1860)]

EVANS, Dame Edith (1888–1976)

When a woman behaves like a man, why doesn't she behave like a nice man?

[*The Observer*, 1956]

FAIRBAIRN, Lady Sam

Behind every great man is an exhausted woman.

[*The Independent*, 1994]

FORD, Anna (1943–)

It is men who face the biggest problems in the future, adjusting to their new and complicated role.

[Attr.]

FRANCIS, Clare (1946–)

I think men are intimidated by my independence and wonder what they have to offer me when I already have a house in Kensington and a career. Men of my generation still need to feel needed.

[*Daily Mail*, 1995]

FRANKLIN, Miles (1879–1954)

Men are clumsy, stupid creatures regarding little things, but in their right place they are wonderful animals.

[*My Brilliant Career* (1901)]

FRENCH, Marilyn (1929–)

Whatever they may be in public life, whatever their relations with men, in their relations with women, all men are rapists, and that's all they are. They rape us with their eyes, their laws and their codes.

[*The Women's Room* (1977)]

FRIEDAN, Betty (1921–)

Men weren't really the enemy – they were fellow victims suffering from an outmoded

masculine mystique that made them feel unnecessarily inadequate when there were no bears to kill.

[*Christian Science Monitor*, 1974)]

GABOR, Zsa-Zsa (1919–)

Never despise what it says in the women's magazines: it may not be subtle but neither are men.

[*The Observer*, 1976]

GASKELL, Elizabeth (1810–1865)

A man ... is so in the way in the house!

[*Cranford* (1853)]

GAY, John (1685–1732)

Man may escape from rope and gun;
Nay, some have out-liv'd the doctor's pill;
Who takes a woman must be undone,
That basilisk is sure to kill.
The fly that sips treacle is lost in the sweets,
So he that tastes woman, woman, woman,
He that tastes woman, ruin meets.

[*The Beggar's Opera* (1728)]

GREER, Germaine (1939–)

Probably the only place where a man can feel really secure is in a maximum security prison, except for the imminent threat of release.

[*The Female Eunuch* (1970)]

A woman becomes the extension of a man's ego like his horse or his car.

[*The Female Eunuch* (1970)]

HALL, Jerry (1956–)

My mother said it was simple to keep a man, you must be a maid in the living room, a cook in the kitchen and a whore in the bedroom. I said I'd hire the other two and take care of the bedroom bit.

[*The Observer*, 1985]

HARLOW, Jean (1911–1937)

I like to wake up feeling a new man.

[In Simon Rose, *Classic Film Guide* (1995)]

HENRY, O. (1862–1910)

If men knew how women pass the time

when they are alone they'd never marry.

[*'Memoirs of a Yellow Dog'* (1906)]

HILL, Reginald (1936–)

He created a man who was hard of head, blunt of speech, knew which side his bread was buttered on, and above all took no notice of women. Then God sent him forth to multiply in Yorkshire.

[*Pictures of Perfection* (1994)]

HOLMES, Oliver Wendell (1809–1894)

Man has his will, – but woman has her way.

[*The Autocrat of the Breakfast-Table* (1858)]

JONG, Erica

Men and women, women and men. It will never work.

KEILLOR, Garrison (1942–)

Years ago, manhood was an opportunity for achievement, and now it is a problem to be overcome.

[*The Book of Guys* (1994)]

KENNEDY, Florynce R. (1916–)

If men could get pregnant, abortion would be a sacrament.

[In Steinem, *The Verbal Karate of Florynce R. Kennedy, Esq.* (1973)]

KIPLING, Rudyard (1865–1936)

Take my word for it, the silliest woman can manage a clever man; but it needs a very clever woman to manage a fool.

[*Plain Tales from the Hills* (1888)]

For a man he must go with a woman, which women don't understand –
Or the sort that say they can see it, they aren't the marrying brand.

[*'The Mary Gloster'* (1894)]

Open and obvious devotion from any sort of man is always pleasant to any sort of woman.

[*Plain Tales from the Hills* (1888)]

LAVER, James (1899–1975)

Man in every age has created woman in the image of his own desire.

[In Neustater, *Hyenas in Petticoats: a Look at 20 Years of Feminism* (1989)]

LAWRENCE, D.H. (1885–1930)

There is no comradeship between men and women, none whatsoever, but rather a condition of battle, reserve, hostility.

[*Twilight in Italy* (1916)]

One realizes with horror, that the race of men is almost extinct in Europe. Only Christ-like heroes and woman-worshipping Don Juans, and rabid equality-mongrels.

[*Sea and Sardinia* (1921)]

LERNER, Alan Jay (1918–1986)

Why can't a woman be more like a man?
Men are so honest, so thoroughly square;
Eternally noble, historically fair.

[*My Fair Lady* (1956)]

LONGFELLOW, Henry Wadsworth (1807–1882)

As unto the bow the cord is,
So unto the man is woman;
Though she bends him, she obeys him,
Though she draws him, yet she follows;
Useless each without the other!

[*The Song of Hiawatha* (1855)]

MARX, Groucho (1895–1977)

A man is only as old as the woman he feels.

[Attr.]

MAUGHAM, William Somerset (1874–1965)

Men have an extraordinarily erroneous opinion of their position in nature; and the error is ineradicable.

[*A Writer's Notebook* (1949)]

MEAD, Margaret (1901–1978)

Women want mediocre men, and men are working to be as mediocre as possible.

[*Quote Magazine*, 1958]

MENCKEN, H.L. (1880–1956)

Every normal man must be tempted, at times, to spit on his hands, hoist the black flag, and begin slitting throats.

[*Prejudices* (1922)]

Women hate revolutions and revolutionists. They like men who are docile, and well-regarded at the bank, and never late at meals.

[Prejudices (1922)]

Men have a much better time of it than women. For one thing, they marry later. For another thing, they die earlier.

[A Mencken Chrestomathy (1949)]

MEREDITH, George (1828–1909)

I expect that Woman will be the last thing civilized by Man.

[The Ordeal of Richard Feverel (1859)]

NORRIS, Kathleen (1880–1966)

There are men I could spend eternity with. But not this life.

[The Middle of the World (1981)]

O'BRIEN, Conan

A study in the Washington Post says that women have better verbal skills than men. I just want to say to the authors of that study: *Duh.*

PALACIO VALDÉS, Armando (1853–1938)

Cuando un hombre deja de ser un dios para su esposa, puede tener la seguridad de que ya es menos que un hombre.

When a man stops being a god for his wife, he can be sure that he's now less than a man.

[Doctor Angélico's Papers (1911)]

PARKER, Dorothy (1893–1967)

Men seldom make passes
At girls who wear glasses.

[Not So Deep as a Well (1937)]

PATMORE, Coventry (1823–1896)

A woman is a foreign land,
Of which, though there he settle young,
A man will ne'er quite understand
The customs, politics, and tongue.

[The Angel in the House (1854–1862)]

PIZZEY, Erin (1939–)

Men are gentle, honest and straightforward. Women are convoluted, deceptive and dangerous.

[Attr. in The Observer, 1996]

POPE, Alexander (1688–1744)

Men, some to business, some to pleasure take;
But every Woman is at heart a rake:
Men, some to quiet, some to public strife;
But every lady would be queen for life.

['Epistle to a Lady' (1735)]

RAMEY, Estelle (1917–)

More and more it appears that, biologically, men are designed for short, brutal lives and women for long miserable ones.

[The Observer, 1985]

RHONDDA, Viscountess (1883–1958)

Women must come off the pedestal. Men put us up there to get us out of the way.

[The Observer, 1920]

ROCHESTER, Earl of (1647–1680)

What vain, unnecessary things are men!
How well we do without 'em!

['Fragment' (published 1953)]

ROWLAND, Helen (1875–1950)

Never trust a husband too far, nor a bachelor too near.

[The Rubaiyat of a Bachelor (1925)]

SCHREINER, Olive (1855–1920)

It is delightful to be a woman; but every man thanks the Lord devoutly that he isn't one.

[The Story of an African Farm (1884)]

SHAKESPEARE, William (1564–1616)

O heaven, were man
But constant, he were perfect!

[The Two Gentlemen of Verona, V.iv]

SHAW, George Bernard (1856–1950)

A man who has no office to go to – I don't care who he is – is a trial of which you can have no conception.

[The Irrational Knot (1905)]

SPARK, Muriel (1918–)

Do you think it pleases a man when he looks into a woman's eyes and sees a reflection of the British Museum Reading Room?

[In Cowan, The Wit of Women (1969)]

STANTON, Elizabeth Cady (1815–1902)

Men are uniformly more attentive to women of rank, family, and fortune, who least need their care, than to any other class.

[In Anthony and Gage (eds), *History of Woman Suffrage* (1881)]

STEINEM, Gloria (1934–)

A woman needs a man like a fish needs a bicycle.

[Attr.]

TENNYSON, Alfred, Lord (1809–1892)

Man is the hunter; woman is his game:
The sleek and shining creatures of the chase,
We hunt them for the beauty of their skins;
They love us for it, and we ride them down.

[*The Princess* (1847)]

Man for the field and woman for the hearth:
Man for the sword and for the needle she:
Man with the head and woman with the heart:
Man to command and woman to obey;
All else confusion.

[*The Princess* (1847)]

TROLLOPE, Anthony (1815–1882)

How I did respect you when you dared to speak the truth to me! Men don't know women, or they would be harder to them.

[*The Claverings* (1867)]

TUCHOLSKY, Kurt (1890–1935)

Die Frauen haben es ja von Zeit zu auch nicht leicht. Wir Männern aber müssen uns rasieren.
Women from time to time don't have it easy either. But we men have to shave.

[*Scraps* (1973))]

TURNBULL, Margaret (fl. 1920s–1942)

When a man confronts catastrophe on the road, he looks in his purse – but a woman looks in her mirror.

[*The Left Lady* (1926)]

TWAIN, Mark (1835–1910)

[Responding to the question 'In a world without women what would men become?']

Scarce, sir. Mighty scarce.

[Attr.]

VAIL, Amanda (1921–1966)

Sometimes I think if there was a third sex men wouldn't get so much as a glance from me.

[*Love Me Little* (1957)]

WEST, Dame Rebecca (1892–1983)

[Defining an anti-feminist]
The man who is convinced that his mother was a fool.

[*The Clarion*]

WEST, Mae (1892–1980)

A man in the house is worth two in the street.

[*Belle of the Nineties*, film, 1934]

When women go wrong, men go right after them.

[In Weintraub, *The Wit and Wisdom of Mae West* (1967)]

WHITEHORN, Katherine (1926–)

No nice men are good at getting taxis.

[*The Observer*, 1977]

WHITTON, Charlotte (1896–1975)

Whatever women do they must do twice as well as men to be thought half as good. Luckily, this is not difficult.

[*Canada Month*, 1963]

WILDE, Oscar (1854–1900)

Women represent the triumph of matter over mind, just as men represent the triumph of mind over morals.

[*The Picture of Dorian Gray* (1891)]

Men can be analysed, women ... merely adored.

[*An Ideal Husband* (1895)]

All women become like their mothers. That is their tragedy. No man does. That's his.

[*The Importance of Being Earnest* (1895)]

Men play the game; women know the score.

[*The Observer*, 1982]

WOOLF, Virginia (1882–1941)

It is the masculine values that prevail. Speaking crudely, football and sport are 'important'; the worship of fashion, the buying of clothes 'trivial'… This is an important book, the critic assumes, because it deals with war. This is an insignificant book because it deals with feelings of women in a drawing-room … everywhere and much more subtly the difference of values persists.

[*A Room of One's Own* (1929)]

Why are women … so much more interesting to men than men are to women?

[*A Room of One's Own* (1929)]

See FEMINISM; HOMOSEXUALS; HUMANITY AND HUMAN NATURE; MARRIAGE; WOMEN

MERIT

BENNY, Jack (1894–1974)

[Said on receiving an award]
I don't deserve this, but I have arthritis, and I don't deserve that either.

[Attr.]

MELBOURNE, Lord (1779–1848)

[On the Order of the Garter]
I like the Garter; there is no damned merit in it.

[In H. Dunckley, *Lord Melbourne* (1890)]

POPE, Alexander (1688–1744)

Good-humour can prevail,
When airs, and flights, and screams, and scolding fail.
Beauties in vain their pretty eyes may roll;
Charms strike the sight, but merit wins the soul.

[*The Rape of the Lock* (1714)]

RICHARDSON, Samuel (1689–1761)

Desert and reward, I can assure her, seldom keep company.

[*Clarissa* (1747–1748)]

THATCHER, Margaret (1925–)

[Said after receiving school prize, aged nine]
I wasn't lucky. I deserved it.

[Attr.]

WESTMORLAND, John Fane, Tenth Earl of (1759–1841)

Merit, indeed! … We are come to a pretty pass if they talk of merit for a bishopric.

[In C. Oman, *The Gascoyne Heiress* (1968)]

MILLENNIUM

WAUGH, Auberon (1939–)

All the signs are that the millennium is going to be one of the greatest flops of British social history.

[*The Observer*, 1999]

MIND

BERKELEY, Bishop George (1685–1753)

All the choir of heaven and furniture of earth – in a word, all those bodies which compose the mighty frame of the world – have not any subsistence without a mind.

[*A Treatise Concerning the Principles of Human Knowledge* (1710)]

BETHELL, Richard (1800–1873)

His Lordship says he will turn it over in what he is pleased to call his mind.

[In Nash, *Life of Westbury*]

BRADLEY, F.H. (1846–1924)

His mind is open; yes, it is so open that nothing is retained; ideas simply pass through him.

[Attr.]

BURKE, Edmund (1729–1797)

The march of the human mind is slow.

[*Speech on Conciliation with America* (1775)]

CHESTERTON, G.K. (1874–1936)

There is a road from the eye to the heart that does not go through the intellect.

[*The Defendant* (1901)]

DOSTOEVSKY, Fyodor (1821–1881)

The mind is a tool, a machine, moved by
spiritual fire.

[Letter to his brother, 1838]

DYER, Sir Edward (c.1540–1607)

My mind to me a kingdom is,
Such present joys therein I find,
That it excels all other bliss
That earth affords or grows by kind.
Though much I want which most
    would have,
Yet still my mind forbids to crave.

['In praise of a contented mind' (1588). Attr.]

GAY, John (1685–1732)

Give me, kind heav'n, a private station,
A mind serene for contemplation.

[Fables (1738)]

HAMILTON, Sir William (1788–1856)

[Quoting Phavorinus]
On earth there is nothing great but man; in
man there is nothing great but mind.

[Lectures on Metaphysics and Logic (1859)]

HOPKINS, Gerard Manley (1844–1889)

O the mind, mind has mountains; cliffs of fall
Frightful, sheer, no-man-fathomed.

['No Worst, there is None' (1885)]

HUBBARD, Elbert (1856–1915)

Little minds are interested in the
extraordinary; great minds in the
commonplace.

[A Thousand and One Epigrams (1911)]

JUNG, Carl Gustav (1875–1961)

Das geistige Pendel schwingt zwischen Sin und
Unsinn und nicht zwischen richtig und unrichtig.
The pendulum of the mind swings between
sense and nonsense, and not between what
is right and what is wrong.

[Memories, Dreams, Thoughts
(1962)']

LA ROCHEFOUCAULD (1613–1680)

L'esprit est toujours la dupe du coeur.
The mind is always fooled by the heart.

[Maximes (1678)]

PIRSIG, Robert (1928–)

That's the classical mind at work, runs fine
inside but looks dingy on the surface.

[Zen and the Art of Motorcycle Maintenance (1974)]

PRIOR, Matthew (1664–1721)

Be to her virtues very kind;
Be to her faults a little blind;
Let all her ways be unconfin'd;
And clap your padlock – on her mind.

['An English Padlock' (1705)]

PUNCH

What is Matter? – Never mind.
What is Mind? – No matter.

[1855]

RADCLIFFE-BROWN, Alfred Reginald (1881–1935)

[On the anthropologist and reformer, Daisy Bates]
The contents of her mind … were somewhat
similar to the contents of a well-stored
sewing-basket after half a dozen kittens had
been playing there undisturbed for a few
days.

[In E.L. Grant Watson, But to What Purpose]

RYLE, Gilbert (1900–1976)

The dogma of the Ghost in the Machine.

[The Concept of Mind (1949)]

SALLUST (86–c.34 BC)

Dux atque imperator vitae mortalium animus est.
The mind is the guide and ruler of men's
lives.

[Jugurtha]

SHAW, George Bernard (1856–1950)

One man that has a mind and knows it can
always beat ten men who haven't and don't.

[The Apple Cart (1930)]

SHERRINGTON, Sir Charles Scott (1857–1952)

If it is for mind that we are searching the
brain, then we are supposing the brain to be
much more than a telephone-exchange. We
are supposing it a telephone-exchange
along with the subscribers as well.

[Man on his Nature]

SMITH, Sydney (1771–1845)

Not body enough to cover his mind decently with; his intellect is improperly exposed.

[In Holland, *A Memoir of the Reverend Sydney Smith* (1855)]

SNYDER, Gary (1930–)

A clear, attentive mind
Has no meaning but that
Which sees is truly seen.

[*Riprap* (1959)]

SPARK, Muriel (1918–)

A short neck denotes a good mind … You see, the messages go quicker to the brain because they've shorter to go.

[*The Ballad of Peckham Rye* (1960)]

WALPOLE, Horace (1717–1797)

When people will not weed their own minds, they are apt to be overrun with nettles.

[Letter to the Countess of Ailesbury, 1779]

WELCH, Raquel (1940–)

The mind can also be an erogenous zone.

[Attr.]

WILLIAMS, William Carlos (1883–1963)

Minds like beds always made up,
(more stony than a shore)
unwilling or unable.

[*Paterson* (1958)]

See IDEAS; INTELLIGENCE; THOUGHT

MIRACLES

AGNELLI, Giovanni (1921–)

I miracoli si possono fare, ma con il sudore.
Miracles can be made, but only by sweating.

[*Corriere della Sera*, 1994]

ARNOLD, Matthew (1822–1888)

Miracles do not happen.

[*Literature and Dogma* (1883 edition)]

HUME, David (1711–1776)

The Christian religion not only was at first attended with miracles, but even at this day cannot be believed by any reasonable person without one. Mere reason is insufficient to convince us of its veracity: and whoever is moved by Faith to assent to it, is conscious of a continued miracle in his own person, which subverts all the principles of his understanding, and gives him a determination to believe what is most contrary to custom and experience.

[*Philosophical Essays Concerning Human Understanding* (1748)]

No testimony is sufficient to establish a miracle, unless the testimony be of such a kind that its falsehood would be more miraculous than the fact which it endeavours to establish.

[*Philosophical Essays Concerning Human Understanding* (1748)]

RICE, Tim (1944–)

[Herod to Christ]
Prove to me that you're no fool,
Walk across my swimming pool.

['King Herod's Song', 1970, from Jesus Christ Superstar!]

MODERATION

ARISTOTLE (384–322 BC)

Blessed is the state in which those in power have moderate and sufficient means since where some are immoderately wealthy and others have nothing, the result will be extreme democracy or absolute oligarchy, or a tyranny may result from either of these extremes.

[*Politics*]

AUGUSTINE, Saint (354–430)

Multi quidem facilius se abstinent ut non utantur, quam temperent ut bene utantur.
Many find it easier to abstain totally than to use moderation.

[*On the Good of Marriage*]

PROVERB

Moderation in all things.

TERENCE (c.190–159 BC)

Id arbitror

Adprime in vita esse utile, ut nequid nimis.

My view is that the golden rule in life is never to have too much of anything.

[*Andria*]

WILDE, Oscar (1854–1900)

Moderation is a fatal thing, Lady Hunstanton. Nothing succeeds like excess.

[*A Woman of No Importance* (1893)]

See EXCESS

MODESTY

BARRIE, Sir J.M. (1860–1937)

I'm a second eleven sort of chap.

[*The Admirable Crichton* (1902)]

BUCHANAN, Robert Williams (1841–1901)

She just wore

Enough for modesty – no more.

['White Rose and Red' (1873)]

CHURCHILL, Sir Winston (1874–1965)

[Of Clement Attlee]

He is a modest man who has a good deal to be modest about.

[In *Chicago Sunday Tribune Magazine of Books*, 1954]

CONGREVE, William (1670–1729)

Ah! Madam, … you know every thing in the world but your perfections, and you only know not those, because 'tis the top of perfection not to know them.

[*Incognita* (1692)]

GILBERT, W.S. (1836–1911)

Wherever valour true is found,

True modesty will there abound.

[*The Yeoman of the Guard* (1888)]

RUSSELL, Bertrand (1872–1970)

… the nuns who never take a bath without wearing a bathrobe all the time. When asked why, since no man can see them, the reply

'Oh, but you forget the good God.'

[*The Basic Writings of Bertrand Russell* (1961)]

STEELE, Sir Richard (1672–1729)

These Ladies of irresistible Modesty are those who make Virtue unamiable.

[*The Tatler*, 1710]

MONARCHY AND ROYALTY

ABELARD, Peter (1079–1142)

Quis rex, quae curia, quale palatium,

Quae pax, quae requies, quod illud gaudium.

What a king, what a court, how fine a palace, what peace, what repose, what joy is there!

[*Hymnus Paraclitensis*]

ALTRINCHAM, Lord (John Grigg) (1924–)

[On Queen Elizabeth II's style when speaking in public]

The personality conveyed by the utterances which are put into her mouth is that of a priggish schoolgirl, captain of the hockey team, a prefect, and a recent candidate for confirmation. It is not thus that she will be able to come into her own as an independent and distinctive character.

[*National and English Review*, August 1958]

AMES, Fisher (1758–1808)

A monarchy is a merchantman which sails well, but will sometimes strike on a rock, and go to the bottom; a republic is a raft which will never sink, but then your feet are always in the water.

[Attr.]

ANDREWS, Elizabeth

[Said when an intruder was found in Queen Elizabeth II's bedroom]

Bloody hell, Ma'am, what's he doing here?

[*Daily Mail*, 1982]

ARCHER, Lord Jeffrey (1940–)

An entire family of divorcees, and they're head of the Church of England. It's going to make the person out there wonder if it's all worth it.

[Comment on the Royal Family, 1992]

BAGEHOT, Walter (1826–1877)

[The Monarchy] gives now a vast strength to the entire Constitution, by enlisting on its behalf the credulous obedience of enormous masses.

[*The English Constitution* (1867)]

The sovereign has, under a constitutional monarchy such as ours, three rights – the right to be consulted, the right to encourage, the right to warn.

[*The English Constitution* (1867)]

The mystic reverence, the religious allegiance, which are essential to a true monarchy, are imaginative sentiments that no legislature can manufacture in any people.

[*The English Constitution* (1867)]

The best reason why Monarchy is a strong government is, that it is an intelligible government. The mass of mankind understand it, and they hardly anywhere in the world understand any other.

[*The English Constitution* (1867)]

It has been said, not truly, but with a possible approximation to truth, 'that in 1802 every hereditary monarch was insane.'

[*The English Constitution* (1867)]

BEAVERBROOK, Lord (1879–1964)

[Remark to Winston Churchill during the abdication crisis, 1936]
Our cock won't fight.

[In Frances Donaldson, *Edward VIII* (1974)]

BENTLEY, Edmund Clerihew (1875–1956)

George the Third
Ought never to have occurred.
One can only wonder
At so grotesque a blunder.

[*More Biography* (1929)]

BLACKSTONE, Sir William (1723–1780)

That the king can do no wrong, is a

necessary and fundamental principle of the English constitution.

[*Commentaries on the Laws of England* (1765–1769)]

The king never dies.

[*Commentaries on the Laws of England* (1765–1769)]

BURCHILL, Julie (1960–)

[Of Princess Diana]
She is Madonna crossed with Mother Theresa – a glorious totem of Western ideals.

[*Sex and Sensibility* (1992)]

CAMPBELL, David (1915–1979)

'Hop in,' said the Queen Mother. In I piled
Between them to lie like a stick of wood.
I couldn't find a thing to say. My blood
Beat, but like rollers at the ebb of tide.
'I hope Your Majesties sleep well,' I lied.
A hand touched mine and the Queen said, 'I am
Most grateful to you, Jock. Please call me
Ma'am.'

['The Australian Dream' (c. 1965)]

CARNEGIE, Andrew (1835–1919)

A king is an insult to every other man in the land.

[Letter, 1887]

CHARLES FRANCIS JOSEPH, Emperor of Austria (1887–1922)

[On hearing of his accession to emperor]
What should I do? I think the best thing is to order a new stamp to be made with my face on it.

[In H. Hoffmeister, *Anekdotenschatz*]

CHARLES X (1757–1836)

I would rather hew wood than be a king under the conditions of the King of England.

[Attr.]

CORNEILLE, Pierre (1606–1684)

Et enfin la clémence est la plus belle marque
Qui fasse à l'univers connaître un vrai monarque.
For in the end, mercy is the greatest sign by which the world may recognise a true king.

[*Cinna* (1641)]

CUNNINGHAM, Allan (1784–1842)

Wha the deil hae we got for a King,
But a wee, wee German lairdie!

['The Wee, Wee German Lairdie' (1825)]

DISRAELI, Benjamin (1804–1881)

[To Queen Victoria]
Your Majesty is the head of the literary
profession.

[Attr.]

[In answer to Gladstone's taunt that Disraeli could
make a joke of any subject, including Queen Victoria]
Her Majesty is not a subject.

[Attr.]

[Asked if Queen Victoria should visit him during
his last illness]
No, it is better not. She would only ask me to
take a message to Albert.

[Attr.]

[To Matthew Arnold]
Everyone likes flattery; and when you come
to Royalty you should lay it on with a trowel.

[Attr.]

EDWARD VIII (later Duke of Windsor) (1894–1972)

[On receiving a large bill from a luxury hotel]
Now what do I do with this?

[Attr.]

I have found it impossible to carry the heavy
burden of responsibility and to discharge my
duties as King as I would wish to do without
the help and support of the woman I love.

[Abdication speech, 1936]

ELIZABETH I (1533–1603)

I am your anointed Queen. I will never be by
violence constrained to do anything. I thank
God I am endued with such qualities that if I
were turned out of the Realm in my petticoat
I were able to live in any place in Christome.

[Attr. Speech, 1566]

The queen of Scots is lighter of a fair son, and
I am but a barren stock.

[In F. Chamberlin, *The Sayings of Queen Elizabeth*
(1923)]

[Of Mary Queen of Scots]
The daughter of debate, that eke discord
doth sow.

[In F. Chamberlin, *The Sayings of Queen Elizabeth*
(1923)]

[Of the approaching Armada]
I know I have the body of a weak and feeble
woman, but I have the heart and stomach of
a king, and of a king of England too; and
think foul scorn that Parma or Spain, or any
prince of Europe, should dare to invade the
borders of my realm.

[Speech, 1588]

Though God hath raised me high, yet this I
count the glory of my crown: that I have
reigned with your loves.

[The Golden Speech, 1601]

ELIZABETH II (1926–)

[Comment about Princess Michael of Kent]
She's more royal than we are.

[Attr., in *Sunday* magazine, 1985]

ELIZABETH, the Queen Mother (1900–)

[On whether, after the bombing of Buckingham
Palace, her children would leave England]
The children will not leave unless I do. I shall
not leave unless their father does, and the
King will not leave the country in any
circumstances whatever.

[Attr.]

FABYAN, Robert (d. 1513)

King Henry [I] being in Normandy, after some
writers, fell from or with his horse, whereof
he caught his death; but Ranulphe says he
took a surfeit by eating of a lamprey, and
thereof died.

[*The New Chronicles of England and France*
(1516)]

FAROUK I (1920–1965)

[Remark made to Lord Boyd-Orr, 1948]
There will soon be only five kings left – the
Kings of England, Diamonds, Hearts, Spades
and Clubs.

[Attr.]

FERDINAND I, Emperor of Austria (1793–1875)

I am the emperor, and I want dumplings.

[In E. Crankshaw, *The Fall of the House of Habsburg* (1963)]

FREDERICK THE GREAT (1712–1786)

Une couronne n'est qu'un chapeau qui laisse passer la pluie.

A crown is merely a hat that lets the rain in.

[Remark on declining a formal coronation, 1740]

GEORGE III (1738–1820)

Born and educated in this country I glory in the name of Briton.

[Speech, 1760]

GEORGE V (1865–1936)

[Having just asked Ramsay MacDonald to form the first Labour Government]

Today, 23 years ago, dear Grandmama died. I wonder what she would have thought of a Labour Government.

[Diary, 22 January 1924]

GEORGE VI (1895–1952)

We're not a family; we're a firm.

[Attr. in Lane, *Our Future King*]

GILMOUR, Sir Ian (1926–)

The monarch is a person and a symbol. He makes power and state both intelligible and mysterious.

[*The Times*, 1992]

HAMILTON, William (Willie) (1917–)

The tourists who come to our island take in the Monarchy along with feeding the pigeons in Trafalgar Square.

[*My Queen and I* (1975)]

HANOVER, Ernst August, Elector of (1629–1698)

[On seeing Louis XIV's stables at Versailles]
Les chevaux du roi de France sont mieux logés que moi.
The king of France's horses are better housed than I am.

[Attr.]

HARDIE, Keir (1856–1915)

From his childhood onward this boy [the future Edward VIII] will be surrounded by sycophants and flatterers by the score – [Cries of 'Oh, oh!'] – and will be taught to believe himself as of a superior creation. [Cries of 'Oh, oh!'] A line will be drawn between him and the people whom he is to be called upon some day to reign over. In due course, following the precedent which has already been set, he will be sent on a tour round the world, and probably rumours of a morganatic alliance will follow – [Loud cries of 'Oh, oh!' and 'Order!'] – and the end of it all will be that the country will be called upon to pay the bill. – [Cries of 'Divide!'].

[Speech, House of Commons, 1894]

HENRI IV (1553–1610)

Je veux qu'il n'y ait si pauvre paysan en mon royaume qu'il n'ait tous les dimanches sa poule au pot.

It is my wish that in my kingdom there should be no peasant so poor that he cannot have a chicken in his pot every Sunday.

[In Hardouin de Péréfixe, *Histoire du Roy Henry le Grand* (1681)]

[Of James VI and I]
The wisest fool in Christendom.

[Attr.; also attributed to Sully]

JAMES V OF SCOTLAND (1512–1542)

[On the rule of the Stuart dynasty in Scotland]
It cam' wi' a lass, and it'll gang wi' a lass.

[Remark, 1542]

JEFFERSON, Thomas (1743–1826)

There is not a single crowned head in Europe whose talents or merit would entitle him to to be elected a vestryman by the people of any parish in America.

[Attr.]

JOHNSON, Lionel (1867–1902)

The saddest of all Kings
Crown'd, and again discrown'd …
Alone he rides, alone,
The fair and fatal king.

['By the Statue of King Charles I at Charing Cross' (1895)]

JONSON, Ben (1572–1637)

They say princes learn no art truly, but the art of horsemanship. The reason is, the brave beast is no flatterer. He will throw a prince as soon as his groom.

[*Timber, or Discoveries made upon Men and Matter* (1641)]

KIPLING, Rudyard (1865–1936)

He wrote that monarchs were divine,
And left a son who – proved they weren't!

[Songs written for C.R.L. Fletcher's *A History of England* (1911), 'James I']

LANDOR, Walter Savage (1775–1864)

George the First was always reckoned
Vile, but viler George the Second;
And what mortal ever heard
Any good of George the Third?
When from earth the Fourth descended
God be praised, the Georges ended!

[*The Atlas*, 1855]

LAWSON, Henry (1867–1922)

The Queen has lived for seventy years, for seventy years and three;
And few have lived a flatter life, more useless life than she;
She never said a clever thing or wrote a clever line,
She never did a noble deed, in coming times to shine;
And yet we read, and still we read, in every magazine,
The praises of that woman whom the English call 'the Queen',
Whom the English call 'the Queen',
Whom the English call 'the Queen' –
That dull and brainless woman whom the English call 'the Queen'.

['The English Queen: A Birthday Ode']

LEOPOLD II (1835–1909)

[Instructing Prince Albert, the heir apparent, to pick up some papers from the floor]
A constitutional king must learn to stoop.

[In Kelen, *The Mistress*]

LOUIS XIV (1638–1715)

J'ai failli attendre.

I almost had to wait.

[Attr.]

MACHIAVELLI (1469–1527)

Debbe, pertanto, uno principe non si curare della infamia di crudele, per tenere li suddili suoi uniti e in fede.

In order to keep his people united and faithful, a prince must not be concerned with being reputed as a cruel man.

[*The Prince* (1532)]

MARVELL, Andrew (1621–1678)

[Of Charles II]
For though the whole world cannot shew such another,
Yet we'd better by far have him than his brother.

['The Statue in Stocks-Market' (1689)]

MELBOURNE, Lord (1779–1848)

[Advising Queen Victoria against granting Prince Albert the title of King Consort]
For God's sake, ma'am, let's have no more of that. If you get the English people into the way of making kings, you'll get them into the way of unmaking them.

[In Lord David Cecil, *Lord M.* (1954)]

PEGLER, Westbrook (1894–1969)

[On the abdication of Edward VIII]
He will go from resort to resort getting more tanned and more tired.

[In Alistair Cooke, *Six Men*]

PLATO (c.429–347 BC)

Debbe, pertanto, uno principe non si curare della infamia di crudele, per tenere li suddili suoi uniti e in fede.
Every king springs from a race of slaves, and every slave has had kings among his ancestors.

[*Theaetetus*]

PRIOR, Matthew (1664–1721)

What is a King? – a man condemn'd to bear
The public burden of the nation's care.

[*Solomon* (1718)]

ROCHESTER, Earl of (1647–1680)

A merry monarch, scandalous and poor.

['A Satire on King Charles II' (1697)]

Here lies our sovereign lord the King
Whose word no man relies on,
Who never said a foolish thing,
Nor ever did a wise one.
[Epitaph written for Charles II (1706)]

ROOSEVELT, Theodore (1858–1919)
Kings and such like are just as funny as
politicians.
[In John Dos Passos, *Mr Wilson's War* (1963)]

**SCHILLER, Johann Christoph Friedrich
(1759–1805)**
Die Könige sind nur Sklaven ihres Standes,
Dem eignen Herzen dürfen sie nicht folgen.
Kings are but slaves of their rank,
They may not follow their own heart.
[*Maria Stuart* (1800)]

SELDEN, John (1584–1654)
A king is a thing men have made for their
own sakes, for quietness' sake. Just as in a
family one man is appointed to buy the
meat.
[*Table Talk* (1689)]

SELLAR, Walter (1898–1951) and
YEATMAN, Robert Julian (1897–1968)
Charles II was always very merry and was
therefore not so much a king as a Monarch.
[*1066 And All That* (1930)]

SHAKESPEARE, William (1564–1616)
Uneasy lies the head that wears a crown.
[*Henry IV, Part 2*, III.i]

I think the King is but a man as I am: the
violet smells to him as it doth to me.
[*Henry V*, IV.i]

For God's sake let us sit upon the
  ground
And tell sad stories of the death of kings:
How some have been depos'd, some
  slain in war,
Some haunted by the ghosts they have
  depos'd,
Some poison'd by their wives, some
  sleeping kill'd,
All murder'd – for within the hollow
  crown

That rounds the mortal temples of a
  king
Keeps Death his court.
[*Richard II*, III.ii]

**THOMPSON, William Hale 'Big Bill'
(1867–1944)**
[If ever King George V were to set foot in Chicago]
I'd punch him in the snoot.
[Attr.]

TWAIN, Mark (1835–1910)
All kings is mostly rapscallions.
[*The Adventures of Huckleberry Finn* (1884)]

The institution of monarchy in any form is an
insult to the human race.
[*Notebook*, 1888]

VICTORIA, Queen (1819–1901)
We are not amused.
[Attr. in Holland, *Notebooks of a Spinster Lady*
(1919)]

WILSON, Harold (1916–1995)
The monarchy is a labour-intensive industry.
[*The Observer*, 1977]

WORSTHORNE, Sir Peregrine (1923–)
A little more willingness to bore, and much
less eagerness to entertain, would do the
monarchy no end of good in 1993.
[*The Sunday Telegraph*, 1993]

Dull men do make the best kings.
[Comment on BBC programme, *George VI – The
Reluctant King*, 1999]

ZAMOYSKI, Jan (1541–1605)
The king reigns, but does not govern.
[Speech, Polish Parliament, 1605]

See GOVERNMENT

MONEY AND WEALTH

ADAMS, Franklin P. (1881–1960)
The rich man has his motor car,
His country and his town estate.
He smokes a fifty-cent cigar
And jeers at Fate …

Yet though my lamp burns low and dim,
Though I must slave for livelihood –
Think you that I would change with him?
You bet I would!

['The Rich Man']

AGASSIZ, Louis (1807–1873)

[On lecturing for fees]
I can't afford to waste my time making money.

[Attr.]

ALLAINVAL, Abbé d' (c.1700–1753)

L'Embarras des Richesses.
The embarrassment of riches.

[Title of play, 1725]

ANONYMOUS

Money no longer talks. It just goes without saying.

[In Lieberman, *3,500 Good Quotes for Speakers* (1983)]

ASQUITH, Margot (1864–1945)

Rich men's houses are seldom beautiful, rarely comfortable, and never original. It is a constant source of surprise to people of moderate means to observe how little a big fortune contributes to Beauty.

[*The Autobiography of Margot Asquith* (1920)]

ASTOR, John Jacob (1763–1848)

A man who has a million dollars is as well off as if he were rich.

[Attr.]

BACON, Francis (1561–1626)

Riches are a good handmaid, but the worst mistress.

[*The Dignity and Advancement of Learning* (1623)]

And money is like muck, not good except it be spread.

['Of Seditions and Troubles' (1625)]

BALDWIN, James (1924–1987)

Money, it turned out, was exactly like sex, you thought of nothing else if you didn't have it and thought of other things if you did.

[*Nobody Knows My Name* (1961)]

BARING, Maurice (1874–1945)

If you would know what the Lord God thinks of money, you have only to look at those to whom He gives it.

[Attr.]

BEHN, Aphra (1640–1689)

Money speaks sense in a language all nations understand.

[*The Rover* (1677)]

BELLOC, Hilaire (1870–1953)

Lord Finchley tried to mend the Electric Light
Himself. It struck him dead: And serve him right!
It is the business of the wealthy man
To give employment to the artisan.

[*More Peers* (1911)]

I'm tired of Love: I'm still more tired of Rhyme.
But Money gives me pleasure all the time.

[*Sonnets and Verse* (1923)]

BENCHLEY, Robert (1889–1945)

[Comment on being told his request for a loan had been granted]
I don't trust a bank that would lend money to such a poor risk.

[Attr.]

BETJEMAN, Sir John (1906–1984)

I've to prostitute myself to live comfortably and I see no point in money except to buy off anxiety. I don't want to be rich. I want to be unanxious.

[Interview with Graham Lord, *Sunday Express*, 1974]

THE BIBLE
(King James Version)

The love of money is the root of all evil.

[*I Timothy*, 6:10]

THE BIBLE
(The New Testament in Scots)

Nae man can sair two maisters: aither he will ill-will the tane an luve the tither, or he will grip til the tane an lichtlifie the tither. Ye canna sair God an Gowd baith.

[*Matthew*, 6:24]

BRENAN, Gerald (1894–1987)
Those who have some means think that the most important thing in the world is love. The poor know that it is money.

[*Thoughts in a Dry Season* (1978)]

BURKE, Edmund (1729–1797)
If we command our wealth, we shall be rich and free: if our wealth commands us, we are poor indeed.

[*Two Letters on the Proposals for Peace with the Regicide Directory of France*]

BUTLER, Samuel (1835–1902)
It has been said that the love of money is the root of all evil. The want of money is so quite as truly.

[*Erewhon* (1872)]

CARNEGIE, Andrew (1835–1919)
Surplus wealth is a sacred trust which its possessor is bound to administer in his lifetime for the good of the com-munity.

[*The Gospel of Wealth*]

DENNIS, Nigel (1912–1989)
But then one is always excited by descriptions of money changing hands. It's much more fundamental than sex.

[*Cards of Identity* (1955)]

FRANCE, Anatole (1844–1924)
Dans tout État policé, la richesse est chose sacrée; dans les démocraties elle est la seule chose sacrée.
In every well-governed state, wealth is a sacred thing; in democracies it is the only sacred thing.

[*Penguin Island* (1908)]

GALBRAITH, J.K. (1908–)
Wealth has never been a sufficient source of honor in itself. It must be advertised, and the normal medium is obtrusively expensive goods.

[*The Affluent Society* (1958)]

Wealth is not without its advantages, and the case to the contrary, although it has often been made, has never proved widely persuasive.

[*The Affluent Society* (1958)]

Money differs from an automobile, a mistress or cancer in being equally important to those who have it and those who do not.

[Attr.]

GETTY, J. Paul (1892–1976)
The meek shall inherit the earth, but not the mineral rights.

[Attr.]

If you can actually count your money you are not really a rich man.

[In A. Barrow, *Gossip*]

GOLDSMITH, Oliver (c.1728–1774)
Ill fares the land, to hastening ills a prey,
Where wealth accumulates, and men decay;.

[*The Deserted Village* (1770)]

GREGORY, Lady Isabella Augusta (1852–1932)
It's a good thing to be able to take up your money in your hand and to think no more of it when it slips away from you than you would of a trout that would slip back into the stream.

[*Twenty-Five*]

HEALEY, Denis (1917–)
I warn you there are going to be howls of anguish from the 80,000 people who are rich enough to pay over 75% on the last slice of their income.

[Speech, Labour Party Conference, 1 October 1973]

HOOGSTRATEN, Nicholas van
[Banning ramblers who claimed their was a public right of way across his land]
The only purpose in creating wealth like mine is to separate oneself from the riff-raff.

[*The Observer*, 1998]

HORACE (65–8 BC)
Rem facias, rem si possis recte, si non, quocumque modo rem.
Make money: make it honestly if possible; if not, make it by any means.

[*Epistles*]

HUGHES, Howard (1905–1976)
[Response when called a 'paranoid, deranged

millionaire' by a newspaper]
Goddammit, I'm a billionaire.

[Attr.]

HUXLEY, Sir Julian Sorell (1887–1975)
We all know how the size of sums of money appears to vary in a remarkable way according as they are being paid in or paid out.

[*Essays of a Biologist*]

ILLICH, Ivan (1926–)
Man must choose whether to be rich in things or in the freedom to use them.

[*Deschooling Society* (1971)]

IRVING, Washington (1783–1859)
The almighty dollar, that great object of universal devotion throughout our land.

[*Wolfert's Roost* (1855)]

JOHNSON, Samuel (1709–1784)
Sir, the insolence of wealth will creep out.

[In Boswell, *The Life of Samuel Johnson* (1791)]

You never find people labouring to convince you that you may live very happily upon a plentiful fortune.

[In Boswell, *The Life of Samuel Johnson* (1791)]

There are few ways in which a man can be more innocently employed than in getting money.

[In Boswell, *The Life of Samuel Johnson* (1791)]

KENNEDY, Joseph P. (1888–1969)
If you want to make money, go where the money is.

[In A.M. Schlesinger Jr, *Robert Kennedy and his Times* (1978)]

LAWRENCE, D.H. (1885–1930)
Money is our madness, our vast collective madness.

['Money-Madness' (1929)]

LENNON, John (1940–1980)
For I don't care too much for money,
For money can't buy me love.

['Can't Buy Me Love', song, 1964, with Paul McCartney]

LIVINGSTONE, Ken (1945–)
The working classes are never embarrassed about money – only the absence of it.

[Comment, 1987]

LOWER, Lennie (1903–1947)
The best way to tell gold is to pass the nugget around a crowded bar, and ask them if it's gold. If it comes back, it's not gold.

[*Here's Another* (1932)]

LUTHER, Martin (1483–1546)
Darum gibt unser Herr Gott gemeiniglich Reichtum den groben Eseln, denen er sonst nichts gönnt.
For that reason our Lord God commonly gives wealth to those coarse asses to whom he grants nothing else.

[*Table Talk* (1531–1546)]

MACAULAY, Lord (1800–1859)
We have heard it said that five per cent is the natural interest of money.

[*Collected Essays* (1843)]

MACNEICE, Louis (1907–1963)
Better authentic mammon than a bogus god.

[*Autumn Journal* (1939)]

It is particularly vulgar to talk about one's money – whether one has lots of it, and boasts about it, or is broke, and says so. Now I myself cannot see why a man should not talk about his money. Everybody is interested in everybody else's finances, and it seems hypocrisy to hush the subject up in the drawing room – as if bank balances were found under gooseberry bushes.

['In Defence of Vulgarity' (1937)]

MILLIGAN, Spike (1918–)
Money can't buy friends, but you can get a better class of enemy.

[*Puckoon* (1963)]

MILNE, A.A. (1882–1956)
For one person who dreams of making fifty thousand pounds, a hundred people dream of being left fifty thousand pounds.

[*If I May*]

MORAVIA, Alberto (1907–1990)

Ma è morto come potrebbe domani morire tanta gente come lui: correndo dietro al denaro e illudendosi che non ci sia che il denaro; e poi, improvvisamente, restando agghiacciato dalla paura alla vista di ciò che sta dietro il denaro.

But he died as many people like him could die tomorrow, running after money, and believing that there is nothing but money; then he was suddenly frozen by the fear of seeing what lies behind money.

[Two Women (1957)]

NICHOLSON, Jack (1937–)

I am in an age group where it is rude to discuss money, and now it is all anyone cares about.

[The Observer, 1999]

PARSONS, Tony (1953–)

There are few things in this world more reassuring than an unhappy Lottery winner.

[The Observer, 1998]

PEPYS, Samuel (1633–1703)

I bless God I do find that I am worth more than ever I yet was, which is £6,200, for which the Holy Name of God be praised!

[Diary, October 1666]

But it is pretty to see what money will do.

[Diary, March 1667]

PINDAR (518–438 BC)

Water is best, but gold like fire blazing in the night shines more brightly than all other lordly wealth.

[Olympian Odes]

PORTER, Cole (1891–1964)

Who Wants to Be a Millionaire? I don't.

[Title song, 1956, from Who Wants to be a Millionaire?]

PROVERBS

A fool and his money are soon parted.

Take care of the pence, and the pounds will take care of themselves.

REINHARDT, Gottfried (1911–)

Money is good for bribing yourself through

the inconveniences of life.

[In L. Ross, Picture]

RUNYON, Damon (1884–1946)

Always try to rub up against money, for if you rub up against money long enough, some of it may rub off on you.

[Furthermore (1938)]

RUSKIN, John (1819–1900)

There is no wealth but life.

[Unto this Last (1862)]

Whereas it has long been known and declared that the poor have no right to the property of the rich, I wish it also to be known and declared that the rich have no right to the property of the poor.

[Unto this Last (1862)]

SCHOPENHAUER, Arthur (1788–1860)

Wealth is like sea-water; the more we drink, the thirstier we become; and the same is true of fame.

[Parerga and Paralipomena (1851)]

SCOTT, William (1745–1836)

The elegant simplicity of the three per cents.

[In Campbell, *Lives of the Lord Chancellors*]

SHAKESPEARE, William (1564–1616)

Well, whiles I am a beggar, I will rail
And say there is no sin but to be rich;
And being rich, my virtue then shall be
To say there is no vice but beggary.

[King John, II.i]

SHAW, George Bernard (1856–1950)

Money is indeed the most important thing in the world; and all sound and successful personal and national morality should have this fact for its basis.

[The Irrational Knot (1905)]

The universal regard for money is the one hopeful fact in our civilization, the one sound spot in our social conscience. Money is the most important thing in the world. It represents health, strength, honour, generosity and beauty as conspicuously and undeniably as the want of it represents illness, weakness, disgrace, meanness and ugliness.

[*Major Barbara* (1907)]

SHERIDAN, Tom (1775–1817)
[To his father, after learning that he was to be cut out of his will with a shilling]
I'm sorry to hear that, sir, you don't happen to have the shilling about you now, do you?

[In L. Harris, *The Fine Art of Political Wit* (1965)]

SICKERT, Walter (1860–1942)
Nothing knits man to man … like the frequent passage from hand to hand of cash.

['The Language of Art']

SMITH, Adam (1723–1790)
With the greater part of rich people, the chief enjoyment of riches consists in the parade of riches, which in their eyes is never so complete as when they appear to possess those decisive marks of opulence which nobody can possess but themselves.

[*Wealth of Nations* (1776)']

SMITH, Logan Pearsall (1865–1946)
I love money; just to be in the room with a millionaire makes me less forlorn.

[*Afterthoughts* (1931)]

To suppose, as we all suppose, that we could be rich and not behave as the rich behave, is like supposing that we could drink all day and keep absolutely sober.

[*Afterthoughts* (1931)]

SWIFT, Jonathan (1667–1745)
If heaven had looked upon riches to be a valuable thing, it would not have given them to such a scoundrel.

[Letter to Miss Vanhomrigh, 1720]

THATCHER, Margaret (1925–)
Pennies do not come from heaven. They have to be earned here on earth.

[*The Sunday Telegraph*, 1982]

TUCKER, Sophie (1884–1966)
From birth to eighteen, a girl needs good parents. From eighteen to thirty-five, she needs good looks. From thirty-five to fifty-five, she needs a good personality. From fifty-five on, she needs good cash.

[In Freedland, *Sophie* (1978)]

I've been poor and I've been rich. Rich is better.

[In Cowan, *The Wit of Women*]

TWAIN, Mark (1835–1910)
[Agreeing with a friend's comment that the money of a particular rich industrialist was 'tainted']
That's right. 'Taint yours, and 'taint mine.

[Attr.]

A banker is a person who lends you his umbrella when the sun is shining and wants it back the minute it rains.

[Attr.]

VANDERBILT, William H. (1821–1885)
I have had no real gratification or enjoyment of any sort more than my neighbor on the next block who is worth only half a million.

[In B. Conrad, *Famous Last Words* (1961)]

VESPASIAN (AD 9–79)
Pecunia non olet.
Money does not smell.

[In Suetonius, *Lives of the Caesars*]

WELLS, H.G. (1866–1946)
I don't 'old with Wealth. What is Wealth? Labour robbed out of the poor.

[*Kipps: the Story of a Simple Soul* (1905)]

WILLIAMS, Tennessee (1911–1983)
You can be young without money but you can't be old without it.

[*Cat on a Hot Tin Roof* (1955)]

See CAPITALISM; EXCESS; GREED; CONSUMER SOCIETY; INCOME

MORALITY

AYER, A.J. (1910–1989)
No morality can be founded on authority, even if the authority were divine.

[*Essay on Humanism*]

MORALITY

GREENE, Graham (1904–1991)

Morality comes with sad wisdom of age.
When the sense of curiosity has withered.

[Attr. in *The Observer*, 1996]

HARDY, Thomas (1840–1928)

I like a story with a bad moral … all true
stories have a coarse touch or a bad moral,
depend upon't. If the story-tellers could ha'
got decency and good morals from true
stories, who'd have troubled to invent
parables?

[*Under the Greenwood Tree* (1872)]

HAWTHORNE, Nathaniel (1804–1864)

Dr Johnson's morality was as English an
article as a beefsteak.

[*Our Old Home* (1863)]

HUXLEY, Aldous (1894–1963)

The quality of moral behaviour varies in
inverse ratio to the number of human beings
involved.

[*Grey Eminence* (1941)]

JOHNSON, Samuel (1709–1784)

We are perpetually moralists, but we are
geometricians only by chance. Our
intercourse with intellectual nature is
necessary; our speculations upon matter are
voluntary, and at leisure.

['Milton']

KANT, Immanuel (1724–1804)

*Endlich gibt es einen Imperativ, der, ohne irgend eine
andere durch ein gewisses Verhalten zu erreichende
Absicht als Bedingung zum Grunde zu legen, dieses
Verhalten unmittelbar gebietet. Dieser Imperativ ist
kategorisch … Dieser Imperativ mag der der
Sittlichkeit heissen.*

Finally, there is an imperative which
immediately dictates a certain mode of
behaviour, without having as its condition
any other purpose to be achieved by means
of that behaviour. This imperative is
categorical … This imperative may be called
that of morality.

[*Outline of the Metaphysics of Morals* (1785)]

Handle so, dass du die Menschheit, sowohl in deiner

*Person, als in der Person eines jeden andern, jederzeit
zugleich als Zweck, niemals bloss als Mittel
brauchest.*

Act in such a way that you treat humanity,
both in your own person as well as in that of
any other, at any time as an end withal, never
merely as a means.

[*Outline of the Metaphysics of Morals* (1785)]

KRAUS, Karl (1874–1936)

*Moral ist die Tendenz, das Bad mit dem Kinde
auszuschütten.*

Morality is the tendency to throw out the
bath along with the baby.

[*Pro domo et mundo* (1912)]

LAWRENCE, D.H. (1885–1930)

Morality which is based on ideas, or on an
ideal, is an unmitigated evil.

[*Fantasia of the Unconscious* (1922)]

MACAULAY, Lord (1800–1859)

We know of no spectacle so ridiculous as the
British public in one of its periodical fits of
morality.

['Moore's Life of Byron' (1843)]

NIETZSCHE, Friedrich Wilhelm (1844–1900)

Es gibt Herren-Moral und Sklaven-Moral.

There is master-morality and slave-morality.

[*Beyond Good and Evil* (1886)]

Moralität ist Herden-Instinkt im Einzelnen.

Morality is the herd-instinct in the individual.

[*The Gay Science* (1887)]

PANKHURST, Emmeline (1858–1928)

Men made the moral code and they expect
women to accept it.

[Speech, 1913]

PROUST, Marcel (1871–1922)

On devient moral dès qu'on est malheureux.

One becomes moral as soon as one is
unhappy.

[*A l'ombre des jeunes filles en fleurs* (1918)]

RUSSELL, Bertrand (1872–1970)

We have, in fact, two kinds of morality side by
side: one which we preach but do not

practise, and another which we practise but seldom preach.

[*Sceptical Essays* (1928)]

SAMUEL, Lord (1870–1963)

Without doubt the greatest injury of all was done by basing morals on myth. For, sooner or later, myth is recognized for what it is, and disappears. Then morality loses the foundation on which it has been built.

[*Romanes Lecture*, 1947]

SHAW, George Bernard (1856–1950)

I'm one of the undeserving poor: that's what I am. Think of what that means to a man. It means that he's up agen middle class morality all the time … What is middle class morality? Just an excuse for never giving me anything.

[*Pygmalion* (1916)]

An Englishman thinks he is moral when he is only uncomfortable.

[*Man and Superman* (1903)]

SPENCER, Herbert (1820–1903)

Absolute morality is the regulation of conduct in such a way that pain shall not be inflicted.

['Prison Ethics' (1891)]

STEVENSON, Robert Louis (1850–1894)

If your morals make you dreary, depend upon it, they are wrong.

[*Across the Plains* (1892)]

WILDE, Oscar (1854–1900)

The moral life of man forms part of the subject matter of the artist, but the morality of art consists in the perfect use of an imperfect medium.

[*The Picture of Dorian Gray* (1891)]

Morality is simply the attitude we adopt towards people whom we personally dislike.

[*An Ideal Husband* (1895)]

WITTGENSTEIN, Ludwig (1889–1951)

Ethics does not treat of the world. Ethics

must be a condition of the world, like logic.

[In Auden, *A Certain World*]

See GOOD AND EVIL; GOODNESS; PRINCIPLES; VIRTUE

MORTALITY

ANONYMOUS

Gaudeamus igitur,
Juvenes dum sumus
Post jucundam juventutem,
Post molestam senectutem,
Nos habebit humus.
Let us be happy while we are young, for after carefree youth and careworn age, the earth will hold us also.

['Gaudeamus Igitur', 13th century]

AURELIUS, Marcus (121–180)

And you will give yourself peace if you perform each act as if it were your last.

[*Meditations*]

Everything is ephemeral, both that which remembers and that which is remembered.

[*Meditations*]

BEHN, Aphra (1640–1689)

Faith, Sir, we are here today and gone tomorrow.

[*The Lucky Chance* (1687)]

THE BIBLE
(King James Version)

All flesh is grass, and all the goodliness thereof is as the flower of the field.

[*Isaiah*, 40:6]

DOWSON, Ernest (1867–1900)

They are not long, the weeping and
    the laughter,
Love and desire and hate:
I think they have no portion in us after
We pass the gate.
They are not long, the days of wine
    and roses;
Out of a misty dream

Our path emerges for a while, then
    closes
Within a dream.

> ['Vitae Summa Brevis Spem Nos Vetat Incohare
> Longam' (1896)]

HERRICK, Robert (1591–1674)

Gather ye Rose-buds while ye may,
Old Time is still aflying:
And this same flower that smiles today,
Tomorrow will be dying.

> [*Hesperides* (1648)]

Faire Daffadills, we weep to see
You haste away so soone:
As yet the early-rising Sun
Has not attain'd his Noone.
Stay, stay,
Untill the hasting day
Has run
But to the Even-song;
And, having pray'd together, we
Will goe with you along.

We have short time to stay, as you,
We have as short a Spring;
As quick a growth to meet Decay,
As you, or any thing.

> [*Hesperides* (1648)]

HOMER (fl. c.8th century BC)

Like Leaves on Trees the Race of Man is
found,
Now green in Youth, now with'ring on the
Ground,
Another Race the following Spring supplies,
They fall successive, and successive rise.

> [*Iliad*]

HORACE (65–8 BC)

Omnem crede diem tibi diluxisse supremum.
Believe every day that has dawned is your
last.

> [*Epistles*]

LEACOCK, Stephen (1869–1944)

I detest life-insurance agents; they always
argue that I shall someday die, which is not
so.

> [*Literary Lapses* (1910)]

MARTIAL (c.AD 40–c.104)

Bonosque
Soles effugere atque abire sentit,
Qui nobis pereunt et imputantur.
Each of us feels the good days hasten and
depart, our days that perish and are counted
against us.

> [*Epigrammata*]

MARVELL, Andrew (1621–1678)

But at my back I always hear
Time's wingèd chariot hurrying near.
And yonder all before us lie
Deserts of vast eternity.
Thy beauty shall no more be found;
Nor, in thy marble vault, shall sound
My echoing song: then worms shall try
That long preserved virginity:
And your quaint honour turn to dust;
And into ashes all my lust.
The grave's a fine and private place,
But none I think do there embrace.

> ['To His Coy Mistress' (1681)]

MILLAY, Edna St Vincent (1892–1950)

Death devours all lovely things:
Lesbia with her sparrow
Shares the darkness, – presently
Every bed is narrow …

After all, my erstwhile dear,
My no longer cherished,
Need we say it was not love,
Just because it perished?

> ['Passer Mortuus Est' (1921)]

MONTAIGNE, Michel de (1533–1592)

Il faut être toujours botté et prêt á partir.
One should always have one's boots on and
be ready to leave.

> [*Essais* (1580)]

MOORE, Thomas (1779–1852)

Oh! ever thus, from childhood's hour,
I've seen my fondest hopes decay;
I never lov'd a tree or flow'r,
But 'twas the first to fade away.
I never nurs'd a dear gazelle,
To glad me with its soft black eye,

But when it came to know me well,
And love me, it was sure to die!

[*Lalla Rookh* (1817)]

SPENSER, Edmund (c.1522–1599)

So passeth, in the passing of a day,
Of mortall life the leafe, the bud, the flowre,
Ne more doth flourish after first decay,
That earst was sought to decke both bed
and bowre,
Of many a Ladie, and many a Paramowre:
Gather therefore the Rose, whilest yet is
prime,
For soone comes age, that will her pride
deflowre:
Gather the Rose of love, whilest yet is time,
Whilest loving thou mayst loved be with
equall crime.

[*The Faerie Queene* (1596)]

STEVENSON, Robert Louis (1850–1894)

Old and young, we are all on our last cruise.

[*Virginibus Puerisque* (1881)]

THOMAS, Dylan (1914–1953)

The force that through the green fuse drives
the flower
Drives my green age; that blasts the roots of
trees
Is my destroyer.
And I am dumb to tell the crooked rose
My youth is bent by the same wintry fever.

['The force that through the green fuse drives the
flower' (1934)]

YOUNG, Edward (1683–1765)

All men think all men Mortal, but themselves.

[*Night-Thoughts on Life, Death and Immortality*
(1742–1746)]

See DEATH; IMMORTALITY; LIFE; TIME

MOTHERS

ACHEBE, Chinua (1930–)

It's true that a child belongs to its father. But
when a father beats his child, it seeks
sympathy in its mother's hut. A man belongs
to his fatherland when times are good and
life is sweet. But when there is sorrow and
bitterness he finds refuge in his motherland.
Your mother is there to protect you. She is
buried there. And that is why we say that
mother is supreme.

[*Things Fall Apart* (1958)]

ALCOTT, Louisa May (1832–1888)

What do girls do who haven't any mothers to
help them through their troubles?

[*Little Women* (1868)]

ANONYMOUS

You can fool all of the people some of the
time, and some of the people all of the time,
but you Can't Fool Mom.

[Captain Penny's Law]

BALLANTYNE, Sheila (1936–)

I acknowledge the cold truth of her death for
perhaps the first time. She is truly gone,
forever out of reach, and I have become my
own judge.

[*Imaginary Crimes* (1982)]

BARKER, George (1913–1991)

Seismic with laughter,
Gin and chicken helpless in her Irish hand,
Irresistible as Rabelais, but most tender for
The lame dogs and hurt birds that surround
her.

['Sonnet: To My Mother' (1944)]

BARZAN, Gerald

Mother always said that honesty was the
best policy, and money isn't everything. She
was wrong about other things too.

[Attr.]

BEHAN, Brendan (1923–1964)

Never throw stones at your mother,
You'll be sorry for it when she's dead,
Never throw stones at your mother,
Throw bricks at your father instead.

[*The Hostage* (1958)]

BOMBECK, Erma (1927–1996)

My mother phones daily to ask, 'Did you just
try to reach me?' When I reply, 'No', she adds,
'So, if you're not too busy, call me while I'm

still alive,' and hangs up.

[*The 1992 Erma Bombeck Calendar*]

CAMPBELL, David (1915–1979)

The cruel girls we loved
Are over forty,
Their subtle daughters
Have stolen their beauty;
And with a blue stare
Of cool surprise
They mock their anxious mothers
With their mothers' eyes.

['Mothers and Daughters' (c. 1965)]

DAWE, (Donald) Bruce (1930–)

Mum, you would have loved the way
    you went!
one moment, at a barbecue in the
    garden
– the next, falling out of your chair,
hamburger in one hand,
and a grandson yelling.

['Going' (1970)]

EDGEWORTH, Maria (1767–1849)

My mother took too much, a great deal too
much, care of me; she over-educated, over-
instructed, over-dosed me with premature
lessons of prudence: she was so afraid that I
should ever do a foolish thing, or not say a
wise one, that she prompted my every word,
and guided my eyes, hearing with her ears,
and judging with her understanding, till, at
length, it was found out that I had no eyes, or
understanding of my own.

[*Vivian* (1812)]

ELLIS, Alice Thomas (1932–)

Claudia … remembered that when she'd had
her first baby she had realised with
astonishment that the perfect couple
consisted of a mother and child and not, as
she had always supposed, a man and woman.

[*The Other Side of the Fire*]

FISHER, Dorothy Canfield (1879–1958)

A mother is not a person to lean on but a
person to make leaning unnecessary.

[*Her Son's Wife* (1926)]

FREUD, Sigmund (1856–1939)

A mother is only brought unlimited
satisfaction by her relation to a son; this is
altogether the most perfect, the most free
from ambivalence of all human relationships.

[*Freud on Women* (1990)]

FRIDAY, Nancy (1937–)

Blaming mother is just a negative way of
clinging to her still.

[*My Mother/My Self* (1977)]

GAY, John (1685–1732)

Where yet was ever found a mother,
Who'd give her booby for another?

[*Fables* (1727)]

GREER, Germaine (1939–)

Mother is the dead heart of the family,
spending father's earnings on consumer
goods to enhance the environment in which
he eats, sleeps and watches the television.

[*The Female Eunuch* (1970)]

HUBBARD, Kin (1868–1930)

The old-time mother who used to wonder
where her boy was now has a grandson who
wonders where his mother is.

[Attr.]

PROVERB

God could not be everywhere, so therefore
he made mothers.

[Jewish proverb]

KEY, Ellen (1849–1926)

The mother is the most precious possession
of the nation, so precious that society
advances its highest wellbeing when it
protects the functions of the mother.

[*The Century of the Child*
(1909)]

LAWRENCE, D.H. (1885–1930)

[On his relationship with his mother]
We have loved each other, almost with a
husband and wife love, as well as filial and
maternal … It has been rather terrible and
has made me, in some respects, abnormal.

[Attr.]

LAZARRE, Jane (1943–)

At her best, she is … quietly receptive and intelligent in only a moderate, concrete way; she is of even temperament, almost always in control of her emotions. She loves her children completely and unambivalently. Most of us are not like her.

[*The Mother Knot* (1976)]

LINDBERGH, Anne Morrow (1906–)

By and large, mothers and housewives are the only workers who do not have regular time off. They are the great vacationless class.

[*Gift From the Sea* (1955)]

MASEFIELD, John (1878–1967)

In the dark womb where I began
My mother's life made me a man.
Through all the months of human birth
Her beauty fed my common earth.
I cannot see, nor breathe, nor stir,
But through the death of some of her.

['C.L.M.' (1910)]

MAUGHAM, William Somerset (1874–1965)

Few misfortunes can befall a boy which bring worse consequences than to have a really affectionate mother.

[*A Writer's Notebook* (1949)]

OLSEN, Tillie (1913–)

More than in any other human relationship, overwhelmingly more, motherhood means being instantly interruptible, responsive, responsible.

[*Silences: When Writers Don't Write* (1965)]

RAYNER, Claire (1931–)

[Motherhood] is a dead-end job. You've no sooner learned the skills than you are redundant.

[*Weekend Guardian*, 1960]

RILEY, Janet Mary

The role of mother is probably the most important career a woman can have.

[*The Times-Picayune*, 1986]

SCOTT-MAXWELL, Florida (1884–1979)

No matter how old a mother is, she watches her middle-aged children for signs of improvement.

[*The Measure of My Days* (1968)]

SHAKESPEARE, William (1564–1616)

Thou art thy mother's glass, and she in thee
Calls back the lovely April of her prime.

[Sonnet 3]

STANTON, Elizabeth Cady (1815–1902)

… mothers of the race, the most important actors in the grand drama of human progress.

[*History of Woman Suffrage* (1881)]

STEAD, Christina (1902–1983)

A mother! What are we really? They all grow up whether you look after them or not.

[*The Man Who Loved Children*]

STEFANO, Joseph (1922–)

A boy's best friend is his mother.

[*Psycho*, screenplay, 1960]

TAYLOR, Jane (1783–1824)

Who ran to help me when I fell,
And would some pretty story tell,
Or kiss the place to make it well?
My Mother.

[*Original Poems for Infant Minds* (1804)]

WALLACE, William Ross (c.1819–1881)

The hand that rocks the cradle
Is the hand that rules the world.

['What Rules the World' (c. 1865)]

WHISTLER, James McNeill (1834–1903)

[Explaining to a snobbish lady why he had been born in such an unfashionable place as Lowell, Massachusetts]
The explanation is quite simple. I wished to be near my mother.

[Attr.]

WILDE, Oscar (1854–1900)

All women become like their mothers. That is

their tragedy. No man does. That's his.

[*The Importance of Being Earnest* (1895)]

WOOD, Mrs Henry (1814–1887)

Dead! and … never called me mother.

[*East Lynne* (stage adaptation, 1874)]

See BABIES; BIRTH; CHILDREN; FAMILY; FATHERS; PREGNANCY

MOURNING

PROUST, Marcel (1871–1922)

On l'enterra, mais toute la nuit funèbre, aux vitrines éclairées, ses livres disposés trois par trois veillaient comme des anges aux ailes éployées et semblaient, pour celui qui n'était plus, le symbole de sa résurrection.

They buried him, but all through the night of mourning, in lighted windows, his books arranged three by three kept watch like angels with outspread wings and seemed, for him who was no more, the symbol of his resurrection.

[*A la recherche du temps perdu, La Prisonnière* (1923)]

ROSSETTI, Christina (1830–1894)

When I am dead, my dearest,
Sing no sad songs for me;
Plant thou no roses at my head,
Nor shady cypress tree:
Be the green grass above me
With showers and dewdrops wet;
And if thou wilt, remember,
And if thou wilt, forget.

['Song: When I am Dead' (1862)]

SITWELL, Dame Edith (1887–1964)

A lady asked me why, on most occasions, I wore black. 'Are you in mourning?'
'Yes.'
'For whom are you in mourning?'
'For the world.'

[*Taken Care Of* (1965)]

See DEATH; REGRET

MURDER

JAMES, Henry (1843–1916)

To kill a human being is, after all, the least injury you can do him.

[*Complete Tales* (1867)]

MARX, Groucho (1895–1977)

My husband is dead.
– I'll bet he's just using that as an excuse.
I was with him to the end.
– No wonder he passed away.
I held him in my arms and kissed him.
– So it was murder!

[*Duck Soup*, film, 1933]

MORTIMER, John (1923–)

Murderers are really very agreeable clients. I do think murderers get a very bad press.

[*The Observer*, 1999]

PORTEUS, Beilby (1731–1808)

One murder made a villain,
Millions a hero.

['Death' (1759)]

SAKI (1870–1916)

'The man is a common murderer.'
'A common murderer, possibly, but a very uncommon cook.'

[*Beasts and Super-Beasts* (1914)]

SEXBY, Edward (d. 1658)

Killing noe Murder. Briefly Discourst in three quaestions.

[Title of pamphlet, 1657]

WAINEWRIGHT, Thomas Griffiths (1794–1847)

[On being asked by a caller at Newgate prison how he could have the barbarity to poison such a 'fair, innocent and trusting creature' as his sister-in-law Helen Abercromby]
Upon my soul, I don't know, unless it was because she had such thick legs.

[In W.C. Hazlitt, *Wainewright's Essays* (1880)]

WEBSTER, John (c.1580–c.1625)

Other sins only speak; murder shrieks out.

[*The Duchess of Malfi* (1623)]

WHITEING, Richard (1840–1928)

'Did you hear that fearful cry?'

'Ah! I 'eerd somethink.'

'There's murder going on – a woman, I think.'

'Dessay. It's Sat'dy night.'

[*No 5 John Street* (1899)]

See CRIME

MUSIC

ADDISON, Joseph (1672–1719)

Music, the greatest good that mortals know,
And all of heaven we have below.

['Song for St Cecilia's Day' (1694)]

ADE, George (1866–1944)

The music teacher came twice a week to bridge the awful gap between Dorothy and Chopin.

[Attr.]

ANDERSEN, Hans Christian (1805–1875)

[Of the music to be played at his funeral]

Most of the people who walk after me will be children; make the beat keep time with little steps.

[In R. Godden, *Hans Christian Andersen* (1955)]

APPLETON, Sir Edward Victor (1892–1965)

I do not mind what language an opera is sung in so long as it is a language I don't understand.

[*The Observer*, 1955]

ARMSTRONG, Louis (1900–1971)

[When asked how he felt about people copying his style]

A lotta cats copy the Mona Lisa, but people still line up to see the original.

[Attr.]

BEECHAM, Sir Thomas (1879–1961)

[On Elgar's A Flat Symphony]

The musical equivalent of the towers of St Pancras station – neo-Gothic, you know.

[In N. Cardus, *Sir Thomas Beecham* (1961)]

The English may not like music – but they absolutely love the noise it makes.

[In L. Ayre, *The Wit of Music* (1966)]

[On Beethoven's 7th Symphony]

What can you do with it? – it's like a lot of yaks jumping about.

[In H. Atkins and A. Newman, *Beecham Stories: Anecdotes, Sayings and Impressions of Sir Thomas Beecham* (1978)]

[On Herbert von Karajan]

[He's a kind] of musical Malcolm Sargent.

[In H. Atkins and A. Newman, *Beecham Stories: Anecdotes, Sayings and Impressions of Sir Thomas Beecham* (1978)]

A musicologist is a man who can read music but can't hear it.

[Attr.]

[Of Bruckner's 7th Symphony]

In the first movement alone, I took note of six pregnancies and at least four miscarriages.

[Attr.]

At a dinner given in honour of his seventieth birthday, when messages of congratulation from great musicians all over the world were being read out, he was heard to murmur, 'What, nothing from Mozart?'.

[In Patricia Young, *Great Performers*]

There are two golden rules for an orchestra: start together and finish together. The public doesn't give a damn what goes on in between.

[In Atkins and Newman, *Beecham Stories* (1978)]

[Of Bach]

Too much counterpoint; what is worse, Protestant counterpoint.

[*The Guardian*, 1971]

The sound of the harpsichord resembles that of a bird-cage played with toasting-forks.

[Attr.]

BEETHOVEN, Ludwig Van (1770–1827)

[Said to a violinist complaining that a passage was unplayable]

When I composed that, I was conscious of

being inspired by God Almighty. Do you think I can consider your puny little fiddle when He speaks to me?

[Attr.]

BELLOC, Hilaire (1870–1953)

It is the best of all trades, to make songs, and the second best to sing them.

[*On Everything* (1909)]

BIRTWISTLE, Harrison (1934–)

I get someone to write the programme notes. Then I know what the piece is about.

[*The Observer*, 1996]

BROWNE, Sir Thomas (1605–1682)

For there is a music wherever there is a harmony, order or proportion; and thus far we may maintain the music of the spheres; for those well ordered motions, and regular paces, though they give no sound unto the ear, yet to the understanding they strike a note most full of harmony.

[*Religio Medici* (1643)]

BURNEY, Fanny (1752–1840)

All the delusive seduction of martial music.

[*Diary*, 1802]

BUTLER, Samuel (1835–1902)

How thankful we ought to feel that Wordsworth was only a poet and not a musician. Fancy a symphony by Wordsworth! Fancy having to sit it out! And fancy what it would have been if he had written fugues!

[*The Note-Books of Samuel Butler* (1912)]

CONGREVE, William (1670–1729)

Music has charms to soothe a savage breast.

[*The Mourning Bride* (1697)]

COWARD, Sir Noël (1899–1973)

Extraordinary how potent cheap music is.

[*Private Lives* (1930)]

DRYDEN, John (1631–1700)

What passion cannot Music raise and quell?

['A Song for St. Cecilia's Day' (1687)]

FORSTER, E.M. (1879–1970)

Beethoven's Fifth Symphony is the most sublime noise that ever penetrated into the ear of man.

[*Howard's End* (1910)]

GASKELL, Elizabeth (1810–1865)

We were none of us musical, though Miss Jenkyns beat time, out of time, by way of appearing to be so.

[*Cranford* (1853)]

GELDOF, Bob (1954–)

I'm into pop because I want to get rich, get famous and get laid.

[Attr.]

GERSHWIN, George (1898–1937)

[On his opera Porgy and Bess]

I think the music is so marvelous – I really can't believe I wrote it.

[Quoted by E. Jablonski in sleeve notes to the RCA Victor recording]

HERBERT, George (1593–1633)

Music helps not the tooth-ache.

[*Jacula Prudentum; or Outlandish Proverbs, Sentences &c.* (1640)]

HOLST, Gustav (1874–1934)

Never compose anything unless the not composing of it becomes a positive nuisance to you.

[Letter to W.G. Whittaker]

HUXLEY, Aldous (1894–1963)

Since Mozart's day composers have learned the art of making music throatily and palpitatingly sexual.

[*Along the Road* (1925)]

JENNINGS, Paul (1918–1989)

Of all musicians, flautists are most obviously the ones who know something we don't know.

[The Jenguin Pennings, 'Flautists Flaunt Afflatus']

JOHNSON, Samuel (1709–1784)

Of music Dr Johnson used to say that it was the only sensual pleasure without vice.

[In *European Magazine*, 1795]

JONSON, Ben (1572–1637)

Slow, slow, fresh fount, keep time with my salt tears:

Yet, slower, yet; O faintly, gentle springs:
List to the heavy part the music bears,
Woe weeps out her division, when she sings.

[*Cynthia's Revels* (1600)]

LANDOWSKA, Wanda (1877–1959)

[Remark to a fellow musician]

Oh, well, you play Bach your way. I'll play him his.

[Attr.]

LEHRER, Tom (1928–)

It is sobering to consider that when Mozart was my age he had already been dead for a year.

[In N. Shapiro, *An Encyclopedia of Quotations about Music*]

LENIN, V.I. (1870–1924)

[Remark made to Gorky, while listening to Beethoven]

I can't listen to music too often. It affects your nerves; you want to say nice, stupid things and stroke the heads of people who could create such beauty while living in this vile hell. And now you must not stroke anyone's head – you might get your hand bitten off. You have to hit them on the head, without any mercy.

[In Lev Trotsky, trans. M. Eastman, *The History of the Russian Revolution* (1933)]

MENCKEN, H.L. (1880–1956)

Opera in English is, in the main, just about as sensible as baseball in Italian.

[Attr.]

NEWMAN, Ernest (1868–1959)

I sometimes wonder which would be nicer – an opera without an interval, or an interval without an opera.

[In Heyworth (ed.), *Berlioz, Romantic and Classic*]

PARKER, Charlie (1920–1955)

Music is your own experience, your thoughts, your wisdom. If you don't live it, it won't come out of your horn.

[In Shapiro and Hentoff, *Hear Me Talkin' to Ya* (1955)]

PARKER, Henry Taylor (1867–1934)

[Rebuking some talkative members of an

audience, near whom he was sitting]

Those people on the stage are making such a noise I can't hear a word you're saying.

[In L. Humphrey, *The Humor of Music*]

PAVAROTTI, Luciano (1935–)

You don't need any brains to listen to music.

PEPYS, Samuel (1633–1703)

Went to hear Mrs Turner's daughter … play on the harpsichon; but, Lord! it was enough to make any man sick to hear her; yet was I forced to commend her highly.

[*Diary*, May 1663]

Music and women I cannot but give way to, whatever my business is.

[*Diary*, 1666]

POUND, Ezra (1885–1972)

Music begins to atrophy when it departs too far from the dance; … poetry begins to atrophy when it gets too far from music.

[*ABC of Reading* (1934)]

PREVIN, André (1929–)

The basic difference between classical music and jazz is that in the former the music is always greater than its performance – whereas the way jazz is performed is always more important than what is being played.

[In Shapiro, *An Encyclopedia of Quotations about Music*]

PROVERB

Music is the food of love.

RANDOLPH, David (1914–)

[On Parsifal]

The kind of opera that starts at six o'clock and after it has been going three hours, you look at your watch and it says 6.20.

[In *The Frank Muir Book* (1976)]

RIMSKY-KORSAKOV, Nikolai (1844–1908)

[Of Debussy's music]

I have already heard it. I had better not go: I will start to get accustomed to it and finally like it.

[In Robert Craft and Igor Stavinsky, *Conversations with Stravinsky* (1959)]

ROSSINI, Gioacchino (1792–1868)

Monsieur Wagner a de beaux moments, mais de mauvais quart d'heures.

Wagner has beautiful moments but awful quarters of an hour.

[In E. Naumann, *Italienische Tondichter* (1883)]

Give me a laundry-list and I will set it to music.

[Attr.]

SANTAYANA, George (1863–1952)

Music is essentially useless, as life is: but both have an ideal extension which lends utility to its conditions.

[*The Life of Reason* (1905–1906)]

SARASATE (Y NAVASCUÉS), Pablo (1844–1908)

[On being hailed as a genius by a critic]
A genius! For thirty-seven years I've practised fourteen hours a day, and now they call me a genius!

[Attr.]

SARGENT, Sir Malcolm (1895–1967)

[Rehearsing a female chorus in 'For Unto Us a Child is Born' from Handel's *Messiah*]
Just a little more reverence, please, and not so much astonishment.

[Attr.]

SATIE, Erik (1866–1925)

[Direction on one of his piano pieces]
To be played with both hands in the pocket.

[Attr.]

SCHNABEL, Artur (1882–1951)

I know two kinds of audience only – one coughing and one not coughing.

[*My Life and Music* (1961)]

The sonatas of Mozart are unique; they are too easy for children, and too difficult for artists.

[In Nat Shapiro (ed.), *An Encyclopaedia of Quotations about Music* (1978)]

[Advice given to the pianist Vladimir Horowitz]
When a piece gets difficult make faces.

[Attr.]

The notes I handle no better than many pianists. But the pauses between the notes – ah, that is where the art resides.

[*Chicago Daily News*, 1958]

SCHOENBERG, Arnold (1819–1849)

[When told that his violin concerto would need a soloist with six fingers]
Very well, I can wait.

[Attr.]

SCHUBERT, Franz (1797–1828)

My compositions spring from my sorrows. Those that give the world the greatest delight were born of my deepest griefs.

[*Diary*, 1824]

SHAKESPEARE, William (1564–1616)

In sweet music is such art,
Killing care and grief of heart
Fall asleep or hearing die.

[*Henry VIII*, III.i]

Music oft hath such a charm
To make bad good and good provoke to harm.

[*Measure For Measure*, IV.i]

The man that hath no music in himself,
Nor is not mov'd with concord of sweet sounds,
Is fit for treasons, stratagems, and spoils;
The motions of his spirit are dull as night,
And his affections dark as Erebus.
Let no such man be trusted.

[*The Merchant of Venice*, V.i]

How sour sweet music is
When time is broke and no proportion kept!
So is it in the music of men's lives.

[*Richard II*, V.v]

SHAW, George Bernard (1856–1950)

At every one of those concerts in England you will find rows of weary people who are there, not because they really like classical music, but because they think they ought to like it.

[*Man and Superman* (1903)]

STEVENS, Wallace (1879–1955)

Just as my fingers on these keys
Make music, so the self-same sounds
On my spirit make a music, too.

Music is feeling, then, not sound.
And thus it is what I feel,
Here in this room, desiring you.

Thinking of your blue-shadowed silk,
Is music.

['Peter Quince at the Clavier' (1923)]

STRAVINSKY, Igor (1882–1971)

Rachmaninov's immortalizing totality was his scowl. He was a six-and-a-half-foot-tall scowl.

[In Igor Stravinsky and Robert Craft, *Conversations with Igor Stravinsky* (1958)]

[On Rachmaninov]

He was the only pianist I have ever seen who did not grimace. That is a great deal.

[In Igor Stravinsky and Robert Craft, *Conversations with Igor Stravinsky* (1958)]

My music is best understood by children and animals.

[*The Observer*, 1961]

TENNYSON, Alfred, Lord (1809–1892)

Music that gentlier on the spirit lies,
Than tir'd eyelids upon tir'd eyes.

['The Lotos-Eaters' (1832)]

THOMAS, Irene (1920–)

The cello is not one of my favourite instruments. It has such a lugubrious sound, like someone reading a will.

[Attr.]

TOSCANINI, Arturo (1867–1957)

[Rebuking an incompetent woman cellist]
Madame, there you sit with that magnificent instrument between your legs, and all you can do is scratch it!

[Attr.]

TWAIN, Mark (1835–1910)

I have been told that Wagner's music is better than it sounds.

[*Autobiography* (1959 edition)]

WHARTON, Edith (1862–1937)

An unalterable and unquestioned law of the musical world required that the German text of French operas sung by Swedish artists should be translated into Italian for the clearer understanding of English speaking audiences.

[*The Age of Innocence* (1920)]

WILLIAMSON, Malcolm (1931–)

Lloyd Webber's music is everywhere, but so is Aids.

[Attr.]

ZAPPA, Frank (1940–1993)

Most people wouldn't know music if it came up and bit them on the ass.

[Attr.]

A composer? What the fuck do they do? All the good music's already been written by people with wigs and stuff.

[Attr.]

See CRITICISM; SONGS AND SINGERS

NAMES

BENÉT, Stephen Vincent (1898–1943)

I have fallen in love with American names,
The sharp gaunt names that never get fat,
The snakeskin-titles of mining-claims,
The plumed war-bonnet of Medicine Hat,
Tucson and Deadwood and Lost Mule Flat.

['American Names' (1927)]

HAZLITT, William (1778–1830)

A nickname is the heaviest stone that the devil can throw at a man.

[*Edinburgh Magazine*, 1818']

HEWITT, John (1923–)

The names of a land show the heart of the race;
They move on the tongue like the lilt of a song.
You say the name and I see the place –
Drumbo, Dungannon, or Annalong.
Barony, townland, we cannot go wrong.

['Ulster Names']

HUXLEY, Aldous (1894–1963)

It's like the question of the authorship of the Iliad … The author of that poem is either Homer or, if not Homer, somebody else of the same name.

[*Those Barren Leaves* (1925)]

JOYCE, James (1882–1941)

I am afraid I am more interested, Mr Connolly, in the Dublin street names than in the riddle of the universe.

[Remark to Cyril Connolly]

LAURENCE, Margaret (1926–1987)

Women have no surnames of their own. Their names are literally sirnames. Women only have one name that is ours, our first or given name.

[*Dance on the Earth: A Memoir* (1989)]

MARX, Groucho (1895–1977)

No, Groucho is not my real name. I'm breaking it in for a friend.

[Attr.]

REID, Sir George Houstoun Reid (1845–1918)

[On being asked at a meeting, apropos of his stomach, 'What are you going to call it, George?']
If it's a boy, I'll call it after myself. If it's a girl I'll call it Victoria after our Queen. But if, as I strongly suspect, it's nothing but piss and wind, I'll call it after you.

[In Humphrey McQueen, *Social Sketches o Australia*]

SITWELL, Dame Edith (1887–1964)

Would you please substitute Dame Edith for Dr Sitwell. The Queen has honoured my poetry by making me a Dame, so that is now my name.

[Letter to G. Singleton, 1955]

SPOONER, William (1844–1930)

I remember your name perfectly, but I just can't think of your face.

[Attr.]

STEIN, Gertrude (1874–1946)

Rose is a rose is a rose is a rose, is a rose.

[*Sacred Emily* (1913)]

VANZETTI, Bartolomeo (1888–1927)

[Statement disallowed at his trial]
Sacco's name will live in the hearts of the people and in their gratitude when Katzmann's and yours bones will be dispersed by time, when your name, his name, your laws, institutions, and your false god are but a deem rememoring of a cursed past in which man was wolf to the man.

[In Frankfurter and Jackson, *Letters of Sacco and Vanzetti* (1928)]

NATIONS

BOLINGBROKE, Henry (1678–1751)
Nations, like men, have their infancy.

[*Letters on Study and Use of History* (1752)]

INGE, William Ralph (1860–1954)
A nation is a society united by a delusion about its ancestry and by a common hatred of its neighbours.

[In Sagittarius and George, *The Perpetual Pessimist*]

KUBRICK, Stanley (1928–1999)
The great nations have always acted like gangsters, and the small nations like prostitutes.

[*The Guardian*, 1963]

MCMILLAN, Joyce (1952–)
… recognition of the suffering inflicted on peoples by their own leaders is undermining the idea of absolute national sovereignty, just as recognition of the unacceptability of domestic violence undermined the idea of absolute patriarchal rights in the family.

[*Scotland on Sunday*, 1992]

PARNELL, Charles Stewart (1846–1891)
No man has a right to fix the boundary of the march of a nation: no man has a right to say to his country – thus far shalt thou go and no further.

[Speech, 1885]

WILSON, Woodrow (1856–1924)
No nation is fit to sit in judgement upon any other nation.

[Speech, 1915]

NATURE

ADDISON, Joseph (1672–1719)
Should the whole frame of nature round him break,
In ruin and confusion hurled,
He, unconcerned, would hear the mighty crack,
And stand secure amidst a falling world.

[Translation of Horace, *Odes*]

AKENSIDE, Mark (1721–1770)
O ye Northumbrian Shades, which overlook
The rocky pavement and the mossy falls
Of solitary Wensbeck's limpid streams;
How gladly I recall your well-known seats
Beloved of old, and that delightful time
When all alone, for many a summer's day,
I wandered through your calm recesses, led
In silence by some powerful hand unseen.

[*The Pleasures of Imagination* (1744)]

BAUDELAIRE, Charles (1821–1867)
La nature est un temple où de vivants piliers
Laissent parfois sortir de confuses paroles;
L'homme y passe á travers des forêts de symboles
Qui l'observent avec des regards familiers.
Nature is a temple in which living columns sometimes utter confused words. Man walks through it among forests of symbols, which watch him with knowing eyes.

[*Les Fleurs du mal* (1857)]

**THE BIBLE
(King James Version)**
While the earth remaineth, seedtime and harvest, and cold and heat, and summer and winter, and day and night shall not cease.

[*Genesis*, 8:22]

BRIDGES, Robert (1844–1930)
Man masters nature not by force but by understanding.

[Attr.]

BROWNE, Sir Thomas (1605–1682)
All things are artificial, for nature is the art of God.

[*Religio Medici* (1643)]

BYRON, Lord (1788–1824)
There is a pleasure in the pathless woods,
There is a rapture on the lonely shore,
There is society, where none intrudes,
By the deep Sea, and music in its roar:
I love not Man the less, but Nature more,
From these our interviews, in which I steal
From all I may be, or have been before,

To mingle with the Universe, and feel
What I can ne'er express, yet cannot all
conceal.

[*Childe Harold's Pilgrimage* (1818)]

CHESTERTON, G.K. (1874–1936)
Is ditchwater dull? Naturalists with
microscopes have told me that it teems with
quiet fun.

[*The Listener*, 1936]

CHURCHILL, Charles (1731–1764)
It can't be Nature, for it is not sense.

['The Farewell' (1764)]

CLARKE, Marcus (1846–1881)
In Australia alone is to be found the
Grotesque, the Weird, the strange scribblings
of nature learning how to write.

[Preface to A.L. Gordon, *Sea Spray and Smoke Drift* (1867)]

COWPER, William (1731–1800)
Nature is but a name for an effect,
Whose cause is God.

[*The Task* (1785)]

CURIE, Marie (1867–1934)
All my life through, the new sights of Nature
made me rejoice like a child.

[*Pierre Curie*]

DARWIN, Charles (1809–1882)
What a book a devil's chaplain might write
on the clumsy, wasteful, blundering, low, and
horribly cruel works of nature!

[Letter to J.D. Hooker, 1856]

DONNE, John (1572–1631)
There is nothing that God hath established in
a constant course of nature, and which
therefore is done every day, but would seem
a Miracle, and exercise our admiration, if it
were done but once.

[*LXXX Sermons* (1640)]

EMERSON, Ralph Waldo (1803–1882)
Nature is full of freaks, and now puts an old
head on young shoulders, and then a young
heart beating under fourscore winters.

[*Society and Solitude* (1870)]

FIELDING, Henry (1707–1754)
All Nature wears one universal grin.

[*Tom Thumb the Great* (1731)]

GRACIÁN, Baltasar (1601–1658)
No es menester arte donde basta la Naturaleza.
Art is not essential where Nature is sufficient.

[*The Hero* (1637)]

GREY OWL (1888–1938)
Civilisation says, 'Nature belongs to man.' The
Indian says, 'No, man belongs to nature.'

[Address at Norwich]

HAWKING, Stephen (1942–)
There are grounds for cautious optimism
that we may now be near the end of the
search for the ultimate laws of nature.

[*A Brief History of Time: From the Big Bang to Black Holes*, 1988]

HORACE (65–8 BC)
Naturam expelles furca, tamen usque recurret.
You may drive out Nature with a pitchfork,
but she always comes hurrying back.

[*Epistles*]

HUGO, Victor (1802–1885)
*La nature est impitoyable; elle ne consent pas á
retirer ses fleurs, ses musiques, ses parfums et ses
rayons devant l'abomination humaine.*
Nature is unforgiving; she will not agree to
withdraw her flowers, her music, her scents
or her rays of light before the abominations
of man.

[*Ninety-three* (1874)]

INGERSOLL, Robert Greene (1833–1899)
In nature there are neither rewards nor
punishments – there are consequences.

[*Some Reasons Why* (1881)]

LINNAEUS, Carl (1707–1778)
Natura non facit saltus.
Nature does not make progress by leaps and
bounds.

[*Philosophia Botanica*]

LOCKE, John (1632–1704)
Nature never makes excellent things for

mean or no uses.

[*Essay concerning Human Understanding* (1690)]

MILTON, John (1608–1674)

In those vernal seasons of the yeer, when the air is calm and pleasant, it were an injury and sullennesse against nature not to go out, and see her riches, and partake in her rejoycing with heaven and earth.

[*Of Education: To Master Samuel Hartlib* (1644)]

NEWTON, Sir Isaac (1642–1727)

Nature is very consonant and conformable to her self.

[*Opticks* (1730)]

Whence is it that nature doth nothing in vain; and whence arises all that Order and Beauty which we see in the World?

[*Opticks* (1730)]

RABELAIS, François (c.1494–c.1553)

Natura abhorret vacuum.
Nature abhors a vacuum.

[*Gargantua* (1534)]

SCHILLER, Johann Christoph Friedrich (1759–1805)

When Nature conquers, Art must then give way.

[Remark to Goethe]

Es gibt Augenblicke in unserm Leben, wo wir der Natur in Pflanzen, Mineralen, Tieren, Landschaften sowie der menschliche Natur in Kindern, in den Sitten des Landvolks und der Urwelt, nicht weil sie unsern Sinnen wohltut, auch nicht weil sie unsern Verstand oder Geschmack befriedigt ... sondern bloss weil sie Natur ist, eine Art von Liebe und von rührender Achtung widmen.

There are moments in our life when we accord a kind of love and touching respect to nature in plants, minerals, the countryside, as well as human nature in children, in the customs of country folk and the primitive world, not because it is beneficial for our senses, and not because it satisfies our understanding or taste either ... but simply because it is nature.

['On Naive and Sentimental Poetry', 1795–1796)]

SHAKESPEARE, William (1564–1616)

In nature's infinite book of secrecy
A little I can read.

[*Antony and Cleopatra*, I.ii]

SMITH, Alexander (1830–1867)

Nature, who makes the perfect rose and bird,
Has never made the full and perfect man.

[*City Poems* (1857)]

SNYDER, Gary (1930–)

My political position is to be a spokesman for wild nature. I take that as a primary constituency.

[*The Real Work, Interviews and Talks 1964–1979* (1980)]

TENNYSON, Alfred, Lord (1809–1892)

So careful of the type she seems,
So careless of the single life ...

[*In Memoriam A. H. H.* (1850)]

Who trusted God was love indeed
And love Creation's final law –
Tho' Nature, red in tooth and claw
With ravine, shrieked against his creed.

[*In Memoriam A. H. H.* (1850)]

THOMAS, R.S. (1913–)

We will listen instead to the wind's text
Blown through the roof, or the thrush's song
In the thick bush that proved him wrong,
Wrong from the start, for nature's truth
Is primary and her changing seasons
Correct out of a vaster reason
The vague errors of the flesh.

[*Song at the Year's Turning* (1955)]

THOREAU, Henry David (1817–1862)

I frequently tramped eight or ten miles through the deepest snow to keep an appointment with a beech-tree, or a yellow birch, or an old acquaintance among the pines.

[*Walden* (1854)]

UVAVNUK

The arch of sky and mightiness of storms
Have moved the spirit within me,
Till I am carried away

Trembling with joy.

[In Rasmussen, *Intellectual Culture of the Igulik Eskimos* (1929)]

VACHELL, Horace Annesley (1861–1955)

In nature there are no rewards or punishments; there are consequences.

[*The Face of Clay* (1906), 10]

VOLTAIRE (1694–1778)

Sachez que le secret des arts
Est de corriger la nature.

Know that the secret of the arts is to correct nature.

[*Épîtres*]

WHISTLER, James McNeill (1834–1903)

Nature is usually wrong.

[*Mr Whistler's 'Ten O'Clock'* (1885)]

WHITMAN, Walt (1819–1892)

After you have exhausted what there is in business, politics, conviviality, and so on – have found that none of these finally satisfy, or permanently wear – what remains? Nature remains.

[*Specimen Days and Collect* (1882)]

WORDSWORTH, William (1770–1850)

I have learned
To look on nature, not as in the hour
Of thoughtless youth; but hearing often-
times
The still, sad music of humanity.

['Lines composed a few miles above Tintern Abbey' (1798)]

Nature never did betray
The heart that loved her.

['Lines composed a few miles above Tintern Abbey' (1798)]

One impulse from a vernal wood
May teach you more of man,
Of moral evil and of good,
Than all the sages can ...

Sweet is the lore which Nature brings;
Our meddling intellect

Misshapes the beauteous forms of things:
We murder to dissect.

['The Tables Turned' (1798)]

See ANIMALS; BIRDS; HUMANITY AND HUMAN NATURE; FLOWERS; SCIENCE

THE NAVY

BERLIN, Irving (1888–1989)

We joined the Navy to see the world,
And what did we see? We saw the sea.

['We Saw the Sea', song, 1936; in film *Follow the Fleet*]

BLACKSTONE, Sir William (1723–1780)

The royal navy of England hath ever been its greatest defence and ornament; it is its ancient and natural strength; the floating bulwark of the island.

[*Commentaries on the Laws of England* (1765–1769)]

CAMPBELL, Thomas (1777–1844)

Britannia needs no bulwarks,
No towers along the steep;
Her march is o'er the mountain waves,
Her home is on the deep.
With thunders from her native oak
She quells the floods below.

['Ye Mariners of England' (1801)]

CHARLES II (1630–1685)

It is upon the Navy under the good Providence of God that the safety, honour, and welfare of this Realm do chiefly depend.

[Preamble to Articles of War, 1652, in Callender, *The Naval Side of British History* (1924)]

CHURCHILL, Sir Winston (1874–1965)

Don't talk to me about naval tradition. It's nothing but rum, sodomy and the lash.

[In Gretton, *Former Naval Person* (1968)]

COVENTRY, Thomas (1578–1640)

The dominion of the sea, as it is an ancient and undoubted right of the crown of England, so it is the best security of the land.

The wooden walls are the best walls of this kingdom.

[Speech in Star Chamber, 1635]

DRAKE, Sir Francis (c.1540–1596)

I must have the gentleman to haul and draw with the mariner, and the mariner with the gentleman … I would know him, that would refuse to set his hand to a rope, but I know there is not any such here.

[In Corbett, *Drake and the Tudor Navy* (1898)]

FISHER, John Arbuthnot (1841–1920)

[On the ruinous cost of the Fleet and those responsible for it]
You must be ruthless, relentless, and remorseless! Sack the lot!

[Letter, *The Times*, 1919]

The British navy always travels first class.

[In W. Churchill, *The Second World War* (1948–1954)]

GARRICK, David (1717–1779)

Come cheer up, my lads! 'tis to glory we steer,
To add something more to this wonderful year;
To honour we call you, not press you like slaves,
For who are so free as the sons of the waves?
Heart of oak are our ships,
Heart of oak are our men:
We always are ready;
Steady, boys, steady;
We'll fight and we'll conquer again and again.

['Heart of Oak' (1759)]

GLOVER, Denis (1912–1980)

[On overcrowding in Royal Navy ships]
With five or six faces in front of a mirror it sometimes becomes a problem just which one to shave.

[In Lehmann, *I Am My Brother* (1960)]

HALSEY, Admiral W.F. ('Bull') (1882–1959)

Our ships have been salvaged and are retiring at high speed toward the Japanese fleet.

[Radio message, 1944, following claims by the Japanese that most of the American Third Fleet had been sunk or were retiring]

MACAULAY, Lord (1800–1859)

There were gentlemen and there were seamen in the navy of Charles the Second. But the seamen were not gentlemen; and the gentlemen were not seamen.

[*History of England* (1849)]

MOUNTBATTEN OF BURMA, First Earl (1900–1979)

In my experience, I have always found that you cannot have an efficient ship unless you have a happy ship, and you cannot have a happy ship unless you have an efficient ship. That is the way I intend to start this commission, and that is the way I intend to go on – with a happy and an efficient ship.

[Address to crew of HMS Kelly, 1939]

VOLTAIRE (1694–1778)

[Referring to the execution of the English Admiral Byng for refusing to attack a French fleet]
Dans ce pays-ci il est bon de tuer de temps en temps un amiral pour encourager les autres.
In this country it is considered a good idea to kill an admiral from time to time, to encourage the others.

[*Candide* (1759)]

See SEA; WAR

NECESSITY

PROVERB

Necessity is the mother of invention.

PUBLILIUS, Syrus (1st century BC)

Necessitas dat legem non ipsa accipit.
Necessity gives the law without itself recognizing any.

[*Sententiae*]

Necessitas non habet legem.
Necessity has no law.

[Attr. proverb]

THOMSON, James (1834–1882)

I find no hint throughout the universe
Of good or ill, of blessing or of curse;
I find alone Necessity Supreme.

[*The City of Dreadful Night* (1880)]

VOLTAIRE (1694–1778)

Le superflu, chose très nécessaire.

The superfluous, a very necessary thing.

[*Le Mondain* (1736)]

NEIGHBOURS

AUSTEN, Jane (1775–1817)

For what do we live, but to make sport for
our neighbours, and laugh at them in our
turn?

[*Pride and Prejudice* (1813)]

THE BIBLE
(King James Version)

Thou shalt love thy neighbour as thyself.

[*Leviticus*, 19:18]

BRADLEY, F.H. (1846–1924)

The propriety of some persons seems to
consist in having improper thoughts about
their neighbours.

[*Aphorisms* (1930)]

CARLYLE, Jane Welsh (1801–1866)

Some new neighbours, that came a month or
two ago, brought with them an
accumulation of all the things to be guarded
against in a London neighbourhood, viz, a
pianoforte, a lap-dog, and a parrot.

[Letter to Mrs Carlyle, 1839]

CHESTERTON, G.K. (1874–1936)

We make our friends, we make our enemies;
but God makes our next-door neighbour.

[*Heretics* (1905)]

CLEESE, John (1939–)

Loving your neighbour as much as yourself is
practically bloody impossible… You might as
well have a Commandment that states, 'Thou
shalt fly'.

[*The Times*, 1993]

HOLMES, Oliver Wendell (1809–1894)

But when our neighbours do wrong, we
sometimes feel the fitness of making them
smart for it, whether they have repented or not.

[*The Common Law* (1881)]

HORACE (65–8 BC)

Nam tua res agitur, paries cum proximus ardet.

For your own safety is at stake, when your
neighbour's wall catches fire.

[*Epistles*]

PROVERBS

Good fences make good neighbours.

Love your neighbour, but don't pull down
the fence.

NEW ZEALAND

ADAMS, Phillip (1939–)

[On attitudes to New Zealanders]
And while we don't exactly hate New
Zealanders, we're not exactly fond of each
other. While they regard us as vulgar
yobboes, almost Yank-like, we think of them
as second-hand, recycled Poms.

[*Age*, 1977]

ALLEN, Dave (1936–)

New Zealanders are the most balanced
people in the world – they have a chip on
each shoulder.

[A regular joke during his New Zealand tour, 1978]

DAVISON, Sir Ronald Keith (1920–)

[Giving judgement in the trial of Alain Mafart and
Dominique Prieur, two French agents charged with
manslaughter and wilful damage over the
Rainbow Warrior bombing]
People who come to this country and
commit terrorist activities cannot expect to
have a short holiday at the expense of our
government and return home as heroes.

[In Michael King, *Death of the Rainbow Warrior*
(1986)]

FREUD, Clement (1924–)

[On being asked his opinion of New Zealand]
I find it hard to say, because when I was there

it seemed to be shut.

[BBC radio, 1978]

NEWS AND NEWSPAPERS

ANONYMOUS

The Times is a tribal noticeboard.

[Remark by a candidate for the editorship of the paper's Woman's Page in the 1960s]

ARNOLD, Harry

[Commenting on the news that the Queen had started to refer privately to Royal reporters as 'scum']

At least we're la crème de la scum.

[*The Observer*, 1995]

ARNOLD, Matthew (1822–1888)

The magnificent roaring of the young lions of the Daily Telegraph.

[*Essays in Criticism* (1865)]

AUSTEN, Jane (1775–1817)

Lady Middleton … exerted herself to ask Mr Palmer if there was any news in the paper. 'No, none at all,' he replied, and read on.

[*Sense and Sensibility* (1811)]

BALDWIN, Stanley (1867–1947)

What the proprietorship of these papers is aiming at is power, and power without responsibility – the prerogative of the harlot through the ages.

[Speech at an election rally, 1931]

BALFOUR, A.J. (1848–1930)

Frank Harris … said …:'The fact is, Mr Balfour, all the faults of the age come from Christianity and journalism.' To which Arthur replied … 'Christianity, of course … but why journalism?'.

[In Margot Asquith, *Autobiography* (1920)]

BENNETT, Arnold (1867–1931)

Journalists say a thing that they know isn't true, in the hope that if they keep on saying it long enough it will be true.

[*The Title* (1918)]

BENNETT, James Gordon (1841–1918)

Deleted by French censor.

[Used to fill empty spaces in his papers during World War I when news was scarce]

BENTLEY, Nicolas (1907–1978)

No news is good news; no journalists is even better.

[Attr.]

BEVAN, Aneurin (1897–1960)

I read the newspapers avidly. It is my one form of continuous fiction.

[*The Observer*, 1960]

BONE, James (1872–1962)

[Referring to C.P. Scott, former editor of The Manchester Guardian]

He made righteousness readable.

[Attr.]

BRADBURY, Malcolm (1932–)

Reading someone else's newspaper is like sleeping with someone else's wife. Nothing seems to be precisely in the right place, and when you find what you are looking for, it is not clear then how to respond to it.

[*Stepping Westward* (1965)]

CANTONA, Eric (1966–)

[Commenting on the interest taken by the press in the outcome of his court case]

When the seagulls follow the trawler, it is because they think sardines will be thrown into the sea.

[*The Observer*, 1995]

CARLYLE, Thomas (1795–1881)

Burke said there were Three Estates in Parliament; but, in the Reporters' Gallery yonder, there sat a Fourth Estate more important far than they all.

['The Hero as Man of Letters' (1841)]

CHESTERTON, G.K. (1874–1936)

It's not the world that's got so much worse but the news coverage that's got so much better.

[Attr.]

COWPER, William (1731–1800)
Thou god of our idolatry, the press …
Thou fountain, at which drink the good and wise;
Thou ever-bubbling spring of endless lies;
Like Eden's dread probationary tree,
Knowledge of good and evil is from thee.
['The Progress of Error' (1782)]

CRABBE, George (1754–1832)
A master-passion is the love of news.
[*The Newspaper* (1785)]

CURZON, Lord (1859–1925)
I hesitate to say what the functions of the modern journalist may be; but I imagine that they do not exclude the intelligent anticipation of facts even before they occur.
[Speech, 1898]

DANA, Charles Anderson (1819–1897)
When a dog bites a man that is not news, but when a man bites a dog that is news.
[*New York Sun*, 1882]

DEVONSHIRE, Duke of (1895–1950)
[Referring to Stanley Baldwin's attack on newspaper proprietors]
Good God, that's done it. He's lost us the tarts' vote.
[Attr.]

DRAYTON, Michael (1563–1631)
Ill news hath wings, and with the wind doth go,
Comfort's a cripple and comes ever slow.
[*The Barrons' Wars* (1603)]

ELDERSHAW, M. Barnard (1897–1987)
Journalists are people who take in one another's washing and then sell it.
[*Plaque with Laurel* (1937)]

FAIRBURN, A.R.D. (1904–1957)
The press: slow dripping of water on mud;
thought's daily bagwash, ironing out opinion,
scarifying the edges of ideas.
[*Collected Poems* (1966)]

FIELDING, Henry (1707–1754)
A newspaper, which consists of just the same number of words, whether there be news in it or not … may, likewise, be compared to a stagecoach, which performs constantly the same course, empty as well as full.
[*Tom Jones* (1749)]

FLAUBERT, Gustave (1821–1880)
Je regarde comme un des bonheurs de ma vie de ne pas écrire dans les journaux. Il en coûte ma bourse – mais ma conscience s'en trouve bien.
I regard the fact that I don't write for the newspapers as a source of happiness in my life. My purse suffers – but my conscience is glad of it.
[Letter, 1866]

GARCÍA MÁRQUEZ, Gabriel (1928–)
El periodismo es un género literario, muy parecido a la novela, y tiene la gran ventaja de que el reportero puede inventar cosas. Y eso el novelista lo tiene totalmente prohibido.
Journalism is a literary genre very similar to that of the novel, and has the great advantage that the reporter can invent things. And that is completely forbidden to the novelist.
[Speech, 1994]

Destructive journalism fosters the belief that politicians routinely evade the truth and break their promises. It creates a climate in which trust in society as a whole dissolves; in which difficulties are magnified beyond all proportion; in which no one is believed to act except for the most self-centred of motives.
[*The Spectator*, May 1996]

HEARST, William Randolph (1863–1951)
[Instruction to artist Frederic Remington, who wished to return from peaceful Havana in spring 1898]
Please remain. You furnish the pictures and I'll furnish the war.
[Attr. in Winkler, *W.R. Hearst* (1928)]

HEPWORTH, John (1921–)
Most journalists of my generation died early,

succumbing to one or other of the two great killers in the craft – cirrhosis or terminal alimony.

[*National Review*, 1974]

IGNATIEFF, Michael (1947–)
News is a genre as much as fiction or drama: it is a regime of visual authority, a coercive organization of images according to a stopwatch.

[*Daedalus*, 1988]

KIPLING, Rudyard (1865–1936)
[Of newspaper barons]
Power without responsibility – the prerogative of the harlot throughout the ages.

[Remark, quoted by Baldwin in 1931]

KRAUS, Karl (1874–1936)
Keinen Gedanken haben und ihn ausdrücken können – das macht den Journalisten.
To have no thoughts and be able to express them – that's what makes a journalist.

[*Pro domo et mundo* (1912)]

LAMB, Charles (1775–1834)
Newspapers always excite curiosity. No one ever lays one down without a feeling of disappointment.

[*Last Essays of Elia* (1833)]

LONGFORD, Lord (1905–)
On the whole I would not say that our Press is obscene. I would say that it trembles on the brink of obscenity.

[*The Observer*, 1963]

MACAULAY, Lord (1800–1859)
The gallery in which the reporters sit has become a fourth estate of the realm.

[*Collected Essays* (1843)]

MACCARTHY, Sir Desmond (1878–1952)
[Journalists are] more attentive to the minute hand of history than to the hour hand.

[In Tynan, *Curtains* (1961)]

MAILER, Norman (1923–)
Once a newspaper touches a story, the facts are lost forever, even to the protagonists.

[*The Presidential Papers* (1976)]

MANKIEWICZ, Herman J. (1897–1953)
I run a couple of newspapers. What do you do?

[*Citizen Kane*, film (1941)]

MARQUIS, Don (1878–1937)
The art of newspaper paragraphing is to stroke a platitude until it purrs like an epigram.

[In Anthony, *O Rare Don Marquis* (1962)]

MILLER, Arthur (1915–)
A good newspaper, I suppose, is a nation talking to itself.

[*The Observer*, 1961]

MURDOCH, Rupert (1931–)
[On the publication of the *Kinsey Report*, a survey of human sexual behaviour]
Family newspapers like ourselves gain great kudos leaving this muck alone.

[Telegram sent to the *Adelaide News*, 1953]

I think the important thing is that there be plenty of newspapers with plenty of people controlling them so there can be choice.

[Film interview, 1967]

MURRAY, David (1888–1962)
A reporter is a man who has renounced everything in life but the world, the flesh, and the devil.

[*The Observer*, 1931]

OCHS, Adolph S. (1858–1935)
All the news that's fit to print.

[Motto of the *New York Times*]

PHILLIPS, Wendell (1811–1884)
We live under a government of men and morning newspapers.

[*Address: The Press*]

PROVERBS
Bad news travels fast.

No news is good news.

SALISBURY, Lord (1830–1903)

[Of the *Daily Mail*]
By office boys for office boys.

[In Fyfe, *Northcliffe, an Intimate Biography* (1930)]

SCOTT, C.P. (1846–1932)

Comment is free, but facts are sacred.

[*Manchester Guardian*, 1921]

SHERIDAN, Richard Brinsley (1751–1816)

The newspapers! Sir, they are the most villainous – licentious – abominable – infernal – Not that I ever read them – No – I make it a rule never to look into a newspaper.

[*The Critic* (1779)]

STOPPARD, Tom (1937–)

Milne: No matter now imperfect things are, if you've got a free press everything is correctable, and without it everything is conceivable.
Ruth: I'm with you on the free press. It's the newspapers I can't stand.

[*Night and Day* (1978)]

[Referring to foreign correspondents]
He's someone who flies around from hotel to hotel and thinks the most interesting thing about any story is the fact that he has arrived to cover it.

[*Night and Day* (1978)]

SWAFFER, Hannen (1879–1962)

Freedom of the press in Britain is freedom to print such of the proprietor's prejudices as the advertisers don't object to.

[In Driberg, *Swaff* (1974)]

TOMALIN, Nicholas (1931–1973)

The only qualities essential for real success in journalism are rat-like cunning, a plausible manner, and a little literary ability.

[*The Sunday Times Magazine*, 1969]

WAUGH, Evelyn (1903–1966)

News is what a chap who doesn't care much about anything wants to read. And it's only news until he's read it. After that it's dead.

[*Scoop* (1938)]

WELLINGTON, Duke of (1769–1852)

Possible? Is anything impossible? Read the newspapers.

[In Fraser, *Words on Wellington* (1889)]

WILDE, Oscar (1854–1900)

As for modern journalism, it is not my business to defend it. It justifies its own existence by the great Darwinian principle of the survival of the vulgarest.

[*Intentions* (1891)]

There is much to be said in favour of modern journalism. By giving us the opinions of the uneducated, it keeps us in touch with the ignorance of the community.

['The Critic as Artist' (1891)]

WOLFE, Humbert (1886–1940)

You cannot hope
To bribe or twist,
thank God! the
British journalist.
But, seeing what
the man will do
unbribed, there's
no occasion to.

['Over the Fire' (1930)]

ZAPPA, Frank (1940–1993)

Rock journalism is people who can't write interviewing people who can't talk for people who can't read.

[In Linda Botts, *Loose Talk* (1980)]

See MEDIA; TELEVISION

NOSTALGIA

ADAMS, Scott (1957–)

Someday we'll look back on this and plow into a parked car.

[*The Dilbert Principle*]

AUGIER, Emile (1820–1889)

La nostalgie de la boue.
Homesickness for the gutter.

[*Le Mariage d'Olympe* (1855)]

BYRON, Lord (1788–1824)

Ah! happy years! once more who would not be a boy?

[*Childe Harold's Pilgrimage* (1818)]

The 'good old times' – all times when old are good –
Are gone.

['The Age of Bronze' (1823)]

CARR, J.L. (1912–1994)

We can ask and ask but we can't have again what once seemed ours forever – the way things looked, that church alone in the fields, a bed on a belfry floor, a loved face … They'd gone, and you could only wait for the pain to pass.

[*A Month in the Country* (1980)]

FITZGERALD, Penelope (1916–)

[Her hopes for the New Year]
Conductors should be back on the buses, packets of salt back in the crisps, clockwork back in clocks and levers back in pens.

[*The Observer*, 1998]

HOUSMAN, A.E. (1859–1936)

Into my heart an air that kills
From yon far country blows:
What are those blue remembered hills,
What spires, what farms are those?

That is the land of lost content,
I see it shining plain,
The happy highways where I went
And cannot come again.

[*A Shropshire Lad* (1896)]

LAMB, Charles (1775–1834)

All, all are gone, the old familiar faces.

['The Old Familiar Faces']

ORWELL, George (1903–1950)

Before the war, and especially before the Boer War, it was summer all the year round.

[*Coming Up for Air* (1939)]

STEINBECK, John (1902–1968)

Cannery Row in Monterey in California is a poem, a stink, a grating noise, a quality of light, a tone, a habit, a nostalgia, a dream.

[*Cannery Row* (1939)]

TENNYSON, Alfred, Lord (1809–1892)

Tears, idle tears, I know not what they mean,
Tears from the depth of some divine despair
Rise in the heart, and gather to the eyes,
In looking on the happy Autumn-fields,
And thinking of the days that are no more.

[*The Princess* (1847)]

THOMAS, Dylan (1914–1953)

Years and years and years ago, when I was a boy, when there were wolves in Wales, and birds the colour of red-flannel petticoats whisked past the harp-shaped hills … when we rode the daft and happy hills bareback, it snowed and it snowed.

[*A Child's Christmas in Wales* (1954)]

USTINOV, Sir Peter (1921–)

The English have an enormous nostalgia for school. There is no other country in the world where you see elderly gentleman dressed like schoolboys.

[*The Observer*, 1998]

VILLON, François (b. 1431)

Mais où sont les neiges d'antan?
But where are the snows of yesteryear?

[*Le Grand Testament* (1461)]

YEATS, W.B. (1865–1939)

In the Junes that were warmer than these are, the waves were more gay,
When I was a boy with never a crack in my heart.

['The Meditation of the Old Fisherman' (1886)]

See MEMORY; PAST; REGRET

NUCLEAR WEAPONS

EINSTEIN, Albert (1879–1955)

[Of his part in the development of the atom bomb]
If only I had known, I should have become a watchmaker.

[*New Statesman*, 1965]

LAURENCE, William L. (1888–1977)

[Referring to the explosion of the first atomic bomb, over Hiroshima, 6 August 1945]

At first it was a giant column that soon took the shape of a supramundane mushroom.

[*New York Times*,1945]

KING, Martin Luther (1929–1968)

Our scientific power has outrun our spiritual power. We have guided missiles and misguided men.

[*Strength to Love*, 1963]

LE BLANC, Jacques

[Describing France's nuclear testing, 1995]

I do not like this word bomb. It is not a bomb; it is a device which is exploding.

MCLUHAN, Marshall (1911–1980)

The hydrogen bomb is history's exclamation point. It ends an age-long sentence of manifest violence.

[Attr.]

OPPENHEIMER, J. Robert (1904–1967)

[On the consequences of the first atomic test]

We knew the world would not be the same.

[In Giovanitti and Freed, *The Decision to Drop the Bomb* (1965)]

OWEN, Dr David (1938–)

It was on this issue, the nuclear defence of Britain, on which I left the Labour Party, and on this issue I am prepared to stake my entire political career.

[*The Observer*, 1986]

RUSSELL, Bertrand (1872–1970)

[On the possibility of nuclear war between the USA and the USSR]

You may reasonably expect a man to walk a tightrope safely for ten minutes; it would be unreasonable to do so without accident for two hundred years.

[In Desmond Bagley, *The Tightrope Men* (1973)]

RUTHERFORD, Ernest (1871–1937)

[Joking about the atom's enormous potential energy]

Some fool in a laboratory might blow up the universe unawares.

[In Mark Oliphant, *Rutherford Recollections of the Cambridge Days* (1972)]

SCHROEDER, Congresswoman Patricia (1940–)

We've got the kind of President who thinks arms control means some kind of deodorant.

[*The Observer*, 1987]

STEVENSON, Adlai (1900–1965)

There is no evil in the atom; only in men's souls.

[Speech, Hartford, Connecticut, 1952]

TIBBET, Paul W. (20th century)

[Description of atomic bomb explosion]

A mushroom of boiling dust up to 20,000 feet.

[Attr.]

TOYNBEE, Arnold (1889–1975)

[Urging the need for a greater British influence in the United Nations Organisation, 1947]

No annihilation without representation.

[Attr.]

WHITE, Patrick (1912–1990)

Today when science has perfected the techniques of destruction, nuclear warfare could mean the immediate annihilation of what we know as civilisation, followed by a slow infection of those who inhabit the less directly involved surface of this globe – as it revolves in space – swathed in its contaminated shroud.

[Speech to public meeting on nuclear disarmament, Melbourne, 1981]

WIGG, George Edward Cecil, Baron (1900–1983)

For Hon. Members opposite the deterrent is a phallic symbol. It convinces them that they are men.

[*The Observer*, 1964]

See WAR

NURSERY RHYMES

(For sources, the reader is referred to the authoritative *Oxford Dictionary of Nursery Rhymes*)

As I was going to St Ives,
I met a man with seven wives.
Each wife had seven sacks,
Each sack had seven cats,
Each cat had seven kits:
Kits, cats, sacks, and wives,
How many were going to St Ives?
[One or none].

Baa, baa, black sheep,
Have you any wool?
Yes, sir, yes, sir,
Three bags full;
One for the master,
And one for the dame,
And one for the little boy who lives down the
lane.

Bobby Shafto's gone to sea,
Silver buckles on his knee;
He'll come back and marry me,
Bonny Bobby Shafto!

Boys and girls come out to play,
The moon doth shine as bright as day.

Bye, baby bunting,
Daddy's gone a-hunting,
Gone to get a rabbit skin
To wrap the baby bunting in.

Cock a doodle doo!
My dame has lost her shoe,
My master's lost his fiddling stick,
And doesn't know what to do.

Come, let's to bed
Says Sleepy-head;
Tarry a while, says Slow;
Put on the pan;
Says Greedy Nan,
Let's sup before we go.

Curly locks, Curly locks,
Wilt thou be mine?
Thou shalt not wash dishes
Nor yet feed the swine;
But sit on a cushion
And sew a fine seam,
And feed upon strawberries,
Sugar and cream.

Ding, dong, bell,
Pussy's in the well.
Who put her in?
Little Johnny Green.
Who pulled her out?
Little Timmy Stout.

Doctor Foster went to Gloucester
In a shower of rain;
He stepped in a puddle,
Right up to his middle,
And never went there again.

Fee, fi, fo, fum,
I smell the blood of an Englishman;
Be he alive or be he dead,
I'll grind his bones to make my bread.

A frog he would a-wooing go,
Heigh ho! says Rowley,
Whether his mother would let him or no.
With a rowley, powley, gammon and spinach,
Heigh ho! says Anthony Rowley.

Georgie Porgie, pudding and pie,
Kissed the girls and made them cry;
When the boys came out to play,
Georgie Porgie ran away.

Goosey, goosey gander,
Whither shall I wander?
Upstairs and downstairs
And in my lady's chamber.

There I met an old man
Who wouldn't say his prayers,
I took him by the left leg
And threw him down the stairs.

Here is the church, and here is the steeple;
Open the door and here are the people.

Hey diddle diddle,
The cat and the fiddle,
The cow jumped over the moon;
The little dog laughed
To see such sport,
And the dish ran away with the spoon.

Hickory, dickory, dock,
The mouse ran up the clock.

The clock struck one,
The mouse ran down,
Hickory, dickory, dock.

Hot cross buns!
Hot cross buns!
One a penny, two a penny,
Hot cross buns!

How many miles to Babylon?
Three score miles and ten.
Can I get there by candle-light?
Yes, and back again.

Humpty Dumpty sat on a wall,
Humpty Dumpty had a great fall.
All the king's horses,
And all the king's men,
Couldn't put Humpty together again.

I had a little nut tree,
Nothing would it bear
But a silver nutmeg
And a golden pear;
The King of Spain's daughter
Came to visit me,
And all for the sake
Of my little nut tree.

I had a little pony,
His name was Dapple Grey;
I lent him to a lady
To ride a mile away.
She whipped him, she lashed him,
She rode him though the mire;
I would not lend my pony now,
For all the lady's hire.

I love little pussy,
Her coat is so warm,
And if I don't hurt her,
She'll do me no harm.

I love sixpence, jolly little sixpence,
I love sixpence better than my life;
I spent a penny of it, I lent a penny of it,
And I took fourpence home to my wife.

I'm the king of the castle,
Get down, you dirty rascal!

I see the moon,

And the moon sees me;
God bless the moon,
And God bless me.

Jack and Jill went up the hill
To fetch a pail of water;
Jack fell down and broke his crown,
And Jill came tumbling after.

Jack Sprat could eat no fat,
His wife could eat no lean,
And so between them both, you see,
They licked the platter clean.

Ladybird, ladybird,
Fly away home,
Your house is on fire
And your children are gone.
All except one
And that's little Ann
And she has crept under
The warming pan.

Lavender's blue, dilly dilly,
Lavender's green;
When I am king, dilly dilly,
You shall be queen.

The lion and the unicorn
Were fighting for the crown;
The lion beat the unicorn
All around the town.

Little boy blue, come blow your horn,
The sheep's in the meadow, the cow's in the
corn.

Little Jack Horner
Sat in the corner,
Eating a Christmas pie;
He put in his thumb,
And pulled out a plum,
And said, What a good boy am I!

Little Miss Muffet
Sat on a tuffet,
Eating her curds and whey;
There came a big spider,
Who sat down beside her
And frightened Miss Muffet away.

Little Polly Flinders

Sat among the cinders,
Warming her pretty little toes;
Her mother came and caught her,
And whipped her little daughter
For spoiling her nice new clothes.

Little Tommy Tucker,
Sings for his supper:
What shall we give him?
White bread and butter
How shall he cut it
Without a knife?
How will he be married
Without a wife?

London Bridge is falling down,
My fair lady.

Mary had a little lamb,
Its fleece was white as snow;
And everywhere that Mary went
The lamb was sure to go.
It followed her to school one day,
That was against the rule;
It made the children laugh and play
To see a lamb at school.

Mary, Mary, quite contrary,
How does your garden grow?
With silver bells and cockle shells,
And pretty maids all in a row.

Monday's child is fair of face,
Tuesday's child is full of grace,
Wednesday's child is full of woe,
Thursday's child has far to go,
Friday's child is loving and giving,
Saturday's child works hard for a living,
And the child that is born on the Sabbath day
Is bonny and blithe, and good and gay.

My mother said that I never should
Play with the gypsies in the wood;
If I did, she would say,
Naughty girl to disobey.

The north wind doth blow,
And we shall have snow,
And what will poor robin do then?
Poor thing.

O dear, what can the matter be?
Dear, dear, what can the matter be,
Oh, dear, what can the matter be?
Johnny's so long at the fair.

He promised he'd buy me a fairing should please me,
And then for a kiss, oh! he vowed he would tease me,
He promised he'd buy me a bunch of blue ribbons
To tie up my bonny brown hair.

Oh! the grand old Duke of York
He had ten thousand men;
He marched them up to the top of the hill,
And he marched them down again.
And when they were up they were up,
And when they were down they were down,
And when they were only half way up.
They were neither up nor down.

Old King Cole
Was a merry old soul,
And a merry old soul was he;
He called for his pipe,
And he called for his bowl,
And he called for his fiddlers three.

Old Mother Hubbard
Went to the cupboard,
To fetch her poor dog a bone;
But when she came there
The cupboard was bare
And so the poor dog had none.

One, two, buckle my shoe;
Three, four, knock at the door;
Five, six, pick up sticks;
Seven, eight, lay them straight;
Nine, ten, big fat hen;
Eleven, twelve, dig and delve;
Thirteen, fourteen, maids a-courting;
Fifteen, sixteen, maids in the kitchen,
Seventeen, eighteen, maids in waiting;
Nineteen, twenty, my plate's empty!

Oranges and lemons,
Say the bells of St Clement's …

You owe me five farthings,
Say the bells of St Martin's.

When will you pay me?
Say the bells of Old Bailey.

When I grow rich
Say the bells of Shoreditch.

Pray, when will that be?
Say the bells of Stepney.

I'm sure I don't know
Says the great bell at Bow.

Here comes a candle to light you to bed,
Here comes a chopper to chop off your
head!

Pat-a-cake, pat-a-cake, baker's man,
Bake me a cake as fast as you can;
Pat it and prick it, and mark it with B,
Put it in the oven for baby and me.

Peter, Peter, pumpkin eater,
Had a wife and couldn't keep her;
He put her in a pumpkin shell
And there he kept her very well.

Peter Piper picked a peck of pickled pepper.
A peck of pickled pepper Peter Piper picked.
If Peter Piper picked a peck of pickled
pepper,
Where's the peck of pickled pepper Peter
Piper picked?

Please to remember
The Fifth of November,
Gunpowder, treason and plot;
We know no reason
Why gunpowder treason
Should ever be forgot.

Polly put the kettle on,
Polly put the kettle on,
Polly put the kettle on,
We'll all have tea.
Sukey take it off again,
Sukey take it off again,
Sukey take it off again,

They've all gone away.

Pussy cat, pussy cat,
Where have you been?
I've been to London
To look at the queen.
Pussy cat, pussy cat,
What did you there?
I frightened a little mouse
Under her chair.

The Queen of Hearts
She made some tarts,
All on a summer's day;
The Knave of Hearts
He stole the tarts,
And took them clean away.

Rain, rain, go away,
Come again another day.

Ride a cock-horse to Banbury Cross,
To see a fine lady upon a white horse;
Rings on her fingers and bells on her toes,
She shall have music wherever she goes.

Ring-a-ring o' roses,
A pocket full of posies,
A-tishoo! A-tishoo!
We all fall down.

Rock-a-bye, baby, on the tree top,
When the wind blows the cradle will rock;
When the bough breaks the cradle will fall,
Down will come baby, cradle, and all.

Round and round the garden
Like a teddy bear;
One step, two step,
Tickle you under there!

Round and round the rugged rock
The ragged rascal ran.

Rub-a-dub-dub,
Three men in a tub,
And how do you think they got there?
The butcher, the baker,
The candlestick-maker.
They all jumped out of a rotten potato,
'Twas enough to make a man stare.

See-saw, Margery Daw,
Jacky shall have a new master;
Jacky shall have but a penny a day,
Because he can't work any faster.

Simple Simon met a pieman,
Going to the fair;
Says Simple Simon to the pieman,
Let me taste your ware.

Sing a song of sixpence,
A pocket full of rye;
Four and twenty blackbirds,
Baked in a pie.

When the pie was opened,
The birds began to sing;
Wasn't that a dainty dish,
To set before the king?

The king was in his counting-house,
Counting out his money;
The queen was in the parlour,
Eating bread and honey.

The maid was in the garden,
Hanging out the clothes,
When down came a blackbird
And pecked off her nose!

Solomon Grundy,
Born on Monday
Christened on Tuesday
Married on Wednesday
Took ill on Thursday
Worse on Friday
Died on Saturday
Buried on Sunday.
This is the end of Solomon Grundy.

Taffy was a Welshman, Taffy was a thief,
Taffy came to my house and stole a piece of
beef.

Tell tale, tit!
Your tongue shall be split,
And all the dogs in town
Shall have a little bit.

There was a crooked man, and he walked a
crooked mile,

He found a crooked sixpence against a
crooked stile;
He bought a crooked cat, which caught a
crooked mouse,
And they all lived together in a little crooked
house.

There was an old woman who lived in a shoe,
She had so many children she didn't know
what to do.
She gave them some broth without any bread,
She whipped them all soundly and put them
to bed.

Thirty days hath September,
April, June and November;
All the rest have thirty-one,
Excepting February alone
And that has twenty-eight days clear
And twenty-nine in each leap year.

This is the horse and the hound and the horn
That belonged to the farmer sowing his corn,
That kept the cock that crowed in the morn,
That waked the priest all shaven and shorn,
That married the man all tattered and torn,
That kissed the maiden all forlorn,
That milked the cow with the crumpled horn,
That tossed the dog,
That worried the cat,
That killed the rat,
That ate the corn,
That lay in the house that Jack built.

This little pig went to market,
This little pig stayed at home,
This little pig had roast beef,
This little pig had none,
And this little pig cried, Wee-wee-wee-wee-wee,
I can't find my way home.

Three blind mice, see how they run!
They all ran after the farmer's wife,
She cut off their tails with a carving knife,
Did ever you see such a thing in your life,
As three blind mice?

Three little kittens they lost their mittens,
And they began to cry.
Oh mother dear, we sadly fear

Our mittens we have lost.
What! lost your mittens,
You naughty kittens!
Then you shall have no pie.

Tinker,
Tailor,
Soldier,
Sailor,
Rich man,
Poor man,
Beggarman,
Thief.

Tom, he was a piper's son,
He learnt to play when he was young,
And all the tune that he could play
Was 'Over the hills and far away'.

Tom, Tom, the piper's son,
Stole a pig and away he run.
The pig was eat,
And Tom was beat,
And Tom went howling down the street.

The twelfth day of Christmas,
My true love sent to me
Twelve lords a-leaping,
Eleven ladies dancing,
Ten pipers piping,
Nine drummers drumming,
Eight maids a-milking,
Seven swans a-swimming,
Six geese a-laying,
Five gold rings,
Four calling birds,
Three French hens,
Two turtle doves, and
A partridge in a pear tree.

Two little dicky birds,
Sitting on a wall;
One named Peter,
The other named Paul,
Fly away, Peter!
Fly away, Paul!
Come back, Peter!
Come back, Paul!

Wee Willie Winkie runs through the town

Upstairs and downstairs and in his
nightgown,
Rapping at the window, crying through the lock,
Are the children all in bed? It's past eight o'clock.

What are little boys made of?
Frogs and snails
And puppy-dogs' tails,
That's what little boys are made of.

What are little girls made of?
Sugar and spice
And all things nice,
That's what little girls are made of.

What are young men made of ?
Sighs and leers,
And crocodile tears,
That's what young men are made of.

What are young women made of?
Ribbons and laces,
And sweet, pretty faces,
That's what young women are made of.

Where are you going to, my pretty maid?
I'm going a-milking, sir, she said.
What is your fortune, my pretty maid?
My face is my fortune, sir, she said.

Who killed Cock Robin?
I, said the Sparrow,
With my bow and arrow,
I killed Cock Robin.

Who saw him die?
I, said the Fly,
With my little eye,
I saw him die.

And all the birds of the air
Fell to sighing and sobbing,
When they heard the bell toll
For poor Cock Robin.

A wise old owl lived in an oak;
The more he saw the less he spoke;
The less he spoke the more he heard.
Why can't we all be like that wise old bird?

O

OBEDIENCE

GIBBON, Edward (1737–1794)
I sighed as a lover, I obeyed as a son.
[Memoirs of My Life and Writings (1796)]

PLATO (c.429–347 BC)
Through obedience learn to command.
[Leges]

SCHILLER, Johann Christoph Friedrich (1759–1805)
Gehorsam ist des Weibes Pflicht auf Erden,
Das harte Dulden ist ihr schweres Los.
Obedience is woman's earthly duty,
Harsh suffering is her sorry fate.
[The Maid of Orleans (1801)]

STORR, Dr Anthony (1920–)
I myself believe that the tendency towards obedience is one of the most sinister of human traits.
[Feet of Clay (1996)]

OBSTINACY

ARISTOTLE (384–322 BC)
Obstinate people may be subdivided into the opinionated, the ignorant, and the boorish.
[Nicomachean Ethics]

BROWNE, Sir Thomas (1605–1682)
Obstinacy in a bad cause, is but constancy in a good.
[Religio Medici (1643)]

MACNEICE, Louis (1907–1963)
One must not dislike people … because they are intransigent. For that could be only playing their own game.
[Zoo (1938)]

MAUGHAM, William Somerset (1874–1965)
Like all weak men he laid an exaggerated stress on not changing one's mind.
[Of Human Bondage (1915)]

PROVERB
None so deaf as those who will not hear.

SHERIDAN, Richard Brinsley (1751–1816)
She's as headstrong as an allegory on the banks of the Nile.
[The Rivals (1775)]

STERNE, Laurence (1713–1768)
'Tis known by the name of perseverance in a good cause, – and of obstinacy in a bad one.
[Tristram Shandy (1759–67)]

OPINIONS

BAEZ, Joan (1941–)
I've never had a humble opinion. If you've got an opinion, why be humble about it.
[Scotland on Sunday, 1992]

BROWNE, Sir Thomas (1605–1682)
I could never divide my self from any man upon the difference of an opinion, or be angry with his judgment for not agreeing with me in that, from which perhaps within a few days I should dissent my self.
[Religio Medici (1643)]

CHESTERTON, G.K. (1874–1936)
Bigotry may be roughly defined as the anger of men who have no opinions
[Heretics (1905)]

CONGREVE, William (1670–1729)
I am always of the opinion with the learned, if they speak first.
[Incognita (1692)]

EMERSON, Ralph Waldo (1803–1882)
Tomorrow a stranger will say with masterly good sense precisely what we have thought and felt all the time, and we shall be forced

to take with shame our own opinion from another.

['Self-Reliance' (1841)]

HALSEY, Margaret (1910–)

… the English think of an opinion as something which a decent person, if he has the misfortune to have one, does all he can to hide.

[*With Malice Toward Some* (1938)]

HOBBES, Thomas (1588–1679)

They that approve a private opinion, call it opinion; but they that mislike it, heresy: and yet heresy signifies no more than private opinion.

[*Leviathan* (1651)]

JAMES, Henry (1843–1916)

The superiority of one man's opinion over another's is never so great as when the opinion is about a woman.

[*The Tragic Muse* (1890)]

JEFFERSON, Thomas (1743–1826)

Error of opinion may be tolerated where reason is left free to combat it.

[First inaugural address, 1801]

LOCKE, John (1632–1704)

New opinions are always suspected, and usually opposed, without any reason but because they are not already common.

[*Essay concerning Human Understanding* (1690)]

MACKINTOSH, Sir James (1765–1832)

Men are never so good or so bad as their opinions.

['Jeremy Bentham' (1830)]

MAISTRE, Joseph de (1753–1821)

Les fausses opinions ressemblent á la fausse monnaie qui est frappée d'abord par de grands coupables, et dépensée ensuite par d'honnêtes gens qui perpétuent le crime sans savoir ce qu'ils font.

Wrong opinions are like counterfeit coins, which are first minted by great wrongdoers, then spent by decent people who perpetuate the crime without knowing what they are doing.

[*Les soirées de Saint-Pétersbourg*]

MILL, John Stuart (1806–1873)

If all mankind minus one, were of one opinion, and only one person were of the contrary opinion, mankind would be no more justified in silencing that one person, than he, if he had the power, would be justified in silencing mankind.

[*On Liberty* (1859)]

PALMERSTON, Lord (1784–1865)

What is merit? The opinion one man entertains of another.

[In Carlyle, 'Shooting Niagara and After?' (1837)]

PERSIUS FLACCUS, Aulus (AD 34–62)

Nec te quaesiveris extra.
Do not look for opinions beyond your own.

[*Satires*]

SPENCER, Herbert (1820–1903)

Opinion is ultimately determined by the feelings, and not by the intellect.

[*Social Statics* (1850)]

STEVENSON, Robert Louis (1850–1894)

All opinions, properly so called, are stages on the road to truth.

[*Virginibus Puerisque*, 'Crabbed Age and Youth']

TERENCE (c.190–159 BC)

Quot homines tot sententiae: suos quoique mos.
There are as many opinions as there are people: each has his own point of view.

[*Phormio*]

TURGENEV, Ivan (1818–1883)

I submit to no man's opinion; I have opinions of my own.

[*Fathers and Sons* (1862), 13]

TWAIN, Mark (1835–1910)

You tell me whar a man gets his corn pone, en I'll tell you what his 'pinions is.

['Corn Pone Opinions']

WEBSTER, Daniel (1782–1852)

Inconsistencies of opinion, arising from changes of circumstances, are often justifiable.

[Speech, 1846]

WENDERS, Wim (1945–)

The more opinions you have, the less you see.

[Attr.]

See IDEAS

OPPORTUNITY

ANONYMOUS

Opportunity always knocks at the least opportune moment.

[Ducharme's Precept]

BACON, Francis (1561–1626)

A wise man will make more opportunities than he finds.

[Essays]

PROVERBS

A bird in the hand is worth two in the bush.

The early bird catches the worm.

God helps them that help themselves.

Opportunity seldom knocks twice.

See CHANCE

OPPOSITION

ROOSEVELT, Eleanor (1884–1962)

I have spent many years of my life in opposition and I rather like the role.

[Letter to Bernard Baruch, 1952]

RUSK, Dean (1909–1994)

[Of the Cuban missile crisis]

We're eye-ball to eye-ball and the other fellow just blinked.

[Remark, 1962]

STEVENS, Wallace (1879–1955)

Two things of opposite natures seem to depend
On one another, as a man depends
On a woman, day on night, the imagined
On the real.

['Notes Toward a Supreme Fiction' (1948)]

See GOVERNMENT; POLITICS

OPTIMISM

CABELL, James Branch (1879–1958)

The optimist proclaims that we live in the best of all possible worlds; and the pessimist fears this is true.

[The Silver Stallion (1926)]

ELIOT, George (1819–1880)

I am not an optimist but a meliorist.

[In L. Housman, A.E.H. (1937)]

MAILER, Norman (1923–)

Being married six times shows a degree of optimism over wisdom, but I am incorrigibly optimistic.

[The Observer, 1988]

MARQUIS, Don (1878–1937)

an optimist is a guy
that has never had
much experience.

[archy and mehitabel (1927)]

O'CASEY, Sean (1880–1964)

A lament in one ear, maybe; but always a song in the other. And to me life is simply an invitation to live.

[In Eileen O'Casey, Eileen]

SHORTER, Clement King (1857–1926)

The latest definition of an optimist is one who fills up his crossword puzzle in ink.

[The Observer, 1925]

USTINOV, Sir Peter (1921–)

I am an optimist, unrepentant and militant. After all, in order not to be a fool an optimist must know how sad a place the world can be. It is only the pessimist who finds this out anew every day.

[Dear Me (1977)]

VOLTAIRE (1694–1778)

Tout est pour le mieux dans le meilleur des mondes possibles.

Everything is for the best in the best of all

possible worlds.

[*Candide* (1759)]

See HOPE; PESSIMISM

ORDER

POPE, Alexander (1688–1744)
Order is Heav'n's first law.

[*Essay on Man* (1734)]

SMILES, Samuel (1812–1904)
A place for everything, and everything in its place. Order is wealth.

[*Thrift* (1875)]

STEVENS, Wallace (1879–1955)
Oh! Blessed rage for order, pale Ramon.
The maker's rage to order words of the sea,
Words of the fragrant portals, dimly-starred,
And of ourselves and of our origins,
In ghostlier demarcations, keener sounds.

['The Idea of Order at Key West' (1936)]

ORIGINALITY

MILL, John Stuart (1806–1873)
All good things which exist are the fruits of originality.

[*On Liberty* (1859)]

TATSUNO, Sheridan M.
[Yoshifumi Nishimura, chemist, in conversation with Stephen Kreider Yoder, former Tokyo correspondent of the Wall Street Journal]
There's no environment where you can do wacky things that end up being creative ... If you're different, you're a minus ... That nips originality in the bud.

[In *Created in Japan*]

WORDSWORTH, William (1770–1850)
Never forget what I believe was observed to you by Coleridge, that every great and original writer, in proportion as he is great and original, must himself create the taste by which he is to be relished.

[Letter to Lady Beaumont, 1807]

P

PARENTS

ALLEN, Woody (1935–)
My parents were very old world. They come from Brooklyn which is the heart of the old world. Their values in life are God, and carpeting.

[In Adler and Feinman, *Woody Allen: Clown Prince of American Humor*]

And my parents finally realize that I'm kidnapped and they snap into action immediately: they rent out my room.

[In Eric Lax, *Woody Allen* (1991)]

BACON, Francis (1561–1626)
The joys of parents are secret, and so are their griefs and fears.

['Of Parents and Children' (1625)]

BUTLER, Samuel (1835–1902)
Parents are the last people on earth who ought to have children.

[Attr.]

COMPTON-BURNETT, Dame Ivy (1884–1969)
Don't be too hard on parents. You may find yourself in their place.

[*Elders and Betters* (1944)]

DE VRIES, Peter (1910–1993)
There are times when parenthood seems nothing but feeding the mouth that bites you.

[*The Tunnel of Love*]

EMERSON, Ralph Waldo (1803–1882)
Respect the child. Be not too much his parent. Trespass not on his solitude.

[Attr.]

FUKUYAMA, Francis
It takes a great deal of effort to separate a mother from her infant, and a fair amount to get a father to be involved with his.

[*The Great Disruption* (1999)]

JENNINGS, Elizabeth (1926–)
Lying apart now, each in a separate bed,
He with a book, keeping the light on late,
She like a girl dreaming of childhood,
All men elsewhere – it is as if they wait
Some new event: the book he holds unread,
Her eyes fixed on the shadows overhead.

Tossed up like flotsam from a former passion,
How cool they lie. They hardly ever touch,
Or if they do it is like a confession
Of having little feeling – or too much.
Chastity faces them, a destination
For which their whole lives were a preparation.

Strangely apart, yet strangely close together,
Silence between them like a thread to hold
And not wind in. And time itself's a feather
Touching them gently. Do they know they're old,
These two who are my father and my mother
Whose fire from which I came, has now grown cold?

[*The Mind has Mountains* (1966)]

LARKIN, Philip (1922–1985)
They fuck you up, your mum and dad.
They may not mean to, but they do.
They fill you with the faults they had
And add some extra, just for you.

['This be the Verse' (1974)]

LEACOCK, Stephen (1869–1944)
The parent who could see his boy as he really is, would shake his head and say: 'Willie is no good: I'll sell him.'

[*Essays and Literary Studies* (1916)]

NASH, Ogden (1902–1971)
Children aren't happy with nothing to ignore,
And that's what parents were created for.

[*Happy Days* (1933)]

POWELL, Anthony (1905–)

All the same, you know parents – especially step-parents – are sometimes a bit of a disappointment to their children. They don't fulfil the promise of their early years.

[*A Buyer's Market*]

SCHMICH, Mary

Get to know your parents. You never know when they'll be gone for good.

['Everybody's Free (To Wear Sunscreen)' (1997)]

SHAW, George Bernard (1856–1950)

Parentage is a very important profession; but no test of fitness for it is ever imposed in the interest of the children.

[*Everybody's Political What's What* (1944)]

SPARK, Muriel (1918–)

Parents learn a lot from their children about coping with life.

[*The Comforters* (1957)]

STERNE, Laurence (1713–1768)

I wish either my father or my mother, or indeed both of them, as they were in duty both equally bound to it, had minded what they were about when they begot me.

[*Tristram Shandy* (1759–1767)]

USTINOV, Sir Peter (1921–)

The young need old men. They need men who are not ashamed of age, not pathetic imitiations of themselves … Parents are the bones on which children sharpen their teeth.

[*Dear Me* (1977)]

WILDE, Oscar (1854–1900)

To lose one parent may be regarded as a misfortune … to lose both seems like carelessness.

[*The Importance of Being Earnest* (1895)]

See CHILDREN; FAMILIES; FATHERS; MOTHERS

AUSTEN, Jane (1775–1817)

The sooner every party breaks up the better.

[*Emma* (1816)]

PORTER, Cole (1891–1964)

He: Have you heard it's in the stars
Next July we collide with Mars?
She: Well, did you evah! What a swell party this is.

['Well, Did you Evah!', song, 1956, from *High Society*]

WHITEHORN, Katherine (1926–)

The Life and Soul, the man who will never go home while there is one man, woman or glass of anything not yet drunk.

[*Sunday Best* (1976)]

See SOCIETY

CHAPMAN, George (c.1559–c.1634)

For one heate (all know) doth drive out another,
One passion doth expell another still.

[*Monsieur D'Olive* (1606)]

CONNOLLY, Cyril (1903–1974)

The man who is master of his passions is Reason's slave.

[In V.S. Pritchett (ed.), *Turnstile One*]

DRYDEN, John (1631–1700)

A man is to be cheated into passion, but to be reasoned into truth.

[*Religio Laici* (1682)]

HUME, David (1711–1776)

We never remark any passion or principle in others, of which, in some degree or other, we may not find a parallel in ourselves.

[*A Treatise of Human Nature* (1739)]

JUNG, Carl Gustav (1875–1961)

Ein Mensch, der nicht durch die Hölle seiner Leidenschaften gegangen ist, hat sie auch nie überwunden.
A man who has not gone through the hell of his passions has never overcome them either.

[*Memories, Dreams, Thoughts* (1962)]

KEMPIS, Thomas à (c.1380–1471)

Passione interdum movemur; et zelum putamus.

We are sometimes moved by passion and think it zeal.

[*De Imitatione Christi* (1892)]

L'ESTRANGE, Sir Roger (1616–1704)

It is with our passions as it is with fire and water, they are good servants, but bad masters.

[Translation of *Aesop's Fables*]

MEREDITH, George (1828–1909)

In tragic life, God wot,
No villain need be! Passions spin the plot:
We are betrayed by what is false within.

[*Modern Love* (1862)]

POPE, Alexander (1688–1744)

The ruling Passion, be it what it will,
The ruling Passion conquers Reason still.

['Epistle to Lord Bathurst' (1733)]

In Men, we various Ruling Passions find,
In Women, two almost divide the kind;
Those, only fix'd, they first or last obey,
The Love of Pleasure, and the Love of Sway.

['Epistle to a Lady' (1735)]

POUND, Ezra (1885–1972)

As a bathtub lined with white porcelain,
When the hot water gives out or goes tepid,
So is the slow cooling of our chivalrous passion,
O my much praised but-not-altogether-satisfactory lady.

['The Bath Tub' (1916)]

RACINE, Jean (1639–1699)

Ce n'est plus une ardeur dans mes veines cachée:
C'est Vénus tout entière à sa proie attachée.
It is no longer an ardour hidden in my veins:
it's Venus in all her power fastening on her prey.

[*Phèdre* (1677)]

RUSSELL, Bertrand (1872–1970)

Three passions, simple but overwhelmingly strong, have governed my life: the longing for love, the search for knowledge, and unbearable pity for the suffering of mankind.

[*The Autobiography of Bertrand Russell* (1967–1969)]

SHAFFER, Peter (1926–)

Passion, you see, can be destroyed by a doctor. It cannot be created.

[*Equus* (1973)]

SHAKESPEARE, William (1564–1616)

A man that Fortune's buffets and rewards
Hast ta'en with equal thanks; and blest are those
Whose blood and judgment are so well comeddled
That they are not a pipe for Fortune's finger
To sound what stop she please. Give me that man
That is not passion's slave, and I will wear him
In my heart's core, ay, in my heart of heart,
As I do thee.

[*Hamlet*, III.ii]

STEELE, Sir Richard (1672–1729)

Women dissemble their Passions better than Men, but … Men subdue their Passions better than Women.

[*The Lover* (1714)]

STERNE, Laurence (1713–1768)

Having been in love, with one princess or other, almost all my life, and I hope I shall go on so till I die, being firmly persuaded, that if ever I do a mean action, it must be in some interval betwixt one passion and another.

[*A Sentimental Journey* (1768)]

STEVENSON, Robert Louis (1850–1894)

You have only to look these happy couples in the face, to see they have never been in love, or in hate, or in any other high passion all their days.

[*Virginibus Puerisque* (1881)]

THACKERAY, William Makepeace (1811–1863)

Yes, I am a fatal man, Madame Fribsbi. To inspire hopeless passion is my destiny.

[*Pendennis* (1848–50)]

See FEELINGS; LOVE

THE PAST

BEERBOHM, Sir Max (1872–1956)
There is always something rather absurd about the past.

[Attr.]

COLETTE (1873–1954)
But the past, the beautiful past striped with sunshine, grey with mist, childish, blooming with hidden joy, bruised with sweet sorrow. … Ah! if only I could resurrect one hour of that time, one alone – but which one?

[*Paysages et portraits* (1958)]

CONGREVE, William (1670–1729)
In hours of bliss we oft have met;
They could not always last;
And though the present I regret
I'm grateful for the past.

['False though she be']

FITZGERALD, F. Scott (1896–1940)
So we beat on, boats against the current, borne back ceaselessly into the past.

[*The Great Gatsby* (1925)]

HARTLEY, L.P. (1895–1972)
The past is a foreign country: they do things differently there.

[*The Go-Between* (1953)]

[Remark just before he died]
I seem to have become part of my past.

[In Wright, *Foreign Country: The Life of L.P. Hartley*]

HUXLEY, Aldous (1894–1963)
One of the evil results of the political subjection of one people by another is that it tends to make the subject nation unnecessarily and excessively conscious of its past … It is to the past – the gorgeous imaginary past of those whose present is inglorious, sordid, and humiliating – it is to the delightful founded-on-fact romances of history that subject peoples invariably turn.

[*Jesting Pilate* (1926)]

ONDAATJE, Michael (1943–)
The past is still, for us, a place that is not yet safely settled.

[*The Faber Book of Contemporary Canadian Short Stories* (1990)]

SANTAYANA, George (1863–1952)
Those who cannot remember the past are condemned to repeat it.

[*The Life of Reason* (1906)]

TERTZ, Abram (1925–1997)
In the past, people did not cling to life quite as much, and it was easier to breathe.

[*A Voice From the Chorus* (1973)]

THOMAS, Edward (1878–1917)
The past is the only dead thing that smells sweet.

['Early One Morning' (1917)]

WAIN, John (1925–1994)
Keep off your thoughts from things
   that are past and done;
For thinking of the past wakes regret
   and pain.

[*Resignation*, translated from the Chinese of Po-Chü-I]

WHITELAW, William (1918–)
I do not intend to prejudge the past.

[*The Times*, 1973]

See EXPERIENCE; FUTURE; HISTORY; MEMORY; NOSTALGIA; PRESENT; REGRET; TIME

PATIENCE

ARNOLD, Matthew (1822–1888)
With close-lipped patience for our only friend,
Sad patience, too near neighbour to despair.

['The Scholar-Gipsy' (1853)]

BIERCE, Ambrose (1842–c.1914)
Patience: A minor form of despair, disguised as a virtue.

[*The Cynic's Word Book* (1906)]

CERVANTES, Miguel de (1547–1616)
I say have patience, and shuffle the cards.

[*Don Quixote* (1615)]

FONTAINE, Jean de la (1621–1695)

Patience et longueur de temps
Font plus que force ni que rage.

Patience and time do more than force and rage.

[*Fables*]

MASSINGER, Philip (1583–1640)

Patience, the beggar's virtue.

[*A New Way to Pay Old Debts* (1633)]

PROVERBS

Everything comes to him who waits.

Patience is a virtue.

SHAKESPEARE, William (1564–1616)

How poor are they that have not patience!
What wound did ever heal but by degrees?

[*Othello*, II.iii]

TAYLOR, Elizabeth (1912–1975)

It is very strange … that the years teach us patience; that the shorter our time, the greater our capacity for waiting.

[*A Wreath of Roses* (1950)]

See PERSISTENCE

PATRIOTISM

ADDISON, Joseph (1672–1719)

What pity is it
That we can die but once to serve our country!

[*Cato* (1713)]

BARRINGTON, George (1755–c.1835)

[Of convicts transported to Botany Bay]
From distant climes, o'er widespread seas we come,
Though not with much éclat or beat of drum;
True patriots we; for be it understood,
We left our country for our country's good.
No private views disgraced our generous zeal,
What urged our travels was our country's weal;
And none will doubt but that our emigration

Has proved most useful to the British nation.

['Prologue' for the opening of the Playhouse, Sydney, 1796]

CAVELL, Edith (1865–1915)

[Said on the eve of her execution]
Standing, as I do, in view of God and eternity I realize that patriotism is not enough. I must have no hatred or bitterness towards anyone.

[*The Times*, 1915]

CHESTERTON, G.K. (1874–1936)

They died to save their country and they only saved the world.

[*The Ballad of Saint Barbara and Other Verses* (1922)]

DECATUR, Stephen (1779–1820)

[Toast during a banquet, 1815]
Our country! In her intercourse with foreign nations, may she always be in the right; but our country, right or wrong.

[In Mackenzie, *Life of Decatur* (1846)]

DRYDEN, John (1631–1700)

Never was patriot yet, but was a fool.

[*Absalom and Achitophel* (1681)]

FARQUHAR, George (1678–1707)

'Twas for the good of my country that I should be abroad. – Anything for the good of one's country – I'm a Roman for that.

[*The Beaux' Stratagem* (1707)]

FORSTER, E.M. (1879–1970)

I hate the idea of causes, and if I had to choose between betraying my country and betraying my friend, I hope I should have the guts to betray my country.

[*Two Cheers for Democracy* (1951)]

GARIBALDI, Giuseppe (1807–1882)

Soldati, io esco da Roma. Chi vuole continuare la guerra contro lo straniero venga con me. Non posso offrirgli né onori né stipendi; gli offro fame, sete, marcie forzate, battaglie e morte. Chi ama la patria mi segua.

Men, I am leaving Rome. If you want to carry on fighting the invader, come with me. I cannot promise you either honours or wages; I can only offer you hunger, thirst, forced marches, battles and death. If you love your country, follow me.

[In Guerzoni, *Garibaldi* (1929)]

GASKELL, Elizabeth (1810–1865)

That kind of patriotism which consists in hating all other nations.

[*Sylvia's Lovers* (1863)]

GOLDSMITH, Oliver (c.1728–1774)

Such is the patriot's boast, where'er we roam,
His first best country ever is at home.

['The Traveller' (1764)]

HALE, Nathan (1755–1776)

[Speech before he was executed by the British]
I only regret that I have but one life to lose for my country.

[In Johnston, *Nathan Hale* (1974)]

HORACE (65–8 BC)

Dulce et decorum est pro patria mori.
It is sweet and honourable to die for one's country.

[*Odes*]

HUNT, G.W. (1829–1904)

We don't want to fight, but, by jingo if we do,
We've got the ships, we've got the men,
we've got the money too.

[Music hall song, 1878]

JOHNSON, Samuel (1709–1784)

Patriotism is the last refuge of a scoundrel.

[In Boswell, *The Life of Samuel Johnson* (1791)]

KINNOCK, Neil (1942–)

[Of nuclear disarmament]
I would die for my country but I could never let my country die for me.

[Speech, 1987]

OWEN, Wilfred (1893–1918)

If you could hear, at every jolt, the blood
Come gargling from the froth-corrupted lungs,
Obscene as cancer, bitter as the cud
Of vile, incurable sores on innocent tongues, –
My friend, you would not tell with such high zest

To children ardent for some desperate glory,
The old Lie: Dulce et decorum est
Pro patria mori.

['Dulce et decorum est' (1917)]

PAINE, Thomas (1737–1809)

My country is the world, and my religion is to do good.

[*The Rights of Man* (1791)]

PLOMER, William (1903–1973)

Patriotism is the last refuge of the sculptor.

[Attr.]

RUSSELL, Bertrand (1872–1970)

Patriots always talk of dying for their country, and never of killing for their country.

[Attr.]

SCHURZ, Carl (1829–1906)

Our country, right or wrong! When right, to be kept right; when wrong, to be put right!

[Speech, 1872]

SCOTT, Sir Walter (1771–1832)

Breathes there the man, with soul so dead,
Who never to himself hath said,
This is my own, my native land!
Whose heart hath ne'er within him burned,
As home his footsteps he hath turned,
From wandering on a foreign strand!

[*The Lay of the Last Minstrel* (1805), VI]

SMOLLETT, Tobias (1721–1771)

True Patriotism is of no Party.

[*The Adventures of Sir Launcelot Greaves* (1762)]

SPRING-RICE, Cecil Arthur (1859–1918)

I vow to thee, my country – all earthly things above –
Entire and whole and perfect, the service of my love.

['I Vow to Thee, My Country' (1918)]

TROTSKY, Leon (1879–1940)

Patriotism to the Soviet State is a revolutionary duty, whereas patriotism to a bourgeois State is treachery.

[In Fitzroy Maclean, *Disputed Barricade*]

WHITTIER, John Greenleaf (1807–1892)

'Shoot if you must, this old grey head,
But spare your country's flag,' she said.

['Barbara Frietchie' (1863)]

WILDE, Oscar (1854–1900)

Patriotism is the virtue of the vicious.

[Attr.]

See WAR

PEACE

ANONYMOUS

Since wars begin in the minds of men, it is in the minds of men that the defences of peace must be constructed.

[Constitution of UNESCO]

BELLOC, Hilaire (1870–1953)

Pale Ebenezer thought it wrong to fight,
But Roaring Bill (who killed him) thought it right.

['The Pacifist' (1938)]

THE BIBLE (King James Version)

They shall beat their swords into plowshares, and their spears into pruninghooks: nation shall not lift up sword against nation, neither shall they learn war any more.

[*Isaiah*, 2:4]

BIERCE, Ambrose (1842–c.1914)

Peace: In international affairs, a period of cheating between two periods of fighting.

[*The Cynic's Word Book* (1906)]

BRECHT, Bertolt (1898–1956)

Sagen sie mir nicht, dass Friede ausgebrochen ist.
Don't tell me that peace has broken out.

[*Mother Courage* (1939)]

CHAMBERLAIN, Neville (1869–1940)

This is the second time in our history that there has come back from Germany to Downing Street peace with honour. I believe it is peace for our time.

[Speech, Downing Street, after Munich Agreement, 1938, in Feiling, *The Life of Neville Chamberlain* (1946)]

CICERO (106–43 BC)

Id quod est praestantissimum maximeque optabile omnibus sanis et bonis et beatis, cum dignitate otium.
The thing which is by far the best and most desirable for all who are sane and good and fortunate is 'peace with honour'.

[*Pro Sestio*, 98]

CROMWELL, Oliver (1599–1658)

It's a maxim not to be despised, 'Though peace be made, yet it's interest that keeps peace.'

[Speech, 1654]

DISRAELI, Benjamin (1804–1881)

Lord Salisbury and myself have brought you back peace – but peace, I hope, with honour.

[Speech, 1878]

EINSTEIN, Albert (1879–1955)

Peace cannot be kept by force. It can only be achieved by understanding.

[*Notes on Pacifism*]

I am an absolute pacifist ... It is an instinctive feeling. It is a feeling that possesses me, because the murder of men is disgusting.

[Interview, 1929]

EISENHOWER, Dwight D. (1890–1969)

The peace we seek, founded upon decent trust and co-operative effort among nations, can be fortified, not by weapons of war but by wheat and by cotton, by milk and by wool, by meat and by timber and by rice. These are words that translate into every language on earth. These are needs that challenge this world in arms.

[Speech, 1953]

I think that people want peace so much that one of these days governments had better get out of the way and let them have it.

[Broadcast discussion, 1959]

GANDHI (1869–1948)

I wanted to avoid violence. Non-violence is the first article of my faith. It is also the last article of my creed.

[Speech, 1922]

GEORGE V (1865–1936)

[On the battlefield cemetries in Flanders, 1922]
I have many times asked myself whether there can be more potent advocates of peace upon earth through the years to come than this massed multitude of silent witnesses to the desolation of war.

[Attr.]

HARDY, Thomas (1840–1928)

'Peace upon earth!' was said. We sing it,
And pay a million priests to bring it.
After two thousand years of mass
We've got as far as poison-gas.

['Christmas: 1924' (1928)]

IZETBEGOVIC, Alija (1865–1936)

[On signing the Balkan peace accord in Paris, December 1995]
I feel like a man who is drinking a bitter but useful medicine.

[The Observer Review, 1995]

JERROLD, Douglas William (1803–1857)

We love peace, as we abhor pusillanimity; but not peace at any price.

['Peace' (1859)]

LIE, Trygve (1896–1968)

Now we are in a period which I can characterize as a period of cold peace.

[The Observer, 1949]

LITVINOV, Maxim (1876–1951)

Peace is indivisible.

[Speech to League of Nations, 1936]

MAYHEW, Christopher (1915–1997)

[On the Munich Agreement]
The peace that passeth all understanding.

[Speech, 1938]

MILTON, John (1608–1674)

Peace hath her victories

No less renowned than war.

['To the Lord General Cromwell' (1652)]

RENDALL, Montague John (1862–1950)

Nation shall speak peace unto nation.

[Motto of BBC]

ROOSEVELT, Franklin Delano (1882–1945)

When peace has been broken anywhere, the peace of all countries everywhere is in danger.

[Radio broadcast, 1939]

RUSSELL, Lord John (1792–1878)

If peace cannot be maintained with honour, it is no longer peace.

[Speech, 1853]

SHAKESPEARE, William (1564–1616)

A peace above all earthly dignities,
A still and quiet conscience.

[Henry VIII, III.ii]

TACITUS (AD c.56–c.120)

Ubi solitudinem faciunt pacem appellant.
They create a desert, and call it peace.

[Agricola]

WALPOLE, Horace (1717–1797)

When will the world know that peace and propagation are the two most delightful things in it?

[Letter to Sir Horace Mann, 1778]

WILSON, Woodrow (1856–1924)

There is a price which is too great to pay for peace, and that price can be put in one word. One cannot pay the price of self-respect.

[Speech, 1916]

It must be a peace without victory ... only a peace between equals can last.

[Speech, 1917]

See WAR; WAR AND PEACE

THE PEOPLE

ALCUIN (735–804)

Nec audiendi qui solent dicere, Vox populi, vox Dei, quum tumultuositas vulgi semper insaniae proxima sit.

Nor should those be heeded who are wont to say 'The voice of the people is the voice of God', since popular uproar is always akin to madness.

[Letter to Charlemagne]

BROWNE, Sir Thomas (1605–1682)

If there be any among those common objects of hatred I do contemn and laugh at, it is that great enemy of reason, virtue, and religion, the multitude; that numerous piece of monstrosity, which, taken asunder, seem men, and the reasonable creatures of God, but, confused together, make but one great beast, and a monstrosity more prodigious than Hydra.

[*Religio Medici* (1643)]

BURKE, Edmund (1729–1797)

It is a general popular error to imagine the loudest complainers for the public to be the most anxious for its welfare.

[Observations on 'The Present State of the Nation' (1769)]

The people never give up their liberties but under some delusion.

[Speech, 1784]

BURNS, Robert (1759–1796)

Who will not sing God save the King
Shall hang as high's the steeple;
But while we sing God save the King,
We'll ne'er forget the People!

['Does Haughty Gaul Invasion Threat?' (1795)]

CARLYLE, Thomas (1795–1881)

The Public is an old woman. Let her maunder and mumble.

[Attr.]

CHAPLIN, Charlie (1889–1977)

I am for people. I can't help it.

[*The Observer*, 1952]

CICERO (106–43 BC)

Salus populi suprema est lex.

The good of the people is the chief law.

[*De Legibus*]

CONFUCIUS (c.550–c.478 BC)

The people may be made to follow a course of action, but they may not be made to understand it.

[*Analects*]

CROMWELL, Oliver (1599–1658)

[Referring to a cheering crowd]
The people would be just as noisy if they were going to see me hanged.

[Attr.]

DE MILLE, Cecil B. (1881–1959)

The public is always right.

[In Colombo, *Wit and Wisdom of the Moviemakers*]

DICKENS, Charles (1812–1870)

'But suppose there are two mobs?' suggested Mr Snodgrass. 'Shout with the largest,' replied Mr Pickwick.

[*The Pickwick Papers* (1837)]

DRYDEN, John (1631–1700)

Nor is the people's judgement always true:
The most may err as grossly as the few.

[*Absalom and Achitophel* (1681)]

If by the people you understand the multitude, the hoi polloi 'tis no matter what they think; they are sometimes in the right, sometimes in the wrong: their judgement is a mere lottery.

[*Essay of Dramatic Poesy* (1668)]

ELLIOTT, Ebenezer (1781–1849)

When wilt thou save the people?
Oh, God of Mercy! when?
The people, Lord, the people!
Not thrones and crowns, but men!

['The People's Anthem' (1850)]

GLADSTONE, William (1809–1898)

All the world over, I will back the masses against the classes.

[Speech, Liverpool, 1886]

HAZLITT, William (1778–1830)

There is not a more mean, stupid, dastardly, pitiful, selfish, spiteful, envious, ungrateful animal than the Public. It is the greatest of cowards, for it is afraid of itself.

[*Table-Talk* (1822)]

HITLER, Adolf (1889–1945)

Die breite Masse eines Volkes … [fällt] einer grossen Lüge leichter zum Opfer als einer kleinen.

The broad mass of a people … falls victim to a big lie more easily than to a small one.

[*Mein Kampf* (1925)]

HOOKER, Richard (c.1554–1600)

He that goeth about to persuade a multitude, that they are not so well governed as they ought to be, shall never want attentive and favourable hearers.

[*Of the Laws of Ecclesiasticall Politie* (1593)]

IBSEN, Henrik (1828–1906)

The majority has the might – more's the pity – but it hasn't right … The minority is always right.

[*An Enemy of the People* (1882)]

JUVENAL (c.60–130)

Duas tantum res anxius optat,
Panem et circenses.

Two things only the people anxiously desire: bread and circuses.

[*Satires*]

KENNEDY, Robert F. (1925–1968)

One fifth of the people are against everything all the time.

[*The Observer*, 1964]

LA BRUYÈRE, Jean de (1645–1696)

Le peuple n'a guère d'esprit et les grands n'ont point d'âme … faut-il opter, je ne balance pas, je veux être peuple.

The people have little intelligence, the great no heart … if I had to choose I should not hesitate: I would be of the people.

[*Les caractères ou les moeurs de ce siècle* (1688)]

LINCOLN, Abraham (1809–1865)

You can fool some of the people all of the time, and all of the people some of the time,
but you cannot fool all of the people all the time.

[Attr.]

MONTESQUIEU, Charles (1689–1755)

Les grands seigneurs ont des plaisirs, le peuple a de la joie.

Great lords have pleasures, but the people have fun.

[*Pensées et fragments inédits* (1899)]

NORTHCLIFFE, Lord (1865–1922)

[Rumoured to have been a notice to remind his staff of his opinion of the mental age of the general public]

They are only ten.

[Attr.]

PARKMAN, Francis (1823–1893)

The public demands elocution rather than reason of those who address it … On matters of the greatest interest it craves to be excited or amused.

[*The Tale of the Ripe Scholar*]

POPE, Alexander (1688–1744)

The People's Voice is odd,
It is, and it is not, the voice of God.

[*Imitations of Horace* (1737–1738)]

ROSCOMMON, Fourth Earl of (1633–1685)

The multitude is always in the wrong.

[*An Essay on Translated Verse* (1684)]

SANDBURG, Carl (1878–1967)

The people will live on.
The learning and blundering people will live on.

[*The People, Yes* (1936)]

SCHULZ, Charles (1922–)

I love mankind – it's people I can't stand.

[*Go Fly a Kite, Charlie Brown*]

SITWELL, Dame Edith (1887–1964)

During the writing … of this book, I realized that the public will believe anything – so long as it is not founded on truth.

[*Taken Care Of* (1965)]

VANDERBILT, William H. (1821–1885)
[When asked whether the public should be consulted about luxury trains]
The public be damned! I'm working for my stockholders.
[Remark, 1883]

WALPOLE, Horace (1717–1797)
Our supreme governors, the mob.
[Letter to Sir Horace Mann, 1743]

WELLINGTON, Duke of (1769–1852)
You must build your House of Parliament upon the river: so … that the populace cannot exact their demands by sitting down round you.
[In Fraser, *Words on Wellington* (1889)]

See HUMANITY AND HUMAN NATURE

PERCEPTION

BLAKE, William (1757–1827)
Mans desires are limited by his perceptions; none can desire what he has not perceiv'd.
[*There is No Natural Religion* (c. 1788)]

If the doors of perception were cleansed every thing would appear to man as it is, infinite.
[*The Marriage of Heaven and Hell* (c. 1790–1793)]

LANGBRIDGE, Frederick (1849–1923)
Two men look out through the same bars:
One sees the mud, and one the stars.
['A Cluster of Quiet Thoughts' (1896)]

RUSKIN, John (1819–1900)
Not only is there but one way of doing things rightly, but there is only one way of seeing them, and that is, seeing the whole of them.
[*The Two Paths* (1859)]

TRUMBULL, John (1750–1831)
But optics sharp it needs I ween,
To see what is not to be seen.
[*McFingal*]

PERFECTION AND IMPERFECTION

DE QUINCEY, Thomas (1785–1859)
Even imperfection itself may have its ideal or perfect state.
['Murder Considered as One of the Fine Arts' (1839)]

HALL, Joseph (1574–1656)
Perfection is the child of Time.
[*Works* (1625)]

MILL, John Stuart (1806–1873)
The great majority of those who speak of perfectibility as a dream, do so because they feel that it is one which would afford them no pleasure if it were realized.
[*Speech on Perfectibility* (1828)]

POPE, Alexander (1688–1744)
Whoever thinks a faultless piece to see,
Thinks what ne'er was, nor is, nor e'er shall be.
[*An Essay on Criticism* (1711)]

Then say not man's imperfect, Heav'n in fault;
Say rather, Man's as perfect as he ought.
[*An Essay on Man* (1733)]

POUND, Ezra (1885–1972)
Come, my songs, let us speak of perfection –
We shall get ourselves rather disliked.
['Salvationists' (1916)]

ROYDON, Matthew (fl. 1580–1622)
Was never eye, did see that face,
Was never ear, did hear that tongue,
Was never mind, did mind his grace,
That ever thought the travel long –
But eyes, and ears, and ev'ry thought,
Were with his sweet perfections caught.
['An Elegy, or Friend's Passion, for his Astrophill' (1593)]

SMITH, Robert (1634–1716)
Powers act but weakly and irregularly, till they are heightened and perfected by their habits. A well radicated habit, in a lively, vegete faculty, is like an apple of gold in a

picture of silver; it is perfection upon perfection, it is a coat of mail upon our armour, and, in a word, it is the raising the soul at least one story higher: for take off but these wheels and the powers of all their operations will drive but heavily.

[Sermon, 30 April 1668]

STEPHENS, James (1882–1950)

Finality is death. Perfection is finality. Nothing is perfect. There are lumps in it.

[*The Crock of Gold* (1912)]

PERSEVERANCE

CHURCHILL, Sir Winston (1874–1965)

[Remark, December 1941]

We must just KBO ('Keep Buggering On').

[In M. Gilbert, *Finest Hour*]

HICKSON, William Edward (1803–1870)

'Tis a lesson you should heed,
Try, try again.
If at first you don't succeed,
Try, try again.

['Try and Try Again']

LATIMER, Bishop Hugh (c.1485–1555)

Gutta cavat lapidem, non vi sed saepe cadendo.
The drop of rain maketh a hole in the stone, not by violence, but by oft falling.

[Sermon preached before Edward VI, 1549]

STEVENSON, Robert Louis (1850–1894)

Surely we should find it both touching and inspiriting, that in a field from which success is banished, our race should not cease to labour.

[*Across the Plains* (1892)]

See PATIENCE

PESSIMISM

BENNETT, Arnold (1867–1931)

Pessimism, when you get used to it, is just as

agreeable as optimism.

[*Things That Have Interested Me*]

BEVERIDGE, William Henry (1879–1963)

Scratch a pessimist, and you find often a defender of privilege.

[*The Observer*, 1943]

KING, Benjamin (1857–1894)

Nothing to do but work,
Nothing to eat but food,
Nothing to wear but clothes
To keep one from going nude.

Nothing to breathe but air,
Quick as a flash 'tis gone;
Nowhere to fall but off,
Nowhere to stand but on!

['The Pessimist']

LOWELL, Robert (1917–1977)

If we see light at the end of the tunnel,
It's the light of the oncoming train.

['Since 1939' (1977)]

MALLET, Robert (1915–)

How many pessimists end up by desiring the things they fear, in order to prove that they are right.

[*Apostilles*]

MEIR, Golda (1898–1978)

Pessimism is a luxury that a Jew can never allow himself.

[*The Observer*, 1974]

PETER, Laurence J. (1919–1990)

A pessimist is a man who looks both ways before crossing a one-way street.

[Attr.]

See OPTIMISM

PHILOSOPHY

ADDISON, Joseph (1672–1719)

It was said of Socrates that he brought philosophy down from heaven to inhabit among men; and I shall be ambitious to have it said of me that I have brought philosophy out of closets and libraries, schools and colleges, to dwell in clubs and assemblies, at tea-tables and in coffee-houses.

[*The Spectator*, March 1711]

AYER, A.J. (1910–1989)

The principles of logic and metaphysics are true simply because we never allow them to be anything else.

[*Language, Truth and Logic* (1936)]

BACON, Francis (1561–1626)

All good moral philosophy … is but an handmaid to religion.

[*The Advancement of Learning* (1605)]

BOWEN, Lord (1835–1894)

On a metaphysician: A blind man in a dark room – looking for a black hat – which isn't there.

[Attr.]

BRADLEY, F.H. (1846–1924)

Metaphysics is the finding of bad reasons for what we believe upon instinct; but to find these reasons is no less an instinct.

[*Appearance and Reality* (1893)]

CHAMFORT, Nicolas (1741–1794)

Je dirais volontiers des métaphysiciens ce que Scalinger disait des Basques, on dit qu'ils s'entendent, mais je n'en crois rien.
I am tempted to say about metaphysicians what Scalinger would say about the Basques: they are said to understand one another, but I don't believe a word of it.

[*Maximes et Pensées* (1796)]

CICERO (106–43 BC)

Sed nescio quo modo nihil tam absurde dici potest quod non dicatur ab aliquo philosophorum.
But somehow there is nothing so absurd that some philosopher has not said it.

[*De Divinatione*]

EDWARDS, Oliver (1711–1791)

I have tried too in my time to be a philosopher; but, I don't know how, cheerfulness was always breaking in.

[In Boswell, *The Life of Samuel Johnson* (1791)]

GOLDSMITH, Oliver (c.1728–1774)

To a philosopher, no circumstance, however trifling, is too minute.

[*The Citizen of the World* (1762)]

This same philosophy is a good horse in the stable, but an errant jade on a journey.

[*The Good Natur'd Man* (1768)]

HUME, David (1711–1776)

Philosophers never balance between profit and honesty, because their decisions are general, and neither their passions nor imaginations are interested in the objects.

[*A Treatise of Human Nature* (1739)]

HUXLEY, T.H. (1825–1895)

I doubt if the philosopher lives, or has ever lived, who could know himself to be heartily despised by a street boy without some irritation.

[*Evolution and Ethics* (1893)]

JOHNSON, Samuel (1709–1784)

[Kicking a stone in order to disprove Berkeley's theory of the non-existence of matter]
I refute it thus.

[In Boswell, *The Life of Samuel Johnson* (1791)]

KAFKA, Franz (1883–1924)

Metaphysisches Bedürfnis ist nur Todesbedürfnis.
A metaphysical need is only a need for death.

[*Diary* (1912)]

KEATS, John (1795–1821)

Do not all charms fly
At the mere touch of cold philosophy?
There was an awful rainbow once in heaven:
We know her woof, her texture; she is given
In the dull catalogue of common things.
Philosophy will clip an Angel's wings.

['Lamia' (1819)]

LAO-TZU (c.604–531 BC)

Acting without design, occupying oneself without making a business of it, finding the great in what is small and the many in the few, repaying injury with kindness, effecting difficult things while they are easy, and managing great things in their beginnings:

this is the method of Tao.

[*Tao Te Ching*]

MACNEICE, Louis (1907–1963)

Good-bye now, Plato and Hegel,
The shop is closing down;
They don't want any philosopher-kings in England,
There ain't no universals in this man's town.

[*Autumn Journal* (1939)]

NIETZSCHE, Friedrich Wilhelm (1844–1900)

Wie ich den Philosophen verstehe, als einen furchtbaren Explosionsstoff, vor dem Alles in Gefahr ist.

What I understand philosophers to be: a terrible explosive, in the presence of which everything is in danger.

[*Ecce Homo* (1888)]

ORTEGA Y GASSET, José (1883–1955)

El placer sexual parece consistir en una súbita descarga de energ'a nerviosa. La fruic'on estética es una súbita descarga de emociones alusivas. Análogamente es la filosofia como una súbita descarga de intelección.

Sexual pleasure seems to consist in a sudden discharge of nervous energy. Aesthetic enjoyment is a sudden discharge of allusive emotions. Similarly, philosophy is like a sudden discharge of intellectual activity.

[*Meditations on Quijote* (1914)]

PASCAL, Blaise (1623–1662)

Se moquer de la philosophie, c'est vraiment philosopher.

To ridicule philosophy is truly to philosophize.

[*Pensées* (1670)]

PEABODY, Elizabeth (1804–1894)

[Giving a Transcendentalist explanation for her accidentally walking into a tree]
I saw it, but I did not realize it.

[In L. Tharp, *The Peabody Sisters of Salem*]

PLATO (c.429–347 BC)

Unless either philosophers become kings in our states, or those who are now called kings and rulers become to a serious and sufficient degree philosophers … there will be no fewer ills afflicting our states or indeed the whole of the human race.

[*Republic*]

RUSSELL, Bertrand (1872–1970)

Matter … a convenient formula for describing what happens where it isn't.

[*An Outline of Philosophy* (1927)]

Organic life, we are told, has developed gradually from the protozoon to the philosopher, and this development, we are assured, is indubitably an advance. Unfortunately it is the philosopher, not the protozoon, who gives us this assurance.

[*Mysticism and Logic* (1918)]

RYLE, Gilbert (1900–1976)

Philosophy is the replacement of category-habits by category-disciplines.

[*The Concept of Mind* (1949)]

SANTAYANA, George (1863–1952)

It is a great advantage for a system of philosophy to be substantially true.

[*The Unknowable* (1923)]

SELDEN, John (1584–1654)

Philosophy is nothing but discretion.

[*Table Talk* (1689)]

SHAKESPEARE, William (1564–1616)

There are more things in heaven and earth, Horatio,
Than are dreamt of in your philosophy.

[*Hamlet*, I.v]

SWIFT, Jonathan (1667–1745)

Philosophy! the lumber of the schools.

['Ode to Sir W. Temple' (1692)]

THOREAU, Henry David (1817–1862)

There are now-a-days professors of philosophy but not philosophers.

[*Walden* (1854)]

VOLTAIRE (1694–1778)

En philosophie, il faut se défier de ce qu'on croit entendre trop trop aisément, aussi bien que des choses qu'on n'entend pas.

In philosophy, we must distrust the things we understand too easily as well as the things we don't understand.

[*Lettres philosophiques* (1734)]

La superstition met le monde entier en flammes; la philosophie les éteint.
Superstition sets the whole world on fire; philosophy quenches the flames.

[*Dictionnaire philosophique* (1764)]

WHITEHEAD, A.N. (1861–1947)

The safest general characterization of the European philosophical tradition is that it consists of a series of footnotes to Plato.

[*Process and Reality* (1929)]

The systematic thought of ancient writers is now nearly worthless; but their detached insights are priceless.

[Attr.]

Philosophy is the product of wonder.

[*Nature and Life* (1934)]

WITTGENSTEIN, Ludwig (1889–1951)

Philosophy is not a theory but an activity.

[*Tractatus Logico-Philosophicus* (1922)]

Philosophy is a struggle against the bewitching of our minds by means of language.

[*Philosophical Investigations* (1953)]

See LOGIC; THOUGHT

PHOTOGRAPHY

ABBOTT, Berenice (1898–1991)

Photography can never grow up if it imitates some other medium. It has to walk alone; it has to be itself.

[*Infinity*, 1951]

ASTOR, Nancy, Viscountess (1879–1964)

[Refusing to pose for a close-up photograph]
Take a close-up of a woman past sixty! You might as well use a picture of a relief map of Ireland!

[Attr.]

HOCKNEY, David (1937–)

[On the death of photography]
Once you can manipulate pictures on a computer you can't believe them any more. There will be no more Cartier-Bressons.

[Interview, *The Observer*, May 1999]

LAWRENCE, D.H. (1885–1930)

The modern pantheist not only sees the god in everything, he takes photographs of it.

[*St Mawr* (1925)]

SONTAG, Susan (1933–)

A photograph is not only an image (as a painting is an image), an interpretation of the real; it is also a trace, something directly stencilled off the real, like a footprint or a death mask.

[*New York Review of Books*, 1977]

Social misery has inspired the comfortably-off with the urge to take pictures, the gentlest of predations, in order to document a hidden reality, that is, a reality hidden from them.

[*New York Review of Books*, 1977]

VIDAL, Gore (1925–)

As much of an art form as interior decorating.

[Attr.]

PLAGIARISM

ANONYMOUS

Copy from one, it's plagiarism; copy from two, it's research.

BIERCE, Ambrose (1842–c.1914)

Plagiarize: To take the thought or style of another writer whom one has never, never read.

[*The Enlarged Devil's Dictionary* (1961)]

MIZNER, Wilson (1876–1933)

When you steal from one author, it's plagiarism; if you steal from many, it's research.

[Attr.]

MONTAIGNE, Michel de (1533–1592)

Quelqu'un pourrait dire de moi que j'ai seulement fait ici un amas de fleurs étrangères, n'y ayant fourni du mien que le filet á les lier.

One could say of me that in this book I have only made up a bunch of other men's flowers, providing of my own only the string to tie them together.

[*Essais* (1580)]

MORE, Hannah (1745–1833)

He lik'd those literary cooks
Who skim the cream of others' books;
And ruin half an author's graces
By plucking bon-mots from their places.

SHERIDAN, Richard Brinsley (1751–1816)

All that can be said is, that two people happened to hit on the same thought – and Shakespeare made use of it first, that's all.

[*The Critic* (1779)]

STEVENSON, Robert Louis (1850–1894)

Of all my verse, like not a single line;
But like my title, for it is not mine,
That title from a better man I stole;
Ah, how much better, had I stol'n the whole!

[*Underwoods* (1887)]

STRAVINSKY, Igor (1882–1971)

A good composer does not imitate; he steals.

[In Yates, *Twentieth Century Music* (1967)]

SULLIVAN, Sir Arthur (1842–1900)

[Accused of plagiarism]
We all have the same eight notes to work with.

[Attr.]

PLANS

BIERCE, Ambrose (1842–c.1914)

Plan: To bother about the best method of accomplishing an accidental result.

[*The Enlarged Devil's Dictionary* (1961)]

BRECHT, Bertolt (1898–1956)

Die schönsten Plän sind schon zuschanden

geworden durch die Kleinlichkeit von denen, wo sie ausführen sollten.

The best plans have always been wrecked by the narrow-mindedness of those who should carry them out.

[*Mother Courage and her Children* (1941)]

BURNS, Robert (1759–1796)

The best-laid schemes o' mice an' men
Gang aft agley,
An' lea'e us nought but grief an' pain,
For promis'd joy!

['To a Mouse' (1785)]

CANETTI, Elias (1905–1994)

It is important what you still have planned at the end. It shows the extent of injustice in your death.

[*The Human Province* (1973)]

DRYDEN, John (1631–1700)

Plots, true or false, are necessary
   things,
To raise up commonwealths and ruin
   kings.

[*Absalom and Achitophel* (1681)]

GILMAN, Charlotte Perkins (1860–1935)

Where young boys plan for what they will achieve and attain, young girls plan for whom they will achieve and attain.

[*Women and Economics* (1898)]

OSLER, Sir William (1849–1919)

When schemes are laid in advance, it is surprising how often the circumstances fit in with them.

[Attr.]

YOUNG, Edward (1683–1765)

For her own breakfast she'll project a scheme,
Nor take her tea without a stratagem.

[*Love of Fame, the Universal Passion* (1725–1728)]

PLEASURE

ALCOTT, Bronson (1799–1888)

A sip is the most that mortals are permitted

from any goblet of delight.

[*Table Talk* (1877)]

AUSTEN, Jane (1775–1817)

'I am afraid,' replied Elinor, 'that the pleasantness of an employment does not always evince its propriety.'

[*Sense and Sensibility* (1811)]

One half of the world cannot understand the pleasures of the other.

[*Emma* (1816)]

BEHN, Aphra (1640–1689)

Variety is the soul of pleasure.

[*The Rover* (1677)]

BIERCE, Ambrose (1842–c.1914)

Debauchee: One who has so earnestly pursued pleasure that he has had the misfortune to overtake it.

[*The Cynic's Word Book* (1906)]

BURKE, Edmund (1729–1797)

I am convinced that we have a degree of delight, and that no small one, in the real misfortunes and pains of others.

[*A Philosophical Enquiry into the Origin of our Ideas of the Sublime and Beautiful* (1757)]

BURNS, Robert (1759–1796)

But pleasures are like poppies spread:
You seize the flow'r, its bloom is shed;
Or like the snow falls in the river,
A moment white – then melts for ever.

['Tam o' Shanter' (1790)]

BYRON, Lord (1788–1824)

There's not a joy the world can give like that it takes away.

['Stanzas for Music' (1815)]

Pleasure's a sin, and sometimes sin's a pleasure.

[*Don Juan* (1824)]

Though sages may pour out their wisdom's treasure,
There is no sterner moralist than Pleasure.

[*Don Juan* (1824)]

CABELL, James Branch (1879–1958)

A man possesses nothing certainly save a

brief loan of his own body: and yet the body of man is capable of much curious pleasure.

[*Jurgen* (1919)]

CAMUS, Albert (1913–1960)

Il semblait être l'ami de tous les plaisirs normaux, sans en être l'esclave.
He seemed to indulge in all the usual pleasures without being a slave to any of them.

[*The Plague*, 1947)]

CLARE, John (1793–1864)

Summer's pleasures they are gone like to visions every one
And the cloudy days of autumn and of winter cometh on
I tried to call them back but unbidden they are gone
Far away from heart and eye and for ever far away.

['Remembrances' (1908)]

CLARK, Manning (1915–1991)

[Of the Australian writer, Henry Lawson]
He said later that the greatest pleasure he ever knew in the world was when his eyes met the eyes of a mate over the top of two foaming glasses of beer.

[*In Search of Henry Lawson* (1987)]

CLOUGH, Arthur Hugh (1819–1861)

The horrible pleasure of pleasing inferior people.

[*Amours de Voyage* (1858)]

COWPER, William (1731–1800)

Remorse, the fatal egg by pleasure laid.

['The Progress of Error' (1782)]

DRYDEN, John (1631–1700)

For present joys are more to flesh and blood
Than a dull prospect of a distant good.

[*The Hind and the Panther* (1687)]

GAY, John (1685–1732)

A miss for pleasure, and a wife for breed.

['The Toilette' (1716)]

HAZLITT, William (1778–1830)

The art of pleasing consists in being pleased.

[*The Round Table* (1817)]

HERBERT, George (1593–1633)

Look not on pleasures as they come, but go.

[*The Temple* (1633)]

HERBERT, Sir A.P. (1890–1971)

People must not do things for fun. We are not here for fun. There is no reference to fun in any Act of Parliament.

[*Uncommon Law* (1935)]

HUNT, Leigh (1784–1859)

A pleasure so exquisite as almost to amount to pain.

[Letter to Alexander Ireland, 1848]

JOHNSON, Samuel (1709–1784)

Pleasure is very seldom found where it is sought; our brightest blazes of gladness are commonly kindled by unexpected sparks.

[*The Idler* (1758–1760)]

The great source of pleasure is variety.

[*The Lives of the Most Eminent English Poets* (1779–1781)]

If I had no duties, and no reference to futurity, I would spend my life in driving briskly in a post-chaise with a pretty woman.

[In Boswell, *The Life of Samuel Johnson* (1791)]

No man is a hypocrite in his pleasures.

[In Boswell, *The Life of Samuel Johnson* (1791)]

KEATS, John (1795–1821)

Ever let the Fancy roam,
Pleasure never is at home.

['Fancy' (1819)]

LAMB, Charles (1775–1834)

The greatest pleasure I know, is to do a good action by stealth, and to have it found out by accident.

['Table Talk by the Late Elia']

LOOS, Anita (1893–1981)

Fun is fun but no girl wants to laugh all of the time.

[*Gentlemen Prefer Blondes* (1925)]

LUTHER, Martin (1483–1546)

Wer nicht liebt Wein, Weib und Gesang,
Der bleibt ein Narr sein Leben lang.

Whoever does not love wine, woman and song,
Remains a fool his whole life long.

[Attr]

MARVELL, Andrew (1621–1678)

Let us roll our strength and all
Our sweetness up into one ball,
And tear our pleasures with rough strife
Thorough the iron gates of life:
Thus, though we cannot make our sun
Stand still, yet we will make him run.

['To His Coy Mistress' (1681)]

MOLIÈRE (1622–1673)

Le ciel défend, de vrai, certains contentements
Mais on trouve avec lui des accommodements.

Heaven forbids certain pleasures, it is true, but one can arrive at certain compromises.

[*Tartuffe* (1664)]

O'ROURKE, P.J. (1947–)

After all, what is your hosts' purpose in having a party? Surely not for you to enjoy yourself; if that were their sole purpose, they'd have simply sent champagne and women over to your place by taxi.

[Attr.]

POPE, Alexander (1688–1744)

Pleasures are ever in our hands or eyes,
And when in act they cease, in prospect rise;
Present to grasp, and future still to find,
The whole employ of body and of mind.

[*An Essay on Man* (1733)]

ROCHESTER, Earl of (1647–1680)

'Is there then no more?'
She cries. 'All this to love and rapture's due;
Must we not pay a debt to pleasure too?'.

['The Imperfect Enjoyment' (1680)]

SELDEN, John (1584–1654)

Pleasure is nothing else but the intermission of pain, the enjoyment of something I am in great trouble for till I have it.

[*Table Talk* (1689)]

SHADBOLT, Tim (1932–)

[On teenage pleasures, c. 1960]

I used to love sitting in the gutter with

barefeet, a chrome-studded chair-covered leather jacket and filthy jeans. Eatin' chips. People look at you with such disgust and hate. It was terrific.

[*Bullshit & Jellybeans* (1971)]

SHAKESPEARE, William (1564–1616)

These violent delights have violent ends.

[*Romeo and Juliet*, II.vi]

SMOLLETT, Tobias (1721–1771)

I consider the world as made for me, not me for the world: it is my maxim therefore to enjoy it while I can, and let futurity shift for itself.

[*The Adventures of Roderick Random* (1748)]

SPENSER, Edmund (c.1522–1599)

And painefull pleasure turnes to pleasing paine.

[*The Faerie Queene* (1596)]

VIRGIL (70–19 BC)

Trahit sua quemque voluptas.
Each one's pleasure draws him on.

[*Eclogues*]

WOOLLCOTT, Alexander (1887–1943)

All the things I really like to do are either immoral, illegal, or fattening.

[In Drennan, *Wit's End* (1973)]

See HAPPINESS

POETRY

ADDISON, Joseph (1672–1719)

[Of The Georgics]
The most complete, elaborate, and finisht piece of all antiquity.

[*Essay on Virgil's Georgics* (1697)]

Nothing which is a phrase or saying in common talk, should be admitted into a serious poem.

[*Essay on Virgil's Georgics* (1697)]

ARISTOTLE (384–322 BC)

The task of the poet is not to describe what actually happened, but the kind of thing that

might happen according to probability or necessity … For this reason poetry is something more philosophical and more worthy of serious attention than history.

[*Poetics, IX*]

ARNOLD, Matthew (1822–1888)

[Of poetry]
A criticism of life under the conditions fixed for such a criticism by the laws of poetic truth and poetic beauty.

[*Essays in Criticism* (1888)]

BACON, Francis (1561–1626)

[Poesy] was ever thought to have some participation of divineness, because it doth raise and erect the mind, by submitting the shows of things to the desires of the mind; whereas reason doth buckle and bow the mind unto the nature of things.

[*The Advancement of Learning* (1605)]

BANVILLE, Théodore Faullain de (1823–1891)

Licences poétiques. Il n'y en a pas.
Poetic licence. There's no such thing.

[*Petit traité de poésie française*]

BARROW, Isaac (1630–1677)

Poetry is a kind of ingenious nonsense.

[In Spence, *Anecdotes*]

BENTLEY, Richard (1662–1742)

It is a pretty poem, Mr Pope, but you must not call it Homer.

[In John Hawkins (ed.), *The Works of Samuel Johnson* (1787)]

BOILEAU-DESPRÉAUX, Nicolas (1636–1711)

Quelque sujet qu'on traite, ou plaisant, ou sublime,
Que toujours le bon sens s'accorde avec la rime.
Be the subject lighthearted or sublime, sense always should agree with rhyme.

[*L'Art Poétique* (1674)]

BOLAND, Eavan (1944–)

Poetry is defined by its energies and its eloquence, not by the passport of the poet or the editor; or the name of the nationality. That way lie all the categories, the separations, the censorships that poetry exists to dispel.

[Review of Seamus Heaney's *An Open Letter*, *The Irish Times*, 1983]

BRADSTREET, Anne (c.1612–1672)

I am obnoxious to each carping tongue,
Who sayes my hand a needle better fits,
A Poet's Pen, all scorne, I should thus wrong;
For such despight they cast on female wits:
If what I doe prove well, it won't advance,
They'll say it's stolne, or else, it was by chance …

Let Greeks be Greeks, and Women what they are,
Men have precedency, and still excell …

This meane and unrefined stuffe of mine,
Will make your glistering gold but more to shine.

['The Prologue' (1650)]

BRONTÉ, Charlotte (1816–1855)

One day, in the autumn of 1845, I accidentally lighted on a MS volume of verse in my sister Emily's handwriting … I looked it over, and something more than surprise seized me, – a deep conviction that these were not common effusions, nor at all like the poetry women generally write. I thought them condensed and terse, vigorous and genuine. To my ear, they had also a peculiar music – wild, melancholy, and elevating.

[Biographical notice]

BYRON, Lord (1788–1824)

Nothing so difficult as a beginning
In poesy, unless perhaps the end.

[*Don Juan* (1819–1824)]

What is poetry? – The feeling of a Former world and Future.

[*Journal*, 1821]

CAGE, John (1912–1992)

I have nothing to say, I am saying it, and that is poetry.

[*Silence* (1961)]

CARROLL, Lewis (1832–1898)

'I can repeat poetry as well as other folk if it comes to that –'
'Oh, it needn't come to that!' Alice hastily said.

[*Through the Looking-Glass (and What Alice Found There)* (1872)]

CHAPMAN, George (c.1559–c.1634)

A Poeme, whose subject is not truth, but things like truth.

[*Revenge of Bussy D'Ambois* (1613)]

COLERIDGE, Samuel Taylor (1772–1834)

In the hexameter rises the fountain's silvery column;
In the pentameter aye falling in melody back.

['Ovidian Elegiac Metre' (1799)]

Trochee trips from long to short;
From long to long in solemn sort
Slow Spondee stalks; strong foot! yet ill able
Ever to come up with Dactyl trisyllable.
Iambics march from short to long; –
With a leap and a bound the swift Anapaests throng.

['Metrical Feet' (1806)]

That willing suspension of disbelief for the moment, which constitutes poetic faith.

[*Biographia Literaria* (1817)]

Poetry is not the proper antithesis to prose, but to science. Poetry is opposed to science, and prose to metre.

[*Lectures and Notes of 1818*]

I wish our clever young poets would remember my homely definitions of prose and poetry; that is prose = words in their best order; poetry = the best words in the best order.

[*Table Talk* (1835)]

Poetry is certainly something more than good sense, but it must be good sense at all events; just as a palace is more than a house, but it must be a house, at least.

[*Table Talk* (1835)]

COPE, Wendy (1945–)

I hardly ever tire of love or rhyme –
That's why I'm poor and have a rotten time.

[*'Variation on Belloc's 'Fatigue'*]

COWPER, William (1731–1800)

There is a pleasure in poetic pains
Which only poets know.

[*The Task* (1785)]

ELIOT, T.S. (1888–1965)

After the erection of the Chinese Wall of
Milton, blank verse has suffered not only
arrest but retrogression.

['Christopher Marlowe' (1919)]

In the seventeenth century a dissociation of
sensibility set in, from which we have never
recovered.

['The Metaphysical Poets' (1921)]

Poetry is not a turning loose of emotion, but an
escape from emotion; it is not the expression of
personality, but an escape from personality.

['Tradition and the Individual Talent' (1919)]

EMERSON, Ralph Waldo (1803–1882)

It is not metres, but a metre-making
argument, that makes a poem.

[*Essays, Second Series* (1844)]

EWART, Gavin (1916–1995)

Good light verse is better than bad heavy
verse any day of the week.

[*Penultimate Poems* (1989)]

FARQUHAR, George (1678–1707)

Poetry's a mere drug, Sir.

[*Love and a Bottle* (1698)]

FROST, Robert (1874–1963)

A poem may be worked over once it is in
being, but may not be worried into being.

[*Collected Poems* (1939)]

Poetry is a way of taking life by the throat.

[In Sergeant, *Robert Frost: the Trial by Existence* (1960)]

GRANVILLE-BARKER, Harley (1877–1946)

Rightly thought of there is poetry in peaches

… even when they are canned.

[*The Madras House*]

HARDY, Thomas (1840–1928)

If Galileo had said in verse that the world
moved, the Inquisition might have let him
alone.

[In F.E. Hardy, *The Later Years of Thomas Hardy* (1930)]

HOPKINS, Gerard Manley (1844–1889)

The poetical language of an age should be
the current language heightened.

[Letter to Robert Bridges, 1879]

HOUSMAN, A.E. (1859–1936)

Experience has taught me, when I am
shaving of a morning, to keep watch over my
thoughts, because, if a line of poetry strays
into my memory, my skin bristles so that the
razor ceases to act.

[The Name and Nature of Poetry' (1933)]

Even when poetry has a meaning, as it
usually has, it may be inadvisable to draw it
out … perfect understanding will sometimes
almost extinguish pleasure.

['The Name and Nature of Poetry' (1933)]

JAMES VI OF SCOTLAND AND I OF ENGLAND (1566–1625)

Dr Donne's verses are like the peace of God;
they pass all understanding.

[Attr.]

JARRELL, Randall (1914–1965)

Some poetry seems to have been written on
typewriters by other typewriters.

[Attr.]

KEATS, John (1795–1821)

Poetry should surprise by a fine excess and
not by Singularity – it should strike the
Reader as a wording of his own highest
thoughts, and appear almost a
Remembrance … Its touches of Beauty
should never be half way, thereby making
the reader breathless instead of content: the
rise, the progress, the setting of imagery
should, like the Sun, come naturally to him.

[Letter to John Taylor, 27 February 1818]

A long Poem is a test of Invention which I take to be the Polar Star of Poetry, as Fancy is the Sails, and Imagination the Rudder.

[Letter to Benjamin Bailey, 1817]

We hate poetry that has a palpable design upon us – and if we do not agree, seems to put its hand in its breeches pocket. Poetry should be great and unobtrusive, a thing which enters into one's soul, and does not startle it or amaze it with itself, but with its subject.

[Letter to J.H. Reynolds, 1818]

If Poetry comes not as naturally as Leaves to a tree it had better not come at all.

[Letter to John Taylor, 1818]

KENNEDY, John F. (1917–1963)

When power narrows the areas of man's concern, poetry reminds him of the richness and diversity of his existence.

[Speech, 1963]

KLOPSTOCK, Friedrich (1724–1803)

[Of one of his poems]
God and I both knew what it meant once; now God alone knows.

[Attr.]

LARKIN, Philip (1922–1985)

I rather think poetry has given me up, which is a great sorrow to me, but not an enormous, crushing sorrow. It's rather like going bald.

[The Observer, 1984]

MACAULAY, Lord (1800–1859)

As civilization advances, poetry almost necessarily declines.

[Collected Essays (1843)]

MACDIARMID, Hugh (1892–1978)

Poetry like politics maun cut
The cackle and pursue real ends,
Unerringly as Lenin, and to that
Its nature better tends.

['Second Hymn to Lenin' (1935)]

MACLEISH, Archibald (1892–1982)

A Poem should be palpable and mute
As a globed fruit,

Dumb
As old medallions to the thumb,

Silent as the sleeve-worn stone
Of casement ledges where the moss has
grown –
A poem should be wordless
As the flight of birds …

A poem should not mean
But be.

['Ars poetica' (1926)]

MENCKEN, H.L. (1880–1956)

Poetry is a comforting piece of fiction set to more or less lascivious music.

[Prejudices (1919–1927)]

MONROE, Harriet (1860–1936)

… poetry, 'The Cinderella of the Arts.'

[In Hope Stoddard, Famous American Women, 'Harriet Monroe']

PATTEN, Brian (1946–)

When in public poetry should take off its clothes and wave to the nearest person in sight; it should be seen in the company of thieves and lovers rather than that of journalists and publishers.

['Prose poem towards a definition of itself']

It should guide all those who are safe into the middle of busy roads and leave them there.

['Prose poem towards a definition of itself']

PAZ, Octavio (1914–)

La poesía no es nada sino tiempo, ritmo perpetuamente creador.
Poetry is nothing but time, ceaselessly creative rhythm.

[The Bow and the Lyre (1956)]

POUND, Ezra (1885–1972)

And give up verse, my boy,

There's nothing in it.

[*Hugh Selwyn Mauberley* (1920)]

PRESTON, Keith (1884–1927)
Of all the literary scenes
Saddest this sight to me:
The graves of little magazines
Who died to make verse free.

['The Liberators']

REICH, Wilhelm (1897–1957)
The few bad poems which occasionally are
created during abstinence are of no great
interest.

[*The Sexual Revolution*]

RICHARDS, I.A. (1893–1979)
[Of poetry]
It is a perfectly possible means of
overcoming chaos.

[*Science and Poetry* (1926)]

ROSSETTI, Dante Gabriel (1828–1882)
A sonnet is a moment's monument, –
Memorial from the Soul's eternity
To one dead deathless hour.

[*The House of Life* (1881)]

SHELLEY, Percy Bysshe (1792–1822)
[Poetry] lifts the veil from the hidden beauty
of the world, and makes familiar objects be
as if they were not familiar.

[*A Defence of Poetry* (1821)]

SITWELL, Dame Edith (1887–1964)
My poems are hymns of praise to the glory
of Life.

[*Selected Poems* (1952)]

SITWELL, Osbert (1892–1969)
Poetry is like fish: if it's fresh, it's good; if it's
stale, it's bad; and if you're not certain, try it
on the cat.

[*The Four Faces* (1936)]

SPRAT, Thomas (1635–1713)
Poetry is the mother of superstition.

[*The History of the Royal Society* (1667)]

STEVENS, Wallace (1879–1955)
Poetry is the supreme fiction, madame.

['A High-Toned old Christian Woman' (1923)]

THOMAS, Dylan (1914–1953)
These poems, with all their crudities, doubts,
and confusions, are written for the love of
Man and in praise of God, and I'd be a damn'
fool if they weren't.

[*Collected Poems* (1952)]

THOREAU, Henry David (1817–1862)
Poetry is nothing but healthy speech.

[*Journal*, 1841]

I do not perceive the poetic and dramatic
capabilities of an anecdote or story which is
told me, its significance, till some time
afterwards … We do not enjoy poetry unless
we know it to be poetry.

[*Journal*, 1856]

VALÉRY, Paul (1871–1945)
Mes vers ont le sens qu'on leur prête.
My poems mean what people take them to
mean.

[*Variety* (1924)]

A poem is never finished, only abandoned.

[In Auden, *A Certain World*]

WAIN, John (1925–1994)
Poetry is to prose as dancing is to walking.

[BBC broadcast, 1976]

WILDE, Oscar (1854–1900)
There seems to be some curious connection
between piety and poor rhymes.

[In Lucas, *A Critic in Pall Mall* (1919)]

**WORDSWORTH, William
(1770–1850)**
I have said that poetry is the spontaneous
overflow of powerful feelings: it takes its
origin from emotion recollected in
tranquillity: the emotion is contemplated till,
by a species of reaction, the tranquillity
gradually disappears, and an emotion,
kindred to that which was before the subject
of contemplation, is gradually produced, and
does itself actually exist in the mind.

[*Lyrical Ballads* (1802)]

YEATS, W.B. (1865–1939)
We make out of the quarrel with others,

rhetoric; but of the quarrel with ourselves, poetry.

['Anima Hominis' (1917)]

See CRITICISM; INSPIRATION; LITERATURE; POETS; WRITING

POETS

ADDISON, Joseph (1672–1719)

[Of Virgil]
He delivers the meanest of his precepts with a kind of grandeur, he breaks the clods and tosses the dung about with an air of gracefulness.

[*Essay on Virgil's Georgics* (1697)]

[Of Milton]
Our language sunk under him, and was unequal to that greatness of soul which furnished him with such glorious conceptions.

[*The Spectator*, February 1712, 297]

[Remark made of the poet Cowley]
He more had pleas'd us, had he pleas'd us less.

[Attr.]

ARNOLD, Matthew (1822–1888)

[Of Wordsworth]
He spoke, and loosed our heart in tears.
He laid us as we lay at birth
On the cool flowery lap of earth.

['Memorial Verses' (1850)]

Wordsworth says somewhere that wherever Virgil seems to have composed 'with his eye on the object', Dryden fails to render him. Homer invariably composes 'with his eye on the object', whether the object be a moral or a material one: Pope composes with his eye on his style, into which he translates his object, whatever it is.

[*On Translating Homer* (1861)]

[Of Wordsworth]
His expression may often be called bald … but it is bald as the bare mountain tops are

bald, with a baldness full of grandeur.

[*Essays in Criticism* (1888)]

[Quoting his own writing on Shelley]
In poetry, no less than in life, he is 'a beautiful and ineffectual angel, beating in the void his luminous wings in vain'.

[*Essays in Criticism* (1888)]

AUBREY, John (1626–1697)

[Of Milton]
He was so fair that they called him the lady of Christ's College.

[*Brief Lives* (c. 1693)]

AUDEN, W.H. (1907–1973)

A poet's hope: to be,
like some valley cheese,
local, but prized elsewhere.

['Shorts II']

It is a sad fact about our culture that a poet can earn much more money writing or talking about his art than he can by practising it.

[*The Dyer's Hand* (1963)]

BAUDELAIRE, Charles (1821–1867)

Le poète est semblable au prince des nuées
Qui hante la tempête et se rit de l'archer;
Exilé sur le sol, au milieu des huées,
Ses ailes de géant l'empêchent de marcher.
The poet is like the prince of the clouds, who haunts the tempest and mocks at the archer. Exiled to the ground, an object of derision, his giant wings prevent him from walking.

[*Les Fleurs du mal* (1857)]

BEER, Thomas (1889–1940)

I agree with one of your reputable critics that a taste for drawing-rooms has spoiled more poets than ever did a taste for gutters.

[*The Mauve Decade* (1926)]

BLAKE, William (1757–1827)

The reason Milton wrote in fetters when he wrote of Angels & God, and at liberty when of Devils & Hell, is because he was a true Poet and of the Devil's party without knowing it.

['The Voice of the Devil']

BOILEAU-DESPRÉAUX, Nicolas (1636–1711)

Enfin Malherbe vint, et, le premier en France,
Fit sentir dans les vers une juste cadence.

At last came Malherbe, and, the first in France, gave poetry a proper rhythm.

[*L'Art Poétique* (1674)]

BURNS, Robert (1759–1796)

I never had the least thought or inclination of turning Poet till I once got heartily in love, and then rhyme and song were, in a manner, the spontaneous language of my head.

[Attr.]

CARLYLE, Jane Welsh (1801–1866)

If they had said the sun and the moon was gone out of the heavens it could not have struck me with the idea of a more awful and dreary blank in the creation than the words: Byron is dead.

[Letter to Thomas Carlyle, May 1824]

CARLYLE, Thomas (1795–1881)

The excellence of Burns is, indeed, among the rarest, ... but ... it is plain and easily recognised: his Sincerity, his indisputable air of Truth.

[*Critical and Miscellaneous Essays* (1839)]

A poet without love were a physical and metaphysical impossibility.

[*Critical and Miscellaneous Essays* (1839)]

Robert Burns never had the smallest chance to get into Parliament, much as Robert Burns deserved, for all our sakes, to have been found there.

[*Latter-Day Pamphlets* (1850)]

CATULLUS (84–c.54 BC)

Nam castum esse decet pium poetam
Ipsum, versiculos nihil necesse est.

For the sacred poet ought to be chaste himself, but it is not necessary that his verses should be so.

[*Carmina*]

COCTEAU, Jean (1889–1963)

Un vrai poète se soucie peu de poésie. De même un horticulteur ne parfume pas ses roses.

A true poet scarcely worries about poetry, just as a gardener does not scent his roses.

[*Professional Secrets* (1922)]

COLERIDGE, Samuel Taylor (1772–1834)

With Donne, whose muse on dromedary trots,
Wreathe iron pokers into true-love knots;
Rhyme's sturdy cripple, fancy's maze and clue,
Wit's forge and fire-blast, meaning's press and screw.

['On Donne's Poetry' (1818)]

To read Dryden, Pope, etc., you need only count syllables; but to read Donne you must measure time, and discover the time of each word by the sense of passion.

[*The Friend* (1818)]

No man was ever yet a great poet, without being at the same time a profound philosopher.

[*Biographia Literaria* (1817)]

CONGREVE, William (1670–1729)

It is the business of a comic poet to paint the vices and follies of human kind.

[*The Double Dealer* (1694]

COPE, Wendy (1945–)

I used to think all poets were Byronic –
Mad, bad and dangerous to know.
And then I met a few. Yes it's ironic –
I used to think all poets were Byronic.
They're mostly wicked as a ginless tonic
And wild as pension plans. Not long ago
I used to think all poets were Byronic –
Mad, bad and dangerous to know.

[*Making Cocoa for Kingsley Amis* (1986)]

CORNFORD, Frances Crofts (1886–1960)

[Of Rupert Brooke]

A young Apollo, golden-haired,
Stands dreaming on the verge of strife,
Magnificently unprepared
For the long littleness of life.

['Youth' (1910)]

COWPER, William (1731–1800)

[Of Pope]

But he (his musical finesse was such,
So nice his ear, so delicate his touch)
Made poetry a mere mechanic art;
And ev'ry warbler has his tune by heart.

[*Table Talk* (1782)]

ELIOT, T.S. (1888–1965)

Tennyson and Browning are poets, and they think; but they do not feel their thought as immediately as the odour of a rose. A thought to Donne was an experience; it modified his sensibility.

['The Metaphysical Poets' (1921)]

The business of the poet is not to find new emotions, but to use the ordinary ones and, in working them up into poetry, to express feelings which are not in actual emotions at all.

['Tradition and the Individual Talent' (1919)]

GOETHE (1749–1832)

Aber Lord Byron ist nur gross, wenn er dichtet; sobald er reflektiert, ist er ein Kind.

Lord Byron is only great as a poet; as soon as he reflects, he is a child.

[*Gespräche mit Eckermann*, 1825]

GRAVES, Robert (1895–1985)

To be a poet is a condition rather than a profession.

[Questionnaire in *Horizon*]

HALDANE, J.B.S. (1892–1964)

Shelley and Keats were the last English poets who were at all up-to-date in their chemical knowledge.

[*Daedalus or Science and the Future* (1924)]

HARDY, Thomas (1840–1928)

Of course poets have morals and manners of their own, and custom is no argument with them.

[*The Hand of Ethelberta* (1876)]

HAZLITT, William (1778–1830)

[Of Coleridge]

He talked on for ever; and you wished him to talk on for ever.

[*Lectures on the English Poets* (1818)]

HEANEY, Seamus (1939–)

To forge a poem is one thing, to forge the uncreated conscience of the race, as Stephen Dedalus put it, is quite another and places daunting pressures and responsibilities on anyone who would risk the name of poet.

[*Preoccupations, Selected Prose 1968–1978*]

JOHNSON, Samuel (1709–1784)

The business of a poet, said Imlac, is to examine, not the individual but the species … he does not number the streaks of the tulip, or describe the different shades in the verdure of the forest.

[*Rasselas* (1759)]

JOYCE, James (1882–1941)

Lawn Tennyson, gentleman poet.

[*Ulysses* (1922)]

KEATS, John (1795–1821)

I think I shall be among the English Poets after my death.

[Letter to George and Georgiana Keats, 1818]

A Poet is the most unpoetical of anything in existence; because he has no Identity – he is continually informing and filling some other Body.

[Letter to Richard Woodhouse, 1818]

LAMB, Charles (1775–1834)

Milton almost requires a solemn service of music to be played before you enter upon him.

[*Last Essays of Elia* (1833)]

LARKIN, Philip (1922–1985)

Deprivation is for me what daffodils were for Wordsworth.

[*The Observer*, 1979]

LEAVIS, F.R. (1895–1978)

The Sitwells belong to the history of publicity rather than of poetry.

[*New Bearings in English Poetry* (1932)]

[Of Rupert Brooke]

His verse exhibits … something that is rather

like Keats' vulgarity with a Public School accent.

[*New Bearings in English Poetry* (1932)]

LEONARDO DA VINCI (1452–1519)

The poet ranks far below the painter in the representation of visible things, and far below the musician in that of invisible things.

[*Selections from the Notebooks of Leonardo da Vinci* (1952)]

LOCKHART, John Gibson (1794–1854)

It is a better and a wiser thing to be a starved apothecary than a starved poet; so back to the shop Mr John, back to 'plasters, pills, and ointment boxes'.

[*Blackwood's Magazine*, 1818, Review of Keats's *Endymion*]

LODGE, David (1935–)

Walt Whitman who laid end to end words never seen in each other's company before outside of a dictionary.

[*Changing Places* (1975)]

LORCA, Federico García (1899–1936)

Ni un solo momento, viejo hermoso Walt Whitman,
he dejado de ver tu barba llena de mariposas.
Not even for a moment, beautiful old Walt Whitman, have I stopped seeing your beard full of butterflies.

[*Poeta en Nueva York* (1929–30)]

MACAULAY, Lord (1800–1859)

Perhaps no person can be a poet, or can even enjoy poetry, without a certain unsoundness of mind.

[*Collected Essays* (1843)]

OWEN, Wilfred (1893–1918)

All the poet can do today is to warn.
That is why the true Poets must be truthful.

[Quoted in *Poems* (1963)]

PESSOA, Fernando (1888–1935)

Ser poeta não é uma ambição minha.
… a minha maneira de estar sozinho.
Being a poet is not an ambition of mine.
It is my way of being alone.

[*The Guardian of Flocks* (1914)]

PLATO (c.429–347 BC)

Poets utter great and wise things which they do not themselves understand.

[*Republic*]

POPE, Alexander (1688–1744)

Poets, like painters, thus, unskill'd to trace
The naked nature and the living grace,
With gold and jewels cover ev'ry part,
And hide with ornaments their want of art.

[*An Essay on Criticism* (1711)]

Sir, I admit your gen'ral Rule
That every Poet is a Fool;
But you yourself may serve to show it,
That every Fool is not a Poet.

['Epigram from the French' (1732)]

SHELLEY, Percy Bysshe (1792–1822)

Poets are … the trumpets which sing to battle and feel not what they inspire …
Poets are the unacknowledged legislators of the world.

[*A Defence of Poetry* (1821)]

SIDNEY, Sir Philip (1554–1586)

Nature never set foorth the earth inso rich Tapistry as diverse Poets have done … her world is brasen, the Poets only deliver a golden.

[*The Defence of Poesie* (1595)]

There have been many most excellent poets that have never versified, and now swarm many versifiers that need never answer to the name of poets.

[*The Defence of Poesie* (1595)]

SPENDER, Sir Stephen (1909–1995)

People sometimes divide others into those you laugh at and those you laugh with. The young Auden was someone you could laugh-at-with.

[Address at W.H. Auden's memorial service, Oxford, 1973]

SQUIRE, Sir J.C. (1884–1958)

But Shelley had a hyper-thyroid face.

['Ballade of the Glandular Hypothesis']

STEVENSON, Robert Louis (1850–1894)

Whitman, like a large shaggy dog, just unchained, scouring the beaches of the world and baying at the moon.

[*Familiar Studies of Men and Books* (1882)]

SWIFT, Jonathan (1667–1745)

Say, Britain, could you ever boast, –
Three poets in an age at most?
Our chilling climate hardly bears
A sprig of bays in fifty years.

['On Poetry' (1733)]

WALLER, Edmund (1606–1687)

Poets lose half the praise they should have got,
Could it be known what they discreetly blot.

['On Roscommon's Translation of Horace']

WATERHOUSE, Keith (1929–)

Why do we need a Poet Laureate at all? We might as well still retain a Court Jester or a Royal Food Taster.

[Comment following the death of Poet Laureate Ted Hughes, November 1998]

WELLINGTON, Duke of (1769–1852)

I hate the whole race … There is no believing a word they say – your professional poets, I mean – there never existed a more worthless set than Byron and his friends for example.

[Attr.]

WILDE, Oscar (1854–1900)

[Of Wordsworth]
He found in stones the sermons he had already hidden there.

[*The Nineteenth Century*, 1889]

WOOLF, Virginia (1882–1941)

I would venture to guess that Anon, who wrote so many poems without signing them, was often a woman.

[*A Room of One's Own* (1929)]

WORDSWORTH, William (1770–1850)

The Poet writes under one restriction only, namely, that of the necessity of giving pleasure to a human Being possessed of that information which may be expected from him, not as a lawyer, a physician, a mariner, an astronomer or a natural philosopher, but as a Man.

[*Lyrical Ballads* (1802)]

Milton! thou shouldst be living at this hour:
England hath need of thee; she is a fen
Of stagnant waters: altar, sword, and pen,
Fireside, the heroic wealth of hall and bower,
Have forfeited their ancient English dower
Of inward happiness …

Thy soul was like a star, and dwelt apart.

['Milton! thou shouldst be living at this hour' (1807)]

YEATS, W.B. (1865–1939)

The poet finds and makes his mask in disappointment, the hero in defeat.

['Anima Hominis']

[Of Keats]
I see a schoolboy when I think of him,
With face and nose pressed to a sweet-shop window,
For certainly he sank into his grave
His senses and his heart unsatisfied,
And made – being poor, ailing and ignorant,
Shut out from all the luxury of the world,
The coarse-bred son of a livery-stable keeper –
Luxuriant song.

[*The Wild Swans at Coole, Other Verses and a Play* (1917)]

[Referring to Wilfred Owen]
He is all blood, dirt and sucked sugar stick.

[In D. Wellesley (ed.), *Letters on Poetry from W.B. Yeats to Dorothy Wellesley* (1940)]

See CRITICISM; POETRY; SHAKESPEARE; WRITERS

POLICE

CONRAD, Joseph (1857–1924)

The terrorist and the policeman both come from the same basket.

[*The Secret Agent* (1907)]

DALEY, Richard J. (1902–1976)

[To the press, concerning riots during Democratic Convention, 1968]
Gentlemen, get the thing straight once and for all. The policeman isn't there to create disorder, the policeman is there to preserve disorder.

[Attr.]

HICKS, Sir Seymour (1871–1949)

You will recognize, my boy, the first sign of old age: it is when you go out into the streets of London and realize for the first time how young the policemen look.

[In Pulling, *They Were Singing* (1952)]

MILLIGAN, Spike (1918–)

Policemen are numbered in case they get lost.

[*The Last Goon Show of All*]

O'BRIEN, Flann (1911–1966)

[Commenting on the fact that policemen always seem to look young]
A thing of duty is a boy for ever.

[Attr.]

O'CASEY, Sean (1880–1964)

The Polis as Polis, in this city, is Null an' Void!

[*Juno and the Paycock* (1924)]

ORWELL, George (1903–1950)

Only the Thought Police mattered.

[*Nineteen Eighty-Four* (1949)]

PEEL, Arthur Wellesley, First Viscount (1829–1912)

[Protesting against his arrest by the police, recently established by his father]
My father didn't create you to arrest me.

[Attr.]

PHILIPPE, Charles-Louis (1874–1909)

On a toujours l'air de mentir quand on parle à des gendarmes.
One always seems to be lying when one speaks to the police.

[*Les Chroniques du canard sauvage*]

ROGERS, E.W. (1864–1913)

Ev'ry member of the force

Has a watch and chain, of course;
If you want to know the time,
Ask a P'liceman!

['Ask a P'liceman', song, 1889]

SHARPE, Tom (1928–)

The South African Police would leave no stone unturned to see that nothing disturbed the even tenor of their lives.

[*Indecent Exposure* (1973)]

POLITICIANS

ADAMS, Franklin P. (1881–1960)

The trouble with this country is that there are too many politicians who believe, with a conviction based on experience, that you can fool all of the people all of the time.

[*Nods and Becks* (1944)]

ALLEN, Dave (1936–)

If John Major was drowning, his whole life would pass in front of him and he wouldn't be in it.

[*On stage*, 1991]

ANONYMOUS

MPs, ministers or otherwise, do not resign because of their integrity. They do so because they have been found out.

[Letter to *The Times*, January 1999]

ASQUITH, Herbert (1852–1928)

[On Bonar Law]
It is fitting that we should have buried the Unknown Prime Minister by the side of the Unknown Soldier.

[Remark supposedly made at Bonar Law's funeral, November 1923]

ASQUITH, Margot (1864–1945)

[Of Lloyd George]
He couldn't see a belt without hitting below it.

[*As I Remember*, 1967]

He [a politician] always has his arm round your waist and his eye on the clock.

[*As I Remember*, 1967]

BAGEHOT, Walter (1826–1877)

[Of Sir Robert Peel]

No man has come so near our definition of a constitutional statesman – the powers of a first-rate man and the creed of a second-rate man.

[*Historical Essays*, The Character of Sir Robert Peel' (1856)]

A constitutional statesman is in general a man of common opinions and uncommon abilities.

[*Historical Essays*, The Character of Sir Robert Peel' (1856)]

BALDWIN, Stanley (1867–1947)

[On becoming Prime Minister]

I met Curzon in Downing Street, from whom I got the sort of greeting a corpse would give to an undertaker.

[Remark, 1933]

[On Churchill]

Then comes Winston with his hundred-horse-power mind and what can I do?

[In G.M. Young, *Stanley Baldwin* (1952)]

[Of the House of Commons, 1918]

A lot of hard-faced men who look as if they had done very well out of the war.

[Attr.]

BALFOUR, A.J. (1848–1930)

[Comment on Winston Churchill in 1899]

I thought he was a young man of promise; but it appears he is a young man of promises.

[In Winston Churchill, *My Early Life* (1930)]

BARNARD, Robert (1936–)

Early on in his stint as a junior minister a newspaper had called him 'the thinking man's Tory', and the label had stuck, possibly because there was so little competition.

[*Political Suicide* (1986)]

BELLOC, Hilaire (1870–1953)

Los jueces se rigen por la legalidad; los políticos por la oportunidad.

Judges are guided by the law; politicians by expediency.

[*El país*, 1994]

BENNETT, Arnold (1867–1931)

Mr Lloyd George spoke for a hundred and seventeen minutes, in which period he was detected only once in the use of an argument.

[*Things That Have Interested Me* (1921–1925)]

BEVAN, Aneurin (1897–1960)

Listening to a speech by Chamberlain is like paying a visit to Woolworths; everything in its place and nothing over sixpence.

[In *Tribune*, 1937]

[Wishing to address the Prime Minister rather than the Foreign Secretary, in the House of Commons]

If we complain about the tune, there is no reason to attack the monkey when the organ grinder is present.

[Speech, 1957]

[On Churchill]

He is a man suffering from petrified adolescence.

[In Brome, *Aneurin Bevan*]

BRIGHT, John (1811–1889)

The right hon Gentleman ... has retired into what may be called his political Cave of Adullam – and he has called about him every one that was in distress and every one that was discontented.

[Speech, House of Commons, 1866]

[Of Disraeli]

He is a self-made man, and worships his creator.

[Remark, c.1868]

BROWN, George (1914–1985)

Most British statesmen have either drunk too much or womanized too much. I never fell into the second category.

[*The Observer*, 1974]

BROWN, Tina (1953–)

[Of Richard Crossman]

[He] has the jovial garrulity and air of witty indiscretion that shows he intends to give nothing away.

[*Loose Talk* (1979)]

BUCHWALD, Art (1925–)

[Of Richard Nixon]

I worship the quicksand he walks in.

[Attr.]

BUTLER, R.A. (1902–1982)

[On Sir Anthony Eden, who had been described as the offspring of a mad baronet and a beautiful woman]

That's Anthony for you – half mad baronet, half beautiful woman.

[Attr.]

CAMERON, Simon (1799–1889)

An honest politician is one who, when he is bought, will stay bought.

[Remark]

CAMPBELL, Menzies (1941–)

[Of John Smith, leader of the Labour Party]

He had all the virtues of a Scottish Presbyterian, but none of the vices.

[*The Guardian*, 1994]

CANNING, George (1770–1827)

Pitt is to Addington
As London is to Paddington.

['The Oracle' (c. 1803)]

CHARMLEY, John (1955–)

What would the man of 1938 have said of the Prime Minister of 1944?

[*Churchill: The End of Glory* (1993)]

CHURCHILL, Lord Randolph (1849–1894)

[Of Gladstone]

For the purposes of recreation he has selected the felling of trees, and we may usefully remark that his amusements, like his politics, are essentially destructive … The forest laments in order that Mr Gladstone may perspire.

[Speech, 1884]

[Of Gladstone]

An old man in a hurry.

[Speech, 1886]

CHURCHILL, Sir Winston (1874–1965)

[Of Lord Charles Beresford]

He is one of those orators of whom it was well said, 'Before they get up they do not know what they are going to say; when they are speaking, they do not know what they are saying; and when they sit down, they do not know what they have said'.

[Speech, House of Commons, December 1912]

[Of Ramsey MacDonald]

I remember, when I was a child, being taken to the celebrated Barnum's circus, which contained an exhibition of freaks and monstrosities, but the exhibit … which I most desired to see was the one described as 'The Boneless Wonder'. My parents judged that that spectacle would be too revolting and demoralising for my youthful eyes, and I have waited 50 years to see the boneless wonder sitting on the Treasury Bench.

[Speech, House of Commons, January 1931]

I have never accepted what many people have kindly said, namely that I inspired the nation. It was the nation and the race dwelling all round the globe that had the lion's heart. I had the luck to be called upon to give the roar.

[Speech at the Palace of Westminster, 1954, on his eightieth birthday]

So they told me how Mr Gladstone read Homer for fun, which I thought served him right.

[*My Early Life* (1930)]

On the night of the tenth of May [1940], at the outset of this mighty battle, I acquired the chief power in the State, which henceforth I wielded in ever-growing measure for five years and three months of world war, at the end of which time, all our enemies having surrendered unconditionally or being about to do so, I was immediately dismissed by the British electorate from all further conduct of their affairs.

[*The Second World War* (1948–1954)]

[Referring to the Soviet statesman Molotov]

I have never seen a human being who more perfectly represented the modern conception of a robot.

[*The Second World War* (1948–1954)]

[Of Clement Attlee]
He is a modest man who has a good deal to be modest about.

[In *Chicago Sunday Tribune Magazine of Books*, 1954]

CLEMENCEAU, Georges (1841–1929)

Politique intérieure: je fais la guerre; politique étrangère: je fais la guerre. Je fais toujours la guerre!
My home policy? I wage war. My foreign policy? I wage war. Always, everywhere, I wage war!

[Speech to the Chamber of Deputies, 8 March 1918]

CLINTON, Bill (1946–)

Any President that lies to the American people should resign.

[Speech as Governor of Arkansas, 1974]

COOK, Peter (1937–1995)

[Giving an impersonation of Harold Macmillan]
We exchanged many frank words in our respective languages.

[*Beyond the Fringe*, 1961]

CRITCHLEY, Julian (1930–)

The only safe pleasure for a parliamentarian is a bag of boiled sweets.

[*Listener*, 1982]

CUMMINGS, e. e. (1894–1962)

a politician is an arse upon which everyone has sat except a man.

[*1 x 1* (1944), no. 10]

CURRAN, John Philpot (1750–1817)

[Of Sir Robert Peel's smile]
… like the silver plate on a coffin.

[Quoted by Daniel O'Connell, *Hansard*, 1835]

CURTIN, John (1885–1945)

[Of R.G. Menzies]
Ah, poor Bob. It's very sad; he would rather make a point than make a friend.

[In Howard Beale, *This Inch of Time* …]

CURZON, Lord (1859–1925)

[Referring to Stanley Baldwin on his appointment as Prime Minister]
Not even a public figure. A man of no experience. And of the utmost insignificance.

[In Harold Nicolson, *Curzon: The Last Phase*]

DE GAULLE, Charles (1890–1970)

Comme un homme politique ne croit jamais ce qu'il dit, il est tout étonné quand il est cru sur parole.
Since a politician never believes what he says, he is quite surprised to be taken at his word.

[Attr.]

In order to become the master, the politician poses as the servant.

[Attr.]

DEVONSHIRE, Duke of (1895–1950)

I dreamt that I was making a speech in the House. I woke up, and by Jove I was!

[In Churchill, *Thought and Adventures*]

DISRAELI, Benjamin (1804–1881)

Though I sit down now, the time will come when you will hear me.

[Maiden Speech in the House of Commons, 1837]

[Of Gladstone]
A sophistical rhetorician, inebriated with the exuberance of his own verbosity.

[Speech, 1878]

DOUGLAS-HOME, Lady Caroline (1937–)

[Referring to her father's suitability for his new role as prime minister]
He is used to dealing with estate workers. I cannot see how anyone can say he is out of touch.

[*Daily Herald*, 1963]

DOUGLAS-HOME, Sir Alec (1903–1995)

There are two problems in my life. The political ones are insoluble and the economic ones are incomprehensible.

[Speech, 1964]

FAIRBAIRN, Sir Nicholas (1933–1995)

[On women MPs]

I can't say I've ever got visually, artistically or sexually excited by any of them. They all look as though they're from the Fifth Kiev Stalinist machine-gun parade.

[*Daily Mail, 1993*]

FOLEY, Rae (1900–1978)

He had the misleading air of open-hearted simplicity that people have come to demand of their politicians.

[*The Hundredth Door* (1950)]

FORD, Gerald R. (1913–)

[On taking the vice-presidential oath]
I am a Ford, not a Lincoln. My addresses will never be as eloquent as Lincoln's. But I will do my best to equal his brevity and plain speaking.

[Speech, published in *Washington Post*, 1973]

[Referring to his own appointment as President]
I guess it proves that in America anyone can be President.

[In Reeves, *A Ford Not a Lincoln*]

GAREL-JONES, Tristan (1941–)

My profession does not allow me to go swanning around buying pints of milk. I wouldn't be of sufficient service to my constituents if I went into shops.

[*The Independent*, 1994]

GINGRICH, Newt (1943–)

I think one of the great problems we have in the Republican Party is that we don't encourage you to be nasty. We encourage you to be neat, obedient, loyal and faithful and all those Boy Scout words, which would be great around a campfire but are lousy in politics.

GOODHART, Sir Philip (1925–)

[On Nicholas Ridley]
I have nothing against Nick's wife or his family but I think it is time he spent more time with them.

[*Sunday Telegraph*, 1990]

GUINAN, Texas (1884–1933)

A politician is a fellow who will lay down

your life for his country.

[Attr.]

HAIG, Alexander (1924–)

[Statement after an assassination attempt on President Reagan]
As of now, I am in charge at the White House.

[*The Times*, 1981]

HAIG, Douglas (1861–1928)

[Of Lord Derby]
A very weak-minded fellow, I'm afraid, and, like the feather pillow, bears the marks of the last person who has sat on him!

[Letter to his wife, 14 January 1918]

HAYDEN, Bill (1933–)

[Gough Whitlam] had many geniuses and one of them was that when he decided we were going to embark on one of the great national disasters, it was done with flair.

[*Sydney Morning Herald*, 1988]

HEALEY, Denis (1917–)

[On Geoffrey Howe's attack on his Budget proposals]
Like being savaged by a dead sheep.

[Speech, 1978]

[Of Mrs Thatcher]
For the past few months she has been charging about like some bargain basement Boadicea.

[*The Observer*, 1982]

HELPS, Sir Arthur (1813–1875)

There is one statesman of the present day, of whom I always say, that he would have escaped making the blunders that he has made if he had only ridden more in omnibuses.

[*Friends in Council* (New Series, 1859)]

HOGGART, Simon (1946–)

Reagan was probably the first modern president to treat the post as a part-time job, one way of helping to fill the otherwise blank days of retirement.

[*America* 1990]

Peter Mandelson is someone who can skulk

in broad daylight.

[*The Observer*, 1998]

HORNE, Donald Richmond (1921–)

Politicians cannot help being clowns. Political activity is essentially absurd. The hopes held for it can be high, the results tragic, but the political art itself must lack dignity: it can never match our ideals of how such things should be done.

[*The Legend of King O'Malley*]

HOWAR, Barbara (1934–)

There are no such things as good politicians and bad politicians. There are only politicians, which is to say, they all have personal axes to grind, and all too rarely are they honed for the public good.

[*Laughing All the Way* (1973)]

JACKSON, Glenda (1936–)

[On career aspirations, 1997]
My only political ambition is to be re-elected.

JARRELL, Randall (1914–1965)

President Robbins was so well adjusted to his environment that sometimes you could not tell which was the environment and which was President Robbins.

[*Pictures from an Institution* (1954)]

JOHNSON, Lyndon Baines (1908–1973)

[Correct version of the frequently-misquoted: 'He couldn't walk and chew gum at the same time']
Gerry Ford is so dumb that he can't fart and chew gum at the same time.

[In R. Reeves, *A Ford, Not a Lincoln* (1975)]

KEATING, Paul (1944–)

[On Andrew Peacock's ambitions to become leader of the Liberal Party following the 1987 elections]
Can a soufflé rise twice?

[ABC television, 1987]

KEYNES, John Maynard (1883–1946)

[Of Lloyd George]
This goat-footed bard, this half-human visitor to our age from the hag-ridden magic and enchanted woods of Celtic antiquity.

[*Essays and Sketches in Biography* (1933)]

[When asked what happened when Lloyd George was alone in a room]
When he's alone in a room, there's nobody there.

[*As I Remember*, 1967]

KHRUSHCHEV, Nikita (1894–1971)

Politicians are the same everywhere. They promise to build a bridge even when there's no river.

[Remark to journalists in the USA, 1960]

LABOUCHERE, Henry (1831–1912)

He [Labouchere] did not object, he once said, to Gladstone's always having the ace of trumps up his sleeve, but only to his pretence that God had put it there.

[In Curzon, *Modern Parliamentary Eloquence* (1913)]

LARDNER, Ring (1885–1933)

[Referring to W.H. Taft, US President 1909–1913]
He looked at me as if I was a side dish he hadn't ordered.

[In A.K. Adams, *The Home Book of Humorous Quotations*]

LE GUIN, Ursula (1929–)

He had grown up in a country run by politicians who sent the pilots to man the bombers to kill the babies to make the world safe for children to grow up in.

[*The Lathe of Heaven* (1971)]

LLOYD GEORGE, David (1863–1945)

[Of Neville Chamberlain]
He saw foreign policy through the wrong end of a municipal drainpipe.

[In Harris, *The Fine Art of Political Wit*]

When they circumcised Herbert Samuel they threw away the wrong bit.

[Attr. in *The Listener*, 1978]

[Speech in Parliament, of Sir John Simon]
The Right Honourable gentleman has sat so long on the fence that the iron has entered his soul.

[Attr.]

[Of Neville Chamberlain]

A good mayor of Birmingham in an off-year.

[Attr.; also attributed to Lord Hugh Cecil]

LONGWORTH, Alice Roosevelt (1884–1980)

[Of John Calvin Coolidge, US President 1923–1929]

He looks as if he had been weaned on a pickle.

[*Crowded Hours* (1933)]

LYNNE, Liz (1948–)

[On the behaviour of MPs]

It was like a bunch of 11-year-olds at their first secondary school.

[*The Independent*, 1992]

LYTTON, Lady Constance (1869–1923)

The first time you meet Winston [Churchill] you see all his faults and the rest of your life you spend in discovering his virtues.

[In Christopher Hassall, *Edward Marsh*]

MACLENNAN, Robert (1936–)

Tony Blair has pushed moderation to extremes.

[*The Observer*, 1996]

MACMILLAN, Harold (1894–1986)

[Of Aneurin Bevan]

He enjoys prophesying the imminent fall of the capitalist system, and is prepared to play a part, any part, in its burial, except that of mute.

[Speech, House of Commons, 1934]

When you're abroad you're a statesman: when you're at home you're just a politician.

[Speech, South African Parliament, 1958]

If people want a sense of purpose they should get it from their archbishop. They should certainly not get it from their politicians.

[In Fairlie, *The Life of Politics* (1968)]

MAJOR, John (1943–)

People with vision usually do more harm than good.

[*The Economist*, 1993]

MAXTON, James (1885–1946)

[Said to Ramsay MacDonald when he made his last speech in Parliament]

Sit down, man. You're a bloody tragedy.

[Attr.]

MENCKEN, H.L. (1880–1956)

[On President Calvin Coolidge]

Here, indeed, was his one really notable talent. He slept more than any other President, whether by day or by night … Nero fiddled, but Coolidge only snored … He had no ideas, and he was not a nuisance.

[*American Mercury*, 1933]

MENZIES, Sir Robert (1894–1978)

[In answer to a woman shouting, 'I wouldn't vote for you if you were the Archangel Gabriel']

If I were the Archangel Gabriel, madam, I'm afraid you would not be in my constituency.

[In Robinson, *The Wit of Sir Robert Menzies* (1966)]

MORLEY, Lord (1843–1905)

I am always very glad when Lord Salisbury makes a great speech … It is sure to contain at least one blazing indiscretion which it is a delight to remember.

[Speech, 1887]

MOSLEY, Sir Oswald (1896–1980)

I am not, and never have been, a man of the right. My position was on the left and is now in the centre of politics.

[Letter to *The Times*, 1968]

MUGGERIDGE, Malcolm (1903–1990)

[Of Anthony Eden]

He was not only a bore; he bored for England.

[*Tread Softly For You Tread on My Jokes* (1966)]

Macmillan seemed, in his very person, to embody the national decay he supposed himself to be confuting. He exuded a flavour of moth-balls.

[*Tread Softly For You Tread on My Jokes* (1966)]

NIXON, Richard (1913–1994)

There can be no whitewash at the White House.

[*The Observer*, 1973]

When the President does it, that means it is

POLITICIANS

[TV interview with David Frost, May 1977]

O'BRIEN, Conor Cruise (1917–)

If I saw Mr Haughey buried at midnight at a cross-roads, with a stake driven through his heart – politically speaking – I should continue to wear a clove of garlic round my neck, just in case.

[*The Observer*, 1982]

PARKER, Dorothy (1893–1967)

[Response to news that President Calvin Coolidge had died]

How could they tell?

[In Keats, *You Might As Well Live* (1970)]

POMPIDOU, Georges (1911–1974)

A statesman is a politician who places himself at the service of a nation. A politician is a statesman who places the nation at his service.

[*The Observer*, 1973]

PRIESTLEY, J.B. (1894–1984)

[Of politicians]

A number of anxious dwarfs trying to grill a whale.

[*Outcries and Asides*]

REAGAN, Ronald (1911–)

[To the surgeons about to operate on him after he was wounded in an assassination attempt]

Please assure me that you are all Republicans!

[In Boller, *Presidential Anecdotes* (1981)]

ROOSEVELT, Franklin Delano (1882–1945)

A radical is a man with both feet firmly planted in the air.

[Radio broadcast, 1939]

ROOSEVELT, Theodore (1858–1919)

The most successful politician is he who says what everybody is thinking most often and in the loudest voice.

[In Andrews, *Treasury of Humorous Quotations*]

RUSSELL, Bertrand (1872–1970)

[Of Anthony Eden]

Not a gentleman; dresses too well.

[In Alistair Cooke, *Six Men* (1977)]

SAHL, Mort (1927–)

Washington could not tell a lie; Nixon could not tell the truth; Reagan cannot tell the difference.

[*The Observer*, 1987]

[Of President Nixon]

Would you buy a second-hand car from this man?

[Attr.]

SALISBURY, 5th Marquess of (1893–1972)

The present Colonial Secretary [Iain Macleod] has been too clever by half. I believe he is a very fine bridge player. It is not considered immoral, or even bad form to outwit one's opponent at bridge. It almost seems to me as if the Colonial Secretary, when he abandoned the sphere of bridge for the sphere of politics, brought his bridge technique with him.

[Speech, House of Lords, 1961]

SHERIDAN, Richard Brinsley (1751–1816)

[Reply to Mr Dundas]

The Right Honourable Gentleman is indebted to his memory for his jests, and to his imagination for his facts.

[Speech, House of Commons]

SHORTEN, Caroline

Most Conservatives believe that a creche is something that happens between two Range Rovers in Tunbridge Wells.

[*The Independent*, September 1993]

SIMON, Guy (1944–)

Jimmy Carter had the air of a man who had never taken any decisions in his life. They had always taken him.

[*The Sunday Times*, 1978]

SMITH, F.E. (1872–1930)

Winston [Churchill] has devoted the best

years of his life to preparing his impromptu speeches.

[Attr.]

STEVENSON, Adlai (1900–1965)

A politician is a statesman who approaches every question with an open mouth.

[In Harris, *The Fine Art of Political Wit*]

TEBBITT, Norman (1931–)

I hope Mrs Thatcher will go until the turn of the century looking like Queen Victoria.

[*The Observer*, 1987]

THATCHER, Carol (1953–)

[Of her mother, Margaret Thatcher]

Reality hasn't really intervened in my mother's life since the seventies.

[*Daily Mail*, 1996]

THATCHER, Margaret (1925–)

U-turn if you want to. The lady's not for turning.

[Speech, 1980]

I don't mind how much my Ministers talk – as long as they do what I say.

[*The Observer*, 1980]

I think I have become a bit of an institution – you know, the sort of thing people expect to see around the place.

[*The Observer*, 1987]

We have become a grandmother.

[*The Observer*, 1989]

THOMAS, Norman M. (1884–1968)

[Referring to his lack of success in presidential campaigns]

While I'd rather be right than president, at any time I'm ready to be both.

[In A. Whitman, *Come to Judgment*]

TROLLOPE, Anthony (1815–1882)

It has been the great fault of our politicians that they have all wanted to do something.

[*Phineas Finn* (1869)]

TRUMAN, Harry S. (1884–1972)

A statesman is a politician who's been dead

ten or fifteen years.

[Attr.]

The President spends most of his time kissing people on the cheek in order to get them to do what they ought to do without getting kissed.

[*The Observer*, 1949]

[Referring to Vice-President Nixon's nomination for President]

You don't set a fox to watching the chickens just because he has a lot of experience in the hen house.

[Speech, 1960]

TWAIN, Mark (1835–1910)

The radical invents the views. When he has worn them out, the conservative adopts them.

[*Notebooks* (1935)]

USTINOV, Sir Peter (1921–)

When Mrs Thatcher says she has a nostalgia for Victorian values I don't think she realises that 90 per cent of her nostalgia would be satisfied in the Soviet Union.

[*The Observer*, 1987]

VICTORIA, Queen (1819–1901)

[On Gladstone's last appointment as Prime Minister]

The danger to the country, to Europe, to her vast Empire, which is involved in having all these great interests entrusted to the shaking hand of an old, wild, and incomprehensible man of 82Ω, is very great!

[Letter to Lord Lansdowne, 1892]

[Of Gladstone]

He speaks to Me as if I was a public meeting.

[In G.W.E. Russell, *Collections and Recollections* (1898), 14]

WALDEN, George (1939–)

[On the Ron Davies affair]

I suspect there is a link between the indiscretions of politicians and the nature of their work.

[*The Observer*, 1998]

WALPOLE, Robert (1676–1745)

[Of fellow-parliamentarians]

All those men have their price.

[In Coxe, *Memoirs of Sir Robert Walpole* (1798)]

WAUGH, Evelyn (1903–1966)

[Of Winston Churchill]

Simply a radio personality who outlived his prime.

[In Christopher Sykes, *Evelyn Waugh*]

WELCH, Joseph

[Army attorney denouncing Senator Joseph McCarthy during the Army-McCarthy Congressional Hearings]

Until this moment, Senator, I think I never really gauged your cruelty or your recklessness … Have you no sense of decency, sir, at long last? Have you left no sense of decency?

[*New York Times*, 1954]

WEST, Dame Rebecca (1892–1983)

Margaret Thatcher's great strength seems to be the better people know her, the better they like her. But, of course, she has one great disadvantage – she is a daughter of the people and looks trim, as the daughters of the people desire to be. Shirley Williams has such an advantage over her because she's a member of the upper-middle class and can achieve that kitchen-sink-revolutionary look that one cannot get unless one has been to a really good school.

[Interview, *The Sunday Times*, 1976]

WHITEHORN, Katherine (1926–)

It is a pity, as my husband says, that more politicians are not bastards by birth instead of vocation.

[*The Observer*, 1964]

WHITELAW, William (1918–)

I am not prepared to go about the country stirring up apathy.

[Attr.]

WILSON, Harold (1916–1995)

Hence the practised performances of latter-day politicians in the game of musical daggers: never be left holding the dagger when the music stops.

[*The Governance of Britain*]

[Of Tony Benn]

He immatures with age.

[Attr., BBC programme, 1995]

See GOVERNMENT; HOUSE OF LORDS; INSULTS; POLITICS

POLITICS

ABBOTT, Diane (1953–)

Being an MP is the sort of job all working-class parents want for their children – clean, indoors and no heavy lifting.

[*The Observer*, 1994]

ADAMS, Douglas (1952–)

Anyone who is capable of getting themselves made President should on no account be allowed to do the job.

[*The Hitch Hiker's Guide to the Galaxy* (1979)]

ADAMS, Gerry (1948–)

[Comment after the referendum on the Good Friday peace proposals]

If no one votes for us, then we'll disappear.

[*The Observer*, 1998]

We have to work to make the Omagh bombing the last violent incident in our country. The violence we have seen must be a thing of the past, over, done with and gone.

[*The Times*, 1998]

ADAMS, Henry (1838–1918)

Politics, as a practice, whatever its professions, has always been the systematic organization of hatreds.

[*The Education of Henry Adams* (1918)]

AGNEW, Spiro T. (1918–1996)

To some extent, if you've seen one city slum you've seen them all.

[Election speech, Detroit, October 1968]

AMERY, Leo (1873–1955)

Speak for England, Arthur!

[Interjection in House of Commons, 1939]

[To Neville Chamberlain, quoting Cromwell's words when he dismissed the Rump of the Long Parliament in 1653]
You have sat too long here for any good you have been doing. Depart, I say, and let us have done with you. In the name of God, go!

[Speech, House of Commons, May 1940]

ANCRAM, Michael

The Liberal Democrats are now so firmly in bed with the Labour Party that they have become little more than a shapeless lump under the Government's duvet.

[*The Observer*, May 1999]

ANDERSON, Bruce (1838–1918)

[Of Tony Blair's New Labour]
The Labour Party has decided to renounce its principles, its policies and its past.

[*The Spectator*, May 1996]

ANONYMOUS

[Pensioner's response to Juliet Peck when she introduced herself as the local Conservative candidate]
Oh, my dear, I know just how you feel. I'm a Jehovah's Witness.

[*The Observer*, 1998]

Don't tell my mother I'm in politics – she thinks I play the piano in a whorehouse.

[American saying from the Depression]

The personal is political.

ARBUTHNOT, John (1667–1735)

He warns the heads of parties against believing their own lies.

[*The Art of Political Lying* (1712)]

ARENDT, Hannah (1906–1975)

Truthfulness has never been counted among the political virtues, and lies have always been regarded as justifiable tools in political dealings.

[*Crises of the Republic* (1972)]

ARISTOTLE (384–322 BC)

Man is by nature a political animal.

[Politics]

ASHDOWN, Paddy (1941–)

Anybody who thinks that the Liberal Democrats are a racist party are staring the facts in the face.

[ITV news, 1993]

ASTOR, Nancy, Viscountess (1879–1964)

Women are young at politics, but they are old at suffering; soon they will learn that through politics they can prevent some kinds of suffering.

[*My Two Countries* (1923)]

BALDWIN, Stanley (1867–1947)

You will find in politics that you are much exposed to the attribution of false motives. Never complain and never explain.

[To Harold Nicolson, 21 July 1943, quoting Disraeli]

There are three groups that no British Prime Minister should provoke: the Vatican, the Treasury and the miners.

[Attr.]

BARNES, Julian (1946–)

One of these days a [British] Prime Minister will have the guts to call an election with the cry 'This is a comparatively unimportant time in our nation's history.'

[*The New Yorker*, 1992]

BARZAN, Gerald

You don't have to fool all the people all of the time; you just have to fool enough to get elected.

[In Lieberman, *3,500 Good Quotes for Speakers* (1983)]

BENN, Tony (1925–)

When I think of Cool Britannia, I think of old people dying of hypothermia.

[*The Observer*, 1998]

BEVAN, Aneurin (1897–1960)

This island is almost made of coal and surrounded by fish. Only an organizing genius could produce a shortage of coal and fish at the same time.

[Speech, Blackpool, 1945]

No amount of cajolery, and no attempts at ethical or social seduction, can eradicate from my heart a deep burning hatred for the Tory Party ... So far as I am concerned they are lower than vermin.

[Speech, 1948]

[Opposing unilateral nuclear disarmament]
If you carry this resolution and follow out all its implications and do not run away from it you will send a Foreign Secretary, whoever he may be, naked into the conference chamber.

[Speech, 1957]

BEVIN, Ernest (1881–1951)

[On foreign policy]
My policy is to be able to take a ticket at Victoria Station and go anywhere I damn well please.

[*Spectator*, 1951]

BIERCE, Ambrose (1842–c.1914)

Nepotism: Appointing your grandfather to office for the good of the party.

[*The Enlarged Devil's Dictionary* (1961)]

BIRCH, Nigel (1906–1981)

For the second time the Prime Minister has got rid of a Chancellor of the Exchequer who tried to get expenditure under control. Once is more than enough.

[Letter to *The Times*, 1962]

BISMARCK, Prince Otto von (1815–1898)

Die Politik ist keine exakte Wissenschaft.
Politics is not a precise science.

[Speech, Prussian House of Deputies, 1863]

Die Politik ist keine Wissenschaft ... sie ist eben eine Kunst.
Politics is not a science ... but an art.

[Speech, Reichstag, 1884]

Die Politik ist die Lehre vom Möglichen.
Politics is the art of the possible.

[Remark, 1863]

BLAIR, Tony (1953–)

If we walk away from Kosovo ... it would be a betrayal of everything this nation stands for.

[*The Independent*, March 1999]

[On the war in the Balkans]
This is not a battle for territory, this is a battle for humanity.

[Speech to Kosovan refugees, May 1999]

BRIGHT, John (1811–1889)

This party of two is like the Scotch terrier that was so covered with hair that you could not tell which was the head and which was the tail.

[Speech, House of Commons, 1866]

BRITTAIN, Vera (1893–1970)

Politics are usually the executive expression of human immaturity.

[*The Rebel Passion* (1964)]

BURCHILL, Julie (1960–)

Green politics, in the final analysis, is so popular with the rich because it contains no race or class analysis at all; politics with everything but the glow of involvement taken out.

[*Sex and Sensibility* (1992)]

BURGESS, Anthony (1917–1993)

The US presidency is a Tudor monarchy plus telephones.

[In Plimpton (ed.), *Writers at Work* (1977)]

BURKE, Edmund (1729–1797)

The conduct of a losing party never appears right: at least it never can possess the only infallible criterion of wisdom to vulgar judgments – success.

[Letter to a Member of the National Assembly (1791)]

Your representative owes you, not his industry only, but his judgement; and he betrays, instead of serving you, if he sacrifices it to your opinion.

[Speech to the Electors of Bristol, 1774]

CALLAGHAN, James (1912–)

Either back us or sack us.

[Speech, Labour Party Conference, 1977]

CALWELL, Arthur Augustus (1894–1973)

[To Arthur Fadden, in the House of Representatives]

I well recall the time when, for forty days and forty nights, you held the destiny of Australia in the hollow of your head.

[In Fred Daly, *The Politician who Laughed*]

CAMUS, Albert (1913–1960)

La politique et le sort des hommes sont formés par des hommes sans idéal et sans grandeur. Ceux qui ont une grandeur ne font pas de politique.

Politics and the fate of mankind are shaped by men without ideals and without greatness. Men who have greatness within them don't concern themselves with politics.

[*Notebooks*, 1935–1942]

CHAMPION, Henry Hyde (1859–1928)

[On the Labour Party of his day]

An army of lions led by asses.

[In R.H. Croll, *I Recall* …]

CHRISTOPHER, Warren (1925–)

Sometimes you have to learn how to give the right answer to the wrong question.

[Remark, 1994]

CLARK, Alan (1928–)

There are no true friends in politics. We are all sharks circling and waiting, for traces of blood to appear in the water.

[*Diary*, 1990]

CLINTON, Bill (1946–)

What we believe in is what works.

[*The Times*, 1999]

COLERIDGE, Samuel Taylor (1772–1834)

In politics, what begins in fear usually ends in folly.

[*Table Talk* (1835)]

COLSON, Charles (1931–)

[To campaign staff, 1972]

I would walk over my grandmother if necessary to get Nixon re-elected!

[*Born Again* (1976)]

CROKER, John Wilson (1780–1857)

[First use of the phrase 'the Conservative Party']

We now are, as we always have been, decidedly and conscientiously attached to what is called the Tory, and which might with more propriety be called the Conservative, party.

[*Quarterly Review*, 1830]

DARROW, Clarence (1857–1938)

When I was a boy I was told that anybody could become President. I'm beginning to believe it.

[In Irving Stone, *Clarence Darrow for the Defence* (1941)]

DE GAULLE, Charles (1890–1970)

I have come to the conclusion that politics are too serious a matter to be left to the politicians.

[Attr.]

DERBY, Earl of (1799–1869)

The Conservatives are the weakest among the intellectual classes: as is natural.

[Letter to Disraeli]

DISRAELI, Benjamin (1804–1881)

A man may speak very well in the House of Commons, and fail very completely in the House of Lords. There are two distinct styles requisite: I intend, in the course of my career, if I have time, to give a specimen of both.

[*The Young Duke* (1831)]

The practice of politics in the East may be defined by one word – dissimulation.

[*Contarini Fleming* (1832)]

A majority is always the best repartee.

[*Tancred* (1847)]

Party is organized opinion.

[Speech, Meeting of Society for Increasing Endowments of Small Livings in the Diocese of Oxford, 1864]

England does not love coalitions.

[Speech, 1852]

Finality is not the language of politics.

[Speech, 1859]

Damn your principles! Stick to your party.

[Attr.]

EINSTEIN, Albert (1879–1955)

An empty stomach is not a good political adviser.

[*Cosmic Religion* (1931)]

EISENHOWER, Dwight D. (1890–1969)

There is one thing about being President – nobody can tell you when to sit down.

[*The Observer*, 1953]

EWING, Winnie (1929–)

[On entering Westminster after winning a 1967 by-election for the SNP]

As I took my seat it was said by political pundits that 'a chill ran along the Labour back benches looking for a spine to run up'.

[Attr.]

The Scottish Parliament, adjourned on 25th March 1707, is hereby reconvened.

[Speech at the opening of the new Parliament on 12th May 1999]

FIELDS, W.C. (1880–1946)

Hell, I never vote for anybody. I always vote against.

[In Taylor, *W. C. Fields: His Follies and Fortunes* (1950)]

FISHER, H.A.L. (1856–1940)

Politics is the art of human happiness.

[*History of Europe* (1935)]

FOUCAULT, Michel (1926–1984)

[In 1966, when Les Mots et les choses appeared, he was attacked for this remark]

Marxism exists in nineteenth-century thought in the same way as a fish exists in water; that is, it stops breathing anywhere else.

[In Eribon, *Michel Foucault* (1989)]

FROST, Robert (1874–1963)

I never dared be radical when young

For fear it would make me conservative when old.

['Precaution' (1936)]

A liberal is a man too broadminded to take his own side in a quarrel.

[Attr.]

GAITSKELL, Hugh (1906–1963)

All terrorists, at the invitation of the Government, end up with drinks at the Dorchester.

[Letter to *The Guardian*, 1977]

GALBRAITH, J.K. (1908–)

Politics is not the art of the possible. It consists in choosing between the disastrous and the unpalatable.

[*Ambassador's Journal* (1969)]

Few things are as immutable as the addiction of political groups to the ideas by which they have once won office.

[*The Affluent Society* (1958)]

There are times in politics when you must be on the right side and lose.

[*The Observer*, 1968]

GARNER, John Nance (1868–1937)

[The Vice-Presidency] isn't worth a pitcher of warm piss.

[Attr.]

HAILSHAM, Quintin Hogg, Baron (1907–)

[On the Profumo affair]

A great party is not to be brought down because of a squalid affair between a woman of easy virtue and a proved liar.

[Interview, BBC TV, 1963]

HAVEL, Václav (1936–)

Ideology is a special way of relating to the world. It offers human beings the illusion of an identity, of dignity, and of morality, while making it easier for them to part with it.

[*Living in Truth* (1987)]

HAYES, Jerry

Conservative party policy is not unlike a Wagner opera. It is not always as bad as it sounds.

[*The Observer*, 'Sayings of the Year', December 1998]

HEALEY, Denis (1917–)

It is a good thing to follow the first law of holes; if you are in one, stop digging.

[*The Observer*, 1988]

HELLMAN, Lillian (1905–1984)

I cannot and will not cut my conscience to fit this year's fashions, even though I long ago came to the conclusion that I was not a political person and could have no comfortable place in any political group.

[Letter to the US House of Representatives Committee on Un-American Activities, 1952]

HIGHTOWER, Jim (1933–)

Only things in the middle of the road are yellow lines and dead armadillos.

[Attr.]

HITLER, Adolf (1889–1945)

Wesentlich ist die politische Willensbildung der gesamten Nation, sie ist der Ausgangspunkt für politische Aktionen.

What is essential is the formation of the political will of the entire nation: that is the starting point for political actions.

[Speech, 1932]

HORNE, Donald Richmond (1921–)

Politics is both fraud and vision.

[*The Legend of King O'Malley*]

ICKES, Harold L. (1874–1952)

[On his resignation as Secretary of the Interior after a dispute with President Truman]

I am against government by crony.

[Remark, 1946]

JACKSON, Glenda (1936–)

[Describing her first impressions of being the new MP for Hampstead and Highgate]

People have said to me that your first week in the Commons is like your first week at school. My school was never like this. People told you what to do, they were less friendly, and there were more girls.

[*The List*, 1992]

JEFFE, Sherry Bebitch

[A definition of the street-car theory of American politics]

To win, a candidate must be standing on the right street corner at the right time when a street-car is going in the right direction, and must have the right amount of change in their pockets.

[*The Independent* on Sunday, 1992]

JENKINS, Roy (1920–)

[Used in connection with the SDP, established in 1981]

Breaking the mould of British politics.

[Attr.]

JOHNSON, Lyndon Baines (1908–1973)

If you're in politics and you can't tell when you walk into a room who's for you and who's against you, then you're in the wrong line of work.

[In B. Mooney, *The Lyndon Johnson Story* (1956)]

JOHNSON, Samuel (1709–1784)

Why, Sir, most schemes of political improvement are very laughable things.

[In Boswell, *The Life of Samuel Johnson* (1791)]

Politics are now nothing more than a means of rising in the world.

[In Boswell, *The Life of Samuel Johnson* (1791)]

JOSEPH, Sir Keith (1918–1994)

We spend more on welfare without achieving well-being, while creating dangerous levels of dependency.

[Speech to Oxford Union, 1975]

JUNIUS (1769–1772)

There is a holy mistaken zeal in politics as well as in religion. By persuading others, we convince ourselves.

[*Letters* (1769–1771)]

KENNEDY, Charles (1959–)

Voting Tory is like being in trouble with the police. You'd rather the neighbours didn't know.

[Speech, Liberal Democrat Conference, 1994]

Paddy Ashdown is the only party leader to be a trained killer. Although, to be fair, Mrs Thatcher was self-taught.

[*The Observer*, 1998]

KINNOCK, Neil (1942–)

[Attacking militant members in Liverpool]

The grotesque chaos of a Labour council – a Labour council – hiring taxis to scuttle around a city handing out redundancy notices to its own workers.

[Speech, Labour Party Conference, Bournemouth, 1985]

KISSINGER, Henry (1923–)

Foreign policy should not be confused with missionary work.

[In *London Review of Books*, 1992, review of *Kissinger: A Biography*]

LA BRUYÈRE, Jean de (1645–1696)

L'esprit de parti abaisse les plus grands hommes jusques aux petitesses du peuple.

Party loyalty brings the greatest of men down to the petty level of the masses.

[*Les caractères ou les moeurs de ce siècle* (1688)]

MACMILLAN, Harold (1894–1986)

Let's be frank about it; most of our people have never had it so good.

[Speech, 1957]

[On the life of a Foreign Secretary]

Forever poised between a cliché and an indiscretion.

[*Newsweek*, 1956]

As usual the Liberals offer a mixture of sound and original ideas. Unfortunately none of the sound ideas is original and none of the original ideas is sound.

[*The Observer*, 1961]

I have never found in a long experience of politics that criticism is ever inhibited by ignorance.

[Attr.]

MAJOR, John (1943–)

[Commenting on the Tories' disastrous results in local government elections]

For those people who may suggest that at the moment the Conservative Party has its back to the wall, I would simply say we will do precisely what the British nation has done all through its history when it had its back to the wall: turn round and fight for the things it believes.

[*The Observer*, May 1996]

MANDELA, Nelson (1918–)

The struggle is my life.

[Letter from underground, 1961]

MANDELSON, Peter

[On the difference between New Labour and the Conservatives]

When was the last time you heard of a Tory Minister resigning to spend more time with his mortgage?

[*The Observer*, 1999]

MAO TSE-TUNG (1893–1976)

All reactionaries are paper tigers.

[*Quotations from Chairman Mao Tse-Tung*]

MARR, Andrew

[On political apathy under New Labour]

Today's ministers are a bit like actors in a huge, dark theatre, initially delighted at the absence of heckling or booing, but beginning uneasily to ask themselves whether anyone is still watching.

[Article in *The Observer*, May1999]

MAXTON, James (1885–1946)

[On a man proposing that the ILP should no longer be affiliated to the Labour Party]

If my friend cannot ride two horses – what's he doing in the bloody circus?

[In G. McAllister, *James Maxton: the Portrait of a Rebel* (1935)]

MAYHEW, Christopher (1915–1997)

[On the Munich Agreement]

A policy of *reculer pour mieux reculer*.

[Speech, Oxford Union, 1938]

MCCARTHY, Senator Eugene (1916–)

Being in politics is like being a football coach. You have to be smart enough to understand the game and dumb enough to think it's important.

[Interview, 1968]

MENZIES, Sir Robert (1894–1978)

A Prime Minister exercises his greatest public influence by creating a public impression of himself, hoping all the time that the people will be generous rather than just.

[In Mayer and Nelson, *Australian Politics: A Third Reader*]

MILL, John Stuart (1806–1873)

The Conservatives ... being by the law of their existence the stupidest party.

[*Considerations on Representative Government* (1861)]

A party of order or stability, and a party of progress or reform, are both necessary elements of a healthy state of political life.

[*On Liberty* (1859)]

MILLIGAN, Spike (1918–)

[Remark made about a pre-election poll]
One day the don't-knows will get in, and then where will we be?

[Attr.]

MITCHELL, Austin

[Description of New Labour]
A children's crusade led by the early middle-aged.

[*The Observer*, 1998]

MORTON, Rogers (1914–1979)

[Refusing to make any last-ditch attempts to rescue President Ford's re-election campaign, 1976]
I'm not going to re-arrange the furniture on the deck of the Titanic.

[Attr.]

NAPOLEON I (1769–1821)

[To Josephine in 1809, on divorcing her for reasons of state]
I still love you, but in politics there is no heart, only head.

[Attr.]

ORWELL, George (1903–1950)

No book is genuinely free from political bias.

The opinion that art should have nothing to do with politics is itself a political attitude.

['Why I Write' (1946)]

In our time, political speech and writing are largely the defence of the indefensible.

[*Shooting an Elephant* (1950)]

PANKHURST, Dame Christabel (1880–1958)

Never lose your temper with the Press or the public is a major rule of political life.

[*Unshackled* (1959)]

PANKHURST, Emmeline (1858–1928)

The argument of the broken pane of glass is the most valuable argument in modern politics.

[Attr.]

PARKINSON, C. Northcote (1909–1993)

The British, being brought up on team games, enter their House of Commons in the spirit of those who would rather be doing something else. If they cannot be playing golf or tennis, they can at least pretend that politics is a game with very similar rules.

[*Parkinson's Law* (1958)]

It is now known ... that men enter local politics solely as a result of being unhappily married.

[*Parkinson's Law* (1958)]

PARRIS, Matthew (1949–)

Being an MP feeds your vanity and starves your self-respect.

[*The Times*, 1994]

[On a particularly sycophantic question to Prime Minister Tony Blair from John Hatton MP]
To call it toadying would be to invite a group libel action from toads.

[*The Times*, 1998]

PAXMAN, Jeremy (1950–)

[Interview with Henry Kissinger]
Didn't you feel a fraud accepting the Nobel Peace Prize?

[BBC radio programme *Start the Week*, 1999]

PEACOCK, Thomas Love (1785–1866)

A Sympathizer would seem to imply a certain degree of benevolent feeling. Nothing of the kind. It signifies a ready-made accomplice in any species of political villainy.

[*Gryll Grange* (1861)]

POWELL, Enoch (1912–1998)

Above any other position of eminence, that of Prime Minister is filled by fluke.

[*The Observer*, 1987]

PRESCOTT, John (1938–)

[During a debate between Prescott, Tony Blair and Margaret Beckett at the time of the contest for the Labour leadership]

We're in danger of loving ourselves to death.

[*The Observer*, 1994]

The Green Belt is a Labour achievement, and we intend to build on it.

[*The Observer*, 'Sayings of the Year', 1998]

RAWNSLEY, Andrew

A British Prime Minister in command of a parliamentary majority is an elected dictator with vastly more domestic power than an American President.

[Article, *The Observer*, May 1999]

REAGAN, Ronald (1911–)

Politics is supposed to be the second oldest profession. I have come to understand that it bears a very close resemblance to the first.

[Remark at a conference, 1977]

Politics is not a bad profession. If you succeed there are many rewards, if you disgrace yourself you can always write a book.

[Attr.]

ROGERS, Will (1879–1935)

The more you read ... about this Politics thing, you got to admit that each party is worse than the other.

[*Autobiography of Will Rogers* (1949)]

England elects a Labour Government. When a man goes in for politics over here, he has no time to labour, and any man that labours has no time to fool with politics. Over there politics is an obligation; over here it's a business.

[*Autobiography of Will Rogers* (1949), 14]

RUSK, Dean (1909–1994)

[Of the Cuban missile crisis]

We're eye-ball to eye-ball and I think the other fellow just blinked.

[Remark, 1962]

SHAW, George Bernard (1856–1950)

He knows nothing; and he thinks he knows everything. That points clearly to a political career.

[*Major Barbara* (1907)]

SHAWCROSS, Lord (1902–)

We are the masters at the moment, and not only at the moment, but for a very long time to come.

[Speech, House of Commons, 1946; usually quoted as 'We are the masters now.']

SHERIDAN, Richard Brinsley (1751–1816)

[On being asked to apologize for calling a fellow MP a liar]

Mr Speaker, I said the honourable member was a liar it is true and I am sorry for it. The honourable member may place the punctuation where he pleases.

[Attr.]

SHERMAN, William Tecumseh (1820–1891)

I would not for a million dollars subject myself and family to the ordeal of a political canvass and afterwards to a four years' service in the White House.

[Letter to his brother, 1884]

SKELTON, Noel (1880–1935)

... to state as clearly as may be what means lie ready to develop a property-owning democracy, to bring the industrial and economic status of the wage-earner abreast of his political and education, to make democracy stable and four-square.

[Article in the *Spectator*, 19 May 1923]

SMITH, Sir Cyril (1928–)
[On the House of Commons]
The longest running farce in the West End.
[Remark to foreign press, 1973]

SOMOZA, Anastasio (1925–1980)
You won the elections. But I won the count.
[*The Guardian*, 1977]

SOPER, Donald (1903–1998)
[On the quality of debate in the House of Lords]
It is, I think, good evidence of life after death.
[*The Listener*, 1978]

SPEIGHT, Johnny (1920–1998)
If Her Majesty stood for Parliament – if the
Tory Party had any sense and made Her its
leader instead of that grammar school twit
Heath – us Tories, mate, would win every
election we went in for.
[*Till Death Do Us Part*, television programme]

STEEL, Sir David (1938–)
Go back to your constituencies and prepare
for government!
[Speech to party conference, 1981]

I sense that the British electorate is now
itching to break out once and for all from the
discredited straight-jacket of the past.
[*The Times*, 1987]

STEVENSON, Adlai (1900–1965)
[Of the Republican Party]
[Needs to be] dragged kicking and
screaming into the twentieth century.
[In K. Tynan, *Curtains* (1961)]

I will make a bargain with the Republicans. If
they will stop telling lies about Democrats,
we will stop telling lies about them.
[Speech, 1952]

**STEVENSON, Robert Louis
(1850–1894)**
Politics is perhaps the only profession for
which no preparation is thought necessary.
[*Familiar Studies of Men and Books* (1882)]

These are my politics: to change what we
can; to better what we can; but still to bear in
mind that man is but a devil weakly fettered

by some generous beliefs and impositions;
and for no word however sounding, and no
cause however just and pious, to relax the
stricture of these bonds.
[*The Dynamiter* (1885)]

STOPPARD, Tom (1937–)
The House of Lords, an illusion to which I
have never been able to subscribe –
reponsibility without power, the prerogative
of the eunuch throughout the ages.
[*Lord Malquist and Mr Moon* (1966)]

THATCHER, Margaret (1925–)
I don't understand Cool Britannia. I believe in
Rule Britannia.
[*The Observer*, 1998]

Let our children grow tall, and some taller
than others if they have it in them to do so.
[Speech, US tour, 1975]

Britain is no longer in the politics of the
pendulum, but of the ratchet.
[Speech, 1977]

Victorian values … were the values when our
country became great.
[Television interview, 1982]

No one would have remembered the Good
Samaritan if he'd only had good intentions.
He had money as well.
[*The Observer*, 1980]

THORPE, Jeremy (1929–)
[Remark on Macmillan's Cabinet purge, 1962]
Greater love hath no man than this, that he
lay down his friends for his life.
[Speech, 1962]

TOCQUEVILLE, Alexis de (1805–1859)
*Il faut une science politique nouvelle á un monde
tout nouveau.*
A new world demands a new political
science.
[*De la démocratie en Amérique* (1835–1840)]

TONER, Pauline Therese (1935–1989)
[The credo of the first woman Minister in the
history of the Victorian Parliament]
Why join a women's group to lobby

government ministers when you can become a minister yourself?

[Australian Women's Weekly, 1982]

TROLLOPE, Anthony (1815–1882)

It is the necessary nature of a political party in this country to avoid, as long as it can be avoided, the consideration of any question which involves a great change … The best carriage horses are those which can most steadily hold back against the coach as it trundles down the hill.

[Phineas Redux (1874)]

TRUMAN, Harry S. (1884–1972)

If you can't stand the heat, get out of the kitchen.

[Mr Citizen (1960), 15]

USTINOV, Sir Peter (1921–)

I could never bear to be a politician. I couldn't bear to be right all the time.

[The Observer, 1998]

VALÉRY, Paul (1871–1945)

La politique est l'art d'empêcher les gens de se mêler de ce qui les regarde.

Politics is the art of preventing people from becoming involved in affairs which concern them.

[As Such 2 (1943)]

VIDAL, Gore (1925–)

Any American who is prepared to run for President should automatically, by definition, be disqualified from ever doing so.

[Attr.]

WALDEN, George (1939–)

[On John Major's policy of non-cooperation with Europe over the export ban on British beef]
Patriots are not supposed to make fools of their own people.

[The Times, May 1996]

WATEN, Judah Leon (1911–1985)

The art of politics is to make more friends than enemies.

[Remark to S. Murray-Smith]

WATERHOUSE, Keith (1929–)

A newspaper poll found that fewer than one in twenty people could explain the government's third way. Some thought it was a religious cult, others a sexual position, and one man asked if it were a plan to widen the M25.

[The Observer, 1998]

WELLINGTON, Duke of (1769–1852)

[On seeing the first Reformed Parliament]
I never saw so many shocking bad hats in my life.

[In Fraser, Words on Wellington (1889)]

WILSON, Harold (1916–1995)

A week is a long time in politics.

[Remark, 1964]

The Labour Party is like a stage-coach. If you rattle along at great speed everybody inside is too exhilarated or too seasick to cause any trouble. But if you stop everybody gets out and argues about where to go next.

[In L. Smith, Harold Wilson, The Authentic Portrait]

ZAPPA, Frank (1940–1993)

Politics is the entertainment branch of industry.

[Attr.]

See COMMUNISM; DEMOCRACY; DIPLOMACY; FASCISM; GOVERNMENT; HOUSE OF LORDS; LIBERALS; MONARCHY AND ROYALTY; OPPOSITION; POLITICIANS; SOCIALISM

POPULARITY

BENNET, Tony

I think one of the reasons I'm popular again is because I'm wearing a tie. You have to be different.

LAMB, Charles (1775–1834)

How I like to be liked, and what I do to be liked!

[Letter to D. Wordsworth, 1821]

MILLER, Arthur (1915–)

He's liked, but he's not well liked.

[*Death of a Salesman* (1949)]

See CELEBRITY; FAME

PORNOGRAPHY

ALLBEURY, Ted (1917–)

The real stuff's inside. Whether you want your porn in black and white, full-colour litho, on film or on gramophone records and in any one of five languages, this is Stockholm's place for connoisseurs. There are no pictures of old slags and tattooed sailors here. The girls in the pictures are young and pretty and even the Great Danes are registered at the Swedish Kennel Club.

[*Snowball* (1976)]

ALLEN, Woody (1935–)

Fielding Mellish: I once stole a pornographic book that was printed in braille. I used to rub the dirty parts.

[Film *Bananas*, (1971)]

CRISP, Quentin (1908–)

What is wrong with pornography is that it is a successful attempt to sell sex for more than it is worth.

[In Kettlehack (ed.), *The Wit and Wisdom of Quentin Crisp*]

HUXLEY, Aldous (1894–1963)

Real orgies are never so exciting as pornographic books.

[*Point Counter Point* (1928)]

LAWRENCE, D.H. (1885–1930)

Pornography is the attempt to insult sex, to do dirt on it.

[*Phoenix* (1936)]

RUSSELL, Bertrand (1872–1970)

Obscenity is what happens to shock some elderly and ignorant magistrate.

[*Look* magazine]

SPEIGHT, Johnny (1920–1998)

Don't be daft. You don't get any pornography on there, not on the telly. Get filth, that's all. The only place you get pornography is in yer Sunday papers.

[*Till Death Do Us Part*, television programme]

See CENSORSHIP; SEX

POVERTY

ANOUILH, Jean (1910–1987)

Moi j'adorerais être pauvre! Seulement, je voudrais être vraiment pauvre. Tout ce qui est excessif m'enchante.

I should love to be poor, as long as I was excessively poor! Anything in excess is quite delightful.

[*Ring Round the Moon* (1948)]

BAGEHOT, Walter (1826–1877)

Poverty is an anomaly to rich people. It is very difficult to make out why people who want dinner do not ring the bell.

[*Literary Studies* (1879)]

BEHN, Aphra (1640–1689)

Come away; poverty's catching.

[*The Rover* (1677)]

**THE BIBLE
(King James Version)**

The poor always ye have with you.

[*John*, 12:8]

BLAKE, William (1757–1827)

Is this a holy thing to see,
In a rich and fruitful land,
Babes reducd to misery,
Fed with cold and usurous hand?

['Holy Thursday' (1794)]

BLUNDEN, Edmund (1896–1974)

All things they have in common being so poor,
And their one fear, Death's shadow at the door.
Each sundown makes them mournful, each sunrise
Brings back the brightness in their failing eyes.

[*The Waggoner and Other Poems* (1920)]

BOOTH, General William (1829–1912)

This Submerged Tenth – is it, then, beyond the reach of the nine-tenths in the midst of whom they live?

[*In Darkest England* (1890)]

CHAMFORT, Nicolas (1741–1794)

Les pauvres sont les nègres de l'Europe.
The poor are the negroes of Europe.

[*Maximes et Pensées* (1796)]

COBBETT, William (1762–1835)

To be poor and independent is very nearly an impossibility.

[*Advice to Young Men* (1829)]

COWPER, William (1731–1800)

[Of a burglar]
He found it inconvenient to be poor.

['Charity' (1782)]

CRABBE, George (1754–1832)

The murmuring poor, who will not fast in peace.

[*The Newspaper* (1785)]

FARQUHAR, George (1678–1707)

'Tis still my maxim, that there is no scandal like rags, nor any crime so shameful as poverty.

[*The Beaux' Stratagem* (1707)]

FRANCE, Anatole (1844–1924)

It is only the poor who pay cash, and that not from virtue, but because they are refused credit.

[In J.R. Solly, *A Cynic's Breviary*]

GAY, John (1685–1732)

No, Sir, tho' I was born and bred in England, I can dare to be poor, which is the only thing now-a-days men are asham'd of.

[*Polly* (1729)]

GELDOF, Bob (1954–)

I'm not interested in the bloody system! Why has he no food? Why is he starving to death?

[In Care, *Sayings of the Eighties* (1989)]

HARDY, Frank (1917–)

Only the poor will help the poor.

[*Legends from Benson's Valley* (1963)]

HORVÁTH, Ödön von (1901–1938)

Wer arm ist, darf sich was vorlügen – das ist sein Recht.
Vielleicht sein einziges Recht.
Whoever is poor may lie to himself – that is his right.
Perhaps his only right.

[*A Child of our Time* (1938)]

JEROME, Jerome K. (1859–1927)

It is easy enough to say that poverty is no crime. No; if it were men wouldn't be ashamed of it. It is a blunder, though, and is punished as such. A poor man is despised the whole world over.

[*Idle Thoughts of an Idle Fellow* (1886)]

JOHNSON, Samuel (1709–1784)

This mournful truth is ev'rywhere confess'd,
Slow rises worth by poverty depress'd.

[*London: A Poem* (1738)]

A man, doubtful of his dinner, or trembling at a creditor, is not much disposed to abstracted meditation, or remote enquiries.

[*The Lives of the Most Eminent English Poets* (1781)]

Resolve not to be poor: whatever you have, spend less. Poverty is a great enemy to human happiness; it certainly destroys liberty, and it makes some virtues impracticable and others extremely difficult.

[Letter to Boswell, 1782]

JUVENAL (c.60–130)

Nil habet infelix paupertas durius in se
Quam quod ridiculos homines facit.
Nothing is harder to bear about luckless poverty than the way it exposes men to ridicule.

[*Satires*]

Cantabit vacuus coram latrone viator.
The poure man when he goth by the weye
Bifore the thieves he may synge and playe.

[*Satires*]

Haud facile emergunt quorum virtutibus obstat
Res angusta domi.
Rarely they rise by virtue's aid, who lie

Plung'd in the depths of helpless poverty.

[*Satires*]

LANDON, Letitia Elizabeth (1802–1838)

Few, save the poor, feel for the poor.

['The Poor']

MARX, Groucho (1895–1977)

Look at me: I worked my way up from nothing to a state of extreme poverty.

[*Monkey Business*, film, 1931]

MEUDELL, George Dick (1860–1936)

Until we partially abolish poverty at home we have no right to burden ourselves with millions of paupers from abroad. What we have, we hold. AUSTRALIA FOR THE AUSTRALIANS.

[*The Pleasant Career of a Spendthrift in London* (1929)]

PEACOCK, Thomas Love (1785–1866)

Respectable means rich, and decent means poor. I should die if I heard my family called decent.

[*Crotchet Castle* (1831)]

PROVERB

When poverty comes in at the door, love flies out of the window.

ROOSEVELT, Franklin Delano (1882–1945)

… the forgotten man at the bottom of the economic pyramid.

[Radio broadcast, 1932]

I see one-third of a nation ill-housed, ill-clad, ill-nourished.

[Second Inaugural Address, 1937]

SAKI (1870–1916)

'No one has ever said it,' observed Lady Caroline, 'but how painfully true it is that the poor have us always with them!'.

[Attr.]

SHAW, George Bernard (1856–1950)

Cusins: Do you call poverty a crime?
Undershaft: The worst of crimes. All the other crimes are virtues beside it: all the other

dishonours are chivalry itself by comparison.

[*Major Barbara* (1907)]

The greatest of our evils and the worst of our crimes is poverty.

[*Major Barbara* (1907)]

SHUTER, Edward (1728–1776)

[Explaining why he did not mend his stocking]
A hole is the accident of a day, but a darn is premeditated poverty.

[*Dictionary of National Biography* (1897)]

SMITH, Adam (1723–1790)

Poverty, though it does not prevent the generation, is extremely unfavourable to the rearing of children. The tender plant is produced, but in so cold a soil and so severe a climate, soon withers and dies.

[*Wealth of Nations* (1776)]

SMITH, Sydney (1771–1845)

Poverty is no disgrace to a man, but it is confoundedly inconvenient.

[In J. Potter Briscoe (ed.), *Sydney Smith* (1900)]

SMOLLETT, Tobias (1721–1771)

Hark ye, Clinker, you are a most notorious offender. You stand convicted of sickness, hunger, wretchedness, and want.

[*The Expedition of Humphry Clinker* (1771)]

TERESA, Mother (1910–1997)

… the poor are our brothers and sisters … people in the world who need love, who need care, who have to be wanted.

[*Time*, 1975]

TRACY, Spencer (1900–1967)

[Of leaner times in his life]
There were times my pants were so thin I could sit on a dime and tell if it was heads or tails.

[In Swindell, *Spencer Tracy*]

WILDE, Oscar (1854–1900)

We are often told that the poor are grateful for charity. Some of them are, no doubt, but the best amongst the poor are never grateful. They are ungrateful, discontented, disobedient, and rebellious. They are quite right to be so.

['The Soul of Man under Socialism' (1891)]

See HUNGER; MONEY AND WEALTH

POWER

ACTON, Lord (1834–1902)
Power tends to corrupt, and absolute power corrupts absolutely. Great men are almost always bad men ... There is no worse heresy than that the office sanctifies the holder of it.

[Letter to Bishop Mandell Creighton, 1887]

ADAMS, Abigail (1744–1818)
I am more and more convinced that man is a dangerous creature and that power, whether vested in many or a few, is ever grasping, and like the grave, cries 'Give, give.'

[Letter to John Adams, 1775]

AMIS, Kingsley (1922–1995)
Generally, nobody behaves decently when they have power.

[*Radio Times*, 1992]

ANDREOTTI, Giulio (1919–)
Il potere logora chi non ce l'ha.
Power wears down the man who doesn't have it.

[In Biagi, *The Good and the Bad* (1989)]

Concepts such as truth, justice, compassion are often the only bulwarks which stand against ruthless power.

[*Index on Censorship*, 1994]

BACON, Francis (1561–1626)
Men in great place are thrice servants: servants of the sovereign or state, servants of fame, and servants of business ... It is a strange desire to seek power and to lose liberty.

['Of Great Place' (1625)]

BEAVERBROOK, Lord (1879–1964)
[Of Lloyd George]

He did not care in which direction the car was travelling, so long as he remained in the driver's seat.

[*New Statesman*, 1963]

BURKE, Edmund (1729–1797)
Those who have been once intoxicated with power, and have derived any kind of emolument from it, even though but for one year, never can willingly abandon it.

[*Letter to a Member of the National Assembly* (1791)]

CLARE, Dr Anthony (1942–)
Apart from the occasional saint, it is difficult for people who have the smallest amount of power to be nice.

[In Care, *Sayings of the Eighties* (1989)]

CRISP, Quentin (1908–)
I expect that rape and murder, either separately or mixed together, fill the fantasies of most men and all stylists. They are the supreme acts of ascendancy over others; they yield the only moments when a man is certain beyond all doubt that his message has been received. Of the few who live out these dreams, some preface rape with murder so as to avoid embracing a partner who might criticize their technique.

[In Guy Kettlehack (ed.), *The Wit and Wisdom of Quentin Crisp*]

DISRAELI, Benjamin (1804–1881)
I repeat ... that all power is a trust – that we are accountable for its exercise – that, from the people, and for the people, all springs, and all must exist.

[*Vivian Grey* (1826)]

EISENHOWER, Dwight D. (1890–1969)
In the councils of government, we must guard against the acquisition of unwarranted influence, whether sought or unsought, by the military-industrial complex. The potential for the disastrous rise of misplaced power exists and will persist.

[Farewell address, 17 January 1961]

FAIRLIE, Henry (1924–1990)

I have several times suggested that what I call the 'Establishment' in this country is today more powerful than ever before. By the 'Establishment' I do not mean only the centres of official power – though they are certainly part of it – but rather the whole matrix of official and social relations within which power is exercised … the 'Establishment' can be seen at work in the activities of, not only the Prime Minister, the Archbishop of Canterbury and the Earl Marshall, but of such lesser mortals as the Chairman of the Arts Council, the Director-General of the BBC, and even the editor of the Times Literary Supplement, not to mention dignitaries like Lady Violet Bonham-Carter.

[*Spectator*, 1955]

FAUST, Beatrice Eileen (1939–)

Women's Liberationists are both right and wrong when they say that rape is not about sex but about power: for men, sex is power, unless culture corrects biology.

[*Women, Sex and Pornography* (1980)]

GIELGUD, Sir John (1904–)

I have never been interested in any power except my own power in the theatre, which I love.

[*The Independent*, 1994]

GOERING, Hermann (1893–1946)

Guns will make us powerful; butter will only make us fat.

[Broadcast, 1936]

HALIFAX, Lord (1633–1695)

There is … no other Fundamental, but that every Supream Power must be Arbitrary.

[*Political, Moral and Miscellaneous Thoughts and Reflections* (1750)]

HITLER, Adolf (1889–1945)

Deutschland wird entweder Weltmacht oder überhaupt nicht sein.

Germany will either be a world power or will not exist at all.

[*Mein Kampf* (1927)]

JONES, Sir William (1746–1794)

My opinion is, that power should always be distrusted, in whatever hands it is placed.

[In Teignmouth, *Life of Sir W. Jones* (1835)]

KISSINGER, Henry (1923–)

Power is the ultimate aphrodisiac.

[Attr.]

KUNDERA, Milan (1929–)

The struggle of man against power is the struggle of memory against forgetting.

[Attr.]

LONG, Huey (1893–1935)

I looked around at the little fishes present and said, 'I'm the Kingfish.'

[In A. Schlesinger Jr, *The Politics of Upheaval* (1961)]

MALCOLM X (1925–1965)

Power never takes a back step – only in the face of more power.

[*Malcolm X Speaks*, 1965]

MAO TSE-TUNG (1893–1976)

Every Communist must grasp the truth. Political power grows out of the barrel of a gun.

[Speech, 1938]

MILL, John Stuart (1806–1873)

The only purpose for which power can be rightfully exercised over any member of a civilized community, against his will, is to prevent harm to others. His own good, either physical or moral, is not sufficient warrant.

[*On Liberty* (1859)]

PITT, William (1708–1778)

Unlimited power is apt to corrupt the minds of those who possess it.

[Speech, House of Commons, 1770]

RENAN, J. Ernest (1823–1892)

'Savoir c'est pouvoir' est le plus beau mot qu'on ait dit.

'Knowledge is power' is the finest idea ever put into words.

[*Dialogues et fragments philosophiques* (1876)]

RUSSELL, Bertrand (1872–1970)

The megalomaniac differs from the narcissist

by the fact that he wishes to be powerful rather than charming, and seeks to be feared rather than loved. To this type belong many lunatics and most of the great men of history.

[*The Conquest of Happiness* (1930)]

STEVENSON, Adlai (1900–1965)

Power corrupts, but lack of power corrupts absolutely.

[*The Observer*, 1963]

TURENNE, Henri, Vicomte (1611–1675)

Dieu est toujours pour les gros bataillons.
God is always on the side of the big battalions.

[Attr.]

See INFLUENCE; LEADERSHIP; RESPONSIBILITY

PRAISE

BACON, Francis (1561–1626)

For as it is said of calumny, 'calumniate boldly, for some of it will stick' so it may be said of ostentation (except it be in a ridiculous degree of deformity), 'boldly sound your own praises, and some of them will stick.'

[*Of the Dignity and Advancement of Learning* (1623)]

BIERCE, Ambrose (1842–c.1914)

Eulogy: Praise of a person who has either the advantages of wealth and power, or the consideration to be dead.

[*The Enlarged Devil's Dictionary* (1961)]

CHURCHILL, Charles (1731–1764)

Greatly his foes he dreads, but more his friends;
He hurts me most who lavishly commends.

['The Apology, addressed to the Critical Reviewers' (1761)]

GAY, John (1685–1732)

Praising all alike, is praising none.

['A Letter to a Lady' (1714)]

JOHNSON, Samuel (1709–1784)

He who praises everybody praises nobody.

[In Boswell, *The Life of Samuel Johnson* (1791)]

All censure of a man's self is oblique praise. It is in order to shew how much he can spare.

[In Boswell, *The Life of Samuel Johnson* (1791)]

KIPLING, Rudyard (1865–1936)

Never praise a sister to a sister, in the hope of your compliments reaching the proper ears … Sisters are women first, and sisters afterward; and you will find that you do yourself harm.

[*Plain Tales from the Hills* (1888)]

LA ROCHEFOUCAULD (1613–1680)

Le refus des louanges est un désir d'être loué deux fois.
Refusal of praise reveals a desire to be praised twice over.

[*Maximes* (1678)]

MARTIAL (c.AD 40–c.104)

Laudant illa sed ista legunt.
They praise those works but they read something else.

[*Epigrammata*]

POPE, Alexander (1688–1744)

Fondly we think we honour merit then,
When we but praise ourselves in other men.

[*An Essay on Criticism* (1711), line 454]

PROVERB

Self-praise is no recommendation.

SHERIDAN, Richard Brinsley (1751–1816)

Yes, sir, puffing is of various sorts; the principal are, the puff direct, the puff preliminary, the puff collateral, the puff collusive, and the puff oblique, or puff by implication.

[*The Critic* (1779)]

SMITH, Sydney (1771–1845)

Praise is the best diet for us, after all.

[In Holland, *A Memoir of the Reverend Sydney Smith* (1855)]

See FLATTERY

PRAYER

ASTLEY, Sir Jacob (1579–1652)
O Lord! thou knowest how busy I must be this day; if I forget thee, do not thou forget me.

[Prayer before the Battle of Edgehill, 1642]

BAYLIS, Lilian (1874–1937)
O God, send me some good actors – cheap.

[The Guardian, 1976]

BECKETT, Samuel (1906–1989)
Let us pray to God … the bastard! He doesn't exist.

[Endgame (1958)]

BETJEMAN, Sir John (1906–1984)
Gracious Lord, oh bomb the Germans.
Spare their women for Thy Sake,
And if that is not too easy
We will pardon Thy Mistake.
But, gracious Lord, whate'er shall be,
Don't let anyone bomb me.

[Old Lights for New Chancels (1940)]

BROWNE, Sir Thomas (1605–1682)
Lord, deliver me from myself.

[Religio Medici (1643)]

BROWNING, Elizabeth Barrett (1806–1861)
God answers sharp and sudden on some prayers,
And thrusts the thing we have prayed for in our face,
A gauntlet with a gift in't.

[Aurora Leigh (1857)]

COLERIDGE, Samuel Taylor (1772–1834)
He prayeth best, who loveth best
All things both great and small;
For the dear God who loveth us,
He made and loveth all.

['The Rime of the Ancient Mariner' (1798), VII]

COWPER, William (1731–1800)
Prayer makes the Christian's armour bright;

And Satan trembles when he sees
The weakest saint upon his knees.

[Olney Hymns (1779), 29]

DUTTON, Geoffrey (1922–)
Those who mumble do not pray.
Prayers grow like windless trees from silence.

['Twelve Sheep']

HALE, Edward Everett (1822–1909)
'Do you pray for the senators, Dr Hale?' 'No, I look at the senators and I pray for the country.'

[In Van Wyck Brooks, New England Indian Summer (1940)]

HERRICK, Robert (1591–1674)
In Prayer the Lips ne're act the winning part,
Without the sweet concurrence of the Heart.

[Noble Numbers (1647)]

LAMB, Charles (1775–1834)
Why have we none [i.e. no grace] for books, those spiritual repasts – a grace before Milton – a grace before Shakespeare – a devotional exercise proper to be said before reading the Faerie Queene?

[Essays of Elia (1823)]

LESSING, Gotthold Ephraim (1729–1781)
Ein einziger dankbarer Gedanke gen Himmel ist das vollkommenste Gebet!
A single grateful thought raised to heaven is the most perfect prayer.

[Minna von Barnhelm (1767)]

MORE, Hannah (1745–1833)
Did not God
Sometimes withhold in mercy what we ask,
We should be ruined at our own request.

[Moses in the Bulrushes (1782)]

NIEBUHR, Reinhold (1892–1971)
God grant me the serenity to accept the things I cannot change, the courage to change the things I can, and the wisdom to distinguish the one from the other.

[Prayer adopted by Alcoholics Anonymous, attributed to but not accepted by Niebuhr]

OTWAY, Thomas (1652–1685)

No praying, it spoils business.

[*Venice Preserv'd* (1682)]

POPE, Alexander (1688–1744)

Teach me to feel another's Woe,
To hide the Fault I see;
That Mercy I to others show,
That Mercy show to me.

['The Universal Prayer' (1738)]

POUND, Ezra (1885–1972)

So many thousand beauties are gone down
to Avernus,
Ye might let one remain above with us.

['Prayer for his Lady's Life' (1908)]

RENAN, J. Ernest (1823–1892)

O Lord, if there is a Lord, save my soul, if I
have a soul.

['A Sceptic's Prayer']

SMITH, Sydney (1771–1845)

[To Monkton Milnes]
I am just going to pray for you at St Paul's,
but with no very lively hope of success.

[In H. Pearson, *The Smith of Smiths* (1934)]

SPYRI, Johanna (1827–1901)

Oh, I wish that God had not given me what I
prayed for! It was not so good as I thought.

[*Heidi* (1880–1881)]

TOLSTOY, Leo (1828–1910)

Let me lie down like a stone, O Lord, and rise
up like new bread.

[*War and Peace* (1868–1869)]

TURGENEV, Ivan (1818–1883)

Whatever a man prays for, he prays for a
miracle. Every prayer reduces itself to this:
'Great God, grant that twice two be not four.'

['Prayer' (1881)]

See CHRISTIANITY; GOD; RELIGION

PREGNANCY

ANNE, the Princess Royal (1950–)

It's a very boring time. I am not particularly

maternal – it's an occupational hazard of
being a wife.

[TV interview, quoted in the *Daily Express*, 1981]

GIBBONS, Stella (1902–1989)

Every year, in the fulness o' summer, when
the sukebind hangs heavy from the wains …
'tes the same. And when the spring comes
her hour is upon her again. 'Tes the hand of
Nature, and we women cannot escape it.

[*Cold Comfort Farm* (1932)]

LETTE, Kathy

I used to rush to the mirror every morning to
see if I had bloomed, but all I did was swell.
My ankles looked like flesh-coloured flares
and my breasts were so huge they needed
their own postcode.

[*The Daily Telegraph*, May 1999]

NICHOLLS, Peter (1927–)

'One advantage of being pregnant,' says a
wife in one of my television plays, 'you don't
have to worry about getting pregnant.'

[*Feeling You're Behind* (1984)]

PARKER, Dorothy (1893–1967)

[Telegram sent to Mary Sherwood after her much-
publicised pregnancy]
Dear Mary, We all knew you had it in you.

[In J. Keats, *You Might As Well Live* (1970)]

[Said on going into hospital for an abortion]
It serves me right for putting all my eggs in
one bastard.

[Attr. in J. Keats, *You Might As Well Live* (1970)]

See BABIES; BIRTH; MOTHERS

PREJUDICE

BELLOC, Hilaire (1870–1953)

I am a Catholic. As far as possible I go to Mass
every day. As far as possible I kneel down
and tell these beads every day. If you reject
me on account of my religion, I shall thank
God that he has spared me the indignity of
being your representative.

[Speech, 1906]

The Anti-Semite is a man so absorbed in his subject that he loses interest in any matter unless he can give it some association with his delusion, for delusion it is.

The Jew cannot help feeling superior, but he can help the expression of that superiority – at any rate he can modify such expression.

['The Jews' (1922)]

FIELDS, W.C. (1880–1946)
I am free of all prejudice. I hate everyone equally.

[Attr.]

LAMB, Charles (1775–1834)
I am, in plainer words, a bundle of prejudices – made up of likings and dislikings.

[*Essays of Elia* (1823), 'Imperfect Sympathies']

NIEMÖLLER, Martin (1892–1984)
In Germany they first came for the Communists, and I didn't speak up because I wasn't a Communist. Then they came for the Jews, and I didn't speak up because I wasn't a Jew. Then they came for the trade unionists, and I didn't speak up because I wasn't a trade unionist. Then they came for the Catholics, and I didn't speak up because I was a Protestant. Then they came for me – and by that time no one was left to speak up.

[*Concise Dictionary of Religious Quotations*]

RUSSELL, Bertrand (1872–1970)
The collection of prejudices which is called political philosophy is useful provided that it is not called philosophy.

[*The Observer*, 1962]

STERNE, Laurence (1713–1768)
Prejudice of education, he would say, is the devil, – and the multitudes of them which we suck in with our mother's milk – are the devil and all. – We are haunted with them, brother Toby, in all our lucubrations and researches; and was a man fool enough to submit tamely to what they obtruded upon him, – what would his book be? … nothing but a farrago of the clack of nurses, and of the nonsense of the old women (of both sexes)

throughout the kingdom.

[*Tristram Shandy* (1759–1767)]

VICTORIA, Queen (1819–1901)
… I too well know its truth, from experience, that whenever any poor Gipsies are encamped anywhere and crimes and robberies &c. occur, it is invariably laid to their account, which is shocking; and if they are always looked upon as vagabonds, how can they become good people?

[*Journal*, 1836]

See EQUALITY; FEMINISM; JEWS; RACE; RELIGION

THE PRESENT

ARNOLD, Matthew (1822–1888)
This strange disease of modern life.

['The Scholar-Gipsy' (1853)]

THE BIBLE (King James Version)
Take therefore no thought for the morrow: for the morrow shall take thought for the things of itself. Sufficient unto the day is the evil thereof.

[*Matthew*, 6:34]

BURKE, Edmund (1729–1797)
To complain of the age we live in, to murmur at the present possessors of power, to lament the past, to conceive extravagant hopes of the future, are the common dispositions of the greatest part of mankind.

[*Thoughts on the Cause of the Present Discontents* (1770)]

CLARE, John (1793–1864)
The present is the funeral of the past,
And man the living sepulchre of life.

['The Past' (1845)]

EMERSON, Ralph Waldo (1803–1882)
Write it on your heart that every day is the best day in the year. No man has learned anything rightly until he knows that every day is Doomsday.

[*Society and Solitude* (1870)]

FITZGERALD, Edward (1809–1883)

Ah, fill the Cup: – what boots it to repeat
How Time is slipping underneath our Feet:
Unborn TOMORROW and dead YESTERDAY,
Why fret about them if TO-DAY be sweet!

[*The Rubáiyát of Omar Khayyám* (1859)]

FRANKLIN, Benjamin (1706–1790)

The golden age never was the present age.

[*Poor Richard's Almanac* (1750)]

HAMMARSKJÖLD, Dag (1905–1961)

Do not look back. And do not dream about
the future, either. It will neither give you back
the past, nor satisfy your other daydreams.
Your duty, your reward – your destiny – are
here and now.

[*Markings* (1965)]

HORACE (65–8 BC)

Carpe diem.
Seize the day.

[*Odes*]

MCLUHAN, Marshall (1911–1980)

The present cannot be revealed to people
until it has become yesterday.

[In Marchand, *Marshall McLuhan*
(1989)]

MALLARMÉ, Stéphane (1842–1898)

Le vierge, le vivace et le bel aujourd'hui.
That virgin, vital, beautiful day: today.

[*Plusieurs sonnets* (1881)]

SHAKESPEARE, William (1564–1616)

Past and to come seems best; things present,
worst.

[*Henry IV, Part 2*, I.iii]

See FUTURE; OPPORTUNITY; PAST; TIME

PRIDE

ADDISON, Joseph (1672–1719)

'Tis pride, rank pride, and haughtiness of
soul;
I think the Romans call it stoicism.

[*Cato* (1713)]

THE BIBLE
(King James Version)

Pride goeth before destruction, and an
haughty spirit before a fall.

[*Proverbs*, 16:18]

BRADSHAW, Henry (d. 1513)

Proude as a pecocke.

[*The Life of Saint Werburge*
(1521)]

COLERIDGE, Samuel Taylor
(1772–1834)

And the Devil did grin, for his darling sin
Is pride that apes humility.

['The Devil's Thoughts' (1799)]

DAVIES, Sir John (1569–1626)

I know my life's a pain and but a span,
I know my sense is mock'd in every thing;
And to conclude, I know myself a man,
Which is a proud and yet a wretched thing.

[*Nosce Teipsum* (1599)]

DOBRÉE, Bonamy (1891–1974)

It is difficult to be humble. Even if you aim at
humility, there is no guarantee that when
you have attained the state you will not be
proud of the feat.

[*John Wesley*]

LANDOR, Walter Savage (1775–1864)

I know not whether I am proud,
But this I know, I hate the crowd.

['With an Album']

MACNEICE, Louis (1907–1963)

Pride in your history is pride
In living what your fathers died,
Is pride in taking your own pulse
And counting in you someone else.

['Suite for recorders' (1966)]

POPE, Alexander (1688–1744)

Pride, the never-failing vice of fools.

[*An Essay on Criticism* (1711)]

RENARD, Jules (1864–1910)

Be modest! It is the kind of pride least likely
to offend.

[*Journal*]

There is false modesty, but there is no false pride.

[*Journal*]

SHAKESPEARE, William (1564–1616)

O world, how apt the poor are to be proud!

[*Twelfth Night*, III.i]

SHELLEY, Percy Bysshe (1792–1822)

But human pride
Is skilful to invent most serious names
To hide its ignorance.

[*Queen Mab* (1813)]

See EGOISM; SELF; VANITY

PRINCIPLES

ADLER, Alfred (1870–1937)

It is easier to fight for one's principles than to live up to them.

[Attr.]

BALDWIN, Stanley (1867–1947)

I would rather be an opportunist and float than go to the bottom with my principles round my neck.

[Attr.]

EBNER-ESCHENBACH, Marie von (1830–1916)

Wenn zwei brave Menschen über Grundsätze streiten, haben immer beide recht.
Whenever two good people argue over principles, both are always right.

[*Aphorisms* (1880)]

HATTERSLEY, Roy (1932–)

Politicians are entitled to change their minds. But when they adjust their principles some explanation is necessary.

[*The Observer*, March 1999]

MACKENZIE, Sir Compton (1883–1972)

I don't believe in principles. Principles are only excuses for what we want to think or what we want to do.

[*The Adventures of Sylvia Scarlett* (1918)]

MAUGHAM, William Somerset (1874–1965)

You can't learn too soon that the most useful thing about a principle is that it can always be sacrificed to expediency.

[*The Circle* (1921)]

MELBOURNE, Lord (1779–1848)

Nobody ever did anything very foolish except from some strong principle.

[Attr.]

ROOSEVELT, Franklin Delano (1882–1945)

To stand upon the ramparts and die for our principles is heroic, but to sally forth to battle and win for our principles is something more than heroic.

[Speech, 1928]

SADE, Marquis de (1740–1814)

All universal moral principles are idle fancies.

[*The 120 Days of Sodom* (1784)]

TODD, Ron (1927–)

You don't have power if you surrender all your principles – you have office.

[Attr.]

See MORALITY; VIRTUE

PRISON

BLAKE, William (1757–1827)

Prisons are built with stones of Law, Brothels with bricks of Religion.

[*The Marriage of Heaven and Hell* (c. 1790–1793)]

BOTTOMLEY, Horatio William (1860–1933)

[When spotted sewing mailbags during his imprisonment for misappropriation of funds]
Visitor: Ah, Bottomley, sewing?
Bottomley: No, reaping.

[Attr.]

BRONTÉ, Emily (1818–1848)

Oh dreadful is the check – intense the agony –
When the ear begins to hear and the eye begins to see;

When the pulse begins to throb, the brain to
think again;
The soul to feel the flesh and the flesh to feel
the chain!

['The Prisoner' (1846)]

DOWLING, Basil Cairns (1777–1834)

[On prisons]
Prisoners and warders – we are all of one
blood.
They're much alike, except for a different
coat
And a different hat;
And they all seem decent, kindly fellows
enough
As they work and chat:
How can it be that men like this have been
hanged
By men like that?

[In O.E. Burton, *In Prison* (1945)]

FRANK, Otto (1889–)

When you have survived life in a
concentration camp you have ceased to
count yourself as a member of the human
race. You will forever be outside the
experience of the rest of mankind.

[In the *Daily Mail*, 1996]

HAWTHORNE, Nathaniel (1804–1864)

The black flower of civilized society, a prison.

[*The Scarlet Letter* (1850)]

What other dungeon is so dark as one's own
heart! What jailer so inexorable as one's self!

[*The House of the Seven Gables* (1851)]

INGRAMS, Richard (1937–)

[On the prospect of going to gaol, 1976]
The only thing I really mind about going to
prison is the thought of Lord Longford
coming to visit me.

[Attr.]

KEENAN, Brian (1950–)

I would be the voyeur of myself. This strategy
I employed for the rest of my captivity. I
allowed myself to do and be and say and
think and feel all the things that were in me,
but at the same time could stand outside

observing and attempting to understand.

[*An Evil Cradling*]

LÉON, Fray Luis de (c.1527–1591)

[Resuming a lecture after five years' imprisonment]
Dicebamus hesterno die.
As we were saying the other day.

[Attr.]

LEVI, Primo (1919–1987)

[Of the Nazi concentration camps]
The worst survived – that is, the fittest; the
best all died.

[*The Drowned and the Saved* (1988)]

LOVELACE, Richard (1618–1658)

Stone walls do not a prison make
Nor iron bars a cage;
Minds innocent and quiet take
That for an hermitage;
If I have freedom in my love,
And in my soul am free;
Angels alone, that soar above,
Enjoy such liberty.

['To Althea, From Prison' (1649)]

RALEIGH, Sir Walter (c.1552–1618)

But now close kept, as captives wonted are:
That food, that heat, that light I find no more;
Despair bolts up my doors, and I alone
Speak to dead walls, but those hear not my
moan.

[Untitled poem]

[Said after his trial for treason, 1603]
The world itself is but a large prison, out of
which some are daily led to execution.

[Attr.]

RAMOS, Graciliano (1892–1953)

*Então mete-se um homem na cadeia porque ele não
sabe falar direito?*
So you put a man in jail because he can't talk
properly?

[*Vidas secas* (*Dry Lives*, 1938)]

SOLZHENITSYN, Alexander (1918–)

Forget the outside world. Life has different
laws in here. This is Campland, an invisible
country. It's not in the geography books, or
the psychology books or the history books.

This is the famous country where ninety-nine men weep while one laughs.

[*The Love-Girl and the Innocent*]

THOREAU, Henry David (1817–1862)
Under a government which imprisons any unjustly, the true place for a just man is also a prison.

[*Civil Disobedience* (1849)]

WAUGH, Evelyn (1903–1966)
Anyone who has been to an English public school will always feel comparatively at home in prison.

[*Decline and Fall* (1928)]

WILDE, Oscar (1854–1900)
The vilest deeds like poison-weeds
Bloom well in prison-air;
It is only what is good in Man
That wastes and withers there.

[*The Ballad of Reading Gaol* (1898)]

[Complaining at having to wait in the rain for transport to take him to prison]
If this is the way Queen Victoria treats her prisoners, she doesn't deserve to have any.

[Attr.]

See CRIME; PUNISHMENT

PRIVACY

DICKINSON, Emily (1830–1886)
I'm Nobody! Who are you?
Are you – Nobody – Too?
Then there's a pair of us?
Don't tell! they'd advertise – you know!

How dreary – to be – Somebody!
How public – like a Frog –
To tell one's name – the livelong June –
To an admiring Bog!

['I'm Nobody! Who are you?' (c. 1861)]

PARKER, Dorothy (1893–1967)
[Pressing a button marked NURSE during a stay in hospital]
That should assure us of at least forty-five

minutes of undisturbed privacy.

[In James R. Gaines, *Days and Nights of the Algonquin Round Table* (1977)]

USTINOV, Sir Peter (1921–)
This is a free country, madam. We have a right to share your privacy in a public place.

[*Romanoff and Juliet* (1956)]

PRIVILEGE

LEVI, Primo (1919–1987)
The ascent of the privileged, not only in the Lager but in all human coexistence, is an anguishing but unfailing phenomenon: only in Utopias are they absent. It is the duty of righteous men to make war on all undeserved privilege, but one must not forget that this is a war without end.

[*The Drowned and the Saved* (1988)]

See ARISTOCRACY; MONEY AND WEALTH

PROBLEMS

ADAMS, Scott (1957–)
There are very few personal problems that cannot be solved through a suitable application of high explosives.

[*The Dilbert Principle*]

ANONYMOUS
All easy problems have already been solved.

Inside every small problem is a large problem struggling to get out.

[Second Law of Blissful Ignorance]

CLEAVER, Eldridge (1935–1998)
If you're not part of the solution, you're part of the problem.

[Attr.]

DICKENS, Charles (1812–1870)
Mr Podsnap settled that whatever he put behind him he put out of existence ... Mr Podsnap had even acquired a peculiar flourish of his right arm in often clearing the world of its most difficult problems, by

sweeping them behind him.

[*Our Mutual Friend* (1865)]

DOYLE, Sir Arthur Conan (1859–1930)

It is quite a three-pipe problem, and I beg that you won't speak to me for fifty minutes.

[*The Adventures of Sherlock Holmes* (1892)]

JOHN XXIII (1881–1963)

It often happens that I wake at night and begin to think about a serious problem and decide I must tell the Pope about it. Then I wake up completely and remember I am the Pope.

[Attr.]

LOVELL, James (1928–)

[After the explosion on board Apollo XIII, which put the crew in serious danger]

OK, Houston, we have had a problem here … Houston, we have a problem.

[Radio message, 11 April 1970]

MARX, Karl (1818–1883)

Mankind always sets itself only those problems it can solve; since, looking at the matter more closely, one will always find that the task itself arises only when the material conditions for its solution already exist or are at least in the process of formation.

[*A Contribution to the Critique of Political Economy* (1859)]

WITTGENSTEIN, Ludwig (1889–1951)

The solution of the problem of life is seen in the vanishing of the problem.

[*Tractatus Logico-Philosophicus* (1922)]

ZEFFIRELLI, Franco (1923–)

All the problems of the world are caused by people who do not listen.

[*The Observer*, 1998]

PROCRASTINATION

ANONYMOUS

Spend sufficient time confirming the need and the need will disappear.

BOYD, William (1952–)

She felt weary and careworn, in the way one often does before the big job of work is tackled; that sense of premature or projected exhaustion that is the breeding-ground of all procrastination.

[*Brazzaville Beach* (1990)]

PROVERBS

Never put off till tomorrow what you can do today.

Put off the evil hour as long as you can.

YOUNG, Edward (1683–1765)

Procrastination is the thief of time.

[*Night-Thoughts on Life, Death and Immortality* (1742–1746)]

PRODUCTION

ANONYMOUS

The Six Stages of Production:

• Wild Enthusiasm
• Total Confusion
• Utter Despair
• The Search for the Guilty
• The persecution of the Innocent
• The Promotion of the Incompetent.

No project was ever completed on time and within budget.

[Cheops Law]

PROGRESS

ANONYMOUS

We've made great medical progress in the last generation. What used to be merely an itch is now an allergy.

BLAKE, William (1757–1827)

Without Contraries is no progression. Attraction and Repulsion, Reason and Energy, Love and Hate, are necessary to Human existence.

[*The Marriage of Heaven and Hell* (c. 1793)]

BORGES, Jorge Luis (1899–1986)

We have stopped believing in progress. What progress that is!

[Ibarra, Borges et Borges]

BUTLER, Samuel (1835–1902)

All progress is based upon a universal innate desire on the part of every organism to live beyond its income.

[*The Note-Books of Samuel Butler* (1912)]

CARLYLE, Thomas (1795–1881)

The progress of human society consists … in … the better and better apportioning of wages to work.

[*Past and Present* (1843)]

CLIFFORD, William Kingdon (1845–1879)

… scientific thought is not an accompaniement or condition of human progress, but human progress itself.

[*Aims and Instruments of Scientific Thought* (1872)]

COMTE, Auguste (1798–1857)

L'Amour pour principe, l'Ordre pour base, et le Progrès pour but.

Love our principle, order our foundation, progress our goal.

[*Système de politique positive*]

CUMMINGS, e. e. (1894–1962)

pity this busy monster, manunkind,

not. Progress is a comfortable disease.

[*1 x 1* (1944), no. 14]

DE KLERK, F.W. (1936–)

A man of destiny knows that beyond this hill lies another and another. The journey is never complete.

[*The Observer*, 1994]

DOUGLASS, Frederick (c.1818–1895)

If there is no struggle, there is no progress.

[Attr.]

DU BOIS, William (1868–1963)

Believe in life! Always human beings will live and progress to greater, broader, and fuller life.

[Last message to the world, read at his funeral]

ELIOT, Charles W. (1834–1926)

In the modern world the intelligence of public opinion is the one indispensable condition of social progress.

[Speech, 1869]

ELLIS, Havelock (1859–1939)

What we call 'Progress' is the exchange of one nuisance for another nuisance.

[Impressions and Comments (1914)]

FREUD, Sigmund (1856–1939)

What progress we are making. In the Middle Ages they would have burned me. Now they are content with burning my books.

[Letter, 1933]

GIBBON, Edward (1737–1794)

All that is human must retrograde if it does not advance.

[*Decline and Fall of the Roman Empire* (1776–88)]

HEGEL, Georg Wilhelm (1770–1831)

The history of the world is none other than the progress of the consciousness of freedom.

[*Philosophy of History*]

HUBBARD, Elbert (1856–1915)

The world is moving so fast these days that the man who says it can't be done is generally interrupted by someone doing it.

[Attr.]

JOHN XXIII (1881–1963)

The social progress, order, security and peace of each country are necessarily connected with the social progress, order, security and peace of all other countries.

[Encyclical letter, April 1963]

LENIN, V.I. (1870–1924)

One step forward, two steps back … It happens in the lives of individuals, and it happens in the history of nations and in the development of parties.

[*One Step Forward, Two Steps Back* (1904)]

LINDBERGH, Anne Morrow (1906–)

Why do progress and beauty have to be so opposed?

[*Hour of Gold, Hour of Lead* (1973)]

SAINT-EXUPÉRY, Antoine de (1900–1944)

Man's 'progress' is but a gradual discovery that his questions have no meaning.

[*The Wisdom of the Sands*]

SANTAYANA, George (1863–1952)

Progress, far from consisting in change, depends on retentiveness. Those who cannot remember the past are condemned to repeat it.

[*The Life of Reason* (1906)]

The cry was for freedom and indeterminate progress: *Vorwärts! Avanti!* Onwards! Full speed ahead!, without asking whether directly before you was not a bottomless pit.

[*My Host the World* (1953)]

SHAW, George Bernard (1856–1950)

The reasonable man adapts himself to the world: the unreasonable one persists in trying to adapt the world to himself. Therefore all progress depends on the unreasonable man.

[*Man and Superman* (1903)]

SPENCER, Herbert (1820–1903)

Progress, therefore, is not an accident, but a necessity … it is a part of nature.

[*Social Statics* (1850)]

STEPHEN, Sir James Fitzjames (1829–1894)

Progress has its drawbacks, and they are great and serious; but whatever its value may be, unity in religious belief would further it.

[*Liberty, Equality and Fraternity* (1873)]

THURBER, James (1894–1961)

Progress was all right; only it went on too long.

[Attr.]

VIGNEAUD, Vincent de (1901–1978)

Nothing holds up the progress of science so much as the right idea at the wrong time.

[*Most Secret War* (1978)]

WALKER, Alice (1944–)

People tend to think that life really does progress for everyone eventually, that people progress, but actually only some people progress. The rest of the people don't.

[In C. Tate (ed.), *Black Women Writers at Work* (1983)]

See CHANGE; CONSERVATISM; TECHNOLOGY

PROMISES

ELIOT, George (1819–1880)

An election is coming. Universal peace is declared, and the foxes have a sincere interest in prolonging the lives of the poultry.

[*Felix Holt* (1866)]

FROST, Robert (1874–1963)

The woods are lovely, dark and deep,
But I have promises to keep,
And miles to go before I sleep,
And miles to go before I sleep.

['Stopping by Woods on a Snowy Evening' (1923)]

KING, Martin Luther (1929–1968)

[Speech given the day before King was assassinated]

… And I've looked over, and I've seen the promised land. I may not get there with you, but I want you to know tonight that we as a people will get to the promised land. So I'm happy tonight. I'm not worried about anything. I'm not fearing any man.

[Speech in Memphis, April 3, 1968]

SERVICE, Robert W. (1874–1958)

A promise made is a debt unpaid.

['The Cremation of Sam McGee' (1907)]

SWIFT, Jonathan (1667–1745)

Promises and pie-crusts are made to be broken, they say.

[*Polite Conversation* (1738)]

TWAIN, Mark (1835–1910)

To promise not to do a thing is the surest way in the world to make a body want to go and do that very thing.

[*The Adventures of Tom Sawyer* (1876)]

PROPERTY

DICKENS, Charles (1812–1870)
Get hold of portable property.
[*Great Expectations* (1861)]

DRUMMOND, Thomas (1797–1840)
Property has its duties as well as its rights.
[Letter to the Earl of Donoughmore, 1838]

EDGEWORTH, Maria (1767–1849)
Well! some people talk of morality, and some
of religion, but give me a little snug property.
[*The Absentee* (1812)]

EMERSON, Ralph Waldo (1803–1882)
A man builds a fine house; and now he has a
master, and a task for life; he is to furnish,
watch, show it, and keep it in repair, the rest
of his days.
[*Society and Solitude* (1870)]

**INGERSOLL, Robert Greene
(1833–1899)**
Few rich men own their own property. The
property owns them.
[Address, 1896]

JAMES, Henry (1843–1916)
The black and merciless things that are
behind the great possessions.
[*The Ivory Tower* (1917)]

LOOS, Anita (1893–1981)
Kissing your hand may make you feel very
very good but a diamond and safire bracelet
lasts forever.
[*Gentlemen Prefer Blondes* (1925)]

MACHIAVELLI (1469–1527)
*Gli uomini sdimenticano più presto la morte del
padre che la perdita del patrimonio.*
Men sooner forget the death of their father
than the loss of their possessions.
[*The Prince* (1532)]

**PROUDHON, Pierre-Joseph
(1809–1865)**
*Si j'avais à répondre à la question suivante: qu'est-ce
que l'esclavage? et que d'un seul mot je répondisse:
c'est l'assassinat, ma pensée serait aussitôt comprise*

*… Pourquoi donc à cette autre demande: qu'est-ce
que la propriété? ne puis-je répondre de même: c'est
le vol!*
If I were asked to answer the following
question: 'What is slavery?' and I replied in
one word, 'Murder!' my meaning would be
understood at once … Why, then, to this
other question: 'What is property?' may I not
likewise answer 'Theft'?
[*Qu'est-ce que la propriété?* (1840)]

RAJNEESH, Bhagwan Shree (1931–)
The more things accumulate the more life is
wasted because they have to be purchased
at the cost of life.
[*The Mustard Seed: Reflections on the Sayings of
Jesus* (1978)]

VANBRUGH, Sir John (1664–1726)
The want of a thing is perplexing enough,
but the possession of it is intolerable.
[*The Confederacy* (1705)]

WILDE, Oscar (1854–1900)
If property had simply pleasures, we could
stand it; but its duties make it unbearable. In
the interest of the rich we must get rid of it.
[*The Fortnightly Review*, 1891]

See CAPITALISM; MONEY AND WEALTH

PROSPERITY

BACON, Francis (1561–1626)
Prosperity doth best discover vice, but
adversity doth best discover virtue.
[*Essays* (1625), 'Of Adversity']

HERBERT, Xavier (1901–1984)
Prosperity is like the tide, being able to flood
one shore only by ebbing from another.
[*Capricornia* (1938), 16]

WEBSTER, John (c.1580–c.1625)
Prosperity doth bewitch men, seeming clear;
As seas do laugh, show white, when rocks are
near.
[*The White Devil* (1612)]

See CONSUMER SOCIETY; MONEY AND WEALTH

PROSTITUTION

ADLER, Polly (1900–1962)
A House Is Not a Home.
[Title of memoirs, 1954]

HARDY, Thomas (1840–1928)
'You left us in tatters, without shoes or socks,
Tired of digging potatoes, and spudding up docks;
And now you've gay bracelets and bright feathers three!'–
'Yes: that's how we dress when we're ruined,' said she.
['The Ruined Maid' (1866)]

PARKER, Dorothy (1893–1967)
[When challenged to compose a sentence using the word 'horticulture']
You can lead a horticulture but you can't make her think.
[In J. Keats, *You Might As Well Live* (1970)]

See SEX

PSYCHIATRY

ANONYMOUS
[Definition of a psychoanalyst]
A Jewish doctor who hates the sight of blood.
[In Leo Rosten, *The Joys of Yiddish* (1968)]

AUDEN, W.H. (1907–1973)
To us he is no more a person
Now but a climate of opinion.
[*In Memory of Sigmund Freud*]

GOLDWYN, Samuel (1882–1974)
Any man who goes to a psychiatrist should have his head examined.
[In Zierold, *Moguls* (1969)]

STOCKWOOD, Mervyn (1913–)
A psychiatrist is a man who goes to the Folies-Bergère and looks at the audience.
[*The Observer*, 1961]

SZASZ, Thomas (1920–)
Psychiatrists classify a person as neurotic if he suffers from his problems in living, and a psychotic if he makes others suffer.
[*The Second Sin* (1973)]

See MADNESS

PUBLICITY

PROVERB
Any publicity is good publicity.

'SIMPLE, Peter' (Michael Wharton) (1913–)
Rentacrowd Ltd, the enterprising firm which supplies crowds for all occasions and has done so much to keep progressive causes in the public eye.
[*Daily Telegraph*, 1962]

WHITLAM, Gough (1916–)
Quite small and ineffectual demonstrations can be made to look like the beginnings of a revolution if the cameraman is in the right place at the right time.
[In Jonathon Green (ed.), *A Dictionary of Contemporary Quotations* (1982)]

See CELEBRITY; FAME; MEDIA; POPULARITY

PUBLISHING

CAMPBELL, Thomas (1777–1844)
Now Barabbas was a publisher.
[Attr. in Samuel Smiles, *A Publisher and his Friends* (1891)]

CONNOLLY, Cyril (1903–1974)
As repressed sadists are supposed to become policemen or butchers so those with irrational fear of life become publishers.
[*Enemies of Promise* (1938)]

INGRAMS, Richard (1937–)
[Referring to his editorship of Private Eye]

My own motto is publish and be sued.

[BBC radio broadcast, 1977]

SLESSOR, Kenneth (1901–1971)

… the principal benefit of publication is that it clears work out of the mind finally, and provides an impulse for new work.

[Letter to Norman Lindsay, 1944]

WELLINGTON, Duke of (1769–1852)

[Reply to a threat of blackmail by Harriette Wilson]

Publish and be damned.

[Attr.]

WILDE, Oscar (1854–1900)

No publisher should ever express an opinion of the value of what he publishes. That is a matter entirely for the literary critic to decide … A publisher is simply a useful middle-man. It is not for him to anticipate the verdict of criticism.

[Letter in St James's Gazette, 1890]

See BOOKS; EDITING

PUNCTUALITY

MITFORD, Nancy (1904–1973)

'Twenty-three and a quarter minutes past,' Uncle Matthew was saying furiously, 'in precisely six and three-quarter minutes the damned fella will be late.'

[Love in a Cold Climate (1949)]

PROVERB

Punctuality is the politeness of princes.

See TIME

PUNISHMENT

ARENDT, Hannah (1906–1975)

No punishment has ever possessed enough power of deterrence to prevent the commission of crimes.

[Eichmann in Jerusalem: A Report on the Banality of Evil (1963)]

BENTHAM, Jeremy (1748–1832)

All punishment is mischief: all punishment in itself is evil.

[An Introduction to the Principles of Morals and Legislation (1789)]

BRAXFIELD, Lord (1722–1799)

[To an eloquent culprit at the bar]

Ye're a vera clever chiel, man, but ye wad be nane the waur o' a hanging.

[In Lockhart, Life of Scott]

DOSTOEVSKY, Fyodor (1821–1881)

Juridical punishment for crime scares a criminal far less than law-makers think, partly because the criminal himself requires it morally.

[Letter to Katkov, 1865]

FISHER, Geoffrey (1887–1972)

The long and distressing controversy over capital punishment is very unfair to anyone meditating murder.

[The Sunday Times, 1957]

GILBERT, W.S. (1836–1911)

My object all sublime
I shall achieve in time –
To let the punishment fit the crime –
The punishment fit the crime.

[The Mikado (1885)]

HALIFAX, Lord (1633–1695)

Men are not hang'd for stealing Horses, but that Horses may not be stolen.

['Of Punishment' (1750)]

HUBBARD, Elbert (1856–1915)

Men are not punished for their sins, but by them.

[A Thousand and One Epigrams (1911)]

JOHNSON, Samuel (1709–1784)

The power of punishment is to silence, not to confute.

[Sermons (1788)]

The rod produces an effect which terminates in itself. A child is afraid of being whipped, and gets his task, and there's an end on't; whereas, by exciting emulation and comparisons of superiority, you lay the foundation of lasting mischief; you make brothers and sisters hate each other.

[In Boswell, *The Life of Samuel Johnson* (1791)]

Depend upon it, Sir, when a man knows he is to be hanged in a fortnight, it concentrates his mind wonderfully.

[In Boswell, *The Life of Samuel Johnson* (1791)]

There is now less flogging in our great schools than formerly, but then less is learned there; so that what the boys get at one end they lose at the other.

[In Boswell, *The Life of Samuel Johnson* (1791)]

JUVENAL (c.60–130)

Prima est haec ultio, quod se ludice nemo nocens absolvitur.

The chief punishment is this: that no guilty man is acquitted in his own judgement.

[*Satires*]

KARR, Alphonse (1808–1890)

Si l'on veut abolir la peine de mort en ce cas, que MM les assassins commencent.

If we want to abolish the death penalty, let our friends the murderers take the first step.

[*Les Guêpes* (1849)]

KEY, Ellen (1849–1926)

Corporal punishment is as humiliating for him who gives it as for him who receives it; it is ineffective besides. Neither shame nor physical pain have any other effect than a hardening one.

[*The Century of the Child* (1909)]

MANN, Horace (1796–1859)

The object of punishment is prevention from evil; it never can be made impulsive to good.

[*Lectures and Reports on Education* (1845)]

PAINE, Thomas (1737–1809)

Lay then the axe to the root, and teach governments humanity. It is their sanguinary punishments which corrupt mankind.

[*The Rights of Man* (1791)]

PEPYS, Samuel (1633–1703)

I went out to Charing Cross, to see Major-

General Harrison hanged, drawn and quartered; which was done there, he looking as cheerful as any man could do in that condition.

[*Diary*, 1660]

RUSSELL, Lord John (1792–1878)

[When asked to describe a suitable punishment for bigamy]

Two mothers-in-law.

[Attr.]

SALMON, George (1819–1904)

[On hearing a colleague claiming to have been caned only once in his life, and that, for telling the truth]

Well, it certainly cured you, Mahaffy.

[Attr.]

SHAKESPEARE, William (1564–1616)

Use every man after his desert, and who shall scape whipping?

[*Hamlet*, II.ii]

Now, as fond fathers,
Having bound up the threat'ning twigs of birch,
Only to stick it in their children's sight
For terror, not to use, in time the rod
Becomes more mock'd than fear'd; so our decrees,
Dead to infliction, to themselves are dead;
And liberty plucks justice by the nose;
The baby beats the nurse, and quite athwart
Goes all decorum.

[*Measure For Measure*, I.iii]

SHAW, George Bernard (1856–1950)

There is no satisfaction in hanging a man who does not object to it.

[*The Man of Destiny* (1898)]

If you strike a child, take care that you strike it in anger, even at the risk of maiming it for life. A blow in cold blood neither can nor should be forgiven.

[*Man and Superman* (1903)']

SHEPHARD, Gillian

My own personal view is that corporal punishment can be a useful deterrent.

[BBC radio interview, 1996]

STOWE, Harriet Beecher (1811–1896)
Whipping and abuse are like laudanum; you have to double the dose as the sensibilities decline.

[*Uncle Tom's Cabin* (1852)]

TROLLOPE, Anthony (1815–1882)
[Of his headmaster]
He must have known me had he seen me as he was wont to see me, for he was in the habit of flogging me constantly. Perhaps he did not recognize me by my face.

[*Autobiography* (1883)]

VIDAL, Gore (1925–)
[When asked for his views about corporal punishment]
I'm all for bringing back the birch, but only between consenting adults.

[TV interview with David Frost]

WILDE, Oscar (1854–1900)
A community is infinitely more brutalised by the habitual employment of punishment than it is by the occasional occurrence of crime.

['The Soul of Man under Socialism' (1891)]

See CRIME; EDUCATION; RETALIATION

PURITANS

BRATHWAITE, Richard (c.1588–1673)
To Banbury came I, O profane one!
Where I saw a Puritane-one

Hanging of his cat on Monday
For killing of a mouse on Sunday.

[*Barnabee's Journal* (1638)]

LAWRENCE, D.H. (1885–1930)
To the Puritan all things are impure, as somebody says.

[*Etruscan Places* (1932), 'Cerveteri']

MACAULAY, Lord (1800–1859)
[Of the Puritans]
On the rich and the eloquent, on nobles and priests, they looked down with contempt: for they esteemed themselves rich in a more precious treasure, and eloquent in a more sublime language, nobles by the right of an earlier creation, and priests by the imposition of a mightier hand.

[*Collected Essays* (1843)]

[Of Puritans and Calvinists]
Persecution produced its natural effect on them. It found them a sect; it made them a faction.

[*History of England* (1849)]

The Puritan hated bear-baiting, not because it gave pain to the bear, but because it gave pleasure to the spectators.

[*History of England* (1849)]

MENCKEN, H.L. (1880–1956)
Puritanism – The haunting fear that someone, somewhere, may be happy.

[*A Mencken Chrestomathy* (1949)]

Q

QUALIFICATIONS

BONO, Sonny (1935–1997)
What is qualified? What have I been qualified for in my life? I haven't been qualified to be a mayor. I'm not qualified to be a songwriter. I'm not qualified to be a TV producer. I'm no qualified to be a successful businessman. And so, I don't know what qualified means. And I think people get too hung up on that in a way, you know?

QUEUES

ANONYMOUS
The other line moves faster.

[Etorre's Observation]

If you change lines, the one you just left will start to move faster than the one you are now in.

[O'Brian's Law]

The longer you wait in line, the greater the likelihood that you are in the wrong line.

[The Queue Principal]

QUOTATIONS

CHURCHILL, Sir Winston (1874–1965)
It is a good thing for an uneducated man to read books of quotations.

[*My Early Life* (1930)]

DUNN, Douglas (1942–)
And, from an open window, Mozart's strings
Encourage echoed songs,
Thrush-throats,
Thrush-wings.
Alluded nature, quoting from a quote,
Returns the symphony
To its wood-note.

[*Northlight* (1988)]

EMERSON, Ralph Waldo (1803–1882)
I hate quotations.

[*Journals*, 1849]

Every man is a borrower and a mimic, life is theatrical and literature a quotation.

[*Society and Solitude* (1870)]

By necessity, by proclivity, – and by delight, we all quote.

[*Letters and Social Aims* (1875)]

Next to the originator of a good sentence is the first quoter of it.

[*Letters and Social Aims* (1875)]

FADIMAN, Clifton (1904–)
We prefer to believe that the absence of inverted commas guarantees the originality of a thought, whereas it may be merely that the utterer has forgotten its source.

[*Any Number Can Play* (1957)]

JOHNSON, Samuel (1709–1784)
[Of citations of usage in a dictionary]
Every quotation contributes something to the stability or enlargement of the language.

[*A Dictionary of the English Language* (1755)]

Classical quotation is the parole of literary men all over the world.

[In Boswell, *The Life of Samuel Johnson* (1791)]

He that tries to recommend him by select quotations, will succeed like the pedant in Hierocles, who, when he offered his house to sale, carried a brick in his pocket as a specimen.

[The Plays of William Shakespeare (1765)]

KAUFMAN, George S. (1889–1961)
Everything I've ever said will be credited to Dorothy Parker.

[Attr.]

MIKES, George (1912–1987)
In England only uneducated people show off their knowledge; nobody quotes Latin or

Greek authors in the course of conversation, unless he has never read them.

[*How to be an Alien* (1946)]

MONTAGUE, C.E. (1867–1928)

To be amused at what you read – that is the great spring of happy quotation.

[*A Writer's Notes on his Trade* (1930)]

PARKER, Dorothy (1893–1967)

How do people go to sleep? I'm afraid I've lost the knack. I might try busting myself smartly over the temple with the nightlight. I might repeat to myself, slowly and soothingly, a list of quotations beautiful from minds profound; if I can remember any of the damned things.

[*Here Lies* (1939)]

PEACOCK, Thomas Love (1785–1866)

A book that furnishes no quotations is, me judice, no book – it is a plaything.

[*Crotchet Castle* (1831)]

PEARSON, Hesketh (1887–1964)

A widely-read man never quotes accurately … Misquotation is the pride and privilege of the learned.

[*Common Misquotations* (1937)]

Misquotations are the only quotations that are never misquoted.

[*Common Misquotations* (1937)]

PRIOR, Matthew (1664–1721)

He rang'd his tropes, and preach'd up patience;
Back'd his opinion with quotations.

['Paulo Purganti and his Wife' (1709)]

RIBBLESDALE, Lord (1854–1925)

It [is] gentlemanly to get one's quotations very slightly wrong. In that way one unprigs oneself and allows the company to correct one.

[In Cooper, *The Light of Common Day* (1959)]

SHAW, George Bernard (1856–1950)

I often quote myself. It adds spice to the conversation.

[*Reader's Digest*, 1943]

STOPPARD, Tom (1937–)

It's better to be quotable than to be honest.

[*The Guardian*]

STRUNSKY, Simeon (1879–1948)

Famous remarks are seldom quoted correctly.

[*No Mean City* (1944)]

WAUGH, Evelyn (1903–1966)

In the dying world I come from quotation is a national vice. It used to be the classics, now it's lyric verse.

[*The Loved One* (1948)]

WILLIAMS, Kenneth (1926–1988)

The nicest thing about quotes is that they give us a nodding acquaintance with the originator which is often socially impressive.

[*Acid Drops* (1980)]

YOUNG, Edward (1683–1765)

Some, for renown, on scraps of learning dote,
And think they grow immortal as they quote.

[*Love of Fame, the Universal Passion* (1725–1728)]

RACISM

BIKO, Steve (1946–1977)

We wanted to remove him [the white man] from our table, strip the table of all the trappings put on it by him, decorate it in true African style, settle down and then ask him to join us if he liked.

[Speech, 1971]

BJELKE-PETERSEN, Florence Isabel (1920–)

[On her husband, Premier of Queensland]
People who criticise Joh unfairly make me angry. They call him 'a racist pig' in Canberra. Joh's not a racist. Why, he's had Aborigines working for him.

[*Woman's Day*, 1975]

BOSMAN, Herman Charles (1905–1951)

Kafirs? (said Oom Schalk Lourens), Yes, I know them. And they're all the same. I fear the Almighty, and I respect His works, but I could never understand why He made the kafir and the rinderpest.

[*Mafeking Road* (1947)]

BRODSKY, Joseph (1940–1996)

Racism? But isn't it only a form of misanthropy?

[*Less Than One* (1986)]

CALWELL, Arthur Augustus (1894–1973)

[Defending the deportation of a Chinese refugee who, Calwell claimed, was not eligible to become a permanent resident of Australia]
There are many Wongs in the Chinese community, but I have to say – and I am sure that the honourable member for Balaclava will not mind me doing so – that 'two Wongs do not make a White'.

[Commonwealth Parliamentary Debates, 1947]

DE BLANK, Joost (1908–1968)

I suffer from an incurable disease – colour blindness.

[Attr.]

DISRAELI, Benjamin (1804–1881)

All is race; there is no other truth.

[*Tancred* (1847)]

EINSTEIN, Albert (1879–1955)

If my theory of relativity is proven successful, Germany will claim me as a German and France will declare that I am a citizen of the world. Should my theory prove untrue, France will say that I am a German and Germany will declare that I am a Jew.

[Address, c. 1929]

FANON, Frantz (1925–1961)

For the black man there is only one destiny. And it is white.

[*Black Skin, White Masks*]

FORSTER, E.M. (1879–1970)

The so-called white races are really pinko-gray.

[*A Passage to India* (1924)]

GOEBBELS, Joseph (1897–1945)

… *mir in Bälde einen Gesamtentwurf über die organisatorischen, sachlichen und materiellen Vorausmassnanahmen zur Durchführung der angestrebten Endlösung der Judenfrage vorzulegen.*
… to place before me soon a complete proposal for the organisational, practical and material preliminary measures which have to be taken in order to bring about the desired Final Solution to the Jewish question.

[Letter to Reinhard Heydrich, 1941]

GORDIMER, Nadine (1923–)

The force of white men's wills, which dispensed and withdrew life, imprisoned and set free, fed or starved, like God himself.

[*Six Feet of the Country* (1956)]

HAGGARD, H. Rider (1856–1925)

[Umbopa to Quatermain]
We are men, you and I.

[*King Solomon's Mines* (1885)]

HITLER, Adolf (1889–1945)

Was nicht gute Rasse ist auf dieser Welt, ist Spreu.
Whoever is not racially pure in this world is chaff.

[*Mein Kampf* (1925)]

KING, Martin Luther (1929–1968)

I want to be the white man's brother, not his brother-in-law.

[*New York Journal – American*, 1962]

We must learn to live together as brothers or perish together as fools.

[Speech at St. Louis, March 22, 1964]

LEE, Spike (1957–)

The only thing I like integrated is my coffee.

[*Malcolm X*, film, 1992]

LESSING, Doris (1919–)

When a white man in Africa by accident looks into the eyes of a native and sees the human being (which it is his chief preoccupation to avoid), his sense of guilt, which he denies, fumes up in resentment and he brings down the whip.

[*The Grass is Singing* (1950)]

[Referring to South Africa]
When old settlers say 'One has to understand the country', what they mean is, 'You have to get used to our ideas about the native.' They are saying, in effect, 'Learn our ideas, or otherwise get out; we don't want you.'

[*The Grass is Singing* (1950)]

MALCOLM X (1925–1965)

If you're born in America with a black skin, you're born in prison.

[Interview, June 1963]

Sitting at the table doesn't make you a diner, unless you eat some of what's on that plate. Being here in America doesn't make you an American. Being born here in America

doesn't make you an American.

[*Malcolm X Speaks*, 1965]

I believe in the brotherhood of all men, but I don't believe in wasting brotherhood on anyone who doesn't want to practise it with me.

[Speech, 1964]

We never made one step forward until world pressure put Uncle Sam on the spot … It has never been out of any internal sense of morality or legality or humanism that we were allowed to advance.

[Speech, 1964]

The Negro problem has ceased to be a Negro problem. It has ceased to be an American problem and has now become a world problem, a problem for all humanity.

[Speech, Harvard Law School, 1964]

MANDELA, Nelson (1918–)

I have fought against white domination, and I have fought against black domination. I have cherished the ideal of a democratic and free society in which all persons will live together in harmony and with equal opportunities. It is an ideal which I hope to live for and achieve. But, if needs be, it is an ideal for which I am prepared to die.

[Statement in the dock, 1964]

MÉNAGE, Gilles (1613–1692)

The evil of modern society isn't that it creates racism but that it creates conditions in which people who don't suffer from injustice seem incapable of caring very much about people who do.

[*The New Yorker*, 1992]

MENAND, Louis (1953–)

The evil of modern society isn't that it creates racism but that it creates conditions in which people who don't suffer from injustice seem incapable of caring very much about people who do.

[*The New Yorker*, 1992]

MENCKEN, H.L. (1880–1956)

One of the things that makes a Negro

unpleasant to white folk is the fact that he suffers from their injustice. He is thus a standing rebuke to them.

[*Notebooks* (1956)]

MILLER, Arthur (1915–)

If there weren't any anti-semitism, I wouldn't think of myself as Jewish.

[*The Observer*, 1995]

PATON, Alan (1903–1988)

I have one great fear in my heart, that one day when they [whites] are turned to loving, they will find we [blacks] are turned to hating.

[*Cry, the Beloved Country* (1948)]

It was on Wednesday 16 June 1976 that an era came to an end in South Africa. That was the day when black South Africans said to white, 'You can't do this to us any more.' It had taken three hundred years for them to say that.

[*Journey Continued* (1988)]

PLOMER, William (1903–1973)

The warm heart of any human that saw the black man first not as a black but as a man.

[*Turbott Wolfe* (1926)]

POWELL, Enoch (1912–1998)

[On race relations in Britain]

As I look ahead I am filled with foreboding. Like the Roman I seem to see 'The River Tiber foaming with much blood.'

[Speech, Birmingham, 1968]

PRINGLE, Thomas (1789–1834)

But I brought the handsomest bride of them all –
Brown Dinah, the bondmaid who sat in our hall …

Shall the Edict of Mercy be sent forth at last,
To break the harsh fetters of Colour and Caste?

[*Poetical Works* (1838)]

SHERIDAN, Philip Henry (1831–1888)

The only good Indian is a dead Indian.

[Attr.]

SMITH, Ian (1919–)

I don't believe in black majority rule in Rhodesia … not in a thousand years.

[Speech, 1976]

SONTAG, Susan (1933–)

The truth is that Mozart, Pascal, Boolean algebra, Shakespeare, parliamentary government, baroque churches, Newton, the emancipation of women, Kant, Marx, and Ballanchine ballets don't redeem what this particular civilisation has wrought upon the world. The white race is the cancer of human history.

[Attr.]

TECUMSEH (d. 1812)

Where today are the Pequot? Where are the Narragansett, the Mohican, the Pokanoket, and many other once powerful tribes of our people? They have vanished before the avarice and the oppression of the White Man, as snow before a summer sun.

[In Brown, *Bury My Heart at Wounded Knee* (1971)]

TOMASCHEK, Rudolphe (b. c.1895)

Modern Physics is an instrument of Jewry for the destruction of Nordic science … True physics is the creation of the German spirit.

[In Shirer, *The Rise and Fall of the Third Reich* (1960)]

TUTU, Archbishop Desmond (1931–)

It is very difficult now to find anyone in South Africa who ever supported apartheid.

[*The Observer*, 1994]

ZANGWILL, Israel (1864–1926)

The law of dislike for the unlike will always prevail. And whereas the unlike is normally situated at a safe distance, the Jews bring the unlike into the heart of every milieu, and must there defend a frontier line as large as the world.

[Speech, 1911]

See EQUALITY; FREEDOM; JEWS; PREJUDICE; SLAVERY; SOUTH AFRICA

READING

AUGUSTINE, Saint (354–430)

Tolle lege, tolle lege.

Take up and read, take up and read!

[*Confessions* (397–398)]

AUSTEN, Jane (1775–1817)

Oh, Lord! not I; I never read much; I have something else to do.

[*Northanger Abbey* (1818)]

BACON, Francis (1561–1626)

Read not to contradict and confute, nor to believe and take for granted, nor to find talk and discourse, but to weigh and consider.

['Of Studies' (1625)]

BAUDELAIRE, Charles (1821–1867)

Hypocrite lecteur, – mon semblable, – mon frère!

Hypocrite reader, my likeness, my brother!

[*Les Fleurs du mal* (1857)]

CHANDLER, Raymond (1888–1959)

All men who read escape from something else … [they] must escape at times from the deadly rhythm of their private thoughts.

[*Atlantic Monthly* (1944)]

COLTON, Charles Caleb (c.1780–1832)

Some read to think, – these are rare; some to unite, – these are common; and some to talk, – and these form the great majority.

[*Lacon* (1820)]

CRABBE, George (1754–1832)

Who often reads, will sometimes wish to write.

[*Tales* (1812)]

DESCARTES, René (1596–1650)

La lecture de tous les bons livres est comme une conversation avec les plus honnêtes gens des siècles passés.

The reading of all good books is like a conversation with the finest men of past centuries.

[*Discours de la Méthode* (1637)]

D'ISRAELI, Isaac (1766–1848)

There is an art of reading, as well as an art of

thinking, and an art of writing.

[*Literary Character* (1795)]

DISRAELI, Benjamin (1804–1881)

[His customary reply to those who sent him unsolicited manuscripts]

Thank you for the manuscript; I shall lose no time in reading it.

[Attr.]

EMERSON, Ralph Waldo (1803–1882)

Tis the good reader that makes the good book.

[*Society and Solitude* (1870)]

FLAUBERT, Gustave (1821–1880)

Mais ne lisez pas, comme les enfants lisent, pour vous amuser, ni comme les ambitieux lisent, pour vous instruire. Non, lisez pour vivre.

Do not read, as children do, for the sake of entertainment, or like the ambitious, for the purpose of instruction. No, read in order to live.

[Letter to Mlle Leroyer de Chantepie, 1857]

FRANKLIN, Benjamin (1706–1790)

[On being asked what condition of man he considered the most pitiable]

A lonesome man on a rainy day who does not know how to read.

[In Shriner, *Wit, Wisdom, and Foibles of the Great*]

GIBBON, Edward (1737–1794)

My early and invincible love of reading, which I would not exchange for the treasures of India.

[*Memoirs of My Life and Writings* (1796)]

HAMERTON, P.G. (1834–1894)

The art of reading is to skip judiciously.

[*The Intellectual Life* (1873)]

HANDKE, Peter (1942–)

Der gedankenloseste aller Menschen: der in jedem Buch nur blättert.

The most unthinking person of all: the one who only flicks through every book.

[*The Weight of the World. A Diary* (1977)]

HELPS, Sir Arthur (1813–1875)

Reading is sometimes an ingenious device

for avoiding thought.

[*Friends in Council* (1849)]

HOBBES, Thomas (1588–1679)

He was wont to say that if he had read as much as other men, he should have knowne no more than other men.

[In Aubrey, *Brief Lives* (c. 1693)]

JOHNSON, Samuel (1709–1784)

A man ought to read just as inclination leads him; for what he reads as a task will do him little good.

[In Boswell, *The Life of Samuel Johnson* (1791)]

KRAUS, Karl (1874–1936)

Man muss alle Schriftsteller zweimal lesen, die guten und die schlechten. Die einen wird man erkennen, die anderen entlarven.

You must read all writers twice, both the good ones and the bad ones. You'll recognize the good ones and you'll unmask the others.

[*Sayings and Contradictions* (1909)]

MAO TSE-TUNG (1893–1976)

To read too many books is harmful.

[*The New Yorker*, 1977]

MILTON, John (1608–1674)

Who reads
Incessantly, and to his reading brings not
A spirit and judgment equal or superior
(And what he brings, what needs he elsewhere seek)
Uncertain and unsettl'd still remains,
Deep verst in books and shallow in himself.

[*Paradise Regained* (1671)]

ORTON, Joe (1933–1967)

Reading isn't an occupation we encourage among police officers. We try to keep the paper work down to a minimum.

[*Loot* (1967)]

PETRONIUS ARBITER (d. AD 66)

Scimus te prae litteras fatuum esse.

We know that you are mad with too much reading.

[*Satyricon*]

QUARLES, Francis (1592–1644)

I wish thee as much pleasure in the reading, as I had in the writing.

[*Emblems* (1635)]

ROSCOMMON, Fourth Earl of (1633–1685)

Choose an author as you choose a friend.

[*An Essay on Translated Verse* (1684)]

RUSKIN, John (1819–1900)

But whether thus submissively or not, at least be sure that you go to the author to get at his meaning, not to find yours.

[*Sesame and Lilies* (1865)]

RUSSELL, Bertrand (1872–1970)

There are two motives for reading a book: one, that you enjoy it, the other that you can boast about it.

[*The Conquest of Happiness* (1930)]

SCHOPENHAUER, Arthur (1788–1860)

To expect a man to retain everything that he has ever read is like expecting him to carry about in his body everything that he has ever eaten.

[*Parerga and Paralipomena* (1851)]

SMITH, Logan Pearsall (1865–1946)

People say that life is the thing, but I prefer reading.

[*Afterthoughts* (1931)]

SMITH, Sydney (1771–1845)

Live always in the best company when you read.

[In Lady Holland, *Memoir* (1855)]

SOLZHENITSYN, Alexander (1918–)

Their teacher had advised them not to read Tolstoy's novels, because they were very long and would only confuse the clear ideas which they had acquired from reading critical studies about him.

[*The First Circle* (1968)]

STEELE, Sir Richard (1672–1729)

Reading is to the Mind, what Exercise is to the Body … But as Exercise becomes tedious and painful when we make use of it only as

REALISM

the Means of Health, so Reading is apt to grow uneasy and burdensome, when we apply our selves to it only for our Improvement in Virtue.

[*The Tatler*, 47, 1710]

STERNE, Laurence (1713–1768)
Digressions, incontestably, are the sunshine; – they are the life, the soul of reading; – take them out of this book for instance, – you might as well take the book along with them.

[*Tristram Shandy*]

WAUGH, Evelyn (1903–1966)
Lady Peabury was in the morning room reading a novel; early training gave a guilty spice to this recreation, for she had been brought up to believe that to read a novel before luncheon was one of the gravest sins it was possible for a gentlewoman to commit.

[*Work Suspended* (1942)]

WILDE, Oscar (1854–1900)
I never travel without my diary. One should always have something sensational to read in the train.

[*The Importance of Being Earnest* (1895)]

See BOOKS; CRITICISM; FICTION; LITERATURE; WRITING

REALISM

ADAMS, Scott (1957–)
My reality check bounced.

[*The Dilbert Principle*]

BACON, Francis (1561–1626)
We are much beholden to Machiavel and others, that write what men do, and not what they ought to do.

[*The Advancement of Learning* (1605)]

BOHM, David (1917–1992)
There are no things, only processes.

CERVANTES, Miguel de (1547–1616)
Mire vuestra merced … que aquellos que allí se

parecen no son gigantes, sino molinos de viento.
Look, your worship … those things which you see over there are not giants, but windmills.

[*Don Quixote* (1605)]

CONNOLLY, Cyril (1903–1974)
Everything is a dangerous drug to me except reality, which is unendurable.

[*The Unquiet Grave* (1944)]

DÜRRENMATT, Friedrich (1921–1990)
Wer dem Paradoxen gegenübersteht, setzt sich der Wirklichkeit aus.
Whoever is faced with the paradoxical exposes himself to reality.

[*The Physicists* (1962)]

ELIOT, T.S. (1888–1965)
Human kind
Cannot bear very much reality.

[*Four Quartets* (1944)]

FRY, Christopher (1907–)
There may always be another reality
To make fiction of the truth we think we've arrived at.

[*A Yard of Sun* (1970)]

HEGEL, Georg Wilhelm (1770–1831)
Was vernünftig ist; das ist wirklich: und was wirklich ist, das ist vernünftig.
What is rational is real, and what is real is rational.

[*Basis of Legal Philosophy* (1820)]

KHRUSHCHEV, Nikita (1894–1971)
If you cannot catch a bird of paradise, better take a wet hen.

[Attr.]

PINDAR (518–438 BC)
Strive not, my soul, for an immortal life, but make the most of the possibilities open to you.

[*Pythian Odes*]

TWAIN, Mark (1835–1910)
Don't part with your illusions. When they are gone, you may still exist, but you have ceased to live.

[*Pudd'nhead Wilson's Calendar* (1894)]

WILDE, Oscar (1854–1900)

The nineteenth century dislike of Realism is the rage of Caliban seeing his own face in a glass.

[*The Picture of Dorian Gray* (1891)]

Cecily: When I see a spade I call it a spade.
Gwendolen: I am glad to say that I have never seen a spade. It is obvious that our social spheres have been widely different.

[*The Importance of Being Earnest* (1895)]

REASON

DRYDEN, John (1631–1700)

Dim, as the borrowed beams of moon and stars
To lonely, weary, wandering travellers
Is reason to the soul.

[*Religio Laici* (1682)]

FRY, Christopher (1907–)

I've begun to believe that the reasonable
Is an invention of man, altogether in opposition
To the facts of creation.

[*The Firstborn* (1945)]

HODGSON, Ralph (1871–1962)

Reason has moons, but moons not hers,
Lie mirror'd on her sea,
Confounding her astronomers,
But, O! delighting me.

['Reason Has Moons' (1917)]

KANT, Immanuel (1724–1804)

Büchergelehrsamkeit vermehrt zwar die Kenntnisse, aber erweitert nicht den Begriff und die Einsicht, wo nicht Vernunft dazukommt.
Book learning certainly increases knowledge, but does not broaden one's ideas and insight when it is not accompanied by reason.

[*Pragmatic Anthropology* (1800)]

KEATS, John (1795–1821)

I have never yet been able to perceive how any thing can be known for truth by consecutive reasoning – and yet it must be.

[Letter to Benjamin Bailey, 22 November 1817]

POWELL, Sir John (1645–1713)

Let us consider the reason of the case. For nothing is law that is not reason.

[In Lord Raymond's *Reports* (1765)]

ROCHESTER, Earl of (1647–1680)

Reason, an ignis fatuus of the mind,
Which leaving the light of nature, sense, behind …

Then Old Age, and Experience, hand in hand,
Lead him to Death, and make him understand,
After a search so painful, and so long,
That all his life he has been in the wrong.
Huddled in dirt the reasoning engine lies,
Who was so proud, so witty, and so wise.

['A Satire Against Reason and Mankind' (1679)]

SHAW, George Bernard (1856–1950)

The man who listens to Reason is lost:
Reason enslaves all whose minds are not strong enough to master her.

[*Man and Superman* (1903)]

VOLTAIRE (1694–1778)

Quand la populace se mêle de raisonner, tout est perdu.
Once the people start to reason, all is lost.

[Letter to Damilaville, 1766]

See ART

REBELLION

ARENDT, Hannah (1906–1975)

The defiance of established authority, religious and secular, social and political, as a world-wide phenomenon may well one day be accounted the outstanding event of the last decade.

[*Crises of the Republic* (1972)]

ARNOLD, Thomas (1795–1842)

As for rioting, the old Roman way of dealing with that is always the right one; flog the rank and file, and fling the ringleaders from the Tarpeian rock.

[Letter, written before 1828]

BERLINGUER, Enrico (1922–1984)

Da ragazzo c'era in me un sentimento di ribellione. Contestavo, se vogliamo usare una parola di moda, tutto.

When I was a young man I felt within me a sentiment of rebellion. I used to challenge, to use a fashionable word, everything.

[*The Geography of Italy* (1975)]

BRADSHAW, John (1602–1659)

Rebellion to tyrants is obedience to God.

[In Randall, *Life of Jefferson* (1865)]

BURKE, Edmund (1729–1797)

Make the Revolution a parent of settlement, and not a nursery of future revolutions.

[*Reflections on the Revolution in France* (1790)]

CAMUS, Albert (1913–1960)

Tout révolutionnaire finit en oppresseur ou en hérétique.

Every revolutionary ends as an oppressor or a heretic.

[*The Rebel* (1951)]

Qu'est-ce qu'un homme révolté? Un homme qui dit non.

What is a rebel? A man who says no.

[*The Rebel* (1951)]

Toutes les révolutions modernes ont abouti á un renforcement de l'Etat.

All modern revolutions have led to a reinforcement of the power of the State.

[*The Rebel* (1951)]

CONRAD, Joseph (1857–1924)

The scrupulous and the just, the noble, humane, and devoted natures; the unselfish and the intelligent may begin a movement – but it passes away from them. They are not the leaders of a revolution. They are its victims.

[*Under Western Eyes* (1911)]

DURRELL, Lawrence (1912–1990)

No one can go on being a rebel too long without turning into an autocrat.

[*Balthazar* (1958)]

ENGELS, Friedrich (1820–1895)

The proletariat has nothing to lose but its chains in this revolution. It has a world to win. Workers of the world, unite!

[*The Communist Manifesto* (1848)]

GEORGE V (1865–1936)

[On hearing Mr Wheatley's life story]
Is it possible that my people live in such awful conditions? … I tell you, Mr Wheatley, that if I had to live in conditions like that I would be a revolutionary myself.

[In MacNeill Weir, *The Tragedy of Ramsay MacDonald* (1938)]

HILL, Reginald (1936–)

The first thing revolutionaries of the left or right give up is their sense of humour. The second thing is other people's rights.

[In Winks (ed.), *Colloquium on Crime* (1986)]

JEFFERSON, Thomas (1743–1826)

A little rebellion, now and then, is a good thing, and as necessary in the political world as storms in the physical.

[Letter to James Madison, January 30, 1787]

KHRUSHCHEV, Nikita (1894–1971)

If you feed people with revolutionary slogans alone they will listen today, they will listen tomorrow, they will listen the day after that, but on the fourth day they will say 'To hell with you!'.

[Attr.]

LEWIS, Wyndham (1882–1957)

The revolutionary simpleton is everywhere.

[*Time and Western Man* (1927)]

SHAKESPEARE, William (1564–1616)

Rebellion lay in his way, and he found it.

[*Henry IV, Part 1*, V.i]

STORR, Dr Anthony (1920–)

It is harder to rebel against love than against authority.

[Attr.]

TROTSKY, Leon (1879–1940)

Insurrection is an art, and like all arts it has its laws.

[*History of the Russian Revolution* (1933)]

VERGNIAUD, Pierre (1753–1793)

[Remark at his trial, 1793]

Il a été permis de craindre que la Révolution, comme Saturne, dévorât successivement tous ses enfants.

There was reason to fear that the Revolution, like Saturn, would eventually devour all her children one by one.

[In Lamartine, *Histoire des Girondins* (1847)]

WEIL, Simone (1909–1943)

On pense aujourd'hui á la révolution, non comme á une solution des problèmes posés par l'actualité, mais comme á un miracle dispensant de résoudre les problèmes.

Nowadays we think of revolution not as the solution to problems posed by current developments but as a miracle which releases us from the obligation to solve these problems.

[*Oppression and Freedom* (1955)]

WELLINGTON, Duke of (1769–1852)

Beginning reform is beginning revolution.

[In Mrs Arbuthnot's Journal, 1830]

See REVOLUTION

RECONCILIATION

MANDELA, Nelson (1918–)

The time for the healing of the wounds has come.

[Speech at his inauguration as President of South Africa, 10 May 1994]

WHITMAN, Walt (1819–1892)

Beautiful that war and all its deeds of carnage must in time be utterly lost,
That the hands of the sisters Death and Night incessantly softly wash again, and ever again, this soil'd world;
For my enemy is dead, a man as divine as myself is dead,
I look where he lies white-faced and still in the coffin – I draw near,
Bend down and touch lightly with my lips the white face in the coffin.

['Reconciliation' (1865)]

REFORM

CARLYLE, Thomas (1795–1881)

All reform except a moral one will prove unavailing.

[*Critical and Miscellaneous Essays* (1839)]

WEBB, Sidney (1859–1947)

The inevitability of gradualness.

[Presidential address to the annual conference of the Labour Party, 1923]

REGRET

CATO THE ELDER (234–149 BC)

In all my life, I have never repented but of three things: that I trusted a woman with a secret, that I went by sea when I might have gone by land, and that I passed a day in idleness.

[In Pliny, *Naturalis Historia*]

MAUGHAM, William Somerset (1874–1965)

It's no use crying over spilt milk, because all the forces of the universe were bent on spilling it.

[*Of Human Bondage* (1915)]

ROSSETTI, Dante Gabriel (1828–1882)

Look in my face; my name is Might-have-been
I am also called No-more, Too-Late, Farewell …

Then shalt thou see me smile, and turn apart
Thy visage to mine ambush at my heart
Sleepless with cold commemorative eyes.

[*The House of Life* (1881)]

THOMPSON, William Hepworth (1810–1886)

[Of Seeley's inaugural lecture as Professor of History at Cambridge, following Charles Kingsley]

I never could have supposed that we should have had so soon to regret the departure of our dear friend the late Professor.

[In A.J. Balfour, *Chapters of Autobiography*]

See APOLOGIES; MEMORY; MOURNING;
    NOSTALGIA; PAST; SORROW

RELIGION

ADDISON, Joseph (1672–1719)
We have in England a particular bashfulness
in every thing that regards religion.
[*The Spectator*, August 1712, 458]

ARNOLD, Matthew (1822–1888)
The true meaning of religion is thus not
simply morality, but morality touched by
emotion.
[*Literature and Dogma* (1873)]

ASHFORD, Daisy (1881–1972)
Bernard always had a few prayers in the hall
and some whiskey afterwards as he was
rarther pious but Mr Salteena was not very
addicted to prayers so he marched up to
bed.
[*The Young Visiters* (1919)]

BARRIE, Sir J.M. (1860–1937)
One's religion is whatever he is most
interested in, and yours is Success.
[*The Twelve-Pound Look*]

BEHAN, Brendan (1923–1964)
Pound notes are the best religion in the
world.
[*The Wit of Brendan Behan* (1968)]

BELLOC, Hilaire (1870–1953)
[Suggested rider to the Ten Commandments]
Candidates should not attempt more than
six of these.
[Attr.]

BLAKE, William (1757–1827)
I went to the Garden of Love,
And saw what I never had seen:
A Chapel was built in the midst,
Where I used to play on the green.

And the gates of this Chapel were shut,
And 'Thou shalt not' writ over the door …

And Priests in black gowns were walking

their rounds,
And binding with briars my joys & desires.
['The Garden of Love' (1794)]

BRENAN, Gerald (1894–1987)
Religions are kept alive by heresies, which
are really sudden explosions of faith. Dead
religions do not produce them.
[*Thoughts in a Dry Season* (1978)]

BROWNE, Sir Thomas (1605–1682)
At my devotion I love to use the civility of my
knee, my hat, and hand.
[*Religio Medici* (1643)]

As for those wingy mysteries in divinity, and
airy subtleties in religion, which have
unhinged the brains of better heads, they
never stretched the *pia mater* of mine.
Methinks there be not impossibilities
enough in Religion for an active faith.
[*Religio Medici* (1643)]

Men have lost their reason in nothing so
much as their religion, wherein stones and
clouts make martyrs.
[*Hydriotaphia: Urn Burial* (1658)]

Persecution is a bad and indirect way to
plant religion.
[*Religio Medici* (1643)]

BURKE, Edmund (1729–1797)
Nothing is so fatal to religion as indifference,
which is, at least, half infidelity.
[Letter to William Smith, 1795]

BURTON, Robert (1577–1640)
One religion is as true as another.
[*Anatomy of Melancholy* (1621)]

BUTLER, Samuel (1835–1902)
To be at all is to be religious more or less.
[*The Note-Books of Samuel Butler* (1912)]

CHARLES II (1630–1685)
He [Charles II] said once to myself, he was no
atheist, but he could not think God would
make a man miserable only for taking a little
pleasure out of the way. He disguised his
popery to the last.
[In Burnet, *The History of His Own Time* (1724)]

[Of Presbyterianism]
The king spoke to him [Lauderdale] to let that [Presbytery] go, for it was not a religion for gentlemen.

[In Burnet, *The History of His Own Time* (1724)]

CHESTERFIELD, Lord (1694–1773)

Religion is by no means a proper subject of conversation in a mixed company … It is too awful and respectable a subject to become a familiar one.

[Letter to his godson, c. 1766]

Putting moral virtues at the highest, and religion at the lowest, religion must still be allowed to be a collateral security, at least, to virtue; and every prudent man will sooner trust to two securities than to one.

[Letter to his son, 1750]

COLERIDGE, Samuel Taylor (1772–1834)

Time consecrates; and what is grey with age becomes religion

[Attr.]

COLTON, Charles Caleb (c.1780–1832)

Men will wrangle for religion; write for it; fight for it; anything but – live for it.

[*Lacon* (1820)]

DALY, Mary (1928–)

Patriarchy is itself the prevailing religion of the entire planet, and its essential message is necrophilia.

[*Gyn/Ecology: the Metaethics of Radical Feminism* (1979)]

DIDEROT, Denis (1713–1784)

Wandering in a vast forest at night, I have only a faint light to guide me. A stranger appears and says to me: 'My friend, you should blow out your candle in order to find your way more clearly.' This stranger is a theologian.

[*Addition aux Pensées Philosophiques*]

DIOGENES (THE CYNIC) (c.400–325 BC)

I do not know whether there are gods, but there ought to be.

[In Tertullian, *Ad Nationes*]

DIX, George Eglington (1901–1952)

It is no accident that the symbol of a bishop is a crook, and the sign of an archbishop is a double-cross.

[Letter to *The Times*, 1977]

DRYDEN, John (1631–1700)

Yet dull religion teaches us content;
But when we ask it where that blessing dwells,
It points to pedant colleges and cells.

[*The Conquest of Granada* (1670)]

EDDY, Mary Baker (1821–1910)

Christian Science explains all cause and effect as mental, not physical.

[*Science and Health, with Key to the Scriptures* (1875)]

ELLIS, Havelock (1859–1939)

The whole religious complexion of the modern world is due to the absence from Jerusalem of a lunatic asylum.

[*Impressions and Comments* (1914)]

EMERSON, Ralph Waldo (1803–1882)

The religions we call false were once true.

['Character' (1866)]

ERASMUS (c.1466–1536)

[Of his failure to fast during Lent]
I have a Catholic soul, but a Lutheran stomach.

[*Dictionnaire Encyclopédique*]

FIELDING, Henry (1707–1754)

When I mention religion, I mean the Christian religion; and not only the Christian religion, but the Protestant religion; and not only the Protestant religion but the Church of England.

[*Tom Jones* (1749)]

FLEMING, Marjory (1803–1811)

I hope I will be religious again but as for reganing my charecter I despare for it.

[In Esdaile (ed.), *Journals, Letters and Verses* (1934)]

FREUD, Sigmund (1856–1939)

Religion is an illusion and it derives its strength from the fact that it falls in with our instinctual desires.

[*New Introductory Lectures on Psychoanalysis* (1933)]

GIBBON, Edward (1737–1794)
The various modes of worship, which prevailed in the Roman world, were all considered by the people as equally true; by the philosopher, as equally false; and by the magistrate, as equally useful.

[*Decline and Fall of the Roman Empire* (1776–88)]

GOLDSMITH, Oliver (c.1728–1774)
As I take my shoes from the shoemaker, and my coat from the tailor, so I take my religion from the priest.

[In Boswell, *The Life of Samuel Johnson* (1791)]

HOOTON, Harry (1908–1961)
Psychology is the theology of the 20th century.

['Inhuman Race']

HOPE, Bob (1903–)
I do benefits for all religions. I'd hate to blow the hereafter on a technicality.

[In Simon Rose, *Classic Film Guide* (1995)]

INGE, William Ralph (1860–1954)
To become a popular religion, it is only necessary for a superstition to enslave a philosophy.

[*Outspoken Essays*]

JERROLD, Douglas William (1803–1857)
Religion's in the heart, not in the knees.

[*The Devil's Ducat* (1830)]

LUCRETIUS (c.95–55 BC)
Tantum religio potuit suadere malorum.
So potent a persuasion to evil was religion.

[*De Rerum Natura*]

MARLOWE, Christopher (1564–1593)
I count religion but a childish toy,
And hold there is no sin but ignorance.

[*The Jew of Malta* (c. 1592)]

MARX, Karl (1818–1883)
Religion … is the opium of the people.

[*A Contribution to the Critique of Hegel's Philosophy of Right* (1844)]

MELBOURNE, Lord (1779–1848)
[On listening to an evangelical sermon]
Things have come to a pretty pass when religion is allowed to invade the sphere of private life.

[In Russell, *Collections and Recollections* (1898)]

MENCKEN, H.L. (1880–1956)
We must respect the other fellow's religion, but only in the sense and to the extent that we respect his theory that his wife is beautiful and his children smart.

[*Notebooks* (1956)]

MONTAIGNE, Michel de (1533–1592)
Notre religion est faite pour extirper les vices; elle les couvre, les nourrit, les incite.
Our religion was made to root out vices; it covers them up, nourishes them, incites them.

[*Essais* (1580)]

NEWMAN, John Henry, Cardinal (1801–1890)
From the age of fifteen, dogma has been the fundamental principle of my religion: I know no other religion; I cannot enter into the idea of any other sort of religion; religion, as a mere sentiment, is to me a dream and a mockery.

[*Apologia pro Vita Sua* (1864)]

O'CASEY, Sean (1880–1964)
There's no reason to bring religion into it. I think we ought to have as great a regard for religion as we can, so as to keep it out of as many things as possible.

[*The Plough and the Stars* (1926)]

RUNCIE, Rosalind (1932–)
Too much religion makes me go pop.

[In M. Duggan, *Runcie: The Making of an Archbishop* (1983)]

RUNCIMAN, Sir Steven (1903–)
Unlike Christianity, which preached a peace that it never achieved, Islam unashamedly

came with a sword.

[*A History of the Crusades* (1954)]

SELDEN, John (1584–1654)

For a priest to turn a man when he lies a-dying, is just like one that has a long time solicited a woman, and cannot obtain his end; at length he makes her drunk, and so lies with her.

[*Table Talk*]

SHAFTESBURY, Earl of (1621–1683)

'People differ in their discourse and profession about these matters, but men of sense are really but of one religion.' … 'Pray, my Lord, what religion is that which men of sense agree in?' 'Madam,' says the earl immediately, 'men of sense never tell it.'

[In Bishop Burnet's *History of His Own Time* (1823)]

SHAW, George Bernard (1856–1950)

There is only one religion, though there are a hundred versions of it.

[*Plays Pleasant and Unpleasant* (1898)]

I can't talk religion to a man with bodily hunger in his eyes.

[*Major Barbara* (1907)]

SHELLEY, Percy Bysshe (1792–1822)

Earth groans beneath religion's iron age,
And priests dare babble of a God of peace,
Even whilst their hands are red with guiltless blood.

[*Queen Mab* (1813)]

STERNE, Laurence (1713–1768)

Whenever a man talks loudly against religion, – always suspect that it is not his reason, but his passions which have got the better of his creed.

[*Tristram Shandy* (1759–67)]

SWIFT, Jonathan (1667–1745)

We have just enough religion to make us hate, but not enough to make us love one another.

[*Thoughts on Various Subjects* (1711)]

WEBB, Beatrice (1858–1943)

Religion is love; in no case is it logic.

[*My Apprenticeship* (1926)]

ZANGWILL, Israel (1864–1926)

Let us start a new religion with one commandment, 'Enjoy thyself'.

[*Children of the Ghetto* (1892)]

See AFTERLIFE; ATHEISM; BELIEF; BIBLE; CHRISTIANITY; CHRISTMAS; CHURCH; DEVIL; GOD; HEAVEN; HELL; PRAYER; SAINTS; SUNDAY

REPENTANCE

DRYDEN, John (1631–1700)

Repentance is the virtue of weak minds.

[*The Indian Emperor* (1665)]

Repentance is but want of power to sin.

[*Palamon and Arcite* (1700)]

SCOTT, Sir Walter (1771–1832)

But with the morning cool repentance came.

[*Rob Roy* (1817)]

REPUTATION

BEAVERBROOK, Lord (1879–1964)

[Of Earl Haig]
With the publication of his Private Papers in 1952, he committed suicide twenty-five years after his death.

[*Men and Power* (1956)]

BURNEY, Fanny (1752–1840)

Nothing is so delicate as the reputation of a woman; it is at once the most beautiful and most brittle of all human things.

[*Evelina* (1778)]

COLETTE (1873–1954)

Ne porte jamais de bijoux artistiques, ça déconsidère complètement une femme.
Never wear artistic jewellery; it ruins a woman's reputation.

[*Gigi* (1944)]

ELIOT, George (1819–1880)

'Abroad', that large home of ruined reputations.

[*Felix Holt* (1866)]

EMERSON, Ralph Waldo (1803–1882)

I trust a good deal to common fame, as we all must. If a man has good corn, or wood, or boards, or pigs, to sell, or can make better chairs or knives, crucibles, or church organs, than anybody else, you will find a broad, hard-beaten road to his house, though it be in the woods.

[*Journals*, 1855]

HILL, Reginald (1936–)

The ultimate stage of reputation would be to have a name so powerful in market terms it would sell anything. Well, the money would be nice, but I don't know yet if I'm ready for the irresponsibility.

[In Winks (ed.), *Colloquium on Crime* (1986)]

KEYNES, John Maynard (1883–1946)

Wordly wisdom teaches that it is better for the reputation to fail conventionally than to succeed unconventionally.

[*The General Theory of Employment, Interest and Money* (1936)]

MITCHELL, Margaret (1900–1949)

Until you've lost your reputation, you never realize what a burden it was or what freedom really is.

[*Gone with the Wind* (1936)]

SHAKESPEARE, William (1564–1616)

Good name in man and woman, dear my lord,
Is the immediate jewel of their souls:
Who steals my purse steals trash; 'tis something, nothing;
'Twas mine, 'tis his, and has been slave to thousands;
But he that filches from me my good name
Robs me of that which not enriches him
And makes me poor indeed.

[*Othello*, III.iii]

The purest treasure mortal times afford

Is spotless reputation; that away,
Men are but gilded loam or painted clay.
A jewel in a ten-times barr'd-up chest
Is a bold spirit in a loyal breast.
Mine honour is my life; both grow in one;
Take honour from me, and my life is done.

[*Richard II*, I.i]

WASHINGTON, George (1732–1799)

Associate yourself with men of good quality if you esteem your own reputation; for 'tis better to be alone than in bad company.

[*Rules of Civility and Decent Behaviour*]

See CELEBRITY; CHARACTER; FAME

RESPECT

ACCIUS, Lucius (170–86 BC)

Let them hate, so long as they fear.

[*Atreus*]

CHURCHILL, Sir Winston (1874–1965)

We do not covet anything from any nation except their respect.

[Broadcast to the French people, October 1940]

VOLTAIRE (1694–1778)

We owe respect to the living; to the dead we owe only truth.

[*Oeuvres*, 'Premiere lettre sur Oedipe']

See COURTESY; MANNERS

RESPONSIBILITY

SAINT-EXUPÉRY, Antoine de (1900–1944)

Tu deviens responsable pour toujours de ce que tu a apprivoisé. Tu es responsable de ta rose.

You become responsible, for ever, for what you have tamed. You are responsible for your rose.

[*The Little Prince* (1943), 21]

SEMPLE, Robert (1873–1955)

[Allegedly said on the occasion of the Fordell tunnel botch, 1944]

As minister I accept the responsibility but

not the blame.

[In Richard Long, *Dominion* (1984)]

TRUMAN, Harry S. (1884–1972)
The buck stops here.

[Sign on his desk]

RETALIATION

MARSDEN, Samuel (1792–1848)
[On Christianity]

A hefty whaler, after some discussion with Marsden, remarked, 'Your religion teaches that if a man is hit on one cheek, he will turn the other.' And hit Marsden on the right cheek. Marsden obediently offered his left cheek and received a second blow. 'Now,' he said, 'I have obeyed my Master's commands. What I do next, he left to my own judgement. Take this.' And knocked the man down.

[From Mrs P.R. Woodhouse, oral tradition]

PARKER, Dorothy (1893–1967)
It costs me never a stab nor squirm
To tread by chance upon a worm.
'Aha, my little dear,' I say,
'Your clan will pay me back one day.'

[*Sunset Gun*, 'Thoughts for a Sunshiny Morning']

See PUNISHMENT; REVENGE

RETIREMENT

ALI, Muhammad (1942–)
[Announcing his retirement]

I want to get out with my greatness intact.

[*The Observer*, 1974]

TAKAYAMA, Hideko
Husbands' inertia at home has made its mark on the language. Wives refer to their menfolk with fond exasperation as 'oversize' trash – and males sheepishly apply the term to themselves. A more recent coinage tags retired husbands as 'wet leaves': no matter how you try to sweep them out the door, they stick to the spot where they landed.

[*Newsweek*, 1990]

THOMSON, James (1700–1748)
An elegant sufficiency, content,
Retirement, rural quiet, friendship, books.

[*The Seasons* (1746)]

See AGE; LONGEVITY

REVENGE

ATWOOD, Margaret (1939–)
An eye for an eye leads only to more blindness.

[*Cat's Eye* (1988)]

BACON, Francis (1561–1626)
Revenge is a kind of wild justice, which the more man's nature runs to, the more ought law to weed it out.

['Of Revenge' (1625)]

A man that studieth revenge keeps his own wounds green.

['Of Revenge' (1625)]

THE BIBLE
(King James Version)
Vengeance is mine; I will repay, saith the Lord.

[*Romans*, 12:19]

CYRANO DE BERGERAC, Savinien de (1619–1655)
Périsse l'Univers, pourvu que je me venge.
The universe may perish, so long as I have my revenge.

[*La Mort d'Agrippine* (1654)]

FORD, John (c.1586–1639)
Revenge proves its own executioner.

[*The Broken Heart* (1633)]

MILTON, John (1608–1674)
Revenge, at first though sweet,
Bitter ere long back on it self recoils.

[*Paradise Lost* (1667)]

PROVERBS
Revenge is sweet.

Revenge is a dish that tastes better cold.

SCOTT, Sir Walter (1771–1832)

Vengeance, deep-brooding o'er the slain,
Had lock'd the source of softer woe.

[The Lay of the Last Minstrel (1805), I]

SHAKESPEARE, William (1564–1616)

Let's make us med'cines of our great revenge
To cure this deadly grief.

[Macbeth, IV.iii]

Heat not a furnace for your foe so hot
That it do singe yourself.

[Henry VIII, I.i]

See RETALIATION

REVOLUTION

ARISTOTLE (384–322 BC)

Revolutions may spring from trifles, but their issues are far from trifling.

[Politics, I]

BOULEZ, Pierre (1925–)

Revolutions are celebrated when they are no longer dangerous.

[The Guardian, 1989]

DISRAELI, Benjamin (1804–1881)

I have been ever of opinion that revolutions are not to be evaded.

[Coningsby (1844)]

EMERSON, Ralph Waldo (1803–1882)

Here once the embattled farmers stood,
And fired the shot heard round the world.

[Poems (1847)]

FOX, Charles James (1749–1806)

[On the Fall of the Bastille]
How much the greatest event it is that ever happened in the world! and how much the best!

[Letter, 1789]

JEFFERSON, Thomas (1743–1826)

To attain all this [universal republicanism], however, rivers of blood must yet flow, and years of desolation pass over; yet the object is worth rivers of blood, and years of desolation.

[Letter to John Adams, 1823]

KAFKA, Franz (1883–1924)

every revolution evaporates, leaving behind only the slime of a new bureaucracy.

[The Great Wall of China: Aphorisms 1917–1919]

LA ROCHEFOUCAULD (1747–1827)

[In reply to Louis XVI's question 'C'est une révolte?' on hearing of the fall of the Bastille]
Non, Sire, c'est une révolution.
No, Sire, it is a revolution.

[Remark, 1789]

LENIN, V.I. (1870–1924)

The substitution of the proletarian for the bourgeois state is impossible without a violent revolution.

[The State and Revolution (1917)]

LEWIS, Wyndham (1882–1957)

The revolutionary simpleton is everywhere.

[Time and Western Man (1927)]

LINKLATER, Eric (1899–1974)

There won't be any revolution in America … The people are too clean. They spend all their time changing their shirts and washing themselves. You can't feel fierce and revolutionary in a bathroom.

[Juan in America (1931)]

ORWELL, George (1903–1950)

Nine times out of ten a revolutionary is merely a climber with a bomb in his pocket.

[New English Weekly, 1939]

PAINE, Thomas (1737–1809)

A share in two revolutions is living to some purpose.

[In Eric Foner, *Tom Paine and Revolutionary America* (1976)]

REED, John (1887–1920)

[Of the October Revolution in Russia]
Ten Days that Shook the World.

[Title of book, 1919]

SEWARD, William (1801–1872)

I know, and all the world knows, that revolutions never go backward.

[Speech at Rochester on the Irrepressible Conflict, 1858]

SIEYÈS, Abbé Emmanuel Joseph (1748–1836)

[Reply when asked what he did during the French Revolution]

J'ai vécu.

I lived.

[In F.A.M. Mignet, *Notice historique sur la vie et les travaux de M. le Comte de Sieyès* (1836)]

TALLEYRAND, Charles-Maurice de (1754–1838)

[Of the French Revolution]

Qui n'a pas vécu dans les années voisines de 1789 ne sait pas ce que c'est que le plaisir de vivre.

He who has not lived during the years around 1789 cannot know what is meant by the joy of living.

[In M. Guizot, *Mémoires pour servir á l'histoire de mon temps* (1858)]

TROTSKY, Leon (1879–1940)

The revolution does not choose its paths, it makes its first steps towards victory under the belly of a Cossack's horse.

[*History of the Russian Revolution* (1933)]

Revolutions are always verbose.

[*History of the Russian Revolution* (1933)]

The fundamental premise of a revolution is that the existing social structure has become incapable of solving the urgent problems connected with the development of the nation.

[*History of the Russian Revolution* (1933)]

USTINOV, Sir Peter (1921–)

Revolutions have never succeeded unless the establishment does three-quarters of the work.

[*Dear Me* (1977)]

WORDSWORTH, William (1770–1850)

Bliss was it in that dawn to be alive,
But to be young was very heaven.

[*The Prelude* (1850)]

See REBELLION

RICH AND POOR

DISRAELI, Benjamin (1804–1881)

'Two nations; between whom there is no intercourse and no sympathy; who are as ignorant of each other's habits, thoughts, and feelings, as if they were dwellers in different zones, or inhabitants of different planets; who are formed by a different breeding, are fed by a different food, are ordered by different manners, and are not governed by the same laws.'
'You speak of –' said Egremont, hesitatingly.
'THE RICH AND THE POOR.'

[*Sybil* (1845)]

PROVERB

There's one law for the rich, and another for the poor.

SHAW, George Bernard (1856–1950)

I am a Millionaire. That is my religion.

[*Major Barbara* (1907)]

SMITH, Adam (1723–1790)

The rich only select from the heap what is most precious and agreeable. They consume little more than the poor, and in spite of their natural selfishness and rapacity … they divide with the poor the produce of all their improvements. They are led by an invisible hand to make nearly the same distribution of the necessaries of life, which would have been made, had the earth been divided into equal portions among all its inhabitants.

[*The Theory of Moral Sentiments* (1759)]

SMITH, Logan Pearsall (1865–1946)

It is the wretchedness of being rich that you have to live with rich people.

[*Afterthoughts* (1931)]

Eat with the rich, but go to the play with the Poor, who are capable of Joy.

[*Afterthoughts* (1931)]

To suppose, as we all suppose, that we could be rich and not behave as the rich behave, is like supposing that we could drink all day and keep absolutely sober.

[*Afterthoughts* (1931)]

STEAD, Christina (1902–1983)

The rich take their time, the rich marry late so that property will be divided little and late, while the poor rush to marry and divide the little pay that one gets.

[*For Love Alone* (1944)]

VIDAL, Gore (1925–)

There's a lot to be said for being *nouveau riche* and the Reagans mean to say it all.

[*The Observer*, 1981]

WILDE, Oscar (1854–1900)

We are often told that the poor are grateful for charity. Some of them are, no doubt, but the best amongst the poor are never grateful. They are ungrateful, discontented, disobedient, and rebellious. They are quite right to be so.

[*The Fortnightly Review*, 1891]

WOOLLCOTT, Alexander (1887–1943)

[On being shown round Moss Hart's elegant country house and grounds]
Just what God would have done if he had the money.

[Attr.]

See MONEY AND WEALTH; POVERTY

RIDICULE

ALBEE, Edward (1928–)

I have a fine sense of the ridiculous, but no sense of humour.

[*Who's Afraid of Virginia Woolf?* (1962)]

HATTERSLEY, Roy (1932–)

In politics, being ridiculous is more damaging than being extreme.

[*The Observer*, 1996]

NAPOLEON I (1769–1821)

Du sublime au ridicule il n'y a qu'un pas.
It is only one step from the sublime to the ridiculous.

[In De Pradt, *Histoire de l'Ambassade dans le grand-duché de Varsovie en 1812* (1815)]

PAINE, Thomas (1737–1809)

The sublime and the ridiculous are often so nearly related, that it is difficult to class them separately. One step above the sublime, makes the ridiculous; and one step above the ridiculous, makes the sublime again.

[*The Age of Reason* (1795)]

SCOTT, Sir Walter (1771–1832)

Ridicule often checks what is absurd, and fully as often smothers that which is noble.

[*Quentin Durward* (1823)]

VOLTAIRE (1694–1778)

I have never made but one prayer to God, a very short one: 'O Lord, make my enemies ridiculous.' And God granted it.

[Letter to Damilaville, 1767]

See CONTEMPT; SATIRE

RIGHT AND WRONG

ANONYMOUS

In simple cases, presenting one obvious right way versus one obvious wrong way, it is often wiser to choose the wrong way so as to expedite subsequent revision.

BUFFETT, Warren (1930–)

It is better to be approximately right than precisely wrong.

[*Fortune*, 1994]

CLAY, Henry (1777–1852)

I had rather be right than be President.

[Remark, 1839]

COLERIDGE, Samuel Taylor (1772–1834)

The innumerable multitude of Wrongs
By man on man inflicted.

['Religious Musings' (1796)]

CONFUCIUS (c.550–c.478 BC)

To see what is right and not to do it is want of courage.

[*Analects*]

COWPER, William (1731–1800)

A noisy man is always in the right.

['Conversation' (1782)]

EMERSON, Ralph Waldo (1803–1882)

No law can be sacred to me but that of my nature. Good and bad are but names very readily transferable to that or this; the only right is what is after my own constitution, the only wrong what is against it.

[*Essays, First Series* (1841)]

GOLDWYN, Samuel (1882–1974)

I am willing to admit that I may not always be right, but I am never wrong.

[Attr.]

JUNIUS (1769–1772)

It is not that you do wrong by design, but that you should never do right by mistake.

[*Letters* (1769–1771)]

KINGSLEY, Charles (1819–1875)

Some say that the age of chivalry is past, that the spirit of romance is dead. The age of chivalry is never past, so long as there is a wrong left unredressed on earth.

[In Mrs C. Kingsley, *Life* (1879)]

LA CHAUSSÉE, Nivelle de (1692–1754)

Quand tout le monde a tort, tout le monde a raison.
When everyone is wrong, everyone is right.

[*La Gouvernante* (1747)]

MELBOURNE, Lord (1779–1848)

[Replying to someone who said he would support Melbourne so long as he was right]
What I want is men who will support me when I am in the wrong.

[In Lord David Cecil, *Lord M.* (1954)]

SOLON (c.638–c.559 BC)

Wrongdoing can only be avoided if those who are not wronged feel the same indignation at it as those who are.

[Attr.]

See GOOD AND EVIL; MORALITY; PRINCIPLES

RIGHTS

CARLYLE, Thomas (1795–1881)

Surely of all 'rights of man', this right of the ignorant man to be guided by the wiser, to be, gently or forcibly, held in the true course by him, is the indisputablest.

[*Chartism* (1839)]

CONDORCET, Antoine-Nicolas de (1743–1794)

Either none of mankind possesses genuine rights, or everyone shares them equally; whoever votes against another's rights, whatever his religion, colour or sex, forswears his own.

[In Vansittart (ed.), *Voices of the Revolution* (1989)]

JEFFERSON, Thomas (1743–1826)

We hold these truths to be self-evident: that all men are created equal; that they are endowed by their Creator with certain unalienable rights; that among these are life, liberty, and the pursuit of happiness.

[Declaration of Independence, 1776]

JOHNSON, Samuel (1709–1784)

I have got no further than this: Every man has a right to utter what he thinks truth, and every other man has a right to knock him down for it. Martyrdom is the test.

[In Boswell, *The Life of Samuel Johnson* (1791)]

MAGNA CARTA (1215)

Nullus liber homo capiatur, vel imprisonetur, aut disseisiatur, aut utlagetur, aut exuletur, aut aliquo modo destruatur, nec super eum ibimus, nec super eum mittemus, nisi per legale judicium parium suorum vel per legem terrae.
No free man shall be taken or imprisoned or dispossessed, or outlawed or exiled, or in any way destroyed, nor will we go upon him, nor will we send against him, except by the lawful judgement of his peers or by the law of the land.

[Clause 39]

PANKHURST, Emmeline (1858–1928)

Women had always fought for men, and for

their children. Now they were ready to fight for their own human rights. Our militant movement was established.

[*My Own Story* (1914)]

UNIVERSAL DECLARATION OF HUMAN RIGHTS

All human beings are born free and equal in dignity and rights.

[Article 1]

VOLTAIRE (1694–1778)

I disapprove of what you say, but I will defend to the death your right to say it.

[Attr.]

See EQUALITY; FEMINISM; FREEDOM; JUSTICE AND INJUSTICE

RULES

CARROLL, Lewis (1832–1898)

'That's not a regular rule: you invented it just now.'
'It's the oldest rule in the book,' said the King.
'Then it ought to be Number One,' said Alice.

[*Alice's Adventures in Wonderland* (1865)]

The rule is, jam to-morrow and jam yesterday – but never jam to-day.

[*Through the Looking-Glass (and What Alice Found There)* (1872)]

CHARLES I (1600–1649)

I will end with a rule that may serve for a statesman, a courtier, or a lover – never make a defence or apology before you be accused.

[Letter to Wentworth, 1636]

CLOUGH, Arthur Hugh (1819–1861)

Thou shalt have one God only; who
Would be at the expense of two? ...

Thou shalt not kill; but need'st not strive
Officiously to keep alive.
Do not adultery commit;
Advantage rarely comes of it.
Thou shalt not steal; an empty feat,
When it's so lucrative to cheat ...

Thou shalt not covet; but tradition
Approves all forms of competition.

['The Latest Decalogue' (1862)]

MAYHEW, Jonathan (1720–1766)

Rulers have no authority from God to do mischief.

[*A Discourse Concerning Unlimited Submission and Non-Resistance to the Higher Powers* (1750)]

MELBA, Dame Nellie (1861–1931)

The first rule in opera is the first rule in life: see to everything yourself.

[*Melodies and Memories* (1925)]

MOLIÈRE (1622–1673)

Je voudrais bien savoir si la grande règle de toutes les règles n'est pas de plaire.
I would like to know if, after all, the greatest rule of all is not to please.

[*L'Ecole des Femmes* (1662)]

RABELAIS, François (c.1494–c.1553)

[Referring to the fictional Abbey of Thélème]
En leur règle n'estoit que ceste clause: 'fay ce que vouldra.'
In their rules there was only this one clause: 'Do what you will.'

[*Gargantua* (1534)]

SHAW, George Bernard (1856–1950)

The golden rule is that there are no golden rules.

[*Man and Superman* (1903)]

See REBELLION

RUSSIA

CHURCHILL, Sir Winston (1874–1965)

I cannot forecast to you the action of Russia. It is a riddle wrapped in a mystery inside an enigma.

[Broadcast, October 1939]

NICHOLAS I, Emperor of Russia (1796–1855)

Russia has two generals in whom she can trust – Generals Janvier and Février.

[Attr.]

NIXON, Richard (1913–1994)

[Urging more generous support for Boris Yeltsin]
Without large-scale outside aid, Russia may turn to a new despotism, which could be a far more dangerous threat to peace and freedom than the old Soviet totalitarianism.

[Remark at a Washington conference, 1992]

REAGAN, Ronald (1911–)

[During a microphone test prior to a radio broadcast]
My fellow Americans, I am pleased to tell you that I have signed legislation to outlaw Russia for ever. We begin bombing in five minutes.

[Audio recording, 1984]

TOLSTOYA, Tatyana

In our country we are all great specialists in the irrational but not yet great specialists in the logical … Today in Russia there are as many sorcerers as militia men.

[Interview, Waterstones, Glasgow]

TROTSKY, Leon (1879–1940)

From being a patriotic myth, the Russian people have become a terrible reality.

[*History of the Russian Revolution* (1933)]

YEVTUSHENKO, Yevgeny (1933–)

No Jewish blood runs among my blood, but I am as bitterly and hardly hated by every anti-semite as if I were a Jew. By this I am a Russian.

['Babi Yar' (1961)]

ZHIRINOVSKY, Vladimir (b. 1946–)

The whole nation, I promise you, will experience an orgasm next year.

[In *Newsweek*, 1994]

See COMMUNISM

S

SACRIFICE

BROOKE, Rupert (1887–1915)
Blow out, you bugles, over the rich Dead!
There's none of these so lonely and poor of
old,
But, dying, has made us rarer gifts than gold.
These laid the world away; poured out the
red
Sweet wine of youth, gave up the years to be
Of work and joy, and that unhoped serene,
That men call age; and those who would
have been,
Their sons, they gave, their immortality.
[*The Dead*' (1914)]

EWER, William Norman (1885–1976)
I gave my life for freedom – This I know:
For those who bade me fight had told me so.
[*Five Souls and Other Verses*
(1917)]

ROSEWARNE, V.A., Pilot Officer (1916–1940)
The universe is so vast and so ageless that
the life of one man can only be justified by
the measure of his sacrifice.
[Letter to his mother, 1940]

YEATS, W.B. (1865–1939)
Too long a sacrifice
Can make a stone of the heart.
[*Easter, 1916* (1916)]

See WAR

SAINTS

BROWNE, Sir Thomas (1605–1682)
There are many (questionless) canonized on
earth, that shall never be Saints in Heaven.
[*Religio Medici* (1643)]

POPE, Alexander (1688–1744)
For Virtue's self may too much zeal be had;

The worst of Madmen is a Saint run mad.
[*Imitations of Horace* (1737–1738)]

PROVERB
All are not saints that go to church.

SAKI (1870–1916)
There may have been disillusionments in the
lives of the mediaeval saints, but they would
scarcely have been better pleased if they
could have foreseen that their names would
be associated nowadays chiefly with
racehorses and the cheaper clarets.
[*Reginald* (1904)]

See BELIEF; CHURCH; MIRACLES;
RELIGION

SATIRE

LEWIS, Wyndham (1882–1957)
In its essence the purpose of satire – whether
verse or prose – is aggression … Satire has a
great big blaring target. If successful, it blasts
a great big hole in the centre.
[*'Note on Verse-Satire'*]

MONTAGU, Lady Mary Wortley (1689–1762)
Satire should, like a polished razor keen,
Wound with a touch that's scarcely felt or
seen.
[*'To the Imitator of the First Satire of Horace'*]

SWIFT, Jonathan (1667–1745)
Satire is a kind of glass, wherein beholders
do generally discover everybody's face but
their own.
[*The Battle of the Books* (1704)]

Satire, by being levelled at all, is never
resented for an offence by any.
[*A Tale of a Tub* (1704)]

See RIDICULE

SCHOLARS

CONFUCIUS (c.550–c.478 BC)

The scholar who cherishes the love of comfort, is not fit to be deemed a scholar.

[*Analects*]

LIPPMANN, Walter (1889–1974)

I doubt whether the student can do a greater work for his nation in this grave moment in its history than to detach himself from its preoccupations, refusing to let himself be absorbed by distractions about which, as a scholar, he can do almost nothing.

[*The Scholar in a Troubled World* (1932)]

SCHOPENHAUER, Arthur (1788–1860)

Die Gelehrten aber, wie sie in der Regel sind, studieren zu dem Zweck, lehren und schreiben zu können. Daher gleicht ihr Kopf einem Magen und Gedärmen, daraus die Speisen unverdaut wieder abgehn.
Scholars, however, as a rule study with the aim of being able to teach and write. That is why their heads are like a stomach and intestines from which food passes out again undigested.

[*Parerga und Paralipomena* (1851)]

SWIFT, Jonathan (1667–1745)

Then, rising with Aurora's light,
The Muse invoked, sit down to write;
Blot out, correct, insert, refine,
Enlarge, diminish, interline …

As learned commentators view
In Homer more than Homer knew.

['On Poetry' (1733)]

YEATS, W.B. (1865–1939)

Bald heads forgetful of their sins,
Old, learned, respectable bald heads
Edit and annotate the lines
That young men, tossing on their beds,
Rhymed out in love's despair
To flatter beauty's ignorant ear.

All shuffle there; all cough in ink;
All wear the carpet with their shoes;
All think what other people think;

All know the man their neighbour knows.
Lord, what would they say
Did their Catullus walk that way?

[In *Catholic Anthology 1914–1915*]

See EDUCATION; KNOWLEDGE; LEARNING; SCHOOL; TEACHERS; WISDOM

SCHOOL

ANTHONY, Susan B. (1820–1906)

And yet, in the schoolroom more than any other place, does the difference of sex, if there is any, need to be forgotten.

[In Theodore Stanton and Harriet Stanton Blatch (eds), *Elizabeth Cady Stanton* (1922)]

BEERBOHM, Sir Max (1872–1956)

Not that I had any special reason for hating school … I was a modest, good-humoured boy. It is Oxford that has made me insufferable.

[*More* (1899)]

CLARK, Lord Kenneth (1903–1983)

[On boarding schools]
This curious, and, to my mind, objectionable feature of English education was maintained solely in order that parents could get their children out of the house.

[*Another Part of the Wood* (1974)]

CONNOLLY, Cyril (1903–1974)

The ape-like virtues without which no one can enjoy a public school.

[*Enemies of Promise* (1938)]

DAVIES, Robertson (1913–1995)

The most strenuous efforts of the most committed educationalists in the years since my boyhood have been quite unable to make a school into anything but a school, which is to say a jail with educational opportunities.

[*The Cunning Man* (1994)]

DICKENS, Charles (1812–1870)

EDUCATION. – At Mr Wackford Squeer's

Academy, Dotheboys Hall, at the delightful village of Dotheboys, near Greta Bridge in Yorkshire, Youth are boarded, clothed, booked, furnished with pocket-money, provided with all necessaries, instructed in all languages, living and dead, mathematics, orthography, geometry, astronomy, trigonometry, the use of the globes, algebra, single stick (if required), writing, arithmetic, fortification, and every other branch of classical literature. Terms, twenty guineas per annum. No extras, no vacations, and diet unparalleled.

[*Nicholas Nickleby* (1839)]

FIELDING, Henry (1707–1754)
Public schools are the nurseries of all vice and immorality.

[*Joseph Andrews* (1742)]

FORSTER, E.M. (1879–1970)
[Of public schoolboys]
They go forth into it [the world] with well-developed bodies, fairly developed minds, and undeveloped hearts.

[*Abinger Harvest* (1936)]

GREENE, Graham (1904–1991)
I had left civilisation behind and entered a savage country of strange customs and inexplicable cruelties: a country in which I was a foreigner and a suspect, quite literally a hunted creature, known to have dubious associates. Was not my father the headmaster? I was like the son of a quisling in a country under occupation.

[*A Sort of Life* (1971)]

LINDSAY, Sir David (c.1490–1555)
We think them verray naturall fules,
That lernis ouir mekle at the sculis.

['Complaynt to the King']

NEIL, A.S. (1883–1973)
'Casting Out Fear' ought to be the motto over every school door.

[*The Problem Child* (1926)]

ORWELL, George (1903–1950)
Probably the Battle of Waterloo was won on the playing-fields of Eton, but the opening battles of all subsequent wars have been lost there.

[*The Lion and the Unicorn* (1941)]

PARSONS, Tony (1953–)
The death of the grammar schools – those public schools without the sodomy – resulted in state education relinquishing its role of nurturing bright young working class kids.

[*Arena*, 1989]

PATTEN, Brian (1946–)
Before playtime let us consider the possibilities of getting stoned on milk.

[*Grinning Jack* (1990)]

RIFKIND, Malcolm (1946–)
Every school needs a debating society far more than it needs a computer. For a free society, it is essential.

[In Kamm and Lean (eds), *A Scottish Childhood* (1985)]

SAKI (1870–1916)
But, good gracious, you've got to educate him first. You can't expect a boy to be vicious till he's been to a good school.

[*Reginald in Russia* (1910)]

SEARLE, Ronald William Fordham (1920–)
Though loaded firearms were strictly forbidden at St Trinian's to all but Sixth-Formers … one or two of them carried automatics acquired in the holidays, generally the gift of some indulgent relative.

[*The Terror of St Trinian's* (1952)]

WAUGH, Evelyn (1903–1966)
That's the public-school system all over. They may kick you out, but they never let you down.

[*Decline and Fall* (1928)]

WELLINGTON, Duke of (1769–1852)
The battle of Waterloo was won on the playing fields of Eton.

[Attr.]

See EDUCATION; KNOWLEDGE; LEARNING; TEACHERS; WISDOM

SCIENCE

AMIS, Martin (1949–)

Not only are all characters and scenes in this book entirely fictitious; most of the technical, medical and psychological data are too. My working maxim here has been as follows: I may not know much about science but I know what I like.

[*Dead Babies* (1975)]

ANONYMOUS

No experiment is reproducible.

[Wyszowski's Law]

When a distinguished but elderly scientist states that something is possible, he is almost certainly right. When he states that something is impossible, he is very probably wrong.

[Clarke's First Law.]

The limits of the possible can only be defined by going beyond them into the impossible.

[Clarke's Second Law]

ARCHIMEDES (c.287–212 BC)

Give me a place to stand, and I will move the Earth.

[*On levers*]

ARNOLD, Thomas (1795–1842)

Rather than have Physical Science the principal thing in my son's mind, I would rather have him think that the Sun went round the Earth, and the Stars were merely spangles set in a bright blue firmament.

[In Alan L. Mackay, *The Harvest of a Quiet Eye* (1977)]

AUDEN, W.H. (1907–1973)

The true men of action in our time, those who transform the world, are not the politicians and statesmen, but the scientists. Unfortunately, poetry cannot celebrate them, because their deeds are concerned with

things, not persons and are, therefore, speechless.

[*The Dyer's Hand* (1963)]

When I find myself in the company of scientists, I feel like a shabby curate who has strayed by mistake into a drawing-room full of dukes.

[*The Dyer's Hand* (1963)]

BAINBRIDGE, Kenneth (1904–)

Now we are all sons of bitches.

[Remark after directing the first atomic test, 1945]

BELLOC, Hilaire (1870–1953)

The Microbe is so very small
You cannot make him out at all ...
Oh! let us never, never doubt
What nobody is sure about!

[*More Beasts for Worse Children* (1897)]

BRIDIE, James (1888–1951)

Eve and the apple was the first great step in experimental science.

[*Mr Bolfry* (1943)]

BRONOWSKI, Jacob (1908–1974)

Physics becomes in those years the greatest collective work of science – no, more than that, the great collective work of art of the twentieth century.

[*The Ascent of Man* (1973)]

That is the essence of science: ask an impertinent question, and you are on the way to the pertinent answer.

[*The Ascent of Man* (1973)]

Science has nothing to be ashamed of, even in the ruins of Nagasaki.

[*Science and Human Values*]

BUSH, Vannevar (1890–1974)

To pursue science is not to disparage things of the spirit.

[Speech, 1953]

CHOMSKY, Noam (1928–)

As soon as questions of will or decision or reason or choice of action arise, human science is at a loss.

[Television interview, 1978]

CLARKE, Arthur C. (1917–)

When a distinguished but elderly scientist states that something is possible, he is almost certainly right. When he states that something is impossible, he is very probably wrong. (Clarke's First Law.).

[*The New Yorker*, 1969]

Technology, sufficiently advanced, is indistinguishable from magic.

[*The Times*, 1996]

COOK, Captain James (1728–1779)

[Following Cook's experiences with the natural historians on his second voyage]
Curse the scientists, and all science into the bargain.

[In J.C. Beaglehole (ed.), *The Voyage of the Resolution* (1961)]

CRICK, Francis (1916–)

[On the discovery of the structure of DNA, 1953]
We have discovered the secret of life!

[In Watson, *The Double Helix* (1968)]

CRONENBERG, David (1943–)

A virus is only doing its job.

[*Sunday Telegraph*, 1992]

CURIE, Marie (1867–1934)

After all, science is essentially international, and it is only through lack of the historical sense that national qualities have been attributed to it.

[*Memorandum*, 'Intellectual Co-operation']

DAGG, Fred (1948–)

I can see ... why a man who lives in Colorado is so anxious for all this nuclear activity to go on in Australia, an area famed among nuclear scientists for its lack of immediate proximity to their own residential areas.

[*Dagshead Revisited* (1989)]

DÜRRENMATT, Friedrich (1921–1990)

Unsere Wissenschaft ist schrecklich geworden, unsere Forschung gefährlich, unsere Erkenntnis tödlich.
Our science has become terrible, our research dangerous, our knowledge fatal.

[*The Physicists* (1962)]

EDDINGTON, Sir Arthur (1882–1944)

We used to think that if we knew one, we knew two, because one and one are two. We are finding that we must learn a great deal more about 'and'.

[In Mackay, *The Harvest of a Quiet Eye* (1977)]

EINSTEIN, Albert (1879–1955)

Why does this magnificent applied science which saves work and makes life easier bring us so little happiness? The simple answer runs: Because we have not yet learned to make sensible use of it.

[Address, California Institute of Technology, 1931]

Science without religion is lame, religion without science is blind.

[*Science, Philosophy and Religion: a Symposium* (1941)]

A theory can be proved by experiment; but no path leads from experiment to the birth of a theory.

[In Mackay, *The Harvest of a Quiet Eye* (1977)]

When a man sits with a pretty girl for an hour, it seems like a minute. But let him sit on a hot stove for a minute – and it's longer than any hour. That's relativity.

[Attr.]

FARADAY, Michael (1791–1867)

[On his scientific research]
It may be a weed instead of a fish that, after all my labour, I may at last pull up.

[Letter, 1831]

HALDANE, J.B.S. (1892–1964)

Einstein – the greatest Jew since Jesus. I have no doubt that Einstein's name will still be remembered and revered when Lloyd George, Foch, and William Hohenzollern share with Charlie Chaplin that ineluctable oblivion which awaits the uncreative mind.

[*Daedalus or Science and the Future* (1924)]

HEISENBERG, Werner (1901–1976)

Natural science does not simply describe and explain nature, it is part of the interplay between nature and ourselves.

[Attr.]

HUXLEY, T.H. (1825–1895)

The great tragedy of Science – the slaying of a beautiful hypothesis by an ugly fact.

[*British Association Annual Report* (1870)]

JEANS, Sir James Hopwood (1877–1946)

Science should leave off making pronouncements: the river of knowledge has too often turned back on itself.

[*The Mysterious Universe* (1930)]

LAMB, Charles (1775–1834)

In everything that relates to science, I am a whole Encyclopaedia behind the rest of the world.

[*Essays of Elia* (1823)]

LEVIN, Bernard (1928–)

Those of our own-day scientists who stir the embers of fires that went out millions of years ago may believe [their theories] but can never know. It would be better for all of us if they said as much.

[*The Times*, 1992]

MEDAWAR, Sir Peter Brian (1915–1987)

Scientific discovery is a private event, and the delight that accompanies it, or the despair of finding it illusory does not travel.

[*Hypothesis and Imagination*]

MONTAIGNE, Michel de (1533–1592)

Science without conscience is but death of the soul.

[In Simcox, *Treasury of Quotations on Christian Themes*]

NEEDHAM, Joseph (1900–1995)

Laboratorium est oratorium.
The place where we do our scientific work is a place of prayer.

[In Alan L. Mackay, *The Harvest of a Quiet Eye* (1977)]

NEWTON, Sir Isaac (1642–1727)

If I have seen further it is by standing on the shoulders of giants.

[Letter to Robert Hooke, 1675–76]

OPPENHEIMER, J. Robert (1904–1967)

[On the consequences of the first atomic test]
The physicists have known sin; and this is a knowledge which they cannot lose.

[Lecture, 1947]

PASTEUR, Louis (1822–1895)

Il n'existe pas de sciences appliquées, mais seulement des applications de la science.
There are no applied sciences, only applications of science.

[Address, 1872]

Dans les champs de l'observation, l'hasard ne favorise que les esprits préparés.
In the field of observation, chance favours only the prepared mind.

[Lecture, 1854]

PEACOCK, Thomas Love (1785–1866)

I almost think it is the ultimate destiny of science to exterminate the human race.

[*Gryll Grange* (1861)]

PIRSIG, Robert (1928–)

Traditional scientific method had always been at the very best, 20-20 hindsight. It's good for seeing where you've been.

[*Zen and the Art of Motorcycle Maintenance* (1974)]

POPPER, Sir Karl (1902–1994)

Science must begin with myths, and with the criticism of myths.

[In C.A. Mace (ed.), *British Philosophy in the Mid-Century* (1957)]

Science may be described as the art of systematic oversimplification.

[*The Observer*, 1982]

PORTER, Sir George (1920–)

Should we force science down the throats of those that have no taste for it? Is it our duty to drag them kicking and screaming into the twenty-first century? I am afraid that it is.

[Speech, 1986]

ROUX, Joseph (1834–1886)

Science is for those who learn; poetry, for those who know.

[*Meditations of a Parish Priest* (1886)]

SALK, Jonas E. (1914–1995)

[On being asked who owned the patent on his antipolio vaccine]
The people – could you patent the sun?

[Attr.]

SANTAYANA, George (1863–1952)

If all the arts aspire to the condition of music, all the sciences aspire to the condition of mathematics.

[*The Observer*, 1928]

SMITH, Sydney (1771–1845)

[Of William Whewell]
Science is his forte and omniscience is his foible.

[In Isaac Todhunter, *William Whewell* (1876)]

SNOW, C.P. (1905–1980)

A good many times I have been present at gatherings of people who, by the standards of the traditional culture, are thought highly educated and who have with considerable gusto been expressing their incredulity at the illiteracy of scientists. Once or twice I have been provoked and have asked the company how many of them could describe the Second Law of Thermodynamics. The response was cold: it was also negative.

[*The Two Cultures and the Scientific Revolution* (1959)]

SPENCER, Herbert (1820–1903)

Science is organized knowledge.

[*Education* (1861)]

STENHOUSE, David (1932–)

[On the conservation of biological resources]
I know a man who has a device for converting solar energy into food. Delicious stuff he makes with it, too. Being doing it for years … It's called a farm.

[*Crisis in Abundance* (1966)]

SUZUKI, David (1936–)

Science is really in the business of disproving its current models or changing them to conform to new information. In essence, we are constantly proving our latest ideas are wrong.

[*Metamorphosis: Stages in a Life* (1987)]

SZENT-GYÖRGYI, Albert von (1893–1986)

Discovery consists of seeing what everybody has seen and thinking what nobody has thought.

[In Good (ed.), *The Scientist Speculates* (1962)]

TOLSTOY, Leo (1828–1910)

The highest wisdom has but one science – the science of the whole – and science explaining the whole creation and man's place in it.

[*War and Peace* (1868–1869)]

VALÉRY, Paul (1871–1945)

Il faut n'appeler 'Science' que l'ensemble des recettes qui réussissent toujours. – Tout le reste est littérature.
The term Science should only be given to the collection of the recipes that are always successful. All the rest is literature.

[*Moralities*, 1932]

VEBLEN, Thorstein (1857–1929)

The outcome of any serious research can only be to make two questions grow where only one grew before.

[*The Place of Science in Modern Civilization* (1919)]

See CULTURE; DISCOVERY; MATHEMATICS; NATURE; PROGRESS; TECHNOLOGY

SCOTLAND

BARRIE, Sir J.M. (1860–1937)

You've forgotten the grandest moral attribute of a Scotsman, Maggie, that he'll do nothing which might damage his career.

[*What Every Woman Knows* (1908)]

There are few more impressive sights in the world than a Scotsman on the make.

[*What Every Woman Knows* (1908)]

BOORDE, Andrew (c.1490–1549)

Trust your no Skott.

[Letter to Thomas Cromwell, 1536]

The devellysche dysposicion of a Scottysh

man, not to love nor favour an Englishe man.

[Letter to Thomas Cromwell, 1536]

BURNS, Robert (1759–1796)

My heart's in the Highlands, my heart is not
here,
My heart's in the Highlands a-chasing the
deer,
A-chasing the wild deer and following the
roe –
My heart's in the Highlands, wherever I go!

['My Heart's in the Highlands' (1790)]

The story of Wallace poured a Scottish
prejudice in my veins which will boil along
there till the flood-gates of life shut in eternal
rest.

[Letter to Dr Moore, 1787]

CLEVELAND, John (1613–1658)

Had Cain been Scot, God would have
changed his doom,
Nor forced him wander, but confined him
home.

['The Rebel Scot' (1647)]

EWART, Gavin (1916–1995)

The Irish are great talkers
Persuasive and disarming,
You can say lots and lots
Against the Scots –
But at least they're never charming!

[The Complete Little Ones (1986)]

FAWKES, Guy (1570–1606)

[On being asked by the King whether he regretted
his proposed plot against Parliament and the royal
family]
A desperate disease requires a dangerous
remedy … one of my objects was to blow
the Scots back again into Scotland.

[Dictionary of National Biography]

FORSYTH, Michael (1954–)

[Attacking Scottish National Party policy on
Europe]
It is difficult to imagine how, if Scotland's
identity is stifled as a nation of five million in
an economic and monetary union of 58
million, it will somehow have more influence,

more authority and more status in a
European Union of 371 million.

[Speech, March 1999]

FREED, Arthur (1894–1973)

[Defending his decision to produce Brigadoon on
the MGM lot]
I went to Scotland and found nothing there
that looks like Scotland.

[In Halliwell, The Filmgoer's Book of Quotes (1973)]

GALT, John (1779–1839)

From the lone shieling of the misty island
Mountains divide us, and the waste of seas –
Yet still the blood is strong, the heart is
Highland,
And we in dreams behold the Hebrides!
Fair these broad meads, these hoary woods
are grand;
But we are exiles from our fathers' land.

[Attr. in Blackwoods Edinburgh Magazine, 1829]

HALLIDAY, J. (1790–1867)

As sure as I'm a Scot
A redshank Norland haggis-eater.

[Rustic Bard, quoted in F. Marian McNeill, The Scots
Kitchen (1929)]

HAMILTON, Ian (1925–)

[On the performance of Scottish National Party
MPs in Westminster]
Courage is a quality Scots lack only when
they become MPs. They should be twisting
the lion's tail until it comes out by the roots.

[Daily Mail, May 1996]

JENKINS, Robin (1912–)

Football has taken the place of religion in
Scotland.

[A Would-Be Saint]

JOHNSON, Samuel (1709–1784)

I know not whether it be not peculiar to the
Scots to have attained the liberal without the
manual arts, to have excelled in ornamental
knowledge, and to have wanted not only the
elegancies, but the conveniences of common life.

[A Journey to the Western Islands of Scotland (1775)]

Boswell: I do indeed come from Scotland, but
I cannot help it …

Johnson: That, Sir, I find, is what a very great many of your countrymen cannot help.

[In Boswell, *The Life of Samuel Johnson* (1791)]

[Of the Scots]
Their learning is like bread in a besieged town: every man gets a little, but no man gets a full meal.

[In Boswell, *The Life of Samuel Johnson* (1791)]

Oats. A grain, which in England is generally given to horses, but in Scotland supports the people.

[*A Dictionary of the English Language* (1755)]

Norway, too, has noble wild prospects; and Lapland is remarkable for prodigious noble wild prospects. But, Sir, let me tell you, the noblest prospect which a Scotchman ever sees, is the high road that leads him to England!

[In Boswell, *The Life of Samuel Johnson* (1791)]

Much may be made of a Scotchman, if he be caught young.

[In Boswell, *The Life of Samuel Johnson* (1791)]

Seeing Scotland, Madam, is only seeing a worse England. It is seeing the flower fade away to the naked stalk.

[In Boswell, *The Life of Samuel Johnson* (1791)]

JOYCE, James (1882–1941)
Poor sister Scotland!
Her doom is fell.
She cannot find any more Stuarts to sell.

[*Chamber Music* (1907)]

KEILLOR, Garrison (1942–)
Lutherans are like Scottish people, only with less frivolity.

[*The Independent*, 1992]

LAMB, Charles (1775–1834)
I have been trying all my life to like Scotchmen, and am obliged to desist from the experiment in despair.

['Imperfect Sympathies' (1823)]

LEACOCK, Stephen (1869–1944)
[Of the Scots]
Having little else to cultivate, they cultivated

the intellect. The export of brains came to be their chief item of commerce.

[*Humour* (1935)]

LINKLATER, Eric (1899–1974)
While swordless Scotland, sadder than its psalms,
Fosters its sober youth on national alms
To breed a dull provincial discipline,
Commerce its god and golf its anodyne.

['Preamble to a Satire']

LOCKIER, Francis (1667–1740)
In all my travels I have never met with any one Scotchman but what was a man of sense. I believe everybody of that country that has any, leaves it as fast as they can.

[In Spence, *Anecdotes* (1858)]

MACDIARMID, Hugh (1892–1978)
A Scottish poet maun assume
The burden o' his people's doom,
And dee to brak' their livin' tomb.

[*A Drunk Man Looks at the Thistle* (1926)]

It's easier to lo'e Prince Charlie
Than Scotland – mair's the shame!

['Bonnie Prince Charlie' (1930)]

The rose of all the world is not for me
I want for my part
Only the little white rose of Scotland
That smells sharp and sweet – and breaks the heart.

['The Little White Rose']

MAUGHAM, William Somerset (1874–1965)
Scotchmen seem to think it's a credit to them to be Scotch.

[*A Writer's Notebook* (1949)]

NASH, Ogden (1902–1971)
No McTavish
Was ever lavish.

['Genealogical Reflection' (1931)]

NICHOLSON, Emma
England treats Scotland as if it was an island off the coast of West Africa in the 1830s.

[*Daily Mail*, 1996]

NORTH, Christopher (1785–1854)

Minds like ours, my dear James, must always be above national prejudices, and in all companies it gives me true pleasure to declare, that, as a people, the English are very little indeed inferior to the Scotch.

[*Blackwood's Edinburgh Magazine*, 1826]

OGILVY, James (1663–1730)

[On signing the Act of Union]

Now there's an end of ane old song.

[Remark, 1707]

PICCOLOMINI, Enea (1405–1464)

[Comment after a visit to Scotland in 1435]

There is nothing the Scots like better to hear than abuse of the English.

[Attr.]

ROBERTSON, Pat

In Europe the big word is tolerance. Homosexuals are riding high in the media … and in Scotland, you can't believe how strong the homosexuals are.

[*The Guardian*, 1999]

SALMOND, Alex (1955–)

There is not an anti-English bone in my body. I have forgotten more about English history than most Tory MPs ever learned.

[*The Observer*, 1998]

SCOTT, Sir Walter (1771–1832)

[Of Pitt]

O Caledonia! stern and wild,
Meet nurse for a poetic child!
Land of brown heath and shaggy wood,
Land of the mountain and the flood,
Land of my sires! what mortal hand
Can e'er untie the filial band,
That knits me to thy rugged strand!

[*The Lay of the Last Minstrel*
(1805)]

Still from the sire the son shall hear
Of the stern strife, and carnage drear,
Of Flodden's fatal field,
Where shiver'd was fair Scotland's spear,
And broken was her shield!

[*Marmion*]

SMITH, Sydney (1771–1845)

It requires a surgical operation to get a joke well into a Scotch understanding. Their only idea of wit … is laughing immoderately at stated intervals.

[In Holland, *A Memoir of the Reverend Sydney Smith* (1855)]

[Of Scotland]

That knuckle-end of England – that land of Calvin, oat-cakes, and sulphur.

[In Holland, *A Memoir of the Reverend Sydney Smith* (1855)]

SMOLLETT, Tobias (1721–1771)

The Scots have a slight tincture of letters, with which they make a parade among people who are more illiterate than themselves; but they may be said to float on the surface of science, and they have made very small advances in the useful arts.

[*Humphry Clinker* (1771)]

VINCENT, John

[On the falling birth rate in Scotland]

The Scottish people will one day become extinct.

[*The Observer*, 1998]

WODEHOUSE, P.G. (1881–1975)

It is never difficult to distinguish between a Scotsman with a grievance and a ray of sunshine.

[*Blandings Castle and Elsewhere* (1935)]

THE SEA

AESCHYLUS (525–456 BC)

The ceaseless twinkling laughter of the waves of the sea.

[*Prometheus Bound*]

ARNOLD, Matthew (1822–1888)

The sea is calm to-night,
The tide is full, the moon lies fair
Upon the straits.

['Dover Beach' (1867)]

Sand-strewn caverns, cool and deep,

Where the winds are all asleep;
Where the spent lights quiver and gleam;
Where the salt weed sways in the stream;
Where the sea-beasts ranged all round
Feed in the ooze of their pasture-ground…
Where great whales come sailing by,
Sail and sail, with unshut eye,
Round the world for ever and aye.

['The Forsaken Merman' (1849)]

BELLOC, Hilaire (1870–1953)

everywhere, the sea is a teacher of truth. I am
not sure that the best thing I find in sailing is
not this salt of reality … There, sailing the
sea, we play every part of life: control,
direction, effort, fate; and there can we test
ourselves and know our state.

[Quoted by Libby Purves, *The Times*, June 1998]

BRIDGES, Robert (1844–1930)

Whither, O splendid ship, thy white sails
crowding,
Leaning across the bosom of the urgent
West,
That fearest not sea rising, nor sky clouding,
Whither away, fair rover, and what thy quest?

['A Passer-by' (1890)]

BYRON, Lord (1788–1824)

Roll on, thou deep and dark blue Ocean –
roll!
Ten thousand fleets sweep over thee in vain;
Man marks the earth with ruin – his control
Stops with the shore.

[*Childe Harold's Pilgrimage* (1818)]

Dark-heaving – boundless, endless, and
sublime,
The image of eternity.

[*Childe Harold's Pilgrimage* (1818)]

CAMPBELL, Alistair Te Ariki (1925–)

Now it is water I dream of,
… lifting
casually on a shore
where yellow lions come out
in the early morning
and stare out to sea.

[*Collected Poems 1947–1981* (1981)]

CARSON, Rachel Louise (1907–1964)

In its mysterious past, it encompasses all the
dim origins of life and receives in the end …
the dead husks of that same life. For all at last
return to the sea – to Oceanus, the ocean
river, like the ever-flowing stream of time, the
beginning and the end.

[*The Sea Around Us* (1951)]

CHOPIN, Kate (1851–1904)

The voice of the sea speaks to the soul. The
touch of the sea is sensuous, enfolding the
body in its soft, close embrace.

[*The Awakening* (1899)]

CLAYTON, Keith (1928–)

[Of sewage]
You can do far worse than putting it into a
deep and well-flushed sea. As far as
poisoning the fish is concerned, that's
rubbish. The sewage has probably kept the
poor fish alive.

[*The Times*, 1992]

COLERIDGE, Samuel Taylor (1772–1834)

The fair breeze blew, the white foam flew,
The furrow followed free;
We were the first that ever burst
Into that silent sea.

['The Rime of the Ancient Mariner' (1798)]

As idle as a painted ship
Upon a painted ocean.

['The Rime of the Ancient Mariner' (1798)]

Water, water, every where,
And all the boards did shrink;
Water, water, every where
Nor any drop to drink.

['The Rime of the Ancient Mariner' (1798)]

CONRAD, Joseph (1857–1924)

This could have occurred nowhere but in
England, where men and sea interpenetrate,
so to speak.

[*Youth* (1902)]

CUNNINGHAM, Allan (1784–1842)

A wet sheet and a flowing sea,
A wind that follows fast

And fills the white and rustling sail
And bends the gallant mast …

['A Wet Sheet and a Flowing Sea' (1825)]

DEKKER, Thomas (c.1570–c.1632)

That great fishpond (the sea).

[*The Honest Whore* (1604)]

DICKENS, Charles (1812–1870)

I want to know what it says … The sea, Floy,
what it is that it keeps on saying?

[*Dombey and Son* (1848)]

'People can't die, along the coast,' said Mr
Peggotty, 'except when the tide's pretty nigh
out. They can't be born, unless it's pretty nigh
in – not properly born, till flood. He's a going
out with the tide.'

[*David Copperfield* (1850)]

DONNE, John (1572–1631)

The sea is as deepe in a calme as in a storme.

[*Sermons*]

FLECKER, James Elroy (1884–1915)

The dragon-green, the luminous, the dark,
the serpent-haunted sea.

[*The Golden Journey to Samarkand*
(1913)]

HOMER (fl. c.8th century BC)

The wine-dark sea.

[*Iliad*]

JOYCE, James (1882–1941)

The snotgreen sea. The scrotumtightening
sea.

[*Ulysses* (1922)]

KEATS, John (1795–1821)

It keeps eternal whisperings around
Desolate shores, and with its mighty swell
Gluts twice ten thousand caverns.

['On the Sea' (1817)]

KIPLING, Rudyard (1865–1936)

What is a woman that you forsake her,
And the hearth-fire and the home-acre,
To go with the old grey Widow-maker?

['Harp Song of the Dane Women' (1906)]

Oh, was there ever sailor free to choose,

That didn't settle somewhere near the sea?

[*The Years Between* (1919)]

LONGFELLOW, Henry Wadsworth (1807–1882)

'Wouldst thou' – so the helmsman
answered –
'Learn the secret of the sea?
Only those who brave its dangers
Comprehend its mystery!'.

['The Secret of the Sea' (1904)]

MASEFIELD, John (1878–1967)

I must go down to the seas again, to the
lonely sea and the sky,
And all I ask is a tall ship and a star to steer
her by,
And the wheel's kick and the wind's song
and the white sail's shaking,
And a grey mist on the sea's face and a grey
dawn breaking …

I must go down to the seas again, for the call
of the running tide
Is a wild call and a clear call that may not be
denied …

I must go down to the seas again, to the
vagrant gypsy life,
To the gull's way and the whale's way where
the wind's like a whetted knife;
And all I ask is a merry yarn from a laughing
fellow rover,
And a quiet sleep and a sweet dream when
the long trick's over.

['Sea Fever' (1902)]

RIMBAUD, Arthur (1854–1891)

Je me suis baigné dans le Poème
De la Mer, infusé d'astres, et lactescent,
Dévorant les azurs verts.
I have bathed in the Poem
Of the Sea, steeped in stars, milky,
Devouring the green azures.

['Le Bâteau ivre' (1870)]

ROSSETTI, Dante Gabriel (1828–1882)

The sea hath no king but God alone.

['The White Ship']

SCOTT, Sir Walter (1771–1832)

It's no fish ye're buying – it's men's lives.

[*The Antiquary* (1816)]

SWINBURNE, Algernon Charles (1837–1909)

I will go back to the great sweet mother,
Mother and lover of men, the sea.
I will go down to her, I and no other,
Close with her, kiss her and mix her with me …
I shall sleep, and move with the moving ships,
Change as the winds change, veer in the tide;
My lips will feast on the foam of thy lips,
I shall rise with thy rising and with thee subside.

['The Triumph of Time' (1866)]

SYNGE, J.M. (1871–1909)

'A man who is not afraid of the sea will soon be drownded,' he said, 'for he will be going out on a day he shouldn't. But we do be afraid of the sea, and we do only be drownded now and again.'

[*The Aran Islands* (1907)]

SYNGE, J.M. (1871–1909)

'A man who is not afraid of the sea will soon be drownded,' he said, 'for he will be going out on a day he shouldn't. But we do be afraid of the sea, and we do only be drownded now and again.'

[*The Aran Islands* (1907)]

UVAVNUK

The great sea
Has set me adrift
It moves me as the weed in the river,
Earth and the great weather
Move me,
Have carried me away
And move my inward parts with joy.

[In Rasmussen, *Intellectual Culture of the Igulik Eskimos* (1929)]

VILLIERS, Alan John (1903–1982)

Only fools and passengers drink at sea.

[*The Observer*, 1957]

WHITING, William (1825–1878)

Eternal Father, strong to save,
Whose arm hath bound the restless wave,
… O hear us when we cry to Thee
For those in peril on the sea.

[Hymn, 1869]

See NAVY

THE SEASONS

ADAMS, Richard (1920–)

Many human beings say that they enjoy the winter, but what they really enjoy is feeling proof against it.

[*Watership Down* (1974)]

ANDREWES, Bishop Lancelot (1555–1626)

It was no summer progress. A cold coming they had of it, at this time of the year; just, the worst time of the year, to take a journey, and specially a long journey, in. The ways deep, the weather sharp, the days short, the sun farthest off in solstitio brumali, the very dead of Winter.

[*Sermon 15, Of the Nativity* (1629)]

CAMPION, Thomas (1567–1620)

The Summer hath his joyes,
And Winter his delights;
Though Love and all his pleasures are but toyes,
They shorten tedious nights.

[*The Third Booke of Ayres* (1617)]

CATULLUS (84–c.54 BC)

Iam ver egelidos refert tepores.
Now Spring brings back her gentle warmth.

[*Carmina*]

COLERIDGE, Samuel Taylor (1772–1834)

Therefore all seasons shall be sweet to thee,
Whether the summer clothe the general earth
With greenness, or the redbreast sit and sing
Betwixt the tufts of snow on the bare branch
Of mossy apple-tree, while the nigh thatch

Smokes in the sun-thaw; whether the eave-drops fall
Heard only in the trances of the blast,
Or if the secret ministry of frost
Shall hang them up in silent icicles,
Quietly shining to the quiet moon.

['Frost at Midnight' (1798)]

Summer has set in with its usual severity.

[*Letters of Charles Lamb* (1888)]

COWPER, William (1731–1800)

Our severest winter, commonly called the spring.

[*Letters and Prose Writings of William Cowper*, Letter to the Rev. W. Unwin, 1783]

HOLMES, Oliver Wendell (1809–1894)

For him in vain the envious seasons roll
Who bears eternal summer in his soul.

['The Old Player' (1861)]

HOOD, Thomas (1799–1845)

I saw old Autumn in the misty morn
Stand shadowless like Silence, listening
To silence.

['Ode: Autumn' (1823)]

JAMES I OF SCOTLAND (1394–1437)

Worshippe, ye that loveris been, this May,
For of your blisse the Kalendis are begun,
And sing with us, away, Winter, away!
Come, Summer, come the sweet seasoun and sun.

[*The Kingis Quair*]

KEATS, John (1795–1821)

Four seasons fill the measure of the year;
There are four seasons in the mind of man.

['The Human Seasons' (1818)]

Where are the songs of Spring? Ay, where are they?
Think not of them, thou hast thy music too.

['To Autumn' (1819)]

LANGLAND, William (c.1330–c.1400)

In a somer seson whan soft was the sonne.

[*The Vision of William Concerning Piers the Plowman*]

NABOKOV, Vladimir (1899–1977)

Yes, I was right, spring and summer did happen in Cambridge almost every year (that mysterious 'almost' was singularly pleasing).

[*The Real Life of Sebastian Knight* (1941)]

RILKE, Rainer Maria (1875–1926)

Frühling ist wiedergekommen. Die Erde ist wie ein Kind, das Gedichte weiss.
Spring has come again. The earth is like a child who knows poems.

[*The Sonnets to Orpheus* (1923)]

SANTAYANA, George (1863–1952)

To be interested in the changing seasons is, in this middling zone, a happier state of mind than to be hopelessly in love with spring.

[*Little Essays* (1920)]

SHAKESPEARE, William (1564–1616)

At Christmas I no more desire a rose
Than wish a snow in May's new-fangled shows;
But like of each thing that in season grows.

[*Love's Labour's Lost*, I.i]

SPENSER, Edmund (c.1522–1599)

Fresh spring the herald of love's mighty king,
In whose cote armour richly are displayd
All sorts of flowers the which on earth do spring
In goodly colours gloriously arrayd.

[*Amoretti, and Epithalamion* (1595), Sonnet 70]

THOMPSON, Francis (1859–1907)

Spring is come home with her world-wandering feet.
And all things are made young with young desires …

Let even the slug-abed snail upon the thorn
Put forth a conscious horn!

['From the Night of Forebeing' (1913)]

TROLLOPE, Anthony (1815–1882)

The comic almanacs give us dreadful pictures of January and February; but, in truth, the months which should be made to look gloomy in England are March and April. Let no man boast himself that he has got through the perils of winter till at least the seventh of May.

[*Doctor Thorne* (1858)]

TUSSER, Thomas (c.1524–1580)

Sweet April showers
Do spring May flowers.

[*Five Hundred Points of Good Husbandry* (1557)]

WALPOLE, Horace (1717–1797)

The way to ensure summer in England is to
have it framed and glazed in a comfortable
room.

[Letter to William Cole, 1774]

See WEATHER

SECRETS

ACTON, Lord (1834–1902)

Everything secret degenerates … nothing is
safe that does not show how it can bear
discussion and publicity.

[Attr.]

AUDEN, W.H. (1907–1973)

At last the secret is out, as it always must
come in the end,
The delicious story is ripe to tell to the
intimate friend;
Over the tea-cups and in the square the
tongue has its desire;
Still waters run deep, my dear, there's never
smoke without fire …

For the clear voice suddenly singing, high up
in the convent wall,
The scent of elder bushes, the sporting prints
in the hall,
The croquet matches in summer, the
handshake, the cough, the kiss,
There is always a wicked secret, a private
reason for this.

[*Collected Poems, 1933–1938*, 'Twelve Songs', VIII]

BEHN, Aphra (1640–1689)

Love ceases to be a pleasure, when it ceases
to be a secret.

[*The Lover's Watch* (1686)

CERVANTES, Miguel de (1547–1616)

*Mucho más dañan a las honras de las mujeres las
desenvolturas y libertades públicas que las maldades
secretas.*

Brazenness and public liberties do much
more harm to a woman's honour than secret
wickedness.

[*Don Quixote* (1615)]

CLARK, Alan (1928–)

[On being asked whether he had any
embarrassing skeletons in the cupboard]
Dear boy, I can hardly close the door.

[*The Observer*, 1998]

CONGREVE, William (1670–1729)

I know that's a secret, for it's whispered
everywhere.

[*Love for Love* (1695)]

CRABBE, George (1754–1832)

Secrets with girls, like loaded guns with boys,
Are never valued till they make a noise.

[*Tales of the Hall* (1819)]

DICKENS, Charles (1812–1870)

We never knows wot's hidden in each other's
hearts; and if we had glass winders there,
we'd need keep the shetters up, some on us, I
do assure you!

[*Martin Chuzzlewit* (1844)]

DRYDEN, John (1631–1700)

For secrets are edged tools,
And must be kept from children and from fools.

[*Sir Martin Mar-All* (1667)]

FRANKLIN, Benjamin (1706–1790)

Three may keep a secret, if two of them are
dead.

[*Poor Richard's Almanac* (1735)]

FRANKS, Oliver, Baron (1905–1992)

It is a secret in the Oxford sense: you may tell
it to only one person at a time.

[*Sunday Telegraph*, 1977]

FROST, Robert (1874–1963)

We dance round in a ring and suppose,
But the Secret sits in the middle and knows.

['The Secret Sits' (1942)]

HALDEMAN, H.R. (1926–1993)

[Comment to John Dean on Watergate affair, 1973]
Once the toothpaste is out of the tube, it is
awfully hard to get it back in.

> [In Hearings Before the Select Committee on
> Presidential Campaign Activities of US
> Senate: Watergate and Related Activities
> (1973)]

SHAKESPEARE, William (1564–1616)

But that I am forbid
To tell the secrets of my prison-house,
I could a tale unfold whose lightest word
Would harrow up thy soul, freeze thy young
blood,
Make thy two eyes, like stars, start from their
spheres,
Thy knotted and combined locks to part,
And each particular hair to stand an end,
Like quills upon the fretful porpentine.
But this eternal blazon must not be
To ears of flesh and blood. List, list, O, list!

> [*Hamlet*, I.v]

STEPHENS, James (1882–1950)

A secret is a weapon and a friend. Man is
God's secret, Power is man's secret, Sex is
woman's secret.

> [*The Crock of Gold* (1912)]

SURTEES, R.S. (1805–1864)

There is no secret so close as that between a
rider and his horse.

> [*Mr Sponge's Sporting Tour* (1853)]

See GOSSIP

SELF

ARNOLD, Matthew (1822–1888)

Resolve to be thyself; and know, that he,
Who finds himself, loses his misery!

> ['Self-Dependence' (1852)]

AUDEN, W.H. (1907–1973)

Some thirty inches from my nose
The frontier of my Person goes,
And all the untilled air between
Is private pagus and demesne.

Stranger, unless with bedroom eyes
I beckon you to fraternize,
Beware of rudely crossing it;
I have no gun, but I can spit.

> [*About the House*, 'Prologue: the Birth of
> Architecture']

AURELIUS, Marcus (121–180)

This whatever this is that I am is flesh and
spirit, and the ruling part.

> [*Meditations*]

BACON, Francis (1561–1626)

It is a poor centre of a man's actions, himself.

> ['Of Wisdom for a Man's Self' (1625)]

BARRIE, Sir J.M. (1860–1937)

The tragedy of a man who has found himself
out.

> [*What Every Woman Knows* (1908)]

BHAGAVADGITA

[On the Self]
He who considers this as a slayer or he who
thinks that this is slain, neither of these
knows the Truth. For it does not slay, nor is it
slain.

> [Ch. II]

BRONTË, Emily (1818–1848)

He is more myself than I am.

> [*Wuthering Heights* (1847)]

BROWNE, Sir Thomas (1605–1682)

There is another man within me, that's angry
with me, rebukes, commands, and dastards
me.

> [*Religio Medici* (1643)]

BURNS, Robert (1759–1796)

O wad some Power the giftie gie us
To see oursels as ithers see us!
It wad frae monie a blunder free us,
An' foolish notion:
What airs in dress an' gait wad lea'e us,
An' ev'n devotion!

> ['To a Louse' (1786)]

CARLYLE, Thomas (1795–1881)

A certain inarticulate Self-consciousness
dwells dimly in us … Hence, too, the folly of

that impossible precept, Know thyself; till it be translated into this partially possible one, Know what thou canst work at.

[*Sartor Resartus* (1834)]

CHAPLIN, Charlie (1889–1977)

You have to believe in yourself, that's the secret. Even when I was in the orphanage, when I was roaming the street trying to find enough to eat, even then I thought of myself as the greatest actor in the world. I had to feel the exuberance that comes from utter confidence in yourself. Without it, you go down to defeat.

[*My Autobiography* (1964)]

CICERO (106–43 BC)

Mens cuiusque is est quisque.
The spirit is the true self.

[*De Republica*]

COMPTON-BURNETT, Dame Ivy (1884–1969)

'Know thyself' is a most superfluous direction. We can't avoid it. We can only hope that no one else knows.

[*A Family and a Fortune* (1939)]

CONNOLLY, Cyril (1903–1974)

I have always disliked myself at any given moment; the total of such moments is my life.

[*Enemies of Promise* (1938)]

EMERSON, Ralph Waldo (1803–1882)

All sensible people are selfish, and nature is tugging at every contract to make the terms of it fair.

[*Conduct of Life* (1860)]

GOETHE (1749–1832)

Ich kenne mich auch nicht und Gott soll mich auch davor behüten.
I do not know myself either, and may God protect me from that.

[*Gespräche mit Eckermann*, 1829]

HILLEL, 'The Elder' (c.60 BC–c.10 AD)

If I am not for myself who is for me; and being for my own self what am I? If not now when?

[In Taylor (ed.), *Sayings of the Jewish Fathers* (1877)]

HUXLEY, Aldous (1894–1963)

There's only one corner of the universe you can be certain of improving, and that's your own self.

[*Time Must Have a Stop* (1944)]

JOAD, C.E.M. (1891–1953)

Whenever I look inside myself I am afraid.

[*The Observer*, 1942]

KEMPIS, Thomas à (c.1380–1471)

Si non potes te talem facere qualem vis, quomodo poteris alium ad tuum habere beneplacitum?
If you cannot mould yourself to such as you would wish, how can you expect others to be entirely to your liking?

[*De Imitatione Christi* (1892)]

Humilis tui cognitio, certior via est ad Deum; quam profunda scientiae inquisitio.
The humble knowledge of thyself is a surer way to God than the deepest search after learning.

[*De Imitatione Christi* (1892)]

LA ROCHEFOUCAULD (1613–1680)

On aime mieux dire du mal de soi-même que de n'en point parler.
One would rather speak ill of oneself than not speak of oneself at all.

[*Maximes*, (1678)]

L'amour-propre est le plus grand de tous les flatteurs.
Self-love is the greatest flatterer of all.

[*Maximes* (1678)]

L'intérêt parle toutes sortes de langues, et joue toutes sortes de personnages, même celui de désintéressé.
Self-interest speaks every kind of language, and plays every role, even that of disinterestedness.

[*Maximes* (1678)]

LOWELL, James Russell (1819–1891)

He's been true to one party – an' thet is himself.

[*The Biglow Papers* (1848)]

MCCARTHY, Mary (1912–1989)

However much we reform our ways, grow a new self, we *are* our past; it lurks behind us, follows us, denounces us, tracks us down.

[*Ideas and the Novel* (1980)]

MANSFIELD, Katherine (1888–1923)

[On human limitations]
To have the courage of your excess – to find the limit of yourself.

[*Journal of Katherine Mansfield* (1954)]

MARRYAT, Frederick (1792–1848)

We always took care of number one.

[*Scenes and Adventures in the Life of Frank Mildmay* (1829)]

MAUGHAM, William Somerset (1874–1965)

I recognize that I am made up of several persons and that the person that at the moment has the upper hand will inevitably give place to another. But which is the real one? All of them or none?

[*A Writer's Notebook* (1949)]

MOLIÈRE (1622–1673)

On doit se regarder soi-même un fort long temps,
Avant que de songer á condamner les gens.
We should look long and carefully at ourselves before we consider judging others.

[*Le Misanthrope* (1666)]

MONTAIGNE, Michel de (1533–1592)

La plus grande chose du monde, c'est de savoir être á soi.
The greatest thing in the world is to know how to belong to oneself.

[*Essais* (1580)]

PASCAL, Blaise (1623–1662)

Le moi est haïssable.
Self is hateful.

[*Pensées* (1670)]

PINTER, Harold (1930–)

[On being asked why he did not include a character representing himself in The Birthday Party]
I had – I have – nothing to say about myself, directly. I wouldn't know where to begin. Particularly since I often look at myself in the mirror and say 'Who the hell's that?'.

[Attr.]

POWELL, Anthony (1905–)

He fell in love with himself at first sight and it is a passion to which he has always remained faithful. Self-love seems so often unrequited.

[*The Acceptance World* (1955)]

PROVERB

Every man for himself and the devil take the hindmost.

ROSSETTI, Dante Gabriel (1828–1882)

I do not see them here; but after death
God knows I know the faces I shall see,
Each one a murdered self, with low last breath.
'I am thyself, – what hast thou done to me?'
'And I – and I – thyself', (lo! each one saith,)
'And thou thyself to all eternity!'.

[*The House of Life*]

RUSSELL, Bertrand (1872–1970)

Man is not a solitary animal, and so long as social life survives, self-realization cannot be the supreme principle of ethics.

[*A History of Western Philosophy* (1946)]

SHAKESPEARE, William (1564–1616)

This above all – to thine own self be true,
And it must follow, as the night the day,
Thou canst not then be false to any man.

[*Hamlet*, I.iii]

SHAW, George Bernard (1856–1950)

It is easy – terribly easy – to shake a man's faith in himself. To take advantage of that to break a man's spirit is devil's work.

[*Candida* (1898)]

Don't fuss, my dear, I'm not unhappy. I am enjoying the enormous freedom of having found myself out and got myself off my mind; it is the beginning of hope and the end of hypocrisy.

[*On the Rocks*]

SITWELL, Dame Edith (1887–1964)

Why not be oneself? That is the whole secret of a successful appearance. If one is a greyhound, why try to look like a Pekingese?

['Why I look the Way I do' (1955)]

TOLSTOY, Leo (1828–1910)

I am always with myself, and it is I who am my own tormentor.

[Memoirs of a Madman (1943)]

TROLLOPE, Anthony (1815–1882)

No man thinks there is much ado about nothing when the ado is about himself.

[The Bertrams (1859)]

Never think that you're not good enough yourself. A man should never think that. My belief is that in life people will take you very much at your own reckoning.

[The Small House at Allington (1864)]

TWAIN, Mark (1835–1910)

When people do not respect us we are sharply offended; yet deep down in his heart no man much respects himself.

[Notebooks (1935)]

WHITE, Patrick (1912–1990)

I have never managed to escape being this thing, Myself.

[The Eye of the Storm (1973)]

WHITMAN, Walt (1819–1892)

I celebrate myself, and sing myself,
And what I assume you shall assume …

['Song of Myself' (1855)]

Behold, I do not give lectures or a little charity,
When I give I give myself.

['Song of Myself' (1855), 40]

WILDE, Oscar (1854–1900)

Other people are quite dreadful. The only possible society is oneself.

[An Ideal Husband (1895)]

See APPEARANCE; PRIDE; VANITY

SENTIMENTALITY

JUNG, Carl Gustav (1875–1961)

Sentimentality is a superstructure covering brutality.

[Reflections]

MAUGHAM, William Somerset (1874–1965)

Sentimentality is only sentiment that rubs you up the wrong way.

[A Writer's Notebook (1949)]

See FEELINGS

SEPARATION

ARNOLD, Matthew (1822–1888)

A God, a God their severance ruled!
And bade betwixt their shores to be
The unplumb'd, salt, estranging sea.

['To Marguerite – Continued' (1852)]

BAYLY, Thomas Haynes (1797–1839)

Absence makes the heart grow fonder,
Isle of Beauty, Fare thee well!

['Isle of Beauty', song, 1830]

BRENNAN, Christopher (1870–1932)

I am shut out of mine own heart
because my love is far from me.

['I Am Shut Out of Mine Own Heart' (1914)]

BROOKE, Rupert (1887–1915)

How that we've done our best and worst,
and parted.

['The Busy Heart' (1913)]

BUSSY-RABUTIN, Comte de (1618–1693)

L'absence est á l'amour ce qu'est au feu le vent; il éteint le petit, il allume le grand.
Absence is to love what the wind is to fire; it extinguishes the small, it kindles the great.

[Histoire Amoureuse des Gaules (1665)]

COPE, Wendy (1945–)

The day he moved out was terrible –
That evening she went through hell.
His absence wasn't a problem
But the corkscrew had gone as well.

['Loss' (1992)]

CORNFORD, Frances Crofts (1886–1960)

How long ago Hector took off his plume,

Not wanting that his little son should cry,
Then kissed his sad Andromache goodbye –
And now we three in Euston waiting-room.

['Parting in Wartime' (1948)]

COWPER, William (1731–1800)

Absence from whom we love is worse than death.

['Hope, like the Short-lived Ray' (1791)]

DICKINSON, Emily (1830–1886)

My life closed twice before its close –
It yet remains to see
If Immortality unveil
A third event to me

So huge, so hopeless to conceive
As these that twice befell.
Parting is all we know of heaven,
And all we need of hell.

['My life closed twice before its close' (1896)]

DONNE, John (1572–1631)

When I died last, and, Dear I die
As often as from thee I go,
Though it be but an hour ago,
And Lovers' hours be full eternity.

[*Songs and Sonnets* (1611)]

ELIOT, George (1819–1880)

In every parting there is an image of death.

[*Scenes of Clerical Life* (1858)]

GAY, John (1685–1732)

O what pain it is to part!

[*The Beggar's Opera* (1728)]

HARAUCOURT, Edmond (1856–1941)

Partir c'est mourir un peu,
C'est mourir á ce qu'on aime:
On laisse un peu de soi-même
En toute heure et dans tout lieu.
Leaving is dying a little,
Dying to one's loves:
One leaves behind a little of oneself
At every moment, everywhere.

[*Seul* (1891)]

JAGO, Rev. Richard (1715–1781)

With leaden foot time creeps along
While Delia is away.

[*Absence*]

KEATS, John (1795–1821)

I wish you could invent some means to make
me at all happy without you. Every hour I am
more and more concentrated in you; every
thing else tastes like chaff in my Mouth.

[Letter to Fanny Brawne, 1820]

KEPPEL, Lady Caroline (b. 1735)

What's this dull town to me?
Robin's not near.
He whom I wished to see,
Wished for to hear;
Where's all the joy and mirth
Made life a heaven on earth?
O! they're all fled with thee,
Robin Adair.

['Robin Adair' (c. 1750)]

KING, Bishop Henry (1592–1669)

We that did nothing study but the way
To love each other, with which thoughts the
day
Rose with delight to us, and with them set,
Must learn the hateful art, how to forget.

['The Surrender' (1651)]

PATMORE, Coventry (1823–1896)

With all my will, but much against my heart,
We two now part.
My Very Dear,
Our solace is, the sad road lies so clear.
It needs no art,
With faint, averted feet
And many a tear,
In our opposed paths to persevere.

[*The Unknown Eros* (1877)]

POUND, Ezra (1885–1972)

And if you ask how I regret that parting:
It is like the flowers falling at Spring's
    end
Confused, whirled in a tangle.
What is the use of talking, and there is
    no end of talking,
There is no end of things in the heart.

['Exile's Letter' (1915)]

PROUST, Marcel (1871–1922)

It is seldom indeed that one parts on good
terms, because if one were on good terms

one would not part.

[A la recherche du temps perdu, La Prisonnière (1923)]

ROSSETTI, Christina (1830–1894)

Remember me when I am gone away,
Gone far away into the silent land ...

Better by far you should forget and smile
Than you should remember and be sad.

['Remember' (1862)]

SCHOPENHAUER, Arthur (1788–1860)

Jede Trennung gibt einen Vorschmack des Todes, –
und jedes Wiedersehen einen Vorschmack der
Auferstehung.

Every separation gives a foretaste of death, –
and every reunion a foretaste of resurrection.

[Parerga und Paralipomena (1851)]

SHAKESPEARE, William (1564–1616)

Parting is such sweet sorrow
That I shall say good night till it be morrow.

[Romeo and Juliet, II.ii]

STERNE, Laurence (1713–1768)

Every time I kiss thy hand to bid adieu, and
every absence which follows it, are preludes
to that eternal separation which we are
shortly to make.

[Tristram Shandy (1759–1767)]

STEVENSON, Robert Louis (1850–1894)

But all that I could think of, in the darkness
and the cold,
Was that I was leaving home and my folks
were growing old.

[Ballads (1890)]

SWINBURNE, Algernon Charles (1837–1909)

I remember the way we parted,
The day and the way we met;
You hoped we were both broken-hearted,
And knew we should both forget ...

And the best and the worst of this is
That neither is most to blame,
If you have forgotten my kisses

And I have forgotten your name.

['An Interlude' (1866)]

See ABSENCE

SERVANTS

BARHAM, Rev. Richard Harris (Thomas Ingoldsby) (1788–1845)

A servant's too often a negligent elf;
– If it's business of consequence do it
yourself!

[The Ingoldsby Legends (1840–1847)]

BELLOC, Hilaire (1870–1953)

In my opinion, Butlers ought
To know their place, and not to play
The Old Retainer night and day.

[Cautionary Tales (1907)]

BRAXFIELD, Lord (1722–1799)

[To the butler who gave up his place because Lady Braxfield was always scolding him]
Lord! Ye've little to complain o': ye may be
thankfu' ye're no married to her.

[In Cockburn, Memorials (1856)]

MONTAIGNE, Michel de (1533–1592)

Tel a été miraculeux au monde, auquel sa femme et
son valet n'ont rien vu de remarquable. Peu
d'hommes ont été admirés par leurs domestiques.

Many a man has been a wonder to the world,
whose wife and valet have seen nothing in
him that was remarkable. Few men have
been admired by their servants.

[Essais (1580)]

SHAW, George Bernard (1856–1950)

When domestic servants are treated as human
beings it is not worth while to keep them.

[Man and Superman (1903)]

WODEHOUSE, P.G. (1881–1975)

Ice formed on the butler's upper slopes.

[Pigs Have Wings (1952)]

SEX

ALLEN, Woody (1935–)

[On bisexuality]

It immediately doubles your chances for a date on Saturday night.

[*New York Times*, 1975]

Hey, don't knock masturbation! It's sex with someone I love.

[*Annie Hall*, film, 1977]

Is sex dirty? Only if it's done right.

[*Everything You Always Wanted to Know About Sex*, film, 1972]

[Referring to sex]
It was the most fun I ever had without laughing.

[*Annie Hall*, film, 1977]

I finally had an orgasm, and then my doctor told me it was the wrong kind.

[Attr. in *The Herald*, 1998]

ANONYMOUS

Post coitum omne animal triste.
After coition every animal is sad.

[Post-classical saying]

AUBREY, John (1626–1697)

He loved a wench well: and one time getting up one of the maids of honour against a tree in a wood ('twas his first lady) who seemed at first boarding to be somewhat fearful of her honour, and modest, she cried, 'Sweet Sir Walter, what do you ask me? Will you undo me? Nay, sweet Sir Walter! Sir Walter!' At last as the danger and the pleasure at the same time grew higher, she cried in ecstasy, 'Swisser Swatter! Swisser Swatter!' She proved with child and I doubt not but this hero took care of them both, as also that the product was more than an ordinary mortal.

[*Brief Lives* (c. 1693)]

BAGNOLD, Enid (1889–1981)

The great and terrible step was taken. What else could you expect from a girl so expectant? 'Sex,' said Frank Harris, 'is the gateway to life.' So I went through the gateway in an upper room in the Café Royal.

[*Enid Bagnold's Autobiography* (1969)]

BANKHEAD, Tallulah (1903–1968)

[To an admirer]
I'll come and make love to you at five o'clock. If I'm late start without me.

[In Morgan, *Somerset Maugham* (1980)]

BENCHLEY, Robert (1889–1945)

[Comment on an office shared with Dorothy Parker]
One cubic foot less of space and it would have constituted adultery.

[Attr.]

BETJEMAN, Sir John (1906–1984)

[When asked if he had any regrets]
Yes, I haven't had enough sex.

[*Time With Betjeman*, BBC TV, 1983]

BOY GEORGE (1961–)

I'd rather have a cup of tea than go to bed with someone – any day.

[Remark, variously expressed, 1983]

BRADBURY, Malcolm (1932–)

If God had meant us to have group sex, I guess he'd have given us all more organs.

[*Who Do You Think You Are? Stories and Parodies* (1976)]

BROME, Richard (c.1590–1652)

Doctor: But there the maids doe woe
the Batchelors, and tis most probable,
The wives lie uppermost.
Diana: That is a trim,
upside-downe Antipodian tricke indeed.

[*The Antipodes* (1638)]

BROWNE, Sir Thomas (1605–1682)

I could be content that we might procreate like trees, without conjunction, or that there were any way to perpetuate the World without this trivial and vulgar way of coition: it is the foolishest act a wise man commits in all his life; nor is there any thing that will more deject his cool'd imagination, when he shall consider what an odd and unworthy piece of folly he hath committed.

[*Religio Medici* (1643)]

BURCHILL, Julie (1960–)

Sex, on the whole, was meant to be short,

nasty and brutish. If what you want is cuddling, you should buy a puppy.

[*Sex and Sensibility* (1992)]

CAMPBELL, Mrs Patrick (1865–1940)
I don't mind where people make love, so long as they don't do it in the street and frighten the horses.

[Attr.]

CHANDLER, Raymond (1888–1959)
She gave me a smile I could feel in my hip pocket.

[*Farewell, My Lovely* (1940)]

CHESTERFIELD, Lord (1694–1773)
[On sex]
The pleasure is momentary, the position ridiculous, and the expense damnable.

[Attr.]

COMFORT, Alex (1920–)
A woman who has the divine gift of lechery will always make a superlative partner.

[Attr.]

CONNOLLY, Cyril (1903–1974)
In the sex-war thoughtlessness is the weapon of the male, vindictiveness of the female.

[*The Unquiet Grave* (1944)]

COOGAN, Tim Pat (1935–)
[Describing the rulings of the Catholic Church on matters of sexual morality]
It's rather like teaching swimming from a book without ever having got wet oneself.

[*Disillusioned Decades: Ireland, 1966–87* (1987)]

DAVIES, Robertson (1913–1995)
Sex that is not an evidence of a strong human tie is just like blowing your nose; it's not a celebration of a splendid relationship.

[Interview, 1974]

DONNE, John (1572–1631)
Licence my roving hands, and let them go,
Before, behind, between, above, below.
O my America! my new-found-land,
My kingdom, safeliest when with one man mann'd.

['To His Mistress Going to Bed' (c. 1595)]

DURRELL, Lawrence (1912–1990)
No more about sex, it's too boring.

[*Tunc* (1968)]

DWORKIN, Andrea (1946–)
Sex exists on both sides of the law but the law itself creates the sides.

[*Intercourse* (1987)]

Intercourse as an act often expresses the power men have over women.

[*Intercourse* (1987)]

Seduction is often difficult to distinguish from rape. In seduction, the rapist often bothers to buy a bottle of wine.

[*The Independent*, 1992]

EKLAND, Britt (1942–)
I say I don't sleep with married men, but what I mean is that I don't sleep with happily married men.

[Attr.]

EPHRON, Nora (1941–)
Women need a reason to have sex. Men need a place.

[*When Harry Met Sally*, film, 1989]

FAIRBAIRN, Sir Nicholas (1933–1995)
Sex is a human activity like any other. It's a natural urge, like breathing, thinking, drinking, laughing, talking with friends, golf. They are not crimes if you plan them with someone other than your wife. Why should sex be?

[*The Independent*, 1992]

Most cases of rape are reported as an act of vengeance because the fellow has got himself another woman. Or guilt.

[*Daily Mail*, 1993]

FIELDING, Henry (1707–1754)
He in a few minutes ravished this fair creature, or at least would have ravished her, if she had not, by a timely compliance, prevented him.

[*Jonathan Wild* (1743)]

FIGES, Eva (1932–)
When modern woman discovered the

orgasm it was (combined with modern birth control) perhaps the biggest single nail in the coffin of male dominance.

[In Morgan, *The Descent of Woman* (1972)]

FRIEDKIN, William

I really think that sex always looks kind of funny in a movie.

FRY, Stephen (1957–)

A walk, a smile, a gait, a way of flicking the hair away from the eyes, the manner in which clothes encase the body, these can be erotic, but I would be greatly in the debt of the man who could tell me what could ever be appealing about those damp, dark, foul-smelling and revoltingly tufted areas of the body that constitute the main dishes in the banquet of love.

[*Paperweight*]

I gave coitus the red card for utilitarian reasons: the displeasure, discomfort and aggravation it caused outweighed any momentary explosions of pleasure, ease or solace.

[*Paperweight*]

FUKUYAMA, Francis

[Arguing that women were more selective in choosing sexual partners than men (he later excepted certain kinds of seahorses and British women)]

For men, it is a notch on the belt; for women, it is a chance to draw men into a relationship of greater intimacy.

[Lecture, 1997]

GRANVILLE-BARKER, Harley (1877–1946)

But oh, the farmyard world of sex!

[*The Madras House*]

GREER, Germaine (1939–)

No sex is better than bad sex.

[Attr.]

GWYN, Nell (1650–1687)

[On prostitution]

As for me, it is my profession, I do not

pretend to anything better.

[In Miles, *The Women's History of the World* (1988)]

HELLER, Joseph (1923–)

Prostitution gives her an opportunity to meet people. It provides fresh air and wholesome exercise, and it keeps her out of trouble.

[*Catch-22* (1961)]

HERRICK, Robert (1591–1674)

Night makes no difference 'twixt the Priest and Clark;

Jone as my Lady is as good i' th' dark.

[*Hesperides* (1648)]

HILLINGDON, Lady Alice (1857–1940)

I am happy now that Charles calls on my bedchamber less frequently than of old. As it is, I now endure but two calls a week and when I hear his steps outside my door I lie down on my bed, close my eyes, open my legs and think of England.

[*Journal* (1912)]

HUXLEY, Aldous (1894–1963)

People will insist … on treating the *mons Veneris* as though it were Mount Everest.

[*Eyeless in Gaza* (1936)]

A million million spermatozoa,
All of them alive:
Out of their cataclysm but one poor Noah
Dare hope to survive.

['Fifth Philosopher's Song' (1918)]

Mr Mercaptan went on to preach a brilliant sermon on that melancholy sexual perversion known as continence.

[*Antic Hay* (1923)]

'Bed,' as the Italian proverb succinctly puts it, 'is the poor man's opera.'

[*Heaven and Hell* (1956)]

KRISTOFFERSON, Kris (1936–)

Never go to bed with anyone crazier than yourself.

[*The Observer*, 1999]

LANDERS, Ann (1918–)

Women complain about sex more often than

men. Their gripes fall into two major categories: (1) Not enough (2) Too much.

[*Ann Landers Says Truth Is Stranger Than* ... (1968)]

LAWRENCE, D.H. (1885–1930)

'It is sex,' she said to herself. 'How wonderful sex can be, when men keep it powerful and sacred, and it fills the world! Like sunshine through and through one! ...'.

[*The Plumed Serpent* (1926)]

It's all this cold-hearted fucking that is death and idiocy.

[*Lady Chatterley's Lover* (1928)]

LEWIS, Wyndham (1882–1957)

The 'homo' is the legitimate child of the 'suffragette'.

[*The Art of Being Ruled* (1926)]

LONGFORD, Lord (1905–)

No sex without responsibility.

[*The Observer*, 1954]

MACKENZIE, Sir Compton (1883–1972)

From the days of Eve women have always faced sexual facts with more courage and realism than men.

[*Literature in My Time* (1933)]

I told him [D.H. Lawrence] that if he was determined to convert the world to proper reverence for the sexual act ... he would always have to remember one handicap for such an undertaking – that except to the two people who are indulging in it the sexual act is a comic operation.

[*My Life and Times*]

MACLAINE, Shirley (1934–)

The more sex becomes a non-issue in people's lives, the happier they are.

[Attr.]

MAUGHAM, William Somerset (1874–1965)

You know, of course, that the Tasmanians, who never committed adultery, are now extinct.

[*The Bread-Winner*]

MIKES, George (1912–1987)

Continental people have sex life; the English have hot-water bottles.

[*How to be an Alien* (1946)]

MILLER, Henry (1891–1980)

Sex is one of the nine reasons for reincarnation ... The other eight are unimportant.

[*Big Sur and the Oranges of Hieronymus Bosch*]

MILTON, John (1608–1674)

Into thir inmost bower
Handed they went; and eas'd the putting off
These troublesom disguises which wee wear,
Strait side by side were laid, nor turned I weene
Adam from his fair Spouse, nor Eve the Rites
Mysterious of connubial Love refus'd:
Whatever Hypocrits austerely talk
Of puritie and place and innocence,
Defaming as impure what God declares
Pure, and commands to som, leaves free to all.

[*Paradise Lost* (1667)]

MONTGOMERY, Viscount (1887–1976)

[Comment on a bill to relax the laws against homosexuals]
This sort of thing may be tolerated by the French, but we are British – thank God.

[Speech, 1965]

MUGGERIDGE, Malcolm (1903–1990)

An orgy looks particularly alluring seen through the mists of righteous indignation.

[*The Most of Malcolm Muggeridge* (1966)]

The orgasm has replaced the Cross as the focus of longing and the image of fulfilment.

[*The Most of Malcolm Muggeridge* (1966)]

NASH, Ogden (1902–1971)

Home is heaven and orgies are vile
But you need an orgy, once in a while.

['Home, Sweet Home' (1935)]

NEWBOLD, H.L. (1890–1971)

Sex is between the ears as well as between the legs.

[*Mega-Nutrients for Your Nerves*]

NEWBY, P.H. (1918–)

He felt that he could love this woman with the greatest brutality. The situation between them was electric. When he was in a room with her the only thing he could think of was sex.

[*A Journey to the Interior* (1945)]

ORTON, Joe (1933–1967)

You were born with your legs apart. They'll send you to the grave in a Y-shaped coffin.

[*What the Butler Saw* (1969)]

PETRONIUS ARBITER (d. AD 66)

Foeda est in coitu et brevis voluptas
Et taedet Veneris statim peractae.
Pleasure in coupling is gross and brief. Once sated, desire begins to pall.

[In A. Baehrens, *Poetae Latini Minores*]

PHILIP, Prince, Duke of Edinburgh (1921–)

I don't think a prostitute is more moral than a wife, but they are doing the same thing.

[*The Observer*, 1988]

PINTER, Harold (1930–)

I tend to believe that cricket is the greatest thing that God ever created on earth … certainly greater than sex, although sex isn't too bad either.

[Interview in *The Observer*, 1980]

PRIOR, Matthew (1664–1721)

No, no, for my virginity,
When I lose that, says Rose, I'll die;
Behind the elms last night, cry'd Dick,
Rose, were you not extremely sick?

['A True Maid' (1718)]

REUBEN, David (1933–)

Everything You Always Wanted to Know About Sex, But Were Afraid to Ask.

[Title of book, 1969]

SALINGER, J.D. (1919–)

Sex is something I really don't understand too hot. You never know where the hell you are. I keep making up these sex rules for myself, and then I break them right away.

[*The Catcher in the Rye* (1951)]

SAYERS, Dorothy L. (1893–1957)

As I grow older and older,
And totter towards the tomb,
I find that I care less and less
Who goes to bed with whom.

[In Hitchman, *Such a Strange Lady* (1975)]

SCOTT, Valerie

[Toronto prostitute-by-choice]
We don't sell our bodies. Housewives do that. What we do is rent our bodies for sexual services.

[*The Toronto Star*, 1989]

SHAKESPEARE, William (1564–1616)

Is it not strange that desire should so many years outlive performance?

[*Henry IV, Part 2*, II.iv]

SIMENON, Georges (1903–1989)

[His wife later said: 'The true figure is no more than twelve hundred']
I have made love to ten thousand women.

[*Die Tat*, 1977]

SOPHOCLES (496–406 BC)

Someone asked Sophocles, 'How do you stand in matters of love? Are you still able to have sex with a woman?' 'Quiet, man,' he replied, 'I've left all that behind me very gladly, as if I'd escaped from a mad and savage master.'

[In Plato, *Republic*]

STEINEM, Gloria (1934–)

[On transsexualism]
If the shoe doesn't fit, must we change the foot?

[*Outrageous Acts and Everyday Rebellions* (1984)]

STEWART, Rod (1945–)

[On his sexual partners]
The most memorable is always the current one; the rest just merge into a sea of blondes.

[Attr.]

SUCKLING, Sir John (1609–1642)

At length the candle's out, and now
All that they had not done they do:
What that is, who can tell?

But I believe it was no more
That thou and I have done before
With Bridget, and with Nell.

['A Ballad upon a Wedding' (1646)]

SZASZ, Thomas (1920–)

Masturbation: the primary sexual activity of
mankind. In the nineteenth century it was a
disease; in the twentieth, it's a cure.

[*The Second Sin* (1973)]

Traditionally, sex has been a very private,
secretive activity. Herein perhaps lies its
powerful force for uniting people in a strong
bond. As we make sex less secretive, we may
rob it of its power to hold men and women
together.

[*The Second Sin* (1973)]

THURBER, James (1894–1961)

[On being accosted at a party by a drunk woman
who claimed she would like to have a baby by
him]
Surely you don't mean by unartificial
insemination!

[Attr.]

TYNAN, Kenneth (1927–1980)

[When asked on live television if he would allow
sexual intercourse on stage at the National
Theatre]
Oh, I think so, certainly. … I mean, there are
few rational people in this world to whom
the word 'fuck' is particularly diabolical or
revolting or totally forbidden.

[In Paul Ferris, *Sex and the British* (1993)]

VIDAL, Gore (1925–)

[On being asked if his first sexual experience had
been heterosexual or homosexual]
I was too polite to ask.

[*Forum*, 1987]

VOLTAIRE (1694–1778)

*C'est une des superstitions de l'esprit humain d'avoir
imaginé que la virginité pouvait être une vertu.*
It is one of the superstitions of the human
mind to have imagined that virginity could
be a virtue.

['The Leningrad Notebooks' (c. 1735–1750)]

WAUGH, Evelyn (1903–1966)

All this fuss about sleeping together. For
physical pleasure I'd sooner go to my dentist
any day.

[*Vile Bodies* (1930)]

YEATS, W.B. (1865–1939)

The tragedy of sexual intercourse is the
perpetual virginity of the soul.

[Attr. in Jeffares, *W.B. Yeats: man and poet* (1949)]

See ABSTINENCE; ADULTERY;
    CONTRACEPTION; PORNOGRAPHY;
    PROSTITUTION

SHAKESPEARE

ARNOLD, Matthew (1822–1888)

Others abide our question. Thou art free.
We ask and ask – Thou smilest and art still,
Out-topping knowledge.

['Shakespeare' (1849)]

AUBREY, John (1626–1697)

When he killed a calf he would do it in high
style, and make a speech.

[*Brief Lives* (c. 1693)]

He was a handsome, well-shaped man: very
good company, and of a very ready and
pleasant smooth wit.

[*Brief Lives* (c. 1693)]

AUSTEN, Jane (1775–1817)

We all talk Shakespeare, use his similes, and
describe with his descriptions.

[*Mansfield Park* (1814)]

BROWNING, Elizabeth Barrett (1806–1861)

There, Shakespeare, on whose forehead
climb
The crowns o' the world. Oh, eyes sublime,
With tears and laughters for all time!

[*A Vision of Poets* (1844)]

CHESTERFIELD, Lord (1694–1773)

If Shakespeare's genius had been cultivated,
those beauties, which we so justly admire in
him, would have been undisgraced by those

extravagancies and that nonsense with which they are frequently accompanied.

[Letter to his son, 1748]

COLERIDGE, Samuel Taylor (1772–1834)

Our myriad-minded Shakespeare.

[*Biographia Literaria* (1817)]

I believe Shakespeare was not a whit more intelligible in his own day than he is now to an educated man, except for a few local allusions of no consequence. He is of no age – nor of any religion, or party or profession. The body and substance of his works came out of the unfathomable depths of his own oceanic mind: his observation and reading, which was considerable, supplied him with the drapery of his figures.

[*Table Talk* (1835)]

CONDELL, Henry (d. 1627)

Who, as he was a happy imitator of Nature, was a most gentle expresser of it. His mind and hand went together: And what he thought, he uttered with that easiness, that we have scarce received from him a blot.

[Preface to the First Folio Shakespeare, 1623]

DARWIN, Charles (1809–1882)

I have tried lately to read Shakespeare, and found it so intolerably dull that it nauseated me.

[*Autobiography* (1877)]

DICAPRIO, Leonardo (1974–)

Romeo was, like, a gigolo who falls for this girl Juliet, who says, 'Look, if you've got the balls, put them on the table.'

[*The Observer*, 1998]

DRYDEN, John (1631–1700)

[Of Shakespeare]

He was the man who of all modern, and perhaps ancient poets, had the largest and most comprehensive soul ... He was naturally learn'd; he needed not the spectacles of books to read Nature: he looked inwards, and found her there ... He is many times flat, insipid; his comic wit

degenerating into clenches, his serious swelling into bombast. But he is always great.

[*Essay of Dramatic Poesy* (1668)]

ELIOT, T.S. (1888–1965)

We can say of Shakespeare, that never has a man turned so little knowledge to such great account.

[Lecture, 1942]

EMERSON, Ralph Waldo (1803–1882)

When Shakespeare is charged with debts to his authors, Landor replies: 'Yet he was more original than his originals. He breathed upon dead bodies and brought them into life.'

[*Letters and Social Aims* (1875)]

FULLER, Thomas (1608–1661)

[Comparing Shakespeare and Ben Jonson]

Many were the wit-combats betwixt him and Ben Jonson, which two I behold like a Spanish great galleon, and an English man of war; Master Jonson (like the former) was built far higher in learning; solid but slow in his performances. Shakespeare was the English man of war, lesser in bulk, but lighter in sailing, could turn with all tides, tack about and take advantage of all winds, by the quickness of his wit and invention.

[*The History of the Worthies of England* (1662)]

GRAVES, Robert (1895–1985)

The remarkable thing about Shakespeare is that he is really very good – in spite of all the people who say he is very good.

[*The Observer*, 1964]

GRAY, Thomas (1716–1771)

[On Shakespeare]

Far from the sun and summer-gale,
In thy green lap was Nature's Darling laid,
What time, where lucid Avon stray'd,
To him the mighty Mother did unveil
Her aweful face: The dauntless child
Stretch'd forth his little arms, and smiled.

['The Progress of Poesy' (1757)]

GREENE, Robert (1558–1592)

[Of Shakespeare]

For there is an upstart Crow, beautified with

our feathers, that with his Tyger's heart wrapt in a Player's hyde, supposes he is as well able to bombast out a blanke verse as the best of you: and being an absolute Iohannes fac totum, is in his owne conceit the onely Shake-scene in a countrey.

[*Greenes Groats-Worth of witte bought with a million of Repentance* (1592)]

HALSEY, Margaret (1910–)

All of Stratford, in fact, suggests powdered history – add hot water and stir and you have a delicious, nourishing Shakespeare.

[*With Malice Toward Some* (1938)]

JOHNSON, Samuel (1709–1784)

Shakespeare never had six lines together without a fault. Perhaps you may find seven, but this does not refute my general assertion.

[In Boswell, *The Life of Samuel Johnson* (1791)]

JONSON, Ben (1572–1637)

Soul of the Age!
The applause! delight! the wonder of our stage!
My Shakespeare, rise; I will not lodge thee by Chaucer, or Spenser, or bid Beaumont lie
A little further, to make thee a room:
Thou art a monument, without a tomb,
And art alive still, while thy book doth live,
And we have wits to read, and praise to give.

['To the Memory of My Beloved, the Author, Mr William Shakespeare' (1623)]

He was not of an age, but for all time!

['To the Memory of My Beloved, the Author, Mr William Shakespeare' (1623)]

I remember the players have often mentioned it as an honour to Shakespeare that in his writing (whatsoever he penned) he never blotted out a line. My answer hath been 'Would he had blotted a thousand'. Which they thought a malevolent speech. I had not told posterity this, but for their ignorance, who chose that circumstance to commend their friend by wherein he most faulted; and to justify mine own candour: for I loved the man, and do honour his memory,

on this side of idolatry, as much as any. He was (indeed) honest, and of an open and free nature; had an excellent phantasy, brave notions, and gentle expressions; wherein he flowed with that facility, that sometimes it was necessary he should be stopped: sufflaminandus erat, as Augustus said of Haterius. His wit was in his own power, would the rule of it had been so too … But he redeemed his vices with his virtues. There was ever more in him to be praised than to be pardoned.

[*Timber, or Discoveries made upon Men and Matter* (1641)]

KEATS, John (1795–1821)

I have great reason to be content, for thank God I can read and perhaps understand Shakespeare to his depths.

[Letter to John Taylor, 1818]

Shakespeare led a life of Allegory: his works are the comments on it.

[Letter to George and Georgiana Keats, 1819]

LAWRENCE, D.H. (1885–1930)

When I read Shakespeare I am struck with wonder
That such trivial people should muse and thunder
In such lovely language.

[*Pansies* (1929)]

OLIVIER, Laurence, Baron (1907–1989)

Shakespeare – the nearest thing in incarnation to the eye of God.

[Kenneth Harris *Talking To*: 'Sir Laurence Olivier']

PHILIP, Prince, Duke of Edinburgh (1921–)

A man can be forgiven a lot if he can quote Shakespeare in an economic crisis.

[Attr.]

POWYS, John Cowper (1872–1963)

He combined scepticism of everything with credulity about everything … and I am convinced this is the true Shakespearian way wherewith to take life.

[*Autobiography*]

SHAME

SHAW, George Bernard (1856–1950)

With the single exception of Homer, there is no eminent writer, not even Sir Walter Scott, whom I can despise so entirely as I despise Shakespeare when I measure my mind against his ... it would positively be a relief to me to dig him up and throw stones at him.

[*Dramatic Opinions and Essays* (1906)]

TERRY, Dame Ellen (1847–1928)

Wonderful women! Have you ever thought how much we all, and women especially, owe to Shakespeare for his vindication of women in these fearless, high-spirited, resolute and intelligent heroines?

[*Four Lectures on Shakespeare* (1932)]

WALPOLE, Horace (1717–1797)

One of the greatest geniuses that ever existed, Shakespeare, undoubtedly wanted taste.

[Letter to Christopher Wren, 1764]

See CRITICISM; POETS; WRITERS

SHAME

BENTLEY, Edmund Clerihew (1875–1956)

When their lordships asked Bacon
How many bribes he had taken
He had at least the grace
To get very red in the face.

[*Baseless Biography* (1939)]

BLAKE, William (1757–1827)

Shame is Pride's cloke.

[*The Marriage of Heaven and Hell* (c. 1790–1793)]

SHAW, George Bernard (1856–1950)

We are ashamed of everything that is real about us; ashamed of ourselves, of our relatives, of our incomes, of our accents, of our opinions, of our experience, just as we are ashamed of our naked skins ... The more things a man is ashamed of, the more respectable he is.

[*Man and Superman* (1903)]

SWIFT, Jonathan (1667–1745)

I never wonder to see men wicked, but I often wonder to see them not ashamed.

[*Thoughts on Various Subjects* (1711)]

SHOPPING

BRYSON, Bill (1951–)

My first rule of consumerism is never to buy anything you can't make your children carry.

[*The Lost Continent* (1989)]

CATO THE ELDER (234–149 BC)

Do not buy what you want, but what you need; what you do not need is dear at a farthing.

[*Reliquiae* (Remains)]

EVANS, Dame Edith (1888–1976)

[In Fortnum and Mason, to a salesgirl who insisted on giving her threepence change]
Keep the change, my dear. I trod on a grape as I came in.

[In B. Forbes, *Dame Edith Evans: Ned's Girl* (1977)]

GINSBERG, Allen (1926–1997)

[Addressing Walt Whitman]
In my hungry fatigue, and shopping for images, I went into the neon fruit supermarket, dreaming of your enumerations!
What peaches and what penumbras! Whole families shopping at night! Aisles full of husbands! Wives in the avocados, babies in the tomatoes! – and you, Garcia Lorca, what were you doing down by the watermelons?

['A Supermarket in California']

SELFRIDGE, H. Gordon (1858–1947)

The customer is always right.

[Slogan in A.H. Williams, *No Name on the Door; A Memoir of Gordon Selfridge* (1956)]

See CONSUMER SOCIETY

SHOWBUSINESS

ALLEN, Woody (1935–)

Showbusiness is dog eat dog. It's worse than

dog eat dog. It's dog doesn't return other dog's phone calls.

[*Crimes and Misdemeanours*, film, 1989]

ANONYMOUS

Can't act, can't sing, slightly bald. Can dance a little.

[Comment by a Hollywood executive on Fred Astaire's first screen test]

BARNES, Clive (1927–)

[On *Oh, Calcutta!* (1969)]
This is the kind of show that gives pornography a bad name.

[Attr.]

BROOKS, Mel (1926–)

That's it, baby, if you've got it, flaunt it.

[*The Producers*, film, 1968]

CAMERON, James (1954–)

[Accepting the Oscars won by *Titanic*]
Does this prove, once and for all, that size does matter?

[*The Observer*, 1998]

CHANDLER, Raymond (1888–1959)

You can live a long time in Hollywood and never see the part they use in pictures.

[*The Little Sister*]

CHASEN, Dave (1926–)

Bogart's a helluva nice guy until 11.30 p.m. After that he thinks he's Bogart.

[In Halliwell, The *Filmgoer's Book of Quotes* (1973)]

CHER (1946–)

Mother told me a couple of years ago, 'Sweetheart, settle down and marry a rich man.' I said, 'Mom, I am a rich man.'

[*The Observer Review*, 1995]

COCHRAN, Charles B. (1872–1951)

I still prefer a good juggler to a bad Hamlet.

[*The Observer*, 1943]

DAVIS, Bette (1908–1989)

[Of a starlet]
I see – she's the original good time that was had by all.

[In Halliwell, *Filmgoer's Book of Quotes* (1973)]

DAVIS, Sammy, Junior (1925–1990)

Being a star has made it possible for me to get insulted in places where the average Negro could never hope to get insulted.

[*Yes I can* (1965)]

DILLINGHAM, Charles Bancroft (1868–1934)

[Said at the funeral of Harry Houdini, the escapologist, while carrying his coffin]
I bet you a hundred bucks he ain't in here.

[Attr.]

GARBO, Greta (1905–1990)

I never said, 'I want to be alone.' I only said, 'I want to be let alone.' There is all the difference.

[In Colombo, *Wit and Wisdom of the Moviemakers*]

GARLAND, Judy (1922–1969)

I was born at the age of twelve on a Metro-Goldwyn-Mayer lot.

[*The Observer*, 1951]

GOLDWYN, Samuel (1882–1974)

Directors [are] always biting the hand that lays the golden egg.

[In Zierold, *Moguls* (1969)]

I'll give you a definite maybe.

[In Colombo, *Wit and Wisdom of the Moviemakers*]

In two words: im possible.

[Attr.; in Zierold, *Moguls* (1969)]

What we want is a story that starts with an earthquake and works its way up to a climax.

[Attr.]

GRABLE, Betty (1916–1973)

There are two reasons why I'm in show business, and I'm standing on both of them.

[Attr.]

GRADE, Lew (1906–1994)

All my shows are great. Some of them are bad. But they are all great.

[*The Observer*, 1975]

GUINAN, Texas (1884–1933)

[When she and her troupe were refused entry to France in 1931]

It goes to show that fifty million Frenchmen can be wrong.

[Attr.]

HELPMAN, Sir Robert Murray (1909–1986)

[After the opening night of Oh, Calcutta!]
The trouble with nude dancing is that not everything stops when the music stops.

[In *The Frank Muir Book* (1976)]

HOPE, Bob (1903–)

Clint Eastwood is a man who walks softly and carries a big percentage of the gross.

[In Simon Rose, *Classic Film Guide* (1995)]

LEVANT, Oscar (1906–1972)

Strip the phony tinsel off Hollywood and you'll find the real tinsel underneath.

[In Halliwell, *Filmgoer's Book of Quotes* (1973)]

MONROE, Marilyn (1926–1962)

I guess I am a fantasy.

[In Steinem, *Outrageous Acts and Everyday Rebellions* (1984)]

REED, Rex (1938–)

Cannes is where you lie on the beach and stare at the stars – or vice versa.

[Attr.]

RICHARD, Cliff (1940–)

There's no room in my life for drugs, fights, divorce, adultery, sadism, unnecessary fuss and sex.

[*Daily Mail*, 1996]

Stars who debauch themselves, get addicted to drugs then kick them get all the praise. Wouldn't you think that people who have never been addicted should be praised all the more?

[*The Observer Review*, 1996]

SHAW, George Bernard (1856–1950)

The trouble, Mr Goldwyn, is that you are only interested in art and I am only interested in money.

[In Johnson, *The Great Goldwyn* (1937)]

SKELTON, Red (1913–1997)

[Commenting on the large crowds attending the funeral of Hollywood producer Harry Cohn]
It proves what they say, give the public what they want to see and they'll come out for it.

[Remark, 1958]

SOUTHERN, Terry (1924–1995)

She says, 'Listen, who do I have to fuck to get off this picture?'.

[*Blue Movie* (1970)]

THOMAS, Irene (1920–)

It was the kind of show where the girls are not auditioned – just measured.

[Attr.]

TRACY, Spencer (1900–1967)

[Explaining what he looked for in a script]
Days off.

[Attr.]

WELLES, Orson (1915–1985)

I began at the top and I've been working my way down ever since.

[In Colombo, *Wit and Wisdom of the Moviemakers*]

See CELEBRITY; CINEMA; FAME; HOLLYWOOD

SILENCE

AUSTEN, Jane (1775–1817)

From politics, it was an easy step to silence.

[*Northanger Abbey* (1818)]

BACON, Francis (1561–1626)

Silence is the virtue of fools.

[*Of the Dignity and Advancement of Learning* (1623)]

BASHÓ, Matsuo (1644–1694)

The din of cicadas
Seeps into the rock;
the air rings with silence.

['Narrow Roads of Oku', 1703)]

CARLYLE, Thomas (1795–1881)

Under all speech that is good for anything there lies a silence that is better. Silence is deep as Eternity; speech is shallow as Time.

['Memoirs of the Life of Scott' (1839)]

DARK, Eleanor (1901–1985)

Silence ruled this land. Out of silence mystery comes, and magic, and the delicate awareness of unreasoning things.

[*The Timeless Land* (1941)]

ELIOT, George (1819–1880)

Speech is often barren; but silence also does not necessarily brood over a full nest. Your still fowl, blinking at you without remark, may all the while be sitting on one addled nest-egg; and when it takes to cackling, will have nothing to announce but that addled delusion.

[*Felix Holt* (1866)]

FLECKNOE, Richard (d. c.1678)

Still-born Silence! thou that art
Floodgate of the deeper heart.

['Invocation of Silence' (1653)]

HOLMES, Oliver Wendell (1809–1894)

And silence, like a poultice, comes
To heal the blows of sound.

['The Music-Grinders' (1836)]

HOOD, Thomas (1799–1845)

There is a silence where hath been no sound,
There is a silence where no sound may be,
In the cold grave – under the deep, deep sea,
Or in the wide desert where no life is found.

['Sonnet: Silence' (1823)]

HUXLEY, Aldous (1894–1963)

Silence is as full of potential wisdom and wit as the unhewn marble of great sculpture.

[*Point Counter Point* (1928)]

JONSON, Ben (1572–1637)

Calumnies are answered best with silence.

[*Volpone* (1607)]

LA ROCHEFOUCAULD (1613–1680)

Le silence est le parti le plus sûr de celui qui se défie de soi-même.
Silence is the safest policy for the man who distrusts himself.

[*Maximes* (1678)]

LINCOLN, Abraham (1809–1865)

Better to remain silent and be thought a fool than to speak out and remove all doubt.

[Attr.]

MANDELSTAM, Nadezhda (1899–1980)

If nothing else is left, one must scream. Silence is the real crime against humanity.

[*Hope Against Hope* (1970)]

PASCAL, Blaise (1623–1662)

Le silence éternel de ces espaces infinis m'effraie.
The eternal silence of these infinite spaces terrifies me.

[*Pensées* (1670)]

PROVERB

Silence is golden.

ROSSETTI, Christina (1830–1894)

Silence more musical than any song.

['Rest' (1862)]

ROSSETTI, Dante Gabriel (1828–1882)

'Tis visible silence, still as the hour-glass …

Deep in the sun-searched growths the dragon-fly
Hangs like a blue thread loosened from the sky: –
So this winged hour is dropt to us from above.
Oh! clasp we to our hearts, for deathless dower,
This close-companioned inarticulate hour
When twofold silence was the song of love.

[*The House of Life* (1881)]

SAINTE-BEUVE, Charles-Augustin (1804–1869)

Le silence seul est le souverain mépris.
Silence is the supreme contempt.

['Mes Poisons']

SARTRE, Jean-Paul (1905–1980)

You get the impression that their normal condition is silence and that speech is a slight fever which attacks them now and then.

[*Nausea* (1938)]

SCHLEIERMACHER, F.E.D. (1768–1834)

[Of a celebrated philologist]
He could be silent in seven languages.

[Attr.]

SIDNEY, Sir Philip (1554–1586)

Shallow brookes murmur moste, Depe sylent slyde away.

[*Old Arcadia* (1581), 'The Firste Eclogues']

SMITH, Sydney (1771–1845)

[Of Macaulay]
He has occasional flashes of silence, that make his conversation perfectly delightful.

[In Holland, *A Memoir of the Reverend Sydney Smith* (1855)]

SWINBURNE, Algernon Charles (1837–1909)

For words divide and rend;
But silence is most noble till the end.

[*Atalanta in Calydon* (1865)]

TUCHOLSKY, Kurt (1890–1935)

Es gibt vielerlei Lärme, aber es gibt nur eine Stille.
There are many sorts of noises, but there is only one silence.

[*Scraps* (1973)]

TUPPER, Martin (1810–1889)

Well-timed silence hath more eloquence than speech.

[*Proverbial Philosophy* (1838)]

VEGA CARPIO, Félix Lope de (1562–1635)

El más discreto hablar
no es santo como el silencio.
The most wise speech
is not as holy as silence.

[*The Stupid Lady* (1613)]

VIGNY, Alfred de (1797–1863)

Seul le silence est grand; tout le reste est faiblesse …
Fais énergiquement ta longue et lourde tâche …
Puis, après, comme moi, souffre et meurs sans parler.
Silence alone is great; all else is weakness …
Perform with all your heart your long and heavy task …
Then, afterwards, as do I, suffer and die

without a word.

['The Death of the Wolf', 1843)]

VIRGIL (70–19 BC)

Tacitae per amica silentia lunae.
Through the friendly silence of the soundless moonlight.

[*Aeneid*]

WITTGENSTEIN, Ludwig (1889–1951)

What can be said at all can be said clearly;
and whereof one cannot speak, thereon one must keep silent.

[*Tractatus Logico-Philosophicus* (1922)]

See CONVERSATION

SIN

AUDEN, W.H. (1907–1973)

All sin tends to be addictive, and the terminal point of addiction is what is called damnation.

[*A Certain World* (1970)]

THE BIBLE (King James Version)

Be sure your sin will find you out.

[*Numbers*, 32:23]

He that is without sin among you, let him first cast a stone.

[*John*, 8:7]

The wages of sin is death.

[*Romans*, 6:23]

BULGAKOV, Mikhail (1891–1940)

Cowardice is, without a doubt, one of the greatest sins.

[*The Master and Margarita* (1967)]

BUNYAN, John (1628–1688)

One leak will sink a ship, and one sin will destroy a sinner.

[*The Pilgrim's Progress* (1678)]

CAMPBELL, Thomas (1777–1844)

An original something, fair maid, you would win me
To write – but how shall I begin?

For I fear I have nothing original in me –
Excepting Original Sin.

> ['To a Young Lady, Who Asked Me to Write
> Something Original for Her Album'
> (1843)]

COOLIDGE, Calvin (1872–1933)

[On being asked what had been said by a
clergyman who preached on sin]
He said he was against it.

> [Attr.]

COWLEY, Abraham (1618–1667)

Lukewarmness I account a sin
As great in love as in religion.

> ['The Request' (1647)]

DONNE, John (1572–1631)

Wilt thou forgive that sin, where I begun,
Which is my sin, though it were done before?
Wilt thou forgive those sins through which I
run
And do them still, though still I do deplore?
When thou hast done, thou hast not done,
For I have more.

Wilt thou forgive that sin, by which I have
won
Others to sin, and made my sin their door?
Wilt thou forgive that sin which I did shun
A year or two, but wallowed in a score?
When thou hast done, thou hast not done,
For I have more.

> ['Hymn to God the Father' (1623)]

EDDY, Mary Baker (1821–1910)

Sin brought death, and death will disappear
with the disappearance of sin.

> [Science and Health (1875)]

HERBERT, Sir A.P. (1890–1971)

Don't tell my mother I'm living in sin,
Don't let the old folks know:
Don't tell my twin that I breakfast on gin,
He'd never survive the blow.

> [Laughing Ann (1925)]

JUVENAL (c.60–130)

Summum crede nefas animam praeferre pudori
Et propter vitam vivendi perdere causas.

Count it the greatest sin to put life before
honour, and for the sake of life to lose the
reasons for living.

> [Satires]

LAWRENCE, D.H. (1885–1930)

There's nothing so artificial as sinning
nowadays. I suppose it once was real.

> [St Mawr (1925)]

MOLIÈRE (1622–1673)

Le scandale du monde est ce qui fait l'offense,
Et ce n'est pas pécher que pécher en silence.
Public scandal is what constitutes offence; to
sin in secret is no sin at all.

> [Tartuffe (1664)]

PLOMER, William (1903–1973)

On a sofa upholstered in panther skin
Mona did research in original sin.

> ['Mews Flat Mona' (1960)]

QUEVEDO Y VILLEGAS, Francisco Gómez de (1580–1645)

Tan ciego estoy a mi mortal enredo
que no te oso llamar, Señor, de miedo
de que querrás sacarme de pecado.
So blind am I to my mortal entanglement
that I dare not call upon thee, Lord, for fear
that thou wouldst take me away from my sin.

> [Christian Heraclitus (1613)]

ROOSEVELT, Theodore (1858–1919)

The worst sin towards our fellow creatures is
not to hate them, but to be indifferent to
them: that's the essence of inhumanity.

> [The Devil's Disciple (1901)]

SHAKESPEARE, William (1564–1616)

Plate sin with gold,
And the strong lance of justice hurtless
breaks;
Arm it in rags, a pigmy's straw does pierce it.

> [King Lear, IV.vi]

Few love to hear the sins they love to act.

> [Pericles, Prince of Tyre, I.i]

Nothing emboldens sin so much as mercy.

> [Timon of Athens, III.v]

SMITH, Sydney (1771–1845)

[Of boring sermons]

They are written as if sin were to be taken out of man like Eve out of Adam – by putting him to sleep.

[In J. Larwood, *Anecdotes of the Clergy*]

THOMAS, Dylan (1914–1953)

You just wait, I'll sin till I blow up!

[*Under Milk Wood* (1954)]

WILDE, Oscar (1854–1900)

There is no sin except stupidity.

[*Intentions* (1891), 'The Critic as Artist']

It has been said that the great events of the world take place in the brain. It is in the brain, and the brain only, that the great sins of the world take place.

[*The Picture of Dorian Gray* (1891)]

See EVIL; VICE

SLAVERY

BURKE, Edmund (1729–1797)

Slavery they can have anywhere. It is a weed that grows in every soil.

[*Speech on Conciliation with America* (1775)]

GANDHI (1869–1948)

The moment the slave resolves that he will no longer be a slave, his fetters fall. He frees himself and shows the way to others. Freedom and slavery are mental states.

[*Non-Violence in Peace and War* (1949)]

GARRISON, William Lloyd (1805–1879)

The compact which exists between the North and the South is 'a covenant with death and an agreement with hell'.

[Resolution adopted by the Massachusetts Anti-Slavery Society, 1843]

GILL, Eric (1882–1940)

That state is a state of Slavery in which a man does what he likes to do in his spare time and in his working time that which is required of him.

['Slavery and Freedom' (1929)]

JOHNSON, Samuel (1709–1784)

How is it that we hear the loudest yelps for liberty among the drivers of negroes?

[*Taxation No Tyranny* (1775)]

LINCOLN, Abraham (1809–1865)

In giving freedom to the slave, we assure freedom to the free – honourable alike in what we give and what we preserve.

[Speech, 1862]

MACKENZIE, Sir Compton (1883–1972)

The slavery of being waited upon that is more deadening than the slavery of waiting upon other people.

[*The Adventures of Sylvia Scarlett* (1918)]

STANTON, Elizabeth Cady (1815–1902)

The prolonged slavery of woman is the darkest page in human history.

[In Anthony and Gage, *History of Woman Suffrage* (1881)]

WEDGWOOD, Josiah (1730–1795)

Am I not a man and a brother?

[Motto adopted by Anti-Slavery Society]

See RACISM

SLEEP

BROWNE, Sir Thomas (1605–1682)

[Sleep is] in fine, so like death, I dare not trust it without my prayers.

[*Religio Medici* (1643)]

Nor will the sweetest delight of gardens afford much comfort in sleep; wherein the dullness of that sense shakes hands with delectable odours; and though in the bed of Cleopatra, can hardly with any delight raise up the ghost of a rose.

[*The Garden of Cyrus* (1658)]

Sleep is a death, O make me try,
By sleeping what it is to die.
And as gently lay my head

On my grave, as now my bed.

[*Religio Medici* (1643)]

Half our days we pass in the shadow of the earth; and the brother of death exacteth a third part of our lives.

[*Pseudodoxia Epidemica* (1646)]

CERVANTES, Miguel de (1547–1616)

Bien haya el que inventó el sueño, capa que cubre todos los humanos pensamientos, manjar que quita la hambre, agua que ahuyenta la sed, fuego que calienta el frío, frío que templa el ardor, y, finalmente, moneda general con que todas las cosas se compran, balanza y peso que iguala al pastor con el rey y al simple con el discreto.

God bless whoever invented sleep, the cloak that covers all human thoughts. It is the food that satisfies hunger, the water that quenches thirst, the fire that warms cold, the cold that reduces heat, and, lastly, the common currency which can buy anything, the balance and compensating weight that makes the shepherd equal to the king, and the simpleton equal to the sage.

[*Don Quixote* (1615)]

COLERIDGE, Samuel Taylor (1772–1834)

Oh sleep! it is a gentle thing
Beloved from pole to pole!
To Mary Queen the praise be given!
She sent the gentle sleep from Heaven,
That slid into my soul.

['The Rime of the Ancient Mariner' (1798)]

DANIEL, Samuel (1562–1619)

Care-charmer Sleep, son of the sable Night,
Brother to Death, in silent darkness born:
Relieve my languish, and restore the light,
With dark forgetting of my care return
And let the day be time enough to mourn
The shipwreck of my ill adventured youth:
Let waking eyes suffice to wail their scorn,
Without the torment of the night's untruth.

[*Delia* (1592)]

DE LA MARE, Walter (1873–1956)

I met at eve the Prince of Sleep,
His was a still and lovely face,

He wandered through a valley steep,
Lovely in a lonely place.

['I Met at Eve' (1902)]

DEKKER, Thomas (c.1570–c.1632)

Golden slumbers kiss your eyes,
Smiles awake you when you rise:
Sleep, pretty wantons, do not cry,
And I will sing a lullaby:
Rock them, rock them, lullaby.

['Patient Grissil' (1603)]

DICKENS, Charles (1812–1870)

It would make any one go to sleep, that bedstead would, whether they wanted to or not.

[*The Pickwick Papers* (1837)]

FIELDS, W.C. (1880–1946)

The best cure for insomnia is to get a lot of sleep.

[Attr.]

FLETCHER, John (1579–1625)

Care-charming Sleep, thou easer of all woes,
Brother to Death.

[*The Tragedy of Valentinian* (1647)]

HENRI IV (1553–1610)

Les grands mangeurs et les grands dormeurs sont incapables de rien faire de grand.
Great eaters and great sleepers are not capable of doing anything great.

[Attr.]

KEATS, John (1795–1821)

O soft embalmer of the still midnight,
Shutting, with careful fingers and benign,
Our gloom-pleas'd eyes.

['To Sleep' (1819)]

NIETZSCHE, Friedrich Wilhelm (1844–1900)

Keine geringe Kunst ist schlafen: es tut schon not, den ganzen Tag darauf hin zu wachen.
Sleeping is no mean art: it is necessary to stay awake for it all day.

[*Thus Spake Zarathustra* (1884)]

PROVERB

There will be sleeping enough in the grave.

RACINE, Jean (1639–1699)

Elle s'endormit du sommeil des justes.

She fell asleep and slept the sleep of the just.

[*Abrégé de l'Histoire de Port Royal* (1742)]

SASSOON, Siegfried (1886–1967)

Why do you lie with your legs ungainly
huddled,
And one arm bent across your sullen, cold
Exhausted face? …

You are too young to fall asleep for ever;
And when you sleep you remind me of the
dead.

['The Dug-Out' (1918)]

SHAKESPEARE, William (1564–1616)

Weariness
Can snore upon the flint, when resty sloth
Finds the down pillow hard.

[*Cymbeline*, III.vi]

Methought I heard a voice cry 'Sleep no more;
Macbeth does murder sleep' – the innocent
sleep,
Sleep that knits up the ravell'd sleave of care,
The death of each day's life, sore labour's bath,
Balm of hurt minds, great nature's second
course,
Chief nourisher in life's feast.

[*Macbeth*, II.ii]

Not poppy, nor mandragora,
Nor all the drowsy syrups of the world,
Shall ever medicine thee to that sweet sleep
Which thou owed'st yesterday.

[*Othello*, III.iii]

SIDNEY, Sir Philip (1554–1586)

Come, Sleepe, O Sleepe, the certaine knot of
peace,
The bathing place of wits, the balm of woe,
The poore man's wealth, the prysoner's
release,
The indifferent Judge betweene the hie and
lowe.

[*Astrophel and Stella* (1591), 38]

SOUTHEY, Robert (1774–1843)

Thou hast been call'd, O Sleep! the friend of
Woe,
But 'tis the happy who have called thee so.

[*The Curse of Kehama* (1810)]

TERTZ, Abram (1925–1997)

Sleep is the watering place of the soul to
which it hastens at night to drink at the
sources of life.
In sleep we receive confirmation … that we
must go on living.

[*A Voice From the Chorus* (1973)]

THOMAS, Edward (1878–1917)

I have come to the borders of sleep,
The unfathomable deep
Forest where all must lose
Their way, however straight,
Or winding, soon or late;
They cannot choose.

['Lights Out' (1917)]

THOMSON, James (1700–1748)

A pleasing land of drowsyhead it was.

[*The Castle of Indolence*
(1748)]

YOUNG, Edward (1683–1765)

Tir'd nature's sweet Restorer, balmy Sleep!
He, like the World, his ready visit pays
Where Fortune smiles; the wretched he
forsakes.

[*Night-Thoughts on Life, Death and Immortality*
(1742–1746)]

See BED; DEATH; DREAMS

SMOKING

CALVERLEY, C.S. (1831–1884)

How they who use fusees
All grow by slow degrees
Brainless as chimpanzees,
Meagre as lizards:
Go mad, and beat their wives;
Plunge (after shocking lives)
Razors and carving knives
Into their gizzards.

['Ode to Tobacco' (1861)]

COWPER, William (1731–1800)

The pipe, with solemn interposing puff,
Makes half a sentence at a time enough;
The dozing sages drop the drowsy strain,
Then pause, and puff – and speak, and pause
again.

['Conversation' (1782)]

Pernicious weed! whose scent the fair
annoys,
Unfriendly to society's chief joys,
Thy worst effect is banishing for hours
The sex whose presence civilizes ours.

['Conversation' (1782)]

DOYLE, Sir Arthur Conan (1859–1930)

A little monograph on the ashes of one
hundred and forty different varieties of pipe,
cigar, and cigarette tobacco.

['The Boscombe Valley Mystery' (1892)]

ELIZABETH I (1533–1603)

[To Sir Walter Raleigh]
I have known many persons who turned
their gold into smoke, but you are the first to
turn smoke into gold.

[In Chamberlin, *The Sayings of Queen Elizabeth*
(1923)]

HELPS, Sir Arthur (1813–1875)

What a blessing this smoking is! perhaps the
greatest that we owe to the discovery of
America.

[*Friends in Council* (1859)]

JAMES VI OF SCOTLAND AND I OF ENGLAND (1566–1625)

A branch of the sin of drunkenness, which is
the root of all sins.

[*A Counterblast to Tobacco* (1604)]

Herein is not only a great vanity, but a great
contempt of God's good gifts, that the
sweetness of man's breath, being a good gift
of God, should be wilfully corrupted by this
stinking smoke.

[*A Counterblast to Tobacco* (1604)]

A custom loathsome to the eye, hateful to
the nose, harmful to the brain, dangerous to
the lungs, and in the black, stinking fume

thereof, nearest resembling the horrible
Stygian smoke of the pit that is bottomless.

[*A Counterblast to Tobacco* (1604)]

JONSON, Ben (1572–1637)

Neither do thou lust after that tawney weed
tobacco.

[*Bartholomew Fair* (1614)]

I do hold it, and will affirm it before any
prince in Europe, to be the most sovereign
and precious weed that ever the earth
rendered to the use of man.

[*Every Man in His Humour* (1598)]

Ods me, I marvel what pleasure or felicity
they have in taking their roguish tobacco. It
is good for nothing but to choke a man, and
fill him full of smoke and embers.

[*Every Man in His Humour* (1598)]

KIPLING, Rudyard (1865–1936)

And a woman is only a woman, but a good
cigar is a Smoke.

['The Betrothed' (1886)]

LAMB, Charles (1775–1834)

This very night I am going to leave off
tobacco! Surely there must be some other
world in which this unconquerable purpose
shall be realized. The soul hath not her
generous aspirings implanted in her in vain.

[Letter to Thomas Manning, 1815]

Dr Parr … asked him, how he had acquired
his power of smoking at such a rate? Lamb
replied, 'I toiled after it, sir, as some men toil
after virtue.'

[In Talfourd, *Memoirs of Charles Lamb* (1892)]

LINDSAY, Norman (1879–1969)

'You ain't got any tobacco,' he said scornfully
to Bunyip Bluegum. 'I can see that at a
glance, You're one of the non-smoking sort,
all fur and feathers.'

[*The Magic Pudding* (1918)]

NAPOLEON III (1808–1873)

[On being asked to ban smoking]
This vice brings in one hundred million
francs in taxes every year. I will certainly

forbid it at once – as soon as you can name a virtue that brings in as much revenue.

[In Hoffmeister, *Anekdotenschatz*]

SATIE, Erik (1866–1925)

[Mon médecin m'a toujours dit de fumer. Il ajoute à ses conseils: 'Fumez, mon ami: sans cela, un autre fumera à votre place.]

' My doctor has always told me to smoke. He explains himself thus: 'Smoke, my friend. If you don't, someone else will smoke in your place.'

[*Mémoires d'un amnésique* (1924)]

SHIELDS, Brooke (1965–)

Smoking kills. If you're killed, you've lost a very important part of your life.

[Remark, quoted in *The Observer*, 1998]

TWAIN, Mark (1835–1910)

[Saying how easy it is to give up smoking]
I've done it a hundred times!

[Attr.]

WILDE, Oscar (1854–1900)

A cigarette is the perfect type of a perfect pleasure. It is exquisite, and it leaves one unsatisfied. What more can one want?

[*The Picture of Dorian Gray* (1891)]

See ABSTINENCE

SNOBBERY

LYNES, J. Russel (1910–1991)

The true snob never rests: there is always a higher goal to attain, and there are, by the same token, always more and more people to look down upon.

THACKERAY, William Makepeace (1811–1863)

It is impossible, in our condition of Society, not to be sometimes a Snob.

[*The Book of Snobs* (1848)]

He who meanly admires mean things is a Snob.

[*The Book of Snobs* (1848)]

WILDE, Oscar (1854–1900)

Never speak disrespectfully of Society, Algernon. Only people who can't get into it do that.

[*The Importance of Being Earnest* (1895)]

See ARISTOCRACY; CLASS

SNOW

BRIDGES, Robert (1844–1930)

When men were all asleep the snow came flying,
In large white flakes falling on the city brown,
Stealthily and perpetually settling and loosely lying,
Hushing the latest traffic of the drowsy town …

All night it fell, and when full inches seven
It lay in depth of its uncompacted lightness,
The clouds blew off from a high and frosty heaven;
And all woke either for the unaccustomed brightness
Of the winter dawning, the strange unheavenly glare …

Or peering up from under the white-mossed wonder,
'O look at the trees!' they cried, 'O look at the trees!'.

['London Snow' (1890)]

EMERSON, Ralph Waldo (1803–1882)

The frolic architecture of the snow.

[*Poems* (1847),'The Snow-storm']

HARDY, Thomas (1840–1928)

Every branch big with it,
Bent every twig with it;
Every fork like a white web-foot;
Every street and pavement mute:
Some flakes have lost their way, and grope back upward, when
Meeting those meandering down they turn

and descend again.

['Snow in the Suburbs' (1925)]

SOUTHEY, Robert (1774–1843)

Their wintry garment of unsullied snow
The mountains have put on.

[*The Poet's Pilgrimage* (1816)]

THOMAS, Dylan (1914–1953)

I can never remember whether it snowed for six days and six nights when I was twelve or whether it snowed for twelve days and twelve nights when I was six.

[*A Child's Christmas in Wales* (1954)]

THOMPSON, Francis (1859–1907)

What heart could have thought you? –
Past our devisal
(O filigree petal!)
Fashioned so purely,
Fragilely, surely,
From what Paradisal
Imagineless metal,
Too costly for cost?

['To a Snowflake' (1913)]

See SEASONS; WEATHER

SOCIALISM

BENN, Tony (1925–)

[On Tony Blair]
The paradox at the moment is that the Labour Party is cheering the leader because they think he'll win. The City and the press are cheering him because they think he's going to destroy socialism.

[*The Observer*, 1995]

BENNETT, Alan (1934–)

Why is it always the intelligent people who are socialists?

[*Forty Years On* (1969)]

BEVAN, Aneurin (1897–1960)

The language of priorities is the religion of Socialism.

[Attr.]

CONNELL, James M. (1852–1929)

The people's flag is deepest red;
It shrouded oft our martyred dead,
And ere their limbs grew stiff and cold,
Their heart's blood dyed its every fold.
Then raise the scarlet standard high!
Within its shade we'll live or die.
Tho' cowards flinch and traitors sneer,
We'll keep the red flag flying here.

['The Red Flag' (1889)]

DUBCEK, Alexander (1921–1992)

In the service of the people we followed such a policy that socialism would not lose its human face.

[Attr.]

DURANT, Will (1885–1982)

There is nothing in Socialism that a little age or a little money will not cure.

[Attr.]

EDWARD VIII (later Duke of Windsor) (1894–1972)

[Quoting Sir William Harcourt]
We are all socialists now.

[Attr.]

KEYNES, John Maynard (1883–1946)

Marxian Socialism must always remain a portent to the historians of opinion – how a doctrine so illogical and so dull can have exercised so powerful and enduring an influence over the minds of men, and, through them, the events of history.

['The End of Laissez-Faire' (1926)]

KINNOCK, Neil (1942–)

The idea that there is a model Labour voter, a blue-collar council house tenant who belongs to a union and has 2.4 children, a five-year-old car and a holiday in Blackpool, is patronizing and politically immature.

[Speech, 1986]

LENIN, V.I. (1870–1924)

We shall now proceed to construct the socialist order.

[Speech, 1917]

Under socialism all will govern in turn and

will soon become accustomed to no one governing.

[*The State and Revolution* (1917)]

LINDSAY, Norman (1879–1969)

[On Melbourne socialists]

They were a bloodthirsty lot, those sentimentalists who wept for the sad lot of the working classes.

[*Bohemians of the Bulletin* (1965)]

ORWELL, George (1903–1950)

As with the Christian religion, the worst advertisement for Socialism is its adherents.

[*The Road to Wigan Pier* (1937)]

To the ordinary working man, the sort you would meet in any pub on Saturday night, Socialism does not mean much more than better wages and shorter hours and nobody bossing you about.

[*The Road to Wigan Pier* (1937)]

STOPPARD, Tom (1937–)

Socialists treat their servants with respect and then wonder why they vote Conservative.

[*Lord Malquist and Mr Moon* (1966)]

STRETTON, Hugh (1924–)

Most capacities for love develop (or don't) in childhood; the largest quantity of willing human cooperation occurs within and between households; cooperation there is the pattern, and has to be the continuing basis, for cooperation anywhere else. To put it in the most shocking possible language, socialism should cease to be the factory-floor and chicken-battery party, and become the hearth-and-home, do-it-yourself party.

[*Capitalism, Socialism and the Environment* (1976)]

THATCHER, Margaret (1925–)

State socialism is totally alien to the British character.

[*The Times*, 1983]

VIERA GALLO, José Antonio (1943–)

Socialism can arrive only by bicycle.

[In Ivan Illich, *Energy and Equity* (1974)]

WARREN, Earl (1891–1974)

Many people consider the things which government does for them to be social progress, but they consider the things government does for others as socialism.

[*Peter's Quotations*]

See COMMUNISM

SOCIETY

ARISTOTLE (384–322 BC)

A person who cannot live in society, or does not need to because he is self-sufficient, is either a beast or a god.

[*Politics*]

AURELIUS, Marcus (121–180)

What is not good for the beehive, cannot be good for the bees.

[*Meditations*]

BACON, Francis (1561–1626)

Man seeketh in society comfort, use, and protection.

[*The Advancement of Learning* (1605)]

BERLIN, Isaiah (1909–1997)

The history of society is the history of the inventive labours that alter man, alter his desires, habits, outlook, relationships both to other men and to physical nature, with which man is in perpetual physical and technological metabolism.

[*Karl Marx* (1978)]

CICERO (106–43 BC)

O tempora! O mores!
What times! What manners!

[In Catilinam]

CLAUDEL, Paul (1868–1955)

The only living societies are those which are animated by inequality and injustice.

[*Conversations dans le Loir-et-Cher*]

COUNIHAN, Noel Jack (1913–1986)

In human society the warmth is mainly at the bottom.

[*Age*, 1986]

CURRY, George

[On the young people involved in the 1991 riots in Tyneside]

It's not sex and drug advice these kids need, so much as help in acquiring a world view, in motivating them to take responsibility and enabling them to build proper relationships. But if you say that sort of thing to the social work agencies, they just turn off and say: 'Oh, those are moral issues – we can't be going into those.' But we have to! Otherwise, we shall simply be raising generations of animals, of Calibans.

[Daily Mail, 1996]

EMERSON, Ralph Waldo (1803–1882)

The virtues of society are the vices of the saint.

[Essays, First Series (1841)]

Society everywhere is in conspiracy against the manhood of every one of its members.

['Self-Reliance' (1841)]

GALBRAITH, J.K. (1908–)

In the affluent society, no sharp distinction can be made between luxuries and necessaries.

[The Affluent Society (1958)]

HAZLITT, William (1778–1830)

I do not think there is anything deserving the name of society to be found out of London.

[Table-Talk (1822)]

HOWKINS, Alun (1947–)

The English pub is, we are told from childhood, a unique institution. Nothing 'quite like it' exists anywhere else. That's true. The pub uniquely represents, even in metropolitan England, the precise inequalities of gender, race and class that construct our society. From the inclusive white, male and proletarian 'public' of many northern pubs to the parasitic blazer and cotton dress 'locals' of the home counties, our unique institution divides our society and our social life.

[New Statesman and Society, 1989]

HUME, Basil (1923–1999)

[On the killing of London headmaster Philip Lawrence]

We have really lost in our society the sense of the sacredness of life.

[The Observer Review, 1995]

JENKINS, Roy (1920–)

The permissive society has been allowed to become a dirty phrase. A better phrase is the civilized society.

[Speech, 1969]

JOSPIN, Lionel

Yes to the market economy. No to the market society.

[The Observer, 1998]

MANDELA, Nelson (1918–)

We enter into a covenant that we shall build the society in which all South Africans, both black and white, will be able to walk tall, without any fear in their hearts, assured of their inalienable right to human dignity – a rainbow nation at peace with itself and the world.

[Inaugural Address, 1994]

MENCKEN, H.L. (1880–1956)

A society made up of individuals who were all capable of original thought would probably be unendurable. The pressure of ideas would simply drive it frantic.

['Minority Report' (1956)]

MILL, John Stuart (1806–1873)

When society requires to be rebuilt, there is no use in attempting to rebuild it on the old plan.

[Dissertations and Discussions (1859)]

ROOSEVELT, Theodore (1858–1919)

The men with the muck-rakes are often indispensable to the well-being of society; but only if they know when to stop raking the muck.

[Speech, 1906]

SMITH, Adam (1723–1790)

No society can surely be flourishing and happy, of which the far greater part of the members are poor and miserable.

[*Wealth of Nations* (1776)]

SPENCER, Herbert (1820–1903)

No one can be perfectly free till all are free; no one can be perfectly moral till all are moral; no one can be perfectly happy till all are happy.

[*Social Statics* (1850)]

SPINOZA, Baruch (1632–1677)

Homo sit animale sociale.

Man is a social animal.

[*Ethics* (1677)]

TAWNEY, R.H. (1880–1962)

As long as men are men, a poor society cannot be too poor to find a right order of life, nor a rich society too rich to have need to seek it.

[*The Acquisitive Society* (1921)]

THACKERAY, William Makepeace (1811–1863)

It is impossible, in our condition of Society, not to be sometimes a Snob.

[*The Book of Snobs* (1848)]

THATCHER, Margaret (1925–)

There is no such thing as society. There are individual men and women and there are families.

[Attr.]

THOREAU, Henry David (1817–1862)

Wherever a man goes, men will pursue him and paw him with their dirty institutions, and, if they can, constrain him to belong to their desperate oddfellow society.

[*Walden* (1854)]

WILDE, Oscar (1854–1900)

[Of society]

To be in it is merely a bore. But to be out of it simply a tragedy.

[*A Woman of No Importance* (1893)]

WILSON, Harold (1916–1995)

[Referring to Christine Keeler]

There is something utterly nauseating about a system of society which pays a harlot 25

times as much as it pays its Prime Minister, 250 times as much as it pays its Members of Parliament, and 500 times as much as it pays some of its ministers of religion.

[Speech, 1963]

See HUMANITY AND HUMAN NATURE; PARTIES; PEOPLE

SOLITUDE

BACON, Francis (1561–1626)

It had been hard for him that spake it to have put more truth and untruth together, in a few words, than in that speech: 'Whosoever is delighted in solitude is either a wild beast, or a god.'

['Of Friendship' (1625)]

COWPER, William (1731–1800)

I praise the Frenchman, his remark was shrewd –

How sweet, how passing sweet, is solitude!

But grant me still a friend in my retreat,

Whom I may whisper – solitude is sweet.

['Retirement' (1782)]

ECO, Umberto (1932–)

Solitude is a kind of freedom.

[*The Observer Review*, 1995]

GIBBON, Edward (1737–1794)

I was never less alone than when by myself.

[*Memoirs of My Life and Writings* (1796)]

MANN, Thomas (1875–1955)

Einsamkeit zeitigt das Originale, das gewagt und befremdend Schöne, das Gedicht. Einsamkeit zeitigt aber auch das Verkehrte, das Unverhältnismässige, das Absurde und Unerlaubte.

Solitude gives rise to what is original, to what is daringly and displeasingly beautiful, to poetry. Solitude however also gives rise to what is wrong, excessive, absurd and forbidden.

[*Death in Venice* (1912)]

MONTAIGNE, Michel de (1533–1592)

Il se faut réserver une arrière boutique toute nôtre,

toute franche, en laquelle nous établissons notre vraie liberté et principale retraite et solitude.
We should keep for ourselves a little back shop, all our own, untouched by others, in which we establish our true freedom and chief place of seclusion and solitude.

[Essais (1580)]

POPE, Alexander (1688–1744)
Thus let me live, unseen, unknown;
Thus unlamented let me die;
Steal from the world, and not a stone
Tell where I lie.

['Ode on Solitude' (c. 1700)]

ROSTAND, Jean (1894–1977)
Etre adulte, c'est être seul.
To be an adult is to be alone.

[Thoughts of a Biologist (1939)]

SARTON, May (1912–)
Loneliness is the poverty of self; solitude is the richness of self.

[Mrs Stevens Hears the Mermaids Singing (1993)]

SASSOON, Siegfried (1886–1967)
Alone … The word is life endured and known.
It is the stillness where our spirits walk
And all but inmost faith is overthrown.

[The Heart's Journey (1928)]

SCHOPENHAUER, Arthur (1788–1860)
Einsamkeit ist das Los aller hervorragenden Geister: sie werden solche bisweilen beseufzen; aber stets sie als das kleinere von zwei ‹beln erwählen.
Solitude is the fate of all outstanding minds: it will at times be deplored; but it will always be chosen as the lesser of two evils.

['Aphorisms for Wisdom' (1851)]

SCHREINER, Olive (1855–1920)
She thought of the narrowness of the limits within which a human soul may speak and be understood by its nearest of mental kin, of how soon it reaches that solitary land of the individual experience in which no fellow footfall is ever heard.

[The Story of an African Farm (1884)]

THOREAU, Henry David (1817–1862)

I never found the companion that was so companionable as solitude.

[Walden (1854)]

See LONELINESS

SONGS AND SINGERS

COLERIDGE, Samuel Taylor (1772–1834)
Swans sing before they die –'twere no bad thing
Should certain persons die before they sing.

['Epigram on a Volunteer Singer' (1800)]

DYLAN, Bob (1941–)
[On being asked if he could say something about his songs]
Yeah, some of them are about ten minutes long, others five or six.

[Interview]

FLETCHER, Andrew, of Saltoun (1655–1716)
I knew a very wise man who believed that … if a man were permitted to make all the ballads, he need not care who should make the laws of a nation. And we find that most of the ancient legislators thought they could not well reform the manners of any city without the help of a lyric, and sometimes of a dramatic poet.

[Letter to the Marquis of Montrose, 1704]

FREED, Arthur (1894–1973)
I'm singing in the rain, just singing in the rain;
What a wonderful feeling, I'm happy again.

['Singing in the Rain', 1929]

LANDOR, Walter Savage (1775–1864)
There is delight in singing, tho' none hear
Beside the singer.

['To Robert Browning' (1846)]

MAUGHAM, William Somerset (1874–1965)
Music-hall songs provide the dull with wit,

just as proverbs provide them with wisdom.

[*A Writer's Notebook* (1949)]

MUSSET, Alfred de (1810–1857)

Les plus désespérés sont les chants les plus beaux
Et j'en sais d'immortels qui sont de purs sanglots.
The most despairing songs are the most beautiful, and I know of immortal ones which are pure tears.

['La Nuit de mai' (1840)]

SAINT-LAMBERT, Jean François, Marquis de (1716–1803)

Souvent j'écoute encor quand le chant a cessé.
Often I am still listening when the song has ended.

[*Les Saisons*, 'Le Printemps']

SASSOON, Siegfried (1886–1967)

Everyone suddenly burst out singing;
And I was filled with such delight
As prisoned birds must find in freedom
Winging wildly across the white
Orchards and dark green fields; on – on – and out of sight.

['Everyone Sang' (1919)]

The song was wordless;
The singing will never be done.

['Everyone Sang' (1919)]

SCOTT, Sir Walter (1771–1832)

The way was long, the wind was cold,
The Minstrel was infirm and old;
His wither'd cheek, and tresses gray,
Seemed to have known a better day.

[*The Lay of the Last Minstrel* (1805), Introduction]

STEVENS, Wallace (1879–1955)

For she was the maker of the song she sang.
The ever-hooded, tragic-gestured sea
Was merely a place by which she walked to sing.

['The Idea of Order at Key West' (1936)]

THOMPSON, Francis (1859–1907)

Go, songs, for ended is our brief sweet play;
Go, children of swift joy and tardy sorrow:
And some are sung, and that was yesterday,
And some unsung, and that may be to-morrow.

['Envoy' (1913)]

WORDSWORTH, William (1770–1850)

Behold her, single in the field,
Yon solitary Highland lass! ...

Will no one tell me what she sings? –
Perhaps the plaintive numbers flow
For old, unhappy, far-off things,
And battles long ago.

['The Reaper' (1807)]

YEATS, W.B. (1865–1939)

I made my song a coat
Covered with embroideries
Out of old mythologies
From heel to throat;
But the fools caught it,
Wore it in the world's eye
As though they'd wrought it.
Song, let them take it
For there's more enterprise
In walking naked.

[*Responsibilities* (1914)]

See MUSIC

THE SOUL

ARNOLD, Matthew (1822–1888)

We cannot kindle when we will
The fire which in the heart resides,
The spirit bloweth and is still,
In mystery our soul abides.

['Morality' (1852)]

BERNARD, Saint (1091–1153)

Liberavi animam meam.
I have freed my soul.

['Epistle 371']

THE BIBLE
(King James Version)

What is a man profited, if he shall gain the whole world, and lose his own soul?

[*Matthew*, 16:26]

CRABBE, George (1754–1832)

It is the soul that sees; the outward eyes
Present the object, but the mind descries.

[*The Lover's Journey*]

DICKINSON, Emily (1830–1886)

The Soul selects her own Society –
Then – shuts the Door –
To her divine Majority –
Present no more …

I've known her – from an ample nation –
Choose One –
Then – close the Valves of her attention –
Like Stone.

['The Soul selects her own Society' (c. 1862)]

DONNE, John (1572–1631)

Poor intricated soul! Riddling, perplexed,
labyrinthical soul!

[*LXXX Sermons* (1640)]

EMERSON, Ralph Waldo (1803–1882)

When divine souls appear men are
compelled by their own self-respect to
distinguish them.

[*Journals*]

HADRIAN (AD 76–138)

Ah fleeting Spirit! wand'ring Fire,
That long hast warm'd my tender Breast,
Must thou no more this Frame inspire?
No more a pleasing, cheerful Guest?

['Ad Animam Suam', trans. Pope]

JUVENAL (c.60–130)

Mors sola fatetur
Quantula sint hominum corpuscula.
Death only this mysterious truth unfolds,
The mighty soul, how small a body holds.

[*Satires*]

KEATS, John (1795–1821)

A man should have the fine point of his soul
taken off to become fit for this world.

[Letter to J.H. Reynolds, 1817]

LEWIS, Wyndham (1882–1957)

The soul started at the knee-cap and ended
at the navel.

[*The Apes of Gods* (1930)]

LUCRETIUS (c.95–55 BC)

Nil igitur mors est ad nos neque pertinet hilum,
Quandoquidem natura animi mortalis habetur.
What has this bugbear death to frighten man

If souls can die as well as bodies can?

[*De Rerum Natura*]

MCAULEY, James Philip (1917–1976)

The soul must feed on something for its
dreams,
In those brick suburbs, and there wasn't
much:
It can make do with little, so it seems.

['Wisteria' (1971)]

MEREDITH, George (1828–1909)

There is nothing the body suffers the soul
may not profit by.

[*Diana of the Crossways* (1885)]

RIMBAUD, Arthur (1854–1891)

O saisons, ô châteaux!
Quelle âme est sans défauts?
O seasons, O castles! What soul is without
faults?

['O saisons, ô châteaux' (1872)]

SHELLEY, Percy Bysshe (1792–1822)

The soul of man, like unextinguished fire,
Yet burns towards heaven with fierce
reproach.

[*Prometheus Unbound* (1820)]

SMITH, Logan Pearsall (1865–1946)

Most people sell their souls, and live with a
good conscience on the proceeds.

[*Afterthoughts* (1931)]

SOCRATES (469–399 BC)

A man should feel confident concerning his
soul, who in his life has rejected those
pleasures and fineries that go with the body
as being alien to him, considering them to
result more in harm than in good, and has
eagerly sought the pleasures that go with
learning and adorned his soul with no alien
but rather with its own proper refinements,
moderation and justice and courage and
freedom and truth; thus he awaits his
journey to the world below, ready whenever
fate calls him.

[Attr. in Plato, *Phaedo*]

STERNE, Laurence (1713–1768)

I am positive I have a soul; nor can all the

books with which materialists have pestered the world ever convince me to the contrary.

[*A Sentimental Journey* (1768)]

SWIFT, Jonathan (1667–1745)

The Manner whereby the Soul and Body are united, and how they are distinguished, is wholly unaccountable to us. We see but one Part, and yet we know we consist of two; and this is a Mystery we cannot comprehend, any more than that of the Trinity.

['On the Trinity']

SWINBURNE, Algernon Charles (1837–1909)

A little soul for a little bears up this corpse which is man.

['Hymn to Proserpine' (1866)]

WEBSTER, John (c.1580–c.1625)

My soul, like to a ship in a black storm, Is driven, I know not whither.

[*The White Devil* (1612)]

WORDSWORTH, William (1770–1850)

Our birth is but a sleep and a
    forgetting.
The Soul that rises with us, our life's Star,
Hath had elsewhere its setting,
And cometh from afar.

['Ode: Intimations of Immortality' (1807)]

See IMMORTALITY

SOUTH AFRICA

CAMPBELL, Roy (1901–1957)

South Africa, renowned both far and wide
For politics and little else beside:
Where, having torn the land with shot and shell,
Our sturdy pioneers as farmers dwell,
And, 'twixt the hours of strenuous sleep, relax
To shear the fleeces or to fleece the blacks.

[*The Wayzgoose* (1928)]

MANDELA, Nelson (1918–)

Let there be justice for all. Let there be peace for all. Let there be bread, water and salt for all. Let freedom reign. The sun shall never set on so glorious a human achievement.

[*Independent on Sunday*, 14 May 1994]

O'ROURKE, P.J. (1947–)

[On white South Africans]
They've never learned to stand up and lie like white men.

[*The Weekend Guardian*, 1993]

PATON, Alan (1903–1988)

It was on Wednesday 16 June 1976 that an era came to an end in South Africa. That was the day when black South Africans said to white, 'You can't do this to us any more.' It had taken three hundred years for them to say that.

[*Journey Continued* (1988)]

PRINGLE, Thomas (1789–1834)

Afar in the desert I love to ride,
With the silent Bush-boy alone by my side;
Away, away in the wilderness vast,
Where the white man's foot hath never passed …

Man is distant, but God is near.

[*African Sketches* (1834)]

SPACE

ADDISON, Joseph (1672–1719)

The spacious firmament on high,
With all the blue ethereal sky,
And spangled heavens, a shining frame,
Their great Original proclaim.

[*The Spectator*, 1712]

ALFONSO X (1221–1284)

[On the Ptolemaic system of astronomy]
If the Lord Almighty had consulted me before embarking upon Creation, I should have recommended something simpler.

[Attr.]

ARMSTRONG, Neil (1930–)

[First words on lunar touch-down of space module during Apollo XI mission]

Tranquillity Base here – the Eagle has landed.

[TV coverage, 20 July 1969]

[On stepping on to the moon]
That's one small step for a man, one giant leap for mankind.

[New York Times, 1969)]

THE BIBLE
(King James Version)
The heavens declare the glory of God; and the firmament sheweth his handywork.

[Psalms, 19:1]

BRENNAN, Christopher (1870–1932)
Where star-cold and the dread of space
in icy silence bind the main
I feel but vastness on my face
I sit, a mere incurious brain,
under some outcast satellite.

[Poems (1914)]

BYRON, Lord (1788–1824)
Ye stars! which are the poetry of heaven!

[Childe Harold's Pilgrimage (1812–18)]

CAMPBELL, Thomas (1777–1844)
The sentinel stars set their watch in the sky.

['The Soldier's Dream']

CHESTERTON, G.K. (1874–1936)
The cosmos is about the smallest hole that a man can hide his head in.

[Orthodoxy (1908)]

DE VRIES, Peter (1910–1993)
Anyone informed that the universe is expanding and contracting in pulsations of eighty billion years has a right to ask, 'What's in it for me?'.

[The Glory of the Hummingbird (1974)]

FROST, Robert (1874–1963)
They cannot scare me with their empty spaces
Between stars – on stars where no human race is.
I have it in me so much nearer home
To scare myself with my own desert places.

['Desert Places' (1936)]

FULLER, Richard Buckminster (1895–1983)
I am a passenger on the spaceship, Earth.

[Operating Manual for Spaceship Earth (1969)]

GALILEO GALILEI (1564–1642)
[Remark made after he was forced to withdraw his assertion that the Earth moved round the Sun]
Eppur si muove.
But it does move.

[Attr., 1632]

HARDY, Thomas (1840–1928)
The sovereign brilliancy of Sirius pierced the eye with a steely glitter, the star called Capella was yellow, Aldebaran and Betelgueux shone with a fiery red.
To persons standing alone on a hill during a clear midnight such as this, the roll of the world eastward is almost a palpable movement.

[Far From the Madding Crowd (1874)]

HOLMES, Rev. John H. (1879–1964)
This universe is not hostile, nor yet is it friendly. It is simply indifferent.

[A Sensible Man's View of Religion (1932)]

HOPKINS, Gerard Manley (1844–1889)
Look at the stars! look, look up at the skies!
Oh look at all the fire-folk sitting in the air!
The bright boroughs, the circle-citadels there!

['The Starlight Night' (1877)]

JOYCE, James (1882–1941)
The heaventree of stars hung with humid nightblue fruit.

[Ulysses (1922)]

O'CASEY, Sean (1880–1964)
I often looked up at the sky an' assed meself the question – what is the stars, what is the stars?

[Juno and the Paycock (1924)]

SHAKESPEARE, William (1564–1616)
Look how the floor of heaven
Is thick inlaid with patines of bright gold;
There's not the smallest orb which thou behold'st

But in his motion like an angel sings,
Still quiring to the young-ey'd cherubins.

[*The Merchant of Venice*, V.i]

SIDNEY, Sir Philip (1554–1586)

With how sad steps O Moone thou clim'st the skyes,
How silently, and with how meane a face,
What may it be, that even in heavenly place,
That busie Archer his sharpe Arrowes tryes?

[*Astrophel and Stella* (1591)]

VIDAL, Gore (1925–)

The astronauts! … Rotarians in outer space.

[*Two Sisters* (1970)]

VIRGIL (70–19 BC)

Nosque ubi primus equis Oriens adflavit anhelis,
Illic sera rubens accendit lumina Vesper.

And when the rising sun has first breathed on us with his panting horses, over there the glowing evening-star is lighting his late lamps.

[*Georgics*]

WOOLLEY, Richard

[In 1956, one year before Sputnik]
Space travel is utter bilge.

[In Martin Moskovits *Science and Society*, 1995]

YOUNG, Andrew John (1885–1971)

But moon nor star-untidy sky
Could catch my eye as that star's eye;
For still I looked on that same star,
That fitful, fiery Lucifer,
Watching with mind as quiet as moss
Its light nailed to a burning cross.

['The Evening Star' (1922)]

See DISCOVERY; SCIENCE; STARS; TECHNOLOGY; UNIVERSE

SPORT AND GAMES

ALI, Muhammad (1942–)

Float like a butterfly, sting like a bee.

[Catchphrase]

ALLISON, Malcolm

Professional football is no longer a game. It's

a war. And it brings out the same primitive instincts that go back thousands of years.

[*The Observer*, March 1973]

ANONYMOUS

Say it ain't so, Joe. Please say it ain't so.

[Plea to 'Shoeless' Joe Jackson, when he and seven other US baseball players were banned for life after being found guilty of throwing the World Series in 1920]

Shooting is a popular sport in the countryside … Unlike many other countries, the outstanding characteristic of the sport has been that it is not confined to any one class.

[The Northern Ireland Tourist Board, 1969]

They'll be dancing in the streets of Raith tonight.

[Falsely attributed to both Kenneth Wolstenholme and David Coleman, this reference to Raith Rovers fans dancing in a non-existent Scottish town – the team plays in Kirkcaldy – almost certainly originated in a BBC radio broadcast from London in 1963, after Raith Rovers defeated Aberdeen in a Scottish Cup tie]

'Well, what sort of sport has Lord –– had?'
'Oh, the young Sahib shot divinely, but God was very merciful to the birds.'

[In Russell, *Collections and Recollections* (1898)]

In the case of almost every sport one can think of, from tennis to billiards, golf to skittles, it was royalty or the aristocracy who originally developed, codified and popularised the sport, after which it was taken up by the lower classes.

[*The Spectator*, 1996]

[After making a substitution which enabled his team to win a key relegation battle]
I thought if we were going to lose it, we might as well lose it by trying to win it.

[*Daily Mail*, 1996]

ATKINSON, Ron

I would not say he [David Ginola] is the best left winger in the Premiership, but there are none better.

He dribbles a lot and the opposition don't like it – you can see it over their faces.

I never comment on referees and I'm not going to break the habit of a lifetime for that prat.

An inch or two either side of the post and that would have been a goal.

[Sky Sports]

BARBARITO, Luigi (1922–)

[Papal emissary, commenting on a sponsored snooker competition at a convent]
Playing snooker gives you firm hands and helps to build up character. It is the ideal recreation for dedicated nuns.

[*The Daily Telegraph*, 1989]

BARDOT, Brigitte (1934–)

[Comment on the 1998 World Cup, hosted by France]
It's a pity to see Paris, the world capital of thinking, devoting so much interest to a game played with feet.

[*The Scotsman*, June 1998]

BARNES, Simon (1951–)

[On the use of drugs in sport]
Showbiz brings us people who change their superficial appearance, but sport brings us people who … change their bodies as we might change a shirt.

[*The Times*, 1999]

Sport is something that does not matter, but is performed as if it did. In that contradiction lies its beauty.

[*The Spectator*, 1996]

BELASCO, David (1853–1931)

Boxing is showbusiness with blood.

[Attr., 1915]

BENNETT, Alan (1934–)

If you think squash is a competitive activity, try flower arrangement.

[*Talking Heads* (1988)]

BERNHARDT, Sarah (1844–1923)

[Remark while watching a game of football]

I do love cricket – it's so very English.

[Attr.]

BEST, George (1946–)

[On being named Footballer of the Century]
It's a pleasure to be standing up here. It's a pleasure to be standing up.

[Speech, 1999]

BLAINEY, Geoffrey Norman (1930–)

We forget that the nineteenth century often turned work into sport. We, in contrast, often turn sport into work.

[*Victorian Historical Journal*, 1978]

BROWN, Rita Mae (1944–)

Sport strips away personality, letting the white bone of character shine through.

[*Sudden Death* (1983)]

BYRON, H.J. (1834–1884)

Life's too short for chess.

[*Our Boys*]

CANTERBURY, Tom

The trouble with referees is that they just don't care which side wins.

[*The Guardian*, 1980]

COLEMAN, David (1926–)

That's the fastest time ever run – but it's not as fast as the world record.

[In Fantoni, *Private Eye's Colemanballs (3)* (1986)]

CONNOLLY, Billy (1942–)

I love fishing. It's like transcendental meditation with a punch-line.

[*Gullible's Travels*]

CONNORS, Jimmy (1952–)

New Yorkers love it when you spill your guts out there. Spill your guts at Wimbledon and they make you stop and clean it up.

[*The Guardian*, 1984]

COWPER, William (1731–1800)

[Of hunting]
Detested sport,
That owes its pleasures to another's pain.

[*The Task* (1785)]

CROOKS, Garth (1958–)

Football is football; if that weren't the case, it wouldn't be the game it is.

[In Fantoni, *Private Eye's Colemanballs (2)* (1984)]

DAVIS, Steve (1957–)

Sport is cut and dried. You always know when you succeed … You are not an actor: you don't wonder 'did my performance go down all right?' You've lost.

[Remark]

DEMPSEY, Jack (1895–1983)

Kill the other guy before he kills you.

[Motto]

DISRAELI, Benjamin (1804–1881)

Yesterday at the racket court, sitting in the gallery among strangers, the ball … fell at my feet. I picked it up, and observing a young rifleman excessively stiff, I humbly requested him to forward its passage into the court, as I really had never thrown a ball in my life.

[Letter to his father, quoted by André Maurois in *Disraeli: A Picture of the Victorian Age* (1927)]

DUFFY, Jim

[Of goalkeeper Andy Murdoch]
He has an answerphone installed on his six-yard line and the message says: 'Sorry, I'm not in just now, but if you'd like to leave the ball in the back of the net, I'll get back to you as soon as I can.'

[In *Umbro Book of Football Quotations* (1993)]

DUROCHER, Leo (1905–1991)

[Remark at a practice ground, 1946]
Nice guys finish last.

[Attr.]

EUBANK, Chris (1804–1881)

Any boxer who says he loves boxing is either a liar or a fool. I'm not looking for glory … I'm looking for money. I'm looking for readies.

[*The Times*, 1993]

FITZSIMMONS, Robert (1862–1917)

[Remark before a boxing match, 1900]
The bigger they come, the harder they fall.

[Attr.]

FORD, Henry (1863–1947)

Exercise is bunk. If you are healthy, you don't need it: if you are sick, you shouldn't take it.

[Attr.]

FOX, Dixon Ryan

I listened to a football coach who spoke straight from the shoulder – at least I could detect no higher origin in anything he said.

[Attr.]

GASCOIGNE, Paul (1967–)

I get on a train and sit in second class and people think, 'tight bastard. Money he's got and he sits in second class.' So I think,' them' and I go in first class and then they say,'look at that ing flash bastard in first class'.

[*The Herald*, 1995]

GRACE, W.G. (1848–1915)

[Refusing to leave the crease after being bowled first ball in front of a large crowd]
They came to see me bat not to see you bowl.

[Attr.]

GREAVES, Jimmy (1940–)

The only thing that Norwich didn't get was the goal that they finally got.

[In Fantoni, *Private Eye's Colemanballs (2)* (1984)]

HEMINGWAY, Ernest (1898–1961)

Bullfighting is the only art in which the artist is in danger of death and in which the degree of brilliance in the performance is left to the fighter's honour.

[*Death in the Afternoon* (1932)]

HUGHES, Thomas (1822–1896)

[Of cricket]
It's more than a game. It's an institution.

[*Tom Brown's Schooldays* (1857)]

HUISTRA, Peter (1967–)

Soccer in Japan is interesting, in Glasgow it's a matter of life and death.

[*Daily Mail*, 1996]

HUMPHRIES, Barry (1934–)

Sport is a loathsome and dangerous pursuit.

[*Sydney Morning Herald*, 1982]

INGHAM, Bernard (1932–)

Blood sport is brought to its ultimate
refinement in the gossip columns.

[Remark, 1986]

JACOBS, Joe (1896–1940)

[Remark made after Max Schmeling, whom he
managed, lost his boxing title to Jack Sharkey in 1932]
We was robbed!

[Attr.]

JERROLD, Douglas William (1803–1857)

The only athletic sport I ever mastered was
backgammon.

[In W. Jerrold, *Douglas Jerrold* (1914)]

JOHN PAUL II (1920–)

[Replying to the suggestion that it was
inappropriate for a cardinal to ski]
It is unbecoming for a cardinal to ski badly.

[Attr.]

JOHNSON, Samuel (1709–1784)

I am sorry I have not learned to play at cards.
It is very useful in life: it generates kindness
and consolidates society.

[In Boswell, *Journal of a Tour to the Hebrides* (1785)]

Fly fishing may be a very pleasant
amusement; but angling or float fishing I can
only compare to a stick and a string, with a
worm at one end and a fool at the other.

[Attr. in Hawker, *Instructions to Young Sportsmen*
(1859)]

JOHNSTON, Brian (1912–1994)

The bowler's Holding, the batsman's Willey.

[Quoted in his obituary, *Sunday Times*]

We're going to see Afaq to Knight at the
Nursery End.

[Quoted in his obituary, *Sunday Times*]

KEEGAN, Kevin

Gary always weighed up his options,
especially when he had no choice.

[Radio 5 live]

Ardiles strokes the ball like it is part of his
own anatomy.

[RTE]

KING, Billie-Jean (1943–)

It's really impossible for athletes to grow up.
As long as you're playing, no one will let you.
On the one hand, you're a child, still playing a
game … But on the other hand, you're a
superhuman hero that everyone dreams of
being. No wonder we have such a hard time
understanding who we are.

[*Billie-Jean* (1982)]

KINGLAKE, Edward (1864–1935)

Every Australian worships the Goddess of
Sport with profound adoration, and there is
no nation in the world which treats itself to
so many holidays.

[*The Australian at Home*]

LAMB, Charles (1775–1834)

Man is a gaming animal. He must always be
trying to get the better in something or
other.

['Mrs Battle's Opinions on Whist' (1823)]

LANG, Andrew (1844–1912)

Golf is a thoroughly national game. It is as
Scotch as haggis, cockie-leekie, high cheek-
bones, or rowanberry jam.

[In W. Pett Ridge (ed.), *Daily News, Lost
Leaders*,1889]

LEACOCK, Stephen (1869–1944)

Golf may be played on Sunday, not being a
game within the view of the law, but being a
form of moral effort.

[*Over the Footlights* (1923)]

LOUIS, Joe (1914–1981)

[Referring to the speed of an opponent, Billy Conn]
He can run, but he can't hide.

[Attr.]

MACDONALD, Charles Blair (1855–1939)

[Remark by a caddy at St Andrews to a professor
who was having difficulty learning the game]
When ye come to play golf ye maun hae a
heid!

[*Scotland's Gift – Golf* (1928)]

MCENROE, John (1959–)

[To an umpire; this remark became a catchphrase

in the early 1980s]
You cannot be serious.

[Attr.]

MCGUIGAN, Barry (1961–)
The gladiators and champions through the
ages confirm quite clearly that aggressive
competition is part of the human makeup.
For the sport of professional boxing to be
banned would be the most terrible error.

[*The Observer*, 1994]

MOURIE, Graham (1952–)
Nobody ever beats Wales at rugby, they just
score more points.

[In Keating, *Caught by Keating*]

MUIR, Edwin (1887–1959)
[On hunting trophies]
To find these abominations on the walls of
Highland hotels, among people of such
delicacy in other things, is peculiarly
revolting.

[*Scottish Journey*]

O'REILLY, Tony (1936–)
[Commenting on the voice of Winston McCarthy,
the noted rugby commentator]
The love call of two pieces of sandpaper.

[*New Zealand Listener*, 1984]

O'ROURKE, P.J. (1947–)
The sport of skiing consists of wearing three
thousand dollars' worth of clothes and
equipment and driving two hundred miles in
the snow in order to stand around at a bar
and get drunk.

[*Modern Manners* (1984)]

ORWELL, George (1903–1950)
Serious sport has nothing to do with fair
play. It is bound up with hatred, jealousy,
boastfulness, disregard for all rules and
sadistic pleasure in witnessing violence; in
other words it is war minus the shooting.

[*Shooting an Elephant* (1950)]

OSGOOD, Peter
Women are around all the time but the World
Cups come only every four years.

[*The Times*, 1998]

OVETT, Steve (1955–)
There is no way sport is so important that it
can be allowed to damage the rest of your
life.

[Remark at the Olympic Games, 1984]

PALMER, Arnold (1929–)
[Replying to an onlooker who observed that he
was playing so well he must have plenty of luck on
his side]
The more I practise the luckier I get.

[Attr.]

PARRIS, Matthew (1949–)
And now the worst news of all. Gay men are
getting interested in football … What a
catastrophe. One became homosexual to get
away from this sort of thing.

[*The Times*, 1998]

POTTER, Stephen (1900–1969)
Gamesmanship or, The Art of Winning Games
without actually Cheating.

[Title of book, 1947]

RICE, Grantland (1880–1954)
For when the One Great Scorer comes to
mark against your name,
He marks – not that you won or lost – but
how you played the Game.

['Alumnus Football' (1941)]

RIDER, Steve
The match will be shown on *Match of the
Day*. If you don't want to know the result,
look away now as we show you Tony Adams
lifting the cup for Arsenal.

[BBC announcement, 1998]

ROBSON, Bobby (1933–)
The first ninety minutes are the most
important.

[Quoted as the title of a TV documentary,
1983]

SEAL, Christopher (1880–1954)
Hunting people tend to be churchgoers on a
higher level than ordinary folk. One has a
religious experience in the field.

[*The Times*, 1993]

SHANKLY, Bill (1914–1981)

Some people think football is a matter of life and death. I don't like that attitude. I can assure them it is much more serious than that.

[Remark on BBC TV, 1981]

SHAW, George Bernard (1856–1950)

[An R.S.V.P. to an invitation to attend an athletic meeting at the Wangamui Domain]
I take athletic competitive sports very seriously indeed … as they seem to produce more bad feeling, bad manners and international hatred than any other popular movement.

[Auckland Star, 1934]

SNAGGE, John (1904–1996)

I don't know who's ahead – it's either Oxford or Cambridge.

[Radio commentary on the Boat Race, 1949]

SOMERVILLE, William (1675–1742)

My hoarse-sounding horn
Invites thee to the chase, the sport of kings;
Image of war, without its guilt.

[The Chase (1735)]

SOUNESS, Graeme

How could I carry out a policy where I won't sign a Catholic but I'll go home and live with one?

[In Kenny MacDonald, Scottish Football Quotations (1994)]

SPENCER, Herbert (1820–1903)

It was remarked to me … that to play billiards well was a sign of an ill-spent youth.

[In Duncan, Life and Letters of Spencer (1908)]

STUBBES, Philip (c.1555–1610)

Football … causeth fighting, brawling, contention, quarrel picking, murder, homicide and great effusion of blood, as daily experience teacheth.

[Anatomy of Abuses (1583)]

SURTEES, R.S. (1805–1864)

'Unting is all that's worth living for – all time is lost wot is not spent in 'unting – it is like the hair we breathe – if we have it not we die

– it's the sport of kings, the image of war without its guilt, and only five-and-twenty per cent of its danger.

[Handley Cross (1843)]

Tell me a man's a fox-hunter, and I loves him at once.

[Handley Cross (1843)]

TEMPLE, William (1881–1944)

[Remark to parents when headmaster of Repton School]
Personally, I have always looked on cricket as organized loafing.

[Attr.]

TOSATTI, Giorgio (1740–1778)

Lo sport è sempre stato strumento di lotta politica.
Sport has always been an instrument for political strife.

[Corriere della Sera, 1994]

TWAIN, Mark (1835–1910)

Golf is a good walk spoiled.

[Attr.]

VIERA, Ondina

Other nations have history. We have football.

[The Spectator, 1996]

VUKOVICH, Bill (1918–1955)

[Explaining his success in the Indianapolis 500]
There's no secret. You just press the accelerator to the floor and steer left.

[Attr.]

WALTON, Izaak (1593–1683)

Sir Henry Wotton … was also a most dear lover, and a frequent practiser of the art of angling; of which he would say, 'it was an employment for his idle time, which was then not idly spent … a rest to his mind, a cheerer of his spirits, a diverter of sadness, a calmer of unquiet thoughts, a moderator of passions, a procurer of contentedness; and that it begat habits of peace and patience in those that professed and practised it.'

[The Compleat Angler (1653)]

We may say of angling as Dr Boteler said of strawberries: 'Doubtless God could have made a better berry, but doubtless God never did'; and so (if I might be judge) God never did make a more calm, quiet, innocent recreation than angling.

[*The Compleat Angler* (1653)]

As no man is born an artist, so no man is born an angler.

[*The Compleat Angler* (1653)]

WHITE, Andrew Dickson (1832–1918)

[Refusing to allow the Cornell football team to visit Michigan to play a match]
I will not permit thirty men to travel four hundred miles to agitate a bag of wind.

[In D. Wallechinsky, *The People's Almanac*]

WILDE, Oscar (1854–1900)

The English country gentleman galloping after a fox – the unspeakable in full pursuit of the uneatable.

[*A Woman of No Importance* (1893)]

WODEHOUSE, P.G. (1881–1975)

While they were content to peck cautiously at the ball, he never spared himself in his efforts to do it a violent injury.

[*The Heart of a Goof* (1926)]

The least thing upset him on the links. He missed short putts because of the uproar of the butterflies in the adjoining meadows.

[*The Clicking of Cuthbert* (1922)]

THE STATE

ARISTOTLE (384–322 BC)

Blessed is the state in which those in power have moderate and sufficient means since where some are immoderately wealthy and others have nothing, the result will be extreme democracy or absolute oligarchy, or a tyranny may result from either of these extremes.

[*Politics*]

AUDEN, W.H. (1907–1973)

There is no such thing as the State
And no one exists alone.
Hunger allows no choice

To the citizen or the police;
We must love one another or die.

[*Collected Poems, 1939–1947*, 'September 1, 1939']

BOUTROS-GHALI, Boutros (1922–)

… the time of absolute and exclusive national sovereignty has passed.

[*Scotland on Sunday*, 1992]

BURKE, Edmund (1729–1797)

A state without the means of some change is without the means of its conservation.

[*Reflections on the Revolution in France* (1790)]

CROMWELL, Oliver (1599–1658)

The State, in choosing men to serve it, takes no notice of their opinions. If they be willing faithfully to serve it, that satisfies.

[Said before the Battle of Marston Moor, 1644]

DÜRRENMATT, Friedrich (1921–1990)

Wir haben durch die Jahrhunderte hindurch so viel dem Staat geopfert, dass es jetzt Zeit ist, dass sich der Staat für uns opfert.
Through the centuries we have sacrificed so much for the state that it is now time for the state to sacrifice itself for us.

[*Romulus the Great* (1964)]

ENGELS, Friedrich (1820–1895)

Der Staat wird nicht 'abgeschafft', er stirbt ab.
The state is not abolished, it dies away.

[*Anti-Dühring* (1878)]

INGE, William Ralph (1860–1954)

The nations which have put mankind and posterity most in their debt have been small states – Israel, Athens, Florence, Elizabethan England.

[*Outspoken Essays: Second Series* (1922)]

LANDOR, Walter Savage (1775–1864)

States, like men, have their growth, their manhood, their decrepitude, their decay.

[*Imaginary Conversations* (1876)]

LENIN, V.I. (1870–1924)

So long as the state exists there is no freedom. When there is freedom there will be no state.

[*The State and Revolution* (1917)]

LOUIS XIV (1638–1715)

L'État c'est moi.
I am the State.

[Attr.]

MILL, John Stuart (1806–1873)

A State which dwarfs its men, in order that they may be more docile instruments in its hands even for beneficial purposes – will find that with small men no great thing can really be accomplished.

[*On Liberty* (1859)]

The worth of a State, in the long run, is the worth of the individuals composing it.

[*On Liberty* (1859)]

PLATO (c.429–347 BC)

Our object in the establishment of the state is the greatest happiness of the whole, and not that of any one class.

[*Republic*]

It is the rulers of the state, if anybody, who may lie in dealing with citizens or enemies, for reasons of state.

[*Republic*]

RUSKIN, John (1819–1900)

I hold it for indisputable, that the first duty of a State is to see that every child born therein shall be well housed, clothed, fed and educated, till it attain years of discretion.

[*Time and Tide by Weare and Tyne* (1867)]

SHELLEY, Percy Bysshe (1792–1822)

The rich have become richer, and the poor have become poorer; and the vessel of the state is driven between the Scylla and Charybdis of anarchy and despotism.

[*A Defence of Poetry* (1821)]

STALIN, Joseph (1879–1953)

The state is a machine in the hands of the ruling class for suppressing the resistance of its class enemies.

[*Foundations of Leninism* (1924)]

TEMPLE, William (1881–1944)

In place of the conception of the Power-State we are led to that of the Welfare-State.

[*Citizen and Churchman* (1941)]

See DEMOCRACY; GOVERNMENT

STATISTICS

ASQUITH, Herbert (1852–1928)

[On the reason for the three sets of figures kept by the War Office]
One to mislead the public; another to mislead the Cabinet, and the third to mislead itself.

[In Alastair Horne, *The Price of Glory* (1962)]

AUDEN, W.H. (1907–1973)

Thou shalt not sit
With statisticians nor commit
A social science.

[*Collected Poems, 1939–1947*, 'Under Which Lyre']

Out of the air a voice without a face
Proved by statistics that some cause was just
In tones as dry and level as the place.

[*The Shield of Achilles* (1955)]

CARLYLE, Thomas (1795–1881)

A witty statesman said, you might prove anything by figures.

[*Chartism* (1839)]

DISRAELI, Benjamin (1804–1881)

There are three kinds of lies: lies, damned lies and statistics.

[Attr.]

LLOYD GEORGE, David (1863–1945)

[Advocating Tariff Reform]
You cannot feed the hungry on statistics.

[Speech, 1904]

NIGHTINGALE, Florence (1820–1910)

To understand God's thoughts we must study statistics, for these are the measure of his purpose.

[Attr.]

STOUT, Rex Todhunter (1886–1975)

There are two kinds of statistics, the kind you look up and the kind you make up.

[*Death of a Doxy*]

STUPIDITY

ANONYMOUS

Never attribute to malice that which is adequately explained by stupidity.

[Hanlon's Razor]

The probability of someone watching you is proportional to the stupidity of your action.

[Hartley's First Law]

DICKENS, Charles (1812–1870)

He'd be sharper than a serpent's tooth, if he wasn't as dull as ditch water.

[Our Mutual Friend (1866)]

MARX, Groucho (1895–1977)

You've got the brain of a four-year-old boy, and I bet he was glad to get rid of it.

[Horse Feathers, film, 1932]

MUIR, Frank (1920–1998)

I've examined your son's head, Mr Glum, and there's nothing there.

[Take it from Here, with Dennis Norden, 1957]

O'ROURKE, P.J. (1947–)

Earnestness is just stupidity sent to college.

[Attr. in The Observer, 1996]

PROVERB

Ask a silly question and you'll get a silly answer.

WILDE, Oscar (1854–1900)

There is no sin except stupidity.

[Intentions (1891), 'The Critic as Artist']

See FOOLISHNESS; IGNORANCE

STYLE

ARNOLD, Matthew (1822–1888)

Nothing has raised more questioning among my critics than these words – noble, the grand style … I think it will be found that the grand style arises in poetry, when a noble nature, poetically gifted, treats with simplicity or with severity a serious subject.

[On Translating Homer (1861)]

BAILEY, David (1938–)

[Commenting on dumbed-down Cool Britannia]
The avant-garde has gone to Tescos.

[The Times, 1999]

BUFFON, Comte de (1707–1788)

Ces choses sont hors de l'homme, le style est l'homme même.
These things [subject matter] are external to the man; style is the essence of man.

['Discours sur le Style' (1753)]

CAMUS, Albert (1913–1960)

Le style, comme la popeline, dissimule trop souvent de l'eczéma.
Style, like sheer silk, too often hides eczema.

[The Fall (1956)]

COLMAN, the Younger, George (1762–1836)

Johnson's style was grand and Gibbon's elegant; the stateliness of the former was sometimes pedantic, and the polish of the latter was occasionally finical. Johnson marched to kettle-drums and trumpets; Gibbon moved to flutes and hautboys: Johnson hewed passages through the Alps, while Gibbon levelled walks through parks and gardens.

[Random Records (1830)]

CONNOLLY, Cyril (1903–1974)

An author arrives at a good style when his language performs what is required of it without shyness.

[Enemies of Promise (1938)]

The Mandarin style … is beloved by literary pundits, by those who would make the written word as unlike as possible to the spoken one. It is the style of those writers whose tendency is to make their language convey more than they mean or more than they feel.

[Enemies of Promise (1938)]

RENARD, Jules (1864–1910)

Un mauvais style, c'est une pensée imparfaite.

Poor style reflects imperfect thought.

[*Journal*, 1898]

SWIFT, Jonathan (1667–1745)
Proper words in proper places, make the true definition of a style.

[*Letter to a Young Gentleman Lately Entered Into Holy Orders* (1720)]

VOLTAIRE (1694–1778)
Tous les genres sont bons hors le genre ennuyeux.
All styles are good except the tedious kind.

[*L'Enfant prodigue* (1738)]

WESLEY, Samuel (1662–1735)
Style is the dress of thought; a modest dress,
Neat, but not gaudy, will true critics please.

['An Epistle to a Friend concerning Poetry' (1700)]

WILDE, Oscar (1854–1900)
In matters of grave importance, style, not sincerity, is the vital thing.

[*The Importance of Being Earnest* (1895)]

See FASHION; TASTE

SUCCESS

ADDISON, Joseph (1672–1719)
'Tis not in mortals to command success,
But we'll do more, Sempronius; we'll deserve it.

[*Cato* (1713)]

BARRIE, Sir J.M. (1860–1937)
Every man who is high up loves to think that he has done it all himself; and the wife smiles, and lets it go at that. It's our only joke. Every woman knows that.

[*What Every Woman Knows* (1908)]

BROOKNER, Anita (1928–)
[On the myth of the tortoise and the hare]
In real life, of course, it is the hare who wins. Every time. Look around you. And in any case it is my contention that Aesop was writing for the tortoise market … Hares have no time to read. They are too busy winning the game.

[*Hotel du Lac* (1984)]

BROWNING, Robert (1812–1889)
A minute's success pays the failure of years.

['Apollo and the Fates' (1887)]

BURKE, Edmund (1729–1797)
The only infallible criterion of wisdom to vulgar minds – success.

[*Letter to a Member of the National Assembly* (1791)]

CAGNEY, James (1904–1986)
Made it, Ma! Top of the world!

[*White Heat*, film, 1949]

CHURCHILL, Charles (1731–1764)
Where he falls short, 'tis Nature's fault alone;
Where he succeeds, the merit's all his own.

[*The Rosciad* (1761)]

CONFUCIUS (c.550–c.478 BC)
In all things, success depends upon previous preparation, and without such preparation there is sure to be failure.

[*Analects*]

DEWAR, Lord Thomas Robert (1864–1930)
The road to success is filled with women pushing their husbands along.

[*Epigram*]

DICKINSON, Emily (1830–1886)
Success is counted sweetest
By those who ne'er succeed.
To comprehend a nectar
Requires sorest need.

['Success is counted sweetest' (c. 1859)]

EBNER-ESCHENBACH, Marie von (1830–1916)
Die stillstehende Uhr, die täglich zweimal die richtige Zeit angezeigt hat, blickt nach Jahren auf eine lange Reihe von Erfolgen zurück.
The clock which has stopped but has twice daily indicated the right time can years later look back on a long line of successes.

[*Aphorisms* (1880)]

HUXLEY, Aldous (1894–1963)
Success – 'The bitch-goddess, Success,' in William James's phrase – demands strange

sacrifices from those who worship her.

[*Proper Studies* (1927)]

JAMES, William (1842–1910)

The moral flabbiness born of the exclusive worship of the bitch-goddess success. That – with the squalid cash interpretation put on the word success – is our national disease.

[Letter to H.G. Wells, 1906]

LA ROCHEFOUCAULD (1613–1680)

Pour s'établir dans le monde, on fait tout ce que l'on peut pour y paraître établi.

To succeed in the world we do all we can to appear successful.

[*Maximes* (1678)]

LEHMAN, Ernest (1920–)

Sweet Smell of Success.

[Title of novel and film, 1957]

MEIR, Golda (1898–1978)

I can honestly say that I was never affected by the question of the success of an undertaking. If I felt it was the right thing to do, I was for it regardless of the possible outcome.

[In Syrkin, *Golda Meir: Woman with a Cause* (1964)]

PATER, Walter (1839–1894)

To burn always with this hard, gemlike flame, to maintain this ecstasy, is success in life.

[*Studies in the History of the Renaissance* (1873)]

PROVERBS

If at first you don't succeed, try, try, try again.

Nothing succeeds like success.

RENOIR, Jean (1894–1979)

Is it possible to succeed without betrayal?

[*My Life and My Films* (1974)]

SASSOON, Vidal (1928–)

The only place where success comes before work is a dictionary.

[Quoting one of his teachers in a BBC radio broadcast]

VIDAL, Gore (1925–)

It is not enough to succeed. Others must fail.

[In Irvine, *Antipanegyric for Tom Driberg* (1976)]

VIRGIL (70–19 BC)

Hos successus alit: possunt, quia posse videntur.

To these success gives heart: they can because they think they can.

[*Aeneid*]

See ACHIEVEMENT; FAILURE; VICTORY

SUFFERING

ADAMS, Scott (1957–)

I don't suffer from stress – I'm a carrier …

[*The Dilbert Priniciple*]

ÁLUARD, Paul (1895–1952)

Adieu tristesse
Bonjour tristesse
Tu es inscrite dans les lignes du plafond.

Sadness, adieu, sadness, hello, you are engraved in the lines of the ceiling.

['Slightly Disfigured', 1932)]

ANONYMOUS

Three things one does not recover from – oppression that knows the backing of brute force,
poverty that knows the destitution of one's home,
and being deprived of children.

[Somali poem]

AUDEN, W.H. (1907–1973)

About suffering they were never wrong,
The Old Masters: how well they understood
Its human position; how it takes place
While someone else is eating or opening a window or just walking dully along …

They never forgot
That even the dreadful martyrdom must run its course
Anyhow in a corner, some untidy spot
Where the dogs go on with their doggy life
and the torturer's horse
Scratches its innocent behind on a tree.

['Musée des Beaux Arts']

AUSTEN, Jane (1775–1817)

One does not love a place the less for having

suffered in it, unless it has all been suffering, nothing but suffering.

[*Persuasion* (1818)]

BACON, Francis (1561–1626)

It is a miserable state of mind to have few things to desire and many things to fear.

['Of Empire' (1625)]

BOETHIUS (c.475–524)

In omni adversitate fortunae, infelicissimum est genus infortunii, fuisse felicem.

At every blow of fate, the worst kind of misfortune is to have been happy.

[*De Consolatione Philosophiae* (c. 522–524)]

Nihil est miserum nisi cum putes; contraque beata sors omnis est aequanimitate tolerantis.

Nothing is miserable unless you think it so; conversely, every lot is happy to one who is content with it.

[*De Consolatione Philosophiae* (c. 524)]

BONO, Edward de (1933–)

Unhappiness is best defined as the difference between our talents and our expectations.

[*The Observer*, 1977]

BROWNING, Elizabeth Barrett (1806–1861)

For frequent tears have run
The colours from my life.

[*Sonnets from the Portuguese* (1850)]

CARLYLE, Thomas (1795–1881)

Man's Unhappiness, as I construe, comes of his Greatness; it is because there is an Infinite in him, which with all his cunning he cannot quite bury under the Finite.

[*Sartor Resartus* (1834)]

CHAUCER, Geoffrey (c.1340–1400)

For of fortunes sharpe adversitee
The worste kynde of infortune is this,
A man to han ben in prosperitee,
And it remembren, whan it passed is.

[*Troilus and Criseyde*]

CONGREVE, William (1670–1729)

Millamant: I believe I gave you some pain.

Mirabel: Does that please you?
Millamant: Infinitely; I love to give pain.

[*The Way of the World* (1700)]

CORNEILLE, Pierre (1606–1684)

A raconter ses maux, souvent on les soulage.

Telling one's sorrows often brings comfort.

[*Polyeucte* (1643)]

COWPER, William (1731–1800)

But misery still delights to trace
Its semblance in another's case.

['The Castaway' (1799)]

DANTE ALIGHIERI (1265–1321)

Nessun maggior dolore,
Che ricordarsi del tempo felice
Nella miseria.

No sorrow is deeper than the remembrance of happiness when in misery.

[*Divina Commedia* (1307)]

DICKINSON, Emily (1830–1886)

After great pain, a formal feeling comes –
The Nerves sit ceremonious, like Tombs –
The stiff Heart questions was it He, that bore,
And Yesterday, or Centuries before? …

This is the Hour of Lead –
Remembered, if outlived,
As Freezing persons, recollect the Snow –
First – Chill – then Stupor – then the letting go.

['After great pain, a formal feeling comes' (c. 1862)]

DIX, Dorothy (1870–1951)

It is only the women whose eyes have been washed clear with tears who get the broad vision that makes them little sisters to all the world.

[*Dorothy Dix, Her Book* (1926)]

GAY, John (1685–1732)

A moment of time may make us unhappy forever.

[*The Beggar's Opera* (1728)]

HAZLITT, William (1778–1830)

The least pain in our little finger gives us more concern and uneasiness, than the

destruction of millions of our fellow-beings.
[*Edinburgh Review*, 1829]

HEMINGWAY, Ernest (1898–1961)

The world breaks everyone and afterward many are strong at the broken places.
[*A Farewell to Arms* (1929)]

HOGG, James (1770–1835)

How often does the evening cup of joy lead to sorrow in the morning!
[Attr.]

HOPKINS, Gerard Manley (1844–1889)

No worst, there is none. Pitched past pitch of grief,
More pangs will, schooled at forepangs, wilder wring.
Comforter, where, where is your comforting? …

O the mind, mind has mountains; cliffs of fall
Frightful, sheer, no-man-fathomed …

Here! creep,
Wretch, under a comfort serves in a whirlwind: all
Life death does end and each day dies with sleep.
['No Worst, there is None' (1885)]

HUGO, Victor (1802–1885)

Souffrons, mais souffrons sur les cimes.
Let us suffer if we must, but let us suffer on the heights.
[*Contemplations* (1856)]

JAMES, William (1842–1910)

There is no more miserable human being than one in whom nothing is habitual but indecision.
[*Principles of Psychology* (1890)]

JOHNSON, Samuel (1709–1784)

I shall long to see the miseries of the world, since the sight of them is necessary to happiness.
[*Rasselas* (1759)]

There is no wisdom in useless and hopeless sorrow.
[Letter to Mrs. Thrale, 1781]

Depend upon it that if a man talks of his misfortunes there is something in them that is not disagreeable to him; for where there is nothing but pure misery there never is any recourse to the mention of it.
[In Boswell, *The Life of Samuel Johnson* (1791)]

KEATS, John (1795–1821)

Is there another Life? Shall I awake and find all this a dream? There must be, we cannot be created for this sort of suffering.
[Letter to Charles Brown, 1820]

KEMPIS, Thomas á (c.1380–1471)

Si libenter crucem portas portabit te.
If you bear the cross willingly, it will bear you.
[*De Imitatione Christi* (1892)]

KIERKEGAARD, Søren (1813–1855)

The Two Ways: One is to suffer; the other is to become a professor of the fact that another suffered.
[In W.H. Auden, *Kierkegaard*]

LA ROCHEFOUCAULD (1613–1680)

On n'est jamais si malheureux qu'on croit, ni si heureux qu'on espère.
One is never as unhappy as one thinks, or as happy as one hopes to be.
[*Maximes* (1664)]

Nous avons tous assez de force pour supporter les maux d'autrui.
We are all strong enough to bear the sufferings of others.
[*Maximes* (1678)]

LOWELL, James Russell (1819–1891)

The misfortunes hardest to bear are those which never come.
['Democracy' (1887)]

MILLER, Arthur (1915–)

Years ago a person, he was unhappy, didn't know what to do with himself – he'd go to church, start a revolution – something. Today you're unhappy? Can't figure it out? What is the salvation? Go shopping.

[*The Price* (1968)]

MONTAIGNE, Michel de (1533–1592)

Qui craint de souffrir, il souffre déjà de ce qu'il craint.
A man who fears suffering is already
suffering from what he fears.

[*Essais* (1580)]

NEAVES, Charles, Lord (1800–1876)

We can't for a certainty tell
What mirth may molest us on Monday;
But, at least, to begin the week well,
Let us all be unhappy on Sunday.

[*Songs and Verses*]

NIETZSCHE, Friedrich Wilhelm (1844–1900)

*Was eigentlich gegen das Leiden empört, ist nicht das
Leiden an sich, sondern das Sinnlose des Leidens.*
What actually fills you with indignation as
regards suffering is not suffering in itself but
the pointlessness of suffering.

[*On the Genealogy of Morals* (1881)]

PARKER, Dorothy (1893–1967)

Sorrow is tranquillity remembered in
emotion.

[*Here Lies* (1939)]

PASCAL, Blaise (1623–1662)

*Tout le malheur des hommes vient d'une seule chose,
qui est de ne savoir pas demeurer en repos dans une
chambre.*
All the troubles of men are caused by one
single thing, which is their inability to stay
quietly in a room.

[*Pensées* (1670)]

POPE, Alexander (1688–1744)

I never knew any man in my life, who could
not bear another's misfortunes perfectly like
a Christian.

[*Miscellanies* (1727)]

SAKI (1870–1916)

He's simply got the instinct for being
unhappy highly developed.

[*The Chronicles of Clovis* (1911)]

SHAKESPEARE, William (1564–1616)

When sorrows come, they come not single
spies,
But in battalions.

[*Hamlet*, IV.v]

In sooth I know not why I am so sad.
It wearies me; you say it wearies you;
But how I caught it, found it, or came by it,
What stuff 'tis made of, whereof it is born,
I am to learn;
And such a want-wit sadness makes of me
That I have much ado to know myself.

[*The Merchant of Venice*, I.i]

Misery acquaints a man with strange
bedfellows.

[*The Tempest*, II.ii]

SHAW, George Bernard (1856–1950)

The secret of being miserable is to have
leisure to bother about whether you are
happy or not.

[*Misalliance* (1914)]

SINATRA, Frank (1915–1998)

I'm for anything that can get you through the
night, be it prayer, tranquillizers or a bottle of
Jack Daniels.

[Attr. in *The Herald*, 1998]

THOMPSON, Francis (1859–1907)

Nothing begins and nothing ends
That is not paid with moan;
For we are born in others' pain,
And perish in our own.

['Daisy' (1913)]

TOLSTOY, Leo (1828–1910)

Pure and complete sorrow is just as
impossible as pure and complete joy.

[*War and Peace* (1869)]

VERLAINE, Paul (1844–1896)

*Il pleure dans mon coeur
Comme il pleut sur la ville.*
Tears fall in my heart as rain falls on the city.

[*Romances sans paroles* (1874)]

VIGNY, Alfred de (1797–1863)

I love the majesty of human suffering.

[*The Shepherd's House* (1844)]

SUICIDE

WHITTIER, John Greenleaf (1807–1892)

For all sad words of tongue or pen,
The saddest are these:'It might have been!'.

['Maud Muller' (1854)]

WILDE, Oscar (1854–1900)

Where there is sorrow, there is holy ground.

[*De Profundis* (1897)]

WOLPERT, Lewis

A useful … way of thinking about depression is in terms of malignant sadness. Sadness is to depression what normal growth is to cancer.

[*Malignant Sadness* (1999)]

See DESPAIR

SUICIDE

BUDGELL, Eustace (1686–1737)

[Lines found on his desk after his suicide]
What Cato did, and Addison approved
Cannot be wrong.

[Attr.]

GREER, Germaine (1939–)

Suicide is an act of narcissistic manipulation and deep hostility.

[*The Observer Review*, 1995]

IBSEN, Henrik (1828–1906)

[Judge Brack, on Hedda Gabler's suicide]
People don't do such things!

[*Hedda Gabler* (1890)]

NIETZSCHE, Friedrich Wilhelm (1844–1900)

Der Gedanke an den Selbstmord ist ein starkes Trostmittel: mit ihm kommt man gut über manche böse Nacht hinweg.
The thought of suicide is a great comfort: it's a good way of getting through many a bad night.

[*Beyond Good and Evil* (1886)]

PARKER, Dorothy (1893–1967)

Razors pain you;
Rivers are damp;
Acids stain you;

And drugs cause cramp.
Guns aren't lawful;
Nooses give;
Gas smells awful;
You might as well live.

['Résumé' (1937)]

PARKES, Sir Henry (1815–1896)

[On William Nicholas Willis]
Ho! the honourable member for Bourke, who is believed to have committed every crime in the calendar, – except the one we could so easily have forgiven him – suicide.

[In Wannan, *With Malice Aforethought*]

RHYS, Jean (1894–1979)

Next week, or next month, or next year I'll kill myself. But I might as well last out my month's rent, which has been paid up, and my credit for breakfast in the morning.

[*Good Morning, Midnight* (1939)]

SANDERS, George (1906–1972)

Dear World, I am leaving you because I am bored. I am leaving you with your worries. Good luck.

[Suicide note]

SWIFT, Jonathan (1667–1745)

In Church your grandsire cut his throat;
To do the job too long he tarry'd,
He should have had my hearty vote,
To cut his throat before he marry'd.

['Verses on the Upright Judge' (1724)]

TENNYSON, Alfred, Lord (1809–1892)

Nor at all can tell
Whether I mean this day to end myself,
Or lend an ear to Plato where he says,
That men like soldiers may not quit the post
Allotted by the Gods.

['Lucretius' (1868)]

See DEATH

SUNDAY

ABELARD, Peter (1079–1142)

O quanta qualia sunt illa sabbata,

Quae semper celebrat superna curia.
O how great and how glorious are those
sabbaths which the heavenly court for ever
celebrates!

[*Hymnus Paraclitensis*]

ADDISON, Joseph (1672–1719)
Sunday clears away the rust of the whole week.

[*The Spectator*, July 1711, 112]

CAREY, Henry (c.1687–1743)
Of all the days that's in the week
I dearly love but one day –
And that's the day that comes betwixt
A Saturday and Monday.

['Sally in our Alley' (1729)]

DE QUINCEY, Thomas (1785–1859)
It was a Sunday afternoon, wet and
cheerless: and a duller spectacle this earth of
ours has not to show than a rainy Sunday in
London.

[*Confessions of an English Opium Eater* (1822)]

HOBAN, Russell (1925–)
Sometimes there's nothing but Sundays for
weeks on end. Why can't they move Sunday
to the middle of the week so you could put it
in the OUT tray on your desk?

[*The Lion of Boaz-Jachin and Jachin-Boaz*]

RHYS, Jean (1894–1979)
The feeling of Sunday is the same
everywhere, heavy, melancholy, standing still.
Like when they say, 'As it was in the
beginning, is now, and ever shall be, world
without end.'

[*Voyage in the Dark* (1934)]

SWIFT, Jonathan (1667–1745)
I always love to begin a journey on Sundays,
because I shall have the prayers of the
church, to preserve all that travel by land, or
by water.

[*Polite Conversation* (1738)]

SUPERSTITION

AUBREY, John (1626–1697)
Anno 1670, not far from Cirencester, was an
apparition; being demanded whether a good
spirit or a bad? returned no answer, but
disappeared with a curious perfume and
most melodious twang. Mr W. Lilly believes it
was a fairy.

[*Miscellanies* (1696)]

BACON, Francis (1561–1626)
There is a superstition in avoiding
superstition.

['Of Superstition' (1625)]

BARRIE, Sir J.M. (1860–1937)
Every time a child says 'I don't believe in
fairies,' there is a little fairy somewhere that
falls down dead.

[*Peter Pan* (1904)]

BERLIN, Isaiah (1909–1997)
What men call superstition and prejudice are
but the crust of custom which by sheer
survival has shown itself proof against the
ravages and vicissitudes of its long life; to
lose it is to lose the shield that protects
men's national existence, their spirit, the
habits, memories, faith that have made them
what they are.

['The Counter-Enlightenment']

BOHR, Niels Henrik David (1885–1962)
[Explaining why he had a horseshoe on his wall]
Of course I don't believe in it. But I
understand that it brings you luck whether
you believe in it or not.

[Attr.]

BROWNE, Sir Thomas (1605–1682)
For my part, I have ever believed, and do now
know, that there are witches.

[*Religio Medici* (1643)]

BURKE, Edmund (1729–1797)
Superstition is the religion of feeble minds.

[*Reflections on the Revolution in France* (1790)]

GOETHE (1749–1832)
Der Aberglaube ist die Poesie des Lebens.
Superstition is the poetry of life.

['Literature and Language' (1823)]

HUME, David (1711–1776)

We soon learn that there is nothing mysterious or supernatural in the case, but that all proceeds from the usual propensity of mankind towards the marvellous, and that, though this inclination may at intervals receive a check from sense and learning, it can never be thoroughly extirpated from human nature.

['Of Miracles' (1748)]

Opposing one species of superstition to another, set them a quarrelling; while we ourselves, during their fury and contention, happily make our escape into the calm, though obscure, regions of philosophy.

[*The Natural History of Religion* (1757)]

JOHNSON, Samuel (1709–1784)

[Of ghosts]

All argument is against it; but all belief is for it.

[In Boswell, *The Life of Samuel Johnson* (1791)]

See LUCK

SURPRISE

DIAGHILEV, Sergei (1872–1929)

[Reply after Jean Cocteau's accusation that he rarely gave praise or encouragement …tonne-moi.]

Surprise me.

[*The Journals of Jean Cocteau* (1956)]

PRIESTLEY, J.B. (1894–1984)

I am always surprised when I am told that somebody likes me.

[*Instead of the Trees: A Final Chapter of Autobiography* (1977)]

TREMAIN, Rose (1951–)

There is something about the unexpected that moves us. As if the whole of existence is paid for in some way, except for that one moment, which is free.

[*Sacred Country*]

WEBSTER, Noah (1758–1843)

[Responding to his wife's comment that she had been surprised to find him embracing their maid] No, my dear, it is I who am surprised; you are merely astonished.

[Attr.]

See ACCIDENTS; CHANCE; LUCK

SURVIVAL

ARNOLD, Matthew (1822–1888)

Friends who set forth at our side,
Falter, are lost in the storm,
We, we only are left!

['Rugby Chapel' (1867)]

BENSON, E. F. (1867–1940)

[Speaking of a fellow of King's College, Cambridge, who never emerged from his rooms except in the evening gloaming]

He then shuffled out on to the big lawn, with a stick in his hand, and he prodded with it at the worms in the grass, muttering to himself, 'Ah, damn ye: haven't got me yet.'

[*As We Were* (1930)]

MEIR, Golda (1898–1978)

We intend to remain alive. Our neighbours want to see us dead. This is not a question that leaves much room for compromise.

[*Reader's Digest*, 1971]

SCOTT, Ridley

This is Ripley – last survivor of the *Nostromo* – signing off.

[*Alien*, film, 1979]

See EVOLUTION

SUSPICION

DICKENS, Charles (1812–1870)

It was a maxim with Foxey – our revered father, gentlemen – 'Always suspect everybody.'

[*The Old Curiosity Shop* (1841)]

MACAULAY, Lord (1800–1859)

Ye diners-out from whom we guard our spoons.

[Letter to Hannah Macaulay, 1831]

MTSHALI, Oswald (1940–)

I trudge the city pavements
side by side with 'madam'
who shifts her handbag
from my side to the other.

[*Sounds of a Cowhide Drum* (1971)]

ROCHE, Sir Boyle (1743–1807)

Mr Speaker, I smell a rat; I see him forming in
the air and darkening the sky; but I'll nip him
in the bud.

[Attr.]

THURBER, James (1894–1961)

Her own mother lived the latter years of her
life in the horrible suspicion that electricity
was dripping invisibly all over the house.

[*My Life and Hard Times* (1933)]

TOLSTOY, Leo (1828–1910)

Don't trust your horse in the field, or your
wife in the house.

[*The Kreutzer Sonata* (1890)]

VIRGIL (70–19 BC)

Equo ne credite, Teucri.
Quidquid id est, timeo Danaos et dona ferentis.
Trust not the horse, Trojans. Whatever it is, I
fear the Greeks even when they bring gifts.

[*Aeneid*]

SWITZERLAND

COREN, Alan (1938–)

[Of Switzerland]
Since both its national products, snow and
chocolate, melt, the cuckoo clock was
invented solely in order to give tourists
something solid to remember it by.

[*The Sanity Inspector* (1974)]

NICHOL, Dave (1222–1282)

[Said at the Summit on the Environment, Toronto,
1989]
Incidentally, I've always heard what a
practical people the Swiss are – I finally
understood these comments when I found
out how they dispose of their mercury
batteries. They collect them, and then dump
them down an abandoned mine shaft – in
France!

[Attr.]

RUSSELL, John (1919–)

Certain phrases stick in the throat, even if
they offer nothing that is analytically
improbable. 'A dashing Swiss officer' is one
such.

[*Paris* (1960)]

SMITH, Sydney (1771–1845)

I look upon Switzerland as an inferior sort of
Scotland.

[*Letters*, To Lord Holland, 1815]

STOPPARD, Tom (1937–)

What a bloody country! even the cheese has
got holes in it!

[*Travesties* (1975)]

WELLES, Orson (1915–1985)

In Italy for thirty years under the Borgias they
had warfare, terror, murder, bloodshed – they
produced Michelangelo, Leonardo da Vinci
and the Renaissance. In Switzerland they had
brotherly love, five hundred years of
democracy and peace, and what did they
produce …? The cuckoo clock.

[*The Third Man*, film, 1949]

T

TALENT

BRONTË, Anne (1820–1849)
All our talents increase in the using, and every faculty, both good and bad, strengthens by exercise.

[*The Tenant of Wildfell Hall* (1848)]

DEGAS, Edgar (1834–1917)
Everybody has talent at twenty-five. The difficult thing is to have it at fifty.

[In Gammell, *The Shop-Talk of Edgar Degas* (1961)]

LERNER, Alan Jay (1918–1986)
Back home everyone said I didn't have any talent. They might be saying the same thing over here, but it sounds better in French.

[*An American in Paris*, film, 1951]

See GENIUS

TASTE

ADAMS, Henry (1838–1918)
Every one carries his own inch-rule of taste, and amuses himself by applying it, triumphantly, wherever he travels.

[*The Education of Henry Adams* (1918)]

BENNETT, Arnold (1867–1931)
Good taste is better than bad taste, but bad taste is better than no taste.

[*The Observer*, 1930]

FITZGERALD, Edward (1809–1883)
Taste is the feminine of genius.

[Letter to J.R. Lowell, 1877]

HUXLEY, Aldous (1894–1963)
The aristocratic pleasure of displeasing is not the only delight that bad taste can yield. One can love a certain kind of vulgarity for its own sake.

[*Vulgarity in Literature* (1930)]

JOHNSON, Samuel (1709–1784)
Our tastes greatly alter. The lad does not care for the child's rattle, and the old man does not care for the young man's whore.

[In Boswell, *The Life of Samuel Johnson* (1791)]

REYNOLDS, Sir Joshua (1723–1792)
Taste does not come by chance: it is a long and laborious task to acquire it.

[In Northcote, *Life of Sir Joshua Reynolds* (1818)]

VALÉRY, Paul (1871–1945)
Le goût est fait de mille dégoûts.
Taste is created from a thousand distastes.

[*Unsaid Things*]

See INDIVIDUALITY

TAXES

BURKE, Edmund (1729–1797)
To tax and to please, no more than to love and to be wise, is not given to men.

[*Speech on American Taxation* (1774)]

CAMDEN, Lord (1714–1794)
[Arguing that the British parliament had no right to tax the Americans]
Taxation and representation are inseparable … whatever is a man's own, is absolutely his own; no man hath a right to take it from him without his consent either expressed by himself or representative; whoever attempts to do it, attempts an injury; whoever does it, commits a robbery; he throws down and destroys the distinction between liberty and slavery.

[Speech, House of Lords, 1766]

CAPONE, Al (1899–1947)
[Objecting to the US Bureau of Internal Revenue claiming large sums in unpaid back tax]
They can't collect legal taxes from illegal money.

[In Kobler, *Capone* (1971)]

DICKENS, Charles (1812–1870)

'It was as true,' said Mr Barkis,'… as taxes is. And nothing's truer than them.'

[*David Copperfield* (1850)]

FRANKLIN, Benjamin (1706–1790)

But in this world nothing can be said to be certain, except death and taxes.

[Letter to Jean Baptiste Le Roy, 1789]

GIBBON, Edward (1737–1794)

All taxes must, at last, fall upon agriculture.

[*Decline and Fall of the Roman Empire* (1776–88)]

HELMSLEY, Leona (1920–)

[Hotel tycoon during her trial for tax evasion]
We don't pay taxes. Only the little people pay taxes.

[Remark, 1989]

JOHNSON, Samuel (1709–1784)

Excise. A hateful tax levied upon commodities.

[*A Dictionary of the English Language* (1755)]

LOWE, Robert (Viscount Sherbrooke) (1811–1892)

The Chancellor of the Exchequer is a man whose duties make him more or less of a taxing machine. He is intrusted with a certain amount of misery which it is his duty to distribute as fairly as he can.

[Speech, 1870]

OTIS, James (1725–1783)

Taxation without representation is tyranny.

[Attr.]

REAGAN, Ronald (1911–)

[To the American Business Conference]
I have my veto pen drawn and ready for any tax increase that Congress might even think of sending up. And I have only one thing to say to the tax increasers. Go ahead – make my day.

[*Time*, 1985]

ROGERS, Will (1879–1935)

Income tax has made more liars out of American people than golf.

[*The Illiterate Digest* (1924)]

SHAW, George Bernard (1856–1950)

A government which robs Peter to pay Paul can always depend on the support of Paul.

[*Everybody's Political What's What* (1944)]

SMITH, Adam (1723–1790)

In England the different poll-taxes never produced the sum which had been expected of them, or which, it was supposed, they might have produced, had they been exactly levied.

[*Wealth of Nations* (1776)]

There is no art which one government sooner learns of another than that of draining money from the pockets of the people.

[*Wealth of Nations* (1776)]

SMITH, Sydney (1771–1845)

The schoolboy whips his taxed top – the beardless youth manages his taxed horse, with a taxed bridle, on a taxed road: – and the dying Englishman, pouring his medicine, which has paid seven per cent., into a spoon that has paid fifteen per cent. – flings himself back upon his chintz bed, which has paid twenty-two per cent. – and expires in the arms of an apothecary who has paid a licence of a hundred pounds for the privilege of putting him to death.

[*Edinburgh Review*, 1820, 'America']

TEA

ADDISON, Joseph (1672–1719)

The infusion of a China plant sweetened with the pith of an Indian cane.

[*The Spectator*,1711]

ARMOUR, G.D. (1864–1949)

Look here, Steward, if this is coffee, I want tea; but if this is tea, then I wish for coffee.

[*Punch*, cartoon caption, July 1902]

CHESTERTON, G.K. (1874–1936)

Tea, although an Oriental,
Is a gentleman at least;
Cocoa is a cad and coward,

Cocoa is a vulgar beast.

[*The Flying Inn* (1914)]

COBBETT, William (1762–1835)

Resolve to free yourselves from the slavery of the tea and coffee and other slop-kettle.

[*Advice to Young Men* (1829)]

COWPER, William (1731–1800)

Now stir the fire, and close the shutters fast,
Let fall the curtains, wheel the sofa round,
And, while the bubbling and loud-hissing urn
Throws up a steamy column, and the cups,
That cheer but not inebriate, wait on each,
So let us welcome peaceful ev'ning in.

[*The Task* (1785)]

GLADSTONE, William (1809–1898)

The domestic use of tea is a powerful champion able to encounter alcoholic drink in a fair field and throw it in a fair fight.

[Budget Speech, 1882]

JOHNSON, Samuel (1709–1784)

A hardened and shameless tea-drinker, who has for twenty years diluted his meals with only the infusion of this fascinating plant; whose kettle has scarcely time to cool; who with tea amuses the evening, with tea solaces the midnight, and with tea welcomes the morning.

[Review in the *Literary Magazine*, 1757]

JOYCE, James (1882–1941)

When I makes tea I makes tea, as old mother Grogan said. And when I makes water I makes water … Begob, ma'am, says Mrs. Cahill, God send you don't make them in the one pot.

[*Ulysses* (1922)]

PAIN, Barry (1864–1928)

The cosy fire is bright and gay,
The merry kettle boils away
And hums a cheerful song.
I sing the saucer and the cup;
Pray, Mary, fill the teapot up,
And do not make it strong.

[*The Poets at Tea*, 'Cowper']

Pour, varlet, pour the water,

The water steaming hot!
A spoonful for each man of us,
Another for the pot!

[*The Poets at Tea*, 'Macaulay']

As the sin that was sweet in the sinning
Is foul in the ending thereof,
As the heat of the summer's beginning
Is past in the winter of love:
O purity, painful and pleading!
O coldness, ineffably gray!
O hear us, our handmaid unheeding,
And take it away!

[*The Poets at Tea*, 'Swinburne']

'Come, little cottage girl, you seem
To want my cup of tea;
And will you take a little cream?
Now tell the truth to me.'
She had a rustic, woodland grin
Her cheek was soft as silk,
And she replied, 'sir, please put in
A little drop of milk.'

[*The Poets at Tea*, 'Wordsworth']

PINERO, Sir Arthur Wing (1855–1934)

While there's tea there's hope.

[*The Second Mrs Tanqueray* (1893)]

PRIESTLEY, J.B. (1894–1984)

Our trouble is that we drink too much tea. I see in this the slow revenge of the Orient, which has diverted the Yellow River down our throats.

[*The Observer*, 1949]

SMITH, Sydney (1771–1845)

Thank God for tea! What would the world do without tea? How did it exist? I am glad I was not born before tea.

[Attr.]

TEACHERS

ANONYMOUS

[Headmaster's reference for a teacher he dismissed]
He left us as he came to us, fired with enthusiasm.

[*The Times*, 1998]

ARMSTRONG, Dr John (1709–1779)

Of right and wrong he taught
Truths as refin'd as ever Athens heard;
And (strange to tell!) he practis'd what he
preach'd.

[*The Art of Preserving Health* (1744)]

AUDEN, W.H. (1907–1973)

A professor is one who talks in someone
else's sleep.

[Attr.]

A professor is one who talks in someone
else's sleep.

[Attr.]

BERLIOZ, Hector (1803–1869)

Time is a great teacher, but unfortunately it
kills all its pupils.

[Attr.]

BROUGHAM, Lord Henry (1778–1868)

The schoolmaster is abroad, and I trust more
to him, armed with his primer, than I do to
the soldier in full military array, for upholding
and extending the liberties of his country.

[Speech, 1828]

CARLYLE, Thomas (1795–1881)

It were better to perish than to continue
schoolmastering.

[In Wilson, *Carlyle Till Marriage* (1923)]

CARROLL, Lewis (1832–1898)

'We called him Tortoise because he taught
us,' said the Mock Turtle angrily.'Really you
are very dull!'.

[*Alice's Adventures in Wonderland* (1865)]

The Drawling-master was an old conger-eel,
that used to come once a week: he taught
Drawling, Stretching, and Fainting in Coils.

[*Alice's Adventures in Wonderland* (1865)]

CHURCHILL, Sir Winston (1874–1965)

Headmasters have powers at their disposal
with which Prime Ministers have never yet
been invested.

[*My Early Life* (1930)]

DARLING, Sir James (1899–)

If you are going to be any good, you have

got to like the little swine.

[Attr.]

DEFOE, Daniel (c.1661–1731)

We lov'd the doctrine for the teacher's sake.

['Character of the late Dr S. Annesley' (1697)]

FARQUHAR, George (1678–1707)

Charming women can true converts make,
We love the precepts for the teacher's sake.

[*The Constant Couple* (1699)]

HUXLEY, T.H. (1825–1895)

Some experience of popular lecturing had
convinced me that the necessity of making
things plain to uninstructed people was one
of the very best means of clearing up the
obscure corners of one's own mind.

[*Man's Place in Nature* (1894)]

MONTESSORI, Maria (1870–1952)

We teachers can only help the work going
on, as servants wait upon a master.

[*The Absorbent Mind*]

SENECA (c.4 BC–AD 65)

Homines dum docent discunt.
Even while they teach, men learn.

[*Epistulae Morales*]

SHAW, George Bernard (1856–1950)

He who can, does. He who cannot, teaches.

[*Man and Superman* (1903)]

TROLLOPE, Anthony (1815–1882)

[Of his headmaster]
He must have known me had he seen me as
he was wont to see me, for he was in the
habit of flogging me constantly. Perhaps he
did not recognize me by my face.

[*Autobiography* (1883)]

WAUGH, Evelyn (1903–1966)

I expect you'll be becoming a schoolmaster,
sir. That's what most of the gentlemen does,
sir, that gets sent down for indecent
behaviour.

[*Decline and Fall* (1928)]

We schoolmasters must temper discretion
with deceit.

[*Decline and Fall* (1928)]

Assistant masters came and went … Some liked little boys too little and some too much.

[*A Little Learning* (1964)]

WILDE, Oscar (1854–1900)

Everybody who is incapable of learning has taken to teaching.

['The Decay of Lying' (1889)]

YEATMAN, Robert Julian (1897–1968)

For every person wishing to teach there are thirty not wanting to be taught.

[*And Now All This* (1932)]

See EDUCATION; LEARNING; SCHOLARS; SCHOOL; UNIVERSITY

TECHNOLOGY

CARLYLE, Thomas (1795–1881)

Man is a tool-using animal.

[*Sartor Resartus* (1834)]

CLARKE, Arthur C. (1917–)

Any sufficiently advanced technology is indistringuisable from magic.

[*Technology and the Future*]

FRISCH, Max (1911–1991)

Technology is the knack of so arranging the world that we do not experience it.

[In Rollo May, *The Cry for Myth*]

RILKE, Rainer Maria (1875–1926)

The machine threatens all achievement.

[*The Sonnets to Orpheus* (1923)]

VERNE, Jules (1828–1905)

Captain Nemo: I wonder if you are familiar with utensils, Mr. Land?
Ned Land: I'm indifferent to 'em.

[*20,000 Leagues Under the Sea*, film, 1954]

See ARTIFICIAL INTELLIGENCE; COMPUTERS; INTERNET; PROGRESS; SCIENCE

TELEVISION

ALLEN, Woody (1935–)

Life doesn't imitate art. It imitates bad television.

[*Husbands and Wives*, film, 1992]

ANONYMOUS

The human race is faced with a cruel choice: work or daytime television.

BAKEWELL, Joan (1933–)

The BBC is full of men appointing men who remind them of themselves when young, so you get the same back-grounds, the same education, and the same programmes.

[*The Observer*, 1993]

BARNES, Clive (1927–)

Television is the first truly democratic culture – the first culture available to everybody and entirely governed by what the people want. The most terrifying thing is what people do want.

BIAGI, Enzo (1920–)

La televisione ha fatto per la nostra unità più di Garibaldi e Cavour, ha dato un linguaggio e un costume comuni.
Television has done more for the unification of Italy than Garibaldi and Cavour did; it has given us a communal custom and language.

[*The Good and the Bad* (1989)]

BIRT, John (1944–)

There is a bias in television journalism. It is not against any particular party or point of view – it is a bias against *understanding*.

[*The Times*, 1975]

CHAYEFSKY, Paddy (1923–1981)

Television is democracy at its ugliest.

COREN, Alan (1938–)

Television is more interesting than people. If it were not, we should have people standing in the corners of our rooms.

[Attr.]

COWARD, Sir Noël (1899–1973)

Television is for appearing on, not looking at.

[Attr.]

CRISP, Quentin (1908–)

If any reader of this book is in the grip of some habit of which he is deeply ashamed, I advise him not to give way to it in secret but to do it on television. No-one will pass him with averted gaze on the other side of the street. People will cross the road at the risk of losing their own lives in order to say 'We saw you on the telly'.

[*How to Become a Virgin*]

DEBRAY, Régis (1942–)

The darkest spot in modern society is a small luminous screen.

[*Teachers, Writers, Celebrities*]

ECO, Umberto (1932–)

La TV non offre, come ideale in cui immedesimarsi, il superman ma l'everyman. La TV presenta come ideale l'uomo assolutamente medio.

Television doesn't present, as an ideal to aspire to, the superman but the everyman. Television puts forward, as an ideal, the absolutely average man.

[*Diario Minimo*]

ELIOT, T.S. (1888–1965)

It is a medium of entertainment which permits millions of people to listen to the same joke at the same time, and yet remain lonesome.

FROST, David (1939–)

Television is an invention that permits you to be entertained in your living room by people you wouldn't have in your home.

[Remark, 1971]

HANSON, Lord James

Television exacerbates the concentration on personality and trivia at the expense of serious discussion and analysis, but its tendency to unbalance and to displace what really matters goes much further and is potentially very damaging to our lives and beliefs. It tends to destroy public trust.

[*The Spectator*, 1996]

HITCHCOCK, Alfred (1899–1980)

Television has done much for psychiatry by spreading information about it, as well as contributing to the need for it.

Television has brought murder back into the home – where it belongs.

[*The Observer*, 1965]

KOVACS, Ernie

Television – a medium. So called because it is neither rare nor well-done.

[Attr.]

LANDERS, Ann (1918–)

Television has proved that people will look at anything rather than each other.

MCLUHAN, Marshall (1911–1980)

Television brought the brutality of war into the comfort of the living room. Vietnam was lost in the living rooms of America – not on the battle fields of Vietnam.

[Montreal *Gazette*, 1975]

MARX, Groucho (1895–1977)

I find television very educating. Every time somebody turns on the set, I go into the other room and read a book.

MUGGERIDGE, Malcolm (1903–1990)

I have had my [TV] aerials removed – it's the moral equivalent of a prostate operation.

[In *Radio Times*, 1981]

PARRIS, Matthew (1949–)

Television lies. All television lies. It lies persistently, instinctively and by habit
… A culture of mendacity surrounds the medium, and those who work there live it, breathe it and prosper by it …
I know of no area of public life – no, not even politics – more saturated by professional cynicism.

[*The Spectator*, 1996]

SCOTT, C.P. (1846–1932)

Television? The word is half Latin and half Greek. No good can come of it.

[Attr.]

THOMSON, Roy (1894–1976)

[To an Edinburgh neighbour just after the opening of Scottish Television, which Thomson had founded, in 1957]

You know, it's just like having a licence to print your own money.

[In R. Braddon, *Roy Thomson of Fleet Street* (1965)]

WILDER, Billy (1906–)

It used to be that we in film were the lowest form of art. Now we have something to look down on.

[In A. Madsen, *Billy Wilder* (1968)]

See MEDIA

TEMPTATION

ANONYMOUS

The trouble with resisting temptation is it may never come your way again.

[Korman's Law]

BECKFORD, William (1760–1844)

I am not over-fond of resisting temptation.

[*Vathek* (1787)]

BELLOC, Hilaire (1870–1953)

The Devil, having nothing else to do,
Went off to tempt My Lady Poltagrue.
My Lady, tempted by a private whim,
To his extreme annoyance, tempted him.

[*Sonnets and Verse* (1923)]

DRYDEN, John (1631–1700)

Thou strong seducer, opportunity!

[*The Conquest of Granada* (1670)]

GRAHAM, Clementina Stirling (1782–1877)

The best way to get the better of temptation is just to yield to it.

[*Mystifications* (1859)]

HOPE, Anthony (1863–1933)

'You oughtn't to yield to temptation.'
'Well, somebody must, or the thing becomes absurd.'

[*The Dolly Dialogues* (1894)]

JERROLD, Douglas William (1803–1857)

Honest bread is very well – it's the butter

that makes the temptation.

[*The Cat's Paw* (1930)]

SHAW, George Bernard (1856–1950)

I never resist temptation, because I have found that things that are bad for me do not tempt me.

[*The Apple Cart* (1930)]

WILDE, Oscar (1854–1900)

The only way to get rid of a temptation is to yield to it.

[*The Picture of Dorian Gray* 1891)]

I couldn't help it. I can resist everything except temptation.

[*Lady Windermere's Fan* (1892)]

THEATRE

ADAMOV, Arthur (1908–1970)

[Remark at the International Drama Conference, Edinburgh, 1963]
The reason why Absurdist plays take place in No Man's Land with only two characters is primarily financial.

[Attr.]

ADDISON, Joseph (1672–1719)

A perfect tragedy is the noblest production of human nature.

[*The Spectator*, 1711]

AGATE, James (1877–1947)

Theatre director: a person engaged by the management to conceal the fact that the players cannot act.

[Attr.]

Long experience has taught me that in England nobody goes to the theatre unless he or she has bronchitis.

[Attr.]

ARISTOTLE (384–322 BC)

Tragedy, then, is the imitation of an action that is serious, has magnitude, and is complete in itself … through incidents arousing pity and fear it effects a catharsis of these and similar emotions.

[*Poetics*]

The plot is the first principle and, as it were, the soul of tragedy; character comes second.

[*Poetics*]

ASKEY, Arthur (1900–1982)
[On pantomime]
Pantomimes – the smell of oranges and wee-wee.

[Attr.]

BANKHEAD, Tallulah (1903–1968)
It's one of the tragic ironies of the theatre that only one man in it can count on steady work – the night watchman.

[*Tallulah* (1952)]

BERNARD, Tristan (1866–1947)
In the theatre the audience want to be surprised – but by things that they expect.

[Attr.]

BOILEAU-DESPRÉAUX, Nicolas (1636–1711)
Qu'en un lieu, qu'en un jour, un seul fait accompli
Tienne jusqu'á la fin le théâtre rempli.
Let a single complete action, in one place, in one day, keep a full house till the end of the play.

[*L'Art Poétique* (1674)]

BROOKS, Mel (1926–)
Tragedy is if I cut my finger. Comedy is if I walk into an open sewer and die.

[*The New Yorker*, 1978]

BUCKINGHAM, Duke of (1628–1687)
What the devil does the plot signify, except to bring in fine things?

[*The Rehearsal* (1663)]

BURNEY, Fanny (1752–1840)
'Do you come to the play without knowing what it is?' 'Oh, yes, sir, yes, very frequently. I have no time to read play-bills. One merely comes to meet one's friends, and show that one's alive.'

[*Evelina* (1778)]

BYRON, Lord (1788–1824)
All tragedies are finish'd by a death,

All comedies are ended by a marriage.

[*Don Juan* (1824)]

COOK, Peter (1937–1995)
You know, I go to the theatre to be entertained … I don't want to see plays about rape, sodomy and drug addiction … I can get all that at home.

[*The Observer*, cartoon caption, 1962]

COWARD, Sir Noël (1899–1973)
[On child star Bonnie Langford in a musical version of *Gone with the Wind* (1972) when a horse defecated on stage]
If they'd stuffed the child's head up the horse's arse, they would have solved two problems at once.

[In N. Sherrin, *Cutting Edge, or, Back in the Knife Box Miss Sharp* (1984)]

[On a poor portrayal of Queen Victoria]
It made me feel that Albert had married beneath his station.

[In D. Richards, *The Wit of Noël Coward*]

CRAIG, Sir Gordon (1872–1966)
Farce is the essential theatre. Farce refined becomes high comedy: farce brutalized becomes tragedy.

[Attr.]

DENNIS, John (1657–1734)
[Remark at a production of *Macbeth*, which used his new technique for producing stage thunder]
See how the rascals use me! They will not let my play run and yet they steal my thunder!

[Attr.]

EVELYN, John (1620–1706)
I saw Hamlet Prince of Denmark played: but now the old playe began to disgust this refined age.

[*Diary*, 1661]

GARRICK, David (1717–1779)
Prologues precede the piece – in mournful verse;
As undertakers – walk before the hearse.

[Prologue to Arthur Murphy's *The Apprentice* (1756)]

GOSSE, Sir Edmund (1849–1928)

[Referring to one of Swinburne's plays]
We were as nearly bored as enthusiasm
would permit.

[In C. Hassall, *Biography of Edward Marsh*]

GUINNESS, Sir Alec (1914–)

[Vowing never to perform again in the West End
when he saw the blank faces of uncomprehending
tourists]
I'd rather go to the provinces where they still
speak English and not Japanese.

[*Scotsman*, 1992]

HITCHCOCK, Alfred (1899–1980)

What is drama but life with the dull bits cut
out?

[*The Observer*, 1960]

HOPE, Anthony (1863–1933)

[On the first night of J. M. Barrie's play Peter Pan]
Oh, for an hour of Herod!

[In Birkin, *J. M. Barrie and the Lost Boys*]

HUXLEY, Aldous (1894–1963)

We participate in a tragedy; at a comedy we
only look.

[*The Devils of Loudun* (1952)]

KEMBLE, John Philip (1757–1823)

[Said during a play which was continually
interrupted by a crying child]
Ladies and gentlemen, unless the play is
stopped, the child cannot possibly go on.

[Attr.]

LLOYD WEBBER, Andrew (1948–)

[On the success of his *Phantom of the Opera*, 1995]
It doesn't stand up to huge intellectual
scrutiny.

PAVLOVA, Anna (1881–1931)

Although one may fail to find happiness in
theatrical life, one never wishes to give it up
after having once tasted its fruits.

[In Franks (ed.), *Pavlova: A Biography*]

PETER, John

Political theatre is by definition subversive:
anything else is only propaganda.

[Review, *Sunday Times*, 1998]

PINTER, Harold (1930–)

I've never regarded myself as the one
authority on my plays just because I wrote
the damned things.

[*The Observer*, 1993]

RATTIGAN, Terence (1911–1977)

A nice, respectable, middle-class, middle-
aged, maiden lady, with time on her hands
and the money to help her pass it … Let us
call her Aunt Edna … Aunt Edna is universal,
and to those who might feel that all the
problems of the modern theatre might be
solved by her liquidation, let me add that …
she is also immortal.

[*Collected Plays* (1953)]

REYNOLDS, Frederic (1765–1841)

Now do take my advice, and write a play – if
any incident happens, remember, it is better
to have written a damned play, than no play
at all – it snatches a man from obscurity.

[*The Dramatist* (1789)]

SHAFFER, Peter (1926–)

Rehearsing a play is making the word flesh.
Publishing a play is reversing the process.

[*Equus* (1973)]

SHAW, George Bernard (1856–1950)

An all-night sitting in a theatre would be at
least as enjoyable as an all-night sitting in
the House of Commons, and much more
useful.

[*Saint Joan* (1924)]

You don't expect me to know what to say
about a play when I don't know who the
author is, do you? … If it's by a good author,
it's a good play, naturally. That stands to
reason.

[*Fanny's First Play* (1911)]

[Responding to a solitary boo amongst the mid-
act applause at the first performance of Arms and
the Man in 1894]
I quite agree with you, sir, but what can two
do against so many?

[*Oxford Book of Literary
Anecdotes*]

STOPPARD, Tom (1937–)

We do on the stage the things that are supposed to happen off. Which is a kind of integrity, if you look on every exit being an entrance somewhere else.

[*Rosencrantz and Guildenstern Are Dead* (1967)]

I can do you blood and love without the rhetoric, and I can do you blood and rhetoric without the love and I can do you all three concurrent or consecutive but I can't do you love and rhetoric without the blood. Blood is compulsory – they're all blood you see.

[*Rosencrantz and Guildenstern Are Dead* (1967)]

The bad end unhappily, the good unluckily. That is what tragedy means.

[*Rosencrantz and Guildenstern Are Dead* (1967)]

VICTORIA, Queen (1819–1901)

[Giving her opinion of *King Lear*]
A strange, horrible business, but I suppose good enough for Shakespeare's day.

[Attr.]

VOLTAIRE (1694–1778)

[When asked why no woman had ever written a tolerable tragedy]
The composition of a tragedy requires testicles.

[In a letter from Byron to John Murray, 1817]

WINCHELL, Walter (1897–1972)

[Referring to a show starring Earl Carroll]
I saw it at a disadvantage – the curtain was up.

[In A. Whiteman, *Come to Judgement*]

See ACTING; ACTORS; CENSORSHIP; CRITICISM; LITERATURE; SHAKESPEARE

THEFT

BALZAC, Honoré de (1799–1850)

[Remark made on waking to find a burglar in his room]
I am laughing to think what risks you take to try to find money in a desk by night where the legal owner can never find any by day.

[Attr.]

CIBBER, Colley (1671–1757)

Stolen sweets are best.

[*The Rival Fools* (1709)]

HUNT, Leigh (1784–1859)

Stolen sweets are always sweeter,
Stolen kisses much completer,
Stolen looks are nice in chapels,
Stolen, stolen, be your apples.

['Song of Fairies Robbing an Orchard' (1830)]

MORAVIA, Alberto (1907–1990)

Ho avuto la malattia del ladro … m'è venuta una crisi di furto. Cosa vuol dire una parola! Tirai avanti qualche giorno, disgustato e smanioso, finché una mattina, ricordai, ad un tratto: cleptomane. E mi sentii innocente.

I had the thief's sickness … I had a thieving crisis. How much meaning there can be in a word! I went along for a few days feeling disgusted and restless, until one morning I suddenly remembered: kleptomaniac. And I felt innocent.

[*Roman Tales* (1954)]

PATTEN, Brian (1946–)

When I went out I stole an orange
It was a safeguard against imagining there was nothing
bright or special in the world.

['The stolen orange']

PEACOCK, Thomas Love (1785–1866)

The mountain sheep are sweeter,
But the valley sheep are fatter;
We therefore deemed it meeter
To carry off the latter.

[*The Misfortunes of Elphin* (1823)]

See CRIME

THOUGHT

BALZAC, Honoré de (1799–1850)

Je préfère la pensée á l'action, une idée á une affaire, la contemplation au mouvement.

I prefer thought to action, ideas to events, meditation to movement.

[*Louis Lambert* (1832)]

Penser, c'est voir.
Thinking is seeing.

[*Louis Lambert* (1832)]

BIERCE, Ambrose (1842–c.1914)
Brain: An apparatus with which we think that we think.

[*The Cynic's Word Book* (1906)]

BLAKE, William (1757–1827)
One thought fills immensity.

[*The Marriage of Heaven and Hell* (c. 1790–1793)]

CONFUCIUS (c.550–c.478 BC)
Learning without thought is labour lost; thought without learning is perilous.

[*Analects*]

DESCARTES, René (1596–1650)
Cogito, ergo sum.
I think, therefore I am.

[*Discours de la Méthode* (1637)]

EMERSON, Ralph Waldo (1803–1882)
Beware when the great God lets loose a thinker on this planet. Then all things are at risk.

['Circles' (1841)]

GOETHE (1749–1832)
Alles Gescheite ist schon gedacht worden, man muss nur versuchen, es noch einmal zu denken.
Everything worth thinking has already been thought, our concern must only be to try to think it through again.

['Thought and Action' (1829)]

HAZLITT, William (1778–1830)
The most fluent talkers or most plausible reasoners are not always the justest thinkers.

[*Atlas* (1830)]

HEATH, Sir Edward (1916–)
The real problem in life is to have sufficient time to think.

[*The Observer*, 1981]

HOLMES, Oliver Wendell (1809–1894)
A thought is often original, though you have

uttered it a hundred times.

[*The Autocrat of the Breakfast-Table* (1858)]

HORVÁTH, Ödön von (1901–1938)
Denken tut weh.
Thinking hurts.

[*A Child of our Time* (1938)]

HUXLEY, Aldous (1894–1963)
Thought must be divided against itself before it can come to any knowledge of itself.

[*Do What You Will* (1929)]

JAMES, William (1842–1910)
A great many people think they are thinking when they are merely rearranging their prejudices.

[Attr.]

JOHNSON, Samuel (1709–1784)
Whatever withdraws us from the power of our senses; whatever makes the past, the distant, or the future, predominate over the present, advances us in the dignity of thinking beings.

[*A Journey to the Western Islands of Scotland* (1775)]

LUTHER, Martin (1483–1546)
Gedanken sind zollfrei.
Thoughts are not subject to duty.

[*On Worldly Authority* (1523)]

MILL, John Stuart (1806–1873)
No great improvements in the lot of mankind are possible, until a great change takes place in the fundamental constitution of their modes of thought.

[*Autobiography* (1873)]

NEWTON, Sir Isaac (1642–1727)
If I have done the public any service, it is due to patient thought.

[Letter to Dr Bentley, 1713]

ORTEGA Y GASSET, José (1883–1955)
Pensar es el afán de captar mediante ideas la realidad.
Thinking is the desire to gain reality by means of ideas.

[*The Dehumanization of Art* (1925)]

REITH, Lord (1889–1971)

You can't think rationally on an empty stomach, and a whole lot of people can't do it on a full one either.

[Attr.]

RUSKIN, John (1819–1900)

The purest and most thoughtful minds are those which love colour the most.

[*The Stones of Venice* (1853)]

RUSSELL, Bertrand (1872–1970)

People don't seem to realize that it takes time and effort and preparation to think. Statesmen are far too busy making speeches to think.

[In Harris, *Kenneth Harris Talking To:* (1971)]

Many people would sooner die than think. In fact they do.

[In Flew, *Thinking about Thinking* (1975)]

SAINTE-BEUVE, Charles-Augustin (1804–1869)

[On the habit of literary men and politicians of constantly improvising and expressing their thoughts in public]

Thoughts which are born in front of everyone are like beautiful women who spend their lives at balls … they have no colouring. Try to produce thoughts which have their natural colour, their true colour, which is red.

[*Notebooks, 1834–1847*]

SARTRE, Jean-Paul (1905–1980)

My thought is me: that is why I cannot stop. I exist by what I think … and I can't prevent myself from thinking.

[*Nausea* (1938)]

SHAKESPEARE, William (1564–1616)

There is nothing either good or bad, but thinking makes it so.

[*Hamlet*, II.ii]

SHELLEY, Mary Wollstonecraft (1797–1851)

Mrs Shelley was choosing a school for her son, and asked the advice of this lady, who gave for advice … Just the sort of banality, you know, one does come out with:'Oh, send him somewhere where they will teach him to think for himself!' … Mrs Shelley answered: 'Teach him to think for himself? Oh, my God, teach him rather to think like other people!'.

[In Matthew Arnold, *Essays in Criticism, Second Series'* (1888)]

SHELLEY, Percy Bysshe (1792–1822)

A single word even may be a spark of inextinguishable thought.

[*A Defence of Poetry* (1821)]

SHERIDAN, Richard Brinsley (1751–1816)

I don't know any business you have to think at all – thought does not become a young woman.

[*The Rivals* (1775)]

SIDGWICK, Henry (1838–1900)

We think so because other people think so, Or because – or because – after all we do think so, Or because we were told so, and think we must think so, Or because we once thought so, and think we still think so, Or because having thought so, we think we will think so.

[' Lines Composed in his Sleep']

SMITH, Sydney (1771–1845)

I never could find any man who could think for two minutes together.

[*Sketches of Moral Philosophy* (1849)]

THACKERAY, William Makepeace (1811–1863)

There are a thousand thoughts lying within a man that he does not know till he takes up the pen to write.

[*The History of Henry Esmond* (1852)]

THOMSON, James (1834–1882)

… to cure the pain Of the headache called thought in the brain.

['L'Ancien Régime' (1880)]

THOMSON, Roy (1894–1976)

Thinking is work.

[*After I Was Sixty: A Chapter of Autobiography*]

VALÉRY, Paul (1871–1945)

A gloss on Descartes: Sometimes I think: and sometimes I am.

[*The Faber Book of Aphorisms* (1962)]

VANBRUGH, Sir John (1664–1726)

Thinking is to me the greatest fatigue in the world.

[*The Relapse, or Virtue in Danger* (1696)]

VAUVENARGUES, Marquis de (1715–1747)

Les grandes pensées viennent du cœur.

Great thoughts come from the heart.

[*Réflexions et Maximes* (1746)]

VOLTAIRE (1694–1778)

Ils ne servent de la pensée que pour autoriser leurs injustices, et n'emploient les paroles que pour déguiser leurs pensées.

People use thought only to justify their injustices, and they use words only to disguise their thoughts.

[*Dialogues* (1763)]

WEBSTER, John (c.1580–c.1625)

There's nothing of so infinite vexation
As man's own thoughts.

[*The White Devil* (1612)]

WITTGENSTEIN, Ludwig (1889–1951)

In order to draw a limit to thinking, we should have to be able to think both sides of this limit.

[*Tractatus Logico-Philosophicus* (1922)]

See BELIEF; IDEAS; INTELLECTUALS; INTELLIGENCE; MIND; PHILOSOPHY

THREATS

CALIGULA (12–41)

Utinam populus Romanus unam cervicem haberet!

I wish that the Roman people had only one neck!

[In Suetonius, *Lives of the Caesars*]

CROMPTON, Richmal (1890–1969)

Violet Elizabeth dried her tears. She saw that they were useless and she did not believe in wasting her effects. 'All right,' she said calmly, 'I'll thcream then. I'll thcream, an' thcream, an' thcream till I'm thick.'

[*Still William* (1925)]

ELIZABETH I (1533–1603)

[To the leaders of her Council when they opposed her policy on Mary Queen of Scots]

I will make you shorter by the head!

[In F. Chamberlin, *The Sayings of Queen Elizabeth* (1923)]

PUZO, Mario (1920–)

We'll make him an offer he can't refuse.

[*The Godfather*, film, 1972]

TIME

ANONYMOUS

The only things that start on time are those that you're late for.

[Cayo's Law]

It always takes longer than you expect, even when you take Hofstadter's Law into account.

[Hofstadter's Law]

AUDEN, W.H. (1907–1973)

O let not Time deceive you,
You cannot conquer Time.

In the burrows of the Nightmare
Where Justice naked is,
Time watches from the shadow
And coughs when you would kiss.

In headaches and in worry
Vaguely life leaks away,
And Time will have his fancy
To-morrow or to-day.

Into many a green valley
Drifts the appalling snow;
Time breaks the threaded dances
And the diver's brilliant bow.

O plunge your hands in water,
Plunge them in up to the wrist;
Stare, stare in the basin
And wonder what you've missed.

The glacier knocks in the cupboard,
The desert sighs in the bed,
And the crack in the tea-cup opens
A lane to the land of the dead …

O stand, stand at the window
As the tears scald and start;
You shall love your crooked neighbour
With your crooked heart.

[Collected Poems, 1933–1938]

AURELIUS, Marcus (121–180)

Time is like a river made up of the things
which happen, and its current is strong; no
sooner does anything appear than it is
carried away, and another comes in its place,
and will be carried away too.

[Meditations]

BACON, Francis (1561–1626)

He that will not apply new remedies, must
expect new evils; for time is the greatest
innovator.

['Of Innovations' (1625)]

BASHÓ, Matsuo (1644–1694)

Days and months are itinerants on an eternal
journey; the years that pass by are also
travellers.

['Narrow Roads of Oku'
(1703)]

BECKETT, Samuel (1906–1989)

Vladimir: That passed the time.
Estragon: It would have passed in any case.
Vladimir: Yes, but not so rapidly.

[Waiting for Godot (1955)]

BELLOC, Hilaire (1870–1953)

I am a sundial, and I make a botch
Of what is done far better by a watch.

[Sonnets and Verse (1938)]

BERLIOZ, Hector (1803–1869)

Time is a great teacher, but unfortunately it
kills all its pupils.

[Attr.]

THE BIBLE
(King James Version)

To every thing there is a season, and a time
to every purpose under the heaven:
A time to be born, and a time to die …
A time to love, and a time to hate; a time of
war, and a time of peace.

[Ecclesiastes, 3:1–8]

BOUCICAULT, Dion (1822–1890)

Men talk of killing time, while time quietly
kills them.

[London Assurance (1841)]

BROWNE, Sir Thomas (1605–1682)

The night of time far surpasseth the day, and
who knows when was the equinox?

[Hydriotaphia: Urn Burial (1658)]

CARLYLE, Thomas (1795–1881)

The illimitable, silent, never-resting thing
called Time, rolling, rushing on, swift, silent,
like an all-embracing ocean-tide, on which
we and all the Universe swim like
exhalations, like apparitions which are, and
then are not.

['The Hero as Divinity' (1841)]

CHESTERFIELD, Lord (1694–1773)

I recommend to you to take care of minutes;
for hours will take care of themselves.

[Letter to his son, 1747]

COMPTON-BURNETT, Dame Ivy
(1884–1969)

'Time has too much credit,' said Bridget. 'I
never agree with the compliments paid to it.
It is not a great healer. It is an indifferent and
perfunctory one. Sometimes it does not heal
at all. And sometimes when it seems to, no
healing has been necessary.'

[Darkness and Day (1951)]

COWARD, Sir Noël (1899–1973)

Time is the reef upon which all our frail
mystic ships are wrecked.

[Blithe Spirit (1941)]

DISRAELI, Benjamin (1804–1881)

Time is the great physician.

[*Henrietta Temple* (1837)]

DOBSON, Henry Austin (1840–1921)

Time goes, you say? Ah no!
Alas, Time stays, we go.

['The Paradox of Time' (1877)]

EMERSON, Ralph Waldo (1803–1882)

[To a person complaining that he had not enough time]
'Well,' said Red Jacket, 'I suppose you have all there is.'

['Works and Days' (1870)]

A day is a miniature eternity.

[*Journals*]

FRAME, Janet (1924–)

There is no past present or future. Using tenses to divide time is like making chalk marks on water.

[*Faces in the Water* (1961)]

FRANKLIN, Benjamin (1706–1790)

Remember that time is money.

[*Advice to a Young Tradesman* (1748)]

GOETHE (1749–1832)

Mein Erbteil wie herrlich, weit und breit!
Die Zeit ist mein Besitz, mein Acker ist die Zeit.
How marvellous, wide and broad is my inheritance!
Time is my property, my estate is time.

[*Wilhelm Meister's Wandering Years* (1821)]

HODGSON, Ralph (1871–1962)

Time, you old gypsy man,
Will you not stay,
Put up your caravan,
Just for one day?

['Time, You Old Gypsy Man' (1917)]

MACAULAY, Dame Rose (1881–1958)

Decades have a delusive edge to them. They are not, of course, really periods at all, except as any other ten years would be. But we, looking at them, are caught by the different name each bears, and give them different attributes, and tie labels on them, as if they

were flowers in a border.

[*Told by an Idiot* (1923)]

MARX, Groucho (1895–1977)

Time wounds all heels.

[Attr.]

MAXWELL, Gavin (1914–1969)

Yet while there is time, there is the certainty of return.

[*Ring of Bright Water* (1960)]

MCLUHAN, Marshall (1911–1980)

For tribal man space was the uncontrollable mystery. For technological man it is time that occupies the same role.

[*The Mechanical Bridge* (1951)]

MUIR, Edwin (1887–1959)

Over the sound a ship so slow would pass
That in the black hill's gloom it seemed to lie
The evening sound was smooth like sunken glass
And time seemed finished ere the ship passed by.

['Childhood' (1952)]

PERICLES (c.495–429)

Wait for that wisest of counsellors, Time.

[In Plutarch, *Life*]

PLATO (c.429–347 BC)

Time brings everything.

[*Greek Anthology*]

PROVERBS

An hour in the morning is worth two in the evening.

No time like the present.

Time is a great healer.

RALEIGH, Sir Walter (c.1552–1618)

[Written the night before his execution]
Even such is Time, which takes in trust
Our youth, our joys, and all we have,
And pays us but with age and dust;
Who in the dark and silent grave,
When we have wandered all our ways,
Shuts up the story of our days.

[Untitled poem (1618)]

ROGERS, Will (1879–1935)

Half our life is spent trying to find something to do with the time we have rushed through life trying to save.

[*New York Times*, 1930]

SARTRE, Jean-Paul (1905–1980)

Trois heures, c'est toujours trop tard ou trop tôt pour ce qu'on veut faire.

Three o'clock is always too late or too early for anything you want to do.

[*Nausea* (1938)]

SERVICE, Robert W. (1874–1958)

Ah! the clock is always slow;
It is later than you think.

['It is Later than You Think' (1921)]

SHAKESPEARE, William (1564–1616)

But thoughts, the slaves of life, and life, time's fool,
And time, that takes survey of all the world,
Must have a stop.

[*Henry IV, Part 1*, V.iv]

Come what come may,
Time and the hour runs through the roughest day.

[*Macbeth*, I.iii]

I wasted time, and now doth time waste me.

[*Richard II*, V.v]

SITWELL, Osbert (1892–1969)

In reality, killing time is only the name for another of the multifarious ways by which time kills us.

['Milordo Inglese' (1958)]

SLESSOR, Kenneth (1901–1971)

All through the night-time, clock talked to clock,
In the captain's cabin, tock-tock-tock,
One ticked fast and one ticked slow,
And Time went over them a hundred years ago.

['Five Visions of Captain Cook' (1931)]

SPENCER, Herbert (1820–1903)

Time: That which man is always trying to kill,

but which ends in killing him.

[*Definitions*]

STOPPARD, Tom (1937–)

Eternity's a terrible thought. I mean, where's it all going to end?

[*Rosencrantz and Guildenstern Are Dead* (1967)]

THOMAS, Dylan (1914–1953)

Oh as I was young and easy in the mercy of his means,
Time held me green and dying
Though I sang in my chains like the sea.

['Fern Hill' (1946)]

THOREAU, Henry David (1817–1862)

Time is but the stream I go a-fishing in.

[*Walden* (1854)]

VIRGIL (70–19 BC)

Sed fugit interea, fugit inreparabile tempus.

But time meanwhile is flying, flying beyond recall.

[*Georgics*]

WATTS, Isaac (1674–1748)

Time, like an ever-rolling stream,
Bears all its sons away;
They fly forgotten, as a dream
Dies at the opening day.

[*The Psalms of David Imitated* (1719)]

YOUNG, Edward (1683–1765)

We take no note of Time
But from its Loss.

[*Night-Thoughts on Life, Death and Immortality* (1742–1746)]

Procrastination is the Thief of Time.

[*Night-Thoughts on Life, Death and Immortality* (1742–1746)]

See CHANGE; ETERNITY; FUTURE; LIFE; PAST; PRESENT

TOLERANCE

THE BIBLE
(King James Version)

For ye suffer fools gladly, seeing ye

yourselves are wise.

[Paul, 3:67]

BROWNE, Sir Thomas (1605–1682)

No man can justly censure or condemn another, because indeed no man truly knows another.

[Religio Medici (1643)]

BURKE, Edmund (1729–1797)

There is, however, a limit at which forbearance ceases to be a virtue.

[Observations on 'The Present State of the Nation' (1769)]

ROSTAND, Jean (1894–1977)

Il est dans la tolérance un degré qui confine á l'injure.
There is a degree of tolerance which borders on insult.

[Thoughts of a Biologist (1939)]

SADE, Marquis de (1740–1814)

La tolérance est la vertu du faible.
Tolerance is the virtue of the weak.

[La nouvelle Justine (1797)]

SMITH, Thorne (1892–1934)

Steven's mind was so tolerant that he could have attended a lynching every day without becoming critical.

[The Jovial Ghosts (1933)]

STAËL, Mme de (1766–1817)

Tout comprendre rend très indulgent.
Understanding everything makes one very tolerant.

[Corinne (1807)]

STERNE, Laurence (1713–1768)

So long as a man rides his hobby-horse peaceably and quietly along the King's highway, and neither compels you or me to get up behind him, – pray, Sir, what have either you or I to do with it?

[Tristram Shandy (1759–1767)]

TROLLOPE, Anthony (1815–1882)

It is because we put up with bad things that hotel-keepers continue to give them to us.

[Orley Farm (1862)]

TRADE

CANNING, George (1770–1827)

[Of a Jacobin]
In matters of commerce the fault of the Dutch
Is offering too little and asking too much.
The French are with equal advantage content,
So we clap on Dutch bottoms just twenty per cent.

[Dispatch, in Cipher. To Sir Charles Bagot, English Ambassador to the Hague, 1826]

HOOVER, Herbert Clark (1874–1964)

[Predicting the outcome if tariff protection were removed]
The grass will grow in the streets of a hundred cities, a thousand towns; the weeds will overrun the fields of millions of farms if that protection is taken away.

[Speech, 1932]

SAKI (1870–1916)

A woman whose dresses are made in Paris and whose marriage has been made in heaven might be equally biased for and against free imports.

[The Unbearable Bassington (1912)]

SCHUMACHER, E.F. (1911–1977)

After all, for mankind as a whole there are no exports. We did not start developing by obtaining foreign exchange from Mars or the moon. Mankind is a closed society.

[Small is Beautiful, A Study of Economics as if People Mattered (1973)]

See ECONOMICS; BUYING AND SELLING

TRAGEDY

ARISTOTLE (384–322 BC)

[Of the dramatic form of tragedy]
A whole is that which has a beginning, a middle, and an end.

[Poetics]

AUSTEN, Jane (1775–1817)

One of Edward's Mistresses was Jane Shore,

who has had a play written about her, but it is a tragedy and therefore not worth reading.

[*The History of England* (1791)]

CHAUCER, Geoffrey (c.1340–1400)

Tragedie is to seyn a certeyn storie,
As olde bookes maken us memorie,
Of hym that stood in greet prosperitee
And is yfallen out of heigh degree
Into myserie, and endeth wrecchedly.

[*The Canterbury Tales* (1387)]

FYFE, Alistair (b.1961)

[Explaining the obscurity of Glasgow architect Alexander 'Greek' Thomson compared with Charles Rennie Mackintosh]
Thomson was guilty of not having enough tragedy in his life.

[*The Guardian*, June 1999]

SCOTT, Sir Walter (1771–1832)

The play-bill, which is said to have announced the tragedy of Hamlet, the character of the Prince of Denmark being left out.

[*The Talisman* (1825)]

TRANSLATION

BORGES, Jorge Luis (1899–1986)

[On Henley's translation of Beckford's Vathek]
El original es infiel a la traducción.
The original is not faithful to the translation.

[*Sobre el 'Vathek' de William Beckford* (1943)]

BORROW, George (1803–1881)

Translation is at best an echo.

[*Lavengro* (1851)]

CAMPBELL, Roy (1901–1957)

Translations (like wives) are seldom strictly faithful if they are in the least attractive.

[*Poetry Review*, 1949]

DENHAM, Sir John (1615–1669)

Such is our pride, our folly, or our fate,
That few, but such as cannot write, translate.

['To Richard Fanshaw' (1648)]

FROST, Robert (1874–1963)

Poetry is what is lost in translation.

[In Untermeyer, *Robert Frost: a Backward Look* (1964)]

JOHNSON, Samuel (1709–1784)

A translator is to be like his author; it is not his business to excel him.

[Attr.]

SHERIDAN, Richard Brinsley (1751–1816)

Not a translation – only taken from the French.

[*The Critic* (1779)]

Egad, I think the interpreter is the hardest to be understood of the two!

[*The Critic* (1779)]

TRAVEL

ANONYMOUS

When the plane you are on is late, the plane you want to transfer to is on time.

[The Airplane Law]

When you are served a meal aboard an aircraft, the aircraft will encounter turbulence.

[Gunter's First Law of Air Travel]

The strength of the turbulence is directly proportional to the temperature of your coffee.

[Gunter's Second Law of Air Travel]

ARNOLD, Matthew (1822–1888)

And see all sights from pole to pole,
And glance, and nod, and bustle by;
And never once possess our soul
Before we die.

['A Southern Night' (1861)]

A wanderer is man from his birth.
He was born in a ship
On the breast of the river of Time.

['The Future']

ATWOOD, Margaret (1939–)

The north focuses our anxieties. Turning to

face north, we enter our own unconscious. Always, in retrospect, the journey north has the quality of dream.

[*Saturday Night*, 1987, 'True North']

BAXTER, James K. (1926–1972)

Upon the upland road
Ride easy, stranger:
Surrender to the sky
Your heart of anger.

['High Country Weather' (1945)]

BOONE, Daniel (1734–1820)

[Reply on being asked if he had ever been lost]
I can't say I was ever lost, but I was bewildered once for three days.

[Attr.]

BRIEN, Alan (1925–)

I have done almost every human activity inside a taxi which does not require main drainage.

[*Punch*, 1972]

BUCHAN, William (1822–1888)

Canadian trains did not rush and rock. They pounded steadily along, every so often giving a warning blast on their sirens. I remember those sirens blowing in the icy darkness of winter nights in Ottawa, the most haunting sound, at once melancholy and stirring, like the mourning of some strange, sad beast.

[*A Memoir*]

CHERRY-GARRARD, Apsley (1886–1959)

Polar exploration is at once the cleanest and most isolated way of having a bad time which has been devised.

[*The Worst Journey in the World* (1922)]

CHESTERTON, G.K. (1874–1936)

Chesterton taught me this: the only way to be sure of catching a train is to miss the one before it.

[In P. Daninos, *Vacances à tous prix* (1958), 'Le supplice de l'heure']

CLARKSON, Jeremy

To argue that a car is simply a means of conveyance is like arguing that Blenheim Palace is simply a house.

[*Sunday Times*, 1999]

COLERIDGE, Samuel Taylor (1772–1834)

From whatever place I write you will expect that part of my 'Travels' will consist of excursions in my own mind.

[*Satyrane's Letters* (1809)]

COOK, Captain James (1728–1779)

[Of the Endeavour expedition]
Altho' the discoveries made in this Voyage are not great, yet I flatter myself that they are such as may merit the attention of their Lordships, and altho' I have failed in discovering the so much talk'd of southern Continent (which perhaps do not exist) and which I myself had so much at heart, yet I am confident that no part of the failure of such discovery can be laid at my Charge.

[Letter, 1770]

COWPER, William (1731–1800)

How much a dunce that has been sent to roam
Excels a dunce that has been kept at home.

['The Progress of Error' (1782)]

DIDION, Joan (1934–)

Certain places seem to exist mainly because someone has written about them.

[*The White Album* (1979)]

DREW, Elizabeth (1887–1965)

Too often travel, instead of broadening the mind, merely lengthens the conversation.

[*The Literature of Gossip* (1964)]

ELIOT, T.S. (1888–1965)

The first condition of understanding a foreign country is to smell it.

[Attr.]

EMERSON, Ralph Waldo (1803–1882)

Travelling is a fool's paradise. Our first journeys discover to us the indifference of places.

['Self-Reliance' (1841)]

FLANDERS, Michael (1922–1975) and SWANN, Donald (1923–1994)

If God had intended us to fly, he'd never have given us the railways.

['By Air', 1963]

GALBRAITH, J.K. (1908–)

The Great Wall, I've been told, is the only man-made structure on earth that is visible from the moon. For the life of me I cannot see why anyone would go to the moon to look at it, when, with almost the same difficulty, it can be viewed in China.

[*The Sunday Times Magazine*]

GEORGE VI (1895–1952)

Abroad is bloody.

[In Auden, *A Certain World* (1970)]

GRAHAME, Kenneth (1859–1932)

[Toad's reaction to the motor-car which destroyed his gypsy caravan]
The real way to travel! Here today – in next week tomorrow! Villages skipped, towns and cities jumped – always somebody else's horizon! O bliss! O poop-poop! O my! O my!

[*The Wind in the Willows* (1908)]

HAZLITT, William (1778–1830)

One of the pleasantest things in the world is going a journey; but I like to go by myself.

[*Table-Talk* (1822)]

Give me the clear blue sky over my head, and the green turf beneath my feet, a winding road before me, and a three hours' march to dinner – and then to thinking! It is hard if I cannot start some game on these lone heaths.

['On Going a Journey' (1822)]

JOHNSON, Amy (1903–1941)

Had I been a man I might have explored the Poles or climbed Mount Everest, but as it was my spirit found an outlet in the air …

[In Margot Asquith (ed.), *Myself When Young*]

JOHNSON, Samuel (1709–1784)

A man who has not been in Italy, is always conscious of an inferiority, from his not having seen what it is expected a man should see. The grand object of travelling is to see the shores of the Mediterranean.

[In Boswell, *The Life of Samuel Johnson* (1791)]

KILVERT, Francis (1840–1879)

Of all noxious animals, too, the most noxious is a tourist. And of all tourists, the most vulgar, ill-bred, offensive and loathsome is the British tourist.

[*Diary*, 1870]

KIPLING, Rudyard (1865–1936)

Down to Gehenna or up to the Throne,
He travels the fastest who travels alone.

['The Winners' (1888)]

MACAULAY, Dame Rose (1881–1958)

The great and recurrent question about abroad is, is it worth getting there?

[Attr.]

MANSFIELD, Katherine (1888–1923)

Whenever I prepare for a journey I prepare as though for death. Should I never return, all is in order. That is what life has taught me.

[*Journal of Katherine Mansfield* (1954)]

MARX BROTHERS

Captain Jeffrey Spaulding: You are going Uruguay, and I'm going my way.

[Film *Animal Crackers*, 1930]

MASEFIELD, John (1878–1967)

It is good to be out on the road, and going one knows not where,
Going through meadow and village, one knows not whither nor why.

['Tewkesbury Road' (1902)]

MCLUHAN, Marshall (1911–1980)

The car has become the carapace, the protective and aggressive shell, of urban and suburban man.

[*Understanding Media* (1964)]

MOORE, George (1852–1933)

A man travels the world over in search of what he needs and returns home to find it.

[*The Brook Kerith* (1916)]

PEARY, Robert Edwin (1856–1920)

The Eskimo had his own explanation. Said

he: 'The devil is asleep or having trouble with his wife, or we should never have come back so easily.'

[*The North Pole* (1910)]

[Explaining how he knew he had reached the North Pole]
Nothing easier. One step beyond the pole, you see, and the north wind becomes a south one.

[Attr.]

PROVERBS

He travels fastest who travels alone.

Travel broadens the mind.

RUSKIN, John (1819–1900)

There was a rocky valley between Buxton and Bakewell, … divine as the vale of Tempe; you might have seen the gods there morning and evening, – Apollo and the sweet Muses of the Light … You enterprised a railroad, … you blasted its rocks away … And now, every fool in Buxton can be at Bakewell in half-an-hour, and every fool in Bakewell at Buxton.

[*Praeterita* (1889)]

SACKVILLE-WEST, Vita (1892–1962)

Travel is the most private of pleasures. There is no greater bore than the travel bore. We do not in the least want to hear what he has seen in Hong-Kong.

[*Passenger to Tehran* (1926)]

SANTAYANA, George (1863–1952)

[On being asked why he always travelled third class]
Because there's no fourth class.

[In Thomas, *Living Biographies of the Great Philosophers*]

SCOTT, Captain Robert (1868–1912)

[Of the South Pole]
Great God! this is an awful place.

[*Journal*, 1912]

Had we lived, I should have had a tale to tell of the hardihood, endurance, and courage of my companions which would have stirred the heart of every Englishman. These rough notes and our dead bodies must tell the tale.

[Message to the Public, 1912]

SHENSTONE, William (1714–1763)

Whoe'er has travell'd life's dull round,
Where'er his stages may have been,
May sigh to think he still has found
The warmest welcome, at an inn.

['At an Inn at Henley' (1758)]

SLESSOR, Kenneth (1901–1971)

… The dark train shakes and plunges;
Bells cry out; the night-ride starts again.
Soon I shall look out into nothing but blackness,
Pale, windy fields. The old roar and knock of the rails
Melts into dull fury. Pull down the blind.
Sleep. Sleep.
Nothing but grey, rushing rivers of bush outside.
Gaslight and milk-cans. Of Rapptown I recall nothing else.

['The Night-Ride']

STARK, Dame Freya (1893–1993)

The beckoning counts, and not the clicking latch behind you.

[*Sunday Telegraph*, 1993]

STERNE, Laurence (1713–1768)

The whole circle of travellers may be reduced to the following Heads:
Idle Travellers,
Inquisitive Travellers,
Lying Travellers,
Proud Travellers,
Vain Travellers,
Splenetic Travellers,
Then follow The Travellers of Necessity,
The delinquent and felonious Traveller,
The unfortunate and innocent Traveller,
The simple Traveller,
And last of all (if you please)
The Sentimental Traveller.

[*Sentimental Journey* (1768)]

I pity the man who can travel from Dan to Beersheba, and cry, 'tis all barren.

[*Sentimental Journey* (1768)]

A man should know something of his own country too, before he goes abroad.

[*Tristram Shandy* (1767)]

STEVENSON, Robert Louis (1850–1894)

Give to me the life I love,
Let the lave go by me,
Give the jolly heaven above
And the byway nigh me.
Bed in the bush with stars to see,
Bread I dip in the river –
There's the life for a man like me,
There's the life for ever.

[*Songs of Travel* (1896)]

Let the blow fall soon or late,
Let what will be o'er me;
Give the face of earth around
And the road before me.
Wealth I seek not, hope nor love,
Nor a friend to know me;
All I seek, the heaven above
And the road below me.

[*Songs of Travel* (1896)]

For my part, I travel not to go anywhere, but to go. I travel for travel's sake. The great affair is to move.

[*Travels with a Donkey in the Cévennes* (1879)]

To travel hopefully is a better thing than to arrive, and the true success is to labour.

[*Virginibus Puerisque* (1881)]

But all that I could think of, in the darkness and the cold,
Was that I was leaving home and my folks were growing old.

['Christmas at Sea' (1890)]

There's nothing under Heav'n so blue
That's fairly worth the travelling to.

['A Song of the Road' (1896)]

THOMSON, Joseph (1858–1895)

[His reply when J.M. Barrie asked what was the most hazardous part of his expedition to Africa]
Crossing Piccadilly Circus.

[In Dunbar, *J.M. Barrie*]

TWAIN, Mark (1835–1910)

You feel mighty free and easy and comfortable on a raft.

[*The Adventures of Huckleberry Finn* (1884)]

VINE, David

Here we are in the Holy Land of Israel – a Mecca for tourists.

VIZINCZEY, Stephen (1933–)

I was told I am a true cosmopolitan. I am unhappy everywhere.

[*The Guardian*, 1968]

WHITE, E.B. (1899–1985)

Commuter – one who spends his life
In riding to and from his wife;
A man who shaves and takes a train,
And then rides back to shave again.

[*Poems and Sketches*, 1982]

See FOREIGNERS

TREES

KEATS, John (1795–1821)

In drear-nighted December,
Too happy, happy tree,
Thy branches ne'er remember
Their green felicity.

['In drear-nighted December' (1817)]

As when, upon a trancèd summer-night,
Those green-rob'd senators of mighty woods,
Tall oaks, branch-charmèd by the earnest stars,
Dream, and so dream all night without a stir.

['Hyperion. A Fragment (1818)']

KILMER, Joyce (1886–1918)

I think that I shall never see
A poem lovely as a tree …

Poems are made by fools like me,
But only God can make a tree.

['Trees' (1914)]

MORRIS, George Pope (1802–1864)

Woodman, spare that tree!
Touch not a single bough!

In youth it sheltered me,
And I'll protect it now.

['Woodman, Spare That Tree' (1830)]

POUND, Ezra (1885–1972)

The difference between a gun and a tree is a difference of tempo. The tree explodes every spring.

[*Criterion* (1937)]

See COUNTRY; NATURE

TRUST

ANONYMOUS

Trust in Allah, but tie your camel.

[Old Muslim Proverb]

CAINE, Michael (1933–)

Never trust anyone who wears a beard, a bow tie, two-toned shoes, sandals or sunglasses.

[*The Times, 1992;* quoting his father]

CAMUS, Albert (1913–1960)

It is very true that we seldom confide in those who are better than ourselves.

[*The Fall* (1956)]

CHRISTIE, Dame Agatha (1890–1976)

Where large sums of money are concerned, it is advisable to trust nobody.

[*Endless Night* (1967)]

FIELDING, Henry (1707–1754)

Never trust the man who hath reason to suspect that you know that he hath injured you.

[*Jonathan Wild* (1743)]

GREENE, Graham (1904–1991)

His smile explained everything; he carried it always with him as a leper carried his bell; it was a perpetual warning that he was not to be trusted.

[*England Made Me* (1935)]

JEFFERSON, Thomas (1743–1826)

When a man assumes a public trust, he should consider himself as public property.

[Remark, 1807]

PITT, William (1708–1778)

I cannot give them my confidence; pardon me, gentlemen, confidence is a plant of slow growth in an aged bosom: youth is the season of credulity.

[Speech, 1766]

RUBIN, Jerry (1936–)

Don't trust anyone over thirty.

[In S.B. Flexner, *Listening to America*]

SANTAYANA, George (1863–1952)

Trust the man who hesitates in his speech and is quick and steady in action, but beware of long arguments and long beards.

[*Soliloquies in England* (1922)]

SHERIDAN, Richard Brinsley (1751–1816)

There is no trusting appearances.

[*The School for Scandal* (1777)]

THEODORIC (c.445–526)

[Explaining why he had a trusted minister, who had said he would adopt his master's religion, beheaded]
If this man is not faithful to his God, how can he be faithful to me, a mere man?

[In E. Guérard, *Dictionnaire Encyclopédique*]

WILLIAMS, Tennessee (1911–1983)

We have to distrust each other. It's our only defence against betrayal.

[*Camino Real* (1953)]

TRUTH

ADLER, Alfred (1870–1937)

The truth is often a terrible weapon of aggression. It is possible to lie, and even to murder, for the truth.

[*Problems of Neurosis* (1929)]

AGAR, Herbert Sebastian (1897–1980)

The truth which makes men free is for the most part the truth which men prefer not to hear.

[*A Time for Greatness* (1942)]

ANONYMOUS

Speak the truth, but leave immediately after.

[Slovenian Proverb]

Se non è vero, è molto ben trovato.

If it is not true, it is a happy invention.

[16th century]

ARISTOTLE (384–322 BC)

Amicus Plato, sed magis amica veritas.

Plato is dear to me, but dearer still is truth.

[Greek original attributed to Aristotle]

ARNOLD, Matthew (1822–1888)

Truth sits upon the lips of dying men.

['Sohrab and Rustum' (1853)]

BACON, Francis (1561–1626)

What a man had rather were true he more readily believes.

[*The New Organon* (1620)]

Some in their discourse desire rather commendation of wit, in being able to hold all arguments, than of judgement in discerning what is true.

['Of Discourse' (1625)]

This same truth is a naked and open daylight, that doth not show the masques and mummeries and triumphs of the world half so stately and daintily as candlelights.

['Of Truth' (1625)]

BALDWIN, Stanley (1867–1947)

A platitude is simply a truth repeated until people get tired of hearing it.

[Attr.]

BALFOUR, A.J. (1848–1930)

It is unfortunate, considering that enthusiasm moves the world, that so few enthusiasts can be trusted to speak the truth.

[Letter to Mrs Drew, 1891]

BERKELEY, Bishop George (1685–1753)

Truth is the cry of all, but the game of the few.

[*Siris* (1744)]

THE BIBLE
(King James Version)

Magna est veritas et praevalet.

Great is Truth, and mighty above all things.

[*Apocrypha, I Esdras*, 4:41]

And ye shall know the truth, and the truth shall make you free.

[*John*, 8:32]

BLAKE, William (1757–1827)

Truth can never be told so as to be understood, and not be believ'd.

['Proverbs of Hell' (c. 1793)]

A truth thats told with bad intent
Beats all the Lies you can invent.

['Auguries of Innocence' (c. 1803)]

When I tell any Truth it is not for the sake of Convincing those who do not know it but for the sake of defending those who Do.

[Public address, from the *Notebook*, c. 1810]

BOLINGBROKE, Henry (1678–1751)

Plain truth will influence half a score of men at most in a nation, or an age, while mystery will lead millions by the nose.

[Letter, 1721]

They make truth serve as a stalking-horse to error.

[*Letters on Study and Use of History* (1752)]

BOWEN, Elizabeth (1899–1973)

Nobody speaks the truth when there's something they must have.

[*The House in Paris* (1935)]

BRAQUE, Georges (1882–1963)

La vérité existe; on n'invente que le mensonge.

Truth exists; only lies are invented.

[*Day and Night, Notebooks* (1952)]

BROOKS, Thomas (1608–1680)

For (*magna est veritas et praevalebit*) great is truth, and shall prevail.

[*The Crown and Glory of Christianity* (1662)]

BROWNE, Sir Thomas (1605–1682)

A man may be in as just possession of truth

as of a city, and yet be forced to surrender.

[*Religio Medici* (1643)]

CARROLL, Lewis (1832–1898)

What I tell you three times is true.

['The Hunting of the Snark' (1876)]

CHAUCER, Geoffrey (c.1340–1400)

Trouthe is the hyeste thyng that man may kepe.

[*The Canterbury Tales* (1387)]

COWPER, William (1731–1800)

And diff'ring judgments serve but to declare
That truth lies somewhere, if we knew but where.

['Hope' (1782)]

DARLING, Charles (1849–1936)

Much truth is spoken, that more may be concealed.

[*Scintillae Juris* (1877)]

Perjury is often bold and open. It is truth that is shamefaced – as, indeed, in many cases is no more than decent.

[*Scintillae Juris* (1877)]

DICKINSON, Emily (1830–1886)

Tell all the Truth but tell it slant –
Success in Circuit lies
Too bright for our infirm Delight
The Truth's superb surprise.

['Tell all the Truth but tell it slant' (c. 1868)]

DONNE, John (1572–1631)

On a huge hill,
Cragged, and steep, Truth stands, and he that will
Reach her, about must, and about must go;
And what the hill's suddenness resists, win so.

[*Satire*, no. 3 (c. 1594)]

DOYLE, Sir Arthur Conan (1859–1930)

It is an old maxim of mine that when you have excluded the impossible, whatever remains, however improbable, must be the truth.

['The Beryl Coronet' (1892)]

DRYDEN, John (1631–1700)

I never saw any good that came of telling truth.

[*Amphitryon* (1690)]

FINEY, George (1895–1987)

The truth is always libellous.

[*Sydney Morning Herald*, 1981]

FRAME, Janet (1924–)

In an age of explanation one can always choose varieties of truth.

[*Living in the Maniototo* (1979)]

HAMILTON, Sir William (1788–1856)

Truth, like a torch, the more it's shook it shines.

[*Discussions on Philosophy* (1852)]

HARE, Augustus (1792–1834)

Truth, when witty, is the wittiest of all things.

[*Guesses at Truth* (1827)]

HELLMAN, Lillian (1905–1984)

Cynicism is an unpleasant way of saying the truth.

[*The Little Foxes* (1939)]

HUXLEY, T.H. (1825–1895)

Irrationally held truths may be more harmful than reasoned errors.

[*Science and Culture, and Other Essays* (1881)]

It is the customary fate of new truths to begin as heresies and to end as superstitions.

[*Science and Culture, and Other Essays* (1881)]

IBSEN, Henrik (1828–1906)

A man should never have his best trousers on when he goes out to battle for freedom and truth.

[*An Enemy of the People* (1882)]

JOHNSON, Samuel (1709–1784)

[On sceptics]

Truth, Sir, is a cow which will yield such people no more milk, and so they are gone to milk the bull.

[In Boswell, *The Life of Samuel Johnson* (1791)]

LA BRUYÈRE, Jean de (1645–1696)

[Il y a quelques rencontres dans la vie où la vérité

et la simplicité sont le meilleur manège du monde.]

There are some circumstances in life where truth and simplicity are the best strategy in the world.

[*Les caractères ou les moeurs de ce siècle* (1688)]

LEACOCK, Stephen (1869–1944)

A half truth in argument, like a half brick, carries better.

[In Flesch, *The Book of Unusual Quotations*]

LE GALLIENNE, Richard (1866–1947)

[Of Oscar Wilde]

Paradox with him was only Truth standing on its head to attract attention.

[*The Romantic 90s*]

MILL, John Stuart (1806–1873)

History teems with instances of truth put down by persecution … It is a piece of idle sentimentality that truth, merely as truth, has any inherent power denied to error, of prevailing against the dungeon and the stake.

[*On Liberty* (1859)]

MILTON, John (1608–1674)

Beholding the bright countenance of truth in the quiet and still air of delightfull studies.

[*The Reason of Church-government Urg'd against Prelaty* (1642)]

NIXON, Richard (1913–1994)

Let us begin by committing ourselves to the truth, to see it like it is and to tell it like it is, to find the truth, to speak the truth and live with the truth. That's what we'll do.

[Nomination acceptance speech, 1968]

PATMORE, Coventry (1823–1896)

For want of me the world's course will not fail:
When all its work is done, the lie shall rot;
The truth is great, and shall prevail,
When none cares whether it prevail or not.

[*The Unknown Eros* (1877)]

PLATO (c.429–347 BC)

But, my dearest Agathon, it is truth which you cannot contradict; you can easily contradict Socrates.

[*Symposium*]

PROUST, Marcel (1871–1922)

Une vérité clairement comprise ne peut plus être écrite avec sincérité.

A truth which is clearly understood can no longer be written with sincerity.

['Senancour c'est moi']

PROVERBS

Craft maun hae claes, but truth goes naked.

[Scots proverb]

Many a true word is spoken in jest.

Truth is stranger than fiction.

Truth will out.

SAMUEL, Lord (1870–1963)

A truism is on that account none the less true.

[*A Book of Quotations* (1947)]

SAND, George (1804–1876)

Le vrai est trop simple, il faut y arriver toujours par le compliqué.

The truth is too simple, it must always be arrived at through complication.

[Letter to Armand Barbès, 1867]

SCHILLER, Johann Christoph Friedrich (1759–1805)

Die Wahrheit lebt in der Täuschung fort.

Truth lives on in deception.

[*On the Aesthetic Education of Man* (1793–1795)]

SHAW, George Bernard (1856–1950)

All great truths begin as blasphemies.

[*Annajanska* (1919)]

SMITH, Sydney (1771–1845)

It is the calling of great men, not so much to preach new truths, as to rescue from oblivion those old truths which it is our wisdom to remember and our weakness to forget.

[Attr.]

SOLZHENITSYN, Alexander (1918–)

When truth is discovered by someone else, it loses something of its attractiveness.

[*Candle in the Wind*]

If decade after decade the truth cannot be told, each person's mind starts to roam irretrievably. One's fellow countrymen become harder to understand than Martians.

[*Cancer Ward* (1968)]

THOREAU, Henry David (1817–1862)
It takes two to speak the truth, – one to speak, and another to hear.

[*A Week on the Concord and Merrimack Rivers* (1849)]

TWAIN, Mark (1835–1910)
When in doubt, tell the truth.

[*Pudd'nhead Wilson's New Calendar*]

There was things which he stretched, but mainly he told the truth.

[*The Adventures of Huckleberry Finn* (1884)]

WHITEHEAD, A.N. (1861–1947)
There are no whole truths; all truths are half-truths. It is trying to treat them as whole truths that plays the devil.

[*Dialogues* (1954)]

WILDE, Oscar (1854–1900)
If one tells the truth, one is sure, sooner or later, to be found out.

[*The Chameleon*, 1894]

The truth is rarely pure and never simple. Modern life would be very tedious if it were either, and modern literature a complete impossibility!

[*The Importance of Being Earnest* (1895), I]

WRIGHT, Frank Lloyd (1869–1959)
The truth is more important than the facts.

[In Simcox, *Treasury of Quotations on Christian Themes*]

WYCLIFFE, John (c.1329–1384)
[To the Duke of Lancaster, 1381]
I believe that in the end the truth will conquer.

[In J.R. Green, *Short History of the English People*]

XENOPHANES (c.570–480 BC)
And of course the clear and certain truth no man has seen.

[In J.H. Lesher, *Xenophanes of Colophon* (1992)]

YELTSIN, Boris (1931–)
Truth is truth, and the truth will overcome the left, the right and the centre.

[Interview in *Newsweek*, 1994]

ZOLA, Emile (1840–1902)
[Article on the Dreyfus affair]
La vérité est en marche, et rien ne l'arrêtera.
Truth is on the move and nothing can stop it.

[In *La Vérité en marche* (1901)]

See ERROR; FACTS; HONESTY; LIES

TYRANNY

ARENDT, Hannah (1906–1975)
Under conditions of tyranny it is far easier to act than to think.

[In Auden, *A Certain World* (1970)]

BELLOW, Saul (1915–)
It is not inconceivable that a man might find freedom and identity by killing his oppressor. But as a Chicagoan, I am rather skeptical about this. Murderers are not improved by murdering.

['A World Too Much With Us' (1975)]

BLAKE, William (1757–1827)
One law for the Lion & Ox is Oppression.

[*Marriage of Heaven and Hell* (c. 1790–1793)]

BROWNING, Robert (1812–1889)
Oppression makes the wise man mad.

[*Luria* (1846)]

BURKE, Edmund (1729–1797)
Bad laws are the worst sort of tyranny.

[*Speech at Bristol* (1780)]

CHURCHILL, Sir Winston (1874–1965)
Dictators ride to and fro upon tigers which they dare not dismount. And the tigers are getting hungry.

[*While England Slept* (1936)]

DEFOE, Daniel (c.1661–1731)
And of all plagues with which mankind are curst,
Ecclesiastic tyranny's the worst.

[*The True-Born Englishman* (1701)]

Nature has left this tincture in the blood,
That all men would be tyrants if they could.

['The Kentish Petition' (1713)]

HERRICK, Robert (1591–1674)

'Twixt Kings & Tyrants there's this difference known;
Kings seek their Subjects good: Tyrants their owne.

[*Hesperides* (1648)]

INGE, William Ralph (1860–1954)

The enemies of Freedom do not argue; they shout and they shoot.

[*End of an Age* (1948)]

JUNG CHANG (1952–)

Mao had managed to turn the people into the ultimate weapon of dictatorship. That was why under him there was no real equivalent of the KGB in China. There was no need. In bringing out and nourishing the worst in people, Mao had created a moral wasteland and a land of hatred.

[*Wild Swans* (1991)]

MANDELA, Nelson (1918–)

Never, never and never again shall it be that this beautiful land will again experience the oppression of one by another and suffer the indignity of being the skunk of the world.

[Inauguration speech, 1994]

MILL, John Stuart (1806–1873)

Whatever crushes individuality is despotism, by whatever name it may be called.

[*On Liberty* (1859)]

Protection, therefore, against the tyranny of the magistrate is not enough: there needs protection also against the tyranny of the prevailing opinion and feeling.

[*On Liberty* (1859)]

NIEMÖLLER, Martin (1892–1984)

In Germany, the Nazis came for the Communists and I didn't speak up because I was not a Communist. Then they came for the Jews and I didn't speak up because I was not a Jew. Then they came for the trade unionists and I didn't speak up because I was not a trade unionist. Then they came for the Catholics and I was a Protestant so I didn't speak up. Then they came for me … By that time there was no one to speak up for anyone.

[In Neil, *Concise Dictionary of Religious Quotations*]

PLATO (c.429–347 BC)

Tyranny comes from no other form of government but democracy.

[*Republic*]

SENECA (c.4 BC–AD 65)

Victima haud ulla amplior
Potest magisque opima mactari Iovi
Quam rex iniquus.
There can be slain
No sacrifice to God more acceptable
Than an unjust and wicked king.

[*Hercules Furens*]

THOMAS, Dylan (1914–1953)

The hand that signed the paper felled a city;
Five sovereign fingers taxed the breath,
Doubled the globe of death and halved a country;
These five kings did a king to death …

The hand that signed the treaty bred a fever,
And famine grew, and locusts came;
Great is the hand that holds dominion over
Man by a scribbled name.

['The hand that signed the paper' (1936)]

TROTSKY, Leon (1879–1940)

Lenin's method leads to this: the party organization at first substitutes itself for the party as a whole. Then the central committee substitutes itself for the party organization, and finally a single dictator substitutes himself for the central committee.

[In N. McInnes, *The Communist Parties of Western Europe*]

See CENSORSHIP

U

UNCERTAINTY

BARNFIELD, Richard (1574–1627)
Nothing more certain than incertainties;
Fortune is full of fresh variety:
Constant in nothing but inconstancy.
[*The Affectionate Shepherd* (1594)]

BISSELL, Claude T. (1916–)
I prefer complexity to certainty, cheerful
mysteries to sullen facts.
[Address, University of Toronto, 1969]

BOYD, William (1952–)
What now? What next? All these questions.
All these doubts. So few certainties. But then
I have taken new comfort and refuge in the
doctrine that advises one not to seek
tranquillity in certainty, but in permanently
suspended judgement.
[*Brazzaville Beach* (1990)]

See DOUBT; INDECISION

UNIVERSE

CARLYLE, Thomas (1795–1881)
Margaret Fuller: I accept the universe.
Carlyle: Gad! she'd better!
[In William James, *Varieties of Religious Experience*
(1902)]

[To Wm Allingham]
I don't pretend to understand the Universe –
it's a great deal bigger than I am … People
ought to be modester.
[In D.A. Wilson and D. Wilson MacArthur, *Carlyle in
Old Age* (1934)]

COOK, Peter (1937–1995)
I am very interested in the Universe – I am
specializing in the universe and all that
surrounds it.
[*Beyond the Fringe*, 1962]

HALDANE, J.B.S. (1892–1964)
My own suspicion is that the universe is not
only queerer than we suppose, but queerer
than we can suppose.
[*Possible Worlds and Other Essays* (1927)]

See SPACE; WORLD

UNIVERSITY

**ARCHIBALD, John Feltham
(1856–1919)**
I have nothing against Oxford men. Some of
our best shearers' cooks are Oxford men.
[In R. H. Croll, *I Recall* …]

BACON, Francis (1561–1626)
Universities incline wits to sophistry and
affectation.
[*Valerius Terminus of the Interpretation of Nature*
(1603)]

BATESON, Mary Catherine (1939–)
Most higher education is devoted to
affirming the traditions and origins of an
existing elite and transmitting them to new
members.
[*Composing a Life* (1989)]

BETJEMAN, Sir John (1906–1984)
Balkan Sobranies in a wooden box,
The college arms upon the lid; Tokay
And sherry in the cupboard; on the shelves
The University Statutes bound in blue,
Crome Yellow, Prancing Nigger, Blunden,
Keats.
[*Summoned by Bells*
(1960)]

CHEKHOV, Anton (1860–1904)
Liubov Andreevna: Are you really still a
student?
Trofimov: I shall probably be a student
forever.
[*The Cherry Orchard* (1904)]

CARLYLE, Thomas (1795–1881)

The true University of these days is a Collection of Books.

[*On Heroes, Hero-Worship, and the Heroic in History* (1841)]

CONGREVE, William (1670–1729)

Aye, 'tis well enough for a servant to be bred at an University. But the education is a little too pedantic for a gentleman.

[*Love for Love* (1695)]

ESSON, Louis (1879–1943)

[On Melbourne University]

If the science professors knew as little about their jobs as the literary ones the University would have been blown up long ago!

[In Vance Palmer, *Louis Esson and the Australian Theatre* (1948)]

EWART, Gavin (1916–1995)

After Cambridge – unemployment. No one wanted much to know.
Good degrees are good for nothing in the business world below.

['The Sentimental Education']

FRY, Stephen (1957–)

The competitive spirit is an ethos which it is the business of universities … to subdue and neutralise.

[*Paperweight* (1992)]

GIBBON, Edward (1737–1794)

To the University of Oxford I acknowledge no obligation; and she will as cheerfully renounce me for a son, as I am willing to disclaim her for a mother. I spent fourteen months at Magdalen College: they proved the fourteen months the most idle and unprofitable of my whole life.

[*Memoirs of My Life and Writings* (1796)]

HODSON, Peregrine

He probably doesn't understand what he's looking at but he's reluctant to ask, because this is Japan and the student doesn't ask questions but waits to be told by the teacher.

[*A Circle Round The Sun – A Foreigner in Japan*]

ILLICH, Ivan (1926–)

Any attempt to reform the university without attending to the system of which it is an integral part is like trying to do urban renewal in New York City from the twelfth storey up.

[*Deschooling Society* (1971)]

JOHNSON, Paul (1928–)

In a growing number of countries everyone has a qualified right to attend a university … The result is the emergence of huge caravanserais … where higher education is doled out rather like gruel in a soup kitchen.

[*The Spectator*, 1996]

LODGE, David (1935–)

Rummidge … had lately suffered the mortifying fate of most English universities of its type (civic redbrick): having competed strenuously for fifty years with two universities chiefly valued for being old, it was, at the moment of drawing level, rudely overtaken in popularity and prestige by a batch of universities chiefly valued for being new.

[*Changing Places* (1975)]

Universities are the cathedrals of the modern age. They shouldn't have to justify their existence by utilitarian criteria.

[*Nice Work*]

MCLUHAN, Marshall (1911–1980)

The reason universities are so full of knowledge is that the students come with so much and they leave with so little.

[*Antigonish Review*, 1988]

MELVILLE, Herman (1819–1891)

A whale ship was my Yale College and my Harvard.

[*Moby Dick* (1851)]

NABOKOV, Vladimir (1899–1977)

Like so many ageing college people, Pnin had long ceased to notice the existence of students on the campus.

[*Pnin* (1957)]

NEWMAN, John Henry, Cardinal (1801–1890)

A university is an *alma mater*, knowing her children one by one, not a foundry, or a mint, or a treadmill.

[Attr.]

O'CONNOR, Flannery (1925–1964)

Everywhere I go I'm asked if I think the university stifles writers. My opinion is that they don't stifle enough of them. There's many a bestseller that could have been prevented by a good teacher.

[In Fitzgerald, *The Nature and Aim of Fiction*]

OSBORNE, John (1929–1994)

I don't think one 'comes down' from Jimmy's university. According to him, it's not even red brick, but white tile.

[*Look Back in Anger* (1956)]

OZICK, Cynthia (1928–)

It is the function of a liberal university not to give the right answers, but to ask right questions.

['Women and Creativity' (1969)]

PEACOCK, Thomas Love (1785–1866)

He was sent, as usual, to a public school, where a little learning was painfully beaten into him, and from thence to the university, where it was carefully taken out of him.

[*Nightmare Abbey* (1818)]

SMITH, Adam (1723–1790)

[Of universities]

Several of those learned societies have chosen to remain … the sanctuaries in which exploded systems and obsolete prejudices found shelter and protection, after they had

been hunted out of every other corner of the world.

[*Wealth of Nations* (1776)]

SPOONER, William (1844–1930)

Sir, you have tasted two whole worms; you have hissed all my mystery lectures and have been caught fighting a liar in the quad; you will leave Oxford by the town drain.

[Attr.]

SPRING-RICE, Cecil Arthur (1859–1918)

I am the Dean of Christ Church, Sir:
There's my wife; look well at her.
She's the Broad and I'm the High;
We are the University.

[In Hiscock (ed.), *The Balliol Rhymes* (1939)]

TRAPP, Joseph (1679–1747)

The King, observing with judicious eyes,
The state of both his universities,
To Oxford sent a troop of horse, and why?
That learned body wanted loyalty;
To Cambridge books, as very well discerning,
How much that loyal body wanted learning.

[Epigram on George I's donation of Bishop Ely's Library to Cambridge University]

WALKER, Alice (1944–)

Ignorance, arrogance and racism have bloomed as Superior Knowledge in all too many universities.

[*In Search of our Mothers' Gardens* (1983)]

See EDUCATION; KNOWLEDGE; LEARNING; SCHOLARS; SCHOOL; TEACHERS

V

VALUES

MONTHERLANT, Henry de (1896–1972)

Les valeurs nobles, á la fin, sont toujours vaincues; l'histoire est le récit de leurs défaites renouvelées.
Noble values, in the end, are always overcome; history tells the story of their defeat over and over again.

[*Le Maître de Santiago* (1947)]

STERNE, Laurence (1713–1768)

Honours, like impressions upon coin, may give an ideal and local value to a bit of base metal; but Gold and Silver will pass all the world over without any other recommendation than their own weight.

[*Tristram Shandy* (1759–1767)]

THATCHER, Margaret (1925–)

Victorian values … were the values when our country became great.

[Television interview, 1982]

USTINOV, Sir Peter (1921–)

When Mrs Thatcher says she has a nostalgia for Victorian values I don't think she realises that 90 per cent of her nostalgia would be satisfied in the Soviet Union.

[*The Observer*, 1987]

WOOLF, Virginia (1882–1941)

It is the masculine values that prevail. Speaking crudely, football and sport are 'important'; the worship of fashion, the buying of clothes 'trivial'… This is an important book, the critic assumes, because it deals with war. This is an insignificant book because it deals with feelings of women in a drawing-room … everywhere and much more subtly the difference of values persists.

[*A Room of One's Own* (1929)]

See PRINCIPLES

VANITY

THE BIBLE (King James Version)

Vanity of vanities, saith the Preacher, vanity of vanities; all is vanity.

[*Ecclesiastes*, 1:2]

COWLEY, Hannah (1743–1809)

Vanity, like murder, will out.

[*The Belle's Stratagem* (1780)]

EBNER-ESCHENBACH, Marie von (1830–1916)

Wir sind so eitel, dass uns sogar an der Meinung der Leute, an denen uns nichts liegt, etwas gelegen ist.
We are so vain that we are even concerned about the opinion of those people who are of no concern to us.

[*Aphorisms* (1880)]

STEVENSON, Robert Louis (1850–1894)

Vanity dies hard; in some obstinate cases it outlives the man.

[*Prince Otto*]

SWIFT, Jonathan (1667–1745)

'Tis an old maxim in the schools,
That vanity's the food of fools;
Yet now and then your men of wit
Will condescend to take a bit.

['Cadenus and Vanessa' (c. 1712)]

THACKERAY, William Makepeace (1811–1863)

Ah! *Vanitas Vanitatum*! Which of us is happy in this world? Which of us has his desire? or, having it, is satisfied? – Come, children, let us shut up the box and the puppets, for our play is played out.

[*Vanity Fair* (1847–1848)]

Oh, Vanity of vanities!
How wayward the decrees of Fate are;
How very weak the very wise,

How very small the very great are!

['Vanitas Vanitatum']

UNAMUNO, Miguel de (1864–1936)

Cúrate de la afección de preocuparte cómo aparezcas a los demás. Cuídate sólo de cómo aparezcas ante Dios, cuídate de la idea que de ti Dios tenga.
Cure yourself of the disease of worrying about how you appear to others. Concern yourself only with how you appear before God, concern yourself with the idea which God has of you.

[*Vida de Don Quijote y Sancho* (1914)]

See APPEARANCE; PRIDE; SELF

VEGETARIANISM

CAMPBELL, Mrs Patrick (1865–1940)

[To Bernard Shaw, a vegetarian]
Some day you'll eat a pork chop, Joey, and then God help all women.

[In Woollcott, *While Rome Burns* (1934)]

DAVIS, Miles (1926–1991)

[On vegetarianism]
I figure if horses can eat green shit and be strong and run like motherfuckers, why shouldn't I?

[In Ian Carr, *Miles Davis: a Critical Biography* (1982)]

LANG, K.D (1961–)

If you knew how meat was made, you'd probably lose your lunch. I'm from cattle country. That's why I became a vegetarian.

OBIS, Paul

[Founder of *Vegetarian Times* on his decision to start eating meat, 1997]
Twenty-two years of tofu is a lot of time.

See DIETS; DINING; FOOD

VICE

CRISP, Quentin (1908–)

Vice is its own reward.

[*The Naked Civil Servant* (1968)]

PROVERB

Vice is often clothed in virtue's habit.

See CRIME; EVIL; SIN; VIRTUE

VICTORY

CHURCHILL, Sir Winston (1874–1965)

You ask, what is our aim? I can answer that in one word: victory at all costs, victory in spite of all terror, victory however long and hard the road may be; for without victory there is no survival.

[Speech, House of Commons, May 1940]

DUVAL, Robert

[As Colonel Killgore in *Apocalypse Now*, 1977]
I love the smell of Napalm in the morning … smells like victory.

KENNEDY, John F. (1917–1963)

Victory has a thousand fathers but defeat is an orphan.

[Attr.]

KHRUSHCHEV, Nikita (1894–1971)

[Of the Cuban missile crisis]
People talk about who won and who lost. Human reason won. Mankind won.

[*The Observer*, 1962]

MACARTHUR, Douglas (1880–1964)

In war there is no substitute for victory.

[Speech to Congress, 1951]

MARCY, William (1786–1857)

[On the politicians of New York]
They see nothing wrong in the rule, that to the victor belong the spoils of the enemy.

[Speech, 1832]

MCLENNAN, Murdoch (fl. 1715)

There's some say that we wan, some say that they wan,
Some say that nane wan at a', man;
But one thing I'm sure, that at Sheriffmuir
A battle there was which I saw, man:
And we ran, and they ran, and they ran, and we ran,

And we ran; and they ran awa', man!

[In J. Woodfall Ebsworth (ed.), *Roxburghe Ballads* (1889)]

NELSON, Lord (1758–1805)

[At the Battle of the Nile, 1798]

Victory is not a name strong enough for such a scene.

[In Robert Southey, *The Life of Nelson* (1860)]

SOUTHEY, Robert (1774–1843)

'And everybody praised the Duke,
Who this great fight did win.'
'But what good came of it at last?'
Quoth little Peterkin.
'Why that I cannot tell,' said he,
'But 'twas a famous victory.'

['The Battle of Blenheim' (1798)]

See SUCCESS; WAR

VIOLENCE

ALI, Muhammad (1942–)

Fighting is not the answer to frustration and hate. It is a sport, not a philosophy of life.

[Interview, *TV Guide* magazine, 1999]

ASCHERSON, Neal (1932–)

Rioting is at least as English as thatched cottages and honey still for tea.

[*The Observer*, 1985]

ASIMOV, Isaac (1920–1992)

Violence is the last refuge of the incompetent.

[*Foundation* (1951)]

BRIEN, Alan (1925–)

Violence is the repartee of the illiterate.

[*Punch*, 1973]

BRIGHT, John (1811–1889)

Force is not a remedy.

[Speech, 1880]

BRONOWSKI, Jacob (1908–1974)

The wish to hurt, the momentary intoxication with pain, is the loophole through which the pervert climbs into the minds of ordinary men.

[*The Face of Violence* (1954)]

BURKE, Edmund (1729–1797)

The use of force alone is but temporary. It may subdue for a moment; but it does not remove the necessity of subduing again: and a nation is not governed, which is perpetually to be conquered.

[*Speech on Conciliation with America* (1775)]

EAMES, Dr Robin (1940–)

[Referring to the Enniskillen bombing, 8 November 1987]

'... I see,' he said with emphasis, 'the faces of the little children who have lost a father, as they walk behind the coffin with roses in their hands. I see the faces of good, honest, decent people who have never done wrong to anyone else, who have lost a loved one, blown to bits by a terrorist bomb. And of course I weep.'

[*The Observer*, 1992]

FONTAINE, Jean de la (1621–1695)

La raison du plus fort est toujours la meilleure.
The reason of the strongest is always the best.

['Le loup et l'agneau']

HORACE (65–8 BC)

Vis consili expers mole ruit sua.
Brute force without judgement collapses under its own weight.

[*Odes*]

INGE, William Ralph (1860–1954)

A man may build himself a throne of bayonets, but he cannot sit upon it.

[*Philosophy of Plotinus* (1923)]

KING, Martin Luther (1929–1968)

A riot is at bottom the language of the unheard.

[*Chaos or Community* (1967)]

KORAN

Let there be no violence in religion.

[Chapter 2]

LAING, R.D. (1927–1989)

We are effectively destroying ourselves by violence masquerading as love.

[*The Politics of Experience* (1967)]

MACKENZIE, Sir Compton (1883–1972)

There is little to choose morally between beating up a man physically and beating him up mentally.

[*On Moral Courage* (1962)]

MILTON, John (1608–1674)

… who overcomes
By force, hath overcome but half his foe.

[*Paradise Lost* (1667)]

READING, the Dowager Duchess of

We are a nation of yobs. Now that we don't have war, what's wrong with a good punch-up?

[*The Observer*, 1998]

TROTSKY, Leon (1879–1940)

Where force is necessary, one should make use of it boldly, resolutely, and right to the end. But it is as well to know the limitations of force; to know where to combine force with manoeuvre, assault with conciliation.

[*What Next?* (1932)]

UNAMUNO, Miguel de (1864–1936)

[Of Franco's supporters]
Vencer no es convencer.
To conquer is not to convince.

[Speech, 1936]

See CRUELTY; FORCE; WAR; WEAPONS

VIRTUE

ALDA, Alan (1936–)

It's too bad I'm not as wonderful a person as people say I am, because the world could use a few people like that.

ARISTOTLE (384–322 BC)

Moral virtue is the child of habit.

[*Nicomachean Ethics*]

Moral virtues we acquire through practice like the arts.

[*Nicomachean Ethics*]

BACON, Francis (1561–1626)

Virtue is like a rich stone, best plain set.

['Of Beauty' (1625)]

BAGEHOT, Walter (1826–1877)

Nothing is more unpleasant than a virtuous person with a mean mind.

[*Literary Studies* (1879)]

BRECHT, Bertolt (1898–1956)

Wenn es wo so grosse Tugenden gibt, das beweist, dass da etwas faul ist.
Whenever there are such great virtues, it's proof that something's fishy.

[*Mother Courage and her Children* (1941)]

BROWNE, Sir Thomas (1605–1682)

There is no road or ready way to virtue.

[*Religio Medici* (1643)]

BUTLER, Samuel (1835–1902)

Virtue and vice are like life and death, or mind and matter: things which cannot exist without being qualified by their opposite.

[*The Way of All Flesh* (1903)]

COLETTE (1873–1954)

My virtue's still far too small, I don't trot it out and about yet.

[*Claudine at School* (1900)]

CONFUCIUS (c.550–c.478 BC)

Fine words and an insinuating appearance are seldom associated with true virtue.

[*Analects*]

To be able to practise five things everywhere under heaven constitutes perfect virtue … gravity, generosity of soul, sincerity, earnestness, and kindness.

[*Analects*]

Virtue is not left to stand alone. He who practises it will have neighbours.

[*Analects*]

CONGREVE, William (1670–1729)

For 'tis some virtue, virtue to commend.

['To Sir Godfrey Kneller']

FLETCHER, John (1579–1625)

'Tis virtue, and not birth that makes us noble:
Great actions speak great minds, and such
should govern.

[The Prophetess (1647)]

GOLDSMITH, Oliver (c.1728–1774)

The virtue which requires to be ever
guarded, is scarce worth the sentinel.

[The Vicar of Wakefield (1766)]

HAZLITT, William (1778–1830)

The greatest offence against virtue is to
speak ill of it.

[London Weekly Review, 1828]

HERBERT, George (1593–1633)

Onely a sweet and vertuous soul,
Like season'd timber, never gives;
But though the whole world turn to coal,
Then chiefly lives.

[The Temple (1633)]

JUVENAL (c.60–130)

Nobilitas sola est atque unica virtus.
The one and only true nobility is virtue.

[Satires]

KINGSLEY, Charles (1819–1875)

To be discontented with the divine
discontent, and to be ashamed with the
noble shame, is the very germ and first
upgrowth of all virtue.

[Health and Education (1874)]

LA ROCHEFOUCAULD (1613–1680)

Il faut de plus grandes vertus pour soutenir la bonne
fortune que la mauvaise.
Greater virtues are needed to sustain good
fortune than bad.

[Maximes (1678)]

MARLOWE, Christopher (1564–1593)

Virtue is the fount whence honour springs.

[Tamburlaine the Great (1590)]

MILTON, John (1608–1674)

Most men admire

Vertue, who follow not her lore.

[Paradise Regained (1671)]

MOLIÈRE (1622–1673)

Il faut, parmi le monde, une vertu traitable.
Virtue, in this world, should be
accommodating.

[Le Misanthrope (1666)]

MONTAIGNE, Michel de (1533–1592)

La vertu refuse la facilité pour compagne … elle
demande un chemin âpre et épineux.
Virtue shuns ease as a companion. It needs a
rough and thorny path.

[Essais (1580)]

PERSIUS FLACCUS, Aulus (AD 34–62)

Virtutem videant intabescantque relicta.
Let them see virtue and pine away for having
lost it.

[Satires]

POPE, Alexander (1688–1744)

When men grow virtuous in their old age,
they only make a sacrifice to God of the
devil's leavings.

[Miscellanies (1727)]

SHAKESPEARE, William (1564–1616)

Dost thou think, because thou art virtuous,
there shall be no more cakes and ale?

[Twelfth Night, II.iii]

SHAW, George Bernard (1856–1950)

What is virtue but the Trade Unionism of the
married?

[Man and Superman (1903)]

SKINNER, Cornelia Otis (1901–1979)

Woman's virtue is man's greatest invention.

[Attr.]

STEELE, Sir Richard (1672–1729)

Will Honeycomb calls these over-offended
Ladies the outrageously virtuous.

[The Spectator, 266, 1712]

TAINE, Hippolyte Adolphe (1828–1893)

Le vice et la vertu sont des produits comme le vitriol
et le sucre.
Vice and virtues are products like sulphuric

acid and sugar.

[*History of English Literature*, 1863)]

WALPOLE, Horace (1717–1797)

Tell me, ye divines, which is the most virtuous man, he who begets twenty bastards, or he who sacrifices an hundred thousand lives?

[Letter to Sir Horace Mann, 1778]

Virtue knows to a farthing what it has lost by not having been vice.

[In Kronenberger, *The Extraordinary Mr. Wilkes* (1974)]

WALTON, Izaak (1593–1683)

Good company and good discourse are the very sinews of virtue.

[*The Compleat Angler* (1653)]

WASHINGTON, George (1732–1799)

Few men have virtue to withstand the highest bidder.

[*Moral Maxims*]

WHITE, Patrick (1912–1990)

Virtue is … frequently in the nature of an iceberg, the other parts of it submerged.

[*The Tree of Man* (1955)]

WILLIAMS, William Carlos (1883–1963)

no woman is virtuous

who does not give herself to her lover

– forthwith.

[*Paterson* (1946–1958)]

WOTTON, Sir Henry (1568–1639)

Virtue is the roughest way,
But proves at night a bed of down.

['Upon the Imprisonment of the Earl of Essex']

See GOOD AND EVIL; GOODNESS; MORALITY; PRINCIPLES; VICE

W

WALES

THOMAS, Dylan (1914–1953)
[Referring to Wales]
The land of my fathers. My fathers can have it.

[In John Ackerman, *Dylan Thomas* (1991)]

THOMAS, Edward (1878–1917)
Make me content
With some sweetness
From Wales
Whose nightingales
Have no wings.

['Words']

THOMAS, Gwyn (1913–1981)
I wanted a play that would paint the full face of sensuality, rebellion and revivalism. In South Wales these three phenomena have played second fiddle only to the Rugby Union which is a distillation of all three.

[*Jackie the Jumper* (1962)]

There are still parts of Wales where the only concession to gaiety is a striped shroud.

[*Punch*, 1958]

WAUGH, Evelyn (1903–1966)
'The Welsh,' said the Doctor, 'are the only nation in the world that has produced no graphic or plastic art, no architecture, no drama. They just sing,' he said with disgust, 'sing and blow down wind instruments of plated silver.'

[*Decline and Fall* (1928)]

WAR

ACHESON, Dean (1893–1971)
[Of the Vietnam war]
It is worse than immoral, it's a mistake.

[Quoted on Alistair Cooke's radio programme *Letter from America*]

ADAMS, Charles Francis (1807–1886)
It would be superfluous in me to point out to your lordship that this is war.

[Dispatch to Earl Russell, September 1863]

ANGELL, Norman (1872–1967)
The Great Illusion.

[Title of book, 1910, which argued against the concept that war was economically advantageous to a nation]

ANONYMOUS
Friendly fire isn't.

The most dangerous thing in the combat zone is an officer with a map.

The quartermaster has only two sizes, too large and too small.

[American officer on the town of Ben Tre, Vietnam, during the Tet offensive, 1968]
To save the town, it became necessary to destroy it.

ARMISTEAD, Lewis (1817–1863)
[Spoken at Gettysburg, 1863]
Give them the cold steel, boys!

[Attr.]

ARNOLD, Matthew (1822–1888)
But now in blood and battles was my youth,
And full of blood and battles is my age;
And I shall never end this life of blood.

['Sohrab and Rustum' (1853)]

ASQUITH, Herbert (1852–1928)
We shall never sheath the sword which we have not lightly drawn until Belgium recovers in full measure all and more than she has sacrificed, until France is adequately secured against the menace of aggression, until the rights of the smaller nationalities of Europe are placed upon an unassailable foundation, and until the military domination of Prussia is wholly and finally destroyed.

[Speech, 1914]

AUDEN, W.H. (1907–1973)

O what is that sound which so thrills the ear
Down in the valley drumming, drumming?
Only the scarlet soldiers, dear,
The soldiers coming …

O it's broken the lock and splintered the door,
O it's the gate where they're turning, turning;
Their boots are heavy on the floor
And their eyes are burning.

[*Collected Poems, 1933–1938*]

AUSTEN, Jane (1775–1817)

[Of the Battle of Albuera in 1811]
How horrible it is to have so many people
killed! – And what a blessing that one cares
for none of them!

[*Letter to Cassandra Austen, 1811*]

BALDWIN, Stanley (1867–1947)

I think it is well also for the man in the street
to realise that there is no power on earth
that can protect him from being bombed.
Whatever people may tell him, the bomber
will always get through. The only defence is
in offence, which means that you have to kill
more women and children more quickly than
the enemy if you want to save yourselves.

[*Speech, 1932*]

BARUCH, Bernard M. (1870–1965)

Let us not be deceived – we are today in the
midst of a cold war.

[*Speech, 1947*]

BEERS, Ethel Lynn (1827–1879)

All quiet along the Potomac to-night,
No sound save the rush of the river,
While soft falls the dew on the face of the
dead –
The picket's off duty forever.

[In *Harper's Magazine*, 1861, 'The Picket Guard']

BELL, Martin

[Comment on NATO's accidental bombing of the
Chinese Embassy in Belgrade]
The greatest military alliance in the world is
becoming 'the gang that cannot shoot
straight'.

[*Speech, House of Commons, May 1999*]

BELLOC, Hilaire (1870–1953)

Whatever happens, we have got
The Maxim Gun, and they have not.

[*Modern Traveller* (1898)]

BENNETT, Alan (1934–)

I have never understood this liking for war. It
panders to instincts already catered for
within the scope of any respectable
domestic establishment.

[*Forty Years On* (1969)]

BETHMANN HOLLWEG, Theobald von (1856–1921)

Just for a word – 'neutrality', a word which in
wartime has so often been disregarded, just
for a scrap of paper – Great Britain is going
to make war.

[*Letter, 1914*]

BETHUNE, Frank Pogson (1877–1942)

Special Orders to No. 1 Section

• The position will be held, and the section
  will remain here until relieved.

• The enemy cannot be allowed to interfere
  with the programme.

• If the section cannot remain here alive, it
  will remain here dead, but in any case it will
  remain here.

• Should any man, through shell shock or
  other cause, attempt to surrender, he will
  remain here dead.

• Should all guns be blown out, the section
  will use Mills grenades, and other novelties.

• Finally, the position, as stated, will be held.

[An order issued by Bethune to his machine gun
section in France, 13 March 1918]

THE BIBLE
(King James Version)

All they that take the sword shall perish with
the sword.

[*Matthew*, 26:52]

BLACKER, Valentine (1778–1823)

Put your trust in God, my boys, and keep
your powder dry.

[*Oliver's Advice* (1856)]

BORGES, Jorge Luis (1899–1986)

[On the Falklands War of 1982]

The Falklands thing was a fight between two bald men over a comb.

[*Time*, 1983]

BOSQUET, Pierre François Joseph (1810–1861)

[Remark on witnessing the Charge of the Light Brigade, 1854]

C'est magnifique mais ce n'est pas la guerre.

It is magnificent, but it is not war.

[Attr.]

BRADLEY, Omar Nelson (1893–1981)

[On General MacArthur's proposal to carry the Korean war into China]

The wrong war, at the wrong place, at the wrong time, and with the wrong enemy.

[Senate inquiry, 1951]

The way to win an atomic war is to make certain it never starts.

[*The Observer*, 1952]

BRECHT, Bertolt (1898–1956)

Hier ist zu lang kein Krieg gewesen.

It's too long since there's been a war here.

[*Mother Courage and her Children* (1941)]

Einen vollkommenen Krieg, wo man sagen könnt: an dem ist nix mehr auszusetzen, wirds vielleicht nie geben.

There'll perhaps never be a perfect war where you could say that there was nothing wrong with it.

[*Mother Courage and her Children* (1941)]

Der Krieg findet immer einen Ausweg.

War always finds a solution.

[*Mother Courage and her Children* (1941)]

BRIGHT, John (1811–1889)

[Comment on the American Civil War]

My opinion is that the Northern States will manage somehow to muddle through.

[Attr.]

[Referring to the Crimean War]

The angel of death has been abroad throughout the land; you may almost hear the beating of his wings.

[Speech, 1855]

BROOKE, Rupert (1887–1915)

Now, God be thanked Who has matched us with His hour,
And caught our youth, and wakened us from sleeping ...

Leave the sick hearts that honour could not move,
And half-men, and their dirty songs and dreary,
And all the little emptiness of love ...

Naught broken save this body, lost but breath;
Nothing to shake the laughing heart's long peace there
But only agony, and that has ending;
And the worst friend and enemy is but Death.

['Peace' (1914)]

CARLYLE, Thomas (1795–1881)

[Referring to the American Civil War]

There they are cutting each other's throats, because one half of them prefer hiring their servants for life, and the other by the hour.

[Attr.]

CHAMBERLAIN, Neville (1869–1940)

In war, whichever side may call itself the victor, there are no winners, but all are losers.

[Speech, Kettering, 1938]

This morning the British Ambassador in Berlin handed the German Government a final note, stating that, unless the British Government heard from them by eleven o'clock that they were prepared at once to withdraw their troops from Poland, a state of war would exist between us. I have to tell you now that no such undertaking has been received, and that consequently this country is at war with Germany.

[Radio broadcast, 3 September 1939]

We have resolved to finish it. It is the evil things we shall be fighting against – brute force, bad faith, injustice, oppression and persecution and against them I am certain that the right will prevail.

[Radio broadcast, 3 September 1939]

[On the annexation by Germany of the Sudetenland]
How horrible, fantastic, incredible, it is that we should be digging trenches and trying on gas-masks here because of a quarrel in a far-away country between people of whom we know nothing.

[Speech, 1938]

CHRISTIE, Dame Agatha (1890–1976)

One is left with the horrible feeling now that war settles nothing; that to win a war is as disastrous as to lose one!

[*An Autobiography* (1977)]

CHURCHILL, Sir Winston (1874–1965)

We shall not flag or fail. We shall go on to the end. We shall fight in France, we shall fight on the seas and oceans, we shall fight with growing confidence and growing strength in the air, we shall defend our island, whatever the cost may be, we shall fight on the beaches, we shall fight on the landing grounds, we shall fight in the fields and in the streets, we shall fight in the hills; we shall never surrender.

[Speech, June 1940]

Let us therefore brace ourselves to our duties, and so bear ourselves that, if the British Empire and its Commonwealth last for a thousand years, men will still say, 'This was their finest hour'.

[Speech, June 1940]

The battle of Britain is about to begin.

[Speech, July 1940]

No one can guarantee success in war, but only deserve it.

[*The Second World War* (1948–1954)]

[Referring to Dunkirk]
Wars are not won by evacuations.

[*The Second World War* (1948–1954)]

[On the ceremonial form of the declaration of war against Japan, 8 December 1941]
When you have to kill a man it costs nothing to be polite.

[*The Second World War* (1948–1954)]

Before Alamein we never had a victory. After Alamein we never had a defeat.

[*The Second World War* (1948–1954)]

[On RAF pilots in the Battle of Britain]
Never in the field of human conflict was so much owed by so many to so few.

[Speech, 1940]

CICERO (106–43 BC)

Silent enim leges inter arma.
Laws are silent in war.

[*Pro Milone*]

Nervos belli, pecuniam infinitam.
The sinews of war, unlimited money.

[*Philippic*]

CLAUSEWITZ, Karl von (1780–1831)

Der Krieg ist nichts als eine Fortsetzung des politischen Verkehrs mit Einmischung anderer Mittel.
War is nothing but a continuation of politics by other means.

[*On War* (1834)]

CLEMENCEAU, Georges (1841–1929)

La guerre! C'est une chose trop grave pour la confier á des militaires.
War is much too serious a thing to be left to the military.

[In Suarez, *Sixty Years of French History: Clemenceau*]

DALY, Dan (1874–1937)

[Remark during Allied resistance at Belleau Wood, 1918]
Come on, you sons of bitches! Do you want to live for ever?

[Attr.]

DAWE, (Donald) Bruce (1930–)

All day, day after day, they're bringing them home,
they're picking them up, those they can find, and bringing them home,
they're bringing them in, piled on the hulls of

Grants, in trucks, in convoys,
they're zipping them up in green plastic
bags,
they're tagging them now in Saigon, in the
mortuary coolness,
they're giving them names, they're rolling
them out of
the deep-freeze lockers – on the tarmac at
Tan Son Nhut
the noble jets are whining like hounds,
they are bringing them home …

telegrams tremble like leaves from a
wintering tree
and the spider grief swings in his bitter
geometry
– they're bringing them home, now, too late,
too early.

['Homecoming' (1971)]

DRYDEN, John (1631–1700)

All delays are dangerous in war.

[*Tyrannic Love* (1669)]

War is the trade of kings.

[*King Arthur* (1691)]

EDEN, Anthony (1897–1977)

We are not at war with Egypt. We are in
armed conflict.

[Speech, 1956]

ELIZABETH, the Queen Mother (1900–)

[After Buckingham Palace was bombed during the
Blitz in 1940]
I'm glad we've been bombed. It makes me
feel I can look the East End in the face.

[Attr.]

ELLIS, Havelock (1859–1939)

In many a war it has been the vanquished,
not the victor, who has carried off the finest
spoils.

[*The Soul of Spain* (1908)]

ERASMUS (c.1466–1536)

Dulce bellum inexpertis.
War is sweet to those who do not fight.

[*Adagia* (1500)]

FOCH, Ferdinand (1851–1929)

[Dispatch during the Battle of the Marne, 1914]
*Mon centre cède, ma droite recule, situation
excellente. J'attaque!*
My centre is giving way, my right is
retreating; situation excellent. I shall attack.

[Attr.]

FONTENELLE, Bernard (1657–1757)

I detest war: it ruins conversation.

[In Auden, *A Certain World* (1970)]

FORGY, Howell (1908–1983)

[Remark at Pearl Harbour, 1941]
Praise the Lord and pass the ammunition.

[Attr.]

GOLDWATER, Barry (1909–1998)

You've got to forget about this civilian.
Whenever you drop bombs, you're going to
hit civilians.

[Speech, 1967]

GORKY, Maxim (1868–1936)

[On Germany's declaration of war against Russia]
One thing is clear; we are entering the first
act of a world-wide tragedy.

[Attr., 1914]

GREY, Edward, Viscount of Fallodon (1862–1933)

[To a caller at the Foreign Office in August 1914]
The lamps are going out all over Europe; we
shall not see them lit again in our lifetime.

[In *Twenty-five Years*]

HAIG, Douglas (1861–1928)

Every position must be held to the last man:
there must be no retirement. With our backs to
the wall, and believing in the justice of our
cause, each one of us must fight on to the end.

[Order to British forces on the Western Front, 1918]

HANRAHAN, Brian (1949–)

[Reporting the British attack on Port Stanley
airport, during the Falklands war]
I'm not allowed to say how many planes
joined the raid but I counted them all out
and I counted them all back.

[BBC report, 1 May 1982]

HARKIN, Thomas (1939–)

The Gulf War was like teenage sex. We got in too soon and we got out too soon.

[*Independent on Sunday*, 1991]

HIROHITO, Emperor (1901–1989)

The war situation has developed not necessarily to Japan's advantage.

[Announcing Japan's surrender, 15 August 1945]

HITLER, Adolf (1889–1945)

[Said in 1939]

In starting and waging a war it is not right that matters, but victory.

[In Shirer, *The Rise and Fall of the Third Reich* (1960)]

HOBBES, Thomas (1588–1679)

Force, and fraud, are in war the two cardinal virtues.

[*Leviathan* (1651)]

HOFFMAN, Abbie

I believe in compulsory cannibalism. If people were forced to eat what they killed, there would be no more wars.

HOOVER, Herbert Clark (1874–1964)

Older men declare war. But it is youth that must fight and die.

[Speech, 1944]

JACKSON, Andrew (1767–1845)

[Order given during the Battle of New Orleans, American War of Independence]

Elevate them guns a little lower.

[Attr.]

JARRELL, Randall (1914–1965)

From my mother's sleep I fell into the State,
And I hunched in its belly till my wet fur froze.
Six miles from earth, loosed from its dream of life,
I woke to black flak and the nightmare fighters.
When I died they washed me out of the turret with a hose.

['The Death of the Ball Turret Gunner' (1969)]

JOHNSON, Hiram (1866–1945)

The first casualty when war comes is truth.

[Speech, US Senate, 1917]

KEY, Ellen (1849–1926)

Everything, everything in war is barbaric … But the worst barbarity of war is that it forces men collectively to commit acts against which individually they would revolt with their whole being.

[*War, Peace, and the Future* (1916)]

Formerly, a nation that broke the peace did not trouble to try and prove to the world that it was done solely from higher motives … Now war has a bad conscience. Now every nation assures us that it is bleeding for a human cause, the fate of which hangs in the balance of its victory … No nation will admit that it was only to insure its own safety that it declared war. No nation dares to admit the guilt of blood before the world.

[*War, Peace, and the Future* (1916)]

KHRUSHCHEV, Nikita (1894–1971)

[Of the Cuban missile crisis]

Only lunatics or suicides, who themselves want to perish and to destroy the whole world before they die, could want an atomic war.

[*The Independent*, 1992]

LAO-TZU (c.604–531 BC)

To joy in conquest is to joy in the loss of human life.

[*Tao Te Ching*]

LAW, Bonar (1858–1923)

I said [in 1911] that if ever war arose between Great Britain and Germany it would not be due to inevitable causes, for I did not believe in inevitable war. I said it would be due to human folly.

[Speech, House of Commons, 1914]

LAWRENCE, D.H. (1885–1930)

We have all lost the war. All Europe.

[*The Ladybird* (1923)]

LEE, Robert E. (1807–1870)

It is well that war is so terrible – we would grow too fond of it.

[Remark after the Battle of Fredericksburg, 1862]

LLOYD GEORGE, David (1863–1945)

[Referring to the popular opinion that World War I

would be the last major war]
This war, like the next war, is a war to end war.

[Attr.]

LOW, Sir David (1891–1963)
I have never met anybody who wasn't against war. Even Hitler and Mussolini were, according to themselves.

[In Jonathon Green (ed.), *A Dictionary of Contemporary Quotations* (1982)]

MACAULAY, Lord (1800–1859)
[Of John Hampden]
He knew that the essence of war is violence, and that moderation in war is imbecility.

[*Collected Essays* (1843)]

MACDONALD, Ramsay (1866–1937)
We hear war called murder. It is not: it is suicide.

[*The Observer*, 1930]

MANNING, Frederic (1882–1935)
War is waged by men; not by beasts, or by gods. It is a peculiar human activity. To call it a crime against mankind is to miss half its significance; it is also the punishment of a crime.

[*Her Privates We* (1929)]

MAO TSE-TUNG (1893–1976)
We are advocates of the abolition of war, we do not want war; but war can only be abolished through war, and in order to get rid of the gun it is necessary to take up the gun.

[*Quotations from Chairman Mao Tse-Tung*]

MARLOWE, Christopher (1564–1593)
Accurs'd be he that first invented war!

[*Tamburlaine the Great* (1590)]

MARY, Queen Consort (1867–1953)
[Remark to soldier who had exclaimed 'No more bloody wars for me']
No more bloody wars, no more bloody medals.

[Attr.]

MCAULIFFE, Anthony C., Major-General
[Response when surrounded by Germans and ordered to surrender during World War II]
Nuts!

MCCLELLAN, George (1826–1885)
[Said during the American Civil War]
All quiet along the Potomac.

[Attr.]

MEIR, Golda (1898–1978)
A leader who doesn't hesitate before he sends his nation into battle is not fit to be a leader.

[I. and M. Shenker, *As Good as Golda* (1943)]

MENCKEN, H.L. (1880–1956)
War will never cease until babies begin to come into the world with larger cerebrums and smaller adrenal glands.

[*Notebooks* (1956)]

MICHAELIS, John H. (1912–1985)
[Said to the 27th Infantry (Wolfhound) Regiment during the Korean War]
You're not here to die for your country. You're here to make those – die for theirs.

[Attr.]

MILOSEVIC, Slobodan
[Warning NATO of the consequences of invading Serbia]
The earth itself will burn under the occupiers' feet.

[*The Times*, April 1999]

MILTON, John (1608–1674)
For what can Warr, but endless warr still breed.

['On the Lord Generall Fairfax at the seige of Colchester' (1648)]

MIRABEAU, Comte de (1749–1791)
La guerre est l'industrie nationale de la Prusse.
War is Prussia's national industry.

[Attr.]

MOLTKE, Helmuth von (1800–1891)
Der ewige Friede ist ein Traum, und nicht einmal ein schöner und der Krieg ein Glied in Gottes

Weltordnung … Ohne den Krieg würde die Welt in Materialismus versumpfen.
Eternal peace is a dream, and not even a pleasant one; and war is an integral part of the way God has ordered the world … Without war, the world would sink in the mire of materialism.

[Letter to Dr J.K. Bluntschli, 1880]

MONASH, Sir John (1865–1931)
[In France, 1917]
[War] is not a business in which one can take any pride or pleasure, or even pretend to. Its horror, its ghastly inefficiency, its unspeakable cruelty and misery has always appalled me, but there is nothing to do but to set one's teeth and stick it out as long as one can.

[In Geoffrey Serle, *John Monash* (1982)]

MONTAGUE, C.E. (1867–1928)
War hath no fury like a non-combatant.

[*Disenchantment* (1922)]

MONTGOMERY, Viscount (1887–1976)
[On American policy in Vietnam]
The US has broken the second rule of war. That is, don't go fighting with your land army on the mainland of Asia. Rule One is don't march on Moscow. I developed these two rules myself.

[Speech, 1962]

NAPOLEON I (1769–1821)
A la guerre, les trois quarts sont des affaires morales, la balance des forces réelles n'est que pour un autre quart.
In war, three-quarters depends on matters of character and morale; the balance of manpower and equipment counts only for the remaining quarter.

[*Correspondance de Napoléon I* (1854–1869)]

[Referring to the carnage at the Battle of Borodino, 1812]
It's the most beautiful battlefield I've ever seen.

[Attr.]

NAPOLEON III (1808–1873)
[After the narrow and bloody French victory at

Solferino, 1859]
I don't care for war, there's far too much luck in it for my liking.

[In E. Crankshaw, *The Fall of the House of Habsburg*]

NELSON, Lord (1758–1805)
[At the Battle of Copenhagen, 1801]
Leave off action? Now, damn me if I do! … I have only one eye – I have a right to be blind sometimes … I really do not see the signal! … Damn the signal!

[In Southey, *The Life of Nelson* (1860)]

ORWELL, George (1903–1950)
The quickest way of ending a war is to lose it.

[*Polemic* (1946)]

OWEN, Wilfred (1893–1918)
What passing-bells for these who die as cattle?
Only the monstrous anger of the guns.
Only the stuttering rifles' rapid rattle
Can patter out their hasty orisons.

['Anthem for Doomed Youth' (1917)]

My subject is War, and the pity of War. The Poetry is in the pity.

[Quoted in *Poems* (1963), Preface]

PANKHURST, Sylvia (1882–1960)
I could not give my name to aid the slaughter in this war, fought on both sides for grossly material ends, which did not justify the sacrifice of a single mother's son. Clearly I must continue to oppose it, and expose it, to all whom I could reach with voice or pen.

[*The Home Front*]

PLOMER, William (1903–1973)
Out of that bungled, unwise war
An alp of unforgiveness grew.

['The Boer War' (1932)]

PRESCOTT, William (1726–1795)
[Command given at the Battle of Bunker Hill, 1775]
Don't fire until you see the whites of their eyes.

[Attr]

PYRRHUS (319–272 BC)
[After a hard-won battle]
If we are victorious against the Romans in

one more battle we shall be utterly ruined.

[In Plutarch, *Lives*]

RABELAIS, François (c.1494–c.1553)

Guerre faicte sans bonne provision d'argent n'a qu'un souspirail de vigueur. Les nerfs des batailles sont les pécunes.
The strength of a war waged without a good supply of money is as fleeting as a breath. Money is the sinews of battle.

[*Gargantua* (1534)]

RAE, John (1931–)

War is, after all, the universal perversion. We are all tainted: if we cannot experience our perversion at first hand we spend our time reading war stories, the pornography of war; or seeing war films, the blue films of war; or titillating our senses with the imagination of great deeds, the masturbation of war.

[*The Custard Boys* (1960)]

REED, Henry (1914–1986)

In a civil war, the general must know – and I'm afraid it's a thing rather of instinct than of practice – he must know exactly when to move over to the other side.

[*Not a Drum was Heard: The War Memoirs of General Gland* (1959)]

REPINGTON, Lieut-Col. Charles A'Court (1858–1925)

I saw Major Johnstone, who is here to lay the bases of an American History. We discussed the right name of the war. I said that we called it now The War, but that this could not last. The Napoleonic War was The Great War. To call it The German War was too much flattery for the Boche. I suggested The World War as a shade better title, and finally we mutually agreed to call it The First World War in order to prevent the millennium folk from forgetting that the history of the world was the history of war.

[Diary entry for 10 September 1918, published in *The First World War 1914–18* (1920)]

ROOSEVELT, Franklin Delano (1882–1945)

More than an end to war, we want an end to the beginnings of all wars.

[Speech, 1945]

RUBENS, Paul Alfred (1875–1917)

We don't want to lose you but we think you ought to go.

['Your King and Country Want You', song, 1914]

SALLUST (86–c.34 BC)

Omne bellum sumi facile, ceterum aegaerrime desinere, non in ejusdem potestate initium ejus et finem esse.
Every war is easy to begin but difficult to stop; its beginning and end are not in the control of the same person.

[*Jugurtha*]

SANDBURG, Carl (1878–1967)

Sometime they'll give a war and nobody will come.

[*The People, Yes* (1936)]

SASSOON, Siegfried (1886–1967)

Safe with his wound, a citizen of life,
He hobbled blithely through the garden gate,
And thought: 'Thank God they had to amputate!'.

['The One-Legged Man' (1916)]

I'd like to see a Tank come down the stalls,
Lurching to rag-time tunes, or 'Home, sweet Home,' –
And there'd be no more jokes in Music-halls
To mock the riddled corpses round Bapaume.

['Blighters' (1917)]

If I were fierce and bald and short of breath,
I'd live with scarlet Majors at the Base,
And speed glum heroes up the line to death …

And when the war is done and youth stone dead
I'd toddle safely home and die – in bed.

['Base Details' (1917)]

[From the statement sent to his commanding officer, July 1917]
I am making this statement as an act of wilful

defiance of military authority, because I believe that the War is being deliberately prolonged by those who have the power to end it … I have seen and endured the sufferings of the troops, and I can no longer be a party to prolong these sufferings for ends which I believe to be evil and unjust.

[*Memoirs of an Infantry Officer* (1930)]

SCHWARTZKOPF, Norman

[Describing Saddam Hussein of Iraq, 1991]
He is neither a strategist nor is he schooled in the operational arts, nor is he a tactician, nor is he a general. Other than that he's a great military man.

SERVICE, Robert W. (1874–1958)

When we, the Workers, all demand:'What are we fighting for?' …
Then, then we'll end that stupid crime, that devil's madness – War.

['Michael' (1921)]

SHAKESPEARE, William (1564–1616)

Once more unto the breach, dear friends, once more;
Or close the wall up with our English dead.
In peace there's nothing so becomes a man
As modest stillness and humility;
But when the blast of war blows in our ears,
Then imitate the action of the tiger:
Stiffen the sinews, summon up the blood,
Disguise fair nature with hard-favour'd rage;
Then lend the eye a terrible aspect.

[*Henry V*, III.i]

We few, we happy few, we band of brothers;
For he to-day that sheds his blood with me
Shall be my brother; be he ne'er so vile,
This day shall gentle his condition;
And gentlemen in England now a-bed
Shall think themselves accurs'd they were not here,
And hold their manhoods cheap whiles any speaks
That fought with us upon Saint Crispin's day.

[*Henry V*, IV.iii]

SHERMAN, William Tecumseh (1820–1891)

There is many a boy here today who looks on war as all glory, but, boys, it is all hell.

[Speech, 1880]

SPOCK, Dr Benjamin (1903–1998)

To win in Vietnam, we will have to exterminate a nation.

[*Dr Spock on Vietnam* (1968)]

STRACHEY, Lytton (1880–1932)

[Reply when asked by a Tribunal what he, as a conscientious objector, would do if he saw a German soldier trying to rape his sister]
I should try and come between them.

[In Holroyd, *Lytton Strachey: A Critical Biography* (1968)]

STRUTHER, Jan (1901–1953)

To abolish shooting before you had abolished war was rather like flecking a speck of dust off the top of a midden.

[*Mrs Miniver*, quoted in *The Times*, 1993]

SWIFT, Jonathan (1667–1745)

Hobbes clearly proves, that every creature Lives in a state of war by nature.

['On Poetry' (1733)]

TABER, Robert (20th century)

The guerrilla fights the war of the flea, and his military enemy suffers the dog's disadvantages: too much to defend; too small, ubiquitous, and agile an enemy to come to grips with.

[*The War of the Flea*]

TALLEYRAND, Charles-Maurice de (1754–1838)

War is much too serious to be left to the generals.

[Attr.]

TELLER, Edward (1908–)

Could we have avoided the tragedy of Hiroshima? Could we have started the atomic age with clean hands? No one knows. No one can find out.

UREY, Harold (1893–1981)

The next war will be fought with atom bombs and the one after that with spears.

[*The Observer*, 1946]

VIRGIL (70–19 BC)

Bella, horrida bella,
Et Thybrim multo spumantem sanguine cerno.
I see wars, dreadful wars, and the Tiber foaming with much blood.

VON SCHLIEFFEN, Alfred, Graf (1833–1913)

[Referring to the Schlieffen plan, a German military strategy to enter France by first going through Belgium]
When you march into France, let the last man on the right brush the Channel with his sleeve.

[In Barbara Tuchman, *The Guns of August 1914* (1964)]

VULLIAMY, Ed

[A pacifist until the war in Bosnia forced him to change his convictions]
Ironically, the horrors of war have taught me that there are things that are worse than war, and against them determined and careful war should be waged, in the name of the innocent and the weak.

[*The Weekend Guardian*, 1992]

WAUGH, Evelyn (1903–1966)

When the war broke out she took down the signed photograph of the Kaiser and, with some solemnity, hung it in the menservants' lavatory; it was her one combative action.

[*Vile Bodies* (1930)]

[Giving his opinions of warfare after the battle of Crete, 1941]
Like German opera, too long and too loud.

[Attr.]

WELLINGTON, Duke of (1769–1852)

All the business of war, and indeed all the business of life, is to endeavour to find out what you don't know by what you do; that's what I called 'guessing what was at the other side of the hill'.

[*The Croker Papers* (1885)]

I always say that, next to a battle lost, the greatest misery is a battle gained.

[In Rogers, *Recollections* (1859)]

[Refusing permission to shoot at Napoleon during the Battle of Waterloo]
It is not the business of generals to shoot one another.

[Attr.]

WHITE, Patrick (1912–1990)

But bombs are unbelievable until they actually fall.

[*Riders in the Chariot* (1961)]

WILSON, Woodrow (1856–1924)

Once lead this people into war and they'll forget there ever was such a thing as tolerance.

[In Dos Passos, *Mr Wilson's War* (1917)]

YOUNG, Edward (1683–1765)

One to destroy, is murder by the law;
And gibbets keep the lifted hand in awe;
To murder thousands, takes a specious name,
War's glorious art, and gives immortal fame.

[*Night-Thoughts on Life, Death and Immortality*]

See ARMY; DEFEAT; NAVY; NUCLEAR WEAPONS; PATRIOTISM; SACRIFICE; VICTORY; WAR AND PEACE

WAR AND PEACE

BLAKE, William (1757–1827)

Sweet Prince! the arts of peace are great,
And no less glorious than those of war.

[*Poetical Sketches* (1783)]

CHURCHILL, Sir Winston (1874–1965)

Peace with Germany and Japan on our terms will not bring much rest … As I observed last time, when the war of the giants is over the wars of the pygmies will begin.

[*The Second World War* (1948–1954)]

Those who can win a war well can rarely

make a good peace and those who could make a good peace would never have won the war.

[*My Early Life* (1930)]

In war, resolution; in defeat, defiance; in victory, magnanimity; in peace, goodwill.

[*The Gathering Storm*]

CLEMENCEAU, Georges (1841–1929)

[To General Mordacq, 11 November 1918]
We have won the war: now we have to win the peace, and it may be more difficult.

[In D.R. Watson, *Georges Clemenceau: a Political Biography* (1974)]

Il est plus facile de faire la guerre que la paix.
It is easier to make war than to make peace.

[Speech, 1919]

COWPER, William (1731–1800)

War lays a burden on the reeling state,
And peace does nothing to relieve the weight.

['Expostulation' (1782)]

FRANKLIN, Benjamin (1706–1790)

There never was a good war, or a bad peace.

[Letter to Josiah Quincy, 1783]

HARDY, Thomas (1840–1928)

My argument is that War makes rattling good history; but Peace is poor reading.

[*The Dynasts* 1903]

HERBERT, George (1593–1633)

He that makes a good war, makes a good peace.

[*Jacula Prudentum; or Outlandish Proverbs, Sentences &c.*,(1640)]

KELLOGG, Frank B. (1856–1937)

The high contracting parties solemnly declare in the names of their respective peoples that they condemn recourse to war for the solution of international controversies, and renounce it as an instrument of national policy in their relations with one another. The high contracting parties agree that the settlement or solution of all disputes or conflicts of

whatever nature or of whatever origin they may be, which may rise among them, shall never be sought except by pacific means.

[Peace Pact, 1928; possibly based on original text by Aristide Briand]

KETTLE, Thomas (1880–1916)

If I live, I mean to spend the rest of my life working for perpetual peace. I have seen war and faced artillery and know what an outrage it is against simple men.

[*Poems and Parodies*]

LAWRENCE, D.H. (1885–1930)

Loud peace propaganda makes war seem imminent.

[*Pansies* (1929)]

SHAKESPEARE, William (1564–1616)

Let me have war, say I; it exceeds peace as far as day does night; it's spritely, waking, audible, and full of vent. Peace is a very apoplexy, lethargy; mull'd, deaf, sleepy, insensible; a getter of more bastard children than war's a destroyer of men.

[*Coriolanus*, IV.v]

STEVENSON, Adlai (1900–1965)

Making peace is harder than making war.

[Address to Chicago Council on Foreign Relations, 1946]

TUCHOLSKY, Kurt (1890–1935)

Aber der Frieden ist undankbar, und weiss nie, dass er seinen Bestand nur dem Krieg dankt.
But peace is ungrateful and never knows it only owes its continued existence to war.

[To Arno Holz (1913)]

VEGETIUS RENATUS, Flavius (fl. c.AD 375)

Qui desiderat pacem, praeparet bellum.
Let him who desires peace be prepared for war.

[*Epitoma Rei Militaris*]

WILDER, Thornton (1897–1975)

When you're at war you think about a better life; when you're at peace you think about a more comfortable one.

[*The Skin of Our Teeth* (1942)]

See ARMY; DEFEAT; NAVY; NUCLEAR WEAPONS; PATRIOTISM; VICTORY; WAR

WATER

CHESTERTON, G.K. (1874–1936)

And Noah he often said to his wife when he sat down to dine,
'I don't care where the water goes if it doesn't get into the wine.' …

And water is on the Bishop's board and the Higher Thinker's shrine,
But I don't care where the water goes if it doesn't get into the wine.

[The Flying Inn (1914)]

COLERIDGE, Samuel Taylor (1772–1834)

Water, water, every where,
And all the boards did shrink;
Water, water, every where
Nor any drop to drink.

['The Rime of the Ancient Mariner' (1798)]

FIELDS, W.C. (1880–1946)

[His reason for not drinking water]
Fish fuck in it.

[Attr.]

HERBERT, Sir A.P. (1890–1971)

For any ceremonial purposes the otherwise excellent liquid, water, is unsuitable in colour and other respects.

[Uncommon Law (1935)]

LAWRENCE, D.H. (1885–1930)

Water is H2O, hydrogen two parts, oxygen one,
but there is also a third thing, that makes it water
and nobody knows what it is.

[Pansies (1929)]

ROBBINS, Tom (1936–)

Human beings were invented by water as a device for transporting itself from one place to another.

[Another Roadside Attraction (1971)]

SLESSOR, Kenneth (1901–1971)

The character and the life of Sydney are shaped continually and imperceptibly by the fingers of the Harbour, groping across the piers and jetties, clutching deeply into the hills, the water dyed a whole paint-box's armoury of colour with every breath of air, every shift of light or shade, according to the tide, the clock, the weather and the state of the moon. The water is like silk, like pewter, like blood, like a leopard's skin, and occasionally merely like water.

[Bread and Wine (1970)]

SMITH, Sydney (1771–1845)

I am better in health … and drinking nothing but London water, with a million insects in every drop. He who drinks a tumbler of London water has literally in his stomach more animated beings than there are men, women, and children on the face of the globe.

[Letter to Countess Grey, 1834]

THE WEATHER

AUSTEN, Jane (1775–1817)

What dreadful hot weather we have! It keeps me in a continual state of inelegance.

[Letter, 1796]

CHEKHOV, Anton (1860–1904)

He who doesn't notice whether it is winter or summer is happy. I think that if I were in Moscow, I wouldn't notice what the weather was like.

[The Three Sisters (1901)]

CONGREVE, William (1670–1729)

Is there in the world a climate more uncertain than our own? And, which is a natural consequence, is there any where a people more unsteady, more apt to discontent, more saturnine, dark and melancholic than our selves? Are we not of all people the most unfit to be alone, and most unsafe to be trusted with our selves?

[Amendments of Mr Collier's False and Imperfect Citations (1698)]

ELLIS, George (1753–1815)

Snowy, Flowy, Blowy,
Showery, Flowery, Bowery,
Hoppy, Croppy, Droppy,
Breezy, Sneezy, Freezy.

['The Twelve Months']

FISH, Michael (1944–)

[Said during the weather forecast just prior to the storm of October 1987 which proved him disastrously wrong]

A woman rang to say she'd heard there was a hurricane on the way – well don't worry, there isn't.

[Sunday Telegraph, 1989]

GOGARTY, Oliver St John (1878–1957)

In my best social accent I addressed him. I said, 'It is most extraordinary weather for this time of year!' He replied, 'Ah, it isn't this time of year at all.'

[It Isn't This Time of Year at All (1954)]

HARDY, Thomas (1840–1928)

This is the weather the cuckoo likes,
And so do I;
When showers betumble the chestnut spikes,
And nestlings fly:
And the little brown nightingale bills his best,
And they sit outside at 'The Travellers' Rest'.

['Weathers' (1922)]

JOHNSON, Samuel (1709–1784)

When two Englishmen meet, their first talk is of the weather.

[The Idler (1758–1760)]

KEATS, John (1795–1821)

[Of Devon]

It is impossible to live in a country which is continually under hatches … Rain! Rain! Rain!

[Letter to J.H. Reynolds, 1818]

LODGE, David (1935–)

The British, he thought, must be gluttons for satire: even the weather forecast seemed to be some kind of spoof, predicting every possible combination of weather for the next twenty-four hours without actually committing itself to anything specific.

[Changing Places (1975)]

MACAULAY, Dame Rose (1881–1958)

Owing to the weather, English social life must always have largely occurred either indoors, or, when out of doors, in active motion.

['Life Among The English' (1942)]

POUND, Ezra (1885–1972)

Winter is icummen in,
Lhude sing Goddamn,
Raineth drop and staineth slop,
And how the wind doth ramm!
Sing: Goddamn.

['Ancient Music' (1916)]

RUSKIN, John (1819–1900)

There is really no such thing as bad weather, only different kinds of good weather.

[Attr.]

SMITH, Logan Pearsall (1865–1946)

Thank heavens, the sun has gone in, and I don't have to go out and enjoy it.

[All Trivia (1933)]

SMITH, Sydney (1771–1845)

[Discussing the recent hot weather]

Heat, Ma'am! It was so dreadful here, that I found there was nothing left for it but to take off my flesh and sit in my bones.

[In Holland, A Memoir of the Reverend Sydney Smith (1855)]

SWIFT, Jonathan (1667–1745)

Plaguy twelvepenny weather.

[Journal to Stella, 1710]

TWAIN, Mark (1835–1910)

everybody talks about the weather but nobody does anything about it.

[Attr.]

See SEASONS

WEDDINGS

BEHAN, Brendan (1923–1964)
I think weddings is sadder than funerals, because they remind you of your own wedding. You can't be reminded of your own funeral because it hasn't happened. But weddings always make me cry.

[*Richard's Cork Leg* (1972)]

LAMB, Charles (1775–1834)
I was at Hazlitt's marriage, and had like to have been turned out several times during the ceremony. Anything awful makes me laugh. I misbehaved once at a funeral.

[Letter to Southey, 1815]

LAMPTON, William James (1859–1917)
Same old slippers,
Same old rice,
Same old glimpse of Paradise.

['June Weddings']

LERNER, Alan Jay (1918–1986)
I'm getting married in the morning!
Ding dong! the bells are gonna chime.
Pull out the stopper!
Let's have a whopper!
But get me to the church on time!

[*My Fair Lady* (1956)]

MUIR, Frank (1920–1998)
It has been said that a bride's attitude towards her betrothed can be summed up in three words: Aisle. Altar. Hymn.

[*Upon My Word!*, 'A Jug of Wine', with Dennis Norden]

See MARRIAGE

WIDOWS

DICKENS, Charles (1812–1870)
Take example by your father, my boy, and be wery careful o' widders all your life.

[*The Pickwick Papers* (1837)]

GAY, John (1685–1732)
The comfortable estate of widowhood, is the only hope that keeps up a wife's spirits.

[*The Beggar's Opera* (1728), I]

I think, you must do like other widows – buy your self weeds, and be cheerful.

[*The Beggar's Opera* (1728)]

GUITRY, Sacha (1885–1957)
[Responding to his fifth wife's jealousy of his previous wives]
The others were only my wives. But you, my dear, will be my widow.

[Attr.]

HOFFNUNG, Gerard (1925–1959)
There is a French widow in every bedroom (affording delightful prospects).

[Speech, Oxford Union debating society, 1958]

IBÁRRURI, Dolores ('La Pasionaria') (1895–1989)
It is better to be the widow of a hero than the wife of a coward.

[Speech, Valencia, 1936]

WYCHERLEY, William (c.1640–1716)
Well, a widow, I see, is a kind of sinecure.

[*The Plain Dealer* (1677)]

WISDOM

AESCHYLUS (525–456 BC)
It is a fine thing even for an old man to learn wisdom.

[*Fragments*]

ARISTOPHANES (c.445–385 BC)
One may learn wisdom even from one's enemies.

[*Birds*]

BACON, Francis (1561–1626)
A wise man will make more opportunities than he finds.

['Of Ceremonies and Respects' (1625)]

THE BIBLE (King James Version)
Wisdom is the principal thing; therefore get

wisdom: and with all thy getting get understanding.

[*Proverbs*, 4:7]

BLAKE, William (1757–1827)

I care not whether a Man is Good or Evil; all that I care
Is whether he is a Wise Man or a Fool. Go! put off Holiness
And put on Intellect.

[*Jerusalem* (1820)]

CAXTON, William (c.1421–1491)

It is notoriously known through the universal world that there be nine worthy and the best that ever were. That is to wit three paynims, three Jews, and three Christian men. As for the paynims they were … the first Hector of Troy … the second Alexander the Great; and the third Julius Caesar … As for the three Jews … the first was Duke Joshua … the second David, King of Jerusalem; and the third Judas Maccabaeus…. And sith the said Incarnation… was first the noble Arthur…. The second was Charlemagne or Charles the Great … and the third and last was Godfrey of Bouillon.

[In Malory, *Le Morte d'Arthur* (1485)]

CHAUCER, Geoffrey (c.1340–1400)

Ful wys is he that kan hymselven knowe!

[*The Canterbury Tales* (1387)]

CHESTERFIELD, Lord (1694–1773)

Be wiser than other people if you can; but do not tell them so.

[Letter to his son, 1745]

CONFUCIUS (c.550–c.478 BC)

Gravity is only the bark of wisdom's tree, but it preserves it.

[*Analects*]

The heart of the wise, like a mirror, should reflect all objects without being sullied by any.

[*Analects*]

COWPER, William (1731–1800)

Knowledge dwells
In heads replete with thoughts of other men;

Wisdom in minds attentive to their own.

[*The Task* (1785)]

Knowledge is proud that he has
learn'd so much;
Wisdom is humble that he knows no more.

[*The Task* (1785)]

EMERSON, Ralph Waldo (1803–1882)

The wise through excess of wisdom is made a fool.

[*Essays, Second Series* (1844)]

Now that is the wisdom of a man, in every instance of his labor, to hitch his wagon to a star, and see his chore done by the gods themselves.

[*Society and Solitude* (1870)]

FITZGERALD, Edward (1809–1883)

With them the Seed of Wisdom did I sow,
And with mine own hand wrought to make it grow;
And this was all the Harvest that I reap'd –
'I came like Water, and like Wind I go'.

[*The Rubáiyát of Omar Khayyám* (1859)]

FULLER, Thomas (1608–1661)

Many have been the wise speeches of fools, though not so many as the foolish speeches of wise men.

[*The Holy State and the Profane State* (1642)]

HORACE (65–8 BC)

Dimidium facti qui coepit habet: sapere aude.
To have made a beginning is half of the business; dare to be wise.

[*Epistles*]

HUTCHESON, Francis (1694–1746)

Wisdom denotes the pursuing of the best ends by the best means.

[*An Inquiry into the Original of our Ideas of Beauty and Virtue* (1725)]

LÉVI-STRAUSS, Claude (1908–)

Le savant n'est pas l'homme qui fournit les vraies réponses; c'est celui qui pose les vraies questions.
The wise man is not the man who gives the right answers; he is the one who asks the right questions.

[*The Raw and the Cooked*]

MARQUIS, Don (1878–1937)

How often when they find a sage
As great as Socrates or Plato
They hand him hemlock for his wage
Or take him like a sweet potato.

[*Taking the Longer View*]

MEREDITH, George (1828–1909)

In action Wisdom goes by majorities.

[*The Ordeal of Richard Feverel* (1859)]

PLATO (c.429–347 BC)

That man is wisest who, like Socrates, has
realized that in truth his wisdom is worth
nothing.

[*The Apology of Socrates*]

PROVERB

It is easy to be wise after the event.

QUARLES, Francis (1592–1644)

Be wisely worldly, not worldly wise.

[*Emblems* (1635)]

ROOSEVELT, Theodore (1858–1919)

Nine-tenths of wisdom is being wise in time.

[Speech, 1917]

SMOLLETT, Tobias (1721–1771)

Some folks are wise, and some are otherwise.

[*The Adventures of Roderick Random* (1748)]

SWIFT, Jonathan (1667–1745)

No wise man ever wished to be younger.

[*Thoughts on Various Subjects* (1711)]

SZASZ, Thomas (1920–)

The stupid neither forgive nor forget; the
naive forgive and forget; the wise forgive but
do not forget.

[*The Second Sin* (1973)]

THOREAU, Henry David (1817–1862)

It is a characteristic of wisdom not to do
desperate things.

[*Walden* (1854)]

TROLLOPE, Anthony (1815–1882)

It may almost be a question whether such
wisdom as many of us have in our mature
years has not come from the dying out of the
power of temptation, rather than as the

results of thought and resolution.

[*The Small House at Allington* (1864)]

WORDSWORTH, William (1770–1850)

Wisdom is oftimes nearer when we stoop
Than when we soar.

[*The Excursion* (1814)]

YOUNG, Edward (1683–1765)

Be wise today, 'tis madness to defer.

[*Night-Thoughts on Life, Death and Immortality*
(1742–1746)]

See INTELLIGENCE; KNOWLEDGE; WIT

WIT

JOHNSON, Samuel (1709–1784)

[Of Lord Chesterfield]
This man I thought had been a Lord among
wits; but, I find, he is only a wit among Lords.

[In Boswell, *The Life of Samuel Johnson* (1791)]

MAHAFFY, Sir John Pentland (1839–1919)

My dear Oscar, you are not clever enough for
us in Dublin. You had better run over to
Oxford.

[In H. Montgomery Hyde, *Oscar Wilde: A Biography*
(1975)]

MAUGHAM, William Somerset (1874–1965)

Impropriety is the soul of wit.

[*The Moon and Sixpence* (1919)]

POPE, Alexander (1688–1744)

Some have at first for Wits, then Poets pass'd,
Turned Critics next, and proved plain fools at
last.

['An Essay on Criticism* (1711)]

You beat your Pate, and fancy Wit will come;
Knock as you please, there's nobody at home.

['Epigram' (1732)]

ROGERS, Thorold (1823–1890)

Sir, to be facetious it is not necessary to be
indecent.

[In John Bailey, *Dr Johnson and his Circle* (1913)]

RUSSELL, Lord John (1792–1878)
A proverb is one man's wit and all men's wisdom.

[In R.J. Mackintosh, *Sir James Mackintosh* (1835)]

SHADWELL, Thomas (c.1642–1692)
And wit's the noblest frailty of the mind.

[*A True Widow* (1679)]

SKELTON, Robin (1925–)
Anything said off the cuff has usually been written on it first.

[Attr.]

STERNE, Laurence (1713–1768)
An ounce of a man's own wit is worth a ton of other people's.

[*Tristram Shandy* (1759–1767)]

See WISDOM

WOMEN

ADDAMS, Jane (1860–1935)
Old-fashioned ways which no longer apply to changed conditions are a snare in which the feet of women have always become readily entangled.

[*Newer Ideals of Peace* (1907)]

ADDISON, Joseph (1672–1719)
The woman that deliberates is lost.

[*Cato* (1713)]

I consider woman as a beautiful, romantic animal, that may be adorned with furs and feathers, pearls and diamonds, ores and silks.

[*Trial of the Petticoat*]

ALCOTT, Louisa May (1832–1888)
… girls are so queer you never know what they mean. They say No when they mean Yes, and drive a man out of his wits for the fun of it …

[*Little Women* (1869)]

ALEXANDER, Sir William, Earl of Stirling (c.1567–1640)
The weaker sex, to piety more prone.

[*Doomsday* (1614)]

ANONYMOUS
In particular, the State recognises that by her life within the home, woman gives to the State a support without which the common good cannot be achieved.

[The Irish Constitution]

ARNOLD, Matthew (1822–1888)
With women the heart argues, not the mind.

[*Merope* (1858)]

AUSTEN, Jane (1775–1817)
Next to being married, a girl likes to be crossed in love a little now and then.

[*Pride and Prejudice* (1813)]

Where people wish to attach, they should always be ignorant. To come with a well-informed mind, is to come with an inability of administering to the vanity of others, which a sensible person would always wish to avoid. A woman especially, if she have the misfortune of knowing any thing, should conceal it as well as she can.

[*Northanger Abbey* (1818)]

In nine cases out of ten, a woman had better show more affection than she feels.

[Letter]

BACALL, Lauren (1924–)
I'm not a member of the weaker sex.

[In Simon Rose, *Classic Film Guide* (1995)]

BAGEHOT, Walter (1826–1877)
Women – one half the human race at least – care fifty times more for a marriage than a ministry.

[*The English Constitution* (1867)]

BEAUVOIR, Simone de (1908–1986)
On ne naît pas femme: on le devient.
One is not born a woman: one becomes a woman.

[*The Second Sex* (1950)]

BEERBOHM, Sir Max (1872–1956)
Most women are not so young as they are painted.

[*The Works of Max Beerbohm* (1896)]

'After all,' as a pretty girl once said to me,

'women are a sex by themselves, so to speak.'

[*The Works of Max Beerbohm* (1896)]

Women who love the same man have a kind of bitter freemasonry.

[*Zuleika Dobson* (1911)]

BEHN, Aphra (1640–1689)

The soft, unhappy sex.

[*The Wandering Beauty* (c. 1694)]

THE BIBLE
(King James Version)

And the rib, which the Lord God had taken from man, made he a woman.

[*Genesis*, 2:22]

Who can find a virtuous woman? for her price is far above rubies.

[*Proverbs*, 31:10]

All wickedness is but little to the wickedness of a woman.

[*Ecclesiasticus*, 25:19]

BRIDGES, Robert (1844–1930)

All women born are so perverse
No man need boast their love possessing.
If nought seem better, nothing's worse:
All women born are so perverse.
From Adam's wife, that proved a curse
Though God had made her for a blessing,
All women born are so perverse
No man need boast their love possessing.

['Triolet' (1890)]

BURNET, Sir Frank Macfarlane (1899–1985)

In an affluent society most healthy women would like to have four healthy children.

[*Dominant Mammal* (1970)]

BURNS, Robert (1759–1796)

Auld nature swears, the lovely dears
Her noblest work she classes, O:
Her prentice han' she try'd on man,
An' then she made the lasses, O.

['Green Grow the Rashes' (1783)]

BUTLER, Samuel (1612–1680)

The souls of women are so small,

That some believe they've none at all.

[*Miscellaneous Thoughts*]

BUTLER, Samuel (1835–1902)

Brigands demand your money or your life; women require both.

[Attr.]

BYRON, Lord (1788–1824)

There is something to me very softening in the presence of a woman, – some strange influence, even if one is not in love with them – which I cannot at all account for, having no very high opinion of the sex.

[*Journal*, 1814]

CATULLUS (84–c.54 BC)

Sed mulier cupido quod dicit amanti,
In vento et rapida scribere oportet aqua.
But what a woman says to her eager lover, she ought to write in the wind and the running water.

[*Carmina*]

CERVANTES, Miguel de (1547–1616)

La mujer honrada, la pierna quebrada, y en casa; y la doncella honesta, el hacer algo es su fiesta.
An honest woman and a broken leg should be at home; and for a decent maiden, working is her holiday.

[*Don Quixote* (1615)]

CHANDLER, Raymond (1888–1959)

It was a blonde. A blonde to make a bishop kick a hole in a stained glass window.

[*Farewell, My Lovely* (1940)]

CHAUCER, Geoffrey (c.1340–1400)

What is bettre than wisedoom? Womman. And what is bettre than a good womman? Nothyng.

[*The Canterbury Tales* (1387)]

CHEKHOV, Anton (1860–1904)

Women don't forgive failure.

[*The Seagull* (1896)]

CHESTERFIELD, Lord (1694–1773)

Women, then, are only children of a larger growth; they have an entertaining tattle and sometimes wit; but for solid, reasoning good-sense, I never in my life knew one that had it, or who reasoned or acted consequentially for four-and-twenty hours together.

[Letter to his son, 1748]

[Of women]
A man of sense only trifles with them, plays with them, humours and flatters them, as he does with a sprightly, forward child; but he neither consults them about, nor trusts them with, serious matters; though he often makes them believe that he does both.

[Letter to his son, 1748]

Women are much more like each other than men; they have, in truth, but two passions, vanity and love; these are their universal characteristics.

[Letter to his son, 1749]

CHESTERTON, G.K. (1874–1936)
She [the elegant female] was maintaining the prime truth of woman, the universal mother: that if a thing is worth doing, it is worth doing badly.

[What's Wrong with the World (1910)]

CHISHOLM, Caroline (1808–1877)
For all the churches you can build, and all the books you can export, will never do much good without what a gentleman in that Colony very appropriately called 'God's police' – wives and little children – good and virtuous women.

[Emigration and Transportation Relatively Considered (1847)]

CONGREVE, William (1670–1729)
Women are like tricks by slight of hand, Which, to admire, we should not understand.

[Love for Love (1695)]

Heav'n has no rage, like love to hatred turned,
Nor Hell a fury, like a woman scorn'd.

[The Mourning Bride (1697)]

COWARD, Sir Noël (1899–1973)
Certain women should be struck regularly, like gongs.

[Private Lives (1930)]

COWLEY, Hannah (1743–1809)
But what is woman?–only one of Nature's agreeable blunders.

[Who's the Dupe? (1779)]

DELANEY, Shelagh (1939–)
Women never have young minds. They are born three thousand years old.

[A Taste of Honey (1959)]

DONNE, John (1572–1631)
Women are like the Arts, forc'd unto none,
Open to all searchers, unpriz'd if unknown.

[Elegies (c. 1595)]

EKLAND, Britt (1942–)
As a single woman with a child, I would love to have a wife.

[The Independent, 1994]

ELIOT, George (1819–1880)
I should like to know what is the proper function of women, if it is not to make reasons for husbands to stay at home, and still stronger reasons for bachelors to go out.

[The Mill on the Floss (1860)]

A woman can hardly ever choose … she is dependent on what happens to her. She must take meaner things, because only meaner things are within her reach.

[Felix Holt (1866)]

FARQUHAR, George (1678–1707)
There's some diversion in a talking blockhead; and since a woman must wear chains, I would have the pleasure of hearing 'em rattle a little.

[The Beaux' Stratagem (1707)]

FITZGERALD, Edward (1809–1883)
Mrs Browning's death is rather a relief to me, I must say: no more Aurora Leighs, thank God! A woman of real genius, I know; but what is the upshot of it all? She and her sex had better mind the kitchen and their children; and perhaps the poor: except in such things as little novels, they only devote themselves to what men do much better, leaving that which men do worse or not at all.

[Letter to W.H. Thompson, 1861]

FRAYN, Michael (1933–)
No woman so naked as one you can see to be naked underneath her clothes.

[Constructions]

FREUD, Sigmund (1856–1939)
The great question … which I have not been able to answer, despite my thirty years of research into the feminine soul, is 'What does a woman want?'.

[In Robb, Psychiatry in American Life]

GAY, John (1685–1732)
Woman's mind
Oft' shifts her passions, like th' inconstant wind;
Sudden she rages, like the troubled main,
Now sinks the storm, and all is calm again.

[Dione (1720)]

I must have women. There is nothing unbends the mind like them.

[The Beggar's Opera (1728)]

GORMAN, Theresa
The Conservative establishment has always treated women as nannies, grannies and fannies.

[The Observer, 1998]

GRANVILLE, George (1666–1735)
Of all the plagues with which the world is curst,
Of every ill, a woman is the worst.

[The British Enchanters]

HAKIM, Catherine
The unpalatable truth is that a substantial proportion of women still accept the sexual division of labour which sees home-making as women's principal activitiy and income-earning as men's principal activity in life.

[The Observer Review, 1996]

HARMAN, Sir Jeremiah (1930–)
I've always thought there were only three kinds of women: wives, whores and mistresses.

[Daily Mail, 1996]

HOME, John (1722–1808)
He seldom errs
Who thinks the worst he can of womankind.

[Douglas (1756)]

IRVING, Washington (1783–1859)
A woman's whole life is a history of the affections.

[The Sketch Book (1820)]

JAMES I OF SCOTLAND (1394–1437)
[On being introduced to a young girl proficient in Latin, Greek, and Hebrew]
These are rare attainments for a damsel, but pray tell me, can she spin?

[Attr.]

JOHNSON, Samuel (1709–1784)
Sir, a woman's preaching is like a dog's walking on his hinder legs. It is not done well; but you are surprised to find it done at all.

[In Boswell, The Life of Samuel Johnson (1791)]

KIPLING, Rudyard (1865–1936)
'Tisn't beauty, so to speak, nor good talk necessarily. It's just IT. Some women'll stay in a man's memory if they once walked down a street.

[Traffics and Discoveries (1904)]

KNOX, John (1505–1572)
The First Blast of the Trumpet Against the Monstrous Regiment of Women.

[Title of pamphlet, 1558]

To promote a Woman to bear rule, superiority, dominion or empire, above any Realm, Nation, or City, is repugnant to Nature; contumely to God, a thing most contrarious to his revealed will and approved ordinance; and finally it is the subversion of good Order, of all equity and justice.

['The First Blast of the Trumpet Against the Monstrous Regiment of Women', 1558]

KNOX, Vicesimus (1752–1821)
Can anything be more absurd than keeping women in a state of ignorance, and yet so

vehemently to insist on their resisting temptation?

[*Liberal Education* (1780)]

LERNER, Alan Jay (1918–1986)

There is no greater fan of the opposite sex than me, and I have the bills to prove it.

[Attr.]

I'd be equally as willing
For a dentist to be drilling
Than to ever let a woman in my life.

[*My Fair Lady* (1956)]

LOOS, Anita (1893–1981)

So this gentleman said a girl with brains ought to do something with them besides think.

[*Gentlemen Prefer Blondes* (1925)]

MACKENZIE, Sir Compton (1883–1972)

Women do not find it difficult nowadays to behave like men; but they often find it extremely difficult to behave like gentlemen.

[*Literature in My Time* (1933)]

MAILER, Norman (1923–)

You don't know a woman until you've met her in court.

[*The Observer*, 1983]

MARLOWE, Christopher (1564–1593)

Like untun'd golden strings all women are
Which long time lie untouch'd, will harshly jar.

[*Hero and Leander* (1598)]

MASEFIELD, John (1878–1967)

To get the whole world out of bed
And washed, and dressed, and warmed, and fed,
To work, and back to bed again,
Believe me, Saul, costs worlds of pain.

['The Everlasting Mercy' (1911)]

MAUGHAM, William Somerset (1874–1965)

A woman will always sacrifice herself if you give her the opportunity. It is her favourite form of self-indulgence.

[*The Circle* (1921)]

MCCARTHY, Abigail (c.1914–)

For those of us whose lives have been defined by others – by wifehood and motherhood – there is no individual achievement to measure, only the experience of life itself.

[*Private Faces/Public Places* (1972)]

MENCKEN, H.L. (1880–1956)

When women kiss, it always reminds me of prize-fighters shaking hands.

[Attr.]

MILTON, John (1608–1674)

… nothing lovelier can be found
In Woman, than to studie household good,
And good works in her Husband to promote.

[*Paradise Lost* (1667)]

O why did God,
Creator wise, that peopl'd highest Heav'n
With Spirits Masculine, create at last
This noveltie on Earth, this fair defect
Of Nature?

[*Paradise Lost* (1667)]

[Reply when asked if he would allow his daughters to learn foreign languages]
One tongue is sufficient for a woman.

[Attr.]

MORISSETTE, Alanis (1974–)

I want to walk through life instead of being dragged through it.

MULKERNS, Val (1925–)

On the last day of his life Dan decided that women who haunted you were not those whom you had enjoyed or even known remotely well, but strangers who had at one time or another troubled you with the most transient flicker of desire.

[*Loser*]

NASH, Ogden (1902–1971)

Women would rather be right than reasonable.

['Frailty, Thy Name is a Misnomer' (1942)]

NIETZSCHE, Friedrich Wilhelm (1844–1900)

Alles am Weibe ist ein Rätsel, und alles am Weibe hat eine Lösung: sie heisst Schwangerschaft.

Everything to do with women is a mystery, and everything to do with women has one solution: it's called pregnancy.

[*Thus Spake Zarathustra* (1884)]

NIN, Anais (1903–1977)

Women (and I, in this Diary) have never separated sex from feeling, from love of the whole man.

[*Delta of Venus* (1977)]

OTWAY, Thomas (1652–1685)

What mighty ills have not been done by woman!
Who was't betrayed the Capitol? – A woman!
Who lost Mark Antony the world? – A woman!
Who was the cause of a long ten years' war,
And laid at last old Troy in ashes? – Woman!
Destructive, damnable, deceitful woman!

[*The Orphan* (1680)]

Oh woman! lovely woman! Nature made thee
To temper man: we had been brutes without you;
Angels are painted fair, to look like you;
There's in you all that we believe of heav'n,
Amazing brightness, purity, and truth,
Eternal joy, and everlasting love.

[*Venice Preserv'd* (1682)]

OVID (43 BC–AD 18)

Quae dant, quaeque negant, gaudent tamen esse rogatae.

Whether they give or refuse, women are glad that they have been asked.

[*Ars Amatoria*]

PAGLIA, Camille (1947–)

There is no female Mozart because there is no female Jack the Ripper.

[Attr. in *The Observer*, 1996]

PERICLES (c.495–429)

The greatest glory of a woman is to be least talked about by men, in praise or blame.

[In Thucydides, *Histories*]

POPE, Alexander (1688–1744)

Most Women have no Characters at all.

['Epistle to a Lady' (1735)]

Woman's at best a Contradiction still.

['Epistle to a Lady' (1735)]

RACINE, Jean (1639–1699)

Elle flotte, elle hésite; en un mot, elle est femme.

She wavers, she hesitates; in a word, she is a woman.

[*Athalie* (1691)]

RENAN, J. Ernest (1823–1892)

La femme nous remet en communication avec l'éternelle source où Dieu se mire.

Woman puts us back into communication with the eternal spring in which God looks at his reflection.

[*Souvenirs d'enfance et de jeunesse* (1883)]

ROWLAND, Helen (1875–1950)

It takes a woman twenty years to make a man of her son, and another woman twenty minutes to make a fool of him.

[*Reflections of a Bachelor Girl* (1909)]

RUBINSTEIN, Helena (c.1872–1965)

There are no ugly women, only lazy ones.

[*My Life for Beauty* (1965)]

SCHOPENHAUER, Arthur (1788–1860)

One needs only to see the way she is built to realise that woman is not intended for great mental labour.

[Attr.]

SCOTT, Sir Walter (1771–1832)

O Woman! in our hours of ease,
Uncertain, coy, and hard to please,
And variable as the shade
By the light quivering aspen made;
When pain and anguish wring the brow,
A ministering angel thou!

[*Marmion* (1808)]

Woman's faith, and woman's trust –
Write the characters in dust.

[*The Betrothed* (1825)]

SHAKESPEARE, William (1564–1616)

Do you not know I am a woman? When I think, I must speak.

[*As You Like It*, III.ii]

Frailty, thy name is woman!

[*Hamlet*, I.ii]

She's beautiful, and therefore to be woo'd;
She is a woman, therefore to be won.

[*Henry VI, Part 1*, V.iii]

A woman mov'd is like a fountain troubled –
Muddy, ill-seeming, thick, bereft of beauty.

[*The Taming of the Shrew*, V.ii]

SHARIF, Omar (1932–)

The truth is I worship women … the kind who can use both intelligence and femininity. The woman must give the impression that she needs a man.

[In Spada, *Streisand: The Intimate Biography* (1995)]

SHAW, George Bernard (1856–1950)

The fickleness of the women I love is only equalled by the infernal constancy of the women who love me.

[*The Philanderer* (1898)]

The one point on which all women are in furious secret rebellion against the existing law is the saddling of the right to a child with the obligation to become the servant of a man.

[*Getting Married* (1911)]

SHERIDAN, Richard Brinsley (1751–1816)

Here's to the maiden of bashful fifteen;
Here's to the widow of fifty;
Here's to the flaunting, extravagant quean;
And here's to the housewife that's thrifty.
Let the toast pass –
Drink to the lass –
I'll warrant she'll prove an excuse for the glass!

[*The School for Scandal* (1777)]

SOUTHEY, Robert (1774–1843)

What will not woman, gentle woman, dare,
When strong affection stirs her spirit up?

[*Madoc* (1805)]

STEINEM, Gloria (1934–)

One day, an army of grey-haired women may quietly take over the earth.

[*Outrageous Acts and Everyday Rebellions* (1984)]

STOCKS, Mary, Baroness (1891–1975)

It is clearly absurd that it should be possible for a woman to qualify as a saint with direct access to the Almighty while she may not qualify as a curate.

[Attr.]

TENNYSON, Alfred, Lord (1809–1892)

The woman is so hard
Upon the woman.

[*The Princess* (1847)]

VANBRUGH, Sir John (1664–1726)

Once a woman has given you her heart you can never get rid of the rest of her.

[*The Relapse, or Virtue in Danger* (1696)]

WAUGH, Auberon (1939–)

It is one of the tragedies of our time to see women making a nuisance of themselves as welfare officers when they could be employed as nursery maids.

[*The Independent on Sunday*, 1994]

WELLS, H.G. (1866–1946)

There's no social differences – till women come in.

[*Kipps: the Story of a Simple Soul* (1905)]

WOLFF, Charlotte (1904–1986)

Women have always been the guardians of wisdom and humanity which makes them natural, but usually secret, rulers. The time has come for them to rule openly, but together with and not against men.

[*Bisexuality: A Study*]

WOOLF, Virginia (1882–1941)

Women have served all these centuries as looking-glasses possessing the magic and delicious power of reflecting the figure of man at twice its natural size.

[*A Room of One's Own* (1929)]

WYNNE-TYSON, Esme (1898–1972)

Scheherazade is the classical example of a

woman saving her head by using it.

[Attr.]

See FEMINISM; MEN AND WOMEN

WORDS

AESCHYLUS (525–456 BC)

Words are physic to the distempered mind.

[*Prometheus Bound*]

ASHDOWN, Paddy (1941–)

Lord, make my words sweet and reasonable. Some day I may have to eat them.

[*The Observer*, 1998]

BACON, Francis (1561–1626)

The ill and unfit choice of words wonderfully obstructs the understanding.

[*The New Organon* (1620)]

BROWN, George MacKay (1921–1996)

We who deal in words must strive to keep language pure and wholesome; and it is hard work, as hard almost as digging a stony field with a blunt spade.

[*Time in a Red Coat* (1984)]

CARLYLE, Thomas (1795–1881)

Be not the slave of Words.

[*Sartor Resartus* (1834)]

CARROLL, Lewis (1832–1898)

'When I use a word,' Humpty Dumpty said in rather a scornful tone, 'it means just what I choose it to mean – neither more nor less.'

[*Through the Looking-Glass (and What Alice Found There)* (1872)]

You see it's like a portmanteau – there are two meanings packed up into one word.

[*Through the Looking-Glass (and What Alice Found There)* (1872)]

CONFUCIUS (c.550–c.478 BC)

Without knowing the force of words, it is impossible to know men.

[*Analects*]

DE LA MARE, Walter (1873–1956)

Until we learn the use of living words we

shall continue to be waxworks inhabited by gramophones.

[*The Observer*, 1929]

ELIOT, T.S. (1888–1965)

Words strain,
Crack and sometimes break, under the burden,
Under the tension, slip, slide, perish,
Decay with imprecision, will not stay in place,
Will not stay still.

[*Four Quartets* (1944)]

EMERSON, Ralph Waldo (1803–1882)

Words are also actions, and actions are a kind of words.

['The Poet' (1844)]

FARQUHAR, George (1678–1707)

Grant me some wild expressions, Heavens, or I shall burst … Words, words or I shall burst.

[*The Constant Couple* (1699)]

FRANCE, Anatole (1844–1924)

Il fut des temps barbares et gothiques où les mots avaient un sens; alors les écrivains exprimaient des pensées.

It was in the times, barbarous and gothic, when words had a meaning; in those days, writers would express thoughts.

[*La Vie Littéraire* (1888)]

HARDY, Thomas (1840–1928)

Dialect words – those terrible marks of the beast to the truly genteel.

[*The Mayor of Casterbridge* (1886)]

HOBBES, Thomas (1588–1679)

Words are wise men's counters, they do but reckon by them; but they are the money of fools.

[*Leviathan* (1651)]

HOLMES, Oliver Wendell (1809–1894)

I am omniverbivorous by nature and training. Passing by such words as are poisonous, I can swallow most others, and chew such as I cannot swallow.

[*The Autocrat of the Breakfast-Table* (1858)]

HUXLEY, Aldous (1894–1963)

Thanks to words, we have been able to rise above the brutes; and thanks to words, we have often sunk to the level of the demons.

[*Adonis and the Alphabet* (1956)]

JAMES, Henry (1843–1916)

Summer afternoon – summer afternoon; to me those have always been the two most beautiful words in the English language.

[In Edith Wharton, *A Backward Glance* (1934)]

JOYCE, James (1882–1941)

I fear those big words, Stephen said, which make us so unhappy.

[*Ulysses* (1922)]

KIPLING, Rudyard (1865–1936)

Words are, of course, the most powerful drug used by mankind.

[Speech, 1923]

LANDOR, Walter Savage (1775–1864)

How many verses have I thrown
Into the fire because the one
Peculiar word, the wanted most,
Was irrevocably lost.

['Verses Why Burnt']

I hate false words, and seek with care, difficulty, and moroseness, those that fit the thing.

[*Imaginary Conversations* (1853)]

LYDGATE, John (c.1370–c.1451)

Woord is but wynd; leff woord and tak the dede.

['Secrets of Old Philosophers']

MADDEN, Samuel (1686–1765)

Words are men's daughters, but God's sons are things.

[*Boulter's Monument* (1745)]

MASSINGER, Philip (1583–1640)

All words,
And no performance!

[*The Parliament of Love* (1624)]

OGDEN, C.K. (1889–1957) and
RICHARDS, I.A. (1893–1979)

The belief that words have a meaning of

their own account is a relic of primitive word magic, and it is still a part of the air we breathe in nearly every discussion.

[*The Meaning of Meaning* (1923)]

PARKER, Dorothy (1893–1967)

[Giving her version of the two most beautiful words in the English language]
Check enclosed.

[Attr.]

POPE, Alexander (1688–1744)

Words are like leaves; and where they most abound,
Much fruit of sense beneath is rarely found.

[*An Essay on Criticism* (1711)]

ROSCOMMON, Fourth Earl of (1633–1685)

But words once spoke can never be recall'd.

[*Horace's Art of Poetry Made English* (1680)]

SCOTT, Sir Walter (1771–1832)

There is a southern proverb, – fine words butter no parsnips.

[*A Legend of Montrose* (1819)]

SHAKESPEARE, William (1564–1616)

But words are words: I never yet did hear
That the bruis'd heart was pierced through the ear.

[*Othello*, I.iii]

SHERIDAN, Richard Brinsley (1751–1816)

You shall see them on a beautiful quarto page, where a neat rivulet of text shall murmur through a meadow of margin.

[*The School for Scandal* (1777)]

SPENCER, Herbert (1820–1903)

How often misused words generate misleading thoughts.

[*Principles of Ethics* (1879)]

SPENDER, Sir Stephen (1909–1995)

The word bites like a fish.
Shall I throw it back, free
Arrowing to that sea
Where thoughts lash tail and fin?
Or shall I pull it in

To rhyme upon a dish?

['Word']

See CONVERSATION; LANGUAGE

WORK

ACHESON, Dean (1893–1971)

[Remark made on leaving his post as Secretary of State, 1952]
I will undoubtedly have to seek what is happily known as gainful employment, which I am glad to say does not describe holding public office.

[Attr.]

ALLEY, Rewi (1897–1987)

[The motto of the Chinese Industrial Co-operatives Association]
Gung Ho!
Work Together!

[In Chapple, *Rewi Alley of China* (1980)]

ANONYMOUS

Laborare est orare.
Work is prayer.

[Unknown origin]

If you tell the boss you were late for work because you had a flat tyre, the next morning you will have a flat tyre.

[Cannon's Law]

It is usually impractical to worry beforehand about interferences – if you have none, someone will make one for you.

The working class can kiss my arse – I've got the boss's job at last.

[Australian Labor movement, traditional folk saying, sung to the tune of the 'Red Flag']

BACON, Francis (1909–1993)

How can I take an interest in my work when I don't like it?

[Attr.]

BALDWIN, James (1924–1987)

The price one pays for pursuing any profession or calling is an intimate

knowledge of its ugly side.

[*Nobody Knows My Name* (1961)]

BENCHLEY, Robert (1889–1945)

I do most of my work sitting down; that's where I shine.

[Attr.]

BENNETT, Arnold (1867–1931)

The test of a first-rate work, and a test of your sincerity in calling it a first-rate work, is that you finish it.

[*Things That Have Interested Me* (1921–1925)]

Habit of work is growing on me. I could get into the way of going to my desk as a man goes to whisky, or rather to chloral.

[*Journals* (1932)]

THE BIBLE (King James Version)

The labourer is worthy of his hire.

[*Luke*, 10:7]

If any would not work, neither should he eat.

[*II Thessalonians*, 3:10]

BURNS, Robert (1759–1796)

We labour soon, we labour late,
To feed the titled knave, man,
And a' the comfort we're to get,
Is that ayont the grave, man.

['The Tree of Liberty' (1838)]

BUTLER, Samuel (1835–1902)

Every man's work, whether it be literature or music or pictures or architecture or anything else, is always a portrait of himself.

[*The Way of All Flesh* (1903)]

CARLYLE, Thomas (1795–1881)

Be no longer a Chaos, but a World, or even Worldkin. Produce! Produce! Were it but the pitifullest infinitesimal fraction of a Product, produce it, in God's name! 'Tis the utmost thou hast in thee: out with it, then. Up, up! Whatsoever thy hand findeth to do, do it with thy whole might.

[*Sartor Resartus* (1834)]

Blessed is he who has found his work; let him

ask no other blessedness.

[*Past and Present* (1843)]

Work is the grand cure of all the maladies and miseries that ever beset mankind.

[*Speech*, 1886]

CERVANTES, Miguel de (1547–1616)

La diligencia es madre de la buena ventura; y la pereza, su contraria, jamás llegó al término que pide un buen deseo.
Diligence is the mother of good fortune; and the goal of a good intention was never reached through its opposite, laziness.

[*Don Quixote* (1615)]

CHEKHOV, Anton (1860–1904)

The time has come, something huge is approaching us, a refreshing, powerful storm is brewing … Soon it will blow away all the laziness, indifference, prejudice against work and decaying boredom from our society … I'm going to work, and in some twenty-five or thirty years' time every one will be working. Every one!

[*The Three Sisters* (1901)]

CHURCHILL, Jennie Jerome (1854–1921)

You seem to have no real purpose in life and won't realize at the age of twenty-two that for a man life means work, and hard work if you mean to succeed.

[Letter to Winston Churchill, 1897]

CICERO (106–43 BC)

Vulgo enim dicitur: 'iucundi acti labores'.
For it is commonly said: 'hard tasks are pleasant when they are finished'.

[*De Finibus*]

CLARKE, John (fl. 1639)

He that would thrive
Must rise at five;
He that hath thriven
May lie till seven.

[*Paraemiologia Anglo-Latina* (1639)]

CLUFF, Algy

[On the controversy over whether the inhabitants of Hong Kong should be allowed to enter Britain]

Energy, brains and hard work made Hong Kong. If only a few of its people would come here.

[*Daily Mail*, 1996]

COGHILL, Anna Louisa (1836–1907)

Work, for the night is coming,
When man works no more.

[*Hymn*, 1854]

COLERIDGE, Samuel Taylor (1772–1834)

Work without hope draws nectar in a sieve,
And hope without an object cannot live.

['Work Without Hope' (1828)]

COLLINGWOOD, Robin George (1889–1943)

Perfect freedom is reserved for the man who lives by his own work and in that work does what he wants to do.

[*Speculum Mentis* (1924)]

COWARD, Sir Noël (1899–1973)

Work is much more fun than fun.

[*The Observer*, 1963]

CUMBERLAND, Bishop Richard (1631–1718)

It is better to wear out than to rust out.

[In Horne, *The Duty of Contending for the Faith* (1786)]

CURIE, Marie (1867–1934)

One never notices what has been done; one can only see what remains to be done …

[Letter to her brother, 1894]

DAVIDSON, John (1857–1909)

'My time is filched by toil and sleep;
My heart,' he thought, 'is clogged with dust;
My soul that flashed from out the deep,
A magic blade, begins to rust.'

['A Ballad of a Workman' (1894)]

DAVIS, Bette (1908–1989)

This became a credo of mine…attempt the impossible in order to improve your work.

EDWARD VIII (later Duke of Windsor) (1894–1972)

[Of steel works in South Wales where 9,000 men

had been made unemployed]
These works brought all these people here.
Something must be done to find them work.

[Speech, 1936]

EMMONS, Margaret
If while you are in school, there is a shortage
of qualified personnel in a particular field,
then by the time you graduate with the
necessary qualifications, that field's
employment market is glutted.

[Attr.]

FRANCE, Anatole (1844–1924)
Man is so made that he can only find
relaxation from one kind of labour by taking
up another.

[The Crime of Sylvestre Bonnard (1881)]

GEORGE, Henry (1839–1897)
The man who gives me employment, which I
must have or suffer, that man is my master,
let me call him what I will.

[Social Problems (1884)]

**GILMAN, Charlotte Perkins
(1860–1935)**
There's a whining at the threshold
There's a scratching at the floor.
To work! To work! In Heaven's name!
The wolf is at the door.

[Attr.]

HOOD, Thomas (1799–1845)
With fingers weary and worn,
With eyelids heavy and red,
A Woman sat, in unwomanly rags,
Plying her needle and thread –
Stitch! stitch! stitch!
In poverty, hunger, and dirt …

O! Men with Sisters dear!
O! Men with Mothers and Wives!
It is not linen you're wearing out,
But human creatures' lives! …

Oh! God! that bread should be so dear,
And flesh and blood so cheap! …

No blessed leisure for Love or Hope,

But only time for Grief!

['The Song of the Shirt' (1843)]

JEROME, Jerome K. (1859–1927)
I like work; it fascinates me. I can sit and look
at it for hours. I love to keep it by me: the
idea of getting rid of it nearly breaks my
heart.

[Three Men in a Boat (1889)]

**JERROLD, Douglas William
(1803–1857)**
The ugliest of trades have their moments of
pleasure. Now, if I were a grave-digger, or
even a hangman, there are some people I
could work for with a great deal of
enjoyment.

[Wit and Opinions of Douglas Jerrold (1859)]

JOHNSON, Samuel (1709–1784)
I have protracted my work till most of those
whom I wished to please have sunk into the
grave, and success and miscarriage are
empty sounds; I therefore dismiss it with
frigid tranquillity, having little to fear or hope
from censure or praise.

[In Boswell, The Life of Samuel Johnson (1791)]

JOLIOT-CURIE, Irène (1897–1956)
[Recalling the advice of her mother, Marie Curie]
That one must do some work seriously and
must be independent and not merely amuse
oneself in life – this our mother has told us
always, but never that science was the only
career worth following.

[In Mary Margaret McBride, A Long Way from
Missouri, 10]

KATZENBERG, Jeffrey
If you don't show up for work on Saturday,
don't bother coming in on Sunday.

[Attr.]

KEROUAC, Jack (1922–1969)
We're really all of us bottomly broke. I haven't
had time to work in weeks.

[On the Road (1957)]

KOLLWITZ, Käthe (1867–1945)
For the last third of life there remains only
work. It alone is always stimulating,

rejuvenating, exciting and satisfying.

[*Diaries and Letters* (1955)]

LANG, Ian (1940–)

Job insecurity is a state of mind.

[*The Observer Review*, 1995]

LARKIN, Philip (1922–1985)

Why should I let the toad work
Squat on my life?
Can't I use my wit as a pitchfork
And drive the brute off?

['Toads' (1955)]

LONDON, Jack (1876–1916)

In an English ship, they say, it is poor grub,
poor pay, and easy work; in an American ship,
good grub, good pay, and hard work. And
this is applicable to the working populations
of both countries.

[*The People of the Abyss* (1903)]

LOWELL, James Russell (1819–1891)

No man is born into the world, whose work
Is not born with him; there is always work,
And tools to work withal, for those who will:
And blessèd are the horny hands of toil!

['A Glance Behind the Curtain' (1844)]

NEILSON, John Shaw (1872–1942)

Work should begin with wine and generous
joking,
And in the place of penalties for smoking
Let us have fines for platitudes and croaking.

[*Collected Poems* (1934), 'To a Blonde Typist']

PARKINSON, C. Northcote (1909–1993)

Work expands so as to fill the time available
for its completion.

[*Parkinson's Law* (1958)]

The rise in the total of those employed is
governed by Parkinson's Law and would be
much the same whether the volume of work
were to increase, diminish or even disappear.

[*Parkinson's Law* (1958)]

PETER, Laurence J. (1919–1990)

In a hierarchy every employee tends to rise
to his level of incompetence.

[*The Peter Principle – Why Things Always Go Wrong* (1969)]

PHILIP, Prince, Duke of Edinburgh (1921–)

[Replying to a query as to what nature of work he
did]
I am self-employed.

[Attr.]

PROVERBS

All work and no play makes Jack a dull boy.

Many hands make light work.

REAGAN, Ronald (1911–)

They say hard work never hurt anybody, but I
figure why take the chance.

[Attr.]

REYNOLDS, Sir Joshua (1723–1792)

If you have great talents, industry will
improve them: if you have but moderate
abilities, industry will supply their deficiency.

[*Discourses on Art* (1769)]

RHODES, Zandra (1940–)

I was lucky to always have a work ethic.
Relationships end, men fail, but your work
will never let you down.

[*The Observer*, 1998]

ROOSEVELT, Theodore (1858–1919)

I wish to preach not the doctrine of ignoble
ease, but the doctrine of the strenuous life.

[*Speech*, 1899]

No man needs sympathy because he has to
work … Far and away the best prize that life
offers is the chance to work hard at work
worth doing.

[*Address*, 1903]

ROWLAND, Helen (1875–1950)

When you see what some girls marry, you
realize how they must hate to work for a
living.

[*Reflections of a Bachelor Girl* (1909)]

RUSKIN, John (1819–1900)

Which of us … is to do the hard and dirty
work for the rest – and for what pay? Who is

to do the pleasant and clean work, and for what pay?

[*Sesame and Lilies* (1865)]

Labour without joy is base. Labour without sorrow is base. Sorrow without labour is base. Joy without labour is base.

[*Time and Tide by Weare and Tyne* (1867)]

Life without industry is guilt, and industry without art is brutality.

[*Lectures on Art* (1870)]

RUSSELL, Bertrand (1872–1970)

One of the symptoms of approaching nervous breakdowns is the belief that one's work is terribly important. If I were a medical man, I should prescribe a holiday to any patient who considered his work important.

[Attr.]

SARGESON, Frank (1903–1982)

[A notice to callers, said to be on his house door] Frank Sargeson works in the mornings. Do you?

[*Islands*, 1978]

SCOTT, Sir Walter (1771–1832)

I live by twa trades, sir, … fiddle, sir, and spade; filling the world, and emptying of it.

[*The Bride of Lammermoor* (1819)]

SHAKESPEARE, William (1564–1616)

The labour we delight in physics pain.

[*Macbeth*, II.iii]

SHAW, George Bernard (1856–1950)

A day's work is a day's work, neither more nor less, and the man who does it needs a day's sustenance, a night's repose, and due leisure, whether he be painter or ploughman.

[*An Unsocial Socialist* (1887)]

SMITH, Adam (1723–1790)

It is the interest of every man to live as much at his ease as he can; and if his emoluments are to be precisely the same whether he does, or does not perform some very laborious duty, it is certainly his interest, at least as interest is vulgarly understood, either to neglect it altogether, or, if he is subject to

some authority which will not suffer him to do this, to perform it in as careless and slovenly a manner as that authority will permit.

[*Wealth of Nations* (1776)]

SOUTHERNE, Thomas (1660–1746)

And when we're worn,
Hack'd, hewn with constant service, thrown aside
To rust in peace, or rot in hospitals.

[*The Loyal Brother* (1682)]

SPOONER, William (1844–1930)

You will find as you grow older that the weight of rages will press harder and harder upon the employer.

[In W. Hayter, *Spooner* (1977)]

STANTON, Elizabeth Cady (1815–1902)

Woman has been the great unpaid laborer of the world.

[In Anthony and Gage, *History of Woman Suffrage* (1881)]

TEBBITT, Norman (1931–)

[Of his father who had grown up during the 1930s] He didn't riot. He got on his bike and looked for work and he kept looking till he found it.

[Speech, 1981]

THOREAU, Henry David (1817–1862)

For more than five years I maintained myself thus solely by the labor of my hands, and I found, that by working about six weeks in a year, I could meet all the expenses of living.

[*Walden* (1854)]

TWAIN, Mark (1835–1910)

Work consists of whatever a body is obliged to do.

[*The Adventures of Tom Sawyer* (1876)]

VOLTAIRE (1694–1778)

Le travail éloigne de nous trois grand maux: l'ennui, le vice et le besoin.
Work keeps away those three great evils: boredom, vice, and poverty.

[*Candide* (1759)]

WATTS, Isaac (1674–1748)

In works of labour, or of skill,
I would be busy too;
For Satan finds some mischief still
For idle hands to do.

['Against Idleness and Mischief' (1715)]

WHITEHORN, Katherine (1926–)

The best careers advice to give to the young is 'Find out what you like doing best and get someone to pay you for doing it.'

[*The Observer*, 1975]

WILDE, Oscar (1854–1900)

Work is the curse of the drinking classes.

[In Pearson, *Life of Oscar Wilde* (1946)]

YEATS, W.B. (1865–1939)

The intellect of man is forced to choose
Perfection of the life, or of the work.

['The Choice' (1933)]

See CAREERS

THE WORLD

ARNOLD, Matthew (1822–1888)

Ah, love, let us be true
To one another! for the world, which seems
To lie before us like a land of dreams,
So various, so beautiful, so new,
Hath really neither joy, nor love, nor light,
Nor certitude, nor peace, nor help for pain;
And we are here as on a darkling plain
Swept with confused alarms of struggle and flight
Where ignorant armies clash by night.

['Dover Beach' (1867)]

BALFOUR, A.J. (1848–1930)

This is a singularly ill-contrived world, but not so ill-contrived as all that.

[Attr.]

BENNETT, Arnold (1867–1931)

Well, my deliberate opinion is – it's a jolly strange world.

[*The Title* (1918)]

BRETON, Nicholas (c.1545–c.1626)

A Mad World, My Masters.

[Title of dialogue, 1603]

BRONOWSKI, Jacob (1908–1974)

The world is made of people who never quite get into the first team and who just miss the prizes at the flower show.

[*The Face of Violence* (1954)]

BRONTË, Anne (1820–1849)

There is always a 'but' in this imperfect world.

[*The Tenant of Wildfell Hall* (1848)]

BROWNE, Sir Thomas (1605–1682)

For the world, I count it not an inn, but an hospital, and a place, not to live, but to die in.

[*Religio Medici* (1643)]

BUCKINGHAM, Duke of (1628–1687)

The world is made up for the most part of fools and knaves.

['To Mr. Clifford, on his Humane Reason']

BUTLER, Samuel (1835–1902)

The world will, in the end, follow only those who have despised as well as served it.

[*The Note-Books of Samuel Butler* (1912)]

CARLYLE, Thomas (1795–1881)

But the world is an old woman, and mistakes any gilt farthing for a gold coin; whereby being often cheated, she will thenceforth trust nothing but the common copper.

[*Sartor Resartus* (1834)]

CHAUCER, Geoffrey (c.1340–1400)

This world nys but a thurghfare ful of wo,
And we been pilgrymes, passynge to and fro.
Deeth is an ende of every worldly soore.

[*The Canterbury Tales* (1387)]

CLOUGH, Arthur Hugh (1819–1861)

This world is bad enough, may-be,
We do not comprehend it;
But in one fact can all agree,
God won't, and we can't mend it.

[*Dipsychus* (1865)]

COWLEY, Abraham (1618–1667)

The world's a scene of changes, and to be
Constant, in Nature were inconstancy.

[*The Mistress: or … Love Verses* (1647)]

DICKINSON, Emily (1830–1886)

How much can come
And much can go,
And yet abide the World!

['There came a Wind' (c. 1883)]

DIDEROT, Denis (1713–1784)

Oh! que ce monde-ci serait une bonne comédie si l'on n'y faisait pas un rôle.

What a fine comedy this world would be if one did not play a part in it!

[Letters to Sophie Volland]

EMERSON, Ralph Waldo (1803–1882)

As there is a use in medicine for poisons, so the world cannot move without rogues.

[*Conduct of Life* (1860)]

FIRBANK, Ronald (1886–1926)

The world is disgracefully managed, one hardly knows to whom to complain.

[*Vainglory* (1915)]

GRACIÁN, Baltasar (1601–1658)

La metad del mundo se está riendo de la otra metad, con necedad de todos.

Half the world is laughing at the other half, which shows how foolish everyone is.

[*Handbook-Oracle and the Art of Prudence* (1647)]

HARDY, Thomas (1840–1928)

Well, World, you have kept faith with me,
Kept faith with me;
Upon the whole you have proved to be
Much as you said you were.

['He Never Expected Much, A Consideration on My Eighty-Sixth birthday (1928)']

HAZLITT, William (1778–1830)

If the world were good for nothing else, it is a fine subject for speculation.

[*Characteristics* (1823)]

HEMINGWAY, Ernest (1898–1961)

The world is a fine place and worth the fighting for.

[*For Whom the Bell Tolls* (1940)]

JOHNSON, Samuel (1709–1784)

This world where much is to be done and little to be known.

[In G.B. Hill (ed.), *Johnsonian Miscellanies* (1897)]

KAFKA, Franz (1883–1924)

Im Kampf zwischen dir und der Welt sekundiere der Welt.

In the struggle between you and the world, support the world.

[*Reflections on Sin, Sorrow, Hope and the True Way* (1953)]

KEATS, John (1795–1821)

Call the world if you Please 'The vale of Soul-making'.

[Letter to George and Georgiana Keats, 1819]

KOESTLER, Arthur (1905–1983)

One may not regard the world as a sort of metaphysical brothel for emotions.

[*Darkness at Noon* (1940)]

LLOYD GEORGE, David (1863–1945)

The world is becoming like a lunatic asylum run by lunatics.

[*The Observer*, 1953]

MACNEICE, Louis (1907–1963)

World is crazier and more of it than we think,
Incorrigibly plural. I peel and portion
A tangerine and spit the pips and feel
The drunkenness of things being various.

['Snow' (1935)]

MARQUIS, Don (1878–1937)

Ours is a world where people don't know what they want and are willing to go through hell to get it.

[In *Treasury of Humorous Quotations*]

O'CASEY, Sean (1880–1964)

Th' whole worl's in a terrible state o' chassis!

[*Juno and the Paycock* (1924)]

OPPENHEIMER, J. Robert (1904–1967)

The optimist thinks that this is the best of all possible worlds and the pessimist knows it.

[*Bulletin of Atomic Scientists*, 1951]

OWEN, Robert (1771–1858)

[To W. Allen, on dissolving their business partnership]

All the world is queer save thee and me, and

even thou art a little queer.

[Attr., 1828]

PATTEN, Brian (1946–)

and I understood
how there is nothing complicated in the
world
that is not of my own making.

['turning the pages']

SARTRE, Jean-Paul (1905–1980)

Le monde peut fort bien se passer de la littérature.
Mais il peut se passer de l'homme encore mieux.
The world can survive very well without
literature. But it can survive even more easily
without man.

[*Situations*]

SCOTT, Sir Walter (1771–1832)

The ae half of the warld thinks the tither daft.

[*Redgauntlet* (1824)]

SHAKESPEARE, William (1564–1616)

I hold the world but as the world, Gratiano –
A stage, where every man must play a part,
And mine a sad one.

[*The Merchant of Venice*, I.i]

How many goodly creatures are there here!
How beauteous mankind is! O brave new
world
That has such people in't!

[*The Tempest*, V.i]

SHAW, George Bernard (1856–1950)

Nothing is ever done in this world until men
are prepared to kill one another if it is not
done.

[*Major Barbara* (1907)]

SMITH, Sydney (1771–1845)

Bishop Berkeley destroyed this world in one
volume octavo; and nothing remained, after
his time, but mind; which experienced a
similar fate from the hand of Mr Hume in
1739.

[*Sketches of Moral Philosophy* (1849)]

SMOLLETT, Tobias (1721–1771)

I consider the world as made for me, not me
for the world: it is my maxim therefore to

enjoy it while I can, and let futurity shift for
itself.

[*The Adventures of Roderick Random* (1748)]

STEVENS, Wallace (1879–1955)

In my room, the world is beyond my
understanding;
But when I walk I see that it consists of three
or four hills and a cloud.

['Of the Surface of Things' (1923)]

STEVENSON, Robert Louis (1850–1894)

The world is so full of a number of things,
I'm sure we should all be as happy as kings.

[*A Child's Garden of Verses* (1885), 'Happy Thought']

THATCHER, Margaret (1925–)

It's a funny old world.

[*The Sunday Telegraph*, 1990]

THOMPSON, Francis (1859–1907)

O world invisible, we view thee,
O world intangible, we touch thee,
O world unknowable, we know thee,
Inapprehensible, we clutch thee!

['The Kingdom of God' (1913)]

TRAHERNE, Thomas (c.1637–1674)

You never enjoy the world aright, till the sea
itself floweth in your veins, till you are
clothed with the heavens, and crowned with
the stars: and perceive yourself to be the sole
heir of the whole world, and more than so,
because men are in it who are every one sole
heirs as well as you. Till you can sing and
rejoice and delight in God, as misers do in
gold, and kings in sceptres, you can never
enjoy the world.

[*Centuries of Meditations*]

WALPOLE, Horace (1717–1797)

This world is a comedy to those that think,
and a tragedy to those that feel.

[Letter to Anne, Countess of Upper Ossory, 1776]

WARD, Nathaniel (1578–1652)

The world is full of care, much like unto a
bubble;
Women and care, and care and women, and

women and care and trouble.

[*Epigram* (1647)]

WORDSWORTH, William (1770–1850)

The world is too much with us; late and soon,
Getting and spending, we lay waste our
powers.

['The world is too much with us'
(1807)]

WOTTON, Sir Henry (1568–1639)

When we meet, all the world to nothing we
shall laugh; and, in truth Sir this world is
worthy of nothing else.

[Letter to Sir Edmund Bacon, 1614]

YEATS, W.B. (1865–1939)

This pragmatical, preposterous pig of a
world.

[In *The Exile*, 1928]

YOUNG, Edward (1683–1765)

To know the World, not love her, is thy point;
She gives but little, nor that little long.

[*Night-Thoughts on Life, Death and Immortality*
(1742–45)]

See UNIVERSE

WORRYING

ASAF, George (1880–1951)

What's the use of worrying?
It never was worth while,
So, pack up your troubles in your old kit-bag,
And smile, smile, smile.

['Pack up Your Troubles in Your Old Kit-bag', song,
1915]

MIDDLETON, Thomas (c.1580–1627)

I never heard
Of any true affection, but 'twas nipt
With care.

[*Blurt, Master-Constable* (1602)]

SCHULZ, Charles (1922–)

I've developed a new philosophy – I only
dread one day at a time.

[Attr.]

WRITERS

ADDISON, Joseph (1672–1719)

Thus I live in the world rather as a spectator
of mankind, than as one of the species, by
which means I have made myself a
speculative statesman, soldier, merchant, and
artisan, without ever meddling with any
practical part in life.

[*The Spectator*, March 1711]

ANONYMOUS

[A member of the Soviet Writers' Union, after the
decision to urge publication of *The Gulag
Archipelago*, in reply to Vladimir Karpov's comment
'I have never seen such unanimity among us']
At least, not since we voted to expel
Solzhenitsyn.

[*The Independent*, 1989]

ARNOLD, Matthew (1822–1888)

[Of Chaucer]
He lacks the high seriousness of the great
classics, and therewith an important part of
their virtue.

[*Essays in Criticism* (1888)]

Dryden and Pope are not classics of our
poetry, they are classics of our prose.

[*Essays in Criticism* (1888)]

AUBREY, John (1626–1697)

How these curiosities would be quite forgot, did
not such idle fellows as I am put them down.

[*Brief Lives* (c. 1693)]

AUDEN, W.H. (1907–1973)

No poet or novelist wishes he were the only
one who ever lived, but most of them wish
they were the only one alive, and quite a
number fondly believe their wish has been
granted.

[*The Dyer's Hand* (1963)]

AUSTEN, Jane (1775–1817)

I think I may boast myself to be, with all
possible vanity, the most unlearned and
uninformed female who ever dared to be an
authoress.

[Letter to James Stanier Clarke, 1815]

BAGEHOT, Walter (1826–1877)

Writers, like teeth, are divided into incisors and grinders.

['The First Edinburgh Reviewers' (1858)]

A man who has not read Homer is like a man who has not seen the ocean. There is a great object of which he has no idea.

[*Literary Studies* (1879)]

BARLOW, Jane (1860–1917)

That old yahoo George Moore … His stories impressed me as being on the whole like gruel spooned up off a dirty floor.

[Letter, 1914]

BEAUVOIR, Simone de (1908–1986)

L'écrivain original, tant qu'il n'est pas mort, est toujours scandaleux.

Writers who stand out, as long as they are not dead, are always scandalous.

[*The Second Sex* (1950)]

BELLOW, Saul (1915–)

If one yearns to live dangerously, is it not as dangerous to persist in the truth as to rush to the barricades? But then it is always more agreeable to play the role of a writer than to be a writer. A writer's life is solitary, often bitter. How pleasant it is to come out of one's room, to fly about the world, make speeches, and cut a swath.

[*Critical Enquiry*, 1975]

BENNETT, Alan (1934–)

We were put to Dickens as children but it never quite took. That unremitting humanity soon had me cheesed off.

[*The Old Country* (1978)]

BERNARD, Jeffrey (1932–1997)

Writers as a rule don't make fighters, although I would hate to have to square up to Taki or Andrea Dworkin.

[*The Spectator*, 1992]

BRENAN, Gerald (1894–1987)

[Of Henry Miller]

Miller is not really a writer but a non-stop talker to whom someone has given a

typewriter.

[*Thoughts in a Dry Season* (1978)]

BRONTË, Charlotte (1816–1855)

Novelists should never allow themselves to weary of the study of real life.

[*The Professor* (1857)]

BRONTË, Rev. Patrick (1777–1861)

Girls, do you know Charlotte has been writing a book, and it is much better than likely?

[In Elizabeth Gaskell, *Life of Charlotte Brontë* (1857)]

BROWNE, Coral (1913–1991)

[To a Hollywood writer who had criticized the work of Alan Bennett]

Listen, dear, you couldn't write fuck on a dusty venetian blind.

[Attr., in *The Sunday Times Magazine*, 1984]

CAMPBELL, Roy (1901–1957)

You praise the firm restraint with which they write –

I'm with you there, of course:

They use the snaffle and the curb all right,

But where's the bloody horse?

[*Adamastor* (1930)]

CANETTI, Elias (1905–1994)

Er legt Sätze wie Eier, aber er vergisst, sie zu bebrüten.

He lays sentences like eggs, but he forgets to incubate them.

[*The Human Province. Notes from 1942 to 1972*]

CARLYLE, Thomas (1795–1881)

O thou who art able to write a Book, which once in the two centuries or oftener there is a man gifted to do, envy not him whom they name City-builder, and inexpressibly pity him whom they name Conqueror or City-burner!

[*Sartor Resartus* (1834)]

Literary men are … a perpetual priesthood.

[*Critical and Miscellaneous Essays* (1839)]

[On Ralph Waldo Emerson]

A hoaryheaded and toothless baboon.

[*Collected Works* (1871)]

CAXTON, William (c.1421–1491)

The worshipful father and first founder and

embellisher of ornate eloquence in our English, I mean Master Geoffrey Chaucer.

[Epilogue to Caxton's edition (c. 1478) of Chaucer's translation of Boethius, *The Consolacion of Philosophie*]

CHATEAUBRIAND, François-René (1768–1848)

L'écrivain original n'est pas celui qui n'imite personne, mais celui que personne ne peut imiter.

The original writer is not the one who refrains from imitating others, but the one who can be imitated by none.

[*The Beauties of Christianity* (1802)]

CHESTERTON, G.K. (1874–1936)

Mr Shaw is (I suspect) the only man on earth who has never written any poetry.

[*Orthodoxy* (1908)]

Jane Austen was born before those bands which (we are told) protected woman from truth, were burst by the Brontës or elaborately untied by George Eliot. Yet the fact remains that Jane Austen knew much more about men than either of them.

[*The Victorian Age in Literature* (1913)]

Hardy went down to botanise in the swamp, while Meredith climbed towards the sun. Meredith became, at his best, a sort of daintily dressed Walt Whitman: Hardy became a sort of village atheist brooding and blaspheming over the village idiot.

[*The Victorian Age in Literature* (1913)]

CLARK, Manning (1915–1991)

All writers are liars, and there is not the slightest chance that any writer will get into heaven.

[Speech, Melbourne, 1987]

COCTEAU, Jean (1889–1963)

Victor Hugo … un fou qui se croyait Victor Hugo.

Victor Hugo … a madman who thought he was Victor Hugo.

[*Opium* (1930)]

COLERIDGE, Samuel Taylor (1772–1834)

Until you understand a writer's ignorance,

presume yourself ignorant of his understanding.

[*Biographia Literaria* (1817)]

Swift was *anima Rabelaisii habitans in sicco* – the soul of Rabelais dwelling in a dry place.

[*Table Talk* (1835)]

When I was a boy, I was fondest of Aeschylus; in youth and middle-age I preferred Euripides; now in my declining years I prefer Sophocles. I can now at length see that Sophocles is the most perfect. Yet he never rises to the sublime simplicity of Aeschylus – a simplicity of design, I mean – nor diffuses himself in the passionate outpourings of Euripides.

[*Table Talk* (1835)]

I believe the souls of five hundred Sir Isaac Newtons would go to the making up of a Shakespeare or a Milton.

[Letter to Thomas Poole, 1801]

CONDON, Richard (1915–)

Writers are too self-centred to be lonely.

[Attr.]

CONNOLLY, Cyril (1903–1974)

An author arrives at a good style when his language performs what is required of it without shyness.

[*Enemies of Promise* (1938)]

Better to write for yourself and have no public, than write for the public and have no self.

[In Pritchett (ed.), *Turnstile One*]

[Of George Orwell]
He would not blow his nose without moralizing on conditions in the handkerchief industry.

[*The Evening Colonnade* (1973)]

DELILLO, Don (1936–)

Years ago I used to think it was possible for a novelist to alter the inner life of the culture. Now bomb-makers and gunmen have taken that territory. They make raids on human consciousness. What writers used to do before we were all incorporated.

[*Mao II*]

DISRAELI, Benjamin (1804–1881)

An author who speaks about his own books is almost as bad as a mother who talks about her own children.

[Speech at Banquet given in Glasgow on his installation as Lord Rector, 1873]

DRYDEN, John (1631–1700)

Our author by experience finds it true,
'Tis much more hard to please himself than you.

[*Aureng-Zebe* (1675)]

EMERSON, Ralph Waldo (1803–1882)

Talent alone cannot make a writer. There must be a man behind the book.

['Goethe; or, the Writer' (1850)]

FAULKNER, William (1897–1962)

The writer's only responsibility is to his art … If a writer has to rob his mother, he will not hesitate; the 'Ode on a Grecian Urn' is worth any number of old ladies.

[*Paris Review*, 1956]

[On Henry James]
The nicest old lady I ever met.

[In E. Stone, *The Battle and the Books* (c. 1964)]

[Of Ernest Hemingway]
He has never been known to use a word that might send the reader to the dictionary.

[Attr.]

FROST, Robert (1874–1963)

No tears in the writer, no tears in the reader.

[*Collected Poems* (1939)]

GOLDSMITH, Oliver (c.1728–1774)

As writers become more numerous, it is natural for readers to become more indolent.

[*The Bee* (1759)]

GORDIMER, Nadine (1923–)

The tension between standing apart and being fully involved; that is what makes a writer.

[*Selected Stories* (1975)]

GUEDALLA, Philip (1889–1944)

The work of Henry James has always seemed divisible by a simple dynastic arrangement into three reigns: James I, James II, and the Old Pretender.

[*Collected Essays* (1920)]

HAZLITT, William (1778–1830)

[Of Sir Walter Scott]
He writes as fast as they can read, and he does not write himself down.

[*The Spirit of the Age* (1825)]

His worst is better than any other person's best.

[*The Spirit of the Age* (1825)]

His works (taken together) are almost like a new edition of human nature. This is indeed to be an author!

[*The Spirit of the Age* (1825)]

HEMINGWAY, Ernest (1898–1961)

[Of James Joyce]
And when you saw him he would take up a conversation interrupted three years before. It was nice to see a great writer in our time.

[*Green Hills of Africa* (1935)]

[In response to a jibe by William Faulkner]
Poor Faulkner. Does he really think big emotions come from big words? He thinks I don't know the ten-dollar words. I know them all right. But there are older and simpler and better words, and those are the ones I use.

[Attr.]

HILL, Reginald (1936–)

[When asked in America why all the great crime writers of the 1920s were female]
Because the men were all dead.

HOBBES, Thomas (1588–1679)

The praise of ancient authors, proceeds not from the reverence of the dead, but from the competition, and mutual envy of the living.

[*Leviathan* (1651)]

HUGHES, Ted (1930–1998)

The progress of any writer is marked by

those moments when he manages to outwit his own inner police system.

[In Wendy Cope, *Making Cocoa for Kingsley Amis* (1986)]

IRVING, Washington (1783–1859)

I am always at a loss to know how much to believe of my own stories.

[*Tales of a Traveller* (1824)]

JOHNSON, Samuel (1709–1784)

The greatest part of a writer's time is spent in reading, in order to write: a man will turn over half a library to make one book.

[In Boswell, *The Life of Samuel Johnson* (1791)]

The chief glory of every people arises from its authors.

[*A Dictionary of the English Language* (1755)]

It is the fate of those who toil at the lower employments of life … to be exposed to censure, without hope of praise; to be disgraced by miscarriage, or punished for neglect … Among these unhappy mortals is the writer of dictionaries … Every other author may aspire to praise; the lexicographer can only hope to escape reproach.

[*A Dictionary of the English Language* (1755)]

JOSEPH, Michael (1897–1958)

Authors are easy to get on with – if you're fond of children.

[*The Observer*, 1949]

KOESTLER, Arthur (1905–1983)

A writer's ambition should be … to trade a hundred contemporary readers for ten readers in ten years' time and for one reader in a hundred years' time.

[*New York Times Book Review*, 1951]

LAMB, Lady Caroline (1785–1828)

[Of Byron]

Mad, bad, and dangerous to know.

[*Journal*, 1812]

LANDOR, Walter Savage (1775–1864)

Clear writers, like clear fountains, do not seem so deep as they are; the turbid look the most profound.

[*Imaginary Conversations* (1824)]

LINCOLN, Abraham (1809–1865)

[On meeting Harriet Beecher Stowe]

So you're the little woman who wrote the book that made this great war!

[Attr.]

MACDIARMID, Hugh (1892–1978)

Our principal writers have nearly all been fortunate in escaping regular education.

[*The Observer*, 1953]

MACMANUS, Michael (1888–1951)

But my work is undistinguished
And my royalties are lean
Because I never am obscure
And not at all obscene.

['An Author's Lament']

PASCAL, Blaise (1623–1662)

Quand on voit le style naturel, on est tout étonné et ravi, car on s'attendait de voir un auteur, et on trouve un homme.

When we see a natural style, we are quite surprised and delighted, for we expected to see an author and we find a man.

[*Pensées* (1670)]

SAKI (1870–1916)

Sherard Blaw, the dramatist who had discovered himself, and who had given so ungrudgingly of his discovery to the world.

[*The Unbearable Bassington* (1912)]

SARTRE, Jean-Paul (1905–1980)

The writer, a free man addressing free men, has only one subject – freedom.

[*What Is Literature?*]

SINGER, Isaac Bashevis (1904–1991)

When I was a little boy they called me a liar but now that I am a grown up they call me a writer.

[*The Observer*, 1983]

SOLZHENITSYN, Alexander (1918–)

No regime has ever loved great writers, only minor ones.

[*The First Circle* (1968)]

STEVENSON, Robert Louis (1850–1894)

Though we are mighty fine fellows nowadays, we cannot write like Hazlitt.

[*Virginibus Puerisque* (1881)]

TYNAN, Kenneth (1927–1980)

William Congreve is the only sophisticated playwright England has produced; and like Shaw, Sheridan, and Wilde, his nearest rivals, he was brought up in Ireland.

[*Curtains* (1961)]

VIDAL, Gore (1925–)

American writers want to be not good but great; and so are neither.

[*Two Sisters* (1970)]

WAUGH, Evelyn (1903–1966)

No writer before the middle of the 19th century wrote about the working classes other than as grotesque or as pastoral decoration. Then when they were given the vote certain writers started to suck up to them.

[*Paris Review*, 1963]

WHITLAM, Gough (1916–)

The challenge for the writer is to adapt his ancient and difficult craft to a generation that is largely insensitive to its virtues and to a popular audience increasingly distracted by the pace, immediacy and materialism of contemporary life.

[Speech, 1975]

YEATS, W.B. (1865–1939)

It's not a writer's business to hold opinions.

[Attr.]

A good writer should be so simple that he has no faults, only sins.

[*The Death of Synge and other Passages from an Old Diary* (1928)]

See CRITICISM; POETS; WRITING

WRITERS (individual)

ANONYMOUS

[Of Irvine Welsh]

'… he is quite distinctive being bald, Scottish and ugly.'

[*Daily Record*, 1999]

JOHNSON, Samuel (1709–1784)

Why, Sir, if you were to read Richardson for the story, your impatience would be so much fretted, that you would hang yourself. But you must read him for the sentiment, and consider the story as only giving occasion to the sentiment.

[In Boswell, *The Life of Samuel Johnson* (1791)]

[Of Thomas Gray]

He was dull in a new way, and that made many people think him great.

[In Boswell, *The Life of Samuel Johnson* (1791)]

[Of Goldsmith]

No man was more foolish when he had not a pen in his hand, or more wise when he had.

[In Boswell, *The Life of Samuel Johnson* (1791)]

LAMB, Mary (1764–1847)

[Of Henry Crabb Robinson]

He says he never saw a man so happy in three wives as Mr Wordsworth is.

[Letter to Sarah Hutchinson, 1816]

LEHMANN, Rosamond (1901–1990)

The trouble with Ian [Fleming] is that he gets off with women because he can't get on with them.

[Borrowing a line from Elizabeth Bowen, quoted in J. Pearson, *The Life of Ian Fleming* (1966)]

LENIN, V.I. (1870–1924)

[Of Bernard Shaw]

A good man fallen among Fabians.

[In Arthur Ransome, *Six Weeks in Russia in 1919* (1919)]

LEVERSON, Ada Beddington (1862–1936)

[Of Oscar Wilde]

The last gentleman in Europe.

[*Letters to the Sphinx* (1930)]

MITFORD, Mary Russell (1787–1855)

I have discovered that our great favourite, Miss Austen, is my country-woman … with whom mamma before her marriage was acquainted. Mamma says that she was then the prettiest, silliest, most affected, husband-hunting butterfly she ever remembers.

[Letter to Sir William Elford, 1815]

[Of Jane Austen]
Perpendicular, precise and taciturn.

[In *Life and Letters of Mary R. Mitford* (1870)]

MUGGERIDGE, Malcolm (1903–1990)

[Of Evelyn Waugh]
He looked, I decided, like a letter delivered to the wrong address.

[*Tread Softly For You Tread on My Jokes* (1966)]

O'CASEY, Sean (1880–1964)

[Of P.G. Wodehouse]
English literature's performing flea.

[In P.G. Wodehouse, *Performing Flea* (1953)]

O'CONOR, Roderic (1860–1940)

[On Somerset Maugham]
A bedbug on which a sensitive man refuses to stamp because of the smell and squashiness.

[Attr. in Larry Powell, 'The Discovery of a New Master, Roderic O'Conor', *Etudes Irlandaises*, 1933]

RUSKIN, John (1819–1900)

Thackeray settled like a meat-fly on whatever one had got for dinner, and made one sick of it.

[*Fors Clavigera* (1871–1884)]

SCOTT, Sir Walter (1771–1832)

The blockheads talk of my being like Shakespeare – not fit to tie his brogues.

[*Journal*, 11 December 1826]

SHERWOOD, Robert Emmet (1896–1955)

It is disappointing to report that George Bernard Shaw appearing as George Bernard Shaw is sadly miscast in the part. Satirists should be heard and not seen.

[Reviewing a Shaw play]

SHORTHOUSE, J.H. (1834–1903)

In all probability 'Wordsworth's standard of intoxication was miserably low.'

[Remark]

SITWELL, Dame Edith (1887–1964)

[Of Virginia Woolf]
I enjoyed talking to her, but thought nothing of her writing. I considered her 'a beautiful little knitter'.

[Letter to G. Singleton, 1955]

WALPOLE, Horace (1717–1797)

Lord Rochester's poems have much more obscenity than wit, more wit than poetry, more poetry than politeness.

[*Catalogue of Royal and Noble Authors* (1758)]

WARD, Artemus (1834–1867)

It is a pity that Chawcer, who had geneyus, was so unedicated. He's the wuss speller I know of.

[*Artemus Ward in London* (1867)]

WAUGH, Evelyn (1903–1966)

[Remark to Graham Greene, who was planning to write a political novel]
I wouldn't give up writing about God at this stage if I was you. It would be like P.G. Wodehouse dropping Jeeves half-way through the Wooster series.

[In Christopher Sykes, *Evelyn Waugh*]

I put the words down and push them a bit.

[Obituary, *New York Times*, 11 April 1966]

WELLS, H.G. (1866–1946)

[Of Henry James]
The thing his novel is about is always there. It is like a church lit but without a congregation to distract you, with every light and line focused on the high altar. And on the altar, very reverently placed, intensely there, is a dead kitten, an egg-shell, a bit of string.

[*Boon* (1915)]

YEATS, W.B. (1865–1939)

[Of George Eliot]
She is magnificently ugly – deliciously hideous … now in this vast ugliness resides a most powerful beauty which, in a very few minutes steals forth and charms the mind.

[Attr.]

See CRITICISM; POETS; SHAKESPEARE;
WRITING

WRITING

ADDISON, Joseph (1672–1719)
[Of the difference between his conversational and writing abilities]
I have but ninepence in ready money, but I can draw for a thousand pounds.

[In Boswell, *The Life of Samuel Johnson* (1791)]

ANONYMOUS
Inspiration is the act of drawing up a chair to the writing desk.

ARNOLD, Matthew (1822–1888)
People think that I can teach them style. What stuff it all is! Have something to say, and say it as clearly as you can. That is the only secret of style.

[In Russell, *Collections and Recollections* (1898)]

ASCHAM, Roger (1515–1568)
He that will write well in any tongue, must follow this counsel of Aristotle, to speak as the common people do, to think as wise men do; and so should every man understand him, and the judgment of wise men allow him.

[*Toxophilus* (1545)]

ATWOOD, Margaret (1939–)
Once upon a time I thought there was an old man with a grey beard somewhere who knew the truth, and if I was good enough, naturally he would tell me that this was it. That person doesn't exist, but that's who I write for. The great critic in the sky.

[In Earl G. Ingersoll (ed.), *Margaret Atwood: Conversations* (1990)]

Writing … is an act of faith: I believe it's also an act of hope, the hope that things can be better than they are.

[Attr.]

AUSTEN, Jane (1775–1817)
… the little bit (two inches wide) of ivory on which I work with so fine a brush, as

produces little effect after much labour.

[Letter, 1816]

Let other pens dwell on guilt and misery.

[*Mansfield Park* (1814)]

BENTHAM, Jeremy (1748–1832)
Prose is when all the lines except the last go on to the end. Poetry is when some of them fall short of it.

[In Packe, *Life of John Stuart Mill* (1954)]

BOILEAU-DESPRÉAUX, Nicolas (1636–1711)
Qui ne sait se borner ne sut jamais écrire.
He who does not know how to limit himself does not know how to write.

[*L'Art Poétique* (1674)]

BRITTAIN, Vera (1893–1970)
The idea that it is necessary to go to a university in order to become a successful writer, or even a man or woman of letters (which is by no means the same thing), is one of those phantasies that surround authorship.

[*On Being an Author* (1948)]

BULWER-LYTTON, Edward (1803–1873)
Beneath the rule of men entirely great
The pen is mightier than the sword.

[*Richelieu* (1839)]

CARLYLE, Thomas (1795–1881)
After two weeks of blotching and blaring I have produced two clear papers.

[Attr.]

DICKENS, Charles (1812–1870)
I hold my inventive faculty on the stern condition that it must master my whole life, often have complete possession of me … and sometimes for months together put everything else away from me.

[*The Letters of Charles Dickens*]

ELIOT, T.S. (1888–1965)
[On his ideal of writing]
The common word exact without vulgarity, the formal word precise but not pedantic,

the complete consort dancing together.

[*Sunday Telegraph*, 1993]

ETHEREGE, Sir George (c.1635–1691)

Writing, Madam, is a mechanic part of wit; a gentleman should never go beyond a song or a billet.

[*The Man of Mode* (1676)]

FANON, Frantz (1925–1961)

[On 'native' writers trying to rid themselves of European influences]

It is always easier to proclaim rejection than to reject.

[*Les damnées de la terre* (1961)]

FROST, Robert (1874–1963)

Writing free verse is like playing tennis with the net down.

[*Address*, 1935]

GALSWORTHY, John (1867–1933)

I do wish I had the gift of writing. I really think that it is the nicest way of making money going.

[Letter to Monica Sanderson, c. 1894]

GORKY, Maxim (1868–1936)

You must write for children just as you do for adults, only better.

[Attr.]

GRAY, Thomas (1716–1771)

Any fool may write a most valuable book by chance, if he will only tell us what he heard and saw with veracity.

[Letter to Horace Walpole, 1768]

HEMINGWAY, Ernest (1898–1961)

Prose is architecture, not interior decoration, and the Baroque is over.

[*Death in the Afternoon* (1932)]

JOHNSON, Samuel (1709–1784)

A man may write at any time, if he will set himself doggedly to it.

[In Boswell, *The Life of Samuel Johnson* (1791)]

What is written without effort is in general read without pleasure.

[In William Seward, *Biographia* (1799)]

The only end of writing is to enable the readers better to enjoy life, or better to endure it.

[*Works* (1787)]

No man but a blockhead ever wrote, except for money.

[In Boswell, *The Life of Samuel Johnson* (1791)]

JUVENAL (c.60–130)

Tenet insanabile multos
Scribendi cacoethes et aegro in corde senescit.
The incurable itch for writing takes hold of many and becomes chronic in their distempered brains.

[*Satires*]

KEATS, John (1795–1821)

I have come to this resolution – never to write for the sake of writing or making a poem, but running over with any little knowledge or experience which many years of reflection may perhaps give me; otherwise I will be dumb.

[Letter to B.R. Haydon, 8 March 1819]

I am convinced more and more day by day that fine writing is next to fine doing, the top thing in the world.

[Letter to J. H. Reynolds, 1819]

LA BRUYÈRE, Jean de (1645–1696)

Tout est dit, et l'on vient trop tard depuis plus de sept mille ans qu'il y a des hommes et qui pensent.
Everything has been said already; we come too late after more than seven thousand years in which men have lived and thought.

[*Les caractères ou les moeurs de ce siècle* (1688)]

LAWRENCE, D.H. (1885–1930)

I like to write when I feel spiteful: it's like having a good sneeze.

[Letter to Lady Cynthia Asquith, 1913]

LERNER, Alan Jay (1918–1986)

You write a hit the same way you write a flop.

[Attr.]

LYNES, J. Russel (1910–1991)

Every journalist has a novel in him, which is an excellent place for it.

MANSFIELD, Katherine (1888–1923)

Better to write twaddle, anything, than nothing at all.

[Attr.]

MAUGHAM, William Somerset (1874–1965)

You don't just get a story … You have to wait for it to come to you. I've never written a story in my life. The story has come to me and demanded to be written.

[In Robin Maugham, *Conversation with Willie* (1978)]

MENCKEN, H.L. (1880–1956)

I write in order to attain that feeling of tension relieved and function achieved which a cow enjoys on giving milk.

[*The Delights of Reading*]

MURDOCH, Iris (1919–1999)

Writing is like getting married. One should never commit oneself until one is amazed at one's luck.

[*The Black Prince* (1989)]

ORWELL, George (1903–1950)

Good prose is like a window pane.

['Why I Write' (1946)]

PASCAL, Blaise (1623–1662)

La dernière chose qu'on trouve en faisant un ouvrage, est de savoir celle qu'il faut mettre la première.
The last thing one finds out when constructing a work is what to put first.

[*Pensées* (1670)]

PINTER, Harold (1930–)

Writing is for me a completely private activity, a poem or a play, no difference … What I write has no obligation to anything other than to itself.

[Speech to student drama festival, 1962]

PIRON, Alexis (1689–1773)

[Discussing Voltaire's *Sémiramis* with him after its poor reception on the first night]
I think you would have been very glad if I had written it.

[In K. Arvine, *Cyclopaedia of Anecdotes*]

POPE, Alexander (1688–1744)

'Tis hard to say, if greater want of skill
Appear in writing or in judging ill.

[*An Essay on Criticism* (1711)]

True ease in writing comes from art, not chance,
As those move easiest who have learn'd to dance.
'Tis not enough no harshness gives offence,
The sound must seem an echo to the sense.

[*An Essay on Criticism* (1711)]

POUND, Ezra (1885–1972)

O God, O Venus, O Mercury, patron of thieves,
Give me in due time, I beseech you, a little tobacco-shop …
And a pair of scales not too greasy,
And the whores dropping in for a word or two in passing,
For a flip word, and to tidy their hair a bit.

O God, O Venus, O Mercury, patron of thieves,
Lend me a little tobacco-shop,
or install me in any profession
Save this damn'd profession of writing,
where one needs one's brains all the time.

['The Lake Isle' (1916)]

RENARD, Jules (1864–1910)

The profession of letters is, after all, the only one in which one can make no money without being ridiculous.

[*Journal*]

SCOTT, Sir Walter (1771–1832)

[On Jane Austen]
The Big Bow-Wow strain I can do myself like any now going; but the exquisite touch, which renders ordinary commonplace things and characters interesting, from the truth of the description and the sentiment, is denied to me.

[*Journal*, 14 March 1826]

But no one shall find me rowing against the stream. I care not who knows it – I write for the general amusement.

[*The Fortunes of Nigel* (1822)]

SHERIDAN, Richard Brinsley (1751–1816)

You write with ease, to show your breeding;
But easy writing's vile hard reading.

['Clio's Protest' (1771)]

SIDNEY, Sir Philip (1554–1586)

Byting my tongue and penne, beating my
selfe for spite:
'Foole,' saide My muse to mee, 'looke in thy
heart and write'.

[*Astrophel and Stella* (1591)]

SIMENON, Georges (1903–1989)

Writing is not a profession but a vocation of
unhappiness.

[*Writers at Work* (1958)]

STEPHEN, James Kenneth (1859–1892)

Will there never come a season
Which shall rid us from the curse
Of a prose which knows no reason
And an unmelodious verse …
When there stands a muzzled stripling,
Mute, beside a muzzled bore:
When the Rudyards cease from kipling

And the Haggards ride no more.

[*Lapsus Calami* (1891)]

STERNE, Laurence (1713–1768)

Writing, when properly managed, (as you
may be sure I think mine is) is but a different
name for conversation.

[*Tristram Shandy* (1759–1767)]

STOPPARD, Tom (1937–)

You can only write about what bites you.

[*The Observer*, 1984]

STOWE, Harriet Beecher (1811–1896)

[Of *Uncle Tom's Cabin*]
I did not write it. God wrote it. I merely did
his dictation.

[Attr.]

TROLLOPE, Anthony (1815–1882)

Three hours a day will produce as much as a
man ought to write.

[*Autobiography* (1883)]

See BOOKS; CRITICISM; FICTION;
INSPIRATION; LITERATURE; POETRY;
READING; WRITERS

Y

YOUTH

ASQUITH, Herbert (1852–1928)

Youth would be an ideal state if it came a little later in life.

[*The Observer*, 1923]

BORROW, George (1803–1881)

Youth will be served, every dog has his day, and mine has been a fine one.

[*Lavengro* (1851)]

BULWER-LYTTON, Edward (1803–1873)

In the lexicon of youth, which Fate reserves For a bright manhood, there is no such word As – fail!

[*Richelieu* (1839)]

CHANEL, Coco (1883–1971)

Youth is something very new: twenty years ago no one mentioned it.

[In Haedrich, *Coco Chanel, Her Life, Her Secrets* (1971)]

CONRAD, Joseph (1857–1924)

I remember my youth and the feeling that will never come back any more – the feeling that I could last for ever, outlast the sea, the earth, and all men; the deceitful feeling that lures us on to perils, to love, to vain effort – to death; the triumphant conviction of strength, the heat of life in the handful of dust, that glow in the heart that with every year grows dim, grows cold, grows small, and expires – and expires, too soon, too soon – before life itself.

[*Youth* (1902)]

CRISP, Quentin (1908–)

The young always have the same problem – how to rebel and conform at the same time. They have now solved this by defying their parents and copying one another.

[*The Naked Civil Servant* (1968)]

CUNARD, Lady (Maud) 'Emerald' (1872–1948)

[Reply to Somerset Maugham, when said he was leaving early 'to keep his youth']

Then why didn't you bring him with you? I should be delighted to meet him.

[In D. Fielding, *Emerald and Nancy: Lady Cunard and her Daughter* (1968)]

DENHAM, Sir John (1615–1669)

Youth, what man's age is like to be doth show;
We may our ends by our beginnings know.

['Of Prudence' (1668)]

DISRAELI, Benjamin (1804–1881)

Almost everything that is great has been done by youth.

[*Coningsby* (1844)]

The Youth of a Nation are the Trustees of Posterity.

[*Sybil* (1845)]

Youth is a blunder; Manhood a struggle; Old Age a regret.

[*Coningsby* (1844)]

FITZGERALD, Edward (1809–1883)

Alas, that Spring should vanish with the Rose!
That Youth's sweet-scented Manuscript should close!
The Nightingale that in the Branches sang,
Ah, whence, and whither flown again, who knows!

[*The Rubáiyát of Omar Khayyám* (1859)]

GAY, John (1685–1732)

Youth's the season made for joys,
Love is then our duty.

[*The Beggar's Opera* (1728)]

HERBERT, Edward (1583–1648)

Now that the April of your youth adorns The Garden of your face.

['Ditty in imitation of the Spanish Entre tantoque L'Avril' (1665)]

IBSEN, Henrik (1828–1906)

Youth will come here and beat on my door, and force its way in.

[*The Master Builder* (1892)]

JOHNSON, Samuel (1709–1784)

Young men have more virtue than old men; they have more generous sentiments in every respect.

[In Boswell, *The Life of Samuel Johnson* (1791)]

JOWETT, Benjamin (1817–1893)

Young men make great mistakes in life; for one thing, they idealize love too much.

[*Life and Letters of Benjamin Jowett* (1897)]

KINGSLEY, Charles (1819–1875)

When all the world is young, lad,
And all the trees are green;
And every goose a swan, lad,
And every lass a queen;
Then hey for boot and horse, lad,
And round the world away:
Young blood must have its course, lad,
And every dog his day.

[Song from *The Water Babies* (1863), 'Young and Old']

MEDICI, Lorenzo de' (1449–1492)

Quant'è bella giovinezza
che si sfugge tuttavia!
Chi vuol esser lieto, sia:
di doman non c'è certezza.

How lovely is youth, which is always slipping away! Let him be glad who will be so: for tomorrow has no certainty.

['Trionfo di Bacco ed Arianna']

MELVILLE, Herman (1819–1891)

In youth we are, but in age we seem.

[*Pierre* (1852)]

OSBORNE, John (1929–1994)

I keep looking back, as far as I can remember, and I can't think what it was like to feel young, really young.

[*Look Back in Anger* (1956)]

PARSONS, Tony (1953–)

Funky royals, coked-out old men and streaking BA stewardesses make me nostalgic for an age when people knew youth was just a stage you passed through, like acne.

[*The Observer*, May 1999]

PITT, William (1708–1778)

The atrocious crime of being a young man … I shall neither attempt to palliate nor deny.

[Speech, House of Commons, 1741]

PORTER, Cole (1891–1964)

They have found that the fountain of youth Is a mixture of gin and vermouth.

PORTER, Hal (1911–1984)

How ruthless and hard and vile and right the young are.

[*The Watcher on the Cast-iron Balcony* (1963)]

SHAKESPEARE, William (1564–1616)

He capers, he dances, he has eyes of youth, he writes verses, he speaks holiday, he smells April and May.

[*The Merry Wives of Windsor*, III.ii]

I would there were no age between ten and three and twenty, or that youth would sleep out the rest; for there is nothing in the between but getting wenches with child, wronging the ancientry, stealing, fighting.

[*The Winter's Tale*, III.iii]

SHAW, George Bernard (1856–1950)

Youth, which is forgiven everything, forgives itself nothing: age, which forgives itself everything, is forgiven nothing.

[*Man and Superman* (1903)]

It's all that the young can do for the old, to shock them and keep them up to date.

[*Fanny's First Play* (1911)]

[On youth]
Far too good to waste on children.

[Attr. in Copeland, *10,000 Jokes, Toasts, & Stories* (1939)]

SMITH, Logan Pearsall (1865–1946)

The old know what they want; the young are sad and bewildered.

['Last Words' (1933)]

STEVENSON, Robert Louis (1850–1894)

Youth is the time to go flashing from one end of the world to the other both in mind and body; to try the manners of different nations; to hear the chimes at midnight; to see sunrise in town and country; to be converted at a revival; to circumnavigate the metaphysics, write halting verses, run a mile to see a fire, and wait all day long in the theatre to applaud *Hernani*.

[*Virginibus Puerisque* (1881)]

THATCHER, Margaret (1925–)

Young people ought not to be idle. It is very bad for them.

[*The Times*, 1984]

THOMAS, Dylan (1914–1953)

Now as I was young and easy under the apple boughs
About the lilting house and happy as the grass was green …

Oh as I was young and easy in the mercy of his means,
Time held me green and dying
Though I sang in my chains like the sea.

['Fern Hill' (1946)]

THOMPSON, William Hepworth (1810–1886)

[Comment on Junior Fellow of Trinity]

We are none of us infallible – not even the youngest.

[Attr.]

VIRGIL (70–19 BC)

In youth alone, unhappy mortals live;
But oh! the mighty bliss is fugitive:
Discoloured sickness, anxious labours, come,
And age and death's inexorable doom.

[*Georgics*]

WEVER, Robert (fl. 1550)

In a harbour grene aslepe whereas I lay,
The byrdes sang swete in the middes of the day,
I dreamèd fast of mirth and play:
In youth is pleasure, in youth is pleasure.

['Lusty Juventus']

WHITMAN, Walt (1819–1892)

Youth, large, lusty, loving – youth full of grace, force, fascination,
Do you know that Old Age may come after you with equal grace, force, fascination?

['Youth, Day, Old Age and Night' (1855)]

WILDE, Oscar (1854–1900)

The old-fashioned respect for the young is fast dying out.

[*The Importance of Being Earnest* (1895)]

WILSON, Woodrow (1856–1924)

Generally young men are regarded as radicals. This is a popular misconception. The most conservative persons I ever met are college undergraduates.

[Speech, 1905]

See AGE; CHILDREN

BIOGRAPHIES

A

Abbott, Diane (1953–) British Labour politician

Accius, Lucius (170–86 BC) Roman poet

Ace, Jane (1905–1974) American comedian and radio personality

Achebe, Chinua (1930–) Nigerian writer, poet and critic

Acheson, Dean (1893–1971) American Democratic politician

Acton, Lord (1834–1902) English historian and moralist

Adamov, Arthur (1908–1970) Russian-born French political dramatist

Adams, Douglas (1952–) English writer

Adams, Franklin P. (1881–1960) American writer, poet, translator and editor

Adams, Gerry (1948–) President of Sinn Fein

Adams, Henry (1838–1918) American historian and memoirist

Adams, John Quincy (1767–1848) American lawyer, diplomat and President

Adams, Richard (1846–1908) Irish journalist, barrister and judge

Adams, Richard (1920–) English writer

Addams, Jane (1860–1935) American sociologist and writer

Addison, Joseph (1672–1719) English essayist, poet, playwright and statesman

Ade, George (1866–1944) American fabulist and playwright

Adenauer, Konrad (1876–1967) German Chancellor

Adler, Alfred (1870–1937) Austrian psychiatrist and psychologist

Adler, Freda (1934–) American educator and writer

Aeschylus (525–456 BC) Greek dramatist and poet

Aesop (6th century BC) Greek fabulist

Aga Khan III (1877–1957) Muslim leader

Agate, James (1877–1947) English drama critic and writer

Agathon (c.445–400 BC) Athenian poet

Ailesbury, Maria, Marchioness of (d.1902) English aristocrat

Aitken, Jonathan (1942–) English Conservative politician

Alain (Emile–Auguste Chartier) (1868–1951) French philosopher, teacher and essayist

Albee, Edward (1928–) American dramatist

Albert, Prince Consort (1819–1861) German-born husband of Queen Victoria

Albertano of Brescia (c. 1190–c. 1270) Jurist, philosopher, magistrate and politician

Alcott, Bronson (1799–1888) American educator, reformer and transcendentalist

Alcott, Louisa May (1832–1888) American writer

Alcuin (735–804) English theologian, scholar and educationist

Aldiss, Brian (1925–) English writer

Aldrich, Henry (1647–1710) English scholar, divine and composer of songs

Alexander the Great (356–323 BC) Macedonian king and conquering army commander

Alfonso X (1221–1284) King of Castile and Leon; legal reformer

Ali, Muhammad (Cassius Clay) (1942–) American heavyweight boxer

Allen, Dave (1936–) Irish comedian and television personality

Allen, Fred (1894–1956) American vaudeville performer and comedian

Allen, Woody (1935–) American film director, writer, actor and comedian

Alley, Rewi (1897–1987) New Zealand reformer and educationist

Allingham, William (1824–1889) Irish poet and diarist

Allison, Malcolm (1927–) English footballer, coach and manager

Altman, Robert (1922–) American film director

Ambrose, Saint (c. 34–397) French-born churchman; writer of music and hymns

Ames, Fisher (1758–1808) American statesman and essayist

Amiel, Henri–Frédéric (1821–1881) Swiss philosopher and writer

Amis, Kingsley (1922–1995) English writer, poet and critic

Amis, Martin (1949–) English writer

Andersen, Hans Christian (1805–1875) Danish writer and dramatist

Anderson, Bruce British journalist

Andreotti, Giulio (1919–) Italian statesman and Prime Minister

Andrewes, Bishop Lancelot (1555–1626) English churchman

Angelou, Maya (1928–) American writer, poet and dramatist

Anka, Paul (1941–) American pop singer and songwriter

Annan, Kofi (1938–) Ghanaian Secretary-General of the UN

Anouilh, Jean (1910–1987) French dramatist and screenwriter

Anthony, Susan B. (1820–1906) American reformer, feminist and abolitionist

Antrim, Minna (1861–1950) American writer

Apollinaire, Guillaume (1880–1918) French poet and writer

Appius Claudius Caecus (4th–3rd century BC) Roman censor and writer

Appleton, Sir Edward (1892–1965) English physicist

Appleton, Thomas Gold (1812–1884) American epigrammatist

Arbuthnot, John (1667–1735) Scottish physician, pamphleteer and wit

Archer, Lord Jeffrey (1940–) British Conservative MP and popular novelist

Arendt, Hannah (1906–1975) German-born American theorist

Aristophanes (c.445–385 BC) Greek dramatist and satirist

Aristotle (384–322 BC) Greek philosopher

Armstrong, Dr John (1709–1779) Scottish physician, poet and writer

Armstrong, Louis (1900–1971) American jazz trumpeter, singer and bandleader

Armstrong, Neil (1930–) American astronaut and first man on the moon

Arnold, Harry British journalist

Arnold, Matthew (1822–1888) English poet, critic, essayist and educationist

Arnold, Thomas (1795–1842) English historian and educator

Artley, Alexandra British writer

Ascham, Roger (1515–1568) English scholar, educationist and archer

Ascherson, Neal (1932–) Scottish journalist

Ashdown, Paddy (1941–) Leader of the UK Social and Liberal Democrat Party

Ashford, Daisy (1881–1972) English child author

Asimov, Isaac (1920–1992) Russian-born American scientist, academic and writer

Asquith, Herbert (1852–1928) English Liberal statesman and Prime Minister

Asquith, Margot (1864–1945) Scottish political hostess and writer

Astor, John (1763–1848) German-born American fur-trader and financier

Astor, Nancy (1879–1964) American-born British Conservative politician and hostess

Atkinson, Surgeon–Captain E.L. (1882–1919) British polar explorer, doctor and naval officer

Atkinson, Ti–Grace (c. 1938–) American feminist

Attlee, Clement (1883–1967) English statesman and Prime Minister

Atwood, Margaret (1939–) Canadian writer, poet and critic

Auber, Daniel (1782–1871) French opera composer

Aubrey, John (1626–1697) English antiquary, folklorist and biographer

Auden, W.H. (1907–1973) English poet, essayist, critic, teacher and dramatist

Augier, Emile (1820–1889) French dramatist and poet

Augustine, Saint (354–430) Numidian-born Christian theologian and philosopher

Aung San Suu Kyi (1945–) Burmese politician

Aurelius, Marcus (121–180) Roman emperor and Stoic philosopher

Austen, Jane (1775–1817) English writer

Austin, Alfred (1835–1913) English poet and journalist

Austin, Warren Robinson (1877–1962) First US ambassador to the UN

Ayckbourn, Alan (1939–) English dramatist and theatre director

Ayer, A.J. (1910–1989) English philosopher

Aykroyd, Dan (1952–) American film actor

Aytoun, W.E. (1813–1865) Scottish poet, ballad writer and satirist

B

Bacon, Francis (1561–1626) English philosopher, essayist, politician and courtier

Bacon, Francis (1909–1993) Irish painter

Baez, Joan (1941–) American folksinger and songwriter

Bagehot, Walter (1826–1877) English economist and political philosopher

Baillie, Joanna (1762–1851) Scottish dramatist and poet

Bailly, Jean Sylvain (1736–1793) French astronomer and politician

Bainbridge, Kenneth (1904–) American nuclear physicist

Bakewell, Joan (1933–) British journalist and television presenter

Bakunin, Mikhail (1814–1876) Russian anarchist and writer

Baldwin, James (1924–1987) American writer, dramatist, poet and civil rights activist

Baldwin, Stanley (1867–1947) English Conservative statesman and Prime Minister

Balfour, A.J. (1848–1930) British Conservative Prime Minister

Ball, Alan (1943–) English footballer

Ballantyne, Sheila (1936–) US writer

Balzac, Honoré de (1799–1850) French writer

Bancroft, Richard (1544–1610) English churchman

Banda, Dr Hastings (1905–1997) Malawian politician and President

Bankhead, Tallulah
(1903–1968) American
actress

Banville, Théodore de
(1823–1891) French poet,
lyricist and dramatist

Barbarito, Luigi (1922–)
Papal emissary

**Barbour, John (c.
1316–1395)** Scottish poet,
churchman and scholar

Bareham, Lindsey (1948–)
Food critic and writer

Barker, George
(1913–1991) English poet
and writer

Barker, Ronnie (1929–)
English comedian

Barnard, Robert (1936–)
English writer

Barnes, Peter (1931–)
English dramatist

Barnes, Simon (1951–)
English writer

Barnfield, Richard
(1574–1627) English poet

Barnum, Phineas T.
(1810–1891) American
showman and writer

Barrie, Sir J.M. (1860–1937)
Scottish dramatist and writer

Barrington, George
(1755–c.1835) Irish
pickpocket and writer;
transported to Australia

Barth, John (1930–)
American writer

Barth, Karl (1886–1968)
Swiss Protestant theologian

Barton, Bruce (1886–1967)
American advertising agent
and writer

Baruch, Bernard M.
(1870–1965) US financier,
government advisor and
writer

Bashó, Matsuo (1644–1694)
Japanese haiku poet

Bates, Daisy May
(1863–1951) Irish-born
journalist, anthropologist
and reformer

Bateson, Mary (1939–)
American anthropologist
and writer

Baudelaire, Charles
(1821–1867) French poet,
translator and critic

Bax, Sir Arnold
(1883–1953) English
composer

Baxter, James K.
(1926–1972) New Zealand
poet and playwright

Baylis, Lilian (1874–1937)
English theatrical manager

Bayly, Thomas Haynes
(1797–1839) English
songwriter, writer and
dramatist

Beaumarchais (1732–1799)
French dramatist, essayist,
watchmaker and spy

Beaumont, Francis
(1584–1616) English
dramatist and poet

Beauvoir, Simone de
(1908–1986) French writer,
feminist critic and
philosopher

Beaverbrook, Lord
(1879–1964) Canadian-born
British newspaper owner

Beckett, Samuel
(1906–1989) Irish dramatist,
writer and poet

Beckford, William
(1760–1844) English writer,
collector and politician

Becon, Thomas
(1512–1567) English
Protestant divine

Bede, The Venerable
(673–735) English monk,
historian and scholar

Beecham, Sir Thomas
(1879–1961) English
conductor and impresario

Beecher, Henry Ward
(1813–1887) US clergyman,
lecturer, editor and writer

Beeching, Rev. H.C.
(1859–1919) English
theologian, poet and essayist

Beer, Thomas (1889–1940)
American writer

Beerbohm, Sir Max
(1872–1956) English satirist,
cartoonist, critic and essayist

Beethoven, Ludwig van
(1770–1827) German
composer

Behan, Brendan
(1923–1964) Irish dramatist,
writer and Republican

Behn, Aphra (1640–1689)
English dramatist, writer,
poet, translator and spy

Belasco, David (1853–1931)
American theatre producer
and playwright

Bell, Alexander Graham (1847–1922) Scottish-born US inventor and educator of the deaf

Bell, Clive (1881–1964) English art critic

Belloc, Hilaire (1870–1953) English writer of verse, essayist and critic; Liberal MP

Bellow, Saul (1915–) Canadian-born American Jewish writer

Benchley, Robert (1889–1945) American essayist, humorist and actor

Benn, Tony (1925–) English Labour politician

Bennett, Alan (1934–) English dramatist, actor and diarist

Bennett, Arnold (1867–1931) English writer, dramatist and journalist

Bentham, Jeremy (1748–1832) English writer and philosopher

Bentley, Edmund Clerihew (1875–1956) English writer

Bentley, Nicolas (1907–1978) English publisher and artist

Berkeley, Bishop (1685–1753) Irish philosopher and scholar

Berlin, Irving (1888–1989) Russian-born US musical and songwriter

Berlin, Sir Isaiah (1909–1997) Latvian-born British philosopher

Berlioz, Hector (1803–1869) French composer; founder of modern orchestration

Bernard, Jeffrey (1932–1997) British columnist

Bernard, Tristan (1866–1947) French writer and dramatist

Bernhardt, Sarah (1844–1923) French actress

Betjeman, Sir John (1906–1984) English poet laureate

Betterton, Thomas (1635–1710) English actor and dramatist

Bevan, Aneurin (1897–1960) Welsh Labour politician, miner and orator

Beveridge, William (1879–1963) British economist and social reformer

Biagi, Enzo (1920–) Italian writer

Bickerstaffe, Isaac (c.1773–c.1808) Irish dramatist and author of ballad operas

Bierce, Ambrose (1842–c.1914) American writer, verse writer and soldier

Biko, Steve (1946–1977) Black South African civil rights leader; murdered in police custody

Billings, Josh (1818–1885) American writer, philosopher and lecturer

Bing, Rudolf (1902–) Director of the New York Metropolitan Opera

Bingham, Sir Thomas (1933–) English Master of the Rolls

Binyon, Laurence (1869–1943) English poet, art historian and critic

Bion (fl. 280 BC) Greek poet

Birley, Mark London nightclub owner

Birt, John (1944–) British television producer and Director-General of the BBC

Birtwistle, Sir Harrison (1934–) English composer

Bismarck, Prince Otto von (1815–1898) First Chancellor of the German Reich

Bissell, Claude T. (1916–) Canadian writer

Bjelke–Petersen, Sir Johannes (1911–) New Zealand-born Australian politician

Blackstone, Sir William (1723–1780) English judge, historian and politician

Blackwell, Antoinette Brown (1825–1921) American writer

Blainey, Geoffrey Norman (1930–) Australian writer

Blair, Tony (1953–) British Labour Prime Minister

Blake, Eubie (1883–1983) American jazz performer and songwriter

Blake, William (1757–1827)
English poet, engraver, painter and mystic

Blücher, Prince (1742–1819) Prussian field marshal

Blue, Rabbi Lionel (1930–)
English lecturer, writer and broadcaster

Blythe, Ronald (1922–)
English writer

Bocca, Giorgio (1920–)
Italian writer

Boethius (c. 475–524)
Roman statesman, scholar and philosopher

Bogarde, Dirk (1921–1999)
British actor and writer

Bohr, Niels (1885–1962)
Danish nuclear physicist

Boileau–Despréaux, Nicolas (1636–1711) French poet, satirist and critic

Boleyn, Anne (1507–1536)
Wife of Henry VIII and mother of Elizabeth I

Bolingbroke, Henry (1678–1751) English statesman, historian and actor

Bolitho, William (1890–1930) South African-born British writer

Bombeck, Erma (1827–1996) US humorist and writer

Bone, James (1872–1962)
Scottish journalist

Bongay, Amy President of the Models Guild

Bonhoeffer, Dietrich (1906–1945) German theologian, executed by the Nazis

Bono, Edward de (1933–)
British physician and writer

Boorde, Andrew (c.1490–1549) English traveller, physician and writer

Boorstin, Daniel (1914–)
American librarian, historian, lawyer and writer

Booth, General William (1829–1912) English founder of the Salvation Army

Borges, Jorge Luis (1899–1986) Argentinian writer, poet and librarian

Borovoy, A. Alan Canadian writer and civil liberties advocate

Borrow, George (1803–1881) English writer and linguist

Bosman, Herman (1905–1951) South African writer

Bosquet, Pierre (1810–1861) French general

Bossidy, John Collins (1860–1928) US oculist

Bottomley, Gordon (1874–1948) English poet and verse dramatist

Bottomley, Horatio William (1860–1933) English journalist, politician and bankrupt

Boucicault, Dion (1822–1890) Irish dramatist, actor and theatrical manager

Boulay de la Meurthe, Antoine (1761–1840)
French statesman and revolutionary

Boutros–Ghali, Boutros (1922–) Egyptian Secretary-General of the United Nations

Bowen, Elizabeth (1899–1973) Irish writer

Bowen, Lord (1835–1894)
English judge and scholar

Bowra, Sir Maurice (1898–1971) English scholar

Boyd, Robin (1919–1971)
Australian architect

Boyd, William (1952–)
Scottish writer

'Boy George' (1961–)
English singer-songwriter and DJ

Brack, (Cecil) John (1920–)
Australian artist

Bradbury, Malcolm (1932–)
English writer, critic and academic

Bradford, John (c. 1510–1555) English Protestant martyr and writer

Bradley, F.H. (1846–1924)
English philosopher

Bradley, Omar Nelson (1893–1981) American general

Bradshaw, Henry (d.1513)
Monk and theologian

Bradshaw, John (1602–1659) English judge and republican

Bradstreet, Anne (c. 1612–1672) English-born American poet

Brahms, Johannes (1833–1897) German composer, pianist and conductor

Brando, Marlon (1924–) American actor

Braque, Georges (1882–1963) French painter

Brasch, Charles Orwell (1909–1973) New Zealand poet and editor

Braxfield, Lord (1722–1799) Scottish judge

Bray, John Jefferson (1912–) Australian lawyer and poet

Brecht, Berthold (1898–1956) German dramatist and poet

Brenan, Gerald (1894–1987) English writer

Brennan, Christopher (1870–1932) Australian poet

Breton, Nicholas (c. 1545–c. 1626) English writer and poet

Bridges, Robert (1844–1930) English poet, dramatist, essayist and doctor

Bridie, James (1888–1951) Scottish dramatist, writer and physician

Brien, Alan (1925–) British writer

Bright, John (1811–1889) English Liberal politician and social reformer

Brittain, Vera (1893–1970) English writer and pacifist

Broderick, John (1927–) Irish writer

Brodsky, Joseph (1940–1996) Russian poet, essayist, critic and exile

Brome, Richard (c.1590–1652) English dramatist

Bronowski, Jacob (1908–1974) British mathematician, writer and TV presenter

Brontë, Anne (1820–1849) English writer and poet

Brontë, Charlotte (1816–1855) English writer

Brontë, Emily (1818–1848) English poet and writer

Brooke, Rupert (1887–1915) English poet

Brookner, Anita (1928–) English writer

Brooks, Mel (1926–) American film actor and director

Brough, Robert (1828–1860) English journalist and writer

Brougham, Lord Henry (1778–1868) Scottish politician, abolitionist and journalist

Brown, Ford Madox (1821–1893) French-born English painter and designer

Brown, Geoff (1949–) Film critic and writer

Brown, Gordon (1951–) British Chancellor of the Exchequer

Brown, Helen Gurley (1922–) American writer and editor

Brown, Rita Mae (1944–) American writer and poet

Brown, Thomas Edward (1830–1897) Manx poet, teacher and curate

Brown, Tina (1953–) English journalist and editor

Browne, Sir Thomas (1605–1682) English physician, author and antiquary

Browne, William (c. 1591–1643) English poet

Browning, Elizabeth Barrett (1806–1861) English poet; wife of Robert Browning

Browning, Robert (1812–1889) English poet

Bruce, Robert (1554–1631) Scottish cleric

Brummel, Beau (1778–1840) English dandy and wit

Bryan, William Jennings (1860–1925) US Democratic politician and editor

Bryson, Bill (1951–) US travel writer

Buchan, John (1875–1940) Scottish writer, lawyer and Conservative politician

Buchanan, Robert Williams (1841–1901) British poet, writer and dramatist

Büchner, Georg (1813–1837) German playwright

Buchwald, Art (1925–) American humorist

Buck, Pearl S. (1892–1973) American writer and dramatist

Buckingham, Duke of (1628–1687) English courtier and dramatist

Buddha (c. 563–483 BC) Indian religious teacher; founder of Buddhism

Budgell, Eustace (1686–1737) English writer

Buffon, Comte de (1707–1788) French naturalist

Bulgakov, Mikhail (1891–1940) Russian writer and dramatist

Bullet, Gerald (1893–1958) English writer, poet and critic

Bullock, Alan (1914–) English historian

Bulmer–Thomas, Ivor (1905–1993) Welsh politician and writer

Bulwer–Lytton, Edward (1803–1873) English writer and politician

Bunn, Alfred (1796–1860) English theatrical manager, librettist and poet

Buñuel, Luis (1900–1983) Spanish film director

Bunyan, John (1628–1688) English preacher, pastor and writer

Burchill, Julie (1960–) English writer

Burgess, Anthony (1917–1993) English writer, linguist and composer

Burgon, John William (1813–1888) English churchman

Burke, Edmund (1729–1797) Irish-born British statesman and philosopher

Burnet, Sir Frank Macfarlane (1899–1985) Australian medical researcher

Burney, Fanny (1752–1840) English diarist

Burns, Robert (1759–1796) Scottish poet and song writer; Scotland's national bard

Burton, Robert (1577–1640) English clergyman and writer

Bussy–Rabutin, Comte de (1618–1693) French soldier, writer and memoirist

Butler, Bishop Joseph (1692–1752) English philosopher and divine

Butler, Nicholas Murray (1862–1947) US teacher, lecturer, politican and writer

Butler, R.A. (1902–1982) Indian-born British Conservative politician

Butler, Samuel (1612–1680) English poet

Butler, Samuel (1835–1902) English writer, painter, philosopher and scholar

Bygraves, Max (1922–) English singer and entertainer

Byron, H.J. (1834–1884) English dramatist and actor

Byron, Lord (1788–1824) English poet satirist and traveller

C

Cabell, James Branch (1879–1958) US writer, poet, genealogist and historian

Caesar, Gaius Julius (c. 102–44 BC) Roman statesman, historian and army commander

Cage, John (1912–1992) American composer and writer

Caillavet, Arman de (1869–1915) French playwright

Calderón de la Barca, Pedro (1600–1681) Spanish dramatist and poet

Caligula (12–41) Roman emperor

Callaghan, James (1912–) English Labour statesman and Prime Minister

Calment, Jeanne (1875–1997) Frenchwoman, renowned for her longevity

Calverley, C.S. (1831–1884) English poet, parodist, scholar and lawyer

Calwell, Arthur Augustus (1894–1973) Australian Labour politician

Cambridge, Duke of (1819–1904) Commander-in-chief of the British army

Camden, William (1551–1623) English scholar, antiquary and historian

Cameron, Simon (1799–1889) American statesman and newspaper editor

Campbell, David (1915–1979) Australian poet, rugby player and wartime pilot

Campbell, Joseph (1879–1944) Irish poet and republican

Campbell, Menzies (1941–) Scottish politician, lawyer and athlete

Campbell, Mrs Patrick (1865–1940) English actress

Campbell, Roy (1901–1957) South African poet and journalist

Campbell, Thomas (1777–1844) Scottish poet, ballad writer and journalist

Campbell–Bannerman, Sir Henry (1836–1908) British Liberal Prime Minister

Camus, Albert (1913–1960) Algerian-born French writer

Canetti, Elias (1905–1994) Bulgarian-born English writer, dramatist and critic

Canning, George (1770–1827) English Prime Minister, orator and poet

Canterbury, Tom American basketball player

Cantona, Eric (1966–) French footballer

Capone, Al (1899–1947) Chicago gangster

Carew, Thomas (c. 1595–1640) English poet, musician and dramatist

Carlyle, Jane Welsh (1801–1866) Scottish letter writer, literary hostess and poet

Carlyle, Thomas (1795–1881) Scottish historian, biographer, critic, and essayist

Carnegie, Andrew (1835–1919) Scottish-born US millionaire and philanthropist

Carr, J.L. (1912–1994) English writer and publisher

Carroll, Lewis (1832–1898) English writer and photographer

Carson, Rachel (1907–1964) American marine biologist and writer

Carswell, Catherine (1879–1946) Scottish writer

Carter, Angela (1940–1992) English writer

Carter, Jimmy (1924–) US President

Carter, 'Miz' Lillian (1902–) Mother of US President Jimmy Carter

Cartland, Barbara (1902–) English writer

Casson, Sir Hugh (1910–) English architect and writer

Castellani, Maria (fl. 1930s) Italian educator and writer

Cather, Willa (1873–1947) US writer

Catherine the Great (1729–1796) German-born Empress of Russia

Cato the Elder (234–149 BC) Roman statesman, writer and orator

Catullus (84–c. 54 BC) Roman poet

Cavell, Edith (1865–1915) English nurse, executed by the Germans

Cecil, Lord David (1902–1986) English critic and writer

Cernuda, Luis (1902–1963) Spanish poet

Cervantes, Miguel de (1547–1616) Spanish writer and dramatist

Chamberlain, Neville (1869–1940) English Conservative Prime Minister

Chamfort, Nicolas (1741–1794) French writer

Chandler, Raymond (1888–1959) American crime writer

Chanel, Coco (1883–1971) French couturier and perfumer

Chaplin, Charlie (1889–1977) English comedian, film actor, director and satirist

Chapman, George (c. 1559–c. 1634) English poet, dramatist and translator

Charles I (1600–1649) British king

Charles II (1630–1685) British king

Charles X (1757–1836) King of France

Charles, Prince of Wales (1948–) Son and heir of Elizabeth II and Prince Philip

Chase, Ilke (1905–1978) American writer, actress and broadcaster

Chasen, Dave Hollywood restaurateur

Chateaubriand, François–René (1768–1848) French writer and statesman

Chaucer, Geoffrey (c. 1340–1400) English poet, public servant and courtier

Chekhov, Anton (1860–1904) Russian writer, dramatist and doctor

Cher (1946–) US singer and actress

Cherry–Garrard, Apsley (1886–1959) English polar explorer and writer

Chesterfield, Lord (1694–1773) English politician and letter writer

Chesterton, G.K. (1874–1936) English writer, poet and critic

Chevalier, Maurice (1888–1972) French singer and actor

Chifley, Ben (1885–1951) Australian politician

Child, Lydia M. (1802–1880) American writer, abolitionist and suffragist

Childers, Erskine (1870–1922) English writer and historian; Irish revolutionary

Chillingworth, William (1602–1644) English theologian and scholar

Chisholm, Caroline (1808–1877) English-born Australian humanitarian

Chomsky, Noam (1928–) American linguist and political critic

Chopin, Kate (1851–1904) US writer

Christie, Dame Agatha (1890–1976) English crime writer and playwright

Chuang Tse (c. 369–286 BC) Chinese Taoist philosopher

Churchill, Charles (1731–1764) English poet, political writer and clergyman

Churchill, Sir Winston (1874–1965) English Conservative Prime Minister

Ciano, Count Galeazzo (1903–1944) Italian politician

Cicero (106–43 BC) Roman orator, statesman, essayist and letter writer

Clare, Dr Anthony (1942–) Irish professor, psychiatrist and broadcaster

Clare, John (1793–1864) English rural poet; died in an asylum

Clark, Alan (1928–) British Conservative politician and historian

Clark, Lord Kenneth (1903–1983) English art historian

Clarke, Arthur C. (1917–) English writer

Clarke, John (fl. 1639) English scholar

Clarke, Marcus (1846–1881) English-born Australian writer

Claudel, Paul (1868–1955) French dramatist, poet and diplomat

Clausewitz, Karl von (1780–1831) German general and military philosopher

Clayton, Keith (1928–) Professor of Environmental Sciences

Cleese, John (1939–) British comedian, actor and writer

Clemenceau, Georges (1841–1929) French Prime Minister and journalist

Cleveland, John (1613–1658) English poet

Clifford, William Kingdon (1845–1879) English mathematician

Clinton, Bill (1946–) Democrat President of the USA

Clive, Lord (1725–1774) English general, statesman and Indian administrator

Clough, Arthur Hugh (1819–1861) English poet and letter writer

Cluff, Algy British businessman

Cobbett, William (1762–1835) English politician, reformer, writer, farmer and army officer

Cochran, Charles B. (1872–1951) English showman and theatrical producer

Cocteau, Jean (1889–1963) French dramatist, poet, film writer and director

Cody, Henry (1868–1951) Anglican churchman

Coetzee, J.M. (1940–) South African writer

Cohen, Sir Jack (1898–1979) Supermarket magnate

Coke, Sir Edward (1552–1634) English judge, writer and politician

Colby, Frank Moore (1865–1925) American editor, historian and economist

Coleman, David (1926–) English sports commentator and broadcaster

Coleridge, Hartley (1796–1849) English poet and writer

Coleridge, Samuel Taylor (1772–1834) English poet, philosopher and critic

Colette (1873–1954) French writer

Collingwood, Robin (1889–1943) English philosopher, archaeologist and historian

Collins, Michael (1890–1922) Irish revolutionary leader

Collins, Mortimer (1827–1876) English poet and writer

Colman the Elder, George (1732–1794) English dramatist and theatrical manager

Colman the Younger, George (1762–1836) English dramatist and Examiner of Plays

Colton, Charles Caleb (c. 1780–1832) English clergyman and satirist

Coltrane, Robbie (1950–) Scottish comedian and actor

Comfort, Alex (1920–) British medical biologist and writer on sex

Compton–Burnett, Dame Ivy (1884–1969) English writer

Comte, Auguste (1798–1857) French philosopher and mathematician

Condorcet, Antoine–Nicolas de (1743–1794) French mathematician and academician

Confucius (c. 550–c. 478 BC) Chinese philosopher and teacher of ethics

Congreve, William (1670–1729) English dramatist

Connolly, Cyril (1903–1974) English literary editor, writer and critic

Connolly, James (1868–1916) Irish labour leader

Connors, Jimmy (1952–) US tennis player

Conrad, Joseph (1857–1924) Polish-born British writer, sailor and explorer

Conran, Shirley (1932–) English writer

Constable, John (1776–1837) English painter

Constant, Benjamin (1767–1834) Swiss-born French writer and politician

Coogan, Tim Pat (1935–) Irish writer

Cook, A.J. (1885–1931) English miners' leader

Cook, Peter (1937–1995) English comedian and writer

Coolidge, Calvin (1872–1933) US President

Cooper, Roger British hostage in Iran

Cope, Wendy (1945–) English poet

Coren, Alan (1938–) British humorist, writer and broadcaster

Corneille, Pierre (1606–1684) French dramatist, poet and lawyer

Cornford, F.M. (1874–1943) English Platonic scholar

Cornford, Frances Crofts (1886–1960) English poet and translator

Cornuel, Madame de (1605–1694) French society hostess

Cory, William (1823–1892) English poet, teacher and writer

Coubertin, Pierre de (1863–1937) French educationist and sportsman

Counihan, Noel (1913–1986) Australian cartoonist and artist

Coventry, Thomas (1578–1640) English Attorney-General and politician

Coward, Sir Noël (1899–1973) English dramatist, actor, producer and composer

Cowley, Abraham (1618–1667) English poet and dramatist

Cowley, Hannah (1743–1809) English dramatist and poet

Cowper, William (1731–1800) English poet, hymn and letter writer

Cozzens, James Gould (1903–1978) American writer

Crabbe, George (1754–1832) English poet, clergyman, surgeon and botanist

Craig, Sir Gordon (1872–1966) English actor, artist and stage designer

Craig, Maurice James (1919–) Poet and historian

Cranmer, Thomas (1489–1556) English Protestant martyr

Crashaw, Richard (c. 1612–1649) English religious poet

Creighton, Mandell (1843–1901) English churchman, historian and biographer

Crick, Francis (1916–) British biologist

Crisp, Quentin (1908–) English writer, publicist and model

Critchley, Julian (1930–) English writer, broadcaster, journalist and politician

Crompton, Richmal (1890–1969) English writer and teacher

Cromwell, Oliver (1599–1658) English general, statesman and Puritan leader

Cronenberg, David (1943–) Canadian film director

Crooks, Garth (1958–) English footballer

Crowfoot (1821–1890) Blackfoot warrior

Cumberland, Bishop Richard (1631–1718) English philosopher, divine and translator

cummings, e.e. (1894–1962) US poet, noted for his typography, and painter

Cummings, William Thomas (1903–1945) American priest

Cunningham, Allan (1784–1842) Scottish poet, reporter and biographer

Cunningham, Peter Miller (1789–1864) Surgeon-superintendent on convict ships

Curie, Marie (1867–1934) Polish-born French physicist

Curnow, Allen (1911–) New Zealand poet and editor

Curran, John Philpot (1750–1817) Irish judge, orator, politician and reformer

Curry, George English churchman

Curtiz, Michael (1888–1962) Hungarian film director

Curzon, Lord (1859–1925) English statesman and scholar

Cuvier, Baron (1769–1832) French anatomist and politician

Cyprian, Saint (c. 200–258) Carthaginian churchman, theological writer and martyr

Cyrano de Bergerac, Savinien de (1619–1655) French writer, soldier and duellist

D

Dagg, Fred (1948–) Australian writer, actor and broadcaster

Dahl, Roald (1916–1990) British writer

Dali, Salvador (1904–1989) Spanish painter and writer

D'Alpuget, Blanche (1944–) Australian writer

Daly, Mary (1928–) American feminist and theologian

Damien, Father (1840–1889) Belgian Roman Catholic missionary

Dana, Charles Anderson (1819–1897) American newspaper editor and reformer

Daniel, Samuel (1562–1619) English poet, historian and dramatist

Danton, Georges (1759–1794) French revolutionary leader

Darling, Charles (1849–1936) English judge and Conservative politician

Darrow, Clarence (1857–1938) American lawyer, reformer and writer

Darwin, Charles (1809–1882) English naturalist

Darwin, Charles Galton (1887–1962) English physicist; grandson of Charles Darwin

David, Elizabeth (1913–1992) British cookery writer

Davies, David (1742–1819) Welsh cleric

Davies, Sir John (1569–1626) English poet and politician

Davies, Robertson (1913–1995) Canadian playwright, writer and critic

Davies, Scrope Berdmore (c.1783–1852) English conversationalist

Davies, William Henry (1871–1940) Welsh poet, writer and tramp

Davis, Bette (1908–1989) US film actress

Davis, Sammy, Junior (1925–1990) African-American entertainer and singer

Davis, Steve (1957–) Snooker player

Davison, Frank Dalby (1893–1970) Australian writer

Davy, Sir Humphry (1778–1829) English chemist and inventor

Dawe, (Donald) Bruce (1930–) Australian poet and lecturer

Day, Clarence Shepard (1874–1935) American essayist and humorist

Day Lewis, C. (1904–1972) British poet

De Blank, Joost (1908–1968) Dutch-born British churchman

Debray, Régis (1942–) French writer

Debussy, Claude (1862–1918) French composer and critic

Decatur, Stephen (1779–1820) American naval commander

Defoe, Daniel (c. 1661–1731) English writer and critic

Degas, Edgar (1834–1917) French painter and sculptor

De Gaulle, Charles (1890–1970) French statesman and general

De Klerk, F.W. (1936–) South African politician

De La Mare, Walter (1873–1956) English poet and writer

Delaney, Shelagh (1939–) English dramatist, screenwriter and writer

Delbanco, Andrew Writer and academic

Delille, Abbé Jacques (1738–1813) French poet and translator

Delors, Jacques (1925–)
French politician

Demosthenes (c. 384–322 BC) Athenian statesman and orator

Dempsey, Jack (1895–1983) American boxer

Denham, Sir John (1615–1669) English poet, royalist and Surveyor-General

Denning, Lord (1899–1999) English Master of the Rolls

Dennis, C.J. (1876–1938) Australian writer and poet

Dennis, John (1657–1734) English critic and dramatist

Dennis, Nigel (1912–1989) English writer, dramatist and critic

Dent, Alan (1905–1978) Scottish writer and critic

De Quincey, Thomas (1785–1859) English essayist and opium addict

Descartes, René (1596–1650) French philosopher and mathematician

Desmoulins, Camille (1760–1794) French pamphleteer, orator and revolutionary

Destouches, Philippe Néricault (1680–1754) French dramatist

De Valera, Eamon (1882–1975) American-born Irish statesman

Devlin, Bernadette (1947–) Irish politician

Devonshire, Duke of (1833–1908) English statesman

Devonshire, Duke of (1895–1950) English politician

De Vries, Peter (1910–1993) US writer and humorist

Dewar, Lord (1864–1930) Scottish Conservative politician and writer

Dewey, John (1859–1952) American educationist, philosopher and reformer

De Wolfe, Elsie (1865–1950) English actress, society leader and writer

Díaz, Porfirio (1830–1915) Mexican general and statesman

Dibdin, Charles (1745–1814) English songwriter, dramatist and actor

Dickens, Charles (1812–1870) English writer

Dickinson, Angie (1932–) US actress

Dickinson, Emily (1830–1886) US poet

Diderot, Denis (1713–1784) French philosopher, encyclopaedist, writer and dramatist

Didion, Joan(1934–) US writer

Dietrich, Marlene (1901–1992) German-born American actress and singer

Diller, Phyllis (1917–1974) American comedian

Dillingham, Charles Bancroft (1868–1934) American theatrical producer

Diodorus Siculus (c. 1st century BC) Sicilian-born Greek historian

Diogenes (the Cynic) (c. 400–325 BC) Greek philosopher

Dionysius of Halicarnassus (fl. 30–7 BC) Greek historian, critic and rhetorician

Disney, Walt (1901–1966) American film-maker and pioneer of animated films

Disraeli, Benjamin (1804–1881) English statesman and writer

Dix, Dorothy (1870–1951) American writer

Dix, George (1901–1952) English Anglican monk, historian and scholar

Dobbs, Kildare (1923–) Canadian writer

Dobrée, Bonamy (1891–1974) English academic, critic and editor

Dobson, Henry Austin (1840–1921) English poet, essayist and biographer

Dodd, Ken (1931–) English comedian, singer, entertainer and actor

Donatus, Aelius (fl. 4th century BC) Roman Latin grammarian and teacher

Donleavy, J.P. (1926–) American-born Irish writer and dramatist

Donne, John (1572–1631) English poet

Dostoevsky, Fyodor (1821–1881) Russian writer

Douglas, Lord Alfred (1870–1945) English poet; intimate of Oscar Wilde

Douglas, James, Earl of Morton (c. 1516–1581) Regent of Scotland

Douglas, Kirk (1916–) US actor

Douglas, Norman (1868–1952) Austrian-born Scottish writer

Douglas–Home, Sir Alec (1903–1995) Scottish statesman

Douglass, Frederick (c.1818–1895) US anti-slavery activist

Dowling, Basil Caims New Zealand poet and pacifist

Dowson, Ernest (1867–1900) English poet

Doyle, Sir Arthur Conan (1859–1930) Scottish writer and war correspondent

Doyle, Roddy (1958–) Irish writer

Drake, Sir Francis (c. 1540–1596) English navigator

Drayton, Michael (1563–1631) English poet

Dreiser, Theodore (1871–1945) US writer

Drew, Elizabeth (1887–1965) English-born American writer and critic

Dring, Philip American preacher

Drummond, Thomas (1797–1840) Scottish statesman and engineer

Dryden, John (1631–1700) English poet, satirist, dramatist and critic

Du Bellay, Joachim (1522–1560) French poet

Du Belloy, P–L.B. (1727–1775) French dramatist and merchant

Du Bois, William (1868–1963) African-American sociologist, writer and political activist

Duffy, Jim Scottish football pundit

Duhamel, Georges (1884–1966) French writer, poet, dramatist and physician

Dulles, John Foster (1888–1959) American statesman and lawyer

Dunbar, William (c. 1460–c. 1525) Scottish poet, satirist and courtier

Duncan, Isadora (1878–1927) American modern dance pioneer

Dundy, Elaine (1927–) American writer

Dunne, Finley Peter (1867–1936) American writer

Duppa, Richard (1770–1831) English artist and writer

Durant, Will (1885–1982) American philosopher and writer

Durrell, Lawrence (1912–1990) Indian-born British poet and writer

Dürrenmatt, Friedrich (1921–1990) Swiss dramatist and writer

Dworkin, Andrea (1946–) American writer and feminist

Dyer, Sir Edward (c. 1540–1607) English poet and courtier

E

Eames, Emma (1865–1952) Chinese-born American opera singer

Earhart, Amelia (1898–1937) US aviator

Eastman, Max (1883–1969) American writer, editor and critic

Eastwood, Clint (1930–) American actor and film director

Eban, Abba (1915–) South African-born Israeli statesman and writer

Ebner–Eschenbach, Marie von (1830–1916) Austrian writer

Eco, Umberto (1932–)
Italian critic and writer

**Eddington, Sir Arthur
(1882–1944)** English
astronomer, physicist and
mathematician

**Eddy, Mary Baker
(1821–1910)** American
founder of Christian Science

**Eden, Anthony
(1897–1977)** English
Conservative Prime Minister

**Edgeworth, Maria
(1767–1849)** English-born
Irish writer

**Edison, Thomas Alva
(1847–1931)** American
inventor and industrialist

**Edmond, James
(1859–1933)** Scottish-born
Australian writer and editor

Edward VII (1841–1910)
King of Great Britain and
Ireland

**Edward VIII (later Duke of
Windsor) (1894–1972)**
Uncrowned British king;
abdicated

**Edwards, Oliver
(1711–1791)** English lawyer

Einstein, Albert (1879–1955)
German-born American
mathematical physicist

**Eisenhower, Dwight D.
(1890–1969)** American
President and general

Ekland, Britt (1942–)
Swedish actress

**Eldershaw, M. Barnard
(1897–1987)** Australian
writer, critic and librarian

**Eliot, Charles W.
(1834–1926)** President of
Harvard University

Eliot, George (1819–1880)
English writer and poet

Eliot, T.S. (1888–1965)
American-born British poet,
verse dramatist and critic

Elizabeth I (1533–1603)
Queen of England, scholar
and letter writer

**Elizabeth, the Queen
Mother (1900–)** Queen of
the United Kingdom and
mother of Elizabeth II

Elliot, Jean (1727–1805)
Scottish lyricist

**Elliott, Ebenezer
(1781–1849)** English poet
and merchant

Ellis, Alice Thomas (1932–)
British writer

Ellis, Bob (1942–)
Australian dramatist

Ellis, George (1753–1815)
West Indian-born British
satirist and poet

Ellis, Havelock (1859–1939)
English sexologist and
essayist

**Emerson, Ralph Waldo
(1803–1882)** US poet,
essayist, transcendentalist
and teacher

**Emmet, Robert
(1778–1803)** Irish patriot

**Engels, Friedrich
(1820–1895)** German
socialist and political
philosopher

Epicurus (341–270 BC)
Greek philosopher and
teacher

Erasmus (c. 1466–1536)
Dutch scholar and humanist

Ertz, Susan (1894–1985)
English writer

**Estienne, Henri
(1531–1598)** French scholar,
lexicographer and publisher

**Etherege, Sir George (c.
1635–1691)** English
Restoration dramatist

Eubank, Chris (1966–)
British boxer

Euclid (fl. c. 300 BC) Greek
mathematician

Euripides (c. 485–406 BC)
Greek dramatist and poet

Evans, Abel (1679–1737)
English churchman, poet and
satirist

**Evans, Dame Edith
(1888–1976)** English actress

Evans, Harold (1928–)
English journalist and
newspaper editor

**Evarts, William Maxwell
(1818–1901)** American
lawyer and statesman

Evelyn, John (1620–1706)
English writer and diarist

Ewart, Gavin (1916–1995)
English poet

Ewer, William (1885–1976)
English journalist

Eyre, Richard (1943–)
English film, theatre and
television director

F

Fadiman, Clifton (1904–)
American writer, editor and broadcaster

Fairbairn, Sir Nicholas (1933–1995) Scottish Conservative MP and barrister

Fairbairn, Lady Sam Wife of Conservative MP, Sir Nicholas Fairbairn

Fairburn, A.R.D. (1904–1957) New Zealand poet

Falkland, Viscount (c. 1610–1643) English politician and writer

Fanon, Frantz (1925–1961) West Indian psychoanalyst and philosopher

Faraday, Michael (1791–1867) English chemist and physicist

Farmer, Edward (c. 1809–1876) English poet and writer

Farquhar, George (1678–1707) Irish dramatist

Farrell, J.G. (1935–1979) English novelist

Faulkner, William (1897–1962) US writer

Faust, Beatrice (1939–) Australian writer and feminist

Feather, Vic, Baron (1906–1976) English trade unionist

Ferdinand I, Emperor (1503–1564) Spanish-born King of Hungary and Bohemia

Fergusson, Sir James (1832–1907) Scottish Conservative statesman

Ferlinghetti, Lawrence (1920–) American publisher, painter, poet and writer

Fern, Fanny (1811–1872) American writer

Ferrier, Kathleen (1912–1953) English singer

Feuerbach, Ludwig (1804–1872) German philosopher

Field, Eugene (1850 1895) American columnist, children's poet, translator and humorist

Fielding, Henry (1707–1754) English writer, dramatist and journalist

Fields, W.C. (1880–1946) American film actor

Figes, Eva (1932–) German-born British writer and critic

Firbank, Ronald (1886–1926) English writer

Fisher, Dorothy Canfield (1879–1958) American writer

Fisher, H.A.L. (1856–1940) English historian

FitzGerald, Edward (1809–1883) English poet, translator and letter writer

Fitzgerald, F. Scott (1896–1940) American writer

Fitzsimmons, Robert (1862–1917) New Zealand world champion boxer

Flanders, Michael (1922–1975) English actor and lyricist

Flaubert, Gustave (1821–1880) French wnter

Flecker, James Elroy (1884–1915) English poet, orientalist and translator

Flecknoe, Richard (d. c. 1678) Irish priest, poet and dramatist

Fleming, Marjory (1803–1811) Scottish child diarist

Flers, Marquis de (1871–1927) French playwright

Fletcher, John (1579–1625) English dramatist

Fletcher, Phineas (1582–1650) English poet and clergyman

Florian, Jean–Pierre Claris de (1755–1794) French writer

Fo, Dario (1926–) Italian playwright and actor

Foch, Ferdinand (1851–1929) French marshal

Foley, Rae (1900–1978) American writer

Fonda, Jane (1937–) American actress, political activist and aerobics pioneer

Fontaine, Jean de la (1621–1695) French poet and fabulist

Fontenelle, Bernard (1657–1757) French librettist, philosopher and man of letters

Foot, Michael (1913–) British Labour politician

Foote, Samuel (1720–1777) English actor, dramatist and wit

Forbes, Miss C.E (1817–1911) English writer

Ford, Anna (1943–) English television newscaster and reporter

Ford, Gerald R. (1913–) American politician and President

Ford, Henry (1863–1947) American car manufacturer

Ford, John (c. 1586–1639) English dramatist and poet

Ford, John (1895–1973) Irish-American film director

Forgy, Howell (1908–1983) American nave chaplain

Forster, E.M. (1879–1970) English writer, essayist and literary critic

Foucault, Michel (1926–1984) French philosopher

Fourier, François (1772–1837) French social theorist

Fowles, John (1926–) English writer

Fox, Charles James (1749–1806) English statesman and abolitionist

Fox, Henry Stephen (1791–1846) English diplomat

Foyle, Christina (1911–1999) Member of famous British bookselling family

Frame, Janet (1924–) New Zealand writer

France, Anatole (1844–1924) French writer and critic

Francis, Clare (1946–) English yachtswoman and writer

Frank, Anne (1929–1945) Jewish diarist; died in Nazi concentration camp

Frank, Otto (1889–1980) Dutch concentration camp survivor and father of Anne Frank

Franklin, Benjamin (1706–1790) American statesman, scientist, political critic and printer

Franklin, Miles (1879–1954) Australian writer

Franks, Oliver, Baron (1905–1992) English diplomat, lecturer and banker

Frayn, Michael (1933–) English dramatist and writer

Frazer, Sir James (1854–1941) Scottish anthropologist and writer

Frederick the Great (1712–1786) King of Prussia and patron of the arts

French, Marilyn (1929–) American writer and critic

Freud, Clement (1924–) British Liberal politician, broadcaster and writer

Freud, Sigmund (1856–1939) Austrian physicist; founder of psychoanalysis

Friday, Nancy (1937–) American writer

Friedan, Betty (1921–) American feminist leader and writer

Friedman, Milton (1912–) American economist

Friel, Brian (1929–) Irish dramatist and writer

Frisch, Max (1911–1991) Swiss dramatist, writer and architect

Frost, Sir David (1939–) English television personality and writer

Frost, Robert (1874–1963) American poet

Froude, James Anthony (1818–1894) English historian and scholar

Fry, Christopher (1907–) English verse dramatist, theatre director and translator

Fry, Elizabeth (1780–1845) English social and prison reformer

Fry, Roger (1866–1934) English art critic, philosopher and painter

Fry, Stephen (1957–) British comedian and writer

Frye, Marilyn American feminist and writer

Frye, Northrop (1912–1991) Canadian critic and academic

Fuller, Richard Buckminster (1895–1983) American architect and engineer

Fuller, Thomas (1608–1661) English churchman and antiquary

Furphy, Joseph (1843–1912) Australian writer and poet

Fyfe, Alistair (b.1961) Scottish artist

G

Gabor, Zsa–Zsa (1919–) Hungarian-born American actress

Gaisford, Rev. Thomas (1779–1855) Dean of Christ Church, Oxford

Gaitskell, Hugh (1906–1963) English Labour politician

Galbraith, J.K. (1908–) Canadian-born American economist, diplomat and writer

Galileo Galilei (1564–1642) Italian mathematician, astronomer, physicist, inventor and teacher

Gallacher, William (1881–1965) Scottish Communist politician

Galsworthy, John (1867–1933) English writer and dramatist

Galt, John (1779–1839) Scottish writer and Canadian pioneer

Gambetta, Léon (1838–1882) French statesman and Prime Minister

Gandhi (1869–1948) Indian political leader

Gandhi, Indira (1917–1984) Indian statesman and Prime Minister

Garbo, Greta (1905–1990) Swedish-born American film actress

García Márquez, Gabriel (1928–) Colombian writer

Gardiner, Richard (b. c. 1533) English writer

Garel–Jones, Tristan (1941–) English politician

Garibaldi, Giuseppe (1807–1882) Italian soldier and patriot

Garland, Judy (1922–1969) American film actress and singer

Garrick, David (1717–1779) English actor and theatre manager

Garrod, Heathcote William (1878–1960) English scholar, academic and essayist

Gascoigne, Paul (1967–) English footballer

Gaskell, Elizabeth (1810–1865) English writer

Gautier, Théophile (1811–1872) French poet, writer and critic

Gay, John (1685–1732) English poet, dramatist and librettist

Geldof, Bob (1954–) Irish rock musician and charity fund raiser

George II (1683–1760) British king

George V (1865–1936) British king

George VI (1895–1952) British king

George, Eddie (1938–) Governor of the Bank of England

George, Henry (1839–1897) American economist, editor and lecturer

Gerrish, Theodore American soldier

Gerry, Elbridge (1744–1814) US Vice-President

Getty, J. Paul (1892–1976) American oil billionaire and art collector

Gibbon, Edward (1737–1794) English historian, politician and memoirist

Gibbons, Orlando (1583–1625) English organist and composer of church music

Gibbs, Sir Philip (1877–1962) British journalist

Gibran, Kahlil (1883–1931) Lebanese poet, mystic and painter

Gide, André (1869–1951) French writer, critic, dramatist and poet

Gilbert, W.S. (1836–1911) English dramatist, humorist and librettist

Gill, Eric (1882–1940) English stonecarver, topographer and writer

Gilman, Charlotte Perkins (1860–1935) US writer, social reformer and feminist

Gilmour, Sir Ian (1926–) Scottish Conservative politician

Ginsberg, Allen (1926–1997) US poet

Giraudoux, Jean (1882–1944) French dramatist, poet, writer and satirist

Gladstone, William (180–1898) English statesman and reformer

Glover, Denis (1912–1980) New Zealand poet and printer

Godard, Jean–Luc (1930–) French film director and writer

Goebbels, Joseph (1897–1945) Nazi politician

Goering, Hermann (1893–1946) Nazi leader and military commander

Goethe (1749–1832) German poet, writer, dramatist and scientist

Gogarty, Oliver St John (1878–1957) Irish poet, dramatist, writer, politician and surgeon

Gogol, Nicolai (1809–1852) Russian writer and soldier

Golding, William (1911–1993) English writer and poet

Goldman, Emma American anarchist

Goldsmith, Sir James (1933–1997) British business magnate and French MEP

Goldsmith, Oliver (c. 1728–1774) Irish dramatist, poet and writer

Goldwater, Barry (1909–1998) US presidential candidate and writer

Goldwyn, Samuel (1882–1974) Polish-born American film producer

Gonne, Maud (1865–1953) Irish patriot and philanthropist

Gordimer, Nadine (1923–) South African writer

Gordon, Adam Lindsay (1833–1870) Australian poet and ballad writer

Gorky, Maxim (1868–1936) Russian writer, dramatist and revolutionary

Gorton, John (1911–) Australian parliamentarian

Goulburn, Edward (1818–1897) English divine and teacher

Gowers, Sir Ernest (1880–1966) English civil servant, champion of plain language

Grable, Betty (1916–1973) American film actress and wartime 'pin-up'

Grace, W.G. (1848–1915) English cricketer, physician and surgeon

Gracian, Baltasar (1601–1658) Spanish Jesuit writer, philosopher and preacher

Grade, Lew (1906–1994) Russian-born British film, TV and theatrical producer.

Graham, Clementina (1782–1877) Scottish writer, lyricist and translator

Graham, James, Marquis of Montrose (1612–1650) Scottish Covenanter, soldier, poet and Royalist

Grainger, James (c. 1721–1766) Scottish poet, army surgeon and editor

Grant, Bruce Alexander (1925–) Australian writer, critic and civil servant

Grant, Cary (1904–1986) English-born American film actor

Grant, Ulysses S. (1822–1885) US President, Civil War general and memoirist

Granville, George (1666–1735) English poet, dramatist and politician

Granville–Barker, Harley (1877–1946) English actor, dramatist, producer and critic

Graves, Robert (1895–1985) English poet, writer, critic, translator and mythologist

Gray, John British academic

Gray, Patrick, Lord (d. 1612) Scottish courtier, ambassador at the court of Elizabeth I of England

Gray, Thomas (1716–1771) English poet and scholar

Greaves, Jimmy (1940–) English footballer and television commentator

Green, Michael (1927–) English writer and playwright

Greene, Graham (1904–1991) English writer and dramatist

Greer, Germaine (1939–) Australian feminist, critic, English scholar and writer

Gregory VII (c. 1020–1085) Italian Pope, saint and church reformer

Gregory, Lady Isabella (1852–1932) Irish dramatist, writer and translator

Grellet, Stephen (1773–1855) French missionary

Greville, Fulke (1554–1628) English poet, dramatist, biographer, courtier and politician

Grey Edward (1862–1933) English statesman and writer

Grey Owl (1888–1938) Canadian writer and naturalist

Griffith, D.W. (1874–1948) US film director

Griffith–Jones, Mervyn (1909–1979) British lawyer

Griffths, Trevor (1935–) British dramatist and screenwriter

Groening, Matt American cartoonist

Grossmith, George (1847–1912) English singer, songwriter and writer

Grossmith, Weedon (1854–1919) English writer, painter and actor

Guedalla, Philip (1889–1944) English historian, writer and lawyer

Guinan, Texas (1884–1933) Canadian actress

Guinness, Sir Alec (1914–) British actor

Guitry, Sacha (1885–1957) Russian-born French actor, dramatist and film director

Gulbenkian, Nubar (1896–1972) British industrialist, diplomat and philanthropist

Gurney, Dorothy (1858–1932) English poet

Gwenn, Edmund (1875–1959) English actor

Gwyn, Nell (1650–1687) English actress and mistress of Charles II

H

Hadrian (76–138) Roman emperor and patron of the arts

Hague, William (1961–) English politician; leader of the Conservative Party

Hahnemann, C.F.S. (1755–1843) German physician and founder of homeopathy

Haig, Douglas, Earl (1861–1928) Scottish military commander

Hailsham, Quintin Hogg, Baron (1907–) English Conservative politician and Lord Chancellor

Hakim, Catherine British academic

Haldane, J.B.S. (1892–1964) British biochemist, geneticist and popularizer of science

Hale, Sir Matthew (1609–1676) English judge and writer

Hale, Nathan (1755–1776) American soldier and revolutionary

Halifax, Lord (1633–1695) English politician, courtier, pamphleteer and epigrammatist

Hall, Jerry (1956–) US fashion model

Hall, Rodney (1935–) US poet and writer

Halleck, Fitz–Greene (1790–1867) American poet, satirist and banker

Halsey, Margaret (1910–) US writer

Hamerton, P.G. (1834–1894) British artist and writer

Hamilton, Ian (1925–)
Lawyer and Scottish
Nationalist

Hamilton, Sir William
(1788–1856) Scottish
metaphysical philosopher

Hamilton, William (Willie)
(1917–) British politician,
teacher and antiroyalist

Hammarskjöld, Dag
(1905–1961) Swedish
statesman, Secretary-General
of the United Nations

Hampton, Christopher
(1946–) English dramatist

Hancock, Sir William
(1898–1988) Australian
historian

Handke, Peter (1942–)
Austrian playwright

Hanrahan, Brian (1949–)
Television news
correspondent and reporter

Hanson, Lord James
(1922–) English millionaire
businessman

Hardwicke, Earl of
(1690–1764) English judge
and Lord Chancellor

Hardy, Rev. E.J.
(1849–1920) Irish army
chaplain and writer

Hardy, Thomas
(1840–1928) English writer
and poet

Hare, Augustus
(1792–1834) English
clergyman and writer

Hare, Maurice Evan
(1886–1967) English
limerick writer

Harlech, Lord (1918–1985)
English politician, and TV
company chairman

Harman, Sir Jeremiah
(1930–) British High Court
judge

Harney, Bill (1895–1962)
Australian writer

Harris, George (1844–1922)
American churchman and
educator

Harris, Max (1921–1995)
Australian critic, poet and
publisher

Harris, Sydney J. (1917–)
US journalist

Hartley, L.P. (1895–1972)
English writer and critic

Harwood, Gwen (1920–)
Australian poet and music
teacher

Haskins, Minnie Louise
(1875–1957) English
teacher and writer

Hattersley, Roy (1932–)
British Labour politician and
writer

Havel, Václav (1936–)
Czech President

Hawke, Bob (1929–)
Australian Premier

Hawthorne, Nathaniel
(1804–1864) American
allegorical writer

Hazlitt, William
(1778–1830) English writer
and critic

Hazzard, Shirley (1931–)
Australian writer

Healey, Denis (1917–)
English Labour politician

Hearst, William Randolph
(1863–1951) American
newspaper proprietor

Heath, Sir Edward (1916–)
English Conservative Prime
Minister

Hegel, Georg Wilhelm
(1770–1831) German
philosopher

Heine, Heinrich
(1797–1856) German lyric
poet, essayist and journalist

Heisenberg, Werner
(1901–1976) German
theoretical physicist

Heller, Joseph (1923–)
American writer

Hellman, Lillian
(1905–1984) American
dramatist and screenwriter

Helpman, Sir Robert
Murray (1909–1986)
Australian choreographer
and director

Helps, Sir Arthur
(1813–1875) English
historian and writer

Hemingway, Ernest
(1898–1961) American
writer and war
correspondent

Henderson, Hamish
(1919–) Scottish folklorist,
composer, translator and
poet

Hendrix, Jimi (1942–1970)
American rock singer,
songwriter and guitarist

Henley, W.E. (1849–1903) English poet, dramatist and critic

Henri IV (1553–1610) French Huguenot leader, became Catholic King (1589-1610)

Henry, O. (1862–1910) American short-story writer

Henry, Patrick (1736–1799) American lawyer, orator and statesman

Henshaw, Bishop Joseph (1603–1679) English churchman and writer

Hepworth, Dame Barbara (1903–1975) English sculptor

Hepworth, John (1921–) Australian writer

Heraclitus (c. 540–c. 480 BC) Greek philosopher

Herbert, Sir A.P. (1890–1971) English humorist, writer, dramatist and politician

Herbert, George (1593–1633) English poet and priest

Herrick, Robert (1591–1674) English poet, royalist and clergyman

Hervey, Lord (1696–1743) English politican and memoirist

Hewart, Gordon (1870–1943) English Liberal politician and Lord Chief Justice

Hewett, Dorothy (1923–) Australian dramatist and poet

Hewitt, John (1907–1987) Irish poet and museum and art gallery director

Hightower, Jim (1933–) Texan agriculture commissioner

Higley, Brewster (19th century) American songwriter

Hill, Joe (1879–1914) Swedish-born American songwriter and workers' organizer

Hill, Reginald (1936–) British writer and playwright

Hill, Rowland (1744–1833) English preacher and hymn writer

Hillary, Sir Edmund (1919–) New Zealand mountaineer, explorer and apiarist

Hillel 'The Elder', (c. 60 BC–c. AD 10) Babylonian rabbi and doctor of Jewish law

Hillingdon, Lady Alice (1857–1940) English aristocrat

Hilton, James (1900– 1954) English writer and screenwriter

Hippocrates (c. 460–357 BC) Greek physician

Hirohito, Emperor (1901–1989) Emperor of Japan

Hirst, Damien(1965–) British artist

Hitchcock, Alfred (1899–1980) English film director

Hitler, Adolf (1889–1945) German Nazi dictator, born in Austria

Hobbes, Thomas (1588–1679) Political philosopher

Hobson, Sir Harold (1904–1992) British critic and writer

Hodgson, Ralph (1871–1962) English poet, illustrator and journalist

Hodson, Peregrine British author

Hoffer, Eric (1902–1983) American writer, philosopher and longshoreman

Hoffmann, Max (1869–1927) German general

Hoffnung, Gerard (1925–1959) British artist, illustrator and musician

Hogg, James (1770–1835) Scottish poet, ballad writer and writer

Hogg, Quintin (1907–) see Hailsham, Baron

Hoggart, Simon (1946–) British journalist

Hokusai (1760–1849) Japanese artist

Holland, Lord (1705–1774) English politician

Holland, Canon Henry Scott (1847–1918) English cleric, Professor of Divinity and Christian social reformer

Holmes, Hugh (Lord Justice Holmes) (1840-1916) Irish judge

Holmes, Rev. John H.
(1879–1964) American
Unitarian minister

Holmes, Oliver Wendell
(1809–1894) US physician,
poet, writer and scientist

Holmes, Oliver Wendell Jr.
(1841–1935) American jurist
and judge

Holst, Gustav (1874–1934)
English composer

Holt, Harold Edward
(1908–1967) Australian
statesman and Prime
Minister

Hood, Thomas (1799–1845)
English poet, editor and
humorist

Hooker, Richard (c.
1554–1600) English
theologian and churchman

Hooper, Ellen Sturgis
(1816–1841) American poet
and hymn wnter

Hooton, Harry (1908–1961)
Australian philosopher and
poet

Hoover, Herbert
(1874–1964) US President

Hope, Alec (1907–)
Australian poet and critic

Hope, Anthony
(1863–1933) English writer,
dramatist and lawyer

Hopkins, Gerard Manley
(1844–1889) English Jesuit
priest, poet and classicist

Hopkins, Jane Ellice
(1836–1904) English social
reformer and writer

Hopper, Hedda
(1890–1966) American
actress and writer

Horace (65–8 BC) Roman
lyric poet and satirist

Home, Donald Richmond
(1921–) Australian writer
and lecturer

Horváth, Ödön von
(1901–1938) German-
Hungarian writer

Household, Geoffrey
(1900–1988) English writer

Housman, A.E. (1850–1936)
English poet and scholar

Howar, Barbara (1934–)
American television
correspondent and writer

Howard, Michael (1922–)
English historian and writer

Howard, Philip (1933–)
English journalist

Howells, W.D. (1837–1920)
American writer, critic, editor
and poet

Howkins, Alun (1947–)
British historian and writer

Hubbard, Elbert
(1856–1915) American
printer, editor, writer and
businessman

Hubbard, 'Kin' (1868–1930)
American humorist and
writer

Hudson, Louise(1958–)
English poet and editor

Hughes, Howard
(1905–1976) US millionaire
industrialist, aviator and film
producer

Hughes, Sean (1966–) Irish
comedian

Hugo, Victor (1802–1885)
French poet, writer, dramatist
and politician

Huistra, Peter (1967–)
Dutch footballer

Hull, Josephine
(1886–1957) US actress

Hume, Basil (1923–1999)
English Cardinal, Archbishop
of Westminster

Hume, David (1711–1776)
Scottish philosopher and
political economist

Humphries, Barry (1934–)
Australian entertainer

Hunt, G.W. (1829–1904)
British song-writer and
painter

Hunt, Leigh (1784–1859)
English writer, poet and
literary editor

Hunter, John (1728–1793)
British surgeon

Hurst, Fannie (1889–1968)
American writer and
playwright

Huss, Jan (c. 1370–1415)
Bohemian religious reformer,
preacher and martyr

Hutcheson, Francis
(1694–1746) Scottish
philosopher

Huxley, Aldous
(1894–1963) English writer,
poet and critic

Huxley, Henrietta
(1825–1915) English writer
and poet; wife of T.H. Huxley

Huxley, Sir Julian (1887–1975) English biologist and Director-General of UNESCO

Huxley, T.H. (1825–1895) English biologist, Darwinist and agnostic

I

Ibárruri, Dolores ('La Pasionara') (1895–1989) Basque Communist leader

Ibsen, Henrik (1828–1906) Norwegian writer, dramatist and poet

Ignatieff, Michael (1947–) Canadian wnter and media personality

Illich, Ivan (1926–) Austrian-born US educator, sociologist, writer and priest

Inge, William Ralph (1860–1954) English divine, writer and teacher

Ingersoll, Robert Greene (1833– 1899) American lawyer, soldier and writer

Ingham, Sir Bernard (1932–) Chief Press Secretary to Margaret Thatcher

Ingrams, Richard (1937–) British journalist and editor of Private Eye

Ingres, J.A.D. (1780–1867) French painter

Iphicrates (419–353 BC) Athenian general

Irvine, Lord (1940–) UK Lord Chancellor

Irving, Washington (1783–1859) American writer and diplomat

Izetbegovic, Alija (1925–) President of Bosnia

J

Jackson, F.J. Foakes (1855–1941) English divine and church historian

Jackson, Robert (1946–) English Conservative politician and writer

Jacobs, Joe (1896–1940) American boxing manager

Jago, Rev. Richard (1715–1781) English poet

James I of Scotland (1394–1437) King of Scots

James VI of Scotland and I of England, (1566–1625) Son of Mary, Queen of Scots; essayist and patron of poetry

James, Brian (1892–1972) Australian writer

James, Henry (1843–1916) American-born British writer, critic and letter writer

James, William (1842–1910) American psychologist and philosopher

Jarrell, Randall (1914–1965) American poet, critic and translator

Jay, Douglas (1907–1996) British economist and writer

Jeans, Sir James Hopwood (1877–1946) English mathematician, physicist and astronomer

Jefferson, Thomas (1743–1826) US President (Democrat)

Jenkins, David (1925–) English Bishop of Durham

Jenkins, Roy (1920–) Welsh politician and writer

Jerome, Jerome K. (1859–1927) English writer and dramatist

Jerrold, Douglas William (1803–1857) English dramatist, writer and wit

Jespersen, Otto (1860–1943) Danish philologist

Joad, C.E.M. (1891–1953) English popularizer of philosophy

John XXIII (1881–1963) Italian Pope, proponent of ecumenicalism

Saint John of the Cross (1542–1591) Spanish mystic

John Paul II (1920–) First Polish pope

Johnson, Amy (1903–1941) English aviator

Johnson, Hiram (1866–1945) American Republican politician

Johnson, Paul (1928–) British editor and writer

Johnson, Samuel (1709–1784) English lexicographer, poet, critic, conversation-alist and essayist

Johnston, Brian (1912–1994) British broadcaster

Johnston, Jill (1929–) English-born American dancer, critic and feminist

Jones, Sir William (1746–1794) English orientalist, translator and jurist

Jonson, Ben (1572–1637) English dramatist and poet

Joseph, Michael (1897–1958) English publisher and writer

Jowett, Benjamin (1817–1893) English scholar, translator, essayist and priest

Joyce, James (1882–1941) Irish writer

Julia (39 BC–AD 14) Daughter of the Emperor Augustus

Junell, Thomas Host of Finland's seaborne drinking championships

Jung, Carl Gustav (1875–1961) Swiss psychiatrist and pupil of Freud

Jung Chang (1952–) Chinese author, based in London

Junius (fl. 1769–1772) Penname of anonymous author

Justinian, Emperor (c. 482–565) Byzantine emperor

Juvenal (c. 60–130) Roman verse satirist and Stoic

K

Kael, Pauline (1919–) US film critic

Kafka, Franz (1883–1924) Czech-born Germanspeaking writer

Kant, Immanuel (1724–1804) German idealist philosopher

Karr, Alphonse (1808–1890) French writer and editor

Kaufman, Gerald (1930–) English Labour politician

Kaufman, George S. (1889–1961) US scriptwriter, librettist and journalist

Kautman, Sue (1926–) US writer and editor

Keats, John (1795–1821) English poet

Keenan, Brian (1950–) Irish journalist and hostage in Lebanon

Keillor, Garrison (1942–) American writer and broadcaster

Keith, Penelope (1940–) English actress

Keller, Helen (1880–1968) US writer and educator of the blind and deaf

Kelman, James (1946–) Scottish novelist

Kelly, Bert (1912–1997) Australian politician

Kelly, Ned (1855–1880) Australian outlaw folk hero

Kemble, John Philip (1757–1823) English Shakespearian actor

Kempis, Thomas à (c. 1380–1471) German mystic, monk and writer

Keneally, Thomas (1935–) Australian writer and screenwriter

Kennedy, A.L. (1965–) Scottish novelist

Kennedy, Florynce R. (1916–) US lawyer, feminist and civil rights activist

Kennedy, John F. (1917–1963) US President

Kennedy, Robert F. (1925–1968) US Attorney General and Democrat politician

Kenny, Mary (1944–) Irish writer and broadcaster

Kerouac, Jack (1922–1969) American writer and poet

Kerr, Jean (1923–) US writer and dramatist

Kettle, Thomas (1880–1916) Irish writer and academic

Key, Ellen (1849–1926) Swedish feminist, writer and lecturer

Keynes, John Maynard (1883–1946) English economist

Khrushchev, Nikita (1894–1971) Russian statesman and Premier of the USSR

Kierkegaard, Sören (1813–1855) Danish philosopher and theologian

Kilvert, Francis (1840–1879) English curate and diarist

King, Billie–Jean (1943–) US tennis player

King, Bishop Henry (1592–1669) English royal chaplain; poet and sermonist

King, Martin Luther (1929–1968) American civil rights leader and Baptist minister

Kingsley, Charles (1819–1875) English writer, poet, lecturer and clergyman

Kingsmill, Hugh (1889–1949) English critic and writer

Kinnock, Neil (1942–) Welsh Labour politician

Kipling, Rudyard (1865–1936) Indian-born British poet and writer

Kissinger, Henry (1923) German-born US Secretary of State

Kitchener, Lord (1850–1916) British War Minister, 1914-1916

Klee, Paul (1879–1940) Swiss painter, engraver and teacher

Klopstock, Friedrich (1724–1803) German poet

Knox, Philander Chase (1853–1921) US lawyer and Republican politician

Knox, Ronald (1888–1957) English Catholic priest and biblical translator

Knox, Vicesimus (1752–1821) English churchman and writer

Koestler, Arthur (1905–1983) British writer, essayist and political refugee

Kollwitz, Käthe (1867–1945) German painter, sculptor and graphic artist

Kraus, Karl (1874–1936) Austrian scientist, critic and poet

Kübler–Ross, Elisabeth (1926–) Swiss-born pioneer in the care of the dying

Kubrick, Stanley (1928–1999) American screenwriter, producer and director

Kundera, Milan (1929–) Czech writer and critic

Kurtz, Irma (1935–) British writer and 'agony aunt'

Kyd, Thomas (1558–1594) English dramatist and poet

L

La Bruyère, Jean de (1645–1696) French moralist and satirist

Laing, R.D. (1927–1989) Scottish psychiatrist, psychoanalyst and poet

Lamartine, Alphonse de (1790–1869) French poet, historian, royalist and statesman

Lamb, Lady Caroline (1785–1828) English writer and poet

Lamb, Charles (1775–1834) English essayist, critic and letter writer

Lancaster Sir Osbert (1908–1986) English writer, cartoonist and stage designer

Landers, Ann (1918–) Famous 'agony aunt' and columnist

Landor, Walter Savage (1775–1864) English poet and writer

Landseer, Sir Edwin Henry (1802–1873) English painter, engraver and sculptor

Lang, Andrew (1844–1912) Scottish poet, writer, mythologist and anthropologist

Lang, Ian (1940–) Scottish Conservative politician

Langland, William (c. 1330–c. 1400) English poet

Lardner, Ring (1885–1933) US humorist and writer

Larkin, Philip (1922–1985) English poet, writer and librarian

La Rochefoucauld (1613–1680) French moralist and epigrammatist

Latimer, Bishop Hugh (c.1485–1555) English Protestant churchman

Laver, James (1899–1975) English art, costume and design historian

Law, Bonar (1858–1923) Canadian-born British statesman and Conservative MP

Lawrence, D.H. (1885–1930) English writer, poet and critic

Lawrence, Frances Widow of Philip Lawrence, murdered schoolmaster

Lawrence, T.E. (1888–1935) British soldier, archaeologist, translator and writer; known as 'Lawrence of Arabia'

Lawson, Henry (Hertzberg) (1867–1922) Australian writer and poet

Lazarre, Jane (1943–) US journalist

Lazarus, Emma (1849–1887) American poet and translator

Leach, Sir Edmund (1910–1989) English social anthropologist

Leacock, Stephen (1869–1944) English-born Canadian humorist, writer and economist

Leavis, F.R. (1895–1978) English critic, lecturer and writer

Le Corbusier (1887–1965) Swiss-born French architect and town planner

Ledru–Rollin, Alexandre Auguste (1807–1874) French lawyer and politician

Lee, Nathaniel (c.1653–1692) English dramatist

Lee, Robert E. (1807–1870) Confederate general during American Civil War

Lee, Spike (1957–) US film director

Lefèvre, Théo (1914–1973) Belgian Prime Minister

Le Gallienne, Richard (1866–1947) English poet, writer and critic

Le Guin, Ursula (1929–) American writer and critic

Leith, Prue (1940–) English cookery writer and businesswoman

Le Mesurier, John (1912–1983) English actor

Lenin, V.I. (1870–1924) Russian revolutionary, Marxist theoretician and first leader of the USSR

Lennon, John (1940–1980) English pop singer-songwriter; member of The Beatles

Léon, Fray Luis de (c. 1527–1591) Spanish Augustinian monk, poet and translator

Leonard, Hugh (1926–) Irish dramatist and screenwriter

Leopold II (1835–1909) King of Belgium

Lermontov, Mikhail (1814–1841) Russian poet and writer

Lerner, Alan Jay (1918–1986) American lyricist and screenwriter

Lesage, Alain–René (1668–1747) French writer and dramatist

Lessing, Doris (1919–) British writer, brought up in Zimbabwe

Lessing, Gotthold Ephraim (1729–1781) German dramatist, critic and theologian

L'Estrange, Sir Roger (1616–1704) English writer, royalist, translator and politician

Levant, Oscar (1906–1972) American pianist and autobiographer

Levi, Primo (1919–1987) Italian writer, poet and chemist; survivor of Auschwitz

Lévi–Strauss, Claude (1908–) French structuralist and anthropologist

Levin, Bernard (1928–) British writer

Lévis, Duc de (1764–1830) French writer and soldier

Lewes, G.H. (1817–1878) English writer, philosopher, critic and scientist

Lewis, C.S. (1898–1963) Irish-born English academic, writer and critic

Lewis, D.B. Wyndham (1891–1969) British writer and biographer

Lewis, Sir George Cornewall (1806–1863) English Liberal politician and writer

Lewis, Sinclair (1885–1951) US writer

Lewis, Wyndham (1882–1957) American-born British painter, critic and writer

Liberace (1919–1987) American pianist and showman

Lichtenberg, Georg (1742–1799) German physicist, satirist and writer

Lie, Trygve (1896–1968) Norwegian politician and Secretary-General of the UN

Lightner, Candy (1946–) US estate agent and founder of MADD (Mothers Against Drunk Driving)

Lincoln, Abraham (1809–1865) US President; assassinated

Lindbergh, Anne Morrow (1906–) American aviator, poet and writer

Lindsay, Norman (1879–1969) Australian artist and writer

Linklater, Eric (1899–1974) Welsh-born Scottish writer and satirist

Linnaeus, Carl (1707–1778) Swedish botanist

Linton, W.J. (1812–1897) English wood engraver, editor and printer

Lloyd George, David (1863–1945) British Liberal Prime Minister

Locke, John (1632–1704) English philosopher

Lockhart, John Gibson (1794–1854) Scottish writer, critic, and translator

Lockier, Francis (1667–1740) English churchman

Lodge, David (1935–) English writer, satirist and literary critic

Logau, Friedrich von (1605–1655) German epigrammatist

London, Jack (1876–1916) American writer, sailor, socialist and goldminer

Longfellow, Henry Wadsworth (1807–1882) American poet and writer

Longford, Lord (1905–) British politician, social reformer and biographer

Longworth, Alice Roosevelt (1884–1980) American writer

Loos, Anita (1893–1981) American writer and screenwriter

Louis XIV (1638–1715) French monarch, the 'Sun King', and patron of the arts

Louis XVIII (1755–1824) King of France

Louis, Joe (1914–1981) US champion boxer

Lovelace, Richard (1618–1658) English poet

Lover, Samuel (1797–1868) Irish songwriter, painter, writer and dramatist

Low, Sir David (1891–1963) New Zealand-born British political cartoonist

Lowe, Robert (1811–1892) English Liberal politician and lawyer

Lowell, James Russell (1819–1891) US poet, editor, abolitionist and diplomat

Lowell, Robert (1917–1977) US poet and writer

Lowry, Malcolm (1909–1957) English writer and poet

Luce, Clare Boothe (1903–1987) US diplomat, politician and writer

Lucretius (c. 95–55 BC) Roman philosopher

Lunt, Alfred (1892–1977) American actor

Luther, Martin (1483–1546) German Protestant theologian and reformer

Lutyens, Sir Edwin Landseer (1869–1944) English architect

Lydgate, John (c. 1370–c. 1451) English monk, poet and translator

Lyly, John (c. 1554–1606) English dramatist and politician

Lynne, Liz (1948–) English politician

M

McAlpine, Sir Alfred (1881–1944) Scottish building contractor

Macaulay, Lord
(1800–1859) English Liberal
statesman, essayist and poet

Macaulay, Dame Rose
(1881–1958) English writer

McAuley, James (1917–1976)
Australian poet and critic

MacCaig, Norman
(1910–1996) Scottish
lecturer and poet

MacCarthy, Cormac
(1933–) US writer

MacCarthy, Sir Desmond
(1878–1952) English critic

**McCarthy, Abigail (c.
1914–)** US writer

McCarthy, Senator Eugene
(1916–) US politician,
lecturer and writer

McCarthy, Senator Joseph
(1908–1957) American
Republican politician

McCarthy, Mary
(1912–1989) American
writer and critic

McCartney, Paul (1942–)
English singer-songwriter,
guitarist and Beatle

McDermott, John W.
Hawaiian travel writer

McDiarmid, Hugh
(1892–1978) Scottish poet
and wnter

MacDonald, George
(1824–1905) Scottish writer,
poet and preacher

MacDonald, Ramsay
(1866–1937) Scottish
Labour politician, Prime
Minister

**McGonagall, William (c.
1830–1902)** Scottish poet,
tragedian and actor

McGough, Roger (1937–)
English poet and teacher

McGregor, Craig (1933–)
Australian writer

McGuigan, Barry (1961–)
British boxer

Machiavelli (1469–1527)
Florentine statesman,
political theorist and
historian

MacInnes, Colin
(1914–1976) English writer

McIver, Charles D.
(1860–1906) American
educationist

McKenney, Ruth
(1911–1972) US writer

Mackenzie, Sir Compton
(1883–1972) Scottish writer
and broadcaster

Mackintosh, Sir James
(1765–1832) Scottish
philosopher, historian, lawyer
and politician

Maclaine, Shirley (1934–)
US actress

McLean, Joyce Canadian
writer

Macleod, Iain (1913–1970)
English Conservative
politician and writer

McLuhan, Marshall
(1911–1980) Canadian
communications theorist

Macmillan, Harold
(1894–1986) British
Conservative Prime Minister

McMillan, Joyce(1952–)
Scottish critic

MacNally, Leonard
(1752–1820) Irish lawyer,
dramatist and political
informer

MacNeice, Louis
(1907–1963) Belfast-born
poet, writer, radio producer,
translator and critic

Madan, Geoffrey
(1895–1947) English
bibliophile

Madariaga, Salvador de
(1886–1978) Spanish writer,
diplomat and teacher

Maeterlinck, Maurice
(1862–1949) Belgian poet,
playwright and essayist

Mailer, Norman (1923–)
American writer

Maistre, Joseph de
(1753–1821) French
diplomat and political
philosopher

Major, John (1943–)
English Conservative Prime
Minister

Mallarmé, Stéphane
(1842–1898) French poet

Mallet, Robert (1915–)
French university rector, poet
and writer

Malouf, David (1934–)
Australian writer and poet

Malthus, Thomas Robert
(1766–1834) English
political economist

Mandela, Nelson (1918–)
President of South Africa,
lawyer and political prisoner

Mandelstam, Nadezhda (1899–1980) Russian writer, translator and teacher

Mankiewicz, Herman (1897–1953) American journalist and screenwriter

Mann, Horace (1796–1859) American educationist, politician and writer

Mann, Thomas (1875–1955) German writer and critic

Mann, W. Edward (1918–) Canadian sociologist

Manners, Lord John (1818–1906) English Conservative politician and writer

Manning, Frederic (1882–1935) Australian writer

Mansfield, Earl of (1705–1793) Scottish judge

Mansfield, Katherine (1888–1923) New Zealand writer

Mantel, Hilary (1952–) English writer

Mao Tse–Tung (1893–1976) Marxist revolutionary and leader of the Chinese Communist Party

Markham, Beryl (1902–1986) English aviator and writer

Marlowe, Christopher (1564–1593) English poet and dramatist

Marmion, Shackerley (1603–1639) English dramatist and poet

Maron, Monika (1941–) German writer

Marquis, Don (1878–1937) American columnist, satirist and poet

Marryat, Frederick (1792–1848) English naval officer and writer

Marshall, Alan (Jock) (1911–1968) Australian zoologist and explorer

Martial (c. 40–c. 104) Spanish-born Latin epigrammatist and poet

Martineau, Harriet (1802–1876) English writer

Marvell, Andrew (1621–1678) English poet and satirist

Marx, Groucho (1895–1977) US comedian

Marx, Karl (1818–1883) German political philosopher and economist; founder of Communism

Mary, Queen of Scots (1542–1587) Daughter of James V, mother of James VI and I; executed by Elizabeth I of England

Masefield, John (1878–1967) English poet, writer and critic

Massinger, Philip (1583–1640) English dramatist and poet

Matthews, Brander (1852–1929) US critic, lecturer, dramatist and writer

Maugham, William Somerset (1874–1965) English writer, dramatist and physician

Maxwell, Gavin (1914–1969) British writer and naturalist

Mayakovsky, Vladimir (1893 1930) Russian poet, dramatist and artist

Mayer, Louis B. (1885–1957) Russian-born American film executive

Mayhew, Christopher (1915–1997) British parliamentarian and writer

Maynard, Sir John (1602–1690) English judge, politician and royalist

Mead, Margaret (1901–1978) US anthropologist, psychologist and writer

Medawar, Sir Peter (1915–1987) British zoologist and immunologist

Medici, Cosimo de' (1389–1464) Member of Medici family, rulers of Tuscany and Florence

Meir, Golda (1898–1978) Russian-born Israeli stateswoman and Prime Minister

Melba, Dame Nellie (1861–1931) Australian opera singer

Melbourne, Lord (1779–1848) English statesman

Mellon, Andrew (1855–1937) American, banker, public official and art collector

Melville, Herman (1819–1891) American writer and poet

Mencken, H.L. (1880–1956) American writer, critic, philologist and satirist

Menzies, Sir Robert (1894–1978) Australian statesman

Meredith, George (1828–1909) English writer, poet and critic

Meredith, Owen (1831–1891) English statesman and poet

Merritt, Dixon Lanier (1879–1972) US editor

Meudell, George Dick (1860–1936) Australian writer, traveller and social commentator

Meyer, Agnes (1887–c. 1970) American writer and social worker

Meynell, Hugo (1727–1780) Frequenter of London society, acquaintance of Dr Johnson

Michaelis, John H. (1912–1985) American army officer

Mikes, George (1912–1987) Hungarian-born British writer

Mill, John Stuart (1806–1873) English philosopher, economist and reformer

Millay, Edna St Vincent (1892–1950) American poet and dramatist

Miller, Alice Swiss-born American psychotherapist and writer

Miller, Arthur (1915–) American dramatist and screenwriter

Miller, Henry (1891–1980) American writer

Miller, Jonathan (1934–) English writer, director, producer and physician

Milligan, Spike (1918–) Irish comedian and writer

Milne, A.A. (1882–1956) English writer, dramatist and poet

Milner, Alfred (1854–1925) British statesman and colonial administrator

Milton, John (1608–1674) English poet, libertarian and pamphleteer

Minifie, James M. (1900–1974) Canadian broadcaster

Mitchell, George (1933–) US politician and peacebroker in Northern Ireland

Mitchell, Margaret (1900–1949) American author of Gone With The Wind

Mitford, Nancy (1904–1973) English writer

Mizner, Wilson (1876–1933) American writer, wit and dramatist

Molière (1622–1673) French dramatist, actor and director

Moltke, Helmuth von (1800–1891) German field marshal

Monash, Sir John (1865–1931) Australian military commander

Monmouth, Duke of (1649–1685) Illegitimate son of Charles II

Monroe, Marilyn (1926–1962) American film actress and model

Montagu, Lady Mary Wortley (1689–1762) English letter writer, poet, traveller and introducer of smallpox inoculation

Montague, C.E. (1867–1928) English writer and critic

Montaigne, Michel de (1533–1592) French essayist and moralist

Montesquieu (1689–1755) French philosopher and jurist

Montessori, Maria (1870–1952) Italian doctor and educationist

Montgomery, Viscount (1887–1976) English field marshal

Mooney, Bel British journalist

Moore, Brian (1921–) Canadian writer

Moore, George (1852–1933) Irish writer, dramatist and critic

Moran, Lord (1924–) British diplomat and politician

Moravia, Alberto (1907–1990) Italian writer

Mordaunt, Thomas (1730–1809) British officer

More, Hannah (1745–1833) English poet, dramatist and religious writer

More, Sir Thomas (1478–1535) English statesman and humorist

Morell, Thomas (1703–1784) English scholar, librettist, editor and clergyman

Morito, Akio Japanese Chairman of Sony

Morley, John British writer

Morley, Robert (1908–1992) British actor

Morris, Charles (1745–1838) English songwriter and soldier

Morris, Desmond (1928–) English anthropologist and broadcaster

Morris, William (1834–1896) English poet, designer, craftsman, artist and socialist

Morrison, Danny (1950–) Irish Republican activist

Mortimer, John (1923–) English lawyer, dramatist and writer

Morton, Rogers (1914–1979) American government official

Moses, Grandma (1860–1961) US painter

Mosley, Sir Oswald (1896–1980) English founder of the British Union of Fascists

Mountbatten of Burma, Earl (1900–1979) British naval commander; killed by IRA

Mourie, Graham (1952–) New Zealand rugby player

Mtshali, Oswald (1940–) South African poet

Muggeridge, Malcolm (1903–1990) English writer

Muir, Edwin (1887–1959) Scottish poet, critic, translator and writer

Muir, Frank (1920–1998) English writer, humorist and broadcaster

Mumford, Ethel (1878–1940) American writer, dramatist and humorist

Mumford, Lewis (1895–1990) American sociologist and writer

Murdoch, Iris (1919–1999) Irish-born British writer, philosopher and dramatist

Murdoch, Rupert (1931–) Australian-born publisher and international businessman

Murdoch, Sir Walter (1874–1970) Australian writer and broadcaster

Murray, David (1888–1962) British writer

Murray Les A. (1938–) Australian poet and writer

Murrow, Edward R. (1908–1965) US reporter and war correspondent

Mussolini, Benito (1883–1945) Italian fascist dictator

N

Nabokov, Vladimir (1899–1977) Russian-born US writer, poet, translator and critic

Naipaul, Sir V.S. (1932–) Trinidadian writer

Nairn, Ian (1930–1983) English writer on architecture and journalist

Napier, Sir William (1785–1860) British general and historian

Napoleon I (1769–1821) French emperor

Napoleon III (1808–1873) French emperor

Narayan, R.K. (1907–) Indian writer and translator

Narváez, Ramon Maria (1800–1868) Spanish general and statesman

Nash, Ogden (1902–1971) American poet

Naylor, James Ball (1860–1945) American physician and writer

Neaves, Lord (1800–1876) English jurist

Nelson, Lord (1758–1805) English admiral

Nero (37–68) Roman emperor

Nerval, Gérard de (1808–1855) French poet and writer

Newby, P.H. (1918–) English writer and Director of the BBC

Newcastle, Margaret, Duchess of (c.1624–1674) English poet, dramatist and woman of letters

Newman, Ernest (1868–1959) English music critic and writer

Newman, John Henry (1801–1890) English Cardinal, theologian and poet

Newman, Paul (1925–) American actor

Newton, Sir Isaac (1642–1727) English scientist and philosopher

Nicholson, Sir Bryan (1932–) British businessman

Nicholson, Emma (1941–) British Liberal Democrat politician

Niebuhr, Reinhold (1892–1971) American Protestant theologian and writer

Niemöller, Martin (1892–1984) German Lutheran theologian

Nietzsche, Friedrich (1844–1900) German philosopher, critic and poet; famed for his concept of the 'Superman'

Nin, Anaïs (1903–1977) American writer

Nixon, Richard (1913–1994) US President, forced to resign (1974)

Nolan, Sir Sidney (1917–1992) Australian artist

Norris, Kathleen (1880–1966) American writer, pacifist and activist

North, Christopher (1785–1854) Scottish poet, writer, editor and critic

Northcliffe, Lord (1865–1922) Irish-born British newspaper proprietor

Novello, Ivor (1893– 1951) Welsh actor, composer, songwriter and dramatist

O

Oates, Captain Lawrence (1880–1912) English Antarctic explorer

O'Brian, Patrick Irish writer

O'Brien, Edna (1936–) Irish writer and dramatist

O'Casey, Sean (1880–1964) Irish dramatist

Ochs, Adolph S. (1858–1935) American newspaper publisher and editor

O'Connell, Daniel (1775–1847) Irish nationalist politician

O'Connor, Flannery (1925–1964) US writer

Ogden, C.K. (1889–1957) English linguist

Ogilvy, James (1663–1730) Scottish politician and lawyer

O'Keeffe, Georgia (1887–1986) US artist

Olivier, Laurence, Baron (1907–1989) English actor and director

Olsen, Tillie (1913–) US writer

Onassis, Aristotle (1906–1975) Turkish-born Greek shipping magnate

Ondaatje, Michael (1943–) Canadian writer

O'Neill, Eugene (1888–1953) US dramatist

Oppenheimer, J. Robert (1904–1967) American nuclear physicist

O'Reilly, Tony (1936–) Irish entrepreneur and international rugby player

O'Rourke, P.J. (1947–) American writer

Ortega y Gasset, José (1883–1955) Spanish philosopher and critic

Ortega Spottorno, José Spanish writer

Orton, Joe (1933–1967) English dramatist and writer

Orwell, George (1903–1950) English writer and critic

Osborne, John (1929–1994) English dramatist and actor

Osgood, Peter English footballer

Osler, Sir William (1849–1919) Canadian physician

O'Sullivan, John L. (1813–1895) American editor and diplomat

Otis, James (1725–1783) US lawyer, politician and pamphleteer

Otway, Thomas (1652–1685) English dramatist and poet

Ouida (1839–1908) English writer and critic

Ovett, Steve (1955) English athlete

Ovid (43 BC–AD 18) Roman poet

Owen, John (c. 1560–1622) Welsh epigrammatist and teacher

Owen, Wilfred (1893–1918) English poet

Ozick, Cynthia (1928–) American writer

P

Paglia, Camille (1947–) US academic

Paine, Thomas (1737–1809) English-born US political theorist and pamphleteer

Palacio Valdés, Armando (1853–1938) Spanish writer

Paley, Rev. William (1743–1805) English theologian and philosopher

Palmer, Amold (1929–) American golfer

Palmerston, Lord (1784–1865) British Prime Minister

Pankhurst, Dame Christabel (1880 1958) English suffragette

Pankhurst, Emmeline (1858–1928) English militant suffragette

Pankhurst, Sylvia (1882–1960) English suffragette, pacifist and internationalist

Park, Mungo (1771–1806) Scottish explorer, writer and physician

Parker, Charlie (1920–1955) American jazz musician and composer

Parker, Dorothy (1893–1967) American writer, poet, critic and wit

Parkes, Sir Henry (1815–1896) Australian politician, writer and poet

Parkinson, C. Northcote (1909–1993) English political scientist and historian

Parnell, Anna (1852–1911) Irish politician

Parnell, Charles Stewart (1846–1891) Irish nationalist politician

Parris, Matthew (1949–) British Conservative politician and journalist

Parsons, Tony (1953–) British journalist and broadcaster

Parton, Dolly (1946–) American country and western singer

Pascal, Blaise (1623–1662) French philosopher and scientist

Pasteur, Louis (1822–1895) French chemist, bacteriologist and immunologist

Pater, Walter (1839–1894) English critic, writer and lecturer

Paton, Alan (1903–1988) South African writer

Patten, Brian (1946–) British poet

Patton, General George S. (1885–1945) American general

Pavese, Cesare (1908–1950) Italian writer and translator

Pavlova, Anna (1881–1931) Russian ballet dancer

Paxman, Jeremy (1950–) English journalist, writer and broadcaster

Payne, J.H. (1791–1852) American dramatist, poet and actor

Paz, Octavio (1914–1998) Mexican poet and critic

Peacock, Thomas Love (1785–1866) English writer and poet

Pearson, Hesketh (1887–1964) English biographer

Pearson, Lester B. (1897–1972) Canadian diplomat and politician

Peary, Robert Edwin (1856–1920) American Arctic explorer, admiral and writer

Peck, Gregory (1916–) American actor

Péguy, Charles (1873–1914) French Catholic socialist, poet and writer

Penn, William (1644–1718) English Quaker, founder of state of Pennsylvania

Pepys, Samuel (1633–1703) English diarist, naval administrator and politician

Perelman, S.J. (1904–1979) American humorist, writer and dramatist

Pericles (c. 495–429) Athenian statesman, general, orator and cultural patron

Pessoa, Fernando (1888–1935) Portuguese poet

Peter, Laurence J. (1919–1990) Canadian educationist and writer

Peters, Ellis (1913–1995) English writer

Pheidippides (d. 490 BC) Athenian athlete

Philip, Prince, Duke of Edinburgh (1921–) Greek-born consort of Queen Elizabeth II

Philips, Ambrose (c. 1675–1749) English poet and politician

Picasso, Pablo (1881–1973) Spanish painter, sculptor and graphic artist

Piggy, Miss Character from The Muppets

Pindar (518–438 BC) Greek lyric poet

Pinter, Harold (1930–) English dramatist, poet and screenwriter

Pirsig, Robert (1928–) American author

Pitt, William (1708–1778) English politician and Prime Minister

Pitt, William (1759–1806) English politician and Prime Minister

Plath, Sylvia (1932–1963) American poet, writer and diarist

Plato (c. 429–347 BC) Greek philosopher

Pliny the Elder (23–79) Roman scientist, historian and soldier

Plomer, William (1903–1973) South African-born British writer and editor

Plutarch (c. 46– c. 120) Greek biographer and philosopher

Poe, Edgar Allan (1809–1849) American poet, writer and editor

Polo, Marco (c.1254–1324) Venetian merchant, traveller and writer

Pompidou, Georges (1911–1974) French statesman, Premier and President

Pope, Alexander (1688–1744) English poet, translator and editor

Popper, Sir Karl (1902–1994) Austrian-born British philosopher

Porson, Richard (1759–1808) English scholar

Porter, Sir George (1920–) English chemist

Porter, Hal (1911–1984) Australian writer, dramatist and poet

Portland, Duke of (1857–1943) British aristocrat and writer

Post, Emily (1873–1960) American writer

Potter, Stephen (1900–1969) English writer, critic and lecturer

Pound, Ezra (1885–1972) US poet

Powell, Anthony (1905–) English writer and critic

Powell, Enoch (1912–1998) English politician and scholar

Power, Marguerite, Countess of Blessington (1789–1849) English writer

Powys, John Cowper (1872–1963) English writer and poet

Preston, Keith (1884–1927) American poet, writer and teacher

Previn, André (1929–) German-born American conductor and composer

Priestland, Gerald (1927–1991) English writer and broadcaster

Priestley, J.B. (1894–1984) English writer, dramatist and critic

Pringle, John (1912–) Scottish-born Australian writer

Pringle, Thomas (1789–1834) Scottish poet

Propertius, Sextus Aurelius (c. 50– c. 15 BC) Roman poet

Proudhon, Pierre–Joseph (1809–1865) French social reformer, anarchist and writer

Proust, Marcel (1871–1922) French writer and critic

Puzo, Mario (1920–) American writer

Pyrrhus (319–272 BC) King of Epirus and army commander

Q

Quarles, Francis (1592–1644) English poet, writer and royalist

Quevedo y Villegas, Francisco Gómez de (1580–1645) Spanish poet and writer

Quiller–Couch, Sir Arthur ('Q') (1863–1944) English writer, poet, critic and academic

R

Rabelais, François (c. 1494– c. 1553) French monk, physician, satirist and humanist

Racine, Jean (1639–1699) French tragedian and poet

Rae, John (1931–) English educationist and writer

Rainborowe, Thomas (d. 1648) English parliamentarian and soldier

Rains, Claude (1889–1967) British actor

Rajneesh, Bhagwan Shree (1931–) Indian guru and teacher

Raleigh, Sir Walter (c. 1552–1618) English courtier, explorer, military commander, poet, historian and essayist

Ramey, Estelle (1917–) American physiologist, educator and feminist

Rattigan, Terence (1911–1977) English dramatist and screenwriter

Reagan, Ronald (1911–) US President

Reed, Henry (1914–1986) English poet, radio dramatist and translator

Reed, Rex (1948–) American film and music critic and columnist

Reger, Max (1873–1916) German composer, conductor, teacher and pianist

Reinhardt, Gottfried (1911–) Austrian film producer

Reith, Lord (1889–1971) Scottish wartime minister, administrator, diarist and Director-General of the BBC

Renan, J. Ernest (1823–1892) French philologist, writer and historian

Renard, Jules (1864–1910) French writer and dramatist

Renoir, Jean (1894–1979) French film director

Renoir, Pierre–Auguste (1841–1919) French painter

Revson, Charles (1906–1975) American cosmetic company executive

Reynolds, Sir Joshua (1723–1792) English portrait painter

Reynolds, Malvina (1900–1978) American singer-songwriter

Rhodes, Cecil (1853–1902) English imperialist, financier and South African statesman

Rhondda, Viscountess (1883–1958) English magazine editor and suffragette

Rhys, Ernest (b.1859) British poet

Rhys, Jean (1894–1979) West Indian-born British writer

Ribblesdale, Lord (1854–1925) British army officer and courtier

Rice, Grantland (1880–1954) US writer

Richard, Sir Cliff (1940–) English singer

Richards, I.A. (1893–1979) English critic, linguist, poet and teacher

Richardson, Sir Ralph (1902–1983) English actor

Richelieu, Cardinal (1585–1642) Prime Minister to Louis XIII, 1624–1642

Richelieu, Duc de (1766–1822) French courtier, soldier and Prime Minister

Rifkin, Jeremy American bioethicist

Rifkind, Malcolm (1946–) Scottish barrister and Conservative politician

Riley, Janet (1915–) American lawyer, educator and civil rights activist

Rilke, Rainer Maria (1875–1926) Austrian poet, born in Prague

Rimbaud, Arthur (1854–1891) French poet

Rippon, Geoffrey (1924–) English Conservative politician

Robertson, George (1946–) British Labour Cabinet minister

Robespierre, Maximilien (1758–1794) French revolutionary

Robinson, Mary (1944–) President of Ireland, 1990-1997, and barrister

Robinson, Roland (1912–1992) Irish-born Australian poet

Rochester, Earl of (1647–1680) English poet, satirist, courtier and libertine

Rogers, Will (1879–1935) American humorist, actor, rancher, writer and wit

Roland, Madame (1754–1793) French revolutionary and writer

Roosevelt, Franklin Delano (1882–1945) US President (Democrat)

Roosevelt, Theodore (1858–1919) US President (Republican)

Ross, Harold (1892–1951) American editor

Ross, Nick (1947–) British broadcaster

Rossetti, Christina (1830–1894) English poet

Rossetti, Dante Gabriel (1828–1882) English poet, painter, translator and letter-writer

Rossini, Gioacchino (1792–1868) Italian composer

Rostand, Jean (1894–1977) French biologist

Rosten, Leo (1908–1997) Polish-born American social scientist, writer and humorist

Roth, Philip (1933–) American writer

Rousseau, Jean–Jacques (1712–1778) Swiss-born French philosopher educationist and essayist

Rousselot, Fabrice French journalist

Roux, Joseph (1834–1886) French priest and epigrammatist

Rowbotham, David (1924–) Australian journalist, critic and poet

Rowland, Helen (1875–1950) US writer

Rowland, Richard (1881–1947) American film executive

Rubin, Jerry (1936–) US political activist

Rubinstein, Helena (c. 1872–1965) Polish-born US cosmetician and businesswoman

Rückriem, Ulrich (1938–) German sculptor

Runciman, Sir Steven (1903–) British scholar, historian and archaeologist

Runyon, Damon (1884–1946) American writer

Rushdie, Salman (1946–) Indian-born writer, resident in Britain; subject of a fatwa issued by the Ayatollah Khomeini

Rusk, Dean (1909–1994) American politician and diplomat

Ruskin, John (1819–1900) English art critic, philosopher and reformer

Russell, Bertrand (1872–1970) English philosopher, mathematician, essayist and social reformer

Russell, Lord John (1792–1878) English Liberal Prime Minister and writer

Rutskoi, Alexander (1947–) Russian politician

Ryle, Gilbert (1900–1976) English philosopher

S

Saatchi, Charles (1943–) co-founder of Saatchi & Saatchi advertising agency

Sabia, Laura Canadian feminist writer

Sackville–West, Vita (1892–1962) English writer, poet and gardener

Sade, Marquis de (1740–1814) French soldier and writer

Sagan, Françoise (1935–) French writer

Sahl, Mort (1927–) Canadian-born American comedian

Saikaku, Ihara (1642–1693) Japanese writer and poet

Sainte–Beuve (1804–1869) French critic, essayist and poet

Saint–Exupéry, Antoine de (1900–1944) French writer and aviator

Saint–Pierre, Bernardin de (1737–1814) French writer

Saintsbury, George (1845–1933) English critic and historian

Saki (1870–1916) Burmese-born British writer

Salinger, J.D. (1919–) American writer

Salisbury, Lord (1830–1903) English Conservative Prime Minister

Salk, Jonas E. (1914–1995) US virologist

Sallust (86– c. 34 BC) Roman historian and statesman

Salmon, George (1819–1904) Provost of Trinity College, Dublin

Sampson, Anthony (1926–) British writer

Samuel, Lord (1870–1963) English Liberal statesman, philosopher and administrator

Sand, George (1804–1876) French writer and dramatist

Sandburg, Carl (1878–1967) American poet, writer and song collector

Sanders, George (1906–1972) Russian-born British film actor

Santayana, George (1863–1952) Spanish-born American philosopher and writer

Sappho (fl. 7th–6th centuries BC) Greek poet

Sarasate (y Navascués) Pablo (1844–1908) Spanish violinist and composer

Sargent, John Singer (1856–1925) American painter

Sargent, Sir Malcolm (1895–1967) English conductor

Saro–Wiwa, Ken (1941–1995) Nigerian writer and human rights activist

Saroyan, William (1908–1981) American writer and dramatist

Sarton, May (1912–1995) US poet and writer

Sartre, Jean–Paul (1905–1980) French philosopher, writer, dramatist and critic

Sassoon, Siegfried (1886–1967) English poet and writer

Satie, Erik (1866–1925) French composer

Saunders, Ernest (1935–) British businessman and company director

Sayers, Dorothy L. (1893–1957) English writer, dramatist and translator

Sayle, Alexei (1952–) British actor, comedian and writer

Scanlon, Hugh, Baron (1913–) British trade union leader

Scargill, Arthur (1941–) English trade union official

Scarron, Paul (1610–1660) French dramatist, writer and poet

Schelling, Friedrich von
(1775–1854) German
philosopher

Schiller, Johann
(1759–1805) German writer,
dramatist, poet and historian

Schlegel, Friedrich von
(1772–1829) German critic
and philosopher

Schnabel, Artur
(1882–1951) Austrian
pianist and composer

Schopenhauer, Arthur
(1788–1860) German
philosopher

Schreiner, Olive
(1855–1920) South African
writer

Schubert, Franz
(1797–1828) Austrian
composer

Schulz, Charles (1922–) US
cartoonist

Schumacher, E.F.
(1911–1977) German-born
British economist and essayist

Schurz, Carl (1829–1906)
German-born American
lawyer, soldier, Republican
politician and writer

Scott, C.P. (1846–1932)
English newspaper editor
and Liberal politician

Scott, Capt. Robert
(1868–1912) English naval
officer and Antarctic explorer

Scott, Valerie Canadian
prostitute and feminist

Scott, Sir Walter
(1771–1832) Scottish writer
and historian

Scott–Maxwell, Florida
(1884–1979) US writer,
suffragist, psychologist,
playwright and actress

Seal, Christopher British
churchman

Sedgwick, Catharine Maria
(1789–1867) American
writer and feminist

Seeley, Sir John
(1834–1895) English
historian, essayist and
scholar

Segal, Erich (1937–) US
academic

Selden, John (1584–1654)
English historian, jurist and
politician

Sellar, Walter (1898–1951)
British writer

Seneca (c. 4 BC–AD 65)
Roman philosopher, poet,
dramatist, essayist,
rhetorician and statesman

Sévigné, Madame de
(1626–1696) French letter-
writer

Sexton, Anne (1928–1974)
US poet

Shahn, Ben (1898–1969)
Lithuanian-born American
painter and muralist

Shakespeare, William
(1564–1616) English
dramatist, poet and actor

Shankly, Bill (1914–1981)
Scottish football player and
manager

Sharif, Omar (1932–)
Egyptian film actor

Sharpe, Tom (1928–)
English writer

Shaw, George Bernard
(1856–1950) Irish socialist,
writer, dramatist and critic

Sheen, J. Fulton
(1895–1979) American
Catholic bishop, broadcaster
and writer

Shelley, Percy Bysshe
(1792–1822) English poet,
dramatist and essayist

Sheridan, Philip Henry
(1831–1888) American
general

Sheridan, Richard Brinsley
(1751–1816) Irish dramatist,
politician and orator

Sherman, Alfred (1919–)
British journalist

**Sherman, William
Tecumseh (1820–1891)**
American Civil War general

Shinwell, Emanuel
(1884–1986) British Labour
politician

Shirley, James (1596–1666)
English poet and
dramatist

Shorten, Caroline British
spokesperson for Social and
Liberal Democrat party

Shorter, Clement King
(1857–1926) English writer
and critic

Shuter, Edward
(1728–1776) English actor
and wit

Sibelius, Jean (1865–1957)
Finnish composer

Sickert, Walter (1860–1942) German-born British painter and writer

Sidney, Sir Philip (1554–1586) English poet, critic, soldier, courtier and diplomat

Sigismund (1368–1437) King of Hungary, Bohemia and Holy Roman Emperor

Simenon, Georges (1903–1989) Belgian writer

Simon, Neil (1927–) US playwright

Simonides (c. 556–468 BC) Greek poet and epigrammatist

Simpson, N.E (1919–) English dramatist

Singer, Isaac Bashevis (1904–1991) Polish-born American Yiddish writer

Sinyavsky, Andrei: see Tertz, Abram

Sitwell, Dame Edith (1887–1964) English poet, anthologist, critic and biographer

Sitwell, Sir Osbert (1892–1969) English poet and writer

Skelton, Red (1913–1997) US comedian

Slater, Nigel Food writer

Smart, Christopher (1722–1771) English poet and translator

Smith, Adam (1723–1790) Scottish economist, philosopher and essayist

Smith, Alexander (1830–1867) Scottish poet and writer

Smith, Sir Cyril (1928–) British politician

Smith, Delia (1941–) Cookery writer

Smith, F.E. (1872–1930) English politician and Lord Chancellor

Smith, Ian (1919–) Prime Minister of what was Rhodesia (now Zimbabwe)

Smith, Joseph (1805–1844) Founder of the Mormon Church

Smith, Logan Pearsall (1865–1946) US-born British epigrammatist, critic and writer

Smith, Stevie (1902–1971) English poet and writer

Smith, Sydney (1771–1845) English clergyman, essayist, journalist and wit

Smith, Sir Sydney (1883–1969) New Zealand-born British forensic scientist and writer

Smollett, Tobias (1721–1771) Scottish writer, satirist, historian, traveller and physician

Snagge, John (1904–1996) British television broadcaster and commentator

Snow, C.P. (1905–1980) English writer, critic, physicist and public administrator

Soames, Nicholas (1948–) English Conservative politician

Socrates (469–399 BC) Athenian philosopher

Solanas, Valerie (1940–1998) US artist

Solon (c. 638–c. 559 BC) Athenian statesman, reformer and poet

Solzhenitsyn, Alexander (1918–) Russian writer, dramatist and historian

Somoza, Anastasio (1925–1980) President of Nicaragua

Sontag, Susan (1933–) American critic and writer

Soper, Donald, Lord (1903–1998) Methodist churchman and writer

Southern, Terry (1924–) American writer and screenwriter

Southerne, Thomas (1660–1746) Irish dramatist

Southey, Robert (1774–1843) English poet, essayist, historian and letterwriter

Spalding, Julian (1948–) English art administrator

Spark, Muriel (1918–) Scottish writer, poet and dramatist

Sparrow, John (1906–1992) English lawyer and writer

Spencer, Herbert (1820–1903) English philosopher and journalist

Spencer, Sir Stanley (1891–1959) English painter

Spender, Sir Stephen (1909–1995) English poet, editor, translator and diarist

Spenser, Edmund (c. 1522–1599) English poet

Spinoza, Baruch (1632–1677) Dutch philosopher and theologian

Spooner, William (1844–1930) English churchman and university warden

Squire, Sir J.C. (1884–1958) English poet, critic, writer and editor

Stacpoole, H. de Vere (1863–1951) Irish writer and physician

Staël, Mme de (1766–1817) French writer, critic, memoirist and hostess

Stalin, Joseph (1879–1953) Soviet Communist leader

Stanton, Elizabeth Cady (1815–1902) American suffragist, abolitionist, feminist, editor and writer

Stapledon, Olaf (1886–1950) British philosopher and writer

Stark, Dame Freya (1893–1993) French-born traveller and writer

Stassinopoulos, Ariana (1950–) Greek writer

Stead, Christina (1902–1983) Australian writer

Steele, Sir Richard (1672–1729) Irish-born English writer, dramatist and politician

Stefano, Joseph (1922–) US screenwriter

Steffens, Lincoln (1866–1936) American political analyst and writer

Stein, Gertrude (1874–1946) American writer, dramatist, poet and critic

Stein, Jock (1922–1985) Scottish football player and manager

Steinbeck, John (1902–1968) American writer

Steinem, Gloria (1934–) American writer and feminist activist

Stendhal (1783–1842) French writer, critic and soldier

Stenhouse, David (1932–) English-born New Zealand zoologist and educationist

Stephen, Sir James Fitzjames (1829–1894) English judge and essayist

Stephen, James Kenneth (1859–1892) English writer and poet

Stephens, James (1882–1950) Irish poet and writer

Sterne, Laurence (1713–1768) Irish-born English writer and clergyman

Stevens, Wallace (1879–1955) American poet, essayist, dramatist and lawyer

Stevenson, Adlai (1900–1965) American lawyer, statesman and United Nations ambassador

Stevenson, Robert Louis (1850–1894) Scottish writer, poet and essayist

Stewart, Rod (1945–) English rock singer

Stocks, Mary, Baroness (1891–1975) English educationist, broadcaster and biographer

Stockwood, Mervyn (1913–1995) English Anglican churchman

Stone, I.F (1907–1989) American writer

Stone, Judith American science writer

Stoppard, Tom (1937–) British dramatist

Storr, Dr Anthony (1920–) British writer and psychiatrist

Stowe, Harriet Beecher (1811–1896) American writer and reformer

Strachey, Lytton (1880–1932) English biographer and critic

Stravinsky, Igor (1882–1971) Russian composer and conductor

Streatfield, Sir Geoffrey (1897–1978) British judge

Stretton, Hugh (1924–) Australian political scientist and historian

Stromme, Sigmund Norwegian publisher

Stubbes, Philip (c.1555–1610) English Puritan pamphleteer and writer

Sturges, Preston (1898–1959) US film director and scriptwriter

Su Tung–P'o (Su Shih) (1036–1101) Chinese poet, writer, painter and public official

Sullivan, Annie (1866 1936) American lecturer, writer and teacher

Sullivan, Sir Arthur (1842–1900) English composer, particularly of operettas

Sully, Duc de (1559–1641) French statesman and financier

Surtees, R.S. (1805–1864) English writer

Suzuki, D.T. (1870–1966) Japanese Buddhist scholar and main interpreter of Zen to the West

Swaffer, Hannen (1879–1962) English writer

Swann, Donald (1923–1994) English composer and pianist

Swift, Jonathan (Dean Swift) (1667–1745) Irish satirist, poet, essayist and cleric

Swinburne, Algernon Charles (1837–1909) English poet, critic, dramatist and letter writer

Synge, J.M. (1871–1909) Irish dramatist, poet and letter writer

Szasz, Thomas (1920–) Hungarian-born American psychiatrist and writer

Szent–Györgyi, Albert von (1893–1986) Hungarian-born American biochemist

T

Taber, Robert (20th century) US writer

Tacitus (c. 56–c. 120) Roman historian

Talleyrand, Charles–Maurice de (1754–1838) French statesman, memoirist and prelate

Tannen, Deborah (1945–) American linguist and academic

Tarkington, Booth (1869–1946) American writer and dramatist

Tawney, R.H. (1880–1962) British economic historian and Christian socialist

Taylor, A.J.P. (1906–1990) English historian, writer, broadcaster and lecturer

Taylor, Bert Leston (1866–1921) US journalist

Taylor, Elizabeth (1912–1975) English writer

Taylor, Bishop Jeremy (1613–1667) English divine and writer

Tebbitt, Norman, Lord (1931–) English Conservative politician

Tecumseh (d. 1812) Leader of the Shawnee Indians

Teilhard de Chardin, Pierre (1881–1955) French priest, palaeontologist and philosopher

Temple William (1881–1944) Anglican prelate, social reformer and writer

Tennyson, Alfred, Lord (1809 1892) English lyric poet

Terence (c. 190–159 BC) Carthaginian-born Roman dramatist

Teresa, Mother (1910–1997) Catholic missionary in India

Terry, Dame Ellen (1847–1928) English actress, theatrical manager and memoirist

Tertullian (c. 160–225) Carthaginian theologian

Tertz, Abram (Andrei Sinyavsky) (1925–1997) Russian writer and dissident

Tessimond, A.S.J. (1902–1962) English poet

Thackeray, William Makepeace (1811–1863) Indian-born English writer

Thales (c. 624–547 BC) Ionian philosopher, mathematician and astronomer

BIOGRAPHIES

Thatcher, Carol (1953–) English writer and broadcaster; daughter of Margaret Thatcher

Thatcher, Sir Denis (1915–) British businessman, husband of Margaret Thatcher

Thatcher, Margaret, Baroness (1925–) English Conservative Prime Minister

Theroux, Paul (1941–) American writer

Thiers, Louis Adolphe (1797–1877) French statesman and historian

Thomas, Dylan (1914–1953) Welsh poet, writer and radio dramatist

Thomas, Gwyn (1913–1981) Welsh writer, dramatist and teacher

Thomas, Irene (1920–) English writer and broadcaster

Thomas, Lewis (1913–) American pathologist and university administrator

Thomson, James (1700–1748) Scottish poet and dramatist

Thomson, Joseph (1858–1895) Scottish explorer, geologist and writer

Thoreau, Henry (1817–1862) American essayist, social critic and writer

Thorpe, Jeremy (1929–) English Liberal politician

Thurber, James (1894–1961) American humorist, writer and dramatist

Thurlow, Edward (1731–1806) English lawyer, politician and Lord Chancellor

Tibullus (c. 54–19 BC) Roman poet

Tichborne, Chidiock (c. 1558–1586) English Catholic conspirator against Elizabeth I

Tindal, Matthew (1657–1733) English deist and writer

Titus Vespasianus (39–81) Roman emperor and public benefactor

Tocqueville, Alexis de (1805–1859) French historian, politician, lawyer and memoirist

Todd, Ron (1927–) British trade unionist

Tolstoy, Leo (1828–1910) Russian writer, essayist, philosopher and moralist

Tomalin, Nicholas (1931–1973) English journalist

Tomaschek, Rudolphe (b. c.1895) German scientist

Tomlin, Lily (1939–) American actress

Toner, Pauline (1935–1989) Australian politician

Toynbee, Arnold (1889–1975) English historian and scholar

Tracy, Spencer (1900–1967) US film actor

Traherne, Thomas (c. 1637–1674) English religious writer and clergyman

Trapp, Joseph (1679–1747) English poet, pamphleteer, translator and clergyman

Tree, Sir Herbert Beerbohm (1853–1917) English actor and theatre manager

Trevelyan, G.M. (1876–1962) English historian and writer

Trollope, Anthony (1815–1882) English writer, traveller and post office official

Trotsky, Leon (1879–1940) Russian revolutionary and Communist theorist

Truman, Harry S. (1884–1972) US President

Tuchman, Barbara W. (1912–1989) American journalist and historian

Tucholsky, Kurt (1890–1935) German satirist and writer

Tucker, Sophie (1884–1966) Russian-born American vaudeville singer

Tupper, Martin (1810–1889) English writer, lawyer and inventor

Turenne, Henri, Vicomte (1611–1675) French marshal

Turgenev, Ivan (1818–1883) Russian writer and dramatist

Turgot, A–R–J. (1727–1781) French economist and statesman

Turnbull, Margaret (fl. 1920s–1942) Scottish-born US writer and dramatist

Tusser, Thomas (c. 1524–1580) English writer, poet and musician

Tutu, Archbishop Desmond (1931–) South African churchman and anti-apartheid campaigner

Twain, Mark (1835–1910) American humorist, writer, journalist and lecturer

Tynan, Kenneth (1927–1980) English drama critic, producer and essayist

U

Unamuno, Miguel de (1864–1936) Spanish philosopher, poet and writer

Updike, John (1932–) American writer, poet and critic

Urey, Harold (1893–1981) American chemist

Ustinov, Sir Peter (1921–) English actor, director, dramatist, writer and raconteur

Uvavnuk Inuit singer and shaman

V

Vail, Amanda (1921–1966) US writer

Valéry, Paul (1871–1945) French poet, mathematician and philosopher

Vanbrugh, Sir John (1664–1726) English dramatist and baroque architect

Vanderbilt William H. (1821–1885) American financier and railway magnate

Van der Post, Sir Laurens (1906–1996) South African writer, soldier and explorer

Vaughan, Henry (1622–1695) Welsh poet and physician

Vauvenargues, Marquis de (1715–1747) French soldier and moralist

Veblen, Thorstein (1857–1929) American economist and sociologist

Vega Carpio, Félix Lope de (1562–1635) Spanish dramatist, poet and writer

Vegetius Renatus, Flavius (fl. c. 375) Military writer

Vergniaud, Pierre (1753–1793) French politician and revolutionary

Verlaine, Paul (1844–1896) French poet and autobiographer

Vespasian (9–79) Roman emperor

Victoria, Queen (1819–1901) British Queen, Empress of India; diarist and writer

Vidal, Gore (1925–) American writer, critic and poet

Viera, Ondina Uruguayan football manager

Vigneaud, Vincent de (1901–1978) Canadian biochemist

Villiers de l'Isle–Adam, Philippe Auguste (1838–1889) French poet, writer and dramatist

Virgil (70–19 BC) Roman poet

Vizinczey, Stephen (1933–) Hungarian-born writer, editor and broadcaster

Voltaire (1694–1778) French philosopher, dramatist, poet, historian writer and critic

Vorster, John (1915–1983) South African Nationalist politician, Prime Minister and President

Vulliamy, Ed British writer

W

Waddell, Helen (1889–1965) Irish scholar and writer

Wain, John (1925–1994) English poet, writer and critic

Walden, George (1939–) British Conservative politician and diplomat

Wales, Princess of (1961–1997) Diana Spencer, wife of Charles, Prince of Wales

Walker, Alice (1944–) American writer and poet

Wallace, Edgar (1875–1932) English writer and dramatist

Wallace, William Ross (c.1819–1881) American lawyer and poet

Wallach, Eli (1915–) American actor

Waller, Edmund (1606–1687) English poet and politician

Walpole, Horace (1717–1797) English writer and politician

Walpole, Sir Hugh (1884–1941) New Zealand-born English writer

Walpole, Robert (1676–1745) English statesman and first British Prime Minister

Walsh, William (1663–1708) English critic, poet and politician

Walton, Izaak (1593–1683) English writer

Ward, Artemus (1834–1867) American humorist, journalist, editor and lecturer

Warhol, Andy (c. 1926–1987) American painter, graphic designer and filmmaker

Warren, Earl (1891–1974) American lawyer and politician

Washington, George (1732–1799) American general, statesman and President

Watts, Isaac (1674–1748) English hymn-writer, poet and minister

Waugh, Auberon (1939–) English writer and critic

Waugh, Evelyn (1903–1966) English writer and diarist

Wax, Ruby (1953–) US comedienne

Webb, Beatrice (1858–1943) English writer and reformer

Webb, Sidney (1859–1947) English reformer, historian and socialist

Webster, Daniel (1782–1852) American statesman, orator and lawyer

Webster, John (c. 1580–c. 1625) English dramatist

Wedgwood, Josiah (1730–1795) English potter, manufacturer and pamphleteer

Wedgwood, Veronica (1910–1997) English historian

Weil, Simone (1909–1943) French philosopher, essayist and mystic

Weiss, Peter (1916–1982) German dramatist, painter and film producer

Welch, Joseph US attorney

Welch, Raquel (1940–) American actress

Weldon, Fay (1931–) British writer

Welles, Orson (1915–1985) American actor, director and producer

Wellington, Duke of (1769–1852) Irish-born British military commander and statesman

Wells, H.G. (1866–1946) English writer

Wenders, Wim (1945–) German film director

Wesley, John (1703–1791) English theologian and preacher

Wesley, Samuel (1662–1735) English churchman and poet

West, Mae (1892–1980) American actress and scriptwriter

West, Dame Rebecca (1892–1983) English writer, critic and feminist

Wharton, Edith (1862–1937) American writer

Whately, Richard (1787–1863) English philosopher, theologian, educationist and writer

Whistler, James McNeill (1834–1903) American painter, etcher and pamphleteer

White, E.B. (1899–1985) American humorist and writer

White, Patrick (1912–1990) English-born Australian writer and dramatist

BIOGRAPHIES

Whitehead, A.N.
(1861–1947) English mathematician and philosopher

Whitehorn, Katherine
(1926–) English writer

Whitelaw, William, Viscount
(1918–) English Conservative politician

Whiting, William
(1825–1878) English teacher, poet and hymn writer

Whitlam, Gough (1916–)
Australian Labor statesman and Prime Minister

Whitman, Walt
(1819–1892) American poet and writer

Whittier, John Greenleaf
(1807–1892) American poet, abolitionist and journalist

Whorf, Benjamin
(1897–1941) American anthropological linguist and engineer

Wilberforce, Bishop Samuel (1805–1873)
English divine and writer

Wilcox, Ella Wheeler (1850–1919) American poet and writer

Wilde, Lady Jane
(1826–1896) Irish poet and society hostess, mother of Oscar Wilde

Wilde, Oscar (1854–1900)
Irish poet, dramatist, writer, critic and wit

Wilder, Billy (1906–)
Austrian-born American film director, producer and screenwriter

Wilder, Thornton
(1897–1975) American dramatist, writer and teacher

Wilhelm I, Kaiser
(1797–1888) King of Prussia and first Emperor of Germany

William of Wykeham
(1324–1404) English churchman and Chancellor of England

Williams, Kenneth
(1926–1988) English actor and comedian

Williams, Tennessee
(1911–1983) American dramatist and writer

Williams, William Carlos
(1883–1963) American poet, writer and paediatrician

Williamson, Malcolm
(1931–) Master of the Queen's Music

Williamson, Nicol (1938–)
Scottish actor

Wilikie, Wendell
(1892–1944) American lawyer, industrialist and Republican politician

Wilson, Charles E.
(1890–1961) American industrialist, car manufacturer and politician

Wilson, Harold, Baron
(1916–1995) English Labour Prime Minister

Wilson, Woodrow
(1856–1924) American Democrat President

Winchell, Walter
(1897–1972) American drama critic, columnist and broadcaster

Wittgenstein, Ludwig
(1889–1951)
Austrian–born British philosopher

Woddis, Roger British poet and scriptwriter

Wodehouse, P.G.
(1881–1975) English humorist and writer

Wolfe, Humbert
(1886–1940) Italian-born British poet, critic and civil servant

Wolfe, James (1727–1759)
English major-general

Wolff, Charlotte
(1904–1986) German-born British psychiatrist and writer

Wollstonecraft, Mary
(1759–1797) English feminist, writer and teacher

Wolsey, Thomas (c. 1475–1530) English Cardinal and statesman

Wood, Mrs Henry
(1814–1887) English writer and editor

Woolf, Virginia
(1882–1941) English writer and critic

Woollcott, Alexander
(1887–1943) US writer, drama critic and anthologist

Wordsworth, Dame Elizabeth (1840–1932) English educationist and wnter

Wordsworth, William (1770–1850) English poet

Worsthorne, Sir Peregrine (1923–) English journalist

Wotton, Sir Henry (1568–1639) English diplomat, traveller and poet

Wren, Sir Christopher (1632–1723) English architect and mathematician and astronomer

Wright, Frank Lloyd (1869–1959) American architect and writer

Wright, Judith (1915–) Australian poet, critic and writer

Wycherley, William (c. 1640–1716) English dramatist and poet

Wyllie, George (1921–) Scottish artist

Wynne–Tyson, Esme (1898–1972) British actress, dramatist and writer

X

Xerxes (c. 519–465 BC) King of Persia

X, Malcolm (1925–1965) African-American activist

Y

Yankwich, Leon R. (1888–1975) Romanian-born American judge and writer

Ybarra, Thomas Russell (b. 1880) American writer and poet

Yeatman, Robert (1897–1968) British writer

Yeats, W.B. (1865–1939) Irish poet, dramatist, editor, writer and senator

Yeltsin, Boris (1931–) Russian President

Yevtushenko, Yevgeny (1933–) Russian poet

Young, Andrew (1885–1971) Scottish poet, churchman and botanist

Young, Andrew (1932–) US politician and civil rights campaigner

Young, Edward (1683–1765) English poet, dramatist, satirist and clergyman

Young, George W. (1846–1919) British writer

Z

Zamoyski, Jan (1541–1605) Polish Chancellor and army leader

Zangwill, Israel (1864–1926) English writer and Jewish spokesman

Zappa, Frank (1940–1993) American rock musician, songwriter and record producer

Ze Ami (1363–1443) Japanese playwright, theorist and director of Noh theatre

INDEX OF THEMES

INDEX OF SOURCES

BERKELEY COLLEGE LIBRARY / WESTCHESTER

3 6615 4000 0866 3

REF 080 COL

Collins quotation finder